Foreword

This volume on "Women and Children as Victims and Offenders: Background, Prevention, Reintegration. Suggestions for Succeeding Generations" takes an interdisciplinary approach to the situation of women and children involved with the criminal justice system, placing a special emphasis on them as offenders and victims of crime.

Over past decades, the international community has adopted important standards to safeguard the rights of women and children who come into contact with the criminal justice system, including as victims and offenders. These include the right to access justice, to legal aid and assistance, to protection from unlawful or arbitrary detention, to social reintegration as well as to freedom from violence.

Unfortunately, the gap between these critical commitments and reality remains wide, compromising the rights of countless children and women around the world. Children and women involved with the criminal justice system remain surrounded by stigma, and their situation is seldom a priority on the national agenda. Awaiting trial for months or even years, denied access to legal aid, placed in overcrowded and unsuitable facilities and deprived of health services, education and vocational training, children and women are also often exposed to humiliating treatment by staff and at risk of harassment, torture, rape and abuse.

As a result of disturbing reports on serious violations of their rights, including human trafficking, sexual violence and homicide, the plight of women and children has gained increasing visibility on the domestic and international justice and security agenda. The urgency of safeguarding their fundamental rights and the need to identify and address the root causes leading to their exposure to violence have helped to generate increasing attention and action across regions. Yet, implementation on the ground remains a serious challenge.

This publication is designed to overcome this challenge and thus promote the effective realisation of the rights of children and women. Risk diagnoses, trust, fairness, justice and restorative justice approaches, the roles of the family, the education system and the media as well as the impact of urban planning in the life of girls are some of the important questions discussed in depth. Another important dimension considered is the implementation of the right to education from preschool to university level, and the attacks against schools that seriously compromise the opportunity to promote children's education and personal development and have been condemned in significant resolutions by the United Nations Security Council.

Taking into consideration intergenerational, intercultural and socio-economic perspectives, this multidisciplinary volume also discusses a wide range of other topics such as bioethics, the promotion of interfaith dialogue, the reintegration and rehabilitation of young offenders, the abolition of the death penalty, the need to counter online abuse of children and women as well as tackling corruption, in which women and children may have an as-yet unexplored preventive role.

As the Special Representative of the UN Secretary General on Violence against Children, I have urged Member States to spare no efforts in mobilising governmental departments, national institutions, civil society partners, faith-based organisations, communities and families at large to build nations free from violence. Violence against children is never justified and all violence against children can be effectively prevented. Strong political will, strategic alliances, sound knowledge and unshakable action can bring violence to an end. This volume makes a significant contribution to this goal and is a useful reminder of the values of the United Nations and its unwavering resolve to build peaceful societies and strong institutions, guided by human rights, committed to justice and fairness, and respectful of the dignity and worth of every person.

UN Special Representative of the Secretary General on Violence against Children
New York, NY, USA

Marta Santos Pais

Women and Children as Victims and Offenders: An Introduction

In criminological and public discussions, women and children are often seen as victims rather than as offenders—a view that has not much changed over time. In times of war and armed conflict, they still are the group that has to bear the most suffering: they are displaced, misused, raped and even killed.

It was the founding purpose of UNICEF in 1946, after the horrors of World War II, to protect children from the effects of war. This task is today as necessary as it was then.

The UNICEF Report 2015 ("Children between the Lines") documents this vividly: "We are currently experiencing one of the worst phases of conflicts since the end of World War II. UNICEF estimates that in 2014 about 230 million children grew up worldwide in war and crisis zones. Their everyday life is marked by violence and hatred – often for years ... Wars and armed conflicts have forced nearly 60 million people to leave their homes. More than half of these refugees and the internally displaced are women and children. They are particularly affected by the consequences of war, characterized by poor supply and lack of educational opportunities. Moreover, cases of serious violence have increased dramatically against boys and girls in the war" (p. 1). According to UNICEF one in ten children grows up in a country or region affected by crises and violent conflicts (UNICEF 2015).

Many children do not have adequate supplies of essentials, including food, water and medical assistance. Most are only able to attend school infrequently, if at all. "In the civil wars raging in Syria, Iraq, South Sudan and the Central African Republic children are also targets of the worst form of abuse" (ibid., p. 2). Groups such as ISIS in Syria and Iraq and Boko Haram in Nigeria blatantly disregard the principles of international humanitarian law. The UN Security Council lists for 2014 a total of 23 conflict situations in which children were exposed to serious human rights violations (UNICEF 2015). They were kidnapped, abused as sex slaves or child soldiers or sent to death as suicide bombers. In the first 7 months of 2015, UN officials reported 27 suicide bombings by Boko Haram. In at least three-quarters of the blast, the bombers were women or children (UNICEF 2015).

Why are young people attracted to terror organisations such as IS, even to the extent to give their lives? UNICEF gives the following answer: "The cynical use and display of children as victims makes them an object of political propaganda ... Ideologies like those propagated by IS promise adventure, social inclusion and the feeling to be able to get past the limitations imposed on young people in their everyday life. They make the youngsters feel important, make them believe that they can influence world events and impose their ideas on the whole world" (UNICEF Report 2015, p. 4).

Phenomena such as IS make it clear "that general humanitarian principles are not automatically part of human traditions. They will never be because in times of war they are contrary to many primary instincts. The only way to entrench humanitarian values in the mind of each person – as a civilian, potential fighter, actual combatant or policy maker – is education" (ibid., p. 5).

According to UNICEF, in 2015 more than 62 million children in conflict areas will urgently need food, clean water, medical aid, the possibility to continue their education and protection from exploitation and violence. The realisation of the post-2015 UN sustainable development goals will depend to a large extent on whether we succeed in caring for and protecting children in such situations.

In its "Core Commitments for Children in Humanitarian Action", UNICEF spelled out its main obligations to children in war situations: providing life-saving measures for pregnant women, newborns and children; facilitating school attendance even in emergency situations; help in searching for dispersed family members; and care for victims (UNICEF Report 2015, p. 6). As far as the creation of a durable peace is concerned, UNICEF gives children and adolescents a major role as "natural agents of change", and mediators between the generations. There shall be no more "lost generations", but instead all children shall have access to education and a better economic future. These are ambitious aims. Their realisation will need a greater commitment of wealthier nations and much work at persuasion. This work wants to make a small contribution.

As far as the situation of women is concerned, their equality in society has improved in many countries, but not to an extent that would allow us to speak of true gender equality (Kury and Obergfell-Fuchs 2005). It is not that long ago that the old legal tradition giving the husband dominion over his wife has been abolished in western countries, and it is still alive in many Muslim countries and other countries with a strong tribal tradition.

Recent research on women as victims presents the following picture (Lundgren et al. 2002; McGee et al. 2002; Medina and Barberet 2003; Müller and Schröttle 2004; Rodriguez Menés and Safranoff 2013): "The key findings include confirmation that violence against women is a universal phenomenon and occurs in every age and economic group although at different rates; there is indication that between 35 and 60 % of women in the surveyed countries have experienced violence by a man during their lifetime and that less than one third of women reported their experience of violence to the police (and where they do report, women are more likely to report stranger violence than intimate partner violence)" (Gelsthorpe and

Larrauri 2014, p. 193). A study covering nine countries of the European Union concluded that in roughly 25 % of all sexual aggressions, the offenders were either partners or ex-partners of the victim and that in these cases the level of violence was higher (Burman et al. 2009; see also Gelsthorpe and Larrauri 2014, p. 194; Müller and Schröttle 2004).

Hester (2013, p. 634) demonstrated in her study that women are not only more frequently victims of domestic and partner violence, but that the victimisation is more serious and that if they retaliate, the courts treat them worse than the male offenders: "While cases were very varied, there were significant differences between male and female perpetrators of domestic violence in many respects. Men were the perpetrators in a much greater number of incidents; the violence used by men against female partners was much more severe than that used by women against men; violence by men was most likely to involve fear by and control of female victims; women were more likely to use weapons, often in order to protect themselves; and female perpetrators were more likely to be alcoholic, or mentally ill, although alcohol misuse by men had a greater impact on severity on outcomes. Despite these patterns, however, women were three times as likely to be arrested per incident, indicating gendered injustice in the approach. There was little evidence that cases involving dual perpetration might generally be categorised as 'mutual' and men were in the main the primary aggressors".

Not only women, but also children, become victims of domestic violence. As Levi and Maguire (2002, p. 818) point out, there are many reasons that may lead to child abuse, not the least the incessant crying of a baby. "Situational opportunity variables are also salient to baby battering; modern nuclear families are far more isolated than the extended families found in many Third World Countries, where parents are seldom alone in the house". But more than situational opportunities, it is societal factors such as unemployment, poverty or isolation that lead to problems in a family and may expose children to violent reactions from frustrated parent. The fault in such cases is usually attributed only to the offender and society feels no blame. If anything, it is up to "the politicians" to do something about it. Moser (1972, p. 289) says it clearly: "It is astonishing to what extent society gives these children time to develop into full-fledged delinquents. It hardly cares about them, as long as they are the victims. Only when society itself is victimized or at least can present itself as victim, does it decide to act. And then [they act] like neglected and immature parents that hit blindly when the crying and the pranks of their neglected children exasperated them, when the angry need to have peace becomes the main motive of their intervention".

The social cost of domestic violence is very high. In Finland, for instance, it has been estimated that the annual financial cost amounts to approximately 91 million euro (Heiskanen and Piispa 2002, p. 36; see also Walby 2004; Haller and Dawid 2006; Brzank 2009). Such cost are however difficult to estimate and we should not forget that the financial aspect is only one part of "social costs". Numerous studies have shown that "Children who are physically abused or neglected tend to become offenders later in life" (Farrington 2002, p. 674; see also the chapter by Farrington in volume 1; Widom 1989; Widom and Ames 1994). Already in 1951, Bowlby developed the theory that there is a strong connection between broken homes and delinquency (see also Farrington 2002, p. 675; McCord 1983).

Much of domestic violence remains hidden, as many women are reluctant to denounce their partners. In order to get some more precise figures of actual victimisations, victim studies include now specific questions on domestic violence (see, for instance, the British Crime Survey). Many countries have also introduced special legislation to protect women and children from domestic violence. According to Gelsthorpe and Larrauri (2014, p. 194): "European responses to IPV (Intimate Partner Violence) and domestic violence have revolved around civil or criminal protection orders in each country (http://ec.europa.eu/justice/fundamental-rights/document/index_en.htm as well as the Directive 2011/99/EU of the European Parliament and of the Council of 13 December 2011 on the European protection order); additionally all European countries have created new specific public offences or increased penalties, and domestic violence courts; and all have some form of victim support and protection mechanisms".

There is no doubt that there has been considerable progress, especially in the West, concerning equal rights for women and the protection of children, but much still needs to be done. As Gelsthorpe and Larrauri (2014, p. 198) put it: "There is still a need for wider recognition of violence against women (including attention to sub-cultural gender violence such as 'forced marriages', and to women in different structural positions, immigrant women, women with multiple social needs or disability, drugs or alcohol problems, for example). Additionally we need consistent monitoring and evaluation of changing policies in relation to domestic violence and sexual assault across countries, and attention to the high rates of attrition in regard to the prosecution of violence against women, for instance".

The growing increase of refugees fleeing from wars and persecutions creates new problems concerning their integration. Most come from different cultural backgrounds and bring with them traditions and attitudes that may be at odds with those of their host countries, especially their attitudes towards women and children as well as their perception of what constitutes legitimate violence. Stamatel, in her study of female homicide victimisation rates across Europe from 1985 to 2010, calculated time series over four time periods for 33 countries and came to the following conclusion (2014, p. 596): "Better economic conditions reduce female homicide victimization, as they do for violence more generally. Gender dynamics play a contradictory role: less traditional gender roles increase the risk of victimization, whereas improving the collective status of women in society reduces that risk. Most importantly, controlling for these known predictors of female homicide victimization, the historical legacies and socio-historical contexts of nations matter greatly for explaining variation across Europe".

When women turn to offending, they do so considerable less often than men. In his international comparison of crime rates, Heidensohn (2002, p. 496) underlines that "such differences [in crime rates] seem to be common across a variety of nations and cultures. In surveying material on Europe, I found that crime is still an activity overwhelmingly dominated by men in all European countries" (see also Heidensohn and Farrell 1991). The same is true for countries such as Brasil or India

(Lemgruber 2001; Patkar 2001). The author continues (Heidensohn 2002, p. 496): "This apparently consistent pattern has led some commentators to suggest that women offenders are 'only 10 % of the trouble'. Considering different types of offences and changes over time, a more complex and qualified picture emerges. Women contribute to all types of offending, but their share varies considerably". Austin gives a similar assessment of the situation in the United States (2003, p. 560): "I have calculated that if the males behaved like females, violent crime rates would drop by 2/3 and the 2 million people in the prison and jail population would not exceed 200,000. The associated costs of a 112 billion dollar criminal justice system would shrink to less than 20 billion dollars".

Some authors claim however that the situation is changing: female crime rates are rising faster than those of males, and the gap is narrowing. Adler (1975) commented already in the 1970s on this rise and explained it with a change in female behaviour: women, according to him, have become more aggressive and violent, and therefore their offending resembles increasingly that of their male counterparts. Responsible for this change, in Adler's view, is primarily the strengthening of the women's movement and the greater freedom women enjoy today. But the topic remains controversial. Heidensohn puts it as follows: "Arguments about whether female crime was rising at a faster rate than male, and that thus the female share was going up, have been a highly contended criminological issue since the 1970s. Indeed, this is one of the few topics to do with women and crime to excite widespread attention" (Heidensohn 2002, p. 496).

Gelsthorpe and Larrauri (2014, p. 188) refer to another important aspect: "At the beginning of the twenty-first century new crimes and concerns have emerged: terrorism, cyber-crime, human trafficking and other human rights violations for instance, all of which have produced new ways of women being involved in crime as offenders, or as victims". The authors underline further (p. 188): "Women certainly have a much higher profile than they once did, but it can still be argued that there is a general neglect of women in relation to crime and criminal justice". Even if we have more information about crime than ever before, there are still very few empirical studies on gender-related differences and their causes. Crime is still seen as a "male domain".

The situation of women in prison was also for many years a neglected theme in criminology—their number was too small to be noteworthy. Whereas the number of rehabilitation programmes for male offenders was increasing, it didn't seem "worthwhile" to elaborate such programmes for the small number of female prisoners. Only recently more attention has been paid to the collateral damage of female imprisonment, for instance, on children, and the special victimisation risks women are exposed to in prison.

The percentage of female inmates is relatively low: only 4–5 % of the total number of inmates, with little variations between countries. Most of them fit exactly into the category described by Moser (1972, p. 291) already 40 years ago: "Most misfits, in particular those who are locked up, belong to those minorities, who cannot speak for themselves, who have no public voice, can't organise themselves, and can't defend their interests. They depend on an enlightened public that pit their fate, and not just their actual fate but their whole life against the ideal – so dear to society – of the right of each person to personal development; the public will then have to ponder if the kind of punishment meted out today is a just reward for their deeds or if it is not rather help that should be given greater importance".[1] The role of proper public information in this context cannot be underestimated and is a focal concern of this work.

In the quest to improve the plight of women and children, the United Nations has played a most important role. After the horrors of two world wars in the twentieth century, it has made an invaluable contribution to pave the way for a durable peace. The goal, admittedly difficult to reach, is already clearly set out in the Preamble of its foundational Treaty of 1945[2]: "We the Peoples of the United Nations are determined to save succeeding generations from the scourge of war, which twice in our lifetime has brought untold sorrow to mankind"...and "to unite our strength to maintain international peace and security" (1 UNTS 16). Women and children (girls and boys)—now roughly half of the present world's population—determine any "succeeding generation".

The concept of "generations" was formulated in the beginning of the twentieth century (Nora 1997, p. 2992). Combined with the UN Charter's Preamble term "succeeding", it means parents, children and grandchildren succeed each other at more or less regular intervals (Suleiman 2002, p. 278).[3] It is for the "succeeding generations" that the Charter calls for the promotion of "social progress and better standards of life in larger freedom", including full employment, and conditions of economic and social progress and development (art. 55).

This two-volume book responds to this call by focusing on the intergenerational, international and intercultural transmission of values through learning. Yet the main focus of the book is on justice issues with global commonalities. The work blends academic with UN considerations, findings and recommendations on justice. A common thread is the prevention of crime/delinquency and victimisation of women and children. The most glaring form of crime and delinquency is violence. As repeatedly emphasised by the UN leadership, violence against women and children must be countered effectively. Ban Ki-moon, the present Secretary-General has appealed to "break the silence" concerning violence against women,[4] and also the UN Special Representative of the Secretary-General on Violence against Children has underscored that "violence against children is never justified

[1] Free translation by Evelyn Shea.

[2] The Charter of the United Nations was signed in San Francisco, California, on 26 June 1945, by 50 of the 51 original member countries.

[3] It is this a broader context in which the concept of "1.5 generation" originally emerged: of child survivors of the Holocaust "too young to have had an adult understanding of what was happening to them but old enough to have been there during the Nazi persecution of Jews" (Suleiman 2002, p. 277).

[4] http://www.un.org/en/women/endviolence/about.shtml.

and all violence against children can be effectively prevented. With strong political will, wide mobilization and steady action, it can be brought to an end".[5]

While the emphasis on physical component of violence is understandable, violence against children can also be "mental" (art. 19 of the Convention on the Rights of the Child, 1577 UNTS 3). However improper and detrimental, this or that form of violence may be for the future conduct of a child, let us not forget that child's conduct can also be mishandled in many other forms. From a criminological perspective, subtly manipulating child's sense of trust, disorienting a child about his/her entitlements, mishandling mental anguish or facilitating emotional deprivations is likewise important for crime prevention. This work caters also to this broader crime prevention function and vision.

The UN has joined that vision 45 years after the Second World War (1939–1945), when the concept of "succeeding generations" (up to that point faintly related to war prevention) did receive some more attention. In 1990 "The United Nations Guidelines for the Prevention of Juvenile Delinquency" ("The Riyadh Guidelines", A/RES/45/112) emphasised in paragraph 15 the socialisation function of family in the prevention of delinquency: "Special attention should be given to children of families affected by problems brought about by rapid and uneven economic, social and cultural change, in particular the children of indigenous, migrant and refugee families. As such changes may disrupt the social capacity of the family to secure the traditional rearing and nurturing of children, often as a result of role and culture conflict, innovative and socially constructive modalities, for the socialization of children have to be designed".

Ten years later, in the "Guidelines for the prevention of urban crime", the UN Economic and Social Council (ECOSOC) explicitly recommended Member States to "Consider the relevance to the crime prevention action plan of such factors as . . . relationships in the family, between generations or between social groups etc." (ECOSOC resolution 1995/9). Finally, in 2002, the Council adopted the "Guidelines for the Prevention of Crime" (ECOSOC resolution 2002/13). They emphasise how crime prevention action should be developed, with a focus on local communities, where crime is experienced, as well as those with high needs, and that it be conducted through partnerships across government sectors and with civil society and the participation of communities, that it be sustained and accountable, rather than short term, and be based on sound evidence-based practice.

A set of eight basic principles is involved for pursuing these approaches (articles 7–14 in the Guidelines):

1. *Government leadership*: All levels of government should play a leadership role in developing effective and humane crime prevention strategies and in creating and maintaining institutional frameworks for their implementation and review.
2. *Socio-economic development and inclusion*: Crime prevention considerations should be integrated into all relevant social and economic policies and

[5] Political will, 'steady action' can end violence against children, UN envoy tells Indonesia, www.un.org/apps/news/story.asp?NewsID=50207.

programmes, including those addressing employment, education, health, housing and urban planning, poverty, social marginalisation and exclusion. Particular emphasis should be placed on communities, families, children and youth at risk.
3. *Cooperation/partnerships*: Cooperation/partnerships should be an integral part of effective crime prevention, given the wide-ranging nature of the causes of crime and the skills and responsibilities required to address them. This includes partnerships working across ministries and between authorities, community organisations, non-governmental organisations, the business sector and private citizens.
4. *Sustainability/accountability*: Crime prevention requires adequate resources, including funding for structures and activities, in order to be sustained. There should be clear accountability for funding, implementation and evaluation and for the achievement of planned results.
5. *Knowledge base*: Crime prevention strategies, policies, programmes and actions should be based on a broad, multidisciplinary foundation of knowledge about crime problems, their multiple causes and promising and proven practices.
6. *Human rights/rule of law/culture of lawfulness*: The rule of law and those human rights which are recognised in international instruments to which Member States are parties must be respected in all aspects of crime prevention. A culture of lawfulness should be actively promoted in crime prevention.
7. *Interdependency*: National crime prevention diagnoses and strategies should, where appropriate, take account of links between local criminal problems and international organised crime.
8. *Differentiation*: Crime prevention strategies should, when appropriate, pay due regard to the different needs of men and women and consider the special needs of vulnerable members of society.

All these UN guidelines adopted for women and children as one of the vulnerable groups with special crime prevention needs are summarised in the subsequent UN handbook, as follows: "In essence, the principles laid out in the 2002 and the 1995 guidelines, establish the normative basis with the importance of the rule of law and respect for human rights, of the social and economic inclusion of populations, whatever their status and background, and the importance of ensuring that the particular needs of vulnerable minorities, as well as gender differences, are taken into account" (UN Handbook 2010, p. 23).

On balance, in the 70 years since the founding of the United Nations, it has paid more attention to "succeeding generations" in its ideology than in its legal instruments. The specific crime prevention needs of women and children, as the succeeding generation, are only nominally addressed. Generally, so far, the balance of the UN's mandate and functions involving "prevention" and "control" has remained negative, not only regarding the needs of "succeeding generations" pointed out above but also demographically and politically—despite the proclamation of the UN Secretary-General that "prevention is the first imperative of justice" (S/2004/616, para. 4). Notwithstanding this imbalance, academic and UN criminology studies have accumulated and reviewed evidence for diagnosing and countering crime not only for the current but also for the succeeding generation. The goal of this work is to widen this perspective.

Before presenting the individual chapters, it may be helpful to clarify the concept of "succeeding generations": First, on a demographical note, the expected lifespan of the present generation is, globally, over 67 years (over 65 for males and 70 for females). In 1945, at the time of the creation of the UN, the expectancy was five years shorter (ST/ESA/SER.A/313). In years 2045–2050 it should increase to 74 years (Cohen 2003, p. 1173). Of course, between one and the other generation, there are overlapping generations, and within one generation, there are smaller decimal-point generations. They may be differently (sub-)divided and named. However, certainly the division between "Generation-C" ("connect, communicate, change") or "Digitally Native" generation (Palfrey et al. 2009; Matvyshyn 2012, p. 1979) and others is worth mentioning, because of the fundamentally different childhood than that of their parents, hence different attitudes to law and ensuing effects (violation and victimisation).

Second, in this work, "education" is a broad term. It "comprise[s] all deliberate and systematic activities designed to meet learning needs [and] involve [s] organized and sustained communication designed to bring about learning" (UNESCO 1997). It includes formal (preschool, primary, secondary, tertiary) and non-formal, i.e. outside the formal education system[6]—both mutually complimentary and necessary for a socio-economic development and the implementation of the right to education (Hausler et al. 2012, pp. 72–77).

Third, education is negatively correlated with women's fertility—"a uniquely universal negative relation between female education and fertility" (Basu 2002, p. 1779)—and positively correlated with infants' health (Krueger and Lindhal 2001, p. 1107). In turn, girls born into smaller families are more likely to be sent to school and to complete more years of education (Basu 2002, p. 1788). This, coupled with the fact that already more than half of the world population experiences fertility rates below the replacement level of two surviving children per woman (exactly 2.1 by a conventional estimate, Wilson 2004), begs the question of the sustainability of our present culture. In particular, as far as the topic of this work is concerned, it begs the question of the sustainability of a culture of lawfulness. This axiologically Western concept—the culture of lawfulness—(Redo 2014) nominally entered the UN crime prevention agenda through the 2002 Guidelines. Only very recently the Declaration of the Thirteenth UN Congress on Crime Prevention and Criminal Justice (Doha, Qatar, 2015) made it a fully-fledged UN concept (A/CONF.222/L.6) with emphasis on education for all children and youth, including the eradication of illiteracy. Education and the eradication of illiteracy are both fundamental to the prevention of crime and corruption and to the promotion of a culture of lawfulness that supports the rule of law and human rights

[6] Education provided through nursing, kindergarten care, human rights training sessions, workshops, seminars and webinars is a non-formal education. Informal education is acquired through other life and work experience.

while respecting cultural identities. Finally, the Declaration stressed the fundamental role of youth participation in crime prevention efforts.

In 1992, in paragraph 21 of the Rio Declaration, Member States of the UN urged that "The creativity, ideals and courage of the youth of the world should be mobilized to forge a global partnership in order to achieve sustainable development and ensure a better future for all" (A/CONF.151/26: Vol. I). But only now, with the forthcoming Rio+20 post-2015 UN sustainable development goals, particularly "Goal 4. Ensure inclusive and equitable quality education and promote lifelong learning opportunities for all" (A/68/970), the organisation took a comprehensive and incisive look into the role of culture in sustainable development. We read there, that by 2030, Member States and other stakeholders should "ensure that all learners acquire the knowledge and skills needed to promote sustainable development, including, among others, through education for sustainable development and sustainable lifestyles, human rights, gender equality, promotion of a culture of peace and non-violence, global citizenship and appreciation of cultural diversity and of culture's contribution to sustainable development" (ibid., p. 13/24).[7]

Fourth, it follows that non-violence is a recognised element of any legal culture. And so is anti-corruption about which the framers of the UN post-2015 sustainable development agenda speak as a part of the envisioned goal 16—the promotion of peaceful and inclusive societies for sustainable development, the provision of access to justice for all and building effective, accountable and inclusive institutions at all levels. A global culture of lawfulness for the succeeding generation will have on its agenda such moral universals.

Interculturally universalising morality by dignifying our partners, children and others is not automatic. Bringing up children in the spirit of universal moral values starts in our bedrooms and homes, becomes public in the nurseries, kindergartens, schools and then goes into the streets, businesses and other governance. Universal morality rather than once and for all "given", every now and then, needs to be revived to keep humanity on the track of progress. Franklin D. Roosevelt, one of the fathers of the UN Charter, said that "the test of our progress is not whether we add more to the abundance of those who have much; it is whether we provide enough for those who have too little" (quoted after Grafton 1999, p. 61).

Since the inception of the UN, Roosevelt's ideas have had a considerable impact on it and in the world. The organisation has witnessed a four-fold increase in the world's quality of life, as measured by the GDP per capita. More precisely, in comparison with 1945, there are now respectively 4 rich to 1 poor *vis à vis* 4 poor to 1 rich in terms of average income per capita in the constant purchasing power parity (PPP) (Acemoglu 2012, p. 5). This considerable improvement concurs with the one

[7] As this book goes to print, the United Nations General Assembly finalised its action on the draft sustainable development goals 2016–2030, now reflected in resolution A/69/L. 85 (pending A/RES/70/?), unanimously adopted on 25 September 2015, with unamended wording. Therefore, the references to them or quotations drawn by the contributors to this book from various earlier UN source documents are fully compatible with A/69/L. 85.

hundred year projection to that effect in 1930 by John Maynard Keynes in his *Economic Possibilities for Our Grandchildren* (Keynes 1935).

As comforting as the factual corroboration of Keynes' projection may now be, those economic possibilities have currently been monopolised by 1 % of the adult population in the world. According to Oxfam, as of 2016, 1 % will proportionally own more than 50 % of global wealth (possessions) than the 99 % of the adult population of the world (Oxfam 2015). Is this moral? In many Western industrialised countries like Germany in the last decades, more people got extremely rich and more poor; the difference between both groups is obviously not decreasing but increasing.

This two-volume book originated with the latent premise that excessive socio-economic inequality is immoral. It reduces opportunities in education, especially in quality education. Notwithstanding the different professional backgrounds of the editors of the work, and even more diverse professional backgrounds of its contributors, we believe we all share in the idea that evidence-based, quality crime prevention and education are the prerequisites for a successful Culture of Lawfulness anywhere in the world. We also believe that to achieve this goal, partnerships of all kinds will become ever more important. They should involve government agencies, the private sector, civil society, academia, philanthropic foundations and faith-based organisations. Their collaboration will prove critical to the implementation of the UN's new sustainable development agenda that stresses inclusiveness as the core vehicle for poverty amelioration and peaceful non-violent societies.

We expose this idea to the critical scrutiny of the readers in the academic spirit of "organized criticism" (Robert Merton). We are keenly aware that this interdisciplinary work covers only some criminological and other aspects of a more equitable, effective and humane treatment of women and children as victims and offenders and that much remains to be said. Yet, we still trust that the various chapters will open new visions how to reduce the victimisation of women and children as well as their offending.

The contributions to this work are opened by *Santos Pais*, the United Nations Special Representative of the Secretary-General on Violence against Children, and closed by H.E. Ambassador *Martin Sajdik*, the 70th President of the United Nations Economic and Social Council. We very much appreciate the contributions of these eminent representatives. These contributions both demonstrate that a strong political will, partnerships, sound knowledge and decisive action can help to counter violence, corruption and other crimes and their negative impact on sustainable development and the fortunes of succeeding generations.

As to the contributors, some of them are academics, some of them practitioners and still others are both academics and practitioners. We hope that this diversified authorship adds to the value of this work that aims at providing suggestions for succeeding generations to deal more effectively and humanely with women and children as victims and offenders. Some of these suggestions are explicit, others implicit. Some articles explicitly and some other implicitly invoke the UN values embodied in the UN crime prevention and criminal justice standards and norms. The five questions at the end of each text were added to stimulate discussion about possible solutions for the problems raised. Since the two volumes are written by academics and policy-makers, scholars and practitioners, their action profile involves more often strategic than tactical work of a "manual" kind.

On the understanding of these limits, in the *Post Scriptum* we roughly outline and envision the implementation of the work's suggestions until 2030. However, the floor is open to alternative recommendations, to a more visionary and incisive discourse, to closer fieldwork and follow-up. When the UN ideas about sustainable development and crime prevention interact with those of the academic world, in the next 15 years the academic world will have a unique opportunity to contribute to improve crime prevention for women and children. In this context we thank all the authors for their generous contributions and sincerely hope that their texts will advance "social progress and better standards of life in larger freedom" (art. 55 of the UN Charter) and the "Future We Want for All".

These texts are grouped in six parts. **Part I "UN Principles for Crime Prevention-Treatment of Women and Children"** starts with "International Human Rights Law on Violence Against Women and Children and Its Impact on Domestic Law and Action", examined by *Goldfarb and Goldscheid*, two US scholars. They examine the impact and potential of international human rights law as a component of efforts to prevent and redress violence against women and children. Other components, such as laws, policies and community-driven initiatives, countering violence against women and children has made important inroads internationally and in several countries domestically. The chapter's authors not only document the scope of these various initiatives, but discuss particular legal cases and other actions against parties of the UN and regional treaties, whose residents complained about gender violence and the lack of due diligence by State authorities to protect them or their children from such a form of violence.

Dussich, an international victimologist, notes in his chapter about "Blue Victimology and Femicide: The UN Response to Victims and Female Victims of Gender Killings" that since its beginning the UN championed the rights of women and children. In the face of the fact that across the globe every day female children and adults are being killed by men ("femicide"), usually with impunity just because they are females, one of the UN's central goals is to reaffirm faith in fundamental human rights, in the dignity and worth of the human person, in the equal rights of men. The author gives a detailed account of the enormity of the problem in different parts of the world and puts his main hopes on the UN as the most significant forum to take unified action. It has the obligation, the resources and the will to bring about the necessary changes across the globe.

Mwenifumbo and Fuentes, two UN officers, present a chapter about "In the Pursuit of Justice for Women and Children and the Right to Development: A Review of Concluding Observations of the United Nations Human Rights Treaty Bodies". The authors discuss relevant to the UN treaties human rights regime criminal and preventive aspects of "justice" and "the right to development", as far as women and children are concerned. The article analyses the intergenerational issues from, both, the local and global perceptions of justice. It looks into how the UN human rights treaty bodies advance the global justice standards and norms for the treatment of women and children, particularly with regard to victims. In the light of the concluding observations by the UN treaty bodies and the right to development in general, the article makes recommendations concerning gender mainstreaming in formal and informal education.

The final contribution to Part I is provided by *Wintersteiner*. His "International Strategies for Building a Culture of Peace Through Access to Good Education" connects this part of the book with the subsequent ones. He stresses that education may be the only instrument for creating and maintaining democratic, just and peaceful societies. Moreover, education is the cornerstone of a strategy towards a culture of peace and describes what happens when this cornerstone is undermined and education comes under attack (for a specific case, see *Carapic* and *Dönges* in Part II). Wintersteiner emphasises that whilst education is a fundamental human right and essential for the exercise of all other human rights, other human rights have to be guaranteed to be able to make use of the right to education. Education is a prerequisite for the economically and socially marginalised adults and children to lift themselves out of poverty and participate fully as citizens. The author concludes with a brief note on the preparation of the post-2015 education agenda in the framework of the UN sustainable development goals that marks a new step in integrating the human rights approach.

Part II "Education and Social Learning: Their Impact on the Development of Children and Adolescents" is composed of 11 chapters.

Carapic and Dönges present a chapter about "Attacks on Education in Conflict, Post-conflict and Non-conflict Settings". The authors discuss the need for a more informed implementation of the right to education. They note that not much is known about the actual prevalence of attacks on education, the perpetrators involved, the circumstances under which it takes place, for what purpose it is used and how it is regulated. They suggest that understanding attacks on education requires disaggregating the phenomenon along four dimensions: frequency, targeting, repertoire and purpose. After discussing the four dimensions, the authors then show the utility of the proposed framework by examining attacks on education carried out by the Nigerian militant group Boko Haram. In conclusion, they note that despite a number of initiatives to provide more and better monitoring and reporting, the mechanisms necessary for systematic data collection have been found wanting.

In their chapter "The Role of Early Childhood Education in Social behaviour of Children", *Nores and Barnett* discuss the importance of the first five years in the development of children and consequently the need for public investments into early childhood care and education. A large body of evidence on early childhood interventions has found short- and medium-term effects that extend beyond narrowly academic or cognitive outcomes to improvements in pro-social behaviours and skills such as self-regulation, commitment to schooling, employment and earnings, as well as mental and physical health (see also Farrington in his chapter). Given the importance of the early years in child development, the chapter focuses on summarising the evidence of the impact of early childhood interventions on children's social and emotional behaviour in the United States and globally; it describes which aspects of these interventions are associated with larger short-term and long-term social and emotional effects and identifies which types of programs have been found to affect parenting and households in ways that matter for children's behavioural development.

Kanngiesser, Schmidt and Rossano write on "Young Children's Understanding of Social Norms and Social Institutions" at the early preschool level. The authors remind us that as adults we typically navigate our social world effortlessly and mostly unaware of the intricate web of social norms and institutions shaping our behaviour. Children are born into this web that defines (mis-)behaviour. Social norms also form the basis of more complex social institutions such as ownership that create obligations, rights and duties. The authors use the example of ownership to argue that it is one of the first social institutions that young children understand. The chapter seeks to broaden our crime prevention perspectives by going beyond "mental violence" that victimises children (Art. 19 of the Convention on the Rights of the Child) to the question of children's understanding of ownership—an issue that may be at the core of early anti-corruption education (see also *Redo* in Part V).

Farrington ("Family Influences on Offending and Family-Based Intervention") discusses the aspect of intergenerational transmission. Mindful that "cold, rejecting parents tend to have delinquent children" and that "parental warmth could act as a protective factor against the effects of physical punishment", he reviews the insights obtained by cross-national research on the effectiveness of family-based interventions (about emotions see also *Kury* in Part V). The author concludes that a great deal still has to be learnt about family influences on offending and effective family-based programmes in order to further corroborate the present research. He points out that the time is ripe to establish national agencies in all countries willing to participate to advance our knowledge about family risk factors (from longitudinal studies) and about effective family-based interventions (from randomised experiments and cost-benefit analyses).

In "Women's Substance Abuse and Its Impacts on Children's Early Development and Deviant Behaviors", *Gao and Liu* examine from an international perspective the root causes of women's substance abuse, including women's victimisation. The authors focus on the intergenerational sociolegal consequences and impacts of women's drug abuse on children's early development. Like other authors in this work, they conclude that with the continued global growth of female substance abuse, the research and discussion in the international arena should focus not only on implementing meaningful gender-specific programmes for women, their children and families, but should also test whether programmes that were successful in other countries fit into their specific cultural needs.

The moral development of children is a complex problem, which has rather been neglected in criminology. Little attention has been paid, for example, to the relationship between justice and trust. *Brugman, Out and Gibbs* ("Fairness and Trust in Developmental Psychology") point out the importance of this relationship. They emphasise that fairness or justice is central to moral development, but without relating it to trust, there is little cooperation among people. This interpersonal relationship starts in early childhood and foreshadows the close social relationship individuals develop later in life. These essential developments have not been sufficiently studied. The authors review them from a theoretical and empirical perspective, both of which bring new insights. They conclude that a successful mutual moral understanding, difficult in practice as it always has been, depends to a large extent on sensitive parenting and a long process of education and schooling.

Marshall discusses in her chapter "Results of the Second Round of the International Self Report Delinquency (ISRD2) Study: Importance of Education and Social Learning for 12–15-Year Olds" criminological aspects of education and schooling. She notes that, typically, policymakers tend to be more concerned about those youth who are involved in frequent, repeated delinquent behaviour. Although repeating classes and below-average performance of pupils may be warning signs, other school-related factors (such as truancy and type of school, e.g. egalitarian/quality-focused) appear to be more strongly linked to delinquent behaviour. Like *Bokil and Raghavan* (Part IV), Marshall notes the importance of social learning (SL) in understanding effective prevention of delinquency. Pupils with higher acceptance levels of violence also tend to have significantly higher levels of involvement in delinquency. Finally, she presents recommendations that may counter delinquency through early education, better training and pay for teachers who work in low-income areas and greater flexibility in allowing students to gradually move to higher tracks.

In "The Role of Justice and Fairness as Global Values: Promoting Public International Law at the (Pre-)university Level"), *Clark* looks into the avenues and precepts of inculcating an appreciation for international law and international principles (especially justice and fairness) through education at the university level, particularly at the pre-university level, based on the UN Charter and other international instruments that promote justice and international law as cornerstones of peace and security. The chapter discusses ways in which relevant learning takes place both in the regular curriculum and in such extra-curricular activities as Model United Nations Conferences, which involve both high school and university students. Various efforts by the UN and its specialised agencies to stimulate such education are noted, such as the "United Nations Academic Impact Initiative". The author also points out the dearth both of curricular requirements and of teaching materials suitable for teaching the subject at the pre-university level.

Pływaczewski and Kraśnicka's chapter "Legal Education in Transition: Is the Bologna Process Responding to Europe's Place in the World?" looks into the implications of the Bologna Process (a series of ministerial meetings and agreements between European countries aimed at harmonising the standards and quality of higher education qualifications) for the region and beyond. The authors regret that the Bologna Process is exclusively centred on Europe and has left out from its purview other regions of the world, such as North America. Europe could, for instance, benefit from the US system of legal education, which promotes not only an effective teaching mechanisms but core fundamental principles such as rule of law and human rights. The authors show how the North American approach could be integrated into European legal education, but that also US universities could learn from the Bologna Process.

Stanners ("A Critical Examination of the Contention of the Existence of a Culture Justice Education at the Vienna International School, Austria") deals with international justice education at the secondary level, exemplified by the curriculum choices of the Vienna International School. She explores research on justice and democracy in education in the context of a school which "gives no message of gender differences in any of its approaches or teaching" and asks which of the characteristics identified as being necessary for justice and democracy to be present exist in the school. The author thinks that whilst the curriculum plays a strong part in providing a context in which justice and democracy can be nurtured, this by itself is insufficient to guarantee a culture of justice but that the real key to the presence of such a culture in the school can be found in the relationships that exist between all the stakeholders.

Barberet writes about college-level "Education for Justice: Experiences and Prospects for Further Internationalization". She discusses in her article the internationalisation of criminal justice education in the United States, highlighting the experiences of John Jay College of Criminal Justice (JJC) of the City University of New York (USA), a leader in international criminal justice education. The author reviews the development of the most recent JJC program, the Master of Arts program: its curriculum, faculty, the undergraduate and graduate students it attracts and the prospects of these programs for the future. The chapter then moves on to international curricular initiatives concerning women, crime and criminal justice. It ends with a discussion of why and how nations around the world might encourage similar curricular development and how the work of intergovernmental organisations such as the UN could contribute to such developments as well as benefit from them.

In **Part III "Children/Juveniles and Women as Victims and Offenders"** (18 chapters), *van Dijk* discusses "The Criminal Victimization of Children and Women in International Perspective". The author presents an overview of the results of the national and international victims surveys regarding the distribution of victimisation according to age and gender with a focus on violent crime. The results show a consistent inverse relationship between age and criminal victimisation for all types of crime. The relationship between gender and victimisation is less straightforward. Men are more exposed to various types of non-sexual violence by strangers, including homicide. Cross-national analyses suggest that violence by intimates against females is most prevalent in countries where gender equality is low. However, self-reported victimisation rates of violence against women by intimates are also relatively high in countries where gender equality is the highest, such as in the Scandinavian countries, presumably because of increased sensitivity to acts of lesser violence among female respondents in those countries. The author ends on a practical note, recommending the expansion of special services for female victims of domestic violence and the provision of similar services tailored to the needs of male victims.

Lappi-Seppälä and Lehti analyse "Global Homicide Mortality Trends by Gender 1950–2010". Historical data series show that the higher the level of violence, the smaller the share of female victims and perpetrators. This chapter tests the current differences in male and female homicide mortality levels with the most extensive available data today. In spite of various differences between male and female homicide mortality, the authors find that social control and economic factors have very similar effects on lethal violence regardless of the gender of victims: High male and female homicide mortality rates as well as female/male homicide ratio correlate with the same socio-economic factors and in almost an equal manner. Increasing gender equality seems to increase the *relative* homicide victimisation risk for women. This is due to the fact that gender equality seems to go along with general welfare indicators, which reduce all types of lethal violence in society; male victimisation decreases in this case even faster than female victimisation. The authors conclude that well-governed, legitimate and prosperous democracies are safe—and equal—societies.

Schröttle and Vogt ("Women as Victims and Perpetrators of Violence: Empirical Results from National and International Quantitative Violence Research") discuss empirical findings on the extent, causes and consequences of violence against women from national and international empirical research. These studies show that if women are victims of physical, sexual and/or psychological violence, it is most often a case of domestic violence by intimate partners. The two authors evaluate the value and effectiveness, as well as the limitations, of violence prevalence studies from a methodological and gender-critical perspective. They conclude that there is still a lack of empirically well-founded analyses that focus on the construction and deconstruction of violence, gender, disability, migration and other aspects. In this respect, a targeted expansion of qualitative research, which would also aim at deepening representative quantitative violence prevalence studies, would be a great gain, in order to be able to better portray contexts of occurrence and causality, as well as the significance of violence.

Lysova presents data about "Victims but also Perpetrators: Women's Experience of Partner Violence". The chapter opens with an analysis of major negative health consequences of partner violence (PV) for women around the world: homicide, suicide, injury, antenatal and postnatal mental disorders and HIV/AIDS. The author then reports on studies analysing why women themselves become active participants in PV. The author concludes that because a "one size fits all" approach does not seem to work for addressing such a complex and multidimensional phenomenon as PV, carefully tailored interventions at various levels for different types of violence and violent types/incidents should be considered. Integrating attention to the dynamics of partner violence with elements of the "violence against women" framework would allow global research to recognise and give voice to women's diverse experiences of partner violence, help reveal its intrinsic, interactional nature and, as a result, promote a more effective approach to crime prevention at the international and domestic level.

Alvazzi del Frate in her text "A Reflection on Women, Girls and Armed Violence" discusses aspects of (lethal) violence against women and girls, with special emphasis on firearm violence. The author presents international data on armed violence against women and girls in different settings. Although there is a correlation between high levels of violence and high numbers of females killed, most of the violent deaths of women and girls occur in settings where there is no declared armed conflict. Whether firearms are used in fatal killings very much depends on the ease of access to such weapons. In conclusion, the author express the hope that the UN Sustainable Development Goals and recent developments in the policy and research agendas on ending violence against women may represent a unique opportunity for a more effective prevention and reduction of many forms of violence impacting on women and girls, including firearm violence.

Nikolic-Ristanovic and Stevkovic's chapter "Women and Children as Victims and Offenders: The Impact of Armed Conflict and Post-conflict Period Challenges" assess the role played by the State, civil society and international actors concerning domestic violence and trafficking in persons in the aftermath of armed conflict. The brutalisation effect of war on crime lasts longer than the war itself, as the factors that drive up crime during armed conflicts continue in the post-war period. Once violence has been legitimised by war and the settling of interpersonal differences by force, these attitudes carry over to the period immediately after. After describing in detail the Serbian experience concerning the victimisation of women and children during the war (1991–1999), the authors acknowledge many important changes in post-war Serbia but note that the lack of timely and adequate protection and support of victims during the war has still not been remedied. They recommend therefore shifting the attention of scholars and policymakers from treating victimisation and offending of women and children merely as a legal problem to that of a social problem.

In their chapter "A Biopsychosocial Model of Female Criminality: Implications for Assessment and Evidence-Based Treatment Approaches", *Peper, Krammer and Klecha* present their cross-disciplinary research findings on offending behaviour by women and indicate how the complex factors underlying female criminality could be integrated in a multilevel model. For this purpose, the authors interlink clinical and other criminological information with recent results from the cognitive, social and affective neurosciences. In the opinion of the authors, because of the anthropological and biological antecedents of early criminology, the contemporary way of dealing with a biopsychosocial model of female criminality may be still short of taking their new approach into account, and it is hence unable to contribute to that multilevel model.

Chesney-Lind and Hadi discuss the important topic of "Criminalizing Women: Global Strategies for Denying Female Victimization". Their chapter opens with the staggering statistics that nearly one-third of the world's female population will become victims of violence and not only that, in many cases, they will also be blamed for it. The authors address the problem of victim blaming from four angles: the merging of religion and law to criminalise female sexuality and sexual expression, the demonisation and sexualisation of "enemy" women as a justification for mass rape in wartime, the criminalisation of reproductive rights and the use of courts to punish victims of sexual abuse who run away from their abusers. The authors suggest that the pattern of criminalising women and girls' victimisation requires both research to document and action to challenge the "legal" abuse of women and enforcement of patriarchal privilege. They try to establish that there is a direct interface between women's victimisations globally and systems that both punish the victim and avoid punishing the assailants.

Krahé addresses a related topic, "Societal Responses to Sexual Violence Against Women: Rape Myths and the 'Real Rape' Stereotype", from a socio-psychological perspective. Her chapter examines the role of stereotypes and myths about rape in understanding societal responses to victims of sexual violence. She notes that there is a widely shared stereotype of the "real rape" that is squarely at odds with the reality of the sexual victimisation of women yet serves to inform the social perception of victims and their credibility. After presenting prevalence rates of sexual assault worldwide, the author analyses the attrition process from the initial police investigation to eventual court proceedings and a verdict. She provides strong evidence of the impact of rape myths and stereotypes on the handling of rape complaints and concludes with a review of potential strategies for challenging rape myths and stereotypes and reducing their influence in the criminal justice system.

Pakzad and Alipour write from an Iranian perspective about "Justice and Family Issues in the Shiite: Confronting with the Domestic Violence in Shiite Communities". The authors incisively discuss domestic violence against children and women in Shia communities and point out the great differences that exist across the Muslim world. Looking at the various approaches of Islamic sects makes it clear that religion is not inflexible in the face of social changes, or regional and cultural components. Since family issues in the Shia tradition depend on a dynamic jurisprudence, some jurisprudents have attempted to interpret religious laws in an up-to-date manner and have brought about legal changes improving the status of women, such as giving women preference over men as primary caretakers of children or introducing sanctions for the ill-treatment of women by men. The chapter also deals with women as offenders, in particular with women who consider it their right to use violence themselves and justify such acts in the light of religion and regional cultures.

Asli and Amrollahi Byouki, also Iranian academics, comment on "Forced Marriage in Islamic Countries: The Role of Violence in Family Relationships". In their chapter, the authors make a clear argument for equality of women and men by contending the custom of forced marriage that deprives both sexes of their fundamental rights and in the case of women often leads to their victimisation. The authors point out that forced marriages have been a persistent issue in most societies, not only in Islamic countries, and have more to do with customs and traditions than with religious rules. In order suggest to eradicate this tradition, Islamic countries must insist that the religious ordinances prohibiting this kind of marriage are followed, fulfil their international obligations in terms of proper legislations for proscribing forced marriage and use the mass media and all public and private resources to raise public awareness about its harmful effects.

Bokil and Raghwawan discuss "The Case of De-notified Tribes in India". Their text renews our interest in the fate of "Indian criminal tribes" under the British colonial rule, the study of which provides material for the social learning theory of criminal behaviour through the intergenerational transmission of values. The two authors review the history of British legislation regulating the conduct of those tribes and point out the incorrect colonial understanding of the Indian caste system. This lack of understanding led to the marginalisation and social exclusion of the de-notified tribes (DNTs) and their eventual de-citizenship and criminalisation. Women and children had to bear the brunt of this process, in terms of institutional and structural violence—poor access to food security, education, healthcare, social protection and justice delivery. The authors argue that the vicious circle forcing the DNTs to remain in the criminal nexus can still be broken through concerted efforts by the state, community associations and individual members of DNTs, and civil society.

Klaus, Rzeplińska and Woźniakowska-Fajst describe "Victimization and Delinquency of Minors in Central-European Countries". The authors note that despite the considerable differences among the individual countries, Central Europe still takes a fairly patronising and paternalistic approach to children. Their research takes a closer look at the situation in Hungary, Poland and the Czech Republic—three former post-socialist countries that have a great deal in common, both from a historical and a socio-economic perspective. The Czech Republic has the fewest juvenile issues, whilst Hungary has the highest level of crime in the region. Hungary, Poland and the Czech Republic also differ in their juvenile justice systems and the ideology underpinning their response to juvenile offences. The authors conclude their chapter by emphasising that Poland, Hungary, and the Czech Republic have been continually striving for higher standards of caring for children and protecting their rights at every stage of criminal trials in the 25 years or more that have elapsed since these countries set out on the road to democracy and during their 10 years as EU members.

Selmini's chapter examines "Sexual Abuse of Children in Comparative and International Perspective". Child sexual abuse (CSA) is a chronic problem that can occur in any family or any country. In recent times, it has increasingly become a priority topic of the European Union, the UN and other intergovernmental and non-governmental organisations. Scholars have also given CSA greater attention, even though more at clinical case study than at policy levels. The author analyses national and international quantitative violence studies which show that if women are the victims of physical, sexual and/or psychological violence, it is most often a case of domestic violence by intimate partners—in contrast to men, who are more often victims of violence in public spaces at the hands of persons known or unknown to them. Both women and men are primarily victims of violence by male perpetrators. Women comparatively rarely act as perpetrators of severe violence.

Kangaspunta, Sarrica and Johansen report on "Trafficking in Persons: The Involvement of Women and Children" from the perspective of the UN "Global Report on Trafficking in Persons". The authors analyse the global dynamics and patterns of trafficking in persons, especially of women and children, who are disproportionately involved, both as victims and as offenders. Women comprise a majority of the detected trafficking victims, but women are also prosecuted and convicted of trafficking in persons in a far larger proportion than for nearly any other crime. Children are frequently victims. The authors draw particularly on findings from the 2012 "Global Report on Trafficking in Persons" and examine some of the patterns of trafficking in persons as detected and reported by countries worldwide. They report that the share of women has somewhat declined during the last years. At the same time, the share of detected girl victims has increased which could indicate that the traffickers are turning to the exploitation of younger victims.

Shirwadkar's chapter "Exploring Hidden Spaces: Sexual Abuse of Girl Children in India" describes different aspects of sexual abuse of girls, focusing largely on an Indian context. In spite of progress and new opportunities of education, social and structural divides, traditional cultural practices and gender inequality are some factors that make girl children particularly vulnerable and easy victims for sexual abuse. The measures taken by the state to control this danger as well as the limitations to address the issue are discussed in the context of the changing social situation in India. The author analyses the different factors underlying the sexual abuse of children and stresses the need to strengthen the effort to improve education and awareness and make every possible effort to control the threat.

In "Sexual Abuse Within the Family: The Intergenerational Transmission of Victimhood and Offending", *Bijleveld, Hill and Hendriks* address a related topic in a European context. Their chapter provides an overview of research carried out on 185 juvenile male sex offenders who received treatment in a residential centre in the Netherlands. In their study, the authors examined both the offenders' and their parents' history of sexual abuse. Specifically they tested hypotheses relating to the mechanisms linking offender and victim status in cases of sexual abuse within families, i.e. intra-familial abuse. Their findings offer support for the theory of social learning of sexual abuse. Juvenile sex offenders either from families where intra-familial abuse has occurred or who have a father with a history of sexual abuse against children occurring during their childhood have an increased risk of abusing children themselves. Also juvenile sex offenders who themselves have been the victim of intra-familial abuse, or who have a sibling that has suffered intra-familial abuse, have an increased risk of committing such an offence themselves.

In his chapter "'Violence Against Children Sells Very Well'. Reporting Crime in the Media and Attitudes to Punishment", *Hestermann* critically evaluates the role of the media in crime reporting. In order to reach a wide audience, the media stir up emotions, especially sympathy with the victim and fear of violence. Whilst children generate a lot of attention as victims of violence, whilst older people are ignored. The more dramatic a crime, the more closely associated it is with sexual violence, the greater the chance of its being presented in detail. The media contrasts a dark image of the perpetrator ("real scum") with a bright iconic image of an idealised victim, preferably childlike and female. Against the background of international findings from Brazil, Colombia, India, Spain and USA, the author finds this dichotomy corroborated by the results of his research in Germany. The contrast between the villain and the innocent victim facilitates the calls for tough sentencing. In effect, politicians come under pressure to introduce stiffer penalties—not as a reaction to a real increase in criminality but as a reaction to assumptions about criminality fed by the media.

Part IV "The Role of Crime Prevention: Punishment–Imprisonment–Alternative Sanctions" opens with a chapter by *Hermann and Dölling*, "General Prevention: Does It Work?" To answer this question the authors present the results of a meta-analysis of 700 international empirical studies on negative general prevention with more than 7800 effect estimates. The questions asked were two in particular: whether deterrent effects are dependent on the age of the target group and whether they also depend on the type of offence. The results vary, depending on the econometric or criminological approach taken to measure those effects. If an economic theory of behaviour is used, the deterrence hypothesis is refuted less often than with a recourse to criminological-sociological theories. The deterrent effects are also confirmed relatively rarely for young people, and they vary depending on the offence. In the light of their very comprehensive research, the authors conclude that "A high discovery probability and consistent prosecution of crimes are more important than severe punishment". This conclusion us shared by the UN penal policy recommendations.

Zapatero's chapter deals with "Actors, Factors and Processes on the Road to the Abolition of the Death Penalty". He addresses the degree of compliance with two UN initiatives: the 2000–2015 Millennium Development Goals (MDGs) and the 2007 General Assembly resolution calling for a universal moratorium on the application of the death penalty. The author sees both UN initiatives as the product of political and academic work of people who have a leading role in the life of the organisation as diplomats, staff members, experts and members of non-governmental organisations that construct a cultural and political heritage of humanity. The author vigorously supports the objective of the eventual abolition of death penalty, stipulated in Art. 6 para. 6 of the International Covenant on Civil and Political Rights. Through Zapatero's contribution we learn that in genuinely inclusive societies, someone's exclusion by the death penalty is not an option. His text supports the further expansion and implementation of the right to life.

Huber in her chapter "Women Prisoners: Women in Criminal Justice Systems and the Added Value of the UN Bangkok Rules", ask various questions. For instance, do prosecutors and judges deal more leniently with female offenders? Should prison conditions, treatment in detention and rehabilitation programmes be equal for all prisoners, and aren't they in correctional facilities nowadays anyway? Her answers outline aspects of discrimination faced by female suspects, defendants and prisoners in criminal justice systems, their number, profile and characteristics, and the offences they are typically charged with or convicted for. The chapter covers key conditions in detention as well as programmes in place with regard to rehabilitation and reintegration. In doing so, it draws on data, country examples and findings from a number of research studies. The findings show that there are usually fewer educational and training opportunities for women and those that are available are less varied and of poorer quality than those offered to male detainees. She concludes that women undeniably face discrimination in the criminal justice system, mirroring discrimination in society as a whole.

Beichner and Hagemann write about "Incarcerated Women: Their Situation, Their Needs and Measures for Sustainable Reintegration". Their chapter centres on incarcerated women offenders worldwide, their experiences, specific problems and needs, as well as correctional programmes intended to help them reintegrate back into society. It provides a theoretical understanding of the general marginalisation of women in almost every modern society and an overview of theories that have been developed to explain why women commit offences. Next, the authors provide statistical information on the prevalence of women prisoners in various parts of the world and the ways in which policy changes in the war on drugs and mandatory sentencing have impacted women's incarceration rates. The chapter then explores the gender-specific differences in women's pathways to prison and their distinct problems and needs, including the detrimental effects of mothers' incarceration on children. Based on experiences of several countries, the authors conclude with suggestions for promising approaches that involve sustainable reintegration.

Gelsthorpe and Durnescu discuss "Probation Supervision for Women and Young Offenders". The authors note that ever since the question of probation has entered the international arena through the Eighth International Penitentiary Congress in Washington, DC (1910), the topic of probation supervision for women and young offenders can be located in a number of theoretical and practice contexts. The focus in this chapter is on the risk/need/responsivity model (RNR): the intensity of the intervention should match the level of risk; interventions should target so-called criminogenic needs such as antisocial attitudes, antisocial cognition, antisocial associates, substance abuse, etc. and, finally, the programme delivery has to be in a style and mode that is consistent with the learning and the ability of the offender. The authors recall in this context the United Nations Rules on the Treatment of Women Offenders and Prisoners and conclude that there is emerging evidence that provision for women offenders in the community should be even more gender-oriented, i.e. on women only.

In her chapter "Release Management for Female and Juvenile Prisoners. How Important Is Release Management in Prison for Crime Prevention?" *Pruin,* in looking for answer to this question, first takes a closer look at the recommendations and results from the debate on prisoner "resettlement" that pertain to pre-release preparation, how these recommendations have been put into practice, and whether we can identify good or promising practices in the literature. Among the most important legal instruments the author lists the United Nations Standard Minimum Rules for the Treatment of Prisoners ("The Mandela Rules") and the Convention on the Rights of the Child. Her findings suggest that the use of open institutions and of strategies that allow women and juveniles to leave the prison temporarily has not yet reached satisfactory levels. Also the provision of gender-specific education, vocational training and work opportunities is greatly lacking in Europe. The author concludes that research does not paint a particularly satisfying picture of release management for women and juveniles, but that there are a number of promising approaches worth monitoring.

Allen analyses "The Impact of Sanctions on Child and Female Offenders". The author notes that meeting basic practical needs in prisons remains crucial. Research on young offenders has shown that supervisors in whatever setting are effective if they are clear about their role show positive social values and behaviour themselves and are prepared to challenge the young persons consistently and fairly about their delinquency. Effectiveness is also enhanced if offenders are helped with problems, which they themselves identify, particularly if these are related to their offending. Tackling substance misuse, lack of employment and damaging relationships with family and peers may be particularly important. Similar factors are likely to be significant for women too. The inappropriateness of custodial sentences for juveniles and women is increasingly recognised, but developing the legal framework, policy and practice, which can reduce and ultimately eliminate its use, has proved difficult in a social climate which places a greater value on punishment than is justified by evidence.

A team of NGOs, *Robertson, Christmann, Sharratt, Manby, Ayre, Berman, Foca, Asiminei, Philbrick, Koivumaa and Garvriluta* write about "Children of Prisoners: Their Situation and Role in Long-Term Crime Prevention". They review an innovative EU-funded project that addresses the distress caused by a parent's imprisonment and the reaction of others to it (especially if it is stigmatising—"your dad's a criminal"). Such responses can result in the children becoming isolated, angry and/or scared, and in some cases developing physical or mental health problems. Studies suggest that whilst parental imprisonment can increase a child's likelihood to offend, positive responses to the situation can aid the children's well-being, attitudes and attainment. Drawing on findings from the project, the chapter explores the factors that help a child to cope with parental imprisonment and the actions that different stakeholders can take to strengthen such factors. It identifies some of the mental health impacts at different stages of parental imprisonment, the roles played by non-imprisoned parents/carers and by schools, and suggests options for further clarifying the factors that help and hinder children of prisoners in the short and long term.

Wemmers and Cyr discuss "Gender and Victims' Expectations Regarding Their Role in Criminal Justice System: Towards Victim-Centred Prosecutorial Policies". These policies include therapeutic jurisprudence—an interdisciplinary approach to law that to study the extent to which legal rules, procedures or practice promote the psychological well-being of the people it affects. Law is a tool and people who engage the criminal justice system do so for a reason. Against a historical background depicting the various ways in which victims are involved in pursuing justice, the authors examine the extent to which current legal procedures meet victims' expectations. Following a discussion of recent international policy developments regarding victims of crime and victims of violence against women in particular, the authors consider how victims' relationship with the offender affects their expectations, including the awareness of possible future victimisation.

Kury discusses in his chapter "Mediation, Restorative Justice and the Social Integration of Offenders: The Effects of Alternative Sanctions on Punishment" the background and development of alternatives to "classical" criminal sanctions. Whereas in traditional societies procedures like victim-offender-reconciliation were common, in modern societies criminal justice, and with it the punishment of the offender, has been taken over by the State. Compensation that formerly was given to the victim is now collected by the state in the form of fines, and the victim is left on the sidelines. Criminological research during the last decades has increasingly shown that victims are more interested in restitution than in harsh punishment of the offenders. This has revived in many countries a discussion about alternatives to punishment. Empirical results show that mediation is not only more successful in re-establishing social peace but also much cheaper than the classical handling of crime.

Dandurand's chapter "Alternative Approaches to Preventing Recidivism: Restorative Justice and the Social Reintegration of Offenders" reviews the original promises of the restorative justice approach as an alternative to the conventional criminal justice response to juvenile crime and seeks to recast mediation and restorative justice programmes as a form of reconciliation between the juvenile offender and the community and a frequent prerequisite to the offender's successful social reintegration. The author emphasises that very few restorative justice elements have been integrated systematically into community-based sentences or into post-release programmes and the capacity of existing restorative justice programmes to achieve social reintegration objectives tends to be quite limited. Some good practices have been identified, but they need to be both better understood and more systematically evaluated. Proponents of restorative justice typically deplore the lack of progress in implementing restorative justice within the juvenile justice system and will continue to do so unless new ways are found to develop restorative justice's full potential in contributing to the social reintegration of offenders.

Hamilton and Yarrow write about "Preventing and Addressing Youth Offending: Restorative Justice and Family Focused Programming". They remind us that "the primary purpose of restorative justice is just that – to restore justice", i.e. the purpose stated by the United Nations Special Representative of the Secretary-General on Violence Against Children, who also provided the Foreword to this volume. This purpose is already reflected in the 1989 Convention on the Rights of the Child, which stipulates that children who come into conflict with the law should be treated in a manner which promotes their own dignity and worth as well as their understanding of the rights and freedoms of others. Restorative justice has, however, limitations. The authors point out that restorative mechanisms often prioritise healing and reparation for victims over addressing the root causes of child offending. They conclude that restorative justice mechanisms may be most valuable where they complement, rather than replace the work done by a wide range of social agencies tackling the risk factors associated with child offending.

Ehret, Szego and Dhondt add to the restorative justice paradigm their own expertise in "Peacemaking Circles, Their Restorative and Crime Prevention Capacities for Women and Children: Insights from a European Pilot Study". Peacemaking circles are a restorative justice approach to conflict resolution that is inclusive and non-hierarchical with long historical roots in indigenous cultures going back to their so-called talking circles. Particularly, the circle traditions of First Nation people of Canada have been further developed for dealing with crime and have spread across the border to the Northern USA, Hawaii and as far as Australia. These traditions aim to repair the harm done by crime through focusing on the effects crime has on relationships between victims, offenders, their families and their communities. The authors emphasise that it is this primary focus that requires a substantially different response to crime by moving away from the adversarial "win or lose" logic of the traditional distributive justice system towards a "win-win" approach aimed at restoring societal peace through the means of dialogue, conflict resolution, amends or redress.

In **Part V "Crime Prevention: Proactive Strategies"** (ten chapters), *Walsh* discusses "Justice, Faith and Interfaith: The Relevance of Faith and Interfaith Relations to Crime Prevention". The chapter opens with an estimate: of the seven billion people living on this earth, the majority identify themselves as belonging to a particular religious tradition, such as Christianity, Judaism, Islam, Hinduism, Buddhism, indigenous traditions, and others. With a global resurgence of religion, along with an increase in religious plurality in many societies, the author sees the growing awareness of religion as a significant factor—sometimes positive, sometimes negative—in the lives of individuals, families, societies and nations. Consequently, we also need an increased awareness of religion as it functions in society and its potential impact on justice. In the latter context, this chapter explores the relevance of religion in particular for crime prevention.

Corrado, Peters, Hodgkinson and Mathesius comment on "Crime Reduction, Reduction of Imprisonment and Community Crime Prevention Programs: Risk Factors and Programs Implemented to Reduce Them". The chapter reviews the general research on this subject focussing on three topics: (1) the typical victim profile, (2) factors associated with serious/violent young offending and victimisation and their distinct developmental pathways and (3) key examples of current intervention programmes that have successfully reduced serious/violent youth offending and victimisation. The authors conclude that treatment interventions will accelerate with breakthroughs in brain imaging technology, which will identify more completely the neurological bases for serious offending. Therapeutic interventions will include pharmacological approaches to target aggression/violence. More controversial therapies may regard stem cell breakthroughs concerning neurologically based disorders related to serious violence.

Lee's chapter "Evaluating Children and Adolescents in Contact with the Justice System" focusses on developmentally sensitive, evidence-based instruments and approaches for evaluating child and adolescent offenders and victims. The author first addresses the assessment of adolescent offenders, with the main emphasis on tools designed to measure risks and needs. Secondly, she looks at the evaluation of child victims, with a focus on investigative interviewing. Once developmentally appropriate, evidence-based instruments and approaches have been established; an important next step is to illustrate whether their use contributes to changes in policy and practice. This is arguably the ideal standard for assessing whether science translates meaningfully into practice to encourage the transformation of the juvenile justice system into a system that applies a developmental framework to all decisions.

Alex and Feltes analyse "The Problem of Risk Assessment: Can Better Crime Prognosis Reduce Recidivism?" They note that every society has to face the fact that there is a very small group of people who do not respect elementary rules of human behaviour and who repeatedly commit very serious violent crimes. But how do we know who belongs to this group and who does not? In order to find answer to this question, the authors review recidivism studies and conclude that the task of assessing the probability of serious re-offending is very difficult, and the risk of erring on the side of caution (false negatives) real. Given the fact that it will hardly ever be possible to predict human behaviour with complete certainty, Alex and Feltes recommend that other means than unlimited imprisonment of offenders labelled as very dangerous be used to manage the problem of crime prevention in a way that considers both human rights' aspects as well as public needs.

Redo writes about "Anti-corruption Education as a Form of Early Prevention of Conflict with the Law for Women and Children: Making the United Nations Law Work 2016–2030". He does so from three perspectives (Western, Eastern and UN) by reviewing some recent measures reported by the State Parties to the 2003 United Nations Convention against Corruption. The author argues that the UN anti-corruption education for women and children is a promising path to follow. In his view, against the intercultural background of anti-corruption challenges, two educational issues may decide about the character and effectiveness of an anti-corruption strategy: the prevalence of patriarchal or contractual features in any legal culture and its accommodation of the sustainable development ideology provided that both engage personal responsibility. The implementation of the UN goal of "peaceful and inclusive societies" in which countering bribery and corruption is included will depend on how well in contractual and sustainable development terms the present and succeeding generation will muster anti-corruption ethical education for women and children.

Beier's chapter "Proactive Strategies to Prevent Child Sexual Abuse and the Use of Child Abusive Images: Experiences from the German Dunkelfeld Project" describes proactive strategies used in Germany to protect children from sexual exploitation though online offences and from direct sexual abuse. These strategies include research on individuals at risk to commit first or persistent sexual offences against children, at the same time offering preventive assessment and treatment. As many offenders in this category remain undetected by legal authorities in the "*Dunkelfeld*" (literally "dark field"), this program focusses on those who admit a longstanding sexual interest in prepubescent and/or pubescent children, self-motivated by the distress experienced due to their sexual preference. The author shows that these people are reachable as long as they can rely on the professional pledge of confidentiality. Public Health Services have then a real chance of encouraging the concerned persons to seek professional help before any kind of sexual offences against children are committed.

Wößner's chapter deals with "Women and Children as Victims of Sex Offences: Crime Prevention by Treating the Offenders?" The author provides an overview of the number of sex crimes in comparison to other crimes and discusses how valid these data are given the problem of considerable underreporting. As a measure of victim protection, one of the most important aspects of offender treatment is crime prevention. Given the tremendous traumatising effects sexual victimisation can have on victims, it is undoubtedly justified to do as much as possible to prevent sexual crimes and to respond to sexual violence appropriately. The author discusses in this context treatment programmes for sex offenders and their impact on recidivism. Even if as yet no unambiguous conclusion on the effectiveness of such treatment programmes can be drawn, they should not be abandoned in favour of more punitive solutions. Long-term imprisonment or lifelong detention can only present an alternative for the most dangerous offenders. For less serious offences, a treatment approach may be a better way to protect the victim and at the same time open for the offender a way back into society.

Dobovšek and Slak discuss "Women and Children at the Centre of Preventing Organized Crime". In their chapter, the authors advance the thesis that the emancipation of women is partly responsible for the greater involvement of women in crime (see also *Gao and Liu* in volume 1 in support of this view and for a different assessment *Beichner and Hagemann* in volume 2). But they also acknowledge that in egalitarian societies women are active in business and politics, which opens up new possibilities for their involvement in organised white-collar crime. The authors see education and information as the most important factor for prevention. Yet in the end, it all depends on the integrity of policymakers. The authors recommend that governments should seriously consider imposing that policymakers include criminologists, fraud experts and other social scientists on their staff.

Howell discusses "Systemic Vulnerabilities on the Internet and the Exploitation of Women and Girls: Challenges and Prospects for Global Regulation". The Internet, as a global phenomenon, has increasingly become host to pervasive forms of cybercrime, among them sexual abuse. Women and girls are, often as a result of underlying socio-economic and political disparities, more vulnerable to many of these forms of cybercrime. This is especially true in lower-income countries. The Internet's "new frontier" is the developing world, where its growth has been extraordinary. In this context, the author points out the "uncomfortable truth" that cybercrimes are also committed by women and even children. Using examples drawn from Africa, the author argues that global regulation is both urgent and needed, but that the development of such a framework will continue to be fraught with difficulties and needs to be contextually and strategically specific to the areas and places in which it is applied. As such, these responses, whether domestic or international, will need to draw on the intellectual capital and resources of multiple state and non-state actors, ranging from local police forces to transnational regulatory agencies, including the UN.

Quirchmayr, Buchegger and Gerö write about a related topic: "Protecting Children and Women Against Online Dangers". The authors argue for increasing domestic and international efforts to protect children from online dangers in a rapidly changing technology-driven world. Whilst criminals usually have to make considerable efforts in the real world, the Internet is a prime platform for such activity at comparatively low costs. After briefly describing the current situation and identifying the resulting challenges for education (especially recommending a holistic approach, i.e. involving families, children, schools, crime prevention specialists, and suitable educational material), the authors present a few case studies, introduce one of the leading European-based computer networks dedicated to this task and look at efforts aimed at online protection of female users. The chapter concludes with arguments for a truly international solution, in which the involvement of many partners, local/domestic and interstate (e.g. Council of Europe and the UN), is essential. At the same time, it is essential to empower children and young people to use the Internet safely.

In **Part VI "Final Discussion"** (seven chapters) *Zhang* writes from a Chinese perspective about "The United Nations, Equal and Inclusive Society and Crime Prevention: Chinese Philosophical Contributions to the Idea of Sustainable Development for Women and Children, and the Current Practice in China". Her chapter takes the reader into another legal culture (see also *Reichel and Albanese* below) and points out the great difference between Chinese and Western legal thought in terms of concepts and methods for dealing with the question of crime prevention for women and children. In Western criminology very little is known in this regard. Recalling Lawrence Sherman's saying that for the practitioners of crime prevention it should not only be an art, but also a science, her article highlights the relevant connotations of sustainable development in traditional Chinese philosophy. With a few strokes the author paints the richness of that philosophy in which Confucian thought already anticipated some of the United Nation's ideas on inclusive and equitable education and on gender equality.

Platzer contributes "Some Insights on the Rights to a Safe City of Women and Girls". He shows the need for such rights by giving the example of gang rapes in India, the murder of "streetwalkers" in the Americas or the kidnapping, trafficking and enslavement of girls in Africa and the Middle East. He then puts those examples in the context of a draft UN sustainable development Goal 11.7 that reads: "by 2030, provide universal access to safe, inclusive and accessible, green and public spaces, particularly for women and children, older persons and persons with disabilities" (A/68/970, p. 18/24). Yet so far, the rights of women and girls to safe cities have been painfully slow to be recognised. By bringing the policies of city officials and the urban planning concerns of adolescent girls together, this can create a real opportunity to create sustainable economic and social change that will benefit all. This means the provision of adequate, safe and affordable housing and infrastructure, but more than that, access to good education, health, transport, human development and social and recreational services. But most importantly, it should involve making cities safe.

Shaw's chapter "Women as Actors in Community Safety: Taking Action Worldwide" approaches the topic of safety from a different angle. The author notes that it has been customary to refer to women's involvement in the criminal justice system and in the field of crime prevention as either victims or offenders, or sometimes as professionals, but that it is much less common to think of the role, which women and girls themselves play in actively promoting safer cities or preventing the violence and crime, which affects them because of their gender. Yet an increasing number of women do assume this role, as demonstrated by the author through concrete examples of such "hands-on" women's participatory approaches in crime prevention, and how they are helping to increase the role of women and girls in decision-making, especially at the local level. The importance of this movement is helping to change policies, attitudes and behaviours towards women and girls in both public and private spaces. The final section of the chapter reflects on the ways in which the Doha Declaration of the Thirteenth United Nations Congress on Crime Prevention and Criminal Justice (12–19 April 2015) aims to strengthen and support this work.

Dünkel discusses "Juvenile Justice and Human Rights: European Perspectives". He underlines that international human rights standards and in particular the Convention on the Rights of the Child (CRC) have had a major impact on juvenile justice reforms in Europe during the last 25 years. The general orientation towards the ideal of education has further been developed in Europe. The development of human rights standards has played a major role in this context. The UN 1985 Beijing-Rules on juvenile justice administration and the CRC have been landmarks in the juvenile justice human rights movement. This chapter evaluates youth justice policies and practice in Europe from a comparative perspective. The focus is on tendencies in youth justice legislation and on the sentencing practice of prosecutors and judges in youth courts. The chapter explains why continental European countries generally have succeeded in resisting "penal populism" in youth crime.

Mitrofanenko writes about "Intergenerational Practice: An Approach to Implementing Sustainable Development and Environmental Justice". She observes that "sustainable development" is a concept hardly pursued in criminal justice, even less so when it comes to the respective role of women and children. The concept is also only nascent in crime prevention, but the elaboration of the post-2015 UN sustainable development agenda may fundamentally change this picture. In line with this agenda, the chapter introduces the idea of intergenerational practice (IP) as a way to operationalise sustainable development and environmental justice (EJ) principles on the local level. Mitrofanenko emphasises that younger people living today are the link between the current and the future society. Yet different generations living today do not always enjoy equitable access to resources and opportunities to engage in the development process. IP has been shown to equalise that access, enhance community cohesion, improve understanding among the younger and older population and diminish the fear of crime in communities.

Breczko and Oliwniak write from a Polish perspective about "Biopolitics, Ethics and the Culture of Lawfulness. Implications for the Next Generation?" Europe is ageing faster than any other continent. The regional demographic crisis and the replacement of generations are currently among the problems most frequently discussed on this continent. This chapter describes the process of the formation of pastoral biopower (Foucault's concept of biopolitics) within the framework of the European culture of lawfulness. It shows how the schools of pronatalism, antinatalism and environmental ethics have shaped the policies of European countries with regard to procreation, as well as people's behaviours in that area. It also describes how demographic policy has evolved under the influence of progress in biotechnology. There is a failure of replacement of generations—successive generations are found to be less populous than the preceding ones; hence the interregionally emanating culture of lawfulness will not be sustained in future.

The authors bring to this volume important philosophical considerations broadening the concept of succeeding generations by including in it humankind's natural environment.

Finally, *Reichel and Albanese* write about "Comparing and Delivering Juvenile Justice Across the World". Their chapter offers a brief historical review of the question of recognition of childhood as an innocent life period followed by a discussion of the nature of formal procedures for handling juvenile offenders and specific governmental and multilateral responses to juvenile delinquency. The chapter considers the variation in attitudes and approaches used over time and place when governments respond to misbehaving young people. The similarities and differences among these approaches are evaluated to assess their contribution to fairness, justice, crime control and delinquency prevention. The authors conclude that the promise of justice for juveniles has not yet been met. Despite international consensus codified in important and universally acclaimed international agreements, the implementation of indicators and procedures to ensure justice for juveniles has lagged, largely because of a shortage of resources. The authors stress the importance to keep the attention focussed on the problem to avoid belated reactions to grave incidents, violence and crises in juvenile justice.

The work closes with the editors following up on the closing statement by H.E. Ambassador *Martin Sajdik*, 70th President of the United Nations Economic and Social Council tasked with the elaboration of the 2016–2030 sustainable development goals for the world. We complement his statement with our Post Scriptum that stresses the need for education in order to arrive at a culture of lawfulness that mirror the United Nations crime prevention and criminal justice values emanating from the United Nations Charter.

Given the size of this collective work, it is published in two separate volumes, each containing the preface, introduction, conclusions and the full index of the work. The editors would like to thank first and foremost all the authors for bearing with us through the long editorial process and attending to our many queries on points of detail. Without their fruitful and interesting cooperation, it would have been impossible to edit this collective work on a very important topic. We also thank the publisher, Springer, and especially Ms. Seyfried for their excellent advice and prompt and efficient publication.

Freiburg, Germany Helmut Kury
Wien, Austria Sławomir Redo
Zürich, Switzerland Evelyn Shea
August 2015

References

A/CONF.151/26 (Vol. I) Report of the United Nations Conference on Environment and Development (Rio de Janeiro, 3–14 June 1992).

A/CONF.222/L.6 Draft Doha Declaration on integrating crime prevention and criminal justice into the wider United Nations agenda to address social and economic challenges and to promote the rule of law at the national and international levels, and public participation, Therteent United Nations Congress on Crime Prevention and Criminal Justice (Doha, Qatar, 12–19 April 2015).
A/RES/45/112 (Annex) United Nations Guidelines for the Prevention of Juvenile Delinquency (The Riyadh Guidelines), 14 December 1990.
A/68/970 Report of the Open Working Group of the General Assembly on Sustainable Development Goals, 12 August 2014.
Acemoglu, D. (2012). *The world our grandchildren will inherit: the rights revolution and beyond.* NBER Working Paper No. 17994. http://www.nber.org/papers/w17994
Adler, F. (1975). *Sisters in crime*. New York: McGraw Hill.
Annan, K. (2004). *Letter.* Reprinted in Reuterswaärd CF, Stil aär bedraägeri [Style is Deception]. Vaärnamo: Area.
Austin, J. (2003). Why criminology is irrelevant. *Criminology & Public Policy, 2*, 557–565.
Basu, A. M. (2002). Why does education lead to lower fertility? A Critical review of some of the possibilities. *World Development, 30*(10), 1779–1790.
Behringer, W. (Ed.). (1988). *Hexen und Hexenprozesse in Deutschland.* München: Deutscher Taschenbuch Verlag.
Bloom, P. (2013). *Just babies. The origins of good and evil.* New York: Crown Publishers.
Bowlby, J. (1951). *Maternal care and mental health.* Geneva: World Health Organization.
Brzank, P. (2009). (Häusliche) Gewalt gegen Frauen: sozioökonomische Folgen und gesellschafliche Kosten. *Einführung und Überblick, 52*, 330–338.
Buggle, F. (1992). *Denn sie wissen nicht, was sie glauben. Oder warum man redlicherweise nicht mehr Christ sein kann.* Reinbek b. Hamburg: Rowohlt.
Burman, M., Lovett, J., & Kelly, L. (2009). *Different systems, similar outcomes? Tracking attrition in reported rape cases in eleven countries.* London: Child and Woman Abuse Studies Unit, London Metropolitan University.
BusinessDictionary.Com. http://www.businessdictionary.com/definition/handbook.html
Charter of the United Nations, 1 UNTS 16.
Cohen, J. E. (2003). Human population: the next half century. *Science, 302*, 1172–1175.
Coleman, K., Jansson, K., Kaiza, P., & Reed, E. (2007). *Homicides, firearm offences and intimate violence 2005/6: Supplementary volume 1 to crime in England and Wales 2005/6.* London: Home Office Statistical Bulletin 02/07, Office for National Statistics.
Convention on the Rights of the Child, 1577 UNTS 3.
Cressey, D. R. (Ed.). (1961). *The prison.* New York: Holt, Rinehart and Winston.
Daly, K. (2002). Sexual assault and restorative justice. In H. Strang & J. Braithwaite (Eds.), *Restorative justice and family violence* (pp. 62–88). Cambridge: Cambridge University Press.
Daly, K., & Stubbs, J. (2006). Feminist engagement with restorative justice. *Theoretical Criminology, 10*, 9–28.
ECOSOC resolution 1995/9 (Annex) Guidelines for the prevention of urban crime, 24 July 1995.
ECOSOC resolution 2002/13 (Annex) Guidelines for the Prevention of Crime, 24 July 2002.
Farrington, D. (2002). Developmental criminology and risk-focused prevention. In M. Maguire, R. Morgan, & R. Reiner (Eds.), *The Oxford handbook of criminology* (pp. 657–701). Oxford: Oxford University Press.
Gelsthorpe, L., & Larrauri, E. (2014). Gender and crime in Europe. In S. Body-Gendrot, M. Hough, K. Kerezsi, R. Lévy, & S. Snacken (Eds.), *The Routledge handbook of European criminology* (pp. 188–203). London/New York: Reoutledge.
Grafton, J. (Ed.). (1999). *Great speeches by Franklin Delano Roosevelt.* Mineola, NY: Dover Publications.
Haller, B., & Dawid, E. (2006). *Kosten häuslicher Gewalt in Österreich.* Wien: Institut für Konfliktforschung.

Hausler. K., Urban, N., & McCorqodale, R. (2012). *Protecting education in insecurity and armed conflict: an international law handbook*. London/Doha: British Institute of International and Comparative Law/Education Above All.
Heidensohn, F. (2002). Gender and crime. In M. Maguire, R. Morgan, & R. Reiner (Eds.), *The Oxford handbook of criminology* (pp. 491–530). Oxford: Oxford University Press.
Heidensohn, F. M., & Farrell, M. (Eds.). (1991). *Crime in Europe*. London: Routledge.
Heiskanen, M., & Piispa, M. (2002). *The costs of violence in a municipality. A case study of violence against women and its costs in the city of Hämeenlinna 2001, based on estimates provided by authority representatives*. Helsinki: Ministry of Social Affairs and Health.
Heitmeyer, W., & Schröttle, M. (Eds.). (2006). *Gewalt. Beschreibungen, Analysen, Prävention*. Bonn: Bundeszentrale für politische Bildung.
Hester, M. (2013). Who does what to whom? Gender and domestic violence perpetrators in English police records. *European Journal of Criminology, 10*, 623–637.
Hestermann, T. (2010). *Fernsehgewalt und die Einschaltquote. Welches Publikumsbild Fernsehschaffende leitet, wenn sie über Gewaltkriminalität berichten*. Baden-Baden: Nomos.
Hoffman, M. L. (2000). *Empathy and moral development. Implications for caring and justice Cambridge*. Cambridge: University Press.
Keynes, J. M. (1935). Economic possibilities for our grandchildren. In J. M. Keynes (Ed.), *Essays in persuasion*. London: Macmillan.
Hinckeldey, C., & Kriminalmuseum Rothenburg ob der Tauber (Ed.). (1980). *Strafjustiz in alter Zeit*. Mittelalterliches Kriminalmuseum: Rothenburg ob der Tauber.
Krueger, A. B., & Lindhal, M. (2001). Education for growth: why and for whom? *Journal of Economic Literature, 39*, 1101–1136.
Kury, H. (2003). Wie werden Opfer von Straftaten gesehen? Zur Stigmatisierung von Verbrechensopfern. In S. Lamnek & M. Boatca (Eds.), *Geschlecht – Gewalt – Gesellschaft* (pp. 418–443). Opladen: Leske + Budrich.
Kury, H., & Obergfell-Fuchs, J. (2005). *Gewalt in der Familie. Für und Wider den Platzverweis*. Freiburg: Lambertus.
Lahlah, E., Van der Knaap, L. M., & Bogaerts, S. (2013). Dangerous boys or boys in danger? Esamining the relationship between ethnicity, child abuse and violent offending. *European Journal of Criminology, 10*, 641–658.
Leder, K. B. (1986). *Todesstrafe. Ursprung, Geschichte, Opfer*. München: Deutscher Taschenbuch Verlag.
Lemgruber, J. (2001). Women in the criminal justice system. In N. Ollus & S. Nevala (Eds.), *Women in the criminal justice system: International examples and national responses*. Helsinki: HEUNI.
Levi, M., & Maguire, M. (2002). Violent crime. In M. Maguire, R. Morgan, & R. Reiner (Eds.), *The Oxford handbook of criminology* (pp. 795–843). Oxford: Oxford University Press.
Lewis, H. (2005). Justice from the victim's perspective. *Violence Against Women, 11*, 571–602.
Lundgren, E., Heimer, G., Westerstrand, J., & Kalliokoski, A. (2002). *Captured queen: Men's violence against women in ‚equal Sweden – a prevalence study*. Umea: Astrom trykeri AB.
Matvyshyn, A. M., & Generation, C. (2012). Childhood, code, and creativity. *Notre Dame Law Review, 87*, 9–49.
McCord, J. (1983). A forty year perspective on effects of child abuse and neglect. *Child Abuse and Neglect, 7*, 265–270.
McGee, H., Garavan, R., de Berra, M., Byrne, J., & Conroy, R. (2002). *The SAVI report: Sexual abuse and violence in Ireland. A national study of Irish experiences, beliefs and attitudes concerning sexual violence*. Dublin: Liffey Press. http://epubs.rcsi.ie/psycholre/10/
Medina, J., & Barberet, R. (2003). Intimate partner violence in Spain. *Violence Against Women, 9*, 302–322.
Morris, A., & Gelsthorpe, L. (2000). Revisioning men's violence against female partners. *Howard Journal of Criminal Justice, 39*, 412–428.

Moser, T. (1972). *Jugendkriminalität und Gesellschaftsstruktur. Zum Verhältnis von soziologischen, psychologischen und psychoanalytischen Theorien des Verbrechens*. Frankfurt/M.: Fischer.
Müller, U., & Schröttle, M. (2004). *Lebenssituation, Sicherheit und Gesundheit von Frauen in Deutschland. Eine repräsentative Untersuchung zu Gewalt gegen Frauen in Deutschland.* Bielefeld: Interdisziplinäres Frauenforschungs-Zentrum der Universität Bielefeld. www.bmfsfj.de/BMFSFJ/Service/Publikationen/publikationen,did=20560.html
Newburn, T. (2002). Young people, crime, and youth justice. In M. Maguire, R. Morgan, & R. Reiner (Eds.), *The Oxford handbook of criminology* (pp. 531–578). Oxford: Oxford University Press.
Nora, P. (1997). La génération [Generation]. In P. Nora (Ed.), *Les Lieux de mémoire [Sites of memory]* (Vol. 2, Quarto edition). Paris: Gallimard.
Oxfam. (2015, January). Wealth: Having it all and wanting more. Issue Briefing.
Packalén, S. (2010). Culture and sustainability. *Corporate Social Responsibility and Environmental Management, 17*, 118–121.
Palfrey, J., & Gasser, U. (2009). *Born digital*. New York: Basic Books.
Patkar, P. (2001). Consolidating protection against ever-escalating violation. In N. Ollus & S. Nevala (Eds.), *Women in the criminal justice system: International examples and national responses*. Helsinki: HEUNI.
Redo. (2014). Education for succeeding generations in culture of lawfulness. In E. W. Pływaczewski (Ed.), *Current problems of the penal law and criminology* (pp. 698–722). Warszawa: Wydawnictwo C. H. Beck.
Rodriguez-Menés, J., & Safranoff, A. (2013). Violence against women in intimate relations: a contrast of five theories. *European Journal of Criminology, 10*, 584–603.
S/2004/616 Rule of Law and Transitional Justice in Conflict and Post-Conflict Societies. Report of the Secretary-General to the Security Council, 3 August 2004.
Schlesinger, S. E. (2004). *Act of creation: the founding of the United Nations: A story of superpowers, secret agents, wartime allies and enemies, and their quest for a peaceful world*. Cambridge, MA: Westview, Perseus Books Group.
Simon, R. J. (1975). *Women and crime*. Toronto: Lexington Books.
Smart, C. (1977). *Women, crime and criminology*. London: Routledge and Kegan Paul.
Stamatel, J. P. (2014). Explaining variations in female homicide victimization rates across Europe. *European Journal of Criminology, 11*, 578–600.
ST/ESA/SER.A/313 Department of Economic and Social Affairs, Population Division. (2011). *World population prospects: The 2010 revision, Volume I: Comprehensive tables*. New York: United Nations.
Stubbs, J. (2007). Beyond apology? Domestic violence and critical questions for restorative justice. *Criminology and Criminal Justice, 7*, 169–187.
Suleiman, S. R. (2002). The 1.5 generation: thinking about child survivors and the Holocaust. *American Imago, 59*, 277–295.
Sykes, G. (1956). *Society of captives*. Princeton: Princeton University Press.
UNICEF-Report 2015. (2015). Kinder zwischen den Fronten. Frankfurt/M.: Fischer (http://www.unicef.de/report2015; http://www.unicef.de/presse/2015/unicef-report--jedes-zehnte-kind-waechst-im-krieg-auf/80378; Summary: http://www.unicef.de/blob/80400/54134727140bd27763126edb7360f25f/zusammenfassung-unicef-report-2015-data.pdf)
Walby, S. (2004). *The cost of domestic violence*. London: Women & Equality Unit, National Statistics. www.statistics.gov.uk
Widom, C. S. (1989). The cycle of violence. *Science,* 244, 160–166.
Widom, C. S., & Ames, M. A. (1994). Criminal consequences of childhood sexual victimization. *Child Abuse and Neglect, 18*, 303–318.
Wilson, C. (2004). Fertility below replacement level. *Science, 304*(5668), 207–209.
United Nations. (1945). *Charter of the United Nations*. http://www.un.org/en/documents/charter/preamble.shtml

United Nations Scientific and Cultural Organization. (1997). *International standard classification of education*. Paris: UNESCO.

United Nations Office on Drugs and Crime. (2010). *Handbook on the crime prevention guidelines*. New York: Making them Work, United Nations.

Woźniakowska-Fajst, D. (2015). Criminality and the media. In K. Buczkowski, B. Czarnecka-Dzialuk, W. Klaus, A. Kossowska, I. Rzeplinska, P. Wiktorska, D. Woźniakowska-Fajst, & D. Wójcik (Eds.), *Criminality and criminal justice in contemporary Poland: Sociopolitical perspectives* (pp. 159–169).

Yanay, U., & Borowski, A. (2013). From a court orientation to a victim orientation: the paradigm shift in Israel's Juvenile Probation Service. *European Journal of Criminology*, *10*, 675–689.

Contents of Volume 2

Contents of Volume 1

About the Authors

Jay S. Albanese, Professor of Criminology in the Wilder School of Government and Public Affairs at Virginia Commonwealth University (Richmond, VA, USA). Dr. Albanese served as Chief of the International Center at the National Institute of Justice, the research arm of the U.S. Department of Justice. He has written and edited 17 books, 70 articles and book chapters, and has made keynote and invited presentations in 18 countries. He is recipient of the *Elske Smith Distinguished Lecturer Award* from Virginia Commonwealth University, the *Scholar Award in Criminal Justice* from the Virginia Social Science Association, and the *Gerhard Mueller Award* from the International Section of the Academy of Criminal Justice Sciences. He is a past president and fellow of the Academy of Criminal Justice Sciences. He is currently a member of the Executive Board of the American Society of Criminology.

Dr. Michael Alex, Attorney at Law. He studied law and psychology. His main topics of research/publication are criminal policies and preventive detention. He published several essays on social-therapeutic measures in prison and conducted a study on the legal probation of former prisoners who had been released from prison, although they were still assumed to be very dangerous.

Hassan Alipour, Ph.D. in Criminal Law and Criminology (Shahid Beheshti University, Tehran, Iran, 2009); Assistant Professor of Criminal Law and Criminology at Shahrekord University and Visiting Professor at Isfahan University (Isfahan, Iran). His research interests involve cybercrime, corporate criminal law and national security law. His main articles about family and women issues are: *Women Trafficking: A Crime against Women's Dignity* (2009), *Feminism and Criminology* (2006), *Content-Related Crime*; *the Black Content of Information Technology* (2005).

Charles Robert Mason Allen, Co-Director Justice and Prisons (London, UK); Associate in Penal Reform International; former Director of International Centre for Prison Studies. Main areas of research and publication are youth justice, criminal justice policy, prisons and alternatives to custody. He has authored a number of articles about justice reinvestment and also has an interest in public attitudes to sentencing. He has undertaken assessments of prison systems in various countries and independent investigations into life-threatening incidents of self-harm in UK prisons. He writes a regular blog at http://reformingprisons.blogspot.com/.

Dr. Anna Alvazzi del Frate, Research Director of the *Small Arms Survey* (an independent research project located at the Graduate Institute of International and Development Studies in Geneva, Switzerland) which she joined in 2010, after more than twenty years spent with the United Nations, at UNODC (Vienna, Austria), and earlier at UNICRI (Turin, Italy), and in Angola. A social scientist with vast experience in applied research for evidence-based policymaking, she is a specialist in the application of quantitative and qualitative research methods—especially surveys on crime and violence—in developing and post-conflict settings. Her interests include firearm violence, prevention, monitoring and evaluation, with particular attention to gender aspects.

Mojgan Amrollahi Byouki, Ph.D. Candidate in Criminal Law and Criminology (Albert Ludwigs University, Freiburg im Brsg., Germany). Her research centres on the problems of child abuse and domestic violence; she is an attorney at law, Grade I, Bar Association (Tehran, Iran) and member of the Association for Support of Children against Child Labour.

Dr. Romeo Asiminei, Senior Lecturer, Alexandru Ioan Cuza University of Iaşi (Iaşi, Romania). his main research topics are electoral sociology, political communication and sociological methodology. He is the author of *Electoral Sociology. Elections, Voters and Voting Behavior* (2013) and coauthor of the *Electoral Atlas of Romania 1990 – 2009* (2013).

Dr. Elizabeth V. Ayre, Director of Children of Prisoners Europe (formerly Eurochips), an action research network active in 17 countries across Europe; Research Fellow in European Studies, Maastricht University (Maastricht, The Netherlands). Her research is about policy processes for children affected by parental incarceration in EU Member States from a frame-analytical perspective. Her relevant publications include consultation response to *Strengthening Mutual Trust in the European Judicial Area – a Green Paper on the Application of EU Criminal Justice Legislation in the Field of Detention* (2011); and *Children with Imprisoned Parents: European Perspectives on Good Practice* (co-ed., 2006, 2013), Paris: Eurochips.

Prof. Rosemary Barberet, Professor, (John Jay College of Criminal Justice, City University of New York, New York, NY, USA). She is the Editor of *Feminist Criminology*; author of *Women, Crime and Criminal Justice: A Global Enquiry* (2014); 2014 Recipient of the Distinguished Book Award of the Division of International Criminology, American Society of Criminology; and Recipient of the 2015 Outstanding Book Award, International Section, Academy of Criminal Justice Sciences.

W. Steve Barnett, Ph.D., Director, National Institute for early Educational Research, Board of Governors Professor, Graduate School of Education, Rutgers University (New Brunswick, NJ, USA). His research includes studies of the economics of early care and education including costs and benefits, the long-term effects of preschool programmes on children's learning and development, and the distribution of educational opportunities. His best known works include reviews of the research on long-term effects; benefit-cost analyses of the Perry Preschool and Abecedarian programmes; randomised trials comparing alternative approaches to educating children including length of day, monolingual versus dual-language immersion, the Tools of the Mind curriculum; and the series of State Preschool Yearbooks providing annual state-by-state analyses of progress in public pre-K.

Dawn Beichner, Associate Professor in the Criminal Justice Sciences Department at Illinois State University Normal, Ill, USA; she is a core faculty member in Women's and Gender Studies at that university. She is also a co-director of Peace and Conflict Resolution Studies. Her current research centres on incarcerated mothers in jails and prisons and their transitions home to their families and communities. Recent publications on women as victims, offenders and practitioners in the criminal justice system, include the following which she was a co-author: *"I don't want to go back to that town" : Incarcerated mothers and their return home to rural communities*; *An analysis of advertisements: A lens to view the social exclusion of women in police imagery*; *Examining charging agreement between police and prosecutors in rape cases*; *A Comparison of Civil and Criminal Orders of Protection as Remedies for Domestic Violence Victims in a Midwestern County.*

Dr. Klaus M. Beier, M.D., Ph.D., Professor of Sexology and Sexual Medicine at the Charité—Universitätsmedizin Berlin (Berlin, Germany). He specialises in sexual medicine. Since 1997 he has been organising official post-graduate training for physicians and psychologists in this field. His main focus in research is forensic sexology, in particular follow-up studies of previously expert evaluated sex offenders. His current research focuses on the prevention of child sexual abuse. The goal is to encourage self-identified undetected pedophiles and hebephiles to seek professional help in order to avoid committing child sexual abuse or the use of child abusive images (www.dont-offend.org). This project has been awarded in Germany several national prizes. Professor Beier is in charge of the Outpatient Clinic of the Institute of Sexology which deals with the full range of sexual disorders and gender dysphoria. His last English co-authored book publication was *Sexual Medicine in Clinical Practice* (Springer: New York 2013).

Dr. Anne H. Berman, Associate Professor of Clinical Psychology at Karolinska Institutet (Stockholm, Sweden); Licensed clinical psychologist and psychotherapist; chief author of a 2010 Swedish-language textbook *Kriminalvården i praktiken: Strategier för att minska återfall i brott och missbruk [Correctional Work in Practice: Strategies for Minimizing Relapse in Crime and Substance Abuse]*. She is involved in e-health interventions for problematic substance use as well as issues related to criminal justice.

Prof. Dr. Catrien C.J.H. Bijleveld, Director of *Het Nederlands Studiecentrum Criminaliteit en Rechtshandhaving*—NSCR Institute for the Study of Crime and Law Enforcement (Amsterdam, Netherlands); Professor of Research Methods in Criminology at the Vrije Universiteit Amsterdam (VU Amsterdam, Netherlands). Main research interests are criminal careers, female offenders, the intergenerational transmission of offenders, genocide and sex offending. She is the author of several textbooks as well as of edited books, on crime and justice in the Netherlands and on the association between employment and offending.

Dr. Milind Bokil, Freelance writer and Sociologist, Marathi (one of 23 official languages of India) writer from Pune, India. He has been associated with civil society organisations for more than 25 years. He has done extensive work with tribal communities in Maharashtra, and his other research interests centre on natural resource management, rural development, education, gender issues, migrant children and disaster management. He has been writing fiction and non-fiction in Marathi and has published more than ten books: short story volumes, novels, travelogues and socio-anthropological studies.

Prof. Dr. Anetta Breczko, (Habil.), Department of Theory of Law and Philosophy of Law, Institute of Philosophy of Law and Ethics of Law, Faculty of Law, University of Białystok (Białystok, Poland). Fields of study: Philosophy of Law, Theory of Law, Bioethics. From this perspective, she recently published articles on the problem of the legal discourse ethics and the axiology of law in the context of universally recognised moral values (2011), and one article on the question of legalisation of torture, in *War and Peace, Philosophical, Political and Legal Aspects,* co-edited by her (Temida 2, 2013).

Prof. Dr. Daniel Brugman, Emeritus; his professional interests cover the meaning, measurement and conditions of sociomoral functioning, in particular in children and adolescents with externalising problem behaviour. His research focuses on sociomoral development, including moral judgement, moral identity, perception of contextual moral atmosphere, and moral disengagement through self-serving cognitive distortions. His applied research concerns interventions to reduce externalising behaviour in schools and residential settings by stimulating sociomoral development.

Barbara Buchegger, M.Ed. is pedagogical manager of the awareness-raising initiative Saferinternet.at (www.saferinternet.at) based in Vienna, Austria. She is currently developing awareness-raising material on the safe and responsible use of the Internet and mobile devices for the target group of children and young people. She is a teacher trainer and educates parents, young people and children, as well as senior citizens on the safe and responsible Internet use. She is an expert on online behaviour of young people, on social media for NPO, cyber-bullying, sexting, cyber-grooming, online-safety, e-learning, new apps and online tools, as well as on organisational development and large group facilitation for all age groups. She is part of the European network insafe (www.saferinternet.org).

Dr. Jovana Carapic, Political Science; Gender Focal Point in *Small Arms Survey*, an independent research project located at the Graduate Institute of International and Development Studies in Geneva, Switzerland. Her research focuses on the conceptualisations of "authority" with respect to various types of armed groups and what this means for how they interact with the state. Since completing her doctorate, she has been increasingly motivated to extend the insights obtained during her studies to gender-based violence, urbanisation and urban violence mainly through various professional and academic engagements.

Prof. Dr. Meda Chesney-Lind, Chair and Professor of Women's Studies at the University of Hawaii at Manoa (Hawaii, USA); She is nationally recognised for her work on women and crime. Her books include *Girls, Delinquency and Juvenile Justice* awarded by the American Society of Criminology's with the *Michael J. Hindelang Award* for the "outstanding contribution to criminology, 1992" and *The Female Offender: Girls, Women and Crime* (1997, Sage). Her most recent book is an edited collection entitled *Female Gangs in America* (2014, Lakeview Press).

Kris Christmann, Research Fellow, Applied Criminology Centre, University of Huddersfield (Huddersfield, UK). His research is about the effects on children's mental health and well-being when a caretaker is imprisoned (the COPING project); children of prisoners worldwide; political and religious violence, specifically youth radicalisation; hate crime; anti-minority mobilisation; policing of gang-involved young people; and the policing of transnational events.

Prof. Roger S. Clark, Board of Governors Professor, Rutgers University School of Law (Camden, NJ, USA). His scholarship is mostly in the areas of International Criminal Law, International Organizations, Human Rights and the Abolition of Nuclear Weapons. Between 1986 and 1990 he was elected by the United Nations Economic and Social Council as a member of the UN Committee on Crime Prevention and Control. In 1995 he represented the Government of Samoa in the International Court of Justice in the Advisory Proceedings on the use and threat of use of nuclear weapons. He represented Samoa between 1995 and 2010 in the negotiations to create the International Criminal Court and to bring the crime of aggression within its effective jurisdiction. He is currently a member of the team representing the Marshall Islands at the ICJ in its cases against the states possessing nuclear weapons.

Raymond R. Corrado, Professor at the School of Criminology at Simon Fraser University (SFU, Burnaby, BC, Canada). He was an associate SFU faculty member in the Psychology Department and the Faculty of Health Sciences. He is a Visiting Professor in the Faculty of Law at the University of Bergen (Bergen, Norway) and a Visiting Fellow at Clare Hall College and the Institute of Criminology, University of Cambridge (Cambridge, UK). He is a Founding Member of the Mental Health, Law, and Policy Institute at SFU. He also was a former Co-director of the BC Centre for Social Responsibility and former Director of the Centre for Addictions Research British Columbia, SFU site. He is on the editorial boards of 6 major criminology and forensic mental health journals. He has co-authored 9 edited books including, *Multi-Problem Violent Youth*; *Issues in Juvenile Justice*; *Evaluation and Criminal Justice Policy*; and *Juvenile Justice in Canada*, as well as having published over 150 articles, book chapters and reports on a wide variety theory and policy issues, including youth/juvenile justice, violent young offenders, mental health, adolescent psychopathy, Aboriginal victimisation, child/adolescent case management strategies, and terrorism. Currently, he is a principal investigator and co-principal investigator of several research projects including three large-scale studies on incarcerated serious and violent young offenders, on comprehensive risk management instrument for violent children and youth and on early childhood aggression.

Katie Cyr, Ph.D. She is a Researcher at the Université du Québec en Outaouais (Gatineau, Québec, Canada) and a Member of the *Groupe de recherche et d'action sur la victimisation des enfants* (GRAVE). She conducted research on victim's empowerment, on their experience with the criminal justice system and restorative justice. She now conducts research in the mechanisms and dynamics involved in repeat victimisation and in child victimisation, including its effects on child trauma symptoms and delinquent behaviour.

Prof. Yvon Dandurand, Fellow, International Centre for Criminal Law Reform & Faculty, School of Criminology and Criminal Justice, University of the Fraser Valley (Abbotsford, BC, Canada). Specialises in comparative criminal law and criminal justice research and has been extensively involved in juvenile justice reform and policy development projects in Canada and abroad. He recently worked as the UNODC lead consultant for the development of the United Nations Model Strategies and Practical Measures on the Elimination of Violence against Children in the Field of Crime Prevention and Criminal Justice.

Davy Dhondt, Professional Mediator at Suggnomè (the umbrella organisation for victim-offender mediation for adults in the Flemish part of Belgium) with years of experience with different models of mediation and different types of conflicts. For the time of that research project (2 years), he also worked at the Katholieke University of Leuven (Leuven, Belgium) as a researcher of the Criminology Department. In 2013 he co-published *Implementing Peacemaking Circles in a European Context: Additional Findings from a European Research Project.*

Bojan Dobovšek, Professor at Faculty of Criminal Justice and Security, University of Maribor (Maribor, Slovenia). He is also a Member of Parliament of the Republic of Slovenia (from 2014 onwards). His main fields of research are organised crime, corruption, State capture, economic crime, art crime, criminal investigations and lately informal economy researched from a criminological stand point.

Prof. Dr. Dieter Dölling, Director of the Institute of Criminology at the University of Heidelberg (Heidelberg, Germany). His main topics of research include juvenile delinquency, corruption, crime prevention, empirical research on criminal proceedings, and criminal sanctions. His main publications include: *Polizeiliche Ermittlungstätigkeit und Legalitätsprinzip* (1987); *Empfehlen sich Änderungen* *des Strafrechts und des Strafprozessrechts, um der Gefahr von Korruption in Staat, Wirtschaft und Gesellschaft wirksam zu begegnen? Gutachten für den 61. Deutschen Juristentag* (1996); Co-editor: *Jugendgerichtsgesetz. Kommentar*, 12. Edition (2011).

Hannah Dönges, she has a Master of Arts in International Relations/Political Science and is a Ph.D. candidate in International Relations/Political Science. She is pursuing a doctorate at the Graduate Institute of International and Development Studies in Geneva, Switzerland. Her dissertation investigates norms and practices of protecting civilians in armed conflict. She has previously worked with the *Small Arms Survey* (an independent research project located at the Graduate Institute of International and Development Studies in Geneva, Switzerland), in the African regional office of the Centre for Humanitarian Dialogue, the Brookings Institution, the European Council on Foreign Relations, among others. During her research and work, she focuses on aspects of armed violence and conflict analysis, particularly in sub-Saharan Africa.

Prof. Dr. Frieder Dünkel is a Professor of Criminology and Head of the Department of Criminology at the University of Greifswald (Greifswald, Germany). He is author of 36 books and about 500 articles which cover a wide range of empirical studies in juvenile criminology, penology, prisons and community sanctions, alcohol and drunk driving, human rights, etc. He and the other staff of the department conducted several empirical international comparative projects on men's prisons in the states of the Baltic Sea, on women's imprisonment in Europe, on long-term imprisonment in ten European countries and on youth violence in the states of the Baltic Sea. His most recent project involved *Restorative Justice in Penal Matters* in 36 European countries (funded by the Criminal Justice—Programme of the EU, 2015).

Dr. Ioan Durnescu is a Senior Lecturer at the University of Bucarest, Bucarest, Romania; he teaches comparative probation, social work in prison and rehabilitation methods of offenders. He also conducts research on probation or prison issues. He is the co-editor of the *European Journal of Probation* and also of the *Probation in Europe* (2008).

Prof. Dr. John Peter Joseph Dussich is a Master's of Science in Criminology and Corrections; Doctor of Philosophy in Criminology and Sociology; and Professor Emeritus of Criminology and Victimology. His main topics of research are criminology, corrections, work release, parole, coping juvenile delinquency, victimology, victim assistance, child abuse victims, elder abuse victims, sexual assault victims, family violence victims, victims' rights, abuse of power victims, disaster victimization and recovery, psycho-social coping theory; and human trafficking victims and femicide victims.

Prof. Dr. Beate Ehret, she is a Professor at the Federal College of Public Administration (Wiesbaden, Germany), a Researcher, sociologist and criminologist. Her career progression reflects her experience in research of more than 15 years on a variety of topics related to juvenile delinquency, its formal and informal control, recidivism, risk assessment and restorative justice. From 2011 to 2013 she was the Research Coordinator of a pilot study funded by the European Commission on the implementation of Peacemaking Circles in the European Union. Currently she teaches criminology and sociology at the Federal College of Public Administration and conducts a research project with the goal of developing a "best practice" model for police investigators dealing with victims of international and war crimes or human rights violations.

David Philip Farrington, Professor Emeritus of Psychological Criminology, Cambridge University (Cambridge, UK) and Leverhulme Trust Emeritus Fellow, Cambridge University. His main research interest is in developmental and life-course criminology and prospective longitudinal studies of offending. He is Director of the Cambridge Study in Delinquent Development, a prospective longitudinal survey of over 400 London males from age 8 to age 56. He is also very interested in experimental evaluations of crime prevention programmes and in cost-benefit analysis.

Prof. Dr. Thomas F. Feltes, M.A., Chair of Criminology and Police Science, Law Faculty, Ruhr-University Bochum (Bochum, Germany). His main fields of research are in all aspects of law enforcement and justice. Since 1998 he is the editor of the *Police Newsletter*, a monthly published E-mail- and Internet-newsletter on police and criminology, in German, English, French and Spanish (www.police-newsletter.com). He published 15 books and over 160 articles on juvenile law, sentencing, alternative sanctions, public prosecution, policing.

Liliana Foca, Project Manager, Mental health of Romanian children of prisoners. She also consults on family relations; problems faced by partners of prisoners; policies aiming for the wellbeing of vulnerable children in general and of children with parents in prison in particular.

Diana Harumi Fuentes Furuya, Human Rights Officer, United Nations Office of the High Commissioner for Human Rights in Geneva, Switzerland. Main topics of research include the United Nations treaty bodies, multiple and intersecting forms of discrimination, and the human rights of migrant workers. Her current focus is the right to education for persons with disabilities.

Huan Gao, Associate Professor of Criminal Justice, California State University, Stanislaus, CA, USA. She received her Ph.D. from the School of Criminal Justice at Rutgers University. Her areas of expertise include substance abuse and crime, gender, crime and justice, and juvenile criminal gangs. She published a book *Women and Heroin Addiction in China's Changing Society* (Routledge, 2011). She also has publications on drug trafficking, drug control policy, criminological theory and organised crime etc.

Cristina Gavriluta, Professor of Sociology at the Alexandru Ioan Cuza University, Faculty of Philosophy and Social Work (Iaşi, Romania). Main topics of research are prisons; reintegration of prisoners through labour; mental health of children of prisoners. Author of 5 books and more than 50 articles and studies, including: *Human Trafficking. Secularization and Public Policy Intervention* (2013), *The Social Construction of Justice* (2010), *Sacred Rituals, the Body's Religious Symbolism and Human Trafficking* (2013).

Loraine Gelsthorpe, Professor of Criminology and Criminal Justice at the Institute of Criminology, University of Cambridge (Cambridge, UK); President of the British Society of Criminology (2011–2015). She has international expertise in a range of criminological topics, including: Youth justice, gender, crime and justice, and community sanctions. She teaches research methods, ethics, critical criminological theories, and socio-critical perspectives on crime and justice. Her current research includes: Anti Human Trafficking Measures, Migration and Crime, the Arts in Criminal Justice contexts, and the links between Criminal and Social Justice.

Aleksandra Sandra Gerö, M.A., Psychologist in private practice, Trainer for Media Education, Expert Team Member of the Office of Ombudsman for victims of violence and abuse in the Catholic Church, Management Team Member of the Section Psychotraumatology and the Arbitration Board at the Professional Association of Austrian Psychologists (BÖP), former Member of the Expert Commission of the Austrian Ombudsman Board (2012–2015) and the Human Rights Advisory Board of the Ministry of the Interior (2009–2012). For many years she has been working with victims of domestic and/or institutional violence and in the training of professionals in the victim consultation. She has publications in the field of Knowledge Management, Learning and Reflexivity in Teams, Online Counselling, Media Education for Counsellors.

Prof. John C. Gibbs, Ph.D., His work has concerned developmental theory, assessment of social cognition and moral judgement development, and interventions with conduct-disordered individuals. His authored or co-authored books include *Moral Development and Reality: Beyond the Theories of Kohlberg, Hoffman, and Haidt*; *Moral Maturity: Measuring the Development of Sociomoral Reflection*; and *The EQUIP Program: Teaching Youth to Think and Act Responsibly through a Peer Helping Program.*

Sally Goldfarb, Professor of Law at Rutgers University School of Law (Camden, NJ, USA), where she has earned several teaching awards. She has also taught at Harvard Law School, New York University School of Law, and University of Pennsylvania Law School. Before joining the Rutgers faculty, she was a staff attorney at Legal Momentum (formerly NOW Legal Defense and Education Fund). Whilst at NOW LDEF, she was instrumental in the drafting and passage of the federal Violence Against Women Act of 1994. She is the author of many articles and book chapters on violence against women, family law, and other topics. She has served on several boards and commissions, including the New Jersey Supreme Court Committee on Women in the Courts, the Board of Advisers for the American Law Institute's Principles of the Law of Family Dissolution, and three expert groups on violence against women convened by the United Nations Division for the Advancement of Women or UN Women.

Julie Goldscheid, Associate Dean for Academic Affairs and Professor of Law at the City University of New York (CUNY) School of Law (New York, USA), where she teaches subjects including civil procedure, lawyering, and courses on gender and law. Her scholarship focuses on gender equality, with a particular focus on gender-based violence and economic equality. Before joining the CUNY faculty, she held positions including senior staff attorney and acting legal director at Legal Momentum (formerly NOW Legal Defense and Education Fund), where her litigation and policy work included defending the constitutionality of the civil rights remedy of the 1994 Violence Against Women Act in courts nationwide, and before the U.S. Supreme Court in *United States v. Morrison*. She has served on the Board of Directors of the Stonewall Community Foundation and other NGOs, and has been active in bar association committees and task forces. She has taught at Columbia Law School, NYU School of Law, Penn State Law School and Brooklyn Law School. She received her law degree from NYU School of Law, a master's in social work from Hunter College School of Social Work, and her undergraduate degree from Cornell University.

Dr. Syeda Tonima Hadi, Associate Protection Officer, Division of International Protection, United Nations High Commissioner for Refugees (Geneva, Switzerland). Recently published in *The Routledge Handbook of International Crime and Justice Studies* on the criminalisation of women worldwide and the need for an International Feminist Criminology. For her dissertation, she conducted research on people's perceptions about Intimate Partner Violence (IPV) in the context of Bangladesh. Previously, she has written on gender issues such as patriarchal attitudes of Bangladeshi couples regarding domestic violence.

Prof. Dr. Otmar Hagemann, Kiel University of Applied Sciences (Germany). His main research topics are Restorative Justice at various levels, Victimology, Criminology, Peacebuilding and Action Research in Social Work. His publications include: co-edited: *Victimology, Victim Assistance and Criminal Justice. Perspectives Shared by International Experts at the Inter-University Centre of Dubrovnik*. Mönchengladbach: Hochschule Niederrhein (2009). Hagemann, O. (2010) *Restorative Justice – A European and Schleswig-Holsteinian Perspective. Restorative Justice – Aus der europäischen und Schleswig-Holsteinischen Perspektive*. Kiel: SH Verband für Soziale Strafrechtspflege (2011). Other publications are: *Restorative Justice in the Context of Victim Needs and Coping Strategies of Victims*. In: Lummer, R./Nahrwold, M./Süß, B. (eds) (2012). *Restorative Justice - A Victim Perspective and Issues of Co-operation*. Kiel: SH Verband für Soziale Strafrechtspflege, pp. 46–67. *Exploring and Understanding Victim Empathy*. In: Schäfer, Peter and Weitekamp, Elmar (eds.). *Establishing Victimology. Festschrift for Prof. Dr. Gerd Ferdinand Kirchhoff. 30th Anniversary of Dubrovnik Victimology Course*. Mönchengladbach: Hochschule Niederrhein (2014).

Carolyn Hamilton is Professor Emeritus of Law at the University of Essex, a Fellow of the Human Rights Centre and Director of Coram International at Coram Children's Legal Centre UK. She was also the Senior Legal Adviser to the Children's Commissioner and served as the Children and Families Commissioner to the Legal Services Commission. She is an internationally known child rights lawyer who has published widely on issues of children's rights. Her latest research on Legal Protection for Violence: Analysis of Domestic Laws Related to Violence Against Children in ASEAN Member States was shortlisted for the best of UNICEF research award 2015. She has worked with the UN, in over 20 different countries on issues of juvenile justice, child protection and access to justice.

Prof. Dr. Jan Hendriks, Clinical psychologist at the forensic outpatient treatment centre De Waag in The Hague (The Netherlands) as well as Professor in Forensic Psychiatry and Psychology and Professor in Forensic Orthopedagogics at Vrije Universiteit Amsterdam (University of Amsterdam, The Netherlands). He specialises in the treatment of and research on juvenile sex offenders. He also conducts research on (juvenile) female sex offenders and treatment programmes designed for juvenile delinquents.

Prof. Dr. Dieter Hermann, University Lecturer, Adjunct Professor of Sociology (University of Heidelberg, Heidelberg, Germany); Research in sociology of crime, empirical methods and statistics, sociology of culture, ethics. Publications include: *Posttraditionale Ethik. Empirische Analysen und theoretische Reflexionen*. Hamburg 2008; *Werte und Kriminalität. Konzeption einer allgemeinen Kriminalitätstheorie*. Wiesbaden 2003; *Die Abschreckungswirkung der Todesstrafe – ein Artefakt der Forschung?* In: Dölling, D. et al. (Hrsg.): *Verbrechen – Strafe – Resozialisierung. Festschrift für Heinz Schöch*. Berlin, New York 2010.

Prof. Thomas Hestermann, Ph.D., Media School, Macromedia University of Applied Sciences, Hamburg and Berlin (Germany). He researches on the reporting of violence and media effects. His major topics are changes in journalism, new formats on television, online journalism and media ethics. Before, he worked at the Criminological Research Institute of Lower Saxony, Hannover (Germany). He published numerous articles on the situation of crime victims, especially second victimisation, coping strategies and media coverage of crime victims. He researched also on human trafficking. Besides his academic activities, he works as a journalist for German public television stations.

Jessica M. Hill, M.Sc., Ph.D. candidate at *Het Nederlands Studiecentrum Criminaliteit en Rechtshandhaving* - NSCR Institute for the Study of Crime and Law Enforcement (Amsterdam, The Netherlands). Her Ph.D. research focusses on emerging adulthood, looking at young people aged 18–29 years old. She examines how changes in their lives affect their delinquent and antisocial behaviour, testing criminological theories relating to desistance from crime in adulthood.

Tarah Kathleine Hodgkinson, Ph.D. Student in the School of Criminology at Simon Fraser University (Barnaby, BC, Canada). Her research areas include crime prevention, neighbourhood safety and sustainability, victimisation, policing, political protest, and violence. She currently works with community members of high-crime neighbourhoods to improve safety and social cohesion. She is also working with a national research group focused on the sustainability of policing in Canada.

Dr. Simon Peter Howell, Research Fellow at the Centre of Criminology, University of Cape Town (Cape Town, The Republic of South Africa). He has engaged with and published on a diverse selection of topics pertinent to contemporary South Africa. Recent publications include, for instance, critiques of the legislative framework in which illegal substances have been regulated, gangsterism, youth violence, gender issues and racial conflict. All of these topics share a core concern with questions of identity, and the manner in which they intersect with the structural and legislative frameworks that continue to define the country.

Andrea Huber, Policy Director at Penal Reform International (London, UK) since 2011, responsible for advocacy at a regional and international level and the development of policy. A lawyer by training, research of human rights issues and advocacy for the implementation and advancement of international human rights law have been at the core of her work. Starting as a legal counsellor for asylum seekers in 1997, subsequently she headed the department for refugees and migration of Caritas Austria with a focus on advocacy and policy development. After a one-year engagement in the judiciary as a legal assistant to judges of the Regional Higher Court Vienna she joined Amnesty International, tasked with research and advocacy in different functions in the Vienna office, the EU office in Brussels and as Deputy Director for Europe and Central Asia at Amnesty International's headquarters in London. She published two books and contributed to several evaluation reports and comparative analyses in the European context. She participated in field missions to DR Congo, Ukraine, Syria and Georgia and has got varied experience in trainings.

Raggie Johansen, Research Officer, Researcher for the Global Report on Trafficking in Persons, is part of the small team that produces the biennial UNODC Global Report on Trafficking in Persons. She has focused on analysing case briefs of prosecuted cases of trafficking in persons around the world to learn more about the organisation of trafficking in persons and the modus operandi of traffickers. She is also involved in data collection through in-depth interviews with experienced criminal justice system personnel. She has contributed to UNODC research on illicit drug markets and a broad range of transnational organised criminal activities, in its publications such as the annual World Drug Report and the Transnational Organized Crime Threat Assessment.

Kristiina Kangaspunta, Chief, Global Report on Trafficking in Persons Unit, UNODC. She has been involved with international crime prevention and criminal justice work for more than 20 years. For the last 13 years, she has been working with the United Nations. She is currently heading the preparation of the biennial

Global Report on Trafficking in Persons at UNODC (Vienna, Austria). Previously, she was the Deputy Director of UNICRI, leading the Research Programme. Before UNICRI, she worked with UNODC, as the Chief of the Anti-Human Trafficking Unit. She moved to UNODC from the Ministry of Justice of Finland where she worked at the European Institute for Crime Prevention and Control, affiliated with the United Nations (HEUNI). She has participated in the planning and coordination of several research projects on crime trends and victimisation. She has been involved in the development of the International Violence against Women Survey and she was the chair of the research section of the National Project on Eliminating Violence against Women as well as the chair of the working group to develop the first national violence against women survey in Finland.

Patricia Kanngiesser, Ph.D., Marie Curie Research Fellow, Department of Developmental and Comparative Psychology, Max Planck Institute for Evolutionary Anthropology (Leipzig, Germany). She completed a Ph.D. in Psychology at the University of Bristol in 2012 and was a visiting researcher at Harvard University and Kyoto University. Her research is in the area of social cognition and social interactions, focusing on questions relating to social norms. She has conducted research on the development of ownership norms in young children and adults, and on norms of fairness and promise keeping. In her work she combines a developmental and comparative approach, studying non-human primates and human children from Western and non-Western (small-scale) populations. She has published numerous, peer-reviewed articles and regularly participates in international conferences.

Witold Klaus, Assistant Professor at the Department of Criminology, Institute of Law Studies, Polish Academy of Sciences (Warsaw, Poland); President of the Polish Association for Legal Intervention and Secretary of the Board of the Polish Society of Criminology. Graduate of the School of Human Rights at the Helsinki Foundation for Human Rights. Holds a Post-Graduate Diploma in Evaluating Social Programmes at the Institute of Sociology, University of Warsaw. Main academic interests: the problems of criminality and the victimisation of immigrants; issues related to social exclusion and criminality, juvenile delinquency and restorative justice. Works with migration, the rights of foreigners, and the functioning of the principle of non-discrimination and equal treatment. Currently works on problems of violence against immigrant women and criminalisation of immigration (crimmigration).

Dorothee Klecha, Dr. Med., Dipl.-Psych.; Consultant for Psychiatry and Psychotherapy; Forensic Psychiatry Certificate SGFP; Head of Forensic Psychiatric Service (FPD), University of Bern (Bern, Switzerland). Studied medicine and psychology at the University of Göttingen, Germany, training as a clinical psychiatrist at the University Hospital Freiburg (Freiburg im Brsg., Germany). Since 2012 Head of Forensic Psychiatric Service (FPD), University of Bern, Switzerland. Since 2012 board member of the Swiss Society of Forensic Psychiatry (SGFP). Lectures in Forensic Therapy and Milieu Therapy at the Institut für Opfer- und Täterschutz

(IOT Zurich). Publications on general and forensic psychiatry issues including mental health issues in Africa, problem solving, cognitive behavioural and interpersonal psychotherapy, depressive disorder, effectiveness of offender rehabilitation and psychotherapy programmes, schema therapy in forensic settings and women offenders. Special interests in the development of services and the implementation of forensic treatment programmes for offenders with mental disorders.

Barbara Krahé, Professor of Social Psychology, University of Potsdam, Germany. Her research interests lie in the domain of applied social psychology, in particular aggression research (media violence and aggression, sexual aggression) and social cognition research applied to legal decision-making (rape myths and biases in judgments about sexual assault). Her co-authored book *Sexual Assault and the Justice Gap: A Question of Attitude* was published in 2008.

Sandy Krammer, Dr. Phil., Psychologist. He studied psychology at the University of Zurich (Zurich, Switzerland). Research assistant and doctoral student at the Department of Psychopathology and Clinical Intervention at the University of Zurich, Switzerland (2010–2012). He defended Ph.D. thesis on "Studies on classic and complex PTSD and the role of social-interpersonal factors". Since 2012 he has been research assistant at the Forensic-Psychiatric Service (FPD), University of Bern, Switzerland. He completed postgraduate training at the School of Criminology, International Criminal Law and Psychology of Law, University of Bern. Main topics of research include complex PTSD, psychotraumatology, incarcerated women, forensic therapy evaluation, criminal psychology.

Dr. Izabela Anna Kraśnicka, she holds a doctoral degree in law and is an Associate Professor in the Department of Public International Law of the Faculty of Law at the University ofBialystok (Białystok, Poland). Her research and teaching fields include three main areas: international law of aviation, constitutional law of the United States in comparative perspective, as well as modern challenges of legal education. In addition to her academic responsibilities she acts as the Dean's Representative for International Relations who runs exchange programmes at the Faculty, including the Erasmus Plus programme of the European Union. She has been a member of the board of the Polish Legal Clinics Foundation since its establishment and thus has been involved in the development of the clinical educational programmes nationwide and abroad.

Helmut Kury, Prof. h.c. Mult., Dr. Dipl.-Psych. He studied Psychology at the University of Freiburg (Freiburg im Brsg., Germany), Diploma, Dr. in Psychology and Habilitation at the Unviersity of Freiburg. Between 1970 and 1973 Assistant Teacher at the University of Freiburg, Institute for Psychology, between 1973–1980 and from 1989 to 2006 Senior Researcher at the Max-Planck-Institute for Foreign and International Penal Law in Freiburg im Brsg, Department of Criminology, 1980–1988. First and Founding Director of the Criminological Research Institute of Lower Saxony (KFN). Research in offender rehabilitation, crime prevention, attitudes to punishment, fear of crime, punitivity, alternatives to punishment, methodological problems of empirical social science research, international comparison of crime and punishment. Most recent publications: Kury, H., Ferdinand, T.N. (Eds.) (2008). *International Perspectives on Punitivity*. Bochum: Universitätsverlag Dr. Brockmeyer; Kury, H. (Ed.)(2008). *Fear of Crime – Punitivity. New Developments in Theory and Research*. Bochum: Universitätsverlag Dr. Brockmeyer. Kury, H., Shea, E. (Eds.)(2011). *Punitivity – International Developments*. 3 Vols., Bochum: Universitätsverlag Dr. Brockmeyer.

Dr. Tapio Lappi-Seppälä, Director of the Institute of Criminology and Legal Policy, member of the Finnish Academy of Sciences (Helsinki, Finland) with a long career as a researcher and senior legislative advisor in the Ministry of Justice. He has taken actively part in international research co-operation in several international organisations. His publications cover over 250 titles including books, research reports and articles in several languages in the field of criminal law, criminology and penal policy. His recent research activities are focused on comparative criminal justice and penal policy, on which he has lectured widely in Europe and overseas. Selected writings: Tapio Lappi-Seppälä. *Changes in Penal Policy in Finland*. In Punitivity. International Developments. Vol. 1: *Punitiveness - a global Phenomenon*?, In H. Kury and E. Shea (eds), Universitätsverlag Dr. Brockmeyer. Bochum, Germany, 2011; *Explaining imprisonment in Europe*. European Journal of Criminology, 2011; Co-authored and/or co-edited: *Crime and Justice in Scandinavia. Crime and Justice: A Review of Research*, vol. 40, Chicago: University of Chicago Press, 2011; *The development of crime in light of Finnish and Swedish criminal justice statistics, ca. 1750–2010*. European Journal of Criminology, 2013; *Cross-Comparative Perspectives on Global Homicide Trends*. In: *Crime and Justice: A Review of Research*, vol. 43, Chicago: University of Chicago Press, 2015.

Zina Lee, Assistant Professor School of Criminology (University of the Fraser Valley, Abbotsford, BC, Canada). Her primary research interests include the assessment and development of psychopathic personality traits and aggression in youth. Other research interests include deception, false confession, and programme evaluation. Recent publications examine the challenge of assessing aggression in youth and distinct profiles of high-risk youth. Her recent research focuses on risk and protective factors for youth cybercrime and the development of policies and laws to address youth cybercrime.

Martti Lehti, LL.D., Senior Researcher, Institute of Criminology and Legal Policy, University of Helsinki (Helsinki, Finland). Current projects: Finnish Homicide Monitor. Selected publications in English: *Homicide Trends in Estonia in 1971–1996. In Five Centuries of Violence in Finland and the Baltic Area*. History of Crime and Criminal Justice Series. Columbus: Ohio State University Press, 2001; *Homicide Trends in Finland and Estonia in 1880–1940*. Journal of Scandinavian Studies in Criminology and Crime Prevention, 2011. Co-author of: *Trafficking for Sexual Exploitation*. In: *Crime and Justice* (ed. Michael Tonry), Vol. 34. Chicago: The University of Chicago Press, 2006; *Homicide in Finland, the Netherlands and Sweden. A First Study on the European Homicide Monitor Data. The*

Swedish National Council for Crime Prevention Research Report 2011, Stockholm: Brå., 2011; *Homicide in Finland and Sweden*. In: *Crime and Justice in Scandinavia* (eds. Michael Tonry & Tapio Lappi-Seppälä), Volume 40. Chicago: The University of Chicago Press, 2011; *Social Correlates of Intimate Partner Homicide in Finland: Distinct or Shared with Other Homicide Types?. Homicide Studies*, 2012; *The Declining Number of Child Homicides in Finland, 1960–2009. Homicide Studies*, 2012. Author of *Homicide Drop in Finland, 1996–2012. Journal of Scandinavian Studies in Crime Prevention and Criminology*, 2014.

Jianhong Liu, Professor at University of Macau (Taipa, Macau, China), President, Scientific Commission of International Society for Criminology; President, Asian Criminological Society, Editor-in-Chief, Asian Journal of Criminology. His primary interest is in comparative criminology and criminal justice. His major contribution is in the area of Asian Criminology. He is the author, editor, or co-editor of 19 books, and chief editor of a book series on *Criminal Science and Drug Crimes in China*. He has authored, co-authored more than 60 journal articles and book chapters, many appeared in journals such as *Justice Quarterly, Criminology, British Journal of Criminology, Criminology, the Journal of Research in Crime and Delinquency*.

Alexandra V. Lysova, Dr. of Sociology (Russian Academy of Sciences); Ph.D. candidate in Criminology (University of Toronto), Trudeau Scholar at the Centre for Criminology and Sociolegal Studies at the University of Toronto. For over 10 years her main research interests have been in intimate partner violence, homicide, and the intersection of male and female offending and victimisation. The other research interests involve the examination of situational patterns of violence; gender inequality and violence against an intimate partner cross-nationally; corporal punishment of children in the families; and criminalised women in Canada and Russia. Recent publications appeared in the *Aggressive Behavior, Journal of Interpersonal Violence, Nordic Studies on Alcohol and Drugs, and Handbook of European Homicide Research.*

Martin Manby, Ph.D., Affiliate of the University of Huddersfield (Huddersfield, UK). Previously: Director, Nationwide Children's Research Centre, Huddersfield (UK). Main topics of his research are parenting programmes; family support; child protection. His recent articles have included family support provided in a women's prison; and family processes among families of children and prisoners, including re-appraisal of the imprisoned parent and the emergence of family policy for handling parental imprisonment.

Ineke Haen Marshall, Ph.D., Professor of Criminology and Sociology, Northeastern University (Boston, MA, USA). She specialises in comparative and international criminology and crime policy, migration and crime, self-report methodology, juvenile delinquency and criminal careers. Her current research focuses on cross-national surveys of juvenile delinquency and comparative examination of homicide. She is the chair of the Steering Committee of the International Self-Report

Study of Delinquency (ISRD), an international collaborative study with participants from countries all over the globe (www.northeastern.edu/isrd).

Jeff Mathesius, Ph.D. student in the School of Criminology at Simon Fraser University (Burnaby, BC, Canada). His current research interests include the development of violence and sexual aggression, as well as the risk assessment and management of serious violent juvenile offenders.

Tamara Mitrofanenko, Education for Sustainable Development Consultant in the United Nations Environmental Programme (UNEP, United Nations Office at Vienna, Austria); Project manager at Zoi Environment Network. The main topic of her research and practice is involvement of the local population of the rural mountainous regions, especially the younger and the older people, in sustainable development. Currently she focuses on intergenerational practice as a potential approach to engaging the local youth and elderly in protected area management and tourism development. Her research is linked to the UNEP projects, and aims at being transdisciplinary and at facilitating capacity-building of the research partners and local stakeholders. Co-author of: *Potential for Applying Intergenerational Practice to Protected Area Management in Mountainous Regions. Mountain Research and Development*, 2015; *Transferability Tool Kit. Big Foot. Crossing Generations, Crossing Mountains. Project "Big Foot. Crossing Generations, Crossing Mountains*, Vienna, Austria, http://www.bigfoot-project.eu/transferability-tool-kit.html.

Anganile Willie Mwenifumbo, Legal Practitioner, Human Rights Officer, United Nations Office of the High Commissioner for Human Rights (Geneva, Switzerland). She conducted extensive research and has written on biotechnology, biodiversity, climate change, the right to food, ethnicity and the right to development, post-genocide justice mechanisms in Rwanda, the African human rights system and on the United Nations treaty body system. Her main research focus is on the implementation of human rights standards.

Dr. Vesna Nikolić–Ristanović, Professor at Belgrad University (Belgrad, Serbia). Her main fields of experience and research include: violence against women, war victimisation, women's crime, war and crime, domestic violence, trafficking in people, and truth and reconciliation. Among the most important publications are: *Women, violence and war* (ed.), *From victim to prisoner: domestic violence and women's crime, Social Change, Gender and Violence*: *Post-Communist and War-Affected Societies, Surviving Transition: Everyday life and Violence in Post-communist and Post-conflict Societies, Domestic Violence in Serbia* (ed.) *and Domestic Violence in Vojvodina* (ed.).

Milagros Nores, Ph.D., Associate Director of Research, National Institute for Early Education Research (Rutgers University, New Brunswick, NJ, USA). Her research includes early childhood attainment, the economics of education, poverty, and international and comparative education. She currently runs a randomised longitudinal early childhood study in Colombia and another randomised trial on parental-child educational practices for minority children in the U.S. Her best known works include: reviews of the international research on effects of early childhood interventions; benefit-cost analyses of the Perry Preschool, and research on early achievement gaps for Hispanic and bilingual children.

Sławomir Oliwniak, Ph. D., Senior Lecturer at the Department of Law Theory and Philosophy of Law, Faculty of Law, University of Białystok (Białystok, Poland). His main fields of interests are: postmodernism and law, Foucault and Agamben's analysis of law, biopower and biopolitics, surveillance society. He published respective articles on, e.g. *Foucault and Agamben: law as inclusive/exclusive discourse. In: Language, Law, Discourse,* ed. by M. Aleksandrowicz, H. Święczkowska, Studies in Logic, Grammar and Rhetoric, 2011; *Biopolitics and the rule of law.* In: *Axiology of the Modern State Under the Rule of Law. Selected Issues,* ed. by S. Oliwniak, H. Święczkowska, Studies in Logic, Grammar and Rhetoric, 2009.

Christa Out-van Kessel, MSc., Research Assistant, Faculty of Social and Behavioural Sciences, Utrecht University (Utrecht, The Netherlands). As a research assistant her main interest is in applied research on children and adolescents with externalising behaviour and conduct disorder, and in research on moral development. Furthermore, she participated in research on gene x environment interactions, specifically on the concept of differential susceptibility. Alongside her work as research assistant, she also works as a child psychologist in mental health care, with children aged 4–18, with various diagnoses. She is specialised in doing diagnostic research and treating children and their parents by intensive home treatment programmes.

Batoul Pakzad, Ph.D., Assistant Professor in Criminal Law and Criminology at the Islamic Azad University (Tehran, Iran), Head of the Law Department. Dr. Pakzad is also an attorney-at-law and professional and legal adviser in Iran, and is currently serving as a counsellor in the Ministry of Justice. She has been a deputy and the Chair of the Law Commission of the High Council of Provinces in Iran and advisor of women affairs for the local governor in Rafsanjan. Although her primary interest has always been the study of and research in Criminal Law, Criminology, Islamic Law, jurisprudence and comparative law, other topics of her research and publications include cybercrime, cyber-terrorism, family law and criminality and victimisation of women and children in the real world and cyberspace.

Martin Peper, Prof. Dr. rer. medic. Dr. Phil., Clinical Neuropsychologist GNP, Studied psychology at the University of Heidelberg; Dr. phil. at the University of Heidelberg (Heidelberg, Germany), Dr. rer. medic. at the Charité, Medical Faculty of the Humboldt University Berlin (Berlin, Germany); Assistant Professor and Associate Professor (until 2006), Personality Psychology Section, University of Freiburg im Brsg., Germany; Visiting Scholar, Center for Neural Science, New York University, USA (1992). Since 2007 full Professor of Neuropsychology, Faculty of Psychology, University of Marburg (Marburg, Germany). Adjunct Research Associate and forensic psychology expert at the Forensic Psychiatry

Service (FPD), University of Bern (Bern, Switzerland). Associate board member and chairman of the scientific advisory board of the German Neuropsychological Society (GNP). Main topics of research include medical, clinical and experimental neuropsychology, criminology, neurobehavioural toxicology. Publications on emotional and personality disorders in patients with cerebral diseases, emotional and executive dysfunction in offenders with mental disorders, research on forensic psychotherapy effects; psychophysiological assessment in the clinical setting and in everyday life. Co-author of a textbook on emotion psychology (2014); books and articles on neuropsychology, criminology, behavioural toxicology, ambulant psychophysiological monitoring.

Adrienne M.F. Peters, Ph.D., Sessional instructor in the School of Criminology and Criminal Justice and a research assistant for the Centre for Public Safety and Criminal Justice Research at the University of the Fraser Valley (Abbotsford, BC, Canada). She completed her doctoral research at Simon Fraser University, which examined the offending and risk assessment outcomes for severely mentally disordered, serious-violent, and gang-involved young offenders assigned to specialised community supervision programmes. Her research interests include young offenders; serious and violent youth offending; mental health and its association with delinquency; young offender treatment, programming, and rehabilitation; the Youth Criminal Justice Act and young offender policy; best practices in policing; and collaborative crime reduction strategies. She has presented at conferences and co-authored publications in each of these areas. She acts as the research director for the Study on Specialized Community Case Management of Young Offenders and served as a research assistant on a number of other research projects.

Kate Philbrick, OBE, Board member, Children of Prisoners Europe (COPE). She researches on best practices concerning the guidance on how to support and provide for children of prisoners, from the point of arrest through court and sentencing to imprisonment and release. Particular emphasis on provision for children visiting prisons, and training of prison officers in relation to this.

Dr. Michael Platzer, main topics of scientific activities are Human Rights, Rights of Victims, Prisoners Rights, Prison Pastoral Care, Migrant Rights, Juvenile Justice, Death Penalty, Femicide, Social Media, Radicalization of Youth, Development, Climate Change, Sustainable Development Goals. Main Publications are *Jugendliche im Gefängnis? Modelle im Umgang mit straffälligen Jugendlichen, Schriftenreihe des Bundesministeriums für Justiz*. In: *Chancengleichheit für die Jugend; Österreichische und Europäische Initiativen gegen Soziale Ausgrenzung*, Wien, 2009; *Vienna Conference on the Abolition of the Death Penalty: Working Together towards the Universal Abolition of the Death Penalty*, Bundesministerium, ACUNS, 2011; *"Empfehlungen für die Behandlung von Ausländern in Haft", International Commission for Catholic Prison Pastoral Care, "Grundprinzipien: Religion im Gefängnis", International Commission of Catholic Prison Pastoral Care*. In: *Academics Meet UN Practitioners: An Encounter in Vienna*, Favorita Papers, 2010; *UN Agencies Reaching out to Academia and Civil*

Society, Favorita Papers. Diplomatische Akademie, 2013; *Vienna Vision: Peaceful, Inclusive, Prosperous, and Sustainable World,* Academic Council on the United Nations System, 2015. *Femicide: A Global Issue That Demands Action*, Volumes 1–3, Academic Council on the United Nations System, 2013, 2014, 2015.

Emil Walenty Pływaczewski, Prof. Dr. (Habil.) of Penal Law and Criminology; Dean of the Faculty of Law, University of Bialystok (Białystok, Poland); Director, Institute of Criminal Law; Head of the Department of Penal Law and Criminology. His literary output comprises over 370 publications, published in Poland and abroad (70), a dozen of them are monographs. His research interests include organised crime, money laundering, corruption, criminal policy and public security issues. In 1997 he won the Distinguished International Scholar Award of the International Division of the American Society of Criminology. Many times, he was a guest lecturer or visiting professor at the universities in Australia, Austria, Belgium, Brazil, China, the Czech Republic, Germany, Lithuania, Finland, France, Greece, India, Italy, Japan, The Netherlands, New Zealand, The Republic of Korea, Switzerland, Turkey, and in the United States of America. In the years 1994–2012, he had been the representative of Poland in the International Examination Board of the Central European Police Academy. Since 2005 he is Chief Coordinator of the Polish Platform for Homeland Security (PPHS)—a unique initiative in Europe whose activities aim at creating integrated computer tools to support the broadly defined efforts to improve public security.

Dr. Ineke Pruin, Research Associate at the University of Greifswald (Greifswald, Germany). Her main research interests focus on prisoner resettlement, juvenile justice and sentencing practices. Some of her recent publications in English include co-authored *Young Adult Offenders in Europe: Interdisciplinary Research Results and Legal Practices.* Barrow Cadbury Trust, London, 2014, and her own article *Law, Diversion and Community Sanctions in Juvenile Justice.* In: Bruinsma G, Weisburd D (eds), Encyclopedia of Criminology and Criminal Justice. Springer, New York, 2014, and *Conditional release in Germany.* In: Padfield N, van Zyl Smit D, Dünkel F (eds), *Release from Prison: European Policy and Practice.* Willan, Collumpton, 2010; *Recalling conditionally released prisoners in Germany.* European Journal of Probation, 2012, plus the co-edited book: *Juvenile Justice Systems in Europe – current situation, reform developments and good practices*. 2nd edn. Forum Verlag Godesberg, Mönchengladbach, 2011.

Gerald Quirchmayr, Univ.-Prof. DI, Dr. Dr., Faculty of Computer Science, University of Vienna (Vienna, Austria); Adjunct Professor, School of Information Technology & Mathematical Sciences, University of South Australia. His major research focus is on information systems in business and government with a special interest in security, applications, formal representations of decision-making and legal issues. His publication record comprises approximately 150 peer reviewed papers plus several edited books and conference proceedings as well as nationally and internationally published project reports.

Vijay Raghavan, Professor and Chairperson, Centre for Criminology and Justice, School of Social Work, Tata Institute of Social Sciences (Mumbai, India). Primary research interests include custodial justice and prison reforms in post-colonial societies, social work practice in criminal justice regimes, and more recently, youth involvement in organised crime in post-industrial cities.

Mehrdad Rayeijan Asli, Ph.D., in Criminal Law and Criminology, Shahid-Beheshti University (Tehran, Iran); Assistant Professor, Faculty of Law, Tarbiat-Modares University (Tehran, Iran). Research in victimology, criminology, sociology of crime, criminal policy, and criminal law. Experiences in teaching the above topics at several universities in Iran. Over 50 articles published in scientific-research journals. She published: *The Victim in Criminal Justice Process*, Khatte-Sevom Pub., Tehran, 2002; *Assistant-oriented Victimology*, Dadgostar Pub., Tehran, 2002 and 2006; *Design Out Crime* (translated into Persian), Mizan Pub. Tehran, 2009 and 2011; *Victimology*, Vol. I., Shahre-Danesh, Tehran, 2009; *Handbook of Victimology* (translated into Persian), Armane-Hoquq, Tehran, 2012; *Contemporary Critical Criminology* (translated to Persian), Dadgostar, Tehran, 2013; *Victimology*, Vol. II, Shahre-Danesh, Tehran, 2014; Cyber Crime and Victimization of Women, Majd Pub., Tehran, 2014.

Sławomir Redo, Dr. Habil.(Law/Criminology); former UN Senior Crime Prevention and Criminal Justice Expert and staff of the UNODC (ret.); Senior Programme Adviser, Academic Council on the United Nations System (Liaison Office, Austria, Vienna). Now as an independent scholar and lecturer he teaches "The United Nations and Crime Prevention"—a graduate course delivered at the universities in Austria, China and Poland; Member of the editorial boards of: *Asian Journal of Criminology*; *Caribbean Journal of Criminology*, the *Journal of International Organization Studies*. Author of: "*Blue Criminology. The Power of United Nations Ideas to Counter Crime Globally*" (HEUNI, Helsinki, 2012); and three other books; Co-Editor of: *For the Rule of Law: Criminal Justice Teaching and Training @cross the World* (HEUNI, Helsinki, 2008), and of *Global Crime and Justice Report* (Oxford, 1999). About 70 articles and book chapters on various crime and justice issues, mostly covered by United Nations law and practice, including cross-national crime trends, crime prevention, computerisation of criminal justice, cyberspace crime, extradition, policing, principles of prosecution, judicial independence, victim compensation, death penalty, organised crime; international and intercultural crime prevention in education.

Philip Reichel, Ph.D., Emeritus Professor at the University of Northern Colorado (Greeley, CO, USA) and Adjunct Professor at the University of New Hampshire Law School. He is the author of Comparative Criminal Justice Systems (2013): A Topical Approach, co-editor of *Handbook of Transnational Crime and Justice* (2014); and co-editor of *Human Trafficking: Exploring the International Nature, Concerns, and Complexities* (2012). He has authored or co-authored more than 30 articles, book chapters, and encyclopaedia entries. He has lectured at universities in Austria, Germany, and Poland, was a presenter for a United Nations crime prevention webinar, presented papers at side events during the Twelfth United Nations Congress on Crime Prevention and Criminal Justice (Brazil) and the United Nations Commission on Crime Prevention and Criminal Justice (Vienna), and was an invited speaker at Zhejiang Police College in Hangzhou, China.

Oliver Robertson, Project Manager at the Prison Reform International (London, UK) on: death penalty and alternatives, comparative international studies on the rules and realities for children with parents in prison, international human rights related to children of prisoners, children of parents sentenced to death, wider impacts of the death penalty; death penalty.

Federico Rossano, Ph.D. (Linguistics), Radboud University, Nijmegen (Netherlands). Worked at the Max Planck Institute for Psycholinguistics from 2004 to 2008 and as a guest researcher at the Max Planck Institute for Evolutionary Anthropology from 2009 to 2011. Since 2012, he is a post-doctoral researcher in the Department of Developmental and Comparative Psychology at the Max Planck Institute for Evolutionary Anthropology in Leipzig (Germany). His research interests include: social cognition and communication in human infants and non-human primates, ontogeny and phylogeny of property concerns, value perception, distributive and procedural justice, conversation analysis and the role of visible behaviour (gesture and gaze in particular) in face-to-face interaction.

Irena Rzeplińska, Professor of Law and Criminology in the Department of Criminology of the Institute of Law Studies in the Polish Academy of Sciences (Warsaw, Poland); Vice-Director of the Institute of Law Studies; Editor-in-Chief of the oldest Polish criminological journal „Archives of Criminology". Her fields of research are deviance, self-report studies, crime and crime policy—historical and contemporary, foreigners criminality in Poland, youth crime—past and present. Publications (among others) in H. Kury & E. Shea (eds): *Punitivity. International Developments*, Bochum 2011; A. Selih & A. Zavrsnik (eds): *Crime and Transition in Central and Eastern Europe,* Springer 2012; I. Rzeplińska as co-author in: K. Buczkowski and others: *The Sociopolitical Background of Contemporary Criminality in Poland*, Warsaw, ed. SEDNO 2013 in Polish (Ashgate 2015 in English); and author: *An evergreen or forgotten subject: relationship among crime, criminology and criminal policy*—plenary lecture on EUROCRIM 2013, Budapest, published in Proceedings of Criminology, Hungarian Society of Criminology, 2014.

Fabrizio Sarrica, Research Officer for the Global Report on Trafficking in Persons Unit of the UNODC. He holds a Ph.D. in Criminology, a Master degree in Economics and International Relation and a University degree in Economics. Dr. Sarrica has been working as a researcher for UNODC since the year 2002. In this role, he has conducted researches and assessments on corruption, organised crime, smuggling of migrants and trafficking in persons in different parts of the world. He is the co-author of four UNODC *Global Reports on Trafficking in Persons*.

Dr. Marco F.H. Schmidt, Department of Developmental and Comparative Psychology, Max Planck Institute for Evolutionary Anthropology (Leipzig, Germany). He investigates the developmental origins of human normativity and morality, with a particular focus on mechanisms of norm acquisition, norm enforcement, and norm creation. Furthermore, he is interested in interrelations between moral, social-cognitive, and prosocial development.

Dr. Monika Schröttle, Visiting Professor at TU Dortmund (Dortmund, Germany). Since 2013 Project Director at the Institute for Empirical Sociology at the University of Erlangen-Nürnberg (Nürnberg, Germany). Together with Dr. Renate Klein she coordinates the European Network on Gender and Violence (www.engv.org). She was project director for the first large-scale German representative survey on violence against women. The data of the study that was published in 2004 and then was further analysed in relation to questions of risk factors, levels and types of violence, health impact and migration. With a background in political science and interdisciplinary violence research in women's and gender studies, she focuses on the empirical analysis of violence in gender relations. Her newest quantitative study at the University of Bielefeld was concerned with violence against disabled women in Germany and is the first representative survey on violence with disabled women in Europe.

Rossella Selmini, Ph.D., in Social and Political Science of the European University Institute; Associate Professor and Research Associate, Department of Sociology, University of Minnesota (Minneapolis, MN, USA). Her field of work is the analysis of crime phenomena and of criminal public policies. During her career she has directed many research projects, both quantitative and qualitative, on crime, victimisation, crime prevention and violence against women and she is author or co-author of several books and many papers in Italian and international journals and edited books on the same topics. Her recent works focus on trends in rape e in female homicide in a comparative perspective.

Kathryn Sharratt, M.Sc., Lecturer in Criminology (Department of Criminology, Sociology and Politics, University of Huddersfield, Huddersfield, UK). She researches forensic and criminal psychology; offending behaviour and experiences of imprisonment; the role of personality in suicide-related behaviour among prisoners; children's experiences of visiting parents in prison; validation of emotional and behavioural measures among samples of children affected by parental imprisonment; confirmatory factor analysis; latent class analysis; propensity score matching techniques.

Margaret Shaw, Ph.D., sociologist and criminologist. She was Director of Analysis and Exchange at the International Centre for the Prevention of Crime (ICPC, Montreal, Québec, Canada) from 1999 to 2011. She now works as an independent consultant. Before joining ICPC she worked for over 20 years as a research and policy advisor in the Home Office, England. Between 1986 to 1999 she was a lecturer and Associate Professor in the Department of Sociology & Anthropology at Concordia University, Montréal, and undertook research for Federal, Provincial and municipal governments and police organisations in Canada. She has undertaken extensive research internationally including for UNODC, UN-HABITAT, UN WOMEN and WHO and published widely on crime prevention, youth violence, justice and rehabilitation, gender, women's imprisonment and safety, human trafficking, and evaluation. In 2013 she was awarded the *Saltzman Prize for Contributions to Practice* by the Division of Women and Crime, American Society of Criminology, and in 2014 the *G.O.W. Mueller Award for Distinguished Contributions to International Criminal Justice,* from the International Division of the Academy of Criminal Justice Sciences. Recent publications are: 2010 Preparation of *Handbook on the Crime Prevention Guidelines: Making Them Work,* United Nations, New York; 2013 *Building Inclusive Cities*: *Women's Safety and the Right to the City*. (Co-ed.) London: Earthspan; *Too Close to Home: Guns and Intimate Partner Violence*. In: Small Arms Survey Yearbook 2013; *Everyday Dangers*. Geneva and Cambridge: University of Cambridge Press & Small Arms Survey, 2013; *International, national and local government policies to reduce youth violence*. In: Violence: A Global Health Priority. Edited by Donnelly, P.D. and Ward, C. Oxford: Oxford University Press, 2014.

Evelyn Shea, LL.D. (University of Basel), Diploma in Criminology, Institute of Criminology, Cambridge, England, Ph.D. in Law and Criminology (University Robert Schuman, Strasbourg), Her main interest lies in the role of work in prison, and the rehabilitation of prisoners. Her publications include: *Le travail pé nitentiaire: un défi européen* (Paris: L'Harmattan, 2006), *Why Work?* (Berlin: Drucker & Humblot, 2007), *Punitivity, International Developments*, 3 volumes (Bochum: Universitätsverlag Brockmeyer, 2011) co-edited with Helmut Kury, and several articles in academic journals. She is an independent researcher and currently a prison visitor (Zurich, Switzerland).

Prof. Swati Shirwadkar, Ph.D. in Sociology, University of Pune, India, Dr. h.-c. (Tampere University, Finland); Professor & Head, Department of Sociology and Director, Erasmus Mundus Euroculture Program, University of Pune, India. Her research interests and publications are broadly in the field of socio-cultural changes, gender, sexuality and violence, reproductive health, religion, education and development, globalisation, diaspora and identity issues. Engaged in research projects on life-style issues for the IT sector, regional social history, social changes and empowerment of village people, reproductive health challenges for primitive tribe women, international comparisons of dating violence and violence against women.

Boštjan Slak, Researcher and part-time member of the Chair of Criminal Investigation at the Faculty of Criminal Justice and Security, University of Maribor (Maribor, Slovenia). His research interests are issues of integrity, white-collar and organised crime, as well as media portrayal of criminal investigation and its influence on criminal investigation process.

Elisabeth Stanners, Secondary School Principal, Vienna International School (Vienna, Austria). Facilitator of the generation of data for other researchers on topics related to best practice in schools. Research for implementation within a school setting in the areas of language acquisition, additive bilingualism, assessment, character education, educational leadership and service learning.

Ljiljana Stevkovic, M.Sc., Teaching assistant, Faculty of Special Education and Rehabilitation, University of Belgrade (Belgrade, Serbia). Researcher volunteer at the Victimology Society of Serbia, member of the Victimology Society of Serbia, European Society of Criminology (ESC), ESC Working group of young researchers, European Working Group of Researchers on Organized Crime, and the European Working Group on Victimology. She participated in numerous national and international projects on crime victims, victims of domestic violence, victimisation of children, juvenile delinquency, human and victim rights and protection of women victims of violence who are serving prison sentences. In the area of the research interest she published numerous papers dealing with the problem of domestic violence, juvenile delinquency, victimisation of children and the elderly, and trafficking in human organs.

Dora Szego, Researcher, sociologist and Ph.D. student at Corvinus University Budapest (Budapest, Hungary). She is the assistant director of the Central and East-European department of the International Institute for Restorative Practices. She is involved in research projects since 2011 related to Restorative Justice in prisons, in the criminal justice system, and in local communities at Foresee Research Group.

Jan Van Dijk, degree in law from Leiden University (1970) and a Ph.D. in criminology from the University of Nijmegen (1977). He is Emeritus Professor at the International Victimology Institute (INTERVICT) of the University of Tilburg (Tilburg, The Netherlands) and Visiting Professor at Lausanne University, Switzerland. He is a member and vice-president of the *Group of Experts on Action against Trafficking in Human Beings* (GRETA) of the Council of Europe and vice-president of the Dutch State Compensation Fund for Victims of Violent Crime. He published extensively on victims' rights, crime prevention and human trafficking. His latest monograph is *The World of Crime: Breaking the silence on issues of security, justice and development*, Sage, 2008. He co-edited the book *The New Faces of Victimhood; Globalization, Transnational Crimes and Victim Rights* (Springer, 2011) and *The International Drops in Crime* (Palgrave/Mac Millan, 2012). In 2009 he received the Sellin-Glueck Award of the American Society of Criminology and in 2012 the Stockholm Prize in Criminology.

Kathrin Vogt, M.A., Research assistant at the Universities of Bielefeld, Gießen, Nuremberg and Dortmund (Germany). With a background in pedagogics and interdisciplinary violence research in women's and gender studies she was working at the Institute for Interdisciplinary Women's and Gender Studies, University of Bielefeld from 2011–2014. She is currently research assistant for studies on violence against women (with disabilities) at the Gender Studies Unit of the University of Gießen, as well as at the Institute for Empirical Sociology at the University of Nuremberg, Germany. Here she supported different national as well as international projects on women's political issues, as, e.g. the first representative survey on violence against disabled women in Germany and the Daphne Project "Access to specialised victim support services for women with disabilities who experienced violence". Furthermore she assisted in the (re)establishment of a European network on Gender and Violence.

Dr. Thomas Gerald Walsh (Ph.D. in Religion, Vanderbilt University, Nashville, TN); President of the Universal Peace Federation, an international NGO in special consultative status with the United Nations Economic and Social Council. With academic training in the field of Religion and Ethics, he earned his Ph.D. at Vanderbilt University. He has been a teacher, author and editor, with specialisation in areas of interfaith relations, religious studies, religion and peace, philosophy and social theory. He serves on the International Council of the World Association of Non-Governmental Organizations, and on the board of directors of the International Coalition for Religious Freedom and The Washington Times. He serves as Publisher of *UPF Today* magazine and *Dialogue and Alliance*, a scholarly interfaith journal. He has contributed to and edited more than twenty books related to interfaith, peacebuilding and renewal of the United Nations; among these volumes are *Renewing the United Nations and Building a Culture of Peace* and *The Millennium Declaration of the United Nations: A Response from Civil Society*.

Jo-Anne M. Wemmers, Ph.D. (Leiden University, The Netherlands); Professor, School of Criminology, Université de Montréal (Montreal, Quebéc, Canada). Her research interests focus on victims in the criminal justice system in the broadest possible sense. Central themes in my research are victims' justice judgements and therapeutic jurisprudence. She has published widely in the areas of victimology, international criminal law and reparative justice, including: *Reparation for Victims of Crimes against Humanity* (2014), *Therapeutic Jurisprudence and Victim Participation in Justice* (2011); *Introduction to Victimology* (2003).

Prof. Dr. Werner Wintersteiner, Ph.D., Director of Centre for Peace Research and Peace Education, University of Klagenfurt, Austria. Director of the University Master Program (further education) "Global Citizenship Education". His professional interests include development of a complex transdisciplinary peace research with a strong focus on cultural dimensions including post-colonial approaches, development of a comprehensive peace education, linking civic education, conflict resolution, and a culture of remembrance—globalisation, post-colonialism, transculturality and literature (education).

Gunda Wößner, Professor of Psychology at the University of Applied Police Sciences Baden-Wuerttemberg in Villingen-Schwenningen (Germany). From 2006 to 2014 Senior Researcher in the Department of Criminology at the Max Planck Institute for Foreign and International Criminal Law, Freiburg im Brsg., Germany. Her primary research interests include sexual and violent offending, particularly offender treatment and recidivism, evaluation research, effects of electronic monitoring, and restorative justice in cases of sexual violence. Her recent publications focus on correctional treatment outcome in violent and sexual offenders with particular consideration of recidivism, therapeutic change, prison climate, education and employment, on electronic monitoring of offenders in Germany, and on mental health problems in juvenile offenders.

Dagmara Woźniakowska-Fajst, Doctor of Law, Criminologist, Assistant Professor at the Faculty of Criminology, Institute of Law Studies, Polish Academy of Sciences (Warsaw, Poland), and at the Department of Criminology and Criminal Policy at the Institute of Social Prevention and Resocialisation, University of Warsaw. Interests include victimology, harassment issues in an emotional context, deviant behaviour of juveniles and women, crime as presented in the media, and justice system policy. Member of the European Society of Criminology, the Polish Society of Criminology, and the Association for Legal Intervention.

Elizabeth Yarrow, Senior Researcher with the Coram Children's Legal Centre (London, UK). She specialises in conducting applied social and legal research on a range of thematic rights issues, with a particular focus on the nexus between childhood, gender and violence. She has an LLM in International Human Rights Law and MA in Social and Political Sciences from Cambridge University.

Luis Arroyo Zapatero, Professor Dr. h. c. mult., criminal law professor and Director of the Institute of European and International Criminal Law at the University of Castilla-La Mancha, Spain, of which he is Rector Emeritus. Since 2002 he is President of Société Internationale de Défense Sociale with headquarters in Paris and Milan. Scientific Advisory Board member and Vice President thereof from 2009 of the Max-Planck Institute for Foreign and International Criminal Law in Freiburg i. Br. Vice President of the Association Internationale de Droit Pénal (2007), Member of the Board of Directors of the International Society of Criminology (2005) and of International Scientific and Professional Advisory Council of the United Nations Crime Prevention and Criminal Justice Program (ISPAC). His publications have focused mainly on four areas: penal protection of human rights at the workplace, economic criminal law; European criminal law; relations between criminal law and Constitution and death penalty world abolition processes. Last 10 years publications in http://uclm.academia.edu/LuisArroyoZapatero.

Yingjun Zhang, Ph.D., Associate Professor in International Law (Law Faculty, South-Central University for Nationalities, Wuhan, P.R. China), Member of the Chinese Society of International Law (CSIL). In 2011 and 2013 Visiting Scholar at the Max Planck Institute for Foreign and International Criminal Law, Freiburg im Brsg. Germany. Her research focuses on corporate liability under international criminal law. She published *The Legal Issues of International Law on Transnational Corporate Offences (Beijing, 2012), Corporate Criminal Responsibility in China, 2012.*

Abbreviations

ABA	American Bar Association
ACUNS	Academic Council on the United Nations System
ADHD	Attention deficit hyperactivity disorder
APD	Antisocial Personality Disorder
BPD	Borderline Personality Disorder
BWS	Battered Woman Syndrome
CAI	Child abusive images
CAT	Convention against Torture and Other Cruel, Inhuman or Degrading Treatment or Punishment
CAPTA	The Child Abuse Prevention and Treatment Act (US)
CBT	Cognitive-bahavioural therapy
CCPC	Chicago Child–Parent Center
CED	Committee on Enforced Disappearances
CEDAW	Convention on the Elimination of All Forms of Discrimination against Women
CERD	Committee on the Elimination of Racial Discrimination
CESCR	Committee on Economic, Social and Cultural Rights
CIEL	Center for International Environmental Law
CIP	Center for Inergenerational Practice
CIT	Couter Interrogation Tactics
CMW	Committee on the Protection of the Rights of All Migrant Workers and Members of Their Families
ComEDAW	Committee on the Elimination of All Forms of Discrimination against Women
COPING	Children of Prisoners, Interventions and Mitigations to Strengthen Mental Health
CoSA	Circles of Support and Accountability
CRC	Convention on the Rights of the Child
CRPD	Committee on the Rights of Persons with Disabilities
CSA	Child Sexual Abuse

CTA	Criminal Tribes Act
CWS	(US) Child welfare system
DFG	Deutsche Forschungsgemeinschaft (German Research Foundation)
DNA	Deoxyribonucleic acid
DNT	De-notified tribes
DRF	Dynamic risk factors
DSM	Diagnostic and Statistical Manual of Mental Disorders
EC	European Commission
EMIL	European Map of Intergenerational Learning
EPR	European Prison Rules
ECHR	European Court of Human Rights
EMCDDA	European Monitoring Centre for Drugs and Drug Addiction
ENGW	European Network on Gender and Violence
ESCCJ	European Sourcebook of Crime and Criminal Justice
FBI	Federal Bureau of Investigation
FGC	Family Group Conference
FGM	Female genital mutilation
FRA	Agency for Fundamental Rights (EU)
GBAV	Global Burden of Armed Violence
GCPEA	Global Coalition to Protect Education from Attack
GTD	Global Terrorism Data Base
HOA	Habitual Offenders Act
HRC	Human Rights Committee
IACHR	Inter-American Commission on Human Rights
ICC	Iranian Civil Code
ICCPR	International covenant on Civil and Political Rights
ICD	International Classification of Mental and Behavioural Disorders
ICD	International Criminal Law
ICERD	International Convention on the Elimination of All Forms of Racial Discrimination
ICESCR	International Covenant on Economic, Social and Cultural Rights
ICIP	The International Consortium for Intergenerational Programmes
ICMW	International Convention on the Protection of the Rights of All Migrant Workers and Members of Their Families
ICPED	International Convention for the Protection of All Persons from Enforced Disappearance
ICPS	International Centre for Prison Studies
ICRPD	Convention on the Rights of Persons with Disabilities
ICT	Information and Communication Technology
ICVS	International Crime Victims Surveys
IHDP	Infant Health and Development Program (US)
IHL	International Humanitarian Law
IHTL	International Human Rights Law
IL	Intergenerational Learning

ILO	International Labour Organisation
IOM	International Organisation for Migration
IP	Intergenerational Practice
IPJJ	Interagency Panel on Juvenile Justice
IPV	Intimate Partner Violence
ISRD2/3	International Self Report Delinquency Study
JGG	Jugendgerichtsgesetz (Youth Court Law)
MDG	Millennium Development Goals
MST	Multi-systemic therapy
MTCT	Mother to child transmission of HIV/AIDS
NAFTA	North American Free Trade Agreement
NGO	Nongovernmental Organisation
NIC	National Institute of Correction (US)
NICHD	National Institute of Child Health and Human Development (US)
NIDA	National Institute on Drug aBuse (US)
NSCAW (US)	National Survey of Child and Adolescent Well-Being
OECD	Organization for the Economic Cooperation and Development
OBC	Other Backward Classes
OSRSG	United Nations Office of the Special Representative of the Secretary-General on Violence against Children
PAHO	Pan American Health Organization
PFC	Prefrontal Cortex
PPD	Prevention Project Dunkelfeld
PTE	Potentially Traumatic Events
PTSD	Post-traumatic stress disorder
PV	Partner violence
RAD	Reactive attachment disorders
RJ	Restorative justice
RNR	Risk/Need/Responsivity Model
SC	Schedule of Castes
SCR	(UN) Security Council Resolutions
SD	Sustainable Development
SDGs	Sustainable Development Goals
SDQ	Strength and Difficulties Questionnaire
SES	Self Esteem Scale
SPT	Subcommittee on Prevention of Torture
SRH	Sexual and Reproductive Health
ST	Schedules of Tribes
STAC	Strategies Towards Active Citizenship
STD	Sexually Transmitted Disease
STI	Sexually transmitted infections
TFC	Treatment foster Care
TOA	Täter-Opfer-Ausgleich

ToM	Theory of Mind
TWP	Together Women Programme
UN	United Nations
UNEA	United Nations Environmental Assembly
UNECE	United Nations Economic Commission for Europe
UNDAW	United Nations Division for the Advancement of Women
UNICEF	United Nations Children's Fund
UNICTI	Interregional Crime and Justice Research Institute (UNICRI)
UNiTE	UN Secretary-General's Campaign to end violence against women
UNODC	United Nations Office on Drugs and Crime
UNRISD	United Nation's Research Institute for Social Development
US EPA	United States Environmental Protection Agency
VOM	Victim-offender mediation
WAVE	Women Against Violence Europe
WHO	World health Organization
WCED	United Nations World Commission on Environment and Development
YLS/CMI	Youth Level of Service/Case Management Inventory

Part IV
The Role of Crime Prevention: Punishment–Imprisonment–Alternative Sanctions

General Prevention: Does It Work?

Dieter Hermann and Dieter Dölling

Abstract A meta-analysis based on 700 international empirical studies on negative general prevention with 7822 effect estimates investigates whether deterrent effects are dependent on the age of the target group, and with which criminal offences deterrent effects exist. Differences in the study design and the consideration of theoretical principles are also included in the analysis. It is shown that the latter in particular has a significant impact on the study result: if an economic theory of behavior is used as a basis, the deterrence hypothesis is refuted less often than with a recourse to criminological-sociological theories. Another result is that deterrent effects are confirmed relatively rarely for young people, and that deterrent effects vary depending on the criminal offence. They are relatively low in the case of homicide, and are higher—and significant on average—in the case of property damages and theft of more expensive goods. The probability of punishment has a deterrent effect which may, however, hardly be expected of more severe penalties.

1 Introduction

The idea of controlling behavior through deterrent measures is found not just in law but also e.g. in military deterrence plans and educational concepts.[1] The concept of deterrence is anchored in the legal systems of many societies, and the establishment of international criminal courts is legitimized, among others, by the consideration that international criminal prosecutions serve to deter the commission of genocide, crimes against humanity, and war crimes.[2] The idea that criminal penalties can have a deterrent effect and contribute to reducing crime was developed as a theory particularly in Europe towards the end of the 18th and the beginning of the 19th century. It was assumed that the threat of sanctions and the sanctions themselves

[1] Catudal (1985); Fuhrer (2009); Hinz and Becker (2012); Ogilvie-White (2011).

[2] Wippmann (1999), p. 473.

D. Hermann (✉) • D. Dölling
University of Heidelberg, Heidelberg, Germany
e-mail: hermann@krimi.uni-heidelberg.de; doelling@krimi.uni-heidelberg.de

H. Kury et al. (eds.), *Women and Children as Victims and Offenders: Background, Prevention, Reintegration*, DOI 10.1007/978-3-319-28424-8_1

prevent potential perpetrators from committing criminal offences. Similar considerations were expressed by Cesare Beccaria and Jeremy Bentham, among others.[3] Both assume that societies are constituted on the basis of fictitious contracts between its citizens and by societal consensus, whereby utilitarian philosophy holds that the objective of all government measures is to achieve the highest possible level of happiness for all members of the community.[4]

It is true that punishment will do harm to the person it is inflicted on, which will have a negative effect on the general level of happiness. However, according to the theory of negative general prevention, the deterring effect of the threat of punishment and the punishment itself also prevent criminal offences, which has a positive effect on the level of happiness. Therefore punishment can be justified, according to the principle of "the greatest happiness of the greatest number", precisely if it improves the societal level of happiness.[5]

Deterrence exists mainly through the knowledge that breaches of the law will be punished. The certainty of moderate punishment has a greater deterrent effect than the fear of more severe punishment, if there is sufficient hope that the punishment will not be applied[6]; it is important that the suffering associated with the punishment exceeds the benefit obtained from the offence.[7] The legal scholar Johann Anselm Feuerbach also developed a general preventative deterrence theory and took a closer look at the psychological aspects of deterrence. According to his theory of psychological coercion, all humans search for pleasure and try to avoid unpleasantness. Thus illegal acts can be prevented if every person knows that the pleasure gained from breaking the law is followed by something more unpleasant. Therefore Feuerbach argues in favor of criminal law that is based on the deterrence principle and thus guarantees the protection of mutual freedom.[8]

More recently, Gary S. Becker and Isaac Ehrlich transferred the general preventative theories of deterrence to the operationalizable level of mathematical/economic and econometric models.[9] Becker in particular addresses the concept of "expected punishment", whereby "expected" must be understood in terms of the mathematical expected value. Put in simplified terms, the expected punishment will depend on the severity of the punishment and the probability that the perpetrator will be held responsible for his action in the case of a criminal offence. In this sense, even less severe punishment can already have a deterrent effect in principle, if it is assumed that each offence will be discovered. Therefore the consideration that deterrence depends not solely on the severity of the punishment but also on the probability that the punishment will be inflicted is of central importance both to the

[3] Beccaria (1766); Bentham (1823).

[4] Beccaria (1766), p. 167; Müller (1996), p. 18.

[5] Baurmann (1981), p. 19; Burns (2005), p. 46.

[6] Beccaria (1766).

[7] Baurmann (1981); Bentham (1823).

[8] Feuerbach (1799), pp. 38–45.

[9] Becker (1968); Ehrlich (1973); Ehrlich (1975); Ehrlich (1977).

scientific understanding of the deterrence hypothesis as well as to the practical crime-fighting policies.

Prevailing German criminal law is based on the theory of negative general prevention in addition to other penal theories.[10] Court decisions hold that the severity of the punishment may be increased under certain conditions in order to deter the general public.[11] The German Federal Constitutional Court has acknowledged negative general prevention as a purpose of criminal law.[12]

The purpose of negative general prevention in terms of criminal law is discussed mainly with regard to the criminal law that applies to adults. On the other hand, it is generally agreed that criminal law relating to young offenders is mainly tasked with a special preventative mission, which it carries out mainly on the basis of educational initiatives for young offenders.[13] This is underlined by sect. 2 subsect. 1 of the German JGG (Youth Court Act), which was added to the JGG by the Second JGG Amendment law of 13 December 2007.[14] According to sect. 2 subsect. 1 sentence 1 JGG, the application of criminal law relating to young offenders is mainly designed to counteract repeat offences by juveniles or young adults. To attain this objective, sect. 2 subsect. 1 sentence 2 JGG sets out that legal consequences and—taking into account the parent's right to educate the child—also legal proceedings must be primarily aligned to the idea of education.

Penal theories of negative general prevention are normative theories but they also feature an empirical core; they postulate that deterrence prevents criminal activities. Many empirical studies have been conducted with regard to this hypothesis, although they have not been able to answer the question with absolute certainty. This chapter centers on the question whether the current threats of sanctions contained in legal norms pertaining to criminal law have an effect on criminal behavior and levels of crime, with a focus on comparing the deterrent effects for younger and older persons. In addition, the chapter aims to study whether deterrent effects vary depending on the type of criminal offence, whereby it focuses on criminal acts that are perpetrated by juveniles and young adults relatively frequently or rarely, hence criminal offences with significantly different rates of prevalence among younger and older individuals. In addition, criminal offences with a particular propensity to affect women as victims will also be taken into account.

According to data from German police crime statistics for the year 2012,[15] the proportion of children (up to 13 years of age), juveniles (15–17 years) and young

---

[10] Jescheck und Weigend (1996).

[11] Decisions by the Federal Court of Justice in criminal matters, Vol. 17, p. 321, 324; Vol. 20, pp. 264, 267; Vol. 28, pp. 318, 326.

[12] Decisions by the Federal Constitutional Court Vol. 21, pp. 391, 404; Vol. 39, pp. 1, 57; Vol. 45, pp. 187, 253.

[13] Brunner und Dölling 2002: 40 and onward.

[14] Federal Law Gazette (Bundesgesetzblatt) I, p. 2894.

[15] Bundeskriminalamt (2013), p. 69; own calculations.

adults (18–20 years) in the number of suspects depends on the nature of the criminal offence. With regard to the breaches of legal norms included in the police crime statistics, this proportion is 23 % for all criminal offences. It is significantly higher in the case of robbery (45 %), property damages (42 %), theft under aggravating circumstances (36 %), dangerous and serious injury (34 %) and theft without aggravating circumstances (33 %). The proportion of young suspects is very low in the case of willful homicide (17 %), and fraud (17 %). The proportion of female victims also varies considerably. It is 40 % when all criminal offences are taken into account, drops to 32 % in the case of willful homicide, 34 % for robberies, extortionary robbery and robbery attacks on drivers, 37 % for injuries, 49 % for offences against personal freedom, and 93 % for offences against sexual self-determination with the use of force or exploitation of a dependency relationship.[16] Another question concerns the mechanisms of deterrence. Feuerbach points out that already the threat of punishment has a deterrent effect. Becker and Ehrlich postulate that all costs of offences are action-relevant, in particular the expected severity of sanctions and the probability of sanctions. Others expect that especially informal sanctions, e.g. stigmatization by friends, are deterrent.

The questions regarding offence- and age-specific deterrent effects and the mechanisms of deterrence are to be answered with the help of a meta-analysis. The meta-analysis is a statistical study about studies. It concerns the quantitative and systematic study of individual empirical studies with the objective of obtaining the best reliable assessment of current research results for a specific hypothesis. The meta-analysis also aims to ascertain the reasons for the different results reached by the various studies, which may be found in particular in the study design or the frame conditions of the studies, for example the societal situation at the time the study is conducted.[17] To this end, suitable statistical techniques are used for the integration and analysis of individual research results. Meta-analyses generally do not have access to the raw data. Therefore statistical estimates such as correlations or significance are collected from the individual studies and are systematically analyzed. In this chapter, the primary purpose of the meta-analysis is to assess the effectiveness of deterrence in selected framework conditions.

2 Research Status: Meta-Analyses on Deterrence Studies

Numerous studies on the effectiveness of deterrence through criminal punishment are available; they differ not just in the study methods but also in the study results. The discrepancy in results is reflected in the work conducted by Eisele,[18] who

[16] Bundeskriminalamt (2013), p. 41.

[17] See e.g. Farin (1994); Fricke and Treinis (1985); Hedges and Olkin (1985); Rosenthal (1991); Wolf (1986).

[18] Eisele (1999).

considered 28 elaborated studies on negative general prevention as part of a qualitative meta-analysis. Of these, nine studies confirm the deterrence hypothesis, while nine studies refute it. Ten studies modify the original hypothesis and postulate, for example, the dependence of the deterrent effect on the frame conditions.

Nagin takes into account approximately 20 studies, whereby the analysis focuses on the listing of methodological-statistical problems of deterrence studies—including the validity deficits of crime statistics when estimating crime rates, and a lack of distinction between the various effects of imprisonment. In this context, according to Nagin imprisonment has a deterrent effect on the general public, but also promotes crime due to the involvement of prisoners in the prisons' subculture. If the two effects are not isolated, then the results must be incorrect and deterrent effects are underestimated. Therefore Nagin demands more elaborated studies as the available results can only be interpreted with extreme caution.[19]

Similarly, Petrosino's meta-analysis regarding the effects of deterrent measures on perpetrators did not lead to a clear confirmation of the deterrent hypothesis. As part of a meta-analysis, Petrosino considered 150 English-language studies that were published between 1950 and 1993, and which were based on randomized experiments. The objective of the studies was to study the effects of interventions on relapse behavior, whereby only 23 studies were related to deterrent measures. Thus Petrosino's work is a special preventative deterrence study; hence the results can only be transferred to general preventative issues with great reservations. The relapse-reducing effect of deterrent measures was less than that of rehabilitation programs; however, this relationship changed if the analysis took into account a weighting using the number of cases. Seen overall, the results do not point to any stable effects.[20]

Cameron compared approximately 80 econometric studies on the deterrence hypothesis, with a focus on problems of theory, method and statistics. His analysis showed that studies that work with aggregate data had only limited success in confirming the effects of deterrence, while studies with prisoners and victims of crime indicate that deterrent measures do not affect crime at all, or even promote it.[21]

Several meta-analyses exist with regard to capital punishment. Based on a research overview of 74 studies, Chan and Oxley concluded that capital punishment does not have a deterrent effect. This view is confirmed when the number of studies is reduced to 61 studies that use elaborated statistical analytical methods.[22] The meta-analyses conducted by Yang and Lester, on the other hand, leads to the opposite result.[23] This study is based on 95 publications.

[19] Nagin (1978).

[20] Petrosino (1997).

[21] Cameron (1988).

[22] Chan and Oxley (2004).

[23] Yang and Lester (2008).

A meta-analysis by Hermann using 82 studies capital punishment leads to the result that in particular the institutional location of the researchers and the applied action theory have an effect on the research result. Thus studies that use the idea of homo oeconomicus as a basis confirm the deterrence theory much more frequently than other studies.[24]

3 Study Method

The project for the meta-analysis of deterrence studies was conducted by a research group[25] and financially supported by the DFG (Deutsche Forschungsgemeinschaft—German Research Foundation). For the implementation of the meta-analysis, the relevant empirical studies were sought out in literature databases and literature lists of publications. All studies published up to August 2006 were taken into account. The study is based on 700 studies with 7822 effect estimates. The objective of the study was an exhaustive sample, i.e. all relevant studies were to be taken into account, and all published deterrent effects per study were to be included. However, economic deterrent studies are different from others with regard to the type of publication: in economic studies, the robustness of the calculated effect is often tested by varying the underlying model. This means that economic studies frequently result in a large number of reported effect estimates, although they differ only minimally with regard to their framework conditions. For this reason, only one effect estimate per criminal offence was selected in the case of economic studies, on the basis of the random principle. In the case of criminological and social science studies, on the other hand, all relevant estimates were included. To prevent possible distortions due to the different numbers of effect estimates per study, the empirical analyses are weighted in such a way that each study—regardless of the number of its effect estimates—is included in the analysis at the same weight. A differentiated description of the study design can be found at Dölling, Entorf, Hermann and Rupp.[26]

Effect estimates in the various studies are expressed in the form of numerous statistical values, such as correlation coefficients, partial regression coefficients, percentage rate differences, significance levels, F-values and t-values. These statistical variables are usually scaled differently and can thus only be compared with limitations. Thus all effect estimates were converted into t-values for the purpose of establishing comparable statistical values. The use of t-values is a common method

---

[24] Hermann (2012). The study originated as part of the study introduced herein.

[25] Prof. Dr. Dieter Dölling, Prof. Dr. Dieter Hermann and Dr. Andreas Woll (Universität Heidelberg, Institute of Criminology) and Prof. Dr. Horst Entorf and Dr. Thomas Rupp (Universität Frankfurt am Main, Department of Economics).

[26] Dölling et al. (2011); see also Rupp (2008).

in meta-analyses.[27] The t-value is a statistical value that is usually used in inference-statistical analyses for calculating error probabilities. Many association coefficients that may be viewed as benchmarks of the reliableness of drawing conclusions for the entire population from a random sample can be converted into t-values, if the number of degrees of freedom is known.

When converting statistics into t-values, they are coded so that negative values represent a confirmation of the deterrence hypothesis, and positive values refute the same. Moreover, in studies with a small number of cases the t-values were extrapolated as if they were from a larger study ($N > 200$); the effect of this correction ensures that the calculated t-value is independent of the number of cases. There are 7057 t-values out of a total of 7822 measurement values as a result of direct inclusion and conversion. Weighting reduces the number of effect estimates in the analyses to 6530 t-values and 663 studies.

For the analyses at hand, a characteristic that merely makes a distinction whether an effect estimate is consistent with the theory and significant (or not) is used as an indicator of the effectiveness of deterrence. The percentage proportion of effect estimates that are consistent with the theory and significant can be interpreted as a benchmark for the reliableness of the ascertainment of a correlation. If an effect estimate in the population has a value of zero, and if random samples with a sufficient number of cases are drawn from this population, significant estimate values are found in 5 % of samples, whereby half is consistent with the theory, even though the effect estimate for the population is zero. If the value of the effect estimate in the population is so small that it would be just barely significant in a random sample, then effect estimates that are consistent with the theory and significant would be found in 50 % of all random samples. A deterrent effect may be viewed as relevant if at least half of the effect estimates are consistent with the theory and significant. The average t-value can be used as another relevant criterion. For samples with large numbers of cases the critical threshold for separating significant from non-significant t-values is -1.96. According to these criteria, a deterrent effect is relevant if 50 % of effect estimates are both consistent with the theory and also significant, and if the average t-value is at most -1.96.

The result of a meta-analysis always depends on the input. Studies differ in terms of their methodological quality, and a meta-analysis is only as good as the studies that it takes into consideration. A summary can hardly improve the quality if only methodologically problematical studies are used: garbage in—garbage out.[28] The methodological quality of the studies under consideration was assessed in order to address this problem. The following questions in particular were used to assess the quality of the studies: Does the study purport to be representative? Does it include a test for representativity? Have error control or plausibility control been carried out? Have reliability and validity tests been performed? Have significance tests been carried out? If yes, were the criteria for testing significance met? Did the study

[27] Stanley (2001); Antony and Entorf (2003).

[28] Wagner and Weiß (2006).

control for third variables? These indicators were used to identify studies with methodological deficiencies. This analysis only took into account studies that featured no or only minor methodological deficiencies. Hence the number of (weighted) effect estimates was reduced to 5992. Of the effect estimates from methodologically elaborated studies, 41 % are consistent with the theory and significant, compared to 46 % in studies with problems; this difference is significant. It means that the probability that the deterrence hypothesis will be refuted increases with the elaborateness of the studies.

A frequent criticism of meta-analyses is that they compare studies that cannot actually be compared. A meta-analyses is then similar to a method that measures "apples and oranges" in the same manner.[29] Deterrence studies are conducted using different methods and data: crime statistical data, surveys and experiments. Works studying the effectiveness of capital punishment represent another methodological specialty. Some studies work with individual data, while others work with aggregate data. Using the scientific concept of Durkheim, who views the micro and macro level as sui generis realities, whereby phenomena at each level can only be explained by characteristics of this level,[30] deterrence studies at the micro level could not be compared with studies at the macro level. This is supported by the fact that correlations with micro data cannot be transferred to the macro level—and vice versa.[31] Both arguments suggest that studies that refer to different levels should be analyzed separately as part of the meta-analysis. For this reason, the study performs separate analyses for studies that use different study methods: crime statistics studies with 3495 effect estimates, works on the effectiveness of capital punishment with 520 effect estimates, surveys with 1562 effect estimates and experiments with 798 effect estimates.

Another problem associated with meta-analyses, but also all other empirical studies, is that the researcher's view of the world and theory preferences can influence the study result. Max Scheler and Karl Mannheim already pointed out the presence of social processes during the generation of knowledge. In this context, Scheler talks about the social nature of knowledge, while Mannheim refers to knowledge's connection to the being, i.e. the context of the research process.[32] Studies on deterrence research are usually based on either social science crime theories or the rational choice approach. The first theory approach is particularly dominant in criminology, sociology and psychology—where the idea of individuals acting in a purely rational manner is viewed with skepticism.[33] The second approach and the idea of homo oeconomicus are particularly dominant in older works of economy. If the selection of the basic theory for an empirical deterrence

[29] Wagner and Weiß (2006), p. 495.

[30] Durkheim (2002).

[31] Robinson (1950).

[32] Scheler (1926); Mannheim (1970).

[33] Auer (2005); Böckenförde (2001); Dahrendorf (2006); Dietz (2005); Dölling (2007); Dölling (2012).Manstetten (2002); Weber (1980).

study has an effect on the result, it makes sense that studies with a different theoretical basis should be analyzed separately as part of a meta-analysis. In the methodologically elaborated studies, 3931 effect estimates are attributable to studies that use criminal-sociological theories, and 2444 effect estimates to studies based on economic theories.

4 Results

4.1 The Impact of the Studies' Theoretical and Methodological Framework Conditions on the Study Results

The results of deterrence studies depend on how a study was structured, how variables were operationalized, which analytical methods were used, and which data was used as a basis.[34] In this case, only the influence of the study type and underlying theory shall be studied—all subsequent analyses regarding offence-specific and age-specific deterrent effects are differentiated according to these characteristics. The result of the analysis is shown in Table 1.

The results of deterrence studies depend on the study method and underlying theory—the differences are significant. With regard to the type of study, the greatest difference exists between experiments and studies on capital punishment. Both study types differ significantly in terms of the sanctions studied—usually informal sanctions in the case of laboratory experiments, which are imposed in game situations if a player cheats, and typically sanctions imposed on breaches of laws in traffic situations in the case of natural experiments. Compared to capital punishment, these are minor breaches of the law with rather light sanctions, but they seem to be more effective than drastic sanctions such as capital punishment. Survey studies and crime statistics studies do not differ greatly with respect to the number of effect estimates that are consistent with the theory and significant.

In all study types, results will depend on the underlying theory. If an economic theory is used as a basis, the number of effect estimates consistent with the theory and significant is higher than in the other cases. The difference is particularly glaring in the case of studies on capital punishment.

[34] Instead of many: Dölling et al. (2011).

Table 1 Dependence of deterrent effects on the study method and underlying theory

Type of study	Theory	Percentage share of effect estimates that are consistent with the theory and significant	Number of effect estimates
Crime statistics study	Criminal-sociological theory	39	1530
	Economic theory	42	1734
	Total	41	3264
Survey study	Criminal-sociological theory	40	1297
	Economic theory	43	171
	Total	40	1468
Experiment	Criminal-sociological theory	54	628
	Economic theory	61	143
	Total	55	770
Study on capital punishment	Criminal-sociological theory	16	306
	Economic theory	44	184
	Total	27	489
Total	Criminal-sociological theory	40	3760
	Economic theory	43	2232
	Total	41	5992

4.2 *Deterrent Effects Depending on Age*

Only studies whose method allows for a comparison of age groups can be included in a study of this issue. This does not apply to studies on capital punishment and studies with crime statistics data—these studies always used data without making a distinction between age groups. Only survey studies and experiments were conducted with younger and older persons, and take this difference into account. Therefore only survey studies and experiments have been included in the meta-analysis. These studies differ in terms of the object of the study—which may include juveniles and young adults (young persons) or the total population. The deterrent effects in these groups shall be compared. At the same time, this

Table 2 The dependence of deterrent effects on the study method, the underlying theory and the age of the groups studied

Type of study	Theory	Age group	Percentage share of effect estimates that are consistent with the theory and significant	Number of effect estimates
Survey study	Criminal-sociological theory	Total population	47	267
		Young persons	38	565
	Economic theory	Total population	43	81
		Young persons	[a]	[a]
	Total	Total population	46	348
		Young persons	37	575
Experiment	Criminal-sociological theory	Total population	35	190
		Young persons	76	197
	Economic theory	Total population	50	31
		Young persons	74	71
	Total	Total population	37	220
		Young persons	76	268
		Total	58	489

[a]Less than 20 cases

differentiation by age group is not very precise, as studies using the entire population also include younger persons. This means that differences between the age groups under consideration will be underestimated.[35]

The result of the analysis is shown in Table 2. The age group "Young persons" includes juveniles, young adults and students. This table does not include effect estimates if the analysis is based on less than 20 cases.

The analysis yields an apparently contradictory picture. While significant deterrent effects were found more frequently in survey studies relating to the entire population than in survey studies with young persons, the effect is reversed in experiments. This becomes even more noticeable if the average t-value is used as

[35] See also Dölling and Hermann (2012).

the indicator for the deterrent effect. It is −2.2 for survey studies with the total population and −1.0 with young persons. The first value is significantly different from zero at the 0.05 level, the second is not. The average t-value for experimental studies with the total population is −0.9, and −2.9 with young persons. The second value is significant, the first is not.

This situation can be explained as follows: Survey studies and experiments examine deviant behavior at different levels of severity. The first case generally focuses on legal breaches in the area of criminal offences of low to medium severity, hence actions that are linked to criminal penalties. Laboratory experiments, on the other hand, usually involve the imposition of sanctions for cheating in game situations, and even in field experiments sanctions are frequently of an informal kind. In addition, it is not clear whether results from laboratory experiments regarding the deterrent hypothesis can be transferred to real life situations; the problem with experiments is that they offer a high internal but low external level of validity. Therefore deterrent criminal penalties for criminal acts do not appear to be effective, or have only limited effect, with respect to young persons; informal sanctions, on the other hand, appear to be effective.

4.3 Deterrent Effects Depending on the Criminal Offence

The analysis aims to answer the question whether deterrent effects vary by the type of criminal offence, whereby the focus is on such offences that are committed particularly often or rarely by juveniles and young adults, as well as offences that affect women in particular: robbery, property damage, theft, bodily injury, willful homicide and fraud, as well as sexual offences. Moreover, analyses regarding drinking and driving were also included, because this area appears to be particularly suited to legal deterrence measures.[36] The result of the analysis is shown in Table 3. In this context, only those analysis results were taken into account that are based on at least 50 effect estimates. This is designed to ensure the reliability of the results and clarity of the table.

According to the analyses in Table 1, in all study types the result of a deterrence study will depend on the underlying theory. If an economic theory is used, then the number of effect estimates consistent with the theory and significant is higher than in the other cases. This result is confirmed in an offence-specific analysis, whereby economic theories are limited to crime statistics studies and studies on capital punishment, while criminological-sociological theories were used in all study types. For all offences that are taken into account, the proportion of significant deterrent effects is higher when economic theories are used, compared to the use of criminological-sociological theories (see Table 3). As already mentioned, the

[36] Dünkel (2010); Iffland and Balling (1999); Schöch (1991); Spirgath 2013; Vollrath and Krüger (1999).

Table 3 Offence-specific deterrent effects: Percentage portion of effect estimates consistent with the theory and significant (only indicated if more than 50 cases)

Theory	Offence	Percentage share of effect estimates that are consistent with the theory and significant	Number of effect estimates
Crime statistics studies			
Criminal-sociological theory	Homicide, premeditated	34	388
	Sexual assault	29	153
	Bodily injury, premeditated	28	202
	Robbery	33	221
	Theft (non-differentiated)	27	177
	Theft (more expensive)	57	51
	Drunk driving	53	391
Economic theory	Homicide, premeditated	41	353
	Sexual assault	46	182
	Bodily injury, premeditated	40	205
	Bodily injury, negligence	36	82
	Robbery	41	360
	Theft (non-differentiated)	42	356
Survey studies			
Criminal-sociological theory	Bodily injury, premeditated	59	107
	Property damage	64	70
	Theft (non-differentiated)	43	166
	Theft (lower value)	53	105
	Theft (more expensive)	56	95
	Fraud	46	116
	Drunk driving	48	233
Experiments			
Criminal-sociological theory	Homicide, premeditated	43	84
	Sexual assault	41	51
	Fraud	68	71
Studies on capital punishment			
Criminal-sociological theory	Homicide, premeditated	14	284
Economic theory	Homicide, premeditated	49	168

differences are particularly significant in studies on capital punishment.[37] Significant differences can also be found in (crime statistics) studies on rape. If such a study was based on an economic theory, 46 % of effect estimates were consistent with the theory and significant, whereas in the relevant studies based on criminological-sociological theories only 29 % of effect estimates were significant. Because of the strong influence of the underlying theory, offence-specific analyses are examined on a differentiated level based on the theory.

In studies based on an economic theory, the proportion of effect estimates consistent with the theory and significant is always under 50 %. In the criminological-sociological studies that are taken into account, the 50 % threshold is exceeded for some offence types. At the same time, the average t-value is below the critical value of −1.96 for only two offence types. Survey studies on deterrence in the case of property damage resulted in 64 % effect estimates consistent with the theory and significant with an average t-value of −2.0. This value was −2.3 in crime statistics studies on theft of more expensive goods. In survey studies regarding this type of offence, the value was only −1.0 however. Hence the deterrent effects seem to be limited to a few offences, which include property damage and the theft of larger amounts of cash or relatively expensive products.

In the case of rape, the proportion of effect estimates consistent with the theory and significant is relatively low if the studies are based on criminological-sociological theories, but relatively high if economic theories are included. But even in this case the percentage portion of effect estimates that are consistent with the theory and significant is below 50 %. However, deterrence is measured differently in these studies. If the number of police per capita is used as a deterrent factor (78 effect estimates), only 29 % of effect estimates are consistent with the theory and significant, and the average t-value is −0.34. On the other hand, 50 % of the effect estimates are consistent with the theory and significant if the analysis is performed using the rate of arrests (61 effect estimates); in this case the average t-value is −1.97. Therefore imprisonment seems to have a higher deterrent effect in the case of rape than the number of police per capita.

4.4 The Mechanisms of Deterrence

In empirical studies on negative general prevention there is frequently made a distinction between the discovery of an offence and its sanctioning as possible causes of deterrence. The question is whether causes of deterrence differ in their efficiency. The result of the analysis is shown in Table 4. Only those analysis results

[37] The difference in the results on capital punishment between Tables 1 and 3 is based on different case numbers. Table 1 considered all effect estimates from studies on capital punishment, whereby some studies refer not to willful homicides. Table 3, on the other hand, only takes into account such effect estimates from studies on capital punishment that relate to premeditated murder.

Table 4 Mechanisms of deterrence: Percentage of effect estimates that are significant and consistent with the theory (only indicated if more than 50 cases)

Theory	Offence	Percentage share of effect estimates that are consistent with the theory and significant	Number of effect estimates
Crime statistics studies			
Criminal-sociological theory	Clearance rate	48	61
	Conviction rate	43	51
	Imprisonment/ arrest rate	40	245
	Length of prison sentence[a]	27	54
	Police resources	26	194
Economic theory	Clearance rate	48	141
	Conviction rate	45	99
	Imprisonment/ arrest rate	60	170
	Length of prison sentence[a]	35	93
	Police resources	23	246
Total	Clearance rate	48	202
	Conviction rate	44	150
	Imprisonment/ arrest rate	49	414
	Length of prison sentence[a]	32	147
	Police resources	24	440
Survey studies			
Criminal-sociological theory	Risk of discovery by police	55	82
	Severity of criminal sanction	70	54
Economic Theory	Risk of discovery by police	[b]	[b]
	Severity of criminal sanction	[b]	[b]
Total	Risk of discovery by police	55	86
	Severity of criminal sanction	75	64
Experiments			
Criminal-sociological theory	Risk of discovery	67	308
	Severity of the punishment	38	232

(continued)

Table 4 (continued)

Theory	Offence	Percentage share of effect estimates that are consistent with the theory and significant	Number of effect estimates
Economic theory	Risk of discovery	55	68
	Severity of the punishment	[b]	[b]
Total	Risk of discovery	65	376
	Severity of the punishment	40	259
Studies on capital punishment			
Criminal-sociological theory	Legal threat of capital punishment	[b]	[b]
	Rate of executions	16	188
Economic theory	Legal threat of capital punishment	[b]	[b]
	Rate of executions	48	91
Total	Legal threat of capital punishment	12	67
	Rate of executions	26	279

[a]Length of prison sentence inflicted or served
[b]No indications, less than 50 cases

were taken into consideration which were based on at least 50 effect estimates. In addition, only effect estimates were included which refer to serious offences, i.e. homicide, serious injury, burglary, theft of more expensive goods, dealing with illegal drugs, robbery and rape. In the studies on the effectivity of capital punishment, a difference is made between the legal threat of capital punishment and the realization of executions.

According to the criminal-statistical studies which are based on criminological or sociological theories the detection of a crime has a greater deterring effect than a sentence or an imprisonment. Pursuant to criminal-statistical studies based on economic theories, however, the highest deterrent effect is that of imprisonment. Thus there is a contradiction in the results of the studies. It can be assumed that both detection and sanctioning of offences have a (low) deterring effect. However, in the studies on the deterrent effect of the length of imprisonment and the resources of the police, there is no contradiction: The deterrent effect of these variables is small since less of one third of the effect estimates is consistent to the theory and significant. The results do not speak in favor of a deterrent effect of the length of the imprisonment inflicted and served.

Regarding the effect estimates relating to the influence of legal threats of capital punishment on homicides, only 12 % are consistent to theory and significant. The analysis is based on 67 effect estimates, 40 of which are taken from investigations based on criminological or sociological theories—none of these effect estimates is consistent to theory and significant. Out of the remaining 27 effect estimates—those from studies based on economic theories—29 % are consistent to theory and significant. Concerning the effect estimates on the influence of the execution rate, the percentage of estimates consistent to theory and significant is 26. A deterrent effect of the capital punishment can thus not be proven.

5 Conclusion

The studies on the deterrent effect of criminal punishment come to different results. The impact of the underlying theory on the study results is particularly apparent. This highlights a research deficit: The research process itself should be examined more closely, in particular the transfer of theories to study methods, interpretation of results and the selection of results. Despite these methodological problems, the meta-analysis can be used to increase the reliability of results. For example, deterrent criminal penalties appear to be entirely ineffective or only somewhat effective in the case of young persons; and in the case of serious offences such as premeditated murder, deterrent measures apparently fail to have the desired strong effect. The results of the meta-analysis speak in favor of the hypothesis that the threat of punishment as an isolated measure has no deterrent effect; important are discovery of the offence and sanctioning. But even if these two conditions are met, the deterrent effect is not guaranteed.

The theory of negative general prevention is associated with empirical presuppositions. According to this approach, deterrent sanctions can only be considered legitimate if they are actually effective. The meta-analysis of deterrence studies shows that this concept cannot be confirmed as a universal penal theory that can be applied to all groups of persons and types of offences equally. At the same time, the results do not argue against an application as a differentiated penal theory. Since the deterrent effect of penalties is low in the case of young persons, it is recommendable not to react with severe punishment to offences of young persons but to apply pedagogical measures.

It is frequently supposed that severe punishment implies a strong deterrent effect. Deterrence is one of the reasons that national legal systems and Article 77 of the Rome Statute allow life imprisonment for very serious offences. In a number of countries, even capital punishment is applied. However, the deterrent effect of severe punishment should be regarded with skepticism. A deterrent effect of capital punishment is not verifiable.[38] Moreover it holds that a high discovery

[38] Folter (2014).

probability and consistent prosecution of crimes are more important than severe punishment. The required resources must be made available for this purpose. However, reflections on justice and stabilization of the sense of right and wrong may be taken into consideration for severe punishment of serious offences. These reflections may, among others, be relevant for Article 77 of the Rome Statute.

Five Questions

1. Does a connection exist between the theoretical frame of empirical studies on the deterrent effect of criminal law (negative general prevention) and the results of the studies?
2. Is the deterrent effect of criminal law different for younger and older persons?
3. Can differences of the deterrent effects of criminal law be stated according to the type of the criminal offence?
4. Does the probability of punishment have a deterrent effect?
5. Does the length of prison sentence increase the deterrent effect?

References

Antony, J., & Entorf, H. (2003). Zur Gültigkeit der Abschreckung im Sinne der ökonomischen Theorie der Kriminalität: Grundzüge einer Meta-Studie. In H.-J. Albrecht & H. Entorf (Eds.), *Kriminalität, Ökonomie und Europäischer Sozialstaat* (pp. 167–185). Heidelberg: Physica-Verlag.

Auer, K. H. (2005). *Das Menschenbild als rechtsethische Dimension der Jurisprudenz*. Wien: LIT-Verlag.

Baurmann, M. (1981). *Folgenorientierung und subjektive Verantwortungslosigkeit*. Baden Baden: Nomos.

Beccaria, C. (1766). *Über Verbrechen und Strafen*. Übersetzt und herausgegeben von W. Alff, 1988. Frankfurt/Main: Insel-Verlag.

Becker, G. S. (1968). Crime and punishment: An economic approach. *Journal of Political Economy, 76*(2), 169–217.

Bentham, J. (1823). *An introduction to the principles of morals and legislation*. Reprint, 1996. Oxford: Clarendon Press.

Böckenförde, E.-W. (2001). *Vom Wandel des Menschenbildes im Recht*. Münster: Rhema-Verlag.

Brunner, R., & Dölling, D. (2002). *Jugendgerichtsgesetz. Kommentar* (11th ed.). Berlin/New York: De Gruyter.

Bundeskriminalamt (Ed.) (2013). *Polizeiliche Kriminalstatistik für die Bundesrepublik Deutschland, Berichtsjahr 2012*. Wiesbaden: Bundeskriminalamt.

Burns, J. H. (2005). Happiness and utility: Jeremy Bentham's equation. *Utilitas, 17*(1), 46–61.

Cameron, S. (1988). The economics of crime deterrence: A survey of theory and evidence. *Kyklos, 41*(2), 301–323.

Catudal, H. M. (1985). *Nuclear deterrence, does it deter?* Berlin: Berlin-Verl. Spritz.

Chan, J., & Oxley, D. (2004). The deterrent effect of capital punishment: A review of the research evidence. *Crime and Justice Bulletin No., 84*, 1–24.

Dahrendorf, R. (2006). *Homo Sociologicus. Ein Versuch zur Geschichte, Bedeutung und Kritik der Kategorie der sozialen Rolle* (16th ed.). Wiesbaden: VS Verlag für Sozialwissenschaften.

Dietz, A. (2005). *Der homo oeconomicus*. Gütersloh: Gütersloher Verlagshaus.

Dölling, D. (2007). Zur Willensfreiheit aus strafrechtlicher Sicht. *Forensische Psychiatrie, Psychologie, Kriminologie, 1*(1), 59–62.

Dölling, D. (2012). Menschenbilder in der Kriminologie. In M. Hilgert & M. Wink (Eds.), *Menschen-Bilder. Darstellungen des Humanen in der Wissenschaft. Heidelberger Jahrbücher* (pp. 281–289). Berlin, Heidelberg: Springer.

Dölling, D., Entorf, H., Hermann, D., & Rupp, T. (2011). Meta-analysis of empirical studies on deterrence. In H. Kury & E. Shea (Eds.), *Punitivity international developments* (Vol. 3, pp. 315–378). Bochum: Brockmeyer Universitätsverlag.

Dölling, D., Hermann, D. (2012). Zur generalpräventiven Abschreckungswirkung des Strafrechts bei jungen Menschen. In: Deutsche Vereinigung für Jugendgerichte und Jugendgerichtshilfen e.V. (eds) Achtung (für) Jugend! Praxis und Perspektiven des Jugendkriminalrechts. Dokumentation des 28. Deutschen Jugendgerichtstages vom 11. bis 14. September 2010 in Münster (pp. 427–439). Mönchengladbach: Forum.

Dünkel, F. (2010). Greifswalder Forschungen zum Alkohol im Straßenverkehr. In D. Dölling, B. Götting, B.-D. Meier, & T. Verrel (Eds.), *Verbrechen – Strafe – Resozialisierung. Festschrift für Heinz Schöch zum* (Vol. 70, pp. 101–117). Berlin/New York: Geburtstag. De Gruyter.

Durkheim, É. (2002). *Die Regeln der soziologischen Methode.* Hrsg. u. eingel. von René König. -1st edn [reprint]. Frankfurt am Main: Suhrkamp.

Ehrlich, I. (1973). Participation in illegitimate activities: A theoretical and empirical investigation. *Journal of Political Economy, 81*(3), 521–565.

Ehrlich, I. (1975). The deterrent effect of capital punishment: A question of life and death. *American Economic Review, 65*(3), 397–417.

Ehrlich, I. (1977). Capital punishment and deterrence: Some further thoughts and additional evidence. *Journal of Political Economy, 85*(4), 741–788.

Eisele, H. (1999). Die general- und spezialpräventive Wirkung strafrechtlicher Sanktionen. Methoden, Ergebnisse, Metaanalyse. Dissertation, Universität Heidelberg.

Farin, E. (1994). Forschungsperspektive und Methodik der Metaanalyse. Forschungsberichte des Psychologischen Instituts der Albert-Ludwigs-Universität, No. 113. Freiburg i. Br: Albert-Ludwigs-Universität.

Feuerbach, P. J. A. (1799). *Revision der Grundsätze und Grundbegriffe des positiven peinlichen Rechts* (Vol. 1). Erfurt: Henningsche Buchhandlung.

Folter, C. (2014). *Die Abschreckungswirkung der Todesstrafe. Eine qualitative Metaanalyse.* Berlin: LIT.

Fricke, R., Treinis, G. (1985). Einführung in die Metaanalyse. Methoden der Psychologie, Vol. 3. Huber, Bern u.a.

Fuhrer, U. (2009). *Lehrbuch Erziehungspsychologie.* Bern: Huber.

Hedges, L. V., & Olkin, I. (1985). *Statistical methods for meta-analysis.* San Diego: Academic.

Hermann, D. (2012). Menschenbild und Forschung – generalpräventive Untersuchungen zur Todesstrafe. In M. Hilgert & M. Wink (Eds.), *Menschen-Bilder. Darstellungen des Humanen in der Wissenschaft. Heidelberger Jahrbücher* (pp. 291–307). Berlin/Heidelberg: Springer.

Hinz, A., & Becker, B. (2012). Belohnung und Bestrafung. In U. Sandfuchs, W. Melzer, B. Dühlmeier, & A. Rausch (Eds.), *Handbuch Erziehung* (pp. 596–599). Bad Heilbrunn: Klinkhardt.

Iffland, R., & Balling, P. (1999). Erste Auswirkungen der 0,5-Promille-Grenze auf das Fahrverhalten alkoholisierter Verkehrsteilnehmer. *Blutalkohol, 36*(1), 39–43.

Jescheck, H.- H., Weigend, T. (1996). *Lehrbuch des Strafrechts. Allgemeiner Teil* (5th edn). Berlin: Duncker and Humblot.

Mannheim, K. (1970). Wissenssoziologie. Auswahl aus dem Werk (2nd edn), edited by Kurt H Wolff. Luchterhand, Neuwied und Berlin.

Manstetten, R. (2002). *Das Menschenbild in der Ökonomie – Der homo oeconomicus und die Anthropologie von Adam Smith.* Freiburg: Karl Alber Verlag.

Müller, J. (1996). *Ökonomische Grundlagen der Generalprävention.* Frankfurt/Main: Lang.

Nagin, D. (1978). General deterrence: A review of the empirical evidence. In A. Blumstein, J. Cohen, & D. Nagin (Eds.), *Deterrence and incapacitation: Estimating the effects of criminal sanctions on crime rates* (pp. 95–139). Washington D.C.: National Academy Press.

Ogilvie-White, T. (2011). *On nuclear deterrence*. Abingdon, Oxon: Routledge.

Petrosino, A. J. (1997). 'What works?' revisited again: A meta-analysis of randomized experiments in: rehabilitation, deterrence and delinquency prevention. Diss. Rutgers University, Ann Arbor.

Robinson, W. S. (1950). Ecological correlations and the behavior of individuals. *American Sociological Review, 15*(3), 351–357.

Rosenthal, R. (1991). *Meta-analytic procedures for social research*. Revised Edition. Beverly Hills: Sage.

Rupp, T. (2008). Meta-analysis of crime and deterrence: A comprehensive review of the literature. Dissertation, Technische Universität Darmstadt. http://tuprints.ulb.tu-darmstadt.de/1054/2/rupp_diss.pdf (11/2008).

Scheler, M. (1926). *Die Wissensformen und die Gesellschaft*. Leipzig: Der Neue Geist.

Schöch, H. (1991). Kriminologische und sanktionsrechtliche Aspekte der Alkoholdelinquenz im Verkehr. *Neue Zeitschrift für Strafrecht, 11*(1), 11–17.

Spirgath, T. (2013). Zur Abschreckungswirkung des Strafrechts - Eine Metaanalyse kriminalstatistischer Untersuchungen. Reihe: Kriminalwissenschaftliche Schriften, Vol. 39. Berlin: LIT.

Stanley, T. D. (2001). From wheat to chaff: Meta-analysis as quantitative literature review. *Journal of Economic Perspectives, 15*(3), 131–150.

Vollrath, M., & Krüger, H.-P. (1999). Auswirkungen der "Androhung" 0,5-Promille-Grenze im Kontext längerfristiger Entwicklungen. *Blutalkohol, 36*, 349–361.

Wagner. M, Weiß, B. (2006). Meta-Analyse als Methode der Sozialforschung. In: Diekmann A (ed) *Methoden der Sozialforschung. Kölner Zeitschrift für Soziologie und Sozialpsychologie*, Vol. 44 (pp. 479–504). Sonderheft.

Weber, M. (1980). In J. Winckelmann (Ed) Wirtschaft und Gesellschaft. Grundriß der Verstehenden Soziologie (5th edn) (Studienausgabe). Tübingen: Mohr.

Wippmann, D. (1999). Atrocities, deterrence, and the limits of international justice. *Fordham International Law Journal, 23*, 473–488.

Wolf, F. M. (1986). Meta-analysis. Quantitative methods for research synthesis. University Paper Series on Quantitative Applications in the Social Sciences 59. Thousand Oaks: Sage.

Yang, B., & Lester, D. (2008). The deterrent effect of executions: A meta-analysis thirty years after Ehrlich. *Journal of Criminal Justice, 36*(5), 453–460.

Actors, Factors and Processes on the Road to the Abolition of the Death Penalty

Luis Arroyo Zapatero

Abstract In 2015, the UN has reviewed the degree of compliance with two United Nations initiatives: the Millennium Development Goals 2000–2015 and the 2007 Assembly Resolution calling for a Universal Moratorium on the Application of the Death Penalty. These are two different but very closely related matters. The Millennium Development Goals urge the UN member States and the international community to prevent millions of deaths by famine and epidemics of curable illnesses. In the second initiative, the majority of the members of the General Assembly call on its Member States to end the use of death as a punishment in their justice systems, even in legal proceedings. In both cases the ideas of the United Nations, the product of political and academic works of people who have a leading role in the life of the United Nations as diplomats, staff members, experts, and members of non-governmental organizations that construct a cultural and political heritage of humanity. This chapter concentrates on the actors in the processes of abolition and the factors triggering them since the 1948 Universal Declaration of Human Rights and searches for elements that can exert influence over the events.

1 Introduction

In 2015, the degree of compliance with two relevant initiatives of the United Nations has been reviewed: the Millennium Development Goals (MDGs), established in the declaration of the UN General Assembly of 2000 (A/RES/55/1), and another UN resolution (A/RES/62/149), of 2007, calling for a universal moratorium on the application of the death penalty. These are two different but very closely related matters. The Millennium Development Goals urge the UN member States and the international community to prevent millions of deaths by famine and

---

The text is taken from the presentation given in French at the École Normal Supérieure in October 2013, at the colloquium "*Vers l'interdiction absolue de la peine de mort. Perspectives philosophiques et juridiques*", organized by Marc Crépon and Jean Luis Halpérin and by Stefano Manacorda of the Collége de France.

L. Arroyo Zapatero (✉)
University of Castilla-La Mancha, Ciudad Real, Spain
e-mail: Luis.ArroyoZapatero@uclm.es

H. Kury et al. (eds.), *Women and Children as Victims and Offenders: Background, Prevention, Reintegration*, DOI 10.1007/978-3-319-28424-8_2

epidemics of curable illnesses. In the second initiative, the majority of the members of the General Assembly call on its Member States to end the use of death as a punishment in their justice systems, even in legal proceedings. It is in both cases the ideas of the United Nations, the product of political and academic works of people who have a leading role in the life of the United Nations as diplomats, staff members, experts, and members of non-governmental organizations that construct a cultural and political heritage of humanity.[1]

The question of the abolition of the death penalty was not addressed at the founding of the Organization. The symbol of peace was precisely the executions of war criminals at both Nuremberg and Tokyo. The debate only began while preparing the Universal Declaration of Human Rights in 1948, but no consensus was reached and it was preferred to make no mention of the matter when proclaiming the right to life. This lack of consensus was repeated in the preparation of the International Covenant on Civil and Political Rights in 1966: article 6 enshrined the legitimacy of the death penalty, even when it was expressed in such a way that it was subjected to certain restrictions and controls for the countries that maintain that punishment in force, which has allowed notable monitoring by various United Nations bodies, especially by the UN Human Rights Council.

At the time of the adoption of the Universal Declaration of Human Rights in 1948, no more than a dozen countries had abolished the death penalty. By December 2014, more than 106 had done so, and more than a few—39—are countries that do not execute, even though they maintain the death penalty in their laws. At present, however, a relevant group of countries still detain and execute prisoners, some of them as important as the United States, China, and Japan.[2] The study of the data on the abolition in different countries should be completed with a study of the reasons and factors that have promoted the decision in favour of either the legal or the de-facto abolition of capital punishment.

A traditional cartography of the death penalty throughout the world would be of immense utility and might outline the transformation, since the end of the 1950s, of retentionist countries into abolitionist countries. However, the progressive changes to the colours of the political map will not in themselves convey sufficient information to understand the reasons and motives for progress or the obstacles to abolition and its trends. It will not be easy to gather the knowledge needed for a better understanding of the international harmonization of criminal law and to guide it effectively towards the abolition of the death penalty throughout the world. A modern map such as the one developed by Jean-Luis Halperin and Stefano Manacorda, the team formed by jurists from both the *Collège de France* and the *École Normal Superieur* of Paris, seeks to do precisely that: it is intended as a resource for knowledge and understanding, capable of producing guidelines for action. These roads towards harmonization also serve as the model with which to

[1] On this topic, with references, Arroyo Zapatero et al. (2010), pp. 39–50.

[2] See the latest data in Hood and Hoyle (2015), p. 16.

interpret the evolution of the legal, and especially the criminal facts, which Mireille Delmas-Marty, Member and Emeritus Professor of the *Collège de France*, has prepared as a general theory over recent years, at the helm of a remarkable group of researchers.

Mireille Delmas-Marty has developed a model for technical interpretation and construction of the processes of international legal harmonization, which goes by the name of "*Les chemins de l'harmonization*".[3] In my opinion, it is an essential complement to the traditional methods of comparative law. The methodology of *Les Chemins* can be applied to numerous specific matters that today have already been harmonized, constructing new legal realities: terrorism, international criminal law, the trafficking of human beings, money laundering, corruption, etc., but also to questions that de-harmonize or that "harmonize in reverse", such as the issue of the universal abolition of the death penalty, which almost 60 years ago began and continues to uphold a premise of universal validity.

Here, it is a question of analysing the movement towards the abolition of the death penalty, across the whole international context, in countries that have implemented it, in those that retain it without applying it, and in those that retain it and apply it:

(a) An attempt to set out a systematic classification of the singular processes of abolition;
(b) The actors, both organizations and private citizens, who intervene in the processes;
(c) The factors that set abolition in motion and, if applicable, the moratorium. We will examine all of that in the processes already carried out as well as in those in which the issue is still alive. Likewise, the processes of the countries that fiercely cling on to the death penalty will be examined.

The processes of greatest impact on abolition in the modern era that assist us with the analysis may be summarised in three models.

2 Processes of Transition, Evolution and Integration

At the height of the preparation of the Universal Declaration of Human Rights, hardly half-a-dozen countries had adopted abolition.[4] However, it was during the constituent processes after the Second World War, when the most representative abolitions took place: in Germany and Italy. In both countries, abolition represents a reaction against the excesses of Nazism and of Fascism; a strong reaction against their previous experiences leading to a complete rejection of arbitrary and cruel death inflicted by the State. Another relevant moment, without leaving Europe, is

[3] Delmas-Marty et al. 2008.

[4] Ancel (1968). For a European context, see Ancel (1962).

the departure from some countries of the old authoritarian regimes, such as in Spain and Greece, which share the rejection of the numerous capital executions in their relatively recent history, especially in the case of Spain. Similar events did not take place in Portugal, because the dictatorship had not changed the early abolition of the nineteenth century and only on limited occasions did it turn to extrajudicial execution, in order to see its enemies disappear.[5]

Abolition processes are also noted in *stable democratic systems* such as Great Britain and France. Abolition, in the former, is a process that was set in motion by two factors: the works of the Royal Commission of Inquiry on the death penalty and the public disclosure that the last execution of a prisoner, a person called Evans,[6] had been the consequence of a tragic judicial error, as the real perpetrator of the crimes for which Evans had been executed confessed to that and to many other crimes. It was the impact on public opinion that tipped the political balance of the Royal Commission of Inquiry, as its report offered no specific conclusion on retention or abolition.

The French case is a prototype of the political decision against the death penalty, even with a majority public opinion in its favour. It is a question of the *Badinter factor*, a fervent abolitionist, who brought together the "learned" professor and the criminal lawyer specialized in cases of capital punishment. He contended, before juries and in the face of public opinion, that the personality disorders of family origin of the majority of capital punishment cases counter the punishment in its most extreme form, because the accused could not fully assume responsibility for his acts.[7]

Among the political processes of international origin, those of Turkey, Poland and Latvia are of interest. The first, as a significant member of the European Convention on Human Rights, came under pressure from the Human Rights Court at Strasbourg to moderate the Death Penalty, and at a later point in time, in its desire to integrate in the European Union, its legislators opted for abolition. Poland, at the time before it assumed full EU membership, reacted in ways that were contrary to the community viewpoint, for instance, in the case of the death penalty, but this position was reversed by the previous big decision in favour of integration and, subsequently, by the Treaty of Lisbon.[8,9]

---

[5] On the singular history of the first abolitionist country in the world, see Braga da Cruz (1967), p. 423–557; Miranda Rodrigues (2014), pp. 79–84.

[6] A passionate account may be seen in chapter 10 of the *Adventures in Criminology* by Sir Leon Radzinowicz, p. 245 and ff. With full details, likewise, Hood and Radzinowicz (1986), p. 661 and ff. Hood and Hoyle (2015), p. 40 and ff. A presentation in Spanish in Arroyo Zapatero, *La experiencia de la abolición de la pena de muerte en Gran Bretaña*, in Revista de la Facultad de Derecho de la Universidad Complutense de Madrid, 62, Madrid 1981, pp. 47–66, now in Rodriguez Yagüe (2013), p. 471 and ff.

[7] Bandinter (2008).

[8] The **Treaty of Lisbon** is an international agreement which amends the two treaties which form the constitutional basis of the European Union (EU). The Treaty of Lisbon entered into force on 1 December 2009.

[9] Yorke (2008), pp. 43–100.

3 The Actors

The leading role in the national processes of abolition is usually the responsibility of the Government and the parliamentary majorities. At times, no special actor stands out in the process, for example, in the case of Germany, Italy, Spain and France.

On occasions, the leading role is taken by a court, as with the Supreme Court in South Africa,[10] which declared that the death penalty was a cruel, inhuman and degrading punishment. More frequently, it has been a case of regional Courts, both in Europe with the Court of Human Rights at Strasbourg, and in Latin America with the Inter-American Court of Human Rights. International jurisprudence establishes a sort of siege mentality around capital punishment that, without making a direct declaration of a conventional breach, does say as much in an indirect way, especially as a cruel, inhuman and degrading punishment. This is what happened in the cases of Soering and of O'Calan, two persons charged with murder whose extradition, asked by the US and Turkey, was rejected by the ECHR because they could be punished with the death penalty.[11] Their efficacy was very relevant in relation to Turkey. It has been even more relevant in the abolitionist countries, for example, in Chile and in Peru, in which the Inter-American Convention[12] proscribes the reintroduction once it has been abolished. The moratorium in the Russian Republic is in direct relation to the process of its incorporation in the Council of Europe. The only fiercely retentionist country, Belorussia, avoids for this reason and for others its incorporation into the European Convention.

There are very few examples of a solitary President of a Republic in favour of the reform, with a parliament set against it, such as in Mongolia, where President Elbeg was able to ratify the 2° Optional Protocol in his parliament within 2 years.[13]

4 International Bodies

International bodies have and increasingly are accomplishing a starring role in the range of actors in the abolition process. The first great step forward was taken by the Commission on Crime Prevention and Criminal Justice of the United Nations,

---

[10] Chenwi (2007).

[11] Nieto Martín (2010), pp. 51–75.

[12] The American convention on Human Rights, also known as the **Pact of San José**, is an international human rights instrument that was adopted in 1969 and came into forcé on 18 July 1978. The bodies responsable for overseeing compliance with the Convention are the Inter-American Commission on Human Rights and the Inter-American Court of Human Rights. Bourgorge and Ubeda (2011).

[13] Halvorsen (2014), p. 297.

especially at the Sixth United Nations Congress on the Prevention of Crime and the Treatment of Offenders (Caracas, Venezulela, 1980). A proposal on abolition was adopted there, supported by the whole apparatus that we know as *safeguards*, which are found under article 6 of the International Covenant on Civil and Political Rights of 1966 in the years following the aforementioned Congress, and especially in 1989.[14]

The Council of Europe followed a similar but more complete process and closed the question with the adoption of the equivalent of the 2° facultative protocol of the ICCPR, protocol n° 6 to the European Convention of Human Rights, ratified today by every country except Belorussia. The Treaty of Lisbon had the last word with its express abolition of capital punishment.[15]

The process at an international level provisionally concluded with the adoption of the 2nd Facultative Protocol to the International Convention that established abolition except in times of war, although certainly in a year of global optimism: 1989. But subsequently, it has been endorsed with extraordinary legislative and symbolic vigour in the three resolutions from the Security Council and the Assembly General through the rejection of the death penalty as a punishment for the most serious crimes—against humanity and war crimes—in the ad hoc Tribunals of the 1990s. The enshrining has been its inclusion in the Statute of Rome.[16] Its effects on national legislations were especially evident in abolition in Rwanda, but its effects have multiplied since then throughout Africa.

Academics have played a significant role as a group of actors, both in their own university circles as well as their participation in institutions representing political order. As an example of the first, it is worth recalling, in the case of Spain, my mentor Professor Marino Barbero. His inaugural lesson from the 1963–1964 academic year on the death penalty called for its abolition with only a few months after the execution of the Communist leader Julián Grimau, who was the last person executed of the Francoist genocide time (1963). It was the end of the *first* and *second* periods of Francoism that gave way to a "solely" authoritarian version of the Regime and left a long-lasting memory in Spanish life. The maximum academic authority, the Rector of the University of Murcia, wore the uniform of the Francoist "Movement" under his academic attire. He surely shuddered when Marino Barbero Santos shouted that if they made the effort to keep it, because of its great importance, then entrust the executions to the Head of State himself to carry out with his own hands.

Another academic who successfully dedicated a good part of his life to abolition was the President of the International Society for Social Defence (ISSD), Marc Ancel. His reports to the United Nations General Assembly and then for the Council

---

[14] About *safeguards* s. Bernaz (2008).

[15] Yorke (2009), pp. 205–229.

[16] The **Rome Statute of the International Criminal Court** (often referred to as the **International Criminal Court Statute** or the **Rome Statute**) is the treaty that established the International Criminal Court (ICC). It was adopted at a diplomatic conference in Rome on 17 January 1998.

of Europe have been the ashlar blocks of abolitionist thought. Over the last 20 years, leading academics have assumed responsibility for the 5-yearly report for the Secretary General: Roger Hood and William Schabas.[17] Robert Badinter may undoubtedly be positioned mid-way between academia and politics.

NGOs joined the ranks of actors against capital punishment late in the day, but when they did so, on the eve of globalization, their voice was heard everywhere. Amnesty International named its campaign "when the State kills"[18] and started a movement that was assumed monographically at least by the *Ensemble contre la peine de mort*, which gave way to the *World Coalition against the death penalty*, a mobilizing movement that together with other activities has propelled numerous processes, such as the launch, in 2010, of the inter-governmental organization *International Commission Against the Death Penalty*, which is chaired by Federico Mayor Zaragoza.[19] At the time of the Amnesty International report, 1989, it was reported that 70 countries had abolished capital punishment by law or were *de facto* abolitionists, while 100 conserved it.

5 The Events That Brought About the Abolition Processes

In the processes of abolition, factors stand out that help set the abolition processes in motion, although there are some others that tend to have the contrary effect.

Among the factors that drive abolition are judicial errors.[20] The Evans case that led to abolition in Great Britain has previously been mentioned. The numerous cases of judicial error that have occurred in the USA, and were discovered primarily—but not only—on the basis, of the availability of DNA tests, and are today well recognized and systemized in the *Death Penalty Project,* are the propelling factor that has given rise to most progress towards abolition in the USA. As told by lawyer Scott Turow,[21] over 100 people convicted of the death penalty and later declared innocent while they were on death row made Governors shudder such as the Governor of Illinois, George Ryan. Subsequently, seven US States, with or without moratorium, abolished the death penalty as a reaction to the horror of the execution of innocents over the past 5 years.[22]

---

[17] Hood has recently published his 5th edition of the most important work at a global level on the matter, in collaboration with Carolyn Hoyle. William Schabas also held again the responsibility for the report to the Secretary General of the United Nations over the period 2010–2015.

[18] *When the State Kills. The Death Penalty vs. Human Rights.* Edited and published by Amnesty International, 1989.

[19] For a presentation of tasks and objectives of the Commission, see Mayor Zaragoza (2013).

[20] The Death Penalty Project, *The inevitability of error. The administration of justice in death penalty cases*, London 2014.

[21] Turow (2002).

[22] On the effects of wrongful convictions in various countries, see Hood and Hoyle (2015), p. 323 and ff.

The general feeling of social aversion to the death penalty is fundamentally due to the awareness of risk and error and repugnance towards cruelty in the execution, specially the so-called "botched executions".[23] But in 2014, a new factor has recently emerged that has been on the point of helping abolition by referendum in California: the economic cost to the state of the criminal proceedings with requests for capital punishment. *Due process*, surrounded by guarantees in the capital cases, multiplies the procedural costs, which replicated in thousands of cases produces a rejection in people concerned with the public *debt*, which generates strange alliances for abolition in California.

Added to wars, their horror, massacres, and so on, another relevant factor in contemporary times has been the dissolution of military blocks. Their most direct consequences, linked to the optimism of 1989, are those already mentioned in the International Convention on the Rights of the Child, which has managed to exclude children from being candidates for execution in countries that are reluctant to do so, even out of a repugnance towards accepting sources of legal authority in international organs, such as those in the United States. Its signatories also include countries fiercely committed to execution such as Saudi Arabia and China. The approval of the *safeguards* refers to the same process.

Events may also be identified that trigger contrary social processes, favourable to maintaining capital punishment or its reintroduction, which includes recourse to execution in *de facto* abolitionist countries.

Horrible crimes have resulted from *de facto* abolitionism in Gambia. Terrorism is another driving factor that breaks a moratorium. The numerous pitiless violations with or without murders, carried out, or experienced for the first time, in India, is what has reinforced the institutional social impact of capital punishment in a country that had only one execution in the past few years and only because of the terrorist attacks in Bombay that caused over 70 victims. Terrorism was the sad event that triggered the attempts to reintroduce capital punishment in Peru.[24]

Perhaps it is the religious standpoint of certain religions, and the spirit of the Talion, that could be included among the reasons that, rather than triggering, maintain the predominance of capital punishment. The law of Talion is also a typical sociological fact that operates by itself, especially in modern-day society of mass communication.

6 Final Considerations

All of the above shows a lattice work of relevant processes, facts, and authors in the evolution of the abolition process. Completed with other research, it may all serve to develop a cartographic *opus majus*.

[23] Radelet (2014).

[24] Hurtado Pozo (2010), pp. 213–222.

What drives the processes of abolition is not only the positive idea that what we call the right to life but, above all, the idea and feeling of rejection of cruel treatment, causing pain to others. It is the feeling of rejection of torture and harsh cold-blooded murder. The rejection of the death penalty can form part of a contemporary "*ethical-cosmopolitanism strategy*",[25] which radically rejects killing other people.

The most complex question lies in how to define and to transmit the rejection of the death penalty and the grounds of its proscription. Once again, the arts, including photography and literature, appear to be the most appropriate to define the rejection of cold-blooded death that the State inflicts with capital punishment and the solidarity towards whoever suffers such a punishment. Francisco de Goya was the first to denounce cruel and inhuman punishment, as well as the cruelties of war, in illustrated works, in which his rejection of the death penalty is manifest.[26] One has to wait for the modern vanguards to find similar expressions of such values and, most especially, the German expressionists of the 1920s, well represented at the centenary commemoration of the First World War, inspired by Goya in the "Disasters of War".

Many people are today searching for a guide for human action founded on the search for the common good, in solidarity and in the rejection of cruelty based on scientific research beyond Kantian ethical universalism and Christian moral thought, including the programme for an "ethical world" of Hans Küng.[27] Three orientations deserve to be highlighted: the contribution of Richard Rorty in his "*Contingency, Irony and Solidarity*"[28] and that of Von Trotha[29]: the former primarily on solidarity and the latter on cruelty, as well as in favour and against the "*Consentement meurtrier*" *[murderous consent]* an idea developed by Marc Crépon,[30] all inspired like Goya by the "Disasters of War". Those who find themselves searching for guidelines on human actions in favour of the common good are very numerous, goodness in which human rights have a place and among them that of not losing the right to life, not even by the actions of the State in its policy on justice. A task to which the best of the generations that have constructed and developed the United Nations have dedicated themselves.

Five Questions

1. Which are the UN resolutions related to the death penalty and deaths caused by hunger and illness whose compliance will be reviewed in 2015?
2. What kind of political process usually brings about the abolition of death penalty?

---

[25] Held (2010); Charvet (1998), pp. 523–541.

[26] Blas and Matilla (2000). Also Arroyo Zapatero and Bordes (2013).

[27] Küng (1998).

[28] Rorty (1989).

[29] von Trotha and Rösel (2011).

[30] Crépon (2012).

3. Who have been the most outstanding scholars in the international debate against the death penalty?
4. Which kind of factors trigger processes of abolition or reinstatement of death penalty?
5. Which are the main arguments forming the basis of the abolitionists' proposals?

References

Ancel, M. (1962). *La peine de mort dans les pays européens*. Report. Council of Europe.

Ancel, M. (1968). *The death penalty* Part I: *Evolution until 1960* and Part II: *Evolution from 1961 to 1965*. Department of Economic and Social Affairs New York, United Nations.

Arroyo Zapatero, L. & Bordes, J. (2013). *Francisco de Goya. Contra la crueldad de la pena de muerte Against the cruelty of capital punishment*. Madrid: Universidad de Castilla-La Mancha and Real Academia de Bellas Artes. Also on line at www.academicsforabolition.net and at http://www.inacipe.gob.mx/publicaciones/Goya.php.

Arroyo Zapatero, L., Biglino, P. & Schabas, W. (Eds.); Muñoz Aunión, A. (Coord.) (2010). *Towards universal abolition of the death penalty*. Valencia: Tirant lo Blanch. Also full on line at Google books and www.academicsforabolition.net.

Bandinter, R. (2008). *Contre la peine de mort. Écrits 1970–2006*. Paris: Fayard.

Bernaz, N. (2008). *Le droit international et la peine de mort*. Paris: La Documentation Française.

Blas, J. & Matilla, J. M. (2000). *El libro de los Desastres de la Guerra*. Museo Nacional del Prado.

Bourgorge, L., & Ubeda, A. (2011). *The Inter-American court of human rights. Case-law and commentary*. Oxford: Oxford University Press.

Charvet, J. (1998). The possibility of a cosmopolitan ethical order based on the idea of universal human rights, in Millennium. *Journal of International Studies, 27*(3), 523–541.

Chenwi, L. (2007). *Towards the abolition of the death penalty in Africa, a human right perspective*. Pretoria: Pretoria University Law Press.

Crépon, M. (2012). *Le consentement meurtrier*. Paris: Cerf.

Braga da Cruz, G. (1967). O movimento abolicionista e a aboliçao da pena de morte em Portugal: Resenha histórica In P. de Morte (Ed.), Coloquio Internacional comemorativo do Centenário da aboliçao da pena de morte em Portugal, vol. 3 (pp. 423–557). Edit. Faculdade de Direito da Universidade de Coimbra.

Delmas-Marty, M., Pieht, M., & Sieber, U. (2008). *Les chemins de l'harmonisation pénale. Harmonising criminal law*. Paris: Société de Législation Comparée.

Halvorsen, V. (2014). Criminal justice, sustainability and the death penalty. In L. Scherdin (Ed.), *Capital punishment A hazard to a sustainable criminal justice system*. Surrey/Burlington: Ashgate.

Held, D. (2010). *Cosmopolitanism: Ideals, realities, and deficits*. Cambridge: Polity Press.

Hood, R., & Hoyle, C. (2015). *The death penalty* (5th ed.). Oxford: Oxford University Press.

Hood, R., & Radzinowicz, L. (1986). *A history of english criminal law and its administration from 1750. The emergence of penal policy*. London: Stevens and Sons.

Hurtado Pozo, J. (2010) Attempts to reinstate the death penalty in Peru. In L. Arroyo Zapatero, P. Biglino & W. Schabas (Eds.); A. Muñoz Aunión (Coord.), *Towards universal abolition of the death penalty* (pp. 213–222). Valencia: Tirant lo Blanch.

Küng, H. (1998). *A global ethic for global politics and economics*. New York: Oxford University Press.

Mayor Zaragoza, F. (2013). The abolition of the death penalty: a question of respect for human rights. In L. Arroyo & J. Bordes, *Francisco de Goya. Contra la crueldad de la pena de muerte/ Against the cruelty of capital punishment*. Madrid: Universidad de Castilla-La Mancha and

Real Academia de Bellas Artes. On line at http://www.inacipe.gob.mx/publicaciones/Goya.php.

Miranda Rodrigues, A. (2014) Portugal como país pionero en la abolición de la pena de muerte en Europa. In L. Arroyo Zapatero, A. Nieto & W. Schabas; B. García-Moreno (Coord.), *Pena de muerte: Una pena cruel e inhumana y no especialmente disuasoria* (pp. 79–84). Cuenca: UCLM and Tirant lo Blanch.

Nieto Martín, A. (2010) Judicial cooperation in the EU as a means of combating the death penalty and expansion of human rights. In L. Arroyo Zapatero, P. Biglino & W. Schabas (Eds.); A. Muñoz Aunión (Coord.), *Towards universal abolition of the death penalty* (pp. 51–75). Valencia: Tirant lo Blanch.

Radelet, M. (2014) *Some examples of Post-Furman Botched Executions*. Available online at http://www.deathpenaltyinfo.org/some-examples-post-furman-botched-executions.

Rodriguez Yagüe, C. (Ed.); Gargallo, L. (Coord.) (2013). *Clásicos españoles sobre la pena de muerte*. Ciudad Real: UCLM.

Rorty, R. (1989). *Contingency, Irony, and Solidarity*. Cambridge: Cambridge University Press.

Turow, S. (2002). *Ultimate punishment: A lawyer's reflections on dealing with the death penalty*. New York: Picador.

von Trotha, T., & Rösel, J. (2011). *On cruelty, Sur la Cruauté, Über Grausamkeit*. Cologne: R. Köppe.

Yorke, J. (2009). The right to life and abolition of the death penalty in the Council of Europe. *European Law Review, 34*, 205–230.

Yorke, J. (2008). Against the death penalty: international initiatives and implications. *Ashgate*.

Women in Criminal Justice Systems and the Added Value of the UN Bangkok Rules

Andrea Huber

Abstract Many argue that treating women differently in the criminal justice system constitutes discrimination, that women prisons are "nicer" anyway, and that the focus should be on the majority (male) prison population, given the low number of female suspects, defendants and prisoners. Others reason that for decades the attention has been focused entirely on male offenders and prisoners, and that the specific backgrounds and needs of women have been overlooked long enough to justify increased attention on this particularly vulnerable group. Is discrimination against women in the criminal justice system a myth? Are women offenders and prisoners "better off" anyway? Do prosecutors and judges deal more leniently with female offenders? Shouldn't prison conditions and rehabilitation programmes be the same for both men and women, and aren't they in correctional facilities nowadays anyway? This chapter seeks to outline aspects of discrimination faced by female suspects, defendants and prisoners in criminal justice systems, their number, profile and characteristics, and the offences they are typically charged with or convicted for, drawing on findings from a number of recent research studies. Based on the specific characteristics and needs of female offenders and prisoners the chapter highlights the respective standards established by the United Nations Rules for the Treatment of Women Prisoners and Non- custodial Measures for Women Offenders (the Bangkok Rules), adopted by the UN General Assembly in December 2010.

1 Introduction

Many argue that treating women differently in the criminal justice system constitutes discrimination, that women prisons are "nicer" anyway, and that the focus should be on the majority (male) prison population, given the low number of female suspects, defendants and prisoners. Others reason that for decades the attention has

A. Huber (✉)
Penal Reform International, London, UK
e-mail: ahuber@penalreform.org

H. Kury et al. (eds.), *Women and Children as Victims and Offenders: Background, Prevention, Reintegration*, DOI 10.1007/978-3-319-28424-8_3

been focused entirely on male offenders and prisoners, and that the specific backgrounds and needs of women have been overlooked long enough to justify increased attention on this particularly vulnerable group. Is discrimination against women in the criminal justice system a myth? Are women offenders and prisoners 'better off' anyway? Do prosecutors and judges deal more leniently with female offenders? Should prison conditions, treatment in detention and rehabilitation programmes be equal for all prisoners, and aren't they in correctional facilities nowadays anyway?

This chapter seeks to outline aspects of discrimination faced by female suspects, defendants and prisoners in criminal justice systems, their number, profile and characteristics, and the offences they are typically charged with or convicted for. It covers certain key conditions in detention as well as programmes in place with regard to rehabilitation and reintegration.

In doing so, it draws on data, country examples and findings from a number of research studies. It should be emphasised that these examples have not been chosen to "single out" certain countries, but are meant to be illustrative of the aspects covered and in particular to focus on countries where surveys have been conducted most recently. While research methodologies and scope vary, they provide an in-depth and recent insight into the situation in Argentina, Armenia, China, Georgia, Jordan, Kazakhstan, Kyrgyzstan, South Africa and Tunisia.

While some data has been published, mostly on women in prison in Western countries, research into the profile of female offenders and prisoners as well as their pathways to offending is still scarce, particularly in Asia, the Middle East, Africa and Latin America. However, a few studies have been conducted recently, not least inspired by Rule 67 et seq. of the United Nations Rules for the Treatment of Women Prisoners and Non-custodial Measures for Women Offenders (the Bangkok Rules), adopted in December 2010 (GA res. 65/229 of 12 December 2010).

The lack of attention women suspects, defendants and prisoners received has not been limited to research, but was—up until the adoption of these Rules—also mirrored in key international standards relating to the treatment of prisoners. The 1955 UN Standard Minimum Rules for the Treatment of Prisoners (Standard Minimum Rules),[1] still the one comprehensive set of guidelines on the treatment of prisoners and conditions of detention, provide little gender-specific guidance.[2] They do require women and men to be detained in separate facilities and women prisoners to be exclusively supervised and attended to by female prison officers. Otherwise, however, Rules relating to female prisoners were limited to pre- and

[1] Adopted by the First United Nations Congress on the Prevention of Crime and the Treatment of Offenders, and approved by the Economic and Social Council by resolutions 663 C (XXIV) of 31 July 1957 and 2076 (LXII) of 13 May 1977.

[2] Please note that after this article was written, on 17 December 2015 the United Nations General Assembly completed the revision of this standard and adopted the revised Standard Minimum Rules for the Treatment of Prisoners (Nelson Mandela Rules, Resolution 70/175). The review updated nine areas and resulted in a renumbering of the Rules. This article does not reflect the revision.

post-natal care and to nursing of infants. The UN Standard Minimum Rules for Non-custodial Measures (Tokyo Rules),[3] which represent the basic principles relating to the use of non-custodial measures and sanctions, do not contain any provisions specific to female offenders at all.

The adoption of the Bangkok Rules in December 2010 therefore constituted a major step forward in recognising the gender-specific needs of women in the criminal justice system. The Rules were initiated by the government of Thailand, with HRH Princess Bajrakitiyabha of Thailand playing a pivotal role in the development of the Rules, and are therefore known as the Bangkok Rules.

The 70 Rules[4] cover the treatment of women prisoners, but also alternatives to imprisonment by incorporating specific provisions on gender-sensitive non-custodial measures and sanctions, the consideration of gender-specific circumstances in sentencing as well as standards relating to conditions in detention. The Rules do not replace but supplement both the Standard Minimum Rules and the Tokyo Rules, rectifying the gaps related to specific needs of female offenders.[5] This chapter therefore seeks to highlight, where applicable, the added value of this set of international guidance on the treatment of women prisoners and their access to non-custodial measures and sanctions.

2 Discrimination Against Women in the Criminal Justice System

2.1 *Gender-Specific Offences*[6]

In many countries criminal sanctions are used to curb sexual or religious 'immorality' through the use/designation of "offences" such as adultery, extramarital sex, sexual misconduct, violations of dress codes or prostitution. Such offences tend to penalise women exclusively or disproportionately even if they are formulated in a gender-neutral way. Some studies also suggest that females charged on moral offences are treated more harshly than males, presumably for having transgressed their gender role.[7]

In some jurisdictions, women face charges of adultery even where there is clear indication of rape, and criminal procedures place the burden of proof on the female

[3] UN General Assembly, United Nations Standard Minimum Rules for Non-Custodial Measures (The Tokyo Rules): resolution/adopted by the General Assembly, 2 April 1991, A/RES/45/110.

[4] See Penal Reform International Toolbox on the Bangkok Rules: http://www.penalreform.org/priorities/women-in-the-criminal-justice-system/bangkok-rules-2/tools-resources/.

[5] While they do not represent a legally binding treaty, they do express a commitment by the 193 member states, which unanimously adopted them at the UN General Assembly.

[6] Sometimes, the term "status offences" is used, which refers to laws prohibiting certain actions based on their sex, race, nationality, religion, age etc.

[7] UNODC Handbook (2014a), pp. 81, 97.

victim.[8] For example, in Pakistan reports indicate a high number of women in prisons accused of or convicted for violating the prohibition against extramarital sex, including after reporting rape or after filing for divorce.[9] Similarly in Afghanistan approximately 50 % of women in prisons were estimated to have been convicted of moral crimes.[10]

Criminalisation of women also occurs where abortion is illegal or legal only in limited circumstances, again including in cases of rape. In Colombia, for example, abortion is prohibited in all circumstances and women can be imprisoned for up to four and a half years for having abortions even in cases of rape or when their lives were at risk. Only narrow exceptions allow judges to waive penal sentences.[11]

In some countries, women are imprisoned for leaving their homes without permission ("running away"). Many of these women leave in an attempt to escape from forced marriages, forced prostitution or physical or sexual violence by a family member.[12] A study in Afghanistan in 2007 found approximately 20 % of the incarcerated women were charged with the offence of running away, often combined with another offence, such as adultery or theft.[13]

Girls, in particular, tend to be treated more harshly for offences, which are atypical in terms of the behaviour expected of a girl,[14] including "being beyond parental control".[15] Research in juvenile rehabilitation centres in Afghanistan, for example, found that 14 % of girl respondents were in detention, not because of an offence, but because they were without shelter. None of the boys reported being in detention as a result of being lost or without accommodation.[16]

Women who are sex workers, including victims of trafficking, also face imprisonment in numerous countries for offences such as prostitution. International law prohibits discrimination, including discrimination based on sex.[17] States therefore need to review their legislation, policies and practice in order to ensure that women are not penalised exclusively or disproportionately.

---

[8] Special Rapporteur on violence against women, A/68/340 (2013), paras. 16 and 18.

[9] *Ibid.*, para. 17.

[10] UNODC, Afghanistan (2008), para. 14; Human Rights Watch, Afghanistan (2012), p. 1.

[11] Human Rights Watch, Colombia (2005).

[12] Special Rapporteur on violence against women, A/68/340, (2013), paras. 19, 20.

[13] UNODC, Afghanistan (2008), para. 14.

[14] Gelsthorpe (1989).

[15] Penal Reform International/Interagency Panel on Juvenile Justice (2014), p. 5. See, also for example, Human Rights Watch, Afghanistan (2012), which details how girls are convicted and imprisoned for crimes that usually involve flight from unlawful forced marriage or domestic violence.

[16] Penal Reform International/Interagency Panel on Juvenile Justice (2014), p. 5, quoting UNICEF, Justice for Children: The situation for children in conflict with the law in Afghanistan, 2008.

[17] Convention on the Elimination of All Forms of Discrimination against Women, New York, 18 December 1979, Article 2 (f) and (g) and Article 5; see also Human Rights Committee, General Comment No. 21 (1992).

2.2 "Protective" Detention

Again, in some countries detention is used as a form of (alleged) "protection" from threats of honour crime and of victims of rape, to protect them as well as to ensure that they will testify against the perpetrator in court. For example, the UN Special Rapporteur on torture has reported detention of women for their "protection" for up to 14 years because they were at risk of becoming victims of honour crimes.[18] Such practices are also reported in Iraq, where "detention centers sometimes end up serving as protective shelters to prevent families from killing women and girls at risk of honour killing."[19] In Jordan also, women are held in administrative detention as a means of "protection" if they are perceived at risk of being harmed by their family, based on a decision by the local governor.[20]

In response to such practices, Bangkok Rule 59 calls for non-custodial means of protection, for example shelters,[21] and reiterates that any placement of women in detention centres for means of protection, where necessary and expressly requested by the woman concerned, must be temporary and not continued against her will. The Rule also demands respective supervision by judicial and other competent authorities.

2.3 Legal Representation

As a result of unequal access to economic resources in society, women in contact with the law often depend on the willingness of male family members to spend resources on due process of law for them, making them particularly vulnerable to being deprived of their liberty. Eligibility criteria for legal aid can further discriminate against women if they are based on family/household income, which women offenders do not have access to.

Many studies point to disadvantages women face in accessing legal representation. For example, while 65 % of the women offenders surveyed in Albania in 2013 were legally represented in their first judicial hearings by private lawyers, they had to turn to legal aid lawyers later on in the criminal procedure, failing to afford payment. 35 % of the women offenders could not afford legal counsel from the start and had to rely—where applicable at all—on legal aid lawyers, even though many were dissatisfied with the quality of representation.[22] For women detained in

[18] Special Rapporteur on torture on Jordan (2007), A/HRC/4/33/Add.3, paras. 39. and 72 lit. (u).

[19] Heartland Alliance, Iraq.

[20] Penal Reform International, Jordan and Tunisia (2014b), p. 8.

[21] In the light of such practices, Rule 59 of the Bangkok Rules provides that '[g]enerally, non-custodial means of protection, for example in shelters managed by independent bodies, non-governmental organizations or other community services, shall be used to protect women.'

[22] Papavangjeli (2013), p. 13.

Jordan, access to legal representation was the most commonly identified support requirement.[23] In a prison in Afghanistan, it was found that "not a single female prisoner had been provided with legal representation".[24]

However, access to legal counsel is a prerequisite to safeguard a fair trial. Given that most legal systems are complex, access to non-custodial alternatives to imprisonment also often depends on legal representatives putting forward respective motions, such as for bail, diversion, restorative justice or mediation.[25] Lack of access to legal representation faced by women offenders in many countries therefore has a significant impact on the probability of their imprisonment.

Research also suggests that lawyers and judges lack awareness of gender-specific circumstances and their relevance in sentencing. As a consequence, mitigating factors relating to offences committed by women in conflict with the law are neither pleaded by legal representatives nor considered by judges. Such circumstances include a history of (sexual) violence suffered by partners/spouses prior to violence against these perpetrators or coercion to commit or abet an offence. It is likely that in many jurisdictions the interpretation of self-defence and of mitigating factors does not adequately allow for the consideration of prior long-term and systematic abuse by male family members or partners, in particular where the violent response to (sexual) abuse by the female victim is not immediate.

Such disadvantages in criminal procedures are exacerbated in many cultures by the fact that women are socialised in such a way that they do not speak up for themselves at court, and even less so about their experiences of domestic or sexual violence. Research in Albania, for example, has highlighted that women offenders remain "silent" in court, reluctant to reveal their personal experiences.[26]

International human rights standards enshrine the right to legal counsel as a crucial element of the right to defence and fair trial.[27] Yet, the UN Principles and Guidelines on Access to Legal Aid in Criminal Justice Systems[28] constituted the very first set of standards[29] encouraging special measures to ensure meaningful

[23] Penal Reform International, Jordan and Tunisia, (2014b), p. 18.

[24] Amnesty International, Afghanistan (2005a), p. 32.

[25] AdvocAid (2012), p. 13.

[26] Papavangjeli (2013), p. 13.

[27] E.g. Article 14 (3b) of the International Covenant on Civil and Political Rights, Body of Principles for the Protection of All Persons under Any Form of Detention or Imprisonment; Rule 93 of the Standard Minimum Rules for the Treatment of Prisoners; Principle 8 of the Basic Principles on the Role of Lawyers.

[28] The Principles clarify, inter alia, that legal aid is a duty and responsibility of the state, for which it should allocate sufficient resources, and acknowledge that legal aid needs to be provided promptly and effectively at all stages of the criminal process, including unhindered access to legal aid providers for detained persons (UN General Assembly resolution 67/187, 20 December 2012).

[29] Bangkok Rule 26 reiterates that women prisoners' contact with legal representatives shall be encouraged and facilitated by all means. However, the provision is located in the section on treatment in prison, does not address access to legal aid or call for specific measures for women offenders.

access to legal aid for women, including training of legal aid providers on the rights and needs of women.[30]

2.4 Non-Custodial Alternatives to Imprisonment

Alternatives to imprisonment avoid the high social and economic cost of detention and have proven to be more effective than imprisonment in preventing reoffending, in particular for minor, non-violent offences. The percentage of women offenders charged with these types of offences is particularly high. However, both alternatives to pre-trial detention and to prison sentences tend not to be gender-specific, but tailored to the male majority of suspects and offenders, depriving them of equal access to such alternatives.

Women may be unable to meet "standard" bail obligations like regular reporting to authorities. They may not be allowed to leave home without being accompanied by a male, because transport to the respective police station is not affordable or feasible, or because reporting times would jeopardise caretaking responsibilities, for example conflicting with times at which mothers need to pick up their children from school.

At the sentencing stage, women offenders also face disadvantages in accessing non-custodial sanctions. Their typically high level of poverty and dependency on male family members mean that they are often unable to pay fines, which are the most frequently employed alternative to imprisonment for minor, non-violent offences. For instance in Pakistan many women were found to be detained for long periods, even for minor offences, as they had been abandoned by their families and were unable to afford bail.[31] In England, it was found that decision-makers were reluctant to fine women and instead issued more severe community penalties. As a result, in the event of a subsequent conviction, such women could be given even more severe sentences because a step had been skipped on the sentencing ladder.[32]

Moreover, schemes determining the amount of fines tend to disproportionately disadvantage the poor (see high level of poverty amongst female prisoners), and decisions on alternatives, both pre-trial and at the sentencing stage, often overlook the typical background of women offenders, their caring responsibilities, their history of domestic violence and the usually lower security risk they pose to society. The Bangkok Rule 57 therefore promotes the use of alternatives for women suspects, defendants and offenders, recognising the need for gender-specific considerations as well as the impact of imprisonment not only on these women, but also their children and families.

[30] Principles 10 and 37 and Guideline 9.

[31] Law and Justice Commission of Pakistan (2012).

[32] Report by Baroness Jean Corston (2007), p. 18.

Relating to the sentencing stage, Bangkok Rule 61 states that "courts shall have the power to consider mitigating factors such as lack of criminal history and relative non-severity and nature of the criminal conduct, in the light of women's caretaking responsibilities and backgrounds."[33]

The impact of prison sentences on the children of the offender was the focus of a landmark ruling of the Constitutional Court of South Africa in 2007, in which the consequences for the appellants' children aged 8, 12 and 16 lead the Court to suspend the prison sentence for four years.[34]

Good practice has been established in some countries, not least inspired by the (imminent) adoption of the Bangkok Rules—even though most of them are limited to pregnant or breast-feeding women. In China, for example, women are not subjected to detention pending trial, but released on guarantee, placed under residential surveillance or subjected to other non-custodial compulsory measures and courts pronounce a suspension of sentences until the end of the nursing period.[35] In Argentina legislation allows for house arrest for pregnant offenders, women offenders with children of less than 5 years of age living with them and those caring for a child with disabilities. However, lack of awareness about this legal provision means that many children still reside in prison with their mothers and the law has not achieved its potential of providing an alternative.[36]

Cognisant of common problems leading to women's contact with the criminal justice system, Bangkok Rules 60 and 62 call for non-custodial interventions such as therapeutic courses and counselling for victims of domestic violence and sexual abuse, suitable treatment for those with mental disabilities, and gender-sensitive drug dependency programmes. The Rule takes into account the recognised gender differences in substance dependency and related complications that require different treatment approaches. In the delivery of community-based programmes, women may need gynaecological care, skills for negotiating safer sex, and opportunities to discuss issues such as violence and pregnancy.

2.5 Stigmatisation

Gender roles result in a particular stigma attached to women in prison, and while spouses regularly support their husbands in prison and upon release as a matter of course, reciprocally women tend to be shunned by their spouse–and often even by the whole family if they are detained. This also means no or less frequent visits in prison, increasing the sense of isolation and hindering reintegration upon release.

[33] Rule 64 reiterates the preference of non-custodial sentences for pregnant women and women with dependent children.

[34] Constitutional Court of South Africa, S. v. M. (2007).

[35] Lei et al. (2014), p. 30.

[36] Cornell Law School's Avon Global Center for Women and Justice et al. (2013), pp. 5, 32.

Research in China, for example, confirmed the high level of stigmatisation of female offenders, stating that they are abandoned by their loved ones and have no one to visit them for many years.[37] In Jordan, 44 % of the women surveyed in judicial detention stated that they had been stigmatised by their family and community as a consequence of their conviction and imprisonment. In Tunisia, this number was 41 %.[38]

Having fewer or no visits indirectly produces additional disadvantages as for many prisoners visitors provide not only emotional support but also vital material support such as money, or goods such as toiletries, underwear and telephone cards.

3 Characteristics of Women Offenders

The profile and background of women in prison differ significantly from those of men. Research in Europe indicates that women in conflict with the law "are women that have been physically and psychologically abused, and sometimes even sexually abused when they were children", women with drug-dependency issues, women who "had little or no support at all during their childhood, adolescence and adulthood", poor women, women belonging to ethnic minorities who have experienced stigmatisation, social exclusion, direct or indirect discrimination as well as women with health problems.[39]

Concern for the welfare of children acts as a constraint on women's choices and, within circumstances of poverty and poor support systems, provides a rationale for both non-violent and, when combined with other factors, violent crime.[40]

3.1 Poverty

While marginalised groups are overrepresented in the prison population as a whole, research shows that poverty plays a particular role when it comes to women in conflict with the law. Women are twice as likely as men to live in poverty and recent data suggests that their economic and social position is deteriorating relative to men.[41] The Sierra Leone Truth and Reconciliation Commission noted a "feminisation of poverty".[42]

[37] Lei et al. (2014), p. 27.

[38] Penal Reform International, Jordan and Tunisia (2014b), p. 14.

[39] Papavangjeli (2013), p. 2.

[40] Artz et al. (2012), p. xvi; UNODC, Women and HIV, p. 3.

[41] Lawlor et al. (2008), p. 7.

[42] AdvocAid (2012), p. 15.

While the rate of women as family heads is increasing, they face discrimination at the labour market, inequalities of salaries and lack of protection by labour laws.[43] Typically, if employed at all prior to imprisonment, a high percentage worked in precarious/uncertain types of work such as part-time and temporary labour.[44]

Young motherhood, experiencing poverty arising from low levels of education and the breakdown of marriages and families are common features in the profile of women in conflict with the law. Research shows that a high number of female offenders led single-headed households prior to imprisonment, and economic pressure on them was high, having to raise children with no or little financial support from their partners or husbands.[45]

For example, in Tunisia, 66 % of the women surveyed said that they were very poor or poor, and those employed before imprisonment had worked in low-paid jobs.[46] Of the women surveyed in South Africa, those employed (50 %) had only part-time or temporary work, and low wages still made it difficult to survive. This is reflected in women making up the highest percentage of unemployed in the country's overall unemployment rate, alongside young people.[47]

Research in Albania paints a similar picture, showing the high percentage of joblessness among women prisoners and lack of access to social welfare, leaving them economically dependent on their spouses. 45.5 % were unemployed prior to imprisonment and 83 % of those employed had worked in the black market. [48]

3.2 Education

Women offenders are typically characterised by a low educational profile, which cannot be seen in isolation from the usually more limited access to education for girls in the respective countries. For example, in Albania 31.5 % of the women surveyed had only eight years education and 12 % even less.[49] The explanations the women interviewed gave for this were mainly family-related, such as marriage and/or pregnancy at an early age.[50]

In China, poverty and illiteracy rates amongst women prisoners were at high levels, and levels of crimes committed were found to be linked to education

[43] Surt Association (2005), p. 23.

[44] Papavangjeli (2013), p. 9.

[45] Cornell Law School's Avon Global Center for Women and Justice et al. (2013), p. 2.

[46] Penal Reform International, Jordan and Tunisia (unpublished).

[47] Artz et al. (2012), p. 106.

[48] Papavangjeli (2013), p. 9.

[49] National secondary school participation has been reported at 84.3 % for men and 82.4 % for women between 2008 and 2012 (UNICEF, www.unicef.org/infobycountry/albania_statistics.html).

[50] Papavangjeli (2013), p. 10.

status.[51] In the general population, the adult literacy rate in 2000 was 95.5 % for men and 86.5 % for women.[52]

In Mexico, 6.1 % of women detainees were illiterate, compared to 2.4 % amongst men. Illiteracy rates were high amongst women prisoners surveyed in Jordan and Tunisia. Nearly a quarter of the women in judicial detention were illiterate, representing a higher rate than amongst the general female population in Jordan (11 %).[53]

A common reason given by women prisoners surveyed for not continuing their education included lack of financial resources in the family (e.g., for food and electricity necessary for studying) and inability to purchase school supplies, as well as having little encouragement to further their education.[54] Others had to sacrifice their education entirely, or had little time to devote to their studies, because they had to help at home.[55] Women spoke about the numerous household responsibilities they were given as children, which were generally "gendered" and differed from tasks that male siblings were expected to assume.[56] Other reasons stated were traumatic life events, (early) marriage, childcare responsibilities and frequent moving. Two women interviewed had dropped out of school after experiences of rape, two others left after the death of family members.[57]

While this clearly impacted on employment opportunities later on, it also shaped the choices (or absence of choices) women could envision for their lives in other ways, and perpetuated circumstances of poverty.[58]

3.3 *Family Status/Children*

Surveys document, across the globe, the high percentage of women prisoners who are mothers. In the South Caucasus, 78 % of the women prisoners surveyed were mothers.[59] In Central Asia it was 75 % with 45 % of these having children under 18.[60] In Jordan, three quarters of women in judicial detention had children, 78 % of them under 18.[61] In Albania the figure was even higher at 93.2 %, almost all of the mothers imprisoned having two or more children, of which a considerable number

[51] Lei et al. (2014), p. 21.

[52] UNESCO, Background paper (2006), p. 5.

[53] UNESCO, Education for All Global Monitoring Report 2013/14, p. 320.

[54] Artz et al. (2012), pp. 105–106.

[55] *Ibid.*, pp. 105–106.

[56] *Ibid.*, p. 197.

[57] *Ibid.*, pp. 31–32.

[58] *Ibid.*, p. 106.

[59] Penal Reform International, Armenia and Georgia (2013b), pp. 13–14.

[60] Penal Reform International, Kazakhstan and Kyrgyzstan (2014c), p. 11.

[61] Penal Reform International, Jordan and Tunisia (2014b, p. 11).

were placed in an orphanage as a consequence of their mothers' imprisonment.[62] In South Africa, the percentage of mothers in the sample surveyed was 75 %, 45 % of them had their first child between the ages of 16 and 20 years.[63]

While little qualitative research is available, women's social and family roles have been shown to play a relevant role when it comes to explaining pathways to offending, particularly in situations of family breakdown. An in-depth study conducted in South Africa, for instance, shows how the women's familial and relationship histories as well as traumatic events, especially in childhood, shaped their choices—or lack thereof—and was linked to their involvement in crime.[64]

Motherhood, in particular early pregnancies, also appear to play a role in women's pathways to crime. Experiences of abuse during childhood are a factor for early pregnancies, impacting on the women's relationships later in their lives.[65] In Kazakhstan, for example, research indicated a typical pattern where women fell into debt following the breakdown of a marriage and then turned to fraud, drug dealing or theft to raise funds to make repayments. Informal marriages appear to constitute a particular factor for women's vulnerability in this country, with an estimated 30 % of children born into informal marriages.[66]

Alongside low levels of education, responsibility for children, caring for other relatives and aging family members, typically constitute obstacles to employment for these women, contributing to their marginalisation and economic dependency. Often children are used as leverage to trap them in an—often violent—relationship.[67]

3.4 Violence Against Women

According to the WHO, 35 % of women worldwide have experienced either intimate partner violence or non-partner sexual violence in their lifetime.[68] There is a strong link between violence against women and women's incarceration, whether prior to, during or after incarceration.[69] Women have been victims of violence at a much higher rate prior to entering prison than is acknowledged by the

[62] Papavangjeli (2013), p. 10.

[63] Artz et al. (2012), p. vi, 11, 35.

[64] *Ibid.*, p. ix.

[65] See for example Artz et al. (2012), pp. xv, pp. 114–137. Early motherhood plays an important role in women's pathways to crime and in the way in which they experience incarceration. Experiences of childhood victimisation increased the women's vulnerability as young girls to early pregnancies, which impacted heavily on their relationships and support systems (Cornell Law School's Avon Global Center for Women and Justice et al. (2013), p. 30).

[66] Penal Reform International, Kazakhstan and Kyrgyzstan (2014c), footnotes 42, 43.

[67] Artz et al. (2012), p. xv.

[68] World Health Organization, Factsheet N°239 (2013).

[69] Special Rapporteur on violence against women, A/68/340 (2013), p. 4.

legal system generally,[70] partly due to the persistent phenomenon of underreporting of such abuse. In many regions, it is still the victim who is stigmatised rather than the perpetrator and for many women the experience of violence has become normalised.[71]

Anglo-American research has found that female offenders are three times more likely than their male counterparts to have been physically or sexually abused in their past and twice as likely as women in the general public to report childhood histories of physical or sexual abuse.[72] Another study found that a staggering 86 % of incarcerated women had, as children, suffered either sexual or physical abuse or witnessed violence at home.[73]

In Jordan, more than three out of five women surveyed in detention had experienced domestic violence and for 92 % of these women, this was a frequent occurrence. While these figures represent a significant percentage, they are still likely to reflect under-reporting.[74] Of the women who responded to this question in a survey in Argentina, 39.04 % reported experiencing violence from a spouse or family member prior to their imprisonment; 13.6 % had been raped at least once.[75]

The life stories captured in the South African study, where almost 70 % of the women prisoners interviewed had experienced some form of domestic violence,[76] revealed experiences of abuse throughout childhood[77] and adulthood (including witnessing and directly experiencing domestic violence), physical and psychological neglect, exposure to violent communities, witnessing and engaging in substance abuse, and unstable and troubled family lives. 67 % of the women had experienced some form of domestic violence and/or rape in their adult life, which is three times higher than the rate in the general population.[78]

While not intending to characterise women detainees as "passive victims of the criminalisation system",[79] it is important to understand the role trauma and violence has played in the lives of these women[80] and the links between offending and

[70] *Ibid.*, p. 4.

[71] Artz et al. (2012), pp. xiii, 148.

[72] *Ibid.* footnote 96.

[73] Greene et al. (2000), p. 9.

[74] Penal Reform International, Jordan and Tunisia (2014b, p. 17). Under-reporting was established, for example, by the Committee on the Elimination of Discrimination against Women (Committee on the Elimination of Discrimination against women, Jordan, CEDAW/C/JOR/CO/5 (2012), para. 25).

[75] Cornell Law School's Avon Global Center for Women and Justice et al. (2013), p. 2.

[76] Artz et al. (2012), p. xiii, pp. 102–113.

[77] 37 % of the women in the sample reported that they had been physically abused during their childhood, 29 % of respondents reported some form of sexual abuse in their childhood. 62 % of those who experienced childhood sexual abuse were abused by a father figure or male caregiver, with only 12.5 % stating that they did not know the perpetrator (Artz et al., pp. xii, xiii, 125, 132).

[78] Artz et al. (2012), pp. xii, xiii pp. 83–100.

[79] Special Rapporteur on violence against women, A/68/340 (2013), para. 2.

[80] Papavangjeli (2013), p. 4 referring to trauma theory.

histories of prior abuse. For example, the South African study shows that domestic abuse is related to female offending in both direct and indirect ways.[81] Similarly, studies in Australia, Canada and South Africa reveal high rates of violence prior to arrest and possible links with criminal conduct.[82]

In the cases researched of women alleged or convicted of offences against life (assault, manslaughter or murder), experiences of domestic and sexual abuse often were the direct cause of incarceration. Many women surveyed in Argentina, for example, described how they used force against their abuser after suffering severe and ongoing domestic violence, including out of fear for the safety of their children.[83] Such fears are not unfounded. Globally, two thirds of the victims of homicide were female in 2012 and almost half of all female victims (47 %) were killed by their intimate partners or family members, compared to less than 6 % of male homicide victims.[84]

In Kyrgyzstan, a UN report noted that 70 % of women convicted of killing a husband or other family member had experienced a 'longstanding pattern of physical abuse or forced economic dependence'.[85] In Jordan, of the 26 % of women in judicial detention charged with or convicted of violent offences, 98 % of these charges/sentences relating to murder/manslaughter of a male family member.[86] Research conducted in New York State in the US found that more than nine out of ten women convicted of killing an intimate partner had been abused by an intimate partner in the past.[87]

Some studies have suggested that exposure to extreme, traumatic events cause high rates of borderline personality disorder, antisocial personality disorder, substance abuse, and symptoms of post-traumatic stress disorder (PTSD) among women inmates.[88] For others, abuse led to problem behaviours such as drugs, alcohol and gambling as a way of dealing with their experiences.[89]

3.5 Drug and Alcohol Dependence

Due to factors described above, women generally experience more psychological distress than men over their lifetimes, including anxiety, depression and guilt. Maybe not surprisingly, therefore, women prisoners have shown to have higher

---

[81] Artz et al. (2012), p. Xiii, pp. 83–100.

[82] Special Rapporteur on violence against women, A/68/340 (2013), p. 5.

[83] Cornell Law School's Avon Global Center for Women and Justice et al. (2013), p. 19.

[84] UNODC, World crime trends (2014b), para. 10.

[85] Special Rapporteur on violence against women, Kyrgyzstan (2010), para. 26.

[86] Penal Reform International, Jordan and Tunisia (2014b), pp. 12, 13.

[87] Kraft-Stolar et al. (2011), p. 3.

[88] Artz et al. (2012), p. 141.

[89] See for example Artz et al. (2012), p. 162.

rates of mental health issues and histories of substance abuse than their male counterparts.[90]

Research in women prisons in Kazakhstan in 2011, for instance, estimated that over 40 % of the female prison population had been dependent on drugs prior to imprisonment, an increase from 32 % in 2005.[91] Canadian research in federal prisons indicated a percentage as high as 80 %.[92] For the majority of the women surveyed in South Africa with alcohol or drug dependency problems substances had been used as a coping mechanism, including to "escape" childhood abuse and domestic violence.[93]

Alcohol and/or drugs were found to play a central role in women's offending behaviour, both directly and indirectly. Addictions were the cause of their offending in order to finance substance use,[94] excluded them from legal employment and provided an entry into criminal circles.[95] In some cases recorded, it was not the women's own substance abuse that led to their criminal behaviour, but their partner's.[96]

3.6 *First-Time Offenders/Recidivism*

While statistics disaggregated by gender are scarce, studies available on female prisoners show a high percentage of women who are first-time offenders and, in general, a lower rate of recidivism than men. [97]

In Tunisia, for instance, the recidivism rate according to the Directorate General for Prison Administration and Rehabilitation was 22 % for women in 2013 as compared to 44 % for men.[98] A survey in Argentina found that 81.1 % of women interviewed for the study had not been previously detained.[99] In South Africa, 74 % of the women surveyed served a sentence for the first time.[100] In the US a study in 2007 stated, that "female prisoners were more likely than the total sample to have

[90] WHO Regional Office for Europe, Health in Prisons (2007); Moloney et al. (2009), pp. 426–430.

[91] Penal Reform International, Kazakhstan (2011a); Penal Reform International, Kazakhstan and Kyrgyzstan (2014c), p. 17.

[92] Artz et al. (2012), p. 202.

[93] *Ibid.*, p. 206.

[94] In South Africa, for example, of the women with a drug dependency problem, one-third (9 % of total sample) had committed financially-motivated crimes (drug trafficking, robbery, and fraud) as a means of financing their addictions, and in one case, in an attempt to raise enough money to send herself to rehabilitation. (Artz et al., p. 210).

[95] Artz et al. (2012), pp. xvii, 203.

[96] *Ibid.*, p. xvii, pp. 138–145.

[97] Deschenes et al. (2006).

[98] Penal Reform International, Jordan and Tunisia (2014b), p. 3.

[99] Cornell Law School's Avon Global Center for Women and Justice et al. (2013), p. 17.

[100] Artz et al. (2012), pp. viii, 38.

lower rates of recidivism across all four measures (rearrest, reconviction, resentence to prison and return to prison)".[101]

4 Women Offenders and Prisoners

4.1 Statistics

On the basis of figures up to the beginning of 2013 there were more than 660,000 women in prison throughout the world. Women (and girls) comprise the minority of prisoners, constituting an estimated 2–9 % of national prison populations. However, the number of imprisoned women has increased significantly, and at a greater rate than for men.

According to the International Centre for Prison Studies, the number of women in prison increased between 2000 and the beginning of 2013, by over 40 %,[102] compared to 16 % for the world prison population as a whole in the same period. While in 2000 women represented 5.3 % of the global prison population, this figure was 6.5 % in 2013, representing an increase of more than a fifth.[103] The proportion of female pre-trial detainees also rose in all regions from 16.4 % in 2004 to 17.5 % in 2012.[104]

In Mexico, for example, the female prison population has grown by 400 % since 2007.[105] In China, the number of female prisoners (pre-trial and convicted) has risen significantly in the last few years: by 30.53 % since 2004, in particular due to the increase of un-convicted detainees.[106] South African statistics show an increase of approximately 10 % in both the number of sentenced and unsentenced female inmates between January 2007 and February 2011.[107]

Nonetheless, little research has been conducted to understand why there has been such a considerable increase in women's incarceration, in particular amongst certain groups. Some studies highlighted the disproportionate incarceration rates of women from ethnic and minority groups,[108] who in many countries are more likely to be imprisoned.

In Albania, 12.5 % of the female prison population belonged to the Roma minority,[109] while in the last census in 2011 the proportion of the Roma population

[101] Deschenes et al. (2007).

[102] Walmsley (2014).

[103] Penal Reform International, The use and practice of imprisonment (2014a), p. 11.

[104] UNODC, World crime trends (2014b), paras. 15, 16, based on a sample of 40 countries worldwide.

[105] Agren, Female felons swell ranks among Mexican criminals, USA Today, 2 December 2010.

[106] Lei et al. (2014), p. 4, 5.

[107] Artz et al. (2012), p. 10.

[108] Special Rapporteur on violence against women, A/68/340 (2013), p. 5.

[109] Papavangjeli (2013), p. 10.

in the country was only 0.3 %.[110] In the US, a 2005 report noted an increase in the imprisonment rate of African American women of 800 %, compared to 400 % for women of all other racial groupings.[111]

Also, the percentage of convicted girls increased more than the percentage of convicted female adults.[112]

4.2 *Offences*

Research available on women prisoners (pre-trial and sentenced) shows that the majority of offences women are charged with or convicted for are non-violent, while the proportion of charges and convictions for these types of offences in the general prison population is generally much lower. While the overall figure for economic offences globally is 18 %,[113] surveys reviewed for this chapter identified rates between 22 % and almost 50 % of women charged with or convicted for economic offences.

In most countries, a significant number of women are imprisoned on drug-related offences (up to 70 %) while the rate in the overall sentenced prison population is 21 %.[114] Other types of offences that disproportionately affect women are "sex crimes", in particular where prostitution and similar offences are only penalised for "providers" but not for "clients".

Statistics analysed from research in four prisons in China in 2013 show that 86.96 % of the female pre-trial prisoners surveyed had been accused of non-violent offences, compared to 67.35 % of male suspects.[115] For the convicted prison population property crimes such as theft, fraud and extortion represented 22.32 % of offences.[116] In the South Caucasus, too, the majority of women surveyed in pre-trial detention were charged with economic offences. In Georgia, of the convicted female prison population, 42 % had been sentenced for property offences, 29 % for drug-related offences and 6 % for violent crimes.[117] In Armenia, official statistics on convictions of female offenders indicate a proportion of property offences of 33.3 %, followed by drug-related offences (17 %).[118]

---

[110] See information at PAIRS South East Europe at http://www.pairs-see.net/page?view=15, accessed 2 June 2014.

[111] American Civil Liberties Union, Caught in the Net (2005a), p. 1.

[112] UNODC, World crime trends (2014b), para. 16.

[113] *Ibid.*, para. 29.

[114] *Ibid.*, para. 29.

[115] Lei et al. (2014), p. 19.

[116] *Ibid.*, p. 22.

[117] Penal Reform International, Armenia and Georgia (2013b), pp. 8, 9, with reference to Georgia's very strict drug legislation resulting in a high number of imprisonment for drug use or possession.

[118] *Ibid.*, p. 11, noting new legislation implemented in 2009 which de-criminalised the use of illegal drugs and the transfer of small amounts of drugs without purpose of sale (e.g. sharing of small quantities among users).

In Jordan, 26 % were in prison relating to violent offences, while the vast majority of women prisoners were charged with or convicted of offences presumed to be predominantly non-violent. 23 % were detained relating to sexual offences, including prostitution and adultery, punishable with up to three years in prison.[119] In Kazakhstan, non-violent crimes also constituted the largest share of convictions with 41 % of women imprisoned for property offences. 28 % of sentences were drug related, reflecting severe penalties for the sale of drugs in this country.[120] 23 % of the women surveyed had committed violent offences.

Statistics from South Africa, by comparison to other countries, reflect a very high proportion of violent crimes overall, with an unusually high 36.6 % of women having been convicted of "aggressive" crimes. 10 % of women offenders were incarcerated for narcotics crimes, and the largest percentage, yet again for economic crimes (45.2 % for fraud, forgery, shoplifting and theft).[121] In Kyrgyzstan, too, the number of convictions for murder or manslaughter was strikingly high compared to other countries, with 20 % of women offenders convicted of the murder or manslaughter of a male family member and a further 12 % of murder of someone other than a male family member.[122]

A survey in Argentina found over 85 % of women were convicted of economic crimes,[123] and the rate of women being accused or convicted of drug trafficking was particularly high (55.75 %), which appears to be common in Latin America as a whole.[124]

4.3 Drug-Related Offences

Worldwide statistics show that drug-related offending is particularly high among women prisoners, and both domestic and international anti-drug policies have been identified as a leading cause for the rising rates of incarceration of women around the world. For example, according to a recent comprehensive study, over 31,000 women across Europe and Central Asia were imprisoned for drug offences, with almost 70 % of all women prisoners in Tajikistan, 40 % in Georgia, about 50 % in Estonia, Portugal and Spain, almost 70 % in Latvia and 37 % in Italy.[125]

---

[119] Penal Reform International, Jordan and Tunisia (2014b, p. 12).

[120] The European Monitoring Centre for Drugs and Drug Addiction describes Kazakhstan's national drug laws as 'the most rigid criminal legislation on the territory of post-Soviet countries' and reports sentences imposed for the sale of drugs ranging from five to 12 years. (Penal Reform International, Kazakhstan and Kyrgyzstan (2014c), footnote 34.

[121] Artz et al. (2012), p. 11.

[122] Penal Reform International, Kazakhstan and Kyrgyzstan (2014c), p. 14.

[123] Cornell Law School's Avon Global Center for Women and Justice et al. (2013), p. 2.

[124] *Ibid.*, p. 12.

[125] Iakobishvili (2012), p. 5.

In Kazakhstan and Kyrgyzstan too, a high percentage of women prisoners surveyed in 2012 were convicted for drug-related offences (about a third).[126] High rates of incarceration of women for drug-related offences have also been reported in the Russian Federation, with acquittal rates in drug cases of less than 5 %.[127] In China, drug offences by women prisoners accounted for 41.88 % of crimes and 48.17 % of non-violent crimes.[128] In Canada, about a third of women prisoners were convicted of drug-related offences.[129] In Thailand, this figure was 57 %.[130]

Particularly high rates of women imprisoned on drug-related charges are documented in Latin America, with percentages up to 70 %,[131] owing to harsh drug laws. Between 2006 and 2011, the female prison population in the region almost doubled, increasing from 40,000 to more than 74,000 prisoners, usually for low-level trafficking offences.[132] This trend has been attributed to the greater ease with which low-level crimes can be prosecuted[133] and gender disparities in the "war on drugs".[134]

Research in Argentina showed that women's primary role in drug trafficking is that of a mule,[135] which makes them typically easy targets for drug enforcement authorities, even though it does little to disrupt drug trafficking networks. All of the women charged with drug trafficking interviewed in Argentina were transporting small quantities of illegal substances across the border.[136] As a consequence, harsh prison sentences, including for non-violent, low-level drug crimes, appear to affect women disproportionately.[137]

In Ecuador, 77 % of women in prison were incarcerated for drug-offences compared to 33.5 % of the male prison population, indicating a gendered disparity.[138] An older study in the US also found that women were over-represented among low-level non-violent drug offenders, with minimal or no prior criminal

[126] Penal Reform International, Kazakhstan and Kyrgyzstan (2014c), p. 12.

[127] Golichenko (2013).

[128] Lei et al. (2014), pp. 20, 21.

[129] EurekAlert (2011).

[130] Department for Corrections, Ministry of Justice, Thailand, www.correct.go.th/eng/statistics.html.

[131] E. Iakobishvili, Cause for Alarm (2012), p. 5.

[132] Tomasini (2012), cited in OAS, Women and Drugs in the Americas (2014), p. 29.

[133] Cornell Law School's Avon Global Center for Women and Justice et al. (2013), p. 15.

[134] Special Rapporteur on violence against women, A/68/340, (2013), para. 26.

[135] Transporting drugs, often by swallowing them or introducing them into their body cavities.

[136] Cornell Law School's Avon Global Center for Women and Justice et al. (2013), pp. 2, 17, with reference also to Transnational Institute, drug laws and prisons in Latin America, supra note 10, at 97 (studies suggest 'a growing number of women, often the sole providers for their families, enter the drug trade simply to put food on the table for the children.').

[137] Cornell Law School's Avon Global Center for Women and Justice et al. (2013), p. 15, with reference also to a report from the Office of the Human Rights Ombudsman in Buenos Aires.

[138] Special Rapporteur on violence against women, A/68/340 (2013), para. 26.

history and not representing principal figures in criminal organisations or activities. Nevertheless they received sentences similar to high-level drug offenders under the mandatory sentencing policies.[139]

Other research has also indicated that more serious offenders, mainly male, escape imprisonment or have their sentences reduced by entering plea-bargaining deals and providing assistance to the prosecution, which women are usually unable to provide.[140]

4.4 Motives/Causes for Crime

While not seeking to describe women as "passive victims" when in conflict with the law, root causes of offending and the specific contexts in which women commit crimes have to be taken into account. Research is still scarce on pathways of women to and motivations for offending, as well as the gendered nature of poverty. However, findings, for example in South Africa, illustrate the link between women's offending and conditions of structural poverty, education levels, access to employment and the environments in which women lived and were socialised.[141]

Research also demonstrated that prior emotional, physical, and/or sexual abuse contributes to women's criminal behaviour. Reasons for violent offences, captured by research in China, for example, rank domestic violence first, taking "extreme measures to protect themselves".[142] In Kyrgyzstan, 20 % of women cited self-defence or self-protection as the main reason for their offence.[143] In Jordan 6 % of the women in judicial detention identified that they acted in self-defence or self-protection, another 6 % said they sought to protect their children.[144] More research should be undertaken into domestic abuse as a trigger for violent crimes, and on the extent to which such experiences are taken into account by courts.[145]

In some cases, women are incarcerated for illegal activities, which they commit in response to coercion by abusive partners, or as a result of their connection with others engaged in illegal behaviour. A study illustrated how women had been forced to commit offences by physical attacks or even death threats, or following more subtle pressure or provocation. This included being manipulated or "talked

[139] Amnesty International, Women in Prison Factsheet (2005b), citing Department of Justice, Bureau of Justice Statistics, Prisoners (1997).

[140] Special Rapporteur on violence against women, A/68/340 (2013), para. 26.

[141] Artz et al. (2012), p. 118.

[142] Lei et al. (2014), pp. 19, 26. (This affected mainly the female prison population in the age range of 30–50.).

[143] Penal Reform International, Kazakhstan and Kyrgyzstan (2014c), p. 17.

[144] Interview with PRI and SIGI and Adalah Centre for Human Rights Studies, 11 December 2013.

[145] It is likely that in many jurisdictions the interpretation of self-defence and of mitigating factors do not adequately allow for the consideration of prior long-term and systematic abuse by male family members, in particular where the violent response by the female victim is not instant.

into" committing the offence, confessing to an abuser's crime, or committing physical assaults in response to psychological victimisation.[146]

Sometimes called the "girlfriend problem", women are often caught up in the offences of their significant other by participating in crimes minimally, or unknowingly, often drug-related.[147] In Mexico, for example, it has been estimated that at least 40 % of the women convicted of drug-related crimes, such as transporting drugs between cities or smuggling drugs into prisons, were coerced into doing so by their boyfriends or husbands.[148]

5 Prison Conditions[149]

Not least because of their small number amongst the population detained, prisons and prison regimes are almost invariably designed for the majority male prison population. This includes everything from the architecture of prisons and security procedures to staffing, healthcare services, family contact, work and training. As a result, many prisons do not meet the needs of women on multiple levels.

As Debbie Denning, Chief of Programs and Support Services, Department of Corrections in Illinois, put it: "There is a view that when it comes to conditions in prison women get everything and men get nothing. In reality, women get everything that can be provided for free."[150]

The Committee on the Elimination of Discrimination against Women established within an individual complaint in 2001 that discrimination against women encompasses ill-treatment that affects women disproportionately as well as detention conditions which do not address the specific needs of women.[151]

5.1 Location/Allocation

Generally there are far fewer prison facilities for women or they are housed in annexes to male prisons, sometimes with insufficient separation. As a result female prisoners are often detained far from home, limiting their contact with their

[146] Richie (1996), pp. 127–131.

[147] American Civil Liberties Union, 'Girlfriend problem' (2005b).

[148] Agren (2010).

[149] Although rather comprehensive, this chapter does not provide a complete overview of treatment and conditions in prison or of the Bangkok Rules provisions relating to them, but seeks to capture the main areas in which gender-specific attention is required and in which the Rules provide a particular added value.

[150] Report of Expert Group Meeting University of Chicago Law School (2013).

[151] UN Committee on the Elimination of Discrimination Against Women, CEDAW/C/49/D/23/2009 (2011), referring also to the Bangkok Rules.

families. Fewer facilities also often result in women being held at a higher security facility or unit than necessary, corresponding with more restrictions and less access to rehabilitation programmes.

In Kazakhstan, for example, the size of the country and the limited facilities mean that women are imprisoned far from home, family, friends and community, exacerbated by the fact that different prisons have different security categories. The ninth largest country in the world has only six women's prisons, with differing regimes of security, partly in remote areas. Koksun prison in Karaganda for instance is in a very isolated position about an hour and a half drive from the nearest city and with inadequate public transport links. This also impacts on the health of women prisoners since many of them rely on visitors to bring medicine, food, warm clothes and toiletries. Survey findings in 2013 confirmed the high level of social isolation experienced by women prisoners as a result.[152]

In China, of the 36 women's prisons in total, there is only one facility in most provinces, meaning that it is "largely impossible to be allocated to a place of detention near their home".[153] In Albania also, female prisoners were placed far from their communities, family and circle of relatives and friends as they can only be placed in one of the two women's prisons in Tirana, while the majority (71.5 % of pre-trial detainees and 77.5 % of convicted women) come from cities and rural villages in the north and south of Albania.[154] In South Africa, it was established that, while 96.77 % of inmates housed within 30 km of their home and family received visits, 56.10 % of those inmates housed over 100 km away did not.[155]

Bangkok Rule 4 therefore enunciates the considerations that need to be taken into account when allocating female prisoners to certain facilities, including the impact on the woman's ability to maintain links with her family, the potential impact of allocation on her children and the availability of services and rehabilitation programmes.

5.2 *Separation of Prisoners and Staffing*

As women and men being housed together in detention facilities increases the risk of abuse,[156] already the Standard Minimum Rules for the Treatment of Prisoners require that women and men should be detained in separate facilities.[157] For the same reason women prisoners should be supervised only by female prison

[152] Penal Reform International, Kazakhstan and Kyrgyzstan (2014c), p. 20; See also Frances Shehan, Imprisoned far from home (2013).

[153] Lei et al. (2014), pp. 27–28.

[154] Papavangjeli (2013), p. 11.

[155] Cornell Law School's Avon Global Center for Women and Justice et al. (2013), p. 26.

[156] Bastick and Townhead (2008), p. 29.

[157] Rule 8(a) Standard Minimum Rules for the Treatment of Prisoners.

officers.[158] Some countries reflect this principle in their legislation and practice.[159] However, in other countries or prison facilities, even 60 years after the adoption of the Standard Minimum Rules in 1955, women prisoners are still housed together with men and are exposed to sexual abuse by male staff.

A recent investigation in Alabama, US, for example, found that women prisoners at one of the state's prisons "live in a toxic environment with repeated and open sexual behavior" and revealed that "serious systemic operational deficiencies (...) have exposed women prisoners to harm and serious risk of harm from staff-on-prisoner sexual abuse and sexual harassment."[160]

In Honduras, reporting on a "mixed prison" it was highlighted that "according to reliable reports, many of these women, when they first enter, need to find themselves a 'husband' (...) to seek protection and find a place in the social structure of the prison". This was "aggravated by the fact that it is a prison in which internal control is exercised completely by the prisoners and the women find themselves in a particularly vulnerable situation".[161]

5.3 *Protection from Violence and Abuse*

As the Special Rapporteur on violence against women has noted, "The continuum of violence during and after incarceration is a reality for many women globally".[162] In many regards, women have a heightened vulnerability to mental and physical abuse during arrest, questioning and in prison.

They are at particular risk of rape, sexual assault and humiliation, by male fellow prisoners and prison staff. Custody, for many women, includes ill-treatment, such as threats of rape, touching, "virginity testing", being stripped naked, invasive body searches, insults and humiliations of a sexual nature or even rape. Women in prison are routinely monitored under surveillance, including being watched by male guards in various stages of nudity, including while undressing, bathing, using the toilet and during medical examinations.[163] Furthermore, there are cases of dependency of detainees upon prison staff, which lead to increased vulnerability to sexual exploitation, as it drives them to "willingly" trade sex for favours.

---

158 Rule 53 (2) and (3) Standard Minimum Rules for the Treatment of Prisoners.

159 In China, for example, the legal framework requires women and men to be held in separated facilities, and female prisoners to be under the direct supervision of female staff (Lei et al. 2014, p. 14).

160 US Department of Justice (2014).

161 Inter-American Commission (2013), paras. 91–93.

162 Special Rapporteur on violence against women, A/68/340 (2013), p. 4.

163 *Ibid.*, para. 42.

"Virginity tests" constitute a particularly gross form of discrimination and of custodial violence against women.[164] In Paraguay, for example, women reported that they had been asked by policemen to perform oral sex in exchange for better treatment. None of the detainees interviewed had filed complaints (...) stating that they feared reprisals or that the remedies available were ineffective.[165] In women's prisons in Armenia, Azerbaijan and Georgia, male guards had an unobstructed view into the women's showers and regularly watched female prisoners bathing.[166]

A medical screening on entry to prison (Bangkok Rule 6) is one of the essential steps in detecting ill-treatment and torture by law enforcement authorities, and vital also in providing for the psychological and physical needs likely to arise from such abuse. Furthermore, Bangkok Rule 7 details steps to be taken by prison authorities in such cases, beyond the provision of appropriate medical treatment, including full information about their right to issue a complaint, psychological support and protection from retaliation. The principle of confidentiality should be respected during this process, and any tests prescribed need to be voluntary.[167]

5.4 *Hygiene*

Hygiene, including sanitary articles and safe and regular access to hot water, is particularly important for women prisoners, yet remains one of the most common deficiencies in women prisons across the globe.

Women in Argentina reported problems in accessing sufficient sanitary pads while in prison, describing it as "a nightmare for girls within their periods" as they only received one roll of toilet paper per week.[168] Inmates in Russia reported that they could not wash until the next allocated shift for showering when their period started unexpectedly.[169] In South Africa, women prisoners reported that they were rarely supplied with painkillers for menstruation cramps,[170] and due to the lack of lavatories they got up at 2 am or 3 am in order to queue for the shower to be ready for the parade.[171]

Often access to hygiene products depends on women having the means to purchase such items themselves, or on NGOs providing them. This was the case

[164] Special Rapporteur on torture, A/HRC/7/3 (2008), para. 34.

[165] Subcommittee on Prevention of Torture, Paraguay, CAT/OP/PRY/1 (2010), paras. 134, 141.

[166] Council of Europe, Parliamentary Assembly, (2007), para. 53; Special Rapporteur on violence against women, United States of America, A/HRC/17/26/Add.5 and Corr.1. (2011).

[167] See also Istanbul Protocol on the Effective Investigation and Documentation of Torture and Other Cruel, Inhuman or Degrading Treatment or Punishment (2004).

[168] Cornell Law School's Avon Global Center for Women and Justice et al. (2013), p. 22.

[169] European Committee for the Prevention of Torture (2006), para. 31.

[170] Artz et al. (2012), p. 47.

[171] *Ibid.*, p. 54.

in China, for example, where only 3 % of the women surveyed were provided with free sanitary pads, which were donated by women's federations, charitable organisations and other community organisations.[172]

While provisions relating to toiletry articles and items for men to shave regularly are included in the Standard Minimum Rules,[173] for decades provisions have been lacking regarding women's needs, even though a failure to provide a hygienic environment that meets basic health needs infringes the right to health and dignity.

Bangkok Rule 5 therefore fills a crucial gap, finally recognising the specific hygiene needs of women and requiring, explicitly, the provision of free of charge sanitary towels, as well as a regular supply of water for personal care, in particular to those women who are pregnant, breastfeeding or menstruating.

5.5 Health-Care

Provision of adequate healthcare in prison is a major issue faced by prison systems around the globe, even more so because in the prison population (both male and female) individuals with poor health and chronic untreated conditions, mental health problems and health risks related to drug injection are over-represented. The prison environment can exacerbate these preconditions.[174]

Yet, beyond this general situation, women prisoners have different and greater primary healthcare needs in comparison to men. This is partly due to physiological differences, and partly because of their typical backgrounds, which can include drug use, physical or sexual abuse, sex work and unsafe sexual practices. HIV and other sexually transmitted and blood-borne diseases are more prevalent among female prisoners than their male counterparts, due to the combination of gender inequality, stigma and women's vulnerability to contracting sexually transmitted infections and diseases.

Health conditions of women prisoners may have been untreated before admission due to discriminatory practices that prevent women from accessing adequate healthcare in the community.[175] Typically, there is limited reproductive health-care available for women in prison and even less so antiretroviral therapy, even for HIV-positive pregnant women although such treatment could prevent mother-to-

[172] Lei et al. (2014), p. 33.

[173] Rules 15 and 16. Rule 16 reads: 'In order that prisoners may maintain a good appearance compatible with their self-respect, facilities shall be provided for the proper care of the hair and beard, and men shall be enabled to shave regularly.'

[174] International Centre for Prison Studies, Guidance Note (2005).

[175] A study undertaken by the European Fundamental Rights Agency, for instance, on inequalities in accessing healthcare in EU countries has found that financial barriers affect women's access to health-care (European Union Fundamental Rights Agency 2013, p. 41).

child transmission. Many prisons do also not provide adequate substance abuse treatment programmes, or do not tailor programmes to women. Many penitentiary systems also overlook that medical examination by male doctors puts women prisoners at risk of re-traumatisation as a high percentage of them have been victims of violence, including sexual violence.

As the UN Special Rapporteur on violence against women noted, "The mere replication of health services provided for male prisoners is (. . .) not adequate."[176] Yet, most prison facilities do not meet women's medical needs, and prior to the adoption of the Bangkok Rules, standards on health-care for women in prison were limited to pregnancy, pre- and post-natal care. In Argentina, for example, a survey showed that over a third of women prisoners surveyed had never received a Papanicolaou test (PAP) (32.31 %) and almost three quarters reported that they never received breast cancer screening (73.36 %). This number was even higher among pre-trial detainees; 42.11 % and 82.11 % respectively had not received a PAP test or breast cancer screening. 75.53 % of pre-trial detainees versus 53.78 % of convicted women indicated they never received HIV-prevention education.[177]

In China, both initial health-screening and gynaecological care later on during imprisonment were found to fail women's healthcare needs. In the facilities surveyed, medical screening on entry was limited to blood and urine tests, chest X-rays and blood pressure checks, not providing gynaecological examination.[178] Such examinations were found to only be prescribed every one or two years and only for "female workers who enter menopause".[179] 40 % of the surveyed women had never undergone any specific gynaecological health and disease examinations.[180]

Access to substance abuse treatment programmes, in many countries, is discriminating against women. In Kyrgyzstan, for instance, in 2008 a planned methadone programme in women's prisons fell victim to funding cuts, and as a result opioid substitution therapy (OST) was only available in men's prisons.[181] When finally established,[182] contrary to the programme provided in eight men's prisons, no separate 'clean zone' was available with the programme for women, but those undergoing the treatment mixed freely with the other prisoners.[183] In Georgia, too, a survey in 2008 found that methadone as an opioid substitution therapy (OST) was available in some men's prisons but not in women's prisons, a common practice

[176] Quoted in Lines (2008), p. 13.

[177] Cornell Law School's Avon Global Center for Women and Justice et al. (2013), pp. 3, 21.

[178] Lei et al. (2014), p. 37.

[179] *Ibid.*, p. 8.

[180] *Ibid.*, p. 37.

[181] Stoicescu (2012), p. 129.

[182] The programme 'Atlantis' was established in Stepnoye prison in 2009, providing a six month long treatment for up to 12 women at a time on a voluntary basis.

[183] Penal Reform International, Kazakhstan and Kyrgyzstan (2014c), p. 17.

mirrored also in reports on discrimination against women regarding the accessibility of substance abuse programmes in the Russian Federation.[184]

While the principle of non-discrimination in the treatment of prisoners, including on the ground of sex, has already been enshrined in other standards, the common deficiencies in providing adequate health-care to female prisoners underlines the added value of guidance put in place by the Bangkok Rules.

A provision on medical screening upon entry finally spells out the need for a comprehensive examination, explicitly including the reproductive health history, presence of drug dependency, of sexually transmitted or blood-borne diseases and mental health-care needs, and whether sexual abuse or other forms of violence have been suffered prior to admission (Rule 6, Rule 7 details the precautions in case prior abuse is determined). Due to women prisoners' backgrounds it may be the first time in their lives that they have a medical examination or have access to a doctor.[185]

Bangkok Rule 10 (2) requires that women are examined and treated by a woman physician or nurse if she so requests, except for situations of medical urgency. Rule 11 captures that, with limited exceptions, only medical staff should be present during examinations. Conscious of the fact that women feel particularly vulnerable exposing their bodies and of experiences of sexual abuse, the Rules require health-care services to be provided in a culturally and gender-sensitive manner, ensuring privacy and dignity.

Gender-sensitivity and responsiveness to the specific needs and backgrounds of women is one of the common features in all respective provisions, alongside the principle of equivalence of health-care to that delivered in the community, which includes close cooperation between prison and public health services (Bangkok Rule 10).

Bangkok Rule 8 captures the principle of confidentiality of medical information as well as the voluntariness of examination and treatment, not yet included in the 1955 Standard Minimum Rules. As both principles are human rights standard regardless of the sex of the patient or the environment medical examination or treatment are taking place, their first explicit incorporation in the Bangkok Rules is of added value to all prisoners. Women specifically may not wish to share their reproductive health history or status,[186] but the Rule also prohibits 'virginity testing' as exercised in some countries[187] in violation of the right to dignity and the right not to be subjected to ill-treatment.[188]

---

[184] Penal Reform International, Russia (2010).

[185] UNODC, WHO Europe (2009), p. 21.

[186] Research in China, for example, documented mandatory pregnancy tests (Lei et al. 2014, p. 31).

[187] For example, such practice was reported in Egypt in 2011 (Amnesty International, Egypt, 2011).

[188] Special Rapporteur on torture, A/HRC/7/3 (2008), para. 34.

5.6 Specific Health Issues

Gender-specific treatment and care for HIV/AIDS is required by Bangkok Rule 14, acknowledging that medical treatment for women with HIV/AIDS needs to be different than treatment of men. The components of a treatment and prevention strategy include the provision of reproductive health and family planning advice, information on the transmission of sexually transmitted infections and HIV and ways to reduce those risks. Education initiatives and an appropriate diet and nutrient supplements are another important component, with extra care for pregnant or breastfeeding women.[189]

Gendered differences in substance dependencies and related complications are acknowledged by Bangkok Rule 15, which highlights the need for 'specialised treatment programmes designed for women substance abusers'. Access to harm reduction programmes,[190] rehabilitation programmes and drug-free areas must not be discriminating against women. Treatment programmes need to take into account prior victimisation, diverse cultural backgrounds, any history of abuse or domestic violence and mental health problems common among women with substance dependencies as well as the special needs of pregnant women and women with children.

Health-care, for all prisoners, should include preventative health-care measures, but for women these need to comprise pap smears and screening for breast and gynaecological cancer (Bangkok Rule 18). Other preventative health-care measures required by women may include the provision of contraceptive pills, as necessary, for instance in cases of problematic menstruation. Sport activity, for example, is also a key preventative health-care measure to maintain the physical and mental well-being of prisoners. However, in many prisons recreational activities are gender-stereotyped, and often sports facilitated for men are not available for women.

Provision of adequate and healthy food also constitutes a requirement of physical and mental health, and the lack of it—often discriminatory to access granted to male prisoners—can give rise to concerns. For instance, research in South Africa revealed women prisoners' limited diet and poor quality of food, including smelly and rotten vegetables and meat mostly consisting of skin and fat. This appeared to result mainly from the fact that the food was prepared in the men's prison kitchen by male offenders who selected meat and vegetables for themselves, leaving the less desirable food for the women.[191] It was also found that women prisoners rarely had any fruit, because they only received the leftovers when excess was sent over from another male prison.[192]

[189] See more guidance in WHO et al., A Framework for an Effective National Response (2006).

[190] Such as pharmaceutical interventions, for example, opioid substitution therapy (OST).

[191] Artz et al. (2012), pp. 63, 64.

[192] *Ibid.*, p. 64.

5.7 *Mental Health*[193]

Women who are admitted to prison are more likely than men to suffer from mental health problems,[194] often as a result of previous domestic violence, physical and sexual abuse. Mental health issues can be both the cause and consequence of imprisonment, sometimes further exacerbated by overcrowding, inadequate health-care services and abuse. Moreover, family beak-ups and feelings of failure in their parental responsibilities have been found to cause women particular stress, feelings of guilt and anxiety.

Parental concerns have been found to have a significant impact on women's experiences of incarceration, in part emanating from the fact that due to societal gender roles women have a higher sense of guilt for not fulfilling their role as mothers when detained and suffer more from the separation from their children.[195] Research in China, for example, confirmed the greater emotional damage to female prisoners following family breakdown due to detention, resulting in depression, loss of hope, anxiety and other symptoms.[196] Of the women surveyed in Georgia a significant number suffered from post-traumatic stress disorder and various mental health problems.[197]

Half of the women surveyed in Kazakhstan and 38 % in Kyrgyzstan experienced depression as a consequence of their imprisonment.[198] In Jordan, psychological problems as a consequence of imprisonment was the most commonly identified concern. Yet, only 27 % had received treatment for psychological/psychiatric problems.[199] As many as 71 % of the women surveyed in Tunisia said that they experienced depression as a consequence of their imprisonment and 61 % experienced anxiety, but only a third had received treatment for a psychological or psychiatric problem.[200] In the US, nearly 75 % of incarcerated women have been diagnosed with mental illness, a rate much higher than their male counterparts.[201]

Yet, adequate psychological care, counselling and support relating to the causes of mental health problems are often missing, and much too frequently, symptoms are addressed through medication. In Argentina, women surveyed described the common practice of receiving sleeping pills at their appointments with the

[193] 'Mental health' is defined as a state of well-being in which every individual realizes his or her own potential, can cope with the normal stresses of life, can work productively and fruitfully, and is able to make a contribution to her or his community (World Health Organization).

[194] For example according to a study conducted by the Bureau of Justice Statistics in 2002 and 2004. See UNODC Handbook (2014a), p. 9.

[195] Artz et al. (2012), p. 167.

[196] Lei et al. (2014), p. 10.

[197] Penal Reform International, Armenia and Georgia (2013b), p. 18.

[198] Penal Reform International, Kazakhstan and Kyrgyzstan (2014c), p. 18.

[199] Penal Reform International, Jordan and Tunisia (2014b), p. 16.

[200] Penal Reform International, Jordan and Tunisia (2014b), p. 28.

[201] American Civil Liberties Union, Worse than Second Class (2014).

psychiatrist without further inquiry into their specific health issues.[202] In Canada, an investigation found a dramatic spike in prescriptions for all mood-altering medications among female prisoners in the last decade, at least until 2011. So-called psychotropic medications overall surged in 2013 to 63 % of female prisoners, up from 42 % in 2002. Medications prescribed included *quetiapine* as a sleeping aid, although approved only for treating bipolar diseases and schizophrenia. 21 out of 22 women interviewed said that they had been prescribed this drug in either a federal or provincial institution. Health professionals stated that the drugs used have side effects that can be lethal.[203]

5.8 Suicide and Self-Harm

Linked to women prisoners' state of mental health, research has shown a higher risk in comparison to men of women prisoners harming themselves or attempting suicide.[204] This has been attributed, in part, to the higher level of mental health problems and substance dependency and to the harmful impact of isolation from the community due to the distances of women's prisons from their family and community. An Australian report argues that in contrast to male prisoners, who express anger and frustration by engaging in physical violence or initiating riots, women are more likely to turn to self-harm.[205]

A case in Canada, for example, demonstrates the fatal consequences of the failure to address a young woman prisoner's mental health needs. A woman prisoner committed suicide in 2007 while she was under suicide watch. Rather than providing treatment and support, her mental health issues were 'treated' through excessive periods of segregation, use of force and restraints.[206] In his report on the incident, the Federal Prison Ombudsperson found that the death was "the result of individual failures that occurred in combination with much larger systemic issues within ill-functioning and under-resourced correctional and mental health systems."[207]

In Kyrgyzstan, over a quarter of women prisoners surveyed had attempted suicide and 29 % had harmed themselves at some point in their life.[208] In Tunisia

[202] Cornell Law School's Avon Global Center for Women and Justice et al. (2013), p. 22.

[203] CBC News, Prisoners given powerful drugs off-label, allegedly to 'control behaviour', 14 April 2014.

[204] WHO Regional Office for Europe, Health in Prisons (2007).

[205] Special Rapporteur on violence against women, A/68/340 (2013), footnote 119.

[206] Canadian Association of Elizabeth Fry Societies (2013).

[207] Bingham and Sutton (2012).

[208] Penal Reform International, Kazakhstan and Kyrgyzstan (2014c), p. 18. In Kazakhstan authorities had requested four questions to be removed from the questionnaire, which related to the provision of psychological or psychiatric treatment and to suicide and self-harm prior to and during imprisonment, and no research results are therefore available.

40 % of the women surveyed had either harmed themselves and/or attempted suicide.[209] Certain times were highlighted by interviewees as constituting a heightened risk of self-harm and suicide: during the first weeks of admission; the period before and after trial; and following a six months' period of detention.[210] In some countries self-harm and suicide attempts are penalised as criminal offences, rather causing further deterioration than a solution to the problem.

Bangkok Rule 12 acknowledges that successful treatment of mental health issues requires an individualised gender-sensitive approach, addressing the root causes and taking into account any trauma that the female prisoner may have experienced. Rule 16 requires the development of a strategy to prevent suicide and self-harm in consultation with mental health-care and social welfare services.[211]

5.9 *Body Searches*

Body searches,[212] in particular strip and invasive body searches are prone to humiliation and abuse for both, male as well as female prisoners. Yet, given women's background (anatomy, socialisation) and the high rate of prior abuse, the impact of such searches on women is disproportionately greater than on men, in particular where conducted by male staff or in the presence of men. Such searches require prisoners to undress and lift their breasts, bend over at the waist and spread their cheeks. In some countries they are conducted on a more or less routine basis or by male guards.[213] The Special Rapporteur on violence against women described the improper touching of women during searches carried out by male prison staff as 'sanctioned sexual harassment'.[214]

The Rapporteur documented, for example, highly invasive and often traumatic strip searches in Australia, which were not proportional to preventing illegal items from being smuggled into prison.[215] A prisoner described how they were strip

---

[209] Penal Reform International, Jordan and Tunisia (2014b), p. 28.

[210] Penal Reform International, Armenia and Georgia (2013b), p. 18.

[211] For more detailed guidance on the key components of a suicide prevention programme in prison, see Preventing suicide in jails and prisons, Co-produced by WHO and IASP, the International Association for Suicide Prevention, 2007.

[212] Searches include all personal searches, including pat down and frisk searches, as well as strip and invasive searches. A strip search refers to the removal or rearrangement of some or all of the clothing of a person so as to permit a visual inspection of a person's private areas. Invasive body searches involve a physical inspection of the detainee's genital or anal regions. Other types of searches include searches of the property and rooms of prisoners. Visitors to prison are also frequently searched.

[213] Special Rapporteur on violence against women, United States of America, /HRC/17/26/Add.5 and Corr.1, (2011), para. 43; Human Rights Watch, Unjust and Unhealthy (2010); South African Human Rights Commission (1998), p. 67.

[214] Special Rapporteur on violence against women, United States of America, E/CN.4/1999/68/ Add.2, paras. 55, 58.

[215] Penal Reform International, Guidance Document (2013a), p. 62, footnote 209.

searched after every visit, 'naked, told to bend over, touch our toes, spread our cheeks. If we've got our period we have to take the tampon out in front of them. It's degrading and humiliating. When we do urines it's even worse, we piss in a bottle in front of them. If we can't or won't we lose visits for three weeks.'[216]

In Belarus, the search by a male guard of a female arrestee lead to a widely noted complaint to the UN Committee on the Elimination of Discrimination against Women. During the search, one of the guards had poked her buttock with his finger, made humiliating comments and threatened to strip search her.[217] Such practices were also reported, for example, by inmates at a prison in Zambia, which involved prison officers inserting their fingers into women's private parts, on a routine basis on Saturdays, in search of valuables and money.[218] In Greece, reports stated that prisoners who refused to undergo such searches were placed in segregation for several days and forced to take laxatives.[219]

Bangkok Rules 19 and 20 are therefore of particular relevance, even more so as until the revision of the Standard Minimum Rules in December 2015 they provided the only explicit international standard on body searches, differentiating between pat down, frisk and visual searches as compared to invasive and body cavity searches.

The Rules reiterate that strip or invasive body searches should only be carried out by someone of the same gender,[220] only in exceptional circumstances when absolutely necessary, and should be replaced by scans and other alternative screening methods. Where necessary, it should be undertaken in two steps, meaning that the detainee is asked to remove his/her upper clothing at separate times so they are never fully naked.[221]

5.10 *Restraints*

While certain restrictions for the use of restraints were already included, in general, in Rule 33(a) of the 1955 Standard Minimum Rules, Bangkok Rule 24 finally

[216] Australian Human Rights Committee (2012) and George (1993), p. 211.

[217] UN Committee on the Elimination of Discrimination Against Women, CEDAW/C/49/D/23/2009 (2011).

[218] Mweetwa (2013).

[219] Penal Reform International, Guidance Document (2013a), p. 61, footnote 208.

[220] The principle that women prisoners should only be supervised and attended to by female officers is already enshrined in Rule 53 of the Standard Minimum Rules, and has been emphasised by various international and regional bodies in order to prevent sexual abuse and humiliation of prisoners. Yet, increasing use of mixed staff also means that male staff is carrying out searches of women prisoners in some countries, and the Standard Minimum Rules do not include any explicit guidance on body searches.

[221] World Medical Association, Statement on Body Searches of Prisoners (2005). It states, inter alia, that physicians should not participate in prison's security system and that searches should not be conducted by physicians who will subsequently provide medical care to the prisoner.

prohibited the use of any kind of body restraint on women during labour, during birth, and immediately after birth. In the US, for example, the shackling of pregnant prisoners still persists to this day, even though there is no reasonable chance of a woman escaping during labour, while giving birth or after birth.[222]

Such practices have also been documented in the Occupied Palestinian Territory,[223] and have been described by the Special Rapporteur on violence against women as 'representative of the failure of the prison system to adapt protocols to unique situations faced by the female prison population'.[224]

Serious health concerns arise from this practice. As women in labour need to be mobile so as to assume various positions as needed and so they can be moved to an operating room if necessary, shackling of women in labour compromises the mother and baby's health. Lack of mobility can cause hemorrhage or decrease in fetal heart tones. In particular, if complications arise during delivery, a delay of even five minutes can result in permanent brain damage for the baby.[225]

5.11 Solitary Confinement

Disciplinary segregation or solitary confinement[226] in general have been found to be extremely harmful to a person's psychological health and wellbeing. Medical research confirms that the denial of meaningful human contact can cause 'isolation syndrome' the symptoms of which include anxiety, depression, anger, cognitive disturbances, perceptual distortions, paranoia, psychosis, self-harm and suicide, and can destroy a person's personality.[227] Where prolonged or indefinite, such treatment can amount to torture and ill-treatment, as emphasised by the Special Rapporteur on Torture.[228]

Yet, for women, the particular distress experienced when in isolation needs to be taken into account, even more so if they have mental health issues, are pregnant or have recently given birth. Solitary confinement also places women at greater risk

---

[222] American Civil Liberties Union, Briefing Paper (2012).

[223] Special Rapporteur on violence against women, Occupied Palestinian Territory, E/CN.4/2005/72/Add.4 (2005).

[224] Special Rapporteur on violence against women, A/68/340 (2013), para. 57.

[225] Provided to Amnesty International by Chicago Legal Aid to Incarcerated Mothers, December 1998, and printed in Amnesty International, Not part of my sentence (1999).

[226] There is no universally agreed definition of solitary confinement, but authoritative sources such as the Istanbul Statement on the Use and Effects of Solitary Confinement and the Special Rapporteur on Torture have described it as the 'physical (and social) isolation of individuals who are confined to their cells for 22-24 h a day.' *See* Special Rapporteur on torture, A/66/268 (2011), paras. 57–58.

[227] Grassian (2006), pp. 124–156; Haney (2003); Shalev (2008).

[228] See Special Rapporteur on torture, A/66/268 (2011). See also Rules 44 and 45 revised Standard Minimum Rules for the Treatment of Prisoners (Nelson Mandela Rules), General Assembly Resolution A/70/175, adopted on 17 December 2015.

for physical and/ or sexual abuse by prison staff. For example, a report by the American Civil Liberties Union revealed that a number of women perceived to be mentally ill were held in solitary confinement, some of them as a punishment for raising complaints. The isolation has also been found to jeopardise access to pre-natal care.[229]

In May 2014, for instance, a women detainee in Texas was forced to give birth in her solitary cell, resulting in the death of her newborn baby. A respective lawsuit claims that "obvious signs of labor and constant requests for medical assistance" were ignored and she was left unattended in a solitary cell. The woman reported that the nurse on duty had examined her, but said she was not in labour. While in her solitary cell, repeatedly requesting to see a doctor, the guards ignored her until a detention officer walking by her cell saw that she was delivering.[230]

Even though Bangkok Rule 22 is not very far-reaching, at least it incorporates an explicit prohibition of the use of solitary confinement or segregation as a disciplinary measure for pregnant women, women with infants and breastfeeding mothers. Beyond this explicit restriction, due to its harmful and often irrevocable consequences disciplinary segregation or solitary confinement should be used only as a last resort in exceptional circumstances and for the shortest period of time possible.[231]

5.12 *Visits*

In many prisons around the world, women receive fewer visits than men. This is caused by fewer prison facilities for women, resulting in greater distances from family and community and greater logistical difficulties and costs involved in arranging such visits. Women offenders' particular stigma also often means that they are shunned by their families. Prison regulations and institutional barriers may add additional factors in lacking or limited family contact.[232]

For example, in England and Wales (UK) half of all women on remand were reported not to receive visits from their family, compared to one in four for male prisoners.[233] Stigmatisation of female offenders was found to be a reason for isolation in China, with female offenders having no one to visit them for many years, as they were abandoned by their loved ones.[234] In Ghana, research confirmed as contributing factors for fewer visits of female prisoners the smaller number of women prisons and the different gender roles in Ghanaian culture. As a result

---

[229] American Civil Liberties Union, Worse than Second Class (2014).

[230] Counter Current News (2014).

[231] UNODC Handbook (2014a), p. 47.

[232] See for example Artz et al. (2012), p. 52.

[233] The Corston Report (2007), p. 18.

[234] Lei et al. (2014), p. 27.

women prisoners were less likely than their male counterparts to be delivered necessary items, including food.[235]

The subsequent absence of contact with the family, in particular children, is detrimental to women prisoners' mental health as well as to rehabilitation and reintegration efforts,[236] even more so where the legal framework allows for the termination of parental rights in case of disrupted ties. For example, in-depth interviews in South Africa illustrated that for women prisoners, the separation from their children constituted one of the most difficult aspects of imprisonment, and that concern for their children played a crucial role in the determination of these women to resist future offending and substance abuse.[237] In addition to emotional support friends and family often provide vital material support for incarcerated family members, by bringing money or goods such as toiletries, underwear and telephone cards.[238] Those without such support are at a considerable disadvantage.

The UN Standard Minimum Rules for the Treatment of Prisoners therefore provide that prisoners should be allowed to communicate with their family and friends. Yet, the Bangkok Rules add value in the light of the realities in many countries, resulting in increased isolation of women prisoners. Bangkok Rule 4 requires, as far as possible, for women to be allocated close to their home. However, as this is often not the case, Bangkok Rule 26 calls for measures to counterbalance the disadvantages that stem from this. Where visits are not possible or infrequent due to the distances, other means of communication should be facilitated and contact should not be prohibited as a disciplinary sanction (Bangkok Rule 23).[239]

Other measures to compensate for disadvantages caused by farer distances can include extending visiting hours or providing overnight accommodation if family members have to travel a long way. School and standard working hours should be taken into account, even if this is outside regular visiting hours, and families should be provided with information about the location and any transfer of their imprisoned family member. Also the frequency and length of telephone calls should be increased, if families are unable to travel to the prison, and cooperation should be developed with organisations which can facilitate visits.

The conditions and atmosphere of a visit also play a crucial role as they strongly affect the quality of a visit and are likely to impact on the number of visits women receive. Often visitors and prisoners are separated by a wire mesh or glass, and can

---

[235] Amnesty International, Ghana (2012), p. 28.

[236] UNODC, Afghanistan (2007), p. 47. Bangkok Rule 43 recognizes that visits are an important prerequisite to ensuring women prisoners' mental well-being and social reintegration.

[237] Artz et al. (2012), pp. 189, 191.

[238] Ashdown and James (2010), p. 132.

[239] Bangkok Rule 44, conscious of the fact that a significant proportion of women in prison has experienced violence and may not wish to be visited by them, emphasises that women prisoners should be consulted on who is allowed to visit them.

only communicate through an earpiece, even though such precautions are not necessarily based on actual security risks.

Bangkok Rule 28 is therefore supplementary to other prison standards in recognising the strong need for mothers and children to have physical contact and requires a child-friendly environment to reduce any distress felt by the children. It is good practice to allow for visits with physical contact in a comfortable, inviting setting, which provides an opportunity for interaction, bonding and for playing with children.[240]

Humiliating search procedures of visitors are likely to discourage visits, in particular for children. Complaints about such procedures have been documented, for instance, in Brazil, including even elderly women and children,[241] or in Afghanistan. In a men's prison on the edge of Kabul, reportedly a blanket order to conduct invasive body-cavity searches of female visitors was argued as a measure to keep out contraband, while most male visitors got into the prison with a mere pat down search.[242]

While Bangkok Rule 21 does not provide guidance for searches of visitors in general or in a comprehensive manner, at least for children it explicitly refers to the need for any searches of children to be carried out in a way that protects their dignity. Conjugal visits,[243] in some countries, are allowed for male prisoners, but not for their female counterparts. For example in Chile, women prisoners are generally prohibited from having sexual relations with their partners. While two pilot programmes have been introduced, female prisoners are only eligible for conjugal visits if they have already been sentenced and if certain requirements are met, such as having a stable partner, 'good behaviour', and if the absence of sexually transmitted infections has been verified. Male inmates, by comparison, are not required to meet any such criteria, but have the right to conjugal visits.[244]

To address such gender-based discrimination, Bangkok Rule 27 requires that male and female prisoners are allowed conjugal visits on an equal basis.

[240] Currie (2012), p. 16.

[241] Subcommittee on Prevention of Torture, Brazil, CAT/OP/BRA/1.en (2012), para.118.

[242] New York Times, Afghan Prison's Invasive Searches of Female Visitors Stir Fear of Slipping Rights' 16 March 2012; Human Rights Watch, Afghanistan: End Invasive Searches of Women Visiting Prison, 20 March 2012.

[243] A conjugal visit is a scheduled period in which a prisoner can spend time with a visitor in private, usually their spouse or long-term partner. These visits help to maintain a couple's intimate bond, including their sexual relationship. The couple usually spends the visit in a small unit, which contains, at a minimum, a bed, a shower and other sanitary facilities.

[244] Organisation Mondiale contre la Torture (2004), para. 123.

5.13 Children Living in Prison with their Mother/Parent[245]

Almost all countries allow babies and children to live in prison with their mothers, typically until they reach a certain age. For example, Argentina allows children up to the age of four to reside with their mothers in prison.[246] In England and Wales, babies can stay with their mothers until the age of between 9 and 18 months—or longer if the release date is imminent.[247] In contrast, prison rules in most states in India permit imprisoned mothers to keep children with them up to the age of 6, and some state prisons have allowed girls of 10 and 12 who have a disability to remain in prison with their mothers.[248]

While allowing infants and young children to live with their incarcerated parents (co-residence programmes) reduces some risks associated with separation, life in prison is a distressing and traumatic experience for children and has to be implemented with adequate safeguards, proper infrastructure and necessary resources.

The Bangkok Rules therefore include specific provisions tailored to children living in prison with their parent (mother or father).[249] Bangkok Rule 49 stipulates that decisions to allow children to stay with their mothers/fathers in prison need to be based on the best interests of the children. If they co-reside with their parent in prison they should never be treated as prisoners (Bangkok Rule 49), their experience must be as close as possible to life for a child outside (Bangkok Rule 51). Children living in prison with their mothers (or fathers) are likely to also have health-care and psychological support needs, which are recognised in Bangkok Rules 9 and 51.

The conditions in detention inevitably impact on the children living in prison with their parent, in terms of overall conditions as well as due to the lack of infrastructure suitable for children. Sierra Leone prisons, for example, were found to lack dedicated infrastructure for co-residence, and infants frequently became ill due to the conditions in prison and the spread of contagious diseases.[250] Most of the children in prison with their mothers were under two and held in a maximum-

---

[245] Standards relating to children of imprisoned parents, other than in the Bangkok Rules, have been developed by the African Committee on the Rights and Welfare of the Child, General Comment No. 1 (2014) and Committee on the Rights of the Child, Day of General Discussion. (2011). See http://acerwc.org/wp-content/uploads/2013/12/GC-No1-on-Article-30-of-the-African-Charter-on-the-Rights-and-Welfare-of-the-Child.pdf.

[246] Cornell Law School's Avon Global Center for Women and Justice et al. (2013), p. 5.

[247] Penal Reform International, Submission (2011b).

[248] *Ibid.*

[249] Para. 12 of the Bangkok Rules' preliminary observations state that "Some of these rules address (...) both men and women, including (...) parental responsibilities (...)." *See* further recommendations in the Report and Recommendations of the General Discussion on 'Children of Incarcerated Parents', 30 September 2011, UN Committee on the Rights of the Child, and; General Comment 1 on the African Charter on the Rights and Welfare of the Child Comment (2014).

[250] Special Rapporteur on violence against women, A/68/340 (2013), para. 80.

security prison, which was seen to have the best facilities. However, babies were observed to be malnourished, whether breast-feeding or eating on their own, because of the lack of food and basic hygiene.[251]

As most countries provide in their laws for a specific age until which babies and children can live in prison with their parent, inevitably, they will be separated at some point, resulting in emotional stress for both, the parent and the child, and raising questions about alternative child-care arrangements.

In recognition of the difficult situation arising from separation, Bangkok Rule 52 requires that such decisions shall be based on individual assessments and the best interests of the child and that the removal of the child from prison shall be undertaken with sensitivity, and only when alternative care arrangements for the child have been identified.

6 Rehabilitation and Reintegration

6.1 Classification

In order to achieve the rehabilitative purpose of imprisonment, the prison term has to be used to ensure to the extent possible that upon return to society the offender is able to lead a law-abiding and self-supporting life.[252] Classification, usually conducted upon arrival, constitutes a crucial tool to ensure suitable rehabilitative services.[253]

Women prisoners may face discrimination in such classification processes, which can result in the allocation of a security level higher than necessary, usually linked to more restrictions and less access to work and rehabilitation programmes.[254] Common causes are the low number of women prisons and procedures that are not gender-sensitive, in particular with regard to women's experiences of violence and typically poorer state of mental health, which is often misinterpreted as security risk.[255]

In Australia, for example, the insufficient number of women prisons has resulted in women being detained in maximum-security prisons with male prisoners.[256] In the women's section of a prison in Thailand, there was only one male prison guard in charge of classification and all women were classified as high-risk, even though the prison director said that only six of them actually met the criteria.[257] The lack of

[251] Penal Reform International, Submission (2011b).

[252] Rule 58 Standard Minimum Rules.

[253] See Standard Minimum Rules 63 and 67–69.

[254] Ashdown and James (2010), p. 130.

[255] Penal Reform International/Association to Prevent Torture (2013), p. 9.

[256] Australian Human Rights Commission (2012).

[257] Report from East Asia-Pacific Regional Meeting, UNODC/JSDO/BKEGM/2013/1 (2013), para. 39.

gender-sensitive processes is also illustrated in South Africa, where sentence plans are drawn on the basis of an initial admission interview of incoming offenders, including the determination of rehabilitation programmes. The design of the process resulted in women only indicating recent events and issues directly related to their arrest, rather than violence and trauma dating back further.[258]

Taking into account these common problems in classification methods, Bangkok Rules 40 and 41 stipulate the development and implementation of classification methods that are gender-specific and ensure appropriate rehabilitative plans.

6.2 Consequences of Imprisonment

In designing rehabilitation programmes it is important to understand the consequences of imprisonment for detainees in general, and to identify particular obstacles women face in this regard.

Overall, former prisoners will experience loss of employment while they were imprisoned, and the criminal record will make it difficult to find work again. Loss of housing will also be a common feature, although women may be more affected in societies where they face increased stereotypes and are rejected by their families. If they have left a violent relationship, women will have to establish a new life, which is likely to entail additional economic, social and legal difficulties. Already before imprisonment women are likely to have faced discrimination in the labour market, which will be exacerbated following imprisonment.

The low levels of education and vocational skills, which has been identified as a common feature amongst women prisoners, if unaddressed during their prison term, will remain an equally big challenge as prior to imprisonment. Break-up of families tends to affect women more than their male counterparts, and they are likely to have a particular sense of guilt towards their children. In some countries they may lose their parental rights. Confidence and life skills also tend to be lower amongst the female prison population than amongst their male counterparts.

Health problems are a common concern, for both male and female prison population, as a generally poor state of health amongst prison populations is likely to have been further deteriorated by prison conditions, poor nutrition, the prevalence of infectious diseases[259] and poor health services. Yet again, former women prisoners will be affected by discrimination in access to health-care services and social welfare in countries where equality has not been achieved in the respective policies.

---

[258] Artz et al. (2012), p. 46.

[259] There is a heightened risk of mental illness and infection rates for tuberculosis, HIV and hepatitis B and C can be up to a 100 times higher in prisons than in the outside community (International Centre for Prison Studies, Guidance Note: Improving Prison Health Care, January 2005). The TB rate in prisons in Europe in 2002 was 84 times higher than in the general population (UNODC/WHO Europe, Good governance (2013), pp. 1, 2).

The lack of attention for women's particular health issues in many prisons, not least reproductive and preventive health-care needs, may result in a particularly poor state following their release. Mental health problems, typically higher amongst the female prison population, are likely to have worsened in prison rather than improved, and they may have long-term consequences due to isolation and the higher rate of self-harm and suicide.[260]

Other challenges and forms of discrimination in society may equally affect women following their release. Research in China, for example, has revealed that spouses often force their wives in prison to unfair divorce settlements or secretly initiate property transfers, leaving them without financial security when they are released.[261] Women prisoners are therefore likely to face different and additional challenges following release, which need to be addressed in a gender-sensitive way preparing them for release and following discharge from prison.

6.3 Rehabilitation Programmes in Prison

Pre-release preparation and post-release support policies and programmes are typically structured around the requirements of men and rarely address the gender-specific needs of women offenders. There are usually fewer educational and training opportunities for women, and those that are available are less varied and of poorer quality than those offered to male detainees.[262]

Furthermore, in many prisons the types of activities offered to women as part of rehabilitation programmes are gendered,[263] traditionally thought appropriate for women. While skills taught to men are generally framed in terms of preparation for employment on release those taught to women rarely are. Where they are not mirroring domestic work conventionally conducted by women in the household, they equip for the most low-paid jobs in the economy. This reinforces women's dependency on men and the inability to find employment with sufficient income following release.

A UN report on Abomey prison in Benin, for instance, reflects this phenomenon, stating that women prisoners "appeared not to have equal access to the training courses and workshops provided for some male prisoners, nor to the education classes provided to male adolescent detainees."[264] In New Hampshire state prisons,

[260] Suicide attempts are more prevalent compared to women outside of prison, and compared to men in pre-trial detention. (See for example WHO/ISAP, Preventing suicide in jails and prisons, 2007).

[261] Lei et al. (2014), p. 10.

[262] Special Rapporteur on violence against women, A/68/340 (2013), para. 68.

[263] See for example *ibid.* and Report of the Special Rapporteur on the right to education, A/HRC/11/8 (2009), para. 51.

[264] Subcommittee on Prevention of Torture, Benin, CAT/OP/BEN/1 (2001), para. 277.

a report by the State Advisory Committee observed, that "It is noteworthy that the vocational training opportunities made available to incarcerated men reflect the kinds of well-paying work from which women have been traditionally excluded – automotive mechanics, carpentry, and the like while the sole industry available to women at the Goffstown prison is sewing. (...) The facts speak for themselves regarding the state's complicity in sex-based discrimination confronting incarcerated women within the state."[265] The Committee also found that the significant contrast of services offered to women prisoners resulted in exceptionally high recidivism rates for female offenders in New Hampshire. In 2005, the reoffending rate for women was at an unprecedented high of 56 % compared to 49 % for men.[266]

The discrimination of women prisoners in access to rehabilitation programmes is also captured in a report of the UN Special Rapporteur on the Right to Education stating, '[i]n many countries, the quality and range of programmes is poorer than those provided for men and, where they are offered, they often reflect traditional female roles such as sewing, kitchen duties, beauty care, and handicrafts.'[267] The Special Rapporteur on the right to education noted that generally "it is unsurprising that research involving female detainees has uncovered deep expressions of frustration with the extent and quality of education and training they received".[268]

Other support, like social services, counselling, confidence-building and life skills, too often are lacking or ignoring the fact that similar needs operate differently for men and women.[269] For women, interpersonal skills, with a special focus on family, have also been found to be important. A parliamentary review of educational programmes for women in British prisons found that literacy and numeracy were over-emphasised, with insufficient focus on 'emotional literacy'.[270] Criminologists with gender-specific expertise also emphasise the importance of "assertiveness training programmes, anger management and activities, which enhance women's skills and experiences".[271]

Surveys on women's priorities with regard to rehabilitation programmes confirm this approach. Programmes to build confidence and life skills represented the second most important support desired in a survey in the South Caucasus, even before vocational skills training (19 % in Georgia and 21 % in Armenia).[272] Women prisoners interviewed in South Africa also highlighted life skills ('surviving out

---

[265] New Hampshire Advisory Committee to the US Commission on Civil Rights, (2011), see also the Guardian, Discrimination against women in prison keeps them going back, 4 January 2013, accessed 22 January 2013, www.guardian.co.uk/commentisfree/2013/jan/04/discrimination-women-prison-recidivism.

[266] *Ibid.*

[267] Special Rapporteur on the right to education, A/HRC/11/8 (2009), para. 12.

[268] *Ibid.*, para. 51.

[269] Artz et al. (2012), p. 61.

[270] The Corston Report (2007).

[271] Artz et al., p. 61.

[272] Penal Reform International, Armenia and Georgia (2013b), p. 20.

there'), for example how to open a bank account, how to use an ATM, how to get a cell phone contract, how to draft a CV or apply for a job with 'missing years', how to apply for social grants, how to secure housing and handle rental contracts, as highly important for rebuilding their lives.[273] If a variety of rehabilitative programmes are provided in women's correctional facilities, often they are dependent on external funding and volunteers.[274]

Responding to discrimination of women prisoners in access to appropriate rehabilitation programmes, Bangkok Rule 46 requires prison authorities to implement comprehensive, individualised rehabilitation programmes which take into account women's gender-specific needs and aim to address the underlying factors that led to their offence so they can better cope with them following release. Programmes offered should not be limited to skills, which are traditionally considered appropriate for women due to gender-stereotyping and emphasise training and work that increases women's chances of earning a living wage after their release.

In light of the impact of family breakdown and separation from children, maintaining relationships with the family, in particular children, is also of key importance in preparation of successful reintegration of female offenders. Support for child-care and reunification with family was highly ranked in surveys, for example in the South Caucasus. 49 % in Armenia and 50 % in Georgia stated they required this kind of assistance to build a new life.[275]

6.4 Reintegration Support Following Release

Although many problems women face upon release are similar to those of men, the intensity and multiplicity of their post-release needs can be very different. On top of typically having access to fewer and/ or lower quality rehabilitation programmes preparing them for release, "they are commonly burdened with low social and economic status in society and within their own families, and therefore face more difficult conditions upon release than do men."[276]

For women prisoners in Jordan, stigmatisation was the biggest obstacle preventing reintegration (71 %), followed by family abandonment (50 %). Women prisoners in Tunisia had equal anxieties, 69 % of them identifying stigmatisation as the most serious obstacle to reintegration.[277] Obstacles in finding employment despite a criminal record usually constitutes the biggest challenge following release from prison in general, but even more so for women. Confronted

[273] Artz et al. (2012), p. 59.

[274] See for example Artz et al. (2012), p. 59.

[275] Penal Reform International, Armenia and Georgia (2013b), p. 20.

[276] Report of the Special Rapporteur on the Right to Education, A/HRC/11/8 (2009), para.49; Special Rapporteur on violence against women, A/68/340 (2013), para. 67.

[277] Penal Reform International, Jordan and Tunisia (2014b, p. 31).

already with low levels of education and discrimination in access to the labour market, work and rehabilitation activities in prison—if existent—may not have equipped them with the necessary skills.

Help with finding employment was the most common support need expressed by women surveyed in Central Asia and the South Caucasus. For example, nearly 60 % of women in Kyrgyzstan and half of the respondents in Kazakhstan highlighted this as a priority and stated that their criminal record prevented employment.[278] In Georgia, 70 % of the women surveyed indicated that they needed support in finding employment following release, in Armenia this figure was 65 %.[279] In Tunisia, too, support in finding employment lead on the list of support requirements expressed by women prisoners; 56 % highlighted this as a priority.[280]

Finding housing is also a significant challenge for former prisoners, who often lose their accommodation due to imprisonment. Following release, they are likely not to have financial resources to afford housing, in particular to pay rent upfront or make security deposits. Applications may also require the disclosure of criminal records.[281] For women the situation may be exacerbated by being shunned by their families, or not being able to return to their spouses in case of a previous history of domestic abuse. In Australia, research has shown that women are left homeless, or forced to remain in secure custody, due to fear of payback and retaliation by the community.[282] A survey of women prisoners in Afghanistan highlighted that women released from prison cannot sign a property rental agreement without a man's signature, restricting their ability to lead an independent life.[283]

In a survey in Kazakhstan and Kyrgyzstan accommodation was perceived as a problem by 40 % of the women.[284] In England and Wales 30 % of women offenders lost their accommodation while in prison, and of the women who had reoffended following release, 56 % stated that homelessness contributed to their offence.[285]

Another barrier faced by women prisoners following release is to address various health problems, either through denial of access or inability to afford health-care insurance.[286] In the South Caucasus, the majority of women identified treatment for health problems as the most important support to receive as helping them with reintegration following release (48 % in Georgia and 60 % in Armenia).[287] In Jordan as well as Tunisia, the women surveyed indicated that their poor

[278] Penal Reform International, Kazakhstan and Kyrgyzstan (2014c), p. 20.

[279] Penal Reform International, Armenia and Georgia (2013b), p. 20.

[280] *Ibid.*

[281] Special Rapporteur on violence against women, A/68/340 (2013), para 73.

[282] *Ibid.*, para 75.

[283] UNODC, Afghanistan (2007), p. 34.

[284] Penal Reform International, Kazakhstan and Kyrgyzstan (2014c), p. 22.

[285] The Corston Report (2007), p. 3.

[286] Special Rapporteur on violence against women, A/68/340 (2013), para 70.

[287] Penal Reform International, Armenia and Georgia (2013b), p. 20.

psychological state was a major obstacle to reintegration (50 % in Jordan and 61 % in Tunisia).[288]

Absence of substance dependency treatment following release is particularly damaging as the lack of care "means that the conditions that rendered them vulnerable to drug involvement in the first place are sometimes replicated and augmented in prison, and after release".[289] According to a study in Canada women released were 10 times more likely to return to prison within one year when they did not participate in a drug treatment programme.[290]

Attention to mental health problems is equally important following release, as former women prisoners have a propensity to self-harm, including overdosing on drugs. For example, a study in England and Wales found that within one year of being released, former female prisoners were 36 times more likely to die by suicide than the general population.[291]

While the Bangkok Rules could be more specific and detailed on the elements of gender-specific aftercare, Rules 56 and 47 emphasise the requirement to design gender-specific reintegration programmes in cooperation with probation and/or social welfare services, local community groups and NGOs and to provide additional support to released women who need psychological, medical, legal and practical help.

7 Conclusion

Women who come in conflict with the law certainly should not be described as unaccountable passive victims of male making. At the same time, undeniably, they face discrimination in the criminal justice system, to a considerable extent sustaining discrimination in society in general.

Patriarchal structures, perceptions of gender-appropriate behaviour, economic dependence and discrimination in the labour market as well as in access to education in many countries shape women's lives. It is not surprising that these factors leave a trace and directly or indirectly contribute to women offending—or in case of moral crimes and protective detention to their penalisation in the first place. Penitentiary systems are designed for the majority male population of offenders and prisoners, overlooking—often in a misunderstood claim of equality—the specific characteristics and needs of women.

The link between violence against women and imprisonment is particularly striking. What available research there is shows that the pathway of many women offenders is paved with domestic or sexual violence, mostly at the hands of their

[288] Penal Reform International, Jordan and Tunisia (2014b, pp. 19, 31).

[289] Special Rapporteur on violence against women, A/68/340 (2013), para 71.

[290] *Ibid.*, para 71.

[291] *Ibid.*, para. 69.

partners or family members. Once in detention they may easily find themselves, yet again, in a 'toxic environment'[292] of (sexual) abuse and harassment. International standards ignored their needs for too long, maybe most evidently symbolised in the self-evident provision for shaving items in prison standards since 1955, whereas it took until 2010 to incorporate sanitary pads.

The UN Bangkok Rules do not provide guidance on all issues surrounding women in the criminal justice system (discriminatory penal laws or sentencing, gender-specific offences, legal representation are not within their scope). However, they are a truly comprehensive set of standards covering not only conditions in detention but also non-custodial measures and gender-specific considerations in sentencing. In a few areas the Bangkok Rules are not very progressive or far-reaching (e.g. limitations to the use of solitary confinement or restraints) and in others guidance could be more concrete and specific (co-residence, visits, search procedures regarding children for example).

That aside, they are a milestone in the recognition of the need for gender-sensitive penal systems, and have a considerable added value to guide states and authorities on how to rectify their blind spots when it comes to women offenders and prisoners. The call for gender-sensitive justice systems does not mean that attention should suddenly shift from the majority male prison population to their female counterparts. Yet, in the light of the amount of ignorance and neglect vis-à-vis women in contact or conflict with the law for decades counter-balancing is now in order.

Human rights for offenders and prisoners are not only rights for the majority and the mere replication of services provided to men does not produce gender equality.

Five Questions

1. Why is the number of women prisoners and their rate amongst prison populations rising across the globe?
2. To what extent does the 'feminisation of poverty' contribute to the increasing number of women in prison?
3. Has the 'war on drugs' resulted in gendered disparities in the penal system?
4. To what extent do judges take into account systematic domestic or sexual violence as a mitigating factor or plea of self-defence in criminal proceedings against women who have committed violent offences against their abusive husband or spouse?
5. What considerations should be taken into account to decide whether babies/ children should co-reside with their parent in prison?

[292] US Department of Justice (2014).

References

AdvocAid. (2012). Women, Debt & Detention: An Exploratory Report on Fraudulent Conversion and the Criminalisation of Debt in Sierra Leone, July 2012. Available at http://www.advocaidsl.com/wp-content/uploads/2011/03/AdvocAid 2012-Women-Debt-and-Detention-Final-Report.pdf

African Committee on the Rights and Welfare of the Child. (2013). General Comment No. 1 on 'Children of Incarcerated and Imprisoned Parents and Primary Caregivers'. Adopted in November 2013, unpublished.

Agren, D. (2010). Female felons swell ranks among Mexican criminals. USA Today, 2 December 2010.

American Civil Liberties Union. (2005a). Caught in the Net: The Impact of Drug Policies on Women and Families.

American Civil Liberties Union. (2005b). 'Girlfriend problem' harms women and children, impacted families call mandatory sentences unfair and destructive, 14 June 2005.

American Civil Liberties Union. (2012). Briefing Paper, The Shackling of Pregnant Women & Girls in U.S. Prisons, Jails & Youth Detention Centers, 12 October 2012.

American Civil Liberties Union. (2014). Worse than Second Class: Solitary Confinement of Women in the United States, 2014.

Amnesty International. (1999, March). Not part of my sentence: Violations of the Human Rights of Women in Custody. AI Index: AMR 51/01/99.

Amnesty International. (2005a). Afghanistan: Women still under attack—a systematic failure to protect. AI Index: ASA 11/007/2005.

Amnesty International. (2005b). Women in Prison Factsheet, August 2005, citing Department of Justice, Bureau of Justice Statistics, Prisoners in 1997, www.amnestyusa.org/women

Amnesty International. (2011). Egypt: Military 'virginity test' investigation a sham, 9 November 2011.

Amnesty International, Ghana. (2012). Prisoners are bottom of the pile: The human rights of inmates in Ghana. AI Index: AFR 28/002/2012.

Artz, L., Hoffman-Wanderer, Y., & Moult, K. (2012). *Hard time(s): Women's pathways to crime and incarceration*. Cape Town: GHJRU, University of Cape Town.

Ashdown, J., & James, M. (2010, March). Women in detention. *International Review of the Red Cross, 72*(877), available at http://www.icrc.org/eng/assets/files/other/irrc-877-ashdown-james.pdf

Australian Human Rights Commission. (2012). *Australian study tour report: Visit of the UN Special Rapporteur on violence against women*, April 2012, available at https://www.humanrights.gov.au/publications/australian-study-tour-report-visit-un-special-rapporteur-violence-against-women.

Australian Human Rights Committee. (2012). Australian Study Tour Report, Visit of the UN Special Rapporteur on Violence against Women 10–20 April 2012, available at https://www.humanrights.gov.au/publications/australian-study-tour-report-visit-un-special-rapporteur-violence-against-women

Bastick, M., & Townhead, L. (2008). Women in prison: A commentary on the UN Standard Minimum Rules for the Treatment of Prisoners. Human Rights & Refugees Publications (Quaker United Nations Office).

Bingham, E., & Sutton, R. (2012). In R. Mandhane (Ed.), *International human rights program, cruel, inhuman and degrading? Canada's treatment of federally-sentenced women with mental health issues*. University of Toronoto.

Canadian Association of Elizabeth Fry Societies. (2013). Jury rules Ashley Smith's Death a Homicide, December 19, 2013, see http://www.caefs.ca/jury-rules-ashley-smiths-death-a-homocide/

Committee on the Elimination of Discrimination against Women (CEDAW). (2011). Communication No. 23/2009, Inga Abramova v. Belarus, 27 September 2011, UN-Doc. CEDAW/C/49/D/23/200, available at www.unhcr.org/refworld/docid/4fd6f75a2.html

Committee on the Elimination of Discrimination against Women (CEDAW). (2012). Concluding observations on Jordan, 23 March 2012, CEDAW/C/JOR/CO/5.

Committee on the Rights of the Child. (2011). Report and Recommendations of the Day of General Discussion on 'Children of incarcerated parents', 30 September 2011.

Constitutional Court of South Africa, S. v. M., 26 September 2007, Ref. no. [2008] (3) SA 232 (CC) 261, http://www.saflii.org/cgi-bin/disp.pl?file=za/cases/ZACC/2007/18.html&query=%20M%20v%20S

Convention on the Elimination of All Forms of Discrimination against Women, New York, 18 December 1979, Article 2 (f) and (g) and Article 5; see also Human Rights Committee, General Comment No. 21 on Article 10 (Humane treatment of persons deprived of their liberty), 1992.

Cornell Law School's Avon Global Center for Women and Justice and International Human Rights Clinic, Ministry of Defence of Argentina and the University of Chicago Law School International Human Rights Clinic. (2013). Women in prison in Argentina: Causes, conditions, and consequences.

Council of Europe, Parliamentary Assembly. (2007). The situation of women in the South Caucasus, document 11178, 6 February 2007.

Counter Current News. (2014). Jailed Woman Forced to Give Birth in Solitary Confinement, Baby Dies in Cell, 26 May 2014, http://countercurrentnews.com/2014/05/jailed-woman-forced-to-give-birth-in-solitary-confinement-baby-dies-in-cell/

Currie, B. (2012). *Women in prison: A forgotten population*, available at http://www.internetjournalofcriminology.com/Currie_Women_in_Prison_A_Forgotten_Population_IJC_Oct_2012.pdf. Accessed 15 May 2013.

Deschenes, E. P., Owen, B., & Crow, J. (2006). Recidivism among female prisoners: Secondary analysis of the 1994 BJS [Bureau of Justice Statistics] recidivism data set. Unpublished report submitted to the United States Department of Justice.

Deschenes, E. P., Owen, B., & Crow, J. (2007). Recidivism Among Female Prisoners: Secondary Analysis of the 1994 BJS Recidivism Data Set, January 2007, https://www.ncjrs.gov/pdffiles1/nij/grants/216950.pdf

EurekAlert. (2011). Higher return to prison for women without drug abuse programs, 31 May 2011, http://www.eurekalert.org/pub_releases/2011-05/smh-hrt053111.php

European Committee for the Prevention of Torture and Inhuman or Degrading Treatment or Punishment (CPT). (2000). The CPT Standards: Substantive sections, 2006 Extract from the 10th General Report, CPT/Inf (2000) 13.

European Union Fundamental Rights Agency (2013) Inequalities and multiple discrimination in access to and quality of healthcare (p. 41).

Gelsthorpe, L. (1989). *Sexism and the female offender*. Aldershot: Gower.

George, A. (1993). Strip searches: Sexual assault by the state, in without consent: confronting adult sexual violence. Australian institute of Criminology.

Golichenko, M. (2013) Vulnerability of women who use drugs to arbitrary arrest and discriminating sentencing, presentation on behalf of the Canadian HIV/AIDS Legal Network at the expert group meeting, University of Chicago, 14 May 2013.

Grassian, S. (2006). Psychiatric effects of solitary confinement. *Journal of Law and Policy, 22*:325–383.

Greene, S., Haney, C., & Hurtado, A. (2000). Cycles of pain: Risk factors in the lives of incarcerated mothers and their children. *The Prison Journal, 80*(1).

Haney, C. (2003). Mental health issues in long-term solitary and 'Supermax' confinement. *Crime & Delinquency, 49*(1), 124–156.

Heartland Alliance. Iraq: Gender-Based Violence Prevention: Legal, Medical and Psychosocial Services, http://www.heartlandalliance.org/international/wherewework/project-pages/iraq-gender-based-violence.html

http://www.presunciondeinocencia.org.mx/images/stories/hoja_campania_global_mujer_prision_abril2012.pdf (only available in Spanish), cited in OAS, Women and Drugs in the Americas, 2014.

Human Rights Watch. (1998). Unjust and unhealthy, 2010; South African Human Rights Commission. Report of the National Prisons Project.

Human Rights Watch. (2005) Colombia: Women face prison for abortion, 27 June 2005, http://www.hrw.org/news/2005/06/26/colombia-women-face-prison-abortion. Accessed 2 June 2014.

Human Rights Watch. (2012). *I had to run away: The imprisonment of women and girls for 'Moral Crimes' in Afghanistan*. New York: Human Rights Watch.

Iakobishvili, E. (2012). *Cause for alarm: The incarceration of women for drug offences in Europe and Central Asia, and the need for legislative and sentencing reform*. London: Harm Reduction International.

Inter-American Commission on Human Rights. (2013). Report on the Situation of Persons Deprived of Liberty in Honduras, 18 March 2013, OEA/Ser.L/V/II.147 Doc. 6.

International Centre for Prison Studies (2005, January). *Guidance note: Improving prison health care*. London: International Centre for Prison Studies.

Istanbul Protocol on the Effective Investigation and Documentation of Torture and Other Cruel, Inhuman or Degrading Treatment or Punishment (2004).

Kraft-Stolar, T., Brundige, E., Kalantry, S., & Getgen, J. E. (2011). From protection to punishment: Post-conviction barriers to justice for domestic violence survivor-defendants in New York State. Cornell Legal Studies Research Paper No. 11-21, 7 June 2011.

Organisation Mondiale contre la Torture, Joint submission. (2004). State Violence in Chile: An alternative report to the UN Committee against Torture, March 2004, http://www.omct.org/files/2004/03/2360/stateviolence_chile_04_eng.pdf. Accessed 15 May 2013.

Law and Justice Commission of Pakistan. (2012). Releasing the Female Accused on Bail, PKLJC 48, May 2012. Available at http://commonlii.org/pk/other/PKLJC/reports/48.html. Accessed 4 December 2012.

Lawlor, E., Nicholls, J., & Sanfilippo, L. (2008, November). *Unlocking value: How we all benefit from investing in alternatives to prison for women offenders*. London: The New Economics Foundation.

Lei, C., Xiaogang, L., & Jianjun, C. (2014). Research report on the treatment of women detainees in China - Using the Bangkok rules as the starting point of analysis.

Lines, R. (2008). The right to health of prisoners in international human rights law. *International Journal of Prisoner Health, 4*(1).

Moloney, K. P., van den Bergh, B. J., & Moller, L. F. (2009). Women in prison: The central issues of gender characteristics and trauma history. *Public Health, 123*(6).

Mweetwa, S., & Africa, A. (2013). Zambia: Humiliating Searches Unsettle Kabwe Inmates, 25 May 2013, available at http://allafrica.com/stories/201305260053.html. Accessed 4 June 2013.

New Hampshire Advisory Committee to the US Commission on Civil Rights. (2011). Unequal treatment: Women incarcerated in New Hampshire's State prison system, Briefing Report, September 2011. Accessed 22 January 2013, www.usccr.gov/pubs/Unequal_Treatment_WomenIncarceratedinNHStatePrisonSystem.pdf.

Papavangjeli, E., PhD Student. (2013). Women offenders and their re-integration into the society—gender perspective in the criminal justice system, available at www.doktoratura.unitir.edu.al/wp-content/uploads/2014/02/Doktoratura-Edlira-Papavangjeli-Instituti-Studimeve-Europiane.pdf

Penal Reform International. (2010). Women in prison in Russia: At a glance.

Penal Reform International. (2011a). Report on Women's Health in Kazakhstan. Available at: www.penalreform.org/wp-content/uploads/2013/05/Womens-Health-in-Kazakhstan-1.pdf

Penal Reform International. (2011b). Submission for UN Committee on the Rights of the Child, Day of General Discussion, 30 September 2011, Protecting Children in Prison with a Parent—Implement and Develop the Bangkok Rules.

Penal Reform International. (2013a) Guidance Document on the Bangkok Rules, Working Draft.

Penal Reform International. (2013b). Who are women prisoners? Survey results from Armenia and Georgia.

Penal Reform International. (2014a). The use and practice of imprisonment: Current trends and future challenges.

Penal Reform International. (2014b). Who are women prisoners? Survey results from Jordan and Tunisia.

Penal Reform International. (2014c). Who are women prisoners? Survey results from Kazakhstan and Kyrgyzstan.

Penal Reform International/Association to Prevent Torture. (2013). Balancing security and dignity in prisons: A framework for preventive monitoring.

Penal Reform International/Interagency Panel on Juvenile Justice. (2014). Neglected needs: Girls in the criminal justice system.

Penal Reform International Toolbox on the Bangkok Rules, http://www.penalreform.org/priorities/women-in-the-criminal-justice-system/bangkok-rules-2/tools-resources/

Report by Baroness Jean Corston, A review of women with particular vulnerabilities in the Criminal Justice system (The Corston Report), March 2007, available at www.justice.gov.uk/publications/docs/corston-report-march-2007.pdf

Report from East Asia-Pacific Regional Meeting on the Implementation of the United Nations Rules for the Treatment of Women Prisoners and Non-custodial Measures for Women Offenders (the Bangkok Rules) Bangkok, 19–21 February 2013, UNODC/JSDO/BKEGM/2013/1, 14 March 2013.

Report of Expert Group Meeting convened by the International Human Rights Clinic at the University of Chicago Law School on behalf of Rashida Manjoo, the UN Special Rapporteur on Violence against women, 14 May 2013, available at http://www.lawschool.cornell.edu/womenandjustice/Clinical-Projects/upload/Expert-Group-Meeting-FINAL.pdf

Richie, B. E. (1996). *Compelled to crime: The gender entrapment of battered black women.*

Shalev, S. (2008). *A sourcebook on solitary confinement*. London: Mannheim Centre for Criminology, LSE.

Shehan, F. (2013). Imprisoned far from home: The impact of social isolation on women prisoners, at www.penalreform.org/blog/imprisoned-home-impact-social-isolation-women-prisoners/, 9 October 2013.

South African Human Rights Commission. (1998). Report of the National Prisons Project.

Special Rapporteur on the right to education, Vernor Muñoz, Report on The Right to Education of Persons in Detention, UN-Doc. A/HRC/11/8, 2 April 2009, available at http://www2.ohchr.org/english/bodies/hrcouncil/docs/11session/A.HRC.11.8_en.pdf

Special Rapporteur on torture and other cruel, inhuman or degrading treatment or punishment. Addendum to the Report on the Mission to Jordan, 5 January 2007, UN-Doc. A/HRC/4/33/Add.3.

Special Rapporteur on torture and other cruel, inhuman or degrading treatment or punishment. Interim Report to the Human Rights Council, 5 August 2011, A/66/268.

Special Rapporteur on torture and other cruel, inhuman or degrading treatment or punishment. Report to the Human Rights Council, Seventh Session, Manfred Nowak, A/HRC/7/3, 15 January 2008.

Special Rapporteur on violence against women, Report on the mission to the United States of America on the issue of violence against women in state and federal prisons, E/CN.4/1999/68/Add.2.

Special Rapporteur on violence against women, its causes and consequences, Rashida Manjoo, Report to the UN General Assembly, Pathways to, conditions and consequences of incarceration for women, 21 August 2013, UN-Doc. A/68/340.

Special Rapporteur on violence against women, its causes and consequences, Report on the Mission to Kyrgyzstan, 28 May 2010, UN-Doc. A/HRC/14/22/Add.2.

Stoicescu, E. C. (2012). *The global state of harm reduction 2012: Towards an integrated response* (p. 129). Harm Reduction International

Subcommittee on Prevention of Torture. (2012). Report on the visit of the Subcommittee on Prevention of Torture and Other Cruel, Inhuman or Degrading Treatment or Punishment to Brazil, 5 July 2012, CAT/OP/BRA/1.en.

Subcommittee on Prevention of Torture and Other Cruel, Inhuman or Degrading Treatment or Punishment. (2001). Report on the visit to Benin, 15 March 2001, UN-Doc. CAT/OP/BEN/1.

Subcommittee on Prevention of Torture, and Other Cruel, Inhuman or Degrading Treatment or Punishment. (2010). Report on the visit to Paraguay, 7 June 2010, CAT/OP/PRY/1.

Surt Association. (2005, June). *Women integration and prison*. Barcelona: Aurea Editores S.L.

Tomasini, D. (2012) 'Mujeres y Prisión Preventiva: Presuntas inocentes sufriendo castigos anticipados y abusos' Open Society Justice Initiative.

Treatment: Women Incarcerated in New Hampshire's State Prison System, Briefing Report, September 2011, www.usccr.gov/pubs/Unequal_Treatment_WomenIncarceratedinNHStatePrisonSystem.pdf. Accessed 22 January 2013.

UN Commission on Human Rights. (2005). Report on violence against women, its causes and consequences, Mission to Occupied Palestinian Territory, 2 February 2005, UN-Doc. E/CN.4/2005/72/Add.4.

UNESCO. Background paper prepared for the Education for All Global Monitoring Report 2006 Literacy for Life, p. 5, http://unesdoc.unesco.org/images/0014/001461/146108e.pdf

UNESCO. Education for All Global Monitoring Report 2013/14, Table of Adult and Youth Literacy, accessed at http://unesdoc.unesco.org/images/0022/002256/225660e.pdf

UN General Assembly. (1991). United Nations Standard Minimum Rules for Non-Custodial Measures (The Tokyo Rules): Resolution/adopted by the General Assembly, 2 April 1991, A/RES/45/110.

UNICEF. (2008). Justice for children: The situation for children in conflict with the law in Afghanistan.

UNODC. (2007, March). Afghanistan, female prisoners and their social reintegration.

UNODC. (2008). Afghanistan: Implementing alternatives to imprisonment, in line with international standards and national legislation.

UNODC. (2014a). *Handbook for prison managers and policymakers on women and imprisonment*.

UNODC. (2014b). World crime trends and emerging issues and responses in the field of crime prevention and criminal justice, 12 February 2014, UN-Doc. E/CN.15/2014/5.

UNODC/WHO Europe. (2009). *Women's health in prison: Correcting gender inequity in prison health*. London: UNODC, WHO Europe.

UNODC/WHO Europe. (2013). Good governance for prison health in the 21th century.

UNODC. Women and HIV in Prison Settings, HIV/AIDS Unit, available at http://www.unodc.org/documents/hiv-aids/Women_in_prisons.pdf

US Department of Justice. (2014). Justice Department Releases Findings Showing That the Alabama Department of Corrections Fails to Protect Prisoners from Sexual Abuse and Sexual Harassment at the Julia Tutwiler Prison for Women, 22 January 2014, http://www.justice.gov/opa/pr/2014/January/14-crt-061.html

Walmsley, R. (2014). Variation and growth in levels of female imprisonment, www.prisonstudies.org/news/female-imprisonment

World Health Organization. (2013). Factsheet N°239, Violence against women, last updated October 2013, http://www.who.int/mediacentre/factsheets/fs239/en/

World Health Organization and Joint United Nations Programme on HIV/AIDS. (2006). HIV/AIDS Prevention, Care, Treatment and Support in Prison Settings: A Framework for an Effective National Response in this Framework for an effective national response.

World Health Organization and the International Association for Suicide Prevention (IASP). (2007). Preventing suicide in jails and prisons.

World Health Organization Regional Office for Europe. (2007). *Health in prisons: A WHO guide to the essentials in prison health*, EUR/07/5063925 (Copenhagen, 2007); WHO Regional Office for Europe, *Women's health in prison.*

Incarcerated Women: Their Situation, Their Needs and Measures for Sustainable Reintegration

Dawn Beichner and Otmar Hagemann

Abstract This contribution centers on incarcerated women offenders worldwide, their lived experiences, specific problems and needs, as well as correctional programming intended to help them reintegrate back into society. The chapter provides a theoretical understanding of the general marginalization of women in almost every modern society and an overview of theories that have been developed to explain why women commit offenses. Next, statistical information is provided concerning the prevalence of women prisoners in various parts of the world and the ways in which policy changes in the war on drugs and mandatory sentencing have impacted women's incarceration rates. The chapter then explores the gender-specific differences in women's pathways to prison and their distinct problems and needs, including the detrimental effects of mothers' incarceration on children. It concludes with promising approaches from different countries.

1 Introduction

This chapter is a collaborative effort between two scholars: A US American and a German. Although we attempted to gather comprehensive information on the topic of women and aftercare for all regions of the world, the emphasis in the contribution is slightly biased on North America—responsible for more than 30 % of all incarcerated women offenders—and Europe. This chapter is divided into four distinct subsections: Overview of Women's Marginalization, Statistics on Women and Crime Worldwide, Prison and Aftercare Programming, and Conclusions and Recommendations. An overview of each of the subsections is outlined below.

To explain Women's Marginalization (Sect. 2), we refer to Intersectionality Theory originally posited by Crenshaw (1989). The section also provides an overview

D. Beichner (✉)
Illinois State University, Normal, IL, USA
e-mail: dmbeich@ilstu.edu

O. Hagemann
Kiel University of Applied Sciences, Kiel, Germany
e-mail: Otmar.Hagemann@fh-kiel.de

H. Kury et al. (eds.), *Women and Children as Victims and Offenders: Background, Prevention, Reintegration*, DOI 10.1007/978-3-319-28424-8_4

of women's mental health and depression prevalence rates worldwide. Furthermore, the section explores research examining the variety of traumas women experience over their lifetimes, including child abuse and physical and sexual victimizations.

In addition to providing Statistics on Women and Crime Worldwide, Sect. 3 outlines four primary theories that have been developed to describe women's involvement in crime and the gendered patterns in criminal offending. The section provides information on criminal justice policy changes that have contributed to the growth of women in prison globally. The section concludes with a review of world incarceration rates for women.

Section 4, Prison and Aftercare Programming for Women, begins with an examination of maternal incarceration and family-centered programming. The section highlights programs offered in prisons to strengthen and empower women inmates, such as art therapy and theatre. It also synthesizes the literature on the challenges of returning home from prison and promotes gender specific aftercare programming. The section concludes with some best practices from Denmark, Northern Ireland (UK), Germany, England (UK), and the USA.

In the last section of the manuscript, Conclusions and Recommendations, we present four proposals for reform. First, we explore the abolition of prison sentences for non-dangerous women offenders. Second, we call for the conversion of existing correctional institutions into restorative prisons. Third, we provide an overview of Restorative Justice procedures specific to release from prison. Last, we call for sensible transition management, which addresses incarcerated women's personal deficits (e.g., educational/vocational, substance abuse, mental health issues, debt, housing) and provides a detailed plan for successful reentry.

2 Overview of Women's Marginalization

2.1 Intersectionality Theory

Following the conventions set forth in contemporary research on the consequences of incarceration on women and their families (Christian and Thomas 2009; Foster 2011; Henriques and Manatu-Rupert 2001), we use the theory of Intersectionality as the framework through which to explore the individual and systematic oppression of incarcerated women and their access to aftercare programming worldwide. It is important to note that contemporary developments in this area are built from the theoretical perspectives developed by Crenshaw (1989, 1991) and later expanded by Collins (2000). According to Crenshaw (1991), Intersectionality Theory explains how social identities, at both the micro and macro level, overlap and create unique experiences for women.

Intersectionality Theory posits that social identities are interdependent and not mutually exclusive; the identities do not stand-alone and are often complicated and intersecting (Bowleg 2012). Considering that our focus is on women who have been incarcerated and their access to aftercare programming, the micro level social identities of race, ethnicity, sexuality, and gender and the macro level social identities of socioeconomics and poverty are critical. Moreover, as Barberet (2014, p. 7) points out, internationalization contributes other social identities, such as nationality, migratory and refugee status, indigenous status, and postcolonial perspectives. Each woman's lived experiences—before, during, and after prison—are shaped by the social identities that she embodies and the discrimination and oppression that she faces.

When Crenshaw (1989) originally posited Intersectionality Theory, she demonstrated her theory with a USA example, stating that the oppression resulting from being African American and a woman was much more crippling than sexism or racism alone. Today, in the age of globalization, we must also consider how the various layers of women's oppression are further shaped by the larger global, economic, and political forces, as well as women's nationality, migratory and refugee status, and colonialism (Barberet 2014; Mohanty 2003, 2013). In this larger context, we can compare and contrast the African American woman's experience in the USA with that of a Roma woman in an Eastern European state or a Rwandan woman whose family was killed in the genocide. By expanding Intersectionality Theory to include an international perspective, we broaden our scope beyond race, class, and socioeconomic status and achieve a deeper understanding of how women involved in criminal justice systems are more marginalized than any other women in the world.

Women's disadvantaged statuses—especially as manifested in our incarcerated population—also shape the experiences of their respective children and other family members. Maternal incarceration forces immediate changes in children's living arrangements and presents ongoing challenges to family members in the community to provide care for the children left behind. The caregivers face the challenges of raising the children in the mother's absence, including assuming the requisite financial burden. Lastly, the amount and type of support available to families of incarcerated women varies greatly based upon the community; whereas families in urban centers may have access to numerous social services, those in suburban, rural, or underdeveloped areas may not. Given that incarcerated mothers often return to their role as primary care-providers to their children, their pathways home to their communities and families are shaped by the interlocking layers of oppression that they face. We will explore how these varying intersectionalities impact women's access to aftercare programming, as well as how children and families lives are impacted.

2.2 *Women's Mental Health and Depression Prevalence Worldwide*

As the World Health Organization (2014) reports, gender is influential in determining the differential power and control that men and women have over the determinants of their mental health and lives, their positions in society, societal status, treatment in society, and their susceptibility and exposure to specific mental health risks. Worldwide, women experience depression at much higher rates than their male counterparts (Harvard Medical School 2014). According to the World Bank (2014), globally, depression as a serious health risk ranks 6th for women and 16th for men worldwide. Using the lenses of internationalization and Intersectionality Theory, it is important to recognize that women's rates of depression vary worldwide based upon women's position in society; societal attributes such as political power, participation in the labor force, and overall value impact women's prevalence of mental health issues. Considered another way, although women's rates of depression are higher than men's worldwide, in the USA, women experience depression at a rate of two to one to that of men (Harvard Medical School 2014). In the Middle East and North Africa, women experience higher rates of depression than any other area of the world (World Bank Organization 2014). Women's higher rates of depression and mental health issues partially stem from living in patriarchal societies and having reduced levels of social, economic, and political power.

Another reason that women's rates of depression worldwide are greater than men's relates to women's experiences with early childhood or lifetime trauma and victimization. Research examining adolescent women indicates that young women have lower self-concepts and are more likely to attempt suicide than their male peers (Miller et al. 1995). Given what we know regarding the prevalence of past victimizations among incarcerated women, this is critically important to aftercare programming. In a study examining incarcerated women in the USA, more than one out of five women had reported attempting suicide in the past (Holley and Brewster 1996). Contemporary research examining incarcerated women in the USA has estimated that three-quarters or more of the incarcerated women population has been subject to a variety of traumas over their lifetimes, including child abuse and physical and sexual victimizations (Bloom et al. 2004; Green et al. 2005; Lynch et al. 2012; McDaniels-Wilson and Belknap 2008). Exposure to such traumatic experiences greatly increases women's likelihood for post-traumatic stress disorder (PTSD), depression, substance abuse issues, and other mental health problems (Campbell 2002; Dutton et al. 2006; Hedtke et al. 2008; Lynch et al. 2012). The extent of the exposure to traumatic experiences explains why incarcerated women's mental health issues exceed women in the general population, as well as those of incarcerated men (Drapalski et al. 2009; Hills et al. 2004; James and Glaze 2006).

3 Statistics on Women and Crime Worldwide

3.1 Theories Explaining Women's Involvement in Crime

Most of the criminological theories addressing why certain individuals commit crime has centered on men. Despite the important differences that exist between men and women in gender socialization, opportunity, and equality, historically, there were no theories that focused on the differences in male and female offending.

Many feminists have outlined how theories describing criminality have focused only on what motivates men to commit crime (Messerschmidt 1993; Naffine 1996). As Kathleen Daly (1995) remarked, early criminological approaches to studying women's involvement in crime was to take the male-focused theories, add women, and stir. There have, however, been four primary theories developed to describe women's involvement in crime: emancipation hypothesis, economic marginalization, gender inequality, and pathways (Barberet 2014).

The emancipation hypothesis, largely developed by Adler (1975) and Simon (1975), purports that women will become more criminally involved as they gain more gender equality and crossover from the private sphere of home life to the public sphere of employment. According to this theory, as women become emancipated from domestic responsibilities and become more educated and have greater access to employment, they will have greater opportunities and skills to commit offenses. Proponents of the emancipation hypothesis see women's liberation and commensurate gains in economic and political equality as precursors to criminality, whereby increases in power translate into additional opportunities to commit crime.

Economic marginalization, as an explanation of women's criminality, is the opposite of the emancipation hypothesis (Barberet 2014). According to this theory, it is the feminization of poverty and globalization that explains women's decisions to commit crime. For example, a woman who lacks funds to provide for her children's basic needs might be motivated to commit a financial crime, in order to make ends meet. In the global context, examples abound where a woman facing economic marginalization is coerced or recruited to commit crimes (i.e., human or drug trafficking) by males, but in the systems of criminal justice, she is viewed not as a victim, but as an offender.

Gender inequality as a theory to describe women's involvement in crime takes this conceptualization further, by focusing on the lack of women's free will and determination in crime commission, as well as their involvement in secondary or lesser roles than their male counterparts (Barberet 2014). This theory posits that women are involved in crime due to their exploitation and victimization by men. Global gender inequality pushes women into committing such crimes as low-level drug trafficking and recruitment in human trafficking circles, wherein men have more primary roles. Gender inequality also provides a framework for understanding crimes of immorality in Islamic countries (i.e., adultery, running away, eloping), for which only women are arrested or detained. The theory is also useful in understanding young women's disproportionate representation in status offenses (i.e., running away) in the USA.

The final theoretical explanation of women's involvement in crime, pathways, is distinct from the other three theories, in that it is an individual-level theory (Barberet 2014). There is a growing body of literature that examines the many pathways to criminality that women experience, including abuse, poverty, and gender inequality (Brown and Bloom 2009; Covington and Bloom 2006; Few-Demo and Arditti 2013). The most documented pathway to offending for women is that of victimization; women are often victims of trauma and abuse in their childhood home environments and may continue to be abused throughout their lifetimes (Few-Demo and Arditti 2013).

3.2 Policy Changes and the Growth of Women in Prison

Critics of the prison industrial complex criticize harsh drug laws, mandatory sentencing, and policing strategies focused on smaller crimes for the growing population of women in prison (Alleyne 2006). Globally, the policy that has contributed most to the growth in the number of women arrested and detained is the war on drugs. Although this "war" began in the United States of America, it quickly influenced drug interdiction practices in the illicit market globally (Barberet 2014). Due to what Steffensmeier (1983) termed "underworld sexism," women are often given the most visible, lowest paid positions in the criminal underworld. This is certainly the case in the illicit drug market worldwide. Because drug interdiction methods globally are focused on small-scale dealers, women are more likely to be detected and arrested, as this is where women predominate (Barberet 2014). Most often, women involved in the illicit drug economy are low-level dealers and drug mules—the positions which are of central focus to law enforcement.

A second policy that has been highly influential in the increase of incarcerated women is that of presumptive or mandatory arrest in cases of intimate partner violence in the USA (Belknap 2015). In effect, presumptive or mandatory arrest policies eliminate law enforcement officers' discretion; if an assault has taken place, at least one, but sometimes both, of the parties involved are subject to arrest. Since the inception of this policy shift, more women are arrested for assault charges. This is especially important, when we consider that approximately 30% of the world population of incarcerated women is in the USA (Walmsley 2012; Walmsley 2014).

It is important to note that, in the European Union (EU), there have been policy changes intended to reduce the use of incarceration for women. In the late 1990s, the EU introduced the approach of gender mainstreaming (European Institute for Gender Equality 2014). Among other efforts, the strategy of gender mainstreaming includes conducting gender assessments of policies. In some European states and on the transnational level of the Council of Europe, policy initiatives aiming at reducing incarceration have been started. For example, in 2009, the Parliamentary Assembly of the Council of Europe (PACE) passed Resolution 1663, which stated in part, "prison should be used as a last resort only if no other options are available and alternative forms of sentencing, including community service orders and Restorative Justice approaches should be considered first" (Quaker Council for European Affairs 2014). Moreover, the promotion of Restorative Justice practices, such as the efforts by the United Nations, is a step toward reducing the numbers of incarcerated women.

3.3 Women's Involvement in Crime

Globally, the vast majority of crimes are committed by men; women constitute a small minority of offenders in all countries (Walmsley 2012; Walmsley 2014; Belknap 2015). There are stark gendered patterns in the research examining offending; whereas men are more likely to be incarcerated for a violent offense (i.e. murder, rape), women are more likely to be incarcerated for non-violent offenses, such as drug or property crimes (i.e. larceny, fraud, forgery, and embezzlement) (The Sentencing Project 2012). This "gender gap" in offending (Schwartz and Steffensmeier 2008) appears to be rather consistent worldwide.

In the USA, which has the largest number of women incarcerated worldwide, there are both similarities and differences in the patterns of criminal offending by men and women (Schwartz and Steffensmeier 2008). Given the USA's mass incarceration policies, both men and women prisoners are likely to be incarcerated for crimes that would likely not result in incarceration in other parts of the world, such as minor property crimes or offenses related to substance abuse and addiction. The differences in offending among men and women in the USA are most often related to crime seriousness. Men in the USA commit serious offenses, such as murder, robbery, and aggravated assault, at much higher rates than women. In the USA, men's involvement in crime surpasses that of women in all categories except prostitution (Belknap 2015). Moreover, there is only one additional crime—embezzlement—for which there is a gender-neutral pattern of offending. In short, studies of offending in the USA consistently show that women generally commit fewer crimes than men and also that their offenses are much less serious.

The European Sourcebook on Crime and Criminal Justice Statistics is a compilation of statistical information from European countries. The most recent published edition from 2010 contains data on convicted females and women prisoners. Very high percentages (>16 % of all convicted persons) for females have been observed in Denmark, Finland, Germany, Sweden and England & Wales (as part of the United Kingdom); the lowest percentages (<8 %) are observed in Albania, Armenia, Cyprus, Romania, The Former Yugoslav Republic of Macedonia and Turkey. The average is 12 %, which is true for The Netherlands (WODC 2010, Table 3.2.2.1, page 195). Considered together, the average percentage of the female prison population was 5 %, which is close to the more recent data published by Walmsley (2012). Countries where women form the biggest proportion of inmates (between 6.2 and 6.7 %) are Finland, Hungary and Portugal; the lowest proportions could be found in Albania, Armenia, Bulgaria, France, Lithuania, Turkey and Northern Ireland, ranging between 2.6 and 3.8 % (WODC 2010, Table 4.2.3.1, page 309).

3.4 Global Numbers of Women Arrested and Detained

Although the rate at which women are involved in the criminal justice system varies widely across the world, in all geographic areas, women's involvement is much less than their male counterparts. The United Nations Office on Drugs and Crime publishes annual data on the number of individuals who have had formal contact with the police and/or criminal justice system, which includes information on individuals suspected, arrested, or cautioned. In 2012, there were 38 countries/ territories reporting data on women (UNODC 2012). The percentage of women reported to have had formal contact with the police or other criminal justice authority ranged from a low of 1 % in Grenada to a high of 27 % in the Hong Kong Special Administration Region of China (UNODC 2014), with an average of 12 %. Although 20 of the 38 reporting countries and territories reported rates of formal contact of women at or below 10 %, seven places reported that women comprised 20 % or more of the total individuals in formal contact (Hong Kong, Australia, New Zealand, Columbia, Guyana, England/Wales, and Northern Ireland (UK)).

When we examine women's incarceration globally, there are two important trends: although women make up a small proportion of the total world imprisonment population, the rate at which they are being incarcerated is increasing, sometimes exceeding the growth in the world population of incarcerated men (Belknap 2015). According to the World Female Imprisonment List, which includes incarceration data for 212 prison systems worldwide, the percentage of women prisoners is growing on all five continents (Walmsley 2012). Whereas the population of women prisoners increased 6 % in Europe between 2006 and 2012, the increase in the same 6 year period was 23 % in the Americas.

Worldwide, there are 625,000 women and girls being held in penal institutions, either as pre-trial detainees or serving incarceration sentences (Walmsley 2012). Not surprisingly, almost one-third (32 %) of all women incarcerated worldwide are in prisons and jails in the USA. In the USA alone, 201,200 women are detained or incarcerated (equals 8.8 % of all inmates). Considered another way, the incarceration of women and girls in the USA exceeds that of the 27 European Union Member States by a factor of 6, even though the USA has only two-thirds of the European female population (Moloney et al. 2009). Other countries with relatively high rates of incarcerated women are China (84,600 = 5.1 %), Russia (59,200 = 7.8 %), Brazil (35,596 = 6.9 %), and Thailand (29,175 = 14.6 %). Of the 212 independent countries and dependent territories represented in the World Female Imprisonment List, only five others incarcerate more than 7000 women: India, Vietnam, Mexico, Ukraine, and the Philippines.

Consistent with the variation in rates of incarceration across world regions, the numbers of women incarcerated also varies considerably from place to place. On average, women comprise between 2 and 9 % of the total prison population in most countries. Whereas women in the USA make up approximately 9 % of the total incarcerated population, the rate is much higher in Hong Kong (20 %), Bahrain (18.5 %), Qatar (15 %), and Thailand (15 %). Moreover, although the median level of women's incarceration is 4.45 % worldwide, levels are significantly higher in Asia (5.95 %), the Americas (5.15 %), and Europe (4.9 %) and lower in Africa (3.1 %) and Oceania (3.9 %) (Walmsley 2012).

4 Prison and Aftercare Programming for Women

Women prisoners are among the most neglected, oppressed, and misunderstood groups in society (Belknap 2015). As mentioned in the previous sections, although women make up a small proportion of offenders globally, their incarceration has a distinct impact on the children that are left behind. Moreover, given women offenders' unique victimization, mental health, and substance abuse histories, educational/vocational backgrounds, as well as their likelihood of resuming the role as primary care provider to their children following incarceration, women face a number of unique challenges in the journey home from prison. Despite the critical nature of women's reentry into their home communities and reunification with their children, there is a dearth of prison-based programs and aftercare programming that centers on women globally. In this section, we provide an overview of available programming.

4.1 Maternal Incarceration and Family-Centered Programming

In terms of the magnitude of the effects on children, there is compelling evidence to suggest that women's incarceration is much more disruptive for children than men's (Jones and Wainaina-Woźna 2013; Murray and Farrington 2008; Prison Reform Trust 2013; Bloom 1993). There are a number of important gendered patterns in the research. First, incarcerated women are somewhat more likely to have children under the age of 18 than their male counterparts; recent figures indicate that three-quarters of incarcerated women leave at least one child under the age of 18 behind, compared with two-thirds of incarcerated men (Murray 2005; Prison Reform Trust 2013; Bloom and Steinhart 1993; Morton and Williams 1998; Pollock 2002). Additionally, approximately one quarter of all recently incarcerated women have delivered a child in the past year or are currently pregnant (Fogel 1995; Clarke 2013). Research studies also reveal that incarcerated women are far more likely than incarcerated men to be the primary care providers for their children (Quaker Council for European Affairs 2007; Bloom and Steinhart 1993; Hairston 1991; LaPoint et al. 1985; McGowan and Blumenthal 1978; Pollock 2002; Snell and Morton 1994) and the majority believe that they will be the primary care providers upon their release from prison (Crawford 1990; Pollock 2002).

The negative consequences of parental incarceration have been well documented over the past 3 decades. In their comprehensive examination of the negative effects of incarceration on children, McGowan and Blumenthal (1978) asked the question, *Why Punish the Children*? Subsequent studies examining the disruption caused by parental incarceration confirm that the detrimental impact of parental incarceration meets or exceeds that posed by death or divorce; whereas support is readily available in situations of the latter, the negative stigma attached to deviance precludes open dialogue and support for families and children of incarcerated persons (Kazura 2001).[1] Moreover, children of incarcerated parents often suffer from emotional and behavior problems; research confirms that children of incarcerated parents are more likely than other children to exhibit sleep disruptions, depression, anger, poor school performance, delinquent behavior, and juvenile detention (Jones and Wainaina-Woźna 2013; Bloom and Steinhart 1993; Hairston 1988, 1991; Hannon et al. 1984; LaPoint et al. 1985; Kazura 2001).

Parent and family-centered programming presents many potential advantages for both incarcerated women and their children. The research examining women enrolled in parenting programs reveals that women participants are less likely than non-participants to engage in institutional misconduct (Carlson 2001). Similarly, studies examining prisoners' reintegration back into society have consistently revealed that family support has an enormous influence on a person's successful transition back into society. Formerly incarcerated persons who were enrolled in family-centered programming during confinement and had family support following their incarceration demonstrate an increased commitment to goals, as well as lower rates of recidivism, drug usage, and relapse (Carlson 2001; LaPoint et al. 1985; Martin 1997; Stöver and Thane 2011; Vera Institute of Justice 2004). In fact, respondents from a recent study examining former prisoners' experiences reintegrating into Chicago land area, identified family as the most important factor in helping them stay out of prison (Lynch and Sabol 2001).

The benefit of reduced criminality also applies to the children of incarcerated persons; there is a reduced likelihood of juvenile delinquency when family bonds are maintained and fostered throughout the period of incarceration (Hairston 1988, 1991). Findings such as these have spawned the creation of a variety of parenting programs for incarcerated individuals, as well as family-centered prisoner reintegration programs (Vera Institute of Justice 2004).

---

[1] This is exactly the starting point for the German project TAKT, which is named from the connotation with tact or tactfulness. Central to this project, social workers assist relatives of male and female prisoners and their family members in finding a variety of services, support and advocacy. The project has developed material to be used for educative purpose in schools and institutions of child and youth welfare, as well as for all persons with close contact to families where a parent is or has been incarcerated. Furthermore it has implemented a network approach, focusing on sensitizing police officers and professionals working in the youth welfare service, in schools and kindergartens for questions related to incarcerated parents. (https://www.treffpunkt-nbg.de/projekte/takt.html accessed 18.7.2014).

There is a wide range of parenting programs made available to incarcerated women in the USA and globally (See Barberet 2014 and Pollock 2002 for a review). Although many women's correctional facilities provide some form of parenting courses, there is institutional variation in the types of visitation permitted with children and the overall comprehensiveness and intensity of programming. Whereas less intensive programs provide for classroom-based parenting courses only, more intensive programs provide for additional parenting amenities, such as special visiting areas for mothers and children,[2] reading programs, and day camps. Most correctional facilities in the USA provide programs that are consistent with the latter, whereas programs in other countries tend to focus more on fostering bonds between mothers and children.

Globally, women do not have an automatic right to have their children in prison with them (Barberet 2014). Instead, when granted, co-habitation with children is viewed as a privilege, determined by authorities to be in the best interest of the children. Worldwide, the vast majority of countries permit some women to have their children with them during incarceration (Barberet 2014). The most comprehensive study examining children residing with mothers in prison included 76 countries and was conducted by a Quaker nongovernmental organization (Robertson 2011). For most countries that permit children to live with incarcerated mothers, the child age limit ranges from newborn to 6 years. It is important to note, however, that in the USA, the global leader in women's incarceration, only a small number of facilities have intensive mother-child programs which permit inmates to have overnight visitations with their children. Some countries, such as Spain, have taken great efforts to accommodate motherhood in prison, including child care centers (which follow national standards for daycare facilities), arrangements for outside childcare, weekend furloughs, and parenting cells, in which parents who are both incarcerated can live together in a cell with their child(ren) (Barberet 2014). Only three other countries—Denmark, Sweden, and Finland—allow children to stay with both incarcerated fathers and mothers.

Thirteen of the 76 countries in the Quaker study (Bulgaria, Cuba, Democratic Republic of the Congo, France, Germany, Ghana, Kiribati, Mongolia, Spain, Sweden, Tanzania, United Kingdom, and the United States of America) permit newborn children to reside with mothers. In several countries, the period of cohabitation is limited to the time period in which the infant is nursing. In others, no such limit is placed. In the USA, New York, Nebraska, Indiana, and Illinois are among a small number of states which provide a prison nursery program, in which expectant mothers complete a parenting course and are permitted to keep their newborn babies with them until they have been released from the institution, generally for a period of up to 2 years following birth. In Mongolia, pregnant

[2] In some Italian provinces, the project Spazio Giallo (yellow room) of the child lobby organization "Bambinisenzasbarre" supports children visiting an incarcerated parent. The organization found that in Italy about 100,000 children are visiting their parents every year, sometimes suffering from traumatic experiences as a consequence of the emotional impact of these visit (See Sacerdote 2014).

mothers are temporary released for the birth of their children and remain in the community for 18 months, at which time mother and infant return to the correctional facility (Robertson 2011).

Research examining family-centered programs and moms and babies units is quite sparse. For example, although mother and baby units have existed in Finland since 1881, there is very little data about them (Poso et al. 2010). Moreover, much of the extant research in this area is rather dated. Despite these issues, research tends to confirm that parenting programs that include expanded visitation between mothers and children are more effective in offsetting the negative consequences of incarceration than those that do not (Pollock 2002). Parenting programs in which mothers are able to have ongoing contact and communication with their child(ren) throughout the period of incarceration appear to produce the most positive results for both mothers and children (Hairston 1991; LaPoint et al. 1985; Snyder et al. 2001). The prospective benefits of the program are impacted by both the quantity and quality of mother-child visits. McPeek and Tse (1988) found that children who were only able to visit their mother once per month or less were at an increased risk of developing emotional problems. Furthermore, the authors found that the overall quality of the visit had an even more profound effect: negative effects were not offset by weekly visits alone; only those children who were given adequate time for parental bonding during the weekly visits were at a lower risk of developing emotional problems (McPeek and Tse 1988). One recent study, comparing levels of attachment among babies and mothers—incarcerated and not—found secure attachment levels (Byrne et al. 2010).

4.2 *Healing Past Trauma Through Art and Theatre Programming in Prisons*

Women's pathways to prison are often marked with victimizations and damaged childhoods, including intimate partner violence, sexual abuse, familial estrangement, addiction, and violence (See Beichner and Rabe-Hemp 2014 for a review). Art therapy and educational theater are effective forms of rehabilitation for incarcerated persons; these programs serve a bridging function to open up the inmates for further therapeutic offers. The literature[3] on art and theatre programming for incarcerated women promotes the potential advantages of such programming on offender rehabilitation. Art and theatre programs for incarcerated women exist in several countries around the world. In this subsection, we provide an overview of the relevant research.

Much of the research examining art therapy for incarcerated women finds favorable results. Gussak (2008) found improvement in mood, behavior, and

[3] There is a dearth in the literature examining prison art programs; although many examples abound, few programs have been empirically researched.

problem solving among participants in a prison art program. Merriam's (1998) research with incarcerated women survivors[4] revealed that art images enabled women to contain potentially destructive thoughts and feelings associated with the traumatic experiences that they had experienced across their lifetimes. Another pilot program, which used visual art, storytelling, music, and journaling to heal and empower incarcerated women with histories of abuse, centered on re-conceptualization of their identities from victims to survivors (Johnson 2008, p. 103).

Art therapy may be used to respond to several types of traumatic life events experienced by incarcerated women. For example, Ferszt et al. (2004), evaluated an art therapy program used with incarcerated women who were grieving the death of a loved one, with promising results. Moreover, an evaluation of the women's art and wellness education program revealed improvements in women's personal and interpersonal growth, including improvements in self-esteem, self-concept, and relationships with others (Mullen 1999). Marian Liebmann (2007) of the United Kingdom has worked extensively with prisoners and edited four books on using art therapy for restorative purpose in addition to her book on Restorative Justice.

Similar to art programming, theatre programming has many rehabilitative applications for incarcerated women. The transformative power of theatre been touted for healing from past abuse and trauma (Salas 2002; Schrader 2012; Wilson 2013), empowering women by giving them voice (Clark 2004; Davies 2012) and reclaiming their bodies (Clark 2004), as well as building community within the prison environment (Fraden 2001; Wilson 2013). With regard to healing, The Playback Theatre, which has troops in over thirty countries, uses the method of storytelling as a method of healing (Salas 2002). The connections that are achieved through sharing personal stories can serve as a counterforce to isolation and alienation (Salas 2002: 290), making this especially useful in a prison environment. In the USA, Wilson (2013) worked with incarcerated women on a theatrical production that included a symbolic burial scene, in which women placed items that represented their old selves inside a coffin (i.e, victimization, pain, drug use, abandonment, anger, self-hatred). Not only did the play address the underlying causes of the incarcerated women's oppression, it also included a reinvention of the women as survivors, imparting wisdom to their incarcerated peers in the audience.

Clark (2004), who spent 20 years working with incarcerated women in Melbourne, Australia, is a proponent of prison theatre as a tool of empowerment in restoring women's voices and bodies. Incarcerated women are often subject to others—lawyers, judges, psychologists, and policymakers—defining who they are and speaking about them (Clark 2004: 104). Through theatre, and participation in a collective creative process, incarcerated women are able to discover the power of

[4] In therapeutic circles, the term "survivor" is commonly used to replace the term "victim." Whereas the former term centers on empowerment by acknowledging survival of past serious victimizations, the latter often has a connotation with weakness or being a loser. The term "survivor" is regularly used in feminist literature (See, among others, Chesney-Lind 1989).

their own voices (Wilson 2013). The Lebanese actress and drama therapist, Zeina Daccache of Catharsis—Lebanese Center for Drama Therapy (NGO), has set up a theatre project in the women's Baabda Prison in Beirut. During the project, which led to a publicly sold film of the play on DVD, the women described how they felt free for the first time in their life. A quote from a 28-year-old woman serving a 3-year jail term for fraud illustrates the rise in self-confidence: "I was so worried about appearing in front of the camera, then after thought if I hide my face I'd be only contributing to hiding myself, my voice, the women and human being within me. I'm taking off my mask and showing (myself) as I wish to" (Davies 2012). Beyond the empowerment of voice, participation in theatre and acting provides incarcerated women an opportunity to reclaim their bodies, which are often handcuffed, observed through camera observations and strip searched in penal institutions (Clark 2004: 104). As Clark (2004) notes, this can be quite empowering in a prison environment, where an incarcerated women's bodies are not their own.

4.3 The Challenges of Returning Home from Prison and the Call for Gender Specific Programming

The research examining prisoner reentry has confirmed that the formerly incarcerated confront many challenges in assimilating back into their communities. They confront barriers in their attempts to find housing, gainful employment, health care, and substance abuse and mental health treatment. Research also confirms that the consequences of incarceration are not confined to the ex-offender alone; incarceration produces detrimental effects on the ex-offender's neighborhood, family, and children. Another important finding from the literature is that the ex-offender's family plays an important role in the reentry process; ex-offenders who have supportive families are more likely to abstain from substance use and criminal offending (Zurhold et al. 2011; Stöver and Thane 2011; World Health Organization (WHO)/United Nations Office on Drugs and Crime (UNODC 2009). We posit, however, that although women share *some* of the same needs returning home from prison as men, women's reentry or aftercare needs are distinctly unique (Krucsay 2007; Hedderman et al. 2011).

The concept of gender-responsive programming is a relatively new concept, which has only received attention for the past 15 years (White 2012). Women who enter prison have been characterized as socially and economically marginalized individuals who have unique needs pertaining to their histories of traumatic victimizations, substance abuse histories, and mental health issues (Wright et al. 2012; Fretz et al. 2007; WHO 2001; WHO and UNODC 2009). Research on women offenders consistently reveals low levels of educational attainment and poor job skills, both of which relegate them into low-paying, low-skilled occupations. Prior to incarceration, they are often financially dependent on others (i.e., significant others, family members, or public assistance) and many have spent some of their lives homeless or living in shelters. Moreover, women are more likely than men to be responsible for young children prior to incarceration and immediately following release. Considered together, these factors demonstrate the overall need for women-centered programming.

Advocates of gender-responsive aftercare programming have identified five primary areas of need of special importance to women: childcare and parenting skills development; healthcare, mental health counseling, substance abuse treatment; housing and transportation services; education, employment and job training services; and social support programs (Scroggins and Malley 2010). Generally, proponents recommend that aftercare programming provide a continuum of services in three phases (Garcia and Ritter 2012; Holliday et al. 2012). Phase one, or the institutional phase of programming, centers on identification of offenders' needs and acquisition of institutional programming. Phase two, which generally takes place in the weeks leading to the offender's return home from prison, focuses on offender's plans for return home to their families and communities. The third phase, community reintegration, includes a follow-up phase, in which a caseworker meets with the client in the immediate period following incarceration.

"Transition management" (Matt 2014) or "through the gate care" (Prison Reform Trust 2011) are two expressions for more comprehensive programs, combining phase two and three into one program. Transition management involves inter-agency collaboration for the social reintegration of people returning home from prison. The collaborative effort includes judicial authorities, institutions of offender support, and health and human service providers (see Wirth 2010: 81). Matt (2014) argues that "transition work" would be a more appropriate term, referring to actions and processes which are necessary to achieve transition and to cope with it on the individual level as well as on organizational and societal level.

Worldwide, there are a limited number of gender-specific programs available to women in prison and as they return home to their families. Many of the programs were developed for men, but have expanded focus to include women prisoners. In the section that follows, we provide some examples of what we consider to be some of the best practices around the globe. Prior to this exploration, however, it is necessary to understand some general background information on available programs. After reviewing the extant literature on gender-specific aftercare programming, three important trends emerge. First, aftercare or reentry programming not only varies widely from country-to-country, but also within specific countries. Meaning, it is difficult to identify country-wide trends in programming. Second, consistent with the discussion of women's invisibility in global justice systems, some of the programs that exist for incarcerated mothers and most programs for women returning home from prison began as programs for males, but have expanded over time to include women. Third, there is a paucity of research in this area; few women-centered programs have been evaluated to date. This is an important trend, given that research in England and Wales suggests that women have different predictors of program completion than males (Martin et al. 2009).

4.4 Examples of Gender-Specific Parenting and Aftercare Programming Around the Globe

Gender-specific programming and—to a lesser extent, family reunification programs—are relatively new in justice systems globally. Our hope is that programming in this area will continue to expand and evolve over the next decades, as will the evaluative research in this area. The program summaries that follow are some of what we believe to be the best practices for women offenders and their children. We give special attention to those programs that have been evaluated.

4.4.1 Denmark: "Familie Huset Engelsborg" (Family House of Engelsborg)

Worldwide, one of the most progressive and unique reunification programs that exists for children of incarcerated parents is the "Family House" in Lyngby, Denmark (Bundesarbeitsgemeinschaft für Straffälligenhilfe e.V., Chance e.V. Münster und Der Paritätische Landesverband NRW e.V. 2013). To date, this is the only prison based on the needs of the children of incarcerated parents. If the social services of the Danish prison system deem that it is in the child's best interest, an inmate will be permitted to live with his/her children and partner, during the parent's final period of incarceration. Whereas the inmate's mobility is restricted during the period of cohabitation, the children and partners are not confined and may travel freely. Not only does the program provide incarcerated parents and children a unique opportunity for cohabitation, it also provides services from a family therapist and a social worker. In order to be eligible for the program, parents must meet a number of risk assessments and be nearing completion of their incarceration. During the last segment of the offender's incarceration, s/he may live in an apartment setting with her/his family. Since the project's inception in 2005, there have been 89 inmates in the program, 39 of whom are women (information gathered by telephone call with director in August 2014 from co-author Hagemann). Preliminary evaluative research on this project reveals positive developments of the families involved; trends include strengthening of self-efficacy, self-consciousness, and sense of responsibility of the parents (Halmø 2008).

4.4.2 Northern Ireland: The Inspire Women's Project

In Northern Ireland, women comprise only about 3 % of all offenders, but research on women offenders in this area reveals significant mental health and substance abuse issues (O'Neill 2011). Accordingly, the Probation Board of Northern Ireland created the gender-specific program, The Inspire Women's Project. The project began as a pilot in 2008, but has been sustained through Department of Justice funding to date. The program is designated for women probationers sentenced to community supervision. The program provides childcare for participants and includes five subprograms: (1) a life coaching subprogram, aimed at increasing self-esteem and responsibility, (2) anger management, (3) alcohol and drug counseling, (4) Job Track, a subprogram that provides clients with employment advice, and (5) a mentoring program which links participants to women mentors in the community. There is also an enhanced program for habitual women offenders with more than three prior convictions, which provides a cognitive behavior curriculum. A preliminary evaluation of the program in 2010 revealed success in clients' self-esteem, as well as an overall reduction in recidivism for program participants.

4.4.3 Germany: Women's Prison at Preungesheim

One of the most comprehensive programs for incarcerated women and their children is in Frankfurt, Germany.[5] In the Preungesheim prison, high-security inmates are permitted to stay with their newborns through age 3, and lower-security inmates may reside with their children up to age 6 (Kauffman 2001; Einsele and Rothe 1982). Mothers and children reside in a separate, "mother-child house," on the prison grounds. Generally, children in the toddler through preschool age go to a neighborhood preschool, while incarcerated mothers work. Moreover, in this prison, motherhood is recognized as an occupation and therefore one of the options for work-release in the community. Mothers who have school-age children outside of the correctional facility and are eligible for the family work-release program take public transportation to their children's homes and assist children with their morning routines. Once the children leave for school, mothers are responsible for completing other household tasks, such as grocery shopping and other household management activities. When the children return from school, the mothers assist them with homework, provide them with dinner, and carry out any other tasks related to their children's needs. At the children's bedtime, the mothers return to the prison to sleep. There is a long-lasting close cooperation with an exclusively feminine non-government organization, specifically centered on the care of the women, as they are released from prison (See Einsele and Rothe 1982 and Geiger and Steinert 1993).

4.4.4 England: The Feminist Organization Together Women and Women Centres

The positive role of the England-based Feminist Organization Together is emphasized in the final report of the Women's Justice Taskforce (Prison Reform Trust

[5] Although the passage focuses on one prison's model, there are similar programs in five other German prisons.

2011). Women Centres, inspired by the feminist movement, have quite a long tradition; the Centre in Nottingham was founded in 1971. The Together Women Programme (TWP) was developed to establish and assess gender-specific approaches for women offenders—namely, identifying the causes of crime and re-offending among this group and reducing the need for custody. Facilities include one stop centres, crèches, and support for finding housing.

TWP aims to meet the needs of women at all stages of their involvement with the criminal justice system, including prevention and diversion, custody, and reentry planning following prison. By offering a low-threshold institution not solely focusing on crime-related problems, the TWP women centers have effectively assisted former offenders and met their needs in the community. Assessments of the TWP indicate success in reducing recidivism; only 3 % of women using the services commited further offenses and only 7 % breached their community order (Prison Reform Trust 2011: 1). Often the threshold to contact a professional case manager or social worker is quite high, especially taking the shame into account if someone has failed again. The women centres offer a continuous contact and opportunity to get support while clients are awaiting therapy. This problem can be met by proactive social work arising in a setting of confidentiality where the client and the professional know each other but their relationship is not restricted to official apointments.

4.4.5 The United States of America: Examples from Delaware, Maine, and Illinois

As mentioned in previous sections, the USA is the world leader in incarceration of both men and women. In recent years, there has been national attention focused on reducing recidivism through reentry programming. Since the inception of the Second Chance Act of 2008, the federal government has provided competitive federal grants to governmental agencies and nonprofit organizations to provide support, strategies, and services to individuals returning home from prison. Accordingly, there are a number of emerging gender-specific family and aftercare programs in the USA, centered on incarcerated women and their children. Three such programs have yielded favorable outcomes in improving relationships with children and/or reducing recidivism.

Delaware One of the most comprehensive aftercare programs for women returning home from prison is the CREST Outreach Treatment Center in the state of Delaware (Robbins et al. 2009). The program, although originally designed for men, is now open to all individuals with histories of substance abuse returning home from prison. Clients in the work-release, therapeutic environment complete a 6 month program, during which time they either work or attend educational classes in the community. The CREST program provides a comprehensive treatment environment, designed to transform behavior, attitudes, emotions, and values of clients. The treatment center employs trained counselors and former CREST graduates, who guide clients through a program of mutual self-help. After successful completion of several weeks in the treatment program, clients may either have their children visit them in the treatment facility or request a home furlough to visit children in their place of residence. Preliminary research on program participants revealed that clients who completed the CREST program were more likely to be arrest free in the 18-month follow-up period, than individuals who did not complete the program.

Maine Transitional programming for women in the state of Maine's prison system begins 6 months prior to release and extends up to 6 months after release, and provides a comprehensive transition plan for returning home from prison (Fortuin 2007). The program is part of the Women's Center at the Maine Correctional Center. The programming phase that takes place inside the correctional institution is based on an individual assessment tool completed jointly by the woman inmate and the correctional staff. The assessment is a strengths-based approach, which emphasizes skill-building, treatment, self-efficacy, and family reunification plans for each of the women. A holistic, integrated approach is used to match each woman's identified needs (i.e., financial, family reunification, housing, mental health, substance abuse, medical, employment/vocational/educational, and mentoring) to natural supports in the community, including mentors and community providers. Following release, the women continue to work with transition case managers, program staff, and community mentors for a minimum of 90 days and a maximum of 180 days. Follow-ups in the post-release months are conducted face-to-face and by telephone contact. Preliminary research of program participants reveals that women returning home from the Women's Center at the Maine Correctional Center have a significantly lower rate (17 %) or recidivism, compared to national figures (33 %).

Illinois A third USA example that warrants coverage in this section is the Decatur Correctional Center in the state of Illinois (TASC 2013; IDOC 2014). This premiere correctional facility offers both a family reunification program and a prison nursery program, through a partnership of the Illinois Department of Corrections (IDOC), Treatment Alternatives for Safe Communities (TASC), and a team of community-based partners. Both programs are available to women who meet a strict set of criteria: non-violent offenders who have no cases with the Illinois Department of Children and Family Services. Women in both the Family Reunification and Moms & Babies programs are housed in a separate wing of the prison and are required to participate in comprehensive educational/vocational training and counseling. The curriculum in the special wing focuses on five core areas: (1) facilitation of support networks, (2) parenting classes, (3) healing from past abuse and trauma, (4) substance abuse counseling, and (5) preparation for transition home to families and communities. Whereas women in the family reunification program are granted contact visits with children for up to 8 h per day, the women in the prison nursery program reside with their infants from birth through age 2 Acquisition of Second Chance Act funding in 2011 has made enhanced aftercare programming available for women in the prison nursery program. As Moms and Babies participants transition home from prison, they are provided ongoing case management and home visits by TASC staff who assist them in referrals to services and support in the community. From the Moms and Babies program's inception in 2007 to the present, 59 mothers have resided with their newborns in the Decatur Correctional Center and only one has returned to prison within 3 years following release.

In summary, incarcerated women have unique needs—namely, substance addiction histories, exposure to past abuse and trauma, low self-esteem, limited vocational training, and familial responsibilities—which require gender-specific programming. The prison and aftercare programs that we have highlighted are comprehensive in approach, addressing women's past histories and focusing on skill-building for successful reunification with families and reintegration with communities. It is critical to have sustainable reentry service systems on the formal level and informal networks of care, so that women returning home from prison do not return. Restorative Justice, as a philosophy of connectedness and community-building, has much to offer in this critical transition home from prison. This concept is addressed in the final section, as one of several recommendations.

5 Conclusions and Recommendations

Thus far, we have demonstrated that incarcerated women are at a disadvantage to men; their needs are hardly taken into account and they have fewer programming opportunities to prepare them for better life circumstances after release from prison. We have to find answers to how reintegration after release can be achieved and how relapses can be prevented. Furthermore, we must address how we can offset the consequences of maternal incarceration on children and disrupt patterns of intergenerational incarceration. In this section, we present four recommendations, three of which take the prison as a starting point.

5.1 Abolition of Prison Sentences

Committed feminists (e.g. Radosh 2008 and Chesney-Lind 1989, 2002) have demonstrated convincingly that the vast majority of incarcerated women have endured abuse and trauma that have led them into committing offenses; they are offenders, but also survivors. Other research describes how abuse and trauma are common pathways into criminality for women offenders (See Beichner and Rabe-Hemp 2014 for a review). Radosh's (2008) research provides an overview of the cognitive dissonance that this situation presents for incarcerated women. Many of the women, who were severely victimized by their intimate partners or fathers, see that their perpetrators either are not punished at all or are punished only minimally for their abusive acts. At the same time, when these women commit non-dangerous offenses, they are severely punished by the criminal justice system.

Therefore, our first recommendation, which is consistent with a demand of the Women's Justice Taskforce (Prison Reform Trust 2011: 3) in the UK, is to abolish prisons and prison sentences for women offenders. Thus, both the cognitive dissonance situation (Radosh 2008) and the collateral consequences of maternal incarceration on the minor children would be eliminated. Of course the measure would be extended to remand imprisonment (see Edgar 2004 for gender-specific misuse in UK) and to imprisonment for failure to pay a fine (jail sentence in lieu of a criminal fine) (see Swedish imprisonment avoidance model, von Hofer 2002). Although the abolition of prison is the main premise of this recommendation, this must be coupled with treatment for victims. Victims must receive support in coping with their past victimization and trauma, through individual or group therapy. We propose that this might be funded through compensation to victims for crime induced costs.

It is important to note that the abolition of imprisonment for women could be regarded as a violation of legal equality principles, if the imprisonment of men continues unabated. It is not merely a question of women receiving equal treatment to men. In the prison system, equality is everywhere conflated with uniformity; women are treated as if they *are* men" (Home Office 1997, paragraph 3.46). Especially in conjunction with the current "discourse about dangerousness," we see no realistic general abolitionist perspective, but the possibility of abolishing imprisonment for at least "non-dangerous" offenders or for certain offenses, such as crimes without the use of weapons or property and drug offenses below a certain monetary threshold (See WHO and UNDOC 2009; Prison Reform Trust 2011, among others). With the abolition of prison for "non-dangerous" offenses, female prisoners would comprise about 10 % of the current female prison population, which would simultaneously reduce the number of children impacted by incarceration. If all of the money saved by incarcerating only "dangerous" men and women would be spent on support actions (see Waller 2008), it would be a cost-neutral proposal. Moreover, in the long term, the proposal might even lead to considerable savings, since many of the affected children would grow up to become taxpayers rather than marginalized outsiders. Nevertheless, for the remaining violent perpetrators, all the considerations presented in the previous section are true because in at least a large part of these cases the offense evolved from a deprived social status or from the position of a victim.

5.2 *Converting Existing Institutions into Restorative Prisons*

If the abolitionist strategy cannot be implemented,[6] then women's prisons must be fundamentally redesigned through a Restorative Justice approach. The "Restorative

[6] Bianchi (1994), in his work on sanctuaries, has shown that the prison for offenders is a relatively new institution and that historic societies were able to handle serious crime in a way we would now call restorative.

Prison" model is centered on a "culture of respect," in which a victim-focused perspective is used within the prison, including victim awareness training and mediation (van Ness 2007; Hagemann 2003). Since 1998, this model has been used in Belgium prisons (Robert and Peters 2003; Mariën 2010) and since 2000 in the UK, it has been used in several male and female prisons (Newell 2002; Edgar and Newell 2006). "Restorative Prisons" are characterized by an orientation on victims' issues, a greater permeability between the prison and the community (e.g., prisoners offering services for the community; community access to the prison), and an openness to outside advocacy (e.g., Victim Support, Restorative Justice organizations, community or church-related organizations). Restorative Justice consultants in Belgium, however, faced some problems with staff and with the traditional prison hierarchy in their pursuits to change past practices (see also Correctional Service Canada 2011).

Although the philosophy of Restorative Justice is already successfully implemented in criminal justice practices around the world, it is most commonly implemented as a diversionary program at the pre-sentence level, enabling the conflicting parties involved to solve relevant criminal (or civil) disputes themselves in the form of a mediated dialogue before formal court proceedings are required. In some countries, Restorative Justice methods exist on the post-sentencing level. That is, victims and perpetrators—possibly supported by caring others from their informal networks—attempt to restore social peace despite, after or in addition to punishment in a dialogic process. Participation in Restorative Justice processes is voluntary. Therefore, the idea of "ownership" (Christie 1977) is a core feature; participants determine how such a process takes place and who will be involved. The focus is on life-world actors,[7] the informal network of key stakeholders. Professionals (system-actors) are included for specific questions, but neither determines the process nor the outcome. The central figure—in this case: the woman prisoner—along with her caring others, develop a plan and take responsibility for its implementation. The professionals may consider this plan and they are asked to accept parts explicitly, if costs are to be borne by public authorities or the community or if specific decisions require their consent (e.g. release from prison, certain bail conditions).

[7] The term "life world actors" has been derived from Husserl's (1977) notion of the life world or "Lebenswelt," further developed by Schütz and Luckmann (1979). The concept of life world gives people the autonomy to act using a common sense base, following subjective convictions or traditional customs, whereas the system concept (see Habermas 1981) is organized by a different logic of rationality. Thus, "life world actors" denotes ordinary people, not professionals or experts in the criminal justice system.

5.3 Restorative Justice Procedures Specific to Release from Prison

Due to the ownership concept of Restorative Justice, aftercare plans will be developed that are tailored to the individual needs and abilities of the incarcerated woman and the specific conditions in the life-world. Since the prisoner is at the center of the effort and the composition of its participants largely self-determined, she is taken seriously; her contributions are appreciated and her needs are acknowledged. Due to this setting, there is no reason to neutralize the result later as something that others have imposed on one-self. On the contrary, she agrees to all points of the plan explicitly; in the ideal case, most aspects go back to the woman's own suggestion. This type of Restorative Justice programming has shown very good results (Sherman and Strang 2007; Shapland et al. 2011). In our opinion, this model should be offered in all cases in which women prisoners are amenable, because the informal network (e.g., friends, family members, colleagues, neighbors) can be integrated. It has also been found that the self-determined plans are more targeted, detailed, realistic and appropriate to the specific situation than plans that have been devised by professionals (e.g. regular prison treatment and discharge planning staff). The Restorative Justice approach is based on considerations of bonding and control theories; reintegration into a social network (e.g. family, neighbors, friends) provides a tighter control with the possibility of a more timely intervention.

If a situation emerges in which a prisoner wishes to engage in a Restorative Justice process, but there is no informal network, or members of the informal network want no more contact, the approach must be modified. One of the co-authors visited a so-called faith-based unit in Rimutaki Prison for male prisoners in New Zealand (Workman 2007). In this case, a Christian community carried out intensive volunteer work with the prisoners and assisted with their reintegration into the community after release, providing employment assistance, housing, and support in various problem situations. We advocate that this same approach be used with the women returning home from prison; meaning, in the absence of an informal support network, we would call on volunteers from the community.

5.4 Sensible Transition Management

The fourth recommendation centers on the idea of transition management, which addresses incarcerated women's personal deficits (e.g., employment, education, substance abuse, mental health issues, debt, housing). In contrast to the Restorative Justice-based interventions, this approach is morally neutral and mainly provided by criminal justice practitioners, in conjunction with health and human service professionals. The only requirement for the prisoner is a willingness to change, by desisting from illicit substance abuse and criminal behavior (see Maruna 2006;

Matt 2014). The approach requires a basis of trust with the responsible case manager and it is therefore recommended, if possible, to have the same contact person(s) throughout the process, which begins several months before release and lasts usually until about 6 months after release. Whereas a relationship of trust with friends and family is cultivated over years of time, this approach requires a great deal of bonding in a short time frame. Moreover, because most transitional management programs operate over a limited timeframe, the professional person disappears from the life of the target person after about 1 year. This could be problematic, especially for people with negative attachment experiences, who might be reluctant to invest much personal energy into a short-term relationship.

We propose that transition management be implemented using the Restorative Justice approach of relying on involvement of the informal network. Past research suggests that the traditional, formal approach to transition management is more suitable for male offenders and ex-prisoners than for females (Holst 2004; German Expert Committee 2012). The transition management does not seem to be so different from other traditional approaches with offenders. The specificity lies in the coordination and pooling of once very scattered resources, which had to be integrated by the formerly incarcerated person. It remains the case that formerly incarcerated persons often lack self-confidence and take a more passive stance in their aftercare plans. The offender's informal network is sometimes not included and the—albeit incomplete—formal control is experienced only as such, not as a way of support. By using a Restorative Justice approach to transition management, we can more fully support offenders and prisoners and help them to invest in their futures after prison. Meaning, as McNeill (2006: 47) observed, "It is not just the events and changes that matter, it is what these events and changes *mean* to the people involved." Although there is a risk that undesirable developments may be detected too late, traditional transition management is the only promising option for individuals without a social network or without an openness to participate in Restorative Justice.

In conclusion, far too many women are forced to spend years of their lives behind bars, even though they have not committed dangerous crimes. On the contrary, they have been subject to serious victimizations in childhood and in adult life. Compared with incarcerated men, incarcerated women receive much less attention and because of their marginalization, they get fewer opportunities to prepare for reintegration following imprisonment. Programs addressing incarcerated women's specific needs are rare. Moreover, there is a dearth in women's aftercare programming. Women leaving prison typically have access to the general—predominantly male—support organizations, which often focus on control.

This societal neglect is especially problematic, given that women prisoners are often the primary care providers for their children. Indirectly, these children are collaterally punished by their mothers' incarceration and society should be aware that they might follow in their mothers' footsteps later in life. Instead of punishment and formal control, the mothers and their children need assistance in this very challenging life experience. This support can be offered by professionals from social work and health services. Because many of the women have had bad experiences in a male-dominated world, it should preferably be offered by gender-specific institutions, such as the Women Centres in England or the project in Frankfurt-Preungesheim prison. Both gender-specific approaches seem to be very successful in establishing trustful relationships and assisting women in their desistance from crime. Currently, the concept of transition management also offers a promising outlook.

Although professional support is necessary, it covers only a part of life. Restorative Justice initiatives, aimed at reconciling the ex-prisoner with her community—to the extent that it is possible—and reintegrating her into a community of care, built by relatives, friends, and neighbors, could be even more important. In criminological theory terms, the focus should be on *informal* social control structures, which are available around the clock and are not primarily about control, but rather care and support. Often the persons involved have had lasting relationships over time and can build or reestablish a trustful relationship in which to plan aftercare. These long term relationships are much more conducive to aftercare programming than short-term relationships with professionals alone. Members of this informal network, however, also need to be supported by health and human service providers.

Studying women's crime generally does not lead to an argument in favor of incarceration, at least not for 90 % of the women currently imprisoned. As long as imprisonment exists, we need to focus on aftercare and reintegration, but it would make much more sense not to exclude these women from society by putting them into prisons. The exclusion posed by incarceration is often a result of a preceding societal exclusion by being female in a male-dominated world. It would save a lot of money and suffering—for both incarcerated mothers and their children—if the primary exclusion from education, the labor market, community, and justice were prevented by more gender adequate policies.

Five Questions

1. Programs and practices that embody the Restorative Justice (RJ) approach can be effective alternatives to incarceration, promising better reintegration for individuals who commit crime and offsetting the negative side effects of incarceration. What potential RJ practices are especially suited for women offenders?
2. Some state (e.g. Council of Europe, World Health Organization, UNODC) and non-governmental (e.g. Prison Reform Trust, Quaker Council for European Affairs) transnational organizations have acknowledged the plight of women prisoners and developed elaborate recommendations. How can these recommendations, which are consistent with results of scientific research, be implemented in binding laws and criminal justice policies?
3. Currently, the US seems to be the (negative) trend setter when it comes to the development of prison sentences. How could examples of countries with low incarceration rates contribute to a trend reversal?
4. Many women prisoners, who were severely victimized by their intimate partners or fathers, see that their perpetrators either are not punished at all or are punished only minimally for their abusive acts. At the same time, when these women commit non-dangerous offenses, they are severely punished by the criminal

justice system. How can we achieve both sensitivity and justice within the criminal justice system?
5. Of the four reforms proposed—abolition of prison sentences for non-dangerous offenders, converting existing institutions into restorative prisons, restorative aftercare programming, and transition management—which is the most practical for affecting change for women offenders?

References

Adler, F. (1975). *Sisters in crime: The rise of the new female criminal*. New York, NY, USA: McGraw Hill.

Alleyne, V. (2006). Locked up means locked out: Women, addiction, and incarceration. *Women and Therapy, 29*, 181–194.

Barberet, R. L. (2014). *Women, crime and criminal justice: A global enquiry*. London and New York: Routledge.

Beichner, D., & Rabe-Hemp, C. (2014). "I don't want to go back to that town:" Incarcerated mothers and their return home to rural communities. *Critical Criminology, 22*, 527–543.

Belknap, J. (2015). *The invisible woman: Gender, crime, and justice* (4th ed.). Belmont, CA: Thomson Wadsworth.

Bianchi, H. (1994). *Justice as sanctuary: Toward a new system of crime control*. Bloomington: Indiana Univ. Press.

Bloom, B. (1993). Incarcerated mothers and their children: Maintaining family ties. In *Female Offenders: Meeting the Needs of a Neglected Population*. Laurel, MD: American Correctional Association.

Bloom, B., Owen, B., & Covington, S. (2004). Women offenders and the gendered effect of public policy. *Review of Public Policy, 21*(1), 31–48.

Bloom, B., & Steinhart, D. (1993). *Why punish the children? A reappraisal of the children of incarcerated mothers in America*. San Francisco, CA: National Council on Crime and Delinquency.

Bowleg, L. (2012). The problem with the phrase women and minorities: Intersectionality – an important theoretical framework for public health. *American Journal of Public Health, 102*(7), 1267–1273.

Brown, M., & Bloom, B. (2009). Reentry and renegotiating motherhood: Maternal identity and success on parole. *Crime and Delinquency, 55*, 313–336.

Bundesarbeitsgemeinschaft für Straffälligenhilfe e.V., Chance e.V. Münster and Der Paritätische Landesverband NRW e.V. (Hrsg.) (2013). Das Familienhaus Engelsborg. Verantwortung für die Kinder Inhaftierter. Münster: Eigenverlag Chance e.V.

Byrne, M., Goshin, L., & Joestl, S. (2010). Intergenerational transmission of attachment for infants raised in a prison nursery. *Attachment and Human Development, 12*, 375–393.

Campbell, J. C. (2002). Health consequences of intimate partner violence. *The Lancet, 359*(9314), 1331–1336.

Carlson, J. R. (2001). Prison nursery 2000: A five-year review of the prison nursery at the Nebraska Correctional Center for Women. *Journal of Offender Rehabilitation, 33*(3), 75–97.

Chesney-Lind, M. (1989). Girls' crime and woman's place: Toward a feminist model of female delinquency. In: *Crime and Delinquency* (Pp. 6–29). SAGE.

Chesney-Lind, M. (2002). Imprisoning women. The unintended victims of mass imprisonment. In M. Mauer & M. Chesney-Lind (Eds.), *Invisible punishment. The collateral consequences of mass imprisonment* (pp. 79–94). New York: New Press.

Christian, J., & Thomas, S. S. (2009). Examining intersections of race, gender, and mass imprisonment. *Journal of Ethnicity in Criminal Justice, 7*, 69–81.

Christie, N. (1977). Conflicts as property. *The British Journal of Criminology, 17*, 1–15.

Clark, M. (2004). Somebody's daughter theatre: Celebrating the difference with women in prison. In M. Balfour (Ed.), *Theatre in prison: Theory and practice* (pp. 101–106). Bristol: Intellect Books.

Clarke, J.G. (2013). Prenatal care for incarcerated women. Retrieved from www.uptodate.com/centents/prenatal-care-for-incarcerated-women on April 7, 2014.

Collins, P. H. (2000). Gender, black feminism, and black political economy. *Annals of the American Academy, 568*, 41–53.

Correctional Service Canada (2011). Restorative justice. International perspectives on restorative corrections: A review of the literature. Retrieved from http://www.csc-scc.gc.ca/text/rj/litrvw-eng.shtml on January 24, 2013.

Covington, S. S., & Bloom, B. E. (2006). Gender responsive treatment and services in correctional settings. *Women and Therapy, 29*(3-4), 9–33.

Crawford, J. (1990). *The female offender: What does the future hold?* Laurel, MD: American Correctional Association.

Crenshaw, K. (1989). Demarginalizing the intersection of race and sex: A black feminist critique of antidiscrimination doctrine, feminist theory and antiracist politics (pp. 139–167). The University of Chicago Legal Forum.

Crenshaw, K. (1991). Mapping the intersectionality, identity politics, and violence against women of color. *Stanford Law Review, 43*(6), 1241–1299.

Daly, K. (1995). Looking back, looking forward: The promise of feminist transformation. In B. Raffel Price & N. J. Sokoloff (Eds.), *The criminal justice system and women: Offenders, victims, and workers* (2nd ed., pp. 443–457). New York, NY: McGraw Hill, Inc.

Davies, C. (2012). Lebanon's women prisoners find freedom behind bars. Retrieved from http://www.cnn.com/2012/01/11/world/meast/lebanon-womens-prison/ on May 12, 2014.

Drapalski, A. L., Youman, K., Stuewig, J., & Tangney, J. (2009). Gender differences in jail inmates' symptoms of mental illness, treatment history and treatment seeking. *Criminal Behaviour and Mental Health, 19*(3), 193–206.

Dutton, M. A., Green, B. L., Kaltman, S. I., Roesch, D. M., Zeffiro, T. A., & Krause, E. D. (2006). Intimate partner violence, PTSD, and adverse health outcomes. *Journal of Interpersonal Violence, 21*(7), 955–968.

Edgar, K. (2004). Lacking conviction: The rise of the women's remand population. London: Prison Reform Trust. Retrieved from http://www.prisonreformtrust.org.uk/Portals/0/Documents/Lacking%20Conviction%20the%20rise%20of%20the%20women's%20remand%20population.pdf on July 24, 2014

Edgar, K., & Newell, T. (2006). *Restorative justice in prisons. A guide to making it happen.* Winchester: Waterside Press.

Einsele, H., & Rothe, G. (1982). *Frauen im Strafvollzug*. Reinbek bei Hamburg: Rowohlt.

European Institute for Gender Equality (2014). Gender mainstreaming: A strategy to achieve equality between men and women. Retrieved from http://eige.europa.eu/content/activities/gender-mainstreaming-methods-and-tools on November 2, 2014.

Ferszt, G., Hayes, P. M., DeFedele, S., & Horn, L. (2004). Art therapy with incarcerated women who have experienced the death of a loved one. *Journal of the American Art Therapy Association, 21*, 191–199.

Few-Demo, A.L., & Arditti, J.A. (2013). Relational vulnerabilities of incarcerated and reentry mothers: therapeutic implications. *International Journal of Offender Therapy and Comparative Criminology*. Online First: http://ijo.sagepub.com/content/early/2013/07/09/0306624X13495378.

Fogel, C. (1995). Pregnant prisoners: Impact of incarceration on health and health care. *Journal of Correctional Health Care, 2*(2), 169–190.

Fortuin, B. (2007). Maine's female offenders are reentering – and succeeding. *Corrections Today, 69*, 34–37.

Foster, H. (2011). The influence of incarceration on the children at the intersection of parental gender and race/ethnicity: A focus on child living arrangements. *Journal of Ethnicity in Criminal Justice, 9*, 1–21.

Fraden, R. (2001). *Imagining media: Rhodessa Jones and theatre for incarcerated women*. Chapel Hill/London: The University of North Carolina Press.

Fretz, R., Erickson, J., & Mims, A. (2007). Reentry Programming and female offenders: The case for a gender-responsive approach. *Journal of Community Corrections, 16*(3), 9–21.

Garcia, M., & Ritter, N. (2012). Improving access to services for female offenders returning to the community. *NIJ Journal, 269*, 18–23.

Geiger, M., & Steinert, E. (1993). *Straffällige Frauen und das Konzept der Durchgehenden sozialen Hilfe*. Kohlhammer: Stuttgart u.a.

German Expert Committee (Fachausschuss, Straffällig gewordene Frauen). (2012). Werkstattpapier zur frauenspezifischen Straffälligenhilfe. In: BAG-S Informationsdienst Straffälligenhilfe, 20, 2, S. 4–8

Green, B. L., Miranda, J., Daroowalla, A., & Siddique, J. (2005). Trauma exposure, mental health functioning and program needs of women in jail. *Crime and Delinquency, 51*(1), 133–151.

Gussak, D. (2008). The effects of art therapy on male, female inmates: Advancing the research base. *The Arts in Psychotherapy*. doi:10.1016/j.aip.2008.10.002.

Habermas, J. (1981). *Theorie des kommunikativen Handelns. 2 Bände*. Frankfurt/M.: Suhrkamp.

Hagemann, O. (2003). Restorative justice in prisons? In L. Walgrave (Ed.), *Repositioning restorative justice* (pp. 221–236). Collumpton: Willan Publishing.

Hairston, C. F. (1988). Family ties during imprisonment: Do they influence future criminal activity? *Federal Probation, 52*(1), 48–51.

Hairston, C. F. (1991). Mothers in jail: Parent-child separation and jail visitation. *AFFILIA, 6*(2), 9–27.

Halmø, I. (2008). Resocialisering med familiebehandling i utraditionelle og hidtil uprøvede rammer. Afrapportering over erfaringerne med implementering af Familiebehandling i Kriminalforsorgen. Lyngby: Kriminalforsorgens Pension Engelsborg.

Hannon, G., Martin, D., & Martin, M. (1984). Incarceration in the family: Adjustments to change. *Family Therapy, 11*, 253–260.

Harvard Medical School. (2014). Women and Depression. Retrieved from http://www.health.harvard.edu/newsweek/Women_and_depression.htm on May 28, 2014.

Hedderman, C., Gunby, C., & Shelton, N. (2011). What women want: the importance of qualitative approaches in evaluating work with women offenders. *In: Criminology and Criminal Justice (February 2011), 11*(1), 3–19.

Hedtke, K. A., Ruggiero, K. J., Fitzgerald, M. M., Zinzow, H. M., Saunders, B. E., Resnick, H. S., et al. (2008). A longitudinal investigation of interpersonal violence in relation to mental health and substance use. *Journal of Consulting and Clinical Psychology, 76*(4), 633–647.

Henriques, Z. W., & Manatu-Rupert, N. (2001). Living on the outside: African American women before, during, and after imprisonment. *Prison Journal, 81*(1), 6–19.

Hills, H., Siegfried, C., & Ickowitz, A. (2004). *Effective prison mental health services: Guidelines to expand and improve treatment*. Retrieved from http://nicic.gov/Library/ 018604.

Holley, P. D., & Brewster, D. (1996). The women at Eddie Warrior Correctional Center. *Journal of the Oklahoma Criminal Justice Research Consortium, 3*, 107–114.

Holliday, S., Heilbrun, K., & Fretz, R. (2012). Examining improvements in criminogenic needs: The risk reduction potential of a structured re-entry program. *Behavioral Science and Law, 30*, 431–447.

Holst, B. (2004). Herstellung von Chancengleichheit von Männern und Frauen auf dem Arbeitsmarkt: EU-Querschnittsthema Gender Mainstreaming auch in MABiS.NeT. In: MABiS.NeT Report Juni/2004, S. 2-3.

Home Office (1997). Her Majesty's Chief Inspector of Prisons. Women in Prison: A Thematic Review. London: Home Office. Retrieved from: http://www.justice.gov.uk/downloads/publications/inspectorate-reports/hmipris/thematic-reports-and-research-publications/woman_in_prison-1996-rps.pdf on August 16, 2014.

Husserl, E. (1977). *Grundprobleme der Phänomenologie 1910/11*. Den Haag: Martinus Nijhoff.

Illinois Department of Corrections. (2014). *Women and Family Services*. Retrieved from: http://www2.illinois.gov/idoc/programs/Pages/WomenFamilyServices.aspx on August 4, 2014.

James, D. J., & Glaze, L. E. (2006). *Mental health problems of prison and jail inmates* (NCJ Report 213600). Retrieved from http://bjs.ojp.usdoj.gov/content/pub/pdf/mhppji.pdf on August 4, 2014.

Johnson, L. M. (2008). A place for art in prison: Art as a tool for rehabilitation and management. *The Southwest Journal of Criminal Justice, 5*(2), 100–120.

Jones, A. D., & Wainaina-Woźna, A. E. (2013). *Children of prisoners. Interventions and mitigations to strengthen mental health*. Huddersfield: University of Huddersfield.

Kauffman, K. (2001). Mothers in Prison. *Corrections Today, 63*, 62–65.

Kazura, K. (2001). Family programming for incarcerated parents: a needs assessment among inmates. *Journal of Offender Rehabilitation, 32*(4), 67–83.

Krucsay, B. (2007). Bedürfnisse männlicher und weiblicher Strafgefangener vor und nach der Entlassung. Bericht zur Fragebogenerhebung im Rahmen des Projekts Schritt für Schritt. Wien (Manuskript).

LaPoint, V., Pickett, M., & Harris, B. (1985). Enforced family separation: A descriptive analysis of some experiences of black imprisoned mothers. In M. Spencer (Ed.), *Beginnings: The social and affective development of black children* (pp. 239–255). Hillsdale, NJ: Lawrence Erlbaum, Associates.

Liebmann, M. (2007). *Restorative justice. How it works*. London/Philadelphia: Jessica Kingsley Publishers.

Lynch, S. M., Fritch, A., & Heath, N. M. (2012). Looking beneath the surface: The nature of incarcerated women's experiences of interpersonal violence, treatment needs, and mental health. *Feminist Criminology, 7*, 381–400.

Lynch, J. P., & Sabol, W. J. (2001). Prisoner reentry in perspective. Crime Policy Report, vol. 3. Washington, D.C.: Urban Institute Press.

Mariën, K. (2010). Restorative justice in Belgian prisons. In K. Lanyi & M. Gyokos (Eds.), *European best practices of restorative justice in criminal Procedure* (pp. 225–229). Budapest: Ministry of Justice and Law Enforcement, Republic of Hungary.

Martin, J., Kautt, P., & Gelsthorpe, L. (2009). What works for women? A comparison of community-based general offending programme completion. *British Journal of Criminology, 49*, 879–899.

Martin, M. (1997). Connected mothers: A follow-up study of incarcerated women and their children. *Women and Criminal Justice, 8*(4), 1–23.

Maruna, S. (2006). *Making good. How ex-convicts reform and rebuild their lives*. Washington, DC: American Psychological Association.

Matt, E. (2014). *Übergangsmanagement und der Ausstieg aus Straffälligkeit. Wiedereingliederung als gemeinschaftliche Aufgabe*. Herbolzheim: Centaurus.

McDaniels-Wilson, C., & Belknap, J. (2008). The extensive sexual violation and sexual abuse histories of incarcerated women. *Violence Against Women, 14*(10), 1090–1127.

McGowan, B., & Blumenthal, K. (1978). *Why punish the children? A study of the children of women prisoners*. Hackensack, NJ: National Council on Crime and Delinquency.

McNeill, F. (2006). A desistance paradigm for offender management. *Criminology and Criminal Justice, 6*, 39–62.

McPeek, S., & Tse, S. (1988). *Bureau of prisons parenting programs: Use, costs, and benefits*. Washington, D.C.: Federal Office of Research and Evaluation.

Merriam, B. (1998). To find a voice: Art therapy in a women's prison. *Women and Therapy, 21*(1), 157–171.

Messerschmidt, J. W. (1993). *Masculinities and crime*. Lanham, MD, USA: Rowman and Littlefield.

Miller, D., Trapani, C., Fejes-Mendoza, K., Eggleston, C., & Dwiggins, D. (1995). Adolescent female offenders: Unique considerations. *Adolescence, 30*, 429–435.

Mohanty, C. T. (2003). *Feminism without borders: Decolonizing theory, practicing solidarity*. Durham, NC/London: Duke University Press.

Mohanty, C. T. (2013). Transnational feminist crossings: On neoliberalism and radical critique. *Signs, 38*, 967–991.

Moloney, K. P., van den Bergh, B. J., & Moller, L. F. (2009). Women in prison: The central issues of gender characteristics and trauma history. *Public Health, 123*(6), 426–430.

Morton, J. B., & Williams, D. M. (1998). Incarcerated women struggle to maintain meaningful relationships with children. *Corrections Today, 60*(7), 98–104.

Mullen, C. A. (1999). Reaching inside out: Arts-based educational programming for incarcerated women. *Studies in Art Education, 40*(2), 143–161.

Murray, J. (2005). The effects of imprisonment on families and children of prisoners. In A. Liebling & S. Maruna (Eds.), *The effects of imprisonment* (pp. 442–462). Cullompton, Devon: Willan. Retrieved from http://www.bgsu.edu/downloads/cas/file77089.pdf on December 16, 2013.

Murray, J., & Farrington, D. P. (2008). The effects of parental imprisonment on children. In M. Tonry (Ed.), *Crime and justice: A review of research* (Vol. 37, pp. 133–206). Chicago: University of Chicago Press.

Naffine, N. (1996). *Feminism and criminology*. Philadelphia, PA, USA: Temple University Press.

Newell, T. (2002). Restorative practice in preparing prisoners for resettlement, integration and return to their communities. In: Restorative Justice in Prisons. Resource Book and Report. Arising out of a conference held in Friends House, London on Monday 11th February 2002 and a project of work in three prisons -Bristol, Norwich and Winchester pp. 81–83.

O'Neill, J. (2011). The inspire women's project: Managing women offenders within the community. *Irish Probation Journal, 8*, 93–108.

Pollock, J. M. (2002). Parenting programs in women's prisons. *Women and Criminal Justice, 14* (1), 131–154.

Poso, T., Enroos, R., & Vierula, T. (2010). Children residing in prison with their parents. *Prison Journal, 90*, 516–533.

Prison Reform Trust. (2011). Reforming women's justice: Final report of the Women's Justice Taskforce. London.

Prison Reform Trust. (2013). *Bromley briefings prison factfile*. London: Prison Reform Trust.

Quaker Council for European Affairs (2014). Women in prison. Retrieved November 2, 2014, from http://www.qcea.org/work/human-rights/women-in-prison/.

Quaker Council for European Affairs (QCEA) (2007). *Women in prison. A review of the conditions in member states of the Council of Europe*. Brussels: The Quaker Council for European Affairs.

Radosh, P. F. (2008). Reflections on women's crime and mothers in prison: A peacemaking approach. In J. F. Wozniak, M. C. Braswell, R. E. Vogel, & K. R. Blevins (Eds.), *Transformative justice. Critical and peacemaking themes influenced by Richard Quinney* (pp. 191–206). Plymouth: Lexington Books.

Robbins, C., Martin, S., & Surratt, H. (2009). Substance abuse treatment, anticipated maternal roles, and reentry success of drug-involved women prisoners. *Crime and Delinquency, 55*, 388–411.

Robert, L., & Peters, T. (2003). How restorative justice is able to transcend the prison walls: a discussion of the "restorative detention" project. In E. G. M. Weitekamp & H.-J. Kerner (Eds.), *Restorative justice in context: International practice and directions* (pp. 95–122). Cullompton: Willan Publishing.

Robertson, O. (2011). Collateral convicts: Children of incarcerated parents: Recommendations and good practice from the UN Committee on the Rights of the Child Day of General Discussion 2011. Geneva: Quaker United Nations Office.

Sacerdote, L. (2014). Spazio Giallo. Pfade für Kinder durchs Gefängnis. In: Informationsdienst Straffälligenhilfe, 22 Jg., Heft 1, S. 31–33.

Salas, J. (2002). Playback theatre: A frame for healing. In D. Johnson & R. Emunah (Eds.), *Current approaches in drama therapy* (pp. 288–302). Springfield, IL USA: Charles C. Thomas.

Schrader, C. (2012). *Ritual theatre: The power of dramatic ritual in personal development groups and clinical practice*. London/Philadelphia: Jessica Kingsley.

Schütz, A., & Luckmann, T. (1979). Strukturen der Lebenswelt, Bd. 1 und 2. Frankfurt.

Schwartz, J., & Steffensmeier, D. (2008). The nature of offending: Patterns and explanation. In R.T. Zaplin (ed) (pp. 43–75).

Scroggins, J., & Malley, S. (2010). Reentry and the (Unmet) Needs of Women. *Journal of Offender Rehabilitation, 49*, 146–163.

Shapland, J., Robinson, G., & Sorsby, A. (2011). *Restorative justice in practice. Evaluating what works for victims and offenders*. London/New York: Routledge.

Sherman, L., & Strang, H. (2007). *Restorative justice. The evidence*. London: The Smith Institute.

Simon, R. (1975). *Women and crime*. Lexington, MA, USA: D.C. Heath.

Snell, T.L., & Morton, D.C. (1994). *Survey of State Prison Inmates, 1991: Women in Prison*. Washington, DC: Bureau of Justice Statistics.

Snyder, Z., Carlo, T., & Coats Mullins, M. M. (2001). Parenting from prison: An examination of a children's visitation program at a women's correctional facility. *Marriage and Family Review, 32*, 33–61.

Steffensmeier, D. (1983). Organization properties and sex-segregation in the underworld: Building a sociological theory of sex differences in crime. *Social Forces, 61*(4), 1010–1032.

Stöver, H., & Thane, K. (2011). *Towards a continuum of care in the EU criminal justice system. A survey of prisoners' needs in four countries (Estonia, Hungary, Lithuania, Poland)*. Oldenburg: BIS-Verlag der Carl von Ossietzky Universität.

The Sentencing Project. (2012). Incarcerated Women Factsheet. Retrieved from http://www.sentencingproject.org/doc/publications/cc_Incarcerated_Women_Factsheet_Sep24sp.pdf on December 16, 2013.

Treatment Alternatives for Safe Communities (TASC). (2013). News and views: Women's prison program fosters family unity, community reentry. Retrieved from: http://www2.tasc.org/program/moms-and-babies-program on August 4, 2014.

UNODC (2012). *Global Report. Proportion of offenders convicted of all crimes who are women, select countries, 2006-2009*. Vienna: United Nations Office on Drugs and Crime.

UNODC (2014). *Statistics on criminal justice. Total persons brought into contact with the police and/or criminal justice system, select countries, 2003-2012*. Retrieved from http://www.unodc.org/unodc/en/data-and-analysis/statistics/crime.html on June 30, 2014.

Van Ness, D. W. (2007). Prison and restorative justice. In W. Daniel, G. Johnstone, & D. W. Van Ness (Eds.), *Handbook of restorative justice* (pp. 312–324). Cullompton: Willan.

Vera Institute of Justice. (2004). In M. Bobbitt & M. Nelson (Eds.), *The front line: Building programs that recognize families' role in reentry (Issues in brief, September)*. New York, NY: The Urban Institute 2001.

von Hofer, H. (2002). Die Ersatzfreiheitsstrafe in Schweden. In: Baechtold, Andrea and Senn, Ariane (Hrsg.). Brennpunkt Strafvollzug. Regards sur la prison. Bern: StàmpfliVerlagAG.

Waller, I. (2008). *Less law more order. The truth about reducing crime*. Ontario: Manor House Publishing Inc.

Walmsley, R. (2012). *World female imprisonment list* (2nd Ed.). London: International Centre for Prison Studies, Kings College London. Retrieved from https://www.prisonlegalnews.org/media/publications/international_centre_for_prison_studies_world_female_imprisonment_list_2nd_ed.pdf on June 30, 2014.

Walmsley, R. (2014). World prison population list (10th Ed.). London: International Centre for Prison Studies, Kings College London. Retrieved from http://prisonstudies.org/sites/prisonstudies.org/files/resources/downloads/wppl_10.pdf on July 4, 2014.

White, G. (2012). Gender-responsive programs in U.S. prisons: Implications for change. *Social Work in Public Health, 27*, 283–300.

Wilson, J. (2013). Agency through collective creation and performance: Empowering incarcerated women on and off stage. *Making Connections, 14*(1), 1–15.

Wirth, W. (2010). Übergangsmanagement aus dem Strafvollzug: Fokus „Arbeitsmarktintegration". In: DVJJ Landesgruppe Baden-Württemberg Jahrestagung 2010: Jugendliche Gewaltdelinquenz. Stuttgart. S. 77–96.

WODC. (2010). *European sourcebook of crime and criminal justice statistics - 2006* (4th ed.). Den Haag: Wetenschapelijk Onderzoek en Documentie Centrum.

Workman, K. (2007). Resolving conflict and restoring relationships: Experiments in community justice within a New Zealand faith-based prison. In G. Maxwell & J. H. Liu (Eds.), *Restorative justice and practices in New Zealand: Towards a restorative society* (pp. 139–161). IPS: Wellington.

World Bank Organization. (2014). The surprising rates of depression among MENA's women. Retrieved from http://blogs.worldbank.org/arabvoices/surprising-rates-depression-among-mena%E2%80 %99 s-women on June 10, 2014.

World Health Organization. (2014). Gender and women's mental health. Retrieved from http://www.who.int/mental_health/prevention/genderwomen/en/ on June 26, 2014.

World Health Organization/United Nations Office on Drugs and Crime (WHO/UNODC). (2009). Projektbericht. Gesundheit von Frauen im Strafvollzug. Beseitigung von Ungleichheiten zwischen den Geschlechtern im Strafvollzug. Kopenhagen WHO_UNDOC_2009.pdf http://www.euro.who.int/__data/assets/pdf_file/0005/76514/E92347G.pdf (8.8.2014)

World Health Organization-Europe (WHO) (2001). Health in prisons project. HIV in prisons: A reader with particular relevance to the newly independent states.

Wright, E., Van Voorhis, P., Salisbury, E., & Bauman, A. (2012). Gender-responsive lessons learned and policy implications for women in prison: A review. *Criminal Justice and Behavior, 39*, 1612–1632.

Zurhold, H., Moskalewicz, J., Sanclemente, C., Schmied, G., Shewan, D., & Verthein, U. (2011). What affects reintegration of female drug users after prison release? Results of a European follow-up study. *Journal of Offender Rehabilitation, 50*(2), 49–65.

Probation Supervision for Women and Young Offenders

Loraine Gelsthorpe and Ioan Durnescu

Abstract The issue of how to work effectively with offenders has long since been of concern. There is evidence that the risk principle, the need principle and the responsivity principle are useful in determining ways of reducing reoffending, but it has not always been clear how far this tri-partite model applies to women and young offenders. Thus the chapter reviews the evidence on what seems to facilitate effective supervision—including cognitive-behavioural and cognitive social learning strategies—but also looks at other evidence to see what might optimize returns in young people's and women's rehabilitation and reintegration.

1 Introduction

Ever since the question of probation entered the international arena through the Eighth International Penitentiary Congress in Washington, D.C. (1910), the topic of probation supervision for women and young offenders can be located in a number of theoretical and practice contexts (UNICRI 1997). For the purpose of this chapter, we consider these two groups of people on probation and under parole supervision from a "what works" perspective and also from legitimacy and "justice as fairness" points of view.

Probation supervision generally means supervision provided by a statutory Probation Service. Parole supervision (post prison release supervision) is similarly provided by the same service. However, there is different nomenclature in different countries, and different services may be fulfilling the function of supervision. For example, in England and Wales, the supervision of young offenders—under 18—is undertaken by local Youth Offending Teams/Services.[1]

[1] The cut off may vary from area to area—with some Probation Services taking over the supervision of offenders at 16 as opposed to 18 years of age. Moreover, the Probation Service is being

L. Gelsthorpe (✉)
University of Cambridge, Cambridge, UK
e-mail: lrg10@cam.ac.uk

I. Durnescu
University of Bucarest, Bucarest, Romania
e-mail: idurnescu@gmail.com

H. Kury et al. (eds.), *Women and Children as Victims and Offenders: Background, Prevention, Reintegration*, DOI 10.1007/978-3-319-28424-8_5

In Scotland, the supervision of young offenders is undertaken by criminal justice social work services.[2]

The issue of how to work effectively with offenders has long since been of concern, but rather than focus on the history here we focus on more recent developments and particularly from the time when the *risk/need/responsivity model* (RNR) entered mainstream practice almost everywhere around the world. In short, the RNR paradigm suggests that interventions that follow the risk principle, the need principle and the responsivity principle are the most effective in reducing reoffending (Andrews et al. 1990). The *risk principle* suggests that the intensity of the intervention should match the level of risk: low risk of reoffending should be met with minimum intervention while high level of risk of reoffending should be matched with high intensity intervention. Later, Andrews and Bonta (2010) suggested that treatment services (interventions) should be delivered almost exclusively to moderate and higher-risk offenders[3] so as to maximize impact. Indeed, it is suggested that interventions are more effective with this group and least effective with lower risk offenders. The *need principle* emphasizes that interventions should target so-called criminogenic needs (that is, crime-related needs) such as: antisocial attitudes, antisocial cognition, antisocial associates, substance abuse and so on. The *responsivity principle* refers to the delivery of a programme in a style and mode that is consistent with the learning and the ability of the offender.

According to Andrews and Bonta (2010) the most powerful influence strategies are (a) cognitive-behavioural and (b) cognitive social learning strategies, although it is recognized that this does not necessarily take account of gender differences. Nevertheless, this practice paradigm emphasized for the first time in systematic fashion that not all offenders have the same criminogenic needs (that is, crime needs relating to their pathways into crime) and that they do not learn the same way. Therefore, women and young offenders may have specific criminogenic needs that are different from those of other groups of offenders. Moreover, they might be open to some specific learning strategies. In other words, no one model of intervention works for all offenders. In the next two sections of this chapter we discuss the specific needs of young offenders and women. We also provide examples of how these needs are met within some probation services.

---

restructured in England and Wales so that from the latter part of 2014, there has been a single national Probation Service (as opposed to a number of Probation Trusts) responsible for the supervision of tier 3 and 4 offenders (serious offenders); private companies (working in conjunction with voluntary agencies in some cases)—called Community Rehabilitation Companies—are responsible for tier 1 and 2 offenders (the less serious offenders). See: https://www.gov.uk/youth-offending-team.

[2] See, for instance: http://www.scotland.gov.uk/Topics/archive/law-order/offender-management/offender/community/16910.

[3] A conclusion reached on the basis of research evidence, which shows that interventions work best where they are appropriately targeted; less serious offenders can be dealt with via other forms of penalties, such as unpaid work in the community.

2 Young Offenders

The definition of "young offender" is often quite difficult to establish because it is linked to what is defined as "youth" in the general social context. In the criminal justice system a young offender is most often defined as a criminally responsible person under the age of 18 or 21. However, whilst there is some consistency regarding the upper limit of who might be considered to be a "young offender", there is no consistency regarding the lower limit. This is mainly because the age of criminal responsibility varies across the world: it is 10 in England and Wales, 8 in Scotland, 15 in Scandinavian countries and so on. The minimum age of criminal responsibility is different in many North American States: it is 7 in Oklahoma, 14 in California and New Jersey, 10 in Colorado, and 13 in Georgia and Illinois. Interestingly, some USA states do not have a specific age minimum: Alabama, Arizona, Hawaii, Indiana, and Kansas, for instance. Within the category of "young offenders" some countries differentiate even further: in Romania, for instance, the minimum age of criminal liability is 14 but between 14 and 16 the state has to prove that the young person understands the difference between right and wrong. After the age of 16 the person is seen to be fully responsible for their illegal actions. In Sweden and Austria there are separate sentencing options for 18–21 years old (Dünkel and Pruin 2012).

In order to be as comprehensive as possible, but maintaining a focus at the same time, this chapter defines the young offenders as belonging to the 10–21 age group.

2.1 Young Offenders' Needs

Developmental psychologists have pointed out that neurological and psychological research indicates that the brain continues to develop from the childhood, through adolescence and to early adulthood. This development takes place on different levels: the process of myelination continues to happen, the white matter increases, the synapses are pruned etc. The dorsal lateral prefrontal cortex that is responsible for controlling impulses reaches maturity in the early 20s (Giedd 2004). These developments in the prefrontal cortex lead to improvements in the functioning of reasoning, abstract thinking, anticipating consequences, impulse control and planning (Sowell et al. 2001).

In their literature review, Prior et al. (2011) conclude that physical maturity occurs around the age of 12 or 13 whereas the intellectual development matures around the age of 18. However, they also conclude that superior intellectual functions such as planning, verbal memory, impulse control and so on are not fully developed before the age of 25.

From a psychological point of view, it is thought that behavioural controls are fully developed in early adulthood. Steinberg et al. (2009), for example, argue that if the ability to plan ahead and anticipate consequences improves before the age of

20, decision-making, careful risk taking, delay of gratification and resistance to peer pressure mature later, in early adulthood.

After dividing psychological maturity into three different categories (*responsibility*—ability to act independently; *temperance*—ability to control aggression, risk taking and thinking before acting, and *perspective*—the ability to understand another's point of view), Prior et al. (2011) have noted that temperance is most often associated with offending behaviour. If the other two dimensions tend to mature before the age of 18, temperance continue to develop up until the mid 20s.

All these research findings have led Lösel et al. (2012) to conclude that:

> ...juveniles have less mature judgment, poorer emotion-regulation, poorer self-regulation, poorer decision-making abilities, poorer executive functioning, poorer reasoning capacities, less ability to think abstractly and poorer planning skills. (p. 1)

The authors continue to state that, due to these characteristics, juveniles are more likely to take risks and commit crimes for a sense of excitement rather than on any rational cost-benefit calculation. They tend to be more open to peer influence, more changeable and less set in their offending behaviour.

Changes in modern life styles and in the labour market in different countries make these psychological developments even more important. If we look at youth as a transition period towards an independent life, we will note that in modern times this period tends to become longer and longer. As mentioned by Dünkel and Pruin (2012), in the 1950s more than 70 % of German juveniles finished school at the age of 14 or 15 and entered the labour market. Nowadays, in Germany financial independence is achieved at about the age of 25. Furthermore, the labour market becomes more and more sophisticated, with an increasing number of knowledge-based jobs. This structural change requires young people to spend more time in education and therefore postpone the moment of independence from their own families. The same applies to family life. The average age of a man at the time of getting married has increased considerably in Europe from 26 in the 1970s to over 30 in the twenty-first century (Dünkel and Pruin 2012). And the average age of marriage for women in Western Europe and in other developed countries is similarly above 25, although a quarter of women in developing regions will be married between 15 and 19 years of age (United Nations 2000). (This leaves aside the difficult issue of non-consensual marriage, of course).

All these psychological and sociological factors have led international organizations and states around the world to redefine youth—in the sense of raising the upper age limit of those who can be still considered young or a young adult.

2.2 *International Responses to Youth Crime*

Due to these developmental features relating to juveniles, states have adopted different measures to adapt their official reactions. One of the first measures triggered by Art. 40 of the United Nations Convention on the Rights of the Child

(1989) was the establishment of the minimum age of criminal responsibility. As we outline above, this minimum age varies quite widely between 7 and 10 years to 18 or 21 years. From a criminal justice point of view, the age of criminal responsibility is important because only after that age can the person be prosecuted. Before that age, the juvenile is considered to be *doli incapax*—that is, not to be held fully responsible for any wrongdoing.

The second important measure promoted by the same article (inter alia with Article 3), was the adoption of the principle of the need to act in the "best interest of the child". According to this principle the state response to a criminal infringement committed by a young offender takes the interest of the child as the first priority. The second priority of any criminal justice system is to "do justice". Most of the criminal justice systems for juvenile or young offenders can be placed on this continuum between the best interest of the child and the delivery of justice (Yates 2007). Some states are very committed to the principle of the best interests of the child (see, for instance, the Nordic states—Hesbaek 2011). Some other states are dominated by neoliberal ideologies and tend to be more punitive towards children who come in conflict with the law. A simple analysis of the juvenile prison rates will help the reader identify which these countries are (see for example: http://www.t2a.org.uk/wp-content/uploads/2011/09/T2A-International-Norms-and-Practices.pdf).

Anticipating these principles and based on various psychological and sociological studies, the United Nations General Assembly, adopted in 1985 "The United Nations Minimum Rules for the Administration of Juvenile Justice" (the Beijing Rules, UN doc. A/RES/45/113). Directly related to probation and community sanctions (or alternatives to custody in UN language), this document is important because it recommends that member states:

1. use custody as the last resort;
2. emphasize the "well-being" of young people (provide education, vocational training, employment and other rehabilitative measures);
3. ensure that sentences are proportionate to the circumstances of both offenders and the offence;
4. use social inquiry reports (pre-sentence reports) to identify the services needed by the juveniles;
5. use as much as possible measures such as counseling, probation, and community service;
6. use diversion as much as possible;
7. use restorative justice measures;
8. extend the rules which apply to juveniles also to young adults;
9. use conditional release as much as possible.

Later, in 1990, the United Nations adopted another set of rules dealing mostly with the prevention of juvenile offending—The UN Guidelines for Prevention of Juvenile Delinquency (The Riyadh Guidelines, UN. doc. A/RES/45/112). Apart from emphasizing again the principles of child-oriented justice mentioned also in the Beijing Rules, the Riyadh Guidelines make concrete recommendations regarding both general and special prevention. As for the correctional segment of justice which makes the object of the present chapter, this document is relevant because it stresses the importance of a non-stigmatizing treatment of juveniles, suggests special training for correctional staff and also urges states to consider the establishment of an office of ombudsman or similar independent organ which would ensure that the status and the interests of juveniles are upheld. With the adoption of the Convention of the Rights of the Child (1989) and the establishment of the Committee on the Rights of the Child the United Nations set a very high standard for youth justice.

These principles are adopted and enhanced in Council of Europe recommendations such as the Council of Europe Rec. (1997) 20 on social reactions to juvenile delinquency, Rec. (2003) 20 concerning new ways of dealing with juvenile delinquency and the role of juvenile justice and Rec. (2008) 11 on the European rules for juvenile offenders subject to sanctions and measures.

More recently, the European Union has become very active in regard to the juvenile justice sector. The Year of 2010 was declared by the European Parliament and the member states of EU to be “the European year for combating poverty and social exclusion”.[4] Pan-European or international Non-Government Organizations (NGOs) such as the International Juvenile Justice Observatory and the European Council for Juvenile Justice are very active in setting up standards and recommendations for a child-friendly justice system. The Observatory published a Green Paper on the social reintegration of young offenders as a key factor to prevent recidivism (Jacomy-Vite 2014). Moreover, the 23rd session of the Commission on Crime Prevention and Criminal Justice (Vienna, Austria, 2014) has recommended through the Economic and Social Council to the General Assembly a new set of Guidelines (UN doc E/2014/30). It is expected that these new Guidelines will be adopted in due course. Certainly, there is strong encouragement that those states that have not yet integrated crime prevention and children’s issues into their overall rule of law increased efforts to do so and

> . . .to develop and implement a comprehensive crime prevention and justice system policy, with a view to preventing the involvement of children in criminal activities, promoting the use of alternative measures to detention, such as diversion and restorative justice, adopting reintegration strategies for former child offenders and complying with the principle that deprivation of liberty of children should be used only as a measure of last resort and for the shortest appropriate period of time, as well as to avoid, wherever possible, the use of pre-trial detention for children. . . (E/2014/30. E/CN.15.2104/20. Para. 7)

[4] Documents available at: http://ec.europa.eu/employment_social/2010againstpoverty/ (Accessed at 20th of July 2014).

2.3 *Probation and Parole for Juvenile Offenders*

Based on these international documents (including the recommendations above) and on some recent studies, a number of good principles can be identified in the area of probation and parole for juveniles. In this section we describe some of these principles in the context of probation and parole services. Each principle will be exemplified with one or two examples of best practice.

2.3.1 Special Legislation Dedicated to Juveniles and Young Adults

As suggested in the international and European standards, custody should be the last resort when responding to the juvenile offending. Furthermore, the penal response should be concerned more with the child's well being rather than retribution or deterrence. Therefore, most of the interventions relating to juvenile offenders should be informal, community based and focused on education, training, employment and other rehabilitative activities.

Special emphasis is dedicated to restorative justice in juvenile justice. Indeed, a high number of jurisdictions have developed victim-offender mediation services dedicated especially to juveniles. These are predominantly diversionary procedures and they take different forms: diversion from the entire criminal justice process, diversion from prosecution, diversion from custody and so on. In most of the countries where this diversionary option exists, it is regulated in such a way that the child's best interest, age, and physical and mental development are taken into consideration. One of the advantages of this alternative procedure is that it puts into practice the principle of minimum intervention that is very important for juveniles. Indeed, as evidence suggests (see Farrington et al. 2006; Bowles and Pradiptyo 2005) most juvenile offenders tend to desist around the age of 18. The age-desistance curve declines afterwards steadily up to the age of 30. By diverting juveniles from the criminal justice process or from custody a whole range of side effects are avoided (e.g. stigmatization, socialization into crime, reduced access to high quality education and training, family relationship fragmentation, etc.).

There are lots of examples of how diversion can be organized at the police, prosecution, court- and even at the prison level. Overall, research based on experimental design shows that diverted juveniles are more likely to desist than those dealt with via the ordinary routes of conventional justice systems (see, for instance, Davidson et al. 1990; Gilbert 1977; Wilson and Hoge 2013).

Previous studies and experience show also that diversionary schemes are more effective if they are combined with intensive and comprehensive services (e.g. education, health, accommodation and so on) in a holistic fashion where not only the victim and the offender are involved, but the school, family, friends, workplace and neighborhoods, there are more positive and enduring effects.

A good example of work in this direction is the Adolescent Diversion Project run by the Michigan State University. The project is a strengths-based program that diverts arrested youth from formal processing and provides them with community-based services. The project aims at preventing future delinquency by strengthening youths' attachment to family and other pro-social people, increasing access to resources in the community and keeping youth far away from the stigmatizing social contexts. Apart from mediation, the program involves a caseworker (student volunteer) who spends 6–8 h per week with the juveniles in order to provide them with tailored services. The project emphasises the importance of a well-trained and enthusiastic staff in delivering diversion services to young people. The project has been evaluated by more than one study and consistently found effective.[5]

Regarding the existence and the use of community sanctions for juveniles, Dünkel and Pruin (2012) make a very useful observation:

> ...many community sanctions are available all over Europe although their use varies a lot sometimes due to the lack of financial and organisational infrastructure at the local level. (p. 20)

Indeed, when it comes to juvenile offenders, courts have a wide range of options of which to choose. Most of these forms of social control are of an educational nature—schooling, vocational training, leisure time, social skills etc. Some other sanctions aim at changing the anti-social behaviour—behavioural change programs, anti-drug programs, heath program, supervisory measures etc. Other sanctions carry a more punitive weight—community service, detention, electronic monitoring.

In some jurisdictions, these sanctions and measures are also available to young adults under certain circumstances (e.g. Croatia, The Netherlands, Portugal, Russia). In Germany, for instance, juvenile criminal law can be applied to young adults up to the age of 21 if the court considers that at the time of committing the crime, the moral and psychological development of the young adult was like that of a juvenile. Furthermore, juvenile law can be applied also if the motives and the circumstances of the offence are similar to those typical for a juvenile crime (Dünkel and Pruin 2012). A useful example of how the educative measures and the community sanctions can be used creatively and in a flexible way comes from the Scandinavian countries. Here, the court can mix different measures to fit the juvenile offender's needs (Kyvsgaard 2004).

2.3.2 Special Institutions and Specialized Staff

When it comes to the implementation of the community sanctions and measures the picture is very diverse (van Kalmthout and Durnescu 2008). In some countries, the probation service is in charge of probation activities for both juveniles and adults (e.g. Austria, Bulgaria, Czech Republic, Estonia, Finland). In other states, the probation service deals only with adults (e.g. England and Wales (UK), The

---

[5] For more information, see: http://www.crimesolutions.gov/ProgramDetails.aspx?ID=332.

Netherlands, Sweden). In some areas, the Probation Service takes on young offenders when they are 16 (such as in England and Wales). Even in cases where the probation service deals with both juveniles and adult offenders, there is usually a structural or at least functional distinction between these two. Sometimes, there is a department within the probation service that deals with juveniles. Some other times probation officers themselves are specialized to work only with juveniles. Either way, usually staff working with juveniles or young adults tends to be different from those working with adults.

2.3.3 Dedicated Programs

Extensive systematic reviews and meta-analyses have been conducted to evaluate what works with juvenile and young adult offenders (see Lipsey and Cullen 2007; Lipsey 2009; Lösel 2012). Almost all researchers agree that there are some interventions that make an impact on the future reoffending rates among juvenile and young adult offenders.

Based on this evidence, it seems that cognitive behavioural programs, structured therapeutic communities, multisystemic therapy approaches and other multi-modal interventions make the most significant impact on reoffending. Furthermore, it seems that restorative justice programs, face-to-face meetings between the offenders and the victim in particular, are very effective when they are organized by specialized mediators (Strang et al. 2013). Shapland et al. (2008) have also demonstrated that restorative justice interventions lead to less reoffending overall and reduce the frequency of reoffending. Evidence from the desistance and Good Lives Model literature suggests that issues such as the quality of the relationship between the supervisor and offender, readiness to change, and building on strengths can be also effective in achieving the desirable results (Ward and Fortune 2013).

By way of exemplifying good practices in this area, it is worth mentioning that Lipsey (in Lipsey et al. 2010) has developed a tool called the Standardized Program Evaluation Protocol (SPEP) that compares juvenile justice programs to what has been found to be effective in previous research. The tool is configured to have a maximum overall score of 100 points and includes sections such as: type of programme, amount of treatment, quality of treatment and so on. Although this tool might be too prescriptive and inhibit creativity, it can be used to develop a more evidence-based practice in the area of juvenile justice.

2.3.4 Working with Juvenile Offenders. Conclusion

Although the research literature is now replete with evidence regarding two types of offenders: adolescent limited offenders and life-course persistent offenders (Moffitt 1993; Ezell and Cohen 2005), it is not yet clear enough how the prison or probation services can speed up the process of desistance for the first group and how they can make desistance possible for the second. Minimum intervention, a "whole person" approach, good assessment and so on are all very good principles, but only if they are implemented by sensitive organizations and well trained staff. The importance of the social structures and also of the family and the surrounding community has been also emphasized in the research. However, more should be done in order to understand how correctional agencies might engage with all these significant factors in the desistance process.

3 Women

3.1 Introduction

One immediate question has to be answered: why is there a need for a special focus on women and supervision. Interest in the female offender has ebbed and flowed over the past 100 years, but at the turn of the millennium women have very much been back in the limelight, whether because of increasing awareness of worldwide increases in the use of custody (Snider 2003) or because of concerns about "girl gangs", the "mean girl" or "ladettes" (girls and young women who behave in a boisterously assertive or crude manner and engage in heavy drinking sessions (Alder and Worrall 2004). There has also been discovery of the female sex abuser (women who commit sexual offences) (Matravers 1997) as well as more general attention to the need for gender informed criminal justice system practices and to the neglect of women as victims of domestic (spousal), violent and sexual abuse, and the criminal justice system's limited attempts to address these problems (Silvestri and Crowther-Dowey 2008). Thus a specific focus on women and criminal justice arises because much criminological theorizing and research has revolved around men, and what is known about men (their pathways into crime) and justice (what is "just" and what works for men) and has simply been presumed to be relevant to women too, when this is not necessarily the case. Indeed, women have been described as "correctional afterthoughts" (Ross and Fabiano 1986). This is not just about filling a gap in knowledge, but it is about extending our knowledge so that we can understand more clearly how gender—as a social construction—impacts on the conception, delivery and impact of "justice" through supervision.

Article 7 of the United Nations (UN) Universal Declaration of Human Rights states that: "All are equal before the law and are entitled without any discrimination to equal protection of the law."

However, the notion that all are equal before the law is problematic. Criminal justice practices often affect people in different ways in relation to gender (Ethnicity, age, social class and sexual identity are also factors which can, of course, impact on the operation and impact of the law).

One of the issues here is that dominant definitions of masculinity have affected both men and women in the criminal justice system because it is a system which has been "shaped" and designed according to understandings of men, male offenders and victims, and men's needs (Smart 1976; Heidensohn and Silvestri 2012). This is sometimes justified on the basis that criminology and criminal justice should be "crime led". Indeed, it is certainly the case that men predominate in criminal justice systems across the world. The vast majority of "known offenders" are men, with women making up fewer than one in five arrests in some jurisdictions (Brown and Heidensohn 2000). Moreover, many of the people who administer the criminal justice system are men, whether this be the police, judges, prosecutors, defence lawyers, prison officers or probation officers. This situation is replicated internationally and historically (Martin and Jurik 1996).

The consequences of a gender imbalance in gender distribution across criminal justice systems affects women in two main ways. First, responses to women as offenders are often thought not to be equal in relation to men. Second, they are treated differently as victims; specifically when victims of male violence. These differences broadly reflect cultural and ideological assumptions which operate with regard to women. Indeed, feminist writers such as Carol Smart (1976) and Adrian Howe (1994) have noted that it is important to examine the sites of criminal justice enactment (police services, prosecution services, legal defence services, the courts, probation and prisons) and to consider how gender is constructed in these institutional settings.

Thus the experience of women within the criminal justice system is arguably "gendered". To understand this we perhaps need to look outside the criminal justice system. Indeed, the context of the regulation and control of women (as offenders or victims) has to be located within an examination of "patriarchy" and "patriarchal relations", for it is argued that it is these concepts which determine women's social, political and economic status—alongside other relevant factors such as ethnicity, social class, age and sexual identity—and ultimately shape their experiences as offenders and victims, and how they might experience the criminal justice system, including supervision.

In this vein, we should note that there are many different forms of moral and social regulation over women. In some ways, the study of "deviant" or "delinquent" women and "women law breakers" cannot be separated from the study of how all women are defined and controlled in different societies. Ideas and stereotypes about women abound in regard to sexuality, motherhood, prostitution, abortion, alcoholism, and retirement, for instance, in all societies. Women and girls are disciplined, managed, corrected and punished as probationers, prisoners, partners, patients, mothers, and victims, through imprisonment, medicalization, secure care, and cultural stereotypes (Balfour and Comack 2006).

3.2 Women Offenders and Their Crime related Activities and Needs

In all countries where statistics are collected in routine fashion the majority of convicted offenders and the majority of those given court sentences are men. Broadly speaking, offending by women differs in a number of important ways from offending by men: it is less common, less frequent, and generally less serious. In western countries, including the USA, Australia, Canada and New Zealand, women who offend largely commit property-related offences (bearing in mind different legal terms and definitions in an international context).

As indicated in the introduction, historically, the study of crime has been male-centred and the criminal justice system's treatment of women has been imbued with assumptions about men. When the female offender has not been ignored she has been pathologised and treated as abnormal. It is only recently that we have begun to recognize more nuanced accounts of women's pathways into crime, acknowledging that women do not offend as much as men and that their offending behaviour is largely of a less serious nature. There have been periodic moral panics about women's criminality, particularly in relation to increases in violent crime. There have been indeed concerns about an increase in women's violence (Lauritsen et al. 2009) and "girl gangs" (Alder and Worrall 2004), but we would need an analysis of long term trends in this direction to be certain of major changes in patterns of crime as opposed to changes in responses to women (Steffensmeier et al. 2005). It might be added that we also know very little about the relatively few women who do persist in committing crimes or who are prolific in terms of their patterns of behaviour (see, for instance, Brennan et al. 2012).

One consistent feature in the lives of women who offend relates to experiences of poverty. Moreover, there have been consistent messages from the research literature on women offenders and from experienced service providers and service users that women offenders tend to have a history of unmet needs in relation to sexual and violent victimization, physical and mental health, housing and income, and training and employment. Substance misuse and child-care responsibilities often compound these problems. Desistance studies serve to highlight the complexity of factors relating to women's pathways into crime and in terms of pathways out of crime point to the need for broadly-based provision that can be individually tailored. Service providers in prisons and in probation/community corrections as well as researchers support claims that there may well be indirect relationships between abuse and mental health, labour market participation, and substance abuse, all of which are associated with the risk of reoffending. In other words, "victimization" creates psychological sequelae (long term consequences and difficulties), which can lead to offending behaviour (Hollin and Palmer 2006).

3.3 Risk/Needs Confusions

One particular concern relates to risk/needs confusions in dealing with women offenders. Correctional authorities have become increasingly concerned with assessing the risks and needs of offenders in recent years. This move towards risk/needs assessment can be seen as a contemporary manifestation of two residual concerns: predicting future offending and determining "what works". However, as Canadian researchers Hannah-Moffat and Shaw (2003) have highlighted—with international reverberations[6]—the research behind these assessment tools rarely considers the gendered, racialized, or otherwise stratified characteristics of risk and need. Moreover, women offenders are typically characterized as scoring high on "needs" and low on "risk" but that in practice, sentencers sometimes confuse the two with consequential up-tariffing of women in the sentencing system or in terms of "risk" coming to dominate overall approaches to women offenders. One such example concerns the 1990 Task Force on Federally Sentenced Women in Canada, entitled *Creating Choices.* The Task Force recommended the closure of the only women's penitentiary and replacement with regional facilities, which would recognize the low risk, specific needs and experiences of women, but alongside new initiatives there has been a growth in high security arrangements, and the use of assessment tools based on men (Hannah-Moffat and Shaw 2003; see Blanchette and Brown 2006).

3.4 Women, Community Sanctions and Supervision

There are huge gaps in data relating to women and community based sanctions across Europe (Council of Europe 2012) and elsewhere, and so it is perhaps hard to indicate anything very meaningful. But this said, we might point to relatively well-developed probation systems in Northern and Western Europe and smaller but emerging systems in South and Eastern Europe, and to well developed conceptions of supervision in Australia, Canada, New Zealand, and the USA, but not necessarily elsewhere.

Various studies have suggested that the focus and content of probation practice with women is different from that with men. For example, Stewart et al.'s (1994) analysis of probation revealed that women's offending was often explained as "self-expressive" or "coping behaviour" and probation officers responses typically involved supportive counseling aimed at improving self-esteem or self-image, or work on problems arising from poverty and its associated stresses. In Scotland, McIvor and Barry (1998) found that the supervision of women offenders was more on a traditional welfare model (dealing with practical problems and offering

[6] See, for example, the edited international collections of Sheehan et al. (2007) *What Works with Women Offenders* and Malloch and McIvor (2013) *Women, Punishment and Social Justice.*

emotional support) while the supervision of male offenders was more directly focused upon offending behaviour and related issues.

Notwithstanding the sophistication of probation services in some countries, the struggle to make the provision of services and programs "gender-sensitive" is indisputable, although there have been some advances (Carlen 2002; Sheehan et al. 2007; Sheehan 2011). Therefore it is important to examine to what extent a provision is gender sensitive (Chesney-Lind and Pasco 2013). For example, are women sentenced to community sentences in the same way as men? Do sentencers take into consideration the existence of children and mono parental families when they are thinking about the supervision needs of a woman? Are risk measurement tools sensitive to gender differences? And what kind of rehabilitative or training programs do women receive whilst on supervision?

To illustrate some of these issues, across the UK for instance, women have traditionally been under-represented on community service orders or what is now called "unpaid work" in the community, and over-represented on probation (supervision) (Gelsthorpe and McIvor 2007), arguably reflecting a perception of unpaid work as less suited to women who are regarded as more likely to benefit from more welfare-focused supervision. Such differences have now been reduced to some extent, as local Probation Services have tried to find suitable unpaid work for women and in some cases adapt the "working hours" so that women can undertake the work *and* deliver and pick up their children from school at the same time, rather than the one precluding the other.

Further, in the UK (England and Wales), Patel and Stanley (2008) found that women were more likely than men to have supervision and drug treatment requirements attached to Community Orders[7] and Suspended Sentence Orders,[8] while women were less likely than men to receive requirements involving unpaid work and participation in accredited programs.[9] As indicated, there is some evidence that women may be given community sentences as an alternative to a lesser sentence

[7] The Community Order is a generic community sentence (created in the Criminal Justice Act 2003). It is designed to give sentencers flexibility in choosing "requirements" which are commensurate with the seriousness of the offence in terms of punishment, and suitable for the offender (in terms of what might help). There are 12 different requirements which can be attached to an order (although on average sentencers attach about two). The requirements are: supervision, unpaid work (or what is sometimes described as community payback), curfew, accredited programs, specified activities (for example improving basic skills), prohibition, exclusion (from an activity or geographical area), residence (a requirement to live in a particular place), alcohol treatment, drug rehabilitation, attendance centre (this condition requires offenders under the age of 25 to attend a particular centre during their sentence) or mental health treatment.

[8] A Suspended Sentence means that a prison sentence has been imposed, but the execution has been suspended. In cases where a court imposes a Suspended Sentence Order, then most of the above conditions are also available to the court to impose on the offender as part of his/her suspended sentence.

[9] Accredited Programs are recognized programs designed to address behavioural issues such as general offending, violence, sex offending, drug or alcohol abuse, domestic violence, drink driving and acquisitive crime. There is only one "accredited programme" for women: acquisitive crime.

such as a fine; a long-standing concern is that this might indirectly contribute to the imprisonment of women, in the sense that if they reoffend whilst on a community order, or otherwise indicate non-compliance, they might be (Dowds and Hedderman 1997). Certainly, there is no evidence to suggest that the efforts to create suitable community sentences for women (suitable unpaid work that is) have had any impact on the rate of imprisonment for women (Patel and Stanley 2008).

We should add here that although a relatively high number of women offenders in England and Wales are on probation supervision, relatively few women receive prison sentences of over a year; for this reason not very many women have experienced post prison release supervision, since, to date, only those people serving custodial sentences of over a year are supervised in this way.[10]

Of course, as well as knowing what women offenders receive as community sentences, it is important to learn whether they complete the programs. Might there be any obstacles to the completion of community-based programs such as *community service or unpaid work* because of child care commitments or other demands? Might completion and compliance rates be higher if the programs and activities had been designed with women in mind? These are pressing questions. In a strident critique of parole and supervision in the USA, Morash (2010) thinks that such questions have been neglected.

They are difficult questions to unravel of course because a lower rate of successful completion of a supervision order in the community or a community programme in one area (or country) would not necessarily be a result of higher re-offending, rather than that enforcement procedures in the area or country may be more robust (and clients more quickly returned to court or otherwise penalized if they do not comply with the supervision requirements). As Robinson and McNeill (2008) put it, using blunt measures of "success" can mask underlying difficulties that are experienced by the offender, leading them to feel a loss of legitimacy in the process. This can have the effect of encouraging them to go through the motions, rather than actively engage. Robinson and McNeill (2008) identify two principal types of short-term compliance: *formal* and *substantive*. Formal compliance is characterized by an offender who ensures that his or her behaviour meets the requirement of the conditions, while not necessarily actively engaging. Substantive compliance is characterized by the active engagement of offenders who not only meet the requirements of all conditions of supervision but also seek to address their issues. Thus the aim is normative compliance, that is, changing hearts and minds, behaviour and attitudes.

---

[10] The law on this is changing with the advent of the Offender Rehabilitation Act 2014 (England and Wales) which introduces 12 months supervision for everyone sentenced to more than a day in custody. Arguably this could bring benefits for the many women who receive short custodial sentences, although the need for the custodial sentences is questionable (Hedderman 2012) and it is not clear whether people need statutory supervision or informal mentoring. The former could be seen as intrusive and punitive if not framed in relational and supportive fashion.

Before turning to questions of what we know might work with women then, it is important to address some general points about the quality of supervision and how best to achieve normative compliance.

3.5 What Do We Know About Work with Involuntary Clients?

Chris Trotter and Tony Ward (2012), writing on the basis of research in Australia and New Zealand, go further and suggest very strongly that in regard to work with involuntary clients (a good way to describe offenders) criminal justice workers (including supervisors) consciously or unconsciously influence their clients in both positive and negative ways, depending on the way in which they model and reinforce particular values. As Trotter and Ward put it: "Particular concerns are the degree to which practitioners demonstrate appropriate care and empathy for clients and the degree to which they actively scaffold their agency abilities" (2012, p. 1). Such a stance is acknowledged in an earlier work by Held (2006) in regard to the *ethics of care*. Held suggests that five core features shared by the majority of care theories can be identified. First, there is an explicit analytic focus on relationships and more specifically: "on the compelling moral salience of attending to and meeting the needs of the particular others for whom we take responsibility" (Held, 2006, p. 10). Secondly, persons are viewed in relational terms. Third, acts of caring are most reliably motivated by social or moral emotions such as empathic concern, sympathy and compassion. Fourth, the focus of an ethics of care is on the concrete specific relationships people are in. Fifth, there is a rejection of the distinction between public and private spheres of functioning. All of this points to the need to not only engage in pro-social modeling (offering praise for and reinforcement of pro-social actions or expressions on the part of clients) and to work with offenders *through the relationship* formed, but to do so in a way that *engages offenders*. The next step is to suggest that recognition of and respect for individuality (with due respect for social differences whether these be age, gender, ethnicity, culture or whatever) may serve to maximize effectiveness (Gelsthorpe 2001) because such respect is relational and may enhance the legitimacy of the whole process of being under supervision.[11]

3.6 What Works with Women?

The history of work with offenders is not replete with success, but the research base (particularly the meta-analyses) developed since the early 1990s in the UK and

[11] See Shapland et al. (2012) for a literature review on the quality of probation supervision.

other parts of Europe (drawing especially on work in Canada) now strongly supports the position that effective work with offenders is possible. But there has been hardly any attention to "what works with women offenders" amongst policy-makers in different countries, leading to the claim—as stated in the introduction—that women are "correctional afterthoughts" (Ross and Fabiano 1986). Whilst the focus of campaigns has commonly been on the high numbers of women in prison, the lack of gender sensitivity in prisons, and lack of attention to women's specific needs, in the western world in particular there have been recent attempts to focus more directly on what we know about women offenders and their needs, and based on this, to divert them from crime in general and prison in particular.

3.7 *Gender Responsiveness: Some General Issues*

Notwithstanding various developments in programs designed to address offending behaviour in the 1990s, there are controversies regarding their suitability for all offenders (women, black and ethnic minorities, young offenders, offenders with mental health problems, and very high risk and psychopathic offenders). Offender treatment programs are typically designed for white, male, adult offenders, with only minor adaptations for other groups of offenders. Indeed, the criminogenic needs that have emerged from research on men have typically been applied to women offenders. There have been claims that what works for men will work for women too. But this is not so, and even promoters of the popular cognitive skills programs now acknowledge that there may be an issue around the responsivity of female offenders to cognitive skills programs (see, for example, Cann 2006).

One recent study in England and Wales has tried to take things forward by exploring women's lower rate of completion on the community-based General Offending Behaviour Programme (Martin et al. 2009). Compliance is of course an important step on the way to (but not synonymous with) non-offending, and its promotion is clearly important for everyone. The study indicates that despite some similarities, the predictors of programme completion not only vary for men and women, but also operate differently between them. The findings support the "gender-responsiveness" position that men and women should be approached differently, and suggest, moreover, that men are more likely to engage in instrumental compliance and women more likely to achieve normative compliance (relating to compliance achieved though self-interested calculation and compliance based on values and the legitimacy of interventions respectively) (Martin et al. 2009).[12]

[12] See also consideration of how situational, practical and gender-specific factors may affect how women comply in L. Gelsthorpe (2013) "Working with Women in Probation: Will You, Won't You, Will You, Won't You, Won't You Join the Dance?" in P. Ugwudike and P. Raynor (eds) What works in offender compliance (Basingstoke: Palgrave Macmillan).

Attempts to facilitate gender-responsiveness in programs and interventions have been limited because the state of research and programme development for women generally lags behind that for men, but we are able to deduce what is likely to work with women from educational and other areas of research as well as from emerging research findings. From educational research we learn most women prefer to learn in collaborative, rather than competitive, settings (Belenky et al. 1986). If we put this alongside evidence, which suggests that women-only (or women-focused) environments facilitate growth and development (Zaplin 1998), we can see that the evidence adds up to a need to work with women in non-authoritarian co-operative settings, where women are empowered to engage in social and personal change. In addition, "women-specific" factors such as health care, child care and mental health together with factors relating to race and gender combined need to be addressed (see Gelsthorpe 2010). If these things are in place then this will maximize the potential for effectiveness in terms of reducing re-offending, although there are perennial problems in gathering data on re-offending.

3.8 New Initiatives

On the basis of their analysis of work in Canada, Taylor and Blanchette (2009) take us further in advocating the integration of a number of gender-informed theories and methodologies in responses to women offenders. Specifically, they recommend gendered pathways, the use of relational theory, strengths-based approaches, and the use of positive psychology, all of which are critical frameworks for intervention with women. We might add to this the need for such interventions to be sensitive to 'trauma'. In other words, supervision provision for women in the community should reflect these aspects.

There have been some important new initiatives, which reflect this kind of thinking. In Scotland we can turn to Centre 218, which has its origins in reviews following a series of suicides in Scotland's only prison for women. The Centre is based on the idea that female offenders should be able to get "time out" of their normal (and perhaps chaotic and stressful) environment without resorting to "time in" custody. The Centre thus serves as a diversion from prosecution and as an alternative to custody, and more generally it offers particular support—for detoxification, support and outreach to health, social work or housing services. The ethos is therapeutic in intention and there is much emphasis on providing a safe environment for the women (Beglan 2013).

There have been some interesting developments in relation to women and criminal justice in England and Wales too, including major funding and effort to divert women from both crime and custody (Hedderman 2010; Gelsthorpe 2010). A major review of the criminal justice system for women commissioned by the government in 2007 fuelled the changes (Corston 2007). A number of new community centres for women have been set up in the community providing holistic services in order to support women and there is now a national network of such centres (Women's Breakout: http://www.womensbreakout.org.uk/). These centres are increasingly used as settings in which "community supervision" can take place either in terms of using the centres for "specified activities" which might be required as an attachment to a Community (Supervision) Order, or as place where offender and probation officer or offender management might meet. Of course, there are questions to ask: do the developments reflect a new sense of responsibility towards disadvantaged women or might they be interpreted as an extension in the network of control and regulation. What is perhaps at issue now is how the centres can be sustained in a market economy of justice and how they can provide hard evidence of positive impact beyond clients' views (Gelsthorpe and Hedderman 2012).

This said, consumer feedback has been very positive. As Hedderman et al. (2011) indicate in their evaluation of *Together Women* the Government's pilot scheme for such centres, one client returned to a centre after not attending for some time and found:

> It's nice to know that somebody thinks about you and that, you know, there is somebody there to turn to...I thought it'd be like another authority. I thought it'd be like ...police, probation, social services kind of...making these rules, setting down I must do this, and I must do that, and it's not been anything like that....obviously, they're not gonna put up with my bloomin' nonsense, and all that sort of thing – but they just tell me what I should be doing, really, and then leave it to me whether I take it on board, or 'phone me and try to encourage me... (Hedderman et al. 2011, p. 11).

Such claims have been repeated in evaluations of women's community centres. In the *Turnaround* Project in Wales, the clients were unanimously positive about their experiences (Holloway and Brookman 2008). Issues that were highlighted as being particularly positive included: the range of support that was offered, the flexible pace of working, the confidential nature of discussions, the non-judgemental nature of the staff and the ability of staff to uplift them and instil them with confidence and self-esteem.

As Hedderman et al. (2011) note, the key themes which emerge are that what matters to women as service users is experience of key workers (and supervisors) who see service users "as people, not cases", "being accepted and respected", "being in a women only environment" and "being in a quality environment" (by which is meant a good physical environment where colour schemes were bright and furniture modern and comfortable). In many ways this takes us back to the important principles or ethics of care.

What developments have there been elsewhere? In the USA, the National Institute of Corrections (NIC) in cooperation with the University of Cincinnati (UC) (University of Cincinnati, 2013) has created a series of new gender specific risk/need assessments for adult women offenders. The assessments include: (1) a full instrument, the Women's Risk/Needs Assessment, which assesses both gender-neutral and gender-responsive factors and affords separate forms for probation, prison, and pre-release; and (2) the Women's Supplemental Risk/Needs Assessment which is designed to supplement existing risk/needs assessments such as the Level of Supervision Inventory—Revised (LSI-R) (Andrews and Bonta 1995).

The Women's Supplemental Risk/Needs Assessment is also available in separate forms for probation, prison, and pre-release populations.

The NIC/UC project was developed from two perspectives on offender rehabilitation: (1) research by Canadian scholars which stresses the importance of treating dynamic risk factors; and (2) work by feminist criminologists stressing the importance of women's unique "pathways to crime". Both paradigms stress the importance of programming for dynamic risk factors. However, the pathways model asserts that women's unique needs are not adequately tapped by currently used risk/needs assessments. In response, the new women's assessments identify such needs as: trauma and abuse; unhealthy relationships; parental stress; depression; self-efficacy, and current mental health symptoms.

Elsewhere in the USA there are developments relating to gender responsive programming in prisons and in the community (Lawston 2013), and in Victoria, Australia, developments regarding diversion from prison and better community provision in relation to drug and alcohol support, family reunification, debt management and independent living skills for example (Sheehan 2013).

Altogether, whilst it is obviously impossible to provide illustration of all the new developments across different jurisdictions, there is emerging evidence that provision for women offenders in the community should be women-only to foster safety and a sense of community and to enable staff to develop expertise in work with women; integrate offenders with non-offenders so as to normalise women offenders' experiences and facilitate a supportive environment for learning; foster women's empowerment so they gain sufficient self-esteem to directly engage in problem-solving themselves, and feel motivated to seek appropriate employment. Thus what is required is the utilization of what is known about effective learning styles with women; a holistic and practical stance to helping women to address social problems which may be linked to their offending; links with mainstream agencies, especially health, debt advice and counselling; capacity and flexibility to allow women to return to a community centre or supportive relationship for "top ups" or continued support and development where required; and arrangements for women to have a supportive milieu or mentor to whom they can turn when they have completed any offender-related programs, since personal care is likely to be as important as any direct input addressing offending behaviour. In addition it is important to provide women with practical help with transport and childcare so that they can maintain their involvement in the centre or programme (Gelsthorpe 2010).

Whilst the position of a number of countries is very unclear, the US Department of Justice National Institute of Corrections (Sydney 2005) has certainly acknowledged the need for gender-responsiveness in community corrections (including supervision). As indicated in a strategy paper (Sydney 2005) in addition to examining community corrections policies, procedures, philosophies, and attitudes to determine whether they promote successful outcomes for women offenders, gender-responsiveness requires intervention processes that "acknowledge and accommodate differences between men and women, assess women's risk levels, needs, and strengths and construct supervision case plans accordingly, acknowledge the different pathways through which women enter the community corrections system, recognize the likelihood that women offenders have a significant history of victimization, build on women's strengths and values, including recognizing that relationships are important to women, and acknowledge and accommodate the likelihood that women are primary caregivers to a child or other dependent." Various re-entry coaching programs (involving supervision in the community) reflect similar principles (see, for instance, Modley and Giguere 2010). In Connecticut, USA, the *Women Offender Case Management Model* is used throughout the system, built on relational theory, strengths-based, trauma-informed, holistic and culturally sensitive approaches. In Canada, Women's Supervision Units employ a gender-sensitive, multi-disciplinary team approach to the case management of women offenders. Indeed, the Correctional Service of Canada provides women-centred training alongside refresher courses for parole staff working in the women's supervision units. This is a way of ensuring that front-line staff receive adequate gender-specific training, alongside continued opportunities for learning while working (Correctional Service of Canada 2002).

In New Zealand, a holistic model of case management means that women offenders are supervised in a gender-informed way at every step of their involvement with the criminal justice system. Turner et al (2010) outline a similar gender informed approach in Australia. In 2009 Corrections Victoria developed the Dedicated Women's Case Management Model which resulted from the *Better Pathways* report (Corrections Victoria 2006). These are just examples of initiatives of course. And whilst we may wish to assume widespread adoption of good practice, there is a need for further primary research to ensure that good ideas and policies have been well-implemented and sustained.

3.9 Conclusion: Gender Informed Supervision

By unanimously voting in 2010 for the Treatment of Women Prisoners and Non-custodial Measures for Women Offenders ("The Bangkok Rules", A/RES/65/229, Annex), all countries who were members of the United Nations at the time acknowledged that women in the criminal justice system do have gender-specific characteristics and needs, and agreed both to respect and meet them. Rule 60 reads:

> *"Appropriate resources shall be made available to devise suitable alternatives for women offenders in order to combine non-custodial penalties with interventions to address the most common problems leading to women's contact with the criminal justice system. These may include therapeutic courses and counseling for victims of domestic violence and sexual abuse; suitable treatment for those with mental disability; and educational and training programs to improve employment prospects. Such programs shall take account of the need to provide care for children and women-only services."* (United Nations Rules for the Treatment of Women Prisoners and Non-custodial Measures for Women Offenders, 2010, Rule 60).

Certainly there has been an increased awareness of and concern about the direct applicability of research findings from studies conducted predominantly with men to the development and implementation of supervision approaches and community programs for women in the criminal justice system.

In sum, there has been substantial debate about the requirement for and efficacy of gender-responsive approaches in addressing the needs of women offenders (Andrews and Dowden 1999; Bloom et al. 2002). Countries vary as to how far they address gender-specific needs in supervision, but there is certainly a good range of possibilities and encouraging signs of change. At the same time, there are huge gaps in knowledge; we know very little indeed about gender issues in supervision beyond the western hemisphere, and more generally we need more empirical evidence to measure the impact of policy aspirations.

Five Questions

1. Why should probation or parole practice pay attention to the age or the gender of the offenders?
2. What is the evidence to suggest that these two factors are important when designing or implementing a correctional intervention?
3. In what ways do the needs of males and females differ in relation to supervision?
4. What research questions remain in relation to the supervision of young offenders and young adults?
5. What research questions remain in relation to the supervision of women?

References

Alder, C., & Worrall, A. (2004). *Girls' violence: Myths and realities*. New York: SUNY.

Andrews, D. A., & Bonta, J. (1995). *The LSI-R: The level of service inventory–Revised*. Toronto: Multi-Health Systems.

Andrews, D. A., & Bonta, J. (2010). *The psychology of criminal conduct* (5th ed.). Cincinnati: Anderson Publishing.

Andrews, D. A., Bonta, J., & Hoge, R. D. (1990). Classification for effective rehabilitation: Rediscovering psychology. *Criminal Justice and Behaviour, 17*, 19–52.

Andrews, D., & Dowden, G. (1999). A meta-analytic investigation into effective correctional intervention for female offenders. *Forum on Corrections Research, 11*(3), 18–21.

Balfour, G., & Comack, E. (2006). *Criminalising women*. Halifax: Fernwood Publishing.

Beglan, M. (2013). The 218 experience. In M. Malloch & G. McIvor (Eds.), *Women, punishment and social justice*. Abingdon: Routledge.

Belenky, M., Clinchy, B., Goldberger, N., & Tarule, J. (1986). *Women's ways of knowing*. New York: Basic Books.

Blanchette, K., & Brown, S. (2006). *The assessment and treatment of women offenders*. Chichester: John Wiley & Sons.

Blanchette, K., & Taylor, K. (2009). Reintegration of female offenders: Perspectives on 'what works'. *Corrections Today, 71*(6)

Bloom, B., Owen, B., & Covington, S. (2002). *Gender-responsive strategies: Research, practice, and guiding principles for women offenders*. Washington, DC: National Institute of Corrections.

Bowles, R., & Pradiptyo, R. (2005). *Young adults in the criminal justice system: Cost and benefit considerations*. York: Centre for Criminal Justice Economics and Psychology, University of York.

Brennan, T., Breitenbach, M., Dieterich, W., Salisbury, E., & Van Voorhis, P. (2012). Women's Pathways to Serious and Habitual Crime. A Person-Centred analysis Incorporating Gender Responsive Factors'. *Criminal Justice and Behaviour, 39*(9), 1481–1508.

Brown, J., & Heidensohn, F. (2000). *Gender and policing*. Basingstoke: Palgrave-Macmillan.

Cann, J. (2006). *Cognitive Skills Programs: Impact on Reducing Reconviction Among a Sample Of Female Prisoners*. Home Office Research Findings 276. London: Home Office Research Study.

Carlen, P. (2002). *Women and punishment. The struggle for justice*. Cullompton: Willan.

Chesney-Lind, M., & Pasco, L. (2013). *The female offender*. Thousand Oaks, CA: Sage.

Council of the European Union (2012). Report from the Commission to the Council and the European Parliament on the implementation, results and overall assessment of the 2010 European Year for Combating Poverty and Social Exclusion, Brussels.

Council of Europe Recommendation, Rec. (1997). 20, Adopted by the Committee of Ministers on 30 October 1997, at the 607th meeting of the Minister's Deputies, at: http://www.coe.int/t/dghl/standardsetting/media/doc/cm/rec(1997)020&expmem_EN.asp.

Council of Europe Recommendation Rec. (2003). 20 of the Committee of Ministers to member states concerning new ways of dealing with juvenile delinquency and the role of juvenile justice, Adopted by the Committee of Ministers on 24 September 2003 at the 853rd meeting of the Ministers' Deputies, at: https://wcd.coe.int/ViewDoc.jsp?id=70063.

Council of Europe Recommendation Rec. (2008). 11 of the Committee of Ministers to member states on the European Rules for juvenile offenders subject to sanctions or measures, Adopted by the Committee of Ministers on 5 November 2008 at the 1040th meeting of the Ministers' Deputies, at: https://wcd.coe.int/ViewDoc.jsp?id=1367113&Site=CM.

Correctional Service Canada (2002). Community Strategy for Women Offenders, Available at: http://www.csc-scc.gc.ca/publications/fsw/wos22/wos22-eng.shtml.

Corrections Victoria (2005–2006). *Better Pathways - Integrated Response to Women's Offending and Reoffending*, Department of Justice - Corrections Victoria, Melbourne, Policy Document, http://assets.justice.vic.gov.au/corrections/resources/ca8d074b-69494a2a9870f9614a821ef7/better_pathways_integrated_response_womens_offending_reoffending_policy%2bdocument.pdf. Accessed 20 June 2014.

Corston, J. (2007). *The Corston Report: A report by Baroness Jean Corston of a review of women with particular vulnerabilities in the criminal justice system*. London: Home Office.

Davidson, W. S., II, Redner, R., Admur, R., & Mitchell, C. (1990). *Alternative treatments for troubled youth: The case of diversion from the justice system*. New York, NY: Plenum Press.

Dowds, L. & Hedderman, C. (1997). The sentencing of men and women. In: C. Hedderman & L. Gelsthorpe (eds.) *Understanding the sentencing of women*, pp. 7–22. Home Office Research Study 170. London: Home Office.

Dünkel, F., & Pruin, I. (2012). Young adult offenders in juvenile and criminal justice systems in Europe. In F. Losel, A. Bottoms, & D. P. Farrington (Eds.), *Young offenders. Lost in transition?* (pp. 11–38). London: Routledge.

Jacomy-Vite, S. (2014). European Council for Juvenile Justice, NGO Section. *The Social Reintegration of Young Offenders as a Key Factor to Prevent Recidivism, IJJO Green Paper on Child-Friendly Justice, European Juvenile Justice Observatory*, Available at: http://issuu.com/ijjo/docs/green_paper_ngo_section_20012012_en.

Ezell, M., & Cohen, L. (2005). *Desisting from crime*. Oxford: Oxford University Press.

Farrington, D.P., Cold, J.W., Harnett, L., Jolliffe, D., Soteriou., N, Turner, R., et al. (2006). *Criminal careers up to age 50 and life success up to age 48: New findings from the Cambridge Study in Delinquent Development*. London: Home Office (Research Study no. 299).

Forsythe, L., & Adams, K. (2009). Mental health, abuse, drug use and crime: does gender matter? *Trends & Issues in Crime and Criminal Justice*, no. 384.

Gelsthorpe, L. (2001). Accountability: Difference and diversity in the delivery of community penalties. In A. Bottoms, L. Gelsthorpe, & S. Rex (Eds.), *Community penalties. Change and challenges*. Cullompton, Devon: Willan Publishing.

Gelsthorpe, L. (2010). What works with women offenders. In M. Herzog-Evans (Ed.), *Transnational criminology manual* (Vol. 3, pp. 223–235). Nijmegen, NL: Wolf Publishers.
Gelsthorpe, L. (2013). Working with women in probation: Will you, won't you, will you, won't you, wont' you join the dance. In P. Ugwudike & P. Raynor (Eds.), *What works in offender compliance*. Basingstoke: Palgrave Macmillan.
Gelsthorpe, G., & McIvor, G. (2007). Difference and diversity in probation. In L. Gelsthorpe & R. Morgan (Eds.), *Handbook of probation*. Cullompton, Devon: Willan Publishing.
Gelsthorpe, L., & Hedderman, C. (2012). Providing for women offenders: The risks of adopting a payment by results approach. *Probation Journal, 59*(4), 374–390.
Giedd, J. (2004). Structural magnetic resonance imaging of the adolescent brain. *Annals of the New York Academy of Sciences, 1021*, 77–85.
Gilbert, G. (1977). Alternate routes: A diversion project in the juvenile justice system. *Evaluation Quarterly, 1*(2), 301–318.
Government Department, UK, Youth Offending Team, at: https://www.gov.uk/youth-offending-team.
Government Department, Scotland, Local authorities to provide criminal justice social work, at: http://www.scotland.gov.uk/Topics/archive/law-order/offender-management/offender/community/16910.
Hannah-Moffat, K., & Shaw, M. (2003). The meaning of risk in women's prisons. In B. Bloom (Ed.), *Gendered justice. Addressing female offenders*. Durham, North Carolina: Carolina Academic Press.
Hedderman, C. (2010). Policy development in England and Wales. In R. Sheehan, G. McIvor, & C. Trotter (Eds.), *Working with women in the community*. Cullompton, Devon: Willan.
Hedderman, C (2012) *Empty Cells or Empty Words? Government policy on reducing the number of women going to prison*. Report for the Criminal Justice Alliance. London: Criminal Justice Alliance. http://www.criminaljusticealliance.org/docs/CJA_WomenPrisonReportFINAL.pdf.
Hedderman, C., Gunby, C., & Shelton, N. (2011). What women want: The importance of qualitative approaches in evaluating work with women offenders. *Criminology and Criminal Justice, 11*(1), 3–19.
Heidensohn, F., & Silvestri, M. (2012). Gender and crime. In M. Maguire, R. Morgan, & R. Reiner (Eds.), *The Oxford handbook of criminology* (5th ed.). Oxford: Oxford University Press.
Held, V. (2006). *The ethic of care: Personal, political, and global*. Oxford: Oxford University Press.
Hesbaek, A.-D. (2011). Denmark. In N. Gilbert, N. Parton, & M. Skivenes (Eds.), *Child protection systems*. Oxford: Oxford University Press.
Hollin, C., & Palmer, E. (Eds.). (2006). *Offending behaviour programs. Development, application, and controversies*. Chichester: Wiley.
Holloway, K., & Brookman, F. (2008). *An Evaluation of the Women's Turnaround Project*, Report prepared for NOMS Cymru, Centre for Criminology, University of Glamorgan, Pontypridd.
Howe, A. (1994). *Punish and critique. Towards a feminist analysis of penality*. London: Routledge.
Howell, J.C., Feld, B.C., Mears, D.P., Farrington, D.P., Loeber, R., & Petechuk, D. (2013). *Bulletin 5: Young Offenders and an Effective Response in the Juvenile and Adult Justice Systems: What Happens, What Should Happen, and What we need to Know*. U.S. Department of Justice. Available at: http://ncjrs.gov/pdffiles1/nij/grants/242935.pdf.
Kyvsgaard, B. (2004). Youth justice in Denmark. In M. Tonry & A. N. Doob (Eds.), *Youth crime and youth justice- Comparative and cross-national perspectives* (Crime and justice, Vol. 31, pp. 349–391). Chicago: University of Chicago Press.
Lauritsen, J., Heimer, K., & Lynch, J. (2009). Trends in the gender gap in violence: Re-evaluating NCVS and other evidence. *Criminology, 47*(2), 361–400.

Lawston, J. (2013). Prisons, gender responsive strategies and community sanctions: The expansion of punishment in the United States. In M. Malloch & G. McIvor (Eds.), *Women, punishment and social justice*. Abingdon: Routledge.

Lipsey, M. (2009). The primary factors that characterize effective interventions with juvenile offenders: A meta- analytic overview. *Victims and Offenders, 4*, 124–47.

Lipsey, M., & Cullen, F. (2007). The effectiveness of correctional rehabilitation: A review of systematic reviews. *Annual Review of Law and Social Science, 3*, 297–320.

Lipsey, M., Howell, J., Kelly, M., Chapman, G., & Carvr, D. (2010). *Improving the effectiveness of juvenile justice programs. New perspective on evidence-based practice.* Available at: http://cjjr.georgetown.edu/pdfs/ebp/ebppaper.pdf.

Lösel, F. (2012). What works in correctional treatment and rehabilitation for young adults. In F. Lösel, A. Bottoms, & D. Farrington (Eds.), *Young offenders. Lost in transition?* (pp. 74–112). London: Routledge.

Lösel, F., Bottoms, A., & Farrington, D. (2012). Introduction. In F. Lösel, A. Bottoms, & D. Farrington (Eds.), *Young offenders. Lost in transition?* (pp. 1–10). London: Routledge.

Martin, J., & Jurik, N. (1996). *Doing justice. Doing gender*. Thousand Oaks, CA: Sage.

Martin, J., Kautt, P., & Gelsthorpe, L. (2009). What works for women?: A comparison of community-based general offending programme completion. *British Journal of Criminology, 49*, 879–99.

Matravers, A. (1997). Women and the sexual abuse of children. *Forensic Update, 5*(1), 9–13.

McIvor, G., & Barry, M. (1998). *Social work and criminal justice volume 6: Probation*. Edinburgh: Stationery Office.

Modley, P., & Giguere, R. (2010). *Reentry considerations for women offenders*. Silver Spring, MD: Center for Effective Public Policy. http://cjinvolvedwomen.org/sites/all/documents/Ten_Truths.pdf.

Moffitt, T. (1993). 'Life-course persistent' and 'adolescent-limited'antisocial behaviour: A developmental taxonomy. *Psychological Review, 100*, 674–701.

Morash, M. (2010). *Women on probation and parole. A feminist critique of community programs and services*. Boston/Hanover: North Eastern University Press/University Press of New England.

National Institute Of Justice, Adolescent Diversion Project (Michigan State University): http://www.crimesolutions.gov/ProgramDetails.aspx?ID=332.

Patel, S., & Stanley, S. (2008). *The use of the community order and the suspended sentence order for women*. London: Centre for Crime and Justice Studies.

Prior, D., Farrow, K., Hughes, N., Kelly, G., Manders, G., White, S., et al. (2011). *Maturity; young adults and criminal justice*. Birmingham: Institute of Aplied Social Studies, School of Social Policy, University of Birmingham.

Robinson, G., & McNeil, F. (2008). Exploring the dynamics of compliance with community penalties. *Theoretical Criminology, 12*(4), 431–449.

Ross, R., & Fabiano, E. (1986). *Female offenders: Correctional afterthoughts*. Jefferson, NC: McFarland.

Shapland, J., Atkinson, A., Atkinson, H., Dignan, J., Edwards, L., Hibbert, J. et al. (2008). *Does restorative justice affect reconviction? The fourth report from the evaluation of three schemes.* Ministry of Justice Research Series 10/08. London: National Offender Management Service.

Shapland, J., Bottoms, A., Farrall, S., McNeill, F., Priede, C., & Robinson, G. (2012). *The quality of probation supervision A literature review*. University of Sheffield: Centre for Criminological Research.

Sheehan, R. (2011). Policy developments in Australia. In R. Sheehan, G. McIvor, & C. Trotter (Eds.), *Working with women in the community*. Cullompton, Devon: Willan Publishing.

Sheehan, R. (2013). Justice and community for women in transition in Victoria' Australia'. In M. Malloch & G. McIvor (Eds.), *Women, punishment and social justice: Human rights and social*. Abingdon: Routledge.

Sheehan, R., McIvor, G., & Trotter, C. (Eds.). (2007). *What works with women offenders*. Cullompton, Devon: Willan Publishing.

Sherman, L. W., & Strang, H. (2007). *Restorative justice. The evidence*. London: The Smith Institute.

Silvestri, M., & Crowther-Dowey, C. (2008). *Gender & crime*. London: Sage.

Smart, C. (1976). *Women, crime and criminology*. London: Routledge/Kegan Paul.

Snider, L. (2003). Constituting the punishable woman: Atavistic man incarcerates postmodern women. *British Journal of Criminology, 43*(2), 354–78.

Sowell, E. R., Delis, D., Stiles, J., & Jernigan, T. L. (2001). Improved memory functioning and frontal lobe maturation between childhood and adolescence: A structural MRI study. *Journal of the International Neuropsychological Society, 7*, 312–322.

Steffensmeier, D., Schwartz, J., Zhong, H., & Ackerman, J. (2005). An assessment of recent trends in girls' violence using diverse longitudinal sources: Is the gender gap closing? *Criminology, 43*(2), 355–406.

Steinberg, L., O'Brien, L., Kauffman, E., Graham, S., Woolard, J., & Banich, M. (2009). Age differences in future orientation and delay discounting. *Child Development, 80*(1), 28–44.

Stewart, J., Smith, D., & Stewart, G. (1994). *Understanding offending behaviour*. Harlow: Longman.

Strang, H., Sherman, L., Mayo-Wilson, E., Woods, D., & Ariel, B. (2013). *Restorative Justice Conferencing (RJC) Using Face-to-Face Meetings of Offenders and Victims: Effects on Offender Recidivism and Victim Satisfaction. A Systematic Review*. Available at: http://www.campbellcollaboration.org/lib/project/63/.

Sydney, L. (2005). Supervision of women defendants and offenders in the community, *Gender Responsive Strategies for Women Offenders* (pp. 1–23), http://nicic.org/pubs/2005/020419.pdf. Accessed 20 May 2014.

Transition to Adulthood, Young Adults and Criminal Justice: International Norms and Practices, at: http://www.t2a.org.uk/wp-content/uploads/2011/09/T2A-International-Norms-and-Practices.pdf.

Trotter, C., &Ward, T. (2012). Involuntary Clients, Pro-social Modelling and Ethics, *Ethics and Social Welfare*, iFirst Article .Accessed 17 September 2012.

Turner, S., &Trotter, C. (2010). *Case Management With Women Offenders: Literature Review*. Monash University, Aus., Criminal Justice Research Consortium

United Nations (UN). Universal Declaration of Human Rights, http://www.un.org/en/documents/udhr/.

United Nations (1985). United Nations Standard Minimum Rules for the Administration of Juvenile Justice ("The Beijing Rules"), General Assembly A/RES/40/33, 96th plenary meeting.

United Nations (1989). United Nations Convetions on the Rights of the Child, Available at: http://www.unicef.org.uk/Documents/Publication-pdfs/UNCRC_PRESS200910web.pdf.

United Nations (1990). United Nations Guidlines for the Prevention of Juvenile Delinquency (Riyadh Guidelines), General Assembly resolution 45/112. At: http://www.child-abuse.com/childhouse/childrens_rights/dci_del8.html.

United Nations (2000). *The World's Women 2000*, United Nations Statistics Division. United Nations Publications.

United Nations (2010). United Nations Rules for the Treatment of Women Prisoners and Non-custodial Measures for Women Offenders (the Bangkok Rules), General Assembly A/RES/65/229. Sixty-fifth session Agenda Item 105.

United Nations Interregional Crime and Justice Research Institute, Commonwealth Secretariat (1997). Promoting Probation Internationally.In: Ville, R., Zvekic, U., & Klaus, J.F. (Eds.) *Proceedings of the International Training Workshop on Probation* ,2–5 July 1997, Valetta, Malta, Publication No. 58, Rome/London.

Van Kalmthout, A., & Durnescu, I. (Eds.). (2008). *Probation in Europe*. Nijmegen: Wolf Legal Publishers.

Van Voorhis, P. (2010). Women's risk factors and their contributions to existing risk/needs assessment: The current status of a gender-responsive supplement. *Criminal Justice and Behaviour, 37*, 261–288.

Ward, T., & Fortune, C. A. (2013). The good lives model: Aligning risk reduction with promoting offenders' personal goals. *European Journal of Probation, 5*(2), 29–46.

Wilson, H. A., & Hoge, R. D. (2013). The effects of youth diversion programs on recidivism. *Criminal Justice and Behaviour, 40*(5), 497–518.

Women's Breakout: http://www.womensbreakout.org.uk/

Yates, J. (2007). Young offenders. In R. Canton & D. Hancock (Eds.), *Dictionary of probation and offender management* (pp. 331–332). Cullompton: Willan.

Zaplin, R. (Ed.). (1998). *Female offenders. Critical perspectives and effective interventions.* Gaithersburg, MD: Aspen Publishers.

Release Management for Female and Juvenile Prisoners. How Important Is Release Management in Prison for Crime Prevention?

Ineke Pruin

Abstract This chapter focuses on release preparation structures for juvenile and female prisoners that have been found to be an important part of effective resettlement strategies. Research results and international standards call for a holistic approach to resettlement that regards pre-release preparation and post-release aftercare as a uniform challenge that should be governed by the same overall strategic plan. Research often concentrates more on the post-release phase of resettlement, leaving out what has to be done on the inside to support new approaches and ideas, probably oftentimes under the assumption that enough has already been written about what happens in terms of preparation on the inside. Nonetheless, it is worthwhile taking a closer look at the recommendations and results from the prisoner resettlement debate that pertain to pre-release preparation. Regrettably, the literature on this topic is limited. The chapter starts with an overview of the special needs and requirements of female and juvenile offenders with respect to their release preparation. This is followed by a snapshot of the international recommendations relevant to the field of release from prison. The next section focuses on what research has found out about the effectiveness of prison release programmes. Finally, we look at how these findings have been put into practice, and whether we can identify good or promising practices in the literature.

1 Introduction

The issue of prisoner resettlement[1] has gained a lot of attention worldwide in recent years.[2] Debate has been invigorated by developments in the USA. There, a policy of "mass imprisonment" (Garland 2001) has resulted in the highest prisoner rates in

[1] In the US, the term "prisoner reentry" is more common. Terminology is discussed further in section 2 below).

[2] For an overview with a focus on England, see Hedderman (2007).

I. Pruin (✉)
University of Bern, Bern, Switzerland
e-mail: ineke.pruin@krim.unibe.ch

H. Kury et al. (eds.), *Women and Children as Victims and Offenders: Background, Prevention, Reintegration*, DOI 10.1007/978-3-319-28424-8_6

the world.[3] Since the beginning of the new millennium, the USA has been confronted with one consequence of their policy in particular: since most prisoners serve determinate sentences, there has been a continuous flow of people being released; people who need to be reintegrated into society, often after having served lengthy stints in prison. The USA have thus been in search of new concepts and strategies for effectively managing this flow,[4] and it so appears that Canada, Australia and all of Europe have joined in on the conversation.[5]

Criticism of the existing release structures has been rooted primarily in the very high rates of recidivism among persons released from prison. Recent German recidivism studies have found that approximately one in two adults and two in three young persons released from prison re-offend.[6] The risk of recidivism is at its highest in the time immediately following release, as the majority of re-offending occurs within 1 year of leaving custody.[7] These results show that reintegration is not being achieved for a large proportion of offenders released from prisons. Rather, some authors state that re-offending has dynamics of its own ("Eigendynamik der Rückfallkriminalität")[8] due to a very low degree of social integration in freshly released ex-offenders, that shows itself for instance when the label that is attached to "ex-prisoners" makes the search for employment arduous, and a resulting lack of structured routines and economic security make a return to offending much more likely.[9] These findings are particularly concerning in light of the relevant international human rights standards concerning release from prison.

It is obvious that, in many cases, the task of integrating ex-prisoners into society is a difficult one. To prevent new criminality, it is important to minimize possible risk factors that had already existed prior to incarceration. Additionally, imprisonment itself might have produced new risk factors such as homelessness, unemployment or broken social bonds. Prisons therefore face the challenge of preparing prisoners for life on the outside. Depending on the concrete issues or spheres of reintegration (housing, labour, health, debt, documentation, family ties etc.) the

---

[3] The USA regularly lead the table of countries with high prisoner rates. For an up-to-date overview see the respective data from Kings College London and EUROSTAT.

[4] Bumiller (2013), p. 15.

[5] Articles that seek to provide a comparative international overview of a subject are often limited by the terminological and linguistic limitations of their authors. Thus, this chapter covers literature on release preparation that has been published in English or German.

[6] Most recent German recidivism analyses measured a recidivism rate of 48 % for persons who have served unconditional prison sentences, and 69 % for young people who have served a youth prison sentence, see Jehle et al. (2010), p. 60. Similar figures have been measured for England, see Bateman et al. (2013), p. 11. For recidivism studies from Austria, see Bundesministerium für Justiz (2009). For insight into the high methodological standards and requirements for reliable recidivism research, see Jehle (2007).

[7] For Germany, see Jehle (2007), p. 237. In England and Wales in the year 2009, 71.9% of juvenile offenders below the age of 18 years were reconvicted within 1 year of their release, see Gray (2011), p. 239.

[8] Kerner and Janssen (1983), Hermann and Kerner (1988).

[9] See e.g. Wirth (2006) or Matt and Hentschel (2009), each with further references.

time that this preparation needs can be more or less. Research and practice have found that certain conditions are associated with good release preparation, such as providing/supporting vocational training, the (partial) opening of custodial settings or the provision of personal support throughout the whole release process, including cooperation between services inside and outside prisons. Many of these conditions (or factors) have been laid out in international recommendations on imprisonment and/or release. Female and juvenile offenders can be regarded as particularly vulnerable groups in this regard. They have special needs that stem from special, often highly individualized contexts, and release structures have to be adapted to reflect their specific situations. Since women can be seen as "the fastest-growing segment of the U.S. prison population" postulations on "gender responsive" prison programmes have gained more weight.[10]

This chapter focuses on release preparation structures for juvenile and female prisoners that have been found to be an important part of effective resettlement strategies. Research results and international standards call for a holistic approach to resettlement that regards pre-release preparation and post-release aftercare as a uniform challenge that should be governed by the same overall strategic plan. However, the phase and influence of post-release aftercare have been omitted from this chapter for the most part—aftercare, with a special focus on women and juveniles, is covered in detail in another chapter of this handbook (see *Hagemann* in this volume). Focusing on release preparation in the context of resettlement seems justified. Research often focuses more on the post-release phase of resettlement, leaving out what has to be done on the inside to support new approaches and ideas, probably oftentimes under the assumption that enough has already been written about what happens in terms of preparation on the inside. Nonetheless, it is worthwhile taking a closer look at the recommendations and results from the prisoner resettlement debate that pertain to pre-release preparation. It cannot be assumed that there is a deep or wide reservoir of literature that focusses particularly on women and juveniles in this context. Therefore, this chapter starts with an overview of the special needs and requirements of female and juvenile offenders with respect to their release preparation. This is followed by a snapshot of the international recommendations relevant to the field of release from prison. Chapter "Women in Criminal Justice Systems and the Added Value of the UN Bangkok Rules" then focuses on what research has found out about the effectiveness of prison release programmes. In the fourth chapter we look at how these findings have been put into practice, and whether we can identify good or promising practices in the literature.

---

[10] Thompson (2008), p. 45, see also Bumiller (2013), p. 13.

2 Special Needs and Requirements of Juvenile and Female Prisoners with Respect to Their Release

Looking at empirical knowledge about juvenile and female prisoners, the discussion about adequate terminology for describing the aims of the release process becomes especially relevant. The terms commonly used to describe them are "resettlement", "re-entry" or "rehabilitation". This terminology has already been discussed in relation to male adult offenders,[11] with prominent reference to the fact that many adult prisoners had not been "settled" prior to imprisonment, and rarely have adequate social structures to "re-enter". These findings are particularly valid for juvenile and female prisoners, who appear to experience a high degree of social exclusion.[12]

According to empirical research,[13] it is safe to assume that imprisoned women in general have received less schooling and less vocational training[14] compared to non-imprisoned women, and that they had often been unemployed and lacked economic security prior to their imprisonment.[15] Accordingly, vocational training and/or education are particularly important elements of successful release preparation strategies.[16] Due to their (usually) comparatively small number, female prisoners are often placed in small units or small institutions for women, which in turn cannot provide adequate training and educational infrastructures. Ultimately, this results in significant shortcomings in the provision of adequate, targeted and individualized training for imprisoned women.

Furthermore, imprisoned women have oftentimes themselves been victims of violence. A small sample study from Germany[17] revealed almost disturbing results: 91 % of interviewed women had experienced physical violence. 57 % reported to have been victims of sexual violence, of them 72.3 % had been raped.[18] In the majority of cases the aggressor was a partner or ex-partner.[19] These data are similar to findings from other countries,[20] and demonstrate that providing access to

[11] For Europe: Raynor (2004), Bateman et al. (2013), p. 9. For the U.S.: Bumiller (2013), p. 16. A commonly used definition for resettlement is "the process of reintegration back into the community in a positive and managed way" (Mead 2007, p. 268) after serving a prison sentence, see Durnescu (2011), p. 4.

[12] According to Toth (2005), p. 140.

[13] See for an overview, Opsal and Foley (2013), Holtfreter and Wattanaporn (2014), p. 42.

[14] For example for Germany: Schröttle and Müller (2004), p. 17 f.

[15] Cruells and Igareda (2006), p. 5.

[16] See also Gelsthorpe and Sharpe (2007), p. 200 with further references.

[17] Based on a research project conducted by the Ministry of Family, Women and Youth, see BMFSFJ (2004).

[18] See Schröttle and Müller (2004), p. 27 f.

[19] See Schröttle and Müller (2004), p. 33.

[20] See for example for the U.S.: Bumiller (2013), p. 18 and some data for Europe in Cruells and Igareda (2006), p. 12.

qualified psychological treatment is an important element of an individual's preparation for release and successful (re-)integration. In general, imprisoned women seem to have more health problems than the average of women outside prison.[21] Special attention is given in the literature to the "alarming number of women who have hepatitis C and human immunodeficiency virus (HIV)".[22] Different international analyses have revealed that female prisoners are very likely to have drug problems.[23]

It is common to observe that treatment programmes in prisons are designed for men who constitute the absolute majority of prisoners. US American-research however has revealed that some judges have sent female offenders to prison because they regarded prison as the best place for the treatment of women with addiction problems, while community-based programmes have been seen as too difficult for women to comply with.[24] According to a European research project on six countries,[25] only a minority of women prisoners receive adequate psychological treatment.[26] In some countries, there is the somewhat special situation that women are often only sent to prison because alternative sanctions in the community are not available, or are not implemented or designed for women.[27] At the same time, research on recidivism reveals that women are less likely to re-offend regardless of sentence,[28] which would theoretically make them even more suitable for community sentencing.

The literature furthermore makes frequent reference to the significance of family responsibilities as a relevant gender factor for women in prison.[29] Care has to be organized for the children of imprisoned mothers, and prisons face the challenge of allowing imprisoned mothers to adequately maintain family ties while inside, or to recover them during release preparation.[30] Especially when children have been taken into care and after long stays in prison, the reestablishment of relationships between children and their released mothers seems to be particularly difficult.[31] It is

---

[21] See data from Germany in Schröttle and Müller 2004, p. 43, where the interviewed women were younger than the comparison group and were therefore supposed to have had less health-related problems.

[22] Bumiller (2013), p. 18 with further references, Haverkamp (2011), p. 191 with further references.

[23] Thompson (2008) p. 45 with further references, Gelsthorpe and Sharpe (2007), p. 200 with further references.

[24] Bumiller (2013), p. 19 with further references.

[25] Spain, Germany, England and Wales, Italy, France and Hungary, see Toth (2005).

[26] Haverkamp (2011), p. 186 with references to Toth (2005), pp. 26 f., 32 ff.

[27] In this context see Kendall (2013), p. 35 with a citation of the Chief Inspector of Prisons in England and Wales from the year 2012: "There are too many women in prison who simply do not need to be there".

[28] Worrall and Gelsthorpe (2009), p. 335.

[29] Cruells and Igareda (2006), p. 8 ff.; Gelsthorpe and Sharpe (2007), p. 201.

[30] Cruells and Igareda (2006), p. 9.

[31] Gelsthorpe and Sharpe (2007), p. 206.

especially challenging in this respect that women, due to their small numbers, are often in prisons far away from their families and friends.[32] Housing and accommodation seem to pose particular problems for those women who can or should not return to their old places of residence.[33]

The situation for juvenile prisoners seems to be comparably difficult. In general, juvenile offenders in custodial institutions have experienced multiple forms of social exclusion.[34] They often come from families with low socio-economic status, have frequently been excluded from school for deviant behaviour, often exhibit a low level of academic attainment or are school dropouts, and have oftentimes experienced placements in out-of-home care.[35] They may well lack adequate, stable social bonds to which they can return, and are likely to face even more difficult economic circumstances than their adult counterparts as they frequently lack vocational training.

Many juvenile prisoners have experienced social exclusion long before they wind up in prison. This sense of disadvantage might be likely to undermine their motivation to successfully resettle to the community upon release.[36] According to research from England and Wales, "half of young people in custody lived in deprived households" and "nearly 40 % had been on the child protection register and/or had experienced abuse or neglect".[37] Research results show that juveniles often cannot return to their original family after their release from prison.[38] Therefore, housing issues are of particular relevance for preparing those juveniles for release who had lacked adequate accommodation and living circumstances prior their imprisonment.[39] Education and training are vital factors in preparing juveniles for release. It should be known that there are special funding bodies for education/training programmes in prisons and detention centres, for example linked to the educational system or the youth welfare or family law system, so the justice system need not bear the entire financial burden for providing such programmes (e.g. Germany, Sweden, Denmark).

To conclude, the research findings about women and juveniles in prison show in particular that the resettlement of these groups and their preparation for release should even less than in the case of male adults concentrate on the question of how to reconnect them to their old lives. In many cases, release preparation can imply

---

[32] Gelsthorpe and Sharpe (2007), p. 206.

[33] Maguire and Nolan (2007), p. 159 with further references.

[34] Jacomy-Vité (2011), p. 9; Bateman et al. (2013), p. 11.

[35] For the case of England, the Barrow Cadbury Trust (2005) found that almost half of the young prisoners (18–21) had previously been in local authority care.

[36] Gray (2011), p. 236. All internationally compared justice systems worldwide allow juvenile offenders to be sent to at least one form of custody, be it a youth prison (organized by the justice system) or a closed institution (organized by the welfare system). See Dünkel and Stańdo-Kawecka (2011).

[37] Gray (2011), p. 237.

[38] For England, see for example Bateman et al. (2013), p. 15.

[39] Maguire and Nolan (2007), pp.160 ff.

that existing structures need to be reassessed and new perspectives need to be fostered so as to build an adequate social environment. It is highly likely that reflecting on the past of juveniles and women in prison will bring many problems and risk factors to light that can and should be addressed so as to maximize prospects for successful reintegration.

3 International Recommendations

At the international level, several recommendations are devoted to the treatment of prisoners. The Standard Minimum Rules for the Treatment of Prisoners, elaborated by the First United Nations Congress on the Prevention of Crime and the Treatment of Offenders (1955), and subsequently adopted, and amended by the Economic and Social Council (1957 and 1977), are the most prominent in this regard.[40] The most important regulations with respect to release preparation postulate that prisoners have to be prepared for their return to society, either via a pre-release regime or by release on trial (art. 60). "From the beginning of a prisoner's sentence consideration shall be given to his future after release and he shall be encouraged and assisted to maintain or establish such relations with persons or agencies outside the institution as may promote the best interests of his family and his own social rehabilitation" (art. 80). "Services and agencies, governmental or otherwise, which assist released prisoners to re-establish themselves in society shall ensure, so far as is possible and necessary, that released prisoners be provided with appropriate documents and identification papers, have suitable homes and work to go to, are suitably and adequately clothed having regard to the climate and season, and have sufficient means to reach their destination and maintain themselves in the period immediately following their release (art. 81 (1))."

The UN Basic Principles for the Treatment of Prisoners from 1990 (A/RES/45/111 (1990)) add that "conditions shall be created enabling prisoners to undertake meaningful remunerated employment which will facilitate their reintegration into the country's labour market and permit them to contribute to their own financial support and to that of their families" (no. 8). "Prisoners shall have access to the health services available in the country without discrimination on the grounds of their legal situation" (no. 9). "With the participation and help of the community and social institutions, and with due regard to the interests of victims, favourable conditions shall be created for the reintegration of the ex-prisoner into society under the best possible conditions" (no. 10).

The United Nations Rules for the Treatment of Women Prisoners and Non-custodial Measures for Women Offenders (the Bangkok Rules) of 2011 focus especially on women in the criminal justice system. With respect to release issues, they highlight that "prison authorities shall encourage and, where possible,

---

[40] All UN-recommendations can be found under http://www.unodc.org/unodc/en/justice-and-prison-reform/index.html?ref=menuside.

also facilitate visits to women prisoners as an important prerequisite to ensuring their mental well-being and social reintegration" (rule 43). The Rules furthermore highlight options like home leave, open prisons, halfway houses and community-based programmes and services, which should be utilized "to the maximum possible extent for women prisoners, to ease their transition from prison to liberty, to reduce stigma and to re-establish their contact with their families at the earliest possible stage" (rule 45). "Prison authorities, in cooperation with probation and/or social welfare services, local community groups and non-governmental organizations, shall design and implement comprehensive pre- and post-release reintegration programmes which take into account the gender-specific needs of women" (rule 46).

Focusing on child and juvenile offenders, there are several other international standards. The UN Convention on the Rights of the Child (CRC) is the most prominent in this regard.[41] In Art. 40 it sets reintegration as the ultimate goal of juvenile justice.

The United Nations Standard Minimum Rules for the Administration of Juvenile Justice (1985) (The Beijing Rules)[42] do not include special rules for the preparation of prisoners for release, but do refer to the UN Basic Principles for the Treatment of Prisoners (rule 27). They furthermore manifest that "young female offenders placed in an institution deserve special attention as to their personal needs and problems. They shall by no means receive less care, protection, assistance, treatment and training than young male offenders. Their fair treatment shall be ensured" (Rule 26.4) and that "conditional release from an institution shall be used by the appropriate authority to the greatest possible extent, and shall be granted at the earliest possible time" (Rule 28.1).

The United Nations Rules for the Protection of Juveniles Deprived of Their Liberty (The Havana Rules, A/RES/45/113 (1990))[43] highlight the juvenile's right to education, especially in rule 38: "Every juvenile of compulsory school age has the right to education suited to his or her needs and abilities and designed to prepare him or her for return to society. Such education should be provided outside the detention facility in community schools wherever possible and, in any case, by qualified teachers through programmes integrated with the education system of the country so that, after release, juveniles may continue their education without difficulty. Special attention should be given by the administration of the detention facilities to the education of juveniles of foreign origin or with particular cultural or ethnic needs. Juveniles who are illiterate or have cognitive or learning difficulties should have the right to special education." Other recommendations concerning vocational training and work can be found in rules 39–46. Rule 45 emphasizes the relevance of job preparation in the process of release preparation: "Wherever possible, juveniles should be provided with the opportunity to perform remunerated

[41] 1577 UNTS 3, adopted by General Assembly resolution 44/25 of 20 November 1989.

[42] A/RES/40/33, adopted by General Assembly resolution 40/33 of 29 November 1985.

[43] A/RES/45/113.

labour, if possible within the local community, as a complement to the vocational training provided in order to enhance the possibility of finding suitable employment when they return to their communities. The type of work should be such as to provide appropriate training that will be of benefit to the juveniles following release. The organization and methods of work offered in detention facilities should resemble as closely as possible those of similar work in the community, so as to prepare juveniles for the conditions of normal occupational life."

The relevance of contact to the outside world is laid down in rule 59: "Every means should be provided to ensure that juveniles have adequate communication with the outside world, which is an integral part of the right to fair and humane treatment and is essential to the preparation of juveniles for their return to society. Juveniles should be allowed to communicate with their families, friends and other persons or representatives of reputable outside organizations, to leave detention facilities for a visit to their home and family and to receive special permission to leave the detention facility for educational, vocational or other important reasons. Should the juvenile be serving a sentence, the time spent outside a detention facility should be counted as part of the period of sentence." A special paragraph of the Rules is dedicated to the "return to the community" in rules 79 and 80: "All juveniles should benefit from arrangements designed to assist them in returning to society, family life, education or employment after release. Procedures, including early release, and special courses should be devised to this end" (rule 79). "Competent authorities should provide or ensure services to assist juveniles in re-establishing themselves in society and to lessen prejudice against such juveniles. These services should ensure, to the extent possible, that the juvenile is provided with suitable residence, employment, clothing, and sufficient means to maintain himself or herself upon release in order to facilitate successful reintegration. The representatives of agencies providing such services should be consulted and should have access to juveniles while detained, with a view to assisting them in their return to the community" (rule 80).

There are also numerous significant European guidelines and recommendations that in part also make reference to release preparation. The Council of Europe's Recommendation Rec(2006)2 on the European Prison Rules[44] contains a special section on female prisoners (nr. 34.1–34.3), but also statements about release preparation in general, for instance its emphasis on regime relaxations as an element of prison life and sentence planning.[45]

Both Council of Europe Recommendation Rec (2003)22 on conditional release (parole)[46] and Recommendation CM/Rec(2010)1 on the European Probation Rules[47] address issues of release management. The ERJOSSM make detailed

[44] Adopted by the Committee of Ministers on 11 January 2006.

[45] Haverkamp (2011) has empirically researched the situation of female prisoners in Germany against the backdrop of the European Prison Rules.

[46] Adopted by the Committee of Ministers on 24 September 2003.

[47] Adopted by the Committee of Ministers on 20 January 2010.

recommendations for the management of the release of juvenile prisoners that are highlighted in the further course of this chapter.

4 The Importance of Release Preparation According to Criminological Research Results

Although the body of evidence still seems to be far from complete,[48] we can nonetheless speak of validated criminological research results on the effectiveness of offender treatment programmes, which do indeed allow some statements and assumptions to be made about the effectiveness of resettlement strategies. If we concentrate on the question of what this body of research allows us to say about release preparation, we find the following results:

4.1 "What Works": Results with Respect to Release Preparation

After *Martinson's* (1974) results on successful rehabilitation programmes were interpreted as implying that "nothing works", in the US in particular but also in other places, policies were inspired by the "tough on crime" philosophy with its focus on punishment and deterrence instead of treatment.

Ever since, criminological research has felt even more compelled to prove that offender treatment works. The focus on so called "evidence-based" practices in criminal justice organizations started with the work of *Sherman* and his colleagues and their *Maryland Scale of Scientific Methods* (Sherman et al. 1997). This influential research line is very much connected to the terminology of "what works". *Sherman* and his colleagues conducted a meta-analysis on crime prevention programmes in institutional settings, among them criminal justice settings, but also schools, families or labour markets. They looked at the results from prior research studies on crime prevention programmes, and they rated these studies on a scientific methods score of one through five. Level five studies used the "golden standard" of random assignment and large samples, while level one studies show correlation between a type or level of programme and an outcome at a single point in time. The idea was that the scores should help to reflect the level of confidence one can place in the evaluation's conclusions about cause and effect (Petersilia 2004, p. 6). "What works" was defined by at least two level-three evaluations (level three means that the study employed some kind of control or comparison group) and these evaluations had to state that the intervention was effective. What does not

[48] The challenges of research on resettlement have been summarized by Wincup and Hucklesby (2007).

work was defined by at least two level-three evaluations drawing that conclusion, while "what is promising" was identified as findings with low level of certainty but marked by some empirical basis. Everything not fitting into these categories was labelled as "unknown". The idea behind this research was to help policy and practice to focus on programmes or interventions that have been proven as effective in reaching the desired results, and not to make decisions based only on "having a good feeling".[49]

MacKenzie[50] used *Sherman's* methodology and the "what works"-approach for the corrections system. She and her colleagues identified 184 correctional evaluations (conducted between 1978 and 1998) that employed a methodology that could be rated at a level of 3 or higher (which means that the study employed some kind of control or comparison group). She identified some types of programmes for prisoners as "working" to reduce offender recidivism. With respect to the release preparation of prisoners, she highlighted therapeutic programmes in prison using the concept of therapeutic communities and combining it with follow-up treatment in the community as being effective with respect to reductions in recidivism rates. Another important finding with respect to release preparation was that programmes that focussed on finding employment in the community after release were proven to be effective. Preparation through programmes that offer adult basic education and transitional programmes providing individualized employment preparation and services for high risk offenders was categorized as promising.

The research team of *Seiter* and *Kadela* (2003) used a similar approach for the review of evaluations of special re-entry programmes. They looked at re-entry programmes that specifically focus on the transition from prison to the community or initiate treatment in a prison setting and link with a community programme to provide continuity of care. Within this broad definition, they only included programmes that had an outcome evaluation. They found 28 programme evaluations that fit their re-entry definition. 19 of those programme evaluations included a control or comparison group (i.e. they met level 3 criteria as defined by the Maryland Scale). Out of these 19 evaluations, 10 were drug treatment programme evaluations. These numbers show what it means if we limit the "what works" debate to programmes with outcome evaluations using strict criteria—in the same time period, hundreds of work release programmes, halfway houses or pre-release classes must have been implemented in the US that could not come into the focus of that piece of re-entry research because they had not been evaluated at all, or were not evaluated according to the standards.[51]

Seiter and *Kadela*[52] identified vocational training and work release programmes as being effective in reducing recidivism. Another finding with respect to release preparation was that halfway houses that prepare ex-prisoners to a life outside in an

[49] MacKenzie (2014), p. 1472.

[50] See MacKenzie (2006).

[51] Petersilia (2004).

[52] Seiter and Kadela (2003).

open institutional setting and some drug treatment programs combined with intensive aftercare were effective in reducing recidivism. However, the small number of projects within the scope of this evaluation forces the conclusion (made by the researchers themselves) that more evaluations of current programmes are needed for a better analysis.[53]

We can conclude that the "what works" approach provides us with some results in relation to prisoner resettlement that are based on a small percentage of all programmes, but which nonetheless indicate that release preparation works, or is at least promising for reducing recidivism after release.

4.2 Release Preparation in the RNR Model

Another line of criminological research is based on different disciplinary traditions and methodologies and does not focus on programmes as such, but more on the individuals within the programmes and looks at questions like why the programme is more effective for some individuals than for others.[54]

This approach does not restrict its scope to programmes that have been formally evaluated with a high-level evaluation, but looks at the results of evaluations that used different techniques, such as interviews or insights from clinical experience. Researchers following this approach usually do not use the "what works" terminology, and speak instead about "principles" or "guidelines". One conclusion within this line of research is that the effectiveness of treatment programmes is dependent on a variety of so called "moderators" of programme effects that include offender factors (such as risk level or motivation), the treatment context (like staff skills, the continuity of support or the institutional climate) and evaluation methods. This makes it very unlikely that specific programmes or interventions will "work" in any context and in any place.

A very influential piece of research in this context is the well-known risk-need-responsivity approach of *Andrews* and *Bonta* (2010).[55] The RNR-approach is based on three main principles for successful offender treatment: The Risk principle states that the intensity of interventions should match the offenders risk level. Research has found that treatment (especially cognitive behavioural programmes) can have a positive impact on higher-risk offenders, and lower-risk offenders may actually do worse if exposed to treatment with higher-risk offenders. Therefore, low-risk

[53] Petersilia (2004), p. 6.

[54] Geographically, this line of research started in Canada, but is nowadays also strong in Australia and the UK, whereas the "what works" debate is rather influenced and led by researchers from the United States.

[55] According to Lloyd and Serin (2014), p. 3303, the RNR-approach is "the guiding principle worldwide". Meta-analyses have found support for the efficacy of RNR-based treatment programmes in reducing recidivism among general and sexual offenders (e.g. Lösel and Schmucker 2005).

offenders should receive less intense intervention, whereas high-risk offenders should be subjected to intensive treatment. The Needs principle says that interventions should target criminogenic needs, also known as dynamic risk factors. Those factors are causally related to offending and are changeable. They include, for example, negative emotion, pro-offending attitudes, inconsistent employment or substance misuse. The Responsivity principle involves matching the style and mode of interventions to the offender's learning style and abilities. The offender's cognitive abilities, learning styles, and other characteristics have to be considered and treatment has to be delivered accordingly. *Andrews* and *Bonta* confirmed their results both in the context of female[56] and juvenile[57] offenders.

They also conducted a meta-analysis of treatment studies and tried to "translate" the results and the risk-need-responsivity model to the practice of prison and probation work. The "evidence based" principles that have been formulated in this context (Andrews and Bonta 2010, Lowenkamp et al. 2006) have been summarized for the context of reentry by *Petersilia*[58] and allow us to conclude that release preparation as such plays an important role for the successful resettlement of prisoners. The research results demonstrate that programme strategies and the professional approach are an important factor for the effectiveness of those programmes. They clearly state that intensive prison treatment interventions should be used primarily with higher-risk offenders, treatment services should then be behavioural in nature, reinforcements in the programme should be largely positive, not negative, and services should be intensive, lasting 3–12 months (depending on need) and occupying 40–70 % of the offender's time during the course of the programme.

Interventions should, whenever possible, be conducted in the community, because the effects of rehabilitation programmes in the community are higher compared to those inside prison.[59] However, certain aspects of release preparation inside prison are likely to increase the effectiveness of prison programmes: In terms of staffing, there is a need to match styles and modes of treatment service to the learning styles of the offender that in turn are connected with his/her characteristics, for instance his/her intelligence. The specific officer-offender interaction is of great value. The use of empathy, problem-solving strategies and a pro-social approach can reduce recidivism: *Taxman*[60] outlined a special strategy for release preparation and found that recidivism rates of offenders supervised by staff using such methods were about 30 % lower than offenders supervised by staff not trained in this strategy.[61]

[56] Dowden and Andrews (1999a), Andrews and Dowden (1999).

[57] Dowden and Andrews (1999b).

[58] See Petersilia (2004, 2014).

[59] Selection bias has to be observed because community treatment programmes are in general more likely to be offered to offenders with a lower risk of reoffending.

[60] Taxman (2004).

[61] Alexander et al. (2014), p. 3975.

In the context of this research approach, the results of the evaluation of the "Serious and Violent Offender Reentry Initiative (SVORI)" in the USA is of particular interest. SVORI established 89 programmes to improve criminal justice, employment, education, health and housing outcomes for exiting prisoners.[62] The funded projects had to have a three-phase continuum of services that began during the period of incarceration, intensified just before release and during the early months after release and continued for several years after release.

One focus of the evaluation was the question whether the released offenders received the preparation and the services they needed. The results revealed a discrepancy in service delivery between what was intended and what was actually provided at the programme level, and what was needed and what was actually received at the individual level, so that the researchers came to the result that the programmes were not fully implemented (Visher and Travis 2012, p. 698).

With respect to programme outcomes, the evaluations revealed that SVORI participants did better than non-SVORI control groups on self-reported criminal behaviour, employment, substance use and housing. But recidivism outcomes based on official measures were not significantly improved for adult male SVORI participants in the evaluation.

4.3 Release Preparation and Desistance Research

A third line of research that provides some insight into effective release preparation strategies comes from the traditional sociological perspective of attributing crime to social conditions.

Based on desistance research,[63] this research focuses on the conditions for an inner change of an individual. Social bonds or ties to social institutions are assumed to be keys to successful desistance from crime and therefore it is expected that giving people opportunities to form these bonds can reduce their criminal activity. According to *Maruna's* research on desistance, a person must first be cognitively ready to use these social ties and bonds, and in many cases this requires a change in cognitive reasoning and attitudes. According to *Sampson* and *Laub*, human agency plays a major role in the desistance process, because men who desisted played an active role in their desistance process through making explicit choices to disengage from crime.

The so-called "strength based" approaches to working with offenders aim to create competencies in offenders rather than looking for risk factors and criminogenic needs (and aim at reducing risk more indirectly, Ward et al. 2014, p. 1967) and integrate the aim of motivating and engaging offenders in the

[62] Visher and Travis (2012), p. 697.

[63] E.g. Laub and Sampson (2003), Maruna (2001), Giordano et al. (2002), McNeill (2006), Paternoster and Bushway (2009).

rehabilitation process. They furthermore highlight the importance of the relationship between the offender and the person who is working with him, as well as the attitudes the probation officer or the person responsible for the project is offering.

Release preparation should therefore not only focus on criminogenic risks, but should instead provide individual support in achieving personal goals. Supporting the released prisoner with good social structures outside (such as housing, satisfying employment, or drug treatment) is seen as essential for successful resettlement. Likewise, it is vital that the community outside supports and reinforces the desistance process of the released offender (Ward et al. 2014, p. 1970).

As this approach is not really a theory and more a rehabilitation framework, it cannot be evaluated as such. Nonetheless, there have been some evaluations that give support to the notion that inner change is a significant factor for the effectiveness of rehabilitation programmes, and that good social structures have a major impact on recidivism:

For example, research has found that programmes focusing on the formulation of positive goals came to better results than programmes targeting risk-avoidance. A study by *Marshal* and his colleagues showed that a confrontative therapeutic approach had a negative impact on the motivation of offenders to change. In comparison, empathy, warmth, support and a certain degree of directness lead to more positive developments. *Lipsey* (1995) conducted a meta-analysis on treatment programmes for juvenile offenders and concluded that the most effective factor in reducing re-offending rates was employment.[64] In general, many interventions providing increased social opportunities have not been found to have a direct impact on recidivism.[65] But research results raise questions as to whether those results might be attributed to the poor practical implementation of many programmes.

Lewis et al. (2006) concluded the results of seven resettlement projects for short term prisoners in England and Wales (where women are highly represented, see Gelsthorpe and Sharpe 2007, p. 199). The main aim of these projects was to facilitate a successful transition from custody back into the community, for example by assisting them with practical problems (such as lack of accommodation). The study showed that the continuity of services "through the gate" is important to follow up work begun in custody, and that release preparation by professionals trained to address thinking skills and practical problems might be central to an effective resettlement strategy.

[64] See Petersilia (2014), p. 1472.

[65] MacKenzie (2014), p. 1475. According to desistance literature, it is questionable whether a new offence is a sign of ineffectiveness of a strategy, because failures can be regarded as a normal development within the process of desistance.

4.4 Conclusions for the Release Preparation of Women and Juvenile Offenders

If we look at the research results, we find that all different research approaches highlight the importance of release preparation for the effective resettlement of prisoners. We cannot identify release preparation strategies that work universally in all circumstances with all prisoners in all settings. We can, however, formulate factors that, according to today's state of research, make it more likely that release preparation can affect the successful reintegration of offenders in a positive way.[66] Release preparation programmes should be oriented as much as possible towards the life in the community and (as opposed to institutional settings) involve community services and institutions. Intensive in-prison treatment with cognitive-behavioural treatment techniques should be reserved for those prisoners with high risk levels (determined via assessment instruments).

Release preparation programmes should focus on behavioural outcomes, target criminogenic needs and use positive reinforcement. They should match therapist and programme to the specific learning styles and characteristics of individual offenders, begin treatment in prison and provide continuity in the community.[67] "Case management" is regarded as being of particular relevance in this context: sentence planning processes shall identify resettlement needs, and during imprisonment, treatment programmes, including work and training programmes, should be oriented towards those needs.[68] With the involvement of the communities, they should support cognitive transformation and offer environmental opportunities. Institutional relaxations play an important role. The possibilities of prison leave and open prisons should be used from the beginning of the prison sentence onwards, and their use should be intensified in the 6–9 months immediately preceding release, in order to adequately prepare for life on the outside. The selection of staff also seems to be very important. Staff have to be committed to the programmes' aims and have to be able to motivate and to express empathy, warmth and support. Special emphasis should be given to the implementation phase of prison release programmes and strategies.

4.4.1 Specific Conclusions for Women

Gelsthorpe and Sharpe (2007) have combined these general results on release preparation with the special risks and criminogenic needs of female prisoners, and analysed further research results on women and their release from prison.

[66] See also UNODOC (2012), especially chapters 4,7 and 8.

[67] Wincup and Hucklesby (2007) describe, as a consensus, that "the ideal model for the provision of resettlement services is that they are provided "through the prison gate", meaning both in prison and in the community" (p. 44, with further references).

[68] Wincup and Hucklesby 2007, p. 44.

They point out that many released women have accommodation and housing problems, and that state or non-governmental institutions oftentimes focus their programmes on men. Substance misuse problems, inappropriate social networks and a lack of emotional support in particular have to be targeted in the planning and implementation of prison release programmes for women. They also highlighted the importance of training and employment in the release preparation of female prisoners.[69] Their key message is that the specific situation of women offenders needs a coordinated multi-agency response which has to be "gender-informed" or "gender-sensitive"[70] and adapted to women's learning styles.[71]

UNODOC 2008[72] tries to "translate" this theoretical background and the international recommendations concerning work in women's prisons and postulates for prison release preparation programmes that they require "close liaison between social agencies and services, as well as relevant community organizations and prison administrations during sentence. In addition, there needs to be a programme of assistance to prepare for release close to the date of release (often starting 1–2 months prior to the release date), to ensure that the social, psychological and medical support needs of the prisoner are met and continue uninterrupted after prison. Activities undertaken in prison need to be linked to services outside to ensure continuum of care and monitoring of released prisoners. (...) Due to the particular gender related difficulties women are likely to face following imprisonment, prison authorities should cooperate with probation services, social welfare departments and NGOs to design comprehensive pre- and post-release reintegration programmes for women. Assistance provided should cover housing and employment needs, taking into account the parental status and caring responsibilities of the women, parenting skills, psychological support and continued treatment for any substance addiction and other health problems. Efforts to support and strengthen relationships between the released prisoner and her family members (as well as others who may have been caring for her children) are also important to minimize the difficulties likely to be encountered following release, due to the different expectations of both sides. Prison authorities should utilize options such as open prisons and half-way houses, to the maximum possible extent for female prisoners, to ease their transition from prison to liberty and to re-establish contact between female prisoners and their families at the earliest possible stage" (UNODOC 2008, p. 64).

[69] Gelsthorpe and Sharpe (2007), pp. 200 ff. with further references.

[70] Gelsthorpe and Sharpe (2007), p. 200.

[71] Gelsthorpe and Sharpe (2007), p. 208.

[72] See also UNODOC (2012), chapter 8.

4.4.2 Specific Conclusions for Juveniles

The conclusions for juvenile prisoners are comparable to those for women. For this specific group of prisoners, efforts should be devoted in particular to education and vocational training. Providing respective programmes and strategies could in fact be easier for young offenders than for adult offenders, because in many countries, besides the justice system, the youth welfare system is often also responsible, which in turn provides an additional (and in many cases better) source of funding. Since juveniles require support in dealing with public agencies and institutions, the importance of providing them with continuous care and assistance before, during and after release is strongly emphasized. Furthermore, there have been calls for close cooperation between the justice system and the youth welfare system in the context of release and release preparation, and for a holistic approach to sentence and release planning that focusses on adequate future prospects and perspectives for juvenile offenders.[73]

The aforementioned European Rules for Juvenile Offenders Subject to Sanctions and Measures[74] summarize international findings on what constitutes successful release preparation quite well. In the recommendation, preparation for release is regarded as a vital cornerstone of successful reintegration into society. Therefore, a detailed framework of regulations focusses on the principle of "continuous care" (see Basic Principle No. 15) and the continuation upon release of educational and vocational programmes that the juvenile has begun in the institution. The rules stipulate:

> 100.1 All juveniles deprived of their liberty shall be assisted in making the transition to life in the community.
>
> 101.1 Steps shall be taken to ensure a gradual return of the juvenile to life in free society.
>
> 101.2 Such steps should include additional leave, and partial or conditional release combined with effective social support.
>
> 102.1 From the beginning of the deprivation of liberty the institutional authorities and the services and agencies that supervise and assist released juveniles shall work closely together to enable them to re-establish themselves in the community, for example by:
>
> a. assisting in returning to their family or finding a foster family and helping them develop other social relationships,
> b. finding accommodation,
> c. continuing their education and training,
> d. finding employment,
> e. referring them to appropriate social and health-care agencies, and
> f. providing monetary assistance.
>
> 102.2. Representatives of such services and agencies shall be given access to juveniles in institutions to assist them with preparation for release.
>
> 102.3. These services and agencies shall be obliged to provide effective and timely pre-release assistance before the envisaged dates of release.

[73] See for example Matt (2012), pp. 31 ff.

[74] See Dünkel and Stańdo-Kawecka (2011).

5 "Good" Practice for Women and Juveniles?

Some international comparisons on women and juveniles in prison have been conducted that provide some insight into release preparation practices for these groups.

5.1 *Release Preparation for Women: Good Practice?*

European research results do little to spread any optimism when it comes to the degree to which release preparation reflects good practices in the field:

According to a research project that analysed the living conditions of incarcerated women in five European countries, the theoretical approaches that underpin what would constitute good release preparation have been implemented only poorly (if at all) in practice. The results show that the institutions under investigation failed to sufficiently and adequately provide educational training, schooling and work as means of release preparation and improving employability. Often there was simply not enough work to go around, and short sentences, addiction problems and low numbers of working hours proved to be obstacles to the re-integrative measures. Women in mother-child-institutions almost always had only limited access to work or training courses.[75] Furthermore, where work was available, it was, almost without exception, oriented towards outdated traditional roles of women, and did little to provide women with the skills they need in order to access the labour market.[76] Psychological support was described as being "insufficient" in the majority of countries covered in the study, characterized for instance by a lack of assistance for victims of domestic violence and/or psychological counselling.[77] Regarding preparation for release, numerous inmates stated that no such preparation took place.[78] Overall, prisons and detention centres in the countries covered in the study felt that release preparation was not their responsibility, and that their task was merely to help offenders establish contacts with support groups. Special staff dedicated specifically to release preparation appear to be sparse.[79] Expert opinions have stated that the most central reasons for this lack of release preparation lay in

---

[75] Toth (2005), p. 46.

[76] The German report makes a much more promising assessment of the state of affairs in Germany regarding education and vocational training, for instance courses to improve IT-skills, vocational training for call centre agents and desktop-publishers, see *Van den Boogaart* et al. in Cruells and Igareda (2006), p. 221. It needs to be borne in mind, however, that the German respondents were held in comparably large institutions like Vechta and Lübeck. Thus, it cannot be assumed that this positive image also applies to the numerous smaller prison units for women in Germany.

[77] See Toth (2005), p. 41.

[78] By contrast, the majority of interviewed prisoners in Germany appeared to be satisfied with their preparation for release.

[79] See Toth (2005), p. 50, 52, 53, 49.

the fact that: there is no contact to respective organisations; women are often released to a local community other than the one of which the institution is a part, and to which they have not been able to establish any ties or contacts; the time of release is often uncertain and short prison sentences often leave insufficient time to take preparatory action.[80]

Women released from prison had rather varying trajectories and paths following release. Interestingly, women who, via work release, prison leave and/or placement in open institutions, had been able to establish contact with support agencies and organisations prior to their release were more likely to have an easier transition to freedom.[81] Numerous women, however, reported to have been entirely without bearing upon release, and that they had lacked any kind of plan or agenda. What stood out prominently was that the burden of having to find accommodation, secure an income and re-establish family ties, all simultaneously, appeared to be too much for many of the women to carry. Finding employment while bearing the "ex-prisoner" stigma proved virtually impossible, and many women had thus been quickly confronted with an unstable and difficult economic situation. Consequently, there is a clear and present need to design release preparation strategies in a fashion that provides continuous care and support to female prisoners beyond their release.[82]

Another study into the living conditions of female prisoners in 8 European countries[83] revealed that, in practice, prison leaves are not nearly granted as often as they should be in the context of release preparation. In some countries, according to the study, actually leaving the institution prior to being released is a rare exception.[84]

Some positive, regional experiences with release preparation programmes for women can be found in the literature. For example, *Holtfreter* and *Wattanaporn* (2014) report on a programme in the USA, "The Transition from Prison to Community Initiative" (TPCI). While the programme as such is gender-neutral, *Holtfreter/Wattanaporn* nonetheless regard it as appropriate for addressing gender-specific issues during release preparation (and after release). *Cole* et al.[85] describe an approach in England called "PS Plus work with women", a holistic prison-based programme that aims to increase the employability and employment of women at the time of their release. Research has revealed positive effects for this strategy.[86]

---

[80] See Toth (2005), p. 54.

[81] See Toth (2005), p. 54, 59.

[82] See Toth (2005), p. 59. *Einsele* already recognized this problem at the end of the 1970s and founded the 'centre for women who have offended' ("Anlaufstelle für straffällig gewordene Frauen") in Frankfurt a. M., see also Geiger and Steinert (1993), p. 97, 98.

[83] Zolondek (2007).

[84] Zolondek (2007), p. 263.

[85] Cole et al. (2007), p. 132.

[86] Cole et al. (2007), p. 134. For developments in Australia, including some employability programmes, see Bartels and Gaffney (2011).

Experiences of cooperation between prisons and authorities, agencies, services and institutions on the outside are summarized by *Hucklesby/Wincup.*[87] Because prisoners are rarely priorities for these services, they face considerable barriers to accessing them. *Gelsthorpe and Sharpe*[88] have reported on the "Women's Offending Reduction Programme" in England and Wales. It was launched 2004, focuses on coordinating departments and sensitizing them to women's needs and implementing a continued service from the point of arrest to release from prison (based on the success of the Scottish "one stop shop project"). The programme does not focus only on release preparation, but on the whole resettlement process. The interesting findings of *Geltshorpe* and *Sharpe* seem to be valid in general for the context of new strategies in the field of release preparation: the authors criticize that such programmes and initiatives often fail to surpass the status of "demonstration projects"—that show how practice *could be*, but are not continued after the first phase. However, the initiative has led to special accommodation for female ex-offenders or ex-prisoners.

5.2 Release Preparation for Juveniles: Good Practice?

A look at the current state of research shows that education and training are given serious consideration in juvenile prisons at least in Europe, North and South America, Australia and New Zealand. In most of Europe, schooling and/or vocational training constitute important elements of sentence programming for juveniles, and in all 36 countries that were covered by a European juvenile justice research project, juvenile inmates were obliged to participate in schooling and vocational training, often also to work.[89] In terms of release preparation, there appears to be the interesting tendency to delay and externalize training schemes to outside services and institutions. According to *Dünkel* and *Stańdo Kawecka,*[90] in "countries such as the *Netherlands*, *Denmark*, *Norway* or *Sweden*, where prison sentences tend to be relatively short, the provision of training for detainees has largely been taken out of the detention facilities, and instead local communities are more heavily involved in the task of reintegrating offenders."[91] This concept helps to avoid the problem that can arise with shorter prison sentences, namely that prisoners often do not spend enough time in the institution to finish any educational or vocational training programmes they have taken up there. They are thus often released without qualifications, and have difficulties in organising a seamless transition from prison to education in the community themselves. With a view on

[87] Wincup and Hucklesby (2007), p. 45.

[88] Gelsthorpe and Sharpe (2007).

[89] Dünkel and Stańdo-Kawecka (2011), p. 1817.

[90] Dünkel and Stańdo-Kawecka (2011).

[91] Dünkel and Stańdo-Kawecka (2011), p. 1830.

the research results and recommendations for resettlement, these strategies can indeed be regarded as promising.

Data that give some insight into whether release preparation is community-oriented are much less satisfying. According to German analyses "only 10 % of all young prisoners were involved in preparatory release measures like day leaves or prison furloughs of several days that may help adapt to social life outside prison. About 9 % of the young prisoners were accommodated in the two open prisons or one of the (usually small) open units within 17 closed prisons."[92] Young prisoners who are placed in open facilities benefit from comparably superior release preparation: In these open facilities between two thirds and three quarters of the juveniles were granted day leaves, more than 40 % participated in work release, leaving the prison every day for work and coming back for the night.[93] With a view on the results for effective release preparation strategies these practices could therefore be described as promising.

Jacomy-Vité,[94] by contrast, does not agree that opening prisons is a widely used practice in European juvenile penal policy and a confirmed and agreed strategy for release preparation. Instead, gradual or temporary release "serve the purpose of 'deserving' juveniles rather than being a right attached to structured and systematic rehabilitation policy".[95]

Many countries provide strategies, projects and programmes for the preparation of juveniles for their release from prison or detention. Across Europe, the degree of geographical coverage varies from country to country—in some, such programmes are available nationwide, while in others they are limited to certain regions or institutions. The *Work-Wise* methodology in the *Netherlands*, for example, is used in all Dutch youth prisons, and is described as an integrated approach that aims to involve juveniles from custodial institutions in labour, training or day programmes with the support of an adequate social network and a good place to live.[96] "Network and routing consultants" in the Dutch juvenile prisons collect all information relevant for devising, together with the Child Protection Board and the Probation Service, a release plan right from the first weeks in prison onward. Such initiatives can be seen as promising from the perspective of resettlement research. In *Germany* new strategies for release preparation oftentimes concentrate on finding employment or access to vocational training that can begin immediately after release. Some projects have been found to be effective in doing so.[97] In *Denmark*, mentors from outside prison are involved in the release preparation process, an approach that has been described as promising.[98] In *England*, the Youth Justice Board's

[92] Dünkel (2011), p. 607.

[93] Dünkel (2011), p. 607 with further references.

[94] Jacomy-Vité (2011).

[95] Jacomy-Vité (2011), p. 27.

[96] Jacomy-Vité (2011), p. 31.

[97] E.g. Wirth (2009), Pruin (2013).

[98] Decarpes and Durnescu (2012), p. 15.

"Resettlement and Aftercare Provision" (RAP) initiative has produced positive results in preparing juvenile prisoners for their life after release and coordinates different responsible services.[99] On the other hand, research results for England have revealed "poor staffing levels, inadequate funding and shortfalls in both the quality and amount of resources".[100]

6 Conclusions

In the context of ongoing discussions about the resettlement of (ex-)prisoners, release preparation inside prison prior to release has a vital role to play. International research results, compiled in the form of international recommendations, emphasise the need for a community-oriented approach to release preparation that involves open institutions and different forms of temporary release. In particular, improving offenders' employability and thus better preparing them for the labour market is accorded particular emphasis. Prisons should cooperate with institutions, agencies and organisations "on the outside" by releasing prisoners into aftercare that as seamlessly as possible latches onto the preparatory steps that have been taken "on the inside". Another particularly important factor is prison staff and their (positive) attitude and ability to motivate prisoners.

Both the research literature and the international standards and recommendations address the special situations of both female and juvenile prisoners. Women and young people face a comparably higher degree of social marginalization—due to their poorer employability, making a smooth transition and successfully resettling in the community is more difficult to achieve than it is for male adult prisoners. Since numbers of female offenders are generally rather low, institutions only rarely provide individualised release preparation programmes tailored specifically to women and their needs. Research and international recommendations call for special efforts to be devoted to devising special release preparation strategies for women and juveniles that should always be "gender-sensitive", regardless of age.

The conclusions that can be drawn from an analysis of the degree to which these demands have been put into practice are not particularly satisfying. The results from international research into release preparation for juveniles and women are admittedly unlikely to be entirely up to date, as the results from more recent legislative or policy change in this field will not yet have entered into the literature. Against this backdrop, the picture that has been painted is not a particularly pretty one. The use in practice of open institutions and of strategies that allow women and juveniles to leave the prison temporarily has yet to reach satisfactory levels. Furthermore, the provision of gender-specific education, vocational training and work opportunities is greatly lacking in Europe. Where available, training and employment reduce

[99] Bateman et al. (2013), p. 19 ff.

[100] Gray (2011), p. 239 ff.

women to activities that cannot provide a basis on which they can build economic security and independence upon release. Individual projects in certain regions, cities or institutions have been evaluated positively. However, putting them into practice has reportedly been associated with difficult obstacles and constraints.

The chapter at hand shows that there is indeed debate about reforming release preparation policy, and that the results from research have in fact been sufficiently "translated" into corresponding practice recommendations. Even though research does not paint a particularly satisfying or positive picture for women and juveniles as special populations in this context, it nonetheless highlights that there is indeed development in this field that needs to be upheld, fostered and furthered. Future research endeavours into women and juveniles in prison should definitely devote increased attention to aspects relating to preparation for release, and will thus hopefully be able to shed some positive light on the outcomes of the most recent reform developments in law and practice.

Five Questions

1. Why has the discussion about release preparation been intensified in recent years?
2. Why is it discussable to use the terminology of "prisoner resettlement" for the process of prisoner's return to society?
3. What are the special requirements of women with respect to their release from prison?
4. What are the special requirements of juveniles with respect to their release from prison?
5. How should an optimal release preparation for women look like?

References

A/RES/40/33 United Nations Standard Minimum Rules for the Administration of Juvenile Justice ("The Beijing Rules"), 29 November 1985.

A/RES/45/111 United Nations Basic Principles for the Treatment of Prisoners, 14 December 1990.

A/RES/45/113 United Nations Rules for the Protection of Juveniles Deprived of Their Liberty ("The Havana Rules), 14 December 1990.

Alexander, M., Lowenkamp, C. T., & Robinson, C. (2014). Probation and parole practices. In G. Bruinsma & D. Weisburd (Eds.), *Encyclopedia of criminology and criminal justice* (pp. 3973–3978). New York: Springer.

Andrews, D. A., & Bonta, J. (2010). *The psychology of criminal conduct* (5th ed.). New Providence: Matthew Bender and Company.

Andrews, D. A., & Dowden, C. (1999). Meta-analytic investigation into effective correctional intervention for female offenders. *Forum on Corrections Research, 11*, 18–20.

Barrow Cadbury Trust. (2005). *Lost in transition: A report of the Barrow Cadbury Commission on young adults and the criminal justice system*. London: Barrow Cadbury Trust.

Bartels, L., & Gaffney, A. (2011). *Good practice in women's prisons: A literature review*. Canberra: Australian Institute of Criminology.

Bateman, T., Hazel, N., & Wright, S. (2013). *Resettlement of young people leaving custody*. London: Beyond Youth Custody.

Bumiller, K. (2013). Incarceration, welfare state and labour market nexus: The increasing significance of gender in the prison system. In B. Carlton & M. Segrave (Eds.), *Women exiting prison* (pp. 13–33). Oxon, New York: Routledge.

Bundesministerium für Familie, Senioren, Frauen und Jugend (BMFSFJ) (2004). Lebenssituation, Sicherheit und Gesundheit von Frauen in Deutschland. Berlin.

Bundesministerium für Justiz (ed.) (2009). Leistungsdaten für die Kriminaljustiz: die neue Wiederverurteiltenstatistik – and more. Wien: Neuer Wissenschaftlicher Verlag.

Cole, A., Galbraith, I., Lyon, P., & Ross, H. (2007). PS plus: A prison (lately) probation-based employment resettlement model. In A. Hucklesby & L. Hagley-Dickinson (Eds.), *Prisoner resettlement: Policy and practice* (pp. 121–143). Oxon, New York: Willan Publishing.

Cruells, M., & Igareda, N. (2006). *Women, integration and prison. An analysis of the processes of sociolabour integration of women prisoners in Europe.*. Luxembourg: Office for Official Publications of the European Communities.

Decarpes, P., Durnescu, I. (2012). Study regarding the development of an integrated inter-institutional mechanism for the social reintegration of former convicts. Internet-publication. http://undp.ro/libraries/projects/Study_regarding_the_social_reintegration_of_former_convicts.pdf. Accessed 22 December 2014.

Dünkel, F. (2011). Germany. In F. Dünkel, J. Grzywa, P. Horsfield, & I. Pruin (Eds.), *Juvenile justice systems in Europe. Current situation and reform developments* (2nd ed.). Mönchengladbach: Forum Verlag Godesberg.

Dünkel, F., & Stańdo-Kawecka, B. (2011). Juvenile Imprisonment and placement in institutions for deprivation of liberty – Comparative aspects. In F. Dünkel, J. Grzywa, P. Horsfield, & I. Pruin (Eds.), *Juvenile justice systems in Europe. Current situation and reform developments* (2nd ed., pp. 1789–1838). Mönchengladbach: Forum Verlag Godesberg.

Dowden, C., & Andrews, D. A. (1999a). What works for female offenders: A meta-analytic review. *Crime and Delinquency, 45*, 438–452.

Dowden, C., & Andrews, D. A. (1999b). What works in young offender treatment: A meta-analysis. *Forum on Corrections Research, 11*, 21–24.

Durnescu, I. (2011). Resettlement research and practices. An international perspective. http://www.cepprobation.org/uploaded_files/Durnescu-CEP-Resettlement-research-and-practice-final.pdf. Accessed 22 December 2014.

ECOSOC resolutions 663 C(XXIV), 31 July 1957 and 2076 (LXII, 13 May 1977, Standard Minimum Rules for the Treatment of Prisoners.

Garland, D. (Ed.). (2001). *Mass imprisonment*. London/Thousand Oaks/New Delhi: Sage.

Geiger, M., Steinert, E. (1993). Straffällige Frauen und das Konzept der "Durchgehenden sozialen Hilfe", Studie im Auftrag des Bundesministeriums für Frauen und Jugend. Stuttgart/Berlin: Köln.

Gelsthorpe, L., & Sharpe, G. (2007). Women and resettlement. In A. Huckelsby & L. Hagley-Dickinson (Eds.), *Prisoner resettlement- policy and practice* (pp. 199–223). London/New York: Routledge.

Giordano, P., Cernkovich, S., & Rudolph, J. (2002). Gender, crime, and desistance: Toward a theory of cognitive transformation. *American Journal of Sociology, 107*, 990–1064.

Gray, P. (2011). Youth custody, resettlement and the right to social justice. *Youth Justice, 11*, 235–249.

Haverkamp, R. (2011). *Frauenvollzug in Deutschland – Eine empirische Untersuchung vor dem Hintergrund der Europäischen Strafvollzugsgrundsätze*. Berlin: Duncker & Humblot.

Hedderman, C. (2007). Rediscovering resettlement: Narrowing the gap between policy rhetoric and practice reality. In A. Huckelsby & L. Hagley-Dickinson (Eds.), *Prisoner resettlement-policy and practice* (pp. 9–25). London/New York: Routledge.

Hermann, D., & Kerner, H.-J. (1988). Die Eigendynamik der Rückfallkriminalität. *Kölner Zeitschrift für Soziologie und Sozialpsychologie, 40*, 464–484.

Holtfreter, K., & Wattanaporn, K. A. (2014). The transition from prison to community initiative: An examination of gender responsiveness for female offender reentry. *Criminal Justice and Behaviour, 41*, 41–57.

Jacomy-Vité, S. (2011). *The social reintegration of young offenders as a key factor to prevent recidivism*. Brussels: International Juvenile Justice Observatory.

Jehle, J. M. (2007). Methodische Probleme einer Rückfallforschung aufgrund von Bundeszentralregisterdaten. In F. Lösel, D. Bender, & J. M. Jehle (Eds.), *Kriminologie und wissensbasierte Kriminalpolitik* (pp. 227–245). Mönchengladbach: Forum Verlag Godesberg.

Jehle, J. M., Albrecht, H.-J., Hohmann-Fricke, S., & Tetal, C. (2010). *Legalbewährung nach strafrechtlichen Sanktionen*. Berlin: Bundesministerium der Justiz.

Kendall, K. (2013). Post-release support for women in England and Wales: The big picture. In B. Carlton & M. Segrave (Eds.), *Women exiting prison* (pp. 34–55). Oxon, New York: Routledge.

Kerner, H.-J., & Janssen, H. (1983). Rückfall nach Jugendstrafvollzug-Betrachtungen unter dem Aspekt von Lebenslauf und krimineller Karriere. In: Kerner, H.-J., et al. (Eds.), Festschrift für Leferenz (pp. 211–232). Heidelberg.

Laub, J. H., & Sampson, R. J. (2003). *Shared beginnings, divergent lives – delinquent boys to age 70*. Cambridge, MA: Harvard University Press.

Lewis, S., Maguire, M., Raynor, P., Vanstone, M., & Vennard, J. (2006). What works in resettlement? Findings from seven pathfinders for short-term prisoners in England and Wales. *Criminology and Criminal Justice, 7*, 33–53.

Lipsey, M. W. (1995). What do we learn from 400 research studies on the effectiveness of treatment with juvenile delinquents? In J. McGuire (Ed.), *What Works? Reducing reoffending* (pp. 63–78). New York: John Wiley.

Lloyd, C. D., & Serin, R. C. (2014). Offender change in treatment. In G. Bruinsma & D. Weisburd (Eds.), *Encyclopedia of criminology and criminal justice* (pp. 3301–3311). New York: Springer.

Lösel, F., & Schmucker, M. (2005). The effectiveness of treatment for sexual offenders: A comprehensive meta-analysis. *Journal of Experimental Criminology, 1*, 117–146.

Lowenkamp, C. T., Latessa, E. J., & Smith, P. (2006). Does correctional program quality really matter? The impact of adhering to the principles of effective intervention. *Criminal Public Policy, 5*, 575–594.

MacKenzie, D. L. (2006). *What works in corrections? Reducing the criminal activities of offenders and delinquents*. New York: Cambridge University Press.

MacKenzie, D. L. (2014). Examining the effectiveness of correctional interventions. In G. Bruinsma & D. Weisburd (Eds.), *Encyclopedia of criminology and criminal justice* (pp. 1471–1479). New York: Springer.

Maguire, M., & Nolan, J. (2007). Accommodation and related services for ex-prisoners. In A. Hucklesby & L. Hagley-Dickinson (Eds.), *Prisoner resettlement: Policy and practice* (pp. 144–173). Cullompton: Willan.

Maruna, S. (2001). *Making good: How ex-convicts reform and rebuild their lives*. Washington, DC: American Psychological Association Books.

Matt, E. (2012). Überlegungen zum Übergangsmanagement im Jugendbereich. In DBH-Fachverband für Soziale Arbeit, Strafrecht und Kriminalpolitik (Ed.), Übergangsmanagement für junge Menschen zwischen Strafvollzug und Nachbetreuung (pp. 26–40).

Matt, E., & Hentschel, H. (2009). Das KompetenzCentrum an der JVA Bremen. *Forum Strafvollzug, 58*, 71–75.

McNeill, F. (2006). A desistance paradigm for offender management. *Criminology and Criminal Justice, 6*, 39–62.

Mead, J. (2007). Resettlement. In R. Canton & D. Hancock (Eds.), *Dictionary of probation and offender management* (pp. 268–270). Collumpton: Willan.

Opsal, T., & Foley, A. (2013). Making it on the outside: Understanding barriers to women's post-incarceration reintegration. *Sociology Compass, 7*, 265–277.

Paternoster, R., & Bushway, S. (2009). Desistance and the "feared self": Toward an identity theory of criminal desistance. *The Journal of Criminal Law and Criminology, 99*, 1103–1156.

Petersilia, J. (2004). What works in prisoner reentry? Reviewing and questioning the evidence. *Federal Probation, 68*, 4–8.

Petersilia, J. (2014). Parole and prisoner reentry in the United States. In G. Bruinsma & D. Weisburd (Eds.), *Encyclopedia of criminology and criminal justice* (pp. 3440–3450). New York: Springer.

Pruin, I. (2013). Übergangsmanagement im Jugendstrafvollzug: Die Evaluation des Projekts BASIS in der JVA Adelsheim. In: Dölling, D., Jehle, J.-M. (Eds.) Täter Taten Opfer, Grundfragen und aktuelle Probleme der Kriminalität und ihrer Kontrolle. Neue Kriminologische Schriftenreihe (114, pp. 691-714). Mönchengladbach: Forum Verlag Godesberg.

Raynor, P. (2004). Opportunity, motivation and change: some findings from research on resettlement. In R. Burnett & C. Roberts (Eds.), *What works in probation and youth justice: Developing evidence based practice* (pp. 217–233). Cullompton, Devon: Willan.

Schröttle, M., Müller, U. (2004). Teilpopulationen-Erhebung bei Inhaftierten. Bundesministeriums für Familie, Senioren, Frauen und Jugend: "Lebenssituation, Sicherheit und Gesundheit von Frauen in Deutschland". Teilpopulation 3, Berlin.

Seiter, R. P., & Kadela, K. R. (2003). Prisoner reentry: What works, what does not, and what is promising. *Crime and Delinquency, 49*, 360–388.

Sherman, L.W., Gottfredson, D.C., MacKenzie, D.L., Eck, J., Reuter. P., & Bushway, S. (1997). Preventing crime: What works, what doesn't, what's promising. Research in brief. Washington, DC: U.S. National Institute of Justice.

Taxman, F. S. (2004). *Tools of the trade: A guide to incorporating science into practice*. Washington, DC: Maryland Department of Public Safety and Correctional Services.

Thompson, A. C. (2008). *Releasing prisoners, redeeming communities*. New York/London: New York University Press.

Toth, H. (2005). Comparative report. http://pdc.ceu.hu/archive/00006472/01/cps-working-paper-mip-comparative-report-full-version-2005.pdf. Accessed 22 December 2014.

UNODOC. (2008). *Handbook for prison managers and policymakers on women and imprisonment*. New York: United Nations.

UNODOC. (2012). *Introductory handbook on the prevention of recidivism and the social reintegration of offenders*. New York: United Nations.

Visher, C., & Travis, J. (2012). The characteristics of prisoners returning home and effective reentry programs and policies. In J. Petersilia & K. R. Reitz (Eds.), *The Oxford handbook of sentencing and corrections* (pp. 684–703). Oxford/New York: Oxford University Press.

Ward, T., Göbbels, S., & Willis, G. (2014). Good lives model. In G. Bruinsma & D. Weisburd (Eds.), *Encyclopedia of criminology and criminal justice* (pp. 1966–1976). New York: Springer.

Wincup, E., & Hucklesby, A. (2007). Researching and evaluating resettlement. In A. Hucklesby & L. Hagley-Dickinson (Eds.), *Prisoner resettlement: Policy and practice* (pp. 67–94). Oxon/New York: Willan Publishing.

Wirth, W. (2006). Arbeitslose Haftentlassene: Multiple Problemlagen und vernetzte Wiedereingliederungshilfen. *Bewährungshilfe, 53*, 137–152.

Wirth, W. (2009). Aus der Haft in Arbeit oder Ausbildung. *Bewährungshilfe, 56*, 156–164.

Worral, A., & Gelsthorpe, L. (2009). 'What works' with women offenders: The past 30 years. *Probation Journal, 56*, 329–345.

Zolondek, J. (2007). *Lebens- und Haftbedingungen im deutschen und europäischen Frauenstrafvollzug*. Mönchengladbach: Forum Verlag Godesberg.

The Impact of Sanctions on Child and Female Offenders

Charles Robert Allen

Abstract Criminal sanctions do not have a beneficial effect on many of the young people and women made subject to them. Deprivation of liberty may have a particularly negative impact and evidence suggests that keeping both groups out of the formal criminal justice system and away from prison may offer the best chance of addressing the problems, which lead to offending behaviour. For those working with young people and with women lessons from research in the past decade suggest that models based around three elements are most likely to produce positive effects and encourage desistance from crime: motivational and other work prior to release, post-release mentoring, and facilitating access to agencies and organisations that can provide appropriate services. Meeting basic practical needs in prisons remains crucial, in many high-income countries let alone poorer ones. Research on young offenders has found that supervisors in whatever setting are effective if they are clear about their role, show positive social values and behaviour themselves and are prepared to challenge the young persons consistently and fairly about their delinquency. Effectiveness is also enhanced if offenders are helped with problems, which they themselves identify, particularly if these are related to their offending. Tackling substance misuse, lack of employment and damaging relationships with family and peers may be particularly important. Similar factors are likely to be significant for women too. The inappropriateness of custody is increasingly recognised for young people and for women but developing the law, policy and practice, which can reduce and ultimately eliminate its use has proved difficult in a climate of opinion which places a greater value on punishment than is justified by evidence.

1 Introduction

It is widely agreed that the systems for responding both to children and women in conflict with the law are in need of reform in many countries. There are strong international norms governing the treatment of both groups. The United Nations

C.R. Allen (✉)
London, UK
e-mail: rob.allen@justiceandprisons.org

H. Kury et al. (eds.), *Women and Children as Victims and Offenders: Background, Prevention, Reintegration*, DOI 10.1007/978-3-319-28424-8_7

Committee on the Rights of the Child has said that there is "abundant evidence that the placement of children in adult prisons or jails compromises their basic safety, well-being, and their future ability to remain free of crime and to reintegrate"[1] and "that the traditional objectives of criminal justice, such as repression/retribution, must give way to rehabilitation and restorative justice objectives in dealing with child offenders."[2] The United Nations Rules for the Treatment of Women Prisoners and Non-custodial Measures for Women Offenders (the Bangkok Rules) say that "alternative ways of managing women who commit offences, such as diversionary measures and pre-trial and sentencing alternatives, shall be implemented wherever appropriate and possible."[3]

Evidence submitted to UN treaty bodies, academic research and monitoring by civil society organisations shows that the reality of the response to these groups falls way short of meeting these norms. For example, between 2006 and 2012 the UN Committee on the Rights of the Child made concluding observations about juvenile justice in 14 EU member states. In seven of these, recommendations were made to review the legislation with the aim of eliminating the possibility that children can be tried as adults and/or detained with adults and to use detention only as a measure of last resort and for the shortest possible period of time. Six countries were asked to develop a comprehensive policy of alternative sanctions for juvenile offenders; and two to ensure that children deprived of liberty have access to education and to take the necessary measures to provide juvenile detainees with prospects for their future, including their full reintegration into the society.[4] In other parts of the world the need for reform is even greater.

As for women, a recent study of their imprisonment in five countries found that "gender-sensitive international standards on detained women are little known, distributed or implemented among officials, prison administrators, and NGOs working in prison communities".[5]

In order to provide a sound basis for reform efforts, the aim of this chapter is to summarise and discuss what is known about the impact of sanctions on children and on women in conflict with the law. The chapter opens with a general introduction to the topic, which looks first at the purposes which sanctions are designed to achieve and second at some common features of how sanctions impact on these two groups of offenders. The chapter then provides more detailed information first about children and young persons and second about women.

[1] UNCRC 2007, para. 85.

[2] UNCRC 2007 Art 10 http://www2.ohchr.org/english/bodies/crc/docs/CRC.C.GC.10.pdf.

[3] UNGA (2010) Rule 58.

[4] ChildONEurope (2014), pp. 157–8.

[5] Dignity (2014), p. 9.

1.1 The Purpose of Sanctions

In seeking to identify and assess the effect of sanctions on offenders of all kinds, it is important to consider what it is that those sanctions are intended to achieve. By sanctions, we include the whole range of measures that are taken in response to people who have broken the criminal law. These include measures taken by the police, prosecutors and courts and implemented by a range of organisations including prisons, probation, local authorities and non-governmental organisations.

Many discussions about sanctions, particularly in high-income countries, tend to focus on the question of recidivism; that is on the reduction of re-offending. Sanctions are seen to be effective to the extent that the people made subject to them do not commit offences afterwards. This is of course an important question, particularly perhaps in the case of child offenders where the prevention of further offending should be one of the key objectives of the youth justice system. What is known about the way particular sanctions and measures affect recidivism is a central part of this chapter.

It is however worth bearing in mind that the imposition of sanctions serves purposes other than the reduction of re-offending. This is particularly true of sentences imposed by the courts. Indeed, given the often high rates at which people released from prison commit further crimes, it seems unlikely that imprisonment would be imposed as a sanction to the extent that it is, if reducing recidivism were the main aim.

In Uganda for example, where sentencing guidelines have recently been adopted, the courts' overall aim is to promote respect for the law in order to maintain a just, peaceful and safe society and to promote initiatives to prevent crime.[6] Sentences imposed by courts should be aimed at six objectives in all. Two of these objectives—"deterring a person from committing an offence" and "assisting in rehabilitating and re-integrating an offender into society"—are undoubtedly about reducing re-offending. A third objective,—"promoting a sense of responsibility by the offender, acknowledging the harm done to the victim and the community"—is also about producing an attitude, which may be essential if an offender is to stay away from crime. The remaining three objectives are of a different nature. "Providing reparation for harm done to a victim or to the community" may help an offender to desist from crime but it is not the main aim. "Separating an offender from society where necessary" invites the courts to take dangerous and highly persistent offenders out of circulation. "Denouncing unlawful conduct" can be seen to contain elements of deserved punishment for the offender and sending a message to the wider public about what is not acceptable behaviour.

Many jurisdictions have a similar range of sentencing purposes for adult offenders which comprise, alongside the reduction of re-offending, punishment, the protection of the public and reparation to victims. For adult women the framework of sentencing is usually the same as for men. In England and Wales

[6] JLOS (2013).

(UK), a major inquiry into the treatment of women in the criminal justice system did not recommend a separate sentencing framework for women.[7] Sentencing guidelines do however say that "sentencers must be made aware of the differential impact sentencing decisions have on women and men including caring responsibilities for children or elders; the impact of imprisonment on mental and emotional well-being; and the disproportionate impact that incarceration has on offenders who have caring responsibilities if they are imprisoned a long distance from home."[8] Despite this it remains the case that for the most part decisions about the application of sanctions are made on the same basis for women as for men.

For child offenders, usually but not always defined as those under the age of 18, the purposes of sanctions, are often somewhat different, tending to include a greater focus on rehabilitation and reform and a desire to limit the use of incarceration. Many countries, in line with international standards operate a separate juvenile justice system. Canada's youth justice law defines the purpose of youth sentences as being "to hold young people accountable by imposing sanctions that have meaningful consequences for them and that promote their rehabilitation and reintegration into society, thereby contributing to the long-term protection of the public."[9] It goes on to emphasise the need for timely sanctions that reinforce the link between the offending behaviour and its consequences, for promptness and speed in their implementation given young persons' perception of time, and the desirability of involving the parents, the extended family, the community and social or other agencies in the young person's rehabilitation and reintegration.

These requirements leave little room for general deterrence as does South Africa's Child Justice law which requires sentences "to encourage the child to understand the implications of their actions and be accountable for the harm caused; to promote an individualised response which strikes a balance between the circumstances of the child, the nature of the offence and the interests of society; to promote the reintegration of the child into the family and community; to ensure that any supervision, guidance, treatment or services which form part of the sentence assist the child in the process of reintegration and; to use imprisonment only as a measure of last resort and only for the shortest appropriate period of time".[10]

In England and Wales (UK), when sentencing an offender aged under 18, a court must have regard to the principal aim of the youth justice system which is to prevent offending by children and young persons and to the welfare of the young offender. Sentencing guidelines say that "the emphasis should be on approaches that seem most likely to be effective with young people".[11] This has not prevented courts

[7] Corston (2007) http://www.justice.gov.uk/publications/docs/corston-report-march-2007.pdf.

[8] Judicial College (2013), p. 224.

[9] Youth Criminal Justice Act 2002 Section 3.

[10] Child Justice Act S69 (1).

[11] Sentencing Guidelines (2009) 2.11 http://sentencingcouncil.judiciary.gov.uk/docs/web_overarching_principles_sentencing_youths.pdf 2.11.

from imposing sentences that seek to deter young people in general from committing crime rather than rehabilitating the particular young person before them.

Thus while sanctions can provide opportunities for women and, even more so, juveniles in conflict with the law to address the specific problems that cause them to commit crime, these often sit within, or alongside, measures which have other purposes. While repairing the harm to victims may be an important component of taking responsibility which is in turn a pre-requisite for successful rehabilitation, punishment, incapacitation and general deterrence all fit less comfortably with the aim of reducing recidivism.

1.2 Common Considerations in Respect of Children and Women

In thinking about how sanctions impact on young people and on women, it is worth reflecting on a number of special considerations which apply to these two groups of "minorities". They are both categories of offenders that represent a relatively small proportion of people appearing before the courts.

Other chapters in this handbook have catalogued the fact that on the whole offending by both young people and by women is of a less serious nature than the crime committed by adult males—notwithstanding the fact that the peak age for offending in many countries comes during the teenage years.

It is also the case that a high proportion of cases of serious offending by these groups is related to their own experiences of victimisation. In the case of young people we know that abuse and neglect are predictors of criminality—children who became prolific young offenders typically suffered from harsh or neglectful parenting and developed behaviour difficulties at an early age. Many women in prison have themselves been subject to physical and sexual violence. In a UK survey, more than half of female prisoners, compared with a quarter of male prisoners, reported having suffered from violence at home. Furthermore, around one third of women prisoners reported suffering sexual abuse compared to fewer than one in ten men.[12]

As far as sanctions are concerned, there are three common characteristics worth mentioning. First, both young people and women can find themselves subject to sanctions for behaviour, which would not bring adult males before the courts. In jurisdictions of different kinds, children are punished by the courts for so-called "status offences". These are matters such as running away from home, failing to attend school, being incorrigible or consuming alcohol prohibited only because of the age of the child. In the USA in 2008, some 156,000 cases were reported with 13,000 involving a period of secure confinement.[13] In lower income countries,

[12] Williams et al. (2012).

[13] Coalition for Juvenile Justice n.d.

living homeless and on the streets can lead to an appearance in court and punishment.

In a similar way, women in some countries can find themselves made subject to criminal sanctions for behaviour that is not normally prohibited. This includes so called moral crimes such as adultery. Statistics from Afghanistan's Interior Ministry show that the number of women and girls imprisoned for such crimes rose from 400 in October 2011 to 600 in May 2013—a 50 % increase in a year and a half.[14] Such crimes are estimated to account for 95 % of the cases of girls in prison and 50 % of adult women. The Afghan government has rejected calls by the UN to abolish prosecutions of this kind.[15] A range of so-called crimes against patriarchy, which carry no liability in the case of men, can lead to imprisonment, corporal punishment or even death in a number of other countries. Even in jurisdictions with more formal equality, it has been argued that the criminal justice response to women is often coloured by perceptions that women have breached social and cultural expectations about their role as well as the criminal law.

The second issue which affects both juvenile and women offenders is the way in which sanctions can impact on their wider families as well as on them. Of course there is often an impact on families when an offender of any kind is sentenced: paying a fine puts pressure on family budgets and, imprisonment often removes a breadwinner. But when children and women offend, families can be implicated much more directly. In many legal systems, parents can be held responsible for their children's offending by being required to pay fines or made subject to other court orders. Failure to comply can result in imprisonment, usually of the mother. In one tragic case in 2014, a mother of seven died in prison in the USA having been committed there for two days for failing to pay fines imposed in response to her children's truancy. The judge that sent her there complained about a broken system that punishes impoverished parents.[16]

A complementary process arises when women with dependent children are sentenced for offences they themselves have committed. The demands of looking after children can impact on the eligibility of mothers for community based sentences, which involve unpaid work. When a prison sentence is imposed on a woman with an infant child, in almost all countries infants can remain with their mother until they reach a specified age.

Finally and most significantly for the concerns of this chapter, the immediate impact of sanctions, particularly imprisonment, may be harsher for young people and for women than it is for adult males. This is partly because many young offenders and women offenders have needs and vulnerabilities, which make the impact of sanctions more severe than in the case of other types of offenders. The negative impact of removing young people from home may have a particularly

---

[14] Human Rights Watch (2013).

[15] RAWA News 2014 http://www.rawa.org/temp/runews/2014/06/24/afghanistan-end-moral-crimes-prosecutions.html.

[16] Guardian (2014).

adverse impact on their developing physical and psychological maturity; and separating mothers from their children and families can be considered an additional punishment in the case of women causing additional pain to that which is inherent in imprisonment. The generally higher rates of suicide and particularly of self-harm among women prisoners in many western countries suggest that this is the case.[17]

It is also the case that the way in which sanctions are implemented may impose additional hardships or challenges on these two particular groups. In countries where those serving prison sentences are placed in specialist establishments, these may be a long way from where they live. A study in the UK found that the key variable in determining whether prisons worked effectively to ensure reintegration for released prisoners was distance from home. This was found to be "of particular relevance to women and young offenders, where there are fewer prisons."[18]

Wherever they are located, prisons can have a particularly damaging effect on these groups. US research has found that spending time in prison or jail can have profound effects on a young person's future.[19] High rates of recidivism mean that many youth, once in the prison system, will stay there for significant portions of their lives. In some jurisdictions, criminal records obtained while a juvenile can remain with a person well into their adult lives.

The UN Special Rapporteur on Violence against Women has concluded that "the effects of incarceration on women are often longer lasting due to the more dire conditions and deprivations they experience. The consequences of incarceration take a toll on several aspects of women prisoners' lives, including negative outcomes with respect to health, substance abuse, medical insurance, housing, employment, social stability and familial connections. These negative consequences also contribute to recidivism among former female prisoners, even though their recidivism rates, in general, are much lower than those of men."[20]

In the context of these broad similarities, we now turn to some of the specific findings about the effects of sanctions on children and in women.

2 How Sanctions Impact on Child Offenders

Making generalisations about responses to young offenders is very difficult because of the enormous variation in the ways that jurisdictions respond to youth crime. This variation occurs in respect of matters such as the minimum age of criminal responsibility, the upper age limit of the youth justice system, the existence or not

[17] Hawton et al. (2014).

[18] HM Chief Inspector of Prisons (2009), p. 5 The Prison Characteristics That Predict Prisons Being Assessed As Performing. "Well": A Thematic Review January 2009, pp. 5–17.

[19] e.g Geller et al. (2006).

[20] UN doc. A/68/340 (2013), para. 66.

of specialist youth courts and the range of measures available for dealing with young people. The variation arises too in relation to the underlying philosophy of the system, which according UN is "diverse, building from the classical typology of the so-called 'welfare model' and the 'justice model' to more recent typologies including the 'participatory model', the 'modified justice model', the 'crime control model', the 'corporatist model', the 'minimum intervention model', the 'restorative justice model' and the 'neo-correctionalist model'."[21]

There are methodological as well as conceptual difficulties. An American study found "clear communication of program outcomes and system performance in juvenile justice is often hampered by the lack of standard definitions and inconsistent measurement, especially in relation to recidivism".[22] This is even more the case if one seeks to adopt a global perspective on the question. The new Moldova Criminal Code of 2002 distinguishes three forms of recidivism: simple, if a person previously sentenced for an intentional crime repeatedly committed a crime with intent; dangerous, if: (a) a person previously sentenced twice to imprisonment for intentional crimes repeatedly committed an intentional crime; or (b) a person previously convicted of a serious or extremely serious intentional crime repeatedly committed a serious or an extremely serious intentional crime; extremely dangerous, if: (a) a person previously sentenced to imprisonment three or more times for intentional crimes repeatedly committed an intentional crime; or (b) a person previously convicted of an exceptionally serious intentional crime repeatedly committed an extremely serious intentional crime or an exceptionally serious crime.[23]

Whatever their underlying principles, in most systems sanctions range from warnings and admonitions, through fines, community based supervision measures, to institutional placements in welfare, educational or penal establishments.[24] Given the widespread prevalence of minor delinquency among adolescents, in many parts of the world first time offenders can expect to be given a reprimand, warning or caution by the police or prosecutors, with the option of an apology or other restorative disposal increasingly available.

---

[21] UNODC (2013), pp. vi–vii.

[22] Harris et al. (2009) Measuring Recidivism in Juvenile Corrections http://www.journalofjuvjustice.org/jojj0101/article01.htm.

[23] OSF (2010).

[24] The UN Standard Minimum Rules for the Administration of Juvenile Justice require that "a large variety of disposition measures . . . be made available .., allowing for flexibility so as to avoid institutionalization to the greatest extent possible. Such measures include: (a) Care, guidance and supervision orders;(b) Probation; (c) Community service orders; (d) Financial penalties, compensation and restitution; (e) intermediate treatment and other treatment orders; (f) Orders to participate in group counselling and similar activities; (g) Orders concerning foster care, living communities or other educational settings; and(h) Other relevant orders. http://www.un.org/documents/ga/res/40/a40r033.htm.

More serious or repeat offenders are likely to receive a period of supervision or a placement in care or custody. The gravest offences can lead to very long custodial sentences.

In 2005, the United States Supreme Court ruled that the death penalty for those who had committed their crimes at under 18 years of age was cruel and unusual punishment and hence barred by the Constitution.[25] Some countries retain the death penalty for juveniles including Saudi Arabia and Iran.[26] In 2012, the US Supreme Court ruled in Miller v Alabama that mandatory life without parole for juveniles was a violation of the eighth amendment that forbids cruel and unusual punishment. Yet since then only 13 of the 28 states that carry the sentence have amended their laws and about 2000 people sentenced for offences committed while under the age 18 face spending their whole life in prison as a result of mandatory sanctions.[27] A further 8000 people are serving life sentences for offences committed as juveniles; although they have the possibility of parole convicted juveniles are generally "at the back of the parole line" according to a recent study and must wait years for a review.[28]

While most of the available statistics and research needed to draw lessons about the effect of sanctions are from higher income countries, a number of consistent findings have been made.

Perhaps the most important is that the common characteristic of intervention programmes that do not work is an emphasis on punishment and deterrence alone where no attempt is made to resolve the social life problems of young people. On average, sanctions alone are associated with increased offending.[29]

This is because punishment works best with well-socialised, non-impulsive young people with average and above IQs who are cautious and have low arousal thresholds. Most young offenders do not share these characteristics. A report for the Scottish Government's review of the Children's Hearing System concluded that "legal sanctions consistently fail to address criminogenic needs/risks and are insufficient, in themselves to offset the immediacy, frequency and magnitude of rewards from criminal activity which have to be replaced with pro-social alternatives".[30]

[25] Roper v Simmons No. 03-633 see Death Penalty Information Centre n.d.

[26] Amnesty International n.d.

[27] Sentencing Project (2014) (more detailed reference, please).

[28] Sentencing Project (2013).

[29] Lipsey (1992).

[30] Scottish Government (2004), 7.5.

2.1 Diversion

Given this finding it is not surprising that diverting most children and young people away from the formal court system may produce better results than imposing penalties. Findings from a large scale longitudinal study in Scotland indicate that the deeper a youth is carried into the formal processing system, the less likely he or she is to stop offending. The authors argue that the most significant factor in reducing offending is minimal formal intervention and maximum diversion to programming that does not have the trappings of criminal processing.[31]

A systematic review of 29 experiments found that young people with a prior criminal record who were diverted from the criminal justice system to social work were less likely to reoffend compared to those who went to court. Diversion to social work help produced bigger reductions in reoffending compared to simple release that was not combined with some form of intervention.[32] In another meta-analysis, 45 diversion evaluation studies reporting on 73 programs were included in the meta-analysis. The results indicated that diversion is more effective in reducing recidivism than conventional judicial interventions.[33] Unlike the first study, in this one there was no statistical difference between the effectiveness of the 50 programmes that provided positive help or treatment and the 23 that did not.

There are a number of mechanisms that can explain these findings. Keeping people away from formal criminal justice processes may avoid the negative labelling that inevitably attaches to prosecution and conviction whatever the nature of the sanction that may follow. Diversion may allow a speedy, problem solving response which may enable a young person to apologise or make amends for their behaviour or provide the chance to engage them in activities or programmes of work which can help them stay out of further trouble. It may be perceived as a fairer and more legitimate response than court—and one in which young people can participate more actively than in court based processes.

An example of a diversionary programme is the Teen court, which is used in more than 1200 locations across the USA.[34] Using a courtroom setting, a mix of adults and teenagers deal with cases of first time non-violent offenders as an alternative to formal juvenile court processing. They can impose mild sanctions and measures for the teenagers. Research has found Teen courts more effective in terms of recidivism than the juvenile court in three sites but slightly less effective than a police diversion programme in another.[35] In addition to the mechanisms noted above, the Teen Court provides a forum for peer justice through which pro-social influences can take effect on young people. The process also provides

---

[31] McCara and McVie (2007).

[32] Petrosino et al. (2010).

[33] Wilson and Hoge (2013).

[34] Butts and Ortiz (2011).

[35] Butts et al. (2002).

education about the law and the opportunity to learn new skills, both of which may be important in leaving crime behind.[36]

A slightly different philosophy—less elaborate in form though more extensive in application—underpins South Africa's Child Justice Act which aims to divert child offenders from the formal criminal justice system whenever possible. Diversion means that an accused person is not put through formal criminal proceedings but is subjected to an alternative process that does not involve a formal trial, conviction and a criminal record. No sentence is imposed, although the alternative process—which involves an assessment of the child's needs and a plan of action may require the person to perform services or tasks, or to submit to training or other regimes, some of which might be of a punitive nature.

A third example are restorative measures which are used in a variety of formats in the USA, Canada, New Zealand, Northern Ireland and England and Wales (UK). A study of Family Group Conferences[37] in Indianapolis found that participating youths survived longer before being rearrested over a 24-month period and had significantly lower incidence rates.[38]

While evidence about the effectiveness of South Africa's approach is limited, such an approach works well in longer established systems. In the Netherlands, for example, public prosecutors divert the majority of young offenders from court proceedings to a community based reparation project called HALT. The system works well; about 60 % either commit less crime or cease offending altogether.[39]

While diversion is widely accepted as the best first response to youthful offending, there are conflicting views about the most effective types of intervention or if any intervention is needed at all.

For those young people who continue to offend, or whose offences are more serious, continued diversion is not likely to be effective or desirable. More intensive sanctions are likely to be needed and consideration may be given to the use of institutional measures, including the use of custody.

2.2 *Custodial Measures*

Increasingly in the USA and other jurisdictions, interventions with serious child juvenile offenders can involve purely punitive sanctions, with incarceration in a correctional institution as the most common response. Research clearly shows that

---

[36] ibid.

[37] In a family group conference, after admission of responsibility by the offender, they, the victim, and the supporters of both the offender and victim are brought together. They are brought together with a trained facilitator to discuss the incident and the harm brought to the victim. The FGC provides an opportunity for the victim to explain how they have been harmed and ask questions of the offender.

[38] McGarrell and Hipple (2007).

[39] Graham (2011).

punitive sanctions are generally ineffective in reducing criminal activities.[40] There is no evidence that simply being kept in a locked institution will reduce offending. Studies have compared community based versus institutional approaches, in particular locked or incapacitation facilities. 103 published studies involving 267,804 subjects compared the outcomes of these two approaches and showed an average 7 % increase in re-offending associated with institutional approaches.[41]

This is not surprising when one considers the reality of custodial sanctions for young people in most of the world. The suffering and misery experienced by young people goes well beyond the punishment that the institution is intended to provide. International standards, for example, require children to be held separately from adults in custodial establishments. The UN Committee on the Rights of the Child has drawn attention to the "abundant evidence that the placement of children in adult prisons or jails compromises their basic safety, well-being, and their future ability to remain free of crime and to reintegrate."[42] But this most straightforward of requirements is not met in a large number of countries.

In Brazil, the law stipulates that juveniles should not be held together with adults in jails, but according to the US State Department Human Rights report for 2013 this was not always respected. "Multiple sources reported adolescents jailed with adults in poor and crowded conditions. Insufficient capacity in juvenile detention centres was widespread."[43] The State Department report shows that juveniles are kept with adults not only in the poorest countries such as Yemen (where local NGOs reported that children were held with adults and that segregation between adults and juveniles was inconsistent)[44] or in Cambodia, where in most prisons there was no separation of adult and juvenile prisoners (nor indeed of male and female prisoners). In higher income countries too, juveniles were sometimes held with adults; in South Africa (its Child Justice Act notwithstanding) and Serbia where youth and adult populations lacked proper separation at the correctional facility in Valjevo, and there were sporadic reports of mixing youth and adults elsewhere.[45] In India the law requires juveniles to be detained in rehabilitative facilities, although at times they were detained in prisons, especially in rural areas. In China, although the law requires juveniles be held separately from adults, unless facilities are insufficient, children were sometimes held with adult prisoners and required to work.

Even in countries where young people are held separately from adults their experience can be woeful. At best, it might be hoped that secure establishments could provide a safe, structured and caring environment, which might help address the years of neglect, abuse and educational failure that characterise the upbringing

[40] Andrews and Bonta (2006); Lipsey and Wilson (1998).

[41] Andrews et al. (2000).

[42] UN (2007), para. 85t.

[43] US State Department (2013).

[44] Ibid.

[45] ibid.

of many of the most serious and persistent young offenders. This would require an approach that genuinely meets the needs of individual children in small-scale living units, with intensive preparation for release and continuing care once back in the community. When services aimed at meeting individual needs are included in institutional or community-based approaches, the outcomes are more likely to be positive. One review showed modest effects, on average 9 % reduction in re-offending for institutional provision and 14 % for community based provision.[46]

At worst, however institutions can be a frightening interlude in young lives already impoverished by neglect and punishment. Even smaller closed institutions struggle to overcome the hostility and alienation felt by many of the children detained against their will. After all, closed institutions of whatever kind represent an abnormal living experience, which can impair the normal course of adolescent development. As recently as 2004, visitors to Poland found children in small dormitory cells, with no personal items, wearing pyjamas and slippers throughout the day; with no medical screening and no visits for a month.[47]

Whatever the intentions of the law, policymakers and staff, concentrating highly delinquent young people in a closed environment risks reinforcing rather than weakening the attitudes that the justice system is seeking to challenge. The common use of physical restraint in many custodial establishments may further contribute to an 'us and them' attitude towards authority.

The disadvantages of custodial sanctions are reflected in high rates of recidivism. In England and Wales (UK) about seven out of ten juveniles released from custodial establishments are reconvicted within a year.[48] In the USA, re-offending rates are lower among those leaving state incarceration. According to the latest data 55 % were rearrested within a year. 33 % reconvicted and 24 % sent back to custody.[49] This does not necessarily mean that US facilities are more effective. It is more likely to reflect America's greater use of custody which brings into the custodial sector lower risk juveniles than in the UK where more of such offenders would be given community based sanctions.

When considering what can be done to ensure that any custodial experience for a juvenile makes it less rather than more likely that they will reoffend, it is all too easy to overlook the significance of addressing some of the basic quality of life issues with which many custodial establishments struggle. England and Wales's UK's Youth Justice Board (YJB) has recognised, 'reoffending can only be addressed in a safe, secure environment. Effective safeguarding (a term used to refer to the protection of children from abuse and neglect) is therefore important not only in its own right, but also because it is critical to reducing reoffending'.[50]

---

[46] Dowden and Andrews (1999).

[47] Council of Europe (2004), para 38.

[48] MoJ (2014).

[49] OJJDP (2006).

[50] MoJ/YJB (2012).

England and Wales provides an interesting if depressing case study about the realities of custodial treatment in a high-income country. Troublingly, recent independent inspection reports from the UK show that custodial institutions have problems in meeting some of the very basic needs of juveniles, let alone producing more positive outcomes for them.

The Chief Inspector of Prisons reported in 2010/11: "In three establishments, external nutritionists had been consulted but young men said they frequently felt hungry".[51] At one establishment, Feltham, in 2013, residential areas were shabby, graffiti was everywhere, and some areas needed a deep clean.[52] At another, Wetherby, there was inadequate access to showers with the lack of daily showers particularly affecting those who worked in dirty areas.[53]

Annual surveys conducted by prison inspectors have found just under a third of young men and just over a fifth of young women in Young Offender Institutions (YOI's) in England and Wales report that they have felt unsafe at some point while in prison. In 2013, inspectors found that shouting abuse from windows was widespread and saw opportunities for bullying in many areas.[54] They had particularly serious concerns about the safety of young people held at Feltham, in London. Many young people said they were frightened and had little confidence in staff to keep them safe. "There was an average of almost two fights or assaults every day. Some of these were very serious and involved groups of young people in very violent, pre-meditated attacks on a single individual with a risk of very serious injury resulting."[55]

Some of the practices undertaken in custody such as routine strip-searching are seen by some observers to raise questions of decency,[56] and by the Chief Inspector of Prisons to mar efforts by reception staff to reassure new arrivals for whom arriving in custody is a daunting experience. While the inspectors found that most young people said that staff treated them with respect (69 % of young men and 81 % of young women), young men from black and minority ethnic groups reported less favourably: only 57 % said they were treated respectfully. The Chief Inspector noted: "Some young people were very negative about the way they were treated."[57]

It should go without saying that efforts to influence young people to stay out of trouble in the future are likely to be ineffective in institutional environments where some young people do not have enough to eat, cannot keep themselves clean, do not feel safe and are not treated with respect.

But more direct attempts to bring about changes in attitudes and behaviour by young people in custody have also been disappointing. Inspectors found that

---

[51] HMI (2011a), p. 63.

[52] HMI (2013a), p. 6.

[53] HMI (2012), p. 15.

[54] HMI (2013b).

[55] HMI (2013a), p. 5.

[56] National Council for Independent Monitoring Boards (2011).

[57] HMI (2011a).

"support from personal officers or key workers (members of staff given responsibility for a particular group of young people) was generally not rated highly by young people. Sixty-seven per cent of young women said that a member of staff had checked on them within the previous week to see how they were getting on, but for young men this dropped to 39 %."[58] Few personal officers attended important meetings relating to the care of the young people for whom they were responsible. While the overall care of the most vulnerable and troublesome young people, including those who self-harmed or were segregated, had improved and most establishments had a multi-agency forum in which they discussed individual young people and shared information, the co-ordination of a wide range of assessments and care plans for different purposes was poor, resulting in a disjointed approach to caring for the most challenging young people.

The England and Wales experience suggests that particular groups of young people suffer more than others. Without social work expertise to help them interpret relevant legislation and guidance, YOIs have experienced difficulties in identifying, assessing and managing the needs of looked after children—those who are in the care of the local authority because they cannot live with their parents. The provision for foreign nationals (almost a quarter of those in some establishments) is often poor. Further work was also needed in relation to young people with disabilities. There was a failure to identify which young people had learning difficulties or disabilities, yet this could have a significant impact on their experience of custody.

It seems likely that many of the problems identified by Inspectors arise in custodial institutions the world over. The UN Committee for the Rights of the Child reported in 2007 that violence occurs in all phases of the juvenile justice process, from the first contact with the police, during pre-trial detention and during the stay in treatment and other facilities for children sentenced to deprivation of liberty.[59]

The most important lesson about custodial care relates to the need to meet these basic and specific needs —keeping children and people safe, healthy and occupied—before seeking to apply more ambitious programme interventions that aim to produce changes in behaviour and attitude.

Given the strongly negative effects of custodial institutions, there is much to be said for seeking to keep young people out of them as far as possible. The model juvenile law produced by the UN states that detention is a measure of last resort and must not be imposed unless all available sentences other than a custodial sentence have been considered and adjudged inappropriate to meet the needs of the child and provide for the protection of society.[60]

There has been some success in recent years in England and Wales (UK) where the numbers in custody fell from 3000 in April 2008 to 1100 in 2014. This has been brought about by a combination of measures including greater use of diversion,

[58] HMI (2011a).

[59] UN doc. CRC/C/GC/10 (2007) para 13.

[60] UNODC (2013).

more restrictive sentencing criteria, improved communication between social work agencies and the courts and a greater focus on the costs of custodial places.[61] In other countries efforts have been made to reduce the use of custody. In Russia there has been an increase in the use of reconciliation (from 1.4 % of juvenile sentences in 2001 to 25 % in 2005),[62] and in New York State (USA) a number of training schools have been closed.[63] Yet there are counter examples: in Japan juveniles who commit crimes that would earn them life sentences if they had been adults currently face a limit of 15 years in prison. Less severe offences are capped at 10 years. A new law extends these two upper limits to 20 years and 15 years, respectively.

Experience suggests that efforts to reduce the use of custody are not always successful. Introducing demanding alternatives can save young people from the front door of a custodial sentence only to lead them to prison via the back door of breach. Even suspended sentences can have unintended consequences. It has been reported in Russia that because conditional terms of imprisonment are not accompanied by rehabilitation measures such as job or education opportunities, juveniles have few real opportunities to change their way of life. Consequently many, if not most, conditional sentences turn into real terms.

More encouraging are efforts at so-called Justice Reinvestment in which local education, social work and probation agencies are given financial incentives to develop alternatives to prison. While there has been some disappointment that the idea has not lived up to its early promise in the USA, in a number of states a virtuous cycle has been created in which savings from reduced custodial costs are invested in community based prevention and supervision programmes. There are encouraging results from the UK too.[64]

Reducing the use of custodial sanctions requires sentencing reform as well. Uganda's sentencing guidelines require courts to consider, inter alia, the best interests of the child, the rehabilitation of the child, the effect of a custodial sentence on the child, and ensure that the appropriate sentence is the least damaging to the interests of the child. Such criteria should encourage courts to look much more seriously at alternatives. But yet more radical measures may be required. A recent study of Training schools in the US argued "There is nothing —neither investigation, litigation, monitoring, nor oversight; not public censure, court order, or the mandates of the U.S. Constitution—powerful enough to stem the brutality that is part of daily life inside our nation's juvenile prisons, short of the courage to close the places down."[65]

---

[61] Allen (2011).

[62] Hakvag (2009).

[63] Solomon and Allen (2009).

[64] Allen (2014).

[65] Bernstein (2014).

2.3 Treatment

Given the growing acceptance that custodial measures are for the most part ineffective and damaging, recent years have seen a growing interest in devising alternative measures which might prove better at curbing teenage offending. The Washington State Institute for Public Policy analysed a range of measures which might reduce the need to build more prisons in the state.[66] Their work identified a number of programmes for young people which evidence showed would work to reduce re-offending. As well as diversion programmes, restorative justice and Teen Courts for lower risk offenders, these included more intensive programmes such as family and multi systemic therapy for young people who can remain at home, treatment foster care for those placed with other families, specialist programmes for sexual and aggressive offenders and those with chemical dependency and mental illness problems.

These are the kind of programmes which psychological research has shown to be effective in a range of studies over the last 20 years. Effective interventions match the intensity of the intervention to the level of risk posed by the young person and address their specific needs. Weak impulse control, attention deficits, high levels of anger, antisocial attitudes, and poor information-processing are among the factors that treatment programmes commonly try to change in order to reduce the likelihood of re-offending. Although there is a range of programmes that have been shown to produce good results, it has been estimated that only about 15,000 youth in the American juvenile justice system are treated with such evidence-based treatment each year. Since 160,000 youth are placed away from home each year, and an equal number are at high risk of placement, this means that fewer than 5 % of eligible high-risk juvenile offenders in the US are treated with an evidence-based treatment.[67]

There are a number of programmes that have been shown not to work very well; in the Washington study these include some common measures including counselling, education and intensive probation supervision and parole. These are likely to be used much more widely than are evidence based approaches. Other less common yet popular approaches such as Scared Straight (in which juvenile offenders are taken to visit a prison to meet hardened criminals) and Wilderness Challenge have also been found not to work—and in the case of Scared Straight programmes to increase re-offending. Boot camps—explicitly punitive regimes based on military drill and discipline—have also been found not to work well although in many US states they are used in order to shorten the length of sentences. Although they may have value as a short term cost cutting mechanism, they have no benefit in terms of recidivism.

Recent research has focussed less on specific programmes and more on how they are implemented. In a recent analysis only three factors emerged as major correlates

[66] Aos (2006).

[67] Henggeler and Schoenwald (2011).

of program effectiveness: a "therapeutic" intervention philosophy, serving high-risk offenders, and quality of implementation. With other variables statistically controlled, relatively few differences were found in the effectiveness of different types of therapeutic interventions.[68]

High quality implementation of interventions in both custody and the community requires adequate numbers of well-trained and motivated staff. A review of research suggested that a range of skills on the part of the workers are related to reduced offending and increased compliance by those under supervision.[69] Supervisors in whatever setting are effective if they are clear about their role, show pro social values and behaviour themselves and are prepared to challenge the young person consistently and fairly about their delinquency. Effectiveness is also enhanced if they help offenders with problems that are identified by the client rather than the worker, particularly if these are related to the person's offending, e.g. drugs, peers, employment, family issues. "In other words, they work in a collaborative, friendly, optimistic way so that the client develops trust in the worker as someone who can genuinely help them with their problems."[70]

Emphasising the role of staff in implementing sanctions is consistent with the most recent criminological evidence which suggests that treatment must take into account the human processes and social contexts through which change happens, and the meaning offenders attach to the efforts being made to reintegrate them. While it is tempting to want to identify interventions which succeed in stopping offenders from committing crime, it has been argued that the "what works" approach should be replaced by a new "desistance paradigm". This aims to focus on offering opportunities and motivations, and to help ex-offenders discover their capacity to make and enact choices in order to resist and overcome pressures that may lead them back to offending behaviour. This approach seems highly relevant to work with young offenders, including those in custody.[71] The paradigm suggests that a casework approach should be applied in work with young people and attaches priority to the need to engage effectively with young offenders' families, to enlist their support where possible in helping offenders to change their ways.

Thus one important finding from research is to emphasise processes of change rather than simply identify modes of intervention. A second is that interventions should not necessarily be concerned solely with preventing further offending. Encouraging offenders to make amends to victims and to communities through restorative processes and community service can play a part in convincing them that they are managing to become a different person—an essential component of sustained desistance from crime.

Alongside this desistance paradigm, it is important to consider elements of compliance or procedural justice theory, which argue that justice agencies will

[68] Lipsey (2009).

[69] Trotter (2006).

[70] Ibid p. 2.

[71] McNeill (2006).

only command compliance from offenders if they treat them in a way that is transparently fair. Negotiating a shared agenda for change is likely to produce better results than imposing one.

The principle of so called "responsivity"—that different offenders have different learning styles and that work should be tailored to these—is also important. This may be particularly significant in relation to any role played by the police in community based supervision programmes. Evidence from multi agency programmes for persistent offenders in the UK suggests that there can be dissonance between the approach of the police and other partners, underpinned by confusion about the overall aims of the project. From the point of view of some offenders, it is possible that police involvement may be a disincentive to participate in any programme. For others, the key factor will be whether reliable and relevant help is provided, whoever is providing it.

While there is limited evidence about effectiveness, many offenders say that they would prefer to receive help from people who have been through the criminal justice and prison system themselves.

Lessons from research in the past decade suggest that models based around three elements are most likely to produce positive effects: motivational and other work prior to release, post-release mentoring, and facilitating access to agencies and organisations.[72] Meeting basic practical needs remains crucial. The Prison Inspectorate has reported that "barriers such as not having a suitable address, a lack of appropriate courses and not being able to start courses immediately after release meant that many young people did not have an education or training placement to attend and of those that did, few were able to sustain it". A large number of young people had concerns about finding somewhere to live. Resettlement teams identified accommodation problems early, but often accommodation for young people not returning to their families was only confirmed very late in their sentence.[73] A Prison Inspectorate review of training plans for children and young people noted that arrangements for reviewing their progress while in custody were hampered by inadequate targets, infrequent meetings, variable attendance by key contributors and even a lack of appropriate locations for the discussions.[74] In a survey conducted for a thematic inspection report on resettlement provision for children and young people, only a third of young men had an education training or employment place arranged on release, only half were still attending a month later, and only a fifth of those who had not got a placement on release had one confirmed month later: "Overall the outcomes for our sample were very disappointing."[75]

---

[72] Lewis and Vennard (2003).

[73] HMI (2011a).

[74] HMI (2011a).

[75] HMI (2011b).

3 Women

In 1986 Ross and Fabiano published their book titled "Female Offenders Correctional Afterthoughts."[76] Following a period in which the use of imprisonment for women in the US and UK grew more sharply even than it did for men, a UK Supreme Court Judge said in 2005 that "it is now well recognised that a misplaced conception of equality has resulted in some very unequal treatment for the women and girls who appear before the criminal justice system. Simply put, a male ordered world has applied to them its perception of the appropriate treatment for male offenders."[77] Whether or not it is well recognised, in many countries, despite efforts to introduce more appropriate treatment for women, it is still the case that many of the sanctions applied to women are damaging, ineffective and counterproductive.

Two examples help to illustrate this. In October 2007, 19 year old Ashley Smith died by self-strangulation at Grand Valley Prison in Canada. In 2013, an inquest reached a verdict of homicide rather than suicide after their investigation into how it came to pass that a vulnerable young woman on high suicide watch died with a ligature around her neck while guards—who were ordered not to enter her cell if she was breathing —watched and videotaped. "Publicly released surveillance footage gave Canadians a rare window into the way prison staff, at times in full riot gear, wrestled with how to manage a young woman first imprisoned in 2003 after breaching probation for throwing crab apples at a postal worker."[78]

In June 2014, a 19 year old woman from Lancashire in the north of England was sentenced to prison for a violent assault. Natalie Harvey, who was 31 weeks pregnant was herself reportedly taken into care at the age of three. The judge said it was deeply troubling to see what had happened to her and her family in recent years and it may explain why somebody of just 19 had committed 21 offences, a lot of them for violence and it may explain her random, haphazard and chaotic life, not just in the past, but even more recently.

The judge told Natalie that "What's vitally important, it seems to me, in the next two or three months, in your interests, in your child's interests, but more particularly in society's interests, is that there is some stability, some proper medical help and some assistance. Prison provides punishment and it provides a deterrent and these are the main reasons people go to prison. But, prison also has benefits. It can work towards rehabilitation, it can work towards improving somebody's health and it can work towards stabilisation and it seems to me in these circumstances, despite your best endeavours, that stabilisation, at least for a short period of time, ought to be put in place."[79]

These two cases show how prison sanctions have come to fill a gap in society's response to troubled women. We know that female prisoners in many countries

[76] Ross and Fabiano (1986).

[77] Hale (2005).

[78] Globe and Mail (2013).

[79] Lancashire Telegraph (2014).

report higher levels of mental health needs compared with male prisoners. In England and Wales, a quarter revealed symptoms in a recent survey questionnaire that indicated psychotic illness, and 26 % reported having been treated or counselled for a mental health or emotional problem in the year before custody, compared with 16 % of men.[80] Female prisoners are more likely to attempt suicide and self-harm compared to male prisoners. The survey found that a fifth (19 %) of women reported having attempted suicide during the year before custody, nearly three times the rate of men. It was reported in 2014 that two thirds of the women prisoners at Cornton Vale in Scotland were subject to suicide watch.[81]

An earlier survey found histories of childhood abuse, repeated traumatic experiences, ongoing trauma symptoms combined with higher rates of self-harm, mental disorders and substance dependence amongst the sample.[82] A study of women prisons in eight countries carried out by the International Centre for Prison Studies (ICPS) found that "there are similarities in the type of women imprisoned in each country. ... in all countries they are a very disadvantaged group even amongst the disadvantaged and many come from backgrounds of abuse and violence, and have problems of addiction. A higher proportion of physical and mental health problems is noted amongst women prisoners."[83]

It is the case however that the recidivism rates among women leaving prison are lower than those for men. In the USA for example within 3 years of release from prison in 2005, 69.0 % of male and 58.5 % of female inmates had been arrested at least once. Five years after release from prison, more than three-quarters (77.6 %) of males and two-thirds (68.1 %) of females had been arrested. At the end of the first year, the male recidivism rate (44.5 %) was about 10 percentage points higher than the female rate (34.4 %), a difference that remained relatively stable over the following 4 years.[84]

3.1 Sentencing of Women

This very different profile of women offenders, which is found in many countries has led to many proposals for reform and some modifications to the system of sanctions.

In the UK a major review of women with vulnerabilities in the criminal justice system, the Corston review,[85] recommended a distinct approach to tackling

[80] Light et al. (2013).

[81] Scotland (2014).

[82] Borrill et al. (2003).

[83] ICPS (2008).

[84] Bureau of Justice Statistics (2014).

[85] Corston (2007).

women's offending which acknowledges that female offenders may have different problems compared to male offenders.

In practical terms, courts can and do reduce sentences by applying mitigating factors. These may relate to the circumstances relating to the offending—for example by taking into account experience of domestic abuse or violence, and or personal mitigation relating to the mental health care or other needs.

As a result perhaps of such mitigation, sentencing of women can be milder than that of men. In 2011, the latest year for which data is available, in England and Wales (UK), proportionally more females than males were discharged (21 % of females and 11 % of males) or given a community sentence (34 and 29 %, respectively). A greater proportion of males received immediate custodial sentences (27 % compared to 15 % of females) or a fine (17 % compared to 14 % of females).[86] More detailed comparison of the offences would be needed to establish whether these differences reflect different levels of seriousness.

Efforts have also been made to reduce sentence lengths for certain offences, which disproportionately involve women. In England and Wales the Sentencing Council reduced sentence lengths for so called "drug mules"—women who import drugs into the country at the behest of organised criminals. From 2012 the offence has had a starting point of 6 years imprisonment. Interviews with 12 imprisoned "drug mules" carried out as part of the preparation of the guideline demonstrated that a range of different women, with different backgrounds and circumstances, can become involved in operations as "drug mules". Some of these women admit to knowingly transporting drugs in this way, whilst others report travelling with no knowledge of the drugs. What is common amongst most of the women is the involvement of a trusted person in making arrangements or paying for their trips—either a family member, a friend or a friend of a friend. As a result the impact of the offence and sentence on the women was significant, with many reporting family betrayals, relationship breakdowns, health, housing or employment problems.[87]

Many female offenders are of course exclusively, or mainly, responsible for childcare. The Corston Report in the UK recognised that "in trying to break the inter-generational transmission of offending, related at least in part to inconsistent parenting and family breakdown it is recognised as important to divert women who do not present a risk to the public away from custody."[88] In a number of countries specific consideration is given to the impact of sentences on dependent children.

In 2007 South Africa's Constitutional court overturned a 4-year prison sentence imposed on a single mother of three young boys, suspending the sentence and substituting a correctional supervision order. The Court ruled that "the best interests of the child must be a paramount consideration in all proceedings affecting them, and it is clearly in the best interests of the minor children that they continue to

[86] MoJ (2012).

[87] Sentencing Council (2011).

[88] Corston (2007).

receive primary care from their mother. If M. were to be sent to jail, the children would suffer loss of maternal and emotional support, loss of home and community, disruption in school routines and transportation, and potential separation from their siblings, all of which could negatively impact their developmental process."[89] The limitations of the ruling were shown in a subsequent case where the Constitutional Court upheld a 5-year sentence for fraud in the case of a married mother of two. The Court found that although S v M had revolutionised the sentencing process by re-asserting the central role of the interests of young children of someone being sentenced as an independent consideration, where satisfactory alternative care arrangements could be made, there was no reason not to sentence a mother to prison.[90] In Russia, a more systematic approach is adopted: Article 177 of the Code of Criminal Procedure of the Russian Federation (CCPRF) provides the possibility for pregnant women and mothers with young children to defer serving their sentences until the child reaches the age of eight. In Ecuador, there was a one off programme of pardons (*indultos*) for which two categories of prisoner have been able to apply—those with terminal illnesses and also first time offenders convicted of drug trafficking of quantities less than two kilos. Many women benefitted from this. In California (USA), certain women have been allowed to spend the last period of their sentence in house arrest, drug facility or transitional care facility.

3.2 Implementation of Sanctions

Little is known about how different sanctions and measures are used with women across different jurisdictions and how these impact upon aspects of women's lives Elsewhere this handbook describes some of the ways in which prison sentences can be unsuitable for women. International norms require separation but this is not always achieved. In Denmark which prides itself on a philosophy of normalisation in prisons, women and men are held in mixed establishments but sadly, a rising number of sexual harassment cases in Danish prisons has prompted the Justice Ministry to look into whether there is a need for a prison for women only.

Even where women are held separately, they can face the risk of abuse by staff. A recent report alleged that security officials "routinely" rape women in prisons in DR Congo as punishment for their political activities, but this kind of abuse is the tip of an iceberg.

The underlying issue is that almost always prisons are designed and run by men for men. Many have design features and procedures such as security categorisation, which provide unnecessary levels of restriction given the low risks posed by most women in prison. Routine strip searches and constant surveillance may not only be unnecessary but can exacerbate trauma.

---

[89] Constitutional court of South Africa (2007).

[90] Constitutional Court of South Africa (2011).

The ICPS study[91] found the size of the units differs widely across the eight countries studied; the average size of unit in Western European countries has space for 60 women prisoners. The US States studied had the largest unit, with capacity for 2302 prisoners, closely followed by Russia with space for 2000 women.

The countries studied by ICPS found a wide range of approaches to prison design; in New Zealand the "standard" prison design is used even for its at-risk unit for suicidal women. In Canada there are a range of shared houses, in Germany one prison provides flats with balconies whilst Halle prison has a pay-laundry, a piano room and a large garden. In Western Australia at Boronia prison there are "pleasant gardens and well maintained houses that more closely resembled a well-kept suburban landscape than institutional setting."

While it is therefore possible to adapt the physical infrastructure, efforts at gender specific programming have been more controversial, with critics arguing that activities such as dog training in some American prisons are based on a perceived desire to nurture and vulnerability to men. California's proposed Female Rehabilitative Community Correctional Centers were criticised as prisons in all but name and not built. It has been suggested that "there is very little evidence that gender responsive programmes can have a positive impact on meeting women's (rehabilitative) needs and reduce the fast growing population of women in prison. On the contrary, all too often it is precisely this belief in the magic of programming that feeds the rapid growth in women's prison."[92]

As for community based orders, UK evidence suggests that women are slightly more likely to complete probation type orders than men although those women that do not are more likely to have failed to comply with the conditions than men who are more likely to have committed a further offence. It has been suggested that community based sentences are imposed on female offenders who are less serious or persistent than their male counterparts. There is a risk that in the event of further offending, women may be considered by courts to have exhausted these options more quickly than men.

There is some evidence that child care and travel can make it more difficult for women to keep appointments but it may also be that failing to meet some of the other practical, financial and relationship issues that may impact on women's lives increase the risk of non-compliance. There is controversy over whether some of the accredited programmes—particularly those based on cognitive behavioural theory—are as suitable for or as effective with women as men.[93] It has also been suggested that actuarial risk assessment tools are gender blind, and for example "are totally insensitive to South Africa's particular socio- economic and cultural characteristics. They do not take into account economic marginality and structural inequality in the way that it features here."[94]

---

[91] ICPS (2008).

[92] Bosworth and Fili (2013).

[93] Martin et al. (2009).

[94] OSF (2010).

It has been proposed that community based treatment approaches need to be organised in non-authoritarian cooperative settings where women can be empowered to change.[95] Such settings are likely to be for women only and include women who are not offenders. Work should be undertaken to address the full range of a woman's needs and problems—other research has suggested that meeting practical needs for stable accommodation and financial security may be needed before therapeutic help can be successful. Mentoring and the ability to maintain contact with the staff and other women over a period of time are also considered important. Effective relations with staff may be particularly important for women.[96]

The Ministry of Justice in England and Wales has been supporting a network of community based centres for women which apply some of these principles in order to tackle underlying causes of offending and divert those who have not offended, but have a number of risk factors for doing so, away from crime. An outcome evaluation of some of the longer-established centres is under way which will examine their impact on reoffending. This builds on previous research, which found the centres to have been swiftly and efficiently implemented and welcomed by local agencies and sentencers who perceived them to be filling an important gap. Service users who sustained contact valued the support and services offered. A similar project has been operating in Glasgow (Scotland)—the 218 project.

It has been suggested that some sentencers lack knowledge about some of these community services and may be reluctant to send convicted offenders to mixed centres where non-offenders also attend.

4 Conclusion

Sanctions for young people and for women seldom work well and there is a case for a fundamental rethink of the way criminal justice systems deal with both groups. In many cases, diversion away from prosecution and punishment offers a better prospect of reducing recidivism than does formal processing by the courts. The use of imprisonment can have particularly damaging consequences. In the short term poor living conditions and high levels of violence characterise life in institutions the world over. In the longer term, warehousing vulnerable and damaged people without addressing their problems can make it more rather than less likely that they will re-offend. Research has started to identify approaches, which are more effective in encouraging desistance from crime such as support, whether in prison or the community, in tackling substance misuse, employment and relationship problems.

The question remains about whether initiatives such as these are sufficiently widely available to impact on the use of prison. It was recently suggested that "In

[95] Gelsthorpe et al. (2007).

[96] Gelsthorpe (2013).

the last 20 years there has been a growing international recognition that prison is an inappropriate response to women in conflict with the law"[97] Much the same could be said about children. Even if this were true, there is long way to go to turn the recognition into a reality. Developing the law, policy and practice, which can reduce and ultimately eliminate the unnecessary use of imprisonment has proved difficult in a climate of opinion which places a greater value on punishment than is justified by evidence.

Five Questions

1. Under what circumstances is it desirable to divert children and women from the formal justice system?
2. In what ways should emerging knowledge about the impact of sanctions be incorporated into law and policy?
3. 3 Should there be a distinct sentencing system for women offenders?
4. What are the key implications of research for the recruitment and training of staff implementing sanctions?
5. What are likely to be the characteristics of effective institutions for a) children and b) women?

References

Allen, R. (2011). *Last resort: Exploring the reduction in child imprisonment 2008–11*. London: Prison Reform Trust.

Allen, R. (2014). *Justice reinvestment: empty slogan or sustainable future for penal policy?* London: Transform Justice.

Amnesty International undated Executions of juveniles since 1990 International. http://www.amnesty.org/en/death-penalty/executions-of-child-offenders-since-1990 Accessed 28 July 2014.

Dowden, C., & Andrews, D. (1999). What works in young offender treatment: A meta-analysis journal. Forum on Corrections Research Volume:11 Issue 2 Correctional services Canada Ottawa.

Andrews, D., Hollin, C., Raynor, P., Trotter, C., & Armstrong, B. (2000). *Sustaining effectiveness in working with offenders*. Cardiff: Cognitive Centre Foundation.

Andrews, D., & Bonta, J. (2006). *The psychology of criminal conduct* (4th ed.). Newark: Anderson Publishing.

Aos, S. (2006). Evidence-Based Public Policy Options to Reduce Future Prisons Construction, Criminal Justice Costs and Crime Rates http://www.wsipp.wa.gov/ReportFile/952 Accessed July 28 2014.

Bernstein, N. (2014). *Burning down the house. The end of juvenile prison*. New York: The New Press.

Borrill, J., Maden, A., Martin, A., Weaver, T., Stimson, G., Farrell, M., & Barnes, T. (2003). Differential substance misuse treatment needs of women, ethnic minorities and young offenders in prison: prevalence of substance misuse and treatment needs (Home Office Online Report 33/03). Home Office Research, Development and Statistics Directorate. London.

[97] Malloch and McIvor (2012).

Bosworth, M., & Fili, A. (2013). Corrections, gender specific programming and offender re-entry. In C. Renzetti, S. Miller, & G. Routledge (Eds.), *International handbook of crime and gender studies*. London: Routledge.

Bureau of Justice Statistics (2014). Recidivism of Prisoners Released in 30 States in 2005: Patterns from 2005 to 2010. http://www.bjs.gov/content/pub/pdf/rprts05p0510.pdf. Accessed 28 July 2014.

Butts, J., & Ortiz, J. (2011). Teen Courts Do They Work and Why? http://johnjayresearch.org/wp-content/uploads/2011/04/buttsortizjrnjan11.pdf. Accessed 28 July 2014.

Butts, J.A., Buck, J., & Coggeshall, M. (2002). The Impact of Teen Court on Young Offender The Urban Institute Washington DC http://www.urban.org/UploadedPDF/410457.pdf. Accessed 28 July 2014.

ChildONEurope (2014). Survey on the CRC Committee Concluding Observations on the last EU Countries' reports http://www.childoneurope.org/issues/publications/COESeries9-Cocludingobs.pdf.Accessed 28 July 2014.

Coalition for Juvenile Justice (undated). Deinstitutionalisation of Status Offences http://juvjustice.org/sites/default/files/ckfinder/files/dso%20fact%20sheet.pdf. Accessed 28 July 2014.

Constitutional court of South Africa (2007). S v M https://www.crin.org/en/library/legal-database/s-v-m. Accessed 28 July 2014.

Constitutional Court of South Africa (2011). S v the State http://www.saflii.org/za/cases/ZACC/2011/7media.pdf. Accessed 28 July 2014.

Corston, J. (2007). A Report by Baroness Jean Corston of a Review of Women with Particular Vulnerabilities in the Criminal Justice System. Home Office London.

Council of Europe (2004). Report to the Polish Government on the Visit to Poland Carried out by the European Committee for the Prevention of Torture and Inhuman or Degrading Treatment or Punishment (CPT) from 4 to 15 October 2004. Strasbourg.

Death Penalty Information Centre (undated). http://www.deathpenaltyinfo.org/u-s-supreme-court-roper-v-simmons-no-03-633?scid=38&did=885#summary. Accessed 28 July 2014.

Dignity (2014). Conditions for Women in Detention: Needs, vulnerabilities and good practices Danish Institute against Torture Study No. 7 http://www.dignityinstitute.org/media/1991156/no7_women_in_detention_udgave1.pdf.

Geller, A., Garfinkel, I., & Western, B. (2006). *The effects of incarceration on employment and wages: An analysis of the fragile families survey*. Princeton, NJ: The Center for Research on Child Wellbeing.

Gelsthorpe, L., Sharpe, G., & Roberts, J. (2007). Provision for women offenders in the community. *Fawcett Society; London..*

Gelsthorpe, L. (2013). Working with women in probation. In P. Ugwudike & P. Raynor (Eds.), *What works in offender compliance*. London: Palgrave McMillan.

Globe & Mail (2013). Mother 'elated' as Ashley Smith's jail death is ruled a homicide http://www.theglobeandmail.com/news/national/ashley-smith-inquest/article16052548/?page. Accessed 28 July 2014.

Graham, J. (2011). Review of the Youth Justice System in Northern Ireland http://www.dojni.gov.uk/index/publications/publication-categories/pubs-criminal-justice/review-of-youth-justice---large-print-version-of-report.pdf. Accessed 28 July 2014.

Guardian (2014). Do US laws that punish parents for truancy keep their kids in school? 23 June http://www.theguardian.com/education/2014/jun/23/-sp-school-truancy-fines-jail-parents-pun ishment-children. Accessed 28 July 2014.

Hakvag, U. (2009). Juvenile Justice in the Russian Federation University of Oslo https://www.duo.uio.no/bitstream/handle/10852/33991/Hakvaag.pdf?sequence=1. Accessed 28 July 2014.

Hale, B. (2005). The Sinners and the Sinned Against: Women in the Criminal Justice System Longford Lecture http://www.longfordtrust.org/lecture_details.php?id=10. Accessed 28 July 2014.

Harris, P., Lockwood, B., Mengers, L., & Stoodley, B. (2009). Measuring Recidivism in Juvenile Corrections http://www.journalofjuvjustice.org/jojj0101/article01.htm. Accessed 28 July 2014.

Hawton, K., Linsell, L., Adenjii, T., Sariaslan, A., & Fazel, S. (2014). Self-harm in prisons in England and Wales: An epidemiological study of prevalence, risk factors, clustering, and subsequent suicide. *The Lancet, 383*(9923), 1147–1154.

Scotland, H. (2014). Two in three women in Scots prison are on suicide watch 7 February http://www.heraldscotland.com/news/home-news/two-in-three-women-in-scots-prison-are-on-suicide-watch.23368490. Accessed 28 July 2014.

Henggeler, S., & Schoenwald, S. (2011). Evidence-based interventions for juvenile offenders and juvenile justice policies that support them. SRCD Social Policy Report *25*(1), 3–20 http://www.mtfc.com/2011_EB_Interventions_for_Juv_Offenders.pdf. Accessed 28 July 2014.

HMI (2013a). Report on an unannounced inspection of HMP/YOI Feltham (Feltham A – children and young people) 21–25 January 2013 http://www.justiceinspectorates.gov.uk/prisons/wp-content/uploads/sites/4/2014/03/feltham-a-annual-report.pdf. Accessed 28 July 2014.

HMI (2013b). HM Chief Inspector of Prisons for England and Wales Annual Report 2012–13 http://www.justiceinspectorates.gov.uk/prisons/wp-content/uploads/sites/4/2014/04/hm-inspectorate-prisons-annual-report-2012-13.pdf. Accessed 28 July 2014.

HMI (2012). Report on an announced inspection of HMYOI Wetherby 30 January–3 February 2012 http://www.justiceinspectorates.gov.uk/prisons/wp-content/uploads/sites/4/2014/03/wetherby-2012.pdf. Accessed 28 July 2014.

HMI (2011a). Chief Inspector of Prisons for England and Wales Annual Report, 2010/11. http://www.justice.gov.uk/downloads/publications/corporate-reports/hmi-prisons/hmip-annual-report-2010-11.pdf. Accessed 28 July 2014.

HMI (2011b). Resettlement provision for children and young people. http://www.justice.gov.uk/downloads/publications/inspectorate-reports/hmipris/thematic-reports-and-research-publications/Resettlement-thematic-june2011.pdf. Accessed 28 July 2014.

HM Chief Inspector of Prisons (2009). The Prison Characteristics That Predict Prisons Being Assessed As Performing 'Well': A Thematic Review January 2009. http://www.justice.gov.uk/downloads/publications/inspectorate-reports/hmipris/thematic-reports-and-research-publications/prison_performance_thematic-rps.pdf. Accessed 28 July 2014.

Human Rights Watch (2013). Afghanistan Surge in Women Jailed for Moral Crimes. http://www.hrw.org/news/2013/05/21/afghanistan-surge-women-jailed-moral-crimes. Accessed 28 July 2014.

ICPS (2008). International Profile of Women's prisons http://www.prisonstudies.org/sites/prisonstudies.org/files/resources/downloads/20080501_womens_prisons_int_review__final_report_v_2.pdf. Accessed 28 July 2014.

JLOS (2013). The Constitution (Sentencing Guidelines for Courts of Judicature) (Practice) Directions http://www.jlos.go.ug/index.php/component/k2/item/281-sentencing-guidelines-signed-into-law. Accessed 28 July 2014.

Judicial College (2013). Equal Treatment Bench Book http://www.judiciary.gov.uk/wp-content/uploads/JCO/Documents/judicial-college/ETBB_all_chapters_final.pdf. Accessed 28 July 2014.

Lancashire Telegraph (2014). Have your baby in prison http://www.lancashiretelegraph.co.uk/news/11279599.HAVE_YOUR_BABY_IN_PRISON__Judge_sends_pregnant_East_Lancs_attacker_to_jail/. Accessed 28 July 2014.

Lewis, S., & Vennard, J. (2003). *The resettlement of short-term prisoners: An evaluation of seven Pathfinders.*

Light, M., Grant, E., & Hopkins, K. (2013). Gender differences in substance misuse and mental health amongst prisoners Results from the Surveying Prisoner Crime Reduction (SPCR) longitudinal cohort study of prisoners. London: Ministry of Justice.

Lipsey, M. (2009). The primary factors that characterized effective interventions with juvenile offenders: A meta-analytic overview. *Victims & Offenders: An International Journal of Evidence-based Research, Policy, and Practice., 4*(2), 124–147.

Lipsey, M. (1992). Juvenile delinquency treatment: A meta-analytic inquiry into the variability of effects. In T. D. Cook et al. (Eds.), *Meta-analysis for explanation: A casebook*. New York: Russell Sage.

Lipsey, M., & Wilson, D. (1998). Effective intervention for serious juvenile offenders: a synthesis of research. In R. Loeber & D. Farrington (Eds.), *Serious and violent juvenile offenders : Risk factors and successful interventions*. Thousand Oaks, California: Sage.

Malloch, M., & McIvor, G. (2012). Women, punishment and social justice. In M. Malloch & G. McIvor (Eds.), *Women, punishment and social justice: Human rights and penal practices. Routledge frontiers of criminal justice*. London: Routledge.

Martin, J., Kautt, P., & Gelsthorpe, L. (2009). What works for women? A comparison of community-based general offending programme completion. *British Journal of Criminology, 49*(6), 879–899.

McAra, L., & McVie, S. (2007). Youth justice?: The impact of system contact on patterns of desistance from offending. *European Journal of Criminology, 4*(3), 315–345.

McGarrell, E., & Hipple, N. (2007). Family group conferencing and re-offending among first-time juvenile offenders: The Indianapolis experiment. *Justice Quarterly, 24*(2), 221–246.

McNeill, F. (2006). A desistance paradigm for offender management. *Criminology and Criminal Justice, 6*(1), 39–62.

Ministry of Justice (2014). Proven Re-offending Statistics Quarterly Bulletin July 2011 to June 2012, England and Wales https://www.gov.uk/government/uploads/system/uploads/attachment_data/file/305896/proven-reoffending-quarterly-bulletin-jul11-jun12.pdf. Accessed 28 July 2014.

Ministry of Justice. (2012). *Statistics on women and the criminal justice system 2011*. London: Ministry of Justice.

Ministry of Justice/Youth Justice Board (2012). Developing the Secure Estate for Children and Young People in England and Wales: Plans until 2015 http://yjbpublications.justice.gov.uk/en-gb/Scripts/prodView.asp?idproduct=502&eP. Accessed 28 July 2014.

National Council for Independent Monitoring Boards (2011). Behind Closed Doors Annual Report 2011 http://www.justice.gov.uk/downloads/about/imb/imb-national-council-annual-report-2011.pdf. Accessed 28 July 2014.

Office for Juvenile Justice and Delinquency Prevention (2006). Juvenile Offenders and Victims 2006 Report http://www.ojjdp.gov/ojstatbb/nr2006/downloads/NR2006.pdf. Accessed 28 July 2014.

OSF (2010). Report on the Open Society Foundation for South Africa (OSF-SA) conference on recidivism and reoffending in South Africa 29 and 30 November 2010 Sandton Sun Hotel, Johannesburg. http://osf.org.za/wp/wp-content/uploads/2012/09/Meeting-Report_-Recidivism-conference_20101.pdf. Accessed 28 July 2014.

Petrosino, A., Turpin-Petrosino, C., & Guckenberg, S. (2010). Formal System Processing of Juveniles: Effects on Delinquency' Campbell Systematic Review 2010:1 http://www.campbellcollaboration.org/lib/download/761/. Accessed 28 July 2014.

RAWA News (2014). Afghanistan end Moral Crimes Prosecutions http://www.rawa.org/temp/runews/2014/06/24/afghanistan-end-moral-crimes-prosecutions.html. Accessed 28 July 2014.

Ross, R., & Fabiano, E. (1986). *Women offenders correctional afterthoughts*. Jefferson, N.C.: McFarlane.

Scottish Government (2004). International Evidence to Scotland's Children's Hearings Review: Decision Making and Services Relating to Children and Young People Involved in Offending http://www.scotland.gov.uk/Publications/2004/11/20241/46537. Accessed 28 July 2014.

Sentencing Council (2011). Drug 'mules': Twelve case studies http://sentencingcouncil.judiciary.gov.uk/docs/Drug_mules_bulletin.pdf. Accessed 28 July 2014.

Sentencing Guidelines Council (2009). Overarching Principles Sentencing Youths http://sentencingcouncil.judiciary.gov.uk/docs/web_overarching_principles_sentencing_youths.pdf. Accessed 28 July 2014.

Sentencing Project (2014). Slow to Act State Responses to 2012 Supreme Court Mandate on Life without Parole http://sentencingproject.org/doc/publications/jj_State_Responses_to_Miller.pdf. Accessed 28 July 2014.

Sentencing Project (2013). Life Goes on the Historic Rise in Life Sentences in America http://sentencingproject.org/doc/publications/inc_Life%20Goes%20On%202013.pdf. Accessed 28 July 2014.

Solomon, E., & Allen, R. (2009). *Reducing child imprisonment in England and Wales - Lessons from abroad*. London: Prison Reform Trust.

Trotter, C. (2006). Effective community-based supervision of young offenders http://www.aic.gov.au/media_library/publications/tandi_pdf/tandi448.pdf. Accessed 28 July 2014.

UN doc. CRC/C/GC/10 (2007). General Comment, No. 10, Children's rights in juvenile justice.

UN General Assembly resolution 65/229 of 21 December 2010, United Nations Rules for the Treatment of Women Prisoners and Non-custodial Measures for Women Offenders (the Bangkok Rules).

UN doc. A/68/340 (2013). Rashida Manjoo, Special Rapporteur, Pathways to, conditions and consequences of incarceration for women. Note by the Secretary-General http://www.ohchr.org/Documents/Issues/Women/A-68-340.pdf. Accessed 28 July 2014.

UNODC (2013). Justice in Matters Involving Children in Conflict with the Law Model Law on Juvenile Justice and Related Commentary http://www.unodc.org/documents/justice-and-prison-reform/Justice_Matters_Involving-Web_version.pdf. Accessed 28 July 2014.

US State Department (2013). Human Rights Report http://www.state.gov/j/drl/rls/hrrpt/humanrightsreport/index.htm#wrapper. Accessed 28 July 2014.

Williams, K., Papadopolou, V., & Booth, N. (2012). *Prisoners' childhood and family backgrounds Results from the Surveying Prisoner Crime Reduction (SPCR) longitudinal cohort study of prisoners*. London: Ministry of Justice.

Wilson, H., & Hoge, R. (2013). The Effect of Youth diversion programs on recidivism Meta-Analytic Review Criminal Justice and Behaviour Vol. 40, No. 5, May 2013, 497-518 http://www.soc.umn.edu/~uggen/Wilson_CJB_13.pdf. Accessed 28 July 2014.

Children of Prisoners: Their Situation and Role in Long-Term Crime Prevention

Oliver Robertson, Kris Christmann, Kathryn Sharratt, Anne H. Berman, Martin Manby, Elizabeth Ayre, Liliana Foca, Romeo Asiminei, Kate Philbrick, and Cristina Gavriluta

Abstract Studies suggest that maintaining family ties can help reduce the likelihood of reoffending, and that while parental imprisonment can increase a child's likelihood to offend, positive responses to the situation can aid the children's well-being, attitude and attainment. Drawing on findings from the EU-funded COPING Project on the mental health of children of prisoners, this chapter explores the factors that aid a child's ability to cope with parental imprisonment and the actions that different stakeholders can take to support them. It identifies some of the mental health impacts at different stages of parental imprisonment, the roles played by non-imprisoned parents/carers and by schools, and suggests options for further clarifying the factors that help and hinder children of prisoners in the short and long term.

O. Robertson (✉)
Penal Reform International, London, UK
e-mail: orobertson@penalreform.org

K. Christmann • K. Sharratt • M. Manby
University of Huddersfield, Huddersfield, UK
e-mail: k.christmann@hud.ac.uk; k.sharratt@hud.ac.uk; m.manby@hud.ac.uk

A.H. Berman
Karolinska Institutet, Stockholm, Sweden
e-mail: anne.h.berman@ki.se

E. Ayre
Maastricht University, Maastricht, The Netherlands

L. Foca
Alternative Sociale, Bucarest, Romania
e-mail: lilianafoca@alternativesociale.ro

R. Asiminei • C. Gavriluta
Alexandru Ioan Cuza University of Iaşi, Iaşi, Romania
e-mail: romeo.asiminei@uaic.ro; cristina_gavriluta@yahoo.fr

K. Philbrick
Children of Prisoners Europe (COPE), Montrouge, France
e-mail: katephilbrick@uwclub.net

H. Kury et al. (eds.), *Women and Children as Victims and Offenders: Background, Prevention, Reintegration*, DOI 10.1007/978-3-319-28424-8_8

1 Introduction

Children of prisoners have become increasingly visible in academic and policy circles since 2000, though are still widely ignored compared to other situations[1] and marginalised groups. As research has moved on from small-scale or anecdotal accounts to more robust studies, it has been possible to say with more confidence the ways in which children can be affected, as well as highlighting interventions that may assist them in coping with parental imprisonment.

Children can be affected at all stages of a parent's involvement with the criminal justice process, from the point of arrest to the time of reintegration into the community following release. The ways in which they can be affected are also varied and include emotional, psychological, financial, material, physical and social impacts. For example, the loss of a working parent can mean reduced finances and potentially the need to move to a different home, if the current property can no longer be afforded. The parent-child relationship may come under strain because of greatly reduced and highly controlled opportunities for contact. And the distress caused by the parent's imprisonment and the responses of others to it (especially if they are stigmatising—"your dad's a criminal") can mean that children become isolated, angry and/or scared, and in some cases develop physical or mental health problems. It should also be noted that there can be positive effects for children, for example when a dangerous or chaotic parent is removed from the family home.

It immediately becomes clear, when looking at different countries and world regions, that this is not an issue confined to one part of the globe, or that it particularly affects wealthier or poorer countries. Every country has prisons, and it is virtually certain that at least some of the prisoners have children. The range and extent of impacts will vary depending on the country context and the individual child (even children from the same family may react in very different ways), but it is striking that children from many different countries describe the same feelings, with the most universal being loss.

In recent years, the policy and (particularly) academic research on children of prisoners has become increasingly rigorous, with both longitudinal studies (following a group over many years or decades to see the impact of a particular event, in this case parental imprisonment) and large-scale studies (of hundreds or more participants) verifying what previous studies and practitioners have stated, and in

[1] The United Nations Office on Drugs and Crime and the United Nations Children's Fund are among the key global intergovernmental actors who deal with children in conflict with the law and children as victims and witnesses of crime.

a few cases refuting it.[2] One consistent finding across anecdotal and scientifically robust research is that having a parent in prison is generally negative for children, both at a population level (most children report it being a negative experience) and an individual level (most children report more negative impacts than positive).

However, there are a number of interventions that research suggests have positive impacts on children's ability to cope with parental imprisonment. A number of these emerged through the research of the EU-funded COPING Project (Children of Prisoners, Interventions and Mitigations to Strengthen Mental Health), whose methodology and results are detailed and discussed below.

Positive interventions may help in maintaining the relationship with the imprisoned parent, or in supporting the children in other parts of their lives. Research suggests that (at least in some countries) having a parent imprisoned can increase the likelihood of boys going on to exhibit antisocial behaviour later in life. While no research known to the authors has yet been completed identifying whether children that cope better with parental imprisonment have a reduced risk of future antisocial behaviour compared to those that do not, many of the behaviours and factors reported by children of prisoners (including anger, truanting and lack of social ties, as well as having a parent with previous convictions) are recognised risk factors predicting antisocial behaviour and offending (Mortimer 2010; Becroft 2006). Therefore, helping children of prisoners now may reap benefits in terms of future crime prevention. (There is also the long-recognised role played by maintenance of family connections in reducing the probability of reoffending by released prisoners; while not the focus of this chapter, it is relevant to bear in mind as an additional benefit.)

2 Literature Review

Parental imprisonment does not necessarily signal the onset of problems for children; for many, it will represent the continuation of an already difficult family situation. Literature consistently reveals that children of prisoners are more likely than their peers to come from families severely disadvantaged by poverty, unemployment, poor educational outcomes, domestic violence, substance misuse and mental health problems (Social Exclusion Unit 2002). Although the imposition of a custodial sentence might present clear benefits for some children, for example, by

[2] One example is the finding from the COPING study (see below) that children are as affected by a father's imprisonment as by a mother's, which went against previous findings that a mother's imprisonment had more severe effects (due at least in part to the greater likelihood for imprisoned mothers to be raising children on their own, meaning that children would be more likely to change carer and possibly home and school, as well as losing their parent). However, the COPING researchers speculated that this may be due to the cohort of children that participated, almost all of whom were in contact with their imprisoned parent and who were taken to visit by their non-imprisoned parent or carer.

providing a welcome relief from domestic violence and substance misuse, there is considerable evidence to suggest that *most* children suffer following parental imprisonment (Murray 2005). Parental imprisonment has a variety of adverse consequences for children including breakdown of family relationships, disruption to caregiving arrangements, financial hardship, unwelcome adjustments to roles and responsibilities, and stigma and bullying (Smith et al. 2007; Murray 2007).

Children experience a diverse range of negative emotional reactions to parental imprisonment including feelings of rejection, sadness, despair, confusion, depression, withdrawal and symptoms of post-traumatic stress disorder (Hissel et al. 2011; Bocknek et al. 2009; Murray and Farrington 2008). Responses to parental imprisonment are not limited to the aforementioned internalising or 'acting in' problems, but also include externalising or 'acting out' behaviours such as anger, aggression, conduct problems, truancy, sexual promiscuity, and underage smoking and alcohol consumption (Schlafer and Poehlmann 2010; Hanlon et al. 2005; Boswell and Wedge 2002).

3 Criminal and Anti-Social Outcomes

Of particular concern are the numerous studies that indicate a strong association between parental imprisonment and children's involvement in antisocial and criminal behaviour (Barnardos 2014b; see Murray et al. 2009 for a review). For example, USA research identified imprisonment as a powerful determinant of mobility for both former inmates and their children, with children of prisoners suffering reduced educational attainment and lower lifetime income (Pew Charitable Trusts 2010). Although it has been widely recognised that the adverse behavioural outcomes could be attributed to pre-existing disadvantage and might not be a direct result of parental imprisonment, the emergence of more robust methodological approaches provides more convincing evidence that parental imprisonment might actually *cause* criminal behaviour in children. Of particular note is the Cambridge Study of Delinquent Development (UK), which found that children of prisoners are significantly more likely than their peers to engage in criminal and antisocial behaviour both in adolescence and adulthood (Murray and Farrington 2005), suggesting that the effects are both profound and long-lasting.

Adopting similarly robust methodological approaches, the Criminal Career and Life Course Study (Netherlands) found only a weak causal relationship between parental imprisonment and offending behaviour (van de Rakt et al. 2012), and Project Metropolitan (Sweden) found no causal effect (Murray et al. 2007). This is not to suggest that the results are inconclusive, but rather highlight the importance of understanding cross-country differences in the mechanisms underlying the transmission of criminal and antisocial behaviour. The authors suggested that the combination of Scandinavia's more welfare-orientated justice systems, shorter prison sentences, family-friendly prison policies, extensive social support systems, and more sympathetic attitudes towards crime and punishment might explain why children were less affected by parental imprisonment than in the UK.

4 Risk and Protective Factors

The extent to which an individual child might be affected by parental imprisonment will depend greatly on the existence of a range of risk and protective factors. In order to design effective interventions to reduce the likelihood of criminal and antisocial outcomes, it is crucial that we develop an understanding of factors that might mediate the impact of parental imprisonment.

4.1 Individual Differences

Research indicates that boys who have experienced parental imprisonment are at greater risk of developing criminal and antisocial behaviour than girls (Murray et al. 2009). Indeed, there is supporting evidence that boys tend to display more externalising problems in response to parental imprisonment, whereas girls tend to display more internalising problems (Murray and Farrington 2008). As already noted, the effects of parental imprisonment persist throughout the life-course, but have found to be most pronounced in adolescence suggesting that there might be a "critical period" for intervention (Murray et al. 2009). Nevertheless, children's responses to parental imprisonment are highly individualised, and there is evidence that certain temperaments and coping styles can promote more successful adjustment (Hagan et al. 2005).

4.2 The Parent-Child Relationship

Research has also demonstrated that custodial sentences (rather than community sentences), imprisonment since birth (rather than before birth), repeat incarceration, and longer periods of imprisonment all increase the risk of the child engaging in criminal or antisocial behaviour (Murray et al. 2009). This suggests that actual separation due to imprisonment (and not just having a criminal parent) is a significant contributory factor. Secure parent-child attachments are known to be important for development, not least positive behavioural outcomes (Bowlby 1973a), yet children of prisoners are less likely to have secure attachments to their imprisoned parent (Poehlmann 2005). Children variously report feelings of alienation from their parent, problems communicating, difficulties coming to terms with the situation, and shame and embarrassment at their parent's involvement in criminal activity (Tudball 2000; Schlafer and Poehlmann 2010).

There is strong evidence that maintaining frequent contact with the imprisoned parent can act as a significant buffer against the deterioration of the parent-child relationship and adjustment problems on behalf of the child (Lösel et al. 2012; Poehlmann 2005; Murray 2005). Unfortunately there are multiple barriers to sustaining frequent contact, including prison policies governing arrangements for contact, the remaining parent/carer's capacity to facilitate contact, and the distance to prison and associated travel costs (Arditti and Few 2006). Contact that occurs in child-friendly environments or in the context of interventions designed to support positive parent-child interaction also has more positive outcomes for relationships and adjustment (Sharratt 2014; Poehlmann and Schlafter 2010). There is considerable evidence that in the absence of such environments and interventions, many children find the prison environment intimidating and interaction with their parent unsatisfactory (Nesmith and Ruhland 2008; Brown et al. 2001; Tudball 2000).

The maintenance of family relationships also has positive implications for the parent in prison. Enabling prisoners to be actively involved in their child's development is important for their rehabilitation, not least their sense of parental competence and self-esteem (Loper et al. 2009; Clarke et al. 2005). Prisoners who maintain contact also have better resettlement outcomes, for example they are more likely to have accommodation and employment arranged for their release, and are also less likely to reoffend (May et al. 2008; Niven and Stewart 2005).

4.3 Support: Families, Schools and Peers

Research evidence indicates that maternal imprisonment is a greater risk factor for criminal and antisocial outcomes than paternal imprisonment (Murray et al. 2009). Imprisoned mothers tend to be located further from home, presenting greater challenges to visiting and reducing the chances of sustaining parent-child relationships (Robertson 2007; Prison Reform Trust 2013). Maternal imprisonment also causes comparatively more disruption to children's caregiving arrangements, with children being more likely to move in with members of the extended family or to be taken into care (Williams et al. 2012). A change of home might necessitate a change of schools, disrupting children's education and separating them from existing support networks (George and LaLonde 2002). However, positive educational attainment and strong social ties are known to protect against criminal and antisocial outcomes (Social Exclusion Unit 2002).

Research evidence indicates that stable and nurturing caregiving arrangements are critical to ensuring successful adjustment to parental imprisonment, and can protect against the development of behavioural problems (Mackintosh et al. 2006; Poehlmann 2005). The extent to which the non-imprisoned parent/carer successfully copes with parental imprisonment also has a bearing on the child as this can affect their capacity to support the child (Wildeman et al. 2012; Jones and Wainaina-Woźna 2013). Although parents/carers might prefer to provide false explanations or incomplete information regarding the parent's absence with the best interests of protecting the child from harm, there is unequivocal evidence that honest, sensitive and developmentally appropriate communication about the parent's imprisonment facilitates better adjustment on behalf of the child (Poehlmann 2005; King 2002).

It is not uncommon for parents/carers to insist that the child keeps the imprisonment a secret in order to protect them from negative reactions from peers and the community; this denies them the opportunity to seek social support and has been found to be associated with more severe internalising and externalising problems (Hagan and Myers 2003). Conversely, when children share selectively with their closest and most trusted friends, peers can serve as an invaluable source of support and this is associated with more positive emotional and behavioural outcomes (Jones and Wainaina-Woźna 2013).

Families affected by imprisonment can be reluctant to access support from outside agencies due to stigma, lack of information about available support, and in some cases mistrust of statutory services (Pugh and Lanskey 2011). This concern is not unfounded; teachers for example, have been found to hold less favourable expectations of children with a parent in prison (Trice and Brewster 2004; Dallaire et al. 2010). This is unfortunate, since families have an existing relationship with schools, making them a key site of support. Teachers have been observed to be instrumental in supporting children of prisoners to overcome the emotional challenges associated with parental imprisonment and in providing support to enable them to fulfil their academic potential (Roberts 2012). This underscores the need for training and greater understanding of these issues within schools and communities, who can be an invaluable source of support.

5 Methodology[3]

The COPING study included four data collection elements to identify issues related to the mental health and well-being of children of prisoners and their imprisoned and non-imprisoned parents/carers, primarily in Germany, Romania, Sweden and the UK. The children of prisoners and their parents/carers were investigated through a self-reporting questionnaire; and in-depth qualitative interviews were held with a subsection of families who took part in the survey. Other stakeholders, such as prison staff, school staff, social services workers and government officials, were consulted using a qualitative questionnaire; and a mapping of available relevant services inside and outside prison was undertaken in the countries.

[3] The remainder of this chapter draws on the findings of the EU-funded COPING Project (Children of Prisoners, Interventions and Mitigations to Strengthen Mental Health), which was conducted in 2010–2012 by a combination of academic and NGO researchers based in France, Germany, Romania, Sweden, Switzerland and the UK.

The questionnaire was administered to 737 children aged 7–17 and their parents/carers. It included closed and open-ended questions, and had embedded within it four existing instruments: the Strengths and Difficulties Questionnaire (Goodman 1997), the Rosenberg Self Esteem Scale (Rosenberg 1965), the KIDSCREEN-27 (KIDSCREEN Group Europe 2006) and the World Health Organization Quality of Life assessment (World Health Organization 2004). It was administered following pilots in each participating country. Selection methods varied by country and comprised: prison staff identifying prisoners meeting the selection criteria (Germany, Romania, Sweden and UK); meetings with families as they visited prisoners (Germany, Sweden and UK); NGOs identifying families of prisoners (Germany and Sweden); notices via newspapers, radio or websites (Germany, UK); and support from statutory agencies working with children affected by parental imprisonment (Germany, Romania).

In-depth interviews were held with families that completed the survey questionnaire and agreed to take part. Semi-structured interviews were held individually with the children, their parents/carers and their imprisoned parents. Interview guides were constructed, taking into account analysis of data from the surveys as well as feedback from research assistants and available literature. Across the four countries, interviews took place with 161 children (85 boys and 78 girls), 123 non-imprisoned parents/carers and 65 imprisoned parents/carers. Although the initial idea was to recruit equal numbers of children under normal and combined borderline-abnormal ranges according to scores on the Strength and Difficulties Questionnaire, this was only partially met due to refusals from participants. The mean ages of children were: 10.66 years in Romania, 11.60 in the UK, 11.69 in Germany, and 11.83 in Sweden.

Stakeholder consultations comprised interviews and/or focus groups with children of prisoners, imprisoned parents, caregivers, social workers, prison staff, staff within institutional homes, school-related stakeholders, NGO staff, and government staff involved in policy relating to children/families of prisoners in each country. They aimed to identify stakeholders' perceptions regarding the needs of children of prisoners. 122 stakeholders were consulted through in-person meetings, telephone interviews and completion of an online questionnaire with closed and open-ended questions.

The mapping of interventions for children of prisoners in the participating countries included four categories of services and interventions. These were: prison-based specialised interventions for the families of prisoners; community-based specialised services for the families of prisoners; community-based non-specialised services for the families of prisoners; and mental health services for children and adolescents. Questionnaires used for prison and non-prison-based services were sent via email, links to online versions and through telephone conversations with trained NGO volunteers. 289 prisons were involved in the prison-based research. The number of community-based services varied from country to country, from 0 in Romania to 32 in Germany (the UK had 25 services and Sweden 9).

6 Results

6.1 Context

Europe is a small continent, but the national situation, and the context surrounding children of prisoners, varies significantly among its countries. Economic development in 2010 ranged from per capita income (at purchasing power parity) of $16,254 in Romania to $39,569 in Sweden (World Bank 2014). Imprisonment rates (per 100,000 population) also differ greatly, with Romania imprisoning 158 persons per 100,000 of national population, the UK (England & Wales) 148, Germany 77 and Sweden 67 (International Centre for Prison Studies 2014). Precise data on children of prisoners are unavailable: this group is not systematically recorded[4] and existing figures are extrapolations or estimates. For Sweden, the estimate is 10,500 children per year having a parent in prison (Mulready-Jones 2011, p. 5).[5] In the UK, 200,000 children were estimated to have had a parent in prison at some point in 2012 (Barnardos 2014a, p. 2)—more than experienced their parents divorcing (Action for Prisoners' Families et al. 2007, p. 1). Mean imprisonment length varies, with Sweden the shortest at 3.2 years.

None of the four COPING countries had a nationwide governmental agency or department focused on children of prisoners. What provision there was tended to be provided by voluntary agencies or statutory services with a wider or different focus (such as social services).

6.2 Results: Emotional and Mental Health Impacts

While children of prisoners are far from a homogeneous group, the extent to which an individual child might be affected by parental imprisonment will depend greatly on the existence of a range of mediating factors, such as the child's age at separation, the sentence length, the strength of the parent/child bond, the availability of support and the number of previous parent-child separations.

Most children in the COPING Project reported being negatively impacted by the imprisonment of a parent. These mirrored reported impacts from other research, including mental and physical health problems (Hissel et al. 2011; Bocknek et al. 2009; Murray and Farrington 2008), difficulties related to education (Trice and Brewster 2004; Dallaire et al. 2010; Roberts 2012) and stigmatisation by others

---

[4] This is due both to the widespread non-recognition of this group by authorities and that children and parents may hide their status due to stigma or fears about the actions authorities may take upon discovery.

[5] The number is significantly higher than the prison population because many parents, like other prisoners, serve less than a year.

Table 1 Does parental imprisonment have good and/or bad effects on children?

Description	Germany (n = 145)	Romania (n = 251)	Sweden (n = 50)	UK (n = 291)	Overall (n = 737)
% bad effects (reported by parent/carer)	75.0	50.8	79.4	53.7	58.6
% bad effects (reported by child)	54.2	38.4	60.0	51.3	48.0
% good effects (reported by parent/carer)	24.1	19.1	33.3	15.6	19.8
% good effects (reported by child)	18.7	*Not asked*	25.6	9.8	14.3

(Pugh and Lanskey 2011). More children were reported as having negative impacts by parents than self-identified as such (Table 1).

Children reported a range of psychological and mental health impacts. Specific reported impacts included aggressive behaviour, sleeping disorders and nightmares. Emotional support was the issue with which Swedish children of prisoners felt they most needed help. Children in Germany emphasised wanting to live a normal life and were looking forward to their imprisoned parent's return home.

A number of the children in the UK who had been separated from their imprisoned parents for much of their lives appeared to be more vulnerable. Some, mostly boys, had been damaged by their parents' imprisonment, resulting in psychological distress, or displaying anger and disruptive behaviour at school. Children whose parents (fathers in all cases in this study) had been convicted of sexual assaults on other children could also be particularly vulnerable. Of the UK interviewees, four children had been receiving counselling or psychiatric support.

Examining the mental health and well-being (by the SDQ scores[6]) of the children, it is clear that in all countries bar Sweden, children report their well-being more favourably than do their parents (see Tables 2 and 3). In all countries, more children fell within the "normal" range than in the "borderline" or "abnormal" ranges. Additionally, children in all countries scored "reliably higher than the UK norm" (Jones and Wainaina-Woźna 2013, p. 270), meaning they were closer to the 'borderline' or 'abnormal' ranges than UK children generally. The numbers in the abnormal columns indicates that approximately one tenth of the sample (by self-reporting) or one quarter of the sample (by parental report) was at heightened risk of experiencing mental health difficulties.

In all countries bar Germany, older (11+) children had a slightly to moderately higher risk of mental health problems than younger (under 11) children, as

[6] SDQ scores refer to Goodman's (1997) Strengths and Difficulties Questionnaire, which is a behavioural screening instrument eliciting children and young peoples' perceptions of their conduct, concentration, emotions and social relationships. The SDQ incorporates five different subscales (hyperactivity; emotional symptoms; conduct problems; peer problems; and a prosocial scale) which, when summed, provide a total difficulties score (TDS). It is generally agreed that the SDQ instrument provides one means to measure a child's mental health.

Table 2 SDQ categorisation of children by total difficulties score (self-assessment)

Country	Normal (number, %)	Borderline (number, %)	Abnormal (number, %)
Germany	n = 105, 74.5 %	n = 17, 12.0 %	n = 19, 13.5 %
Romania	74.1 %	16.7 %	9.3 %
Sweden	n = 11, 57.9 %	n = 5, 26.3 %	n = 3, 15.8 %
UK	n = 101, 80.8 %	n = 13, 10.4 %	n = 11, 8.8 %

Table 3 SDQ categorisation of children by total difficulties score (parental assessment)

Country	Normal (number, %)	Borderline (number, %)	Abnormal (number, %)
Germany	n = 74, 53.6 %	n = 22, 15.9 %	n = 42, 30.4 %
Romania	49.4 %	15.4 %	35.2 %
Sweden	n = 18, 58.1 %	n = 6, 19.4 %	n = 7, 22.6 %
UK	n = 112, 64.7 %	n = 29, 16.8 %	n = 32, 18.5 %

Table 4 Children scoring high on SDQ total difficulties score, by country

Country	% children aged under 11 scoring high on SDQ total difficulties score	% children aged 11+ scoring high on SDQ total difficulties score
Germany	29	28
Romania	35	47
Sweden	21	27
UK	21	28

measured by parent SDQ ratings (Table 4). (Parent/carer (along with teacher) ratings are considered a more reliable guide to a child's risk of mental health problems than the child's own rating (Goodman et al. 1998)). The children who scored high were doing generally quite poorly.

Furthermore, the SDQ results showed that boys experienced more difficulties than girls, a disparity which was most notable among surveyed children (11+) in the UK and Sweden especially, though children (of both genders) in Romania experienced more difficulties than children in any other country (Table 5).

The self-esteem of children of prisoners varied, with German and Romanian children reporting higher self-esteem than their country norms on the Rosenberg Self Esteem Scale,[7] and UK children scoring lower than the country norm. The authors have found no country norm for Sweden.

[7] The Rosenberg Self Esteem Scale (SES) was devised by Morris Rosenberg (1965) and provides an indication of children and young people's perceived levels of self-esteem (self-evaluation). The scale consists of ten items which are summed to produce an overall score ranging from 10 to 40, where higher scores indicate higher levels of self-esteem. Self-esteem is one aspect of a child's well-being and influences aspirations, personal goals and interaction with others.

Table 5 Difficulties of boys and girls from the SDQ total scale and subscales

	UK	Germany	Romania	Sweden
Girls	n = 48	n = 36	n = 49	n = 9
Boys	n = 77	n = 38	n = 73	n = 6
Total difficulties score (sd)				
Girls	10.5 (6.4)	12.0 (7.1)	14.6 (6.7)	9.8 (6.5)
Boys	13.0 (6.4)	12.6 (7.3)	15.7 (8.0)	13.7 (8.9)
Difference (boys/girls)	B +2.5	B +0.6	B +1.1	B +3.9
Emotions subscale (sd)				
Girls	3.1 (2.7)	3.7 (2.9)	4.9 (2.8)	3.0 (2.4)
Boys	2.6 (2.2)	3.1 (2.8)	4.7 (2.8)	2.5 (1.6)
Difference (boys/girls)	G +0.5	G +0.6	G +0.2	G +0.5
Hyperactivity subscale (sd)				
Girls	3.2 (2.6)	3.4 (2.2)	4.0 (2.3)	3.6 (2.8)
Boys	5.0 (2.0)	4.4 (2.6)	4.6 (2.8)	6.0 (3.9)
Difference (boys/girls)	B +1.8	B +1.0	B +0.6	B +2.4
Peer subscale (sd)				
Girls	2.3 (1.8)	2.4 (2.0)	3.1 (2.0)	1.7 (1.5)
Boys	2.3 (1.8)	2.3 (2.1)	2.9 (2.0)	2.7 (1.5)
Difference (boys/girls)	EVEN	G +0.1	G +0.2	B +1.0
Conduct subscale (sd)				
Girls	2.0 (1.7)	2.5 (1.9)	2.6 (2.1)	1.6 (1.9)
Boys	3.0 (2.2)	2.7 (2.0)	3.5 (2.9)	2.5 (3.3)
Difference (boys/girls)	B +1.0	B +0.2	B +0.9	B +0.9
Prosocial subscale (sd)				
Girls	8.6 (2.0)	7.4 (1.7)	8.4 (1.9)	7.4 (1.9)
Boys	7.3 (2.0)	7.6 (1.8)	7.5 (2.4)	7.3 (2.6)
Difference (boys/girls)	G +1.3	B +0.2	G +0.9	G +0.1

Table 6 KIDSCREEN-27 total scores (untransformed)

	Germany	Romania	Sweden	UK	Overall
Parent	N = 139	N = 245	N = 50	N = 216	N = 650
Child	N = 143	N = 243	N = 50	N = 269	N = 705
KS-27 total: original scale					
Parent	91.4 (11.0)	80.2 (13.8)	90.8 (11.0)	93.6 (14.6)	87.8 (14.7)
Child	93.8 (11.8)	83.2 (15.4)	97.5 (11.8)	98.0 (13.4)	92.0 (15.2)

Table 7 WHOQOL-BREF scores across the four countries (0–100 scale)

	Germany (n = 139)	Romania (n = 244)	Sweden (n = 36)	UK (n = 226)	Overall (n = 645)
QoL-overall	54.9	44.6	66.7	62.6	54.3
QoL-health	51.1	48.0	61.1	65.4	55.4
Physical	63.2	56.5	67.6	71.7	63.8
Psychological	54.1	56.8	61.6	61.7	58.2
Social	53.1	51.8	64.1	58.6	55.2
Environmental	60.0	43.6	63.9	68.1	56.8

Well-being, as captured by the KIDSCREEN survey,[8] varied: while as a whole group, the surveyed children reported lower well-being compared to pan-European norms, with psychological well-being the lowest, the results varied significantly by country and Swedish and UK children scored above the norm in some areas (notably the social support and peers subscale), while Romanian children reported in almost all areas lower well-being than their peers in other countries (Table 6).

Finally, the WHO Quality of Life Scale[9] found that 'Swedish and UK parents/carers judged their [children's] quality of life higher than those in Germany and Romania. Table 7 shows, that on the overall quality of life item, Swedish parents/carers score on average much higher than the others (66.7 on the 0–100 scale) and Romanian parents/carers score much lower than those in other countries (44.6). For the general health item, UK parents/carers score highest and Romanian parents/carers score lowest. Breaking down the total scores into the four specific domains also shows major differences between countries. For the physical domain, German, Swedish and UK parents/carers score quite high, while the Romanian parents/carers score much lower. For the psychological domain, German parents/carers score the lowest, although quite similar to the Romanian parents/carers, with UK and Swedish parents/carers scoring much higher. For the social domain, the Swedish parents/carers score much higher than the others, with the Romanian parents/carers scoring the lowest. For the environmental domain, the UK parents are scoring highest, but not much different from the Swedish and German parents/carers, while the Romanian parents/carers are scoring much lower' (Jones and Wainaina-Woźna 2013, pp. 287–288).

---

[8] The KIDSCREEN instrument elicits children and young peoples' ratings of their health and well-being. This is a self-report instrument and covers five dimensions (physical well-being; psychological well-being; autonomy and parental relation; support and peers; and school environment) with a higher score indicating more positive health and well-being. The KIDSCREEN-27 is a shorter version (27 items) of the original KIDSCREEN-52 questionnaire (Ravens-Sieberer et al. (2007).

[9] The WHO Quality of Life-BREF instrument (WHOQOL) was used to ascertain the non-imprisoned parent/carer's health-related quality of life as well as their aspirations, using a 26-item questionnaire. For more on the WHOQOL-BREF, see Skevington et al. (2004).

Alongside these reports on children's general well-being, quality of life etc. there were also accounts (primarily through in-depth interviews) about times that were particularly difficult for children and could trigger peaks of emotion. These included the arrest and period after arrest, and court appearances at which bail or sentencing were being decided. Arrests were generally sudden and unexpected, and many police operational procedures (such as forced entry into the family home, conducting searches and uprooting belongings, splitting family members and confining children to a room) could be frightening and shocking for children. Children were often not considered at arrest, but "the level of distress could be lessened significantly by sensitive Police practice" (Jones and Wainaina-Woźna 2013, p. 353). One parent in the UK thought their child had been traumatised during their arrest because the parent was unable to explain to them what was happening. Children spoke of their distress at discovering police searching through their personal belongings or becoming emotionally withdrawn since the arrest of the father. In both the UK and Germany, children's rage and helplessness was most intense in the period following arrest: some participants described screaming uncontrollably on discovering the accusations against the parent.

Following arrest, there was often acute uncertainty about whether the arrested parent would be imprisoned while awaiting trial, and the wait for the case to come to court could also leave children and families in a "limbo" state, whether or not the parent was imprisoned while awaiting trial. This could be increasingly difficult as the length of wait increased; the longest example reported was of 3 years for one UK family. Delays in hearings could mean repeated good-byes and reliving the emotional upset these likely caused. When a parent was imprisoned while awaiting trial, the level of contact their children could have with them varied widely between countries, from daily visits for some UK children to no contact at all (in person or by telephone) for some in Sweden, where contact can be denied if it is believed it may result in interference with or may jeopardise the case.

Sentencing following conviction was another particularly difficult period, especially if the child had not been informed about the situation and was not expecting their parent to face a long custodial sentence, or had been unaware of the (alleged) offence. Other difficult times for children would be celebrations such as birthdays and Christmas and other special family occasions where they would often miss the imprisoned parent.

The impact of parental imprisonment on school performance varied significantly among the four countries. School performance declined among half the children in Germany, whereas in Romania the impacts were minimal (except where children had to move home following parental imprisonment). Only in the UK were significant percentages (12 %) suspended or expelled from school; however, this may relate to schools' attitudes more than the extremity of behaviour. School-related issues constituted the second-most important need for Swedish children.

A minority of children in the UK appeared to be more educationally at risk, and this was clearly linked to parental imprisonment in several cases. The interview data also indicated that the school performance of siblings varied considerably, itself influenced by the children's relationship with their imprisoned parent and their emotional development, as well as their age and sex. For some of these children the transition to secondary school can also be difficult for them to manage, although children who struggled here had more complex family circumstances than those who successfully managed moving to secondary school. Communication about the parent's imprisonment appeared to be handled poorly and may have contributed to the child's difficulties. In Germany, nearly half of the parents interviewed did not inform their children's school about their parent's imprisonment; in Romania, the majority did not (and further advised their children not to tell peers at school about the imprisonment).

A significant issue in Romania, the UK and especially Germany, was stigma. It can often result in children who do know about their parent's imprisonment turning inwards and not sharing the reality of their situation outside the family. While about half of the children in Germany spoke to friends, they feared negative consequences, although none of them reported actually experiencing hostility or prejudice. Fear of stigma led to a focus on secrecy and stress. Romania had the highest proportion of children who lied about or were not told the reality about their parent's situation, with the explanation for a parent's absence often being that they had gone abroad to seek work. Lying about the parent's absence is not universally negative: it is one of the most common strategies of resilience and can be employed to protect the family's image and prevent the children being stigmatised.

The UK had the highest proportion of children reporting victimisation or bullying in school as a direct result of having a parent in prison (15 (22 %) self-reporting, 20 (30 %) according to reports from parents). There were several other cases where it was unclear whether bullying had taken place, so this may still be an underestimate. This contrasted with just two Swedish children or parents (7 %) reporting victimisation or bullying due to parental imprisonment.

As might be expected, the main site for bullying was within the school and conducted by other children. In most cases the bullying was a result of secondary social stigma towards the children; bullying usually took the form of verbal abuse through name calling, sarcastic remarks etc. However, there were several cases in the UK where bullying escalated into physical fights, usually as a result of (verbal) retaliation by the child of a prisoner leading to a physical confrontation. There were several other more serious cases of bullying, where a child had been physically attacked and beaten up by peers because of the parent's offence. More usually, children could experience some degree of ostracism, with family friends and acquaintances no longer associating with their parent, usually by ignoring them in the street. On these occasions it was more likely the case that any animosities were levelled by adults against other adults, rather than directed against the children. This was generally driven by negative local media coverage of the case. This could prompt concern by the child for their parent's welfare, causing the child heightened anxiety and stress. The period following a parent's sentence and the ensuing publicity is often reported as one of heightened stress and concern. Over several weeks or months the loss of status, labelling, ostracism and rejection could peak for families. Children could also lose some school friends and be ostracised by others;

Table 8 Reports of good effects of parental imprisonment

Description	Germany	Romania	Sweden	UK
% good effects (reported by child)	18.7	*Not asked*	25.6	9.8
% good effects (reported by parent/carer)	24.1	19.1	33.3	15.6

however, friends who were supportive were an important source of resilience. Indeed, being able to confide in a few close friends (and family members) could buffer some of the negative effects of bullying and stigma, and better enable the child to cope in stressful and challenging circumstances: the majority of Swedish children had done so. Not all schools were supportive of bullied children and there was some evidence of additional stigmatisation from some teachers in Romania and the UK, probably due to the failings of individual staff members. Furthermore, a minority of bullied children reported interpersonal expectancy effects taking place within the school, with some teachers showing lowered expectations for pupils' competency or classroom discipline when they knew the child's parent was imprisoned.

Stakeholders felt that there must be a major change in society's view of detainees so that children do not have to endure a stigma for crimes they did not commit.

Financial concerns were an issue in all countries, but much more so in Romania: "it was not unusual for families to have to choose between visiting prison or meeting basic needs (food and clothing) and purchasing school equipment for children" (Jones and Wainaina-Woźna 2013, p. 357). Material and financial support was the area in which Romanian children most wanted assistance. There were also physical health impacts, which in Romania constituted the greatest risk area for children, according to responses to the WHO Quality of Life Scale.

Not all children found parental imprisonment a negative experience: a quarter of children and a third of parents/carers in Sweden reported good effects from the imprisonment. These centred around improved family relations, and for a minority, how they were feeling, especially where the imprisoned parent had been abusive or had addictions (Table 8).

While a substantial number of children seemed to be quite resilient and seemed to be surviving quite well, it should be stressed that all children suffered some degree of distress. It appears that many from this group of children had mainly strong relationships with their parents, maintained positive relationships with the imprisoned parent, and their parent's sentence was short enough that they could reasonably anticipate the opportunity to resume their relationship upon release. For instance six families in this position described themselves as just "normal families" coping with a difficult period, who managed to adjust to a difficult situation with support from wider family and friends. For others there was a more pronounced period of disruption or crisis followed by a gradual improvement where things got back to normal.

6.3 Results: Relationship and Contact with Imprisoned Parent

Maintaining family ties during imprisonment has been found to reduce the likelihood of reoffending; the COPING research found that the reverse was also true, with children having the best chances if they had strong relationships with both their parents. The evidence from the interview data demonstrates the importance of parental relationships and the quality of caregiving in building the child's resilience. This was the case for both paternal and maternal imprisonment. Maintaining contact only works when both parties are willing to stay in touch (although support for children and parents by psychologically trained volunteers or professionals can in some cases overcome this caveat).

Some of the children in Romania and Germany developed an unrealistic and idealised image of the imprisoned parent. This often had knock-on impacts on the relationships with the remaining parent/carer and meant that emotional and behavioural problems were fought out between parents and children at home. In the UK, children's vulnerability could be higher where their parents' relationship appeared strained, or unbalanced (for example, one parent expecting too much of the other).

A key method of maintaining contact is in-person visits. A majority of children in all countries visited their parent in prison: 81.5 % in Germany, 87.9 % in Romania, 75.9 % in Sweden[10] and 92.9 % in the UK.[11] Barriers to visiting in all countries included travel distance (especially high in Romania, followed by Sweden, with Germany and the UK having shorter average distances) and the high financial cost of visiting. The quality of visits themselves varied widely, with features such as visit length, privacy and possibility of physical contact dictated by the prison regime in the country and the security classification of individual prisons. As reported in Robertson et al. 2012, p. 104:

> *However, stakeholders report that relatively small changes, such as hanging pictures on the walls, painting the walls with bright colours and providing toys or magazines, can make a big difference to children's experience of visiting prison, with children being calmer and more at ease, as well as more positive about returning for subsequent visits. Having special visits shortly after imprisonment can help allay children's fears, while allowing children to meet with parents in special family visiting rooms away from other prisoners can make visits more pleasant. Children can also be helped by being accompanied on prison visits by NGO staff or volunteers or, for children living in institutional settings, by institutional staff. All these accompaniers can provide emotional and practical support, particularly in relation to their fears and how to deal with the parent's imprisonment.*

---

[10] In Sweden, a higher proportion of interviewed parents were entitled to temporary release/home leave, so this may account for the lower prison visiting rate.

[11] Note that participants in the study were almost exclusively recruited during prison visits and through NGOs working with prisoners' families, which almost certainly affected the sample.

When in prison, the amount of contact parents have varies widely, both in terms of visits and in terms of indirect contact (mainly letters and telephone calls). Children's experiences of prison differed greatly depending on the security levels, with Swedish and UK children "acknowledging that as the security rating of the prison decreased, the environment became less intimidating and they were afforded more freedom. As a result, less secure establishments were found to be more conducive towards quality interaction between children and their imprisoned parent" (Jones and Wainaina-Woźna 2013, p. 361). Within England and Wales (UK) prisoners receive as standard between two 1-hour visits and four 2-hour visits a month. Phone calls are permitted but prisoners have to buy phonecards from their own funds. Germany's criminal justice policies prioritise rehabilitation and prisoners, including those convicted of serious offences, have generous home leave entitlements throughout their sentence. Government policies support prisoners' family ties, although there are significant variations between the 16 German states (Länder). The Romanian prison system allows monthly visits depending on the security level.[12] For example, those in maximum security prisons are permitted two visits per month, with only two people allowed to visit and physical contact prohibited. However, there are no child-friendly facilities or arrangements in Romanian prisons: authorities have stated that prison is a hostile environment and lacks facilities for family meetings. Other countries include in-prison programmes and interventions for children and families: these are covered in the next section.

There is also indirect contact. This was particularly important in the UK, where the overwhelming majority (95.9 %) of surveyed children had maintained some contact with their imprisoned parents, most frequently by phone calls (179 children), email or letters (159 children). However, while 90 % of children in Sweden and the UK have frequent telephone contact with their parents in prison, this is very restricted in Germany. Indeed, the importance of telephone contact came across strongly, especially in the UK: regular contact by telephone was found to promote the child/imprisoned parent's relationship as well as supporting the consistent involvement of the imprisoned parent in the upbringing of their children. Early telephone contact not only helped reassure the child the parent was safe and well, but also helped support the child's adjustment in losing a parent to prison, which was an important factor in their continuing resilience. Overall, the evidence from the interview data demonstrated the importance of parental relationships and the quality of caregiving in building the child's resilience. This was the case for both paternal and maternal imprisonment.

The questionnaires and in-depth interviews identified the critical role played by the non-imprisoned parent, in terms of practical and emotional support for the child, but also their role in facilitating contact between the child and imprisoned parent. The relationship between the imprisoned parent and the non-imprisoned parent/carer is extremely important; when the non-imprisoned parent/carer refuses to visit

---

[12] Romania has four levels of security in the prison system: maximum security, closed, semi-open and open.

prison, this can mean the children do not go either, as many prisons require children to be accompanied by an adult. Conversely, when the non-imprisoned parent/carer is committed to maintaining the child-imprisoned parent relationship, they can enable it even when the child may be reluctant to visit. More widely, there is a rule of thumb that if the non-imprisoned parent/carer has a good relationship with both the child and the imprisoned parent, the child-imprisoned parent relationship is likely to be maintained.

6.4 *Results: Positive Effects and Interventions*

The number and effectiveness of interventions varied both between and within countries. Many community-based interventions were small and locally focused, while prison-based ones often operated in a single prison. Services could provide information, advice and practical support for families of prisoners.

COPING found that almost 57 % of prisons surveyed across the four countries had specific interventions for children and families focused on family relations, 47 % on the parent's imprisonment and 34 % on mental health issues. Germany has a broad spectrum of community-based interventions for children of prisoners and their families, including counselling services, youth welfare provision and psycho-therapeutic support. These, as well as prison-based father/child groups, were highly regarded by families taking part in the research. However, the study indicated that community and prison-based interventions available in Sweden today are not sufficient to strengthen children's resilience when they have a parent in custody, even though over 80 % of Swedish children had received some kind of help: a third of all Swedish children indicated that they would like (more) help.

A particularly problematic area was the timing of support for children, which is not adapted to the chain of events associated with a parent's imprisonment: the desire for information about having a parent/carer in prison and available support for children was the top desire of German children. In order for the child to better cope with the situation, it may be crucial that the first parent-child visit occur shortly after detention—parents/carers for the children specifically named the periods immediately after arrest and after release as times when they need the most support.

Sources of economic and personal/emotional support were primarily family members (grandmothers/grandparents were especially likely to be mentioned, particularly in Romania). The care provided by mothers, and grandparent and sibling support, was a key protective factor in Germany. The extended family also plays an important role in the resilience process of Romanian children. However, non-imprisoned mothers in Germany did not always have time to support their children emotionally: they were described as 'over challenged and focusing on pragmatic issues'.

After speaking to the family, children were most likely to confide in teachers or other people in school. Moreover, the interview data strongly suggested that the majority of schools in Germany, Sweden and the UK made an important contribution to reassuring parents and carers, and in maintaining the morale and self-confidence of children while their parent was in prison (Romanian participants reported less school support). This ability to help could be impaired where parents/carers had not openly discussed issues with school staff. Some children did confide in a few trusted teachers (irrespective of the parents informing the school) allowing them to talk through any problems (school or family) they were having and also allowing the school to make adjustments in light of their difficulties.

Interview data from Sweden and the UK showed that the majority of schools were an important source of support and normality for many children and could build their capacity for resilience. This was the case for junior and secondary schools, special schools and private schools, though unsurprisingly only when they knew about the imprisonment. Staff members within schools could work with and complement parents, offering understanding if children were upset as well as dealing firmly with any instances of bullying or inappropriate remarks. A lot of children described particularly valuing support from a staff member whom they trusted and were able to confide in: younger children in Sweden mainly turned to their class teacher, while older children would get support from a school counsellor or school nurse. Girls in the UK tended to talk more openly about their experience of emotional support from school staff, whereas boys tended to say less, but to place an equal value on the support provided. Examples include schools helping children stay calm and to behave properly, as well as providing ongoing emotional support. Schools could also emphasise the importance of academic achievement (doing homework, attending classes and task orientation); the general picture across the four countries was that for most children academic achievement was not strongly adversely affected by imprisonment, and the fact that many children performed well at school itself indicated resilience.

One response that was found to be positive across countries was to have open, honest (and age-appropriate) communication with the child concerning the situation and what was expected to happen. This helped the children to cope when the various stages of the process became a reality. Furthermore, children who chose to tell friends about their imprisoned parent seemed to do well; open discussion helped children to handle their situation; and parents who talked openly with schools received sympathetic responses. Having a trusting and caring relationship between children and school staff when discussing parental imprisonment appeared to function as a protective factor against conduct problems. Indeed, one of the key findings from the COPING research highlights the idea of "community resilience", the importance of social support systems, especially of school, teachers and peer support for children.

7 Discussion

The general picture from the COPING research is that parental imprisonment can have adverse effects for children in a number of areas, but that these effects can be mitigated by formal or (very often) informal support and interventions. This finding reflects and reinforces much previous research, as well as the experience of NGOs in these and other countries. It brings validation that for many children with imprisoned parents there are measurable health impacts and reinforces the understanding that for children the best chance of being resilient to the experience of parental incarceration arises when they have: strong, emotionally capable parents; support from schools; the possibility of good contact with their imprisoned parent; inclusion in society at large; and their needs considered at all stages of the process.

One especially valuable part of the COPING research is the large number of participants compared to most previous studies of children of prisoners (thereby providing some statistical robustness) and the embedding within the survey of the four existing mental health and well-being questionnaires. This provides a quantitative account of children's well-being (the term being used here broadly to include the mental health, self esteem and quality of life aspects recorded by other embedded studies), as well as allowing comparison with other groups who have completed such studies. Such comparisons give evidence of the impact that parental imprisonment has, separate from other factors, and can mean that risk factors for future mental health and well-being can be identified. For example, while only a few UK children were in the lowest group of scores for the Rosenberg Self Esteem Scale (2.7 %, n = 6), such low scores are a concern because low self esteem is a non-specific risk factor in mental ill-health and is involved in the development of a range of internalising and externalising problems.

However, it is important when dealing with such risk factors to consider their likelihood as well as the range of possibilities. So when considering the self-esteem example above, we should remember that the majority of the sample showed higher or intermediate levels of self-esteem, which would assist children of prisoners in negotiating and surviving through the experiences of parental imprisonment and allow them to progress more easily in to a fruitful adult life.

One clear finding was the importance to children of strong, emotionally capable parents or carers, both inside and outside the prison. Given the importance of their role in helping the child, it seems that additional support to non-imprisoned parents/carers (including both practical and emotional support) would benefit the children and build their resilience.

Additionally, imprisoned parents should be supported in building or maintaining a relationship with their children, not least to strengthen an attachment that is often weaker than when the parent has not been imprisoned (Poehlmann 2005), but also (from a crime prevention perspective) because of the impact that good family links have on reducing reoffending. Prisoner-parent support groups such as those offered by the NGO Relais Enfants Parents in France and parental training sessions in Croatia are examples of schemes that help reduce the alienative effects of prison

(Goffman 1961), loss of personal responsibility and diminished agency that can adversely impact parenting capacities. Assisting and enabling parents to talk to children about the imprisonment empowers them as parents and allows children to better process the incarceration.

However, contact with an imprisoned parent can face systemic hurdles, such as a lack of appropriate visiting facilities. Where such facilities and other child-friendly systems do exist (and prison visits do seem to be the area with the most innovation), they are often only in a single or a few prisons. Often they depend on the continued involvement of a concerned staff member or NGO. This is obviously damaging for their sustainability, as the departure of even one key individual could cause the collapse of positive programmes. One recommendation from stakeholders was that more funding be given to organisations that support children of prisoners. However, there also need to be efforts to share good practice between and within prisons and to educate all staff members. Even when child-friendly facilities are available, staff attitudes (down to such things as whether the staff smile or explain what they are doing) can make the difference about whether children report a positive or negative visiting experience (Robertson 2012, p. 35).

As well as examples described in the COPING countries, positive visiting innovations include private visits in Norway (where the family meets without other visitors or guards present[13]), and opportunities for play and creativity (such as puppet shows and painting) in some Italian and Belgian prisons. A major benefit of all child-friendly settings is that children are often more relaxed and can focus more on their relationship with their parent, rather than on fears of the prison. Recent innovations regarding indirect contact include the use of IT to allow children to immediately inform their imprisoned parent about meaningful events, such as Skype in the Czech Republic and in Oregon (USA), and limited mobile phone use by prisoners in some prisons in England and Slovenia. Given the value that many surveyed/interviewed children placed on being able to have regular contact with parents, and the increasing proportion of their communication that is done digitally, such innovations could be expected to be fruitful.

Outside of the family, the next-most important institution in the lives of the children is the school, which plays multiple roles. It is the site of adults and children who can support or stigmatise children of prisoners, and its formal educational role can have both short-term (in terms of being a focus for children) and long-term (in terms of improved employment opportunities and earnings) benefits. 'Children's school performance provides important evidence about their resilience. Their performance is likely to be closely related to their intellectual ability, their motivation and their commitment to their school work. A sudden and potentially traumatic event such as parental arrest and imprisonment is likely to contribute towards a downturn in children's performance at school. This may be only temporary if children adjust to their changed circumstances and receive support where needed' (Jones and Wainaina-Woźna 2013, p. 341). School teachers sensitised to

[13] There are guards outside the room, however.

what a child is experiencing are better equipped to provide support. Examples include a programme run by the NGO Families Outside in Scotland, which raises awareness amongst teachers, and activities by FFP Norway, which sensitise both teachers and students. Outside of families, focus on the school experience may be the most fruitful place to concentrate analysis and support for children of prisoners, because of the long parts of their life they spend in school and the fact that teachers are the non-family adults that children spend most time with and (probably consequently) feel closest to.

Beyond these institutions, many others interact with children of prisoners, whether or not they know it. A key problem is the low level of awareness of children of prisoners, particularly among professionals in the criminal justice system, who can too often maintain a narrow focus on the suspect/offender and not think about the wider impacts of their decisions. Making institutions aware of their existence can itself spur change: after being consulted, stakeholders in Sweden had ideas to facilitate contact with the detained parent, beginning with a child-oriented focus during visits to imprisoned parents. In Romania, there were a series of conclusions related to the improvement of procedures for children's visits in prison, an appropriate space for parent-children meetings, and the development of supporting services—not all of them prison-based (counselling activities, personal development, leisure activities, material support etc.)—for children with parents in prison.

More generally, proposals to systemically improve the situation of children of prisoners generally focus on either compelling consideration of the children by all officials through changes to laws or regulations, or giving a particular individual responsibility for advocating for the children, such as a child's ombudsman in court or prison officer with responsibility for child-friendly visits. The predominant example of considering the children is the landmark judgment of *S v M* (2007) in the Constitutional Court of South Africa. There, the Court ruled that the best interests of the child have to be considered when sentencing a parent (regardless of whether custodial or non-custodial sentences are planned). "If the possible imprisonment will be detrimental to the child, then the scales must tip in favour of a non-custodial sentence, unless the case [is] so serious that that would be entirely inappropriate" (Robertson 2012, p. 15). In the judgment, Justice Albie Sachs said:

> *Every child has his or her own dignity. If a child is to be constitutionally imagined as an individual with a distinctive personality, and not merely as a miniature adult waiting to reach full size, he or she cannot be treated as a mere extension of his or her parents, umbilically destined to sink or swim with them. [...] The sins and traumas of fathers and mothers should not be visited on their children.*
>
> (*S v M* [2007] ZACC 18, at para 18)

Occasionally, though increasingly, laws rather than court judgements include some provision for children of prisoners, whether it is allowing parents who are both sentenced to prison to serve their sentences consecutively to provide continuity of care for children (Egypt and Slovenia) (Robertson 2007), or giving particular importance "to a child's right of access to his or her parents during the execution of a sanction" and ensuring that visits be 'carried out in a room designed for this purpose' (Norway). France is developing national policy for children affected by parental incarceration, and already requires courts to consider alternatives to custody for men and women who are sole carers of children under age 16.

Aside from having adults become more aware of the children, there is also the possibility of involving the children themselves in decision-making. Such an approach was integral to the research design of the COPING study itself. As well as giving the children agency, involving them can also lead to better decisions, as they may be able to identify solutions and potential flaws. In Norway, advisory groups of young people with a parent in prison are consulted to describe their needs, give advice and suggestions, and contribute to UN Convention on the Rights of the Child shadow reports. Relais Enfants Parents Romands in Switzerland works to foster agency in the child during support sessions by letting the child lead the play and the session, rather than forcing them out of their world of imaginary play by imposing adult ideas and realities on them. This interactive approach is characteristic of similar schemes that operate in Luxembourg, Belgium, France and Italy. Swedish children created "10 wishes" of things they wanted done differently (such as being allowed to telephone into prison, not wait for a call from the parent): these were presented at the UN in Geneva in 2010.

It is true that all stakeholders can make changes to support these children, helping them gain an internal sense of what John Bowlby[14] called a 'secure base' in the world (Bowlby 1973b). But it is also the case that even where support is available, it is not always provided in the most efficient way. One concern was that interventions were not linked with the times when the children most needed it, such as the period following arrest. Those providing such support should learn from the results of COPING and other studies to align their interventions to when the need is greatest.

On the specific case of arrest, research from the USA reveals that children can experience violence not only during but also before a parent's arrest. One study found that over 75 % of women imprisoned in South Carolina (USA) said their children had witnessed domestic violence and/or had been victims of physical or sexual violence themselves (DeHart and Altshuler 2009); 20–80 % of these children were likely to have witnessed their parent's arrest (Phillips and Dettlaff 2009). Given that arrest is often a peak time of stress for children, but can be "lessened significantly by sensitive Police practice" (Jones and Wainaina-Woźna 2013, p. 353), the development of detailed protocols on conducting child-friendly arrests are welcome. These protocols, which exist in places including San Francisco (USA), Poland and Denmark, describe how to consider children during arrest, covering such issues as explaining what is happening, and taking children into another room to avoid witnessing their parent being handcuffed. If and when other

[14] Since 1947 his work has inspired the UN and WHO crime prevention and health programmes for children (Redo and Platzer 2013).

police forces develop similar protocols, they should take into account not just good practice, but also research on the impact of a parent's arrest on children.

The other issue that affects the provision of support is the still incomplete knowledge about who is affected by parental imprisonment. The COPING study highlighted the difficulty of knowing what exact percentage of children of prisoners in each country had been surveyed. Few countries record prisoners' parental status and the actual number of affected children is unknown. Countries that do record data often do not systematise the information, basing it on self-reporting by parents, some of whom are wary that their child may be removed from them and taken into care. Were such data recording made mandatory, it would not only help identify the size of the population of prisoners' children, but it would also mean that those recording the information would be sensitised to the children's existence and potentially to their needs.

It should be noted that the COPING study on which most of this chapter is based did not look at children whose parents had been released from prison, though this is both an important area of need and support in itself, and the period in which the longer-term results of any interventions or responses become more clearly seen. These longer-term impacts of interventions can therefore only be surmised, with a presumption that interventions that have a positive effect on the children during a parent's imprisonment will help their coping and resilience in the longer-term also, or at least not damage it.

8 Conclusion

Children of prisoners are slowly shedding their labels as "invisible" and "forgotten" children. Academic and NGO awareness of them is growing, and children affected by parental incarceration now appear on EU and UNICEF lists of vulnerable children. This growing awareness has in turn led to more understanding of both the risks that parental imprisonment has for children's future well-being, and of the effectiveness of certain responses and interventions.

The COPING study of children of prisoners in Germany, Romania, Sweden and the UK is notable in particular for two reasons. Firstly, the large size of the investigated population meant that the impacts and the efficacy of interventions could be studied with some degree of statistical certainty. Secondly, the focus on mental health and well-being meant that there was less emphasis on outputs from interventions (what they did) and more on their outcomes (how they made children feel). Especially relevant findings include the fact that as a population, children of prisoners are more likely than their peers to be at risk from mental ill-health, the importance of non-imprisoned parents/carers and the major support that can come from schools.

It seems clichéd for academic chapters to call for more research into the issue that has just been described at length, but in this case there is more cause than most. Children of prisoners and their needs are still under-recognised, and if many of the major issues (maintaining relationships, stigma, schooling etc.) are known, the specifics, details and (especially) national and regional differences are not. Having a better understanding of how children of prisoners in different countries cope with parental imprisonment is not just helpful in knowing better how to respond to those children; it also helps with sharing good practice. This is an issue where the best answers are not always found in expected places: Uganda and Uruguay have practices that others could learn from, as well as the UK.

However, despite the large gaps in knowledge that remain, there is reason to hope. We do now know what some of the immediate impacts are of parental imprisonment and what the negative long-term consequences can be. We also know of some of the interventions and institutions that can provide support and (to a degree) of their effectiveness. What is not known, and needs to be better understood, is whether and to what extent positive interventions can help prevent negative future outcomes, such as future offending by the children. To get answers with the highest level of confidence, we would need to wait for the outcomes of prospective longitudinal studies comparing (at the least) children of prisoners who receive such interventions with children of prisoners who don't, but in the interim much can be done to find out whether the COPING findings hold for children elsewhere, and to identify further interventions and institutions that appear to have a particularly positive or negative effect on the children.

The other thing that is needed is to continue to raise public and political consciousness about children of prisoners. This should help to reduce stigma towards them and also prevent them falling through the gaps in governmental and non-governmental service provision. Children of prisoners commonly occupy a space between justice and children's ministries in government, with both believing the other should be supporting the children. However, COPING study findings show that there is also a mental and public health dimension to children of prisoners, as well as a significant role that can be played by educational establishments.

Secondary or collateral victims of imprisonment, children of prisoners have committed no crime and should not suffer because of the crimes of others. From the standpoint of fairness, they should be assisted when they face ill-effects caused by another's actions. From the standpoint of expediency, they should be supported in whatever way will most reduce the likelihood of future offending, by the child or their imprisoned parent. But whatever the reason, considering and assisting children of prisoners will most likely benefit the children, those around them and society at large.

Five Questions

1. What can be done to increase awareness and consideration of children of prisoners among criminal justice professionals?
2. What is the best way to ensure governmental provision of support for children of prisoners?
3. What examples of good practice related to children of prisoners can be found in your country/jurisdiction?

4. How would you go about replicating the COPING research in your country/ jurisdiction?
5. How involved are children in designing programmes aimed at supporting them?

References

Action for Prisoners' Families, CLINKS, Prison Advice and Care Trust and Prison Reform Trust (2007), Parliamentary briefing: The children & families of prisoners: recommendations for practice.

Arditti, J. A., & Few, A. L. (2006). Mothers' reentry into family life following incarceration. *Criminal Justice Policy Review, 17*(1), 103–123.

Barnardos. (2014a). *On the outside: identifying and supporting children with a parent in prison.* Ilford: Barnardos.

Barnardos (2014b). Children affected by parental imprisonment. http://www.barnardos.org.uk/what_we_do/our_projects/children_of_prisoners.htm. Accessed 4 June 2014.

Becroft, A.J. (2006). Youth Offending: Factors that Contribute and how the System Responds. Delivered at Symposium Child and Youth Offenders: What Works. http://www.justice.govt.nz/courts/youth/publications-and-media/speeches/youth-offending-factors-that-contribute-and-how-the-system-responds. Accessed 4 June 2014.

Bocknek, E. L., Sanderson, J., & Britner, P. A. (2009). Ambiguous loss and posttraumatic stress in school-age children of prisoners. *Journal of Child and Family Studies, 18*(3), 323–333.

Boswell, G., & Wedge, P. (2002). *Imprisoned fathers and their children.* London: Jessica Kingsley Publishers Ltd.

Bowlby, J. (1973a). *Attachment and loss Vol 2: Separation: Anxiety and anger.* New York: Basic Books.

Bowlby, J. (1973b). *A secure base: Parent-child attachment and healthy human development.* New York: Basic Books.

Brown, K., Dibb, L., Shenton, F., & Elson, N. (2001). *No one's ever asked me: Young people with a prisoner in the family.* London: Federation of Prisoners' Families Support Groups.

Clarke, L., O'Brien, M., Day, R. D., Godwin, H., Connolly, J., Hemmings, J., et al. (2005). Fathering behind bars in English prisons: Imprisoned fathers' identity and contact with their children. *Fathering, 3*(3), 221–241.

Dallaire, D. H., Ciconne, A., & Wilson, L. (2010). Teachers' experiences with and expectations of children with incarcerated parents. *Journal of Applied Developmental Psychology, 31*(4), 281–290.

DeHart, D., & Altshuler, S. (2009). Violence exposure among children of incarcerated mothers. *Child & Adolescent Social Work Journal, 26*(5), 467–479.

George, S.M., & LaLonde, R.J. (2002). Incarcerated mothers in Illinois State Prisons: An analysis of administrative data. Unpublished.

Goffman, E. (1961). *Asylums: Essays on the social situation of mental patients and other inmates.* New York: Doubleday Anchor.

Goodman, R. (1997). The strengths and difficulties questionnaire: A research note. *Journal of Child Psychology and Psychiatry, 38*, 581–586.

Goodman, R., Meltzer, H., & Bailey, V. (1998). The strengths and difficulties questionnaire: A pilot study on the validity of the self-report version. *European Child and Adolescent Psychiatry, 7*, 125–130.

Hagan, K. A., & Myers, B. J. (2003). The effect of secrecy and social support on behavioural problems in children of incarcerated women. *Journal of Child and Family Studies, 12*(2), 229–242.

Hagan, K. A., Myers, B. J., & Mackintosh, V. H. (2005). Hope, social support and behavioral problems in at-risk children. *American Journal of Orthopsychiatry, 75*(2), 211–219.

Hanlon, T. E., Blatchley, R. J., Bennett-Sears, T., O'Grady, K. E., Rose, M., & Callaman, J. M. (2005). Vulnerability of children of incarcerated addict mothers: Implications for preventive intervention. *Children and Youth Services Review, 27*(1), 67–84.

Hissel, S., Bijleveld, C., & Kruttschnitt, C. (2011). The well-being of children of incarcerated mothers: An exploratory study for the Netherlands. *European Journal of Criminology, 8*(5), 346–360.

International Centre for Prison Studies (2014). World Prison Brief. http://www.prisonstudies.org/world-prison-brief. Accessed 17 April 2014.

Jones, A.D., & Wainaina-Woźna, A.E. (Eds.) (2013). *Children of Prisoners. Interventions and mitigations to strengthen mental health*. UK: University of Huddersfield. See also: http://www.coping-project.eu.

KIDSCREEN Group Europe. (2006). *The KIDSCREEN questionnaires: Quality of life questionnaires for children and adolescents*. Germany: Bielefeld University.

King, D. (2002). *Parents, children and prison: Effects of parental imprisonment on children*. Dublin Institute of Technology: Dublin.

Loper, A. B., Carlson, W., Levitt, L., & Scheffel, K. (2009). Parenting stress, alliance, child contact, and adjustment of imprisoned mothers and fathers. *Journal of Offender Rehabilitation, 48*(6), 483–503.

Lösel, F., Pugh, G., Markson, L., Souza, K., & Lanskey, C. (2012). *Risk and protective factors in the resettlement of imprisoned fathers with their families*. Milton: Ormiston Children and Families Trust.

Mackintosh, V. H., Myers, B. J., & Kennon, S. S. (2006). Children of incarcerated mothers and their caregivers: Factors affecting the quality of their relationship. *Journal of Child and Family Studies, 15*(5), 581–596.

May, C., Sharma, N., & Stewart, D. (2008). Factors linked to re-offending: a one-year follow-up of prisoners who took part in the Resettlement Surveys 2001, 2003 & 2004. *Ministry of Justice Research Summary 5*. London: Ministry of Justice.

Mortimer, R. (2010). Risk factors for offending: A developmental approach. Unpublished.

Mulready-Jones, A. (2011). *Hidden children: A study into services for children of incarcerated parents in Sweden and the United States*. London: Winston Churchill Memorial Trust.

Murray, J. (2005). The effects of imprisonment on families and children of prisoners. In S. Maruna & A. Leibling (Eds.), *The effects of imprisonment*. Devon: Willan Publishing.

Murray, J. (2007). The cycle of punishment: Social exclusion of prisoners and their children. *Criminology and Criminal Justice, 7*(1), 55–81.

Murray, J., & Farrington, D. P. (2005). Parental imprisonment: effects on boys' antisocial behaviour and delinquency through the life-course. *Journal of Child Psychology and Psychiatry, 46*(12), 1269–1278.

Murray, J., & Farrington, D. P. (2008). Parental imprisonment: Long-lasting effects on boys' internalizing problems through the life course. *Development and Psychopathology, 20*(1), 273–290.

Murray, J., Janson, C.-G., & Farrington, D. P. (2007). Crime in adult offspring of prisoners: A cross-national comparison of two longitudinal samples. *Criminal Justice and Behavior, 34*(1), 133–149.

Murray, J., Farrington, D.P., Sekol, I., & Olsen, R.F. (2009). Effects of parental imprisonment on child antisocial behaviour and mental health: a systematic review. Campbell Systematic Reviews.

Nesmith, A., & Ruhland, E. (2008). Children of incarcerated parents: Challenges and resiliency, in their own words. *Children and Youth Services Review, 30*(10), 1119–1130.

Niven, S., & Stewart, D. (2005). *Resettlement outcomes on release from prison in 2003. Home Office Findings 248.*. London: Home Office.

Pew Charitable Trusts. (2010). *Collateral Costs: Incarceration's effect on economic mobility*. Washington, D.C.: Pew Charitable Trusts.

Phillips, S. D., & Dettlaff, A. J. (2009). More than parents in prison: The broader overlap between the criminal justice and child welfare systems. *Journal of Public Child Welfare, 3*(1), 3–22.

Poehlmann, J. (2005). Incarcerated mothers' contact with children, perceived family relationships, and depressive symptoms. *Journal of Family Psychology, 19*(3), 350–357.

Prison Reform Trust. (2013). *Bromley briefings prison factfile*. London: Prison Reform Trust.

Pugh, G., & Lanskey, C. (2011). 'Dads Inside and Out': study of risk and protective factors in the resettlement of imprisoned fathers with their families. Conference paper for What's new in Research and Evaluation? Informing our work with prisoners and offenders and their families. Institute of Criminology, University of Cambridge, 19 May 2011.

Ravens-Sieberer, U., Auquier, P., Erhart, M., Gosch, A., Rajmil, L., Bruil, J., et al. (2007). The KIDSCREEN-27 quality of life measure for children and adolescents: Psychometric results from a cross-cultural survey in 13 European countries. *Quality of Life Research, 16*(8), 1347–1356.

Redo, S., & Platzer, M. (2013). The United Nations Role in crime control and prevention: From "what?" to "how?". In P. Reichel & J. Albanese (Eds.), *Handbook of transnational crime and justice* (2nd ed., pp. 283–302). Thousand Oaks: Sage Publications.

Roberts, S. (2012). *The role of schools in supporting families affected by imprisonment*. Families Outside: Edinburgh, Scotland.

Robertson, O. (2012). *Collateral Convicts: Children of incarcerated parents: Recommendations and good practice from the UN Committee on the Rights of the Child Day of General Discussion 2011*. Quaker United Nations Office, Geneva.

Robertson, O. (2007). *The impact of parental imprisonment on children*. Geneva: Quaker United Nations Office.

Robertson, O., Sharratt, K., Pascaru, G., Bieganski, J., Kearney, H., Sommerland, N., Jones, A., Raikes, B., Urban, M., & Cheung, R. (2012). Stakeholder Perspectives on the Needs of Children of Prisoners in Europe, *Analele Ştiinţifice Ale Universităţii "Alexandru Ioan Cuza" Din Iaşi (Serie Nouă), 2012* (2).

Rosenberg, M. (1965). *Society and the adolescent self-image*. Princeton, NJ: Princeton University Press.

Schlafer, R. J., & Poehlmann, J. (2010). Attachment and caregiving relationships in families affected by parental incarceration. *Attachment and Human Development, 12*(4), 395–415.

Sharratt, K. (2014). Children's experiences of contact with imprisoned parents: A comparison between four European countries. *European Journal of Criminology, 11*(6), 760–775.

Skevington, S. M., Lotfy, M., & O'Connell, K. A. (2004). The World Health Organization's WHOQOL-BREF quality of life assessment: psychometric properties and results of the international field trial. A report from the WHOQOL group. *Quality Life Research, 13*(2), 299–310.

Smith, R., Grimshaw, R., Romeo, R., & Knapp, M. (2007). *Poverty and disadvantage amongst prisoners families*. York: Joseph Rowntree Foundation.

Social Exclusion Unit. (2002). *Reducing re-offending by ex-prisoners*. London: Social Exclusion Unit.

Trice, A. D., & Brewster, J. (2004). The effects of maternal incarceration on adolescent children. *Journal of Police and Criminal Psychology, 19*(1), 27–35.

Tudball, N. (2000). *Doing it hard: A study of the needs of children and families in Victoria*. Melbourne, Victoria: VACRO.

van de Rakt, M., Murray, J., & Nieuwbeerta, P. (2012). The long-term effects of paternal imprisonment on criminal trajectories of children. *Journal of Research in Crime and Delinquency, 49*(12), 81–108.

Wildeman, C., Schnittker, J., & Turney, K. (2012). Despair by association? The mental health of mothers with children by recently incarcerated fathers. *American Sociological Review, 77*(2), 216–243.

Williams, K., Papadopoulou, V., & Booth, N. (2012). Prisoners childhood and family backgrounds: Results from the Surveying Prisoner Crime Reduction (SPCR) longitudinal cohort study of prisoners. *Ministry of Justice Research Series 4/12*. Ministry of Justice: London.
World Bank (2014). GDP per capita, PPP (current international $). http://data.worldbank.org/indicator/NY.GDP.PCAP.PP.CD. Accessed 4 June 2014.
World Health Organization. (2004). *The World Health Organization Quality of Life (WHOQOL)-BREF*. Geneva: World Health Organization.

Gender and Victims' Expectations Regarding Their Role in the Criminal Justice System: Towards Victim-Centred Prosecutorial Policies

Jo-Anne Wemmers and Katie Cyr

Abstract Therapeutic jurisprudence is an interdisciplinary approach to law that offers a rich way of looking at law and to study the extent to which legal rules, procedures or practice promote the psychological well-being of the people it affects. Law is a tool and people who engage the criminal justice system do so for a reason. As such it is important to consider the extent to which legal procedures meet victims' expectations. In this chapter, we examine victims' expectations regarding their role in the criminal justice system. Following a discussion of recent international policy developments regarding victims of crime and victims of violence against women in particular, we consider possible gender differences and how the victim's relationship with the offender affects their expectations, including the awareness of possible future victimization.

1 Introduction

Criminal victimization is a global phenomenon. However, only a minority of incidents is reported to the police, and reporting levels have been found to be related to confidence in the police (Van Kesteren et al. 2014). Moreover, in some countries such as Canada, reporting levels have decreased steadily over the last 20 years (Perreault and Brennan 2010; Wemmers 2003). Criminal justice depends largely on victims to report crimes in order to function effectively. While most people are satisfied with the police (Van Kesteren et al. 2014), victims tend to be less satisfied with the police than non-victims (Gannon 2004). Victims are often

J.-A. Wemmers (✉)
École de criminologie, Université de Montréal, Montréal, QC, Canada
e-mail: jo-anne.m.wemmers@umontreal.ca

K. Cyr
Faculté de l'éducation permanente, Université de Montréal, QC, Canada
e-mail: katie.cyr@umontreal.ca

H. Kury et al. (eds.), *Women and Children as Victims and Offenders: Background, Prevention, Reintegration*, DOI 10.1007/978-3-319-28424-8_9

dissatisfied with their role in the criminal justice system and these negative experiences mean that they are less inclined to report to authorities in the future (Shapland et al. 1985; Van Dijk 1999). Victims' expectations regarding the criminal justice system are therefore highly important as they can shape how victims evaluate their experiences, which ultimately can affect the functioning of the justice system. Understanding the importance of victims for the proper functioning of criminal justice has led internationally to efforts to improve the treatment of victims.

Therapeutic jurisprudence studies the law's impact on the wellbeing of individuals who come in contact with it (Wexler and Winick 1991, 1996). It considers how substantive rules of law, legal procedures and the role or actions of legal actors are therapeutic or helpful for people. Conversely, it considers how the same processes can be non-therapeutic or harmful (Erez et al. 2011). This is commonly referred to as "secondary victimization" in the victimological literature, where it refers specifically to the anti-therapeutic effects of criminal justice procedures and criminal justice authorities on crime victims (Maguire 1991; Symonds 1980; Wemmers 2003). However, therapeutic jurisprudence goes beyond secondary victimization in that it applies to all parties affected by the law, not only victims, as well as all types of law. Moreover, therapeutic jurisprudence emphasizes basic legal values such as equity and the presumption of innocence, while addressing the therapeutic impact of the law on all parties involved.

Therapeutic jurisprudence is, however, not a theory. It is a way of looking at the law for all sorts of cases, also non-criminal ones. In order to explain and predict how people are affected by the law, therapeutic jurisprudence relies on procedural justice theory (Waldman 1998). According to procedural justice theory, people are concerned about fairness and in particular, about being treated fairly (Lind and Tyler 1988; Tyler and Lind 1992). Fairness is important because it communicates to people that they are valued and respected members of their group (Tyler and Lind 1992; Van den Bos et al. 2001). Wemmers (1996) has established the relevance of procedural justice for victims of crime and found that victims' fairness judgments affected their confidence in criminal justice authorities. More recently, research on procedural justice and victims has shown that when victims feel they were treated fairly, they also feel better, suggesting that fair treatment has a positive influence on healing or recovery (Orth 2002; Wemmers 2013; Parsons and Bergin 2010; Wemmers 2003). In particular, when victims felt that police and public prosecutors had shown an interest in them, had given them an opportunity to express their wishes and had taken their wishes into consideration, victims were more likely to feel that they had been treated fairly (Wemmers 1996, 2010; Morissette and Wemmers 2016).

In this chapter, we examine victims' expectations regarding their role in the criminal justice system. Following a discussion of recent policy developments regarding victims of crime and victims of violence against women in particular, we consider possible gender differences and how the victim's relationship with the offender affects their expectations.

2 Victims' Role in Criminal Justice

The primary role of victims in the criminal justice system is that of a witness to a crime. In adversarial procedures there are two opposing parties, the accused versus the state. The prosecution represents the state and, while they may rely on victims for evidence, the prosecutor is not the victim's lawyer. This has been a major source of dissatisfaction for victims who want to be recognized as more than a mere witness to a crime and feel that they should have a special status in criminal proceedings (Kilchling 1995; Shapland 1985; Wemmers 1996; Wemmers 2013; Herman 2005).

The role of victims as witnesses has evolved over time. The idea that crime constitutes an act against society rather than an act against the victim is a notion that dates back to the Middle Ages (Viau 1996). Up until the eleventh century, the victim occupied a key position in common law and was responsible for the apprehension, charge and prosecution of offenders. This was known as private prosecution, and victims controlled every aspect of the judicial process including punishment (Kirchengast 2006). The victimologist, Stephan Schafer refers to this period as the "golden age" of the victim because victims exercised such an important role in the criminal justice process (Schafer 1968). From the twelfth century onwards, the state gradually took on an ever-increasing role in keeping the peace and sanctioning offenders until eventually it completely replaced the victim (Doak 2008; Kirchengast 2006). Gradually, the state and its offices and institutions replaced the King but power was never returned to the victim. From the seventeenth century onwards, parliamentary sovereignty grew and the King became less influential personally. As a result, crimes ceased to be considered a violation of the King's peace and instead were viewed as threats to civil society and social interests (Kirchengast 2006, 2011).

The absence of the victim was not even noticed by authors until well into the second half of the twentieth century, following the birth of victimology and a growing interest in victims of crime. In an effort to improve the position of victims in the criminal justice system, both international bodies such as the Council of Europe and the United Nations, as well as national governments developed guidelines regarding the treatment of victims. A milestone in the development of rights for victims is the adoption of the *Declaration of Basic Principles of Justice for Victims of Crime and Abuse of Power* in 1985 by the United Nations General Assembly (UN doc. A/RES/40/34).

The UN *Declaration* takes a victim-centred approach. It includes victim participation and states that victims should be given an opportunity to present "their views and concerns" at "appropriate stages of the proceedings where their personal interests are concerned."[1] In an effort to provide victims with an opportunity for participation, many countries introduced victim impact statements. Victim impact

[1] Article 6b, United Nations *Declaration of Basic Principles of Justice for Victims of Crime and Abuse of Power,* Adopted by the IN General Assembly 29 November 1985.

statements are written statements regarding the impact of the crime, which are submitted to the court at sentencing (Erez 1999). In Canada, for example, victims have the legal right to submit a written statement or read their statement aloud in court.[2] Similar measures exist in other countries including the USA, England and Wales and Australia (Erez and Roberts 2007).

More recently, certain jurisdictions, in the USA and the UK, introduced enforceable rights for victims (Kirchengast 2011). This means that the state has an obligation to respect the victim's rights, and failure to do so is not without consequences (Beloof 2005). For example, as a result of the 2004 *Justice for All Crime Act* in the USA, victims of federal crimes can hire a lawyer to represent their interests in the criminal justice process. In England and Wales, the government launched the Victims' Advocate pilot scheme, which provided a publicly funded lawyer for the family members of homicide victims (Sweeting et al. 2008). These measures give victims a voice in the criminal justice process.

Such victim-centred policies coincide with the literature on therapeutic jurisprudence. Giving victims the opportunity to actively participate in the prosecutorial process enhances their wellbeing (Erez and Hartley 2003; Wemmers 2008; Wemmers 2013; Finn 2013). Moreover, the absence of having a voice and any real influence in criminal proceedings may be harmful to victims' wellbeing (Diesen 2012).

2.1 Protecting Victims

At the same time that governments developed measures in order to give victims a voice in the criminal justice process, they also introduced measures that restrict victim input for certain offences, namely domestic violence. Dempsey (Dempsey 2009, p.4) describes the "radical transformation" of prosecutorial polices over the last 30 years, in which victims have increasingly been given less input, in order to protect them from undue pressure by their offenders. In an effort to better serve and protect victims of domestic violence, throughout the 80s and 90s, many areas in the United States and Canada, introduced mandatory arrest policies (Gouvernement du Québec 1995; Snider 2008). Such policies purposely reduce the victims' voice in the decision whether or not to arrest the offender. The aim is to send a clear message that violence is unacceptable and to protect victims from possible intimidation by the offender by removing victim input into decisions and placing responsibility for the decision to arrest solely in the hands of the state (Hanna 1996; Schneider 2000). Dichter et al. (2011) find that victims of intimate partner violence favour prosecution initiated and driven by the criminal legal system and want the system to take over prosecution without requiring their participation. Mandatory polices are

[2] Article 722, Criminal Code.

thought to deter offenders (Maxwell et al. 2001) and reduce the risk of victim intimidation (Wills 1997).

Mandatory policies have, however, been strongly criticized for disempowering victims (Ford and Regoli 1993a, b; Römkens 2006). While there is a strong degree of support among victims of violence for mandatory charging and arrest, there is a substantial degree of dissatisfaction with the policy of mandatory prosecution (Brown 2000). Several studies indicate that victims use the law as a tool (Fleury-Steiner et al. 2006). According to Ford (1991), victims use prosecution as a rational power strategy for determining the future course of their relationships. Similarly, Lewis et al. (2000) find that victims use the law, purposefully and actively, as a part of a strategic process of challenge and resistance. However, they do so within the confines of the law and of their relationships. Ford (1991) concludes that mandatory arrest and no-drop policies are counterproductive because they disempower victims. Finn (2013) refers to these two distinct policy approaches as *mandatory prosecution* versus *victim-centred prosecution*. Victim-centred prosecution, which allows victim participation in criminal justice procedures, has been found to yield better outcomes for victims of domestic violence in terms of reducing recidivism than mandatory policies (Finn 2013). As Johnson and Dawson (Johnson and Dawson 2011) conclude, debates on the efficacy of these policies are far from over.

The victims of domestic violence are for the most part women and therefore the question of gender is particularly important in this context. Men and women have similar overall rates of victimization but they are susceptible to different types of crime (Perreault and Brennan 2010). Women are more likely than men to be victims of crimes in which there may be a relationship with the offender such as sexual assault (Perreault and Brennan 2010) and domestic violence (Tjaden and Thoennes 2000). Half of violent incidents are committed by someone known to the victim, and victims of sexual and physical assault are more likely to know their offender than victims of other crimes (Gannon and Mihorean 2005).

Hence, there appears to be a dichotomy in public policy on victims, which centres largely on women. On the one hand victims are offered increased possibilities for participation and on the other hand, they are disempowered by mandatory policies regarding domestic violence. As Brown points out, charging and prosecution policies were in part implemented as a response to the perceived need for criminal justice professionals to treat domestic violence like any other crime (Brown 2000). In other words, family violence should be viewed as a threat to civil society rather than a private matter. The irony is that, in fact, these policies differentiated between domestic violence victims and other victims. The question is whether these policy differences correspond with what victims want. Do victims of domestic violence—as no-drop policies suggest—expect the prosecution to take over fully whereas other crime victims seek to retain some influence and control?

In this chapter we examine victims' expectations regarding their role in the criminal justice system. In particular, we consider possible gender differences and whether victims' relationship with the offender impacts their expectations.

3 Method

3.1 Recruitment

Participants were contacted with the help of the Ministry of Justice, Quebec (Canada) All victims whose cases entered the criminal courts of Montreal, Trois-Rivières and Sept-Isles between December 2003 and March 2004 were sent information about the study and invited to participate in it. Victims who wished to participate in the study were asked to contact the researcher. One reminder letter was sent to all victims who had not responded to the original letter. Research shows that crime victims will often move in order to escape crime, which makes it difficult to find them using court data (Xie and McDowell 2008). As a result, this type of study often results in a low rate of response (Brickman 2003; Resick 1988), and this study is no exception with an overall response rate of 8 %. While a more dynamic approach might have generated a larger response, it is unethical to aggressively pursue victims and therefore a more passive approach was favoured.

In all, 188 victims completed an interview. This is a convenience sample and clearly not a representative sample of victims. However, it is interesting none-theless because it is a non-clinical sample and provides insight into the experiences of victims of a wide variety of crimes before the courts.

3.2 Interviews

The interviews were conducted by phone by graduate students in criminology. A closed-questionnaire was developed for the interviews. It included some open-ended questions in order to allow victims to explain their answers. By conducting the interviews by phone the researchers were able to cover a large geographic with limited resources. Research comparing telephone and face-to-face interviewing shows that telephone interviewing can be used productively without reducing the quality of the data (Sturges and Hanrahan 2004). The interviews were conducted in English and French. The questionnaire was made up of 21 different sections, each examining different aspects of the victim, the victimization and their expectations and experiences with the criminal justice system. On average, each interview lasted 1 h.

3.3 Participants

Of the 188 victims who completed an interview, 165 had reported the crime to the police themselves. As the present analyses are based only on victims who chose to report the crime, we will limit our description of the sample to these 165 cases. In all, 60 % of respondents were female and 40 % were male. The victims varied in age from 15 to 77. The median age of the victims was 36. Most (72 %) of the respondents completed secondary school, and 35 % had a college or university degree. Many (44 %) had a family income of $25,000 or less, 19 % earned between $25,001 and $50,000, 27 % earned over $50,000 and 10 % did not know or did not answer this question.

Regarding the type of victimization, almost three-quarters (71 %) of respondents were victims of violent crime. The remaining 29 % were victims of a property crime. In most cases there was just the one victim involved in the offence (66 %) and likewise, most offences involved just one offender (84 %). Most victims (64 %) knew their offender: 40 % were (ex-) partners; 6 % were family members (e.g. brother, brother-in-law); 13 % were neighbours; 9 % were friends; 5 % were colleagues and the remaining 27 % were "other" types of relationships including informal acquaintances.

Half of the victimizations took place less than 4 months prior to the interview (median = 130 days; mean = 190 days; mode = 100 days; SD = 229 days).

4 Results

4.1 What Role Do Victims Expect to Play?

In order to assess victims' expectations, we asked respondents whether, when they reported the crime to the police, they thought that they could influence the criminal justice *process*. Most victims (54.6 %) expected to have a little or some influence on the criminal justice process (See Table 1). Similarly, 53.4 % felt that they would be able to influence the *result* of their case (See Table 4). However, most victims (64.2 %) understood that they would not have a say in *sentencing* (See Table 2). In other words, most victims appear to expect to have some informal influence over the criminal justice process and outcome but they do not expect to have a say regarding the sentence.

4.2 Women and Men Have Different Expectations

Next, we compared men's and women's expectations. Although women tended to be slightly more optimistic than men about their ability to influence the criminal justice process (see Table 3) and their ability to influence the result (see Table 4) these differences were not statistically significant. However, women were much more likely than men to believe that they would have a say regarding the sentence (see Table 5).

Table 1 When you reported the crime to the police, did you think that you could influence the criminal justice process? (N = 165)

	Frequency	%
Not at all	75	45.5
A little	58	35.2
Yes, definitely	32	19.4

Table 2 When you reported the crime to the police, did you think that you would have a say in sentencing? (N = 165)

	Frequency	%
Not at all	106	64.2
A little	42	25.5
Yes, definitely	17	10.3

Table 3 Cross-tabs: gender by victims' expectations when reporting the crime regarding their influence on the criminal justice process (N = 165)

		Did you think that you could influence the criminal justice process when you reported the crime?			
		Not at all	A little	Yes, definitely	Total
Gender	Men	32 (48.5 %)	27 (46.6 %)	7 (10.6 %)	66 (100 %)
	Women	43 (43.4 %)	31 (31.3 %)	25 (25.3 %)	99 (100 %)
Total		75 (45.5 %)	58 (35.2 %)	32 (19.4 %)	165 (100 %)
Chi-sq = 5.6; df = 2; p = 0.060					

Table 4 Victims' expectations to influence the result by gender (N 165)

		Victim expecting to influence the result			
		Not at all	A little	Yes, definitely	Total
Gender	Men	36 (54.5 %)	23 (34.8 %)	7 (10.6 %)	66 (100 %)
	Women	41 (41.4 %)	35 (35.4 %)	23 (23.2 %)	99 (100 %)
		77 (46.7 %)	58 (35.2 %)	30 (18.2 %)	165 (100 %)

Chi-Square = 4.938; df = 2; p = 0.086

Table 5 Gender by victims' expectations regarding having a say regarding the sentence (N = 165)

		Did you expect to have a say in sentencing?			
		Not at all	A little	Yes, definitely	Total
Gender	Men	49 (74.2 %)	10 (15.2 %)	7 (10.6 %)	66 (100 %)
	Women	57 (57.6 %)	32 (32.3 %)	10 (10.1 %)	99 (100 %)
Total		106 (64.2 %)	42 (25.5 %)	17 (10.3 %)	165 (100 %)
Chi-sq = 6.3; df = 2; p = 0.043					

4.3 Women Who Know Their Offender Expect to Maintain Power

We then examined if the relationship between the victim and the offender was related to victims' expectations. Using 2 × 2 × 2 tables, victims' expectations were crossed with gender and their relationship with the offender. When the offender is a stranger, neither men nor women expect to have a say at sentencing ($X^2 = 3.607$; df = 1; p = 0.887). However, when women know their offender, they expect to have a say regarding the sentence (See Table 6) and they are more likely to think that they will be able to influence the result (See Table 7).

These findings warrant a closer look at the relationship between the victim and the offender for the men and women in this sample. While both men (54 %) and women (70 %) in this sample were likely to know their offender, women were more often victimized by their (ex)partner (54 %) than men (14 %). Table 8 provides an overview of the relationship between victims and offenders by gender.

Table 6 2 × 2 × 2 table: victims' expectations to have a say regarding the sentence by gender by relationship with offender (n = 164)[a]

			Victims expecting to have a say regarding the sentence		
Victim-offender relationship			No	Yes	Total
Family/Acquaintance	Gender	Men	27 (75 %)	9 (25 %)	36 (100 %)
		Women	37 (53.6 %)	32 (46.4 %)	69 (100 %)
Chi-square = 3.607; df = 1; p = 0.058					
Stranger	Gender	Men	22 (73.3 %)	8 (26.7 %)	30 (100 %)
		Women	19 (65.5 %)	10 (34.5 %)	29 (100 %)
Total			105 (64 %)	59 (36 %)	164 (100 %)
Chi-square = 0.020; df = 1; p = 0.887					

[a]missing = 1

Table 7 2 × 2 × 2 table: victims' expectations to influence the result by Gender by Relationship with offender (n = 164)[a]

			Victims expecting to influence the result		
Victim-Offender relationship			No	Yes	Total
Family/Acquaintance	Gender	Men	20 (55.6 %)	16 (44.4 %)	36 (100 %)
		Women	25 (36.2 %)	44 (73.3 %)	69 (100 %)
Chi-square = 4.542; df = 1; p = 0.033					
Stranger	Gender	Men	16 (53.3 %)	14 (46.7 %)	30 (100 %)
		Women	16 (55.2 %)	13 (44.8 %)	29 (100 %)
Total			77 (47 %)	87 (53 %)	164 (100 %)
Chi.square = 0.42; df = 1; p = 0.514					

[a]missing = 1

Table 8 Frequency distribution of relationship between victim and offender by gender

Relationship	Men	Women	Total
(Ex-)partener	5 (14 %)	37 (54 %)	42 (40 %)
Family	3 (8 %)	3 (4 %)	6 (6 %)
Friend	4 (11 %)	5 (7 %)	9 (9 %)
Colleague	3 (8 %)	2 (3 %)	5 (5 %)
Neighbour	5 (14 %)	9 (13 %)	14 (13 %)
Other	16 (45 %)	13 (19 %)	29 (27 %)
Total	36 (100 %)	69 (100 %)	105 (100 %)

5 Discussion

Most victims know that they will not have a say in sentencing and many that they will have little to no influence over the criminal justice process. For these victims, their expectations are realistic and correspond with victims' legal role as witnesses to a crime against the state. However, most victims think that while they might not have a say in sentencing, they will retain some influence over the criminal justice process and its outcome. Victims want to be recognized as more than a mere witness to a crime and felt that they should have a special status in criminal proceedings (Herman 2005; Shapland 1985; Wemmers 2013).

Recent efforts to grant victims enforceable rights in the criminal justice process correspond with victims' expectation to play a role in the criminal justice process and should therefore be encouraged. The victim impact statement, which exists in many common law countries, allows victims to express how the crime affected them but it is only introduced at the sentencing stage. This means that victims are excluded from most of the criminal justice process where their only role is that of a witness (Erez 1999; Erez and Roberts 2007; Wemmers 2003). The victim impact statement does not give victims a say in the sentencing of the offender, however, most of the victims in the present study do not expect that either. While most western countries promote victims' rights such as information, consultation and reparation, few actually enforce these rights (Brienen and Hoegen 2000; Groenhuijsen 1999; Kirchengast 2011; Sullivan 1998; Wemmers and Ménard-April 2013). As a result, there is no certainty that victims' rights will actually be recognized and this, in turn, is a source of disappointment and dissatisfaction for victims (Shapland et al. 1985; Wemmers 1996; Herman 2005).

These findings correspond with the research on procedural justice (Lind and Tyler 1988; Tyler 2000). Procedural justice refers to the perceived fairness of decision-making procedures. Research shows that while parties are sometimes willing to cede decision-control to a third-party, they usually want to maintain some influence or voice over the process (Lind et al. 1983; Thibaut and Walker 1975; Tyler 2005; Wemmers 2010). As a result, while victims are willing to give decision-control to criminal justice authorities, they tend to want to retain influence or voice over the process (Wemmers 1996; Van Camp and Wemmers 2011;

Wemmers 2002a; Wemmers 2002b). Most of the victims in this study—both men and women—expect to have some influence over the process but do not expect to have a say at sentencing.

However, women who know their offender have different expectations than other victims. They not only expect to retain some power or influence over the criminal justice process, they also expect to have a say at sentencing. From the victim's perspective, she may believe that because she knows the offender, she has important information for the authorities that will help them make an informed decision (Shapland et al. 1985; (Wemmers and Cousineau 2005). In contrast, victims who do not know their offender may not have something to say about the offender and, therefore, be quite willing to leave it up to the professionals. As for the men who were victimized by someone they knew, very few were victims of intimate partner violence. Hence, the observed differences in victims' expectations may be explained by the high prevalence of intimate partner violence experienced by the women in this sample. The nature of the victimization may indeed be more important in shaping victims' expectations than gender (Felson and Paré 2008). According to the betrayal trauma theory, trauma perpetrated by someone the victim trusts or on whom the victims depends is more psychologically damaging (Freyd 1996). Victimization high in betrayal, in which trust is violated, affects the manner in which victims evaluate their victimization, and is associated with stronger negative appraisals (Gamache et al. 2013). In a recent study, it was found that although women made stronger negative appraisals compared with men, the gender difference became negligible once traumas high in betrayal were considered (Gamache et al. 2013). It is possible that victims who experienced victimization high in betrayal have greater expectations regarding sentencing because the crime had a larger impact or because they perceive more unfairness in the situation and want to restore the balance or regain some power over the situation.

These women's expectations do not correspond with their role in the criminal justice system and, as a result, they will likely be disappointed. Even more than other victims, these women expect to be able to retain some power in the criminal justice system. Yet, the introduction of no-drop policies means that victims of domestic violence have even less power in the criminal justice system than other victims. When victims are excluded and are unable to give their account of the offences, they experience the criminal justice system as unsupportive (Lewis et al. 2000) and they are less satisfied with the criminal justice system (Fleury 2002). Not surprisingly, no-drop policies have been criticized as ineffective and giving rise to new problems (Ford 1991; Landau 2000). The criminalization of family violence provides women with a tool to use in stopping the violence. Several authors (Fischer and Rose 1995; Ford 1991; Hoyle 1998) argue that in many cases victims use the power of the legal system to manage the violence and then disengage from the system. The findings in the present study suggest that women enter the criminal justice system expecting that they will maintain some control or at least have input. Women make choices about the extent of intervention they deem appropriate.

Our findings coincide with those of Lewis et al. (2000) who find that women want to use the system in a more flexible way and often find the court and the prosecution unsupportive. The law should empower victims: helping them to stop victimization and re-establish a sense of control over their lives. No-drop policies should be modified and victims should be given a special status in the criminal justice system, which recognizes them as something more than a mere witness to a crime.

One needs to ask how disappointment with the criminal justice system will impact victims' willingness to go to the police again in the future. Survivors of traumas high in betrayal are less trusting of people in general (Gobin and Freyd in press) and at increased risk of re-victimization (Gobin and Freyd 2009). Repeat victims are less likely to report crime to the police than people with little or no prior victimization experience (Van Dijk 1999). If the criminal justice system essentially discourages victims from collaborating with criminal justice authorities again in the future, how does it protect victims or civil society?

The introduction of rights for victims is, however, very controversial primarily because of concern for the rights of the accused (Ashworth 2000; Roach 1999; Young 2005). Yet, as this study and others have shown, most victims are looking for information and consultation and not decision-making power (Wemmers 1996; Wemmers 2013). Even victims of domestic violence are merely looking for a say in sentencing and not full control. When criminal justice authorities inform victims and consult with them about the developments in their case this does not necessarily jeopardize the rights of the accused (Doak 2008).

Understanding victims' expectations is important in order to avoid that victims will be disappointed and dissatisfied with the criminal justice system. While the present study sheds some light on victims' expectations, the findings are based on a non-representative sample and must be interpreted with caution. Further research is needed in order to enhance our awareness of victims' perspectives across different types of victims and victimizations.

Five Questions

1. What is the *UN Declaration of Basic Principles of Justice for Victims of Crime and Abuse of Power* and why is it important?
2. Why might victim-centred policies yield better outcomes for victims than a protective approach, which mandates prosecution?
3. What is *betrayal trauma theory* and why is it particularly relevant in the context of violence against women?
4. What is the relationship between *Therapeutic jurisprudence* and secondary victimization?
5. According to the research on victims of crime, what role do victims do they appear to want play in the criminal justice process?

References

Ashworth, A. (2000). Victims' rights, defendants' rights and criminal procedure. In A. Crawford & J. Goodey (Eds.), *Integrating a victim perspective within criminal justice* (pp. 185–196). Aldershot: Darmouth Publishing.

Beloof, D. E. (2005). The third wave of crime victims' rights: Standing, remedy and review. *Brigham Young University Law Review, 2005*, 256–370.

Brienen, M., & Hoegen, E. (2000). *Victims of crime in 22 European criminal justice systems.* Nijmegen: Wolf Publishers.

Brickman, E. (2003). *Development of a National Study of Victim Needs and Assistance,* Report submitted to the US Department of Justice, Award no. 98-VF-GX-0011.

Brown, T. (2000). *Charging and prosecution policies in cases of spousal assault: A synthesis of research, academic and judicial responses.* Ottawa: Department of Justice Canada.

Dempsey, M. M. (2009). *Prosecuting domestic violence: A philosophical analysis* (p. 4). New York: Oxford University Press.

Dichter, M. E., Cerulli, C., Kothari, C. L., Barg F. K. and Rhodes K.V. (2011). Engaging with criminal prosecution: The victim' s perspective. *Women and Criminal Justice* (pp. 21–37).

Diesen, C. (2012). Therapeutic jurisprudence and the victim of crime. In T. Oei & M. Groenhuijsen (Eds.), *Progression in forensic psychiatry* (pp. 579–598). Tilburg, NL: Tilburg University.

Doak, J. (2008). *Victims' rights, human rights and criminal justice: Reconceiving the role of third parties.* Oxford: Hart.

Erez, E. (1999). Who's afraid of the big bad victim? Victim impact statements as victim empowerment and enhancement of justice. *Criminal Law Review, 1*, 545–556.

Erez, E., & Hartley, C. C. (2003). Battered immigrant women and the legal system: A therapeutic jurisprudence perspective. *Western Criminology Review, 4*, 155–169.

Erez, E., Kilchling, M., & Wemmers, J. (2011). *Therapeutic jurisprudence and victim participation in justice.* Durham, NC: Carolina Academic Press.

Erez, E., & Roberts, J. (2007). Victim participation in the criminal justice system. In R. Davis, A. Lurigio, & S. Herman (Eds.), *Victims of crime* (3rd ed., pp. 277–296). Los Angeles: Sage Publications.

Felson, R. B., & Paré, P. P. (2008). Gender and the victim's experience with the criminal justice System. *Social Science Research, 37*, 202–219.

Finn, M. A. (2013). Evidence-based and victim-centred prosecutorial policies. Examination of deterrent and therapeutic jurisprudence effects on domestic violence. *Criminology and Public Policy, 12*(3), 443–472.

Fischer, K., & Rose, M. (1995). When "enough is enough": Battered women's decision making around court orders of protection. *Crime & Delinquency, 41*(4), 414–429.

Fleury, R. E. (2002). Missing voices: Patterns of battered women's satisfaction with the criminal legal system. *Violence Against Women, 8*(2), 181–205.

Fleury-Steiner, R. E., Bybee, D., Sullivan, C. M., Belknap, J., & Melton, H. C. (2006). Contextual factors impacting battered women's intentions to reuse the criminal legal system. *Journal of Community Psychology., 34*, 327–342.

Ford, D. (1991). Prosecution as a victim power resource: A note on empowering women in violent conjugal relationships. *Law & Society Review, 25*(2), 313–334.

Ford, D. A., & Regoli, M. J. (1993a). *The Indianapolis domestic violence prosecution experiment: Final report.* Washington, DC: National Institute of Justice.

Ford, D. A., & Regoli, M. J. (1993b). The criminal prosecution of wife assaulters. In N. Z. Hilton (Ed.), *Legal responses to wife assault: Current trends and evaluation.* Newbury Park, CA: Sage.

Freyd, J. J. (1996). *Betrayal trauma: The logic of forgetting childhood abuse.* Cambridge, MA: Harvard University Press.

Gamache, M. C., DeMarni Cromer, L., DePrince, A. P., & Freyd, J. J. (2013). The role of Cumulative trauma, betrayal, and appraisals in understanding trauma symptomatology. *Psychological Trauma: Theory, Research, Practice and Policy, 5*(2), 110–118.

Gannon, M. (2004). *General social survey on victimization cycle 18: An overview of findings*. Ottawa: Statistics Canada.

Gannon M., & Mihorean, K. (2005). Criminal victimization in Canada, 2004. *Juristat 25*, 7.

Gobin, R.L., & Freyd, J.J. (in press). The impact of betrayal trauma on the tendency to trust. *Psychological Trauma: Theory, Research, Practice and Policy*. doi:10.1037/a0032452.

Gobin, R. L., & Freyd, J. J. (2009). Betrayal and revictimization: Preliminary findings. *Psychological Trauma: Theory, Research, Practice and Policy, 1*(3), 242–257.

Gouvernement du Québec (1995). *Politique d'intervention en matière de violence conjugale:pré venir, dépister et contrer la violence conjugale*. Québec: ministère de la Santé et des Ser-vices sociaux, ministère de la Justice, secrétariat à la condition féminine, ministère de la Sécurité publique, ministère de l'Éducation, secrétariat à la famille.

Groenhuijsen, M. (1999). Victims rights in the criminal justice system: A call for more comprehensive implementation theory. In J. M. Van Dijk, R. Van Kaam, & J.-A. Wemmers (Eds.), *Caring for victims of crime* (pp. 85–114). Monsey, NY: Criminal Justice Press.

Hanna, C. (1996). No right to choose: Mandated victim participation in domestic violence prosecution. *Harvard Law Review, 109*, 1849–1910.

Herman, J. L. (2005). Justice from the victim's perspective. *Violence Against Women, 11*, 571–602.

Hoyle, C. (1998). *Negotiating domestic violence: Police, criminal justice and victims*. Oxford, UK: Oxford University Press.

Johnson, H., & Dawson, M. (2011). *Violence against women in Canada: Research and policy perspectives*. Don Mills, Canada: Oxford University Press.

Kilchling, M. (1995). *Opferinteressen und Strafverfolgung* (Victim interests and criminal prosecution). Freiburg im. Br.: Max-Planck-Institut für ausländisches und internationales Strafrecht.

Kirchengast, T. (2006). *The Victim in Criminal Law and Justice*. Basingstoke: Palgrave.

Kirchengast, T. (2011). Les victimes comme parties prenantes d'un procès pénal de type accusatoire. *Criminologie, 44*(2), 99–124.

Landau, T. (2000). Women's experiences with mandatory charging for wife assault in Ontario, Canada: A case against the prosecution. *International Review of Victimology, 7*, 141–157.

Lewis, R., Dobash, R. P., Dobash, R. E., & Cavanagh, K. (2000). Protection, prevention, rehabilitation or justice? Women's use of the law to challenge domestic violence. *International Review of Victimology., 7*(1–3), 179–205.

Lind, E. A., & Tyler, T. (1988). *The social psychology of procedural justice*. New York: Plenum Press.

Lind, E. A., Lissak, R. I., & Conlon, D. E. (1983). Decision control and process control effects on procedural fairness judgements. *Journal of Applied Social Psychology, 13*(4), 338–350.

Maguire, M. (1991). The needs and rights of victims of crime. In M. Tonry (Ed.), *Crime and justice: A review of the research* (pp. 363–433). Chicago, IL: University of Chicago Press.

Maxwell, C. D., Garner, J. H., & Fagan, J. A. (2001). *Effects of arrest on intimate partner violence: New evidence for the souse assault replication program*. Washington, DC: National Institute of Justice.

Morissette, M., & Wemmers, J. (2016). L'influence thérapeutique de la perception de justice informationnelle et interpersonnelle sur le symptômes de stress post-traumatique des victimes d'actes criminels. *Revue canadienne de criminologie et de justice pénale, 58*(1), 31–55.

Orth, U. (2002). Secondary victimization of crime victims by criminal proceedings. *Social Justice Research, 15*(4), 314–325.

Parsons, J., & Bergin, T. (2010). The impact of criminal justice involvement on victims' mental health. *Journal of Traumatic Stress, 23*(2), 182–188.

Perreault, S., & Brennan, S. (2010). *Criminal victimization in Canada, 2009*. Ottawa: Statistics Canada.

Resick, P. (1988). *Reactions of Female and Male Victims of Rape or Robbery*. (Final Report, grant # 85-IJ-CX-0042) Washington, DC: National Institute of Justice.
Roach, K. (1999). *Due process and victims' rights: The new law and politics of criminal justice*. Toronto: University of Toronto Press.
Römkens, R. (2006). Protecting prosecution: Exploring the powers of law in an intervention program for domestic violence. *Violence Against Women, 12*(2), 160–186.
Schafer, S. (1968). *The victim and his criminal: A study in functional responsibility*. New York: Random House.
Schneider, E. M. (2000). *Battered women and feminist lawmaking*. New Haven, CT: Yale University Press.
Shapland, J., Wilmore, J., & Duff, P. (1985). *Victims in the criminal justice system*. Aldershot: Gower Publishing.
Shapland, J. (1985). The criminal justice system and the victim. *Victimology: An International Journal, 10*(1–4), 585–599.
Snider, L. (2008). Criminalising violence against women: solution or dead end? Centre for Crime and Justice Studies. CJM. 74. December.
Sturges, J., & Hanrahan, K. (2004). Comparing telephone and face-to-face qualitative interviewing: A research note. *Qualitative Research, 4*(1), 107–118.
Sullivan, S. (1998). *Equilibrer la balance : L'état des droits des victimes au Canada*. Ottawa, Cendre canadien de ressources pour les victimes de crimes.
Sweeting, A., Owen, R., Turley, C., Rock, P., Garcia-Sanche, M., Wilson, L., et al. (2008). *Evaluation of the victim advocates' scheme pilots*. UK: Ministry of Justice.
Symonds, M. (1980). The Second Injury. *Evaluation and Change*, Special Issue, 36–38.
Thibaut, J., & Walker, L. (1975). *Procedural justice: A psychological analysis*. Hillsdalem, NJ: Wiley.
Tjaden, P., & Thoennes, N. (2000). Prevalence and consequences of male-to-female and female-to-male. Intimate partner violence as measured by the national violence against women survey. *Violence Against Women, 6*, 142–161.
Tyler, T. (2000). Social justice: Outcome and procedure. *International Journal of Psychology, 35* (2), 117–125.
Tyler, T. (2005). *Procedural justice* (Vol. 1). London, UK: Ashgate.
Tyler, T., & Lind, E. A. (1992). A relational model of authority in groups. In M. P. Zann (Ed.), *Advances in experimental social psychology* (Vol. 25, pp. 115–191). San Diego: Academic Press.
UN doc. Declaration of Basic Principles of Justice for Victims of Crime and Abuse of Power, General Assembly Resolution 40/34, 29 November 1985.
Van den Bos, K., Lind, E. A., & Wilke, H. (2001). The psychology of procedural and distributive Justice viewed from the perspective of fairness heuristic theory. In R. Cropanzano (Ed.), *Justice in the workplace: From theory to practice* (Vol. 2, pp. 49–66). Mahwah, NJ: Lawrence Erlbaum Associates Publishers.
Van Camp, T., & Wemmers, J. M. (2011). La justice réparatrice et les crimes graves. *Criminologie, 44*(2), 171–198.
Van Dijk, J. J. M. (1999). Criminal victimization and victim empowerment in an international perspective. In J. J. M. Van Dijk, R. Van Kaam, & J. Wemmers (Eds.), *Caring for victims of crime* (pp. 15–40). Monsey, NY: Criminal Justice Press.
Van Kesteren, J., Van Dijk, J., & Mayhew, P. (2014). The international crime victims surveys: A retrospective. *International Review of Victimology, 20*(1), 49–69.
Viau, L. (1996). Victimes des ambitions royales. *Thémis, 30*, 1.
Waldman, E. A. (1998). The evaluative-facilitative debate in mediation: Applying the lens of therapeutic jurisprudence. *Marquette Law Review, 82*, 155–170.
Wemmers, J. M. (1996). *Victims in the criminal justice system*. Amsterdam: Kugler Publications.
Wemmers, J. M. (2002a). Restorative justice for victims of crime. *International Review of Victimology, 9*, 65–81.

Wemmers, J. M. (2002b). Restorative justice: The choice bilateral decision-making power and third party intervention. In B. Williams (Ed.), *Reparation and victim-focused social work* (pp. 34–44). London: Jessica Kingsley Publishers.

Wemmers, J. (2003). *Introduction à la victimologie*. Montréal: Les Presses de l'Université de Montréal.

Wemmers, J. (2008). Victim participation and therapeutic jurisprudence. *Victims and Offenders, 3*, 165–191.

Wemmers, J. M. (2010). The meaning of fairness to victims. In S. G. Shoham, P. Knepper, & M. Kett (Eds.), *International handbook of victimology* (pp. 27–42). London, UK: CRC.

Wemmers, J. (2013). Victims experiences in the criminal justice system and their recovery from crime. *International Review of Victimology, 19*(3), 221–234.

Wemmers, J., & Cousineau, M. M. (2005). Victims' needs and conjugal violence: Do victims want decision-making power? *Conflict Resolution Quarterly, 22*(4), 493–508.

Wemmers, J.M., & Ménard-April, S. (2013). Consultation on a Bill of Rights for Victims: Brief Submitted to the Minister of Justice, June 29.

Wexler, B., & Winick, D. (1991). *Essays in therapeutic jurisprudence*. Carolina: Carolina Academic Press.

Wexler, D., & Winick, B. (1996). *Law in a therapeutic key: Developments in therapeutic jurisprudence*. Durham, NC: Carolina Academic Press.

Wills, D. (1997). Domestic violence: The case for aggressive prosecution. *UCLA Women's Law Journal, 7*, 173–182.

Xie, M., & McDowall, D. (2008). Escaping crime: The effects of direct and indirect victimization on moving. *Criminology, 46*(4), 809–840.

Young, A. N. (2005). Crime victims and constitutional rights. *Criminal Law Quarterly, 49*, 432–471.

Mediation, Restorative Justice and Social Reintegration of Offenders: The Effects of Alternative Sanctions on Punishment

Helmut Kury

Abstract Empirical criminological research of the last decades has confirmed the validity of previous doubts that punishment may not be the best way of crime prevention. Already Beccaria (Dei Delitti e delle Pene – Von den Verbrechen und von den Strafen. Berlin: Berliner wissenschafts-Verlag, 1764; 2005) discussed the "useless frequency of criminal sentences, which have never made people better" (2005, p. 48). So-called alternative sentences, generally known under the heading of mediation, victim-offender restitution or restorative justice, may actually have greater potential to reduce the conflicts and the harm caused by crime than punishment. This is especially true when the victims are women and children. Yet despite the encouraging results of recent research, traditional criminal justice has a hard time integrating these new possibilities of dealing with offenders because it cannot combine it easily with the principle that justice and the protection of the public require punishment. It would also necessitate changes in the training of the legal profession and a new and expanded perception of the role of judges. This chapter will discuss the recent developments of mediation, its implementation in different countries, and its potential for the solution of societal conflicts such as the victimisation of the most vulnerable: women and children.

1 Introduction

Everywhere and at all times punishment has commonly been considered the most efficient means to correct socially unacceptable, in particular delinquent behaviour. Still today, as soon as there is an increase in registered crime there will invariable be calls for tougher laws and harsher punishment, which are eagerly taken up by politicians, despite the fact that research has consistently shown that tougher punishment is not the most effective way of crime prevention (see Kury and Shea 2011; Dölling et al. 2011). This greater insistence on more punitive laws has to be

H. Kury (✉)
University of Freiburg, Freiburg, Germany
e-mail: helmut.kury@web.de

H. Kury et al. (eds.), *Women and Children as Victims and Offenders: Background, Prevention, Reintegration*, DOI 10.1007/978-3-319-28424-8_10

seen today also in the context of changing social conditions, such as the opening of the national borders inside the European Union, the never ending wave of refugees arriving from war-torn and impoverished countries and the growing uncertainty about our economic future. Citizens get the impression that politicians are unable to cope with the new situation and see thus the only solution in getting tough with those perceived to be responsible for the present malaise. Hassemer (2009, p. 285), a former Judge and Vice-president of the German Constitutional Court summarizes the problem as follows: "Between the two poles of security and freedom, penal law, like other aspects of our life, has for some time been moving toward security. In this movement, penal law becomes tougher, but it does not become better. More and more complicated prohibitions, more severe laws and longer sentences, increased police powers for their investigation, a reduction in guarantees that serve to protect the rights of suspects and to spare the innocents but could slow down the investigation and trial. This answers the increasing fear of modern societies of uncontrollable risks, a larger need for control, processes of normative disorientations, in which certainties fade, on which we previously could blindly rely." Thus, the call for tougher sanctions takes on a substitute function to reduce uncertainties that may have nothing to do with crime.

Given that an increasing number of research result demonstrate the limited and even non-existent preventive effect of criminal sanctions and the possible harmful effects of custodial sentences, particularly on juveniles or imprisoned parents and their children (see Robertson et al. and also Allen in this volume), the search for alternatives has come to the forefront. This search has also been linked to a more intense discussion in the early 1990s of the importance of "emotions" in dealing with offenders. Sherman (2003), for instance, pleaded for a "more emotionally intelligent justice", and Karstedt (2011, p. 3) underlines that we see from the early 1990s onwards a "surprisingly abrupt end of the secular movement and modern project of the 'rationalisation' and 'de-emotionalization of law'" (see also Laster and O'Malley 1996). This development is for instance reflected in the return of "shame" in criminal proceedings, especially in restorative justice, and a greater consideration for victims and their emotional needs. "The main trajectories of the return of emotions seem to have been embedded in the major movements that have changed the face of criminal justice over the past two decades: the victims' movement, restorative justice and the emergence of a highly emotional and mostly punitive public and political discourse on crime and justice" (Karstedt 2011, p. 3). Pratt (2006, p. 64) points out in this context that both the support for restorative justice and at the same time the call for tougher punishments are linked to "decline of the welfare state" and "the particular arrangements of penal power" (see also Karstedt 2011, p. 4; Pratt et al. 2005).

The re-discovery of emotions in the context of crime-related conflicts has also met with some critical appraisals. As Karstedt (2011, pp. 1f.) points out, criminologists as scientists are often cautious about emotions. "Emotions are suspicious to them, and criminology's approach to emotions has been cautious and circumspect. Criminology as a science is a descendant of the Enlightenment, and is as such committed to the ideals of reason and reasonable discourse. This equally applies to modern penal law, and to the practice of criminal justice and its institutions as they developed since the Enlightenment in the late eighteenth century, and within modern liberal democracies. Just as exuberant emotions in the political sphere of democratic societies threaten to disrupt the whole system (and are typically observed in a breakdown of the political system), so the legal system strives to curb the strong emotions that it routinely and inescapably confronts. Yet for a long time it has ignored their undeniable presence and strength. Consequently, the presence of emotions in public debates about criminal justice has deepened the uneasy feelings of criminologists. Collective emotions and their expressions are seen as capable of being manipulated in the interest of politicians and other groups, and in particular by the media, in an irresponsible way. Criminologists tend to deny authenticity to outbursts of collective emotions, and they are more inclined to perceive them as manifestations of popular 'false consciousness'" (see also Burkitt 2005; Loader 2011). Karstedt also underlines that: "The process of 'emotionalization' of law and criminal justice has decisively changed criminological perspectives on the role of emotions in crime and justice during the last decade. 'Reintegrative Shaming' and Restorative Justice have been influential in re-shaping criminal justice around the globe, and the 'return of emotions' into criminological perspectives, theories and research is presently re-configuring notions of the 'rational offender' and criminal justice policies based on these" (2006, p. 223). Already in an earlier work (2002, p. 299) she had pointed out that: "During the last decade, a process of 'emotionalization of law' has spread around the globe, changing the criminal justice system in many ways. Anger, disgust and shame are perceived as 'valuable barometers of social morality' and brought back to criminal procedures. The 'return of emotions' to penal law and criminal justice is linked to and illuminates the moral imagination of late modern societies".

Allowing emotions a stronger place, as has been already done in the context of restorative Justice, produces positive results in finding constructive solutions not only in the courts but also in police interrogations, even in interrogations of terrorists (see Alison et al. 2013, 2014). Based on the analysis of 181 police interrogations of terrorists, Alison and colleagues (2014) could show "that adopting an adaptive rapport based interrogation style in which suspects are treated with respect, dignity and integrity is an effective approach for reducing suspects' use of CITs (Counter Interrogation Tactics)." For decades, psychotherapy research has already convincingly demonstrated the importance of an emotional rapport for the effectiveness of treatment, and this in particular for the rehabilitation of imprisoned offenders. Already Orlinsky and Howard (1986) assigned the "therapeutic bonds" an important role in the success of a therapy. A good therapeutic bond improves not only the feeling of self-worth of the patient and increases his willingness to confront his difficulties; it also makes the patient more open to the therapeutic influences, receptive for the therapeutic interventions, which, without such receptiveness could not achieve much (Grawe et al. 1994, p. 781).

Research results from different fields underline thus the positive effects of giving more considerations to emotions in the resolution of conflicts, even in criminal procedures. Forms of alternative conflict solutions are not new, we have only "rediscovered" them. They were for instance used in medieval Europe, and can still be found in traditional societies as a means of reducing conflicts in society. Today we usually summarize them under the heading of "mediation" or "restorative justice", and there exists now a vast array of procedures and publications (see for example: Hopt and Steffek 2008a; Johnstone and Van Ness 2007a; London 2011; see also Dandurand; Hamilton and Yarrow; Ehret et al. in this volume).

Expanding of research about victims of crime after World War II and the establishment of victimology as an essential and important part of criminology fostered a greater awareness that the victims of crimes did not receive enough attention and support (Braithwaite 1989). During the last decades, many countries have put in place new regulations to ensure better support and help for victims but they often did not translate into practice and the actual changes were few if at all. Even today, in criminal justice procedures the role of victims is reduced to that of witnesses; compensation is given, if at all, seldom by the state or the offender, but mostly by more or less private institutions, in Germany for example by the "White Ring" ("Weißer Ring"; see: https://www.weisser-ring.de).

Yet, international empirical research shows clearly that most victims, except in cases of very severe crimes, are more interested in restitution of the damage than in a severe punishment of the offender (Sessar 1992, 1995). But the interests of the state and the established court system are different: their focus is on "justice", on the re-establishment law and order, thereby disregarding the interests of most victims and large parts of the population in restoring peace in society and reducing the conflict caused by crime. Here measures of mediation can help to establish a bridge between different interests. "Restorative justice presents a different approach to achieving justice than the traditional court system. Whereas court systems depend on punitive measures and do not attend to victim concerns, restorative justice focuses on repairing the harm caused by an offense, bringing the offender back into society, and giving all actors affected by the crime (the offender, the victim and the community) a direct voice in the justice process" (Gromet 2009, p. 40).

In order to have mediation accepted in society as a valid alternative to regular court procedures, it is very important that this measure and its benefits are clearly understood by the population and especially by the courts. Johnstone and Van Ness (2007b, p. 6) still regretfully point out: "Yet, despite its growing familiarity in professional and academic circles, the meaning of the term 'restorative justice' is still only hazily understood by many people." During an international conference in Germany the main reason given for the fact that restorative justice is still today rarely used was that these alternatives are not well known both in society and in the criminal justice systems. Even judges are often poorly informed and share in the general opinion that restorative justice is a "soft" option, and certainly not as effective in crime prevention as proper punishment (Lummer 2011, pp. 240f; Kury and Shea 2011).

In the first part, this chapter will briefly discuss the historical development of mediation and alternative conflict solution. Mediation is a collective term often used in different contexts and different ways. In a second step we will therefore discuss its different definitions. The main part of the chapter will present information about practice and experiences with mediation in Germany and other European countries, with special emphasis on its use in the juvenile justice system (see also Hamilton and Yarrow; Ehret et al. in this volume). A central question concerns the crime prevention effects of mediation, especially in comparison with "classical" punitive reactions of criminal justice, and results of evaluation of these alternatives are presented. In a final discussion we will compare the main results (see also Kury and Kuhlmann 2016) and try to show that alternatives to classical penal procedures have many positive effects in dealing with female and juvenile offenders and victims.

2 Historical Examples of Crime Related Conflict Reduction in Society

Advocates of mediation and restitution in criminal cases often refer to historical examples (see also Kury and Kuhlmann 2016). For example Frühauf (1988, p. 8) discusses the history of restitution and shows that this is one of the most interesting topics in the history of punishment. In earlier times it was a natural part of each sanctioning system and dates back to the beginning of written laws (see also Hagemann 2011). Already the Codex Hamurabi—a Babylonian law code dating back to about 1754 B.C. and one of the earliest law books known—includes next to severe punishments many regulations about restitution to the victim by the offender. Roughly 400 years later, around 1300 B.C., more detailed measures of restitution can also be found in Hittite legislation. Hittite laws were formulated as case laws, starting with a condition, and followed by a ruling, e.g. "If anyone tears off the ear of a male or female slave, he shall pay 3 shekels of silver." Alternative measures to reduce conflicts in societies caused by crime have obviously a long and successful history.

Detailed regulations about restitution seem to have been common in most cultural regions (Frühauf 1988, p. 11). We find them for example in the Old Testament (Burnside 2007), in the Islamic penal system and as an integral part of tribal customs (Zinsstag and Vanfaechem 2012). As Sharpe (2007, p. 26) points out: "Reparation has been a vehicle for justice throughout human history". Rössner (1998, p. 878) concludes that on the basis of behavioural research the aim of establishing peace is part of our biological makeup. Without systematic measures to reduce conflicts, there would be no human community. Until the Middle Ages the restitution of penal peace by social compensation was considered the central part of penal justice.

Frühauf (1988, pp. 13ff.) gives a detailed description of the evolution of restitution over the centuries in German law. From the fifth century A.D. on, we find an increasing number of laws written by the different nations inhabiting these regions. In the "Lex Salica" for example, written between 507 and 511 A.D., a catalogue of penances was defined, which fixed for each crime a restitution to be made by the offender to the victim, even for homicides. The punishment of offenders through restitution was in those times seen as normal and usual (Frühauf 1988, p. 17). The offender was pressured to compensate the damage caused by his criminal act. In the following centuries the principle of restitution was however increasingly replaced by harsher punishment. With the establishment of kingdoms, the distribution of power between state and tribes changed fundamentally (p. 37). In a desire to increase their own power, the rulers of the kingdoms had an interest in abolishing the old legislations in order to take the jurisdiction in their own hands. This was also the beginning of a fundamental change in social control. The new kingdoms established a general penal system, in which law breaking was now increasingly sanctioned by the king, taking it thus away from the people. With the creation of a state penal law in the early Middle Ages private conflict was transformed into a public conflict (Rössner 1998, p. 880). The concept of restitution lo longer fitted into the concept of punishment by State authorities. The re-establishment of a balance impaired by a criminal act was taken away from the community and was managed now by the state in a new power relation between state and offender. The aim was no longer inclusion and integration, but exclusion and separation. Both the conflict and the cooperation in solving or at least reducing it were taken away from the victim (Christie 1977) and the process was more and more formalized and neutralized.

Punishment is used as a measure of power. Especially as far as the use of the death penalty is concerned, it mirrors the interplay between a move to absolute power of the kings and the new authoritarian penal laws (Frühauf 1988, p. 43). After an arrangement, the state began enforcing a *Friedensgeld* (money for peace), which is no other than a fine. Punishment became thus an income for the state. This was the beginning of a problem, which is still with us today: by the end of the reign of the Franks the money to be paid to the state had become the bigger part of the punishment and the damages caused to the victims remained their own private problem (Frühauf 1988, p. 44). This regulation did not substantially change until recently. In Germany, for example, in 1976 a special law was passed regulating the restitution for victims of violent crimes ("Gesetz über die Entschädigung für Opfer von Gewalttaten"; see the overview in Schwind 2011, p. 441 ff.), but in practice only a relatively small part of all victims really receive a (financial) restitution because of too many formal obstacles (see the overviews in Villmow 1988; Villmow and Plemper 1989; Villmow and Savinsky 2013).

Frühauf (1988, p. 45) talks of an all-round "fiscalisation" of penal law on the background of massive financial interests of the kingdoms. Fines were—and still are—a good source of income for the state; only lately restitution to the victims as a task of the state has again become a topic of discussion. Frühauf (1988, p. 59) notes that the regulation and control of justice by the state to control the social behaviour of citizens was and still is the best solution, despite its problems. In the final analysis it guarantees greater justice and a more equal treatment of all penal cases. In this sense, the development beginning in the Middle Ages was a huge progress in civilization. Yet, as Rössner (1998, p. 880) points out that in the absolute theories of punishment propagated by Kant and Hegel—with their continued impact on German politics of punishment and crime control—there is no place for restitution and conflict solution. This might be one of the reasons why in German criminal law the development of victim offender restitution has still not reached the importance it had in earlier times as in practice, victim offender restitution in Germany plays a minor role (Rössner 1998, pp. 880 f.). Even if there is some overall improvement, it is not yet reflected in criminal matters (Schmidt 2012, p. 191). For example in the German *Land* of North Rhine-Westphalia in 2007 we count 4535 cases of victim offender restitutions in comparison to 184,800 "classical" criminal court decisions.

The question to what extent the state needs the principle of punishment was already discussed in the 1980s (Frühauf 1988, p. 60) but has lost nothing of its actuality. Living conditions have changed in society and the restricted use of restitution can be seen as a disadvantage in actual criminal justice, especially in handling crimes of young persons. Dealing with crime means primarily concentrating on the offender; beside penal sanctions there exists today a broad network of treatment and diversion measures, and fines have become the primary sanction but without providing a tangible benefit for the victims of crime. Only modern discussions about victimology have slowly brought about a different way of thinking about crime control (Frühauf 1988, p. 65). Based on the example of other countries, such as the United States, Canada, Australia or New Zealand (see Wemmers and Cyr in this volume; Shearar and Maxwell 2012), also in Germany an increasing number of projects about restitution were implemented.

3 Definition of Mediation

Braithwaite (2009, p. 497) one of the founding fathers of the newer movement in mediation distinguishes between "mediation" and "restorative justice" and points out: "Mediation between just a victim and just an offender can be described as a ‚restorative process', but it does exclude other stakeholders such as the family of the offender". In contrast he defines restorative justice as "a process where all the stakeholders affected by a crime have an opportunity to come together to discuss the consequences of the crime and what should be done to right the wrong and meet the needs of those affected. Of course such an ideal is secured to greater and lesser degrees". On the basis of this process-definition "one on one victim-offender mediation is not as restorative as a conference or a circle to which victims and offenders are encouraged to bring their families and other supporters. In a restorative justice conference both victims and offenders are asked to bring along the people who they most trust and respect to support them during the conference". But restorative justice refers according to Braithwaite (2009, p. 497) not only to processes, "it is also about values. It is about the idea that because crime hurts, justice should heal. The key value of restorative justice is non-domination (see also Braithwaite and Pettit 1990; Braithwaite 2002). The active part of this value is empowerment. Empowerment means preventing the state from 'stealing conflicts' (see Christie 1977) from people who want to hang on to those conflicts and learn from working the through in their own way. Empowerment should trump other restorative justice values like forgiveness, healing and apology, important as they are." In this context to fully accept "empowerment" means also that if a victim wants to react to a victimisation in a more retributive than restorative way, this must also be accepted but, as Braithwaite puts it: "because non-domination is the fundamental value that motivates the operational value of empowerment, people are not empowered to breach fundamental human rights in their pursuit of revenge" (Braithwaite 2009, p. 497 f.).

According to Walgrave (2007, p. 559) the difference between restorative justice and criminal justice can be particularly seen in the following characteristics: "- Crime in restorative justice is defined not as a transgression of an abstract legal disposition, but as social harm caused by the offence. - In criminal justice, the principal collective agent is the state, while collectivity in restorative justice is mainly seen through community. - The response to crime is not ruled by a top-down imposed set of procedures but by a deliberative bottom-up input from those with a direct stake in the aftermath. - Contrary to formalized and rational criminal justice procedures, restorative justice processes are informal, and include emotions and feelings. - The outcome of restorative justice is not a just infliction of a proportionate amount of pain but a socially constructive, or restorative, solution to the problem caused by the crime. - Justice in criminal justice is defined 'objectively', based on legality, while justice in restorative justice is seen mainly as a subjective-moral experience." But the author also emphasizes the fact that the differences between criminal and restorative justice have become smaller over the years. "It is becoming obvious that a clear-cut distinction between restorative justice and criminal justice cannot be sustained as was originally proposed" (Walgrave 2007, p. 560).

There is also no clear and comprehensive definition of mediation and its different forms. As Zernova and Wright (2007, p. 91) point out that there are many different ways how restorative justice can be used in practice. "There is no agreement among restorative justice proponents as to how exactly restorative justice should be implemented and what its relationship to the criminal justice system should be". The authors differentiate between a process-oriented and a result-oriented model. Very often there is a differentiation between court-intern mediation, organized and managed by the judges themselves and included in the penal process, a mediation close to the penal process and more or less included in it and at the same time separate from the penal procedure, and finally mediation completely separated from the court procedure, precisely with the aim to prevent a criminal trial (Hopt and Steffek 2008c, pp. 9 and 19). The two authors found that in the countries included in their research, mediation outside the courts or in cooperation with the courts were the most frequently chosen model (Hopt and Steffek 2008c).

The authors also discovered (2008c, p. 12) that the definitions of mediation varied greatly in the countries included in the project. Given these variations, they chose to use the smallest common denominator for their definition of mediation, which is as follows: "Mediation is a procedure based on voluntary cooperation of the parties, with a mediator without the power to make decisions who facilitates systematically the communication between the parties with the aim to find a solution of a conflict between the parties accepted and produced by the parties." A central element, accepted by all criminal justice systems is that of voluntary cooperation, but again this is defined in different ways in different countries. Also the power to implement the solutions agreed upon is regulated differently and ranges from compulsion (for instance in England, Austria or Portugal) to the free decision of the parties (as in China). Agreement exists to a greater extent about the rule that the mediator has no power to decide, and that conflict resolution is fully in the hands of the parties (p. 12). But again there are differences between the countries concerning the question how far the mediator has the right to propose solutions for conflict regulation (Hopt and Steffek 2008c, p. 13).

It is important to see that mediation is not only used to reduce conflicts of criminal justice matters but also other conflicts, for example in cases linked to social problems. The communities included in Hopt's and Steffeck's research generally agreed that the strength of mediation became particularly visible in the fact that the procedure from the outset aimed at finding a solution of the social conflict, and the legal regulation only had an ancillary function. A systematic promotion of communication by the mediator was a key element, in addition to the confidence in the procedure and the neutrality of the mediator. The definitions of mediation in the different countries included in the project shared in common the following prerequisites: (1). Existence of a conflict, (2). The engagement to solve the conflict on a voluntary basis, (3). The systematic promotion of communication between the different parties, (4). Acceptance of responsibility for the solution found, including the condition that the mediator has no power of decision. Voluntary cooperation is also insofar a very important topic because agreements on the basis of mediation have virtually no chance of being executed by force. In particular with juveniles this approach to handling conflicts works well. They feel more respected (Hopt and Steffek 2008c, p. 13).

An important part of mediation is victim offender restitution (*Täter-Opfer-Ausgleich TOA*) or repairing the damage. Heinz (1993, p. 376) points out that victim offender restitution is strongly correlated with the idea of repairing the damage caused but has, at the same time, a larger scope in the central idea of fairness and satisfaction. By considering the interests and needs of both parties, a fair settlement should be achieved, and in the best cases even reconciliation. This could be arranged by using the possibility of a private-autonomous solution. The offender should learn to see and to accept the effects of the damages caused to the victim and should accept his social responsibility. This idea exceeds the frame of victim offender restitution as practiced today and includes the perspective of the victim as an example of social learning for offenders on parole, probation or in prison (Heinz 1993, p. 376).

In the countries included in the research of Hopt and Steffek (2008c, p. 22) restitution measures receive financial support. As the authors point out, the main reason for the granting financial support has to do with the hope that this will be a cheaper way of solving crime problems: the courts will have to deal with fewer cases and the proceedings will be shortened. The different law systems don't clearly separate mediation from other forms of conflict reducing measures (Hopt and Steffek 2008c, pp. 15 ff.). Related topics may overlap or the title is the same but the procedure different. Some countries ask for special training of the mediators (usually attorneys, social workers or psychologists), others don't. Also the regulations differ strongly between the countries. According to some authors, too rigid regulations may reduce the chances of successful mediation.

A controversial topic in some countries and in the literature is also a division between mediation and retribution. Are they opposites or not? Some authors think that mediation and retribution are very different reactions to deviant behaviour (Braithwaite and Strang 2001). In their view, restitution is hindered if the focus is on punitive measures which exclude the offender from society instead of including him. McCold (2000), for example, refuses all pressures by courts in cases of restorative justice, as this would take the proceedings again in a punitive direction.

Other authors suggest that a combination of mediation and retribution is the best response. Proponents of this concept point out "that retribution is an essential component of addressing wrongdoing, and it is the combination of restoration and retribution that will best achieve justice (see also Barton 1999; Daly 2002; Duff 2003; Robinson 2003). In this view, a pure restorative response is rejected as an acceptable response to wrongdoing. Proponents of this model contend that both the victim and the community have a right to desire retribution for the crimes that wronged them" (Gromet 2009, p. 45). Gromet (ibid. pp. 45 f.) further points out that in an "integrative view of restorative justice … restoration and retribution are not necessarily competing. …The combination of restoration and retribution in fact may provide a better response to wrongdoing than either response on its own, as multiple justice goals can be accomplished. … The justice goals with regard to restoration and retribution are punishment and rehabilitation of the offender, restitution and restoration of the victim, reinforcement of the values of the community and restoration of the community".

Walgrave (2007, p. 565) underlines another important aspect in this discussion: "… restricting restorative justice to voluntary deliberations would limit its scope drastically (see also Dignan 2002). The mainstream response to crime would remain coercive and punitive. The criminal justice system would probably refer only a selection of the less serious cases to deliberative restorative processes, thus excluding the victims of serious crimes who need restoration the most." According to Walgrave (2007, p. 565) restoration and retribution have a lot of commonalities (see also Zehr 2002), "clear censure of reprovable behaviour, an appeal to responsibility and an attempt to restore a balance. Restorative justice scholars, however, should accept the necessity of using coercive power when deliberative processes are impossible."

In some countries, also in Germany, there exists now also online-mediation. This has the advantage to use the procedure in cases where the parties live far away, for example in different countries. Research shows that this procedure is useful especially in minor cases with low amounts of money involved or in cases of online businesses (Hopt and Steffek 2008c, pp. 51 ff.).

4 The Development in Germany

As Frühauf (1988, p. 20) in his historical overview concludes that the displacement of restitution payments from the victim to the State was a big mistake as far as the solution of conflicts in a society and dealing with crime problems in a community are concerned (see also Kury and Kuhlmann 2016). According to Kaiser (1996, p. 1088) the need to solve conflicts by speaking with the other party is still today deeply rooted in society. Yet the potential for dialogue with the other party in penal procedures is not or only poorly used, despite its importance (Bussmann 1986, pp. 158 f.). In Bussmans's view, crime policy should necessarily include victim offender restitution as a more constructive reduction of conflicts in society.

In the middle of last century, after a long period of oblivion (Frühauf 1988, p. 63), the positive effects of mediation became again a subject of international discussion mainly thanks to the interest created by the newly established victimology research (Hentig 1948; Schneider 1975). Also in Germany penal sanctions increasingly included a broad network of treatment and diversion measures, initially however restricted to minor offences (Frühauf 1988, p. 64). The development of mediation in Germany in the 1980s was mainly triggered by reports about its positive effects in the United States, where we find the beginning of an intensive and often controversial discussion about "restorative justice" already in the 1970s (Rössner 1998, p. 889; Rössner and Wulf 1985; Frehsee 1987; Abel 1982; Kaiser 1996, pp. 216 ff.).

"Restorative justice as both a philosophy and an implementation strategy developed from the convergence of several trends in criminal justice: the loss of confidence in rehabilitation and deterrence theory, the rediscovery of the victim as a necessary party, and the rise of interest in community-based justice" (London 2011, p. 13). Even if we do see in the United States from the early 1970s onwards an increase in punitiveness, "along with their interest in punishment, the public's interest in alternative non-punitive solutions has also been recognized" (London 2011, p. 103). If the public is informed about the rather disappointing effectiveness of punishment compared to alternative sanctions, punitiveness decreases; this has been confirmed by several studies (see for instance: Doob and Roberts 1983; Roberts and Hough 2002; Sato 2013). "In sum, while the public's support for punishment is well known, its support for alternatives to punishment and sanctions with a restorative quality is also strong" (London 2011, p. 104). "Punishment alone is an extraordinarily poor way of restoring trust either in an offender or in society" (London 2011, p. 105). This is particularly true for juvenile offenders.

At the beginning of discussions about alternative measures of crime prevention the advantages of mediation were put to the fore, and this for the following reasons: mediation is less formal and more personal, mediation provides greater satisfaction and acceptance of results, can find solutions to conflicts in favour of all parties, is perceived as a more just solution from the point of view of the different parties and the community, offers a better chance to both victims and offenders, alleviates the load of the criminal justice systems and saves costs for the state and the parties (Hopt and Steffek 2008c, p. 7; see also Bush and Folger 2005). Given these advantages, the support for mediation grew steadily, and Germany, like other countries, followed the American example (Hopt and Steffek 2008b, p. 9).

It was the modern victimological research, which led to a new philosophy in criminal justice, even if initially its effects on penal practice were scant. This new interest in victims was also linked to the women's movement, which drew attention to the large number vicitmized women and children. Goodey (2005, p. 102) discussed three main reasons for the sudden attention paid to crime victims and victimology in the United States and Great Britain in the late 1960s and early 1970s—the rise in crime rates and the increasing scepticism about the effectiveness of the treatment of offenders, summarized in Martinson's famous formulation "nothing works" (Martinson 1974; Lipton et al. 1975; Kury 1986)—the beginning of an increasingly right-wing oriented punitive (crime) policy, calling for a harsher treatment of offenders and resulting, particularly in the United States, in a dramatic increase of prisoners—the strengthening of the women's movement and with it the call for more empathy for women and children as victims of mainly male violence. The victims of crime got increasing rights also in criminal trials and could so at least partly overcome the role of being only a witness or spectator. The movement soon spread to other, similar criminal justice systems and also strongly influenced German policy.

Empirical research soon was able to show that restitution and compensation were seen as needs that were widely accepted by both the population and the victims of crime and thus deserved more attention in a modern criminal justice system (Kaiser 1996, p. 1088). In Germany, a model project in mediation in the form of victim offender restitution with juveniles began in 1984/1985 after the German Probation Organisation (*Deutsche Bewährungshilfe e.V.*) had established in 1983/84 a working group "victim offender mediation" (*Täter-Opfer-Ausgleich—TOA*). At about the same time, in 1984, the first German model project in adult criminal law was started (Schmidt 2012, p. 187). After this, the idea took off rapidly (Rössner and Wulf 1985). Already in 1988 victim offender mediation was included in the recommendations of a *Bund/Länder-Adhoc-Kommission* (government/state-adhoc-commision) under the label of "Diversion" (about the discussion of diversion see Kury and Lerchenmüller 1981). In 1991 many new model-projects of victim offender restitution with adults started and enlarged the movement (Delattre 2010, p. 88). As a first official organisation for mediation the *Bundesarbeitsgemeinschaft für Familienmediation* (BAFM) (Governmental working group for mediation in family affairs) was founded in January 1992 (Hopt and Steffek 2008c, p. 7). In September 2008 also the annual conference of German lawyers (*Deutscher Juristentag*) in Erfurt included mediation for the first time (see Heß 2008).

In 1999 the German government voted the "*Gesetz zur Förderung der außergerichtlichen Streitbeilegung*" (Law for out-of court conflict solution). With this law victim offender restitution (TOA) became officially part of penal procedure (Delattre 2010, p. 90). Now, prosecutors and judges at all stages of criminal proceedings should examine the option of solving the cases by mediation (*Bundesministerium des Innern/Bundesministerium der Justiz* 2006, *p. 590*). Experience shows that most of the offenders and victims, when asked and given proper information, are willing to participate in a victim offender restitution program. The results of the cases dealt with TOA between 1993 and 2002 are as follows: in 69 % of cases the offender apologized to the victim for his crime, in 30 % of cases he paid damages, in 19 % he paid punitive damages for causing pain and sufferings, in 13 % of cases there were other benefits, in 7 % no other benefits and in 6 % he did work for the victim (Bundesministerium des Innern/Bundesministerium der Justiz 2006, p. 594). Only 2.5 % of agreements failed.

In juvenile justice legislation (*Jugendgerichtsgesetz—JGG*) education of the offender is the primary goal. From an educational point of view restitution is seen as very important because it makes the offender clearly aware of his wrongdoings. Already in 1923 the court could ask for restitution by the offender on the basis of the JGG. This way the young offender could learn through restitution that he had caused pain and had made a mistake and realise the negative consequences this had caused for himself (Frühauf 1988, p. 76). Victim offender restitution was thus first implemented in juvenile court, and then in 1994 in the criminal code for adults.

To promote victim offender mediation in Germany, since 1999 prosecution offices and the courts have the duty to propose TOA. They must in all cases examine the possibilities and chances of a successful (voluntary) victim offender restitution and must in suitable cases appoint qualified agencies to implement it (Schwind 2011, pp. 438 f.).

The procedures for victim offender restitution is still not the same in all the *Länder* but there is some agreement on what criteria should be applied to use or not to use TOA (see Delattre 2010, p. 93)—TOA should not be used for petty crimes to avoid net widening of social control (see Kury and Lerchenmüller 1981)—the victim must be a person—the facts have to be clear-cut: the offender accepts the charge and confesses his guilt—both parties, victim and offender, accept the procedure and are willing to cooperate. As for the danger of net widening, Johnstone (2007, p. 609) points out that: "Less serious cases will be diverted to informal restorative processes and sanctions. But, because they are less formal and regarded as more benign, these processes will be extended to cases which previously would not have given rise to penal interventions. Overall the reach of the system of penal control will be extended rather than cut back" (see also Zehr 1990, p. 222).

Victim offender mediation is rightly seen as a great pedagogical tool for the offender and a better way to reduce the harm suffered by the victim; yet despite these advantages, it is even now relatively rarely used in Germany (Kilchling 2012; Dünkel and Párosanu 2015). The courts still mostly prefer to punish the offender by a fine payable to a non-profit institution. Even in juvenile law, where the duty of the offender to make restitution was discussed at length on a theoretical level, in praxis it is only used in relatively few cases. That may have to do with the legal training in Germany, especially that of juvenile judges (Frühauf 1988, p. 77).

Based on a decision of the Government and Parliament, the German Probation Organisation (*Deutsche Bewährungshilfe e. V.*) has opened in 1992 a service bureau for victim offender restitution as a supra regional counselling bureau, financed most by the ministry of justice and the *Länder* (http://www.toa-servicebuero.de/) Beundesministerium des Innern/Bundesministeri- um der Justiz 2006, p. 589).

Since then, by order of the ministry of justice more and more neutral bureaus of conflict resolution were established by non-governmental organisations but also by the social services of the justice and social work bureaus.[1] These offices can be used by the prosecution before the trial or by the courts during the trial to promote restitution. The mediators usually are pedagogues or social workers and mostly have an additional specialized training in mediation (Delattre 2010, p. 90). Today roughly 400 of these mediation bureaus exist in Germany (Schwind 2011, p. 439), of which over 300 are staffed with full-time professionals (Germany has approximately 82 Million inhabitants) (Delattre 2010, p. 90). These offices deal today with about 35,000 cases per year, up from roughly 25,000 cases 10 years earlier (Trenczek 2003, p. 104; Delattre 2010, p. 91). This puts Germany in the top bracket of restitution cases in Europe. In comparison with roughly 550,000 criminal charges per year these number is nevertheless relatively low (Schwind 2011, p. 439).

Statistics collected by Kerner et al. (2005) show that in 2002 a majority of cases (47 %) in which victim offender restitution was used were assault cases causing bodily harm (see also Jehle 2005, p. 40), and of these, half concerned conflicts in partnership and other forms of inner-familiar violence (Trenczek 2003, p. 105; Vázquez-Portomene 2012; see also about mediation in cases of partner conflicts: Rössner et al. 1999). Schmidt (2012, p. 189) lists besides bodily injury also damaging of goods, insults, threats, intimidation, trespassing and property crimes. The focus of victim offender restitution is not on the reparation of material damages but of personal conflicts between human beings (Walter 2004, p. 339). In cases of successful victim offender restitution between both parties, the prosecution will in 80 % of all cases close the penal process and the case will not come to court. In other cases the court can reduce the punishment or abstain from it altogether (Jehle 2005, p. 39; for a summary: Schwind 2011, p. 439).

In areas outside the criminal justice system we can also see a growing tendency to regulate conflicts in a non-juridical way. Yet despite this progress and the fact that mediation has become an accepted form of conflict resolution in Germany the possibilities of mediation are still far from being fully exhausted (Hopt and Steffek 2008c, p. 7).

Research in New Zealand and Australia has pointed to conferencing as a particularly helpful form of mediation to reduce conflicts caused by juvenile offending or conflicts in families or partnership. According to Vanfraechem and Zinsstag (2012, p. 1): "Restorative justice in general and conferencing in particular

[1] Source: TOA statistics, which have been collected since 1993 by Kerner and colleagues (2005).

have in the last two decades developed extensively. They have during this time established themselves as valuable potential alternatives to a problematic criminal justice systems, or as an ideal partner through which coordination with a more punitive type of justice attempts to bring a fairer sense of justice to all stakeholders of a crime". Conferencing is a restorative justice practice that is especially helpful to repair the harm caused by the crime to the victim and the community (Walgrave 2008, p. 21). "Family group conferences (FGC) started in New Zealand in 1989, both for youth justice and youth care cases" and this was "the model for various practices throughout the world" (Vanfraechem and Zinsstag 2012, p. 2; see also Morris and Maxwell 2001). As Shearar and Maxwell (2012, p. 101) point out: "New Zealand's youth justice system owes much of its success to the fact that it was based on principles which emphasized constructive outcomes for victims, young offenders, families, and communities through the creation of the family group conference (FGC)". The authors come to the conclusion (2012, p. 114): "New Zealand's youth justice model has provided the world with an important model for youth justice systems. It places emphasis on family and community support for children and young people's pro-social development while making them accountable for their actions. The New Zealand experience has shown the need for widespread commitment from the government, communities, families, and agencies for this model to succeed". That conferencing has its origins in New Zealand and Australia is no accident: this form of conflict resolutions has long been practiced by the aboriginal population of the two countries (see also Daly 2012, pp. 118 ff.; Kury and Kuhlmann 2016).

Daly (2012) discusses the possibilities and risks of using conferences also in cases of gendered violence: "Using conferences in cases of gendered violence (sexual, partner, and family violence) is controversial. Two countries – New Zealand and Australia – have been pioneers in developing appropriate practices. A small body of evidence from the region and elsewhere is available on the topic" (2012, p. 117). The use of appropriate practices is of great importance for a successful outcome in such cases (ibid. p. 130): "Gendered violence offences pose challenges to conferencing and restorative justice, in part because of a charged political context and in part because these offences require serious reflection on the role and place of victims in a justice process. Victim safety and voluntary participation, and facilitators who are knowledgeable about the dynamics of gendered violence offences, are obvious pre-requisites" (see also Cook et al. 2006; Daly and Stubbs 2006).

5 The Development in Other European Countries

Hopt and Steffek (2008b) also give an overview about the development and the actual state of mediation in other countries (see also Rössner 1998, pp. 881 ff.). The volume includes regulations and research from the United States, Austria, France, England, the Netherlands, Japan, Australia, Bulgaria, China, Ireland, Canada,

New Zealand, Norway, Poland, Portugal, Russia, Switzerland, Spain and Hungary, i.e. from western industrialized countries but also from former Soviet Republics. Positive reports about mediation from one country encourage other countries to also include these alternatives in their penal codes. For instance, in their report about the United States, Bush and Folger (2005) praise the introduction of mediation as a "satisfaction story", a "social justice story" and a "transformation story"—praise that had a stimulating effect (see Hopt and Steffek 2008c, p. 10).

Miers (2007, pp. 447ff.) reported about the development of mediation in USA, Belgium, England and Wales and New Zealand. According to his study, in 1996 there existed 289 victim-offender-mediation programs in the United States, albeit only few of them included juveniles (see also Umbreit and Greenwood 1998). Five years later Schiff and Bazemore (2002, p. 180) counted already 773 programs with conferencing. For Canada, Griffiths (1999) counted in 1998 more than 200 programs. Umbreit et al. (2001, p. 121) estimated for the year 2000 worldwide in about 20 countries 1300 programs for juvenile offenders. Mestitz (2005, p. 13) found in Europe strong differences in the distribution of mediation programs, especially concerning juvenile offenders. While in Germany or in France 200 to 300 victim offender restitution programs existed, in other countries like Ireland or Italy there were only very few. Authors link the differences in the programs to the differences in legal systems but to some extent also to the presence or absence of financial support. There were also many differences between "design and delivery" of the programs (Daly 2003b). Restorative justice simply "means different things to different people" (Weitekamp 2002, p. 322). Hopt and Steffek (2008c, pp. 12ff) share this assessment. From a theoretical point of view it is essential that cooperation on a voluntary basis is a key element of mediation yet in some countries the discussion is still going on whether in some cases the parties can be forced to cooperate. There are also differences in the definition of the role of the mediator, for example whether he/she can bring in suggestions and solutions or not. However one positive aspect of mediation shared by all participating countries is the fact that the procedure is centred on the social conflict, and that the legal regulations only have a helping function. This makes it possible that problems outside the juridical sphere, for example in family matters or at the work place, can be handled through mediation as well (see for example Montada 2004, p. 184). There is a common consensus that mediation needs to be handled by trained staff and not by amateurs (Hopt and Steffek 2008c, p. 13). As Hopt and Steffek (2008c, p. 13) point out the definitions of mediation in different countries concentrate on four points: there needs to be a conflict; participation must be voluntary; there has to be systematic support of the communication between the parties; the role of the mediator is to help the parties to come to an agreement, but he has no power to force a decision on them. Also important is the confidentiality of the procedure and the neutrality of the mediator.

One of the reason why most countries report positive results has also to do with the fact that the reduction of conflicts is not from the outset pressed into a rigid corset but that the parties and the mediators have the opportunity to find flexible solutions based on the nature of the conflict (Hopt and Steffek 2008c, p. 42). The flexibility of the concept is a very important aspect the success of which depends to a large extent on the quality of the training of the mediators. In Germany for example, the "*Bundesarbeitsgemeinschaft Täter-Opfer-Ausgleich e. V. (BAG TOA e.V.)*" gives a diploma of quality to qualified mediators which should guarantee high standards in the praxis (Lippelt and Schütte 2010, p. 66). Jung (1998, p. 921) cautions that mediation can lose its specific characteristics and the potential to present a more humane regulation of conflicts as soon as it is incorporated and instrumentalized by the criminal justice system. In this case it can easily degenerate into an inferior variation of the decision making process of the judge. This does not mean that the procedural guarantees of criminal justice should be neglected because, as Walgrave (2007, p. 570) puts it: "It is now almost generally accepted that a state-controlled legal framework is needed to locate restorative justice within the principles of a constitutional democracy."

Tränkle (2007, p. 335) compared the German victim offender mediation procedure and the French model *of médiation pénale* for adults and examined their chances of success under the conditions of the respective criminal procedures. She points out that the mediators would have to bring about a transformation of the classical penal court procedure for an effective mediation (p. 336). Mediation is hindered if the parties are still locked into their roles in the classical penal procedure—this is not a good starting point for open conversation (p. 338). The chances for an open conversation have to be settled before the real mediation can begin. The author comes thus to the conclusion (p. 340) that the structural docking to the penal procedure hinders mediation in its development. And yet, restrictions and structuring on the basis of the classical penal procedure cannot be excluded because the mediation can only partly, if at all, transgress the classical penal court procedure. This analysis is confirmed by Hopt and Steffek who, in their international comparison of penal laws, also show that in some countries the possibilities of free agreements between the parties are substantially reduced (2008c, pp. 70 ff.). Some countries require first special conferences or court decisions, which have to be followed. Coercion for a voluntary solution of conflicts, the so-called Mediation-Paracos, is in any case contra-productive (p. 88).

As far as the training of mediators is concerned, Hopt and Steffek (2008c, pp. 70 ff.) have found in their international analyses great differences between different countries. Only in a few countries have clear training programs been formalized, and also the question which professional groups should be active as mediators finds different answers. Problems with mediation are regularly also linked to the criminal justice regulations of a country. Especially in countries where the concept is new, the authors find problems in the realization, bad conceptualization, little institutional support or even misuse in the sense of a prolongation of penal procedures (Hopt and Steffek 2008c, p. 71). In Germany too there was considerable resistance to mediation in the beginning (see Hammacher 2008, p. 30). Sound information, both for the public and the professionals involved is therefore very important. The better the public is informed, the more mediation will be accepted as an alternative (see for example the development of attitudes to alternatives in the former German Democratic Republic after the reunification of both parts of Germany: Kury et al. 1996; Ludwig and Kräupl 2005).

While in western countries restorative justice is meanwhile largely accepted, at least on a theoretical level, in Eastern European countries such alternatives are less well known, except for those countries that have already adapted their penal policy to western models. Willemsens and Walgrave (2007, p. 491) put it this way: "Although a number of countries in Central and Eastern Europe already have well established victim-offender mediation practices (for example, Poland, the Czech Republic and Slovenia), others are still struggling to take the first steps." On the background of their experiences in the cooperation with Eastern European countries, the authors (2007, p. 491) point out problems and opposition such as: "- a highly punitive attitude among the public and policy makers, - an uncritical reliance on incarceration - strong resistance within the police, prosecutors and judges, who fear competition from alternatives, - a passive civil society and weakened public legitimacy of the state and its institutions, - limited trust in NGOs and in their professional capacities, - lack of information about restorative justice and of restorative justice pilots, - low economic conditions, making it difficult to set up projects, - no tradition of co-operation and dialogue in several sectors and professions, - a general loss of trust in a better future, and a mood of despondency and cynicism, - forms of nepotism and even corruption in parts of the criminal justice system, - heavy administrative and financial constraints on the agencies, preventing investment in qualitative work" (see also Kury and Shea 2011). Chankova and Van Ness (2007, p. 530) emphasize: "The strength of restorative justice as a global reform dynamic is based on more than local dissatisfaction with criminal justice. The recognition that new approaches were being adopted, expanded and evaluated in different parts of the world has encouraged and equipped local practitioners and given them credibility with policy makers." There is therefore hope that also in all Eastern European countries the discussion about restorative justice will rapidly gain ground.

The situation in Russia and Hungary is comparable to that of most Eastern European countries. Kurzynsky-Singer (2008, pp. 837ff.) explains that in Russia mediation is a relatively new development and has not yet been regulated by law. In crime policy discussion, the advantages of the procedure are mainly seen for economic disputes. In 2007 a first draft of a mediation legislation was formulated. The draft also includes disagreements at the workplaces and in family affairs (Kurzynsky-Singer 2008, pp. 837 ff.).

The court has to accept the result of a mediation, the procedure is not confidential and the procedure is not standardized by law. The mediator can be heard by the court as a witness und has to report. Penal proceedings can be ended after a successful mediation. To begin a mediation process, the parties can get information and help from a mediator or a mediation-centre. Anybody can become a mediator and no special training is required. Most mediators have no legal training (Kurzynsky-Singer 2008, p. 846). Some little statistical information is now available, for example from the Saint Petersburg Centre of Conflict Resolution. There, between 1994 and 2006, 520 mediation processes took place of which 364 related to interpersonal problems, 104 to economic disputes and 42 to problems at the work place. In 89 % of these cases an agreement was found, which was voluntarily reached in 69 %. Some of reasons why mediation is in Russia is still rarely used are as follows (p. 846): for one, the costs are not necessarily lower than in classical penal procedures and, secondly, the missing quality standards are deplorable. Mediation develops in Russia especially as an alternative to the classical penal law system. This is seen in the Russian literature as a positive point because it is hoped that with the help of mediation the risk of corruption at the court and the risk of false court decisions can be reduced (Kurzynsky-Singer 2008, p. 848).

Jessel-Holst (2008, pp. 906ff.) reports on the situation of mediation in Hungary. There, in March 2003, a special law was passed concerning mediation. Mediation is only used in civil cases and the main reason for introducing it was to reduce the caseload of the courts, especially for conflicts in the health system. Mediators must have a university diploma, but no further specialized training is required. Mediation is relatively seldom used. The number of mediations increased in 2004 to 721, of which 532 were successful, and 189 had no positive outcome. 254 cases were about family conflicts, 34 about problems at the work place and 433 about other civil disputes. Overall, the mediation procedures are seen as positive.

Mediation is now in many countries not only used in penal or civil law cases but also for other conflicts, for instance inside families (Bannenberg et al. 1999), schools (Morrison 2007), at work, for conflicts in a community (McEvoy and Mika 2002), in commercial companies (Young 2002), in the police (Senghaus 2010; see also the chapters by Delattre 2010 and Röchling 2010) or in prisons (Walter 2002; Matt and Winter 2002; Van Ness 2007; Sasse 2010). But "it is within criminal justice that it is fast becoming most influential" (Green 2007, p. 183).

The Ministry of England and Wales (2013b) reports in a press release from 14 March 2013 that mediation will be used to help in the separation procedures of couples. "The Government strongly supports mediation – a quicker, simpler and more effective way for separating couples to agree how they divide their assets or arrange child contact, which avoids the traumatic and divisive effect of courtroom battles." The Ministry of Justice includes in its annual budget £ 25,000,000 to support mediation programs in this field and develop new binding legislation that couples "must consider mediation to sort out the details of their divorce" before going to court (2013a). The main advantages are seen the reduction of cost and of time: "The average cost of resolving property and financial disputes caused by separation is approximately £ 500 through mediation for a publicly funded client, compared to £ 4000 for issued settled through the courts. The average time for a mediated case is 110 days compared to 435 days for non-mediated cases" (Ministry of Justice 2013a).

Morrison (2007) discusses mediation programs in schools (see also Hopkins 2004). "As the field of restorative justice began to define itself in the 1990s, the role of schools in promoting restorative justice was seen as central to developing a more restorative society as a whole" (Morrison 2007, p. 325). Today, there are many programs internationally, "that focus on developing social and emotional intelligence in schools" (p. 327), in the sense for example of Sherman (2003), who sees restorative justice as "emotionally intelligent justice". Evaluations have shown positive results, "that the use of restorative measures, across a range of levels, is an effective alternative to the use of suspensions and expulsions" (Morrison 2007, p. 340).

Van Ness (2007, p. 314) writes about mediation programs in United States prisons, for example in the context of "victim awareness and empathy programmes" but also for the solution of conflicts between inmates and prison staff. In some programs, victims or substitutes are included but in others the immediate victims don't participate (see for Germany a similar program in Hamburg: Hagemann 2003, p. 225). The use of restorative justice and victim offender mediation in European prisons is on the increase in some countries like Belgium and Germany. For Belgium we can draw on the research by Buntinx (2012). She works for Suggnomè ("ancient Greek word which means looking from different perspectives at the same reality", Buntinx 2012, p. 1), an organisation that uses victim offender mediation in prisons also for very serious cases, for example homicides. On the basis of the Belgian law of 2005, "a mediation process can be started on the demand of everybody who has a direct interest in a criminal procedure, and this is possible during the whole criminal procedure" (Buntinx 2012, p. 2). The beginning of prison mediations dates back to 2001, and since 2008 in each prison an inmate or his victim can ask for mediation (p. 2). In the time from 2008 to 2012, 1792 requests were made, and 614 mediations and 167 face-to-face meetings actually took place. The evaluation of the author is positive: "... the most important conclusion is of course the very great level of satisfaction on the part of the parties that have participated in mediation. This satisfaction is found both on the side of the offender and that of the victim" (Buntinx 2012, p. 6).

In some programs the main aim is the reconciliation with the family members of the inmate or to prepare the community for the re-entry of the prisoner after release. In "prison-community-programmes" the interest is to reduce the separation between inmate and community, a very important element for a successful reintegration after release. Of special importance is also the reduction of prisonisation. "Prison subcultures are typically deviant, making rejection of deviance more difficult for prisoners. Inviting them to participate in a process of restoration and transformation requires tremendous strength on their part to move against the prevailing culture ... Prisons use or threaten physical and moral violence, making adoption of peaceful conflict resolution difficult" (Van Ness 2007, p. 319; see also Gelber 2012, pp. 441 ff.). Very often offenders are themselves victimized by violent crimes as children or juveniles. In the model project "Seehaus Leonberg" in Baden-Württemberg, which was established in 2003 for juvenile offenders, the staff is engaged in a victim-empathy program for the inmates that also includes restitution. In Lower Saxony mediators receive special training to work in prison with a focus on solving conflicts between inmates and staff. According to several authors, more attention should be paid to victims in modern prison systems (Gelber 2012, p. 447; see also Gelber and Walter 2012; Krause and Vogt 2012). Research shows that the victims are more willing to participate in mediation programs as often suggested.

6 Results of Empirical Evaluation of Mediation

Until a few years ago there were, also internationally, relatively few empirical research results available on the evaluation of mediation, in particular of restorative justice This has changed: meanwhile there are many studies that show "the positive impact of restorative practices at multiple levels, with case types ranging from first-time offenders and misdemeanants to more serious chronic and violent offenders" (Bazemore and Elis 2007, p. 397; see also Hayes 2007). Bazemore and Elis (2007, p. 397) point out that in contrast to empirical research about treatment programs for offenders which could also produce negative results, the positive research results about programs of restorative justice are more consistent: "Most studies of restorative programmes, including recent meta-analyses (see also Bonta et al. 2000; Nugent et al. 2003) indicate some positive impact..., and some suggest that restorative programmes may have equal or stronger impacts than many treatment programmes..." The positive effects were particularly evident for the victims, whereby the discussion is still open, if this positive effect is a result of restitution or rather of the experience of a just treatment during the penal process.

Hayes (2007, p. 425) assesses the positive results of restorative justice programs as follows: "It seems clear that restorative justice processes have many benefits for victims, offenders and their communities. Victims benefit from active participation in a justice process. Offenders benefit from the opportunity to repair harms and make amends. Communities (of care) benefit from the negotiation of restorative resolutions to conflict... In this sense, restorative justice has achieved many of its aims (i.e. holding offenders accountable and affording them opportunities to make amends in symbolic and material ways, encouraging reconciliations between offenders, victims and their communities of care)".

While we now have a relatively large number of studies on the immediate impact of mediation, we know little about the question how far the programs also have a positive preventive effect by reducing the recidivism rate of offenders participating in victim offender restitution programs. Such studies exist so far primarily in the United States, Great Britain and Australia (Hayes 2007, p. 433).

The discussion of the results of this research is insofar difficult as there are a lot of methodological problems that can reduce the validity of the studies (Wood 2015). Often it is difficult to generalize the results—the same problems we have seen decades ago in the evaluation of offender treatment programs (see Lipton et al. 1975). Restorative justice is a broad concept, the procedure within the programs may differ and the programs are used in different phases of the penal procedure. Very often the conferences and thus the direct "treatment" of the offender lasts only 60–90 min in one session; the effect may be therefor low, especially if one takes into account the many different factors that can influence recidivism, such unemployment, inclusion in delinquent networks after release, possible drug and alcohol problems, the situation in the family and with relatives, the people they meet. There is also the risk of a "self-selection bias" because offenders and victims have to agree to participate, and motivated offenders with a better prognosis may be overrepresented (Gromet 2009, p. 41). Often the programs are in practice not fully implemented because there may be opposition from the prosecution or the courts, and there may be discrepancies between the written programs and their realisation (Hoyle 2002, p. 116). The realisation of experimental studies is scarcely possible. The fact that the criteria of recidivism are often not clearly defined and comparable adds yet another complication (Menkel-Meadow 2007).

Notwithstanding these problems Hayes (2007, p. 440) sees the future in a positive light: "Despite results that show restorative justice effects no change … or in some cases is associated with increases in offending …, the weight of the research evidence on restorative justice and reoffending seems tipped in the positive direction to show that restorative justice has crime reduction potential. I am not making a definitive claim about restorative justice's ability to prevent crime because, at this stage, we simply do not know enough about how and why suggesting that, on balance, restorative justice 'works'". It could contribute to prevent recidivism, "but post-intervention experiences are important". Johnstone (2007, p. 598) adds a further note of caution by pointing out that most publications about restorative justice are written by experts who support the procedure and this could cause some bias in the evaluation of the results.

The most frequently voiced criticism of restorative justice is about the risk of undermining the deterrent effect of (harsh) punishment. But proponents of restorative justice don't see this as a big risk "It is of course true that the deterrent effects of punishment tend to be greatly overestimated and its tendency to re-enforce criminality underestimated. However, the average citizen will probably find this response unconvincing …, because the idea that without penal sanctions for law-breaking, many people will succumb to temptations to break the law seems self-evident to most people" (Johnstone 2007, p. 601; see also Wilson 1983, p. 117-144).

Some critics point out that restorative justice can be no more than an adjunct to the established punishment by the courts; within criminal justice it has a place but it is no substitute for punishment. Johnstone (2007, p. 610) pleads in his critical appreciation of restorative justice that the programs have to be implemented in a broader pattern of reactions to criminal behaviour. "What is most interesting is that even the most fervent critics tend to regard restorative justice – suitable reformulated and modified – as an extremely valuable contribution to the ongoing debate about how we should understand, relate to, and handle the problem of wrongdoing."

Some authors point out that the reduction of recidivism should not be seen as the only or primary aim of restorative justice (see Morris 2002). The programs concentrate in the first place on the victims and the reduction of damages caused to them. "Rather than focusing empirical scrutiny squarely on reoffending, perhaps researchers should attempt a better understanding of the complex of possible outcomes of restorative processes" (Hayes 2007, p. 440). If the focus of restorative justice is on victims rather than on the offenders, then it makes sense that the preventive effect of restorative justice should not be the only criterion to measure the success of mediation programs but that the positive impact on victims should also be included (Lippelt and Schütte 2010, p. 43).

Yet there are also authors like Braithwaite (1999, 2009) for whom the positive effects of the programs are impressive, also concerning the reduction in recidivism rates. Braithwaite presents results of empirical research from different countries, which consistently show a remarkable reduction in recidivism rates. Other positive effects are a reduction in family violence, in some cases even in the consumption of alcohol. "Restorative justice is more successful in getting offenders to take responsibility for their wrongdoing. This happens because they experience greater remorse than in traditional criminal law process". Also bullying in schools could be substantially reduced through mediation (Olweus 1993).

As Hopt and Steffek (2008a, b, c, p. 77) rightly point out the effects and importance of mediation has to be seen in combination with the legal situation in a country and the culture of dealing with disputes. This is an important point, especially in comparing results from different countries. For example, in the former Soviet republics the legal conditions and the attitudes of people about this form of conflict resolution are different from western countries given their different historical development (Kury and Shea 2011). Western countries have had a longer experience with mediation, are more familiar with the procedures and accept more lenient reactions to crime. The attitudes of the population about punishment are influenced by the actual practice of dealing with crime in a country. When the German government abolished the death penalty in 1949 after World War II, nearly 75 % of the population were in favour of the death penalty in cases of severe crimes. Today this percentage has shrunk to about 20 % (Kury and Shea 2012). In the former Soviet republics the experience of criminal justice professionals and of the population with alternatives to classical punishment is smaller, and public discussion and media reporting still see harsh punishment as the best means for crime prevention (Ludwig and Kräupl 2005). Mediation as a new method to reduce conflicts is not very well known and rarely discussed.

In Norway in 2000, in 20–25 % of civil cases mediation was practiced, and in 70–80 % of these cases a compromise could be found. The greater acceptance of mediation in countries like Great Britain or the United States is probably also based on the high rates of success. This is not the case in Poland and Russia and also in Switzerland and partly in France where empirical research shows a lower acceptance of the procedure.

Empirical research shows increasingly and on an international scale that restorative justice is seen by the victims as advantageous to them, often more so than traditional criminal trials (Green 2007, p. 177). The well-known Thames Valley Police Project in London (see Hoyle and Young 2002) showed, for instance, that "the vast majority of victims felt that the meeting had been valuable in helping them recover from their experiences" (Green 2007, p. 177). The authors also pointed out that two thirds of the victims after participating in the program stated that through the mediation their view of the offenders had changed in a positive way (Hoyle and Young 2002). Comparable results were found in the evaluation of the "Youth Justice Panels" in Great Britain (see Crawford and Newburn 2003, p. 213). These

Youth Justice Panels "received high levels of satisfaction from victims on measures of procedural justice, including being treated fairly and with respect, as well as being given a voice in the process" (Green 2007, p. 178). An important topic is the openness of the victims to mediation and the willingness to cooperate: "... the general conclusion of most restorative justice studies has been that when victims participate in some form of victim-offender mediation the majority find the process helpful...What is evident is that the attitudes of victims who take part in the restorative process are largely positive when compared with those of victims whose cases are tried and sentenced in the conventional way. At this level, at least, restorative justice appears to fulfil its promise to the victims of crime – for the first time in recent history they have been given both a role and status in the resolution of their victimization" (ibid. p. 178). Despite these positive results, restorative justice does not work for all victims and some remain dissatisfied (see for example Daly 2001, 2003a).

Hopt and Steffek (2008a, b, c, S. 79) come to the final conclusion that mediation is a useful and helpful method to reduce conflicts and should be promoted. Mediation has the best positive effects, as the participants see it, if it is included in a system of conflict resolution. The method is also less time consuming and cheaper than conventional trials (2008a, b, c, p. 80). Research results from England and the Netherlands, but also from Germany show that mediation is in comparison to traditional court procedures 33–50 % shorter. The inclusion of mediation into the traditional court proceedings does not lower the positive results (2008a, b, c, p. 82; but see also critically Tränkle 2007). It has a more intensive effect on reconciliation, and agreements are much more often kept than after traditional penal processes without mediation (2008a, b, c, p. 84). These are demonstrable facts that prove the positive effects of mediation, and not, as some critics claim, simple promises by authors in favour of an alternative approach to criminal justice. Even in cases where mediation is not successful the parties report satisfaction with the experience.

Lippelt and Schütte (2010, p. 43) summarize the most important results of German studies, including also the sound methodological studies by Busse (2001) or Dölling et al. (2002) and come to the conclusion that victim offender mediation in most cases shows a lower recidivism rate than classical procedures, and even in unfavourable cases the results were as positive as in classical court procedures. In Germany too the costs were lower, especially in juvenile cases (Kumpmann 2007). A key positive effect of victim offender mediation that was often underlined was the greater satisfaction of both offenders and especially victims compared with the classical procedure. Bals (2006) could show that more than 90 % of the offenders and victims gave mediation a positive vote, and 80 % of victims and 57.1 % of offenders felt treated fairly. Also Delattre (2010, p. 85) points out that most scientific evaluations of victim offender mediation projects show a clearly positive effect. Schmidt (2012, p. 190) gives, however, a more critical appraisal: according to him, the effectiveness of TOA in Germany has only been examined in single projects or in single local regions. According to him, generalizable results are not available today.

Even if a systematic evaluation of alternative reactions to crime is not yet complete, the research results we have today show clearly the limitations of (harsh) punishment in crime prevention and "that punishment alone may not bring about significant improvements to the emotional and psychological recovery of crime victims. On the contrary, the results from the analysis of sentencing models indicate that the 'punitive model' of punishment alone is less conducive to emotional recovery than the 'non-punitive model' of apology and restitution without punishment. When punishment was combined with apology and restitution, however, the resulting model was considered to be the most conducive to victim recovery. Indeed the 'comprehensive model' was the only model that showed a significant increase in victim recovery for all scenarios" (London 2011, p. 115). Gromet (2009, p. 47) too underlines in this context: "The empirical evidence indicates that the best solution is a combined procedure that contains both restorative and retributive elements".

According to London (2011, p. IX), "Restorative justice began as a vision of a better way to do criminal justice and, in hundreds of programs throughout the world, it has proven to be just that. It has helped victims to feel more satisfied with the process and more secure in their personal safety. It has increased offenders' compliance with restitution orders without adversely affecting recidivism rates."

7 Final Discussion

Mediation and restorative justice are no longer a marginal topic. Today we have on an international level and in particular in western industrialized countries an overwhelming number of publications on the subject. The starting point was the legitimate desire for a greater inclusion of victims' interests in criminal justice proceedings. The academic discussion was given a new impetus after World War II, especially from the 1960s and 1970s onward, through the fast growing and rediscovered importance of victimology. Before, and often still today, penal law did not care about the interests of the victims and concentrated only on the sanctions for offenders. It came therefore as no surprise that many victims were dissatisfied with the result of criminal justice. Their only "satisfaction" was to see the offender punished, and this in turn promoted the desire for severe punishment.

Sessar (1992, p. 21) points out that the restitution of "penal peace" ("Rechtsfrieden"), on which modern penal policy is almost exclusively focused, does not bring automatically back social peace. Penal peace is primarily concentrated on control and the prestige of penal law, which means that social peace has to be promoted separately. This includes an effort to avoid shifting the problem to the criminal act alone but to look instead at its origins and find a comprehensive solution. Interpersonal regulations have positive effects on socialisation and peace in a society and once the people understand this, the role of a purely criminal justice can be reduced.

Information is a very important factor in the shaping of people's attitudes and without public support innovations are hard to bring about. As Delattre (2010, p. 91) points out victim offender restitution was promoted as the most important and positive initiative in crime policy of the last 25 years. Yet the possibilities of these new ways of dealing with crime are still not fully exhausted despite their obvious positive aspects. The dialogue with the public is even now a neglected element in promoting mediation and has to be intensified (2010, p. 101). The most important partners here are the police because they are in most cases the first to be in contact with offender and victim.

Young (2002, p. 137) points out that according to the British Crime Survey already 1984, 51 % of the interviewed victims said they would be willing to meet the offender outside the court together with an official "helper" to speak about restitution. Answering a slightly differently formulated question in the British Crime Survey of 1998, 41 % of the respondents accepted a meeting with the offender, in presence of a third person, to ask questions about the background of the crime and to have the opportunity to tell the offender about the effects of the victimization. Sanders (2002, p. 222) emphasizes that research has shown that if offenders understand the penal procedure and perceive it as legitimate, they also can accept the result better, even in cases when they perceive the result as being unjust. The same is the case for the victims. Hopt and Steffek (2008a, b, c, p. 79) underline that the culture of reducing conflicts in a society has to be promoted by clear information given to judges and prosecutors, and especially to the public. The procedure has to be explained, judges and prosecutors have to be informed, mediators have to be well trained and the necessary financial support for mediation has to be assured. Part of the success depends also on accompanying measures that help establish a supporting surroundings in which the mediation program can be implemented.

There is little unanimity about the question how far restoration and retribution should be combined, without risking that restoration is losing out. Sessar (1992, p. 21) speaks about the certainty of the penal law. London (2011, p. 180) emphasizes that "restoration" has to be combined with "retribution" or the public will not accept it. "Neither deterrence, incapacitation, nor retribution offers a strategy for reintegration. Even rehabilitation, by itself, is a poor vehicle for genuine reintegration because it neglects the needs of victims and of society for the satisfaction of justice as a precondition for social acceptance. By subsuming each of these traditional goals to the overall goal of restoring trust, however, criminal sentences can be fashioned that attempt to achieve deterrence, incapacitation, restitution, rehabilitation, and retribution not as ends in themselves, but as part of an overall strategy for repairing the harm of crime" (London 2011, p. 183).

London (2011, p. 315) summarizes the positive results and the challenges of restorative justice as follows: "Restorative justice is a bold and thought-provoking innovation that has engaged the energies and excited the hopes of criminal justice reformers throughout the world over the last several decades. And yet, while it has achieved outstanding results in thousands of programs, it has remained a marginal development because it has failed to articulate a theory and set of practice applicable to serious crimes and adult offenders." He points out that all parties profit from a successful mediation: "For the victim, the restoration of trust approach offers the prospect of genuine repair for the material and emotional harm ... For the community, the restoration of trust offers the prospect of involvement in problem solving toward the goal of achieving safety and resolving ongoing conflicts. For the offender, the restoration of trust approach enhances the likelihood of regaining acceptance into the moral community of law-abiding people by the demonstration of accountability both for the material losses and the moral transgressions involved in the crime" (London 2011, p. 320).

All modern penal law systems are confronted with the question how to relate to victim offender restitution in their systems (Rössner 1998, p. 881). The international comparison by Rössner (p. 894) shows clearly that restitution should be included in all systems of criminal justice. As the victims themselves report in most cases positive effects, mediation cannot be accused of using victims to bring healing to offenders, as it is sometimes criticised, but it is a measure with positive effects for both parts, offenders and victims. We also should also not forget that many victims are women and children.

Initially, mediation was established to help victims, to improve their condition after the victimization and to give them better chances to receive restitution of the damages. The now numerous research results show clearly that this aim can be reached if the measure is handled professionally. Most victims find that their situation has improved after participation in mediation and that they have a better chance to overcome the harm caused by the crime than in classical penal procedures.

Concerning the effects on the offenders, especially on their re-socialization, the results are not as unanimous, which is not surprising. Mediation is usually a short process of a few hours. It would therefore be hoping for too much to see long lasting effects in offenders, especially incarcerated offenders who often have strong social deficits. But as part of a comprehensive rehabilitation program, mediation plays a very important role and its use should therefore be extended. The classical criminal justice approach has obvious disadvantages as far as the reintegration of offenders is concerned which could be, at least partly, reduced by professional mediation.

Five Questions

1. What are the advantages and disadvantages of a traditional criminal justice oriented solution for the sanctioning of offenders?
2. What do we mean by alternatives to criminal sentences? How are they defined?
3. In the search of conflict solutions, why is it important to consider also the damage caused by the crime and the emotional side of both offenders and victims?
4. What do research results on mediation show? How would victims want conflicts and damage solved that are caused by crime?
5. What developments can be seen in different countries concerning mediation and restorative justice and against which background?

Acknowledgement My special thanks go to Dr. Evelyn Shea for her invaluable advice and for her help in translating my text.

References

Abel, R. (1982). *The politics of informal justice*. New York: Acad. Press.

Alison, L., Alison, E., Noone, G., Elntib, S., & Christiansen, P. (2013). Why tough tactics fail and rapport gests results: Observing rapport-based interpersonal techniques (ORBIT) to geanerate useful information from terrorists. *Psychology, Public Policy, Law, 19*, 411–431. http://dx.doi.org/10.1037/a0034564.

Alison, L., Alison, E., Noone, G., Elntib, S., Waring, S., & Christiansen, P. (2014). The efficacy of rapport based techniques for minimizing counter interrogation tactics amongst a field sample of terrorists. Centre for Critical and Major Incident Research, Department of Psychological Sciences, University of Liverpool.

Bals, N. (2006). Täter-Opfer-Ausgleich – Cui bono? Befunde einer Befragung von Geschädigten und Beschuldigten. *Monatsschrift für Kriminologie und Strafrechtsreform, 89*, 131–145.

Bannenberg, B., Weitekamp, E. G. M., Rössner, D., & Kerner, H. -J. (1999). Mediation bei Gewaltstraftaten in Paarbeziehungen. Baden-Baden.

Barton, C. K. B. (1999). *Getting even: Revenge as a form of justice*. Peru, IL: Open Court Publishing.

Bazemore, G., & Elis, L. (2007). Evaluation of restorative justice. In G. Johnstone & D. W. Van Ness (Eds.), *Handbook of restorative justice* (pp. 397–425). Cullompton: Willan.

Beccaria, C. (1764; German Edition 2005). Dei Delitti e delle Pene – Von den Verbrechen und von den Strafen. Berlin: Berliner wissenschafts-Verlag.

Bonta, J., Wallace-Capretta, S., & Rooney, J. (2000). Quasi-experimental evaluation of an intensive rehabilitation supervision program. *Criminal Justice and Behavior, 27*, 312–329.

Braithwaite, J. (1989). *Crime, shame and reintegration*. Cambridge, UK: University Press.

Braithwaite, J. (1999). Restorative justice: Assessing optimistic and pessimistic accounts. In M. Tonry (Ed.), *Crime and justice: A review of research* (Vol. 25, pp. 1–127). Chicago: University of Chicago Press.

Braithwaite, J. (2002). *Restorative justice and responsive regulation*. New York: Oxford University Press.

Braithwaite, J. (2009). Restorativ justice. In H. J. Schneider (Ed.), *Internationales Handbuch der Kriminologie. Band 2: Besondere Probleme der Kriminologie* (pp. 53–98). Berlin: DeGruyter.

Braithwaite, J., & Pettit, P. (1990). *Not just deserts: A republican theory of criminal justice*. Oxford: Oxford University Press.

Braithwaite, J., & Strang, H. (2001). Introduction: Restorative justice and civil society. In J. Braithwaite & H. Strang (Eds.), *Restorative justice and civil society* (pp. 1–13). Cambridge, UK: University Press.

Bundesministerium des Innern/Bundesministerium der Justiz. (Hrsg.), (2006). Zweiter Periodischer Sicherheitsbericht. Berlin: BMI/BMJ.

Buntinx, K. (2012). Victim-offender mediation in homicide cases. Opportunities and risks. Unpublished presenation in Tübingen.

Burkitt, I. (2005). Powerful emotions: Power, government and opposition in the war on terror. *Sociology, 39*, 679–695.

Burnside, J. (2007). Retribution and restoration in biblical texts. In G. Johnstone & D. W. Van Ness (Eds.), *Handbook of restorative justice* (pp. 132–148). Cullompton: Willan.

Bush, R. A. B., & Folger, J. P. (2005). *The promise of mediation – The transformative approach to conflict*. San Francisco: Jossey-Bass.

Busse, J. (2001). Rückfalluntersuchung zum Täter-Opfer-Ausgleich. Eine statistische Untersuchung im Amtsgerichtsbezirk Lüneburg. Diss. Jur. Marburg.

Bussmann, K. -D. (1986). Das Konzept "Versöhnung statt Strafe". Konzept und Praxis von Mediationsprogrammen in Kanada und USA – Bericht einer Studienreise. *Monatsschrift für Kriminologie und Strafrechtsreform, 69*, 152–163.

Chankova, D., & Van Ness, D. W. (2007). Themes. In G. Johnstone & D. W. Van Ness (Eds.), *Handbook of restorative justice* (pp. 529–533). Cullompton: Willan.

Christie, N. (1977). Conflicts as property. *British Journal of Criminology, 17*, 1–26.

Cook, K., Daly, K., & Stubbs, J. (Eds.), (2006). Gender- race, and restorative justice. *Theoretical Criminology, 10*(Special Issue), 5–138.

Crawford, A., & Newburn, T. (2003). *Youth offending and restorative justice: Implementing reform in youth justice*. Cullompton: Willan.

Daly, K. (2001). Conferencing in Australia and New Zealand: Variations, research findings and prospects. In A. M. Morris & G. Maxwell (Eds.), *Restorative justice for Juveniles: Conferencing, mediation and circles*. Oxford: Hart Publishing.

Daly, K. (2002). Restorative justice: The real story. *Punishment and Society, 4*, 5–39.

Daly, K. (2003a). Restorative justice: The real story. In E. McLaughlin, et al. (Eds.), *Restorative justice. Critical issues*. London: Sage.

Daly, K. (2003b). Mind the gap: Restorative justice in theory and practice. In A. von Hirsch, et al. (Eds.), *Restorative justice and criminal justice*. Oxford: Hart Publishing.

Daly, K. (2012). Conferences and gendered violence. Practices, politics, and evidence. In E. Zinsstag & I. Vanfraechem (Eds.), *Conferencing and restorative justice. International practices and perspectives* (pp. 117–135). Oxford: Oxford University Press.

Daly, K., & Stubbs, J. (2006). Feminist engagement with restorative justice. *Theoretical Criminology, 10*, 9–28.

Delattre, G. (2010). Der Täter-Opfer-Ausgleich – die Praxis eines anderen Umgangs mit Straftaten. In P. Senghaus (Ed.), *Mediation und Polizei* (pp. 81–102). Rothenburg/Oberlausitz: Sächsische Polizei.

Dignan, J. (2002). Restorative justice and the law: The case for an integrated, systemic approach. In L. Walgrave (Ed.), *Restorative justice and the law*. Cullompton: Willan.

Dölling, D., Hartmann, A., & Traulsen, M. (2002). Legalbewährung nach TOA im Jugendstrafrecht. *Monatsschrift für Kriminologie und Strafrechtsreform, 85*, 185–193.

Dölling, D., Entorf, H., Hermann, D., & Rupp, T. (2011). Meta-analysis of empirical studies on deterrence. In H. Kury & E. Shea (Eds.), *Punitivity – International developments. Punitiveness and punishment* (Vol. 3, pp. 315–378). Bochum: Universitätsverlag Dr. Brockmeyer.

Doob, A. N., & Roberts, J. (1983). *Sentencing: An analysis of the public's view of sentencing*. Ottawa: Department of Justice.

Duff, R. A. (2003). Restorative punishment and punitive restoration. In G. Johnstone (Ed.), *A restorative justice reader: Texts, sources and context* (pp. 382–397). Portland, OR: Willan.

Dünkel, F., & Părosanu, A. (2015). Germany. In F. Dünkel, J. Grzywa-Holten, & P. Horsfield (Eds.), *Restorative justice and mediation in penal matters. A stock-taking of legal issues, implementation strategies and outcomes in 36 European countries* (Vol. 1, pp. 293–329). Mönchengladbach: Forum Verlag Godesberg.

Frehsee, D. (1987). *Schadenswiedergutmachung als Instrument strafrechtlicher Sozialkontrolle*. Berlin: Duncker & Humblot.

Frühauf, L. (1988). *Wiedergutmachung zwischen Täter und Opfer. Eine neue Alternative in der strafrechtlichen Sanktionspraxis*. Gelsenkirchen: Verlag Dr. Mannhold.

Gelber, C. (2012). Victimologische Ansätze im Strafvollzug. *Monatsschrift für Kriminologie und Strafvollzugsreform, 95*, 441–450.

Gelber, C., & Walter, M. (2012). Über Möglichkeiten einer opferbezogenen Vollzugsgestaltung. *Forum Strafvollzug, 61*, 171–172.

Goodey, J. (2005). *Victims and victimology: Research, policy and practice*. Harlow: Pearson Longman.

Grawe, K., Donati, R., & Bernauer, R. (1994). *Psychotherapie im Wandel. Von der Konfession zur Profession*. Göttingen: Hogrefe.
Green, S. (2007). The victims' movement and restorative justice. In G. Johnstone & D. W. Van Ness (Eds.), *Handbook of restorative justice* (pp. 171–191). Cullompton: Willan.
Griffiths, C. (1999). The victims of crime and restorative justice: The Canadian experience. *International Review of Victimology, 6*, 279–294.
Gromet, D. M. (2009). Psychological perspectives on the place of restorative justice in criminal justice systems. In M. E. Oswald, S. Bieneck, & J. Hupfeld-Heinemann (Eds.), *Social psychology of punishment of crime* (pp. 39–54). Chichester: Wiley-Blackwell.
Hagemann, O. (2003). Restorative justice in prison? In L. Walgrave (Ed.), *Repositioning restorative justice*. Cullompton: Willan.
Hagemann, O. (2011). Restorative justice: Konzept, Ideen und Hindernisse. In R. Lummer, O. Hagemann & J. Tein (Eds.), Restorative Justice – A European and Schleswig-Holsteinian Perspective. Schriftenreihe Soziale Strafrechtspflege, Band 1 (pp. 151–178). http://www.cepprobation.org/uploaded_files/RJ_Band1.pdf
Hammacher, P. (2008). Widerstand gegen Mediation abbauen. *Zeitschrift für Schiedsverfahren 21*, 30–33.
Hassemer, W. (2009). *Warum Strafe sein muss. Ein Plädoyer*. Berlin: Ullstein.
Hayes, H. (2007). Reoffending and restorative justice. In G. Johnstone & D. W. Van Ness (Eds.), *Handbook of Restorative Justice* (pp. 426–444). Cullompton: Willan.
Heinz, W. (1993). Opfer und Strafverfahren. In G. Kaiser, H.-J. Kerner, F. Sack, & H. Schellhoss (Eds.), *Kleines Kriminologisches Wörterbuch* (pp. 372–377). Heidelberg: C.F. Müller.
Heß, H. (2008). Verhandlungen des 67. Deutschen Juristentages Erfurt 2008, Band I: Gutachten, Teil F: Mediation und weitere Verfahren konsensualer Streitbeilegung.
Hopkins, B. (2004). *Just schools: A whole school approach to restorative justice*. London, New York, NY: Jessica Kingsley.
Hopt, K. J., & Steffek, F. (2008b). Vorwort. In K. J. Hopt & F. Steffek (Hrsg.), *Mediation. Rechtstatsachen, Rechtsvergleich, Regelungen* (pp. VII–IX). Tübingen: Mohr Siebeck.
Hopt, K. J., & Steffek, F. (2008c). Mediation – Rechtsvergleich, Regelungsmodelle, Grundsatzprobleme. In K. J. Hopt & Steffek F. (Hrsg.), *Mediation. Rechtstatsachen, Rechtsvergleich, Regelungen* (pp. 3–102). Tübingen: Mohr Siebeck.
Hopt, K. J., & Steffek, F. (Hrsg.), (2008a). Mediation. Rechtstatsachen, Rechtsvergleich, Regelungen. Tübingen: Mohr Siebeck.
Hoyle, C. (2002). Securing restorative justice for the 'Non-participating' victim. In C. Hoyle & R. Young (Eds.), *New visions of crime victims* (pp. 97–131). Oxford, Portland/Oregon: Hart Publishing.
Hoyle, C., & Young, R. (Eds.). (2002). *New visions of crime victims*. Oxford, Portland/Oregon: Hart Publishing.
Jehle, J. -M. (2005). Strafrechtspflege in Deutschland. Berlin: Bundesministerium der Justiz und für Verbraucherschutz.
Jessel-Holst, C. (2008). Mediation in Ungarn. In K. J. Hopt & F. Steffek (Hrsg.), *Mediation. Rechtstatsachen, Rechtsvergleich, Regelungen* (pp. 906–921). Tübingen: Mohr Siebeck.
Johnstone, G. (2007). Critical perspectives on restorative justice. In G. Johnstone & D. W. Van Ness (Eds.), *Handbook of restorative justice* (pp. 598–614). Cullompton: Willan.
Johnstone, G., & Van Ness, D. W. (Eds.). (2007a). *Handbook of restorative justice*. Cullompton: Willan.
Johnstone, G., & Van Ness, D. W. (2007b). The meaning of restorative justice. In G. Johnstone & D. W. Van Ness (Eds.), *Handbook of restorative justice* (pp. 5–23). Cullompton: Willan.
Kaiser, G. (1996). *Kriminologie. Ein Lehrbuch.*. Heidelberg: C.F. Müller.
Karstedt, S. (2002). Emotions and criminal justice. *Theoretical Criminology, 6*, 299–317.
Karstedt, S. (2006). Emotions, crime and Justice: Exploring Durkheimian Themes. In M. Deflem (Ed.), *Sociological theory and criminological research: Views from Europe and the United States* (pp. 223–248). Amsterdam et al.: Elsevier

Karstedt, S. (2011). Handle with care: Emotions, crime and justice. In S. Karstedt, I. Loader, & H. Strang (Eds.), *Emotions, crime and justice* (pp. 1–19). Oxford and Portland/Oregon: Hart Publishing.

Kerner, H. -J., Hartmann, A., & Lenz, S. (2005). Täter-Opfer-Ausgleich in der Entwicklung. Auswertung der bundesweiten Täter-Opfer-Ausgleichs-Statistik 1993 bis 2002. Berlin.

Kilchling, M. (2012). Restorative justice developments in Germany. In D. Miers & I. Aertsen (Eds.), *Regulating restorative justice. A comparative study of legislative provision in European countries* (pp. 158–209). Frankfurt: Verlag für Polizeiwissenschaft.

Krause, M., & Vogt, M. (2012). Gerichtliche Mediation in Strafvollzugssachen. *Betrifft Justiz, 110*, 297.

Kumpmann, S. (2007). Kosten und Kostenersparnis im Täter-Opfer-Ausgleich. Praxisheft Täter-Opfer-Ausgleich Nr. 5. Servicebüro für Täter-Opfer-Ausgleich und Konfliktschlichtung.

Kury, H. (1986). *Die Behandlung Straffälliger. Teilband I: Inhaltliche und methodische Probleme der Behandlungsforschung*. Berlin: Duncker & Humblot.

Kury, H., & Kuhlmann, A. (2016). More severe punishment – or more alternatives? Mediation in Western Countries. Kriminologijos Studijos, in print.

Kury, H., & Lerchenmüller, H. (Hrsg.), (1981). Diversion. Alternativen zu klassischen Sanktionsformen. 2 Bde. Bochum: Studienverlag Dr. N. Brockmeyer.

Kury, H., & Shea, E. (Eds.). (2011). *Punitivity – International developments* (Vol. 3). Bochum: Universtiätsverlag Dr. N. Brockmeyer.

Kury, H., & Shea, E. (2012). Attitudes to punishment – International results. In M. Groenhuijsen, R. Letschert, & S. Hazenbroek (Eds.), *KLM Van Dijk. Liber amicorum prof. dr. mr. J.J.M. van Dijk* (pp. 247–258). Nijmegen: Wolf Legal Publishers.

Kury, H., Dörmann, U., Richter, H., & Würger, M. (1996). *Opfererfahrungen und Meinungen zur Inneren Sicherheit in Deutsachland* (2nd ed.). Wiesbaden: Bundeskriminalamt.

Kurzynsky-Singer, E. (2008). Mediation in Russland. In K. J. Hopt & F. Steffek (Eds.), *Mediation, Rechtstatsachen, Rechtsvergleich, Regelungen* (pp. 837–853). Tübingen: Mohr Siebeck.

Laster, K., & O'Malley, P. (1996). Sensitive new-age laws: The reassertion of emotionality in law. *International Journal of the Sociology of Law, 24*, 21–40.

Lippelt, I., & Schütte, D. (2010). *Innenansichten und Wirkungsforschung zum Täter-Opfer-Ausgleich im Jugendstrafrecht. Die Zufriedenheit von Opfern und Tätern mit "ihrer" Mediation der Jugend- und Konflikthilfe der Landeshauptstadt Hannover*. Frankfurt: Verlag für Polizeiwissenschaft.

Lipton, D. S., Martinson, R., & Wilks, J. (1975). *The effectiveness of correctional treatment: A survey of treatment evaluation studies*. New York: Praeger.

Loader, I. (2011). Playing with fire? Democracy and the emotions of crime and punishment. In S. Karstedt, I. Loader, & H. Strang (Eds.), *Emotions, crime and justice* (pp. 347–360). Oxford: Hart.

London, R. (2011). *Crime, punishment, and restorative justice. From the margins to the mainstream*. London, Boulder: First Forum Press.

Ludwig, H., & Kräupl, G. (2005). *Viktimisierung, Sanktionen und Strafverfolgung. Jenaer Kriminalitätsbefragung über ein Jahrzehnt gesellschaftlicher Transformation*. Möchengladbach: Forum Verlag Godesberg.

Lummer, R. (2011). Restorative justice - EU-Projekt. Konferenz an der Fachhochschule Kiel. Arbeitsgruppen - Ergebnisse. In R. Lummer, O. Hagemann, & J. Tein (Eds.), *Restorative Justice – A European and Schleswig-Holsteinian Perspective. Schriftenreihe Soziale Strafrechtspflege, Band 1* (pp. 235–242). http://www.cepprobation.org/uploaded_files/RJ_Band1.pdf

Martinson, R. (1974). What works? – Questions and answers about prison reform. *The Public Interest 35*, 22–52.

Matt, E., & Winter, F. (2002). Täter-Opfer-Ausgleich in Gefängnissen. *Die Möglichkeiten der restorative justice im Strafvollzug. Neue Kriminalpolitik, 4*, 128–132.

McCold, P. (2000). Toward a holistic vision of restorative juvenile justice: A reply to the maximalist model. *Contemporary Justice Review, 3*, 357–414.

McEvoy, K., & Mika, H. (2002). Restorative justice and the critique of informalism in Northern Ireland. *British Journal of Criminology, 42*, 534–562.

Menkel-Meadow, C. (2007). Restorative justice: What is it and does it work? *Annual Review of Law and Social Science, 3*, 161–187.

Mestitz, A. (2005). A comparative perspective on victim-offender mediation with youth offenders throughout Europe. In A. Mestitz & S. Ghetti (Eds.), *Victim-offender mediation with youth offenders in Europe*. Amsterdam: Springer.

Miers, D. (2007). The international development of restorative justice. In G. Johnstone & D. W. Van Ness (Eds.), *Handbook of restorative justice* (pp. 447–467). Cullompton: Willan.

Ministry of Justice, UK (2013a). More mediation encouraged as divorce hotspots are revealed. Pressemitteilung des englischen Justizministeriums vom 20. 2. 2013. London: Ministry of Justice. http://www.justice.gov.uk/news/features/figures-show-divorce-hot-spots, http://www.justice.gov.uk/news/press-release/moj/more-mediation-encouraged-as-divorce-hotspots-are-revealed.

Ministry of Justice, UK. (2013b). Moving family mediation forward. Pressemitteilung des englischen Justizministeriums vom 14. 3. 2013. London: Ministry of Justice. http://www.justice.gov.uk/news/features.

Montada, L. (2004). Nachhaltaige Beilegung von Familienkonflikten durch Mediation. Familie, Partnerschaft und Recht, 182–187

Morris, A. (2002). Critiquing the critics: A brief response to critics of restorative justice. *British Journal of Criminology, 42*, 596–615.

Morris, A., & Maxwell, G. (Eds.). (2001). *Restorative justice for juveniles. Conferencing, mediation & circles*. Portland: Hart Publishing.

Morrison, B. (2007). Schools and restorative justice. In G. Johnstone & D. W. Van Ness (Eds.), *Handbook of restorative justice* (pp. 325–351). Cullompton: Willan.

Nugent, W., Williams, M., & Umbreit, M. S. (2003). Participation in victim-offender mediation and the prevalence of subsequent delinquent behavior: A meta-analysis. *Utah Law Review 37*, 137–166.

Olweus, D. (1993). Annotation: Bullying at school: Basic facts and effects of a school base intervention program. *Journal of Child Psychology and Psychiatry, 35*, 1171–1190.

Orlinsky, D. E., & Howard, K. I. (1986). Process and outcome in psychotherapy. In S. L. Garfield & A. E. Bergin (Eds.), *Handbook of psychotherapy and behavior change* (pp. 311–384). New York: Wiley.

Pratt, J. (2006). Beyond evangelical criminology: The meaning and significance of restorative justice. In I. Aertsen, T. Dams, & L. Robert (Eds.), *Institutionalizing restorative justice* (pp. 44–67). Cullompton: Willan.

Pratt, J., Brown, D., Brown, M., Hallsworth, S., & Morrison, W. (Eds.). (2005). *The new punitiveness. Trends, theories, perspectives*. Portland/Oregon: Willan.

Roberts, J. V., & Hough, M. (Eds.). (2002). *Changing attitudes to punishment: Public opinion, crime and justice*. Cullompton: Willan.

Robinson, P. H. (2003). The virtues of restorative processes, the vices of restorative justice. *Utah Law Review, 1*, 375–388.

Röchling, A. (2010). Mediation in der Polizei in Baden-Württemberg. In P. Senhaus (Ed.), *Mediation und Polizei* (pp. 149–170). Rothenburg/Oberlausitz: Sächsische Polizei.

Rössner, D. (1998, November). Die Universalität des Wiedergutmachungsgedankens im Strafrecht. In H.-D. Schwind, E. Kube, H.-H. Kühne (Hrsg.), Festschrift für Hans Joachim Schneider zum 70. Geburtstag am 14. Kriminologie an der Schwelle zum 21 (pp. 877–896). Jahrhundert. Berlin.

Rössner, D., & Wulf, R. (1985). *Opferbezogene Strafrechtspflege*. Bonn: Deutsche Bewährungshilfe.

Rössner, D., Bannenberg, B., Kerner, H. -J., & Weitekamp, E. (1999). Mediation und Täter-Opfer-Ausgleich bei Gewaltstraftaten in Paarbeziehungen. Baden-Baden.

Sanders, A. (2002). Victim participation in an exclusionary criminal justice system. In C. Hoyle & R. Young (Eds.), *New visions of crime victims* (pp. 197–222). Oxford, Portland/Oregon: Hart Publishing.

Sasse, A.-K. (2010). *Einbindung der Mediation in die Gerichtsbarkeit. Gerichtliche Mediation in Strafvollzugssachen – ein Projekt.* Hamburg: Dr. Kovac. Diss. Konstanz.

Sato, M. (2013). *Public opinion and the death penalty in Japan: Measuring tolerance for abolition.* Berlin: Springer.

Schiff, M., & Bazemaore, G. (2002). Restorative conferencing for juveniles in the USA: Prevalence, process and practice. In E. Weitekamp & H.-J. Kerner (Eds.), *Restorative justice: Theoretical foundations.* Cullompton: Willan.

Schmidt, A. (2012). *Strafe und Versöhnung. Eine moral- und rechtsphilosophische Analyse von Strafe und Täter-Opfer-Ausgleich als Formen unserer Praxis.* Berlin: Duncker & Humblot.

Schneider, H. J. (1975). *Viktimologie – Wissenschaft vom Verbrechensopfer.* Tübingen: Mohr.

Schwind, H.-D. (2011). *Kriminologie. Eine praxisorientierte Einführung mit Beispielen.* Heidelberg: Kriminalistik Verlag.

Senghaus, P. (Hrsg.), (2010). *Mediation und Polizei.* Rothenburg/Oberlausitz: Sächsische Polizei.

Sessar, K. (1992). *Wiedergutmachen oder Strafen. Einstellungen in der Bevölkerung und der Justiz.* Pfaffenweiler: Centaurus-Verlagsgesellschaft.

Sessar, K. (1995). Restitution or punishment. An empirical study on attitudes of the public and the justice system in Hamburg. *Eurocriminology, 8*, 199–214.

Sharpe, S. (2007). The idea of reparation. In G. Johnstone & D. W. Van Ness (Eds.), *Handbook of restorative justice* (pp. 24–40). Cullompton: Willan.

Shearar, A., & Maxwell, G. (2012). Revolution, decline, and renewal. Restorative youth justice in New Zealand. In E. Zinsstag & I. Vanfaechem (Eds.), *Conferencing and restorative justice. International practices and perspectives* (pp. 101–116). Oxford: Oxford University Press.

Sherman, L. W. (2003). Reason for emotion. Reinventing justice with theories, innovation, and research. *Criminology, 41*, 1–38.

Tränkle, S. (2007). *Im Schatten des Strafrechts. Eine Untersuchung der Mediation in Strafsachen am Beispiel des deutschen Täter-Opfer-Ausgleichs und der französischen médiation pénale auf der Grundlage von Interaktions- und Kontextanalysen.* Berlin: Duncker & Humblot.

Trenczek, T. (2003). Mediation im Strafrecht. *Zeitschrift für Konfliktmanagement, 3*, 105–109.

Umbreit, M., & Greenwood, J. (1998). *National survey of victim offender mediation programs in the United States.* Minneapolis, MN: University of Minnesota Center for Restorative Justice and Peacemaking.

Umbreit, M., Coates, R., & Vos, B. (2001). Victim impact of meeting with young offenders: Two decades of victim offender mediation practice and research. In A. Morris & G. Maxwell (Eds.), *Restorative justice for Juveniles: Conferencing, mediation and circles.* Oxford: Hart Publishing.

Van Ness, D. W. (2007). Prisons and restorative justice. In G. Johnstone & D. W. Van Ness (Eds.), *Handbook of restorative justice* (pp. 312–324). Cullompton: Willan.

Vanfraechem, I., & Zinsstag, E. (2012). Conferencing – setting the scene. In E. Zinsstag & I. Vanfraechem (Eds.), *Conferencing and restorative justice. International practices and perspectives* (pp. 1–8). Oxford: Oxford University Press.

Vázquez-Portomene, F. (2012). Vorgehensweisen und Vermittlungsstandards zur Bearbeitung von TOA-Fällen bei häuslicher Gewalt in Deutschland und Österreich. Ein Modell für Europa? *Monatsschrift für Kriminologie und Strafrechtsreform, 95*, 413–440.

Villmow, B. (1988). Staatliche Opferentschädigung. In G. Kaiser, H. Kury & H. -J. Albrecht (Hrsg.), *Kriminologische Forschung in den 80er Jahren* (pp. 1013–1041). Freiburg: Max-Planck-Institut für ausländisches und internationals Strafrecht.

Villmow, B., & Plemper, B. (1989). *Praxis der Opferentschädigung.* Pfaffenweiler: Centaurus.

Villmow, B., & Savinsky, A. L. (2013). Staatliche Opferentschädigung nach der Jahrtausendwende – statistische Daten, methodische Probleme und einige Anmerkungen zur gegenwärtigen Praxis des OEG. In: Festschrift für Jürgen Wolter. Berlin (im Erscheinen).

von Hentig, H. (1948). *The criminal and his victim*. New Haven: Yale University Press.

Walgrave, L. (2007). Integrating criminal justice and restorative justice. In G. Johnstone & D. W. Van Ness (Eds.), *Handbook of restorative justice* (pp. 559–579). Cullompton: Willan.

Walgrave, L. (2008). *Restorative justice, self-interest and responsible citizenship*. Cullompton: Willan.

Walter, J. (2002). *Möglichkeiten und Perspektiven einer opferbezogenen Gestaltung des Strafvollzugs*. Herbolzheim: Centaurus.

Walter, M. (2004). Mediation im strafrechtlichen Bereich: der Täter-Opfer-Ausgleich. In M. Henssler & L. Koch (Hrsg.), *Mediation in der Anwaltspraxis*. Bonn: Deutscher Anwaltverlag, 327–351.

Weitekamp, E. (2002). Restorative justice: Present prospects and future directions. In E. Weitekamp & H.-J. Kerner (Eds.), *Restorative justice: Theoretical foundations*. Cullompton: Willan.

Willemsens, J., & Walgrave, L. (2007). Europe. In G. Johnstone & D. W. Van Ness (Eds.), *Handbook of restorative justice* (pp. 488–499). Cullompton: Willan.

Wilson, T. (1983). *Thinking about crime*. New York, NY: Basic Books.

Wood, W. R. (2015). Why restorative justice will not reduce incarceration. *British Journal of Criminology, 55*, 883–900.

Young, R. (2002). Testing the limits of restorative justice: The case of corporate victims. In C. Hoyle & R. Young (Eds.), *New visions of crime victims* (pp. 133–172). Oxford, Portland/Oregon: Hart Publishing.

Zehr, H. (1990). *Changing lenses: A new focus for crime and justice*. Scottsdale, PA: Herald Press.

Zehr, H. (2002). *The little book of restorative justice*. Intercourse, PA: Good Books.

Zernova, M., & Wright, M. (2007). Alternative visions of restorative justice. In G. Johnstone & D. W. Van Ness (Eds.), *Handbook of restorative justice* (pp. 91–108). Cullompton: Willan.

Zinsstag, E., & Vanfaechem, I. (Eds.). (2012). *Conferencing and restorative justice. International practices and perspectives*. Oxford: Oxford University Press.

Alternative Approaches to Preventing Recidivism: Restorative Justice and the Social Reintegration of Offenders

Yvon Dandurand

Abstract Mediation and restorative justice are often praised as efficient alternatives to criminal justice proceedings in dealing with juvenile offenders. However, the most powerful feature of such programmes has perhaps not yet been fully examined—their capacity to facilitate and effectively contribute to the social reintegration of offenders. This chapter seeks to recast mediation and restorative justice programmes as a form of reconciliation between the juvenile offender and the community and a frequent pre-requisite to the offender's successful social reintegration.

1 Introduction

Many attempts were made over the last few decades to integrate restorative justice principles into the main-stream criminal justice process for juvenile offenders. Early efforts were inspired by concerns for victims of crime who, it seemed, had been progressively excluded from the criminal justice process, except perhaps as witnesses. The purpose of these initiatives was essentially to increase victim participation and access to redress or compensation. Conciliation was another initial objective of these efforts. Some early programmes indeed focused on victim-offender reconciliation. It was only later that the benefits of these alternative processes for offenders—by contributing to their rehabilitation—and to the justice system itself—by providing an alternative to the time-consuming and costly criminal justice process—were formally acknowledged and progressively turned into their main raison d'être. As I have argued before, the potential appeal and transformative value of these principles were recognized very slowly (Dandurand 2012).

In 1985, the UN Declaration of Basic Principles on Justice for Victims of Crime and Abuse of Power, as it related to access to justice and fair treatment for victims of crime, recommended that "informal mechanisms for the resolution of disputes,

Y. Dandurand (✉)
University of the Fraser Valley, Abbotsford, BC, Canada
e-mail: Yvon.Dandurand@ufv.ca

H. Kury et al. (eds.), *Women and Children as Victims and Offenders: Background, Prevention, Reintegration*, DOI 10.1007/978-3-319-28424-8_11

including mediation, arbitration and customary justice or indigenous practices, should be utilized where appropriate to facilitate conciliation and redress for victims."[1] Also in 1985, the United Nations Standard Minimum Rules for the Administration of Juvenile Justice emphasized the importance of diversion (A/RES/40/33). In 1989, the Convention on the Rights of the Child (CRC,1577 UNTS 3) also called for the use of diversion, or measures for dealing with children without resorting to judicial proceedings, providing that human rights and legal safeguards are fully respected (Article 40 (3) (b)).

In 2007, when the Committee on the Rights of the Child decided to provide some specific guidance on "children's rights in juvenile justice", it recommended the use of alternative measures such as diversion and restorative justice, as measures that provide States with "possibilities to respond to children in conflict with the law in an effective manner serving not only the best interests of these children, but also the short and long-term interest of the society at large." (Committee on the Rights of the Child 2007 (CRC/CGC/10), para 3). The Committee, based on the principle of the primacy of the best interests of the child, concluded that "the traditional objectives of criminal justice, such as repression/retribution, must give way to rehabilitation and restorative justice objectives in dealing with child offenders." (Committee on the Rights of the Child 2007(CRC/C/GC/10), para 10; 2013 (CRC/C/GC/14), para 28).

More recently, in her publication on restorative justice for children, the Special Representative of the Secretary General on Violence against Children (2013) explained the need to promote restorative justice in terms of her observation that "countless children face violent and degrading treatment throughout the criminal justice process".

Restorative justice is essentially presented as an alternative to that process. In May 2014, based on the concern that children who are incarcerated or otherwise institutionalized are at a higher risk of being victimized, the United Nations Model Strategies and Practical Measures on the Elimination of Violence against Children in the Field of Crime Prevention and Criminal Justice[2] recommend the greater use of restorative justice and other diversion programmes.

That thinking led over the years to the development of a host of initiatives, often supported by UNICEF and various international NGOs involved in the field of juvenile justice, to implement diversion programmes based on mediation and other restorative justice models. In most countries, at this point, the vast majority of restorative justice programmes deal principally with young offenders. What is also significant is that the vast majority of these programmes only focus on restorative justice as a means to divert children away from the criminal justice system. They for

[1] Declaration of Basic Principles of Justice for Victims of Crime and Abuse of Power, G. A. resolution 40/34 of 29 November 1985, article 7 (A/RES/40/34, Annex, art. 7).

[2] United Nations Model Strategies and Practical Measures on the Elimination of Violence against Children in the Field of Crime Prevention and Criminal Justice, approved by the U.N. Commission on the Prevention of Crime and Criminal Justice, UN doc. E/2014/30.

the most part, neglect to recognize the intrinsic value of such processes when applied as part of a criminal justice intervention. What is perhaps even more significant is that these diversion programmes, except in rare instances, have essentially failed to transform how States and communities respond to juvenile crime and, if anything, have sometimes often broaden the reach of the justice system and "widened its net".[3]

Restorative justice programmes were first proposed as a means to put the concerns and issues of victims at the centre of the social response to crime.[4] They are now being valued mostly for their participatory characteristics and their ability to involve a few members of the community and various stakeholders in finding an appropriate response to individual crimes.[5] In many countries, the idea of community involvement enjoys a lot of support. Together with problem solving courts and community courts, restorative justice programmes offer communities some means of resolving conflicts. A fundamental challenge for participatory justice is, however, to find ways to effectively mobilize the involvement of civil society, while at the same time protecting the rights and interests of victims and offenders.

This chapter reviews the original promises of the restorative justice approach as an alternative to the conventional criminal justice response to juvenile crime. It also notes some of the model's limitations and the challenges that have shaped and constrained its full implementation. One such promise, the "public safety promise", was that restorative justice approaches would support rehabilitation and prevent recidivism in a way that other forms of interventions did not or could not. That promise, with a few exceptions, is relatively unfulfilled. At the same time, restorative justice programmes are based on the belief that parties to a conflict ought to be actively involved in resolving it and mitigating its negative consequences. They are also based, in some instances, on a will to return to local decision-making and community building (Dandurand 2012, p. 89). These are the characteristics that make restorative justice such a potentially powerful instrument to facilitate the reintegration of offenders. Unfortunately, there have been relatively few applications so far of the restorative justice principles in the offender social reintegration context.

[3] The presence of a "net widening" effect, although a real concern, has not been confirmed in all instances where it has been measured. See: Prichard (2010).

[4] Many proponents of restorative justice approaches see the centrality of the victim's concerns as their main defining characteristic. Van Ness and Heetderks Strong, for example, affirmed that "victim concerns and issues should be at the centre of work for restorative justice, and not ancillary" (2006, p. 141).

[5] See the excellent document of the Law Commission of Canada (2003).

2 Restorative Justice and Its Promises

Restorative justice programmes offer a process for resolving crime by focusing on redressing the harm done to victims, holding offenders accountable for their actions and, often also, engaging the community in the resolution of that conflict. According to the UNODC Handbook on Restorative Justice Programmes, "participation of the parties is an essential part of the process which emphasizes relationship building, reconciliation and the development of agreements around a desired outcome between victims and offender. Restorative justice processes can be adapted to various cultural contexts and the needs of different communities" (UNODC 2006, p. 7).

According to Sherman and Strang (2007), two major claims have usually been made with respect to restorative justice: a procedural claim and an effectiveness claim. The procedural claim is that restorative justice offers victims and offenders a more humane and respectful way to process crimes than conventional justice. The effectiveness claim, or promise, is that restorative justice can produce better outcomes in terms of public safety, victim healing, community heath, and offender rehabilitation and social reintegration. The effectiveness promise, including the public safety promise, is perhaps the hardest one to achieve. It certainly is the hardest one to measure.

As mentioned before, restorative programmes are perceived as an ideal diversion mechanism for children in conflict with the law and dozens of countries have experimented with this approach. However, few of these countries have managed to provide such a diversion alternative on a national scale. In fact, existing programmes rarely achieve the required level of public acceptance and support required for their implementation on a broad scale, and criminal justice resources tend to continue to be channelled towards more traditional criminal justice response mechanisms (Dandurand 2012, p. 90).

So far, the institutionalization of restorative justice has taken many paths in different countries (Artsen et al. 2013). The process of institutionalizing restorative justice principles resists any easy generalization. A frequently expressed concern is that the institutionalization of restorative justice leads to a compromise of restorative justice values and a return to a more retributive focus (Broughton 2012). Notwithstanding that concern, there is a case to be made for expanding the use of the restorative justice model to support the social reintegration of young offenders, and in particular, their successful re-entry into the community after a period of detention or institutionalization. As Bazemore and Maruna argued, "restorative justice interventions are too often focused on the 'soft end' of the justice process, when a growing body of evidence suggests that restorative practices might be more effectively focused on the reintegration process for more serious offenses" (Bazemore and Maruna 2009, p. 375).

2.1 Impact on Offender and Desistence from Crime

The evidence on the impact of restorative justice programmes on reoffending is limited, but recent reviews indicate that restorative justice may be more effective for prolific offenders and even serious offenders than for offenders involved in less serious crimes, and more effective after rather than prior to sentencing. Some programmes seem to have a greater impact than others on preventing recidivism. This is the case, for example, of face-to-face restorative justice conferences. A recent systematic review of these programmes showed that, on average, these programmes cause a modest but highly cost-effective reduction in repeat offending, with substantial benefits for victims (Strang et al. 2013).

Joudo Larsen (2014) who reviewed the outcomes of restorative justice programmes in Australia (mostly for juvenile offenders) concluded that "while the evidence is not overwhelming at present, there is growing body of evidence that supports the assertion that restorative justice can reduce reoffending" (2014, p. 26). Others have reached similar conclusions (Sherman and Strang 2007; Bonta et al. 2009). However, we do not yet have a body of evidence that allows us to conclude that restorative justice, as it is currently implemented, is a less expensive and more efficient way of preventing recidivism than other criminal justice interventions (Weatherburn and Macadam 2013; Weatherburn et al. 2012).

Contrary to assumptions that are often made, a restorative justice process can be quite effective in cases involving serious offences or even offenders entrenched in patterns of serious crime. It can be successfully applied when the offender and victims previously had some form of relationship with each other, even when violence is involved (Sherman and Strang 2012). There is no need to confine our use of restorative justice programmes to cases involving first time offenders or relatively minor offences. (Shapland et al. 2011) Restorative justice may even have a deeper healing impact on serious offenders than on others; it certainly acquires a great significance to the community when violent offences are involved.

Based on their systematic review of available evidence on the impact of restorative strategy, Sherman and Strang (2007) concluded that restorative justice programmes produce the best results, in terms of helping victims and reducing recidivism, when they focus on offences involving a personal victim and a violent offence and intentional harm, rather than a non-violent property offence.

2.2 Impact on Victims

Victim satisfaction with the restorative justice process, at least for those who chose to participate in it, tends to be fairly high. According to the evidence reviewed by Sherman and Strang, "on average, in every test available, victims do better when they participate in RJ than when they do not" (Sherman and Strang 2007, p. 22). However, restorative justice does not always increase victim satisfaction with the justice process and we should try to better understand the reasons why victims are sometimes dissatisfied with the process (Choi et al. 2012).

It is also important to keep in mind that victim participation in a restorative justice process tends to be far more limited that it is usually assumed to be, particularly when dealing with juvenile offenders. A large proportion of children and youth referred to restorative justice programmes are essentially involved in victimless crimes (motor vehicle offences, drug possession, etc.), thus limiting the involvement of a "victim" in the process. Victims' direct involvement is equally limited, or remains largely symbolic, when relatively minor infractions against corporations and businesses (shoplifting) or public agencies (graffiti on the walls of public buildings) are involved. There are also many cases where the offender victimizes a member of his or her own family (Hannem and Leonardi 2014) and where the unmet needs of the offender's family make the participation of the latter in a restorative justice or the offender's social reintegration quite difficult.

2.3 *Community Involvement*

Similarly, the involvement of the community in the vast majority of restorative justice programmes for juvenile offenders tends to be more symbolic than real. The community's involvement remains quite limited and its potential impact on the juvenile offenders' social reintegration is likely to be limited.

The concept of "community" is a central one in both the restorative justice and the social reintegration fields. How a restorative justice programme defines "community" is a critical factor in determining the nature and extent of citizen ownership of and participation in the process (Bazemore and Umbreit 1999, p. 8). However, Hoyle (2010) argued, there is usually quite a gap between the theory and practice.[6] In many ways, restorative justice utopian aspirations are still far away from their realization. The rhetoric of restorative justice often bypasses the "incontrovertible fact that harmony, mutuality, equality, reciprocity and respect are hard won even in our most significant and well-intentioned relationships" (Acorn 2004, p. 9).

Hoyle observed that, in operationalizing the concept of community in restorative justice:

> Only those restorative justice measures established with the explicit aim of responding to crimes against community, such as truth and reconciliation processes, regularly achieve meaningful community integration in the process. For this reason, most restorative processes involve communities of interest around the victims and perpetrators rather than the offence (Hoyle 2010, p. 18).

[6] This is obviously not the only gap between the theory and the practice of restorative justice (Gavrieldes 2007). In fact, the whole area is characterized by lofty discourses and promises and very pedestrian and limited applications.

Furthermore, many of the communities that embrace the promise of restorative justice are among the least able to mobilize the agency necessary to make it work. Ironically, as Dickson-Gilmore and La Prairie (2005) argued, "restorative justice requires successful communities."[7] It is a sad truth that many young offenders neither come from nor are returning to a "successful community". In fact they are more likely to come from communities which are themselves already challenged by poverty, unemployment, social exclusion, alienation and criminality.

The same challenges are present when practitioners are discussing or trying to influence the relationship between young offenders and the "community". In the case of young offenders, particularly, the broader involvement of the community is made even more problematic, no matter how it is defined, because of a legitimate preoccupation with protecting their privacy (as required by international child rights law). In practice, there is often a lot more rhetoric about restorative justice than there is an actual practice that brings together victims, offenders and communities in a genuine healing, transformative and offender reintegration process.

The norms and values of a community are offended and sometimes even threatened by youth crime: "(b)y breaking the bonds of their community, offenders might exclude themselves, or be excluded by others, from the community" (Hoyle 2010 p. 24). The reintegration of the young offender requires that these bonds be re-established while the community is reaasured that those who have transgressed its norms are censured in order to reassert a shared commitment to these norms. However, as Hoyle rightfully argues, it is not always enough for the community to open its arms and reintegrate the young offender. In some cases, it needs to resocialize the young offender and contribute to his or her education and rehabilitation. It is therefore the potential of restorative justice to resocialize the young offender that makes it so powerful as part of the social reintegration process.

A restorative approach, based on the principle that conflicts are a natural part of life and crime and juvenile misconduct are part of growing up, can conceivably play an important part in the social reintegration of young offenders. The extent to which juvenile misconduct and disruptive behaviour negatively affect the community depends to a large extent on how the community responds to them (Pranis et al. 2003, p. 20). To the extent that a restorative justice process responds to youth crime by encouraging young offenders and the community to be respectful, honest, open, and compassionate, it can bring about personal growth in all concerned and repair or deepen the connection between the offenders and the community.

[7] Dickson-Gilmore and La Prairie argued very persuasively that this is often the situation, at least in Canada, of Aboriginal communities wishing to improve their ability to deal with conflict and misconduct among their membership (Dickson-Gilmore and La Prairie 2005).

3 Restorative Justice and Its Challenges

As Chris Cunneen observed, one can hardly escape the observation that restorative justice "is essentially a peripheral add-on to the main workings of the criminal justice system" (Cunneen 2010, p. 184). To talk about the role of restorative justice in the offenders' social reintegration process is not to assume that current restorative justice models will necessarily be equal to that new task. On the contrary, existing models and approaches will likely need to be reconceptualised entirely to create a more genuine opportunity for community involvement and mobilization. In so doing, restorative justice approaches need to re-discover their fundamental commitment to the victims and reconnect with their ability to transform relationships, in particular the relationship between offenders and the community they live in or return to.

3.1 Transformative vs. Problem Solving Interventions

A transformative approach to mediation and restorative justice is what is most likely to contribute to the offender desistence from crime and successful reintegration into the community. The transformative approach refers to an approach which sees conflict as an opportunity to transform human consciousness and behaviour. That approach views the "ideal response to conflict as helping parties take advantage of the opportunities presented to actually achieve transformation." (Baruch Bush and Folger 1994, p. 249) The approach is particularly suited to work with young offenders and communities in facilitating the return and reintegration of the youths who have damaged their relationship with family and community.

Unfortunately, this ideal of restorative justice has largely been replaced by a restorative justice practice focused almost entirely on narrow problem solving and restoration. For example, a recent review of the growth of restorative justice in England and Wales (UK), distinguishing between, on the one hand, approaches based on the offender, victim and community responding together to the aftermath of crime and, on the other hand, programmes more narrowly focused on restoring the harm caused by crime, concluded that criminal justice actors, like the police, tend to be more attracted to the second and much simpler approach (Paterson and Clamp 2012).

Restorative justice should not be equated with conciliation, though the latter can be part of the process. In cases involving young offenders the process labels one party as the wronged and the other as the wrongdoer. It must hold the latter accountable for his or her actions and try to repair the harm caused to the former. It must do so in a manner, which is meaningful to all involved, the offender, the victims and the community. If it does not, it more likely to hinder than help the young offender's social reintegration.

3.2 Best Interests of the Child and Procedural Protections

The United Nations Standard Minimum Rules for the Administration of Justice (Beijing Rules) emphasize the need for a diverse range of services and facilities designed to meet the different needs of young offenders re-entering the community, and to provide them with guidance and support as an important step towards their successful reintegration into society.[8] They call for efforts to "provide semi-institutional arrangements, such as halfway houses, educational homes, daytime training centres and other such appropriate arrangements that may assist juveniles in their proper reintegration into society" (rule 29.1). The Beijing Rules also encourage the frequent and early recourse to conditional release of juvenile offenders in detention. They state that "conditional release from an institution shall be used by the appropriate authority to the greatest possible extent, and shall be granted at the earliest possible time" (rule 28.1), adding that "juveniles released conditionally from an institution shall be assisted and supervised by an appropriate authority and shall receive full support by the community" (rule 28.2).

The Beijing Rules also stress the importance of the cooperation of the community in the rehabilitation of juvenile offenders. They promote the mobilization of volunteers, local institutions and other community resources "to contribute effectively to the rehabilitation of the juvenile in a community setting and, as far as possible, within the family unit" (rule 25.1). Similarly, the United Nations Rules for the Protection of Juveniles Deprived of their Liberty state that all juveniles should benefit from arrangements designed to assist them in returning to society, family life, education or employment after release (Rule 79).[9] Specifically, the rules require competent authorities to ensure that services are available to assist juvenile offenders in re-establishing themselves in society and to lessen prejudice against them and stipulate (rule 80).

Juvenile offenders often belong to families and communities that cannot accommodate them even under the best of circumstances. Therefore, supportive interventions are particularly important. Restorative justice models could be redesigned to ensure that juvenile offenders receive the help and support they need to successfully reintegrate into the community.

Unfortunately, there remains some scepticism, some of it based on experience, about the ability of restorative justice processes to guarantee children's safety, respect their rights and act in a manner consistent with the principle of the best interests of the child. Restorative justice processes do not always offer the procedural guarantees and protection that the conventional system can offer, at least in theory.

[8] United Nations Standard Minimum Rules for the Administration of Justice, General Assembly resolution 40/33 of November 29 1985.

[9] United Nations Rules for the Protection of Juveniles Deprived of their Liberty, General Assembly resolution 45/113 of 14 December 1990.

In 2002, the United Nations Economic and Social Council adopted a resolution calling upon Member States that are implementing restorative justice programmes to be guided by a set of Basic Principles on the Use of Restorative Justice Programmes in Criminal Matters.[10] The resolution accompanying the Basic Principles simply noted that restorative justice was an "evolving response to crime", with some unique benefits, but it stopped short of promoting restorative justice. The strength of these Basic Principles is that the document puts forward a set of procedural conditions and guarantees that could be applied to ensure the proper application of restorative justice principles and avoid practices that might be counter to the rights of participants in a restorative justice process. Unfortunately, the Basic Principles are not well known and they are ignored at least as often as they are respected.

Even as she was writing in support of restorative justice for children, the Special Representative of the Secretary General on Violence against Children, Marta Santos Pais, devoted part of her report to the need to ensure that the necessary procedural safeguards for children are in place in a restorative justice process. She suggested that a competent authority, such as a child justice court, should have effective judicial overview to ensure that the rights of the child are respected at all times and that the process is lawfully conducted. In practice, however, the presence of such an overview mechanism is the exception rather than common practice.

In particular, a reliance on traditional or customary conflict resolution process to apply restorative justice principles to situations involving juvenile offenders is often problematic. These customary dispute resolution mechanisms cannot be assumed to be restorative in nature simply because some form of compensation is ordered. Many of them are not. Although, as we have seen before, the UN Declaration of Basic Principles on Justice for Victims of Crime and Abuse of Power recommended a greater use of alternative mechanisms such as customary and indigenous practices, multilateral organizations have become much more cautious about the role of such traditional conflict resolution mechanisms particularly as it relates to children and young offenders. In its General Comment on indigenous children and their rights under the Convention, the Committee on the Rights of the Child (2009) encouraged States to support indigenous peoples to design and implement traditional restorative justice systems, but only as long as the latter are in accordance with the rights set out in the Convention, notably with the best interests of the child.

For her part, the Special Representative of the Secretary General on Violence against Children, in her report on harmful practices in plural legal systems noted that in countries where national legislation interplays with customary and religious law, the potential tensions between them can be problematic. Traditional conflict resolution mechanisms may present themselves as viable alternatives to the formal justice process in dealing with children. However, as explained by the Special

[10] Basic Principles on the Use of Restorative Justice Programmes in Criminal Matters, Economic and Social Council resolution 2002/12, annex.

Representative, they may allow for the justification of harmful practices on grounds of culture, religion or tradition based on sources of law that may compromise the realization of human rights. Customary law and practices have sometimes placed vulnerable groups, especially women and children at risk of harmful practices (SRSG 2012, p. 17).

4 Restorative Justice and the Reintegration of Juvenile Offenders

Social reintegration refers to various forms of interventions and programmes targeting individuals to prevent them from becoming involved in criminal behaviour or, for those who are already in conflict with the law, to reduce the likelihood that they will reoffend. Social reintegration interventions are therefore attempts by various components of the justice system, in partnership with social agencies, NGOs, educational institutions, communities and the offenders' family, to support the successful social integration of individuals at risk of offending or reoffending (UNODC 2012).

In recent years, there has been a growing emphasis on managing or facilitating the social reintegration of offenders and, in particular, on managing their re-entry into society after a period of incarceration (Borzycki and Makkai 2007; Griffiths et al. 2007; Myers and Olson 2013).

In that context, restorative justice interventions can help offenders take responsibility for their behaviour in a meaningful way, gain insight into the causes of their behaviour and its effects on others, encourage them to desist from crime and help them regain acceptance by their family and community. The rationale behind that kind of intervention is described as follows in a UNODC publication on the social reintegration of offenders:

> Restorative justice is based on the principle that the most effective responses to crime are those which hold offenders accountable for their behaviour in ways that reintegrate them into society rather than increase their sense of isolation and stigma. The objective is to help offenders understand the consequences of their actions and to make amends to the community. By showing offenders the full impact of their behaviour on all those around them, restorative justice can encourage real and lasting change. At the same time, the participation of victims of crime and community members may serve to strengthen ties in the community and to facilitate the development of community-based capacities to assist offenders. (UNODC 2012, p. 101).

In reality, the capacity of current restorative justice programmes to achieve these objectives tends to be quite limited. With a few exceptions directed mostly at violent adult offenders, restorative justice models have not been developed to support social reintegration interventions. However, this is not to say that programmes more directly focused on facilitating the social reintegration of young offenders and their desistence from crime could not be implemented on the basis of genuine restorative justice principles.

Many good practices have been identified that need to be both better understood and more systematically evaluated. For example, some restorative justice elements can be integrated into community-based sentences to facilitate the juvenile offender's social reintegration. In a "restorative probation" model, a judge sentences the offender to probation with a suspended sentence, while a volunteer reparative board meets with the offender and the victim to agree on a contract that the offender agrees to carry out. Fulfilment of the contract is the only condition of probation and the contract is based on restorative goals, namely that the offender understands the effects of the crime and learns how to avoid reoffending, that the victim is restored and healed, and that the community is reassured and offers reintegration to the offender (Kurki 2000; Fox 2010).

4.1 The Social Reintegration of Juvenile Offenders

Facilitating the social reintegration of offenders is a complex task and the impact of specific interventions is often difficult to measure (Griffiths et al. 2007). The primary objective of social reintegration interventions is to provide offenders with the support, assistance and supervision that will help them to lead crime-free lives upon release. However, for such interventions to lead to positive outcomes, the community must obviously also be responsive and engaged in the process (UNODC 2012, p. 81).

Positive reintegration outcomes can be produced when factors predisposing someone to criminal behaviour are addressed in a holistic fashion and when that person's physical and social needs are supported. As part of an aftercare strategy, a number of interventions can be delivered to assist juvenile offenders in reintegrating into their families and the community. The interventions must fit the needs and circumstances of the child, and the choice of an intervention should be based on a realistic assessment of the individual's challenges and needs. When juvenile offenders have been detained, support can be offered at the time of their release to assist them in effecting that difficult transition and to ensure that the community is willing and able to receive them.

As mentioned before, very few restorative justice models actually deliver on the promise to actively involve the community in the rehabilitation, healing and reintegration of offenders. At present, two models are sometimes used to implicate communities more directly in the social reintegration of offenders: sentencing circles and circles of support and accountability (CoSA). In addition, there has been some experimentation with conducting a restorative justice process while the offender (usually an adult) is in prison (e.g., Walker 2009). So far, none of these mechanisms has been used very extensively with juvenile offenders. In fact, a restorative model of re-entry and social reintegration for juvenile offenders has yet to be developed.

4.2 Sentencing Circles and First Nations' Courts

In Canada, sentencing circles and now "First Nations Courts" function as sentencing courts or sentencing-aids, with community participation and at least a nominal commitment to restorative justice principles. Their main purposes is not so much to divert cases from the justice system, but to inform and help shape the criminal justice response in ways that not only consider the offender and the victim, but also the needs, circumstances and capacity of the community to which the offender and the victim belong. These mechanisms represent perhaps the most powerful applications of restorative justice principles in the field of criminal law. They can apply to both juvenile and adult offenders and they challenge communities to accept responsibility for their own safety and development, while considering the need and circumstances of both the offenders and the victims.

Circle sentencing provides for a wide variety of options for restitution and punishment.[11] They can offer flexible solutions that are responsive to the circumstances of each juvenile offender, the requirements of each case and the capacity of the community. Circles are designed to strengthen the collective sense of community and empower the victim, the offender and community members through a healing and problem solving process. The goal is to heal all those affected, but also to facilitate the rehabilitation and social reintegration of the offender by mending the social relationship between the offender and the community.

4.3 Circles of Support and Accountability

The CoSA initiative was originally conceived in Canada as a means to fill a gap in services left by government policy that is, regarding those adult individuals that had served their entire court sentence in prison and were released at the expiration of their warrant. These individuals were being released without a formal process of aftercare and without any assistance or supervision. CoSA was initiated out of necessity to work with released offenders who were most likely to fail to successfully reintegrate society, presumably because of a lack of community support or other resources. Many of these individuals were untreated sex offenders and their return to the community was very likely to attract significant media attention. On release, these offenders faced significant reintegration challenges.

The CoSA Model is an example of community participation and of partnerships between the community and the justice system to promote public safety while actively supporting the reintegration of offenders. Volunteers are carefully selected from the community, professionally trained, and aptly supported; they constitute the inner circle. A covenant or agreement is established between the core member and up to seven circle volunteers. Participation is voluntary on both sides. However,

[11] See for example: Joudo Larsen (2014).

once the covenant is agreed to, it becomes the road map for both the support and the accountability that can be expected by all participants. The outer "professional" circle refers to the support, guidance and interventions that are provided by professionals and official representatives of law enforcement or correctional agencies (Brown and Dandurand 2007).

The CoSA model was evaluated in Canada and elsewhere and it is consistently shown to reduce recidivism and facilitate the reintegration of adult offenders An evaluation of a pilot project based on that model in Ontario suggests that the levels of reoffending in men who were involved in the programme were markedly lower than for similar high-risk offenders who did not participate (Wilson et al. 2009; Wilson et al. 2005; Duwe 2012).

5 Conclusion

Progress has been made in many countries in involving communities in risk management and the management and reintegration of offenders in the community. Community-based interventions and programmes for young offenders have been developed which have significantly contributed to the young offenders' desistance form crime and their successful social reintegration. Many of them are making a good use of professionally trained community volunteers. Positive reintegration outcomes can be produced when factors predisposing a young offender to criminal behaviour are addressed in a holistic fashion and when that person's physical and social needs are supported. As part of an aftercare strategy, a number of interventions can be delivered to assist juvenile offenders in reintegrating into their families and the community. When juvenile offenders are detained, they can be supported after their release and assisted in effecting that difficult transition and to ensure that the community is willing and able to receive them. In all of these instances, restorative justice could play a very beneficial role. If it does not so far, it is because its application in the field of juvenile justice has been largely limited to diversion programmes.

Very few restorative justice elements have been integrated systematically into community-based sentences or into post-release programmes to facilitate the juvenile offender's social reintegration. In fact, this chapter has argued that the capacity of existing restorative justice programmes to achieve social reintegration objectives tends to be quite limited. Some good practices have been identified, but they need to be both better understood and more systematically evaluated. The role of the community in that process has to be operationalized differently and far more concretely. At this point, a restorative model of re-entry and social reintegration for juvenile offenders has yet to be developed.

Proponents of restorative justice typically deplore the lack of progress in implementing restorative justice within the juvenile justice system. In my view, they will still be deploring that problem in 10 years from now unless they find ways to unleash restorative justice full potential in contributing to the social reintegration of offenders, particularly those who have been institutionalized.

Five Questions

1. How can the restorative justice approach be used to actively support the reintegration of offenders?
2. Are there situations in which a victim-offender reconciliation process is a pre-requisite to the offender's successful social integration?
3. How can restorative justice programmes, often valued for their participatory characteristics and their ability to involve community members, be used to promote greater and more positive community involvement in the social reintegration of offenders?
4. What remains to be done to verify the claim of restorative justice programme that they can produce better outcomes in terms of public safety, victim healing, community heath, and offender rehabilitation and social reintegration?
5. Are there examples of programmes focused on facilitating the social reintegration of young offenders and their desistence from crime that integrate genuine restorative justice principles?

References

Acorn, A. (2004). *Compulsory compassion – A critique of restorative justice*. Vancouver: UBC Press.

Artsen, I., Daems, T., & Robert, L. (2013). *Institutionalizing restorative justice*. Cullompton: Willan Publishing.

Baruch Bush, R. A., & Folger, J. P. (1994). *The promise of mediation – Responding to conflict through empowerment and recognition*. San Francisco: Jossey-Bass Publishers.

Bazemore, G., & Maruna, S. (2009). Restorative justice in the reentry context: Building new the-ory and expanding the evidence base. *Victims & Offenders: An International Journal of Evi-dence-based Research, Policy, and Practice, 4*(4), 375–384.

Bazemore, G., & Umbreit, M. (1999). Conference, circles, boards, and mediations: Restorative justice and citizen involvement in the response to youth crime. St Paul, MN: Balanced and Restorative Justice Project.

Bonta, J. R., Jesseman, M., Rugge, T., & Cormier, R. (2009). Restorative justice and recidivism: Promises made, promises kept. In D. A. Andrews & J. Bonta (Eds.), *The psychology of criminal conduct* (5th ed.). Cincinnati, OH: Anderson.

Borzycki, M., & Makkai, T. (2007). *Prisoner reintegration post-release*. Canberra: Australian Institute of Criminology.

Broughton, C. (2012). The institutionalization of restorative justice: A Canadian perspective. Unpublished MA thesis, University of Ottawa, Ottawa.

Brown, R. E., & Dandurand, Y. (2007). Successful strategies that contribute to safer communities. In S. Maio (Ed.), *Selected papers on successful crime reduction and prevention strategies in the urban context* (pp. 77–88). Riyadh, Saudi Arabia: Naif Arab University for Security Sciences (NAUSS).

Choi, J. J., Bazemore, G., & Gilber, M. J. (2012). Review of the research on victims' experiences in restorative justice: Implications for youth justice. *Children and Youth Services Review, 34* (1), 35–42.

Committee on the Rights of the Child (2007). General Comment No. 7 (2007) on children's rights in juvenile justice, CRC/C/GC/10.
Committee on the Rights of the Child (2013). General comment No. 14 (2013) on the right of the child to have his or her best interests taken as a primary consideration (art. 3, para. 1). CRC/C/GC/14.
Cunneen, C. (2010). The limitations of restorative justice. In C. Cunneen & C. Hoyle (Eds.), *Debating restorative justice* (pp. 101–187). Oxford: Hart Publishing.
Dandurand, Y. (2012). Integrating restorative approaches in the criminal justice process: From slow progress to cautious optimism. In S. M. Redo (Ed.), *Blue criminology -The power of United Nations ideas to counter crime globally* (pp. 87–91). Helsinki: HEUNI.
Dickson-Gilmore, J., & La Prairie, C. (2005). *Will the circle be unbroken? Aboriginal communities, restorative justice, and the challenges of conflict and change.* Toronto: University of Toronto Press.
Duwe, G. (2012). Can circles of support and accountability (COSA) work in the United States? Preliminary results from a randomized experiment in Minnesota. *Sexual Abuse: A Journal of Research and Treatment, 25*(2), 143–165.
Fox, K. J. (2010). Second chances: A comparison of civic engagement in offender reentry pro-grams. *Criminal Justice Review, 35*(3), 335–353.
Gavrieldes, T. (2007). *Restorative justice theory and practice: Addressing the discrepancy.* HEUNI: Helsinki.
Griffiths, C. T., Dandurand, Y., & Murdoch, D. (2007). *The social reintegration of offenders and crime prevention.* Ottawa: Public Safety Canada, National Crime Prevention Centre.
Hannem, S., & Leonardi, L. (2014). *Family-victim research: Needs and characteristics.* Kingston, ON: Canadian Families and Corrections Network.
Hoyle, C. (2010). The case for restorative justice. In C. Cunneen & C. Hoyle (Eds.), *Debating restorative justice* (pp. 1–100). Oxford: Hart Publishing.
Joudo Larsen, J. (2014). *Restorative justice in the Australian criminal justice system.* Canberra: Australian Institute of Criminology.
Kurki, L. (2000). Restorative and community justice in the United States. *Crime and Justice: A Review of Research, 27*, 235–303.
Law Commission of Canada. (2003). *Transforming relationships through participatory justice.* Ottawa: Law Commission of Canada.
Myers, D. L., & Olson, J. (2013). Offender re-entry and reintegration: Policy and research. *Criminal Justice Policy Review, 24*(1), 3–8.
Paterson, C., & Clamp, K. (2012). Exploring recent developments in restorative policing in Engalnd and Wales. *Criminology and Criminal Justice, 12*(5), 5893–611.
Pranis, K., Stuart, B., & Wedge, M. (2003). *Peacemaking circles – From crime to community.* St Paul, MN: Living Justice Press.
Prichard, J. (2010). Net-widening and the diversion of young people from court: A Longitudinal analysis with implications for restorative justice. *The Australian and New Zealand Journal of Criminology, 43*(1), 112–129.
Shapland, J., Robinson, G., & Sorsby, A. (2011). *Restorative Justice In Practice: Evaluating what works for victims and offenders.* London/New York: Routledge.
Sherman, L. W., & Strang, H. (2007). *Restorative justice: The evidence.* Canberra: Esmée Fairbarn Foundation and The Smith Institute.
Sherman, L. W., & Strang, H. (2012). Restorative justice as evidence-based sentencing. In J. Pe-tersilia & K. Reitz (Eds.), *The Oxford handbook of sentencing and corrections* (pp. 215–243). NY: Ox-ford University Press.
Special Representative of the Secretary General on Violence against Children. (2012). *Protecting children from harmful practices in plural legal systems.* New York: United Nations & Plan International.
Special Representative of the Secretary General on Violence Against Children. (2013). *Promoting restorative justice for children.* New York: United Nations.

Strang, H., Sherman, L. W., Mayo-Wilson, E., Woods, D., & Ariel, B. (2013). Restorative Justice Conferencing (RJC) using face-to-face meetings of offenders and victims: Effects on of-fender recidivism and victim satisfaction. *A Systematic Review. Campbell Systematic Re-views, 2013*, 12.

United Nations Declaration of Basic Principles of Justice for Victims of Crime and Abuse of Power, G. A. resolution 40/34 of 29 November 1985, article 7 (A/RES/40/34, Annex, art. 7).

United Nations Model Strategies and Practical Measures on the Elimination of Violence against Children in the Field of Crime Prevention and Criminal Justice, Annex, 18 December 2013

United Nations Office on Drugs and Crime (UNODC). (2006). *Handbook on restorative justice programmes*. New York: United Nations.

United Nations Office on Drugs and Crime (UNODC). (2012). *Introductory handbook on the prevention of recidivism and the social reintegration of offenders*. New York: United Nations.

United Nations Standard Minimum Rules for the Administration of Juvenile Justice ("The Beijing Rules", Annex), 29 November 1985 (A/RES/40/33).

Van Ness, D. W., & Heetderks Strong, K. (2010). *Restoring justice – An introduction to restorative justice* (3rd ed.). New Providence, NJ: LexisNexis.

Walker, L. (2009). Modified restorative circles: A reintegration group planning process that pro-motes desistance. *Contemporary Justice Review, 12*(4), 419–431.

Weatherburn, D., McGath, A., & Bartels, L. (2012). Three dogmas of juvenile justice. *University of New South Wales Law Journal, 35*(3), 779–809.

Weatherburn, D., & Macadam, M. (2013). A review of restorative justice responses to offending. *Evidence Base – A Journal of Evidence Review in Key Policy Areas,* (1), 1–19.

Wilson, R., Picheca, J. E., & Prinzo, M. (2005). *Circles of support and accountability: An evaluation of the pilot project in South-Central Ontario*. Ottawa.

Wilson, R. J., Cortoni, F., & McWhinnie, A. J. (2009). Circles of support & accountability: A Canadian national replication of outcome findings. *Sex Abuse: A Journal of Research and Treatment, 21*(4), 412–430.

Preventing and Addressing Youth Offending: Restorative Justice and Family Focused Programming

Carolyn Hamilton and Elizabeth Yarrow

Abstract Restorative justice measures are often presented as the most desirable method for dealing with cases of children who come into conflict with the law. Whilst restorative practices have the potential to contribute to constructive and curative strategies for addressing child offending, there are limitations to these approaches. Restorative mechanisms often prioritise healing and reparation for victims, over addressing the root causes of child offending, and the social and family contexts which underlie children's offending behaviour. They may be most valuable where they complement, rather than replace, the work done by a wide range of social agencies that play a role in tackling the risk factors associated with child offending.

The first half of this chapter evaluates the theory and application of restorative justice methods for preventing and addressing youth offending, while the second half presents a comparative review of a holistic, family-focused model that has been used as a prevention, diversion and sentencing alternative for children in Azerbaijan, Georgia, Kazakhstan, Tajikistan and Tanzania; and provides a series of recommendations for strengthening these programmes, which aim to address both the impacts and causes of juvenile crime.

1 Introduction

It is a fundamental tenet of international law that the primary goal of a juvenile justice system should not be that of punishment, but of rehabilitation and reintegration of the child offender. Recognising children's special needs and vulnerabilities, article 40(1) of the United Nations Convention on the Rights of the Child (UNCRC/1577 UNTS 3) provides that children who come into conflict with the law should be treated in a manner which promotes their own dignity and worth, as well

C. Hamilton (✉) • E. Yarrow
Coram Children's Legal Centre, London, UK
e-mail: Carolyn.Hamilton@coramclc.org.uk; Elizabeth.Yarrow@coramclc.org.uk

H. Kury et al. (eds.), *Women and Children as Victims and Offenders: Background, Prevention, Reintegration*, DOI 10.1007/978-3-319-28424-8_12

as their understanding of the rights and freedoms of others, with a focus on reintegration and assisting the child to assume a constructive role in society (article 40 (1), UNCRC 1989).

Given this, it is unsurprising that 'restorative justice' in its many forms has become an increasingly important concept in juvenile justice practice and reform. It is argued that restorative justice methods have the potential to provide innovative, informal, community based solutions to child offending that avoid exposing already vulnerable children to the adversarial, isolating and punitive operations of formal criminal justice processes. Restorative measures not only provide alternatives to detention and institutionalisation of children *after* offending has occurred, but may also form part of interventions to address the needs of children *at risk* of coming into conflict with the law, contributing to prevention efforts aimed at reducing overall rates of anti-social and criminal behaviour amongst children and young people.

Nevertheless, the principles and strategies of restorative justice are not without their limitations. Whilst the ideals and values espoused by advocates of restorative methods are far reaching and ambitious, there is often a gap between these ideals, and actual practices (Daly 2006). Critics have pointed out that restorative processes demand a level of compassion, emotional maturity and moral responsibility that may be lacking amongst participants, and especially young offenders (Daly 2006). Others have questioned whether a one-off restorative process can address children's offending behaviour, without resolving the complex contexts, circumstances and conditions which drive young people to offend (Levrant et al. 1999).

Recent programmes set up in a range of countries by Coram Children's Legal Centre[1] and UNICEF seek to integrate restorative practices within broader community programmes, which emphasise family and social support, and rehabilitation for children in conflict with the law.[2] These programmes do not take a primarily restorative approach, but rather a 'family focus' and seek to address the underlying drivers of children's offending behaviour, such as family breakdown, poverty, lack of education and other opportunity, and psychosocial distress. This is achieved through the development of tailored programmes which provide children and their families with a range of services, including remedial education; health care; legal services; vocational training and careers advice; sport, drama and art therapy; psycho-social care; family counselling, conferencing and mediation; anger-

[1] Coram Children's Legal Centre is a NGO concerned with law and policy affecting children. The Centre works in the United Kingdom and around the world to protect and promote the rights of children through the reform of law, policy and practice and the provision of direct legal assistance to young people, parents and professionals. The Centre's international department focuses in particular on protecting the rights of children in conflict with the law, and promoting justice for children, in jurisdictions around the world, through: research, law and policy development, advocacy, and the development and implementation of grass roots diversion and alternative sentencing programmes.

[2] See http://www.childrenslegalcentre.com/index.php?page=international_programmes [Accessed 10 Nov. 2014].

management and conflict resolution courses; drug and alcohol rehabilitation support and others.

The first section of this chapter evaluates the theory and application of restorative justice methods for preventing and addressing youth offending. The second half reviews evidence from a number of evaluations of programmes established in Azerbaijan, Georgia, Tajikistan and Tanzania, which have been designed around a holistic, family-focused, service provision model. It considers, whether embedding restorative techniques and practices within a context of 'wrap-around' service provision, can successfully and sustainably curtail both the *impact* and *drivers* of juvenile crime.

2 Understanding Restorative Justice: Core Values, Principles and Justifications

"The primary purpose of restorative justice is just that – to restore justice" (Office of the Special Representative to the Secretary General on Violence Against Children 2013, p. 1).

Restorative justice is a highly contested concept. At its most basic, it is a model of justice which is directed towards the repairing or healing of harm or wrong cause by an offence, to restore individual and community well-being. "Harm" has been understood expansively, to encompass emotional, psychological and relational aspects, as well as financial, material and physical losses. There is significant debate, however, about the content, scope and limits of what can be considered legitimately 'restorative', both in theory and in practice; as Howard Zehr commented recently in an interview: "*Restorative justice as a term has [become] so popular*, that *all kinds of things are being called restorative justice today, some of which...aren't very restorative*".[3]

The debate surrounding the definition of restorative justice, has often been characterised in terms of a tension between those theorists who see restorative justice primarily as a process, and those who focus on the values and outcomes that restorative justice is intended to promote (Braithwaite and Strang 2001). Others have rejected this distinction, pointing out that the desired outcomes of restorative justice derive from the values contained within the process itself (Walgrave 2002; Johnstone 2004). To situate the debate, it is useful to start with Tony Marshall's widely cited definition of restorative justice, which describes it as:

> a process whereby parties with a stake in a specific offence collectively resolve how to deal with the aftermath of the offence and its implications for the future (Marshall 1999).

This definition incorporates many key features of restorative justice models; nevertheless it has been criticised for failing to provide sufficient principled guidance as to the spirit, character and values of the restorative movement (Bazemore

[3] Zehr in Shuck (2014).

and Walgrave 1999). Whilst the idea of 'collective' resolution provides insight into the community-based, cooperative character of restorative justice, it fails to elaborate on how 'collective' decision making should be carried out, and to what ends. Should the priority be consensus building or conversation; resolution or dialogue; presence or participation; peace or transformation? Does it matter whether the process is coercive or voluntary (Doolin 2007)? And what does it mean to 'deal with' the aftermath of an offence and its 'implications for the future' (Van Ness et al. 2001; Doolin 2007)? Without further elaboration on these points there is nothing to prevent restorative processes from becoming oppressive, harmful, or degrading experiences (Doolin 2007). Evidence from a recent study of victim-offender mediation practices in Lao People's Democratic Republic underscores the significance of this point: it revealed (amongst many others) a case where a 15 year old child accused of stealing was physically beaten by the aggrieved adult during mediation, who also repeatedly threatened to kill the child if he ever stole from his house again (Barnes et al. 2013).

On the other hand, a number of restorative justice scholars have set about defining restorative justice in terms of its intended aims or outcomes, or through expounding upon the key values and ideals which form its moral justification and purpose. For example, Gordon Bazemore and Lode Walgrave's 1999 definition of restorative justice characterised it as: "any action that is primarily oriented to doing justice by repairing the harm that is caused by a crime." (Bazemore and Walgrave 1999) Whilst 'outcome' based definitions of this kind are helpful in providing a conceptual framework through which restorative justice interventions can be understood, they lack precision and practical guidance as to how restorative measures can be empirically identified and applied.

Arguably, the most useful and comprehensive definitions of restorative justice combine the two approaches. In 1998, Canadian Susan Sharpe developed a series of five key principles of restorative justice, which were further adapted by Daniel Van Ness, Allison Morris and Gabrielle Maxwell. According to these principles any genuinely restorative process should include: full participation and voluntary involvement of any person affected by a crime; a focus on healing and recovery for both victim and offender; full and direct accountability and responsibility for the offence experienced by the offender; reconciliation of the offender and victim and actions aimed at strengthening community harmony and safety (van Ness et al. 2001).

In practice, restorative justice is typically understood to involve the application of techniques such as victim-offender mediation, family conferencing and circle sentencing. These methods are explored in more detail in Sect. 3 below.

2.1 *Restorative Justice vs. Criminal Justice*

Much literature and debate has sought to define what restorative justice *is*, through opposing it to what it is *not*. The restorative justice movement has been widely celebrated as a 'new paradigm' for how society should respond to crime; a set of ideas that challenge state-sponsored, institutionalised models of criminal justice (Van Ness et al. 2001). Whilst criminal justice treats an offence as a violation of 'the state' and 'the law'—an abstract set of rules designed to legitimise and uphold established systems of power; restorative justice is concerned with the way that crime hurts people, human relationships and the social bonds that define our responsibilities and obligations to others (Zehr 1990, 1995).

Within formal, state-sponsored justice processes both victims and offenders are reduced to passive objects of a detached, adversarial and bureaucratic process of determining guilt and administering penance (Daly 2006). As Daly writes:

> Decisions are made by a distant magistrate or judge, and an overworked duty solicitor and prosecutor with many files to process...in the courtroom, a defendant is typically mute and a victim is not present. State actors do all the work of handling and processing crime. The actual parties to a crime (the persons charged and victim-complainants) are bystanders or absent (Daly 2006).

It is argued that, because criminal justice is owned and administered by the state, it has an essentially punitive character. Punishment constitutes a demonstration of power and authority, which compels offenders into submission, yet it has little (beyond revenge) to offer those who are most affected by crime. As such, Nils Christie had characterised the development of formal, criminal justice as a process by which the state has increasingly sought to 'steal' crimes from their victims; for the primary goal of maintaining social control: a 'King's peace' (Christie 1977). Restorative justice has a more personal focus: the 'state' is no longer the primary stakeholder in justice, but those who are hurt most by an offence. It is a 'community-centred', 'bottom-up' approach to justice, that prioritises maximising input and participation from all those affected by crime. This type of justice searches for solutions beyond vengeful repression and focuses on how to ensure reparation, reconciliation and reassurance (Van Ness et al. 2001; Zehr 1990).

Of course, there is nothing new or original about this conception of justice. 'Restorative justice' as a term is generally thought to have first emerged in criminology in the mid-1970s (Llewellyn and Howse 1998), but the ideas it propounds describe a model of justice that has arguably been dominant "throughout most of human history for all the world's peoples" (Braithwaite 1997).[4] In recognition of this, restorative justice is often characterised as an 'ancient' or 'traditional' conception of justice. The movement is credited with taking justice 'back to its roots'; a 'return' to a primordial understanding of justice, which still has relevance and resonance today (Strang and Sherman 2003). Authors such as Van Ness and Strong have pointed out that restorative conception of justice was prevalent in many

[4] John Braithwaite as quoted in Llewellyn and Howse (1998), prepared for the Law Commission of Canada (p. 4) http://dalspace.library.dal.ca/bitstream/handle/10222/10287/Howse_Llewellyn%20Research%20Restorative%20Justice%20Framework%20EN.pdf?sequence=1 [Accessed 10 Nov 2014].

'pre-colonial African societies' (Van Ness and Strong 1997).[5] Others have argued that restorative justice similarly has roots in 'western' traditions and history (Llewellyn and Howse 1998). Zehr writes:

> For most of our history in the West, non-judicial, non-legal dispute resolution techniques have dominated. People traditionally have been very reluctant to call in the state, even when the state claimed a role. In fact, a great deal of stigma was attached to the state and asking it to prosecute. For centuries the state's role in prosecution was quite minimal. Instead it was considered the business of the community to solve its own disputes (Zehr 1985).[6]

In addition, authors have explored how restorative conceptions of justice can be found today in many aboriginal communities, including the native populations of Canada, New Zealand and Australia (Maxwell and Morris 2001; Alder and Wundersitz 1994); or in the lasting customs of 'traditional' societies across the world (Llewellyn and Howse 1998; UNODC 2006). Therefore, whereas 'criminal justice' is depicted as an essentially 'modern' and 'western' model of justice; restorative justice is conversely characterised as historic, 'indigenous' and 'non-western' in character.

This condensed presentation of the history of justice may be too simplistic. Harry Blag has highlighted that there are dangers associated with 'collap[sing] together a diversity of indigenous justice practices into a singular 'Aboriginality' and assign[ing] the heading 'restorative' to them' (Blagg 2001). At the same time it should be acknowledged that the practice of resolving offending behaviour through the application of collective, community based measures is a contemporary experience of justice that pervades the realities of people affected by crime in diverse communities across the globe today. This may be the case, even in societies characterised by high levels of formal interaction between the state and the population; where some groups may resist, be excluded from, or choose not to use formal mechanisms for a multitude of reasons, including a (state) deficit of political legitimacy, limited legal definitions of rights and protection, institutionalised discrimination, lack of trust in formal systems, high costs of legal services or the personal nature of many crimes (and consequent shame and stigma associated with state-intervention). Addressing offending outside of the formal justice system may be especially common with regards to certain types of abuse, such as sexual and domestic violence (McDonald and Tinsley 2013); or in cases involving particular types of stakeholders, such as, for example, children.

Of course, not all offences are 'resolved' when they are dealt with in the community, and not all informal methods of conflict resolution conform to restorative justice principles and ideals. Nevertheless, it may be deceptive to suppose that

---

[5] Daniel Van Ness and Karen Strong in Llewellyn and Howse (1998), prepared for the Law Commission of Canada (p. 4) http://dalspace.library.dal.ca/bitstream/handle/10222/10287/Howse_Llewellyn%20Research%20Restorative%20Justice%20Framework%20EN.pdf?sequence=1 [Accessed 10 Nov 2014].

[6] Howard Zehr as quoted in Llewellyn and Howse (1998) Restorative Justice: a Conceptual Framework, prepared for the Law Commission of Canada (p. 4) http://dalspace.library.dal.ca/bitstream/handle/10222/10287/Howse_Llewellyn%20Research%20Restorative%20Justice%20Framework%20EN.pdf?sequence=1 [Accessed 10 Nov 2014].

a 'lawful' or 'state-sponsored' understanding of 'crime' and 'punishment' is the dominant model of justice imagined and applied by most people, even in 'modern', 'western' societies. To characterise justice in this way is arguably an exercise in power; an endorsement of an essentially patriarchal and ethno-centric logic of justice, which excludes the experiences of many marginalised groups who have historically been denied access to formal criminal justice systems by pre-eminent, institutionalised structures of power. It is through acknowledgement of this latter point that debate has ensued in the restorative justice movement as to whether restorative justice, as a field of both theory and practice, should sit *within* or *outside of* the paradigm of criminal justice (Wheeldon 2009).[7]

This is not just an abstract concern, but a real practical challenge. Harry Blag has pointed out how attempts to incorporate so-called 'aboriginal' restorative practices into formal legal systems have continued to marginalise aboriginal youth, because, after all, these communities have been historically considered *a priori* criminal (Blagg 2001). Similarly, Gerry Johnstone has argued that many restorative justice advocates concentrate their efforts too narrowly: viewing restorative justice primarily as a new set of mechanisms for dealing with 'crime', as officially defined, instead of engaging with the more transformative aspects of the movement which pose a fundamental challenge to our social and political, as well as legal, institutions (Johnstone 2011). He writes:

> Criminal law is frequently used, not to prevent harmful behaviour, but rather to prohibit behaviour which those with social power find tiresome or distasteful. By the same token, social power is often used to prevent criminal labels and sanctions being applied to behaviour that seems – by many accounts – to be patently harmful to the majority of citizens...To focus narrowly on criminal justice reform, the restorative justice movement leaves itself open to the charge that it is working within and therefore helping to sustain an ideological definition of the problems facing modern societies. (Johnstone 2004, p.14).

Of course this may be the opposite of the intention of many restorative advocates. But this is a risk that comes from viewing restorative justice primarily from a legal standpoint—within the frame of a criminal justice paradigm—that it leads us into the technocratic question of how to 'do' justice better, instead of questioning the very nature of what 'justice' really is.

In his book *Governing Paradoxes of Restorative Justice,* George Pavlich draws on this point to expound a more fundamental critique of the restorative movement, arguing that 'restorative justice' as a philosophical concept is 'unattainable' because its structure and identity is constructed through a 'bifurcation, that simultaneously occasions two logically conflicting strands of thought'. That is to say, the basic concepts of criminal justice—notions of 'crime', 'a victim', 'an offender', 'the community'—are used, but at the same time these ideas are rejected (Pavlich 2005).

---

[7] See Gerry Johnstone's criticism of restorative programmes that focus narrowly on the reform of the criminal justice system, and perceive restorative justice primarily as a method for responding to 'crime' as officially defined, rather than other forms of social harm. Johnstone (2004), pp. 5–15.

In search of a common definition and identity, much of the literature constructs the value and purpose of restorative justice in terms of a series of binary oppositions: restorative justice is presented as 'aboriginal' and 'traditional', and criminal justice as 'mainstream' and 'modern'; restorative justice is 'informal', based within the 'community', whereas criminal justice is 'formal' and owned by the 'state'. Whilst restorative justice is shaped by 'relationships', it is 'rules' that govern criminal justice. Finally, restorative justice is concerned with 'reparation' and healing, whereas criminal justice is preoccupied with the infliction of pain and punishment. This dyadic model is too simplistic; not only because it fails to capture the rich realities and complexities of human experiences of justice, but also because it presents one 'type' of justice as essentially good, and the other as essentially bad (Van Ness et al 2001).

Consider the following passages:

> Restorative justice. . .represents a return to concepts of justice that are ancient and deep-seated, but which have been overshadowed by other approaches. Its contemporary re-emergence, and the widespread interest it has provoked, offers hope for the future of justice (Van Ness et al. 2001).
>
> In Western culture we have come to think of justice as an intervention to punish and correct wrongdoing. But justice has meant something quite different in other cultures and throughout most of human history. In many societies 'justice' has been understood as a state of balance – a system of social cooperation that supports and encourages peaceful coexistence (Sharpe 2004).
>
> Whilst criminal justice asks: what law have been broken? Who did it? What do the offenders deserve? Restorative justice asks: who has been hurt? What are their needs? Whose obligations are these (Zehr 2014)?

These statements have a clear normative message and purpose; but the ideas and distinctions that they present may be ambiguous. Many authors have pointed out that the distinction between retribution and restoration is not always as clear-cut as it has been presented, either in theory or in practice. Some theorists, such as Duff, have argued that retribution in fact forms part of restoration, not to inflict pain as an end in itself, but to evoke the right sort of pain, including remorse and regret, "which crime makes necessary and can only be achieved through punishment" (Doolin 2007, p. 437; Duff 2002). Furthermore, whilst advocates of restorative justice processes anticipate that restorative measures will prompt victims to seek constructive and curative responses to offending, as opposed to punitive ones, there is no guarantee that they will do so: many victims may feel a need or desire to exact punitive retaliation and revenge (Braithwaite 2004; Daly 2002).

Cretney and Davis have argued that: "a victim has an interest in punishment not just restitution or reparation, because punishment can reassure the victim that he or she has public recognition and support" (Daly 2006 p. 6; Cretney and Davis 1995, p. 178).[8] For this reason, some victims may even prefer the public and formal nature of a criminal trial. In a recent interview, a child victim of human trafficking for sexual exploitation spoke of her pleasure at seeing the man who trafficked her

[8] Creteny and Davis as quoted in Daly (2006), pp. 134–137.

systematic, national scale (Weitekamp 2001). Mediation programmes may be operated either by justice or social welfare government departments, or sometimes by not-for-profit organisations, and are delivered at various stages within the criminal justice process, including the pre-charge, pre-trial and post-trial stages. Where mediation occurs during the pre-trial stage it may lead to sentencing recommendations or provides a diversionary alternative to advancement through the criminal justice process. For example, in England and Wales, mediation typically takes place at the pre-trial stage, with a view to securing a negotiated packet of reparation along with a police warning or caution, with the case then being closed (Criminal Justice Review Group 1998).

Victim-offender mediation has typically been utilised in cases where the offender is a child, and in cases of a relatively minor offence, although the practice has also been applied in more serious cases such as murder or sexual abuse (McAlinden 2008). For example, in 1991 Texas prisons began arranging for victims of violent crimes to meet with the offender upon request, provided it was judged safe for them to do so (Van Ness 2010).

3.2 Family Group Conferencing

Family group (or community) conferencing was first developed in New Zealand and Australia in the late 1980s. Designed in the image of a traditional Maori practice—the '*whanau* conference'—this restorative approach was introduced into the New Zealand legal system in response to concerns that existing approaches to juvenile justice were having a disproportionately negative impact on Maori communities (Maxwell and Morris 2001a, b). Subsequently, in 1989, family group conferencing became the *principle* method of dealing with child offending nationwide through the passing of the Children, Young Persons and Their Families Act; and the practice was later extended to adults in 2002 (Maxwell and Morris 2001a, b). Variants on the conference model have since emerged in Australia, Brazil, Canada, England and Wales, Ireland, Lesotho, Northern Ireland, Peru, the Philippines, Thailand, Singapore, South Africa and the USA, amongst others. In different circumstances family group conferences have been used as a diversion approach as well as an alternative sentencing scheme. They have also been applied in non-judicial settings, such as schools and care institutions (SRSG 2013).

Similar to victim-offender mediation, family conferences are led by a trained facilitator, and intended to provide the victim and the offender the opportunity to relay their experiences of the offence and its consequences, with the aim of strengthening learning and understanding about the contexts and impacts of crime. Whilst participation in mediation is typically limited to the offender and the victim, however, conferences include a broader range of participants. These may include family, friends, and other support persons connected to either the victim or the offender, parties affected by the offence or concerned with its aftermath, and professionals who may be able to help with resolution of the harm caused, such as social workers, teachers, coaches, employers, legal advocates, and members of criminal justice agencies, such as police. A typical conference may have around 12 or so participants, though conferences have also been conducted with many more attendants (Van Ness and Strong 1997).

There are two commonly recognised variants of the conferencing model: the New Zealand approach, which is delivered by the social welfare arm of the government and allows for considerable variation in procedure so that participants can opt for the 'style' and framework that they wish; and the 'Waga Waga' approach, which originated in New South Wales, Australia, whereby conferences are carefully scripted and police directed. The 'Waga Waga' style of conference is sometimes referred to as 'restorative policing', and has proved the most influential model globally, providing the basis for programmes reproduced in many other contexts around the world (Criminal Justice Review Group 1998).

Conferences may result in reparations payments, recommendations for sanctions to be imposed, or an agreement that the offender participate in a rehabilitative programme. In some contexts, a conference may proceed without the participation of the victim (or victim representative), and, more rarely, without the participation of the offender. Family group conferences are thought to be particularly effective at ensuring that offenders comply with the agreed reparations plans, because they involve a broad range of concerned persons who may be able to provide ongoing supervision and support to the offenders (McCold and Wachtel 1998).

Family group conferencing has been used as a measure to deal with cases involving children both as victims, including cases of child maltreatment and domestic violence, and as offenders, including arson, minor assault, drug related offences, and vandalism (SRSG 2013).

3.3 Circles: (Sentencing Circles, 'Peacemaking' Circles, Restorative Circles)

The restorative variant typically known as the 'sentencing circle' was inspired by conflict resolution mechanisms practiced amongst the First Nations people of Northern America. 'Sentencing circles' were first applied within the formal criminal justice system in Northern Canada by local judges, and formally introduced into the Canadian Criminal Code in 1996. In the same year, circle sentencing was also adopted into the criminal justice system in the USA through a project piloted in Minnesota (SRSG 2013).

Circles are open to an even more expansive set of participants than family conferences. The victim and offender, their families and supporters, may attend, as well as criminal justice personnel, including prosecutors, defence lawyers, police and judges. Additionally, any person in the community who has an interest in the case may both attend and actively participate in the circle. Participants sit in a circle facing one another, and all attendees are provided the opportunity to speak, if and as they wish. Whilst all participants in the circle have an equal status and position in the process, one attendee will act as a 'keeper' of the circle, whose role is to ensure that the process is safe, relevant and orderly (Van Ness 2010).

Circle discussions need not focus narrowly on the crime that has been committed; participants may choose to explore other issues that may have relevance to 'resolving' the problem presented by the offence. In this way, circle processes are thought to strengthen community relationships and problem solving skills. Through the circle process, justice professionals share authority and decision making power with crime affected communities, meanwhile communities are encouraged to share responsibility with the offender for the crime and its resolution (SRSG 2013).

Usually the focus of the circle process is to develop consensus around a particular sentencing plan. Sentencing plans may include commitments on behalf of the offender, as well as others, including family members or other members of the community. Sentencing may include reparation payments, community service, a commitment to a rehabilitative undertaking, or even a period of incarceration. The circle may also be involved in supporting and monitoring responsible parties' compliance with agreed plans. Where circle sentencing is a formally recognised process within the criminal justice system, the decisions of the circle are typically submitted to the judge who is presiding in the case (who may or may not have participated in the circle). The decision of the circle is not binding on the court: the court must take the circle plan into consideration, but has the choice to adopt the plan, modify it, or reject it completely (Lilles 2001).

In the past, circle sentencing has typically been applied to adult cases. More recently, however, it is a method that has been applied to juvenile cases as well (UNODC 2006). There is relatively little research on the impact of sentencing circles compared to other restorative methods. Some studies have indicated that offenders subject to sentencing circles are less likely to re-offend compared to those who go through the criminal justice system (Umbreit et al. 2002), although others have revealed no difference in rates of reoffending for offenders who undergo circle sentencing as compared to criminal justice disposals (Fitzgerald 2008). A number of authors have further drawn attention to the risks associated with sentencing circles, especially where the offender is in a particularly vulnerable position, or the offence is of a particularly sensitive or taboo character (Cameron 2006).

3.4 Evaluating Restorative Programmes, Impact and Effectiveness

The diverse nature of restorative approaches and their application in different contexts makes it difficult to evaluate their relative benefits in a systematic fashion. Evaluations have been conducted utilising a variety of methodological approaches (with greater and lesser degrees of rigour) and different indicators and outcomes have been used to assess programme success, rendering it difficult to draw comparisons and conclusions across studies (Rodrigez 2007). Nevertheless, there are some common themes that have emerged from a body of empirical research which has set out to explore and evaluate the effectiveness and impact of restorative programmes in practice.

3.4.1 Measuring 'Success'

There are a number of key measures and outcomes that have typically been used as benchmarks for assessing the merit of restorative programmes. First, studies have examined the impact of restorative programmes at the micro or individual level; from the standpoint of those who have participated in restorative justice interventions. Studies have considered subjective indicators such as the level of perceived 'fairness' or 'satisfaction' with the restorative process from the perspectives of both the victim and the offender; or they have sought to identify the extent to which 'restoration' has been achieved in individual cases through analysing levels of remorse, shame and social reintegration displayed by the offender, and levels of 'healing' and understanding, demonstrated by both the victim and offender (e.g. Choi et al. 2011). This has typically involved considering: the degree to which the offender spontaneously expressed remorse, offered an apology, or demonstrated an understanding of the impact of their crime on the victim; the extent to which the process led to an agreement, and the payment of reparations or restitution to the victim (and whether this plan was subsequently completed and adhered to); and an assessment of psychological indicators, such as the levels of post-traumatic distress displayed by the victim and attitudes towards re-offending displayed by the offender both pre- and post-participation in the restorative programme (Daly 2006; Umbreit et al. 2002).

Second, the empirical research has considered the effectiveness of restorative mechanisms at a macro-level, for achieving systems-level goals, such as the desire to divert children out of the criminal justice system, reducing the overall levels of incarceration of children, saving time and costs in administering justice, and reducing overall rates of recidivism and crime within society (Haines 1997).

3.4.2 'Satisfaction' with Restorative Methods

Empirical research has typically revealed positive results in terms of degrees of 'satisfaction' with restorative programmes and perceptions of 'fairness': consistently revealing higher stakeholder satisfaction with restorative programmes in comparison to conventional criminal justice (Doak and O'Mahony 2011). Victims who participate in restorative programmes often report feeling satisfied with the opportunity to express their feelings, to ask questions of the offender (and get answers), and (in some cases) to influence the outcomes of the justice process. Offenders often report feeling satisfied with the opportunity to make amends for their crime, and to tell their personal story (Umbreit et al. 2002).

A 2005 review of 63 empirical studies conducted in five countries concluded that reported rates of 'satisfaction' with restorative justice, and perceptions of 'fairness', have been found to be consistently high amongst victims and offenders who participate in mediation, across research locations, types of programmes, social contexts, and categories of offence; this was also found to be true (although to a lesser extent) in the case of family conferences and circles (Umbreit et al. 2002). In many cases the results have been strikingly positive. A study involving youth offenders in Minnesota, for example, found that as many as 89 % of children believed that they were fairly treated during the restorative process (Fercello and Umbreit 1999).

Significantly, research has often revealed a discrepancy between rates of victim satisfaction compared with offender satisfaction. For example, Latimer et al.'s widely cited meta-evaluation found victim satisfaction with restorative justice programmes to be higher than that of a comparison group (involved in mainstream criminal justice processes) in all but 1 of 13 reviewed studies. Differences in rates of *offender* satisfaction across different disposals, however, were too marginal to be significant (Latimer et al. 2005). Umbreit et al.'s review in 2005 also found higher rates of satisfaction amongst victims compared to offenders for those who participated in victim-offender mediation programmes. Interestingly, however, the results were reversed for family conferences, with offenders reporting higher levels of satisfaction than victims (Umbreit et al. 2002). This may be a consequence of the relatively diminished role for victims in conference processes, given that there are a number of participants present, most of whom are typically connected with the offender, amongst other factors (Umbreit 2000).

Rates of satisfaction amongst young offenders involved in family conferencing have often been associated with their ability to engage actively in the conferencing process and participate in reaching a constructive outcome for all parties. For example, one early study conducted by Maxwell and Morris concerning family group conferencing in New Zealand found that young people are able to play an active part in restorative justice mechanisms, and that many child offenders report feeling involved in decision making and coming up with recommendations (Maxwell and Morris 1993).

These findings have not always been reproduced, however. A study undertaken by Karp et al. in 2004 concluded that young offenders' willingness to participate in restorative programs was variable (Karp et al. 2005). A 2013 evaluation of four restorative programmes in Taiwan found that, contrary to expectations, there has not always been a great deal of space provided for the active participation of young offenders in restorative programmes, which, rather, tend to be dominated by parents, family, law enforcement personnel and judges (Huang and Chang 2013). Christina Stahlkopf's (2009) qualitative study exploring conferencing with young offenders in England concluded that presence at restorative panel meetings does not automatically guarantee meaningful participation in practice. "*I did what they told me*;" "*I had no say. I had to do what I was told*," were typical ways in which children characterised their experiences (Stahlkopf 2009).

Overall the evidence suggests that participants in restorative programmes are more likely to feel satisfied, and fairly treated compared to those who experience formal criminal justice processes. Nevertheless, as many researchers have noted,

these results are likely to be prejudiced by a significant self-selection bias arising from the fact that participation in restorative justice disposals is almost always voluntary. As many commentators have pointed out, it is hardly surprising that participants are more likely to report being 'satisfied' with an activity in which they themselves have actively chosen to participate (Latimer et al. 2005).

Furthermore, as well as being voluntary, restorative meetings and conferences can only take place if the offender has acknowledged guilt for the crime. This is necessarily the case, because there is no fact-finding inquiry or mechanism for determining guilt included in the restorative process (Daly 2006). Thus as Elisabeth MacDonald has pointed out: 'many of those victims who profess satisfaction with restorative processes... would...not go through the experience of a full adversarial trial in any event;' she concludes: 'it may well be a case of comparing apples and pears' (McDonald and Tinsley 2013).

3.4.3 Achieving 'Restoration'

Empirical findings related to 'restoration' are more varied and complex than those that seek to measure 'satisfaction' or perceptions of 'fairness'. Where 'restoration' is measured through the identification of objective measures, such as the payment of reparation or restitution to the victim, restorative process appear (perhaps unsurprisingly) to be more efficacious that criminal justice proposals. Most meetings, conferences and circles do tend to result in agreement; which may take the form of a formal apology, the payment of direct compensation to the victim, work on behalf of the victim, community service, and other undertakings (Daly 2001).

More interestingly, studies have also demonstrated that agreements reached as a consequence of a restorative meeting tend to result in significantly higher rates of *compliance* compared to court-ordered restitution sentences (Gabbay 2005). For example, a 2004 meta-evaluation of 83 restorative projects in the UK found that 83 % resulted in the successful completion of agreed plans (O'Mahony 2012). Another evaluation found that children who participated in victim-offender mediation were over 40 % more likely to complete their programme compared to those who did not (Latimer et al. 2005).

On the other hand, more 'subjective' measures of restoration, including degrees of 'reconciliation', healing and remorse, displayed by participants in restorative programmes are harder to determine. Katherine Daly's research on restorative justice for children in Australia, found that, whilst over 80 % of participants (across different programmes) reported restorative processes as 'fair', indicators of 'restoration' were only present in some 30–60 % of cases, depending on the variable measured. Daly wonders whether restoration is particularly hard to achieve in *juvenile* cases, because of children's relative emotional immaturity, and reduced capacity to consider and understand the perspectives of the victim (Daly 2006).

Christina's Stahlkopf's qualitative research exploring the use of restorative panels for young offenders in the UK is particularly revealing in this respect. Her in-depth study conducted over a period of 17 months examined the functioning of

one of England's leading youth offending teams—the Oxfordshire YOT. Her research revealed that whilst young people may express the view that restorative processes are a 'good idea', and that they are 'fair' in the abstract, this does not necessarily mean that, from a personal perspective, they find them relevant or helpful, or that they are likely to have a positive effect on their behaviour. When asked if participation in the programme had helped them, the majority of young people responded in a neutral or negative manner, with most young people concluding that panel meetings had made no difference to their behaviour. One boy succinctly summarised the discrepancy between young people's general assertions of the 'benefit' of restorative programmes, and their assessments of their own personal experiences: "*referral orders are a good idea and they're better than court....but....well....it wasn't that helpful for me*" (Stahlkopf 2009, p. 236).

Despite these somewhat discouraging findings, there is some evidence of the 'restorative' effects of various programmes. A number of studies, particularly those conducted in the UK, have demonstrated that restorative encounters can reduce victims' levels of post-traumatic stress and help diminish levels of fear and anxiety (Rossner 2008). There may be psycho-social benefits for offenders as well. One 2009 evaluation of a restorative programme implemented in prisons in the UK found that subsequent to participating in the programme, prisoners demonstrated higher levels of 'victim empathy' (higher levels of awareness of the impact of their offending actions on victims). Interestingly, this positive change was found to be marginally greater amongst young offenders (compared with adults) and amongst female (compared with male) offenders (Feasy and Williams 2009).[12]

On the other hand, there is evidence that some participants may even feel *worse* after undergoing restoration (Gal and Moyal 2011). A study of restorative disposals for youth offending in New Zealand found that some victims felt worse after participating in a restorative process for several reasons, including that: they did not feel that the young offender was genuinely sorry; they did not feel able to properly express themselves during the encounter; and/or because they did not feel that their concerns had been appropriately listened to or addressed (O'Mahony 2012; Morris and Maxwell 1998).

Offenders, on the other hand, sometimes report that they feel that victims have sought to 'abuse' the process of restoration: using it as an opportunity to inflict punishment or exact revenge (Umbreit et al. 2002). There are concerns that conferences and circles expose young offenders to a lack of privacy, and arbitrarily subject them to existing conflicts and prejudices that prevail amongst family, friends and other connected persons (Haines 1997). These concerns are even more significant given that a substantial proportion of young offenders have been victim to violence and abuse, often perpetrated by those closest to them (Falshaw 2005). Existing roles, stereotypes, identities and power differentials delineated on the grounds of age, gender, race and class are sometimes reproduced and performed

[12] Since this study did not include a comparison group, however, it failed to establish conclusively that this change was the result of participation in the restorative programme.

in conferencing settings (Haines 1997), with the result that many young offenders are silent and withdrawn throughout restorative proceedings (Stahlkopf 2009). Christina's Stahlkopf's study of youth offending in the UK contains a number of troubling accounts of restorative panellists overstepping their boundaries and abusing their position of power during the restorative process. The following passage from her report is illustrative:

> Jacob...did very well over the course of his order and managed to acquire a full-time job as a postman...However, rather than congratulating Jacob...the panel expressed disappointment in his decision to be a postman. [They] felt that he should have chosen...a more highly paid [position]...[They] proceeded to ridicule Jacob's job, implying that he was lazy and stating that maybe becoming a postman was the perfect job because he would be done by noon. As Jacob continued to talk about his job, he mentioned that he was hoping to transfer his route to work in the area in which he lived. [The] panel members [responded], "*Yeah, good luck trying to transfer before your first 40 years!*" The panel members' comments were inappropriate and only served to alienate the young person at a time when it was crucial to be as reintegrative as possible...Rather than focusing on the positive changes he had made in his life, the panel members instead chose to ridicule him (Stahlkopf 2009).

This evidence evokes Haine's and Braitewaithe's concerns that restorative processes are susceptible to reproducing existing power dynamics and inequalities, especially when children are involved (Haines 1997; Braithwaite 2003a, b).

3.4.4 Reducing Costs

There is evidence that the administration of restorative justice provides for a more proportionate and efficient use of resources compared to traditional criminal justice. Evidence on policing costs in the UK, for example, has found that restorative justice disposals are consistently cheaper and take up less police time compared to criminal justice alternatives (Shewan 2010), and Ministry of Justice research has reportedly estimated that restorative justice saves as much as £9 for every £1 spent on RJ (Restorative Justice Council 2011). Research in Australia has also demonstrated the cost-effective of restorative justice disposals: research conducted by Webber in 2012 concluded that disposing of a youth offending case through conferencing is 18 % cheaper than processing it in in court (Webber 2012); and a 2010 evaluation in Victoria found that conferencing is also less expensive than administering a community based order (Larson 2014). Furthermore, a study in Peru found that restorative justice programmes were almost four times cheaper than holding children in State-run closed detention facilities, and that in one research site the judicial system case load was reduced by 44.2 % as a result of implementing a restorative justice programme (SRSG 2013). A review conducted by the National Commission in Northern Ireland in 2009 concluded that "despite the difficulty in comparing international data, there are clear indications that restorative justice measures are among the less expensive options open to the criminal justice system." (National Commission on Restorative Justice 2009).

3.4.5 Reducing Recidivism

The evidence concerning the effectiveness of restorative justice disposals for preventing juvenile crime and reducing rates of recidivism is highly varied and mixed, and it is difficult to draw general conclusions from the research that has been conducted. Numerous studies have demonstrated lower levels of recidivism for children and youth who have participated in restorative practices in comparison to those within mainstream criminal justice (e.g. Bergseth and Bouffard 2012; Evje and Cushman 2000). A number of random control trials and comparison studies have found that youth who participate in restorative mechanisms, particularly victim-offender mediation, reoffend at a lower rate than youths whose cases are disposed with through the criminal justice system, and where they do reoffend, they commit less serious crimes (Bradshaw and Roseborough 2005; Nugent et al. 2004). For example, a 2000 random control experiment in New Zealand found that young people who were assigned to conferencing were less likely to reoffend than those who attended the youth court (Sherman et al. 2000). Furthermore, research in Australia in 2002 concluded that young offenders who undergo conferencing are between 15 and 20 % less likely to reoffend compared to those who are sentenced in court (Luke and Lind 2002). Similarly a study on rates of reoffending amongst young, violent offenders in the USA found that those children who went through a restorative process were less likely to reoffend after a period of 12 months compared to those whose cases were processed through the criminal justice system (McCold and Wachtel 1998).

On the other hand, a considerable spectrum of research has failed to reproduce these results. Many studies have not detected any discernible impact on recidivism as a result of restorative practices, or have generated results that are too marginal to be significant.[13]

Furthermore, some studies have indicated that some children are *more* likely to re-offend after participating in a restorative process. A meta study in Canada comparing data across 22 studies found that overall restorative justice programmes led to a 7 % reduction in reoffending compared to criminal justice approaches; however, aggregating results across studies conceals vast differences in results; whilst some studies revealed reductions in reoffending of up to 38 %, other studies demonstrated *increases* in child offending subsequent to participation in restorative interventions as high as 23 % (Latimer et al. 2005). A body of research conducted in Australia has indicated that restorative justice disposals may not be as effective in preventing recidivism amongst aboriginal children, as they are amongst children

---

[13] See for example: Niemeyer, M. & Shichor, D. (1996) 'A Preliminary Study of a Large Victim/ Offender Reconciliation Programme'. *Federal Probation,* 60(3):30–34; Bradbury, B. (2002) Deschutes County Delinquent Youth Demonstration Project. Secretary of State Audit Report #2002-29 Salem, OR: Office of the Secretary of State; Roy, S. (1993) Two Types of Juvenile Restitution Programmes in Two Midwestern Counties: A Comparative Study. *Federal Probation,* 57(4): 48–53; Walker, L. (2002) Conferencing: A new approach for juvenile justice in Honolulu. *Federal probation, 66(1),* 38–43; Wilcox, A., Young, R. & Hoyle, C. (2004) An evaluation of the impact of restorative cautioning findings from a reconviction study. Research, Development & Statistics Directorate, Home Office: UK.

from dominant racial groups. For example, a 2011 study examining Australian Reintegrative Shaming Projects found that when data concerning the impact of restorative justice programmes on recidivism was disaggregated by ethnicity, significant differences were detected amongst reoffending rates for white and non-white children: whilst white children were found to be less likely to reoffend after participation in the programme, results were marginal for non-white youth (Kim and Gerber 2012; Centre for Restorative Justice 2011). There is evidence that in some situations the conference process may even be criminogenic for children from minority groups; particularly where conferences are organised by white police officers and/or involve white victims, which can expose children to stigmatisation and discrimination (Luke and Lind 2002; Strang and Sherman 2007). Some studies have indicated that white victims are less likely to agree to participate in a restorative process at all if the offender is from an ethnic minority (Umbreit et al. 2002), evidencing that racial biases do have an influence on the functioning of restorative programmes.

In an addition to ethnicity, other characteristics of offenders may influence rates of recidivism across different justice disposals (O'Mahony 2012). Research undertaken by Rodriguez in 2007 found that restorative justice programmes were significantly more successful in preventing recidivism amongst girls compared to boys. Furthermore, whilst children with no prior offence were considerably less likely to offend after participating in a restorative justice programmeme compared to the control group, this result was *reversed* for cases of children who had offended previously, as well as for those who had committed more "serious" offences (Rodrigez 2007). Similarly, a meta-analysis of 39 restorative justice studies conducted in 2006 found that associations between restorative justice and lower rates of recidivism were stronger amongst low-risk offenders (Bonta et al. 2006). In 2001 Maxwell and Morris conducted a study which demonstrated that amongst children who underwent a restorative justice disposal, those who experienced poverty and parental neglect were more likely to reoffend compared to others (Maxwell and Morris 2001a, b). These results indicate that restorative justice programmes might be less effective for groups of 'high risk' child offenders, who may require more intensive support (compared to 'low risk' offenders) (Kim and Gerber 2012). Interestingly, in 2013 Strang conducted a meta-analysis which found that restorative justice processes had more impact on preventing recidivism amongst *adults* compared to children. These findings contradict popular notions of restorative justice which often presume that restorative disposals are particularly (even only) suitable for children (Strang et al. 2013).

Restorative justice mechanisms may fail to prevent reoffending amongst the most vulnerable groups of children, because the restorative justice model is not oriented toward meaningfully identifying and addressing the root causes of *why* children offend in the first instance. Whilst restorative processes may result in an agreement that a child undergoes a rehabilitative programmeme to address their offending behaviour, this is neither inevitable nor the primary purpose of the restorative process, which is, rather, to repair the harm caused by the offence, most particularly to the victim. Furthermore, even when the restorative process does result in a reparations plan, this is immaterial if suitable referral services are not in place (Haines 1997). Restorative panellists interviewed as part of Stahlkopf's research in the UK emphasised that adequate local facilities and resources are crucial to the success of reintegrating and rehabilitating child offenders, but explained that many panels had difficulty devising a suitable plan for children because necessary services did not exist (Stahlkopf 2009).

For these reason, Haines has argued that restorative principles and methods are "severely limited by their failure to take seriously the needs and troubles of child offenders, and to find constructive solutions to them" (Haines 1997). A succinct analysis of the situation was provided by Morris when he pointed out that even the most restorative of meetings cannot "magically undo the years of social marginalisation and exclusion experienced by so many offenders" (Morris 2002, p. 605; Stahlkopf 2009, p. 240).[14] Even more concerning, there is some evidence that in particular contexts and circumstances the outcomes of restorative practices may not only fail to address a child's offending behaviour, but could even contribute to destabilising a child's situation further. For example, a recent assessment of the use of mediation in juvenile cases in Lao PDR found that: "for [poor] families, the compensation or other financial/material sanction [a typical outcome of mediation cases] was difficult to comply with... Some families had to borrow money, leading to family debt and [a] breakdown in relationships" (Barnes et al. 2013, p.4).

Poverty; poor parental practices (including the failure to provide boundaries, encouragement and support); lack of access to education or other opportunities; experiences of violence and abuse; learning and communication disabilities; mental health problems; social exclusion; and drug and alcohol addiction are some of the complex and challenging issues that underline child offending. Children who offend often require intensive and sustained support to achieve rehabilitation and reintegration into their families and communities. This is the point that perhaps presents the most serious challenge to the claims of the restorative justice movement. While it is argued that restorative techniques provide a rational, just and effective means of addressing and preventing youth offending, the theory and practice of restorative justice fails to grapple with and address the underlying vulnerabilities that drive many young people to offend. Restorative justice cannot address the structural and systemic cycles of disadvantage that so often pervade the realities and experiences of young offenders.

4 An Alternative Model: Family-Focused Programming

"*On the basis of the available evidence one has to question whether [the] failure to draw and agree upon a definition of restorative justice justifies the claims for a foundation of a new theory and approach*" (Haines 1997).

[14] A. Morris as quoted in Stahlkopf (2009), pp. 231–251.

Whilst there is evidence that restorative methods yield positive outcomes for many children, in other cases restorative processes may be at best unhelpful and at worst positively alienating and damaging, especially for the most marginalised, disadvantaged and troubled groups of children. This begs the question as to whether, on the basis of theory and evidence, 'restorative justice' principles and practices, really do provide the most appropriate solution for dealing with cases of child offending.

This section reviews evidence regarding an alternative model for addressing youth offending; sometimes known as the 'family-focused' model, or the 'juvenile justice alternatives programme' (JJAP), which may have potential to address many of the drawbacks and weaknesses of restorative justice mechanisms. These types of programmes are essentially treatment-based: most particularly concerned with understanding and addressing the community, social and family contexts which drive young people to offend. Interventions are focused on tackling the reasons behind, and causes of, a child's offending behaviour; recognising that many children who offend have been affected by poor parenting, and/or have experienced problems in school; many children may come from families deeply affected by poverty; others are runaways or orphans, and may be homeless or vulnerably housed.

This model of justice prioritises rehabilitative work with families, and other caregivers, alongside work with child offenders themselves, to prevent and address youth crime. Interventions aim to restore a child's family stability at home, to build better familial and other relationships, and to improve parenting skills and to raise the child's self-esteem and sense of self-worth. Programmes may incorporate restorative actions, such as mediation and conferencing, but only so far as these measures are likely to serve the primary purpose of reintegrating the child into society. This model is sophisticated in the sense that it recognises that a child's offending behaviour is not simply a matter of individual choice, but the product of broader structural factors which have serious implications for social justice (Haines 1997).

This section draws on (albeit limited) evidence gathered through a number of evaluations of programmes conducted in Azerbaijan, Georgia, Kazakhstan, Tajikistan and Tanzania, to draw tentative and preliminary conclusions about the potentialities and risks of these models for addressing juvenile offending. The studies depended on primarily qualitative methodologies, including the use of semi-structured interviews with children, parents and carers, juvenile justice professionals, social workers and others, and 'participant observation' techniques, such as observing activities at the projects and participating in group therapy and counselling sessions. Where available quantitative data was also collected concerning the number and characteristics of children being referred into the centres (file reviews), and on rates of youth offending and re-offending (data gathered from police departments, justice and social welfare bodies and others).

It is important to acknowledge from the outset, that the evidence that can be drawn from these studies is limited in a number of respects. Firstly, evaluations were conducted only 1–3 years after the projects' inceptions, so there is no evidence on the long-term impacts of the projects. Furthermore, in the light of the reliance on qualitative methodologies, the small samples used, and the absence of any control trials or comparison groups, the results of these studies cannot be used to make scientific claims that can be applied with precision to a broader population. Where relevant, however, reference is made to evaluations of other similar family focused models to determine likely outcomes.[15]

4.1 The Family Focused Programmes

> *"Work with families is very important, as improved family stability, the building of better familial relationships and improved parenting will lower the chances of a child re-offending"* (Anderson 2010, p. 32).

In each country context, the programmes were developed in order to establish a mechanism for the diversion of children out of the formal criminal justice system prior to trial, or as an alternative sentencing measure for child offenders after trial, with the aim of reducing rates of imprisonment and institutionalisation of children. The programmes also admit children who engage in 'anti-social' behaviour, or who are 'at risk' of offending. In each country context the intention was to develop and refine a model that could ultimately be integrated into the national criminal justice system and replicated throughout the country.

The primary function of the programmes is to provide rehabilitation and reintegration support to children and their families to prevent reoffending, through community-based programmes. Initially developed to provide a community-based alternative to custody, the children remain at home, or in provided accommodation (for those who are without parental care) throughout the rehabilitative process. Each project provides individual programmes, based on the needs and interests of each child and their family, identified through a social work assessment. These family focused programmes aim to provide a diverse range of services to children and their families over a sustained period, typically lasting anywhere from 3 to 6 months or if necessary, even longer. These services may include: group and one-to-one counselling for the child, family counselling, family conferences, mediation services, parenting skills training, remedial educational support, legal assistance, vocational training, arts and cultural activities, sports activities, game therapy, and other support. Usually children are able to select which educational courses, vocational training and activities they want to do and their personal programme is developed around this. However, some work, such as counselling, family work and

[15] See for instance, Ross, Duckworth, Smith, Whyness and Schoon, Prevention and Reducation: A review of strategies for intervening early to prevent or reduce youth crime and anti-social behaviour. Centre for Analysis of Youth Transitions DRF-RR111, 2011, UK and Review of Good Practices in Preventing Juvenile Crime in the European Union, European Crime Prevention Network, 2006.

life skills are mandatory. Parents, and other caregivers and guardians are viewed as key partners of the project workers, and their fundamental role in supporting the rehabilitation of the child is reinforced throughout the period that the child remains in the programme.

The programmes usually have a particular focus on supporting children to return to school, and improving their attendance and performance, as well as the child's self-esteem. In the case of older children, staff have endeavoured to link with local NGOs and services that support young people to find paid employment, or offer vocational training.

In each country, projects are being run by local civil society groups with support from local government authorities. All are located within either a youth centre or other similar activity centre. Referral to the projects may be made by police, prosecutors, by the courts, or by law enforcement or social welfare bodies, with a mandate for prevention and response with regard to youth offending.[16] As is the case for restorative justice programmes, in order for a child to be referred to a programme, they must acknowledge their guilt for the offence, and consent to participating in the programme. Consent is also required of the parents or guardian(s) of the offending child. Subsequent to referral, children, parents and guardians must also agree with the programme prepared by the staff, and sign a detailed plan of action.

4.2 *Evaluating Impact and Effectiveness: Family-Focused Model*

The evaluations (reviewed in this section) examined the impact of JJAP programmes in several respects: firstly they explored participants' subjective perceptions, attitudes and experiences of the programmes; secondly they examined the impact of the programmes in terms of reducing rates of recidivism amongst children; thirdly they explored the potential of these programmes to reduce the numbers of children entering the criminal justice system, and being placed in detention, a process commonly known as 'diversion'.

4.2.1 Perceptions and Experiences of JJAP Projects: Children and Their Families

Similar to evaluations of restorative justice programmes, the evaluations of the JJAP projects indicate that young people, as well as other stakeholders (including families of offenders, and criminal justice professionals) are inclined to speak positively about the programmes. Children reported that they were able to

[16] E.g. the Commission on Minors in Tajikistan and Azerbaijan, and social welfare staff Tanzania.

participate in the activities that were most interesting to them, and that that they were involved in developing programme plans; they also reported feeling 'listened to' and 'respected' by project staff. Parents also reported that they felt actively involved in planning the programme for their child and in the assessment process.

Significantly, during the evaluations participants not only expressed their satisfaction with the projects, but also typically identified a series of positive outcomes of the projects, which they directly related to their own feelings, experiences and behaviour. Benefits of the programmes, identified by children and their families, included: improved communication and relationships with others; greater family stability and cohesion; renewed interest in school and education and better performance in school; enhanced livelihoods opportunities through having gained new skills and developed levels of confidence; and overall increased levels of happiness and hope for the future. One child in Tanzania declared: "*when I am here, I feel like I might succeed. I have hope. When I was just at home, I felt like there was no hope*" (Anderson and Ross 2013, p. 38). Similarly another said: "*when I came to the project I gained a direction. Before I did not see a future and did not feel any hope for my life*" (Anderson and Ross, p. 39). As explored in the above sections, this is somewhat different to the evidence gathered from evaluations of restorative justice disposals. In the restorative justice programmes rates of reported 'satisfaction' with the process were typically high, but the research yielded less evidence that restorative measures are thought to actually benefit children on a personal level (Daly 2001; Stahlkopf 2009).

Children enrolled in the rehabilitative programmes were able to articulate clearly the ways in which the programme had a positive impact on their state of mind, behaviour and relationships with others. One boy in Azerbaijan described how having one-to-one counselling sessions had helped to relieve his stress and relax him (Anderson 2010, p. 35); a 17-year-old girl explained that talking to the psychologist 'comforted' her and helped her to 'understand things much better' (Anderson 2010, p. 36). A child in Tanzania told evaluators: "*I had an attitude problem. I was argumentative. Self-awareness classes helped me*" (Anderson and Ross 2013, p. 37), and another child engaged in conflict resolution classes claimed: "*I have changed a lot... now I don't have arguments with people at home, because we sit here and they teach us how not to argue*" (Anderson and Ross 2013, p. 37).

Many children expressed a reduced desire, or tendency to offend. For example, one 15 year old boy in Tanzania explained: "*when I was on the street I was doing nothing. I even stole from my parents and they took me to the police. I am changing my behaviour because I can now see what caused it, and now my environment has changed. I can see the difference in me. I want to get a job*" (Anderson and Ross 2013, p. 36); and another stated: "*I want to stop stealing and learn to read*" (Anderson and Ross 2013, p. 33). A child in Tajikistan described how the programme had made him "*kinder and more respectful of others*"; he said that he had learned how to communicate with others better, and how to make new friends (Ross 2008, p. 17).

Some children in Azerbaijan reported that an excursion to the juvenile colony, arranged by staff at the project, had helped them to understand the potential consequences of any future criminal activity. These findings fit with a recent meta-evaluation study conducted by the Centre for Analysis of Youth Transitions which concluded that programmes which encompass a holistic range of interventions (applied to address a multitude of different 'risk factors') are more likely to be effective at reducing children's offending behaviour than other types of justice disposals that adopt a more singular strategy (Ross et al. 2010, p. 3).

Many children referred to gaining new skills and education as a central positive outcome of the programme; and spoke of how this had led to a change in outlook and renewed positivity about the future: "[*the project*] *has changed my behaviour and has given me skills. I make batik and handcrafts and I like tailoring*" (Anderson and Ross 2013, p. 38). Children in Azerbaijan explained that the JJAP's pedagogue had helped them to achieve better in school, and appreciated access to facilities like computers. One child reported he had been referred by the centre to a hairdressing apprenticeship and spoke favourably of this (Anderson 2010, p. 33). A child enrolled in the JJAP in Tanzania reported: "*it is good here and I am happier. I am learning lessons that I did not understand in school and I have made friends;*" (Anderson and Ross 2013, p. 38) and another told evaluators: "*I used to be rude and I stole a radio, shoes and stuff like that. The project…has created a good environment for me to progress. I am now attending VETA to do a cookery course and I intend to build my future as a cook in a hotel*" (Anderson and Ross 2014, p. 40).

These findings were also backed up from the testimony of parents, grandparents, guardians and others interviewed during the evaluations, such as law enforcement personnel. One police officer in Tajikistan insisted: "*when you see the child after (finishing the programme at) the JJAP, you will immediately notice that this is someone else….someone different now. He visits school again and then he starts to attend school again. You see their intellect, how he behaves, how he or she treats the classmates, peers, teachers. It is very good*" (Ross 2008, p. 20). Many parents reported that following referral to the programme their child had become more motivated to attend school regularly and complete their homework. A parent in Tajikistan explained that prior to referral his son was 'not interested' in school (Ross 2008, p. 18); following attendance at the programme, however, he became motivated to study and particularly developed his skills in writing and drawing (Ross 2008). One parent in Azerbaijan remarked that her son had been having a lot of difficulty at school, but after completing his plan at the programme, he was able to read and write and keep up in class. Another parent reported that her son had an increased understanding of the ramifications of his criminal actions, and his behaviour had noticeably improved (Anderson 2010, p. 35).

Parents also expressed appreciation for the support provided to them through the projects. They reported that social work inputs had helped them care for and communicate more effectively with their children, and learn new parenting skills. Parents receiving support from the programme in Tajikistan explained that they had a renewed understanding of the importance of giving their children regular attention and praise (Ross 2008). In Tanzania, parents reported that the project helped them establish more consistency in disciplining their children, and how to use less harmful disciplinary practices (Anderson and Ross 2013). In Azerbaijan, one

mother described the parenting advice provided to her through the programme as 'invaluable', supporting her to work together with her son to improve his behaviour, and strengthening the relationship between them. Another mother spoke of how the programme had helped her claim the social benefit support she was entitled to; whilst a third reported that the centre had helped her find a job. In general, parents reported that staff contact was regular and supportive, and that it helped them to understand their child better (Anderson 2010).

Children also noted a change in their parents' and guardians' behaviour, and confirmed that relationships at home were considerably improved. One child in Tanzania explained: "*my grandmother has changed. Before, if I refused to do something, she'd deny me food. Now she never denies me food - even if I disobey her*" (Anderson and Ross 2013, p. 35); whilst another reported: "*previously, sitting talking with my parents was difficult. They used to look down on me as a child who was worthless and with nothing to say. Now my parents are eager to spend time with me*" (Anderson and Ross 2013, p. 41). Similarly a child in Azerbaijan reported: "*my father has also changed [as well as me]. He doesn't yell at me or beat me now. Because of the way the staff talk to him*" (Anderson 2010, p. 35).

Despite these encouraging findings, there is need for more evidence on the long term benefits of the programmes. Whilst children and parents may feel positively about the services that they have received whilst they are still enrolled in the programme, or shortly after leaving, it remains to be seen whether these positive effects will last, and what the long term opportunities for these children will be. Several young offenders in Azerbaijan, for example, appeared unsure about their future goals after leaving the programme, and did not appear to have received a good level of assistance in securing further education, vocational training or employment (although these children did speak favourably about the Centre) (Anderson 2010). Furthermore, the majority of programme professionals expressed the view that 3–6 months is not enough time to rehabilitate some of the children referred to the project, especially those with more complex needs, and a number of stakeholders expressed concern that there is little aftercare provided to children following their completion of the programme (Anderson and Ross 2013).

4.2.2 Rates of Recidivism

The evaluations conducted in Azerbaijan, Georgia, Kazakhstan, Tajikistan and Tanzania include information about rates of reoffending amongst children who have attended the programmes. In each case reported rates of reoffending are strikingly low. The evaluation report notes that in Tajikistan, most juvenile justice disposals (within and around the project areas) have a reoffending rate of between 30 and 40 % (Ross 2008) but less than 3 % of the children referred to the rehabilitation programmes were found to have reoffended at the time of conducting the evaluation (2 year after the start of the programme). In Azerbaijan, of the 102 children included in the evaluation, only 2 had reoffended subsequent to leaving the programme (Anderson 2010). Similarly only 2 of the 120 children who participated the Tanzania programme had committed further offences after 2 years (Anderson and Ross 2014). Finally, according to the Kazakhstan evaluation of 150 children enrolled in the programme, *none* went on to reoffend; however, the evaluation report qualifies this finding by acknowledging that this data relies solely on the testimony of judges in the specialised children's court, who would not necessarily be informed about re-offending cases that were disposed with outside of court, or reoffending of children who turned 18 years subsequent to leaving the programme (Syidov 2012). The same low level of reoffending is evident in the programmes in Georgia.

Across all five studies, the evidence in relation to rates of reoffending must be treated with caution: it is incontrovertibly insufficient to draw reliable conclusions about the impact of family focused programmes on reducing recidivism amongst children. Aside from significant methodological limitations presented by the lack of a control trial or comparison group, and the limitations associated with the timings of the evaluations, it is also important to acknowledge that children enrolled in the programmes are not representative of a broader group of children who come into conflict with the law. In each country context, data concerning referrals and enrolment into the programmes revealed that children who attend these programmes are overwhelmingly those who have committed first time, minor offences, and in some cases had not offended at all, but were referred to the projects for being 'at risk' of offending. In Azerbaijan, a number of referring bodies reported that children who had already reoffended, and those who had committed a 'serious' offence would never be considered for referral to the programme; 'serious' offences appeared to be defined very broadly to include even cases of petty theft (Anderson 2010, p. 19). Similarly, the evaluations in Tanzania identified a number of barriers to referral into the project including (amongst others) that the child did not admit guilt, the child did not have a place to live, and that the child had committed an offence that was perceived as 'too serious' for referral to the scheme (Anderson and Ross 2013). This may indicate that those children who may be most likely to reoffend are also those who are least likely to be participating in the programme in the first instance. In other words, as with much of the evidence in relation to restorative justice programmes, there is a significant selection bias which underlies the results in relation to rates of recidivism amongst children participating in the programme. However, it should be acknowledged, that as the programmes have become more experienced they have increasingly taken children who have committed more serious offences, meanwhile, rates of reoffending have (to date) not increased.

4.2.3 Diversion of Children Out of the Formal Criminal Justice System

As with restorative programmes, one of the main goals and justifications for the family focused programmes is to provide a means to ensure that children in conflict with the law are directed out of the criminal justice system, and referred to rehabilitative services; instead of being subject to the formality of an adversarial trial, and a potential custodial sentence.

In all country contexts, the research revealed some evidence that the programmes are playing an important role in this respect; mainly due to the fact that there are few alternative services. The evaluation in Tajikistan revealed that there are very few options that provide an effective response to child offending. Prosecutors and judges interviewed in all regions stated that the only real alternative to referral to the programmes is the imposition of an institutional sentence, including placing children in custody or in a correctional 'school'. The evaluation study concludes therefore, that: 'the lack of effective options for resolving cases of children who come into conflict with the law serves to highlight the importance of the programmes' (Ross 2008). In Tanzania professionals described the project as 'necessary', and noted that it filled a 'gap in the system', providing for children's rehabilitation in the community rather than in custody (Anderson and Ross 2013, p. 13). In Azerbaijan, interviewees reported that if the programmes did not exist, it was likely that 'unmanageable' children would be referred to a closed institution (Anderson 2010). There was also evidence of the project being used as a direct alternative to institutionalisation. For example, one 8 year-old boy, arrested for making a bomb threat to a local hospital, was initially recommended by the prosecutor for referral to a 'special school'. Due to intervention by programme staff, however, in the end a decision was made to refer the boy to the programme. The mother of the child expressed her gratitude for the project staff, and reported that since attending the centre her son had learned to read and write and had "*opened his eyes to the world*" (Anderson 2010, p. 43).

Despite the diversionary purpose of the programmes, it is important to acknowledge that in practice many children are enrolled in the project as a preventative measure, rather than as a means of diversion out of the criminal justice system. In Azerbaijan only 35 % of all children referred to the programme had actually committed an offence, and the majority of these were minor offences, a further 4 % of children had committed an administrative offence, whilst the majority of children (61 %) were referred for 'anti-social' behaviour, truancy from school, running away from home, or because of problems at home (Anderson 2010). Similarly in Tajikistan only 33 % of children referred to the project had committed an offence, with the majority of children, and as many as 80 % in one project site, were referred for 'anti-social behaviour', defined by referred bodies as including truanting or dropping out of school, working in the informal sector (e.g. washing cars or working at the market), children involved in conflict within the family, or children living on the street. Many of these 'at risk' children were affected by poor parenting and poverty and some had previously run away from home (Ross 2008). In this sense the projects are serving an important function: providing secondary and tertiary level preventive services to vulnerable and 'at risk' children to prevent them coming into conflict with the law.

Nevertheless, there is need for caution here: that this shift from a diversionary approach to an increasingly 'interventionist' (preventative) practice does not lend weight to the increasing problematisation, even criminalisation, of childhood and adolescent behaviour. This is a critique that has similarly been levelled against the use of restorative justice for ‘at risk’ children, and those accused of committing minor offences. Haines has expressed concern that the targets of juvenile justice interventionist programmes are often not serious, ‘heavy end’ offenders, but minor offenders and those who may have not yet committed an offence; arguing that this approach feeds into narratives about youth criminality and can lead to culture of ‘zero tolerance’ policing (Haines 1997). There are concerns about whether these sorts of interventions are proportionate, and whether they might result in a ‘net-widening’ effect, drawing increasing numbers of children into contact with law enforcement agencies and the criminal justice system more broadly (O’Mahony 2012).

Of course this is not to say that vulnerable children should not be receiving services; but the question is whether it is appropriate for support services to be delivered through interventions primarily introduced as alternatives and ‘adjuncts’ to the criminal justice system (Haines 1997). As the evaluation in Tajikistan acknowledges, “Children referred [to the programme] for preventative work may benefit from referral to community centres rather than the programme”, and that ‘the programmes were established to deal with the complex needs of children who have committed criminal offences severe enough that they would normally be exposed to the formal criminal justice system’. Some stakeholders in Georgia expressed concern that: “*mixing convicted juveniles with children who have not even entered the justice system [is not necessarily] in the ‘best interests’ of both categories of juveniles.*”[17] They also pointed out that such a perspective assumes ‘at risk’ children will not have access to services through horizontal services focused on delivering child protection services to vulnerable children (Anderson 2009). Finally the Kazakhstan evaluation notes ‘[there may be] a degree of unnecessary ‘problematizing’ of some of the children’ (Syidov 2012).

5 Conclusions and Key Questions for Policy

Restorative approaches to child justice have much to recommend them. A review of the theory and empirical evidence suggests that restorative justice practices do have the potential to provide positive outcomes for those affected by juvenile crime. Whilst there is a need for more evidence from middle and low income countries, a body of research in high income contexts has demonstrated that a range of restorative practices have in many circumstances provided a rational, fair and effective response to juvenile offending.

Nevertheless, these strategies are not without their limitations, particularly in their application to cases of juvenile offending. As Sect. 1 of this chapter explores, there is a subtle tension between the victim-centred character of restorative justice

[17] UNICEF child protection specialist, December, 2009.

theory; and child rights precepts which establish that the best interests of child offenders should be a primary consideration in all decisions concerning the treatment of children in conflict with the law. (A tension which reflects a deeper contradiction contained within the discourse of restorative justice itself: that it draws upon the traditional concepts and values of criminal justice, whilst simultaneously rejecting them) (Johnstone 2004, 2011; Pavlich 2005). Section 2 expounds evidence which suggests that restorative disposals often fail to address the needs of some of the most vulnerable and disadvantaged children who offend; and that there is often considerable gap between the values and ideals of restorative justice, and their realisation in practice.

Section 3 presents an alternative model: which takes a holistic approach, to rehabilitating child offenders, focused on service provision, social work, and therapeutic activities with children, and (most importantly) with their caregivers and broader families. This model is more expensive than common forms of restorative justice and more labour intensive, requiring a far greater level of professional and community input; but it is arguably more useful for addressing the root causes of child offending and finding constructive solutions to these, compared to a typical restorative disposal or approach. The family-focused model is founded on the recognition that juvenile crime is not only a matter of individual choice, but also the consequence of broader social injustices and inequalities, and that these are vital considerations for any (new) model of justice.

The family focussed model of justice is still in its infancy. There are very few examples of these models, and few studies that have sought to evaluate their effectiveness and impact. Nevertheless, the early indications of the empirical evidence are highly encouraging. As international focus shifts towards prevention of crime rather than dealing with its consequences, now is the moment for a systematic study exploring the impact of a family focussed approach, and the extent to which it can complement, and address some of the drawbacks and gaps presented by restorative justice disposals.

Five Questions

1. Is restorative justice theory—with its focus on the needs of victims—an appropriate framework to apply to cases of juvenile offending? Does this framework have the capacity to address the types of offences most commonly committed by children, their causes and their contexts? For example, how would a child from a difficult background make reparations for using illegal drugs?
2. Are there any risks for children associated with the informal nature of restorative justice disposals, and how do we safeguard against these? What measures can be put in place to ensure that restorative disposals do not end up reproducing harmful power dynamics and inequalities between adults and children?
3. Does a 'treatment' based model, such as the family focused model, have more potential to address the root causes of juvenile crime, as well as rehabilitating juvenile offenders? Do we have enough evidence to roll out such a model on a wider scale? Given that these programmes are likely to be more expensive as they last for longer and are more labour intensive than restorative justice

disposals, what outcomes should be required to justify the costs? How do we measure these?

4. Is there likely to be political resistance to the idea of rolling out the family focused model more widely, particularly for children who commit more serious offences? Is there a chance that some actors could perceive these models as 'rewarding' and 'encouraging' criminal behaviour amongst children, especially where part of the programme is to ensure that children participate in activities, such as drama, cultural events and sports activities? If the family focused model is considered to be a rational and constructive means for addressing juvenile offending, how could the type of political resistance be overcome and addressed?
5. As international focus shifts towards the 'prevention' of juvenile crime, how do we ensure that this doesn't lead to an increasingly 'interventionist' approach to juvenile justice which problematises, and even criminalises, ordinary adolescent behaviour. Why are children who end up in alternative justice disposals (restorative justice as well as family focused programmes) so often children who have only committed very minor offences, or who have never offended at all but have been referred for (so-called) 'anti-social' behaviour, or for being 'at risk' of offending? What do we mean by these terms? Is this cause for concern? What are the implications of this, and are any risks (associated with this 'preventative' practice and approach) being seriously considered and addressed at the policy level?

References

Alder, C., & Wundersitz, J. (1994). Family conferencing and juvenile justice: The way forward or misplaced optimism? In C. Alder & J. Wundersitz (Eds.), *Family conferencing and juvenile justice: The way forward or misplaced optimism?* (pp. 15–44). Australian Institute of Criminology: Canberra.

Anderson, A. (2009). *Mid-term evaluation of the juvenile justice support service project (Georgia)*. London: Coram Children's Legal Centre.

Anderson, A. (2010). *Azerbaijan juvenile justice system consultation: Evaluation of Rehabilitation Centre and Legal Clinic*. London: Coram Children's Legal Centre.

Anderson, A., & Ross, G. (2013). *Temeke community rehabilitation programmeme: First year evaluation*. London: Coram Children's Legal Centre.

Anderson, K., & Ross, G. (2014). *Temeke community rehabilitation programmeme: Second year evaluation*. London: Coram Children's Legal Centre.

Apland, K., & Raoof, A. (2014). *Analysis of the justice system in Lao PDR as it relates to children in conflict and in contact with the law*. London: Coram Children's Legal Centre.

Barnes, R., Hamilton, H., & Apland, K. (2013). *Assessment of existing mediation practices involving children in Lao PDR*. London: Coram Children's Legal Centre.

Bazemore, G., & Walgrave, L. (1999). Restorative juvenile justice: In search of fundamentals and an outline for systemic reform. In G. Bazemore & L. Walgrave (Eds.), *Restorative juvenile justice: Repairing the harm of youth crime* (pp. 45–74). Monsey, NY: Criminal Justice Press.

Bergseth, K., & Bouffard, J. (2012). Examining the effectiveness of a restorative justice programme for various types of juvenile offenders. *International Journal of Offender Therapy and Comparative Criminology, 58*(7), 1054–1075.

Blagg, H. (2001). Aboriginal youth and restorative justice: Critical notes from the Australian Frontier. In A. Morris & G. Maxwell (Eds.), *Restorative justice for juveniles: Conferencing, mediation and circles* (p. 230). Oxford: Hart Publishing.

Bonta, J., Jesseman, R., Rugge, T., & Cormier, R. (2006). Restorative justice and recidivism. Promises made, promises kept? In D. Sullivan & L. Tift (Eds.), *Handbook of restorative justice* (pp. 108–120). Oxon, UK: Routledge.

Bradshaw, B., & Roseborough, D. (2005). Restorative justice dialogue: The impact of mediation and conferencing on juvenile recidivism. *Federal Probation, 69*(2), 15–21.

Braithwaite, J. (2004). Restorative justice: Theories and worries. In: UNAFEI (Ed.), *Restorative justice: Theories and worries – resource material series No. 63* (pp. 47–56). Japan: UNAFEI.

Braithwaite, J. (2003). The evolution of restorative justice. In: UNAFEI (Ed.), *Restorative justice: Theories and worries – resource material series No. 63* (pp. 37–46). Japan: UNAFEI.

Braithwaite, J. (1997). Assessing an immodest theory and a pessimistic theory. In M. Tonry (Ed.), *Crime and justice: An annual review of research* (Vol. 25). Chicago: University of Chicago Press.

Braithwaite, J., & Strang, H. (2001). Introduction: Restorative justice and civil society. In H. Strang & J. Braithwaite (Eds.), *Restorative justice and civil society*. Cambridge, UK: Cambridge University Press.

Cameron, A. (2006). Stopping the violence: Canadian feminist debates on restorative justice and intimate violence. *Theoretical Criminology, 10*, 49.

Centre for Restorative Justice (2011). *Reintergrative Shaming Experiments (RISE),* Available at: http://www.aic.gov.au/criminal_justice_system/rjustice/rise.html. Accessed on 12th November 2014.

Choi, J. J., Green, D. L., & Gilbert, M. J. (2011). Putting a human face on crimes: A qualitative study on restorative justice processes for youths. *Child Adolescent Social Work Journal, 28*, 335–355.

Christe, N. (1977). Conflicts as property. *British Journal of Criminology, 17*(1), 1–15.

Coyle, E. M., & Pun, E. (2009). *Withdrawn: Why complainants withdraw rape cases in Namibia*. Namibia: Legal Assistance Centre.

Cretney, A., & Davis, G. (1995). *Punishing violence*. London: Routledge.

Criminal Justice Review Group. (1998). *Review of the criminal justice system in Northern Ireland: A consultation paper*. Belfast: HMSO.

Daly, K. (2001). Conferencing in Australia and New Zealand: Variations, research findings and prospects. In A. Morris & G. Maxwell (Eds.), *Restorative justice for juveniles: Conferencing, mediation and circles* (p. 243). Oxford: Hart Publishing.

Daly, K. (2002). Restorative justice: the true story. *Punishment and Society, 4*(1), 55–79.

Daly, K. (2006). The limits of restorative justice. In D. Sullivan & L. Tifft (Eds.), *Handbook of restorative justice: A global perspective* (pp. 134–145). Oxford: Routeledge.

Doak, J., & O'Mahony, D. (2011). In search of legitimacy: Restorative youth conferencing in Northern Ireland. *Legal Studies, 31*(2), 312.

Doolin, K. (2007). But what does it mean? Seeking definitional clarity in restorative justice. *The Journal of Criminal Law, 71*(5), 427–440.

Duckworth, K., Ross, A., Schoon, I., Smith, D., & Wyness, G. (2011). *Prevention and reduction: A review of strategies for intervening early to prevent or reduce youth crime and anti-social behaviour*. London: Department for Education. available at: https://www.gov.uk/government/uploads/system/uploads/attachment_data/file/182548/DFE-RR111.pdf [accessed 7 October 2014].

Duff, R. (2002). Restorative punishment and punitive restoration. In L. Walgrave (Ed.), *Restorative justice and the law* (pp. 82–100). Cullompton, Devon, UK: Willan Publishing.

Evje, A., & Cushman, R. (2000). *A summary of the evaluations of six California offender reconciliation programmes*. California: The Judicial Council of California.

Falshaw, L. (2005). The link between a history of maltreatment and subsequent offending behaviour. *Probation Journal, 52*, 423–434.

Feasy, S., & Williams, P. (2009). *An evaluation of the Sycamore Tree programmeme: based on an analysis of Crime Pics II data. Project Report.* Sheffield: Sheffield Hallam University, available at: http://shura.shu.ac.uk/1000/1/fulltext.pdf [accessed 14 October 2014].

Fercello, C., & Umbreit, M. (1999). *Client satisfaction with victim-offender conferences in Dakota County, Minnesota.* St. Paul, MN: Center for Restorative Justice & Mediation, University of Minnesota.

Fitzgerald, J. (2008). Does circle sentencing reduce aboriginal offending? *Crime and Justice Bulletin, 115,* 1–12 [Online]. Available at: http://www.bocsar.nsw.gov.au/agdbasev7wr/bocsar/documents/pdf/cjb115.pdf [accessed: 12th November 2014].

Gabbay, Z. (2005). Justifying restorative justice: A theoretical justification for the use of restorative justice practices. *Journal of Dispute Resolution, 2*, 354.

Gal, T., & Moyal, S. (2011). Juvenile victims in restorative justice: Findings from the reintegrative shaming experiments. *British Journal of Criminology, 51*, 1014–1034.

Haines, K. (1997). Some principled objections to a restorative justice approach to working with juvenile offenders. In L. Walgrave (Ed.), *Restorative justice for juveniles: Potentials, risks and problems* (pp. 91–113). Leuven: Leuven University Press.

Huang, H., & Chang, L. (2013). Evaluating restorative justice programmes in Taiwan. *Asian Criminology, 8*, 287–307.

Johnstone, G. (2003). *A restorative justice reader: Texts, sources and context.* Devon: Willan Publishing.

Johnstone, G. (2004). How, and in what terms, should restorative justice be conceived? In H. Zehr & B. Toews (Eds.), *Critical issues in restorative justice* (pp. 5–15). Devon: Criminal Justice Publishing.

Johnstone, G. (Ed.). (2011). *Restorative justice: Ideas, values, debates* (2nd ed.). London: Routledge.

Karp, D., Sweet, D., Kirshenbaum, A., & Bazemore, G. (2005). Reluctant participants in restorative justice? Youthful offenders and their parents. *Contemporary Justice Review, 7*(2), 199–216.

Kim, H. J., & Gerber, J. (2012). The effectiveness of reintegrative shaming and restorative justice conferences: Focusing on juvenile offenders' perceptions in Australian reintegrative shaming experiments. *International Journal of Offender Therapy and Comparative Criminology, 56*(7), 1063–1079.

Larson, J. J. (2014). Restorative Justice in the Criminal Justice System, *AIC Research and Public Policy Series,* Australian Institute of Criminology, available at http://www.aic.gov.au/media_library/publications/rpp/rpp127.pdf [accessed 21 December 2014].

Latimer, J., Dowden, C., & Muise, D. (2005). The effectiveness of restorative justice practices. *The Prison Journal, 85*(2), 127–144.

Levrant, S., Cullen, F., Fulton, B., & Wozniak, J. (1999). Reconsidering restorative justice. The corruption of benevolence revisited. *Crime and Delinquency, 45*(1), 3–27.

Lilles, H. (2001) Circle sentencing: Part of the restorative justice continuum. In: A. Morris, G. Maxwell (ed.) *Restorative justice for juveniles: Conferencing, mediation and circles* (pp. 161–179). Oxford - Portland, Oregon: Hart Publishing.

Llewellyn, J., & Howse, R. (1998). *Restorative justice: A conceptual framework.* Ottawa: Law Commission of Canada.

Luke, G., & Lind, B. (2002).Reducing Juvenile Crime: Conferencing versus Court, *Crime and Justice Bulletin: Contemporary Issues in Crime and Punishment,* 69, available at: http://www.bocsar.nsw.gov.au/agdbasev7wr/bocsar/documents/pdf/cjb69.pdf [accessed 14 October 2013].

Marshall, T. (1999). *Restorative justice: An overview.* London: Research Development and Statistics Directorate.

Maxwell, A., & Morris, A. (1993). Juvenile justice in New Zealand: A new paradigm. *Australian and New Zealand Journal of Criminology, 26*(1), 72–90.

Maxwell, G., & Morris, A. (2001a). Family group conferencing and reoffending. In A. Morris & G. Maxwell (Eds.), *Restorative justice for juveniles: Conferencing* (p. 243). Mediation and Circles, Oxford: Hart Publishing.

Maxwell, G., & Morris, A. (Eds.). (2001b). *Restorative justice for juveniles: Conferencing.* Mediation and Circles, Oxford: Hart Publishing.

McAlinden, A. (2008). Restorative justice as a response to sexual offending – Addressing the failings of current punitive approaches. *Sexual Offender Treatment, 3*(1), 3.

McCold, P., & Wachtel, B. (1998). *Restorative policing experiment: The Bethlehem Pennsylvania police family group conferencing project.* Pipersville, PA: Community Service Foundation.

McDonald, E., & Tinsley, Y. (2013). *From 'real rape' to real justice: Prosecuting rape in New Zealand.* Wellington: Victoria University Press. available at: http://www.lawcom.govt.nz/sites/default/files/restorative_justice_frrtrj_pp_414-423.pdf [accessed 3 October 2014].

Morris, A. (2002). Critiquing the critics. *British Journal of Criminology, 42*, 596–615.

Morris, A., & Maxwell, G. (1998). Restorative justice in New Zealand: Family group conferencing as a case study. *Western Criminology Review, 1*(1), 1–16.

National Commission on Restorative Justice Northern Ireland. (2009). Final Report available at: http://www.justice.ie/en/JELR/NCRJ%20Final%20Report.pdf/Files/NCRJ%20Final%20Report.pdf. Accessed October 2014.

Nugent, W., Williams, M., & Umbreit, M. (2004). Participation in victim-offender mediation and the prevalence of subsequent delinquent behaviour: A meta analysis. *Research on Social Work Practice, 14*(6), 408–416.

O'Mahony, D. (2012). Restorative justice in England and Wales: Two steps forward, one step back. *Nottingham Law Journal, 21*, 86–106.

Office of the Special Representative of SSRG (2013). Promoting Restorative Justice for Children, New York: Office of the Special Representative of SSRG, available at: http://srsg.violenceagainstchildren.org/sites/default/files/publications_final/srsgvac_restorative_justice_for_children_report.pdf [accessed 10 Nov 2014].

Pavlich, G. (2005). *Governing paradoxes of restorative justice* (p. 14). London: Glass House Press.

Restorative Justice Council (2011). *Summary of the Ministry of Justice Restorative Justice Research* available at http://www.restorativejustice.org.uk/resource/mojresearch/ [accessed: 21 December 2014].

Rodrigez, N. (2007). Restorative justice at work: Examining the impact of restorative justice resolutions on juvenile recidivism. *Crime and Delinquency, 53*(3), 359.

Ross, A., Duckworth, K., Smith, D., Wyness, G., Schoon, I. (2010). *Prevention and reduction: A review of strategies for intervening early to prevent or reduce youth crime and anti-social behaviour.* Research Report DFE-RR111.

Ross, G. (2008). *Promoting children's rights in the juvenile justice system in the Republic of Tajikistan: Evaluation of the juvenile justice alternatives projects.* London: Coram Children's Legal Centre.

Rossner, M. (2008). Victims and offenders and reducing crime: A critical assessment of restorative justice practice and theory. *Sociology Compass, 2*(6), 1734–1749.

Syidov, N. (2012) *Assessment of the Pilot Programme operated in Astana by the NGO 'Chance'.* Kazakhstan: UNICEF.

Shapland, J., Atkinson, A., Atkinson, H., Chapman, B., Colledge, E., Dignan, J., et al. (2006). *A restorative justice in practice: The second report from the evaluation of three schemes.* Sheffield: Centre for Criminological Research, University of Sheffield.

Sharpe, S. (2004). How large should the restorative justice 'tent' be? In H. Zehr & B. Toews (Eds.), *Critical issues in restorative justice* (pp. 18–31). Devon: Criminal Justice Publishing.

Sherman, L., Strang, H., & Woods, D. (2000). *Recidivism patterns in the Canberra reintegrative shaming experiments (RISE).* Canberra: Centre for Restorative Justice, Australian National University.

Shewan, G. (2010). The Business Case for Restorative Justice and Policing, Restorative Justice Council. Available at http://www.restorativejustice.org.uk/resource/the_business_case_for_restorative_justice_and_policing/ [accessed: 21 December 2014].

Stahlkopf, C. (2009). Restorative justice, rhetoric, or reality? Conferencing with young offenders. *Contemporary Justice Review, 12*(3), 231–251.

Strang, H., & Sherman, L. (2003). Repairing the harm: Victims and restorative justice. *Utah Law Review, 1*, 15–42.

Strang, H., & Sherman, L. (2007). *Restorative justice: The evidence*. London: The Smith Institute.

Strang, H., Sherman, L., Milson-Mayo, E., Woods, D., & Ariel, B. (2013) Restorative Justice Conferencing (RJC) Using Face-to-Face Meetings of Offenders and Victims: Effects on Offender Recidivism and Victims Satisfaction. A Systematic Review, Available at: http://www.campbellcollaboration.org/lib/project/63/ [accessed 9 October 2014].

Tadesse, B., Tesfaye, Y., & Beyene, F. (2010). Women in conflict and indigenous conflict resolution among the Issa and Gurgura Clans of Somali in Eastern Ethiopia. *African Journal on Conflict Resolution, 10*(1), 85–110.

Umbreit, M. (2000). *Family group conferencing: Implications for crime victims*. USA: DIANE Publishing.

Umbreit, M. (2001). *The handbook of victim offender mediation: An essential guide to practice and research* (p. xliv). San Francisco: Jossey-Bass Inc Publishers.

Umbreit, M., Coates, R., & Vos, B. (2004). Victim-offender mediation: Three decades of practice and research. *Conflict Resolution Quarterly, 22*, 279–303.

Umbreit, M., Coates, R., & Vos, B. (2002) The Impact of Restorative Justice Conferencing: A Review of 63 Empirical Studies in 5 Countries, available at: http://www.cehd.umn.edu/ssw/rjp/resources/rj_dialogue_resources/Restorative_Group_Conferencing/Impact_RJC_Review_63_Studies.pdf [accessed 7 October 2014].

UN General Assembly, *Convention on the Rights of the Child*, 20 November 1989, United Nations, Treaty Series, vol. 1577, p. 3, available at: http://www.refworld.org/docid/3ae6b38f0.html [accessed 12 November 2014].

United Nations High Commissioner for Human Rights (OHCHR). *Access to justice for children*. UNGA A/HRC/25/35, December 16, 2013.

United Nations Office on Drugs and Crime (1999). *Handbook on justice for victims*. United Nations Office for Drug Control and Crime Prevention, Centre for International Crime Prevention.

United Nations Office on Drugs and Crime (2006). *Handbook on Restorative Justice Programmes. Criminal Justice Handbook Series*. New York, available at: http://www.unodc.org/pdf/criminal_justice/06-56290_Ebook.pdf [accessed 3 October 2014].

Van Ness, D. (2010). Encounter. In K. H. Strong (Ed.), *Restoring justice: An introduction to restorative justice* (p. 84). Waltham: Anderson Publishing.

Van Ness, D., Morris, A., & Maxwell, G. (2001). Introducing restorative justice. In A. Morris & G. Maxwell (Eds.), *Restorative justice for juveniles: Conferencing* (pp. 3–12). Mediation and Circles, Oxford: Hart Publishing.

Van Ness, D., & Strong, K. (1997). *Restoring justice*. Ohio: Anderson Publishing Co.

Walgrave, L. (2002). Restorative justice and the law: Socio-ethical and juridical foundations for a systemic approach. In L. Walgrave (Ed.), *Restorative justice and the law* (pp. 191–218). Cullompton: Willan Publishing.

Webber, A. (2012). Youth justice conferences versus children's court: A comparison of cost-effectiveness. *Contemporary Issues in Crime and Justice* no. 164. Sydney: NSW Bureau of Crime Statistics and Research.

Weitekamp, G. (2001). Mediation in Europe: Paradoxes, problems and promises. In A. Morris & G. Maxwell (Eds.), *Restorative justice for juveniles: Conferencing* (pp. 145–160). Mediation and Circles, Oxford: Hart Publishing.

Wheeldon, J. (2009). Finding common ground: Restorative justice and its theoretical construction (s). *Contemporary Justice Review, 12*(1), 91–100.

Zehr, H. (1985). Retributive Justice, Restorative Justice, *New perspectives on Crime and Justice series,* Occasional Paper No. 4, MCC Canada Victim Offender Ministries Programme and MCC US Office of Crime and Justice.

Zehr, H. (1990). *Changing lenses: A new focus for crime and justice*. Canada: Herald Press.

Zehr, H. (1995). *Changing lenses: A new focus for crime and justice*. Scottdale: Herald Press.

Zehr, H. in Shuck, J. (2014). *Restorative Justice.* (podcast) Religion for life. Available at: http://religionforlife.podomatic.com/entry/2014-03-06T09_46_05-08_00 [accessed 10 Nov. 2014].

Peacemaking Circles, Their Restorative and Crime Prevention Capacities for Women and Children: Insights from a European Pilot Study

Beate Ehret, Dora Szego, and Davy Dhondt

Abstract Peacemaking or Healing circles are an approach to conflict resolution with long historical roots in many indigenous cultures going back to their so-called "talking circles." Particularly the circle tradition of First Nation people of Canada has been further developed and cultivated for dealing with crime, leading to their use in juvenile and criminal justice as well as their spread across the border to Northern US, Hawaii and as far as Australia (often referred to as sentencing circles in these contexts). This chapter is based on an international pilot study (This research project took place during the period of September 1st, 2011 to August 31st, 2013 with the Criminology Institute of the University of Tuebingen as the project coordinator and was made possible thanks to the financial support of the European commission's Criminal Justice Framework.) implementing circles for the first time in three European countries: Germany, Belgium and Hungary and offers further insights gained within this framework about their restorative capacities for victims and offenders as well as their crime prevention potentials. These insights are laid out and discussed with a specific focus on the potential benefits of Peacemaking circles for women and children as victims or offenders.

1 Introduction: What's "New" or Different About Restorative Justice?

"Because crime hurts, justice should heal". John Braithwaite (2004)

B. Ehret (✉)
Federal College of Public Administration, Wiesbaden, Germany
e-mail: beate.ehret@gmail.com

D. Szego
Corvinus University Budapest, Budapest, Hungary
e-mail: szegodori@gmail.com

D. Dhondt
Suggnomè and Katholieke University of Leuven, Leuven, Belgium
e-mail: davy.dhondt@suggnome.be

H. Kury et al. (eds.), *Women and Children as Victims and Offenders: Background, Prevention, Reintegration*, DOI 10.1007/978-3-319-28424-8_13

Restorative justice constitutes a paradigm shift in the way societies are dealing with crime. It is based on a fundamentally different perspective on crime by focusing on the harm caused by it instead of the violation of the law and distributive responses to it. The term "harm" subsumes the physical, financial, or psychological consequences of crime for the victim and moreover for relationships between victims and offenders, between them and their communities as well as within the community at large. It is this primary focus that requires a substantially different response to crime by moving away from the adversarial "win or lose" logic of the traditional distributive justice system towards a "win-win" approach aimed at restoring harm and last but not least societal peace through the means of dialogue, conflict resolution, amends or redress. We would emphasize such "win-win" aspects of restorative justice considering that this approach, although initiated by victim's rights movements of the Western world, can mutually benefit both conflict parties: victims and offenders.

Accordingly, in practice, restorative justice also marks a more "practical" shift regarding the responsibility for addressing crime. In the traditional justice system matters are "delegated to experts" such as police officers, lawyers, prosecutors or judges and it is even considered one of civilizations' major achievements that citizens are not taking the law into their own hands for regulating their serious conflicts such as those caused by crimes by themselves considering multiple risks of vigilantism and escalation this would be bearing.

In a restorative justice process, those directly or indirectly affected by a crime are considered to be the ones *best suited* for addressing the harm caused by it, as they are the ones who know best what happened, what consequences it had and what they need to move on or to take responsibility for it by repairing it. Thus they take an active role in its resolution by engaging in dialogue for finding ways of reparation, restitution or making amends which best meet the needs of those harmed and which all conflict parties involved can agree upon. It is this specific trait that has earned restorative justice approaches to crime the recognition for strengthening people's *access to justice* as opposed to demoting them to a subsidiary role by not letting them fully participate in decisions that concern them.

Peacemaking circles, as a specific approach or model of restorative justice, are taking this aspect of granting access to justice to the people harmed by crime into account in the most congruous and coherent way. Compared to other models of conflict resolution such as victim-offender mediation or family group conferences, Peacemaking circles are granting access to justice to the largest extent and on several different levels: First of all by extending the victim-offender mediation process by "widening the circle of participants" through including family members, friends, support persons as well as affected or concerned community members with a sincere interest in repairing the harm caused by a crime. Secondly, Peacemaking circles do so, by applying several methodological techniques for enhancing the degree of equal inclusion of everybody into all phases of the dialogue, the actual decision-making process, as well as the development and support of the resulting resolution or "action plan." These circle traits and their subtle ways of warranting inclusivity and equality are described in more detail below.

How can women and children benefit from restorative justice approaches to crime? Considering the title of this international handbook "women and children as victims and offenders" one might ask the question: Why are these two being put together? What is it in relation to crime that they have in common?

Thinking of women and children as *offenders* one of their "shared" traits is the much observed and prevailing fact that they are to a much lesser degree involved in crime than adult males, that is to say the more offending of the two genders is male and has left his childhood behind. Interestingly, for both women and children rising dynamics regarding their prevalence and frequency of offending have been registered which seem at least partly due to their increased freedom and autonomy compared to more defined and limited roles even decades ago.[1] It does not seem far-fetched to argue that these two groups commit offenses for other reasons and may require a different response than the "typical" criminal offenders: adolescent or young adult males.

When thinking of women and children as *victims of crime*, more commonalities seem in place. At first glance a contrast comes to mind between crime as something threatening or harmful on the one hand and the perceived vulnerability or need for protection of children and (perhaps) women on the other. It seems fair to assume though that many women would disagree with this assertion and may even perceive this notion as an attempt of patronizing them. It seems nevertheless to be part of our mindset related to gender roles within society and has long historical roots as well.

"Women and children first" a phrase, coined in relation to a historic code of conduct from ship evacuations, comes to mind most famously associated with the sinking of the *Titanic*[2] and a maxim to act upon that might have been the exception rather than the rule even in the old times.[3] Aside from the fact that most women do not want any special treatment of this sort or special protection by someone allegedly superior to them, the question remains, why do women and children afford our attention regarding their risk of victimization through crime?

It is an unsettling but nevertheless still present truth that women and children are by far the most common victims of violence around the world.[4] Perhaps more surprisingly but no less unsettling is the realization based on findings of a recently published EU study[5] showing that not even the vast achievements of the women's rights movement towards more gender equality, as indicated for example by higher labor market participation rates of women or efforts towards equal pay for equal

---

[1] Discussing potential reasons for these dynamics would be too far a stretch considering the framework of this chapter but nevertheless an interesting endeavor.

[2] It refers to a historic code of conduct according to which the lives of women and children were to be saved first in a life-threatening situation such as a ship wreck.

[3] A Swedish study analyzing data on ship wrecks by counting survivors could not find supporting evidence of this notion such as many more wrecks with more female survivors than male ones: Elinder and Erixson (2012), *Every man for himself: Gender, norms and survival in maritime disasters*, Uppsala Universitet, Sweden (Archive).

[4] See for example: UNICEF Annual Report (2014).

[5] FRA, European Union Agency for Fundamental Rights, and Study (2014).

work within western welfare states led to much of an improvement regarding this disturbing fact. On the contrary, findings of this EU—wide survey on violence against women, which is based on face-to-face interviews with 42,000 women and funded by the European Union's Agency for Fundamental Rights suggest the opposite: the more equal women are compared to men in these respects the higher the reported victimization rates regarding physical or sexual violence committed by their partners (or other persons). This is reflected by particularly high rates (above the EU average of 33 %) in countries with very well-established welfare states and particularly high gender equality levels such as Finland, Denmark, or Sweden.[6]

These prevailing facts can be so disturbing and unbearable to face that for some it results in a tendency to suppress related facts or turning a blind eye to the pain they do not want to see.

We will leave it up to other contributors of this handbook to shed more light on these issues and will focus on Peacemaking circles in the following, but would like to express our appreciation to the initiators and editors of this handbook for bringing together scientists from different disciplines around the globe to explicitly focus on women and children as victims and offenders for the sake of gaining more insights into these phenomena as well as for developing ideas further for their prevention.

2 What Are Peacemaking Circles?

Peacemaking circles are a restorative justice approach to conflict resolution that is inclusive and non-hierarchical with long historical roots in indigenous cultures going back to their so-called "talking circles." Particularly the circle tradition of First Nation people of Canada has been further developed and cultivated for dealing with crime, leading to their use in juvenile and criminal justice as well as their spread across the border to Northern US, Hawaii and as far as Australia (often referred to as sentencing circles in these contexts). They are applied as a restorative justice model aiming to repair the harm done by crime through focusing on the effects crime has on relationships between victims, offenders, their families and their communities.

This basic philosophy and restorative approach is shared by all three of the most commonly applied models: circles, conferences, and victim-offender mediation:

- "Models of restorative justice can be grouped into three categories: circles, conferences, and victim-offender mediations. Though somewhat distinct in their practices, the principles employed in each model remain similar."[7]

[6] Ibid., p 28.

[7] Latimer et al. (2005), p 128.

Similar to victim-offender mediation or family-group conferencing, the conflict parties come together in a Peacemaking Circle with the goal of resolving their conflict and making amends by talking to each other with the help of a mediator. While this basic idea seems rather simple there is a lot of wisdom in the method or way it is realized and translated into practice by Peacemaking circles. It seems obvious, depending on the seriousness of the crime, that one cannot just put the offender and his or her victim(s) together and they will find a way to work things out. The task at hand is a lot more sensitive and challenging and bears plenty of risks for unwanted escalations, confrontational talking styles, or even re-victimization if not implemented in an informed and careful way.

Interestingly, the First Nation philosophy of "oneness" with our communities, as practiced in their talking circles, comes in nicely for informing us about how to tackle these challenges or avoid such pitfalls by teaching us how to create a safe and comfortable space for walking on the path of peacemaking. It does so by offering plenty of basic but nevertheless rich ideas for facilitating open conversations that enable everyone involved to reach the desired outcome: a resolution everyone can agree with and eventually even "peace," the kind of peace perhaps best translated into German as "Rechtsfrieden". This path is also referred to as the path "from crime to community" by circle proponents (Pranis et al. 2003) since Peacemaking circles, compared to other methods or approaches to conflict resolution make the highest effort of including *everyone* affected by the crime at stake, the victim(s), the offender(s), members of their families or other support persons as well as members of their communities.[8] In our view, Peacemaking circles have the potential to fulfil the aims of restorative justice even more effectively and all-embracing than other RJ approaches for this and several additional reasons. This chapter will focus on such, more general circle traits and their potentially more sustainable crime prevention effects due to select circle qualities.

We set out to conduct a research study[9] for developing a "best practice" model of Peacemaking circles which should fit the conditions of the European legal and institutional framework by exploring its implementation in criminal justice. In doing so we were explicitly taking into account that Peacemaking circles were developed and applied in common law countries whereas Germany, Belgium and

---

[8] Originally, even judicial representatives such as police officers, lawyers, prosecutors or judges are included in the circle process to represent the legal perspective on the crime at stake. However, considering that our pilot study took place in countries governed by the principle of legality, the German and Belgian teams refrained from this idea. In our view, judicial representatives can be included but are not a requirement for implementing circles. We would even argue that they can pose additional risks to the circle dialogue such as their higher status positions as legal experts violating the equality of the circle participants. In addition their legal perspective applies a "win or lose" logic to the process, which was seen as counterproductive for a successful circle dialogue, etc. Our Hungarian colleagues found ways of integrating some judicial representatives in some of their circles. For more information please see the full study report: Weitekamp (Ed.) (2015).

[9] This research project took place during the period of September 1st, 2011 to August 31st, 2013 with the Institute of Criminology of the University of Tuebingen as the project coordinator and was made possible thanks to the financial support of the European Commission.

Hungary are governed by the principle of legality, which required careful consideration and some adaptations of the original model.[10]

According to Bazemore and Umbreit, circles are a flexible "tool" that can be adapted to the needs of the local community (Bazemore and Umbreit 2001). Thus, there is not one clearly defined model that would apply to all methods that could fall under the term "peacemaking circles". Moreover, circles are also more than just a tool. The essence of circles does not lie in their methodological aspects, such as sitting in a circle or using a talking piece (see below), but is embedded in the reasoning behind their use, the circle philosophy. As such, although the uses of circles may differ somewhat depending on the issue at hand and the community in which they are implemented, there are some common elements that can be found in all circles; For the purpose of this handbook, we will focus on two key aspects: *inclusivity* and *equality*. Regarding typical methodological techniques which distinguish peacemaking circles from other models of conflict resolution and serve these two key aspects, we chose to also discuss the use of a talking piece and consensus-based decision making.

2.1 Inclusivity

One of the basic ideas of Peacemaking circles is that you cannot come to a good solution for a conflict, including crime, if you do not *include* everyone who is responsible for and/or affected by it. Thus, circles try not to individualize the conflict by limiting its resolution to victim-offender mediation, hence a meeting between the victim, the offender and a mediator.[11] On the contrary, Peacemaking circles are considering the setting and context of the conflict. In case of crime this means that not only the offender is expected to take responsibility for his or her actions, but this kind of responsibility taking is also expected on the part of the community—both of the offender and the victim and moreover of the broader community. Consequently, "circles invite not a few but everyone to participate" (Pranis et al. 2003, p. 17).

This basic idea is translated into practice by expanding the mediation dialogue through inviting members of these communities to participate in the circle. They are *included* and addressed by asking questions along the lines of: what did the community do or fail to do to let such a crime happen and how can the community contribute to the reparation of the harm caused by it? In doing so, the focus is not on

[10] For this reason, all three study sites included law/legal experts in their implementation teams. For Germany, this was the role of Hans-Jürgen Kerner, for Belgium, Stephan Parmentier, and for Hungary two representatives of the National Institute of Criminology (OKRI), Tünde Barabás and Szandra Windt joined the local team as legal experts and research partners.

[11] While these can certainly also be "extended" to some degree and additional support persons can be added, it is not an explicit goal of the method to aim for such an extension or to even reach out to the community.

blaming or pointing fingers at anyone, rather, the circle dialogue is forward looking by aiming at finding new ways of taking more responsibility in the future and for preventing similar crimes from happening again.

For those readers, who may perceive this idea as too theoretical, abstract or too idealistic, we can provide further insights into the more practical ways community members actually contribute to the conflict resolution process by describing the "added value" of *including* them the way we experienced it. Sometimes it is as simple as them providing additional information about the victim or the offender, such as their skills, interests or personality traits, which can be helpful for developing more holistic, creative and individual ways of repairing the harm done and increasing the potential of more sustainable crime prevention effects. Even specific knowledge about the setting of the crime, such as security gaps, a perceived lack of control or supervisors, or the presence of bad role models displaying undesired behaviours can be helpful in this respect. In addition, our experiences with circles revealed across the three countries that community members contribute their perspective and more neutral positions to the circle dialogue, which helps absorbing or preventing confrontational discussion or escalations.

Furthermore, *including* the community can help making progress because of the outside perspective on the conflict at stake community members are adding to the dialogue. Their contributions can even increase the longer term positive effects of circles; they can do so for example by offering emotional or practical support to the offender for making amends, for remaining strong in future conflicts or simply by giving them additional reasons to care about their community. Of course the victim(s) can benefit from such community support as well, helping them cope with the consequences of the crime.

These community aspects set circles apart from other restorative methods, such as victim-offender mediation (VOM) or conferencing, which both have a more individualising approach to crime. In VOM one can certainly invite others to the dialogue, such as parents or support persons but this is not their explicit goal. While conferencing approaches are more open to this idea, they focus more on strengthening the families of the conflict parties and do not consider the community aspects as much as circles would.

Furthermore, *inclusivity* is also a goal of high importance during the circle dialogue itself and several methodological aspects of circles such as sitting in a circle, using a Talking Piece and the (different and more moderate) role of the circle mediator, or "Circle Keeper" which is what mediators facilitating a circle meeting are called, aim at giving *everybody* a voice as well as granting equal participation rights together with empowering all circle participants to express themselves and their needs. These more methodological means are strongly and closely aimed at making *inclusivity* possible or even taking it to a new level that has not been reached by other RJ methods.[12]

Moreover *inclusivity* refers to the content of the circle dialogue. A conflict brings imbalance to our lives; to restore the balance a holistic perspective is needed that looks at the conflict as one aspect among others of the people concerned and their lives. Phil and Harold Gatensby, two experienced First Nation circle keepers, stated that in Western society too much attention is paid to the *mental* and *physical* dimensions of people and their conflicts (during a training Workshop at the University of Leuven, October 2011).[13] In order to create more balance, more attention is needed for their *emotional* and even *spiritual* dimensions—which are fundamentally part of Peacemaking circles, more so than of other restorative methods. In a way, this more holistic approach *includes* more of us as well as more dimensions of the conflict, which can pave the path to a deeper understanding of the conflict, its causes, and eventually to a more satisfying resolution based on these deeper insights everybody can live with.

2.2 Equality

Another important aspect closely related to inclusivity is that in circles all participants are equal and interact as equals. Everyone participates in the circle dialogue as a human being; titles and professional positions are "left at the door," as it were. This means that no one has more of a right to speak or more decision power in the circle than others, including the circle keepers or judicial representatives if present. While the circle keepers may have some power of "leading the way" or initiating circle rounds by setting the subject or suggesting the question as a starting point, these are all just suggestions and it is up to the circle participants to accept them or to place a different emphasis on certain matters. They can even change the subject if they find other aspects or issues more important. The Keepers remain open and flexible enough for following the circle "flow" as long as the circle ground rules and values are respected. The circle keeper(s) primary role is the preparation of the circle meeting. Once the circle has started, they share the responsibility for the

[12] The main author of this chapter, Dr. Beate Ehret was personally participating in a training program about *Restorative circles*, the way Dominic Barter has developed and implemented them with great success in the *favelas* of Brasil. As a more critical assessment, I learned that while they also strongly adhere to the basic principles of Restorative Justice, they do not use a talking piece and the approach does not make as much of an effort to arrive at full inclusivity and equality as Peacemaking circles would. When applying Barter's approach, a lot more responsibility is in the hands of the mediator, who is in charge of carefully balancing everything out.

[13] While Phil and Harold Gatensby are acknowledged experts of Peacemaking, healing and sentencing circles they did not publish about them. They prefer the traditional First Nation way of spreading the word about these restorative justice models in face to face encounters, by telling stories, and by facilitating circles as role models as well as by providing plenty of opportunity for participants for learning about them via role plays.

course of the dialogue with all circle participants. Hence, their role comes closer to humble guardians of people's needs and the circle philosophy than to superior or privileged participants with more rights than the others. For example, in case participants wander too far off topic or jump ahead without respecting the circle phases by pressing for a solution in a too premature stage, the keepers serve as reminders and may signalize or express this by giving participants the opportunity to remain focussed. They do not impose solutions either, as the solution is found by the circle and developed by all its members applying consensus-based decision making techniques. Though this level of equality may be an aspiration of many restorative methods, it is ensured and warranted in circle meetings by adhering to the circle groundrules, by using the talking piece (as explained in more detail below) and consensus-based decision-making processes. As a result, this increases their *inclusivity* as well.

3 Overview of the European Research Project

Research institutes from each of the three member countries (Germany, Belgium and Hungary) collaborated for this pilot study. For Germany the project initiator and coordinator was the University of Tübingen, the Belgium partner was the Katholieke University of Leuven, and for Hungary two research institutes cooperated closely as the Hungarian partners: Foresee Research Group together with the National Institute of Criminology, OKRI. At all three sites, the research institutes formed partnerships with a mediation service provider, with professional training and experience in victim-offender mediation: for Germany this was Handschlag, Reutlingen, for Belgium: Suggnomè VZW, and for Hungary, the National Probation Service joined them respectively. Together they formed action research teams to get trained in circles, practice what they had learned in mock circles, and then implement Peacemaking circles together based on a multi-method approach using participatory observation, qualitative interviews and questionnaires for documenting and evaluating what they accomplished.

It should be mentioned beforehand, that this European pilot study was not designed and conducted to analyze potential differences in outcomes for specific groups of interest. Rather, its main goal was to implement Peacemaking circles and learn through action research, in a step-by-step approach, which adaptations or changes to the original conceptual model might or might not seem necessary for the European context. The legal system of all three partner countries is dominantly ruled by the principle of legality as opposed to the common law countries of origin of the Peacemaking circle model or other countries where they have been adopted so far. Given that this was the first time Peacemaking circles were introduced in the three countries involved, this constituted pioneering efforts, which tend to come with the risk of not knowing right from the onset what kind of obstacles or challenges we would have to be facing along the way. Not only were there restrictions from the research point of view, we established minimum criteria to count a circle meeting as an actual peacemaking circle, but it was also a challenge for both the mediators and victims and offenders to leave the known route of victim-offender mediation and explore the possibilities of peacemaking circles. In other words, we did not know how many actual Peacemaking circles we would eventually be able to conduct and how generalizable our observations and experiences would ultimately turn out to be in terms of representing the country they were being implemented in.

What we did not know though, was that this restorative justice model or method deserves to be introduced to the European context and has a highly restorative potential together with promising benefits for everyone involved. Based on our research approach of conducting a pilot study for their first implementations, we did not make efforts to arrive at matching samples between the three countries for comparisons, but took the chances we had during the financed implementation period of about a year, to conduct as many circles as seemed suitable and feasible during that timeframe to learn from them as much as we could. Therefore, we arrived at so-called "convenience samples"[14] that were not pulled randomly from a general population. These were not of a representative size or composition, but built up during the process instead. Therefore, we cannot offer final conclusions about circles or their outcomes.

In this light, we are proud to have achieved a total of 30 circles during this research project, spread over the three countries. These peacemaking circles handled a variety of offenses, among them vandalism, assault and battery, and theft. The context of these offenses was also diverse: peacemaking circles were conducted following a crime in a family context, between neighbours or between total strangers. And most importantly, in all of these settings we succeeded to include (a part of) the community, which, as we have described above, was one of the most prominent aims of peace-making circles.

Methodologically, our action research approach permitted us to learn from the data "on the way" and compare our experiences and newly gained insights within our local teams and across the three sites on a regular basis. The following observations and interpretations are based on these experiences, comparisons and reflections and are therefore nevertheless empirically founded and substantiated.

Thus, the goal of this pilot study was to experiment with circles in the three countries. For doing this, a conceptual methodological model for conducting Peacemaking circles was developed, based on information from the pertinent literature in combination with a training provided by the Canadian, First Nation brothers Phil and Harold Gatensby, two experienced Peacemaking circle "keepers", which is what mediators of a circle are called. As background research for collecting data about the "research field", explorative expert-interviews were

[14] Such convenience samples do not provide justifiable grounds for testing hypotheses or drawing generalizations for the population at large. And the small sample size does not warrant any further split of the general sample of participants into specific groups of interest such as men versus women or children versus adults.

conducted with experts from the field of VOM, such as mediators or other closely related relevant stakeholders including but not limited to: youth service providers, mediators, police officers, lawyers, judges, etc. in each country. During the course of the project this conceptual "circle model" was further refined and adapted to the specific needs and conditions of the three European countries. This further developed more refined model consists of two main parts: the *selection/preparation* of cases and the *facilitation* of circle meetings.

3.1 Selecting and Preparing Circles

This was a pilot study and no criteria have been established yet for distinguishing which types of crimes are eligible for Peacemaking circles. In countries where sentencing circles are used, the cases handled vary from alcohol abuse to domestic violence and even sexual abuse cases (Johnson 2010; Lilles 2001; Rieger 2001). In our view, any case suitable for VOM is also suitable for circles and there are no fundamental objections or impediments against this. However, in accordance with our project goal of providing guidelines for circle keepers we started off by outlining basic case selection criteria for finding cases deemed *most suitable* for circles in order to gather as much practical experiences with their implementation as possible. The resulting list of "suitability" criteria can be summarized as follows:

> Cases where the conflict affected multiple victims and/or offenders, or happened within or between groups, or involved people who were not "officially" or "judicially" considered an offender or victim, or the people affected seem emotionally extremely attached to the case, and where they were likely to interact or see each other again in the future.

These circle suitability criteria were applied to cases that had already been preselected and considered for VOM. Thus, other general case selection criteria had already been met, such as voluntary participation of the conflict parties, offender(s) who are willing to take some responsibility for their actions that have led to the crime (conflict), and victim(s) who feel willing and able to meet the offender in person and talk to him/her (otherwise a circle would not make much sense). Moreover, our mediators carefully assessed the risk of re-victimization for the victim and accepted cases for any type of mediation only if this risk could be regarded as limited or bearable, etc.[15]

For preparation, we deemed the following steps crucial for a successful circle meeting: (1) examining if the case was suited for a circle process, (2) informing every participant of the values, goals and basic ground rules of the circle process in personal talks, and (3) giving the conflict parties personal time and space during these preparatory talks to "vent" by listening to them, offering empathy, and preparing them for the actual circle meeting by talking and reflecting about their needs and expectations.

[15] For Germany see TOA Standards (2013), English version.

3.2 The Circle Meeting

The circle meeting is the tip of the iceberg of Peacemaking circles; it is the most visible and apparently the most important aspect of the whole. However, a lot of what is going on is a lot less visible as everything is built upon a set of values and ground rules that resonate from the preparation phase into the circle meeting and its outcomes. Pranis et al. (2003, pp. 33–47) refer to this as the inner framework of circles which consists of the core values agreed upon and practiced in circle of love, respect, honesty, humility, sharing, courage, inclusivity, empathy, trust and forgiveness.

The typical model for a circle meeting delineates four stages:

- Meeting and introduction;
- Building trust;
- Identifying issues; and
- Developing an action plan.

These stages provide a basic orientation to circle participants and help everyone to remind themselves of the goals of the specific current phase, remaining focussed on them as well as preventing them from getting distracted or too far "off track" by jumping ahead or talking about other issues. Our developed model places a high importance on starting the circle through connecting as human beings by not referring to each other based on victim and/or offender roles or going into detail or depth about the conflict at hand during the first two stages. In doing so, all circle participants have the opportunity to speak and listen to each other and a safe setting is developed. By first paying attention to the act of speaking and listening itself, before looking at the conflict, a space is created to then talk about this conflict in a more genuine, respectful and constructive way.

Hence, this lays the foundation for phase three, when the issues, the conflict or crime as well as the harm it caused are identified and reflected upon. Only by understanding all the main dimensions of this harm, an action plan for its repair can be developed that takes these into account.

What matters in this regard is that the action plan is not pre-set. In this last stage, the goal is that all circle participants try to find a way of dealing with the conflict and overcoming it, which may include how to prevent similar conflicts in the future. As mentioned before, all circle participants (and not only the offender) can take the initiative themselves regarding ideas or actions they may want to carry out or support in order to change the circumstances leading up to the conflict or those created by the conflict. Particularly the victim(s) are encouraged to express their needs, give feedback regarding suggestions and ideas or develop their own.

In the circle meeting itself, this "inner" framework is translated into roles and rules, namely the "outer" framework, which consists of five main methodological aspects for the realisation of peacemaking circles (Pranis et al. 2003, pp. 81–125):

- The use of ceremonies;
- The setting of ground rules;

- The role of the circle keeper;
- The use of a talking piece; and
- Consensus-based decision making.

It would take us too far to go into detail about each aspect listed here. For the purpose of this chapter, two of them are selected due to their relevance for our developed model and their potential of increasing participant ***equality*** and circle ***inclusivity*** as well as their potential crime prevention effects: the ***talking piece*** and ***consensus-based decision making***.

Firstly, the ***talking piece*** is an object of symbolic meaning that is used in each circle meeting to maintain the order of speaking and making it visible at the same time. It is passed on in the circle clockwise from person to person and only the person holding it may speak. All the other participants—including the circle keepers—have to listen attentively and wait until the talking piece reaches them before it is their turn to say something. Besides other advantages of using a talking piece and perhaps foremost it is an ***invitation*** to all participants to speak when it is their turn while at the same time it obliges all other participants to ***listen***. As such, it prevents imbalances caused by only the verbally strong getting a chance to speak and others, only listening without paying full attention while waiting for a moment of silence to interrupt for bringing forward their own points of view. Furthermore, the talking piece teaches everyone to remain silent, patiently awaiting their turn and yielding to the circle as a group on its way of finding its own wisdom instead of trying to push their individual thoughts or opinions through.

A much observed response to using a talking piece and the circle experience as a whole during our implementation experiments was that people became a bit impatient wanting to express themselves because they considered something very important and wanted it to be integrated in the conversation. Interestingly, most of them found it though to be a valuable experience to observe how many times other participants expressed rather similar thoughts as the discussion evolved, and addressed their issues/topics just as well—without them having to force it. This can even be a relief or at least an experience that they do not have to take care of everything by themselves but that the group may work some things out for them.

From the perspective of the researchers and our experiences in conducting circles with our mediators, we found this circle aspect particularly valuable as it has trust-building and even community-building capacities if the circles are implemented the right way. However, these capacities take time and effort to be dedicated to the process, which is often limited due to limited resources of mediation providers or due to limited time of the circle participants, who have other interests and obligations as well.

Moreover, the talking piece draws everybody into the circle dialogue by repeatedly inviting them to express their views, needs or concerns. There is no obligation to speak but in a way this repeated invitation has an ***including*** effect on circle members. Interestingly, it also raises everybody's awareness regarding persons in circle, who do not say much or continuously pass on the talking piece without saying anything. The talking piece and repeated circle rounds not only help noticing these persons, who often remain invisible or even ignored in other conversation settings, but also opens up chances for attempts at integrating them by other participants or the circle keepers.

To provide an example, one German circle faced this particular problem, the keeper expressed his concerns about it and asked if maybe the conversation was not going the "right way" from this particular person's kind of view or if there was anything else that might have made her feel uncomfortable or misunderstood. This way, the circle was able to pay attention to a rather silent person and make additional efforts at integrating her by asking her specific questions and offering her additional support. One solution we found this way was the offer of a community member of trying to express her thoughts and perspective on things for her and asking her for her confirmation for this each time she did to make sure she felt represented by it.

Fortunately, most of the time such additional efforts are not necessary and participants benefit from the circle format and the talking piece just by itself, as it is an empowering tool which was noticeable from an observant perspective and was perceived as such across circles and across the three different countries.

Secondly, concerning the conflict resolution process, circles are setting the stakes very high by striving for ***consensus-based decision-making***; the overarching goal to be achieved in circle is finding a solution ***everybody can live*** with, leaving nobody behind in disagreement. To be clear, this does not mean everybody has to be ***happy with it*** and considering the seriousness of the offense or the damage and harm it may have caused, this would indeed be an overambitious or even unrealistic goal. Particularly from the victims' point of view this may simply be too much to ask for in regard of the harm they suffered or are still suffering from. This could even bear the risk of overwhelming or offending them or could negatively affect their motivation and willingness to be there.

Nevertheless, circles are aspiring to reach consensus. In theory, consensus is reached by adhering to the circle ground rules and values as described above as the inner and outer framework. Concerning circle conduction and facilitation, this translates into giving everybody a voice, hearing them out, listening to their doubts, fears or any other objections they may have. The role of the keeper supports this high aspiration by being attentive to everybody and remaining "all-partial" regarding conflicting views or arguments. Most importantly, they empower everybody in the circle to become a "co-keeper" by putting these values into practice and gently reminding others to do the same if they fall short of the rules and values agreed upon at the onset of the circle.

The goal of consensus-based decision-making is translated into practice by taking all points of disagreement into account, considering them carefully and the motivations behind them, spending sufficient time on them by initiating additional circle rounds in case they remain an obstacle for finding a solution and by working them out until nobody disagrees anymore. It is important to note that disagreement is welcome and everybody is encouraged to express it in circle. Circle keepers even ask explicitly if there is anybody in the circle who would disagree with what has been suggested as a potential path towards a solution or action plan. The Gatensby brothers strongly emphasized that "it is o.k. to disagree!" Regarding the goal of consensus this may seem surprising but only at first glance. Upon deeper reflection it becomes obvious that a consensus can only be shared by everyone, if everyone was heard and their objections or doubts were truly considered. After all, it is such objections or doubts that are the barriers or obstacles to finding a solution everybody can live with. Even more so, these barriers can be the source of future conflict or failure of the action plan, and a sustainable peace can only be reached when tackling them.

On the other hand, it becomes clear that on this path to consensus, it is an absolute "no go" to put anyone under pressure for accepting something they are in disagreement with, and this kind of authoritarian behaviour would not be in adherence with circle values. Finally, the difference to majority based decision-making becomes clear, in circles a majority cannot "overrule" a minority because everybody matters and their potential disagreement is considered important and taken into account.

While there are more interesting methodological aspects relevant for circles that contribute their share to their overall restorative impact, we conclude this rather technical discussion at this point in order to remain within the framework of this handbook. The interested reader can find more of this wealth of material in our comprehensive research report at the University of Tübingen.[16]

4 What Are Specific Circle Benefits or Drawbacks for Women?

This work has a specific focus on women and children and the search for alternative responses of dealing with crime and delinquency for succeeding generations. Regarding women, gender would better serve here as the unit of analysis in our view, considering its capacities as a structuring category of society leading to inequalities, differences in social status as well as differential treatment. It is this difference or discrepancy in power relations when comparing the two genders that is of analytical interest and not a limited perspective on women alone. However, as contributors of this work, we can offer the following reflections and thoughts on potential benefits of restorative justice and Peacemaking circles for women in particular as it is the thematical framework for this collection of articles. What should be added from our viewpoint though, is that the benefits outlined in the following can be valid for anyone in a disadvantaged or underprivileged position in society independent of gender or age. For the sake of clarity we will present and explain them with a specific focus on women.

[16] Weitekamp (Ed.) (2015). *Developing Peacemaking Circles in a European Context*. Results of a joint research project in Belgium, Germany and Hungary. University of Tuebingen. The main authors of this report are Ehret, Beate: Szego, Dora, and Dhondt, Davy.

Mediation has been widely criticized by feminist researchers and members of the women's rights movement as being ill-suited or even potentially harmful for women as a means for handling their matters in mixed-gender conflict constellations. The main concern was based on the notion that in a male dominated society, mediation dialogues bear risks of putting women in a disadvantaged position. The main points of criticism of this broad discourse were focussed on concerns that mediation bears potential risks of:

- Perpetuating power imbalances between women and men that are inherent in Western society.
- Providing opportunity for (more powerful) men to coerce or pressure women to settle for "less" than they should or could (without legal safeguards protecting them from it).
- Guiding women towards giving up moral or legal rights for vindication by setting more practical, future oriented priorities (as these are typical goals of mediation).
- Reinforcing the stereotype of the "bad angry woman" by discouraging expressions of anger and placing a higher value on cooperation (as would be common practice in mediation).

Interestingly, this debate was "stirred up" by an article by Grillo (1991) addressing potential dangers for women in case of court-ordered mediation for divorce issues explicitly focussing on this very specific kind of involuntary mediation. However, she stirred up a broad and log-lasting debate about all kinds of mediation in general and this critical perception prevailed over a long period of time.[17]

Domestic violence can be seen as particularly challenging in this regard as these cases represent an extreme form of male domination culminating into violence against women in form of physical or sexual abuse. We know from our national teams of mediators that some practitioners take a strong stand against mediation as inappropriate for dealing with any kind of family/domestic violence cases for this reason. It has been argued that you cannot ensure sufficient safety for these women and that the risk of them becoming re-victimized either during or after the mediation is too high. Considering that prior victimizations can cause psychological damage or even trauma on the part of the victim it seems reasonable to protect them from any risks related to new contact with the perpetrator. However, respecting the fact that cases differ and so do the women involved, their needs may differ too and some may not wish to be "protected" in this way or may even perceive this as paternalistic. They may even need this kind of dialogue in a protected environment and setting to leave things behind and move on with their lives.

[17] See for example in 2004: Acorn, Annalise. Compulsory Compassion: A Critique of Restorative Justice. Vancouver: UBC Press.

During our pilot study we did not conduct circles in domestic violence cases but know from our Belgian colleague, Kristel Buntix,[18] that it has been done successfully and does not put women in additional dangers when applied carefully. In her point of view, it is the women's decision and your role as a mediator is to prepare them, make them aware of potential risks, discuss what they can expect and clarify what they cannot. This way they can make this decision on their own and it remains their choice.

In our view, most of the alleged dangers of mediation for women in general do not apply to victim-offender mediation, particularly not when adhering to basic standards, as participation has to be voluntary, the accused is expected to show some degree of willingness of taking responsibility for his or her actions even to be considered suitable for mediation, and the mediator is specifically trained for "leveling the playing field" by ensuring that everybody is heard and their needs are carefully considered and met.

However, some of these risks may prevail as long as power imbalances between men and women continue to exist, since during mediation these can take on subtle forms that may not always be detected or detectable by mediators. And even if they managed to detect and address them, there comes a time after the circle where they are not there to protect the woman or children and fears or concerns in this regard are beyond their control. Overall it seems difficult to assess the degree or potential harm for women, children or other people in disadvantaged, underprivileged or even subordinate positions.

However, taking victim's matters completely out of their hands and delegating them to legal representatives is not a particularly empowering or satisfactory way of handling this either and completely deprives them of the possibility of finding their voice and asserting their needs. The restorative justice approach grew out of a victim's rights movement that was explicitly aimed at giving them their voice back and addressing their needs in a more holistic way than our traditional justice system would.

Peacemaking circles in particular, take a number of precautions to prevent power imbalances from affecting the mediation dialogue by levelling them out. In addition, several techniques are applied to empower all of their participants. We think that women as well as children can benefit greatly from circles. Some reflections and observations from our pilot study can highlight these benefits and explain some reasons for them, which became clearer during the process. This will be summarized in the following paragraphs:

We agree across all three sites that the ***egalitarian*** nature of Peacemaking circles, as it is a fundamental dimension of their philosophical background and translated into practice by the circle set up and their inner and outer framework, as described above, has many effects that are leveling the playing field, which can be beneficial for everyone involved and of particular benefit to those in disadvantaged,

[18] Presentation during the concluding workshop at the university of Tuebingen, August 2013. Confirmed through personal conversation between her and the main author of this chapter.

weaker or even intimidated positions such as women or children. It should be noted, that males can certainly be in such positions as well depending on the circumstances, and the following arguments seem just as valid for them in these cases.

First of all, circle ***equality*** has empowering effects on their participants. What do we mean by this? The egalitarian circle set up and use of the talking piece enables everybody to speak when it is their turn and express their needs and, even more importantly, to get heard. This way, they have the opportunity of stepping out of potentially subordinate or suppressed positions and getting more space for expressing their thoughts and feelings about the conflict at hand, the harm it has caused to them and others and asserting their resulting needs.

Moreover, this egalitarian set-up manifests itself in several additional ways: the use of the ***talking piece*** also helps limiting the speaking time of those who may otherwise be dominating the dialogue.[19] Immediately from the very beginning of the circle, participants are made aware of the fact that everyone should get their turn and has a right to expect this. As a second step, the talking piece is introduced to them as a means of providing everybody equal opportunity to speak. In addition, the circle keeper assists the circle in adhering to these rules and the circle participants agree by consensus during the starting phase of the circle that this is a rule they want to follow. This agreement in turn serves as an informal means of social control in this regard ensuring a balanced circle dialogue because everybody can count on each others' awareness of it and can claim it based on this.

A good ***circle keeper*** empowers everybody in the circle to become a circle keeper him- or herself as well. Thus, they can all fill the role of a servant of the circle by reminding others of the groundrules or the circle's agreement made at its onset and to adhere to these rules. We experienced several times across sites and circle cases that participants took over this role and found their own individual ways of strengthening these rules by reminding each other of them or by pointing them out again and explaining them. They also did not do this in an authoritarian or rule "enforcing" kind of way but in a collaborate manner, which adhered to the circle values as discussed during the early stages of each circle and was adapted by participants during the process. This keeper role, which differs from the role of the mediator in other mediation settings, reflects a different, more modest and collaborative attitude as a servant of the circle, and the keeper(s) set an example for it by translating it into practice.

Furthermore, circle ***inclusivity*** affects the circle dialogue and can have equalizing effects as well. These effects are a lot more difficult to assess, considering that we cannot know how the circle dialogue would have or could have gone without this aspect. However, we can agree across all three sites, that the ***widening*** of the circle by including additional support persons and/or members of the community

[19] It has been empirically proven in numerous studies that male domination over women can lead to women's speech getting talked over, women getting interrupted more often than men and women getting less time to speak (see for example: Campbell et al. (2001); James and Clarke (1993); Smith-Lovin and Brody (1989)).

creates more ***transparency*** about the underlying conflicts than more private settings such as in VOM. Additional participants from different levels of the community can serve as agents for increasing the degree of informal social control and accountability. This can also help identifying and leveling out power imbalances as more eyes and ears see and hear more.

We also noticed that ***widening*** the circle by including additional persons can lead to "***buffering***" effects regarding the conflict at stake. Given that these additional persons are less involved in the conflict or less affected by its consequences than more immediate or direct victims or offenders, they can offer an outside perspective and bring more emotional distance with them. This can affect the dialogue in many positive ways and can even help prevent escalations. Considering that these persons can be seated between members of the conflict parties and the talking piece is generally used by being handed over from one person to the next, a circle can be planned in a way that direct talk between victim and offender is excluded completely if necessary. This way, immediate spontaneous reactions can be avoided and a slower pace of talking is reached. In escalated or angry discussions or arguments, power imbalances play a much more important role than in mediated talks and therefore theses mechanisms help equalizing circle participants in this respect as well.[20]

These additional participants can also ***increase support*** for women (or children). Supporters can be included from personal and institutional levels upon their request and depending on their needs. They can be intentionally brought in to strengthen the women (or children) and assist them with representing their interests in the circle and beyond. This decision can be based on the victim's expressed needs, on supporters who make additional suggestions who else could be included in the circle, or on the mediators. The German mediators established the rule of always asking the victim during the preparation phase for their consent regarding the invitation of additional people in order to prevent them from being afraid or worried about who they are going to meet and also to make sure they are comfortable with it.

Successful circles can even lead to the creation and strengthening of a supportive network that extends its support beyond the mediation process and assures the follow up of the agreement as well as a supportive kind of control over it after the circle. If needed, this support can even continue after the fulfilment of the action plan. Additional supporters, either community members or social professionals create a bridge between the circle and the time after the circle. They ensure that taking care of the situation is extended and continues on after the circle.

[20] In a way, the circle rhythm teaches patience and the more participants are included, the more patience it takes to go through the motions. However, some participants also voiced criticism about this aspect and were unhappy with the slow pace and the long waiting times before you get your turn to speak. However, in most circles they noticed later on, that the circle managed to make progress and solutions could be generated even if the process of getting there was perceived as too slow.

5 What Are Specific Circle Benefits or Drawbacks for Children?

Our study was implemented within the juvenile or criminal justice system and we did not conduct many circles with children at all. Thus, we cannot offer very specific insights for children or generalizable findings, only a few rather basic or general observations.

One rather basic but nevertheless fundamental child-related aspect of Peacemaking circles to begin with, was that in juvenile or criminal cases child offenders—even if below the age of legal culpability and therefore not officially charged—can be included. Peacemaking circles make it possible to involve child offenders if they wish and therefore provide them with the opportunity of hearing and learning about the consequences of their actions, letting them face other people affected by them, and enabling them to take some level of responsibility. Of course this participation has to be voluntary and the decision has to be made with the informed consent of their parents or legal guardians. This opportunity of involving child offenders is contrary to common mediation practice and seems more likely or feasible in case of Peacemaking circles because circles manage to create a safe environment and atmosphere, they do not privatize the conflict at hand, are open to including additional support persons if needed, or role models the kids can look up to or learn from, peers to balance age differences between participants in addition to all the other safeguards and empowering capacities as they have been discussed in this chapter at length already. Furthermore, children can benefit greatly from their participation because this experience of so many people coming together to listen to them and each other, pay attention and respect and resolve matters together in a circle can have an educational impact on them.

One interesting observation we made concerning PMC and children was that the method itself was picked up easily by children. They seemed to feel comfortable during the circle and they intuitively followed its groundrules. We would even hypothesize that this was easier for them than for adults, since they were more used to following some conversation rules (e.g. in school settings) than adults.

There was a further aspect of circles that fit children very well: circles provide a wide range of opportunity for non-verbal expression. Emotional gestures or signs such as hugs, or even crying are ways of expression in circles that are as equally legitimate as talking. Children were very good at non-verbal expression and helped adults as well to express emotions.

In the few circles with children, the ***egalitarian*** approach of circles and their capacity to create equality between participants by balancing out power discrepancies deriving from differences in maturity, psychological, intellectual and/or communicational skills or different levels of social status was even more tangible and noticeable than in other circles. Observations and reflections by several circle participants and keepers made after the circle, confirmed this notion. For example, they were astounded by the strength of the children, both regarding their position in the circle as well as regarding their contributions to the circle dialogue and what they shared with the circle.

Again, the ***talking piece*** was particularly helpful for achieving this. By providing the possibility to children of expressing themselves as equal members of the dialogue together with adults and, in addition, acknowledging the importance of non-verbal expression of feelings allowed children to participate in a way that differed substantially from their "normal" or everyday experience. Children were truly given an opportunity to speak, while everyone else, including the adults, had to grant them as much time as they wanted or needed, with no possibility to interrupt them. And they actually listened to them. To provide one example, in one of the Belgian circles this seemed to feel so liberating to one of the children, that she talked more than any of her support persons would have ever imagined beforehand.

Of course, a certain degree of social inequality and differences in skills and status will always remain and for children the sheer presence of adults can be intimidating by nature, but Peacemaking circles provide them with an equal opportunity to speak and we were able to observe that the circle experience altogether had an empowering effect on them as participants that seemed helpful for resolving the conflict at hand, no more but no less either.

The ***community*** aspect of circles also mattered greatly for children. Addressing the community is one of the main features distinguishing circles from other restorative justice or mediation methods for conflict resolution. According to the community justice approach of circles, whenever a conflict emerges, micro- and macro-communities are affected by it. However, circumscribing, finding and addressing these communities around the crime, meaning the communities affected by it, associated with it or with other connections to it or the conflict parties was a great challenge for the research and mediation partners at all three sites (in Germany, Hungary and Belgium) to face and take up.

According to the Hungarian and German teams, they experienced that in cases where children were concerned either as victims or as accused, it was easier to make out connections between people, ***find the community*** around the case, and do so on more levels compared to other cases. Especially mobilizing the community of care such as family members, school workers and responsible social services, family supporters, or child protection authorities, etc. seemed less challenging compared to mobilizing supporting communities in other circles concerning conflicts between more grown up or adult parties. Even people who did not have an official obligation to support the child by participating in the circle were more ready to join in and find their role when children were among the victims and/or harm-doers.

The Hungarian analysts formulated the conclusion that social structures of either individual or institutional actors, who are related to each other through a wide range of formal or informal ties are better built and more developed in case of children than in case of adults. Based on this experience they found the PMC method especially useful for handling cases in schools, families (e.g.: physical assaults, abuse) and other forms of child "communities" such as playgrounds (e.g.: vandalism, theft).

The ***inclusion of the community*** of care in circles with children seemed to matter in two major ways. First of all, as emotional support ***for the children*** themselves: The support persons were able to acknowledge what the child had said, compliment or affirm him or her for daring to say it and as such they helped creating a safe environment for the children. In one case, the support person also spoke on behalf of a child, when it was not possible for him to speak for himself.

Secondly, the presence of the support person ***broadened their view of the child*** as a person. During the circle, as mentioned earlier, support persons were at time astounded at what the child said. One support person (a teacher) said for example of a child, who was able to powerfully express her feelings and thoughts: "I do not recognize the shy, little girl from my classroom". Overall, the restorative goal of healing or simply strengthening relationships was noticeable as crime puts a strain on these relationships as well, not just on those between victim and offender.

The presence of members of ***more distant levels of the community***, in cases where children were involved did not seem to be fruitful, especially if they were from the macro-community. At least, it was not perceived as that by the children themselves. This observation was made based on a Belgian circle. One of the children even wrote in the survey after the circle: "they talked too long". This could be linked to the fact that most of the macro-community members in these particular circles tried to remain rather neutral and stay on the middle ground concerning the crime and conflict that was talked about and still going on during the circle. This led to the fact that their contributions tended to be rather nuanced and more at length. This was in stark contrast with the short, but very powerful messages expressed by the children.

6 Conclusion: Peacemaking Circles Have More Sustainable Crime Prevention Effects

Interestingly, the distinct features of circles setting them apart from other models or approaches of restorative justice mediation, such as VOM or conferencing are also additional contributors to more sustainable crime prevention. Given the nature of our project as a pilot study implementing circles for the first time in three European countries, we were not able to collect sufficient data for evaluating crime prevention effects based on an outcome evaluation using indicators such as the level of offending during a follow-up period of time or indicators for an improved social integration or stronger ties (commitment, involvement, attachment, belief) to the community.

What we can offer though, are our shared reflections among the researchers of the three teams on the potential prevention effects of circles.

DFirst of all, and probably the most distinct difference is the strong effort circles make to ***include community members*** who feel affected by the offence (directly or indirectly) or are otherwise interested. This has been discussed at length above as a strong trait of circles that is of benefit for the conflict parties as well as everyone else involved. Assessing these benefits, it becomes clear, that all levels of added value gained by including the community members can also lead to a more balanced dialogue, conflict resolution, and action plan. Particularly in case it has accomplished to include community members into the action plan, the chances of its successful implementation are raised, which can increase victim and offender satisfaction with the outcome, teach the offender a lesson of accountability and may also open their minds for ways they can actively show that they take responsibility and are also capable of making positive contributions to the community and to society as a whole.

Circles also differ from other models as they can *include* ***representatives of the justice system*** such as police, probation officers, or lawyers. This additional option has the potential of improving the mutual perceptions of victims, offenders and their communities on the one hand and members of law enforcement and criminal justice on the other. One could hypothesize that these changed perceptions through personal contacts of a different quality as they are possible in circles could potentially increase the legitimacy of the justice system and the law in general. However, this idea remains speculative at this point.

Considering that circles are geared to addressing ***broader levels of harm*** (harm to secondary victims, to community, including potential causes of crime) than the other models, they also provide more of an opportunity for repairing different levels of harm. Thus such positive outcomes as outlined above become more likely and can potentially be reached on more levels as well. For example, the action plan of one German circle was to repair the harm to the community caused by the repeated vandalization by juveniles of a city fence, by cleaning up a littered city creek close to a playground and a nearby skater park[21] heavily frequented by children and adolescents. This solution did not just address the broken fence but the whole community affected by it and, beyond that, it gave juveniles a chance to make amends for their silly behavior, take responsibility for it, make a contribution to the community and set a good example for others. While this was only a small contribution or attempt of giving back to the community, it exemplifies the rich opportunities Peacemaking circles can help to create for addressing the harmful effects and "ripple" effects crime can have on communities. This way, potentially vicious cycles of harm producing more harm can be interrupted and positive messages and actions can be held against it.

The foundational circle aspects of choosing ***peacemaking values*** **as** guidance for interaction (respect, trust, honesty, etc.), using ***circle structure and ritual*** to create a safe space for dialogue and last but not least applying ***consensus-based*** decision making processes to arrive at a conflict resolution everybody can live with have much potential of creating more sustainable crime prevention effects. If everybody feels included and heard they are more likely to accept, go along and support the solution with their minds, hearts and actions.

[21] A designated site for skaters as well as skateboarders with a half-pipe and jumping ramps, etc.

Five Questions

1. What defines *communities* regarding harmful effects of crime and wrongdoing? In other words: Who is affected and who should be considered for invitation to a Peacemaking circle? (Think of different types of offenses as examples.)
2. How can members of the community/communities be found, reached, approached, and involved in circles and who's responsibility is this?
3. What are potential risks and benefits of involving judicial representatives such as police officers, lawyers, prosecutors, or judges in Peacemaking circles?
4. To what extent should persons who are not legally concerned in criminal cases be involved in decision making processes?
5. Are there any types of crime or wrongdoing where you would deem Peacemaking circles as not suitable or appropriate and why?

References

Acorn, A. (2004). *Compulsory compassion: A critique of restorative justice*. Vancouver: UBC Press.

Bazemore, G., & Umbreit, M. (2001). A comparison of four restorative conferencing models. *Juvenile Justice Bulletin, 21*, 1–20.

Braithwaite, J. (2004). Restorative justice and de-professionalization. *The Good Society, 13*(1), 28–31.

Campbell, K., Kleim, D., & Olson, K. (2001). Conversational activity and interruptions among men and women. *The Journal of Social Psychology, 132*(3), 419–421.

Elinder, M., & Erixson, O. (2012). *Every man for himself: Gender, norms and survival in maritime disasters*. Sweden: Uppsala Universitet (Archive).

FRA, European Union Agency for Fundamental Rights, Study (2014). *Violence against Women: an EU-wide survey*. Luxembourg: Publications Office of the European Union. Retrieved from: http://fra.europa.eu/en/publication/2014/violence-against-women-eu-wide-survey-main-results-report.

Grillo, T. (1991). The mediation alternative: Process dangers for women. *Yale Law Journal, 100* (6), 1545–1610.

James, D., & Clarke, S. (1993). Women, men, and interruptions: A critical review. In D. Tannen (Ed.), *Gender and conversational interaction* (pp. 231–280). New York, NY: Oxford University Press.

Johnson, I.D. (2010). *Restorative justice circles as a method for addressing the impacts of crime on victims, communities and offenders*. BA Honors thesis, University of Alaska, Fairbanks. [Accessed 25.02.2013].

Latimer, J., Dowden, C., & Muise, D. (2005). The effectiveness of restorative justice practices: A meta-analysis. *The Prison Journal, 85*(2), 127–144.

Lilles, H. (2001). Yukon sentencing circles and Elder Panels. *Criminology Aotearoa, NewZealand, 16*, 2–4.

Livingstone, N., Macdonald, G., & Carr, N. (2013). Restorative justice conferencing for reducing recidivism in young offenders (aged 7 to 21). *Cochrane Database of Systematic Reviews*, Issue 2. Art. No.: CD008898.

Pranis, K., Stuart, B., & Wedge, M. (2003). *Peacemaking circles: From crime to community*. St. Paul: Living Justice Press.

Rieger, L. (2001). Circle peacemaking. *Alaska Justice Forum, 17*(4), 1. 6–7.

Servicebüro für Täter-Opfer-Ausgleich und Konfliktschlichtung (2014). *Standards for Victim-Offender-Mediation.* Sixth Revised Edition. Einrichtung des DBH e. V. – Fachverband für Soziale Arbeit, Strafrecht und Kriminalpolitik, Köln.

Smith-Lovin, L., & Brody, C. (1989). Interruptions in group discussions: The effect of gender and group composition. *American Sociological Review, 54*, 424–435.

Weitekamp G.M. (Ed.) (2015). *Developing Peacemaking Circles in a European Context.* Results of a joint research project in Belgium, Germany and Hungary. TüKrim (Vol. 34). University of Tübingen.

Zehr, H. (2005). *Changing lenses – A new focus for crime and justice* (3rd ed.). Scottdale, PA: Herald Press.

Zehr, H. (2002). *The little book of restorative justice.* Intercourse, PA: Good Books.

Part V
Crime Prevention: Proactive Strategies

Justice, Faith, and Interfaith: The Relevance of Faith and Interfaith Relations to Crime Prevention

Thomas G. Walsh

Abstract The concept of justice is both simple and intuitive, and yet also highly complex. In the latter context, this chapter explores the relevance of religion to justice and crime prevention. Among 7 billion human beings, the majority identify themselves as belonging to a particular religious tradition, such as Christianity, Islam, Hinduism, Buddhism, Sikhism, Judaism, Jainism, indigenous traditions, etc. With a global resurgence of religion, along with an increase in religiously plural societies, there is growing awareness of religion as a significant factor—sometimes positive, sometimes negative—in the lives of individuals, families, societies and nations. As such, increased awareness of religion as it functions in society and the world is needed. This is occurring in a variety of fields, such as international relations, conflict mediation, peace studies, and criminology. In addition, there is widespread recognition that interreligious dialogue and cooperation are necessary if we are to build social capital and establish a "radius of trust" on both local and global levels. The UN has become increasingly appreciative of interreligious dialogue, recognizing its relevance to peace, security, human development and the quality of life for succeeding generations.

1 Introduction: The Social Significance of Religion

As has been the case for millennia, religion is a significant force in our world. Despite anticipations that religion might wither away as modernization moved forward, we see no evidence that religion is on the wane globally. Billions of people continue to identify themselves as Christians, Muslims, Hindus, Buddhists, Jews, Sikhs, Jains, mystics, or as members of any number of newer religions and spiritual groups. Such affiliations, for many, are not merely nominal, and are not without substantial relevance to their everyday lives.

T.G. Walsh (✉)
Universal Peace Federation, Tarrytown, NY, USA
e-mail: twalsh@upf.org

H. Kury et al. (eds.), *Women and Children as Victims and Offenders: Background, Prevention, Reintegration*, DOI 10.1007/978-3-319-28424-8_14

Many of the classics in the field of social science have understood the significance of religion, both in terms of its meaning and its function in society. Max Weber (1905/1958), Emile Durkheim (1912), and others were appreciative of religion as an important factor in the lives of many, if not most individuals and societies. While some, such as Durkheim and Marx (1848), understood religion as an outgrowth of social or material forces, others, most notably Max Weber, saw religion as more of an independent force that shaped ideas, worldviews and, consequently, the course of history, including the political and economic spheres.

For millennia, religion was not studied scientifically. However, as an outgrowth of the European Enlightenment, scientific method was developed and the social scientific study of religion distinguished itself from theology. Religion came to be studied objectively and dispassionately, applying principles of "methodological agnosticism", which essentially requires the researcher to try to set aside any positive or negative predispositions toward religion. In this way, the scientific study of religion developed as a discipline, distinct from theology, and a researcher by no means needed to be, although certainly could be, a believer (Eliade 1987; Otto 1923; Smart 1989; Smith 1958).

Despite the development of the scientific study of religion, there has been a slower awakening to an understanding of religion's relevance to other fields of study, for example, political science, international relations, and criminology. Whether a consequence of indifference, illiteracy or an aversion to the subject matter, the religious factor should not be lost in a methodological blind spot. It is simply too relevant. Fortunately, such lacunae are increasingly being overcome.

One obstacle, perhaps, is related to conventional secularization theory, a theory which predicted the decline of religion as human beings developed economically, socially, and intellectually, i.e., secularization is a natural outgrowth of modernization (Berger 1999). However, this theory has been widely called into question by historical developments (Inglehart and Norris 2011). While religion may be on the wane in some highly developed countries, it continues to make its presence felt in most of the world, developed and undeveloped alike (Berger 1999; Taylor 2007; Habermas 2010).

The evidence of religious vitality has been especially pronounced in the post-Cold War era. Consider the devolution of the former Yugoslavia in the post-Soviet era. Cultural roots, ethnicity, and religion were indisputably relevant in the national independence movements in Bosnia, Serbia, Croatia, Montenegro, Macedonia, Kosovo, etc. These forces continue to be relevant in many other regions, often contributing to conflict situations around the world, from Israel and Palestine, to the Philippines, Sri Lanka, Kashmir, Myanmar, Syria, Turkey, Nigeria, the Central African Republic, etc. Religion is a factor in global affairs. Consider terrorism, from the Tamil Tigers in Sri Lanka to Al Qaeda in Afghanistan. Can we understand these phenomena without some appreciation for the role of religion?

This empirical reality has fostered a growing awareness of the relevance of religion to international relations. Political scientists and international relations experts who, even 20 years ago, would have seen religion as deserving of only a minor footnote in discussions of contemporary geopolitical affairs, are increasingly aware of the need to take religion seriously. Religion, after all, is deeply rooted in human cultures, civilizations, and ethnic groups (Huntington 1993; Albright 2006; Thomas 2005; Johnston 1994). As a result, it is one of the primary factors that inform and shape human attitudes and actions.

Along with a global religious resurgence, often manifested in conflict situations, there is also a growing appreciation of the need for interreligious dialogue and cooperation. In other words, religious resurgence, coupled with a tendency toward conflict, has led to the recognition that interreligious understanding and cooperation are necessary if we are to achieve global peace.

These two trends—religious resurgence and interreligious dialogue—are relevant to the wider discussion of the significance of religion *vis-à-vis* society. Religion impacts a wide range of social issues related to marriage, sexuality, violence, war, conflict, crime, economics, justice, humanitarian care for the needy, etc. Hospitals, charities, soup-kitchens, homeless shelters, emergency relief agencies, prison ministries, etc., are often linked to religious organizations. Muslims, Christians, Buddhists, Hindus, and all religions have theological reasons for serving others. Once conceived as entirely "otherworldly" and concerned only with the after-life, religions everywhere are increasingly activist and "socially engaged".

At the same time, religions, more than governments and non-governmental organizations (NGOs), provide a framework of meaning and value for believers, overcoming the sense of alienation, on the one hand, and providing a vision and coherent worldview, on the other hand. As Emile Durkheim (1897) explained, religion often functions to overcome the *anomie* or normlessness that otherwise may characterize modernity. Stated a bit differently, religion's strength lies in its potential to strengthen affective ties with others, civic-mindedness, moral direction, impulse restraint, and a basket of virtues that contribute to empathic and harmonious relations with others.

As is well known, and widely reported, religion has a checkered history. While on the one hand, it may function in ways that uplift, liberate and restore the best virtues and practices of human beings—forgiveness, compassion, unselfish service, care, philanthropy, justice, human rights, etc.—it also may, and often does, function pathologically, giving rise to conflict, violence, and oppression (Kurst-Swanger 2008).

But what does this have to do with crime prevention and criminal justice?

Let's first take a look at the meaning of justice.

2 Theories of Justice: Philosophical and Theological Perspectives

There is a long and lofty history of discussions about justice that can be found throughout the history of philosophy, literature and theology (Sandel 2007; Rawls 1971; MacIntyre 1988; Lebacqz 1986). Plato's *Republic* is often cited as the classic, early philosophical discussion of justice, a tradition carried forward by his student Aristotle and a long line of philosophers, including J. S. Mill, Immanuel Kant, Georg W. F. Hegel, Karl Marx, and John Rawls. Justice is also widely discussed in the scriptures of the various religious traditions, for example, Judaism's Torah, Christianity's New Testament, Hinduism's Bhagavad Gita, Islam's Qur'an or Buddhism's Dhammapada.

The concept of justice is both simple and intuitive, and yet also highly complex. Often justice is described as "treating similar cases similarly" or "giving to each what is due to him or her". The call for justice may seem to be straightforward and simple at first glance. Upon closer inspection, however, one can find a nest of complications.

The Greek word *dikaiosune*, is translated as justice or righteousness. Justice in the classical period was understood as a virtue; moreover, one that would be supported by a family of complementary virtues, such as courage, temperance, generosity and prudence. To be just was to be virtuous in relation to other citizens, giving each what is due to them, what they deserve. In this sense, justice is clearly "distributive" in nature, having to do with giving to others what they deserve. Injustice occurs when one gives or takes from another what they do not deserve to receive or have taken from them. When injustice occurs, some correction is required.

According to Alasdair MacIntyre, in an exposition of Aristotle's conception of justice, good judgment based on wisdom, or *phronesis*, is a prerequisite for justice, that is, for understanding what each is due, according to the situation. MacIntyre writes, "The virtue of justice, like any other moral virtue, cannot be exercised without *phronesis* also being exercised. For truths about what is just are a subclass of truths about what is good, and the ability to embody them in action is the *phronetic* ability to embody these truths in action in the requisite way in particular cases" (MacIntyre 1988, p. 116).

Justice is largely about giving or paying tribute according to what is due, according to a principle of distribution. Closely allied with the concept of justice is the concept of fairness; that is, treat similarly situated persons similarly. The Golden Rule itself, do unto others as you would have them do unto you, is an expression of the essence of justice.

Two central pillars of mainstream theories of justice are the concepts of distribution and retribution. Distributive justice concerns itself with the ways and measure in terms of which to provide or withdraw benefits or goods. Theories of distributive justice are debated in accordance with other principles, namely, equality, liberty and merit. For some, distributions should aim toward equality, while for others the distributions should reward those who are more deserving, or lucky, and not reward those who are undeserving. The principle of liberty suggests that distributive justice is a minimal duty that does not override an individual's freedom to earn what they can and dispose of it as they choose.

Retributive justice is more concerned with re-establishing a lost balance and/or a violation of law. One form of retributive justice is exemplified in the "eye for an eye, tooth for a tooth" theory. What you take from someone unjustly, by committing a crime, must be paid back through some repayment to the victim and to society, through various fines, penalties and other forms of punishment.

The philosophical foundations of modern theories of justice are often linked to two schools of moral philosophy: utilitarianism, based on the ideas of John Stuart Mill (Mill 1863) and Jeremy Bentham (Bentham 1789), and deontological or duty-based ethics, based on the ideas of Emmanuel Kant (Kant 1785). In the case of the former, theories of justice are grounded in an argument that has utility as its primary value or end. If a particular law, rule, principle or punishment yields a "greater good" or "the greatest good for the greatest number," then it is morally legitimate. Mill and Bentham both thought their theories of ethics applicable to the area of crime and punishment, deterrence, and the development of a system of rewards and punishments that would encourage good social behavior that would lead to increased social utility (Sandel 2007, pp. 9–47).

Bentham's first major work, published in 1789, was entitled *The Principles for Morals and Legislation,* and concerned itself with the penal code. Bentham aspired to have a more scientific ethical system guided by a calculus of pleasure and pain, something known as a "hedonic calculus". John Stuart Mill, who published *Utilitarianism* in 1863, also sought to develop a similarly rational system of ethics, based on the principle of utility and the "greatest happiness principle", which affirms an action as morally good if it produces the greatest happiness, or utility, for the greatest number. This approach to ethics is often referred to as consequentialism, owing to the centrality of outcomes in assessing the moral worth of an action.

In contrast to utilitarianism, Kantian theory argues that predictions of the future, that is, anticipating the consequences of actions, are not reliable enough to serve as a foundation for morality. Instead, he argued, we must appeal to those universal principles that any rational person would accept. Discussed in his *Groundwork of the Metaphysic of Morals*, of 1785, Kant's "categorical imperative" yields such maxims as "do not lie unless you can will that all people lie". Moral principles, in other words, are universally applicable and do not admit exceptions. In the Kantian system moral obligations are absolute even when they may possibly or probably yield consequences that seem unacceptable or abhorrent. For example, suicide is wrong because it cannot be universally applied, even though the prospect of continued life for a particular individual may be filled with pain and misery.

John Rawls, author of *A Theory of Justice* (Rawls 1971) is the most prominent advocate of a theory of justice that calls for re-distribution of wealth, insofar as that redistribution yields a greater overall good. Rawls developed the concept of the "veil of ignorance" to represent a realm where rational agents were relieved of knowing anything about their own personal circumstances—wealth, talent, intellect, physical state, age, gender–leading these agents to conclude that the goods of society should be distributed in such a way as to always benefit the least advantaged in some way. Rawls calls this the "difference principle" (Rawls 1971, pp. 52–57).

Justice has not only been of concern to moral philosophers, but also to theologians. Theology is a field of study and inquiry that reflects on the sacred texts and teachings of a religion. It has been referred to as "faith seeking understanding". Many sacred texts refer to justice as a necessary part of a truly spiritual way of life and/or as a divine command.

One of the central concerns of religious thinkers or systematic theologians is the topic of *theodicy*, literally, the justice of God. The discussion of theodicy is related to the question of evil, and, more specifically, the following question: How can a loving, good and all-powerful God create a world with so much suffering and evil? For Max Weber, this was the overriding question that all the great civilizations tried to answer comprehensively and rationally (Weber 1963, pp. 138–150). Within Hinduism, the answer was formulated as the law of karma. Judaism, Christianity and Islam, each in unique ways, developed a doctrine of the Fall of Man. Within Protestant Christianity, and especially Calvinism, the answer was formulated in the doctrine of pre-destination. The concept of justice and fairness is an essential part of the world's religions. Consider the following passages from various scriptures, each speaking to the topic of justice:

> "I hate, I despise your feasts, and I take no delight in your solemn assemblies. Take away from me the noise of your songs; to the melody of your harps I will not listen. But let justice roll down like waters, and righteousness like an ever-flowing stream" (Torah, Amos 5:23–24, Judaism).
>
> "Beware the plea of the oppressed, for he asks God Most High only for his due, and God does not keep the one who has a right from receiving what is due" (Hadith of Bayhaqi, Islam).
>
> "O he who believes! Stand out firmly for justice, as witnesses to God, even as against yourselves, or your parents, or your kin, and whether it concerns rich or poor, for God can best protect both. Follow not the lusts of your heart lest you swerve, and if you distort justice or decline to do justice, verily God is well acquainted with all that you do" (Qur'an 4.135, Islam).
>
> "Someone said, 'What do you say concerning the principle that injury should be recompensed with kindness?' The Master said, 'With what will you then recompense kindness?' Recompense injury with justice, and recompense kindness with kindness" (Analects 14.36, Confucianism).
>
> "Here is my servant whom I uphold; my chosen, in whom my soul delights; I have put my spirit upon him; He will bring forth justice to the nations. . .He will faithfully bring forth justice. He will not grow faint or be crushed until he has established justice in the earth; and the coastlands wait for his teaching" (Isaiah 42.1-4).
>
> "What does God require of you but to do justice, and to love kindness, and to walk humbly with your God?" (Micah 6:8).
>
> "Unless your justice exceeds that of the scribes and Pharisees, you shall not enter the Kingdom of Heaven" (Matthew 5:20).

In Mathew's chapter 25, Jesus calls his disciples to "Love the Lord your God with your whole heart and your neighbor as yourself". He speaks of the two primary commandments, namely, to love God and to love one's neighbor. His "love command" exhorts his followers to go beyond what justice may require, namely, giving what is due, and to practice a higher, sacrificial love, giving more than one owes.

As mentioned previously, within Hinduism there is the doctrine of karma which indicates that every action has its own reward or punishment, and these accrue over a lifetime to determine one's destiny in the next life. Karma is the law of cause and effect that functions as an integral part of a cosmic system of justice; similar to "reaping what you sow". Swami Vivekananda says, "Everything we do, physical or mental, is Karma and it leaves its mark on us" (Vivekananda 1955, p. 5).

The concept of justice is pervasive in religion, from the Book of Job to the Bhagavad Gita, from Isaiah to the Gospels, and from socially activist Christianity, to socially engaged Buddhism.

Of course, religions most often highlight justice in a wider context of other virtues and values, some superior to the call for justice; these include practices such as love, mercy, forgiveness, charity and reconciliation. While most religions affirm the need for justice, it is not the ultimate moral command, and must be understood and practiced in a wider framework of spiritual ideals. Hence the religious path often calls us beyond justice alone, toward a higher calling of forgiveness, self-sacrifice, generosity and "turning the other cheek".

Having endured a bloody and divisive civil war less than 100 years after America's founding, President Abraham Lincoln, in his second Inaugural Address, in March of 1865, stated, "With malice toward none, with charity for all; with firmness in the right, as God gives us to see the right; let us strive on to finish the work we are in; to bind up the nation's wounds; to care for him who shall have borne the battle, and for his widow, and for his orphan; to do all which may achieve and cherish a just and lasting peace among ourselves and with all nations" (Lincoln 1865). These words exemplify a theory of justice that is tempered by "charity for all", and "care" for the downtrodden.

2.1 Forgiveness

Forgiveness is a virtue and a practice extolled in most religions. For example, Jesus' "Our Father" prayer, taken from the New Testament's Book of Matthew, encourages believers to reach out to God, saying "forgive us our debts as we forgive our debtors"(Matthew 6:11–12). The Qur'an teaches, "If you efface and overlook and forgive, then lo! God is forgiving, merciful" (Qur'an 64.14); and in Confucianism's *I Ching* 40, we read, "The superior man tends to forgive wrongs and deals leniently with crimes." The *Adi Granth* of Sikhism states that "Where there is forgiveness, there is God Himself." The *Samanasuttam* 236 of Jainism exhorts us to "subvert anger by forgiveness".

Jesus taught, "Do not resist one who is evil. But if anyone strikes you on the right cheek, turn to him the other also; and if anyone would sue you and take your coat, let him have your cloak as well; and if anyone forces you to go one mile, go with him two miles" (Matthew 5:39-41).

2.2 Restitution

Restitution—to repair or restore what has been damaged, taken, or brought out of balance—is also a well-developed theological concept found in most sacred scriptures. Consider the following:

"O dweller in the body, make reparation for whatever you have done!" (*Garuda Purana* 2.35. Hinduism).

"Whoever by a good deed covers the evil done, such a one illumines this world like the moon freed from clouds" (*Dhammapada* 173 of Buddhism).

"If one has, indeed, done deeds of wickedness, but afterwards alters his way and repents, resolved not to do anything wicked, but to practice reverently all that is good, he is sure in the long run to obtain good fortune—this is called changing calamity into blessing" (*Treatise on Response and Retribution* 5, Taoism).

"If any harm follows, then you shall give life for life, eye for eye, tooth for tooth, hand for hand, foot for foot, burn for burn, wound for wound, stripe for stripe" (Exodus 21:23–25.).

"And we prescribed for them: 'A life for a life, an eye for an eye, a nose for a nose, an ear for an ear, a tooth for a tooth, and for wounds retaliation.' But whoever forgoes it in the way of charity, it shall be expiation for him" (Qur'an 5:45).[1]

2.3 Problematic Aspects of Religion

Of course, the moral guidance found in scripture is at times problematic. For example, in Proverbs 13:24 we read, "He that spareth his rod hateth his son." In Ephesians 5:22–24 we have passages that endorse subordination of women: "Wives be subject to your husbands, as to the Lord. For the husband is the head of the wife as Christ is the head of the Church ... As the Church is subject to Christ, so let wives also be subject in everything to their husbands."

Polygyny was espoused and practiced by early Mormon believers, and is affirmed in Islam as well. Christian Scientist believers have withheld medical treatment from children. In 1978, in Jonestown, Guyana, 900 members of the Peoples Temple committed mass suicide. Christian fundamentalists have blown up abortion clinics and assaulted practitioners. Jihadists engage in suicide missions, leading to the deaths of innocent children, women and men, guided by a belief in eternal bliss in the after-life. The Catholic Church has been plagued by sexual misconduct among priests who sexually abused children, followed by years of inaction and cover-ups. Suffice it to say that religion is prone to all the evils that plague human beings in general, though the sins of the believer stand out against a background of ideals and aspirations that make them appear all the more deviant and disturbing.

Are religious believers more highly inclined toward evil and crime than non-believers, or governments, business professionals, or philosophers? There is no simple answer. Secular governments, and militantly anti-religious governments have also done great damage to humanity. Nevertheless, crimes fostered by or associated with religion are evident throughout history and cannot be ignored. At

[1] For a substantial and useful anthology of passages from scriptures of all religions, and on a variety of topics, see Wilson (1991).

the same time, the regrettable facts of crimes committed in the name of religion should not lead us to throw the baby out with the bathwater.

2.4 *Religion and Restorative Justice*

One theory and practice of justice that has gained ground over the past several decades is known as "restorative justice". Restorative justice stands in contrast to theories of justice and systems of justice that emphasize retribution, adversarial courtroom protocols, and the interests of the state. Restorative justice has roots in indigenous tribal cultures, such as Native Americans, the Maori of New Zealand, and peoples of many of the small island states of the Pacific. These cultures are invariably religious in their worldviews. Certain pacifist Christian groups—Mennonites and Quakers—also advocate practices of restorative justice. In recent times, we can conceive of the Truth and Reconciliation Commission in South Africa as an example of restorative justice at work. The approach is much less adversarial and more focused on human relationships, with dialogical engagement between victim, offender and other stakeholders.

In giving emphasis to mediation between victim and offender, restorative justice often utilizes group processes, "circles of support and accountability". Some argue that restorative justice leads to lower rates of recidivism (Johnson 2011, pp. 105–116).

Practices of restorative justice are generally not sectarian in nature, even though informed and inspired, in many cases, by spiritual ideals, such as honesty, responsibility, repentance, forgiveness, atonement, apology, etc. According to Michael Hadley, the restorative model [of justice] regards crime as a violation of people and relationships; it is concerned with healing the wounds of victim, community and offenders alike (Hadley 2001, p. 9). He adds that restorative justice, with its principles of repentance, forgiveness, and reconciliation, is instead a deeply spiritual process (Hadley 2001, p. 9).

Restorative justice has roots in the spirituality found in indigenous traditions. Roots are also to be found in religions such as Buddhism. David Loy says Buddhist justice grows out of compassion for everyone involved when someone hurts another (Loy 2001, p. 95). According to Howard Zehr,

> Restorative justice is based upon an old, common-sense understanding of wrongdoing ... Underlying this understanding is an assumption about society: we are all interconnected. In the Hebrew scripture, this is embedded in the concept of shalom, the vision of living in a sense of 'all-rightness' with one another, with the creator, and with the environment. Many cultures have a word that represents this notion of the centrality of relationship: for the Maori, it is communicated by *whakapapa*; for the Navaho, *hozho*; for many Africans, the Bantu word *Ubuntu*. Although the specific meanings of these words may vary, they communicate a similar message: all things are connected to each other in a web of relationships. (Zehr 2002, pp. 19–20).

Zehr underscores the point that restorative justice employs a process that is more collaborative, participatory and inclusive than conventional retributivist or utilitarian models. Outcomes, in turn, are based more on consensus than the legalistic imposition of sentences. One might say that restorative justice fits more with a communitarian social model, in contrast to both state-centered and individualistic models. Hence, the emphasis on "circles", victim-offender conferences, family group conferences.

Charles Colson, the Christian evangelical founder of Prison Fellowship International, speaks of restorative justice as a kind of relational justice, one rooted in a biblical worldview. He states that restorative justice grounds justice in the peace of God's created order. Both relational and restorative justice, therefore, offer aspects of the biblical view of shalom, a peace that is intrinsically relationship and righteous (Colson 2001, p. 114). Colson identifies core elements of restorative justice as involving prevention, wise sentencing, judicious use of prisons, community involvement, reintegration programs for offenders, and involvement of crime victims (Colson 2001, pp. 121–143).

Restorative justice offers an approach to criminal justice with potential to benefit from best practices found in many spiritual and religious traditions. Belief that a righteous solution may be found outside a corrupt formal justice system must be one of the reasons why the United Nations in its *Handbook on Restorative Justice Programmes* notes the role of NGOs and faith groups in restorative justice (UNODC 2006, p. 31).

3 Religion, Social Capital and Crime

As stated earlier, the data on the relationship or correlation between religion and crime are not entirely conclusive. Rodney Stark's and Travis Hirschi's landmark hellfire and delinquency research indicated no overwhelmingly positive or negative correlation between religiosity and delinquency (Hirschi and Stark 1969). While religion is clearly a motivating force in the lives of people, and whereas religion counsels a wide range of virtues and principles that lead believers away from criminal activity, human beings do not always act consistently or rationally.

Many times religious people do bad things. As previously mentioned, history is littered with religiously inspired conflicts, crusades, inquisitions, militant jihads, and terrorist acts; not to mention instances of sexual abuse, child neglect and abuse, and other anti-social pathological actions that may be guided by deranged religious inspirations. On the other hand, religion is also often a force for good.

One of the challenges in empirical verification of correlations between religion and crime is that the root causes of crime are themselves complex and plural in nature. Factors such as poverty, parenting, education, involvement in group activity, personality, biology, environment, ideology, etc., are all relevant factors (Ellis and Walsh 2000, pp. 95–99).

A publication of papers presented at the American Society of Criminology in 2010 includes a series of essays on crime and religion. Byron R. Johnson and Sung Joon Jang argue in *Crime and Religion: Assessing the Role of the Faith Factor* that criminologists should be interested in religion not only because it may be useful in explaining why people do or do not commit crime, but because religion may be helpful in understanding why people engage in prosocial activities, something criminologists have tended to ignore (Johnson and Jang 2012, p. 117). Johnson and Jang reviewed 270 religion and crime studies between 1944 and 2010 and conclude that the vast majority of studies report prosocial effects of religion and religious involvement on various measures of crime and delinquency (Johnson and Jang 2012, p. 120). They also cite the work of Durkheim and Bentham, who, as mentioned earlier, saw correlations between religion and pro-social behavior. The authors conclude their essay stating that, "Failure to consider religion variables will cause researchers to be needlessly shortsighted in estimating models designed to explain its direct and indirect influences on antisocial as well as prosocial behavior" (Johnson and Jang 2012, p. 129).

The avoidance of religion within the field of criminology may be attributed in part to the dominance of structural and economic explanations that underscore, for example, the poverty factor. Attention to religion may seem to require a discounting of these social scientific explanations. However, this seems not to be a necessary conclusion, and an anti-reductionistic openness to the religious factor would seem to be called for by a scientific approach. Jeffrey Ulmer argues that, "religion is likely a fundamental and nearly ubiquitous cultural institution that, when present in individual or group life, can shape and condition socialization, identity, learning and opportunity structures, relationship and social bonds, social capital, and coping mechanisms in the face of strains" (Ulmer 2012, p. 168).

In addition to research related to the correlations between religion and crime, it may also be helpful to consider the concept of social capital. There is also compelling evidence suggesting a negative correlation between "social capital" and crime.

The concept of social capital is relevant to our consideration of crime and justice, as scholars such as Robert D. Putnam (Putnam 2000) and Francis Fukuyama (Fukuyama 1999) have indicated, arguing that social relationships and networks may be significant assets in establishing social stability. As M. K. Smith has put it, "There is now a range of evidence that communities with a good 'stock' of 'social capital' are more likely to benefit from lower crime figures, better health, high educational achievement, and better economic growth" (Smith 2013).

According to Fukuyama, "Social capital can be defined simply as a set of informal values or norms shared among members of a group that permits cooperation among them. If members of the group come to expect that others will behave reliably and honestly, then they will come to trust one another. Trust is like a lubricant that makes the running of any group or organization more efficient" (Fukuyama 1999, p. 16).

While there may be many positive outcomes associated with a rise of social capital in a particular social context, there are also potential problems. Social networks that include and bring people together may also lead to forms of exclusion, or "in group" and "out group" tendencies. This is the problem of tribalism, or, within religion, various forms of sectarianism and fundamentalism. While solidarity is established for some, those who are either not welcomed or who simply do not fit may become alienated. For example, the so-called "digital divide" suggests there is a vast difference, even an inequality, between those who are "wired" and those who are not.

Joshua Greene has addressed this problem in his book entitled *Moral Tribes: Emotion, Reason and the Gap between Us and Them*. In discussing tribalism, Greene writes, "Biological accounts of the evolution of cooperation with non-kin involve favoring one's cooperation partners (most or all of whom belong to one's group) over others. Indeed, some mathematical models indicate that altruism within groups could not have evolved without hostility between groups" (Greene 2013, p. 69). In other words, tribal solidarity tends to affirm the members of the tribe and disaffirm those outside of the tribe. Thus, concepts of fairness and justice are often biased in favor of one's tribal affections. Therefore, moral decisions are linked to in-group and out-group mentalities. For this reason, moral philosophers and theologians have sought to universalize the application of moral principles to include all human beings.

If the concept of tribe or community of empathy, trust and cooperation can be expanded, it would seem that a reduction in crime and an increase in prosocial behavior would follow. Fukuyama speaks about the "radius of trust" that may be small and narrow, or large and broad (Fukuyama 1999). He says, "Virtually all forms of traditional culture-social groups like tribes, clans, village associations, religious sects, etc., are based on shared norms and use these norms to achieve cooperative ends" (Fukuyama 1999, p. 3). Thus, there are certain disadvantages to in-group solidarity with a small radius of trust.

However the radius can be extended. International trade and commerce is a good example. While rule of law and contracts are essential for trade and commerce, there are a wide range of informal aspects to cooperation and productivity. Social capital makes such cooperation possible. In other words, social capital helps make commerce and economic transactions work well, perhaps suggesting something of the "invisible hand" or the "moral sentiments" that Adam Smith believed to be the infrastructure of a growing economy (Smith 1993, 2002).

Social capital also applies to the political sphere, and is believed to be an essential ingredient in a successful democratic system. Many have suggested that a thriving civil society is an essential prerequisite for democracy. Quoting Fukuyama, "In the absence of civil society, the state often needs to step in to organize individuals who are incapable of organizing themselves. The result of excessive individualism is therefore not freedom, but rather the tyranny of what Tocqueville saw as a large and benevolent state that hovered over society and, like a father, saw to all of its needs. Low levels of social capital lead to a number of political dysfunctions" (Fukuyama 1999, p. 5). Fukuyama offers the following suggestions to increase social capital (Fukuyama 1999, pp. 11–12):

1. States cannot easily create social capital, for social capital is largely a byproduct of religion, tradition, shared historical experience;
2. Education is the primary area where government can help create and nourish social capital, for example, through moral education, civic education, etc;
3. States can help by protecting property rights and public safety, essentially a safe and secure environment;
4. States should not overstep their legitimate and necessary realm of authority, and should respect the subsidiary authority and value of civil society and the private sector;
5. States should respect the value of religion as an essential source of social capital;
6. Globalization can be a source of growing social capital, through the spread of ideas, innovative, cultural values, etc.

Traditionally, we know that factors of ethnicity, race, class, gender, etc., create not only opportunities for belongingness and trust and solidarity, but also opportunities for racism, ethnocentrism, sexism, classism, etc. Some argue that economic inequality is the decisive factor in creating a decline of social capital and trust for the poor. In this respect the concept of "fairness" is relevant. As populations, minorities, sub-cultures, etc., who are marginalized, alienated or trapped in poverty lose their bonds of affection and trust toward the wider society, social capital declines.

With that caveat, nevertheless, we can also understand the value of communities and relationships which can be characterized by fairness, reciprocity, trust, mutual respect for laws and traditions and values, involvement, interconnectedness, empathy, and pride about one's identity and place in the world. One can easily see that when these factors decline, problems will easily follow.

3.1 Civil Society

One indicator of a higher balance of social capital is the presence of a strong civil society component within a given society or nation. The idea of civil society has classical roots, dating back to Aristotle, and the rise of the concept of a *res publica*, a public thing. It took on its modern understanding with Hegel, whose Philosophy of Right speaks about civil society as a realm that stands in between the family and the state, associated with the rise of capitalism. Marx drew on Hegel's understanding of civil society. Alexis de Tocqueville, in his commentaries on the American and French Revolutions, attributed the relative success of the American Revolution to its robust civil society institutions, including churches (de Tocqueville 1945, Vol. 1, pp. 198–204 and 319–326).

De Tocqueville said, "Americans of all ages, all conditions and all dispositions constantly form associations. They have not only commercial and manufacturing companies, in which all take part, but associations of a thousand other kinds, religious, moral, serious, futile, general or restricted, enormous or diminutive...

Wherever at the head of some new undertaking you see the government in France, or a man of rank in England, in the United States you will be sure to find an association." Continuing, he states, "Among the laws that rule human societies there is one which seems to be more precise and clear than all others. If men are to remain civilized or to become so, the art of associating together must grow and improve in the same ration in which the equality of conditions is increased" (de Tocqueville 1945, Vol. 2, p. 114).

Robert Putnam, a Harvard political scientist, published an article in 1995 called "Bowling Alone: America's Declining Social Capital", and later, in 2000, the book-length version, titled *Bowling Alone: The Collapse and Revival of American Community*, arguing that there was a breakdown of the tradition of voluntary associations, civic associations, etc., including bowling leagues (Putnam 2000). The concept of "social capital" suggests the assets that come with human capacities, strengths, traits, etc., are needed in order to strengthen a nation's capacity to develop a vital and dynamic democracy characterized by the rule of law.

Bernard Lewis, writing in *What Went Wrong: The Clash between Islam and Modernity in the Middle East* (Lewis 2002), argues, in his chapter on "Secularism and Civil Society", that there has been a decline in social capital in a number of Middle Eastern countries which has contributed to instability and a weakness of democratic institutions.

For some the concept of civil society is a neo-liberal or neo-conservative concept that has a built-in anti-state bias. However, it is possible to view this concept without seeing it in a politicized way. For example, some view civil society as a superstructural or consequent factor in social affairs, unrelated to "root causes" such as poverty, class, or race, etc. However, theoreticians on both the left and the right have affirmed the importance of civil society. Non-governmental organizations, for example, represent what we might call both left-wing and right-wing positions and causes.

Citing Fukuyama again, social capital is the "*sine qua non* of stable liberal democracy" and "an instantiated informal norm that promotes cooperation between two or more individuals" (Fukuyama 1999, p. 1). Social capital is cultivated through social networks, civic engagement, and bonded relationships characterized by trust and manifested in some institutional setting, clubs, NGOs, associations, leagues, parties, etc. One way to state the thesis of social capital theory is that "relationships matter". Stated a bit differently, we can say that "civil society matters".

Civil society is often described as a kind of "third sector" distinguished from the realm of the state or government and the realm of the market or the private economic center. Jürgen Habermas, whose work has been focused on the concept of a "public sphere", distinguished between the "system" characterized by bureaucratic rationality and the "lifeworld", where discourse of communicative practices was unfettered by instruments of money and power (Habermas 1984, 1987).

A society with strong civic institutions stands in a better position to both prevent and resolve social epidemics.

3.2 Social Capital and Mediating Institutions

In 1977 Peter Berger and Richard John Neuhaus published a small volume entitled *To Empower the People: From State to Civil Society* (Berger and Neuhaus 1977). At a time in America when there were significant economic problems, rising crime rates, and what President Jimmy Carter called a national "malaise", this volume struck a chord among many, and especially those who had grown skeptical of state-centered solutions to social problems. They called for more focused attention on medium-sized social institutions, particularly family, neighborhood, voluntary associations, and churches or religious affiliations. These institutions are often taken for granted, but serve what Roman Catholic social thought would call essential subsidiary functions. Richard Neuhaus writes, "The several communities to which we each belong require discriminations in moral judgment. . .Church, family, friendships, professional associations, neighborhood, maybe even town or city—these are real communities, made up of touchable face-to-face connections" (Neuhaus 1984, p. 63).

Charles Murray's most recent book, *Coming Apart*, argues that the white population in the USA between 1960 and 2010 experienced a dramatic decline in marriage, down 36 %, an increase in out-of-wedlock births, and growth in dropping out rate of the work force (Murray 2013). Simultaneously crime increased proportionately. Along with these developments, religiosity also declined and secularization rose. Murray points out, in an essay published in *The Wall Street Journal*, "Whatever your personal religious views, you need to realize that about half of American philanthropy, volunteering and associational memberships is directly church-related, and that religious Americans also account for much more nonreligious social capital than their secular neighbors" (Murray 2012).

The white elite have increasingly segregated themselves in what Murray calls "super zips" [ZIP or postal codes], an upper-class culture that may have little if any regular contact with the "lower classes". Murray states, "Changes in social policy in the 1960's made it economically more feasible to have a child without having a husband if you're a woman or to get along without a job if you were a man; safe to commit crimes without suffering consequences; and easier to let the government deal with problems that you and your neighbors formerly had to take care of" (Murray 2012).

Jean Bethke Elshtain speaks of the loss of our "social ecology," attributing this to the deterioration of mediating institutions. "Children", she argues, "bear the brunt of these negative trends," such as growing distrust, individualism and privatization. She says, "Where neighborhoods are intact, drug and alcohol abuse, crime, teenage childbearing, and truancy among the young diminish. But because neighborhoods are less and less likely to be intact, all forms of socially and self-destructive behavior among the young are on the rise" (Elshtain 1996).

3.3 An Upsurge of NGOs and Civil Society Institutions

Beginning in the last century and continuing in this century there has been an explosion of non-governmental organizations, NGOs, sometimes called "civil society" institutions. The term "NGO" emerged at the time of the founding of the United Nations, as a way to differentiate "governmental organizations" from "non-governmental organizations" or NGOs.

We can think of NGOs as non-state actors, and increasingly their voices are being heard and affirmed in many instances. In some respects, NGOs represent more the voice of "we the people" than governments. And, unlike governments, NGOs are easily transnational and unconstrained by the diplomatic traditions and political compromises that limit governments.

But NGOs are not without their critics. Indeed, many NGOs are highly politicized, and behind apparently humanitarian concerns are special interests, or even corrupt or criminal intentions. Indeed NGOs are also not accountable to an electorate in the way that governments are. Moreover, they have often been granted sympathies of which they are not all deserving; for, alongside the many truly humanitarian, authentic NGOs are many unscrupulous and ill-intentioned NGOs.

All things considered, however, NGOs seem to be well suited for generating social capital for many millions of people around the world, fostering solidarity, trust, a sense of belonging, shared values, and the kind of engagement with others that offsets many alienating aspects of post-modern society.

Moreover, efforts to prevent or address destructive social epidemics can be enhanced through NGOs. In turn, there has emerged a term to describe individuals who have made a dramatic impact on society through their NGO efforts. They are called "social entrepreneurs". David Bornstein says, "Social entrepreneurs are uniquely suited to make headway on problems that have resisted considerable money and intelligence. Where governments and traditional organizations look at problems from the outside, social entrepreneurs come to understand them intimately from within...Because they do not have armies or police forces behind them, they work to elicit change rather than impose it, so they build human capacity rather than encouraging dependency. In developing countries where they have engaged at top levels with governments, the results have been impressive" (Bornstein 2007, p. xii).

3.4 Family: The Primary Mediating Institution

The traditional family is another underutilized resource for the development of social capital. Some have coined the term "family capital", arguing that we need to appreciate the multiple ways in which the family is a social asset. It is almost axiomatic, a truism to say that where marriages and families are happy, healthy and harmonious, there is increased potential for stability and prosperity in society.

We know that children, and that includes each one of us, are shaped in profound and irreversible ways by our family experiences, both genetically and socially. For example, just consider religion and the 5 billion believers in our world, and the way in which family has set the course for our religious and spiritual journeys in life.

As with the institutions that foster social capital, the family cuts both ways. It can be a great enhancer, and it can be also the greatest destroyer or damager of human hearts and minds. Families can transmit both the highest ideals to the next generation, or the most tribalistic and regressive ideals. Both can be done by parents or relatives with equal pride and conviction, though with very divergent results.

The Doha Institute for Family Studies and Development published a volume entitled *The Family and the Millennium Development Goals: Using Family Capital to Achieve the 8 Millennium Development Goals* (Roylance 2012). This volume includes articles that cover each of the 8 Millennium Development Goals (MDGs), showing how the family serves as an instrument that has great potential to help in the achievement of the MDGs. The MDGs, outlined by the UN in 2000, are:

1. Overcoming poverty and hunger
2. Universal primary education
3. Gender equality
4. Child mortality
5. Maternal health
6. Combat HIV/AIDS and other diseases
7. Environmental sustainability
8. Global partnerships

In the introduction to the volume, Richard Wilkins says, "Social science data demonstrates two nearly incontestable conclusions: (1) Stable families, founded upon marriage, provide significant benefits for men, women and children, while (2) The breakdown of stable marital structures imposes substantial costs upon individuals and society at large. The family, in short, plays a profoundly important social role. Absent healthy family life, individual and social development suffers" (Roylance 2012, p. iii). The family can and should be a strong bulwark against crime.

Nearing the 2015 conclusion of the Millennium Development Goals, with mixed results, the United Nations community has begun the process of refining, benchmarking, and identifying a set of Sustainable Development Goals, or SDGs, to be launched in 2015. As with the MDGs, the family can and should be seen as a resource and an ally in the effort to promote human development, broadly conceived.

4 Interfaith and the United Nations: Toward an Expanded Radius of Trust

Religion is often described by many as essentially judgmental in nature, continuously pointing out sins and failings of believers and non-believers alike. Religion is also often accused of being largely pathological and a destructive force in the world, citing evils such as religiously inspired terrorism, oppression of women, bigotry, child abuse, intolerant attitudes toward non-believers, fanaticism, and ethnocentrism. This list goes on. One might also add the long list of conflicts which have, in addition to political, economic, social, and ethnic causes at play, a religious component: Israel and Palestine, Sri Lanka, India and Pakistan, Ireland, Mindanao in the Philippines, Syria, Lebanon, Nigeria, Central African Republic, etc.

At the same time, religion is also quite capable of playing a role as an agent of peace and conflict mediation. As we have seen, religion plays a significant role in building "social capital", and while there is not an absolute correlation between religious affiliation and moral uprightness, there are a number of positive associations, evidenced in religious schools, charities, service organizations, disaster relief organizations, hospitals, mentoring, prison ministries, hospice ministries, not to mention religiously inspired social activism that focuses on human rights, women's rights, children's rights, non-violence, hospitality to immigrants, etc.

It is safe to conclude two points about religion. First of all, religions, in ways similar to businesses, NGOs and governments, are capable of doing both great harm and great good. The evils committed by governments over time are enormous, even governments that are militantly anti-religious. Likewise, NGOs, as well as businesses, are prone to various forms of corruption, self-serving agendas, and abuse of public trust. Secondly, religion has great potential and capacity for good. It is this capacity that should be encouraged, strengthened and affirmed.

In this light, I underscore one of the leading developments in the religious sector that has emerged and established positive momentum over the past century. I refer to the interfaith dialogue movement. While there are passages in most of the sacred scriptures of the world's religions that affirm hospitality, generosity and respect toward people of other faiths, these directives have generally not been given adequate emphasis. The focus of most religions, historically, has been on expanding and securing the community within a given territory. However, as the world has grown smaller, and the plurality of the religious landscape—both locally and globally—has become more and more apparent, there has been a corresponding recognition of the need for better understanding and cooperation between, within and among the religions.

The 1893 Parliament of the World's Religions, convened in Chicago, was a turning point in the history of interfaith dialogue, drawing delegations from religions throughout the world (Braybrooke 1992a, pp. 5–42; Sultan 2004, pp. 167–168). A variety of interfaith organizations emerged over the next several decades. Noteworthy among them are the International Association for Religious

Freedom, the World Congress of Faiths, the Temple of Understanding, Religions for Peace, the Council for a Parliament of the World's Religions, the United Religions Initiative, and the Universal Peace Federation (Braybrooke 1992a). Recently, in 2011, a new interfaith institute was established in Vienna, with the backing of Saudi Arabia, together with Spain and Austria, and known as the King Abdullah bin Abdulazziz International Centre for Interreligious and Intercultural Dialogue. These are some of the major interfaith organizations that operate on a global level. There are, at the same time, thousands of interfaith associations and NGOs that serve at the national, metropolitan, local and neighborhood levels.

In addition to the dialogue between or among religions, there is also a growing awareness of the need for intra-faith dialogue. After all, many of the fiercest conflicts have not been between religions, but within religions. Such has been the case within both Christianity—with divisions among Catholics, Orthodox and Protestant traditions—and Islam—with divisions among Sunni, Shiite, and Sufism. Virtually all religions have their divisions, splits and schisms, and these often lead to acrimony and even at times violence. Likewise, most religions have extremist elements, some of which may have a strong tendency toward violence. Thus, as much as interfaith dialogue is important, *intrafaith* dialogue is also urgently needed.

The interfaith dialogue movement is not merely an academic movement or a theological movement. It is closely associated with the ideal of peace. Moreover, it is guided by principles that lie at the heart of most religious traditions, including respect, generosity, hospitality, compassion, and service. While religion has often been a source of conflict and bad, even anti-social behavior, it has also given rise to moments of greatness and sparks of genius. The interfaith dialogue movement works to underscore religion's virtues and its potential to be a source of peace, cooperation, mutual understanding and reconciliation.

The United Nations has taken notice. Various resolutions have been passed in recent years by the General Assembly, including the decision to set up a focal unit within the UN Secretariat for interreligious dialogue. The Economic and Social Council offers NGO consultative status to a number of interfaith NGOs, and the Department of Public Information has many interfaith NGOs on its roster. In 2004 H.E. Jose Luis Rodriguez Zapatero, then president of Spain, proposed to the General Assembly of the United Nations the formation of the Alliance of Civilizations. H.E. Recep Tayyib Erdogan, prime minister of Turkey, joined with President Zapatero as co-sponsor of the initiative, which was presented to the 59th session of the General Assembly. Secretary General Kofi Annan welcomed the initiative and in 2005 the UN Alliance of Civilizations (AOC) was formed.[2] While the Alliance of Civilizations is not exclusively dedicated to interfaith dialogue, it seeks dialogue among peoples around the world, recognizing that civilizations are most often rooted in worldviews that have emerged from and been sustained by religious insights and ethical systems. The UN sense of that dialogue is a religious plurality

[2] For historical background on the United Nations Alliance of Civilizations, see http://www.unaoc.org/who-we-are/history/.

with an attitude of neutrality to the relative claims of religions concerning their priority of one over another.[3]

At its forthcoming 2014 Global Forum, the AOC has sessions dedicated to interfaith dialogue. Religious freedom is also a consistent area of concern. The Vienna Declaration, an outcome of the 5th Global Forum convened in Vienna, recognizes "that all cultures, civilizations and religions contribute to the enrichment of humankind" and stresses the importance of "respect and understanding for cultural and religious diversity" (Alliance of Civilizations 2013). At the center of the AOC vision is the concept of dialogue, a process of bringing people together across the barriers of culture, language, tradition, religion and civilization. The practices of interreligious dialogue have been instrumental in creating a broader culture of dialogue as an alternative to both a lack of civility and an intensification of conflict and distance.

In 2010 the UN General Assembly adopted resolution A/65/5 to dedicate one week each year to the promotion of interfaith dialogue and cooperation; this is known as the World Interfaith Harmony Week (Walsh 2012).

The efforts to promote interfaith dialogue and global ethics are grounded in the premise that there are underlying values and principles that all people share, as human beings with emotion, intellect and will, and regardless of their background or worldview.

These developments are of immense importance, for, through dialogue, they contribute to building a foundation for mutual understanding, respect, and cooperation among people of diverse religious backgrounds. This has the effect of expanding the bonds of trust among the people of the world. As the "radius of trust" expands globally, it impacts positively the relations among nations.

Interfaith efforts aimed at preventing or resolving conflict are often associated with "track two diplomacy". According to Joseph Montville, "...track-two diplomacy is unofficial, informal interaction among members of adversarial groups or nations with the goals of developing strategies, influencing public opinion, and organizing human and material resources in ways that might help resolve the conflict" (Montville 1992, p. 262). We also often hear the use of the term "soft power" to refer to those efforts to improve relations among nations which are focusing on such methods as education, dialogue, people-to-people relations, and civil society activism.

Religion, like other social institutions, has its struggles to avoid polarization. At the opposite end of the spectrum to interfaith and ecumenism lies fundamentalism and sectarianism. These movements are analogous to the contrast between internationalism or cosmopolitanism, on the one hand, and nationalism and identity politics, on the other hand.

[3] See Clark 1997, pp. 141–146 for the balance of the preceding philosophical aspects of the interfaith dialogue.

5 Toward a Global Ethics for a Global Society

There has long been an aspiration among theologians and philosophers alike to establish universal principles grounded in logic and rationality that yield an ethic that can be affirmed and practiced by all people. In recent years, this aspiration has been described as the quest for a global ethic. Moreover, it has been a focus of the interfaith movement in recent years, with an effort to underscore the common ground of morality that characterizes the teachings of the world's religions. The Swiss theologian Hans Küng was an early advocate for a global ethics, and in 1993, at the time of the Parliament of the World's Religions in Chicago, faith leaders from a wide variety of traditions reached consensus on the need to establish a global ethics. At that time the Declaration toward a Global Ethics (Braybrooke 1992b) was produced and affirmed as a statement that illustrated the shared moral values of the world's religious traditions. Values such as non-violence, tolerance, equal rights and justice were upheld.

The attempt to establish a global ethics aims to address issues of human dignity and human rights, the value of the environment, poverty and inequality, and liberty and justice. Hans Küng, a Roman Catholic theologian, has been a strong advocate for both interfaith dialogue and the development of a global ethics. Küng writes, in "The Need for a New World Ethic", that "Constructive engagement with the other religions of this world for the sake of peace in the world is vitally important for survival" (Küng, in Kittrie et al. 2003, p. 1044). He continues:

> It has become clear from beginning to end that a new post-colonial, post-imperialistic, postmodern world constellation is in the making, and thus a polycentric world which is being bound ever closer together by new communication technologies. But at the same time this polycentric world must be a transcultural and multireligious world. In this polycentric, transcultural and multireligious world ecumenical dialogue between the world religions takes on quite a new importance; for the sake of its peace this postmodern world needs more than ever the global religious understanding without which a political understanding will in the last resort no longer be possible (Küng, in Kittrie et al. 2003, p. 2047).

Küng envisions a new ecumenical paradigm, a vision that he sums up as follows: "No human life together without a world ethic for the nations; no peace among the nations without peace among the religions; no peace among the religions without dialogue among the religions" (Küng, in Kittrie et al. 2003, p. 1049).

According to Küng, "The Global Ethic project is based on four fundamental convictions: no peace among nations without peace among religions; no peace among religions without dialogue between the religions; no dialogue between the religions without global ethical standards; no survival of our globe without a global ethic, supported by both religious and non-religious people" (Küng, Global Ethic Foundation, 2008). Küng's proposal was widely affirmed at the 1993 Parliament of the World's Religions, and two core principles were highlighted: first, "the principle of humanity", indicating that each and every human being must be treated humanely; secondly, the "golden rule of reciprocity", namely, "what you do not wish done to yourself, do not do to others" (Küng, Global Ethic Foundation, 2008).

Marcus Braybrooke, in his "A Heart for the World", identifies the four core principles articulated in the declaration that emerged from the Assembly of the 1993 Parliament of the World's Religions:

> Commitment to a culture of non-violence and respect for life.
> Commitment to a culture of solidarity and a just economic order.
> Commitment to a culture of tolerance and a life of truthfulness.
> Commitment to a culture of equal rights and partnership between men and women (Braybrooke 2005, p. 90).

Braybrooke also quotes the recently sainted Pope John Paul II, who stated in 2001, that "As humanity embarks upon the process of globalization, it can no longer do without a common code of ethics ... It is within man as such, within universal humanity sprung from the Creator's hand, that the norms of social life are to be sought ... In all the variety of cultural forms, universal human values exist and they must be brought out and emphasized as the guiding force of all development and progress." Pope John Paul II, Address to the Pontifical Academy of Sciences, on April 27, 2001 (John Paul II 2001).

6 Conclusion

The field of criminology has only very recently begun to appreciate the relevance of religion, recognizing that religion remains a powerful social force in our world. In a variety of fields, such as international relations, political science, peace studies, and business, an awareness of the ongoing relevance of religious ideas and practices is increasingly appreciated. This is most appropriate, given that the conventional theories of secularization as an automatic accompaniment of modernization have been called into question.

One does not have to be a theologian or a believer to appreciate religion's impact on society. Of course, even those who are convinced that religion is necessarily regressive and socially destructive see religion as a social force, albeit one to be marginalized and contained. Others take an affirmative view of religion and its social significance. Still others observe religion non-prejudicially as a social fact. After all, imagine trying to understand Indian society, and its 1 billion plus population, without knowing something about Hinduism; or consider the societies of North Africa, the Middle East and Central Asia without knowing Islam. Therefore, the case can be made for increased attention to religion within the field of criminology.

This is not to suggest that religion is always a decisive or dominating factor in society. Rather, it is simply to suggest that it is an important factor.

We have seen that there is an association between religion and the broader concept of social capital, and that religion can often contribute to the expansion of the radius of trust that defines community. Of course, religion is prone to corruption in the same way that governments, civil society and private sector institutions, and professional communities are. Its ideals and aspirations may be higher, but its practices are sometimes lowly and shameful.

The ideal of a global ethics that is rooted in interfaith dialogue and the search for common ground has promise as an enterprise that can build a strong sense of global community and solidarity. Such ideals are gaining ground within the United Nations, as it also comes to an increased awareness of and appreciation for interreligious dialogue and understanding.

Five Questions

1. What are some of the social effects of religious commitment?
2. To what extent should a "religious factor" be considered in the broader effort to understand the root causes and lasting solutions to crime?
3. Do principles and practices of "restorative justice" have relevance in modern, industrialized, urbanized social environments?
4. Are there any social benefits, such as reduced crime, to be gained through the promotion of interreligious dialogue and understanding?
5. Is a global ethics possible in a highly pluralistic and multi-cultural world?

References

Albright, M. (2006). *The Mighty and the Almighty: Reflections on America, God and World Affairs*. New York: Harper.

Bentham, J. (1789). *An Introduction to the Principles of Morals and Legislation* (p. 2007). Mineola, NY: Dover.

Berger, P. (Ed.). (1999). *The Desecularization of the World: Resurgent Religion and World Politics*. Washington, DC: Ethics and Public Policy Center.

Berger, P., & Neuhaus, R. (1977). *To Empower the People: From State to Civil Society*. Washington, DC: Ethics and Public Policy Center.

Bornstein, D. (Ed.). (2007). *How to Change the World: Social Entrepreneurs and the Power of New Ideas*. Oxford, UK: Oxford University Press.

Braybrooke, M. (1992). *Pilgrimage of Hope: One Hundred Years of Interfaith Dialogue*. New York: Crossroad.

Braybrooke, M. (Ed.). (1992b). *Stepping stones to a global ethic*. London: SCM Press.

Braybrooke, M. (2005). *A heart for the world*. Wincheste, UK: Orca Books.

Clark, J. J. (1997). *Oriental Enlightenment. The Encounter between Asian and Western Thought*. London/New York: Routledge.

Colson, C. (2001). *Justice That Restores*. Wheaton, IL: Tyndale.

Durkheim, E. (1912). *The Elementary Forms of Religious Life*. London: George Allen and Unwin.

Durkheim, E. (1897). *Suicide: A Study in Sociology*. New York: Free Press.

Eliade, M. (1987). *The Sacred and the Profane*. San Diego, USA: Harcourt.

Ellis, L., & Walsh, A. (2000). *Criminology: A global perspective*. Needham Heights, MA: Allyn and Bacon.

Elshtain, J. B. (1996). 'Democracy at Century's End' in National Humanities Center.

Fukuyama, F. (1999). *Social capital and civil society*. Washington, D.C.: Institute of Social Policy/George Mason University/International Monetary Fund.

Greene, J. (2013). *Moral tribes: Emotion, reason and the gap between us and them*. New York: Penguin.

Habermas, J. (1984). *The theory of communicative action* (Vol. I). Boston: Beacon Press.

Habermas, J. (1987). *The theory of communicative action* (Vol. II). Boston: Beacon Press.
Habermas, J. (2010). *An awareness of what is missing: Faith and reason in a post-secular age*. Malden, MA: Polity Press.
Hadley, M. (2001). *The spiritual roots of restorative justice*. Albany, NY: State University of New York Press.
Hirschi, T., & Stark, R. (1969). Hellfire and delinquency. *Social Problems, 17*(2), 202–213.
Huntington, S. (1993). *The clash of civilizations and the re-making of world order*. Foreign Affairs.
Inglehart, R., & Norris, P. (2011). *Sacred and secular: Religion and politics worldwide*. New York: Cambridge University Press.
John Paul II (2001). 'Address of the Holy Father' in Pontifical Academy of Social Sciences, April 27, 2001 in www.vatican.va/holy_father/john_paul.
Johnson, B. R. (2011). *More god, less crime*. West Conshohocken, PA: Templeton Press.
Johnson, B. R., & Jang, S. J. (2012). *Crime and religion: Assessing the role of the faith factor' in contemporary issues in criminological theory and research: The role of social institutions*. Belmont, CA: Wadsworth.
Johnston, D. (1994). *Religion, the missing dimension of statecraft*. New York: Oxford University Press.
Kant, I. (1785). *Groundwork of the metaphysics of morals*. Cambridge: Cambridge University Press.
Kittrie, N., Carazo, R., & Mancham, J. (Eds.). (2003). *The future of peace*. Durham, NC: Carolina Academic Press.
Küng, H. (2003). The need for a new world ethic. In: Kittrie et al. (Eds.), *The future of peace*. Durham, NC: Carolina Academic Press.
Kurst-Swanger, K. (2008). *Worship and sin: An exploration of religion-related crime in the United States*. New York: Peter Lang.
Lebacqz, K. (1986). *Six theories of justice: Perspectives from philosophical and theological ethics*. Minneapolis, MN: Augsberg.
Lewis, B. (2002). *What went wrong: The clash of Islam and modernity in the Middle East*. New York: Oxford University.
Lincoln, A. (1865). Second inaugural address. In: White, R. (2002) (Ed.), *Lincoln's greatest speech: The second inaugural*. New York: Simon & Schuster.
Loy, D. (2001). Healing justice: A Buddhist perspective. In D. Hadley (Ed.), *The spiritual roots of restorative justice*. Albany, NY: State University of New York Press.
MacIntyre, A. (1988). *Whose justice? Which rationality?* South Bend, IN: University of Notre Dame Press.
Marx, K. (1848). *The communist manifesto*. London: Penguin.
Mill, J. S. (1863). *Utilitarianism*. Indianapolis, IN: Hackett Publishing. 2001.
Montville, J. (1992). Transnationalism and the role of track-two diplomacy. In: Thompson, W. S., et al. (Eds.), *Approaches to peace: An intellectual map*. Washington, D.C.: United States Institute of Peace.
Murray, C. (2012). The new American Divide. *Wall Street Journal*.
Murray, C. (2013). *Coming apart*. New York: Random House.
Neuhaus, R. J. (1984). *The naked public square: Religion and democracy in America*. Grand Rapids, MI: Eerdmans.
Otto, R. (1923). *The idea of the holy*. London, Uk: Oxford University.
Putnam, R. (2000). *Bowling alone: The collapse and revival of American community*. New York: Simon and Schuster.
Rawls, J. (1971). *A theory of justice*. Cambridge, MA: Harvard University Press.
Roylance, S. (Ed.). (2012). *The family and the millennium development goals*. Doha, Qatar: Doha Institute for Family Studies and Development.
Sandel, M. (2007). *Justice: A reader*. New York: Oxford University Press.
Smart, N. (1989). *The world's religions*. Cambridge, UK: Cambridge University Press.

Smith, A. (2002). *The theory of moral sentiments*. Cambridge, UK: Cambridge University Press.

Smith, A. (1993). *The wealth of nations*. Oxford, UK: Oxford University Press.

Smith, H. (1958). *The world's religions*. New York: Harper Collins.

Smith, M. K. (2013). Social Capital. In: The Encyclopedia of Informal Education [http://infed.org/mobi/social-capital/] Retrieved 11/8/2013.

Sultan, A. N. (2004). Principal and practical foundations of a global constitutional order. *Washington University Global Studies Law Review, 3*(1), 155–175.

Taylor, C. (2007). *A Secular Age*. Cambridge: Harvard University Press.

Thomas, S. (2005). *The global resurgence of religion and the transformation of international relations: The struggle for the soul of the twenty-first century*. New York: Palgrave Macmillan.

de Tocqueville, A. (1945). *Democracy in America*. New York: Random House.

Ulmer, J. T. (2012). *Religion as a unique cultural influence on crime and delinquency: Expanding on Johnson and Jang's Agenda' in contemporary issues in criminological theory and research: The role of social institutions*. Belmont, CA: Wadsworth.

Vivekananda, S. (1955). *Karma-yoga and Bhakti yoga*. New York: Rmakrishna-Vivekananda Center.

United Nations Office on Drugs and Crime (UNODC). (2006). *Handbook on restorative justice programmes*. New York: United Nations.

Walsh, T. (2012). Religion, Peace and the Post-Secular Public Sphere. *International Journal on World Peace, XXIX*(2), 25–61.

Weber, M. (1905/1958). *The Protestant Ethic and the Spirit of Capitalism*. New York: Scribners.

Weber, M. (1963). *Sociology of Religion*. Boston: Beacon Press.

Wilson, A. (Ed.). (1991). *World Scripture: An Anthology of Sacred Texts*. New York: International Religious Foundation.

Zehr, H. (2002). *The Little Book of Restorative Justice*. Intercourse, PA: Good Books.

Crime Reduction, Reduction of Imprisonment and Community Crime Prevention Programs: Risk Factors and Programs Implemented to Reduce Them

Raymond R. Corrado, Adrienne M.F. Peters, Tarah Kathleine Hodgkinson, and Jeff Mathesius

Abstract A growing body of research has described and documented the risk/protective factors associated with serious/violent offending and victimization. While these two streams of criminology were originally investigated as separate entities, the amassing research in both fields revealed clear overlap in risk factors, leading to the conclusion that the offender is also typically the victim and vice versa. The current chapter seeks to describe this literature and map the conceptual overlap between the offending and victimization of women and children. Specifically, this chapter: (1) describes the typical victim profile; (2) outlines the risk factors associated with serious/violent offending and victimization, and their distinct developmental pathways; and (3) reviews current intervention programs that have successfully reduced serious/violent offending and victimization.

1 Introduction

There has been an extensive increase in the understanding of serious and violent young offending in the last 30 years. In the academic and, later, the United Nations world, there has been an upsurge of victim-centered research and policy recommendations. While there have been few novel theories of these types of crime, existing theories have been elaborated and key hypotheses validated utilizing impressive research designs and statistical analyses. One important theme that continues to be important both theoretically and for policy is the overlap in risk

R.R. Corrado (✉) • T.K. Hodgkinson • J. Mathesius
Simon Fraser University, Burnaby, BC, Canada
e-mail: corrado@sfu.ca; thodgkin@sfu.ca; jrm9@sfu.ca

A.M.F. Peters
University of the Fraser Valley, Abbotsford, BC, Canada
e-mail: adrienne.peters@ufv.ca

H. Kury et al. (eds.), *Women and Children as Victims and Offenders: Background, Prevention, Reintegration*, DOI 10.1007/978-3-319-28424-8_15

factors for serious offending and serious victimization. This chapter reviews the general research on this theme with a focus on three topics: (1) the typical victim profile; (2) factors associated with serious/violent young offending and victimization, and their distinct developmental pathways; and (3) key examples of current intervention programs that have successfully reduced serious/violent youth offending and victimization.

2 Risk Factors for and the Overlap Between Youth Offending and Victimization

Although the majority of young people today who commit crimes are responsible for committing non-violent offences (Perreault 2013), this population is one of the most likely groups to be involved in serious-violent crimes either as the perpetrator or as the victim (Baum 2005; Finkelhor et al. 2009; Perreault and Brennan 2010). According to the routine activities theory (Cohen and Felson 1979), youth who have been the victim of a serious crime may be more likely to commit a violent offence, and, conversely, offenders are more likely to become victims. This theory postulates that this victim-offender cycle occurs based on routine social interactions among delinquent individuals particularly in certain public settings without the supervision of responsible adult supervision. Another related theory, social control/ low self-control asserts that youth caught in this cycle characteristically have low self-control and lack pro-social bonds to key pro-social neighbourhood institutions (Gottfredson and Hirschi 1990; Schreck 1999; Schreck and Fisher 2004). There are several other risk factors such as early and persistent school problems, early onset use of alcohol/drugs and anger/aggression that are associated with serious-violent offending and serious victimization (Chen 2009; Lauritsen et al. 1991; Mustaine and Tewksbury 1998; Shaffer and Ruback 2002). The key theme that has emerged from both theories and research is that adolescent offenders and victims are overwhelming similar in demographic factors, especially age, and ethnicity, as well as in the profile of individual, family, and neighbourhood risk factors that increased the likelihood of serious offending and victimization substantially (Gottfredson 1984; Osgood et al. 1996). Yet regarding the most serious offence and victimization, while youth comprise a very small minority of homicide offenders in advanced industrial countries such as Canada, more than half of young people responsible for homicide in 2011 in this country had a co-accused and the victim was an acquaintance (Perreault 2012). Moreover, and very importantly, youth homicide offenders were associated with a criminal organization or gang in one-third of all of these cases. Although youth crime and victimization rates have declined significantly beginning at the end of the twentieth century in North America (Osofsky 2001), there has been a very small group of young offenders that has continued to commit serious-violent offences and some of whom became serious-violent chronic offenders and victims (Baglivio et al. 2014; Vaughn et al. 2014). Again, even for homicides, there was a high likelihood that the perpetrator and the victim knew each other. The victim experience, therefore, very likely is best explained by the risky lifestyle construct, i.e., both youth and adults who routinely engage in social interactions with peers, usually in public places (e.g., entertainment, transit, parks, school locations), who also use/misuse alcohol and drugs and are part of informal or formal crime-involved groups, are at the highest risk for the most serious victimization (Corrado and Cohen 2014). This construct also involves the theoretical focus on the developmental perspective of serious offending. This entails the identification of the earliest risk factors for and protective factors against involvement in aggression, violence, and other more serious offending, as well as the accumulation of these factors during successive age development stages, e.g., conception to late adulthood across the entire life course. It is important, therefore, to focus on the far greater research available concerning the development of the serious young offender profile in order to better understand both the victimization dynamic for this age group and interventions to reduce this likelihood.

Four key themes have emerged within the developmental criminological perspective: first, the identification of risk and protective factors for serious offending involving individual, neighbourhood, and larger political geographic jurisdictions, e.g., cities and country/nation levels; second, the identification of separate or distinctive pathways of these factors leading to the same serious offences; and, third the identification of specific intervention and treatment programs to reduce the initiation of serious offending or to reduce the likelihood of its continuation, i.e., recidivism; these developmentally based risk factors are also associated with serious and prolific offending into adulthood (see Baglivio et al. 2014; Blumstein et al. 1986; Corrado and Freedman 2011; Farrington 2002; Vaughn et al. 2014; Wolfgang et al. 1972). To begin, youth most at-risk for crime and victimization have been exposed to genetic and prenatal risk factors, and are born into families where there is heavy parental substance use, poor nutrition and health, mental health problems, and high-conflict relationships marred by violence and abuse (Farrington et al. 2008; Lacourse et al. 2002; Lussier et al. 2011). Frequently, the high-risk family consists of a single parent, most commonly a single mother, who either works several low paying jobs, or is unemployed as a result of disability or other health/mental health needs. Youth from single-father families also were at an increased risk for delinquency, likely as a result of lack of supervision and discipline (Demuth and Brown 2004). Another key risk factor involves youth removed from their families because of various forms of abuse who are placed in the care system either temporarily or permanently (National Crime Prevention Centre, Public Safety Canada 2012). Multiple placements because of incompatibilities between the youth and host families often occur for multi-problem needs youth (Smith et al. 2013). Importantly, therefore, early externalizing behaviours in children, such as aggression, are highly predictive of future delinquency and serious violence as well as victimization (Farrington et al. 2008; Nagin and Tremblay 2001). For example, homicide consistently has been the leading risk factor for the death of African American youth (Dahlberg and Mercy 2009).

Several neighbourhood factors including social disorder/low social cohesion and neighbourhood economic disadvantage are strongly associated with the increased risk for serious delinquency or victimization, and even later onset offending (e.g., Sampson et al. 1997; Morenoff et al. 2001; Wikstrom and Loeber 2000). These neighbourhood risk factors also are overwhelmingly predictive of the emergence and persistence of major youth gangs and adult criminal organizations. As mentioned above, both informal and formal gangs are disproportionately the cause of serious victimizations (Esbensen and Huizinga 1993; Esbensen et al. 1993; Huff 1996). Certain urban neighbourhoods, such as those near entertainment and business districts, are also associated with homeless youth. These youth typically have histories of family abuse and rejection, school problems including a high drop-out rate, serious and largely untreated health/mental health needs, poly-substance misuse, and low job skills (Barnaby et al. 2010; Tyler and Johnson 2006; Worthington et al. 2008). Homeless youth are disproportionately at a higher risk of being victimized (Baron 1997, 2003; Cauce et al. 2004; Gaetz 2004; Public Health Agency of Canada 2006). Importantly, though evident for only a minority of youth, many of the risk factors for serious-offending and victimization are precursors to homelessness (Roebuck 2008). The developmental dynamic or process can begin with children raised in multi-needs and problem families who then experience social relationship challenges during elementary and intermediate school. These include peer rejection (Nelson and Dishion 2004), bullying, low academic achievement, which is sometimes related to a learning disability (Sundheim and Voellere 2004), school dismissal or drop-out due to these risks and strains (Nishina et al. 2005; Wolke et al. 2000), and high involvement in a wide range of antisocial behaviours (Hemphill et al. 2006). Youth who drop out, leave home, and associate with high-risk lifestyle peers (i.e., alcohol and drug misuse, property and drug distribution, pimping, fighting) are also at a much higher risk of substance misuse, offending, victimization, and informal criminal groups, including gang involvement (Esbensen and Huizinga 1993; Howell 2010). This high risk lifestyle has been explained partially as a means of coping and the basic human need for a sense of primary group belonging, e.g., providing a family and family substitute. Other than for the latter gang involvement risk, while this dynamic is evident in many neighbourhoods with different income levels, it disproportionately affects youth from the above-described socially disorganized and economically disadvantaged neighbourhoods (Farrington et al. 2008; Henry and Huizinga 2007; Howell 2005; Kempf-Leonard and Johansson 2007).

While it is beyond the scope of this chapter to fully review all the numerous risk factors and multiple pathways identified in the extensive research on serious offending and the related victimization lifestyle cycle, it is important to mention the central role of trauma (Perry 1997). Trauma most obviously has been associated with various forms of abuse including both physical and sexual, as well as neglect. It is only more recently, though, that the enormously complex genetic and epigenetic interactions with environmental risk factors for abuse and its potential causal effect on aggression and violence have been identified. While still largely speculative, the initial theorizing has focused on changes in brain morphology, i.e., brain substructures such as the amygdala and neurological circuits, paralimbic, and executive functions that increase the likelihood for both aggression and violence, but also victimization. Essentially, serious trauma can alter either the brain structures and/or neurological processes involved in prosocial and normative responses to perceived threats and risky behaviours in several ways. Predominantly, however, the two patterns of concern here are characterized by externalizing/fight and internalizing/flight responses. The former simply involves routinely aggressive, including physical, reactions to threats and the former consists of withdrawal or avoidance of the threatening behaviour. Both patterns can involve use of substances and antisocial peers to cope with threatening social environments. In addition, depending on whether fetal alcohol spectrum disorder and/or attention-deficit/ hyperactivity disorder are present, trauma can further affect the two basic response patterns. However, the important theme is that both violence and victimization can involve highly complex and multiple developmental patterns that increasingly are being taken into consideration in interventions directed at reducing these extremely harmful and often tragic phenomena (Corrado and Freedman 2011; Corrado and Lussier 2011).

3 Child and Female Victimization: The Risks and Consequences

Though it is unclear why, crime and victimization have been declining in most western countries for almost a decade (Finkelhor 2011; van Dijk et al. 2012; Waller 2011). Nonetheless, women and children remain both particularly vulnerable to violent victimizations and in need of programs to protect them (Edleson 1999). The following section describes types of victimization, their prevalence, risk factors, consequences, and future directions for related research and policy.

3.1 Child Victimization

3.1.1 Definition

Child victimization, child maltreatment or child abuse consists of an act(s), or the omission of an act(s), by any caregiver that results in the actual, potential, or threat of harm to a person under the age of 18 (Leeb et al. 2008). This definition has been expanded beyond a "caregiver" focus to include *any* type of victimizer, e.g., peers or siblings (Finkelhor 2011). Given that peer-on-peer aggression is so common among youth under 18 years of age (Smokowski and Kopasz 2005) the more recent conceptualization of child victimization now includes severe bullying (Finkelhor 2011; Hawker and Boulton 2000). Nonetheless, research has focused overwhelmingly on victimization, such as neglect, physical abuse, sexual abuse, and emotional abuse perpetrated by parents or caregivers (Edleson 1999).

Because children are particularly vulnerable (more often than not, dependent on the offender) this discussion focuses on child victimization (i.e., that perpetrated by caregivers). Family, adults, and older sibling offenders have easier access to a vulnerable victim, and the child victim, typically, is less likely to report the victimization. This non-reporting tendency is associated frequently with: not wanting a close family member arrested; fear of family disruption and conflict; and skewed perceptions of victimization as normal. Similarly, aware adults can choose to "keep it within the family" and not report officially. While not common, child victimization, on average, is not reported until early adulthood, and, consequently, the attrition of evidence over time often reduces the likelihood of police intervention (i.e., arrest and charges), prosecution, and sentencing (Lamb and Edgar-Smith 1994).

There are four main child victimization types: neglect, physical abuse, emotional abuse, and sexual abuse (Edleson 1999). Neglect involves the failure to meet the basic child needs including proper nutrition, supervision, nurture, and basic, as well as emergency, healthcare (Appleyard et al. 2011; Hildyard and Wolfe 2002). Physical abuse is the actual, or threat, of physical violence, such as hitting, kicking, shaking, choking, burning, or stabbing (Kaplan et al. 1999). Emotional abuse includes verbal cruelty or other psychological punishment (Kaplan et al. 1999). Sexual abuse, the least common type, involves forced sexual contact (Finkelhor 1991).

3.1.2 Prevalence

Prevalence estimates of child victimization have varied substantially for several reasons. First, as explained above, child maltreatment reporting is extremely low and unreliable (Krug et al. 2002). Second, different measures (operational indicators of abuse) and methodologies (e.g., self-report surveys and official criminal justice statistics) have been utilized in abuse studies. Very importantly, official statistics and self-report data generate discrepant findings (e.g., LeBlanc and Fréchette 1989; Lussier et al. 2011; Lussier and Mathesius 2012; Mathesius and Lussier 2014). Regarding operational measure equivalency across studies, several validity issues are common (Finkelhor 2011). Specifically, does "child" victimization occur either before pubescence (<13 years), according to the medical conceptualization of "child," under 18 or within the widely varied maximum legal definition of child across jurisdictions (>16 to >21). For example, a UK study reported a prevalence of 8.9 % under 11 years versus a 21.9 % between 11 and 17 years (Radford et al. 2013). Third, some studies focus on one type of child maltreatment instead of global measures of maltreatment, thus making cross study comparisons difficult.

Nonetheless, there are general themes that have emerged in the studies of the prevalence of child victimization, primarily because of the more recent availability of large-scale victimization surveys and the meta-analytic methodology. For example, global estimates by the World Health Organization (WHO 2006) reported that 40 million children under the age of 14 were victimized. Rates for overall child maltreatment in certain developed countries were 49 per 1000 children in the

U.S. and 90 per 1000 children in the United Kingdom (Jones 2008). In Canada, there were approximately 22 cases of victimization per 1000 children (Trocme et al. 2005), while in the Netherlands, the rate is 30 per 1000 (Euser et al. 2010). Specific types of child victimization, though, were often not available.

However, where included in the studies and, as expected, neglect was the most common form of child victimization with rates as high as 52.7–73.1 % of the child population (Gaudiosi 2005). Yet, neglect is the least detectable and most unreported abuse (Price-Robertson et al. 2010). The widely disparate physical abuse rates range from 29 to 75 % (Krug et al. 2002), while emotional abuse rates only ranged from 70 to 85 %, depending on the type of reporting (Krug et al. 2002). Sexual abuse is the least frequently reported type of child victimization because it frequently occurs in the privacy of a home (Radford et al. 2013). Sexual abuse is most common among females: 20 % of women versus 5–10 % of males (Stoltenborg et al. 2011; Krug et al. 2002). Valid cross national sexual abuse rates are difficult to obtain primarily because of the varied cultural norms involving secrecy and honor concerning sexuality, homosexuality, promiscuity, and respect for parents (Stoltenborgh et al. 2011). One global estimate of combined prevalence of 11.8 %, though, was ascertained from a meta-analysis of studies of sexual abuse. Self-reporting rates were as high as 127 per 1000 (Stoltenborgh et al. 2011).

3.1.3 Risk Factors

While risk factors for child victimization vary by the type of victimization, there are commonalities primarily involving the family domain. Other risk domains include the individual and the neighbourhood levels. Childhood victimization is substantially more prevalent in impoverished and socially disorganized neighbourhoods, i.e., areas that have high levels of minor street crime, such as graffiti, activities related to the sex trade, and vandalism, along with youth gangs, informal and formal, and adult gangs as well. Parents, often single mothers, experienced greater routine emotional stress including depression related to: lack of employment; inadequate housing; inaccessibility of health care; poor quality schools and child recreation facilities; and inability to rely on extended family and friends to assist in the supervision of their children, particularly in public spaces dominated by antisocial and criminal peers (Leventhal and Brooks-Gunn 2000; Sampson et al. 1997; Morenoff et al. 2001, UNODC 2010). This serious and persistent stress affects parenting (McLoyd et al. 1994) even causing mothers' neurological damage that limits their prosocial child rearing practices and increasing child victimization risks (McEwen 1998).

The focus of theories and research on child victimization traditionally, therefore, has been on the familial-level domain risk factors, especially the access to social capital themes mentioned above. However, these same risk factors, historically, have been central to serious and violent offending too. Single-parent households; poverty; lack of parental employment; low levels of parental education, such as not completing high school; being born to a young mother; lack of paternal involvement; large family size; parental mental health problems; and low parental self-control have all been included in the dominant theories of serious crime, especially street located offending, as well as persistent and intergenerational domestic violence (Brown et al. 1998; Euser et al. 2010; Fantuzzo et al. 2011; Hussey et al. 2006; Straus et al. 1990; Thornberry et al. 2014). Furthermore, risk factors have a compounding effect, i.e., the risk of victimization increases exponentially with each additional risk factor (Brown et al. 1998). For example, the risk for sexual abuse increases often because family disruption or lack of parental supervision results in opportunities for misconduct with low risk of intervention (Brown et al. 1998). Furthermore, while females are more at risk than males, males who have been physically or sexually abused as children are at an increased risk of becoming sexual offenders later in life (Seto and Lalumière 2010).

3.1.4 Consequences

There are a multitude of short- and long-term negative consequences to childhood victimization. Most notably, childhood victimization has been linked to childhood externalizing behavioural disorders, including the development of child sexuality (Beitchman et al. 1992), poor academic achievement (Fantuzzo et al. 2011), substance abuse (Appleyard et al. 2011), as well as poor mental health outcomes. The negative mental health outcomes appear to have a gendered effect in which females are more likely to present internalizing disorders (e.g., anorexia [Wonderlich et al. 1997]), while males are more likely to exhibit externalizing behavioural disorders (e.g., sexual offending [Seto and Lalumière 2010]). Critically, these negative outcomes are also key risk factors of serious and violent young offending. This notion that childhood victimization represents one pathway toward serious and violent young offending has been put forth recently by Corrado and Freedman (2011). In addition, early childhood victimization not only places the child at-risk of being incarcerated, but also places them at risk of future victimization via peers, siblings, and by their intimate partner (Radford et al. 2013; Renner and Slack, 2006; Thornberry et al. 2014). Importantly, recent empirical research reveals a link between childhood victimization, the subsequent development of substance abuse, and, finally, culminating in the maltreatment of one's own children as a parent (Appleyard et al. 2011). This finding is critical as it demonstrates the intergenerational transmission of victimization, and, further, suggests the need for proper intervention and support to break the "cycle of violence" (Egeland et al. 1988; Thornberry et al. 2014; Widom 1989).

4 Female Victimization and Intimate Partner Violence

4.1 Definition and Prevalence

Intimate Partner Violence (IPV) is characterized by any physical forms of assault (e.g., pushing, punching, beating, sexual assault) between two intimate partners (Johnson, 1998). Over time, however, definitions of IPV have been extended to include psychological abuse and stalking (American Psychological Association 2002; World Health Organization 2006). IPV is commonly understood as the victimization of women by men. Studies show rates as high as 50–70 % of women being victims of IPV in their lifetimes (Krug et al. 2002; Thompson et al. 2006). More recently, men and women are considered relatively equal in terms of IPV victimization, with lifetime prevalence of 19.3 and 23.1 % respectively (Desmarais et al. 2012). However, women tend to suffer more physical injuries then men, including hospitalization and homicide (Archer 2000; Cunradi 2010; Janssen et al. 2005; Straus 1999; Tjaden and Thoennes 1998; Tjaden and Thoennes 2000). In fact; almost 50 % of female homicides in the United States are a product of IPV compared to less than 5 % of male homicides (Bachman and Saltzman 1995; Kellerman and Mercy 1992). As such, most of the research focuses on the victimization of women by men, in heterosexual intimate partner relationships and will be the focus of this piece.

4.2 Risk Factors

Studies of IPV often emphasize the role of individual-level factors, such as the disposition of the offender or the characteristics of the victim. Consistent individual level risk factors for IPV are membership in a racial/ethnic minority group, lower levels of education, and, consequently lower income levels (Cunradi 2007, 2009; Cunradi et al. 2002; Field and Caetano 2004; Fox et al. 2002; O'Campo et al. 1995; Sorenson et al. 1996). In regards to racial/ethnic minority groups, while collectively all members of minority groups are more likely to experience higher levels of IPV, non-Hispanic blacks experience the highest rates of IPV, followed next by Hispanics (Cunradi 2007, 2009). Young women, between 18 and 30 years of age (U.S. Department of Justice 1994; Wolfner and Gelles 1993), as well as women who are in cohabitating rather than married relationships (e.g., Stets and Straus 1995), are at an increased risk of IPV.

Alcohol misuse is strongly associated with increased IPV. For example, in the United States' 2000 National Household Survey on Drugs and Abuse sample of married or cohabitating Hispanic men ($n = 1148$) and women ($n = 1399$), females who abused alcohol were ten times more likely to have experienced IPV than those who did not abuse alcohol (Cunradi 2009). In an earlier study, women from a drug treatment program had a significantly higher rate of lifetime severe IPV (i.e., hitting with a fist, beating, choking, threats with a weapon), compared to a matched sample on socio-demographic characteristics, without alcohol or drug problems (Miller 1998). There are several explanations of this important relationship. First, alcohol/substance abuse causes IPV (i.e., self-medication to cope with traumatic experiences). Second, according to the indirect effect model, alcohol use leads to marital discord and subsequently IPV. Third, the direct effect model states that chemical properties of the substance produce a psychological/emotional state that causes IPV. To date, the direct hypothesis has had the most empirical support (Cunradi 2010; Klostermann and Fals-Stewart, 2006).

Ecological and structural factors, particularly at the neighbourhood level, have been related to IPV. The most important construct is collective efficacy, which is derived from the classic neighbourhood social disorganization theoretical perspective of crime. Accordingly, the lack of social cohesion and informal social controls among families in chronic socially disorganized and highly concentrated economic disadvantaged neighbourhoods promote all crimes (Sampson et al. 1997). Social cohesion consists of neighbours sharing common values, goals, aspirations, and cooperative interactions. Informal social control refers to the neighbourhood's residents' ability to regulate the antisocial behaviour of residents or visitors, particularly youth. In effect, communities with high collective efficacy reduce all delinquent and criminal behaviours and violent victimizations (e.g., Morenoff et al. 2001; Sampson et al. 1997) by mediating (i.e., lowering) the relationship between individual antisocial propensity (e.g., low self-control) and crime (Zimmerman 2010). Lower levels of collective efficacy were associated with higher rates of IPV, as well as intimate partner homicide (Browning 2002). Collective efficacy is hypothesized to have both a direct and indirect role in moderating the risk of IPV. The direct association involves intervention "at the site" of the IPV, i.e., a bystander witnessing IPV steps in to prevent or stop it. The indirect association involves the community providing social and protective support to the IPV victim that reduces further likelihood of IPV. Benson et al. (2003) utilized neighbourhood-level U.S. Census data to demonstrate that neighbourhood economic deprivation was positively associated with IPV. Earlier, Miles-Doan and Kelly (1997) similarly found that neighbourhoods with severe economic disadvantage had higher rates of IPV. Critically, poverty and neighbourhood disadvantage had increased levels of social isolation within a community (Lee 2000; Lee et al. 2003; Parker and Pruitt 2000), which was related to increased IPV. This relationship was evident previously in the National Survey of Families and Households consisting of cohabitating ($n = 500$) and married ($n = 5000$) couples. Specifically, less frequent ties to groups/organizations, family/friends, and to spouse/partner significantly predicted IPV (Stets 1991).

4.3 A Brief Note on the Male Perpetrators of IPV

Several of the male individual-level risk factors for IPV are the same as the key risk factors for the life-course persistent offender. This is a central developmental criminological theory construct. The individual level IPV predictors include impulsivity (Cunradi et al. 1999; Schafer et al. 2004), high levels of anger (Eckhardt et al. 2002), and alcohol/substances abuse (Cunradi 2007, 2009, 2010; Cunradi et al. 1999; Cunradi et al. 2002). Approval of marital aggression is an additional important risk factor (Caetano et al. 2000). These adult antisocial characteristics typically have been associated with an early criminogenic family environment (e.g., unemployment, criminal behaviour, poor parenting skills) and subsequent IPV (Capaldi and Clark 1998; Farrington 1994; Simons et al. 1998). Critically, this early criminogenic family link was indirect since it was mediated by adolescent antisocial behaviour and neuropsychological deficits (Lussier et al. 2009). Further, problematic childhood behaviour (e.g., defiance, aggression, deceit) was also a strong predictor of later IPV (Moffitt and Caspi 2003). Moffitt et al. (2002) identified a life-course persistent (LCP) trajectory, i.e., childhood onset of problematic behaviours, the LCPs (only 10 % of the Dunedin, New Zealand large cohort), accounted for 62 % of all convictions for IPV by young adulthood.

IPV, therefore, appears to be another manifestation of antisocial behaviour generally. Also, because multiple risk factors were more important than any individual risk factor, prevention or intervention programs attempting to reduce IPV require that most of these risk factors be addressed. This entails the multi-level targeting of both the individual level risk factors (e.g., alcohol/substance use, cognitive distortions surrounding the support of marital aggression) and neighbourhood level risk factors (e.g., building stronger communities through increasing collective efficacy). Given the largely similar risk factors for IPV and the LCP offender, preventative measures more likely need to include an initial early emphasis on LCPs. Traditional intervention programs that target the specific behaviour of adult intimate partner violence have had very limited effectiveness possibly because they have not adequately addressed the earlier developmental stage risk factors in an appropriately age/time manner or not at all (e.g., Babcock et al. 2004; Feder and Wilson 2005).

4.4 Consequences

The financial cost of IPV in the U.S. has been estimated at approximately 67 billion dollars annually (Miller et al. 1996). More importantly, IPV victims suffered numerous health/mental problems including depression, substance abuse, chronic disease, child victimization, suicide and homicide victimization (Appel and Holden 1998; Coker et al. 2002; Fagan and Browne 1994; McCauley et al. 1995; Plichta and Falik 2001). In addition, one-third to one-half of children in women's shelters were also victims (Edleson 1999). Finally, regarding the intergenerational transmission of IPV, witnessing IPV as a child was associated with subsequent IPV victimization (Thornberry et al. 2014).

5 Young Offender Risk Tools and a Discussion of Related Programming for at Risk Children, Youth, and Their Families

Increasingly complex risk assessment and management instruments have been developed to respond to the multiple risks evident across multiple domains for child and youth delinquency and victimization, as well as adult offending and victimization. Ideally, these instruments, first, identify youths' risk profiles, and second, match the corresponding youths' needs profile with appropriate sets of treatment interventions. However, most current standardized assessment tools, typically utilized in youth corrections, have not been sufficiently comprehensive regarding the ever increasingly complex multi-risk and multi-level histories of youth and their families. Lack of comprehensiveness often limits the ability of service providers to provide the necessary range of programing. In contrast, risk management instruments such as the MASPAQ and the CRACOW, though highly complex and difficult to administer, are comprehensive. The latter, for example, includes risks from three broad, comprehensive, and multi-level domains: environmental (e.g., pre-perinatal risk factors, living conditions, peers), familial (e.g., family dynamics, parental characteristics, parent–child relationship), and the individual domain (e.g., psychological, biological) and age developmental stages (e.g., pregnancy to late adolescence) (Corrado 2011). There is preliminary validity research in Canada and Germany concerning the initial developmental stages sections of the CRACOW (Wallner et al. under review; Lussier et al. 2011). However, despite this need for more comprehensive diagnostic instruments to reduce likelihoods of offending and victimizations as discussed above, there is an extensive history of intervention programs. Several model programs have been identified that have undergone rigorous empirical testing and were assessed as either effective, promising, or ineffective. The programs reviewed in this chapter include family-based programs; parenting programs; school-based programs; mentoring strategies; trauma-based interventions; neighbourhood and community-level initiatives; and interventions designed to target specific types of offending and victimization. The latter focus on individuals with psychopathic traits, sexual offending patterns, gang involvement, domestic violence offences (and their victims), and who have been victims of sexual assault.

6 Effective Programs to Reduce Likelihood for Serious-Violent Offending/Recidivism Among Children and Adolescents

6.1 Child- and Family-Centred Programming Interventions

Nurse-Family Partnership (NFP) is among the most effective program types to reduce young people's offending risk and victimization risk. The NFP involves low-income, first-time mothers and provides them with individualized one-on-one support from a nurse who visits the home in the initial pregnancy stages (Olds et al. 1997). The focus is on developing a rapport and trust with the mother that continues until the child reaches the age of 2. The nurse helps the mother identify her needs areas and assists in managing them and/or providing the mother with skills that improve the effectiveness of her parenting practices. Importantly regarding the risk factors discussed above, this program seeks to reduce maternal smoking, substance use, poor nutrition, undesired future pregnancies, and poverty. Regarding the latter risk factor, opportunities for further education and employment are encouraged. Equally important, the nurse fosters intimate, loving, and nurturing attachments between the mother and her child. Family planning includes a healthy life-style during pregnancy; birthing, and the first days following the birth are further emphasized. Finally, parenting strategies for childhood and adolescence too are encouraged.

Various models of nurse-home visitations have been introduced in the United States (Nurse-Family Partnership 2014), Canada (Reiter 2005), and Europe (Barnes et al. 2011) that have been effective in reducing maternal smoking and drinking during pregnancy, early pregnancies, premature birth, and birth complications (Olds et al. 1998). Weekly nurse visits also have reduced maternal stress (Sutton and Glover 2004) and reduced the severity of postpartum depression (Murray et al. 2003). Studies in England have indicated additional positive effects. Nearly two thirds (63 %) of mothers who participated in NFP breast-fed their infants and for a longer time period; had improved relationships with their infant and the infant's father; had confidence in their parenting skills and use of nurturing parenting techniques; participated in educational activities or were employed; and, overall, managed well during their pregnancy, labour, and parenthood (Barnes et al. 2009; Barnes et al. 2011). Several long-term outcomes for children and adolescents included: reduced substance use; fewer serious antisocial behaviours (e.g., arrests, convictions and probation violations); reduced consumption of alcohol; and less running away from home (Olds et al. 1998). However, Barnes et al. (2009) cautioned that successful NFP interventions required stable governmental funding levels and no reduction in the range of services provided. One concern emerging from the research, though, is that reducing subsequent pregnancies did not consistently occur until much later than anticipated (Rubin et al. 2011).

Other programs provide services to assist young people and their families later in the childhood stage. As discussed above, the focus on early intervention is based on the extensive research, which indicated that untreated family related needs increased youth's risks for delinquency, violence, and even mental illness (Gavazzi et al. 2008; Howell 2009; Loeber and Farrington 1998; McWey and Mullis 2004). Secure attachment, in particular, has been identified as a long-standing and critical protective factor; youth with strong attachments to their parents engaged in far fewer delinquent acts and escalating criminal trajectories and victimizations (Hirschi 2002; Maimon et al. 2010; Meeus et al. 2004). Historically, therefore, it is not surprising that certain types of family interventions have been beneficial. These include cognitive-behavioural therapies (CBT), multisystemic therapy (MST), and functional family therapy (FFT). For youth removed from their immediate families, multidimensional treatment foster care (MTFC) has been effective for children and even their families.

Since the early 1970s, Functional Family Therapy (FFT) that targets youth from ages 10–18 (Alexander and Sexton 2000) has been recognized as an effective evidence-based behaviour-modification program. It incorporates the youth's family in the intervention milieu and has been effective with diverse cultural families regarding aggression, offending, and substance abuse issues. FFT therapists create individualized approaches and goals to address multiple needs that have been identified in the family, and then require family members to work as a group. The FFT personnel provide ongoing encouragement and support. However, attrition (i.e., family members dropping out of program participation) is a common challenge for all family-based programs. The more selective or individualized FFT strategies were intended to diminish the likelihood of challenges that can lead to families abandoning the program (Thornton et al. 2002). While family-level risk factors have been the focus, other risk areas are addressed and protective factors strengthened. Based on an examination of individual and family cognitive processes and the family's relational interactions and emotional responses, once the family appears receptive to the program's objectives, the therapist establishes a plan outlining the specific areas that will be targeted for behavioural modifications. The family is provided positive alternative coping and reaction techniques to conflict situations. This also includes new approaches to conflict situations encountered outside home, including school, work, with friends, and the community more generally (Alexander and Sexton 2000; Thornton et al. 2002). Following numerous empirical tests employing rigorous experimental design, numerous FFT evaluation studies have demonstrated reductions in violence, recidivism, and substance use in youth participants (Alexander et al. 2000; Brosnan and Carr 2000; Greenwood and Turner 2011; Mihalic et al. 2001; Waldron and Turner 2008; Welsh and Farrington 2006), as well as decreased likelihood of adult criminality (Gordon et al. 1995). A more recent study found that FFT had to be carefully implemented to have the greatest impact on youth probationer offending, both non-violent and violent, when compared to young offenders who received only traditional probation programing (Sexton and Turner 2010).

Multisystemic Therapy (MST) is another family-focused intervention. As a part of this program, a unique treatment plan is developed for each family to address these areas identified as presenting the greatest challenges within the family. Each plan initiates improved familial attachment, parenting, and communication, and, again, is to be utilized in other domains including school (e.g., improved school performance), peers (e.g., developing relationships with prosocial peer relations), and the community (e.g., involvement in volunteering, community organizations, and extracurricular activities [Burns et al. 2000; Henggeler 1982; Lyons and Rawal 2005]). The therapist also identifies certain patterns or conditions that are barriers (e.g., family stressors, substance use, and mental health conditions) that may hinder positive transformations. Methods to reduce the magnitude of these obstacles becomes the focus of the extended plan (Schoenwald et al. 2000). MST emphasizes the role of the parents; parents are expected to provide consistent supervision and encouragement for the youth regarding their involvement and commitment to pro-social activities, and, conversely, the reduction in interactions with antisocial peers and delinquency (Eddy and Chamberlain 2000; Henggeler and Lee 2003; Leve and Chamberlain 2007). Numerous MST evaluation studies have indicated reductions in anti-social behaviour, recidivism rates (Borduin et al. 1990), severity of delinquent acts, and arrest-rates for violent crimes (Borduin et al. 1995). Other studies have also revealed: lowered out-of-home placements (Kashani et al. 1999), moderated drug use (Henggeler et al. 1999; Waldron and Turner 2008), and improved familial and peer relations (Henggeler et al. 1992).

Family-based role attachment focused therapy programs have also become very important in improving parenting skills and reducing severe behavioural problems in children and adolescents. Connect is an exemplary model program (Larstone and Moretti 2013). By enhancing parents' understanding of their role, and providing them with the confidence and tools to better assist in their child's healthy development, this program significantly improved relationships between parents and their children, and subsequent reductions in adolescent antisocial behaviour.

6.2 *Individual Focused Programming Interventions*

As mentioned briefly above, cognitive-behavioural therapy (CBT) focuses on the youth's behavioural and emotional problems that have been identified as risk factors for delinquency, violence and/or victimization. Once the therapist has met with the young person to assess concerns related to his/her problematic behaviour, CBT focuses on modifying the cognitive patterns involving serious antisociality and criminality. Instead, prosocial cognition and associated behaviours are promoted, especially alternative coping responses to stress and conflict (i.e., social and problem-solving skills [Vaske et al. 2011]). CBT-based anger-management and aggression interventions have been effective for incarcerated or community-based samples. It has as well been utilized in responding to certain mental health disorders associated with violence and victimization. Meta-analysis of CBT programs effect on criminal reoffending concluded that, on average, youth who had undergone the specialized treatment (CBT), had lower risk of recidivating within the 12 months following the therapy, than youth who were assigned to the non-CBT control groups (Lipsey et al. 2001; Lipsey and Landenberger 2006; Lipsey et al. 2007). CBT is most effective when it is based on appropriately implemented program design (e.g., sufficient therapist/staff training, few cases of dropout, "monitoring" the quality and "fidelity" of the intervention) and when it is delivered to high-risk offenders (as compared to low risk). A more recent meta-analysis examined the effects of CBT on violent behaviour more specifically and also revealed preliminary support for the therapy's usefulness in rehabilitating aggressive youth (Özabacı 2011). Other CBT research has also demonstrated transformations in antisocial cognitions and behaviour in young people (Bogestad et al. 2010; Vaske et al. 2011). Importantly, CBT has been effective regarding their managing diverse mental health needs involving anxiety, depression, suicidal ideation, and post-traumatic stress disorder (Schmied and Tully 2009).

6.3 School-Centered Programming Interventions

The Perry Preschool Project (PPP) is considered a classic, and now for over half a century or more, highly effective school-based intervention program with multiple favourable outcomes across the life course for children at high risk for serious criminality and victimization. The PPP was directed towards minority African American preschool-aged children who were identified as high risk for future problems in school and ultimately delinquency, as a result of living in socially disorganized and low income families and neighbourhoods in a Michigan city near Detroit, USA (Schweinhart and Weikart 1997). It consisted of a two and a half hour class format over 30-weeks paired with weekly visits to the child and the family at home to support mothers and assist them in playing a part in their child's learning. The immediate program objectives were to provide young children and their families with the skills and support needed to develop the initial basic school taught skillsets that would prepare them to proceed successfully through the normal education trajectory from elementary, to middle and high school, as well as further to post-secondary education, either university or technical programs. This school-focused success was then hypothesized to translate positively to other areas of their life including employment, health, mental health, stable families and non-criminal life styles. Repeated PPP evaluations consistently indicated that the initial enhanced academic performance of PPP involved children compared to children who were not in the PPP was strongly associated with reduced arrests as youth and adults across the life course into middle adulthood. It has also resulted in healthier adult lives and more stable and happy family lives, and lower levels of substance use (Schweinhart et al. 2005).

Promoting Alternative Thinking Strategies (PATHS) and Life Skills Training (LST) also have been effective in reducing serious antisocial behaviour and victimization. PATHS and LST are both offered in a classroom setting by specially trained teachers and counsellors. The PATHS program's focus provides youth with essential skills indispensable for daily behavioural and emotional management, social interaction, impulse-management, and improved school functioning (Greenberg and Kusché 1993). In contrast, LST focuses on the reduction and cessation of youth's tobacco and drug use (Botvin et al. 1998). Nevertheless, LST does include developing problem-solving skills, social skills, and education concerning the effects of drugs. PATHS evaluations indicated that reduced levels of depression and externalizing behaviours were found in youth who had completed the program, as compared to control group samples. However, although their scores of internalizing behaviours increased over the course of PATHS specialized treatment, this increase was much less when compared with the students' scores for those in the control group (Kam et al. 2004). PATHS participants, though, exhibited reduced levels of anger, greater compliancy and emotional awareness, and improved interpersonal skills (according to teachers' evaluations) (Domitrovich et al. 2007). Substantial reductions in polydrug use, a marginal reduction in smoking, and a general reduction in the use of narcotics, hallucinogens, and inhalants also were evident (Botvin et al. 1998).

6.4 Programming Outside of the Biological Family and Traditional School Setting

Multidimensional Treatment Foster Care (MTFC) programs involve intensive training for foster care regarding skills needed to positively respond to highly complex behavioural and emotional problems for multi-needs and high risk for aggression and violent children and adolescents placed in their care. Caregivers are also in a better position to support children and adolescents in their rehabilitative progress and participation in community-based interventions (Chamberlain and Reid 1998; Leve et al. 2009). The MTFC emphasizes foster parents becoming a positive role model and mentor, and teaches them how to provide close supervision and offer a consistent environment in which clear limits are set and where behaviour is reasonably rewarded and punished. The development of strengths and healthy relationships with family, peers, and school are all central features of these programs. These placements are combined with positive peer interactions, school-focused interventions, and encouragement for strengthening the relationship between the young person and his/her biological parents or long-term guardian.

MTFC seeks to prevent the onset of antisocial behaviours generally, as well as more serious offending. In one study, MTFC-involved adolescent male youth had: fewer incidents of running away; increased program completion; reduced offending, including serious/violent offences; and fewer detention placements, compared to youth who were in traditional group homes (Chamberlain and Reid 1998; Leve et al. 2009). Similar results occurred for girls (Chamberlain et al. 2007). Caregivers who received systematic assistance from various agencies, had reduced stress and feelings of helplessness, which were related to the decreased probability of the youth being removed from the home (Leve et al. 2009). Other residential treatment programs and intensive home-based treatment models have been utilized for youth with mental illness. Care providers provided structured living environments with high intensity supervision in combination with cognitive-behavioural exercises, individual and family counselling (the latter being dependent on the family situation), and schooling. Significant long-term improvements (2 years after intake to the program) in youth's functioning and symptomology were evident, including in relation to substance use problems (Preyde et al. 2011).

One-on-one mentoring programs have been effective for some low-risk and high-risk youth and offenders. Big Brothers/Big Sisters (BB/BS), for example, is a long-standing mentoring program for youth at high risk of offending and reoffending. The young persons are matched with selected positive mentors, or role models (based on sharing similar personalities and interests) who model prosocial behaviours, which assist the youth in developing their social skills and positive peer relations. Mentors expose them to prosocial community and extra-curricular activities, and can work with them as well on improving basic academic performance and coping with substance use. Peer mentors are expected to interact with the adolescents several hours every week in a variety of activities from seeing a film together to writing job applications (Mihalic et al. 2001). One of the most prominent outcomes of mentoring programs is the improvement in academic performance, decision-making, and prosocial attitudes (Henry 2009). BB/BS has also reduced the probability of experimenting with illicit substances, engaging in aggressive conduct, and increased youth's feelings of peer acceptance (Grossman and Tierney 1998).

6.5 *An Integrated Program to Support Multi-Needs Children and the Prevention of Future Criminal Justice Involvement*

The programs outlined above can be effective for children and adolescents who present with problematic behaviours, are at-risk of criminal involvement, or who have already come into contact with the law. One Canadian program that was developed specifically to respond to children who were under the age of criminal responsibility in Canada (i.e., <12 years of age), but who had perpetrated a criminal offence was Stop Now And Plan, most commonly known as SNAP (see Augimeri et al. 2011). Commencing in 1985, several professionals in the field came together to discuss approaches that could be employed to assist these young children who had presented a proclivity towards delinquency (i.e., as a result of their involvement in theft, vandalism, break and enter, or a more serious incident including physical aggression or assault), before they became formally involved in the criminal justice system. The result was SNAP, a multidisciplinary program that was intended to provide much needed support to these children and their families based on skills training, cognitive problem solving, self-control and anger management, cognitive self-instruction, family management skills training, and parent training; the latter which included specifically Social Interactional Learning (SIL), through which children learned positive behaviours through their interactions with their parents (Augimeri et al., under review). Relying on collaboration between police and mental health services, the initial program model was offered to any child aged 6–11 who was identified as a result of their premature "criminal" involvement. It has since evolved to include a separate program for each gender (so that the distinct needs of each group can be met) and is offered under a continuing model rather than the previous session restricted model. The program also relies on the results of structured risk assessments to guide the interventions provided to children and their families. Today, SNAP includes four programs: one that is delivered to boys aged 6–11, one for girls aged 6–11, a school-based program for elementary aged children, and a program designed for older children and adolescents (aged 12–17) who have completed the earlier SNAP program. The expansion of the program to include a follow-up component for youth aged 12–17 occurred as a result of early evidence suggesting that, while most children benefited from the program, there was a small percentage of boys that did not experience the same level of success.

The main objectives of the SNAP program are achieved through a three-step process, in which children learn how to recognize situations that they find difficult, take a moment to calm themselves (STOP), use self-encouragement instead of negative thinking (NOW), and discover solutions to better deal with their negative emotions and challenges (PLAN). In doing this, children learn techniques that can assist them in minimizing their impulsivity and maximizing their planning and decision-making skills. The implementation of the program has produced sustained positive results for both boys and girls, as well as their families, as indicated by reduced externalizing problems (e.g., aggression), delinquency, and ameliorated parenting and home environments (e.g., less rigid family interactions) (Augimeri et al. 2007; Granic et al. 2007; Jiang et al. 2011; Pepler et al. 2010). It has also provided preliminary support in its ability to reduce later criminal involvement in adulthood (Augimeri et al. 2010).

6.6 *Specific Offender-Based Programming Interventions*

There are several programs that target particular types of offending including specifically youth's proclivity towards violence. Violent Offender Treatment Programs (VOTP) have been established in several countries to support the most serious and violent young offenders in the modification of their behaviours (Serin et al. 2009). Components of these strategies often comprise cognitive-behavioural therapy and anger management strategies that have been found to be successful in reducing youth's aggressive and violent conduct (see Serin et al. 2009). Additional research found that youth who successfully participated in a VOTP experienced reductions in violent and non-violent recidivism (Catchpole 2002; Gretton et al. 2003), and that when compared to untreated individuals, there was a lower number of violent offences committed by both males and females subsequent to their treatment (Gretton et al. 2003).

Interventions developed to target the treatment of sex offenders also incorporate strategies from CBT to assist offenders in addressing their behaviours. These interventions are offered in group setting, individual sessions, and in combination with treatment for co-occurring mental health conditions using pharmacological responses (Scalora and Garbin 2003). While a number of factors predict recidivism among adult sex offenders, both general and continued sexual offending (e.g., prior criminal histories, age of first offence, and marital status), multidisciplinary cognitive behavioural approaches have also been associated with reduced recidivism risk. Lösel and Schmucker (2005) examined studies including both adults and adolescents, and highlighted the need to combine hormonal medication treatment with psychosocial interventions, since the risk for recidivism can increase significantly in cases where offenders terminate their medication compliance. They also found that, although not significantly different, interventions that were delivered to adolescent offenders had a somewhat greater impact on recidivism than those that were offered to adult offenders. Although the first researchers (Scalora and Garbin 2003) presented some important caveats—such as whether the program actually impacted re-offending as much as it suggested, or whether the offenders who completed the program were simply more likely to have better outcomes—these studies, for both violent offender and sex offender treatment, supported the application of cognitive-behavioural therapies in diminishing risk for these offences, as well as general youth delinquency and offender recidivism.

While programs designed to treat adolescent sex offenders have been successful in improving these offenders' outcomes, other research has found that, consistent with their hypothesis, adolescent sex offenders who scored high on the PCL:YV prior to completing an adolescent sex offender treatment program (SOTP), had an increased risk of escape, probation violations, and recidivism (including non-violent, sexual, and violent offenses), which also occurred sooner, compared to sex offenders not presenting psychopathic traits (Gretton et al. 2001). The SOTP provided a biopsychosocial intervention strategy that incorporated the youths' parents or caregivers, probation officer, social worker and any additional supports in the young persons' lives. Based on the results of this study, future programming and research in this area should, therefore, take into consideration these findings and recognize the greater complexity in treating these types of young offenders.

Concerning the treatment of adolescent offenders with psychopathic features specifically, one study evaluated the outcomes of offenders who were treated at the Mendota Juvenile Treatment Center (MJTC) compared to the outcomes of a similarly profiled, although not randomly assigned, group of young offenders who were sentenced to a youth detention centre where they received standard treatments available in these custodial settings (Caldwell et al. 2006). The MJTC was a specialized treatment program designed for young offenders with psychopathic features. The intensive treatment group received access to regular mental health professionals with reasonably low offender to psychiatrist and psychologist ratios, and a psychiatric nurse available daily. Alternatively, young offenders detained in the correctional institute typically did not have access to these professionals and instead received only basic assessments to determine medication needs followed by modest monitoring of this. Each intervention model was also rooted in differing philosophical views regarding treatment, in that the Mendota Juvenile Treatment Center model was focused more on trying to rebuild conventional bonds than further damaging these with the use of strictly enforced sanctions. The findings of this study revealed that, following their release from these settings, youth who were treated in the MJTC had significantly lower rates of general recidivism (although this finding dissipated following propensity score matching), and most importantly, led to fewer serious/violent offences, which were also committed at lower rates than by the non-treatment group, including over a longer time frame, homicide. One of the most promising features of the Mendota Juvenile Treatment Center's treatment model was that, despite ongoing behavioural problems among youth undergoing treatment, program providers increased their strategies with these youth, instead of discharging them from the program. While offender dropout and release are common among the most serious young offenders in many of the treatment interventions offered to them, this approach instead encouraged the offenders' continued commitment to the treatment intervention, which may have impacted its positive results (Caldwell et al. 2006).

7 Effective Programs to Prevent Serious Crime Victimization

7.1 Child- and Family-Centred Programming Interventions

For children who develop early defiant and externalizing behaviours, parenting these youth can become incredibly challenging. Sometimes these families, in addition, utilize physical aggression in response to these behaviours, which can further deteriorate the child's behaviour, and also lead to an increased victimization risk through such early incidents of maltreatment and abuse. Parent-Child Interaction Therapy (PCIT) was designed to respond to the needs of these families by helping parents to remodel their interactions with their children so that the likelihood of continued abuse can be tempered (Herschell et al. 2002). Throughout the two phases of the program, parents are guided in how to develop more positive interactions with their child through the use of positive reinforcement and appropriate sanctioning and discipline. These families are also supported by other families who have also been through the program based on their similar experiences. The program relies on role-playing activities so that parents can practice employing new techniques before being expected to relate them to real-life situations. PCIT's model has been found to statistically significantly reduce successive incidents of abuse between parents and their children, thereby reducing reoccurring victimization and in turn modifying youth's likelihood for future victimization and offending (Chaffin et al. 2004). This approach is also being utilized with minority families and is examining its applicability in diverse cultural settings (see Butler and Eyberg 2006).

Similarly, programs such as Triple P—Positive Parenting Program, another comprehensive behavioural family intervention, focus on training parents various techniques to provide a more positive environment for their children using qualified experts and multilevel strategies (see Sanders 2008). Some of the goals of this program include setting manageable expectations and delivering reasonable sanctions and discipline to children with conduct problems, so as to prevent child maltreatment by the parents and persistent behavioural problems in the children. The program is delivered to families with children under the age of 12 and the activities and objectives of the program are offered and reached throughout five levels of intervention. These levels range from the first, which is the media campaign to educate families on the program, to reduce some of parents' pre-conceived notions about parent training programs, and to familiarize parents with the goals of the program. Each stage then builds further on introducing parents to the program, through actual participation in training and guided sessions, with each level building from the previous and addressing increasingly severe behavioural problems (Sanders et al. 2000).

An evaluation of Triple P produced positive results over a 2-year follow-up between families who underwent the program as compared to families who did not receive the intervention. Using a randomized, controlled research design, Prinz et al. (2009) found that while the two groups of families did not differ across their measures of child maltreatment (i.e., substantiated child maltreatment, child out-of-home placements, and hospitalizations or emergency room visits injuries associated with maltreatment) prior to the program implementation, the control group had reduced experiences of the three types of maltreatment as compared to the control group. This supported the utility in this program in reducing experiences of victimization at home for youth from different ethnic backgrounds, many of whom were living in poverty and abusive homes.

7.2 Individual and School-Centered Programming Interventions

Cognitive-behavioural therapies (i.e., Trauma-Focused Cognitive Behavioural Therapy [TF-CBT]) similar to those reviewed earlier have been employed as well in interventions for youth who have experienced traumatic events, such as physical and sexual assault, a car accident, exposure to community violence, and the death/loss of someone they loved. This approach assists youth and their families from diverse backgrounds in overcoming the emotions that are associated with these experiences including anxiety, depression, and post-traumatic stress (e.g., Cohen et al. 2012). These experiences and the resultant feelings can lead to problems for children and adolescents related to sleeping, eating, and even managing social situations. TF-CBT programs have, therefore, been employed and have yielded positive results in reducing youth's scores on scales measuring these feelings and emotions (Cohen et al. 2004; Cohen and Mannarino 1996). These results are encouraging for youth in relation to offending and victimization, since many of these experiences and feelings can result in more severe depression, violence, and/or substance use in adolescents. Furthermore, CBT-based approaches have also positively impacted trauma experienced by young people through the Cognitive Behavioural Intervention for Trauma in Schools (CBITS) strategy. This approach targets schools that have a number of children or young adolescents who may have experienced high levels of trauma or witnessed violence by offering group therapy sessions to teach youth about trauma, relating specifically to its symptoms and mechanisms they can use to manage their feelings (Kataoka et al. 2003; Stein et al. 2003).

7.3 Community Level Crime Reduction Programming and Practices

Beyond early interventions that focus on youth, their families, and schools, at the community level, there are also a series of practices that have been employed to reduce opportunities for crime and victimization, which, in effect, include crime and victimization of children and youth. Although there has not been strong support for neighbourhood watch programs—that rely on community residents to look out for crime and report any incidents to the police—on their impact on victimization, there has been more promising support for its utility in reducing offending based on an extensive meta-analysis (see Bennett et al. 2009). Initiatives in the UK, such as SAFER Cities and those that have re-designed crime prone environments to include improved lighting and visibility, however, have been more successful. SAFER Cities began with the objective of not only reducing crime and victimization and thereby creating safer cities, but also to mediate citizens fears related to crime. The program was able to achieve this based on the development of multiple projects that target hardened countless high-crime areas by introducing lighting, windows, fences, and a series of physical environmental changes that made areas less desirable and/or more visible. Citizens were also involved in this process through educational sessions in which community residents were taught strategies to modify their own homes and environments, so as to reduce the attractiveness of the area for offenders and the likelihood that they would be exposed to crime and victimization. This strategy undoubtedly had an impact on offenders and victims of all ages, especially in relation to property crimes (Ekblom 1996), and in consideration of the high numbers of youth involved in crime and victimization, this inevitably included those crimes and victimization experiences involving young people. Similar strategies have also been used in parks and other areas often frequented by young people, and have reduced underage drinking and other delinquent activities and opportunities for neighbourhood victimization in those areas (Cohen et al. 2014). In all of these cases, there was also limited displacement in projects that implemented strongly designed models; i.e., service providers encouraged the participants to engage in diligent observations and be committed to making their neighbourhoods safer (i.e., moderate to high intensity action). For these properly implemented programs, the crime and disorder problems were neither shifted from one location to another, nor did offenders subsequently engage in different types of offending. Instead, the previous profile of crimes—mainly property-related—were reduced.

7.4 Promising Program Interventions for Bullying and Domestic Violence

In light of all of the positive interventions that exist to reduce young people's risks of involvement in serious offending and victimization, there are additional programs that did not meet with the same degree of success, but that could be promising strategies that would benefit from increased development and research.

7.4.1 Bullying Prevention Programming

Bullying prevention programs have provided mixed evidence concerning their impact on future associated incidents and involvement in these behaviours/activities. With the expanding avenues available to youth today to participate in social exchanges with other young people, it seems as though young people are bullying, being bullied, and/or witnessing bullying more than ever before. Although bullying can be defined in different ways, it is commonly viewed as behaviours that are physical (including hitting, kicking, and punching), verbal (such as taunting and name-calling), or psychological (in the form of rumours or ostracizing actions). Typically, individuals involved with bullying are classified as bullies, peer victims, or bystanders (see Wong 2009). Wong (2009) found that bullying victimization was significantly associated with running away from home, trafficking illegal substances, engaging in vandalism, theft, and other property crimes, and also in committing assault, when this victimization occurred before the age of 12. Her large meta-analytic review also revealed that prevention programs that have been implemented in schools are more successful in reducing students' self-reported experiences of victimization as a result of bullying, than reducing the reported bullying behaviours. This apparent inconsistency in self-reported numbers of victimization and officially reported bullying likely reflects the different types of measurements. Students often are reluctant to report bullying for fear of retaliation or further bullying and the desire to not undermine the positive impacts of these programs in which they were participants. Most importantly, programs that reduce self-reported victimization more validly reflect the impact of the anti-bullying programs. However, Wong (2009) recommends that future research is required to understand why this discrepancy occurs and how to more effectively implement bullying programs. Related to the specific practices themselves, interventions that were delivered in a classroom setting were more effective than those that were offered to the entire school, including anti-bullying policies and that failed to involve one-on-one or group sessions with bullies and/or victims. While it was possible that policies that were implemented school-wide were rejected by students, they may have also provided an environment in which more bullying cases were reported (Wong 2009). Based on these results, she recommends that continued prevention programs targeting bullying also incorporate students' families in the intervention (e.g., through educational sessions or informational bulletins). These recommendations were also made in light of Ttofi and Farrington's (2009) meta-analysis, which produced promising results for bullying and victimization interventions (particularly for those that included peer mentoring and clear classroom rules, provided parents with information and training, provided playground supervision, and were offered over longer periods of time to older students).

7.5 *Intimate Partner Violence*

A large proportion of young people who have a higher risk for criminal justice involvement and victimization come from families and homes that experience high levels of conflict and domestic violence. The above discussion also presented the risks for and consequences of intimate partner violence. As such, interventions have been designed for domestic violence offenders, including the Duluth Model. While some intimate partner violence strategies that incorporate social workers and police (see Davis et al. 2007) and CBT (Babcock et al. 2004) approaches have not had significant effects on future incidents of violence, and in some cases increased these incidents, the Duluth model has experienced greater success based on its focus on domestic violence that occurs as a result of patriarchal ideology and the related power-imbalances between men and women, rather than as a result of anger-management problems, substance abuse, or other factors related to strained relationships. Using the "Power and Control Wheel" (accounting for factors such as intimidation, male privilege, isolation, emotional and economic abuse) group facilitators engage the male in activities that help them to reflect on their preconceived beliefs concerning their role in the relationship and then reframe these ideologies so that healthier relationships can be fostered with their partners (Babcock et al. 2004). Although a meta-analysis produced small effect sizes, the Duluth model significantly reduced domestic violence recidivism among the male partners and reports of victimization from the female partners. Babcock and his colleagues (2004) highlight that for families and children who are exposed to violence and experience its related psychological impacts any positive results should not be diminished.

8 Conclusion

Enormous research and policy advances have been made in understanding and responding to the complex dynamics of offending and victimization for both youth and adults. The focus of this chapter has been on youth, in part, because of the extensiveness of the literature, but also because the offending-victimization relationship frequently can be traced back to risk factors primarily from child and adolescent development stages. This is evident, for example, regarding the pervasive and persistent policy challenges associated with intimate partner violence. Much of the contemporary research reaffirms the continued importance of traditional risk factors primarily involving poverty related risk factors concerning families and child rearing. Intergenerational transmission of risk factors for both violence and victimization has become clearly evident, and raises the key policy issue of how to stop this continuation. Effective programs exist that address this dynamic, for the most part, however, there are certain risk profiles that remain particularly challenging for traditionally vulnerable individuals from certain age groups, i.e., the very young and the elderly, as well as politically and economically marginalized ethnic/racial groups in most countries. An outstanding policy issue is the need to enhance the cooperation necessary to integrate information systems among government and non-government agencies responsible for responding to serious and violent offenders and their victims in order to provide the most effective program interventions at the individual case management level. Clearly funding challenges are integral to this policy theme. Still, confidentiality of deeply sensitive personal information on offenders and victims, ethical concerns centered on aggressive interventions into the lives of already highly vulnerable and marginalized families and individuals, and the shortage of more updated multidisciplinary training of program delivery staff, all limit the ability to provide the most effective individual treatment services. In effect persistent political concerns negatively affect both the types of research and services to serious young offenders (as well as adult serious offenders) and their victims. The encouraging policy trend, though, is that vast increases in the validity of recent research, despite its inherent theoretical complexity, can facilitate progress in implementing effective programs.

9 Future Directions

Research and policy themes for the future will continue to expand on the identification of both risk and protective factors and the development of distinctive pathways for serious and violent offending and vulnerabilities to victimization, respectively. Treatment interventions will accelerate with breakthroughs in brain imaging technology that will likely identify more fully the neurological bases for serious offending. Relatedly, neuro/endocrinology studies will also assist in understanding the biological basis for these phenomena. Therapeutic interventions involving these research trends will include pharmacological approaches to target aggression/violence. More controversial therapies may regard stem cell breakthroughs concerning neurologically-based disorders related to serious violence. Program evaluation research will increasingly be based on random designed studies, which will affect government decisions to implement and/or retain intervention programs.

Five Questions

1. What kind of training would be beneficial for practitioners to assist in identifying and addressing key risk factors?
2. How can agencies improve information sharing practices that maintain confidentiality while allowing for cross-agency collaboration?
3. In what ways can the fragmented research on victimization be better coordinated and how can the learnings from this research be better implemented?
4. A) How can professionals, practitioners, and program providers determine the most appropriate programs to address the individual needs of at-risk and criminally involved youth? B) How can these individuals then ensure that they deliver effective rehabilitative services and treatment to prevent the onset and reduce the continuation of delinquent behaviours?
5. In what ways have cognitive-behavioural therapies been used to address at-risk individuals, as well as specific types of victims and offenders?

References

Alexander, J. F., Robbins, M. S., & Sexton, T. L. (2000). Family-based interventions with older, at-risk youth: From promise to proof to practice. *The Journal of Primary Prevention, 21*, 185–205.

Alexander, J. F., & Sexton, T. L. (2000). *Functional family therapy*. Washington: U.S. Department of Justice, Office of Juvenile Justice and Delinquency Prevention.

American Psychological Association, Intimate Partner Abuse and Relationship Violence Working Groups. (2002). *Intimate partner abuse and relationship violence*. Washington: American Psychological Association. http://www.apa.org/about/division/activities/partner-abuse.pdf.

Appel, A. E., & Holden, G. W. (1998). The co-occurrence of spouse and physical child abuse: A review and appraisal. *Journal of Family Psychology, 12*, 578–599.

Appleyard, K., Berlin, L. J., Rosanbalm, K. D., & Dodge, K. A. (2011). Preventing early child maltreatment: Implications from a longitudinal study of maternal abuse history, substance use problems and offspring victimization. *Prevention Sciences, 12*, 139–149.

Archer, J. (2000). Sex differences in aggression between heterosexual partners: A meta-analytic review. *Psychological Bulletin, 126*, 651–680.

Augimeri, L. K., Farrington, D. P., Koegl, C. J., & Day, D. M. (2007). The SNAP under 12 outreach project: Effects of a community based program for children with conduct problems. *Journal of Child and Family Studies, 16*, 799–807. doi:10.1007/s10826-006-9126-x.

Augimeri, L. K., Walsh, M., & Slater, N. (2011). Rolling out SNAP® an evidence-based intervention: A summary of implementation, evaluation and research. *International Journal of Child, Youth and Family Studies, 2*(1), 330–352.

Augimeri, L. K., Pepler, D., Walsh, M. M., Jiang, D., & Dassinger, C. (2010). Aggressive and antisocial young children: Risk prediction, assessment and clinical risk management. Program evaluation report submitted to The Provincial Centre of Excellence for Child and Youth Mental Health at CHEO. http://www.excellenceforchildandyouth.ca/sites/default/files/gai_attach/RG-976_Final_Outcomes_Report.pdf.

Augimeri, L. K., Walsh, M., Levene, K., & Slater, N. (under review). Scaling deeper: SNAP® model and implementation frameworks. In: R. Corrado, & A, Leschied. (Eds.), *Serious and violent young offenders and youth criminal justice: A Canadian perspective*. Burnaby: Simon Fraser University Press.

Babcock, J. C., Green, C. E., & Robie, C. (2004). Does batterers' treatment work? A meta-analytic review of domestic violence treatment. *Clinical Psychology Review, 23*, 1023–1053.

Bachman, R., & Saltzman, L. E. (1995).Violence against women: A national crime victimization survey (No. JCJ 154348). Washington: U.S. Department of Justice.

Baglivio, M. T., Jackowski, K., Greenwald, M. A., & Howell, J. C. (2014). Serious, violent, and chronic juvenile offenders: A statewide analysis of prevalence and prediction of subsequent recidivism using risk and protective factors. *Criminology and Public Policy, 13*, 83–116. doi:10.1111/1745-9133.12064.

Barnaby, L., Penn, R., & Erickson, P. G. (2010). Drugs, homelessness and health: Homeless youth speak out about harm reduction. The Shout Clinic Harm Reduction Report, 2010. Wellesley Institute, Toronto. http://www.wellesleyinstitute.com/wp-content/uploads/2010/02/homelessyouthspeakout_shoutclinic2010_v2.pdf.

Barnes, J., Ball, M., Meadows, P., Howden, B., Jackson, A., Henderson, J., et al. (2011). *The family nurse partnership programme in England: Wave 1 implementation in toddlerhood and a comparison between Waves 1 and 2a implementation in pregnancy and infancy*. London: Department of Health. https://www.gov.uk/government/uploads/system/uploads/attachment_data/file/215837/dh_123366.pdf.

Barnes, J., Ball, M., Meadows, P., & Belsky, J. (2009). *Nurse-family partnership programme: Second year pilot sites implementation in England: The infancy period*. London: DCSF.

Baron, S. W. (1997). Risky lifestyles and the link between offending and victimization. *Studies on Crime and Crime Prevention, 6*, 53–72.

Baron, S. W. (2003). Street youth violence and victimization Trauma. *Violence and Abuse, 4*, 22–44.

Baum, K. (2005). Juvenile victimization and offending, 1993–2003 (NCJ 209468). Washington: U.S. Bureau of Justice Statistics. http://bjs.ojp.usdoj.gov/content/pub/pdf/jvo03.pdf.

Beitchman, J. H., Zucker, K. J., Hood, J. E., DaCosta, G. A., Akman, D., & Cassavia, E. (1992). A review of the long-term effects of child sexual abuse. *Child abuse and neglect, 16*, 101–118.

Bennett, T., Holloway, K., & Farrington, D. (2009). The effectiveness of neighborhood watch. *Security Journal, 22*, 143–155. doi:10.1057/palgrave.sj.8350076.

Benson, M. L., Fox, G. L., DeMaris, A., & van Wyk, J. (2003). Neighborhood disadvantage, individual economic distress and violence against women in intimate relationships. *Journal of Quantitative Criminology, 19*, 207–235.

Blumstein, A., Cohen, J., Roth, J. A., & Vishner, C. A. (1986). *Criminal careers and career criminals*. Washington: National Academy Press.

Bogestad, A. J., Kettler, R. J., & Hagan, M. P. (2010). Evaluation of a cognitive intervention program for juvenile offenders. *International Journal of Offender Therapy and Comparative Criminology, 54*, 552–565.

Borduin, C. M., Henggeler, S. W., Blaske, D. M., & Stein, T. (1990). Multisystemic treatment of adolescent sexual offenders. *International Journal of Offender Therapy and Comparative Criminology, 34*, 105–114.

Borduin, C. M., Mann, B. J., Cone, L. T., Henggeler, S. W., Fucci, B. R., Blaske, D. M., et al. (1995). Multisystemic treatment of serious juvenile offenders: Long-term prevention of criminology and violence. *Journal of Consulting and Clinical Psychology, 63*, 569–578.

Botvin, G. J., Mihalic, S. F., & Grotpeter, J. K. (1998). Life skills training: Blueprints for violence prevention, book five. In D. S. Elliott (Ed.), *Blueprints for violence prevention series*.

Boulder: Center for the Study and Prevention of Violence, Institute of Behavioral Science, University of Colorado.

Brosnan, R., & Carr, A. (2000). Adolescent conduct problems. In A. Carr (Ed.), *What works with children and adolescents? A critical review of psychological interventions with children, adolescents and their families* (pp. 131–154). UK: Brunner-Routledge.

Brown, J., Cohen, P., Johnson, J. G., & Salzinger, S. (1998). A longitudinal analysis of risk factors for child maltreatment: Findings of a 17-year prospective study of officially recorded and self-reported child abuse and neglect. *Child Abuse and Neglect, 22*, 1065–1078.

Browning, C. R. (2002). The span of collective efficacy: Extending social disorganization theory to partner violence. *Journal of Marriage and Family, 64*, 833–850.

Burns, B. J., Schoenwald, S. K., Burchard, J. D., Faw, L., & Santos, A. B. (2000). Comprehensive community-based interventions for youth with severe emotional disorders: Multisystemic therapy and the wraparound process. *Journal of Child & Family Studies, 9*, 283–314.

Butler, A. M., & Eyberg, S. M. (2006). Parent–child interaction therapy and ethnic minority children. *Vulnerable Children and Youth Studies, 1*, 246–255.

Caetano, R., Cunradi, C. B., Schafer, J., & Clark, C. L. (2000). Intimate partner violence and drinking among white, black and Hispanic couples in the U.S. *Journal of Substance Abuse, 11*, 123–138.

Caldwell, M., Skeem, J., Salekin, R., & van Rybroek, G. (2006). Treatment response of adolescent offenders with psychopathy features: A 2-year follow-up. *Criminal Justice and Behavior, 33*, 571–596. doi:10.1177/0093854806288176.

Capaldi, D. M., & Clark, S. (1998). Prospective family predictors of aggression toward female partners for at-risk young men. *Developmental Psychology, 34*, 1175–1188.

Catchpole, R. E, H. (2002). Empirical findings from two provincial violent offender treatment programs: Risk assessment and treatment outcome. Presented at the American Psychology and Law Society, Biennial Conference, Austin.

Cauce, A. M., Tyler, K. A., & Whitbeck, L. B. (2004). Maltreatment and victimization in homeless adolescents: Out of the frying pan and into the fire. *The Prevention Researcher, 11*, 12–14.

Chaffin, M., Silovsky, J. F., Funderburk, B., Valle, L. A., Brestan, E. V., Balachova, T., et al. (2004). Parent–child interaction therapy with physically abusive parents: Efficacy for reducing future abuse reports. *Journal of Consulting and Clinical Psychology, 72*, 500–510.

Chamberlain, P., Leve, L. D., & DeGarmo, D. S. (2007). Multidimensional treatment foster care for girls in the juvenile justice system: 2-year follow-up of a randomized clinical trial. *Journal of Consulting and Clinical Psychology, 75*, 187–193.

Chamberlain, P., & Reid, J. B. (1998). Comparison of two community alternatives to incarceration for chronic juvenile offenders. *Journal of Consulting and Clinical Psychology, 66*, 624–633. doi:10.1037/0022-006X.66.4.624.

Chen, X. (2009). The link between juvenile offending and victimization: The influence of risky lifestyles, social bonding, and individual characteristics. *Youth Violence and Juvenile Justice, 7*, 119–135. doi:10.1177/1541204008328799.

Cohen, I., Plecas, D., McCormick, A., & Peters, A. (2014). *Eliminating crime: The 7 essential principles of police-based crime reduction*. Abbotsford: Len Garis, University of the Fraser Valley.

Cohen, J. A., Deblinger, E., Mannarino, A. P., & Steer, R. A. (2004). A multisite randomized trial for children with sexual abuse-related PTSD symptoms. *Journal of the American Academy of Child and Adolescent Psychiatry, 43*, 39–402.

Cohen, J. A., & Mannarino, A. P. (1996). A treatment outcome study for sexually abused preschool children: Initial findings. *Journal of the American Academy of Child and Adolescent Psychiatry, 35*, 42–43.

Cohen, J. A., Mannarino, A. P., Kliethermes, M., & Murray, L. A. (2012). Trauma-focused CBT for youth with complex trauma. *Child Abuse and Neglect, 36*, 528–541.

Cohen, L. E., & Felson, M. (1979). Social change and crime rate trends: A routine activity approach. *American Sociological Review, 44*, 588–609.

Coker, A. L., Davis, K. E., Arias, I., Desai, S., Sanderson, M., Brandt, H. M., et al. (2002). Physical and mental health effects of intimate partner violence for men and women. *America Journal of Preventative Medicine, 23*, 260–268.

Corrado, R., & Cohen, I. M. (2014). *A review of the research literature on the socioeconomic contributors to homicide*. Abbotsford: Centre for Public Safety and Criminal Justice Research, University of the Fraser Valley.

Corrado, R. R. (2011). Comprehensive risk management instruments for serious and violent young offenders: Challenges and advantages. In T. Bliesener, A. Beelmann, & M. Stemmler (Eds.), *Antisocial behavior and crime: Contributions of developmental and evaluation research to prevention and intervention* (pp. 239–260). Cambridge: Hogrefe Publishing.

Corrado, R. R., & Freedman, L. (2011). Risk profiles, trajectories and intervention points for serious and chronic young offenders. *International Journal of Child, Youth and Family Studies, 2*, 197–232.

Corrado, R. R., & Lussier, P. (2011). Introduction to the special issue on early developmental prevention of antisocial behaviour. *International Journal of Child, Youth & Family Studies, 2*(1/2), 1–11.

Cunradi, C. B. (2007). Drinking level, neighborhood social disorder, and mutual intimate partner violence. *Alcoholism: Clinical and Experimental Research, 31*, 1012–1019.

Cunradi, C. B. (2009). Intimate partner violence among Hispanic men and women: The role of drinking, neighborhood disorder, and acculturation-related factors. *Violence and Victims, 24*, 83–97.

Cunradi, C. B. (2010). Neighborhoods, alcohol outlets and intimate partner violence: Addressing research gaps in explanatory mechanisms. *International Journal of Environmental Research and Public Health, 7*, 799–813.

Cunradi, C. B., Caetano, R., Clark, C. L., & Schafer, J. (1999). Alcohol-related problems and intimate partner violence among white, black, and Hispanic couples in the U.S. Alcohol Clinical. *Experimental Research, 23*, 1492–1501.

Cunradi, C. B., Caetano, R., & Schafer, J. (2002). Alcohol-related problems, drug use, and male intimate partner violence severity among US couples. *Alcoholism: Clinical and experimental research, 26*, 493–500.

Dahlberg, L. L., & Mercy, J. A. (2009). History of violence as a public health problem. *American Medical Association Virtual Mentor, 11*, 167–172. http://virtualmentory.amassn.org/2009/02/pdf/mhst1-0902.pdf.

Davis, R. C., Weisburd, D. L., & Hamilton, E. E. (2007). *Preventing repeat incidents of family violence: A randomized field test of second responder program in Redlands, California*. Washington: US Department of Justice, National Institute of Justice. https://www.ncjrs.gov/pdffiles1/nij/grants/219840.pdf.

Demuth, S., & Brown, S. L. (2004). Family structure, family processes and adolescent delinquency: The significance of parental absence versus parental gender. *Journal of Research in Crime and Delinquency, 41*, 58–81.

Desmarais, S. L., Reeves, K. A., Nicholls, T. L., Telford, R. P., & Fiebert, M. S. (2012). Prevalence of physical violence in intimate relationships, part 1: Rates of male and female victimization. *Partner Abuse, 3*, 140–169.

Domitrovich, C. E., Cortes, R. C., & Greenberg, M. T. (2007). Improving young children's social and emotional competence: A randomized trial of the preschool "PATHS" curriculum. *The Journal of Primary Prevention, 28*, 67–91.

Eckkardt, C., Jamison, T. R., & Watts, K. (2002). Anger experience and expression among male dating violence perpetrators during anger arousal. *Journal of Interpersonal Violence, 17*, 1102–1114.

Eddy, J. M., & Chamberlain, P. (2000). Family management and deviant peer association as mediators of the impact of treatment condition on youth antisocial behavior. *Journal of Consulting and Clinical Psychology, 68*, 857–863.

Edleson, J. L. (1999). The overlap between child maltreatment and woman battering. *Violence Against Women, 5*, 134–154.

Egeland, B., Jacobvitz, D., & Sroufe, L. A. (1988). Breaking the cycle of abuse. *Child Development, 59*, 1080–1088.

Ekblom, P. (1996). Safer cities and residential burglary. *European Journal on Criminal Policy and Research, 4*, 22–52.

Esbensen, F. A., & Huizinga, D. (1993). Gangs, drugs, and delinquency in a survey of urban youth. *Criminology, 31*, 565–589.

Esbensen, F. A., Huizinga, D., & Weiher, A. W. (1993). Gangs and non-gang youth: Differences in explanatory factors. *Journal of Contemporary Criminal Justice, 9*, 94–116.

Euser, E. M., van Ijzendoorn, M. H., Prinzie, P., & Bakermans-Kranenburge, M. J. (2010). Prevalence of child maltreatment in the Netherlands. *Child Maltreatment, 15*, 5–17.

Fagan, F., & Browne, A. (1994). Violence between spouses and intimates: Physical aggression between women and men in intimate relationships. In A. J. Reiss Jr. & J. A. Roth (Eds.), *Understanding and preventing violence* (Biobehavioural influences, Vol. 2, pp. 115–292). Washington: National Research Council.

Fantuzzo, J. W., Perlman, S. M., & Dobbins, E. K. (2011). Types and timing of child maltreatment and early school success: A population-based investigation. *Child and Youth Services Review, 33*, 1404–1411.

Farrington, D. P., Loeber, R., Jolliffe, D., & Pardini, D. A. (2008). Promotive and risk processes at different life stages. In R. Loeber, D. P. Farrington, M. Stouthamer-Loeber, & H. Raskin White (Eds.), *Violence and serious theft: Development and prediction from childhood to adulthood* (pp. 169–230). New York: Routledge.

Farrington, D. P. (1994). Childhood, adolescent, and adult features of violent males. In L. R. Huesmann (Ed.), *Aggressive behavior: Current perspectives*. New York: Plenum Press.

Farrington, D. P. (2002). Key results from the first forty years of the Cambridge study in delinquent development. In T. P. Thornberry & M. D. Krohn (Eds.), *Taking stock of delinquency: An overview of findings from contemporary longitudinal studies* (pp. 137–183). New York: Kluwer/Plenum.

Feder, L., & Wilson, D. B. (2005). A meta-analytic review of court-mandated batterer intervention programs: Can courts affect abusers' behavior? *Journal of Experimental Criminology, 1*, 239–262.

Field, C. A., & Caetano, R. (2004). Ethnic differences in intimate partner violence in the U.S. general population: The role of alcohol use and socioeconomic status. *Trauma, Violence and Abuse, 5*, 303–317.

Finkelhor, D. (1991). Child sexual abuse. In M. L. Rosenberg & M. A. Fenley (Eds.), *Violence in America: A public health approach* (pp. 79–94). London: Oxford University Press.

Finkelhor, D. (2011). Prevalence of child victimization, abuse, crime, and violence exposure. In J. W. White, M. P. Koss, & A. E. Kazdin (Eds.), *Violence against women and children: Mapping the terrain* (pp. 9–29). Washington: American Psychological Association.

Finkelhor, D., Turner, H., Ormrod, R., Hamby, S., & Kracke, K. (2009). *Children's exposure to violence: A comprehensive national survey*. Washington: US Department of Justice, Office of Justice Programs, Office of Juvenile Justice and Delinquency Prevention. https://www.ncjrs.gov/pdffiles1/ojjdp/227744.pdf.

Fox, G. L., Benson, M. L., Desmaris, A. A., & van Wyk, J. (2002). Economic distress and intimate violence: Testing family stress and resources theory. *Journal of Marriage and Family, 64*, 793–807.

Gaetz, S. (2004). Safe streets for whom? Homeless youth, social exclusion, and criminal victimization. *Canadian Journal of Criminology and Criminal Justice, 46*, 423–455.

Gaudiosi (2005). *Child maltreatment*. U.S. Department of Healh and Human Services.

Gavazzi, S. M., Bostic, J. M., Lim, J., & Yarcheck, C. M. (2008). Examining the impact of gender, race/ethnicity, and family factors on mental health issues in a sample of court-involved youth. *Journal of Marital and Family Therapy, 34*, 353–368.

Gordon, D. A., Graves, K., & Arbuthnot, J. (1995). The effect of functional family therapy for delinquents on adult criminal behavior. *Criminal Justice and Behavior, 22*, 60–73.

Gottfredson, M. R. (1984). Victims of crime: The dimensions of risk (Home Office Research Study No. 81). Her Majesty's Stationery Office, London.

Gottfredson, M. R., & Hirschi, T. (1990). *A general theory of crime*. Stanford, CA: Stanford University Press.

Granic, I., O'Hara, A., Pepler, D., & Lewis, M. D. (2007). A dynamic systems analysis of parent–child changes associated with successful "real-world" interventions for aggressive children. *Journal of Abnormal Child Psychology, 35*, 845–857.

Greenberg, M. T., & Kusché, C. A. (1993). *Promoting social and emotional development in deaf children: The PATHS Project*. Seattle: University of Washington Press.

Greenwood, P. W., & Turner, S. (2011). Juvenile crime and juvenile justice. In J. Q. Wilson & J. Petersilia (Eds.), *Crime and public policy* (pp. 88–129). New York: Oxford University Press.

Gretton, H. M., Mcbride, M., Hare, R. D., O'Shaughnessy, R., & Kumka, G. (2001). Psychopathy and recidivism in adolescent sex offenders. *Criminal Justice and Behavior, 28*, 427–449. doi:10.1177/009385480102800403.

Gretton, H., Arabsky, S., Buchanan, T., & Rajlic, G. (2003). Violent offender treatment program evaluation: Boulder Bay, Prince George and Kamloops executive summary. Presented to the Executive of Youth Forensic Psychiatric Services, Burnaby.

Grossman, J. B., & Tierney, J. P. (1998). Does mentoring work? An impact study of the big brothers big sisters program. *Evaluation Review, 22*, 403–426.

Hawker, D. S., & Boulton, M. J. (2000). Twenty years' research on peer victimization and psychosocial maladjustment: A meta-analytic review of cross-sectional studies. *Journal of child psychology and psychiatry, 41*, 441–455.

Hemphill, S., Toumbourou, J., Herrenkohl, T., McMorris, B., & Catalano, R. (2006). The effect of school suspensions and arrests on subsequent adolescent antisocial behavior in Australia and the United States. *Journal of Adolescent Health, 39*, 736–744.

Henggeler, S. W. (1982). *Delinquency & adolescent psychopathology: A family-ecological systems approach*. Boston: John Wright.

Henggeler, S. W., & Lee, T. (2003). Multisystemic treatment of serious clinical problems. In A. E. Kazdin & J. R. Weisz (Eds.), *Evidence-based psychotherapies for children and adolescents* (pp. 301–322). New York: Guilford Press.

Henggeler, S. W., Melton, G. B., & Smith, L. A. (1992). Family preservation using multisystemic therapy: An effective alternative to incarcerating serious juvenile offenders. *Journal of Consulting and Clinical Psychology, 60*, 953–961.

Henggeler, S. W., Pickrel, S. G., & Brondino, M. J. (1999). Multisystemic treatment of substance-abusing and dependent delinquents: Outcomes, treatment fidelity, and transportability. *Mental Health Services Research, 1*, 171–184.

Henry, K., & Huizinga, D. (2007). Truancy's effect on the onset of drug use among urban adolescents placed at risk. *Journal of Adolescent Health, 40*, 9–17.

Henry, L. (2009). School-based mentoring: Big brothers big sisters. *Educational Digest, 74*, 45–46.

Herschell, A. D., Calzada, E. J., Eyberg, S. M., & McNeil, C. B. (2002). Parent–child interaction therapy: New directions in research. *Cognitive and Behavioral Practice, 9*, 9–16.

Hildyard, K. L., & Wolfe, D. A. (2002). Child neglect: Developmental issues and outcomes. *Child abuse and neglect, 26*, 679–695.

Hirschi, T. (2002). *Causes of delinquency* (2nd ed.). Piscataway: Transaction Publishers.

Howell, J. C. (2005). Moving risk factors into developmental theories of gang membership. *Youth Violence and Juvenile Justice, 3*, 334–354.

Howell, J. C. (2009). *Preventing and reducing juvenile delinquency: A comprehensive framework* (2nd ed.). Thousand Oaks: Sage.

Howell, J. C. (2010). *Gang prevention: An overview of research and programs*. Washington: Office of Juvenile Justice and Delinquency Prevention, US Department of Justice. https://www.ncjrs.gov/pdffiles1/ojjdp/231116.pdf.

Huff, C. R. (1996). The criminal behavior of gang members and nongang at-risk youth. In C. R. Huff (Ed.), *Gangs in America* (2nd ed., pp. 75–102). Thousand Oaks: Sage.

Hussey, J. M., Chang, J. J., & Kotch, J. B. (2006). Child maltreatment in the United States: Prevalence, risk factors, and adolescent health consequences. *Pediatrics, 118*, 933–942.

Janssen, P. A., Nicholls, T. L., Kumar, R. A., Stefanakis, H., Spidel, A. L., & Simpson, E. M. (2005). Of mice and men: Will the intersection of social science and genetics create new approaches for intimate partner violence? *Journal of Interpersonal Violence, 20*, 61–71.

Jiang, D., Walsh, M., & Augimeri, L. K. (2011). The linkage between bullying behaviour and future offending. *Criminal Behaviour and Mental Health, 21*, 128–135. doi:10.1002/cbm.803.

Johnson, H. (1998). Rethinking survey research on violence against women. In R. E. Dobash & R. P. Dobash (Eds.), *Rethinking violence against women* (pp. 23–50). Thousand Oaks: Sage.

Jones, D. P. (2008). Child maltreatment. In M. Rutter, D. Bishop, D. S. Pine, S. Scott, J. Stevenson, E. Taylor & A. Thapar (Eds.), *Rutter's child and adolescent psychiatry* (5th ed.). Wiley-Blackwell Publishers.

Kam, C., Greenberg, M. T., & Kusché, C. A. (2004). Sustained effects of the PATHS curriculum on the social and psychological adjustment of children in special education. *Journal of Emotional and Behavioral Disorders, 12*, 66–78.

Kaplan, S. J., Pelcovitz, D., & Labruna, V. (1999). Child and adolescent abuse and neglect research: A review of the past 10 years. Part I: Physical and emotional abuse and neglect. *Journal of the American Academy of Child and Adolescent Psychiatry, 38*, 1214–1222.

Kashani, J. H., Jones, M. R., Bumby, K., & Thomas, L. A. (1999). Youth violence: Psychosocial risk factors, treatment, prevention, and recommendations. *Journal of Emotional & Behavioral Disorders, 7*, 200–210.

Kataoka, S. H., Stein, B. D., Jaycox, L. H., Wong, M., Escudero, P., Tu, W., et al. (2003). A school-based mental health program for traumatized Latino immigrant children. *Journal of the American Academy of Child and Adolescent Psychiatry, 42*, 311–318.

Kellerman, A. L., & Mercy, J. A. (1992). Men, women, and murder: Gender-specific differences in rates of fatal violence and victimization. *Journal of Trauma, 33*, 1–5.

Kempf-Leonard, K., & Johansson, P. (2007). Gender and runaways: Risk factors, delinquency, and juvenile justice experiences. *Youth Violence and Juvenile Justice, 5*, 308–327.

Klostermann, K. C., & Fals-Stewart, W. (2006). Intimate partner violence and alcohol use: Exploring the role of drinking in partner violence and its implications for intervention. *Aggressive Violent Behavior, 11*, 587–597.

Krug, E. G., Mercy, J. A., Dahlberg, L. L., & Zwi, A. B. (2002). The world report on violence and health. *The Lancet, 360*, 1083–1088.

Lacourse, E., Côte, S., Nagin, D. S., Vitaro, F., Brendgen, M., & Tremblay, R. E. (2002). A longitudinal-experimental approach to testing theories of antisocial behavior development. *Development and Psychopathology, 14*, 909–924.

Lamb, S., & Edgar-Smith, S. (1994). Aspects of disclosure: Mediators of outcome of childhood sexual abuse. *Journal of Interpersonal Violence, 9*, 307–326.

Larstone, R., & Moretti, M. M. (2013). Reaching parents of teens at risk through an attachment based intervention: The connect program. In K. H. Brisch & R. Schmid (Eds.), *Attachment and adolescence*. Munich: Universität München.

Lauritsen, J., Sampson, R., & Laub, J. (1991). The link between offending and victimization among adolescents. *Criminology, 29*, 265–291. doi:10.1111/j.1745-9125.1991.tb01067.x.

LeBlanc, M., & Fréchette, M. (1989). *Male criminal activity from childhood through youth: Multilevel and developmental perspectives*. New York: Springer.

Lee, M. R. (2000). Concentrated poverty, race, and homicide. *Sociological Quarterly, 41*, 189–206.

Lee, M. R., Maume, M. O., & Ousey, G. (2003). Social isolation and lethal violence across the metro/nonmetro divide: The effects of socioeconomic disadvantage and poverty concentration on homicide. *Rural Sociology, 68*, 107–131.

Leeb, R. T., Paulozzi, L., Melanson, C., Simon, T., & Arias, I. (2008). *Child maltreatment surveillance: Uniform definitions for public health and recommended data elements, version 1.0*. Atlanta: Centers for Disease Control and Prevention, National Center for Injury Prevention and Control.

Leve, L. D., & Chamberlain, P. (2007). A randomized evaluation of Multidimensional treatment foster care: Effects on school attendance and homework completion in juvenile justice girls. *Research on Social Work Practice, 17*, 657–663.

Leve, L. D., Fisher, P. H., & Chamberlain, P. (2009). Multidimensional treatment foster care as a preventive intervention to promote resiliency among youth in the child welfare system. *Journal of Personality, 77*, 1869–1902. doi:10.1111/j.1467-6494.2009.00603.x.

Leventhal, T., & Brooks-Gunn, J. (2000). The neighborhoods they live in: The effects of neighborhood residence on child and adolescent outcomes. *Psychological bulletin, 126*, 309–337.

Lipsey, M. W., Chapman, G., & Landenberger, N. A. (2001). Cognitive-behavioral programs for offenders. *The Annals of the American Academy of Political and Social Science, 578*, 144–157.

Lipsey, M. W., & Landenberger, N. A. (2006). Cognitive-behavioral interventions. In B. C. Welsh & D. P. Farrington (Eds.), *Preventing crime: What works for children, offenders, victims, and places* (pp. 57–71). Dordrecht: Springer.

Lipsey, M. W., Landenberger, N. A., & Wilson, S. J. (2007). Effects of cognitive-behavioral programs for criminal offenders. *Campbell Systematic Reviews, 6*, 1–27.

Loeber, R., & Farrington, D. P. (1998). *Serious & violent juvenile offenders: Risk factors and successful interventions*. Thousand Oaks: Sage.

Lösel, F., & Schmucker, M. (2005). The effectiveness of treatment for sexual offenders: A comprehensive meta-analysis. *Journal of Experimental Criminology, 1*, 117–146.

Lussier, P., Bouchard, M., & Beauregard, E. (2011). Patterns of criminal achievement in sexual offending: Unravelling the "successful" sex offender. *Journal of Criminal Justice, 39*, 433–444.

Lussier, P., Farrington, D. P., & Moffitt, T. E. (2009). Is the antisocial child father of the abusive man? A 40-year prospective longitudinal study on the developmental antecedents of intimate partner violence. *Criminology, 47*, 741–780.

Lussier, P., Healey, J., Tzoumakis, S., Deslauriers-Varin, N., & Corrado, R. (2011). *The CRACOW Instrument: A new framework for the assessment of multi-problem violent youth.* Ottawa: Public Safety. http://www.publicsafety.gc.ca/cnt/rsrcs/pblctns/crcw-nstrmnt/index-eng.aspx.

Lussier, P., & Mathesius, J. (2012). Criminal achievement, criminal career initiation, and detection avoidance: The onset of successful sex offending. *Journal of Crime and Justice, 35*, 376–394.

Lyons, J. S., & Rawal, P. H. (2005). Evidence-based treatments for children and adolescents. In C. E. Stout & R. A. Hayes (Eds.), *The evidence-based practice: Methods, models, and tools for mental health professionals* (pp. 177–198). Hoboken: John Wiley & Sons.

Maimon, D., Browning, C. R., & Brooks-Gunn, J. (2010). Collective efficacy, family attachment, and urban adolescent suicide attempts. *Journal of Health and Social Behavior, 51*, 307–325.

Mathesius, J., & Lussier, P. (2014). The successful onset of sex offending: Determining the correlates of actual and official onset of sex offending. *Journal of Criminal Justice, 42*, 134–144.

McCauley, J., Kern, D. E., Kolodner, K., Dill, L., Schroeder, A. F., DeChant, H. K., et al. (1995). The "battering syndrome": Prevalence and clinical characteristics of domestic violence in primary care internal medicine practices. *Annals of Internal Medicine, 123*, 737–746.

McEwen, B. S. (1998). Stress, adaptation, and disease: Allostasis and allostatic load. *Annals of the New York Academy of Sciences, 840*, 33–44.

McLoyd, V. C., Jayaratne, T. E., Ceballo, R., & Borquez, J. (1994). Unemployment and work interruption among African American single mothers: Effects on parenting and adolescent socio-emotional functioning. *Child development, 65*, 562–589.

McWey, L. M., & Mullis, A. (2004). Improving the lives of children in foster care: The impact of supervised visitation. *Family Relations, 53*, 293–300.

Meeus, W., Vollebergh, W., Engels, R. C. M. E., de Graaf, R., & Overbeek, G. (2004). Young adults' recollections of parental bonds. *Social Psychiatry and Psychiatric Epidemiology, 39*, 703–710.

Mihalic, S., Irwin, K., Elliott, D., Fagan, A., & Hansen, D. (2001). *Juvenile justice bulletin: Blueprints for violence prevention*. Washington: U.S. Department of Justice, Office of Juvenile Justice and Delinquency Prevention.

Miles-Doan, R., & Kelly, S. (1997). Geographic concentration of violence between intimate partners. *Scientific Contributions, 112*, 135–141.

Miller, B. A. (1998). Partner violence experiences and women's drug use: Exploring the connections. In C. L. Wetherington & A. B. Roman (Eds.), *Drug addiction research and the health of women*. Rockville: United States Department of Health and Human Services, National Institute of Health, National Institute on Drug Abuse.

Miller, T. R., Cohen, M. A., & Wiersema, B. (1996). *Victim costs and consequences: A new look*. Washington: National Institute of Justice.

Moffitt, A., McClay, J., et al. (2002). Role of genotype in the cycle of violence in maltreated children. *Science, 297*(5582), 851–854.

Moffitt, T. E., & Caspi, A. (2003). Preventing the intergenerational continuity of antisocial behaviour: Implications of partner violence. In D. P. Farrington & J. W. Coid (Eds.), *Early prevention of adult antisocial behaviour*. Cambridge: Cambridge University Press.

Morenoff, J. D., Sampson, R. J., & Raudenbush, S. W. (2001). Neighborhood inequality, collective efficacy, and the spatial dynamics of urban violence. *Criminology, 39*, 517–559.

Murray, L., Cooper, P. J., Wilson, A., & Romaniuk, H. (2003). A controlled trial of the long-term effect of psychological treatment of postpartum depression: Impact on the mother-child relationship and child outcome. *British Journal of Psychiatry, 182*, 420–427.

Mustaine, E. E., & Tewksbury, R. (1998). Predicting risks of larceny theft victimization: A routine activity analysis using refined lifestyle measures. *Criminology, 36*, 829–857. doi:10.1111/j.1745-9125.1998.tb01267.x.

Nagin, D. S., & Tremblay, R. E. (2001). Parental and early childhood predictors of persistent physical aggression in boys from kindergarten to high school. *Archives of General Psychiatry, 58*, 389–394.

National Crime Prevention Centre (NCPC), Public Safety Canada (2012). *A statistical snapshot of youth at risk and youth offending in Canada*. Ottawa: Author.

Nelson, S. E., & Dishion, T. J. (2004). From boys to men: Predicting adult adaptation from middle childhood sociometric status. *Development and Psychopathology, 16*, 441–459.

Nishina, A., Juvonen, J., & Witkow, M. R. (2005). Sticks and stones may break my bones, but names will make me feel sick: The psychosocial, somatic, and scholastic consequences of peer harassment. *Journal of Clinical Child and Adolescent Psychology, 34*, 37–48.

Nurse-Family Partnership (2014). Nurse-Family Partnership locations. http://www.nursefamilypartnership.org/locations.

O'Campo, P., Gielen, A. C., Faden, R. R., Xue, X., Kass, N., & Wang, M. C. (1995). Violence by male partners against women during the childbearing year: A contextual analysis. *American Journal of Public Health, 85*, 1092–1097.

Olds, D. L., Eckenrode, J., Henderson, C. R., Jr., Kitzman, H., Powers, J., Cole, R., et al. (1997). Long-term effects of home visitation on maternal life course and child abuse and neglect. *Journal of the American Medical Association, 278*, 37–43.

Olds, D. L., Henderson, C. R., Jr., Cole, R., Eckenrode, J., Kitzman, H., Luckey, D., et al. (1998). Long-term effects of nurse home visitation on children's criminal and antisocial behavior: 15-year follow-up of a randomized controlled trial. *Journal of the American Medical Association, 280*, 1238–1244.

Osgood, D. W., Wilson, J. K., O'Malley, P. M., Bachman, J. G., & Johnson, L. D. (1996). Routine activities and individual deviant behavior. *American Sociological Review, 61*, 635–655.

Osofsky, J. D. (2001). *Addressing youth victimization*. Washington: US Department of Justice, Office of Justice Programs, Office of Juvenile Justice and Delinquency Prevention. https://www.ncjrs.gov/pdffiles1/ojjdp/186667.pdf.

Özabacı, N. (2011). Cognitive behavioural therapy for violent behaviour in children and adolescents: A meta-analysis. *Children and Youth Services Review, 33*, 1989–1993.

Parker, K. F., & Pruitt, M. V. (2000). How the west was one: Explaining the similarities in race-specific homicide rates in the west and south. *Social Forces, 78*, 1483–1508.

Pepler, D., Walsh, M., Yuile, A., Levene, K., Jiang, D., Vaughan, A., et al. (2010). Bridging the gender gap: Interventions with aggressive girls and their parents. *Prevention Science, 11*, 229–238.

Perreault, S. (2012). Homicide in Canada, 2011. Juristat, 32(1). Ottawa: Statistics Canada. http://www.statcan.gc.ca/pub/85-002-x/2012001/article/11738-eng.htm.

Perreault, S. (2013). Police-reported crime statistics in Canada, 2012. Juristat, 33(1). Ottawa: Statistics Canada. http://www.statcan.gc.ca/pub/85-002-x/2013001/article/11854-eng.htm?fpv=269303#a7.

Perreault, S., & Brennan, S. (2010). Criminal victimization in Canada, 2009. Juristat, 30(2). Ottawa: Statistics Canada. http://www.statcan.gc.ca/pub/85-002-x/2010002/article/11340-eng.htm?fpv=2693.

Perry, B. (1997). Incubated in terror: Neurodevelopmental factors in the "cycle of violence.". In J. Osofsky (Ed.), *Children in a violent society: The search for solutions* (pp. 124–148). New York: Guilford Press.

Plichta, S. B., & Falik, M. (2001). Prevalence of violence and its implications for women's health. *Women's Health Issues, 11*, 244–258.

Preyde, M., Frensch, K., Cameron, G., White, S., Penny, R., & Lazure, K. (2011). Long-term outcomes of children and youth accessing residential or intensive home-based treatment: Three year follow up. *Journal of Child and Family Studies, 20*, 660–668. doi:10.1007/s10826-010-9442-z.

Price-Robertson, R., Bromfield, L., & Vassallo, S. (2010). Prevalence matters: Estimating the extent of child maltreatment in Australia. *Developing Practice, 26*, 13–20.

Prinz, R. J., Sanders, M. R., Shapiro, C. J., Whitaker, D. J., & Lutzker, J. R. (2009). Population-based prevention of child maltreatment: The U.S. Triple P system population trial. *Prevention Science, 10*, 1–12. doi:10.1007/s11121-009-0123-3.

Public Health Agency of Canada (2006). Street youth in Canada: Findings from enhanced surveillance of Canadian street youth, 1999–2003. Ottawa: Public Health Agency of Canada. http://www.phac-aspc.gc.ca/std-mts/reports_06/pdf/street_youth_e.pdf.

Radford, L., Corral, S., Bradley, C., & Fisher, H. L. (2013). The prevalence and impact of child maltreatment and other types of victimization in the UK: Findings from a population survey of caregivers, children and young people and young adults. *Child Abuse and Neglect, 37*, 801–813.

Reiter, J. (2005). Public health nurse: Home visiting for vulnerable families. Report prepared for the Interior Health Authority British Columbia. IHA, Kelowna.

Renner, L. M., & Slack, K. S. (2006). Intimate partner violence and child maltreatment: Understanding intra-and intergenerational connections. *Child Abuse and Neglect, 30*, 599–617.

Roebuck, B. (2008). *Homelessness, victimization and crime: Knowledge and actionable recommendations*. Ottawa: Institute for the Prevention of Crime, University of Ottawa. http://socialsciences.uottawa.ca/ipc/pdf/IPC-Homelessness%20report.pdf.

Rubin, D. M., O'Reilly, A. L. R., Luan, X., Dai, D., Localio, A. R., & Christian, C. W. (2011). Variation in pregnancy outcomes following statewide implementation of a prenatal home visitation program. *Archives of Pediatrics and Adolescent Medicine, 165*, 198–204. doi:10.1001/archpediatrics.2010.221.

Sampson, R. J., Raudenbush, S. W., & Earls, F. (1997). Neighborhoods and violent crime: A multilevel study of collective efficacy. *Science, 277*, 918–924.

Sanders, M. R., Markie-Dadds, C., Tully, L. A., & Bor, W. (2000). The Triple P – positive parenting program: A comparison of enhanced, standard, and self-directed behavioral family intervention for parents of children with early onset conduct problems. *The Journal of Consulting and Clinical Psychology, 68*, 624–640.

Sanders, M. R. (2008). Triple P – positive parenting program as a public health approach to strengthening parenting. *The Journal of Family Psychology, 22*, 506–517.

Scalora, M. J., & Garbin, C. (2003). A multivariate analysis of sex offender recidivism. *International Journal of Offender Therapy and Comparative Criminology, 47*, 309–323. doi:10.1177/0306624X03252396.

Schafer, J., Caetano, R., & Cunradi, C. B. (2004). A path model of risk factors for intimate partner violence among couples in the United States. *Journal of Interpersonal Violence, 19*, 127–142.

Schmied, V., & Tully, L. (2009). *Effective strategies and interventions for adolescents in a child protection context*. Ashfield: Centre for Parenting & Research, NSW Department of Community Services.

Schoenwald, S. K., Brown, T. L., & Henggeler, S. W. (2000). Inside multisystemic therapy: Therapist, supervisory, and program practices. *Journal of Emotional and Behavioral Disorders, 8*, 113–127.

Schreck, C. J. (1999). Criminal victimization and low self-control: An extension and test of a general theory of crime. *Justice Quarterly, 16*, 633–654. doi:10.1080/07418829900094291.

Schreck, C. J., & Fisher, B. S. (2004). Specifying the influence of family and peers on violent victimization: Extending routine activities and lifestyles theories. *Journal of Interpersonal Violence, 19*, 1021–1041. doi:10.1177/0886260504268002.

Schweinhart, L. J., Montie, J., Xiang, Z., Barnett, W. S., Belfield, C. R., & Nores, M. (2005). *Lifetime effects: The High/Scope Perry Preschool Study through age 40* (pp. 194–215). Ypsilanti: High/Scope Press.

Schweinhart, L. J., & Weikart, D. P. (1997). The High/Scope Preschool Curriculum comparison study through age 23. *Early Childhood Research Quarterly, 12*, 117–143. doi:10.1016/S0885-2006(97)90009-0.

Serin, R. C., Gobeil, R., & Preston, D. L. (2009). Evaluation of the persistently violent offender treatment program. *International Journal of Offender Therapy and Comparative Criminology, 53*, 57–73.

Seto, M. C., & Lalumière, M. L. (2010). What is so special about male adolescent sexual offending? A review and test of explanations through meta-analysis. *Psychological Bulletin, 136*, 526–575.

Sexton, T. L., & Turner, C. W. (2010). The effectiveness of functional family therapy for youth with behavioral problems in a community practice setting. *Journal of Family Psychology, 24*, 339–348.

Shaffer, J. N., & Ruback, R. B. (2002). *Violent victimization as a risk factor for violent offending among juveniles*. Washington: US Department of Justice, Office of Justice Programs, Office of Juvenile Justice and Delinquency Prevention. https://www.ncjrs.gov/pdffiles1/ojjdp/195737.pdf.

Simons, R. L., Lin, K. H., & Gordon, L. C. (1998). Socialization in the family of origin and male dating violence: A prospective study. *Journal of Marriage and the Family, 60*, 467–478.

Smith, A., Cox, K., Poon, C., Stewart, D., & McCreary Centre Society (2013). *Time out III: A profile of BC youth in custody*. Vancouver: McCreary Centre Society.

Smokowski, P. R., & Kopasz, K. H. (2005). Bullying in school: An overview of types, effects, family characteristics, and intervention strategies. *Children and Schools, 27*, 101–110.

Sorenson, S., Upchurch, D., & Shen, H. (1996). Violence and injury in marital arguments: Risk patterns and gender differences. *American Journal of Public Health, 86*, 35–40.

Stein, B. D., Jaycox, L. H., Kataoka, S. H., Wong, M., Tu, W., Elliott, M. N., et al. (2003). A mental health intervention for schoolchildren exposed to violence. *Journal of the American Medical Association, 290*, 603–611.

Stets, J. E. (1991). Cohabiting and marital aggression: The role of social isolation. *Journal of Marriage and Family, 53*, 669–680.

Stets, J. E., & Straus, M. A. (1995). The marriage license as a hitting license: A comparison of assaults in dating, cohabitating, and married couples. In M. A. Straus & R. J. Gelles (Eds.), *Physical violence in American families: Risk factors and adaptations to violence in 8,145 families* (pp. 227–244). New Brunswick: Transaction.

Stoltenborgh, M., van Ijzendoorn, M. H., Euser, E. M., & Bakermans-Kranenburg, M. J. (2011). A global perspective on child sexual abuse: Meta-analysis of prevalence around the world. *Child Maltreatment, 16*, 79–101.

Straus, M. A. (1999). The controversy over domestic violence by women: A methodological, theoretical, and sociology of science analysis. In X. B. Arriaga & S. Oskamp (Eds.), *Violence in intimate relationships* (pp. 17–44). Thousand Oaks: Sage.

Straus, M. A., Gelles, R. J., & Smith, C. (1990). *Physical violence in American families: Risk factors and adaptations to violence in 8,145 families* (pp. 29–47). New Brunswick: Transaction Publishers.

Sundheim, S. T. P. V., & Voellere, K. K. S. (2004). Psychiatric implications of language disorders and learning disabilities: Risks and management. *Journal of Child Neurology, 19*, 814–826.

Sutton, C., & Glover, V. (2004). Pregnancy: Risk and protective factors; effective interventions. Support from the start: Working with young children and their families to reduce the risks of crime and anti-social behaviour. Research Report No 524, Department for Education and Skills, London.

Thompson, R. S., Bonomi, A. E., Anderson, M., Reid, R. J., Dimer, J. A., Carrell, D., et al. (2006). Intimate partner violence: Prevalence, types and chronicity across adult women's lifetime. *American Journal of Prevention Medicine, 30*, 447–457.

Thornberry, T. P., Matsuda, M., Greenman, S. J., Augustyn, M. B., Henry, K. L., Smith, C. A., et al. (2014). Adolescent risk factors for child maltreatment. *Child Abuse and Neglect, 38*, 706–722.

Thornton, T. N., Craft, C. A., Dahlberg, D. L., Lynch, B. S., & Baer, K. (2002). *Best practices of youth violence prevention. A sourcebook for community action*. Atlanta: National Center for Injury Prevention and Control. Centers for Disease Control and Prevention.

Tjaden, P., & Thoennes, N. (1998). *Prevalence, incidence, and consequences of violence against women: Findings from the National Violence against Women Survey*. Washington: Institute of Justice.

Tjaden, P. G., & Thoennes, N. (2000). *Extent, nature, and consequences of intimate partner violence*. Washington: US Department of Justice, Office of Justice Programs, National Institute of Justice.

Trocmé, N., Fallon, B., MacLaurin, B., Daciuk, J., Felstiner, C., Black, T., et al. (2005). *Canadian incidence study of reported child abuse and neglect – 2003: Major findings*. Ottawa: Minister of Public Works and Government Services Canada.

Ttofi, M. M., & Farrington, D. P. (2009). What works in preventing bullying: Effective elements of anti-bullying programmes. *Journal of Aggression, Conflict, and Peace Research, 1*, 13–24.

Tyler, K. A., & Johnson, K. A. (2006). Pathways in and out of substance use among homeless-emerging adults. *Journal of Adolescent Research, 21*, 133–157.

U.S. Department of Justice (1994). Criminal victimization in the United States: 1973–1992 trends: A National Crime Victimization Survey Report July 1994 (NCJ-147006). Bureau of Justice Statistics, Washington.

United Nations Office on Drugs and Crime (UNODC) (2010). *Handbook on the crime prevention guidelines. Making them Work*. New York: United Nations.

van Dijk, J., Tsleoni, A., & Farrell, G. (2012). *The international crime drop: New directions in research*. Basingstoke: Palgrave and McMillan.

Vaske, J., Galyean, K., & Cullen, F. T. (2011). Toward a biosocial theory of offender rehabilitation: Why does cognitive-behavioral therapy work? *Journal of Criminal Justice, 39*, 90–102.

Vaughn, M. G., Salas-Wright, C. P., DeLisi, M., & Maynard, B. R. (2014). Violence and externalizing behavior among youth in the United States: Is there a severe 5%? *Youth Violence and Juvenile Justice, 12*, 3–21. doi:10.1177/1541204013478973.

Waldron, H. B., & Turner, C. W. (2008). Evidence-based psychosocial treatments for adolescent substance abuse. *Journal of Clinical Child & Adolescent Psychology, 37*, 238–261.

Waller, I. (2011). *Rights for victims of crime: Rebalancing justice*. Lanham: Rowman and Littlefield Publishers.

Wallner, S., Losel, F., Stemmler, M., Corrado, R. R., & Mathesius, J., (under review). Prediction of antisocial development in preschool children using the Crackow instrument: A follow-up of five years in a community sample. *International Journal of Forensic Mental Health.*

Welsh, B. C., & Farrington, D. P. (2006). Effectiveness of family-based programs to prevent delinquency and later offending. *Psicothema, 18*, 596–602.

Widom, C. S. (1989). The cycle of violence. *Science, 244*, 160–166.

Wikstrom, P. H., & Loeber, R. (2000). Do disadvantaged neighborhoods cause well-adjusted children to become adolescent delinquents? A study of male juvenile serious offending, individual risk and protective factors, and neighborhood context. *Criminology, 38*, 1109–1142.

Wolfgang, M., Figlio, R., & Sellin, T. (1972). *Delinquency in a birth Cohort*. Chicago: University of Chicago Press.

Wolfner, G., & Gelles, R. J. (1993). A profile of violence toward children. *Child Abuse and Neglect, 17*, 197–212.

Wolke, D., Woods, S., Bloomfield, L., & Karstadt, L. (2000). The association between direct and relational bullying behaviour problems among primary school children. *Journal of Child Psychology and Psychiatry, 41*, 989–1002.

Wonderlich, S. A., Brewerton, T. D., Jocic, Z., Dansky, B. S., & Abbott, D. W. (1997). Relationship of childhood sexual abuse and eating disorders. *Journal of the American Academy of Child and Adolescent Psychiatry, 36*, 1107–1115.

Wong, J. S. (2009). No bullies allowed: Understanding peer victimization, the impacts on delinquency, and the effectiveness of prevention programs (Doctoral Dissertation). RAND PRGS Dissertations (RGSD-240).

World Health Organization (2006). WHO facts on intimate partner violence and alcohol. Geneva. http:www.who.int/violence_injury_prevention/violence/world_report/factsheets/fs_intimate.pdf.

World Health Organization. (2006). *Preventing child maltreatment: A guide to taking action and generating evidence*. Geneva: World Health Organization.

Worthington, C., MacLaurin, B., Huffey, D., Dittmann, D., Kitt, O., Patten, S., & Leech, J. (2008). Calgary youth, health and the street: Final report. University of Calgary, Calgary.

Zimmerman, G. M. (2010). Impulsivity, offending, and the neighborhood: Investigating the person-context nexus. *Journal of Quantitative Criminology, 26*, 301–332.

Evaluating Children and Adolescents in Contact with the Justice System

Zina Lee

Abstract The significant social costs associated with child and adolescent offenders and victims underscores the importance of using developmentally-sensitive, evidence-based tools if we are to respond effectively to the unique needs of youth. This chapter reviews some of the important considerations of childhood and adolescence for conducting legal evaluations and some of the essential criteria for determining whether an approach is evidence-based. This is followed by a review of current forensic assessment tools and interview protocols for use with children and adolescents. The goal is to highlight the collaborative work of scholars and practitioners in translating science into practice and encouraging the transformation of the juvenile justice system into a system that applies a developmental framework to all decisions.

1 Introduction

There are significant societal costs associated with child and adolescent offenders and victims across a variety of domains, including legal, medical, and social services. Despite a steady decline in criminal offences committed by youth since the 1990s (Canadian Centre for Justice Statistics 2013; Office of Juvenile Justice and Delinquency Prevention 2014), concerns about adolescent offenders resulted in a number of reforms to the juvenile justice system that focused on accountability, punishment, and retribution (Penney and Moretti 2005; Scott and Steinberg 2008). As such, the nature of youth court evaluations changed (Grisso 2003). In addition to assessments for the purposes of disposition and rehabilitation, the youth criminal justice system required evaluations to assist with legal decisions concerning trial processes, institutional management, and protection of the public. Another significant reform within the criminal justice system developed out of the growing awareness of child maltreatment and the implications of children's involvement

Z. Lee (✉)
University of the Fraser Valley, Abbotsford, BC, Canada
e-mail: Zina.Lee@ufv.ca

H. Kury et al. (eds.), *Women and Children as Victims and Offenders: Background, Prevention, Reintegration*, DOI 10.1007/978-3-319-28424-8_16

as victims and witnesses upon disclosures of abuse (Poole and Dickinson 2013). Despite a lack of consensus concerning whether child maltreatment has declined or remained stable over the years (Canadian Centre for Justice Statistics 2011; Finkelhor and Jones 2012; Gilbert et al. 2012), there is agreement that child maltreatment continues to be a significant concern given that a substantial number of children are victimized each year (Canadian Centre for Justice Statistics 2011; Office of Juvenile Justice and Delinquency Prevention 2013; Spatz Widom and Landry 2011). This chapter will focus on developmentally-sensitive, evidence-based instruments and approaches for evaluating child and adolescent offenders and victims. The first section will address the assessment of adolescent offenders, with a focus on tools designed to measure risks and needs. The second section will address the evaluation of child victims, with a focus on investigative interviewing. In highlighting developmentally appropriate, evidence-based instruments and approaches, the goal is to acknowledge the collaborative work of scholars and practitioners who are motivated to translate science into practice towards the ultimate goal of effectively responding to the needs of children and youth.

2 Assessing Adolescent Offenders

Scholars are increasingly calling for a developmental approach to the juvenile justice system (e.g. Scott and Steinberg 2008; Vincent and Grisso 2005; Vincent et al. 2009). This approach entails an understanding by policy makers and practitioners of developmental issues unique to adolescence that warrants differential approaches to assessment and intervention. Furthermore, consistent with the United Nations Convention on the Rights of the Child, this framework is guided by the best interests of the child and the importance of implementing a juvenile justice system that addresses the root causes of delinquency (United Nations 1989, 2007). First and foremost is acknowledging that adolescence is a period of transition. This is supported by research in biology, cognition, and social development (Scott and Steinberg 2008). In addition to the onset of puberty and brain maturation, adolescents are learning to navigate changes in identity and social roles. As a result, adolescents are more susceptible to the influence of their peers, impulsive, and willing to take risks. Across adolescence and into adulthood, there are improvements in logical reasoning, decision making, and emotion regulation. Second, principles from the field of developmental psychopathology highlight that different pathways lead to the same outcome (referred to as equifinality) and that the same pathway leads to different outcomes (referred to as multifinality; Cicchetti and Rogosch 1996). Put more concretely, adolescent offenders are a heterogeneous group and not all youth identified as high risk possess the same number or type of risk factors. Related to this, risk factor research by developmental psychopathologists notes the importance of interactions between youth and their environments (Kazdin et al. 1997) whereby this developmental period is viewed as dynamic and malleable. Finally, it is well documented that antisocial behavior desists by late adolescence and early adulthood for the vast majority of youth (Burke et al. 2003; Moffitt 1993). A number of large-scale, longitudinal studies indicate that there are two distinct groups of adolescent offenders: one group exhibits problematic behaviors early in childhood and continues to display antisocial and criminal behaviors throughout adolescence and adulthood, and another group begins their antisocial and criminal behavior in adolescence and discontinues these behaviors by early adulthood. The vast majority of youth fall into the latter group, but the former group is responsible for the majority of crime. Furthermore, the causes and correlates of offending for the two groups differ. What these issues illustrate is that context is particularly important to consider when assessing and evaluating youth, and assessments should be conducted more frequently with youth because of the changes that occur during this developmental stage.

Beyond adopting a developmental approach to assessing and evaluating youth, policy makers and practitioners should select instruments and tools that are evidence-based. The following criteria should be present for a measure to be considered evidence-based (Grisso 2005a; Vincent et al. 2009): first, there should be empirical support for the items included in the instrument. Ideally, there will be a published manual accompanying the tool that summarizes this evidence. In the absence of a manual, there should be evidence from peer-reviewed studies that have been conducted by independent researchers (i.e. individuals who did not author the instrument). Second, the instrument should possess an internal structure and reliability. The strongest evidence for this will be factor analytic studies, but more commonly, this criterion is demonstrated through internal consistency, test-retest reliability, and inter-rater reliability. Finally, the instrument should demonstrate validity. There are multiple forms of validity, such as concurrent and predictive, and more weight may be placed on the type(s) of validity relevant to the nature of the tool and its intended use.

Social science research concerning developmental issues and psychometric properties of instruments need to be considered in light of the decisions that criminal justice system personnel must make. Once a youth enters the juvenile justice system, s/he faces a number of assessments conducted at different stages of processing in order to make decisions about treatment amenability, risk for violence, and risk for recidivism (Mulvey 2005; Vincent et al. 2009). As such, any assessment tool should be relevant to answering the primary issue of concern at that point in the juvenile justice system. In other words, the key question faced by criminal justice system personnel will differ at intake, trial, sentencing, and supervision. At intake, decisions typically focus on the appropriateness of diversion. During the trial process, decisions typically focus on pretrial detention and transfer/waiver to adult court. Upon a finding of guilt, decisions typically focus on appropriate placement (community versus custody) and treatment plans. At supervision, decisions typically address questions of appropriate monitoring and interventions within the community. Furthermore, tensions can sometimes arise between theory and practice. On the one hand, scholars and researchers emphasize the need for decision-makers to use evidence-based tools that are developmentally-informed and conform to psychometric test standards. On the other hand, practitioners are faced with difficult decisions concerning individual youths and their decisions may largely be guided by legal requirements concerning rehabilitation and protection of the public. It appears that one way to resolve this, as noted by Mulvey (2005), is for researchers to develop and validate tools focused on a specific decision within the juvenile justice system. The following review summarizes some of the existing assessment tools that policy makers and practitioners may want to consider for use when evaluating youth. To briefly summarize, assessment tools provide a comprehensive, individualized profile of the youth to assist in long-term case management and intervention strategies (Grisso 2005b). In contrast, screening tools are brief and assist in short-term decision-making to address issues that require immediate attention. The decision to focus on assessment tools is guided by the importance of a thorough evaluation in order to most effectively respond to the needs of young persons as individuals.

2.1 Early Assessment Risk Lists for Boys and Girls

The Early Assessment Risk List for Boys (EARL-20B; Augimeri et al. 2001) and the Early Assessment Risk List for Girls (EARL-21G; Levene et al. 2001) are guides designed to assist evaluators with assessing and managing risk for violence and antisocial behavior in children with disruptive behavior problems under the age of 12 years (Augimeri et al. 2010; Augimeri, et al. 2005). The EARL-20B and EARL-21G take approximately 15 min to code following a file review of the child and an interview with the child's parents and collateral informants. The assessments can be completed by a single evaluator or a team of evaluators who are professionals with experience working with high-risk children. Both measures are comprised of risk factors across three domains (Family, Child, and Responsivity). The Family items assess the degree to which the child is nurtured, supported, supervised, and encouraged (e.g. parenting style). The Child items assess the degree to which the child possesses individual risk factors that are associated with future violence and antisocial behavior (e.g. academic performance). The Responsivity items assess the degree to which the child and his/her caregiver are able and willing to engage in and benefit from treatment. The authors devised separate guides for boys and girls based on evidence of gender differences in risk factors. However, there is considerable overlap between the two guides. The only two differences are that one additional item has been included in the Family domain, and one item in the Child domain is distinct in the EARL-21G. The risk factors are rated on a 3-point scale (0 = not present, 1 = somewhat present, 2 = present) and evaluators can indicate whether an item is of particular concern by noting it as a critical risk factor. The items can be summed to yield a total score; the maximum total score is 40 for the EARL-20B and 42 for the EARL-21G. At the same time, given that the EARL instruments adopt a structured professional judgment approach, the evaluator provides an overall risk rating of low, moderate, or high based on a consideration of all risk factors. In general, higher total scores indicate greater risk. If an evaluator's overall risk rating deviates considerably from the total score, s/he should provide an explanation for this divergence. The EARL instruments are designed to identify children at risk for antisocial and violent behavior at an early age in order to inform appropriate interventions. Therefore, in jurisdictions that hold youth criminally liable under the age of 12 years, the EARL instruments are likely best suited for assessing such children for diversion, disposition, and supervision. In jurisdictions whereby the minimum age of criminal liability is 12 years, the instruments are likely best suited for use by police and social service agencies that come into contact with disruptive children and treatment providers who administer interventions to disruptive children.

Existing evidence indicates that the EARL-20B and EARL-21G are reliable and valid tools. Enebrink et al. (2006b) found excellent inter-rater reliability of the EARL-20B total (0.92), Family (0.90), and Child (0.91) scores, and moderate agreement of the overall risk rating (kappa = 0.48). Similarly, there is evidence for good to excellent inter-rater reliability of the EARL-21G total scores, ranging from 0.67 to 0.80 (Augimeri et al. 2010). With respect to concurrent validity, the EARL-20B is associated with reactive and proactive aggression (Enebrink et al. 2006b) and delinquency (Augimeri et al. 2010), and both EARL measures are associated with behavior problems (Augimeri et al. 2010; Enebrink et al. 2006b) and bullying (Jiang et al. 2011). Finally, there is evidence of predictive validity. The EARL-20B predicts aggression and conduct problems (Enebrink et al. 2006a), and both instruments predict criminality (Augimeri et al. 2010; Augimeri et al. 2012). Although this evidence is promising, it is important to note that there are limited studies of the EARL instruments. In particular, there is a need for more independent investigations of the measures, studies examining internal consistency, and stronger evidence for the EARL-21G.

2.2 *Risk-Sophistication-Treatment Inventory*

The Risk-Sophistication-Treatment Inventory (RST-I; Salekin 2004) is a clinical rating scale designed to assist mental health professionals with assessing and managing juvenile offenders between the ages of 9 and 18 years (Salekin et al. 2005). The RST-I ratings are based on an interview with and file review of the youth and collateral informants. Professionals who complete the assessment should have considerable knowledge, skill, and experience with juvenile offenders and hold an advanced professional degree with appropriate training in administering and interpreting psychological tests. The RST-I is comprised of 45 items across three domains (Risk for Dangerousness, Sophistication-Maturity, and Treatment Amenability). The Risk for Dangerousness domain assesses a youth's risk for future violence or recidivism. The Sophistication-Maturity domain assesses a youth's emotional and cognitive maturity. The Treatment Amenability domain assesses a youth's ability to respond to treatment. Each domain is further delineated into three subscales. The Risk for Dangerousness subscales are Violent and Aggressive

Tendencies (e.g. engages in unprovoked violence), Planned and Extensive Criminality (e.g. leadership role in crimes), and Psychopathic Features (e.g. lacks empathy). The Sophistication-Maturity subscales are Autonomy (e.g. internal locus of control), Cognitive Capacities (e.g. foresight), and Emotional Maturity (e.g. ability to delay gratification). Furthermore, a Criminal Sophistication subscale can be derived from the Sophistication-Maturity domain by noting whether the items are used for prosocial or antisocial purposes. The Treatment Amenability subscales are Psychopathology—Degree and Type (e.g. treatability of psychopathology), Responsibility and Motivation to Change (e.g. motivated to engage in treatment), and Consideration and Tolerance of Others (e.g. feels guilt/remorse). Each item is rated on a 3-point scale (0 = absence of the characteristic/ability, 1 = subclinical/ moderate characteristic/ability, 2 = presence of the characteristic/ability) whereby the items are summed to yield domain and subscale scores. These scores can be compared to the norms published in the manual to categorize youth as low, medium, or high; separate norms are reported for boys and girls. The RST-I is designed primarily to assist with decisions concerning transfer to/from adult court and disposition, but can also be utilized during supervision to assist with case management of treatment plans.

Existing evidence indicates that the RST-I is a reliable and valid tool. Inter-rater reliability of the domain scores vary from good to excellent, with reports ranging from 0.60 to 0.94 (Leistico and Salekin 2003; Spice et al. 2010). Similarly, the domain scores possess good to excellent internal consistency, ranging from 0.69 to 0.87 (Spice et al. 2010). Regarding concurrent validity, evidences indicates that risk for dangerousness is positively associated with, whereas treatment amenability is negatively associated, with conduct disorder symptoms (Leistico and Salekin 2003; Spice et al. 2010), psychopathy (Leistico and Salekin 2003), aggression (Leistico and Salekin 2003), criminal history (Leistico and Salekin 2003; Spice et al. 2010), and transfer to adult court (Leistico and Salekin 2003; Spice et al. 2010). In addition, risk for dangerousness is negatively associated with, whereas treatment amenability is positively associated with, institutional treatment compliance (Leistico and Salekin 2003). With respect to sophistication and maturity, evidence indicates this domain is negatively associated with conduct disorder symptoms (Spice et al. 2010). In sum, the evidence for the RST-I is promising. However, more evidence is needed by independent researchers.

2.3 *Structured Assessment of Violence Risk in Youth*

The Structured Assessment of Violence Risk in Youth (SAVRY; Borum et al. 2006) is a guide designed to assist evaluators with assessing and managing violence risk in youth between the ages of 12 and 18 years (Borum et al. 2005; Borum et al. 2010). The SAVRY takes approximately 15 min to code after an interview with and file review of the youth and collateral informants. The assessments can be completed by professionals who are knowledgeable about adolescent development and youth violence, and have expertise in conducting individual assessments. The measure is comprised of 24 risk factors across three domains (Historical, Social/Contextual, and Individual/Clinical) and six protective factors. The Historical risk factors assess past behaviors or experiences (e.g. early initiation of violence). The Social/Contextual risk factors assess the youth's environment and interpersonal relationships (e.g. peer rejection). The Individual/Clinical risk factors assess the youth's psychological functioning (e.g. risk taking/impulsivity). The protective factors are individual and contextual items that buffer the influence of risk factors (e.g. strong social support). The risk factors are rated on a 3-point scale (low, moderate, high) and the protective factors are rated on a binary scale (absent, present). The SAVRY adopts a structured professional judgment approach whereby evaluators provide an overall rating of low, moderate, or high risk for violence based on a consideration of the risk and protective factors. The primary purpose of the SAVRY is to assist evaluators with violence prevention and reduction. As such, the measure can be applied across all stages of the criminal justice system. The specific point at which the SAVRY is administered will depend on legal requirements and assessment policies concerning risk for violence and protection of the public.

Existing evidence indicates that the SAVRY is a reliable and valid guide. Inter-rater reliability of the overall and total risk ratings are excellent, with reports ranging from 0.79 to 0.97 (Hilterman et al. 2014; Lodewijks et al. 2008b; Lodewijks et al. 2008c; Meyers and Schmidt 2008; Penney et al. 2010; Spice et al. 2010; Viljoen et al. 2008; Welsh et al. 2008). Similarly, inter-rater reliability of the domain scores vary from good to excellent, with reports ranging from 0.60 to 0.96 (Hilterman et al. 2014; Lodewijks et al. 2008b, 2008c; Meyers and Schmidt 2008), although one study found low reliability for the Social/Contextual domain (Penney et al. 2010). With respect to internal consistency, the overall score demonstrates excellence, ranging from to 0.83 to 0.98 (Hilterman et al. 2014; Spice et al. 2010; Welsh et al. 2008), whereas the domain scores vary from moderate to excellent, with reports ranging from 0.66 to 0.86 (Hilterman et al. 2014). Finally, there is evidence for predictive validity of the guide. The total scores/summary risk ratings are associated with institutional aggression and violence (Lodewijks et al. 2008c; Viljoen et al. 2008), institutional violations (Lodewijks et al. 2008c), and violent, non-violent, and general recidivism (Gammelgard et al. 2008; Hilterman et al. 2014; Olver et al. 2009; Penney et al. 2010; Schmidt et al. 2011).

2.4 Youth Level of Service/Case Management Inventory

The Youth Level of Service/Case Management Inventory (YLS/CMI; Hoge and Andrews 2003) is a 42-item actuarial risk/need tool that assesses the risks, needs, and responsivity factors of juvenile offenders between the ages of 12 and 17 years (Hoge 2005, 2010). The YLS/CMI takes approximately 30–40 min to score following an interview with and file review of the youth and collateral informants. The assessments can be completed by professionals who have knowledge of child and adolescent psychology, and training in administering and interpreting the tool. Each item is rated on a binary scale (0 = absent, 1 = present) whereby the items are summed to yield eight subscale scores (Prior and Current Offenses, Family Circumstances/Parenting, Education/Employment, Peer Associations, Substance Abuse, Leisure/Recreation, Personality/Behavior, and Attitudes/Orientation) and an overall total score. The YLS/CMI also gives assessors the ability to note the youth's strengths and other concerns. The total score can be used to classify youth into four categories of overall risk/need: low (0–8), moderate (9–22), high (23–34), and very high (35–42). In addition, the measure includes a professional override feature that allows the assessor to estimate the youth's level of risk/need by considering all available information. If the estimate of risk/need arrived at through the professional override feature differs from that arrived at by summing the individual items, the assessor provides the reasons for the difference. The YLS/CMI is designed primarily to assist with the case management of juvenile offenders by identifying the youth's goals and procedures for attaining those goals. Therefore, this measure is best suited to assessing youth for disposition and supervision.

Existing evidence indicates that the YLS/CMI is a reliable and valid tool. Inter-rater reliability of the total scores varies from fair to excellent, with reports ranging from 0.51 to 0.98 (Hilterman et al. 2014; Marshall et al. 2006; Olver et al. 2012; Vieira et al. 2009; Viljoen et al. 2009). However, inter-rater reliability of the subscale scores varies from poor to excellent, with reports ranging from 0.03 to 0.78 (Hilterman et al. 2014; Welsh et al. 2008). With respect to internal consistency, total scores demonstrate excellence, ranging from 0.87 to 0.90 (Hilterman et al. 2014; Olver et al. 2012), whereas the subscale scores vary from poor to excellent, with reports ranging from 0.46 to 0.86 (Hilterman et al. 2014; Olver et al. 2012; Welsh et al. 2008). Finally, there is evidence for concurrent and predictive validity of the tool. The YLS/CMI total score is associated with externalizing, internalizing, and delinquent behavior (Schmidt et al. 2005), official charges and convictions (Marshall et al. 2006), institutional misconduct (Holsinger et al. 2006), and general, serious, and violent recidivism (Bechtel et al. 2007; Hilterman et al. 2014; Olver et al. 2009, 2012; Rennie and Dolan 2010; Schmidt et al. 2011; Schwalbe 2007; Viljoen et al. 2009).

The above review of some of the current evaluation tools illustrates that developmentally-informed, evidence-based measures exist for use with youth who come into contact with the criminal justice system for the purposes of assessment and management. However, as noted earlier, some of these instruments are limited by the small number of independent validation studies. Furthermore, the appropriateness of the tools across gender and ethnicity has not been adequately addressed. Studies of the SAVRY have produced mixed findings, with one study illustrating that the measure is not as effective at predicting recidivism in females (Schmidt et al. 2011) and others concluding that it predicts violent recidivism comparably in males and females (Lodewijks et al. 2008a; Meyers and Schmidt 2008; Penney et al. 2010). Recent studies and meta-analyses indicate that the YLS/CMI predicts recidivism comparably in males and females (Olver et al. 2009, 2012; Schwalbe 2008), and Aboriginals and non-Aboriginals (Olver et al. 2009). However, this is based on a small number of studies and there is evidence that the YLS/CMI is not as effective in predicting recidivism in females (e.g. Onifade et al. 2008; Schmidt et al. 2011) and ethnic minorities (e.g. Onifade et al. 2008).

3 Translating Science into Practice

More importantly, an outstanding issue with respect to youth assessment instruments is that of context. Much of the evidence for the reliability and validity of the tools is based on information obtained in a research context whereby research assistants complete ratings of the youth, and the evaluations do not have implications for placement and services. As such, questions remain concerning the field reliability and validity of the measures. Fortunately, this issue is receiving attention and the emerging findings are promising. In their analysis of YLS/CMI assessments completed by mental health professionals and probation officers, Schmidt et al. (2005) found good to excellent inter-rater reliability of the subscale scores and predictive validity for serious reoffending. Similarly, SAVRY subscale, total, and summary ratings completed by juvenile probation officers possess good to excellent inter-rater reliability (Vincent et al. 2012). With respect to predictive validity, SAVRY total scores completed by youth classification and program officers are associated with violent and non-violent recidivism (Vincent et al. 2011), and SAVRY summary ratings completed by youth probation officers are associated with probation completion and revocation (Childs et al. 2013). In sum, the reliability of juvenile justice system personnel evaluations is comparable to the reliability estimates found in research studies and there is some evidence for the predictive ability of juvenile justice personnel assessments. However, future research is needed in these areas and with other developmentally-informed, evidence-based tools to provide a more optimistic conclusion.

Once the field reliability and validity of evidence-based juvenile instruments are established, an important next step is to illustrate whether their use contributes to changes in policy and practice. This is arguably the ideal standard for assessing whether science translates meaningfully into practice. Emerging evidence examining the SAVRY and YLS/CMI is encouraging. Vincent et al. (2012) conducted a multi-site, pre-post study of six youth probation offices that implemented either the SAVRY or YLS/CMI. Interviews with the juvenile probation officers prior to, 3 months after, and 10 months after implementation of the tools found an increase over time in differential placement/disposition and service recommendations by risk level. In addition, there was a decrease in perceptions of juvenile risk for recidivism and an increase in the use of the tools to assist with decisions concerning disposition, supervision, and services. Similarly, Vincent et al. (2012) compared youth on probation approximately 6 months prior to and 6 months after implementation of the SAVRY, and tracked these youth for approximately 1 year. They found that implementation of the SAVRY resulted in fewer detention dispositions, more probation dispositions, more service referrals, and more youth completing services successfully. Furthermore, risk ratings influenced service referrals and supervision level such that high-risk youth were more likely to receive more service referrals and maximum community supervision. Overall, this resulted in a 30 % reduction in the use of maximum and intensive supervision. It is important to note that these achievements were likely due to a thorough implementation process, which included stakeholder buy-in, comprehensive training, changes in office policy, and standardized procedures for assessment and case management. In sum, developmentally-informed, evidence-based practices can be cost-effective and lead to positive changes in assessing and managing youth.

4 Assessing Child Victims and Witnesses

The use of developmentally-informed, evidence-based instruments is equally important when dealing with child victims and witnesses. This section will review developmental approaches to interviewing children, with a focus on forensic investigative interview protocols to underscore the importance of addressing the needs of child victims and witnesses involved in the criminal justice system. However, the ability to respond to their needs is dependent on society's ability to accurately measure the prevalence of child maltreatment and identify children at risk of maltreatment (for a brief review of some of the assessment methods for determining the prevalence of child maltreatment, please refer to the World Health Organization's (2006) report, Preventing Child Maltreatment). Significant progress has been achieved in developed countries through child protection and mandatory reporting laws, but much work remains to be done in both developed and developing countries due to cultural issues surrounding parenting and the right to privacy within the family, and the lack of systems and structures in place to assist professionals who intervene (Spatz Widom and Landry 2011; World Health Organization 2002, 2006). An important first step in this regard is to encourage collaboration and communication across the social service, medical, and criminal justice systems towards detecting and responding to child victims and witnesses.

Similar to the comments noted earlier concerning juvenile offenders, a developmental approach to addressing child victims and witnesses entails an understanding of the unique characteristics of this population in order to adopt appropriate strategies. Researchers have highlighted a number of important factors that policy makers and practitioners should be mindful of when developing child interview protocols (e.g. Goodman et al. 2011; Lamb et al. 2007c; Poole and Dickinson 2013). One of the most important issues to acknowledge is developmental differences in memory, language, and communication. In general, young children's narratives are shorter than that of older children and adults, but there are no differences in accuracy. This is largely because children have less well developed memory abilities and vocabulary skills. The second important issue concerns fantasy and suggestibility. Existing evidence indicates that children over the age of 6 years are comparable to adults in their ability to distinguish between events that are imagined versus experienced. However, it is not clear to what extent young children have difficulty making this distinction. What researchers have found is that specific interview strategies, such as the use of props, can contribute to imagined details in young children's narratives. With respect to suggestibility, there is considerable evidence that young children are more susceptible to misleading questions. However, a number of studies have also found that children are resistant to suggestion under certain circumstances. The seemingly equivocal statements concerning children's abilities to recount information highlight that a number of external factors contribute to their ability to remember and recall experiences, and influence the quantity and quality of information. As a result, researchers in the fields of child development, cognitive psychology, and forensic psychology have developed a number of guidelines that should be followed when conducting investigative interviews with children and youth, such as rapport building, using free recall questions, and avoiding leading and yes/no questions (Perona et al. 2006; Poole and Dickinson 2013).

There are three interview techniques currently advocated for by scholars that are based on empirical research: the Cognitive Interview (Fisher and Geiselman 1992), the Step-Wise Interview (Yuille et al. 1993), and the National Institute of Child Health and Human Development (NICHD) Investigative Interview Protocol (Lamb et al. 2007a). These protocols possess similar features and guidelines, such as recommending the use of free recall questions to elicit narratives. Importantly, all of the protocols are consistent with the 2005 United Nations guidelines, Justice in Matters Involving Child Victims and Witnesses of Crime (United Nations Office on Drugs and Crime 2009), with respect to advocating for child-sensitive interview techniques that minimize distress and maximize information quality. This section will focus on the NICHD Investigative Interview Protocol as it is incorporates best practices supported by experts and translates these recommendations into an operational guideline for practitioners by providing a detailed script (for a brief review of the Cognitive Interview and Step-Wise Interview, please see Goodman and Melinder 2007). Furthermore, the NICHD Investigative Interview Protocol is a prime example of the translation of science into practice. The developers of the protocol responded to research illustrating that guidelines recommended by scholars for conducting interviews with children are seldom followed, despite awareness of best practices and extensive training. Before moving to a detailed discussion of the NICHD Investigative Interview Protocol, it is important to acknowledge an effort by the state of Michigan's Governor's Task Force on Child Abuse and Neglect, in conjunction with the Department of Human Services (2011), to implement a state-wide forensic interviewing protocol. This protocol is the result of collaborative work between researchers and practitioners. The user-friendly guide is comprehensive and accessible, and is a model example of how stakeholder involvement plays an important role in the translation of science into practice.

4.1 NICHD Investigative Interview Protocol

The NICHD Investigative Interview Protocol is an empirically-based, structured interview protocol for use with child victims (Lamb et al. 2007a). Variations of the protocol have been developed for use with child witnesses (Lamb et al. 2003) and juvenile suspects (Hershkowitz et al. 2004). The NICHD Investigative Interview Protocol includes five phases that address the entire investigative interview process. The first phase is the introduction, whereby the child is introduced to the interviewer, the purpose of the interview is explained to the child, and the rules and expectations of the interview are described. Many jurisdictions address the issue of truth telling in this phase. The second phase is rapport building, whereby the goal is to create a relaxed, supportive environment for the child. The third phrase is training in episodic memory, whereby a recently experienced neutral event is elicited. This is designed to train and familiarize the child with the interview techniques that will be utilized when discussing the incident under investigation. The fourth phase is substantive issues, whereby the incident under investigation is introduced and elicited, and information is obtained concerning the disclosure of the incident. During this phase, the interviewer begins with free recall questions or prompts and only after this is exhausted does the interviewer proceed to focused recall questions. The final phase is the closing, whereby the child is provided with the opportunity to provide any other information and ask questions. This phase ends with the child engaging in a conversation about a neutral topic in order to conclude the process in an emotionally-neutral manner.

Evaluations of the NICHD Investigative Interview Protocol indicate it is an effective strategy for eliciting accounts among children as young as 3 years of age (Cyr and Lamb 2009; Lamb et al. 2007a, 2007c; Sternberg et al. 2002). In addition to improvements in the nature and structure of interviews, adherence to the protocol leads to better quality narratives. For example, the interviews are better organized, interviewers adhere to best practices by using more free recall questions, and children provide more details. Furthermore, there is some evidence to suggest that the protocol facilitates the reporting of accurate information (Brown et al. 2013; Lamb et al. 2007b). A contributing factor in the success of the NICHD Investigative Protocol is likely the manner in which training is administered (Lamb et al. 2007a). Practitioners are provided with an overview of the protocol's theoretical framework to demonstrate how the components of the protocol are supported by research on children's memory, language, communication, and development. This is followed by close supervision in the use of the protocol and monthly workshops, whereby supervision involves analysis and feedback of post-training field interviews. The training procedures were implemented based on empirical evidence illustrating the importance of continued supervision and ongoing feedback (Lamb et al. 2000; Lamb et al. 2002). Importantly, there is emerging evidence that the use of the NICHD Investigative Interview Protocol contributes to the outcome of legal cases. Pipe et al. (2008) found that use of the protocol increased the probability of charges being filed and as a result, more cases were resolved through a guilty plea. In addition, of the cases that proceeded to trial, those that utilized the protocol were more likely to result in a finding of guilt. Together, these findings suggest that translating science into practice involves not only a comprehensive process for implementing and maintaining best practices over time, but also efforts to evaluate whether and how such practices address the ultimate issue at hand.

5 Conclusion

Considerable advancements have been made in the criminal justice system to address the unique needs of child and adolescent offenders and victims. A number of assessment tools and strategies currently exist that are developmentally sensitive and evidence-based. At the same time, improvements can be made with respect to the ability of assessment tools to generalize across gender and ethnicity, and in our understanding of the optimal interview strategies for child and adolescent witnesses. However, these limitations should not detract from the efforts made by researchers and scholars to translate science into practice by addressing how these methods are most effectively utilized by practitioners and whether these tools lead to meaningful changes in policy and practice. In sum, it is important for researchers and practitioners to continue their collaborative work to answer the ultimate legal issues of concern. The hope is that these efforts will transform juvenile justice system policies and practices in such a way that a developmental approach is adopted for all decisions concerning children and youth.

Five Questions

1. What are the advantages and disadvantages of implementing jurisdiction-wide screening tools and/or assessment tools within the juvenile justice system?
2. What can researchers do to encourage the use of developmentally-informed, evidence-based assessment tools with adolescent offenders?
3. What are the necessary components of effective training for practitioners (e.g., police, probation officers, social workers) in the use of youth assessment protocols?
4. Current investigative interview protocols are primarily designed for youth victims of sexual assault. Is an investigative interview protocol specific to youth witnesses required? Why or why not?
5. Is a juvenile justice system that adopts a developmental framework attainable and sustainable? What would this system entail and what factors are necessary to maintain this approach?

References

Augimeri, L. K., Enebrink, P., Walsh, M., & Jiang, D. (2010). Gender-specific childhood risk assessment tools: Early assessment risk lists for boys (EARL-20B) and girls (EARL-21G). In R. K. Otto & K. S. Douglas (Eds.), *Handbook of violence risk assessment* (pp. 43–62). New York, NY: Routledge/Taylor & Francis Group.

Augimeri, L. K., Koegl, C. J., Levene, K. S., & Webster, C. D. (2005). Early assessment risk lists for boys and girls. In T. Grisso, G. Vincent, & D. Seagrave (Eds.), *Mental health screening and assessment in juvenile justice* (pp. 295–310). New York, NY: The Guilford Press.

Augimeri, L. K., Koegl, C. J., Webster, C. D., & Levene, K. S. (2001). *Early assessment risk list for boys: EARL-20B, version 2*. Toronto, Ontario: Earlscourt Child and Family Centre.

Augimeri, L., Walsh, M., Woods, S., & Jiang, D. (2012). Risk assessment and clinical risk management for young antisocial children: The forgotten group. *Universitas Psychologica, 11*(4), 1147–1156.

Bechtel, K., Lowenkamp, C. T., & Latessa, E. (2007). Assessing the risk of re-offending for juvenile offenders using the youth level of service/case management inventory. *Journal of Offender Rehabilitation, 45*(3/4), 85–108. doi:10.1300/J076v45n03_04.

Borum, R., Bartel, P. A., & Forth, A. E. (2005). Structured assessment of violence risk in youth. In T. Grisso, G. Vincent, & D. Seagrave (Eds.), *Mental health screening and assessment in juvenile justice* (pp. 311–323). New York, NY: The Guilford Press.

Borum, R., Bartel, P., & Forth, A. (2006). *Structured assessment of violence risk in youth: Professional manual*. Lutz, FL: Psychological Assessment Resources, Inc.

Borum, R., Lodewijks, H., Bartel, P. A., & Forth, A. E. (2010). Structured assessment of violence risk in youth (SAVRY). In R. K. Otto & K. S. Douglas (Eds.), *Handbook of violence risk assessment* (pp. 63–79). New York, NY: Routledge/Taylor & Francis Group.

Brown, D. A., Lamb, M. E., Lewis, C., Pipe, M., Orbach, Y., & Wolfman, M. (2013). The NICHD investigative interview protocol: An analogue study. *Journal of Experimental Psychology: Applied, 19*(4), 367–382. doi:10.1037/a0035143.

Burke, J. D., Loeber, R., & Lahey, B. B. (2003). Course and outcomes. In C. A. Essau (Ed.), *Conduct and oppositional defiant disorders: Epidemiology, risk factors, and treatment* (pp. 61–94). Mahwah, NJ: Lawrence Erlbaum Associates.

Canadian Centre for Justice Statistics (2011). *Family violence in Canada: A statistical profile* (Catalogue No. 85-224-X). Ottawa, Ontario: Minister of Industry, Statistics Canada. Retrieved from http://www.statcan.gc.ca/pub/85-224-x/85-224-x2010000-eng.htm.

Canadian Centre for Justice Statistics. (2013). *Youth court statistics in Canada, 2011/2012* (Catalogue No. 85-002-X). Ottawa, Ontario: Minister of Industry, Statistics Canada. Retrieved from http://www.statcan.gc.ca/pub/85-002-x/2013001/article/11803-eng.htm

Childs, K. K., Ryals, J., Frick, P. J., Lawing, K., Phillippi, S. W., & Deprato, D. K. (2013). Examining the validity of the structured assessment of violence risk in youth (SAVRY) for predicting probation outcomes among adjudicated juvenile offenders. *Behavioral Sciences and the Law, 31*, 256–270. doi:10.1002/bsl.2060.

Cicchetti, D., & Rogosch, F. A. (1996). Equifinality and multifinality in developmental psychopathology. *Development and Psychopathology, 8*, 597–600.

Cyr, M., & Lamb, M. E. (2009). Assessing the effectiveness of the NICHD Investigative Interview Protocol When interviewing French-speaking alleged victims of child sexual abuse in Quebec. *Child Abuse and Neglect, 33*, 257–268. doi:10.1016/j.chiabu.2008.04.002.

Enebrink, P., Långström, N., & Gumpert, C. H. (2006). Predicting aggressive and disruptive behavior in referred 6- to 12-year-old boys: Prospective validation of the EARL-20B risk/needs checklist. *Assessment, 13*(3), 356–367. doi:10.1177/1073191106290649.

Enebrink, P., Långström, N., Hultén, A., & Gumpert, C. H. (2006). Swedish validation of the early assessment risk list for boys (EARL-20B), a decision aid for use with children presenting with conduct-disordered behaviour. *Nordic Journal of Psychiatry, 60*(6), 438–446. doi:10.1080/08039480601021795.

Finkelhor, D., & Jones, L. (2012). Trends in child maltreatment. *The Lancet, 379*(9831), 2048–2049.

Fisher, R. P., & Geiselman, R. E. (1992). *Memory-enhancing techniques for investigative interviewing: The cognitive interview*. Springfield, IL: Charles C Thomas, Publisher.

Gammelgard, M., Koivisto, A., Eronen, M., & Kaltiala-Heino, R. (2008). The predictive validity of the structured assessment of violence risk in youth (SAVRY) among institutionalized adolescents. *The Journal of Forensic Psychiatry and Psychology, 19*(3), 352–370. doi:10.1080/14789940802114475.

Gilbert, R., Fluke, J., O'Donnell, M., Gonzalez-Izquierdo, A., Brownell, M., Gulliver, P., et al. (2012). Child maltreatment: Variation in trends and policies in six developed countries. *The Lancet, 379*(9817), 758–772. doi:10.1016/S0140-6736(11)61087-8.

Goodman, G. S., & Melinder, A. (2007). Child witness research and forensic interviews of young children: A review. *Legal and Criminological Psychology, 12*, 1–19. doi:10.1348/135532506X156620.

Goodman, G. S., Pipe, M., & McWilliams, K. (2011). Children's eyewitness memory: Methodological issues. In B. Rosenfeld & S. D. Penrod (Eds.), *Research methods in forensic psychology* (pp. 257–282). Hoboken, NJ: John Wiley and Sons, Inc.

Grisso, T. (2003). Forensic evaluation in delinquency cases. In A. M. Goldstein (Ed.), *Handbook of psychology: Forensic psychology, volume 11* (pp. 315–334). Hoboken, NJ: John Wiley and Sons Inc.

Grisso, T. (2005a). Evaluating the properties of instruments for screening and assessment. In T. Grisso, G. Vincent, & D. Seagrave (Eds.), *Mental health screening and assessment in juvenile justice* (pp. 71–94). New York, NY: The Guilford Press.

Grisso, T. (2005b). Why we need mental health screening and assessment in juvenile justice programs. In T. Grisso, G. Vincent, & D. Seagrave (Eds.), *Mental health screening and assessment in juvenile justice* (pp. 3–21). New York, NY: The Guilford Press.

Hershkowitz, I., Horowitz, D., Lamb, M. E., Orbach, Y., & Sternberg, K. J. (2004). Interviewing youthful suspects in alleged sex crimes: A descriptive analysis. *Child Abuse and Neglect, 28*, 423–438. doi:10.1016/j.chiabu.2003.09.021.

Hilterman, E. L. B., Nicholls, T. L., & van Nieuwenhuizen, C. (2014). Predictive validity of risk assessments in juvenile offenders: Comparing the SAVRY, PCL:YV, and YLS/CMI with unstructured clinical assessments. *Assessment, 21*(3), 324–339. doi:10.1177/1073191113498113.

Hoge, R. D. (2005). Youth level of service/case management inventory. In T. Grisso, G. Vincent, & D. Seagrave (Eds.), *Mental health screening and assessment in juvenile justice* (pp. 283–294). New York, NY: The Guilford Press.

Hoge, R. D. (2010). Youth level of service/case management inventory. In R. K. Otto & K. S. Douglas (Eds.), *Handbook of violence risk assessment* (pp. 81–95). New York, NY: Routledge/Taylor & Francis Group.

Hoge, R. D., & Andrews, D. A. (2003). *Youth level of service/case management inventory (YLS/CMI) user's manual*. Toronto, Ontario: Multi-Health Systems.

Holsinger, A. M., Lowenkamp, C. T., & Latessa, E. J. (2006). Predicting institutional misconduct using the youth level of service/case management inventory. *American Journal of Criminal Justice, 30*(2), 267–284.

Jiang, D., Walsh, M., & Augimeri, L. K. (2011). The linkage between childhood bullying behaviour and future offending. *Criminal Behaviour and Mental Health, 21*, 128–135. doi:10.1002/cbm.803.

Kazdin, A. E., Chmura Kraemer, H., Kessler, R. C., Kupfer, D. J., & Offord, D. R. (1997). Contributions of risk-factor research to developmental psychopathology. *Clinical Psychology Review, 17*(4), 375–406.

Lamb, M. E., Orbach, Y., Hershkowitz, I., Esplin, P. W., & Horowitz, D. (2007). A structured forensic interview protocol improves the quality and informativeness of investigative interviews with children: A review of research using the NICHD Investigative Interview Protocol. *Child Abuse and Neglect, 31*, 1201–1231. doi:10.1016/j.chiabu.2007.03.021.

Lamb, M. E., Orbach, Y., Hershkowitz, I., Horowitz, D., & Abbott, C. B. (2007). Does the type of prompt affect the accuracy of information provided by alleged victims of abuse in forensic interviews? *Applied Cognitive Psychology, 21*, 1117–1130. doi:10.1002/acp.1318.

Lamb, M. E., Orbach, Y., Warren, A. R., Esplin, P. W., & Hershkowitz, I. (2007). Enhancing performance: Factors affecting the informativeness of young witnesses. In M. P. Toglia, J. D. Read, D. F. Ross, & R. C. L. Lindsay (Eds.), *The handbook of eyewitness psychology, volume 1: Memory for events* (pp. 429–451). Mahwah, NJ: Lawrence Erlbaum Associates Publishers.

Lamb, M. E., Sternberg, K. J., Orbach, Y., Esplin, P. W., & Mitchell, S. (2002). Is ongoing feedback necessary to maintain the quality of investigative interviews with allegedly abused children? *Applied Developmental Science, 6*(1), 35–41.

Lamb, M. E., Sternberg, K. J., Orbach, Y., Hershkowitz, I., & Horowitz, D. (2003). Differences between accounts provided by witnesses and alleged victims of child sexual abuse. *Child Abuse and Neglect, 27*, 1019–1031. doi:10.1016/S0145-2134(03)00167-4.

Lamb, M. E., Sternberg, K. J., Orbach, Y., Hershkowitz, I., Horowitz, D., & Esplin, P. W. (2000). The effects of intensive training and ongoing supervision on the quality of investigative interviews with alleged sex abuse victims. *Applied Developmental Science, 6*(3), 114–125.

Leistico, A. R., & Salekin, R. T. (2003). Testing the reliability and validity of the risk, sophistication-maturity, and treatment amenability instrument (RST-i): An assessment tool for juvenile offenders. *International Journal of Forensic Mental Health, 2*(2), 101–117.

Levene, K. S., Augimeri, L. K., Pepler, D., Walsh, M., Webster, C. D., & Koegl, C. J. (2001). *Early assessment risk list for girls: EARL-21G, version 1, consultation edition*. Toronto, Ontario: Earlscourt Child and Family Centre.

Lodewijks, H. P. B., de Ruiter, C., & Doreleijers, T. A. H. (2008). Gender differences in violent outcome and risk assessment in adolescent offenders after residential treatment. *International Journal of Forensic Mental Health, 7*(2), 133–146.

Lodewijks, H. P. B., Doreleijers, T. A. H., & de Ruiter, C. (2008a). SAVRY risk assessment in violent Dutch adolescents: Relation to sentencing and recidivism. *Criminal Justice and Behavior, 35*(6), 696–709. doi:10.1177/0093854808316146.

Lodewijks, H. P. B., Doreleijers, T. A. H., de Ruiter, C., & Borum, R. (2008b). Predictive validity of the structured assessment of violence risk in youth (SAVRY) during residential treatment. *International Journal of Law and Psychiatry, 31*, 263–271. doi:10.1016/j.ijlp.2008.04.009.

Marshall, J., Egan, V., English, M., & Jones, R. M. (2006). The relative validity of psychopathy versus risk/needs-based assessments in the prediction of adolescent offending behaviour. *Legal and Criminological Psychology, 11*, 197–210. doi:10.1348/135532505X68719.

Meyers, J. R., & Schmidt, F. (2008). Predictive validity of the structured assessment for violence risk in youth (SAVRY) with juvenile offenders. *Criminal Justice and Behavior, 35*(3), 344–355. doi:10.1177/0093854807311972.

Moffitt, T. E. (1993). Adolescence-limited and life-course-persistent antisocial behavior: A developmental taxonomy. *Psychological Review, 100*, 674–701.

Mulvey, E. P. (2005). Risk assessment in juvenile justice policy and practice. In K. Heilbrun, N. E. Sevin Goldstein, & R. E. Redding (Eds.), *Juvenile delinquency: Prevention, assessment, and intervention* (pp. 209–231). New York, NY: Oxford University Press.

Office of Juvenile Justice and Delinquency Prevention (2013). *2011 Annual Report*. Washington, DC: Office of Justice Programs, U.S. Department of Justice.

Office of Juvenile Justice and Delinquency Prevention (2014). *Delinquency cases in juvenile court, 2010* (Juvenile Offenders and Victims National Report Series Fact Sheet, NCJ 243041). Washington, DC: Office of Justice Programs, U.S. Department of Justice.

Olver, M. E., Stockdale, K. C., & Wong, S. C. P. (2012). Short and long-term prediction of recidivism using the youth level of service/case management inventory in a sample of serious youth offenders. *Law and Human Behavior, 36*(4), 331–344. doi:10.1037/h0093927.

Olver, M. E., Stockdale, K. C., & Wormith, J. S. (2009). Risk assessment with young offenders: A meta-analysis of three assessment measures. *Criminal Justice and Behavior, 36*(4), 329–353. doi:10.1177/0093854809331457.

Onifade, E., Davidson, W., Campbell, C., Turke, G., Malinowski, J., & Turner, K. (2008). Predicting recidivism in probationers with the youth level of service case management inventory (YLS/CMI). *Criminal Justice and Behavior, 35*(4), 474–483. doi:10.1177/0093854807313427.

Penney, S. R., Lee, Z., & Moretti, M. M. (2010). Gender differences in risk factors for violence: An examination of the predictive validity of the structured assessment of violence risk in youth. *Aggressive Behavior, 36*, 390–404. doi:10.1002/ab.20352.

Penney, S. R., & Moretti, M. M. (2005). The transfer of juveniles to adult court in Canada and the United States: Confused agendas and compromised assessment procedures. *International Journal of Forensic Mental Health, 4*(1), 19–37.

Perona, A. R., Bottoms, B. L., & Sorenson, E. (2006). Research-based guidelines for child forensic interviews. *Journal of Aggression, Maltreatment and Trauma, 12*(3–4), 81–130.

Pipe, M., Orbach, Y., Lamb, M., Abbot, C. B., and Stewart, H. (2008). *Do best practice interviews with child abuse victims influence case processing?* Final report submitted to the U.S. Department of Justice (Document No. 224524). Washington, DC: Department of Justice. Retrieved from https://www.ncjrs.gov/pdffiles1/nij/grants/224524.pdf.

Poole, D. A., & Dickinson, J. J. (2013). Investigative interviews of children. In R. E. Holliday & T. A. Marche (Eds.), *Child forensic psychology: Victim and eyewitness memory* (pp. 157–178). New York, NY: Palgrave Macmillan.

Rennie, C., & Dolan, M. (2010). Predictive validity of the youth level of service/case management inventory in custody sample in England. *The Journal of Forensic Psychiatry and Psychology, 21*(3), 407–425. doi:10.1080/14789940903452311.

Salekin, R. T. (2004). *Risk-sophistication-treatment inventory: Professional manual*. Lutz, FL: Psychological Assessment Resources.

Salekin, R. T., Salekin, K. L., Clements, C. B., & Leistico, A. R. (2005). Risk-sophistication-treatment inventory. In T. Grisso, G. Vincent, & D. Seagrave (Eds.), *Mental health screening and assessment in juvenile justice* (pp. 341–356). New York, NY: The Guilford Press.

Schmidt, F., Campbell, M. A., & Houlding, C. (2011). Comparative analyses of the YLS/CMI, SAVRY, and PCL:YV in adolescent offenders: A 10-year follow-up into adulthood. *Youth Violence and Juvenile Justice, 9*(1), 23–42. doi:10.1177/1541204010371793.

Schmidt, F., Hoge, R. D., & Gomes, L. (2005). Reliability and validity analyses of the youth level of service/case management inventory. *Criminal Justice and Behavior, 22*(3), 329–344. doi:10.1177/0093854804274373.

Schwalbe, C. S. (2007). Risk assessment for juvenile justice: A meta-analysis. *Law and Human Behavior, 31*, 449–462. doi:10.1007/s10979-006-9071-7.

Schwalbe, C. S. (2008). A meta-analysis of juvenile justice risk assessment instruments: Predictive validity by gender. *Criminal Justice and Behavior, 35*(11), 1367–1381. doi:10.1177/0093854808324377.

Scott, E. S., & Steinberg, L. (2008). *Rethinking juvenile justice*. Cambridge, MA: Harvard University Press.

Spatz Widom, C., & Landry, E. C. (2011). Research on child abuse and neglect. In B. Rosenfeld & S. D. Penrod (Eds.), *Research methods in forensic psychology* (pp. 487–506). Hoboken, NJ: John Wiley and Sons, Inc.

Spice, A., Viljoen, J. L., Gretton, H. M., & Roesch, R. (2010). Psychological assessment for adult sentencing of juvenile offenders: An evaluation of the RSTI and the SAVRY. *International Journal of Forensic Mental Health, 9*, 124–137. doi:10.1080/14999013.2010.501846.

State of Michigan Governor's Task Force on Child Abuse and Neglect and Department of Human Services. (2011). *Forensic interviewing protocol, third edition* (DHS Pub 779). Lansing, MI: Department of Human Services. Retrieved from http://www.michigan.gov/dhs.

Sternberg, K. J., Lamb, M. E., Esplin, P. W., Orbach, Y., & Hershkowtiz, I. (2002). Using a structured interview protocol to improve the quality of investigative interviews. In M. L. Eisen, J. A. Quas, & G. S. Goodman (Eds.), *Memory and suggestibility in the forensic interview* (pp. 409–436). Mahwah, NJ: Lawrence Erlbaum Associates Publishers.

United Nations (1989). *Convention on the Rights of the Child*. Geneva, Switzerland: Office of the High Commissioner for Human Rights. 1577 UNTS 3. Retrieved from http://www.ohchr.org/en/professionalinterest/pages/crc.aspx.

United Nations (2007). *Convention on the Rights of the Child. General comment no. 10. Children's Rights in Juvenile Justice*. Geneva, Switzerland: Office of the High Commissioner for Human Rights. Retrieved from http://www2.ohchr.org/english/bodies/crc/docs/CRC.C.GC.10.pdf.

United Nations Office on Drugs and Crime. (2009). *Justice in matters involving child victims and witnesses of crime: Model law and related commentary*. New York, NY: United Nations.

Vieira, T. A., Skilling, T. A., & Peterson-Badali, M. (2009). Matching court-ordered services with treatment needs: Predicting treatment success with young offenders. *Criminal Justice and Behavior, 36*(4), 385–401. doi:10.1177/0093854808331249.

Viljoen, J. L., Elkovitch, N., Scalora, M. J., & Ullman, D. (2009). Assessment of reoffense risk in adolescents who have committed sexual offenses: Predictive validity of the ERASOR, PCL: YV, YLS/CMI, and Static-99. *Criminal Justice and Behavior, 36*(10), 981–1000. doi:10.1177/0093854809340991.

Viljoen, J. L., Scalora, M., Cuadra, L., Bader, S., Chávez, V., Ullman, D., et al. (2008). Assessing risk for violence in adolescents who have sexually offended: A comparison of the J-SOAP-II, J-SORRAT-II, and SAVRY. *Criminal Justice and Behavior, 35*(1), 5–23. doi:10.1177/0093854807307521.

Vincent, G. M., Chapman, J., & Cook, N. E. (2011). Risk-needs assessment in juvenile justice: Predictive validity of the SAVRY, racial differences, and the contribution of needs factors. *Criminal Justice and Behavior, 38*(1), 42–62. doi:10.1177/0093854810386000.

Vincent, G., & Grisso, T. (2005). A developmental perspective on adolescent personality, psychopathology, and delinquency. In T. Grisso, G. Vincent, & D. Seagrave (Eds.), *Mental health screening and assessment in juvenile justice* (pp. 22–43). New York, NY: The Guilford Press.

Vincent, G. M., Guy, L. S., Fusco, S. L., & Gershenson, B. G. (2012). Field reliability of the SAVRY with juvenile probation officers: Implications for training. *Law and Human Behavior, 36*(3), 225–236. doi:10.1037/h0093974.

Vincent, G. M., Guy, L. S., Gershenson, B. G., & McCabe, P. (2012). Does risk assessment make a difference? Results of implementing the SAVRY in juvenile probation. *Behavioral Sciences and the Law, 30*, 384–405. doi:10.1002/bsl.2014.

Vincent, G. M., Paiva-Salisbury, M. L., Cook, N. E., Guy, L. S., & Perrault, R. T. (2012). Impact of risk/needs assessment on juvenile probation officers' decision making: Importance of implementation. *Psychology, Public Policy, and Law, 18*(4), 549–576. doi:10.1037/a0027186.

Vincent, G. M., Terry, A. M., & Maney, S. M. (2009). Risk/needs tools for antisocial behavior and violence among youthful populations. In J. T. Andrade (Ed.), *Handbook of violence risk assessment and treatment: New approaches for mental health professionals* (pp. 377–423). New York, NY: Springer Publishing Company.

Welsh, J. L., Schmidt, F., McKinnon, L., Chattha, H. K., & Meyers, J. R. (2008). A comparative study of adolescent risk assessment instruments: Predictive and incremental validity. *Assessment, 15*(1), 104–115. doi:10.1177/1073191107307966.

World Health Organization. (2006). *Preventing child maltreatment: A guide to taking action and generating evidence*. Geneva, Switzerland: World Health Organization. Retrieved from http://www.who.int/violence_injury_prevention/publications/violence/child_maltreatment/en/.

World Health Organization. (2002). *World report on violence and health*. Geneva, Switzerland: World Health Organization. Retrieved from http://www.who.int/violence_injury_prevention/violence/world_report/chapters/en/.

Yuille, J. C., Hunter, R., Joffe, R., & Zaparniuk, J. (1993). Interviewing children in sexual abuse cases. In G. S. Goodman & B. L. Bottoms (Eds.), *Child victims, child witnesses: Understanding and improving testimony* (pp. 95–115). New York, NY: Guilford Press.

The Problem of Risk Assessment: Can Better Crime Prognoses Reduce Recidivism?

Michael Alex and Thomas Feltes

Abstract Every society has to face the situation that there are a very small group of people who do not respect elementary rules of human behavior and who commit very serious violent crimes again and again. But how do we know who belongs to this group and who does not? To predict the probability of people re-offending is one of the most challenging tasks for experts and has become an important part of criminal policy in societies aiming to completely abolish crime. Referring to several studies on recidivism, including an investigation accomplished by the Ruhr-Universität Bochum's Department of Criminology, the limitations of crime prognosis and unjustified promises of crime forecast procedures are pointed out in this chapter. Despite all recent efforts to improve crime prediction, we are unable to predict human behavior precisely. As a result, other means than unlimited imprisonment of people regarded to be very dangerous by psychiatric or psychological experts are recommended to manage the problem of crime prevention in a way that considers both human rights' aspects as well as public needs.

1 Introduction

The English eighteenth-century lawyer William Blackstone once said, "It is better ten guilty persons escape than that one innocent suffer" (quoted in Mangino 2013). Things have changed a lot since that time, and not only in England. After centuries of discussions, which started with Robert Martinson's famous "Nothing Works", and continued on to intensive evaluations and meta-studies, such as by LW Sherman's "What Works and What Doesn't – and What's Promising?" (Sherman et al. 1997), politicians nowadays are promising to eliminate crime completely through preventive measures. Scholars have declared the twenty-first century the century of prevention and analyzed a preventive and punitive turn in penal and police law (Crawford 2009). The idea of "pre-crime" strategies (Zedner 2007) was

M. Alex • T. Feltes (✉)
Ruhr-University Bochum, Bochum, Germany
e-mail: thomas.feltes@rub.de

H. Kury et al. (eds.), *Women and Children as Victims and Offenders: Background, Prevention, Reintegration*, DOI 10.1007/978-3-319-28424-8_17

not only developed by the police (such as in the context of the movie "Minority Report"), but also criticized as "pre-punishment". In the aftermath of 9/11, such ideas have been taken as necessary until the NSA scandal in 2013 when more and more people realized that such pre-crime activities might infringe upon citizen rights. To predict where crime will happen is one thing, but to predict, whether an offender will reoffend is something else entirely.

Whenever a new law is established or—more often—when harsher sentences for certain crimes are demanded, this is done in favor of prevention: to prevent those people who have not yet offended from doing so (usually by asking for more of the same: more laws and harsher sentences), and to stop those who have already committed a crime from doing it again. The prevention of recidivism was and still is in some German states the primary goal in the execution of prison sentences.[1]

The German Criminal Code[2] is one of very few European Criminal Codes that distinguishes between penalties and so-called "measures of correction and prevention" as a state reaction to punish an offender. This twin-track system of sanctions had been considered and discussed since the end of the nineteenth century when Franz von Liszt started the discussion in 1882. The care orders were incorporated into the Criminal Code by the "act of dealing with dangerous habitual offenders and on measures of correction and prevention" (the "Habitual Offenders Act") on November 24, 1933, under Adolf Hitler's Nazi regime. The rules of "Sicherungsverwahrung" (translated as "preventive order/custody" in the following text) remained in force essentially unchanged after 1945 in West Germany, although the allies called for the retraction of this law. But several reforms were enacted by the legislator from 1969 onwards, instead of abolishing the measure of preventive custody.

Penalties in the German Criminal Code (see Articles 38 et seq.) consist mainly of prison sentences and fines. The penalty is fixed according to the defendant's guilt (Article 46 § 1 of the German Criminal Code).

A care order (see Articles 61 et seq. of the German Criminal Code) consists mainly of either a placement in a psychiatric hospital or a detoxification facility (Entzugsanstalt) or assigned a preventive order (Article 66 StGB), according to a proclivity prognosis. Proclivity, in the sense of Article 66 StGB ("Hang"), means the attitude of a person that predisposes him to commit a crime, that is, the intention to commit criminal offenses, or at least the willingness to do so at the earliest opportunity (Müller et al. 2013, p. 9). The purpose of the measures of correction and prevention is to rehabilitate dangerous offenders or to protect the public. They may be ordered for offenders in addition to their punishment (compare Articles 63 et seq. *StGB*). They must, however, be proportionate to the gravity of the offences committed by, or to be expected from, the defendant as well as to his/her[3] dangerousness (Article 62 StGB).

[1] After the right for legislation of the prison law had been moved to the states (formerly it was under the Federal Republic), some states put "security" in first place, and prevention (meaning: preparing the prisoner for not committing crimes after release) second.

[2] There is (contrary to the prison laws) just one criminal code for all of Germany.

[3] Only few female offenders have ever been sentenced to such a preventive measure. In 2011, there have been a total of 84 people in care order, and three female offenders in preventive custody.

The temporal applicability of provisions in the German Criminal Code depends on whether they relate to penalties or measures of correction and prevention. The penalty is determined by the law, which is in force at the time of the act (Article 2 § 1 of the German Criminal Code); if the law in force upon completion of the act is amended before the court's judgment, the more lenient law applies (Article 2 § 3). On the other hand, decisions on measures of correction and prevention are based on the law in force at the time of the decision unless the law provides otherwise (Article 2 § 6) (European Court of Human Rights in the case M v. Germany, application no. 19359/04, judgment of December 17, 2009, p. 11).

The idea of preventive custody was to reduce the risk of relapse of prisoners who had committed severe crimes several times before by keeping them in prison after the time of the sentence was finished. Preventive custody was announced in addition to the sentence in the judgment of the court. In 1934, preventive custody was inflicted against 3723 convicted persons, and in 1939 and 1940, a little less than 2000 convicted persons were sentenced to this additional imprisonment.

In 1954, East Germany cancelled the rules of preventive custody because of their Nazi origin, but in West Germany, the Allies accepted most of the regulations of the so-called "Habitual Delinquents Act." In 1968, preventive custody was imposed on 268 offenders, the largest number since 1945. From 1975 on, preventive custody was not permitted to last longer than ten years when imposed for the first time, but this did not change the tendency of the courts to neglect this additional instrument. The number of persons kept in prison after the end of the regular penalty decreased from 337 in 1975 to 176 in 1996, the lowest rate ever. During the negotiations to accomplish the reunification of Germany in 1990, it was decided to regard the different development in both countries and restrict preventive custody to offences committed on the territory of former West Germany. This agreement was cancelled by the German parliament in 1995.

After singular cases of murder involving children occurred in Belgium and Germany in 1996, efforts were intensified to make it easier for courts to impose preventive orders in addition to the initial penalty, especially against sexual offenders. As a result, in 1998, the number of preceding offenses necessary was lowered and the limit of ten years as the longest time in preventive custody was cancelled by the "Combating of Sexual Offences and Other Dangerous Offences Act" (Gesetz zur Bekämpfung von Sexualdelikten und anderen gefährlichen Straftaten) of January 26, 1998, which came into force on January 31, 1998. In 2002 and 2004, the Criminal Code was amended, establishing the possibility of imposing preventive custody on proviso or even retroactively after the court sentence had been imposed because of new incidents observed afterwards. German courts took care that only extremely severe incidents in prison were suitable to impose preventive custody retroactively, and in most cases applicants had to be released from prison. On December 17, 2009, and in the judgments that followed, the European Court of Human Rights held unanimously that there had been a violation of Art. 5 § 1 (right to liberty and security) of the European Convention on Human Rights by German Courts, retroactively neglecting the 10 year limit for the first period of preventive custody or the retroactive ordering of preventive custody. Due to all these judgments, prisoners had to be released from prison, although prison-officials and psychiatric and psychological experts had argued that there was a high risk they might seriously re-offend.

2 The Risk of Reoffending: Empirical Studies on Recidivism

In Germany, only a few studies have examined the recidivism of small groups released after their court decisions, even though they were still regarded as dangerous. Rusche (2004) examined 32 former inmates from psychiatric-forensic hospitals in East Germany who had to be released after the reunification because their hospital stay was unlawful. Several experts had regarded them as very dangerous. Eight of these reoffended, five of them with severe sexual or violent delinquency. This result is similar to the legal probation of a second group of 31 regularly released patients. Kinzig (2010) studied the records of 22 persons released from preventive custody and found that of the eight of them who had committed new offenses, two of them were registered with severe violent crimes.

Sepejak et al. (1983), Klassen and O'Connor (1988) and Lidz et al. (1993) examined the recidivism rate after release from psychiatric hospitals and found out that in 41–47 % of all cases with negative crime prognosis, no relapse occurred (false positives).

Müller et al. (2013) examined all cases that were finally adjudicated according to the German Federal Supreme Court (Bundesgerichtshof, BGH). 37 decisions by the Federal Supreme Court were available up to the end of the study on June 17, 2008. By May 2010, eight preventive custody decisions of lower courts were confirmed by the Supreme Court and the affected persons were retroactively sent to preventive custody; in 29 cases, the orders were overruled by the Supreme Court and, as a result, the persons affected had to be released immediately. Case files were submitted for 25 of these persons who had been considered to be highly dangerous but ultimately were not taken retroactively into preventive custody because there was not enough evidence that they became dangerous after the original judgment. Although there were only 14 corresponding expert predictions, all 25 cases were included in the study to demonstrate the validity of risk assessment (Müller et al. 2013, p. 9) (Table 1).

A detailed analysis of sex offender recidivism in the state of New York shows that only 6 % of 556 sex offenders released from state prisons in 1986 were returned to prison for a new sex crime (Canestrini 1996). Between 1985 and 2002, a total of 12,863 sex offenders were released from state prisons. Only 272 of these (2.1 %) were returned to prison for new sex crimes within three years of their release (Kellam 2006).

Probation is the most common sentence for sex offenders in New York. Of the 2944 sentences for offenses requiring registration on the Sex Offender Registry

Table 1 Prediction based on determination of proclivity and legal probation

Group	Experts' recommendation: preventive custody, offender dangerous	Experts' recommendation: no preventive custody, no dangerous offense expected
No recidivism/mild recidivism	5/25	4/25
	(20 %)	(16 %)
	False-positive	Correct-negative
Severe recidivism (penalty at least 1 year prison)	5/25	0
	(20 %)	(0 cases)
	Correct-positive	False-negative

Table 2 Proportion of registered offenders rearrested

Proportion of registered sex offenders rearrested (among 19,827 offenders on the registry on March 31, 2005)		
Time from registration date (year)	Any new arrest (%)	Any new registrable sex offense (%)
~1	15	2
~2	24	3
~5	41	6
~8	48	8

Source: DCJS: NYS Sex Offender Registry and NYS Computerized Criminal History Data Base

(SOR) in 2006, 1206 were for probation, representing 41.0 % of the total. Prison sentences accounted for 31.0 % (913) and sentences to local jails accounted for 16.9 % (500). There were 325 offenders in the "other" sentencing category, which includes fines and conditional discharges. A small number of sentences were categorized as unknown (120).

A study that also included those sentenced to probation and county jails examined 19,827 offenders on the New York State Sex Offender Registry on March 31, 2005, see Table 2.

The DCJS data above included probationers, as well as parolees, those under custody, and offenders whose sentence had expired (New York State Division of Probation and Correctional Alternatives 2007).

Utilizing time-series analyses, a study examined differences in sexual offense arrest rates before and after the enactment of New York's Sex Offender Registration Act. Results provided no support for the effectiveness of registration and community notification laws in reducing sexual offending by: (a) rapists, (b) child molesters, (c) sexual recidivists, or (d) first-time sex offenders. Analyses also showed that over 95 % of all sexual offense arrests were committed by first-time sex offenders, casting doubt on the ability of laws that target repeat offenders to meaningfully reduce sexual offending (Sandler et al. 2008).

In a study assessing the practical and monetary efficacy of Megan's Law in New Jersey, 550 released sex offenders were examined. Ultimately, 9 % of them were re-arrested for a sex crime within a time at risk of approximately six and a half years (Zgoba et al. 2008).

In 1999, Margaret A. Alexander examined the utility of sexual offender's treatment, considering that efforts to treat sexual offenders had proliferated over the last 50 years. At that time, several authors had addressed current views of sexual offender treatment efficacy. Some maintained that offenders can benefit from treatment while others argued that the vast majority cannot. Some researchers said that the field of sexual offender treatment was too new to be able to accurately determine whether or not treatment works. This latter group noted that most studies in this field had not yet reached the point at which meta-analytic techniques could be applied; for this reason, no definite statement could be made about the utility of treatment. Alexander's analysis examined the issues from a slightly different perspective. Data from a large group of studies were combined to identify patterns, which could be examined later in more detail. More specifically, 79 sexual offender treatment outcome studies were reviewed, encompassing 10,988 subjects. Recidivism rates for treated versus untreated offenders were investigated according to age of offender, age of victim, offense type, type of treatment, location of treatment, decade of treatment, and length of follow-up. Each study was used as the unit of analysis, and studies were combined according to the number of treated versus untreated subjects who reoffended in each category. The 10,988 subjects were divided into the subtypes shown in Table 3.

Under specific conditions (type of intervention, sexual offender subtype), less than 11 % of treated offenders reoffended, with juveniles responding particularly well to treatment. This led to the conclusion that the question of how best to treat may be as complex as the reasons people offend. Even though research remains in the formative stages, what has been learned so far has practical utility. A variety of treated sexual offenders reoffend at rates below 11 %. This finding suggests that some effective components of the treatment process may have been identified. Practitioners working with offenders should master standard curricula explicating these treatment tools, so they can apply them in a uniform and consistent manner. Future research could then enhance what is already known about how to treat sexual offenders (Alexander 1999, p. 10).

Table 3 Subjects in the data pool

Subject type	Treated recidivism rate	Untreated recidivism rate
Juveniles ($N = 1.025$)	7.1 % (73/1.025)	No data available
Rapists ($N = 528$*)	20.1 % (79/393)	23.7 % (32/135)
Child molesters ($N = 2.137$**)	14.4 % (41/1.676)	25.8 % (119/461)
Exhibitionists ($N = 331$)	19.7 % (61/310)	57.1 % (12/21)
Types not specified ($N = 6.967$)	13.1 % (786/5.979)	12.0 % (119/988)
Totals ($N = 10.988$)	13.0 % (1.240/9.383)	18.0 % (282/1.605)

*Does not include 103 juveniles
**Does not include 47 juveniles

In a meta-analytic review, Hanson et al. (2002) examined the effectiveness of psychological treatment for sex offenders by summarizing data from 43 studies. The 43 studies examined a total of 5078 treated sex offenders and 4376 untreated sex offenders. Averaged across all studies, the sexual offense recidivism rate was lower for the treatment groups (12.3 %) than the comparison groups (16.8 %, 38 studies, unweighted average). A similar pattern was found for general recidivism, although the overall rates were predictably higher (treatment 27.9 %, comparison 39.2 %, 30 studies). These recidivism rates were based on an average 46-month follow-up period using the variety of recidivism criteria reported in the original studies (Hanson et al. 2002, p. 181). The authors came to the conclusion that given the large numbers in their study (9454 offenders in 43 studies), the result that the recidivism rates of treated sex offenders were lower than the recidivism rates of untreated sex offenders cannot be seriously disputed. What can be disputed, in their view, are the reasons for the group differences. "Did the treatment reduce the offenders' recidivism rates, or were the observed differences produced by unintended consequences of the research design? We believe that the balance of available evidence suggests that current treatments reduce recidivism, but that firm conclusions await more and better research" (Hanson et al. 2002, p. 186).

3 Problems of Risk Prediction

Crime prognosis has always been a very controversially discussed matter in the field of psychiatry, psychology, and criminology because in most cases it is almost impossible to predict precisely how a person will actually act in a certain situation. Nevertheless, risk prediction is becoming more and more important in split societies claiming to avoid risks for their members. Politicians promise complete safety from all kinds of threats, and fear of crime is a favorite subject to establish preventive measures. Consequently, the methods of crime prognosis have developed rapidly during the past 20 years. Computer generated models that predict where crime is going to occur are used by the police throughout the United States of America, but as yet they are not a profiling tool to identify who is committing crimes (Mangino 2013). Nevertheless, there is great confidence in the U.S. that the remaining problems can be solved by improving statistical procedures (Berk and Bleich 2013; Perry et al. 2013).

Crime prognosis is fundamentally limited by one of the main methodological problems to predict severe crimes: the mathematical construction of "base rates". The base rate generally refers to the (base) class probabilities unconditioned on featural evidence, also known as "prior probabilities". For purposes of crime prediction, the base rate is supposed to give evidence of the probability that a convicted offender will reoffend. If the base rate was 1 %, only one out of a 100 released prisoners would reoffend. If the base rate was 50 % and the reliability of crime prognosis was about 90 %, one out of two would reoffend. The

Table 4 Prognosis at base rate of 90 %

	Positive prognosis (will reoffend)	Negative prognosis (will not reoffend)	
New offense	True positive: 81	False negative: 9	$N=90$
No offense	False positive: 1	True negative: 9	$N=10$

Table 5 Prognosis at base rate of 10 %

	Positive prognosis (will reoffend)	Negative prognosis (will not reoffend)	
New offense	True positive: 9	False negative: 1	$N=10$
No offense	False positive: 9	True negative: 81	$N=90$

consequences of low and high base rates for crime prediction can be seen in Tables 4 and 5 (reliability 90 %).

The higher the base rate, the more often re-offences are predicted correctly compared to the false positive assumptions, and the more often people reoffend unexpectedly (false negative). These results are a lot more apparent when the base rate is very low, as we can see regarding severe forms of crime. A base rate of 1 ‰ says that, on the average, one of every 1000 people will commit homicide for example, which is close to the actual rate of homicide in Germany (one case per 100,000 population). But it also means that 999 will not commit this offense, even if they were regarded as highly dangerous because of the mathematical limitations (Volckart 2002).

According to global studies of the United Nations Office on Drugs and Crime, 437,000 cases of homicide worldwide were reported to the police in 2012 (UNODC 2014). More than a third of those (36 %) occurred in the Americas, 31 % in Africa, 28 % in Asia, while Europe (5 %) and Oceania (0.3 %) accounted for the lowest shares of homicide at the regional level (UNODC 2014, p. 11). The global average rate was 6.2 homicides per 100,000 population. The annual global rate of sexual violence in 2011 was 36.7 per 100,000, the rate of robbery 138.1, the rate of assault 180.5, the rate of burglary 413.8, and finally, the rate of theft was 981.1 (UN-CTS 2012). All in all, property related crimes are committed much more often than severe violent offenses, and therefore can be predicted much more easily. Severe crimes can hardly be predicted at all without further biographical information about the individual's development.

The idea to predict future crimes (and to prevent them by repressive and/or preventive measures) is not new, but of course very fascinating, as the movie "Minority Report" has shown. In the film, a specialized police department apprehends criminals based on foreknowledge provided by three psychics called "precogs". Although crime forecasting (or predictive policing) in law enforcement has become an important part of policing, especially in the United States, the limits of crime prediction are well known.

> "The key for agencies is to think of the tools as providing situational awareness rather than crystal balls. The system should help agencies understand the where, when, and who of crime and identify the specific problems driving that criminal activity; this information will help support interventions to address these problems and reduce crime" (Perry et al. 2013, p. 136).

While in former times psychiatric experts mostly relied on their professional experience, we now have a wide variety of additional prognostic instruments strengthening the idea that human behavior can be predicted objectively and precisely. Internationally known examples for these instruments of assumed high objectivity, reliability, and validity are the Psychopathy Checklist (Hare 1991), PCL-SV (short version) and PCL-R (revised), Level of Service Inventory—Revised (LSI-R, Andrews and Bonta 1995), the Historical Clinical Risk (HCR-20, Douglas et al. 2013) which is used to predict the risk of violent delinquency, the Sexual Violence Risk (SVR-20, Boer et al. 1997), Rapid Risk Assessment for Sexual Offense Recidivism (RRASOR, Hanson 1997), Static-99 (Harris et al. 2003), Violence Risk Appraisal Guide (VRAG, Quinsey et al. 2006), and the Sex Offender Risk Appraisal Guide (SORAG, Quinsey et al. 2006). Crime forecast is based primarily on these kinds of actuarial assessment instruments in the Anglo-American countries while most European countries, particularly in Germany, regard them as helpful, but not sufficient enough for crime prognosis (Dahle 2006). They suggest that the behavioral instruments should complement a series of other carefully and clinically informed appraisals and should not be used as a substitute for them when making an assessment about a prisoner. What all of these instruments have in common is that there are rather few items relating to demographic characteristics, criminal history and personality variables with a statistically high probability of severe recidivism that can be listed easily and evaluated according to the score that is reached. Because of the statistical background, they are not sufficient to predict the individual's behavior: a high score on a scale does not necessarily indicate a high risk, because there may be a lot of protective variables in the surroundings of the individual (good relationships, satisfying conditions of living) to keep him from committing crimes again. Because there is a strong emphasis on historical events, the instruments also neglect individual developments and changes. Although courts tend to be satisfied with statements as to the degree of dangerousness shown by a test-score, as a high score at first sight is rather convincing, the actual predictive validity is very limited. In fact, a recent German study came to the conclusion that the Psychopathy Checklist is more suited to predict violent delinquency than sexual delinquency (Eher et al. 2012). Therefore, risk prediction without considering the personal situation of the individual is also not a sufficient method. But even with a methodically perfect approach, the prediction of the behavior of a human being will always be a problem without an appropriate solution. This is indicated by former relapse-studies and can also be demonstrated by the results of an examination we performed at the Ruhr-Universität Bochum/Germany. In this study from 2007 to 2013, the actual relapse-rate of 131 released prisoners who were considered to be very dangerous at the end of their sentence and therefore should be taken in permanent custody (preventive custody imposed retroactively) was examined.

4 The Bochum Study on Recidivism in Preventive Custody Cases Was Intended, but not Imposed

The situation in Germany after the decisions of the German Supreme Court and the European Court of Human Rights during the years from 2002 onwards was one of the few opportunities to examine whether the predicted dangerousness by the experts' risk assessment was true or just an assumption that did not correspond with the actual behavior of the prisoners released. As long as people regarded as dangerous are kept in prison, they can never prove that the expectation might have been wrong. The first time a larger group of people had been released from an institution despite of their assumed dangerousness was studied was in 1966. This study is well known as the "Baxtrom Case", when, after a decision of the Supreme Court of the U.S.A., all 967 (920 male, 47 female) inmates of forensic-psychiatric hospitals in the state of New York had to be released, even though they were still regarded as very dangerous. Only nine of them re-offended with severe crimes of violence (Steadman and Cocozza 1974). In 1971, another group of 438 mentally disturbed inmates had to be released in Pennsylvania after a court decision (Dixon vs. Pennsylvania) known as the "Dixon Case." Within four years after release, 14 % of the former inmates showed violent behavior (Thornberry and Jacoby 1979). Such experimental designs are usually quite rare, although the field of experimental criminology is a booming discipline, and some scholars see experimental designs as a kind of "silver bullet" for criminological research.

As German courts rarely imposed preventive custody retroactively since they denied the evidence of high risk concluded from the behavior in prison, about 115 prisoners throughout Germany were released between 2002 and the end of the year 2006, despite expert testimonies that had considered them to be too dangerous to be released. We used this kind of "natural experiment" to study the recidivism rates of those prisoners released from custody. In nearly all of the cases, the prison administration and external experts (psychologists and psychiatrists) had evaluated those people as dangerous. From 2007 to the end of 2009, another group of about 75 prisoners who were considered to be highly dangerous were also released because of court decisions. The recidivism of 121 out of these about 195 released prisoners[4] had been examined in a nation-wide study by the Department of Criminology at the Ruhr-Universität Bochum[5] (Alex 2013; Feltes and Alex 2010). In most cases, in four years after release from prison,[6] 63 people (52 %) had been convicted again for a new offense, but only 38 (31 %) were sentenced to a prison sentence again (see Table 6).

The more severe new offenses (prison terms of one year and longer) compared to the index offense are shown in Table 7 ($N = 11$).

---

[4] Ten released prisoners had already died before the study was finished.

[5] www.rub.de/kriminologie.

[6] Twenty-five people had been released only 2½ up to 4 years before.

Table 6 Sentence in case of recidivism ($N = 63$)

Recidivism					
Fine	Prison on probation	Prison	Prison and additional preventive custody	Other measure (psychiatric hospital)	No recidivism
16	9	19	17	2	58

Table 7 Severe re-offense

Index offense	Re-offense	New penalty
Rape	Theft	1 year and 5 months
Aggravated battery	Fraud, violation of terms of conditioned release	1 year and 8 months
Rape	Stalking	1 year and 9 months, hospital treatment order, Art. 63 StGB
Attempted murder	Theft, violation of terms of conditioned release	1 year and 11 months
Attempted robbery	Breach of narcotic law	2 years
Rape	Robbery	2 years and 2 months
Attempted rape	Theft, fraud	2 years and 9 months
Theft	Breach of narcotic law	3 years and 6 months
Sexual abuse	Burglary	4 years
Attempted aggravated robbery	Theft, fraud	6 years and 9 months
Aggravated robbery	Aggravated robbery	9 years

Two of these new offenses (robbery) can be regarded as cases that reveal the assumed high risk of violent recidivism, but the other nine offenses were less severe. Seventeen further court decisions resulted in imposing additional preventive custody because of very severe recidivism. The most severe new offenses (prison and preventive custody), in comparison to the previous judgment, are shown in Table 8.

All violent or sexual offenses may be regarded as cases where the high risk of serious relapse predicted by the experts came true. Notably, in about 85 % of all cases, the assumed severe recidivism did not occur (Table 9).

Only one of 18 sexual offenders older than 50 years at the time released from prison reoffended with a severe crime (severe sexual abuse), whereas three of the seven former prisoners who had committed other offenses reoffended severely. This demonstrates that sexual offenders in particular become less dangerous with increasing age.

Almost 50 % of the re-offenses with more serious consequences (defined as a sentence of more than two years) were committed during the first six months after discharge, and only five cases of more severe recidivism (22 %) occurred later than 18 months after discharge, as the Table 10 shows.

Table 8 Type of offense and sentence (prison and additional preventive custody) ($N = 17$)

Index offense	Re-offense	New penalty
Rape	Rape	3 years and preventive custody
Robbery	Robbery	3 years and preventive custody
Sexual abuse	Severe sexual abuse	3 years, 2 months and preventive custody
Severe sexual abuse	Severe sexual abuse	3 years, 6 months and preventive custody
Rape	Attempted robbery	3 years, 9 months and preventive custody
Sexual abuse	Sexual abuse	3 years, 9 months and preventive custody
Severe sexual abuse	Severe sexual abuse	4 years, 6 months and preventive custody
Murder	Aggravated battery	4 years, 6 months and preventive custody
Sexual abuse	Sexual abuse	5 years and preventive custody (on reservation)
Severe arson	Attempted arson,	6 years and preventive custody
Aggravated battery	Aggravated battery	6 years, 6 months and preventive custody
Severe sexual abuse	Severe sexual abuse	7 years and preventive custody
Aggravated robbery	Rape, bodily harm	7 years, 3 months and preventive custody
Murder	Aggravated robbery	9 years, 6 months and preventive custody
Aggravated robbery	Aggravated robbery	11 years and preventive custody
Sexual abuse	Rape, severe sexual abuse	11 years, 9 months and preventive custody
Bodily injury	Attempted murder, rape	13 years and preventive custody

Table 9 Age and delinquency ($N = 121$)

Age at release (years)	Sexual index offenses	Recidivism prison > 1 year	Other index offenses	Recidivism prison > 1 year
≤40	23	9 = 39.1 %	32	8 = 25.0 %
≤50	27	4 = 14.8 %	14	3 = 21.4 %
>50	18	1 = 5.6 %	7	3 = 42.9 %
Σ	68	14 = 20.6 %	53	14 = 26.4 %

In 70 cases, experts (psychiatrists, or in some cases psychologists) had given corresponding risk assessment reports. Thirty-nine out of 53 released prisoners (73.6 %) did not commit any new serious offenses, even though they were considered to be very dangerous (Table 11):

Compared to the study of Müller et al. (2013), the group of released prisoners that did not reoffend despite being regarded as very dangerous (false positive) was significantly larger (55.8 % vs. 20 %). This can partly be explained by the different methodological approach, but it also indicates the high rate of false predictions in our study.

Table 10 Time to severe recidivism (persons who were sentenced to imprisonment for more than two years), $N = 23$

	Time after release			
Re-offense	<6 months	<12 months	<18 months	18 months and longer
Sexual abuse	2	1	–	24 months 36 months 45 months 61 months
Rape	–	1	1	–
Other violent offense	5	1	3	–
Non-violent offense	4	–	–	–
Arson	–	–	–	28 months
Σ	11	3	4	5

Table 11 Risk assessment and legal probation

	Experts' recommendation: preventive custody ordered retroactively because of dangerousness		Experts' recommendation: no preventive custody, no probability of serious relapse	
Group	*N*	%	*N*	%
No relapse/mild relapse	39 false positive	55.8	14 correct negative	20.0
Serious relapse (more than 1 year prison	14 correct positive	20.0	Three false negative	4.3
Additional preventive custody	Seven after serious relapse	10.0	One after serious relapse	1.4

In 73.6 % of all 53 cases with negative expectations, this prediction did not end up with serious recidivism, but 82.4 % of 17 cases with positive expectations turned out to be true. Obviously, it is easier to predict positive legal probation than to predict recidivism.

Table 12 with the ICD-10 diagnosis of the 23 people with severe recidivism (penalty of more than two years imprisonment) indicates an expected correlation between dissocial personality disorder and recidivism.

Regarding all 121 examined people with emphasis on dissocial personal disorder and the frequency of reoffending, this result is verified (see Table 13)

Eighteen out of 47 subjects with dissocial personal disorder (38.3 %) were sentenced to imprisonment after reoffending, compared to only ten out of 42 with other diagnoses (23.8 %). Nevertheless, 29 subjects with dissocial personal disorder (61.7 %) did not reoffend at all or not severely.

The number of previous convictions prior to the index offense is also correlated with recidivism as shown in Table 14.

Twenty-eight out of 37 more severe re-offenses (75.7 %) were committed by subjects with five previous convictions or more, although only 50 % of the released prisoners belonged to the group with five previous convictions or more. This

Table 12 ICD-10 diagnosis and recidivism ($N = 23$)

Re-offense	Dissocial personal disorder	Combined personal disorder	Drug addiction	Pedophilia	Mental debility	No risk assessment report
Sexual abuse	2	1	–	1	1	2
Rape	3	–	–	–	–	–
Violence offense	6	–	–	–	–	2
Non-violent offense	2	1	–	–	–	1
Arson	–	–	1	–	–	–

Table 13 Diagnosis and recidivism ($N = 121$)

Penalty	Dissocial personal disorder	All other diagnoses	No risk assessment report
Prison and preventive custody	9	4	4
Prison	9	6	5
Prison on probation	8	2	–
Fine	7	6	3
No relapse	14	24	20
Σ	47	42	32

Table 14 Previous convictions and recidivism

	Number of previous convictions				
Penalty	None	1–4	≥5	≥10	≥15
Prison and preventive custody	0	5	7	4	1
Prison	1	3	2	6	8
Prison on probation	2	2	4	1	1
Fine	5	3	3	3	2
No relapse	16	22	14	5	1
Σ	24	35	30	19	13

illustrates the higher probability of re-offending by people with many previous convictions and also explains the tendency of experts to come to the diagnosis "dissocial personal disorder" just because of the number of previous convictions. Often, the anti-social attitude is only concluded from the number of previous convictions and not by exploring personal traits. On the other hand, 34 out of 62 offenders with five previous convictions or more (54.8 %) did not reoffend severely, which is another evidence for the difficulty of predicting peoples' behavior.

The results of the Bochum study are not very different from the findings of a nationwide survey on recidivism by the German Ministry of Justice. Jehle et al. (2003) observed the legal probation of all persons convicted (fine, sentenced to prison or probation) or released regularly from prison in Germany in 1994 ($N = 947.090$). About 35 % of them reoffended within a follow-up period of four years. 56 % of the released prisoners reoffended, but only half of them ended up in prison again. 27 % of those had previously been convicted for robbery, 19 % for sexual violence, and 10 % for homicide or murder.

In 2008, this study was repeated for the population of convicts or released prisoners in 2004 ($N = 1049.922$) with a slightly different approach (follow-up period of only three years resulting in a lower recidivism-rate), and in 2011 it was extended to the convictions and releases in 2007 ($N = 1049.816$). The general recidivism rates were 36 and 34 %, respectively. After a period of six years after conviction or release (2004–2010), the general recidivism rate increased to 44 %. As in the previous study, most released prisoners reoffended, but less than 50 % ended up in prison again. The highest recidivism-rate was observed after previous convictions for aggravated kinds of theft and robbery (more than 50 %), the lowest rate after previous convictions for homicide or murder. 15 % of all subjects convicted for violent crimes committed new violent crimes, while less than 4 % of previous sexual offenders committed another sexual offense. Recidivism is found only in few cases after more than three years of legal probation. The rate of recidivism with sexual violence increased from 2 to 3 %, the rate of recidivism with any kind of violent or sexual delinquency increased from 9 to 12 %, and the rate of recidivism with sexual abuse increased from 3 to 4 %. Regarding exact corresponding previous convictions only, the recidivism-rate is higher, however. After six years, 7 % of those convicted for sexual violence were again convicted for the same crime, 18 % of those convicted for sexual abuse were again convicted for sexual abuse. The rate of severe recidivism followed by a new sentence to prison varies from 3 % (murder or homicide), 6 % (sexual abuse), 7 % (rape), 20 % (robbery) to 23 % (aggravated battery) (Jehle et al. 2010, 2013). All in all, there is no significant difference concerning the legal probation of regularly released prisoners compared to the results of the Bochum study concerning prisoners considered to be extremely dangerous.

The study of Jehle et al. on recidivism, of which three waves are now available is a result of a development that can be observed throughout the world during the last two decades. The significance of, and the need for collecting comprehensive data on recidivism and its prevention for purposes of research, for judicial decision making, and for criminal policy have been recognized in many European countries and beyond. Similar efforts as in Germany have been made in England/Wales, Scotland, France, the Netherlands, Scandinavian countries, Switzerland, Estonia, and Ireland. Singular studies on recidivism have been conducted in further European countries. Countries in South America, Asia and Africa are also interested in nationwide and systematical studies in recidivism. In North America recidivism statistics based on available information have been established. Australia regards the European development as a milestone for evidence-based criminal policy (Albrecht 2013, p. 401).

"Modern evidence-based criminal policy, which aims to reduce recidivism in general as well as criminal courts which must increasingly deliver individualized decisions on the dangerousness of offenders based on anticipated recidivism are both in need of substantive and reliable information. Yet, the latter task in particular can hardly be fulfilled based on the rudimentary data provided by official statistics in countries such as Germany; likewise, data gathered through specific research studies most often cannot be generalized due to the specific methodological circumstances under which the data have been gathered." (Albrecht 2013, p. 400).

5 Discussion

Every society has to face the situation that there is a very small group of people who do not respect elementary rules of human behavior and commit very serious violent offenses again and again. In Germany these people—who are regarded as so mentally disturbed that they cannot be blamed for their crimes—are kept in psychiatric hospitals for an unlimited period of time until, according to an expert report on crime prognosis, no more serious recidivism is assumed.

Against offenders who were at least partly regarded to be responsible for their delinquency the measure of preventive custody was established in Germany in 1934, but this measure had to be imposed in combination with the judgment and was limited to ten years when ordered for the first time until 1998. This limit was cancelled in 1998 by the "Combating of Sexual Offenses and Other Dangerous Offense Act", and in 2004 a new measure was established for prisoners whose dangerousness was first noticed after judgment during imprisonment. Since 1934 offenders, who were not regarded as mentally disturbed, could not only be punished after previous times of imprisonment, but could be kept in preventive custody after the time of penalty ended. In 2004 the measure of preventive custody was extended to prisoners with penalties of more than five years, if they were assumed to be very dangerous according to events observed during the time of imprisonment.

Single cases of serious recidivism with sexual and/or violent delinquency after release from prison during the last decade of the past century had changed the attitude towards serious crimes in German society and had made the introduction of these new measures possible. On December 17, 2009, the European Court of Human Rights ruled that there had been a violation of Article 5 § 1 (right to liberty and security) and Article 7 § 1 (no punishment without law) of the European Convention on Human Rights by retroactive extension of a prisoner's preventive custody by German courts (M. v. Germany, application no. 19359/04). On January 13, 2011, the court also ruled that there had been a violation of Article 5 § 1 by imposing preventive custody retrospectively, because there had not been a sufficient connection between the conviction and the later decision to impose preventive custody under Article 66b § 1 of the German Criminal Code (H. vs. Germany, application no. 6587/04).

On May 4, 2011, the German Federal Constitutional Court finally accepted this jurisdiction and ruled that the regulations of imposing and executing the measure of preventive custody in the German Criminal Law violated the right to liberty, and as such, Article 2 of the German Constitution had to be changed by May 31, 2013 (judgment from May 4, 2011, no. 2 BvR 2365/09). In the meantime, inmates whose preventive custody had been imposed retrospectively or had been extended over ten years retroactively had to be released from prison, unless they were seen as extremely dangerous (danger to commit most serious sexual or violent crimes because of mental health problems or mental disorder).

The adjusted law was put into force on June 1, 2013, but in a following decision, the European Court of Human Rights from November 28, 2013 doubted whether a dissocial personality alone, which had been found by the German authorities not to be pathological, could be considered as a sufficiently serious mental condition so as to be classified as a "true" mental disorder for the purposes of Article 5 § 1 (e) of the European Convention on Human Rights, providing for detention independent of an offense (G. v. Germany, application no. 7345/12).

It seems that the European debate on preventive custody and the compatibility with human rights standards is not finished yet. Nevertheless, medical, psychological and criminological expertise will often be of much importance to prepare decisions on probation. All over the world, experts are asked in cases of offenders who are assumed to be very dangerous to judge whether these offenders are to be taken into custody or released from prison. It depends on the scientific limits to predict future behavior and on the quality of expert reports to help judges to find an adequate solution. There have been a lot of efforts to improve risk assessments during the last years. Not only have standards with regard to the procedures and contents for risk assessment reports been established, but standardized scales have also been developed to accomplish a more objective prediction of the behavior of offenders expected in the future. Worldwide used actuarial instruments are exemplified by the Psychopathy Check List-Revised (PCL-R), Sexual Violence Risk (SVR-20), Historical Clinical Risk (HCR-20), Static-99, Sex Offender Risk Appraisal Guide (SORAG), Violence Risk Appraisal Guide (VRAG), and the Level of Service Inventory-Revised (LSI-R). What all of these risk assessment instruments have in common is that personal traits and experiences that often correspond with certain kinds of delinquency have to be checked by experts to predict the probability of recidivism.

As to the quality of risk assessment, Müller et al., based on the results of their study, saw the need for improvement in the quality of experts' reports and came to the following conclusion: "Although most forecast reports (87 %) complied with a minimum of requirements, there were gaps, for example, in addressing the initial offense and the conditions with respect to the social support after release. A physical examination was carried out only in one-fifth of the cases, and additional psychological examinations were used only in half of the forecast reports. In addition, one third of the expert's reports only described striking personality traits, without diagnosing a personality disorder in the context of a psychiatric classification system. Around two-fifth of the forecast reports did not use an empirical risk checklist. The discussion about how the residual risk of recidivism might be minimized was missing in about one-third of the forecast reports. By contrast, in the study of interrater reliability, a high correlation in the assignment of psychiatric diagnoses by experts who conducted independent assessments was seen" (Müller et al. 2013, p. 18 with further references). Nevertheless only four out of 25 offenders (16 %) reoffended with crimes that ended up with new imprisonment of more than two years, although in ten cases corresponding experts' reports had assumed severe dangerousness.

The results of the Bochum study on recidivism indicate that, despite of all improvements, risk assessments are still no means to reduce recidivism. Too many subjects are considered to be extremely dangerous, even when they are not (false positive prognosis). Only 19 out of 121 surviving discharged offenders (15.7 %) committed serious sexual and/or violent offenses after they were released from prison. This rate of recidivism of supposedly very dangerous offenders does not differ at all from the relapse-rate of regularly released prisoners. It shows that in almost 85 % of all high-risk cases, no serious new offense is registered after several years.

This result is in accordance with the earlier results and recent studies concerning legal probation of persons released from prison or psychiatric hospital, even though they were regarded as very dangerous. The German studies that we referred to indicate a comparable relapse-rate. The data from New York State indicates that sex offenders have a lower three-year rate of overall recidivism (31 %) than the general prison population (42 %). Only 8 % of sex offenders were returned to prison as a result of a conviction for a new crime. Most were returned for parole violations (Kellam 2006).

The New York Senate Committee on Crime, Crime Victims, and Corrections suggests in their 2009–2010 report to examine the method of assessing risk of re-offense among registered sex offenders currently used by the New York State Board of Examiners and to appoint a commission to choose among the various assessment tools available today one that would provide the most reliable determination of risk. "Assessment guidelines were developed more than fifteen years ago, at a time when experts in the state knew far less about how to measure the risk that someone once convicted of a sex crime would reoffend. It is our belief – one shared by many experts – that there are far too many people in New York who are misclassified in the higher risk level category, and are therefore unnecessarily diverting limited resources away from likely re-offenders" (New York State Senate 2010, p. 28).

The probability that someone who has been convicted for very serious sexual or violent crimes reoffends is much smaller than the chance to become a victim of an offender not having been registered before with similar crimes. In New York, the overwhelming majority (around 95 %) of sex offenses, including rape and child molestation, is committed by those who have never before been convicted of an offense (New York State Senate 2010, p. 29). In Germany, among 25,000 persons convicted of sex offenses, murder/homicide or robbery every year, 85 % have never been registered with offenses like that before (Statistisches Bundesamt: Strafverfolgungsstatistik 2009, 2010, table 2.1.).

Looking at the results of the Bochum study in detail, it is not surprising that, due to the emphasis on sexual delinquency, 71 of the offenders intended to be taken into retrospectively imposed detention had been convicted for a sex offense. Three of them had died soon after release from prison. Eight of the remaining 68 sex offenders relapsed with sexual delinquency (11.8 %), and only one of them was older than fifty years by the time of discharge. The often mentioned idea that sex offenders are liable to relapse with sexual delinquency, even when they are old, can be rejected after the results of our study.

The results also give no evidence that sex offenders often reoffend a long time after discharge. Eighteen of 23 new serious offenses (78.3 %) were committed within one and a half year after release from prison, later than that only four cases of sexual abuse and one case of arson were registered. Concerning experts' risk assessment, there was no difference in the predictability of reoffending with sexual delinquency or violent crimes. The only significant differences between recidivism and non-recidivism were the number of previous convictions and the ICD-10 diagnosis of dissocial personal disorder. This is a self-fulfilling prophecy, though, because people, who have often broken rules tend to do so again more often than people who abide by them.

6 Conclusion

Better crime prognoses will not help to reduce recidivism. Müller et al. come to the conclusion that even though the predictive validity of the experts' reports as a whole still had room for improvement, there was no denying that there were valuable conclusions to be drawn from the experts' reports that do not recommend "subsequent placement in preventive custody" (Müller et al. 2013, p. 18). But the results of the Bochum study show that even in those cases, forecasts do not always come true, although there are more correct predictions than in cases where severe dangerousness is assumed.

Even though the quality of risk-assessment reports may have improved during the last decades, the fundamental difficulties in precisely predicting human behavior cannot be solved. The validity of prediction is limited by methodological problems as well as by unexpected developments in peoples' lives.

Even social scientists who support efforts to use methods of crime forecast in law enforcement activities try to convince people that the nature of predictive policing had nothing to do with "Minority Report": "There is an obvious appeal to being able to prevent crime as opposed to merely apprehending offenders after a crime has been committed. For law enforcement agencies, the ability to predict a crime and stop it before it is committed is tantalizing indeed – as it is to the public. Any hype must be tempered somewhat by considerations of privacy and civil rights, however. Predictive methods, themselves, may not expose sufficient probable cause to apprehend a suspected offender. 'Predictions' are generated through statistical calculations that produce estimates, at best; like all techniques that extrapolate the future based on the past, they assume that the past is prologue. Consequently, the results are probabilistic, not certain." (Perry et al. 2013, p. 8).

We have to accept these limits and must look for other ways to deal with recidivism. One way is to improve treatment of sexual offenders and other persons who have committed severe crimes. As the meta-analyses mentioned above show (Alexander 1999; Hanson et al. 2002), specified types of intervention according to the offenders' personal needs can reduce recidivism significantly. More than 50 % of all prisoners in Germany show personality traits with relevance for psychiatry, or even personality disorders according to ICD-10, F60 (Habermeyer et al. 2012; Konrad 2013), but cannot be classified as "persons of unsound mind" in the sense of Article 5 § 1 (e) of the European Convention of Human Rights (ECHR, judgment of Nov. 28, 2013, application no. 7345/12). Most of them get no treatment during their stay in prison, because they are regarded as being responsible for their offense. Instead of threatening them with preventive detention it is suggested to offer them treatment similar to the treatment in psychiatric hospitals in socio-therapeutic facilities, separated from prison with a staff of psychologists and social workers (Boetticher 2012; Höffler 2013; Konrad 2013). This measure had already been established in the German criminal code in 1969 (§ 65 StGB) but was never put into force and was finally cancelled in 1984, mostly because of the costs for the new institutions. As the extension of preventive detention will also be very expensive, the demand for "recovery" of the former § 65 StGB and a treatment opportunity for prisoners with severe personality disorders is justified and would be a better way to stop violating the European Convention of Human Rights than all past and present efforts to adjust the rules of preventive detention to the Convention (see Arloth 2013 as an example for these efforts).

In addition, positive social surroundings after release from the institution have to be established to reduce recidivism.

Finally, we have to get away from the idea that society could be saved from crime completely. There are many risks in life, and the threat to become victim of a crime is just one of them. This risk cannot be reduced by denouncing discharged prisoners either. Community notification has been found to have no demonstrable impact on sexual recidivism. In fact, some studies suggest that community notification may aggravate stressors that lead to increased recidivism (Freeman 2012), and requiring broad community notification via the internet may discourage some victims of sexual abuse from reporting incidents to the authorities. Victims may be reluctant to report offenses out of concern for a perpetrator who is close to them (a relative, a step-parent), or out of concern for their own privacy (Sandler et al. 2008). There are many examples in the United States of America ("Megan's law", Adam Walsh Act) and in Germany where released prisoners were threatened by their neighbors so severely that integration was about to fail and the risk of recidivism increased (Tewksbury 2005; Tewksbury and Lees 2006). Zevitz and Farkas (2000) also found that a majority of sex offenders reported negative consequences, such as exclusion from residences, threats and harassment, emotional harm to their family members, social exclusion by neighbors, and loss of employment. These problems might even get worse when addresses and biographical data are published on websites. People have to learn that the risk of victimization by reoffending ex-prisoners is much lower than the risk to be attacked by someone who has not been convicted before, and that positive surroundings are very helpful to reduce recidivism. Risk assessment will not prevent society from crime, but will continue to be responsible for a large number of people kept in preventive custody or other means of imprisonment unnecessarily.

Five Questions

1. Can crimes be predicted, and if so, how precisely?
2. How did crime prognosis procedures develop during the last years?
3. Weather forecast vs. crime forecast, what are the problems?
4. Can we avoid re-offending completely?
5. Which measures are useful to prevent re-offending?

References

Albrecht, H.-J. (2013). Rückfallstudien im internationalen Vergleich (an international comparison on the collection of recidivism statistics). *Monatsschrift für Kriminologie und Strafrechtsreform, 96*(5), 400–410.

Alex, M. (2013). *Nachträgliche Sicherungsverwahrung—ein rechtsstaatliches und kriminalpolitisches Debakel* (2nd ed.). Holzkirchen: Felix-Verlag.

Alexander, M. (1999). Sexual offender treatment efficacy revisited. *Sexual Abuse: A Journal of Research and Treatment, 11*, 101–116.

Andrews, D. A., & Bonta, J. (1995). *LSI-R: The level of service inventory-revised.* Toronto.

Arloth, F. (2013). Die Zukunft der Sicherungsverwahrung und der Therapieunterbringung. In A. Dessecker & R. Egg (Eds.), *Justizvollzug in Bewegung* (pp. 205–216). Wiesbaden: KrimZ.

Berk, R., & Bleich, J. (2013). *Statistical procedures for forecasting criminal behavior: A comparative assessment.* Philadelphia, PA: Department of Statistics, Department of Criminology, University of Pennsylvania.

Boer, D. R., Hart, S. D., Kropp, P. R., & Webster, C. D. (1997). *Manual for the sexual violence risk-20.* Burnaby, British Columbia, Canada: The British Columbia Institute against Family Violence, co-published with the Mental Health, Law, and Policy Institute, Simon Fraser University.

Boetticher, A. (2012). Die Idee der Wiederbelebung des alten § 65 StGB. In J. L. Müller, N. Nedopil, N. Saimeh, E. Habermeyer, & P. Falkai (Eds.), *Sicherungsverwahrung—wissenschaftliche Basis und Positionsbestimmung* (pp. 241–263). Berlin: MWV.

Canestrini, K. (1996). *Profile and follow-up of sex offenders released in 1986.* New York: New York State Department of Correctional Services, Division of Program Planning, Research and Evaluation.

Crawford, A. (2009). *Crime prevention policies in comparative perspective.* Cullompton: Willan.

Dahle, K.-P. (2006). Strengths and limitations of actuarial prediction of criminal reoffence in a German prison sample: A comparative study of LSI-R, HCR-20 and PCL-R. *International Journal of Law and Psychiatry, 29*(5), 431–442.

Douglas, K. S., Hart, S. D., Webster, C. D., & Belfrage, H. (2013). *HCR-20V3: Assessing risk of violence—user guide.* Burnaby: Mental Health, Law, and Policy Institute, Simon Fraser University.

Eher, R., Rettenberger, M., Hirtenlehner, H., & Schilling, F. (2012). Dimensionale Struktur und prognostische Relevanz der PCL-R in einer Population österreichischer Sexualstraftäter (factorial structure and predictive validity of the PCL-R in an Austrian sexual offender population). *Monatsschrift für Kriminologie und Strafrechtsreform, 95*(4), 235–251.

Feltes, T., & Alex, M. (2010). Kriminalpolitische und kriminologische Probleme der Sicherungsverwahrung. In D. Dölling, B. Götting, B.-D. Meier, & T. Verrel (Eds.), *Verbrechen—Strafe—Resozialisierung. Festschrift für Heinz Schöch* (pp. 733–754). Berlin: De Gruyter.

Freeman, N. J. (2012). The public safety impact of community notification laws: Rearrest of convicted sex offenders. *Crime & Delinquency, 58*(4), 539–564.

Habermeyer, E., Passow, D., & Vohs, K. (2012). Kriminologische und diagnostische Merkmale von Sicherungsverwahrten. In J. L. Müller, N. Nedopil, N. Saimeh, E. Habermeyer, & P. Falkai (Eds.) *Sicherungsverwahrung—wissenschaftliche Basis und Positionsbestimmung* (pp. 85–97). Berlin: MWV.

Hanson, R. K. (1997). *The development of a brief actuarial risk scale for sexual offense recidivism (user report 1997–04).* Ottawa: Department of the Solicitor General of Canada.

Hanson, R. K., Gordon, A., Harris, A. J. R., Marques, J. K., Murphy, W., Vernon, L., et al. (2002). First report of the collaborative outcome data project on the effectiveness of psychological treatment for sex offenders. *Sexual Abuse: A Journal of Research and Treatment, 14*, 169–194.

Hare, R. D. (1991). *Manual for the hare psychopathy checklist—Revised.* Toronto: Multi Health Systems.

Harris, G. T., Rhenix, A., Hanson, R. K., & Thornton, K. (2003). *Static-99 coding rules revised—2003.* Ottawa: Department of the Solicitor General of Canada.

Höffler, K. (2013). Die Sozialtherapeutische Anstalt als Maßregel—Phoenix aus der Asche? In E. Yundina, S. Stübner, M. Hollweg, & C. Stadtland (Eds.) *Forensische Psychiatrie als interdisziplinäre Wissenschaft* (pp. 103–118). Berlin: MWV.

Jehle, J.-M., Heinz, W., & Sutterer, P. (2003). *Legalbewährung nach strafrechtlichen Sanktionen—eine kommentierte Rückfallstatistik.* Mönchengladbach: Forum-Verlag.

Jehle, J.-M., Albrecht, H.-J., Hohmann-Fricke, S., Tetal, C. (2010). *Legalbewährung nach strafrechtlichen Sanktionen. Eine bundesweite Rückfalluntersuchung 2004 bis 2007.* Mönchengladbach: Forum-Verlag.

Jehle, J.-M., Albrecht, H.-J., Hohmann-Fricke, S., Tetal, C. (2013). *Legalbewährung nach strafrechtlichen Sanktionen. Eine bundesweite Rückfalluntersuchung 2007 bis 2010 und 2004 bis 2010.* Mönchengladbach: Forum-Verlag.

Kellam, L. (2006). *2002 releases: Three year post release follow-up.* New York: New York State Department of Correctional Services, Division of Program Planning, Research and Evaluation.

Kinzig, J. (2010) *Die Legalbewährung gefährlicher Rückfalltäter.* 2nd edn., Berlin: Duncker & Humblot

Klassen, D., & O'Connor, W. A. (1988). A prospective study of predictors of violence in adult male mental health admissions. *Law and Human Behavior, 12*, 142–157.

Konrad, N. (2013). Die Neubewertung psychischer Störungen im Kriminalrecht. In A. Dessecker, & R. Egg (Eds.), *Justizvollzug in Bewegung* (pp. 191–204). Wiesbaden: KrimZ.

Lidz, C. W., Mulvey, E., & Gardner, W. (1993). The accuracy of predictions of violence to others. *Journal of the American Medical Association, 269*, 1007–1011.

Mangino, M. T. (2013). *GateHouse: The perils of crime forecasting.* Available at www.mattmangino.com

Müller, J. L., Haase, K.-A., & Stolpmann, G. (2013). Recidivism and characteristics of highly dangerous offenders being released from retrospectively imposed preventive detention: An empirical study. *Behavioral Sciences and the Law.* Published online in Wiley Online Library (wileyonlinelibrary.com).

New York State Division of Probation and Correctional Alternatives. (2007). *Research bulletin: Sex offender populations, recidivism and actuarial assessment.* New York: New York State Division of Probation and Correctional Alternatives.

New York State Senate (2010). Standing Committee on Crime Victims, Crime and Correction, 2009–2010 Report.

Perry, W. L., McInnis, B., Price, P. C., Smith, S. C., & Hollywood, J. S. (2013). *Predictive policing—The role of crime forecasting in law enforcement operations*. Washington, DC/Santa Monica, CA: National Institute of Justice, Office of Justice Programs, U. S. Department of Justice/Rand Offices.

Quinsey, V. L., Harris, G. T., Rice, M. E., & Cormier, C. A. (2006). *Violent offenders: Appraising and managing risk* (2nd ed.). Washington, DC: American Psychological Association.

Rusche, S. (2004). *In Freiheit gefährlich? Eine Untersuchung zu Häufigkeit und Gründen falscher Kriminalprognosen bei psychisch kranken Gewaltverbrechern*. Regensburg: Roderer.

Sandler, J. C., Freeman, N. J., & Socia, K. M. (2008). Does a watched pot boil? A time-series analysis of New York State's sex offender registration and notification law. *Psychology, Public Policy, and Law, 14*(4), 284–302.

Sepejak, D., Menzies, R., & Webster, C. D. (1983). Clinical predictions of dangerousness. *Bulletin of the American Academy of Psychiatry and the Law, 11*, 171–181.

Sherman, L. W., Gottfredson, D., MacKenzie, D., Eck, J., Reuter, P., & Bushway, S. (1997). *Preventing crime: What works, what doesn't, what's promising*. Internet publication. Available at: www.ncjrs.gov/works/

Statistisches Bundesamt: Strafverfolgungsstatistik (2009). Available at: www.destatis.de.

Statistisches Bundesamt: Strafverfolgungsstatistik (2010). Available at: www.destatis.de.

Steadman, H., & Cocozza, J. (1974). *Careers of the criminally insane*. Lexington, MA: Lexington Book.

Tewksbury, R. (2005). Collateral consequences of sex offender registration. *Journal of Contemporary Criminal Justice, 21*(1), 67–81.

Tewksbury, R., & Lees, M. (2006). Perceptions of sex offender registration: Collateral consequences and community experiences. *Sociological Spectrum, 26*(3), 309–334.

Thornberry, T., & Jacoby, J. (1979). *The criminally insane: A community follow up of mentally ill offenders*. Chicago: University of Chicago Press.

UN-CTS. (2012). *The 2012 United Nations Survey of Crime Trends and Operations of Criminal Justice Systems (2012 UN-CTS)*. New York: United Nations.

UNODC. (2014). *Global study on homicide 2013: Trends, contexts, data*. (United Nations publication, Sales No. 14. IV. 1), New York: United Nations.

Volckart, B. (2002). *Zur Bedeutung der Basisrate in der Kriminalprognose*. Recht und Psychiatrie 20. 2. 105–114

Zedner, L. (2007). Pre-crime and post-criminology? *Theoretical Criminology, 11*(2), 262–281.

Zevitz, R. G., & Farkas, M. A. (2000). *Sex offender community notification: Assessing the impact in Wisconsin*. U.S. Department of Justice, National Institute of Justice, Research in Brief (NCJ 17992).

Zgoba, K., Witt, P., Dalessandro, M., & Veysey, B. (2008). *Megan's law: Assessing the practical and monetary efficacy*. Trenton, NJ: The Research and Evaluation Unit, Office of Policy and Planning, New Jersey Department of Corrections.

Anti-Corruption Education as a form of Early Prevention of Conflict with the Law for Women and Children: Making the United Nations Law Work 2016–2030

Sławomir Redo

Abstract Imprisonment, seizure and confiscation of assets, even the death penalty are invoked as measures to counter corruption. For obvious reasons they are only applicable to adult offenders. The most recent comparative review of the impact of imprisonment on crime rates questions its effectiveness. Even more questionable is the impact of imprisonment and death penalty on corruption, which at best is unknown. Raising the stake in criminal sentencing by handing down these sanctions does not seem to be a decision that ultimately matters in countering crime, let alone corruption. Rampant as corruption is, its countering requires more incisive and tailored measures. This chapter looks from three perspectives (Western, Eastern and United Nations) into some of these measures and reviews respective recent developments reported by the State Parties to the United Nations Convention against Corruption. In conclusion, the author argues that the United Nations anti-corruption education for women and children is a promising path to follow. Two educational issues may decide about the character and effectiveness of that anti-corruption strategy: the prevalence of patriarchal or contractual features in any legal culture, and its accommodation of the sustainable development ideology, if both engage personal responsibility. At the end of the story all corruption acts are choices which do rest on it and on ethics. Accordingly, blending these three perspectives, the implementation of the United Nations goal of "peaceful and inclusive societies" envisioned for 2016–2030 in which countering bribery and corruption is included, will depend on how well in contractual and sustainable development terms the present and succeeding generation will personally muster anti-corruption ethical education for women and children.

> *A true man cannot be corrupted by wealth, subdued by power, or affected by poverty.*
> *People observe moral concepts and codes of behaviour only when they have regular incomes from their property.*
> Meng Zi (327–289 B.C.E.)

S. Redo (✉)
Academic Council on the United Nations System, Liaison Office, Vienna, Austria
e-mail: s@redo.net

H. Kury et al. (eds.), *Women and Children as Victims and Offenders: Background, Prevention, Reintegration*, DOI 10.1007/978-3-319-28424-8_18

1 Introduction

In the most recent analysis of punitivity in the world Professor Helmut Kury, a world authority in this regard, concludes: "Based on the results of international studies, punishment has, if at all, only a very limited deterrent effect, in particular for the prevention of serious crime" (Kury 2013, p. 161).

However, and secondly, he also quotes one of the recent very thorough meta-analysis of 700 methodologically most outstanding studies on harsh penalties that adds:

> Moreover it appears that deterrent effects depend on the risk of being discovered and not on the severity of punishment and that they appear more often with minor infringements of norms...[that is] when administrative offences are investigated as opposed to crimes (Dölling et al. 2011, p. 315).

This finding does not cover sentences for corruption—a clandestine crime on which there is simply too little data anywhere. It thus may only be assumed that the harsh penal policy message on corruption is perfunctory: It hardly demotivates a corrupter and a corrupted to continue unabated their businesses in their habitual manner. Both have no incentive to change it. Neither one nor the other really calculates seriously the harsh penal implications, since corruption is hardly detectable and is not swiftly punishable. Both perpetrators have more to lose when they denounce one another than if they keep silent.

However and by analogy with the comparative effectiveness of administrative over penal measures in preventing serious crime, what about not only advancing anti-corruption into the stage of administrative offences, but—on a crime prevention plane—also for various potential actors and manifestations, that is into early formative stage of personal development when preventive education yields the highest returns to investment? (see in this book: Corrado et al.; Nores and Barnett).

2 Three Perspectives on Early Anti-Corruption Measures[1]

It is not possible to answer this question without first emphasizing that early anti-corruption measures must take account of substantial differences between Western, Eastern and United Nations legal culture. While their point-by-point enumeration here is not possible (see further Glenn 2010; Reichel 2013), two clarifications may be helpful in the further analysis of educational[2] issues involved in the fight against

[1] The text is taken from the lectures delivered in 2014 at the law faculties at the Beijing Normal University, Zhejiang Gongshang University (Hangzhou); South-Central University for Nationalities and Zhongnan University of Economics and Law (Wuhan).

[2] In this article, "education" is a broad term that "comprise[s] all deliberate and systematic activities designed to meet learning needs [and] involve[s] organized and sustained communication designed to bring about learning" (UNESCO 1997). It includes formal education (pre-school,

corruption: the prevalence of patriarchal or contractual features in any legal culture, and its accommodation of the sustainable development ideology.

Regarding "patriarchalism", it is as an interpersonal social justice concept. It includes kinship and tribalism (filial relationships), originating from early law codes based on property/hereditary relationships. It is a transitional form to "an association of service" or "contractualism"—an impersonal social justice concept that involves independent personhood (Hegel 1822-3/2011, pp. 102–103; Heinemann 1964; Walsh 1973; Adler 1994; Mitchell 2004; Sultan 2004; Wong and Tsai 2007; Cumminskey 2008; Stearns 2008; Fassbender 2009; Annan 2014; Bakken 2014). Both concepts, originally restricted to men but presently gender-neutral, appear to capture well the cross-cutting thematic and disciplinary spectra of the interrelated issues.

"Contractualism" is particularly well known in criminology due to Cesare Beccaria's seminal work "*Dei delitti e delle pene*" (1764) to which the UN Crime Prevention and Criminal Justice Programme credits its humanistic crime prevention origin. Now, this concept includes in the UN a moral component: "At the national level, the rule of law is at the heart of the social contract between the State and individuals" (A/66/749, para. 4).

"Patriarchalism" and "contractualism" interplay with the progressive implementation of the UN Charter. They practically contribute to the UN normative way of non-secular modernization set out by art. 55 (international development of economic and social welfare). This provision is subordinated to the provision on the "maintenance of international peace and security" (art. 1), and, next in the same sentence, to "justice and international law", also a subordinate concept in this context (see further Månsson 2007, p. 226).

Regarding "sustainable development",[3] it is now a broad practical and theoretical pursuit (see in this book: Mitrofanenko; Zhang) in which security, the rule of law, justice administration and crime prevention should be treated as renewable resources. Their vital energy is the social energy. That energy is not only produced by each generation for its own use, but also transmitted intergenerationally. Intergenerational transmission of cultural patterns of behaviour, whether positive or negative (crime and violence), is a part of the question of social, people-centred sustainable development and the energy it releases that should drive crime prevention (Redo 2012, pp. 78, 82 and 233).

The above clarifications may help to sort out interculturally the aspects of justice that involve early anti-corruption education for women and children. The following section[4] takes up these anti-corruption aspects. In three subsections it focuses on the

---

primary, secondary, tertiary) and non-formal, i.e. outside the formal education system (i.e. nursing, kindergarten care, human rights training sessions, workshops, seminars and webinars), and informal education through other life and work experience.

[3] The origin of the concept sometimes is credited to the UN Charter (Schrijver 2007, pp. 593–594; Simma et al. 2002, Vol. I, p. 36).

[4] Subsections 2.1-2-3 in their generic early crime prevention points draw on an earlier article by the author (Redo 2014), modified and refocused on anti-corruption.

pre-school intergenerational and intercultural legal education and on governance: from Western, Eastern and United Nations perspective. This is a start-up component for the overall developmental framework of "Culture of Lawfulness". Without that component in the various configurations, subsequent anti-corruption measures for women and children can mostly be reformative, but not formative.

2.1 Western Perspective

From the Western perspective, the following definition of "Culture of Lawfulness" covers anti-corruption education for anybody across various legal cultures, i.e.:

> that the population in general follows the law and has a desire to access the justice system to address their grievances. It does not require that every single individual in that society believe in the feasibility or even the desirability of the rule of law but that the average person believes that formal laws are a fundamental part of justice or can be used to attain justice and that the justice system can enhance his or her life and society in general. Without a Culture of Lawfulness, the population will have no desire to access the system and may resort to violence to resolve grievances. For the rule of law to be fully realized, the population needs to follow the law and support its application voluntarily rather than through coercion (USIP 2009, para. 7.9.1).

Results of various Western early crime prevention projects (starting from the delivery-assistance through nursing schools to tertiary schools) show that helping in the creation of an environment in which equity and fairness are at the core of education is pivotal to a Culture of Lawfulness. Those projects (several from the USA) employed a variety of tailored efforts aimed at reducing the risk of maternal deprivation and gaining taught skillsets that would prepare children to proceed successfully from primary through tertiary education. Depending on the age group of children, all these projects in one way or another aimed to equalize the life chances of economically underprivileged kids, among whom they were many of Hispanic and African-American descent.

The following results should be noted:

First, at the child's delivery stage, criminological birth cohort studies proved a significant correlation between criminal violence and birth complications followed by parental deprivation. They emphasize that in violence reduction biosocial interventions are important through, *inter alia*, obstetrician-assisted reductions in birth complications and nursing because both can reduce maternal rejection (Redo 2014, p. 710).

Second, various other experiments tested this on toddlers and older children who were given or taken an object. In one experiment comparing the respective reaction of toddlers (1–2 years old) and pre-schoolers (3–4 years old), toddlers apparently recognized possession as a basis for asserting control rights but not respecting the same rights of others (Gintis 2009, p. 207). In another experiment among toddlers, children (2–3 years old) and pre-schoolers (3–4 years old), the latter protested much more often than the younger group when the object was taken from them (Rossano et al. 2011). Still another experiment with children between the age of 3–6.5 years showed that their ability to deal with insincerity (cheating) emerges gradually during the preschool years with an increasing level of difficulty, from fantasy to politeness situations, and a notable amount of variability not equally distributed among the tasks (Airenti and Angeleri 2011).

The above suggests that before toddlers become acquainted with bargaining, trade, money and markets, they first start developing a sense of the property rights of others on the basis of their own possession. At the age of 3 children begin to understand the normative dimensions of property rights of others, hence what components of otherness there may be.

Third, at the infant-level, early crime prevention projects involved visits to the child and the family at home to support mothers and assist them in their child's learning. Significant improvement in children's subsequent educational performance was reported (Corrado et al. in this book).

According to one Western developmental psychologist, already at the age of 20 months a child experiences some moral emotions—feelings triggered by right and wrong (Warneken and Tomasello 2008). The critical transition point between a less formative and a more reformative phase of assisting in a child's education occurs in the age bracket of 5–10 years old, with the most critical age being age 8 (Grusec and Redler 1980). At that point reinforcing in a child the right behaviour by emphasizing the child's character ("*You are a helpful person*") rather than the action ("*That was such a helpful thing to do*") may be a viable departure point for a subsequent gradually self-sustaining law-abiding life. Any earlier or later age bracket for the Western view of "Culture of Lawfulness" does not seem to be so viable for forming in the adolescence the sense of right and wrong.

Fourth, at the school-level, assistance additionally focused on reducing prejudice towards others by involving the opposite groups in working for the common good. This was demonstrated by a seminal "Robber's Cave Experiment" (Sherif 1954/1961) that involved highly appealing tasks whose attainment was beyond the resources and efforts of any group alone. Through various methodologies and observational findings (on the connivance at breakfast and lunch through the seating rearrangement, acceptance of performing activities together), the experiment produced an extraordinary increase of friendly relationships between members of the different groups and a dramatic decrease in rejections of out-group members. The "Robber's Cave Experiment" is a very good example of conflict resolution and better mutual understanding and cooperation brought about by attaining agreeable overarching common objectives.

As a follow-up to a successful longitudinal evaluation of several such projects' crime prevention returns to (in)formal education, Professor James J. Heckman (2008), Nobel-Prize winner in Economy (2002), argues that the highest returns are up to 36 months of age (3 years), and then the investment to crime reduction ratio gradually decreases, as it continues through adolescence to adulthood when the crime prevention education returns are the lowest (Fig. 1).

Finally, thanks to this and similar criminological studies on early childhood crime prevention measures, it was found that in terms of cost-benefits ratio,

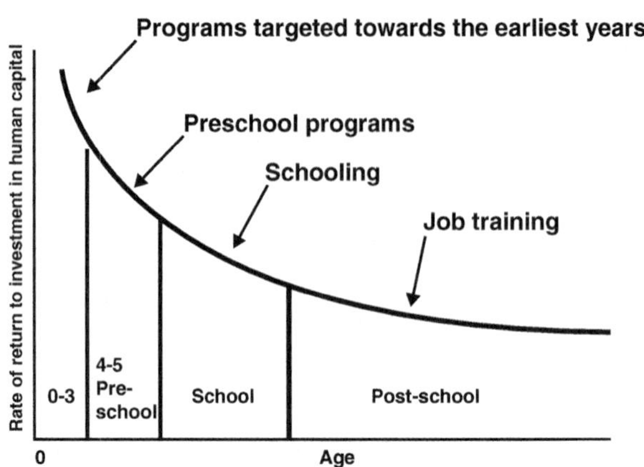

Fig. 1 Crime prevention returns on educational investments. *Source*: Heckman JJ (2008) The Case of Investing in Disadvantaged Young Children. Big Ideas for Children: Investing in Our Nation's Future, First Focus, Washington, D.C. 2008, pp. 49–58

expressed in percentages converted from national monetary units (national currencies), the returns on early crime prevention interventions ranged from 0.38 to 7.16 %, between pre-natal and later (3–4 years) cognitive development stage (Welsh 2003).

While in each and every case these values differed, the lowest return (on - pre-natal and birth planning phase) should not be overlooked. It points to the very start of the development of a normative cognition process which is criminologically relevant because of the afore noted recognition insincerity (cheating) and property rights. Parents who cheat their children may facilitate their children's cheating.

While in each and every situation the effects (returns) and implications will be different in every country and legal culture, the value of those findings cannot lie in their accuracy but in the topicality of questions, like "deterrence", "returns to investment", "formative vs. reformative crime prevention" and so on—questions important for "peaceful and inclusive societies" anywhere in the world.

However, for a long time and squarely, that "anywhere in the world" has mostly been pursued from a Western perspective only.

A case in point is the famous study of Lawrence Kohlberg (1970), US developmental psychologist (1927–1987). He and his research team confronted various groups of young and adult respondents by asking them to determine whether the right to life is above the right to property in the following case:

> a woman was near death from a special kind of cancer. There was one drug that the doctors thought might save her. It was a form of radium that a druggist in the same town had recently discovered. The drug was expensive to make, but the druggist was charging ten times what the drug cost him to make. He paid $200 for the radium and charged $2,000 for a small dose of the drug. The sick woman's husband, Heinz, went to everyone he knew to borrow the money, but he could only get together about $ 1, 000 which is half of what it cost. He told the druggist that his wife was dying and asked him to sell it cheaper or let him pay later. But the druggist said: "No, I discovered the drug and I'm going to make money from it." So Heinz got desperate and broke into the man's store to steal the drug-for his wife. Should the husband have done that? (Kohlberg 1963/2008, p. 12).

Those originally interviewed on the above "Heinz dilemma" were a group of 72 boys aged 10, 13, and 16, from both middle- and lower-class families in Chicago, then the experiment expanded to a sample of younger children, delinquents, and boys and girls from other American cities, and from other countries. In the recurrent exercises, the group of respondents grew to adults from many more countries and cultures, whereby the dilemma was adapted to those cultures.

Generally, there were "yes" responses to the right to life understood in the dilemma as caring for others. Their consolidated analysis of results suggested that on the developed eventually 7-stages scale of upward moral orientation (from the most elementary ("pre-conventional punishment and obedience orientation") through the most advanced ("post-conventional meta-ethical ontological orientation")), the evaluated progress rate favoured Western-minded respondents.

In particular, regarding critical for the difference between patriarchalism and contractualism stage 5 which tested the latter ("social contract legalistic orientation"), the results seemed to indicate that Western respondents scored higher. But this was because that stage of moral development was assessed only on the basis of the Western concept of justice posited by the Heinz dilemma as a binary choice between "life or property". When that dilemma was replaced by a number of non-dilemmatic methods, the statistical re-evaluation of the above study plus a separate meta-analysis of 75 cross-cultural Kohlberg-scale based studies in 23 countries, both showed commonly shared between Eastern and Western respondents stages of moral development and cross-cultural justice values (Gibbs et al. 2007, pp. 454 and 491).

In this connection, the next sub-section considers some of the aspects of Eastern justice values relavant in anti-corruption education.

2.2 *Eastern Perspective*

Unlike in Western legal culture where nowadays filial relationships are for all practical purposes limited to close family (couples, siblings, parents-children), and in other personal configurations individuals are "a mere aggregate" (Ruskola 2013, p. 75), in the 2000-year old Confucian legal culture a broken filial obligation not only is regarded an emotional failure of a filial duty but also violates intergenerational relationships that are far more important than business relationships beyond the family. In all Confucian interpretations the lineage of property involved only male kinsfolk (ibidem). Property is managed by them in the overarching patriarchal spirit of social harmony (benevolence, righteousness, propriety, wisdom and faith), the spirit believed to be the five greatest traditional inspirations for codes of ethics in Asia,[5] like also the five related patriarchal principles of filial piety—a "graded love" continuum of: *Ruler to Ruled*, *Father to Son*, *The Husband to Wife*, *Elder Sibling to Younger Sibling*, *Friend to Friend* (Fan 2010,

[5] Also in Buddhist and Hindu interpretations, see further Glenn 2010, pp. 153–172; Kee 2007.

pp. 203–205). These principles permeated the traditional hierarchical structure of Chinese society with its four social classes, ranked in the following order of priority: officials and intellectuals, peasants, workers, and, finally, businessmen.

In modern China the growth and repositioning of the latter class is now at the focus of public and governmental attention and action because of the growing corruption of the new middle class. Accordingly, those who stress "the moral malaise of the West" that erodes those time-honoured intergenerational relationships urge to resurrect the moral insights of Confucian thought, as if their old strength would suffice to control corruption better (ibidem, p. ix). Presently, this is a serious moral and governance challenge and concern, inter alia, exemplified by various counter-corruption actions—many in vain in the long run.

And, indeed, in the Eastern world "good governance" is a different concept from the Western one. Before sharing some insights how to counter corruption from the United Nations perspective that accommodates the Eastern perspective with its legitimate concern, it should be first acknowledged that, indeed again, the Confucian sense of "good governance" is less contractual and more filial or interpersonal (*ren zheng*—human governance).

Developmental psychologists have documented the source of this difference through cross-cultural parent–child experiments conducted in China and Iceland, as a modification of the "Heinz dilemma". In two such experiments a sizeable group of pre-selected, psychologically, socially and linguistically classified Icelandic and Chinese children was separately interviewed on two dilemmas: a moral one on friendship obligations and another one on interpersonal responsibilities in a parent–child relationship.

In the friendship dilemma a protagonist had to choose between keeping a promise to a best friend or accepting an interesting invitation from another child of the same gender, but new in the class (Keller et al. 2005).[6] The dilemma, experimenters inform, involved an interesting offer made by the friend or the new child (the hedonistic concern), the moral obligation to keep the promise or the arrangement with the friend, interpersonal responsibilities of care (the long-term friendship and the needs and feelings of the close friend) and, finally, the responsibilities towards the third child who is alone. The experimenters concluded that as regards cultural differences in orientation to the principles of justice and care (reasoning about the option who is a "friend"), Icelandic participants were more frequently oriented towards the contractual aspect of the promise. However, the Chinese, apparently prompted by altruism, were more concerned with interpersonal responsibilities towards the friend.

In the parent—child dilemma a mother has promised her daughter that she can spend the money she has earned herself or received as a present on a movie or a concert. At the last minute the mother claims the money from the daughter because

[6] Some aspects made the situation psychologically more complicated. For example, that the meeting with the friend is on their special day or that the old friend appears not to like the new child, and that he or she wants to talk about something that is important for him (Keller et al. 2005).

it is needed to buy things for school. The daughter lies about the amount of money and goes to the movie or concert—with the knowledge of her sister. The dilemma focuses on the sister (first tested at the age of 12, then at the age of 15) who has to decide whether she should tell her mother the truth or be silent about it when the mother asks her about the sister's whereabouts.[7] The interview strategy concentrated exclusively on the moral judgment and the reasons supporting it. In addition, however, respondents were asked for justifications that might support an alternative moral judgment of a fictitious third person.

The experimenters further concluded that in evaluating the results of that dilemma, it turned out that the contractual aspect between the mother and her daughter had for 15-year-old Icelandic students a somewhat greater significance than for the corresponding Chinese group. But, more important, a closer look at the arguments in both groups suggested a bigger significance of fairness over sibling loyalty in the Icelandic parent–child relationship. For the Chinese children it was their preference of parental authority (not fairness, but submissive filial piety) over sibling loyalty—penultimate on the list of the five Confucian bonds. In contrast, for the Icelandic group's conduct it appears that fairness was a part of an emerging moral egalitarian contract between a parent and a child.

The bonding amongst Chinese children and the kinship instinct between them and parents (in short, interpersonal obligations or patriarchal norms) was stronger than in the legal culture of Icelandic families. In Iceland, children's moral sense of intergenerational obligation towards parents seemed to be more contractual, as if driven by a state rather than kinship instinct[8] and motivated by the desire for more intergenerational equity—an idea of delivering fairness or justice in relationships between children, youth, adults and seniors, particularly in terms of treatment and interactions (Marshall et al. 1993, p. 119).

It is this light one may now see the seminal results of moral psychology studies of adolescents (ages 13–18 years) in Canada and China. (Helwig et al. 2003). These studies surprisingly confirmed the similar reasoning about autonomous and authority-based group decision-making in the peer group, family and schools for decisions that involved children, as measured by adolescents' and parent' attitudes to respect the majority rule vs. consensus. In this context, it was surprising to see the adolescents' like-mindedness in favouring consensus in taking decisions in family and by majority rule in larger groups (e.g. school classroom).

Even more surprising was the response to the question whether or not a child in a family should receive special tutoring on weekends (quite a common family practice in China). Chinese parents favoured consensus over exercising their own authority. This was justified by the argument to respect children's autonomy and

[7] Again, the conflict contains different concerns. Beyond the issues of parental authority and the contractual norm of promise keeping the moral norm of truthfulness—not to lie to the mother, and interpersonal responsibilities such as care or loyalty to the sister are important concerns in the situation (Keller et al. 2005).

[8] There is a wide body of well-referenced educational research on children born to Chinese or English parents which basically confirms the above finding (Westbrook 2012).

their right to make academic decisions on their own. Likewise surprising was the difference between Chinese and Canadian adolescents' opinion whether or not to decide by consensus on the educational curricula. While Canadian adolescents favoured that rule, Chinese peers favoured the majority opinion. This striking preference was apparently due to unease and distrust of certain authoritative educational practices involving the standardization of educational curricula and nationwide achievement examinations. Found overly authoritative, these practices were contested as non-participatory.

Other research with adolescents and adults in a non-Druze Islamic patriarchal community in Israel showed similar patterns of judgment about freedoms and rights (Helwig and Turiel 2002).

Finally, researchers have found that ethnic minority groups tend to promote interdependence, and European Americans tend to promote independence. Yet, evidence of both orientations has also been found within each ethnic group. One of the more recent studies of this genre corroborated this evidence for the coexistence of dimensions of independence and interdependence in parents' cultural models among African Americans, Chinese Americans, European Americans and Mexican Americans living in the US (Suizzo 2007).

Thus, in conclusion, the above findings suggest that across diverse cultures the fundamental conception of fair treatment through shared decision-making is appreciated and accepted where patriarchalism mixes with contractualism, albeit not necessarily to the same extent, for the corruptive attitudes are differently embedded in the various family models. Nonetheless, participatory decision-making, whether in property, education or other issues carries a universal moral appeal in the tested models. This appeal transcends the Occidental and Oriental values; therefore a fairer resource distribution ("distributive justice"—material and non-material) through that form of participation may be helpful in anti-corruption education. To some extent, this offers an avenue for modifying a patriarchal perception of justice in favour of a contractual one.

However, there are also clear limits for such modifications on the patriarchalism-contractualism spectrum; limits which show that Occidental and Oriental anti-corruption legal education must account for culture-specific, if not also gender-specific decision-making.

Last but not least, the results of empirical research involving another modification of the Heinz dilemma[9] tested on 9–15 years old randomly sampled students from Beijing primary and secondary schools (Fang et al. 2003) delivered one more interesting finding. Namely, that while certain features of students' moral development are indeed universal in terms of family relationships, other features are more

[9] "Judy's dilemma": "A mother has given a promise to let her daughter Judy go to a rock concert if she paid for the ticket with money she had earned herself. At the last minute, the mother withdrew her permission and requested that Judy used the money to buy a school dress. Judy decided to lie about the money she had earned and to go to the concert anyway. The question was whether her older sister Louise, who was informed about Judy's plan, shoukd tell her mother the truth or not?". (Fang et al. 2003, p. 127).

dependent than in the Western setting on the filial piety between daughter and mother than between the two sisters. Consequently, comparing moral development across such diversified culturally students and countries should account for this Eastern patriarchal and normatively legitimate difference, without locking it through a Western lens into one moral development hierarchy.

This indirectly corroborates the intuitive claim that moral development of women and children is different than of males—overrepresented in the original Heinz dilemma (Gilligan 1982). This claim looks like belabouring the obvious. However, it suggests one important point: apart from these relational subtleties on the right to life in the context of patriarchalism or contractualism, there is otherwise preciously little on the likewise relational issues involved in the right to property, whether understood in the Western or Eastern way. Therefore a similarly intuitive claim that anti-corruption education in property related issues for women and children of different cultures may require more tailored age- and gender-sensitive research and approaches warrants further consideration.

In its light, the following sub-section shows that from the UN perspective only very few inroads have been made into anti-corruption education for women and children, as far as property issues are concerned.

2.3 The United Nations Perspective

Disregard of the law may have various sources: contractual vs. patriarchal attitudes to it, the lack of knowledge of it (e.g. illiteracy is certainly one of the factors), the feeling of impunity—of being "above the law", the feeling of borderless cyberspace with its own virtual law, etc. More often than not, contemporary youth, especially "digitally-native", may be in the last group, while contemporary adult men and women in the other ones.

That little can be said about all people whether from East or West, or—using contemporary UN terminology—South or North. The North–south bridge provided by the United Nations Convention against Corruption/UNCAC (2349 UNTS 41) facilitates cooperation on criminal aspects of countering corruption. Understandably, in this regard it gives priority to any inter-State transfer of anti-corruption expertise relating to the training for the personnel responsible for countering corruption (art. 60), but not to education of the public along the other parameters, and even less to women and children. And yet, art. 13 of UNCAC only addresses (in)formal anti-corruption education in terms of single State-Parties and their territorially limited obligation to include in their public education "school and university curricula" to contribute to non-tolerance of corruption, whoever this public (adults or kids) is. In art. 5 UNCAC obliges State-Parties to collaborate with each other and with relevant international and regional organizations in promoting and developing the measures that promote the participation of society and which reflect the principles of the rule of law, proper management of public affairs and public property, integrity, transparency and accountability. That collaboration may include participation in international programmes and projects aimed at the prevention of corruption.

The UN Secretariat's review of the implementation of this article (CAC/COSP/WG.4/2014/2, paras. 17 and 80–83) shows that in countries which reported on it, its various anti-corruption authorities pursue the relevant work. For example, in France it includes universities and other institutions of higher education. In the Republic of Korea, annual meetings were held to communicate the content of the guidelines to the inspectors of central government agencies, local government bodies and educational institutions, so as to improve consistency and comprehensiveness in the implementation of the national anti-corruption strategy. The guidelines contained the priorities of the national anti-corruption policy for the upcoming year, best practices in implementation by government departments and an overview of the implementation level achieved by each public body in the previous year.

The Bolivarian Republic of Venezuela reported that since 2003 it had been implementing a programme entitled "The Comptroller goes to School", in which school children were required to take action to exercise control over and supervise the correct administration of school resources. The programme, in which over 12,000 students from more than 1000 schools in 23 different states had participated, served to highlight to students the key corruption risks that existed within schools and how to combat those risks.

Similarly, Nigeria noted that it had put in place a number of measures to directly engage children in corruption prevention efforts. The Independent Corrupt Practices and Other Related Offences Commission collaborated with the National Educational and Research Development Council to develop a "national values curriculum" initiative aimed at infusing key anti-corruption ethics and values into the national educational system. The curriculum was integrated into school subjects at all levels of education, and work was in progress to extend the curriculum to polytechnical schools and universities. Additional measures included the introduction of 300 "anti-corruption clubs" in secondary schools, providing a forum in which students could discuss the impact of corruption in Nigeria.

In this regard, the implementation of the Convention on the Rights of the Child/CRC (1577 UNTS 3) lags behind the UNCAC. This is because while the CRC encourages children's right to participation in some decision-making and stresses their right to personal dignity and integrity by obliging the States to take the preventive and educational measures to counter their "mental violence" and other (non) criminal abuses (art. 19), it hardly pays attention elsewhere to more subtle educational aspects, namely how to educate relevant actors in meeting children's right to personal property—a departure point for any anti-corruption education.

The CRC seems to be more geared toward facilitating countering domestic violence than property crime, hence intergenerational equity is somewhat too restrictively interpreted. It stipulates the rights of children to dignified treatment by others through education and health care, the right to privacy, to protection from violence, and to political rights such as freedom of expression and religion, but not to a more participatory resource management.

Overlooking this restrictive interpretation, one CRC commentator applauds it as an impressive document "that not only states the moral sense of the global community, but also potentially creates political structures for fulfilling that view" (Melton 1991, p. 66). Surely, at the time of that writing, exclusively focusing on the prevention of "mental violence" that is at the core of the global moral sense should not be surprising. But as of this writing, no longer one may be so exclusive. Empirical evidence shows (see Kanningiser et al. in this book) that 3 years old children understand some crucial aspects of social norms (e.g. entitlements). Further, already from the age of two they have the ability to relate owners and their property and to make (basic) inferences about who owns what. Moreover, these children correctly assume that stealing does not transfer ownership.

However, even more limited than CRC on anti-corruption education will be the International Covenant on Economic, Social and Cultural Rights of 1966 (993 UNTS 3). In art 13 it only speaks generally of the right to education in terms of its availability, accessibility, acceptability and adaptability (E/C.12/1999/10, Comment 13). Article 5(1)(a) of the UNESCO Convention Against Discrimination in Education of 1960 (429 UNTS 93) is likewise generally relevant because of its emphasis on tolerance. It reads: "Education shall be directed to … the strengthening of respect for human rights and fundamental freedoms; it shall promote understanding, tolerance and friendship among all nations, racial or religious groups, and shall further the activities of the United Nations for the maintenance of peace". In 1974 UNESCO in its "Recommendation concerning Education for International Understanding, Co-operation and Peace and Education relating to Human Rights and Fundamental Freedoms" (see Clark in this book) offered some generic advice on teaching Crime Prevention as part of the UN Peace Studies. In sum, save for the examples of art. 5 UNCAC cited above, in the United Nations legal instruments the new anti-corruption focus is absent.

That particular part of education across the world is left to other devices. However, when the focus is recast, it may be viable for the furthering of early anti-corruption strategies through international exchange.

3 Making the United Nations Anti-Corruption Law Work

While there has already been some UN progress in extending anti-corruption education from adult to children's level, this progress has still been interculturally rather shallow and, at times, attacked. The devastating role of the Nigerian-born "*Boko Haram*" ("Western education is sinful") may be a case in point for countering anti-corruption education, but for each and every country such a point really stands on its own, particularly as regards the impact of contractual and patriarchal relationships on property management. "Property management" by children, that is early prevention educational policies at the core of which that "management" is (and about which little is known or done worldwide) should become a part of anti-corruption strategies across various legal cultures. Be it as it may, paying attention to the property issues with due account of such intricate differences is the key for a more successful countering of corruption anywhere.

Educating in this way in "property issues" is not a technical skill, though. In essence it is eventually the question of good governance for sustainable development skills and effects—global, local and personal (Redo 2012). Researchers, educationists and educators must remember that at the core of these issues are various resource deprivations (material and non-material) which for the purpose of the United Nations sustainable development agenda have been intellectually short-cut to "poverty eradication".

In reality, the post-2015 UN sustainable development agenda as far as anti-corruption education for women and children is concerned, must take account of these various facets of deprivations, including maternal and parental ones. Education starts with intimate contacts at home and school. The post-1945 research, first mandated by the United Nations and then carried out by the World Health Organization and numerous academics ever since, has abundantly documented in this regard the correctness of several earlier fragmentary findings, but also the common wisdom of previous times: Home and school are the places for intergenerational transmission of aspirations, norms, and values—the places for developmental anti-corruption (Redo and Platzer 2013, p. 296).

Since early education builds "the foundational truth" (Westbrook 2012, p. 140)[10] for any young person, in the nascent United Nations treaty exchange of information and experience on early anti-corruption, each and every country deals with its own "truth" concerning formative features for living honestly. However, hardly any has operationalized it in sustainable development terms. This is documented by the afore reported country examples from Europe, Asia, Africa and Latin America regarding the implementation of UNCAC (art. 5). Countries with various legal cultures and socio-economic systems pursue very diversified concepts and methods of countering corruption. Country reports hardly give a sense of anti-corruption education for women and children in sustainable development terms.

In the interest of making this thin blue line more conducive for anti-corruption for women and children globally, the following recommendations may be considered:

First, in the interest of further exchange of information and experience globally, State Parties to UNCAC and others concerned may wish to publish the anti-corruption educational syllabi on the Internet;

Second, at the occasion of biennial conferences of UNCAC State Parties they also may wish to engage directly educationists and academics to discuss that experience through the so called "side events" (i.e. expert meetings organized around the formal conference agenda);

[10] This colloquial expression is an intellectual shortcut for sharing with a child common wisdom, whereby at the very start a bivalent or multivalent way of thinking takes hold in the formative process and makes the headway.

Third, the United Nations publications, including manuals or handbooks, in an operative way should further develop the advice how to counter corruption, taking account of great cultural specificities and developmental challenges of a personal and socio-economic character. An example to follow is the "*ABC of Teaching Human Rights*" (UNHCHR 2000)—the publication which emphasizes that children are human beings whose rights are distinct. They should not be passive objects of care and charity. Such publications underline that children should learn what justice or fairness means through the appropriate methods in education ("equity", fair grading, meeting other anti-corruption educational criteria; empowering of children), in culture (e.g. "a woman is not a property of a man"), and in sports ("fair play"). These are very elementary examples for formative age anti-corruption teaching and other institutional instruction, criminologically relevant because early symptoms of "underachievement" can later be important in terms of delinquency and dropping out of school;

Finally, UNESCO and the United Nations Children's Fund (UNICEF) may here be the leaders with their various anti-corruption country projects, as well as the International Anti-Corruption Academy (IACA)—an authority in a more advanced (academic and non-academic) good governance training and education.

For the less advanced (elementary) level of anti-corruption instruction, there is still more in cross-cultural terms. "Taken together, research on young children's understanding of different ownership rights has revealed that young children already grasp some ownership rights and distinguish between ownership transfers that are temporary (e.g. borrowing, playing with someone's objects) and transfers that are permanent (e.g. gift giving, creating something new). Of course what counts as ownership rights and transfers, who may be entitled to ownership (individuals, groups, etc.), and what entities can and cannot be owned may vary between socio-cultural groups. But... children come prepared with the ability to acquire the specific ownership norms (just as all other norms) of their group" (Kanngiesser et al. in this book).

This research corroborates the viability of practical examples that meet the developmental requirements for countering corruption among older children (10–15 years old). For example, in California (USA) which has in its primary and secondary-level education various minority children, the authorities implemented a 60-lesson curriculum for the intermediate (primary/secondary) junior high school students. This was a follow-up to a shorter curriculum, from which "simply put...the students learned the lessons taught" (Kenney and Godson 2002, p. 439).

This meticulously structured, interactive Californian "*School-based Education to Counter Crime and Corruption*" (Godson and Kenney 2000) is, in fact, adaptable to many other societies. The educational curriculum involves meeting knowledge-based (cognitive) and affective or attitudinal/emotionally-based goals, that is children's non-tolerance to crime and corruption. For those familiar with the researched and reported cultural differences in children's cognition and affection in Eastern and Western legal settings, and how to respond to them constructively in those settings, that curriculum can be a springboard to develop specific domestically and locally-sensitive teaching and learning anti-corruption methods. The curriculum may also help to project relevant anti-corruption instruction into pre-school, primary and university-level activities and classes in a culturally- and psychologically appropriate way. Consequently, and in principle, on the educational continuum one may comprehensively, with expertise and foresight, get at the core of anti-corruption formative and reformative education in every country, with due account of age- and culture-dependent youth features, and other precepts, rule of law ones including.

4 Conclusion: How the United Nations Wants Us to Counter Corruption?

In conclusion, making connections across various legal cultures is important anywhere. The examples of the implementation of art. 5 of UNCAC seem to be inscribed into the above conclusion. Comprehensively and symbolically, this was underscored by the Secretary-General of the United Nations. In 2004 Kofi Annan emphasized that "the 'rule of law' is a concept at the very heart of the Organization's mission". (S/2004/616, para. 6). Two years later, he added that at the very heart of the United Nations is also ensuring that our individual rights must be preserved and respected (Annan 2014, p. 128). Now must be added that good governance for sustainable development should be the main orientation point in anti-corruption education for women and children, and for all.

The UN Culture of Lawfulness has its own multi-level normativity (individual, national and United Nations') and communicates heartfelt universal values of all civilizations. Thus, as far as the UN concept of the Rule of Law is concerned, this normativity, partisan and complex as is, is not only contractual, but also interpersonal and global. This UN normativity owes its further complexity to the formulation of the UN post-2015 development Goal 16. It reads: " Promote peaceful and inclusive societies for sustainable development, provide access to justice for all and build effective, accountable and inclusive institutions at all levels". As one of the sub-goals it envisages to "substantially reduce corruption and bribery in all its forms" (A/68/970, p. 22).

Both formulations seemingly contradict one another: promoting peace and social tolerance and increasing non-tolerance of corruption and bribery. But, in fact, they are flip sides of one coin. An eminent commentator of the UN Charter noted that inserting in it the link between "peace and security" put the Charter ahead of its time (Schrijver 2006, p. 10).

Since then, in the United Nations "justice" has not been at parity with "peace and security". Only when none of the permanent members of the Security Council vetoes, "justice" may subordinately be delivered, e.g. in the fight against corruption or bribery, by this law enforcement arm of the UN, or in other mandated cases may be delivered by its various international criminal tribunals.

Likewise ahead of its time is now the UN 2016–2030 sustainable development agenda. In it countering corruption and bribery is linked to the development of peaceful and inclusive societies. This was first signalled as such at the UN Security Council when its President reaffirmed that corruption is a threat to peace and security (S/PRST/2010/4, p. 2). It appears that the supposedly overarching UN concept of the Rule of Law has been subsumed under "peace and security".

It may thus be generally concluded that the legal and cultural non-tolerance of corruption is the hallmark of a peaceful society, while the hallmark of social inclusion is the further legitimization of otherness in whatever culturally available way it may show itself. Inclusion entails implementing and creating new abiding civic commitments to the essential similarities and, paradoxically, differences everywhere. In essence, the progressive associative impact of contractualism implies pursuing inclusiveness and education, rather than the unbounded tolerance of diversity, especially when it facilitates "uncivil societies" (see further Redo 2012, p. 153). When in such "societies" violence and crime: transnational, organized, modern and traditional; terrorism and the hatred of otherness is manifested in excess, then this fundamentally offends our civic consciousness, may undermine peace and security and the rule of law.

In this connection, other proposed sustainable development goals accordingly emphasize the role of education and life-long learning, both very important for social inclusion (Fig. 2).

It is the above context in which one can now appreciate the two great minds of "the philosophers of the heart", one Chinese—Meng Zi (Latinized as Mencius, 327–289 B.C.E.),[11] and the other—the eighteenth century Swiss Jean-Jacque

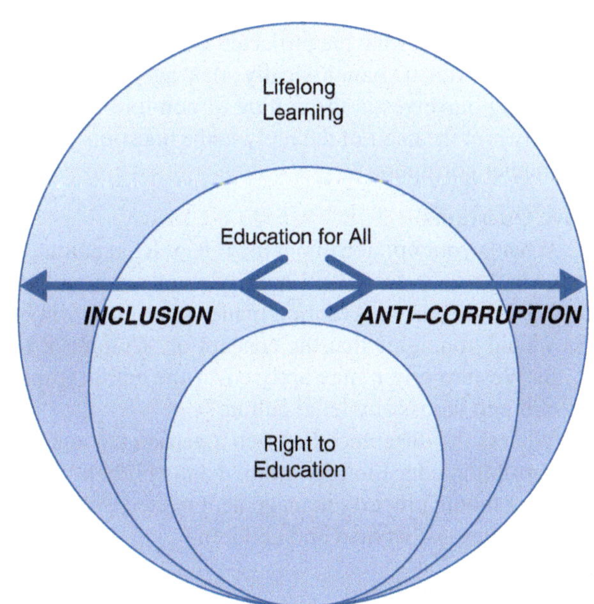

Fig. 2 How the United Nations wants us to counter corruption. *Source*: Adapted from Biermann J (2013) The United Nations Convention on the Rights of persons with Disabilities. Implications and Challenges for National Education Systems. In Platzer M, Idomir ML (Eds.), UN Agencies Reaching out to the Academia and the Civil Society, Favorita Papers 01/2013, ACUNS-UNIDO-CTBTO-Diplomatische Akademie Wien, pp. 237–252

[11] The most accepted date (Wang 2009).

Rousseau (1712–1778),[12] in whose times corruption was still as normal as drinking water and eating rice or bread. Both in their own ways believed in the existence of a natural law (in Chinese *Tien-lei* or *lei*) and *shè huì qì yuē*—a social contract (Shin 1957). Both also provided for their constituencies various arguments for peace and justice as a part of a universal endowment, for empathy as a driver for positive human and international relations, for natural goodness of a person, for governance as an agreement between the ruler and the ruled for the sake of their welfare, and against corruption. As the second motto of this chapter illustrates, Mencius' eventual message on countering corruption is very clear. He has been probably the first one who conveyed in this way the essence of sustainable livelihood (more: Zhang in this book).

But Mencius and Rousseau went even further. Mencius said: "*The great man is he who does not lose his child's heart*" (Book 4, part II in Lau 1970, p. 130). Rousseau who wrote a book on natural education of children ("Emile, or about Education" (1782)), recalled there the thirteenth century Mongol invasion of China. He then warily observed that: "*A philosopher loves the Tartars so as to be spared having to love his neighbours*" (Rousseau 1979, p. 39). By this he meant that personal empathy is in short supply among neighbours, but only with more of it can we appreciate others, and integrate them into our societies.

The welfare of people, their life and, in some cases, the way they die, their honesty and empathy depend on educating ourselves and the succeeding generation in a greater cultural tolerance with more balanced sustainable development whereby excessive economic inequalities are prevented. In this way, indeed, societies can, technically speaking, be less criminogenic and become more peaceful and inclusive. This is what the projected UN post-2015 sustainable development agenda calls for. Even if, paradoxically, that agenda's implementation depends also on educating ourselves in the culture of non-tolerance to corruption. This educational priority is at the heart of the reply to the question "How the United Nations wants us to counter corruption".

Five Questions

1. What is your opinion about the role of legal culture and sustainable development as issues relevant to anti-corruption education of women and children?
2. Why does early prevention matter more than crime prevention later?
3. Would you agree that the concept of "Culture of Lawfulness" notwithstanding its Western origin may aptly cover the anti-corruption education of women and children across any legal culture?
4. What is the difference between a patriarchal and a contractual approach to anti-corruption education for women and children?
5. Why should property management related issues be at the core of anti-corruption education for women and children?

[12] Credited for his contributions to the Universal Declaration of Human Rights (Morsink 1999, pp. 290–291; Høystad 2011, p. 183).

References

A/66/749 Delivering justice: Programme of action to strengthen the rule of law at the national and international levels: Report of the Secretary-General, 16 March 2012.

A/68/970 Report of the Open Working Group of the General Assembly on Sustainable Development Goals, 12 August 2014.

Adler, P. S. (1976/1994), Beyond cultural identity: Reflections on multiculturalism. In Weaver, G. R. (Ed.), *Culture, communication and conflict: Readings on intercultural relations* (pp. 241–259). Needham Heights, MA: Ginn Press.

Annan, K. (2014). Statement, address at an event to mark International Human Rights Day, New York, New York, 8 December 2006. In E. Mortimer (Ed.), *We the peoples: A UN for the twenty-first century*. Boulder, CO: Paradigm Publishers.

Airenti, G., & Angeleri, R. (2011). Situation-sensitive use of insincerity: Pathways to communication in young children. *British Journal of Developmental Psychology, 29*, 765–782.

Bakken, B. (2014). Punishment in China. In L. Cao, I. Y. Sun, & B. Hebenton (Eds.), *The Routledge handbook of Chinese criminology* (pp. 41–46). London/New York: Routledge.

Biermann, J. (2013). The United Nations Convention on the Rights of persons with Disabilities. Implications and challenges for national education systems. In Platzer, M., Idomir, M. L. (Eds.), *UN agencies reaching out to the academia and the civil society*, Favorita Papers 01/2013 (pp. 237–252). ACUNS-UNIDO-CTBTO-Diplomatische Akademie Wien.

CAC/COSP/WG.4/2014/2, Mandates of anti-corruption body or bodies in respect of prevention (article 6 of the United Nations Convention against Corruption), Note by the Secretariat, 25 June 2014.

Convention on the Rights of the Child, 1577 UNTS 3.

Cumminskey, D. (2008). Dignity, contractualism and consequentialism. *Utilitas, 20*(4), 383–408.

Dölling, D., Entorf, H., Hermann, D., & Rupp, T. (2011). Meta-analysis of empirical studies on deterrence. In H. Kury & E. Shea (Eds.), *Punitivity-international developments* (Vol. 3, pp. 315–378). Bochum: Universitäts Verlag Dr. Brockmayer.

E/C.12/1999/10 (1999), Committee on the Economic, Social and Cultural Rights, General Comment No. 13, The right to education.

Fan, R. (2010). *Reconstructionist Confucianism. Rethinking morality after the west.* Dordrecht/ Heidelberg/London/New York: Springer.

Fang, G., Fang, F.-X., Keller, M., Edelstein, W., Kehle, T. J., & Bray, M. A. (2003). Social moral reasoning in Chinese children: A developmental study. *Psychology in the Schools, 40*(1), 125–138.

Fassbender, B. (2009). *The United Nations charter as the constitution of the international community.* Leiden: Brill.

Gibbs, J. C., Basinger, K. S., Grime, L. R., & Snarey, J. R. (2007). Moral judgment development across cultures: Revisiting Kohlberg's universality claims. *Developmental Review, 27*(4), 443–500.

Gilligan, C. (1982). *In a different voice: Psychological theory and women's development.* Harvard: Harvard University Press.

Gintis, H. (Ed.). (2009). *The bounds of reason: Game theory and the unification of the behavioral science.* Princeton: Princeton University Press.

Glenn, P. H. (2010). *Legal traditions of the world.* Oxford: Oxford University Press.

Godson, R., & Kenney, D. J. (2000). Introduction and overview to "School-based education to counter crime and corruption": Evaluation of the initial pilot curriculum for Baja California (Mexico) and San Diego county (USA). *Trends in Organized Crime, 5*(3), 90–101.

Grusec, J. E., & Redler, E. (1980). Attribution, reinforcement, and altruism: A developmental analysis. *Developmental Psychology, 16*(5), 525–534.

Hegel, G. (1822-23/2011). *Lectures on the philosophy of world history- 1: Manuscripts of the introduction and the lectures of 1822–3* (R. F. Brown, & Hodgson P. C., Trans.). Oxford: Clarendon Press.

Heckman, J. J. (2008). *The case of investing in disadvantaged young children. Big ideas for children: Investing in our nation's future* (pp. 49–58). Washington, D.C: First Focus.

Heinemann, B. (1964). *Facets of Indian thought*. New York: Schocken Books.

Helwig, C. C., Arnold, M. L., Tan, D., & Boyd, D. (2003). Chinese adolescents' reasoning about democratic and authority-based decision making in peer, family, and school contexts. *Child Development, 74*, 783–800.

Helwig, C. C., & Turiel, E. (2002). Civil liberties, autonomy, and democracy: Children's perspectives. *International Journal of Law and Psychiatry, 25*, 260–263.

Høystad, O. M. (2011). Hjertets kulturhistorie Frå anttiken til idag (Heart. History of Culture and Symbol).Warszawa, Polish: Bellona.

International Covenant on Economic, Social and Cultural Rights, 993 UNTS 3.

Kee, Y. (2007). Adult learning from a Confucian way of thinking. In S. B. Merriam & Associates (Eds.), *Non-western perspectives on learning and knowing* (pp. 153–172). Malabar, FL: Krieger Publishing Company.

Keller, M., Edelstein, W., Krettenauer, T., Fu-xi, F., & Ge, F. (2005). Reasoning about moral obligations and interpersonal responsibilities in different cultural contexts. In G. Nunner-Winkler & W. Edelstein (Eds.), *Morality in context* (pp. 317–337). Amsterdam: Elsevier.

Kenney, D. J., & Godson, R. (2002). Countering crime and corruption: A school-based program on the US-Mexico border. *Criminology and Criminal Justice, 2*, 409–470.

Kohlberg, L. (1970). Stages of moral development as a basis for moral education. In C. Beck & E. Sullivan (Eds.), *Moral education*. Toronto: University of Toronto Press.

Kohlberg, L. (1963/2008). The development of children's orientations toward a moral order: Sequence in the development of moral thought. What are morals? *Human Development, 51*, 8–20.

Kury, H. (2013). Crime prevention through (harsher) punishment? - Results of international empirical studies. *Acta Criminologiae et Medicinae Japonica, 79*(5), 161.

Lau, L. (1970). *The works of Mencius*. London: Penguin.

Månsson, K. (2007). Reviving the "spirit of San Francisco": The lost proposals on human rights, justice and international law to the UN Charter. *Nordic Journal of International Law, 76*, 217–239.

Marshall, V. W., Cook, F. L., & Marshall, J. G. (1993). Conflict over intergenerational equity: Rhetoric and reality in a comparative context. In W. A. Achenbaum & V. L. Bengtson (Eds.), *The changing contract across generations* (pp. 119–140). New York: A. de Gruyter.

Melton, G. B. (1991). Socialization in the global community. Respect for the dignity of children. *American Psychologist, 46*, 66–67. doi:10.1037/a0033584.

Mitchell, K. (2004). Geographies of identity: Multiculturalism unplugged. *Progress in Human Geography, 28*(5), 641–651.

Morsink, J. (1999). *The universal declaration of human rights: Origins, drafting, and intent*. Philadelphia, PA: University of Pennsylvania Press.

Redo, S. (2012). *Blue criminology: The power of united nations ideas to counter crime globally. A monographic study*. Helsinki, Seoul: European Institute for Crime Prevention and Control, affiliated with the United Nations- Korean Institute of Criminology.

Redo, S. (2014). Education for succeeding generations in culture of lawfulness. In E. W. Pływaczewski (Ed.) (pp. 698–722). Warszawa: Wydawnictwo C.H. Beck.

Redo, S., & Platzer, M. (2013). The United Nations' role in crime control and prevention. In J. Albanese & P. Reichel (Eds.), *Handbook of transnational crime and justice* (pp. 293–294). Los Angeles/London/New Delhi/Singapore/Washington DC: SAGE.

Reichel, P. L. (2013). *Comparative criminal justice systems. A topical approach* (6th ed.). Boston: Pearson.

Rossano, F., Rakoczy, H., & Tomasello, M. (2011). Young children's understanding of violations of property rights. *Cognition, 12*, 219–227.

Rousseau, J. J. (1782/1979). Emile, or about Education (A. Bloom, Trans.). New York: Basic Books.

Ruskola, T. (2013). *Legal orientalism. China, the United States and modern law*. Harvard: Harvard University Press.

S/2004/616 The Rule of Law and Transitional Justice in Conflict and Post-conflict Societies, Report of the Secretary-General, 23 August 2004.

S/PRST/2010/4 Threats to Peace and Security, Statement by the President of the Security Council, 24 February 2010.

Sherif, M. (1954/1961). *The Robber's Cave experiment: Intergroup conflict and cooperation*. Middletown, CONN: Wesleyan University Press.

Shin, P. K. T. (1957). The natural law philosophy of Mencius. *New Scholasticism, 31*(3), 317–337.

Wang, H. (2009). The way of heart: Mencius' understanding of justice. *Philosophy East and West, 59*(3), 317–363.

Schrijver, N. (2006). The future of the Charter of the United Nations. *Max Planck Yearbook of United Nations Law, 10*, 1–34.

Schrijver, N. (2007). Natural resources and sustainable development. In T. G. Weiss & S. Daws (Eds.), *The Oxford handbook on the United Nations*. Oxford: Oxford University Press.

Simma, B. (Ed.) Paulus, A., Chatodou, E. (ass. Eds), In collaboration with Mosler, H., Radelzhofer, A., Tomuschat, Ch., Wolfrum, R. (2002). The Charter of the United Nations. A commentary (second edition). Oxford: Oxford University Press.

Stearns, P. (2008). *World history in documents: A comparative reader*. New York and London: New York University Press.

Suizzo, M.-A. (2007). Parents' goals and values for children dimensions of independence and interdependence across four U.S. ethnic groups. *Journal of Cross-Cultural Psychology, 38*(4), 506–525.

Sultan, A. N. (2004). Principal and practical foundations of a global constitutional order. *Washington University Global Studies Law Review, 3*(1), 155–175.

USIP/United States Institute of Peace. (2009). Guiding Principles for Stabilization and Reconstruction. Washington, D. C.

United Nations Convention against Corruption, 2349 UNTS 41.

United Nations Office of the High Commissioner for Human Rights/UNHCHR. (2000). *ABC of teaching human rights. Human rights topics for upper primary and lower and senior secondary school*. Geneva: United Nations.

UNESCO. (1974). Recommendation concerning education for international understanding, co-operation and peace and education relating to human rights and fundamental freedoms adopted by the General Conference at its eighteenth session Paris, 19 November 1974.

UNESCO. (1997). International Standard Classification of Education, Paris.

UNESCO Convention Against Discrimination in Education, 429 UNTS 93.

Wong, Y., & Tsai, J. L. (2007). Cultural models of shame and guilt. In J. Tracy, R. Robins, & J. Tangney (Eds.), *Handbook of self-conscious emotions* (pp. 210–223). New York: Guilford.

Walsh, J. E. (1973). *Intercultural education in the community of man*. Honolulu: University of Hawaii Press.

Warneken, F., & Tomasello, M. (2008). Extrinsic rewards undermine altruistic tendencies in 20-month-olds. *Developmental Psychology, 44*(6), 1785–1788.

Welsh, B. C. (2003). Economic costs and benefits of primary prevention of delinquency and later offending: A review of the literature. In J. W. Coid & D. P. Farrington (Eds.), *Early prevention of adult antisocial behaviour* (pp. 308–355). Cambridge: Cambridge University Press.

Westbrook, T. P. (2012). An investigation into the effects of Confucian filial piety in the intercultural Christian education experience. *Journal for the Study of Religions and Ideologies, 11*(3), 137–163.

Proactive Strategies to Prevent Child Sexual Abuse and the Use of Child Abuse Images: Experiences from the German Dunkelfeld Project

Klaus M. Beier

Abstract The contribution describes a German prevention approach which aims at improving proactive strategies to protect children from sexual exploitation by online offenses, such as the consumption or distribution of child abuse images (so-called "child pornography"), and hands-on contact child sexual abuse. Prevention strategies include research on individuals at risk to commit first or persistent sexual offenses against children, at the same time offering preventive assessment and treatment. As it is acknowledged that many offenders against children remain undetected by legal authorities in the "Dunkelfeld" (literally "dark field") and are therefore not included in any official statistics, this program focuses on those who admit a longstanding sexual interest in prepubescent and/or early pubescent children, so-called pedophiles and hebephiles, self-motivated by the distress experienced due to their sexual preference (cf. www.dont-offend.org). It will be shown that these groups are reachable (given that they can rely on anonymity and the professional pledge of confidentiality) in order to improve the prevention of child sexual exploitation, because sexually deviant interests have been identified as a major risk factor for first or persistent sexual offending against children. Therefore, public health services have a real chance of encouraging the concerned persons to seek professional help before any kind of sexual offense against children is committed.

Abbreviations

BEDIT	Berlin Dissexuality Therapy
CAI	Child abuse images
CSA	Child sexual abuse
DRF	Dynamic risk factors
DSM	Diagnostic and statistical manual of mental disorders
ICD	International classification of mental and behavioural disorders

K.M. Beier (✉)
Charité – Universitätsmedizin, Berlin, Germany
e-mail: klaus.beier@charite.de

H. Kury et al. (eds.), *Women and Children as Victims and Offenders: Background, Prevention, Reintegration*, DOI 10.1007/978-3-319-28424-8_19

PPD	Prevention Project Dunkelfeld
PPJ	Prevention Project for Juveniles
TUK	ThinkUKnow

1 Introduction

The chapter describes the German prevention approach which aims at improving proactive strategies to protect children from sexual exploitation through online offenses, such as the consumption or distribution of child abuse images (CAI), and hands-on contact child sexual abuse (CSA). Official statistics account for only a fraction of all CSA and the use of CAI, inappropriately called "child pornography offenses". Those cases not reported to the authorities constitute the largest part of sexual offenses against children and are referred to as the "Dunkelfeld" (literally "dark field") in German. Consequently, preventive efforts must consider both primary prevention in the case of potential offenders and secondary prevention for self-referred offenders in the "Dunkelfeld".

Since its beginnings, the German prevention approach was based on the knowledge that in sexual offending against children two groups can be distinguished: On the one hand those showing no sexual preference disorder, but who, for different reasons, sexually abuse children, and on the other hand those showing a sexual preference disorder, namely pedophilia (i.e. the sexual preference for prepubescent minors) and/or hebephilia (i.e. the sexual preference for early pubescent minors).

Sexual preference usually manifests itself during adolescence and remains stable thereafter. This is true for pedophilia and hebephilia. Thus, pedophiles and hebephiles will always be at risk of offending and/or re-offending, mainly in the "Dunkelfeld". Furthermore, empirical data suggest that pedophiles and hebephiles show high levels of co-morbidity and distress due to the problems associated with their sexual preference. As a result, they are more likely than other sexual offenders to seek treatment. However, community-based specialized diagnostics and therapeutic programs for these self-referred individuals remain scarce.

For that reason, the Institute of Sexology and Sexual Medicine in Berlin (Germany) developed a prevention approach to encourage self-identified (but officially not registered) pedophiles and hebephiles to seek professional help to avoid committing CSA and the use of CAI. As part of the project, a media campaign was designed in order to reach the target group.

Between June 2005 and March 2015, on average 15–20 individuals contacted the research office in Berlin per month, resulting in 2,181 applications, 906 assessments, and treatment offers to 459 individuals. The smaller number of assessments was due to geographic distances—the applicants came from all over Germany and many of them were not able to commit to attending treatment sessions on a weekly basis. As expected, the vast majority were either pedophiles or hebephiles. Half of them had already committed child sexual abuse and three quarters admitted to the use of CAI in the "Dunkelfeld".

In a specialized one-year treatment program, the participants learn to ensure impulse control by using cognitive-behavioral techniques, sexological tools (integrating the attachment dimension in terms of an increase in social functioning), and pharmaceutical options (mostly androgen deprivation therapy). The evaluation of the Prevention Project Dunkelfeld (PPD) was performed in a non-randomized waiting list-control design with multiple assessments for 75 participants. It revealed that the primary prevention approach

- reduces risk factors for child sexual abuse,
- prevents sexual offending against minors and reduces the number of contact offenses,
- reduces the frequency and severity of the consumption of CAI.

Currently, the PPD is being expanded. In addition to the one in Berlin, nine further contact points in other German states have been successfully established.

In addition, there are aims of expanding on an international basis, because pedophilia and hebephilia represent a part of human sexuality and can therefore be found in any culture and in any country. Subsequently, a huge "Dunkelfeld" can be assumed in every country, too. Furthermore, particularly the use of child abuse images is a topic of international concern. Despite the fact that the legislation in Germany regarding the non-mandatory reporting practice concerning CSA and the use of CAI is crucial for the success of this preventive program (according to German law, it is considered a breach of confidentiality for the treating therapist to report either committed or planned CSA or use of CAI), the current situation in other countries—even those with mandatory reporting laws—would allow at least to focus on potential or real users of child abuse images in the "Dunkelfeld" for preventive purposes.

The use of child abuse images is an indicator for a pedophilic and/or hebephilic inclination and therefore the user is an important target for prevention. The PPD shows that it is possible to reach pedophiles/hebephiles from the community and to encourage these men to change their habit of using CAI. Furthermore, it indicates the probability of preventing a crossover to hands-on child sexual abuse—which would be a promising primary prevention approach for this cause. But, of course, it will only work, if trust is achieved and confidentiality reliably guaranteed.

2 Child Sexual Exploitation

Child sexual exploitation, i.e. child sexual abuse and the production and consumption of child abuse images, belittlingly and inappropriately called child pornography (even by the United Nations; see United Nations, General Assembly A/55/297), may constitute acute and persistent harm for the victims (Finkelhor et al. 2005). Results of a representative survey within the general public in Germany suggest that 2.8 % of men and 8.6 % of women are sexually traumatized in terms of contact offenses prior to the age of 16 years (Wetzels 1997). A review of 38 prevalence studies in 21 countries resulted in prevalence rates of recalled childhood sexual victimization of approximately 20 % for women and 10 % for men (Pereda et al. 2009). These high prevalence rates of child sexual exploitation go along with a growing understanding that the prevention of CSA and the use of CAI is a critical public health issue (Whitaker et al. 2008). In an American study, 91 % of victims of child sexual abuse had not reported their abuse (Henry and McMahon 2000). According to the United States Department of Justice, over 56,000 cases of child sexual abuse were reported and substantiated in the USA in 2007, but only approximately 30 % of cases were reported to the authorities.[1] Therefore, the majority of actual incidences involving sexual abuse of children is never reported to the police, is thus not registered by the judiciary and criminal prosecution authorities, and remains in the "Dunkelfeld".

In a recent comprehensive meta-analysis combining prevalence figures of child sexual abuse reported in 217 publications published between 1980 and 2008, including 331 independent samples with a total of 9,911,748 participants, the overall estimated CSA prevalence was 127/1000 in self-report studies and 4/1000 in informant studies. Self-reported CSA was more common among female (180/1000) than among male participants (76/1000). Lowest rates for both girls (113/1000) and boys (41/1000) were found in Asia, and highest rates were found for girls in Australia (215/1000) and for boys in Africa (193/1000). The results confirm that CSA is a global problem of considerable extent (Stoltenborgh et al. 2011).

Strong evidence identifies deviant sexual interests as a major risk factor for child sexual exploitation (Hanson and Bussière 1998; Mann et al. 2010). Offenders committing CSA differ from other men (sex offenders with adult victims, non-sex offenders, and non-offending volunteers) in their sexual responses to stimuli depicting prepubescent or early pubescent children in the laboratory (Blanchard et al. 2001; Blanchard et al. 2006). In addition, indicators of sexual interest in children are strong predictors for sexual recidivism among identified sex offenders in clinical or correctional samples (Hanson and Morton-Bourgon 2005). With respect to child abuse images, their use is regarded as a valid indicator of pedophilia (Seto et al. 2006).

3 Terminology and Phenomena

3.1 Sexual Preference

In general, human sexual preference can be described as being sexually attracted towards the gender and body age of one's partner and also the responsiveness concerning certain sexual interaction and practice with the partner. Besides the individual's self-concept, these characteristics are clinically revealed through the

[1] National Sex Offender Public Website (2012), accessed 12/10/2012.

exploration of sexual fantasies and behaviors. Due to cultural norms, self-concept and behavior may differ from sexual fantasies. Social desirability regarding deception of oneself and others is important if characteristics of the sexual preference are socially sanctioned and have to be kept private.

3.2 Characteristic of Preference: Body Age

The relevance of the physical developmental age for the description of sexual preference has been widely accepted (Banse et al. 2010; Freund et al. 1972; Ponseti et al. 2012). Often, this body age preference is determined by mature secondary sexual characteristics of an adult. The sexual preference for the adult, fully developed body age is referred to as teleiophilia (gr. "teleos"—fully grown) (Blanchard et al. 2000). In addition to teleiophilia, there is a distinguishable sexual responsiveness toward the sexually immature or not fully mature developmental age, especially among men.

Since Krafft-Ebing (1912) the sexual preference for prepubescent minors is referred to as pedophilia (gr. "pais"—child). Sexual preference for early pubescent minors was termed hebephilia (from the Greek goddess of youth "Hebe") by Glueck (1955). This sexually preferred physical age is characterized by the stage of transition from the prepubescent to an early pubescent body age, represented by the development of the secondary sexual characteristics (according to Tanner stages 2 and 3; cf. Tanner 1962). Typical for this transition is the incipient breast development with a slight warp in glandular tissue around the areola (so-called breast buds; i.e. "thelarche"). The beginning genital development is characterized by a small amount of pubic hair in form of downy hairs with slight pigmentation around the labia majora or around the root of the penis with no or only little growth of the penis or the labia. The term hebephilia has to be distinguished from ephebophilia (gr. "ephebos"—young man) and parthenophilia (gr. "parthenos"—virgin). Both refer to the sexual preference for male or female adolescents with mostly late pubescent body age (Tanner stages 4 and 5) and are subtypes of teleiophilia (Blanchard et al. 2000; Hirschfeld 1906).

Sixteen years ago, the onset of puberty (male genital development/female breast development) was around the age of 11 in Germany. Recent studies indicate an earlier onset of puberty as well as an acceleration of physical maturation. At the age of 10, half of the girls and more than one third of the boys report a beginning growth of pubic hair. The average age for reaching the late pubescent or adult pubic hair (Tanner stages 4 and 5) was age 12.3 or 13.4 for girls and age 13.4 or 14.1 for boys (Kahl and Schaffrath Rosario 2007). Blanchard and colleagues (2009) were able to distinguish pedophilic, hebephilic and teleiophilic preferences with penile plethysmograph measurement in large groups of delinquent sex offenders (n = 881), but also reported an overlap between these preference patterns. In earlier studies, this work group showed that men with a hebephilic preference had different characteristics (IQ, education, left-handedness, body height, and head injuries before the age of 13), i.e. exactly between the group of pedophiles and teleiophiles (overview cf. Blanchard et al. 2009).

3.3 *The Berlin Classification*

The exploration of the sexual preference for body age based on sexual fantasies often leads to a variety of different preferred ages. In addition to the exclusive types of sexual preference for a prepubescent, an early pubescent, or an adult body age, men report several fantasized body ages, e.g. proportionally existing sexual fantasies regarding the prepubescent and the early pubescent body age in one individual. In Fig. 1, possible combinations of preference are schematically displayed and exemplified in the following case studies (Beier et al. 2013).

3.4 *Sexual Preference Disorder*

Both the DSM and ICD list sexual preference for physically immature sexual partners with different diagnostic criteria in differently headlined groups (APA 2013; WHO 1993). In DSM-5, the term "Pedophilic Disorder" is defined as "sexually arousing fantasies, sexual urges, or behaviors involving sexual activity with a prepubescent child or children (generally age 13 years or younger)" and belongs to the category "Paraphilic Disorders".

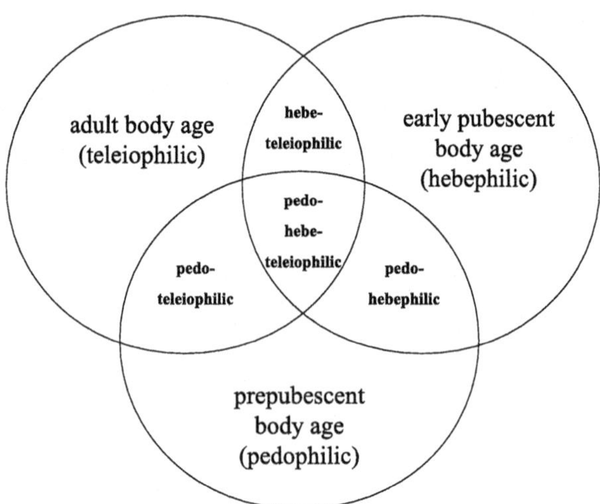

Fig. 1 Sexual preference for body ages according to the Berlin classification: teleiophilic—hebephilic—pedophilic and mixed forms

In ICD-10, pedophilia is defined as a "sexual preference for children, boys or girls, or both, usually of pre-pubertal or early pubertal age" and belongs to the category "Sexual Preference Disorders". A sexual preference for early pubertal children as a separate diagnostic category is not provided in the DSM-5 classification. In ICD-10 this preference is summarized under "pedophilia". The ICD-10 classification has, on the one hand, the advantage of considering prepubescent as well as early pubescent body age, and on the other hand, the disadvantage of not allowing for a terminological differentiation. In the ICD-10 classification, as well as in the DSM-5 classification, a sexual preference or a paraphilic disorder is not diagnosed unless the sexual preference or paraphilia goes along with a clinically significant degree of distress or impairment. It needs to be taken into account that pedophilia fulfills characteristics of a disorder even without the existence of a threat of endangering others (real offenders vs. non-offenders). Comparing pedophilia to other paraphilias, the acting out of the preference can be seen as an idiosyncratic clinically relevant criterion (Blanchard 2010).

The underlying consideration is that refraining from this socially sanctioned form of sexual interaction constitutes sufficient impairment of social functioning inevitably causing psychological distress to the person involved. DSM-5 claims that the individual has to be at least 16 years old and at least 5 years older than the sexually abused child. A significant part of distress in pedophilically inclined persons is the final realization that their often unwanted and internally rejected sexual preference is stable over a longer period of time. According to present knowledge, the sexual preference of a person in its individual characteristics manifests itself during puberty and is marked by constant sexual fantasies over the life span. Therefore, Seto (2012) recently discussed the conceptualization of a sexual preference for minors as a "sexual orientation", similar to gynaephilia (attraction to females) or androphilia (attraction to males). He identified a pubertal onset, associated sexual and romantic behaviors with the desired partner, and the relative stability over the life time as core features of a sexual orientation, and described some relevant empirical data on detected offenders that support this conceptualization. Therapeutic efforts to change characteristics of preference such as the preferred gender of one's partner showed no effects, especially not in the long term (Spitzer 2012). Regarding the ability of therapeutically influencing characteristics such as the body age or the sexual practice preference, there is disagreement concerning the consistency; nonetheless, there has been no evidence so far as to the ability of changing this preference.

Therefore, it needs to be understood that the sexual preference structure of any human in its individual characteristics (standard norm to paraphilic) is established in adolescence and, according to present scientific knowledge, from then on remains manifest and is not categorically changeable, i.e. an orientation toward the adult male gender cannot be transformed into an orientation toward the adult female gender, a fetishist orientation cannot be erased, etc. (cf., e.g., Seto 2012; Spitzer 2012).

This is also expected to be the case in pedophiles, and to date there is no convincing evidence to the contrary.

In a recent study on the stability of sexual preference in pedophilic men (Müller et al. 2014)—implementing phallometric measurements over a course of time in altogether 43 participants-, the authors came to the conclusion that changes would have come about in time (on average there were 50 months between two measurement settings). However, the authors were vehemently criticized due to methodological weaknesses (e.g. unrecorded faulty measurement variance; classification of control groups on the basis of the initial characteristic on the dependent variable; significantly different entry levels of pedophilic arousal of the two groups; a high proportion of convicted offenders), arguing that the generated effects were merely the result of technical faults in measurement within the course of this generally weakly rated study design (Cantor 2014; Lalumière 2014; Bailey 2014).

Analyzing self-reports of participants in the Berlin PPD at different stages in time (three measurements with averagely 1–2 years' time lapse), there was no recording of any significant changes in sexual preference (Grundmann et al. 2016).

With respect to the use of CAI, most self-identified pedophiles reported that CAI is sexually arousing and many acknowledged using these materials at some point in their life (Neutze et al. 2010; Quayle and Taylor 2002; Riegel 2004). Also, detected "child pornography offenders" showed pedophilic patterns of sexual arousal. By comparing phallometric test results of 100 "child pornography offenders" with those of 178 sex offenders with child victims, a group of "child pornography offenders" showed significantly greater sexual arousal to children than did a group of offenders against children. Overall, 61 % of the "child pornography offenders" showed a preference for depictions of children over depictions of adults (Seto et al. 2006). Thus, the use of child abuse images is a valid indicator of pedophilia, because men generally choose to view pornography corresponding to their sexual interests.

On the other hand, the diagnosis of pedophilia is not applicable to all child sexual abusers or the users of child abuse images (Seto 2008). Approximately 60 % of men detained for sexual abuse of children cannot be diagnosed as having a preference disorder in the sense of pedophilia. Offenses are often committed as a substitute activity for sexual interaction with desired adult partners who are, for various reasons (e.g., sexually inexperienced adolescents seeking a surrogate; mentally retarded persons and those with antisocial personality disorders; or perpetrators within generally traumatizing family constellations), not available. By contrast, approximately 40 % of men sentenced for child sexual abuse fulfill the diagnostic criteria for pedophilia (Beier 1998). Pedophilia and offending against children are also not synonymous.

As shown in Fig. 2, there are pedophilic men who manage to restrict their desire for sexual contact with children to fantasies only, as well as others who realize that fantasizing does not satisfy their needs and fear their impulses getting stronger, eventually leading to child sexual abuse. These latter are potential offenders and some of them wish to avoid that their impulses overwhelm them and therefore seek therapeutic help. It is helpful to be aware of the fact that men with this pedophilic inclination have been living with sexual arousal fantasies about children's bodies since puberty, and that they have had to control these impulses in order not to

Fig. 2 Pedophilia and sexual offending against children

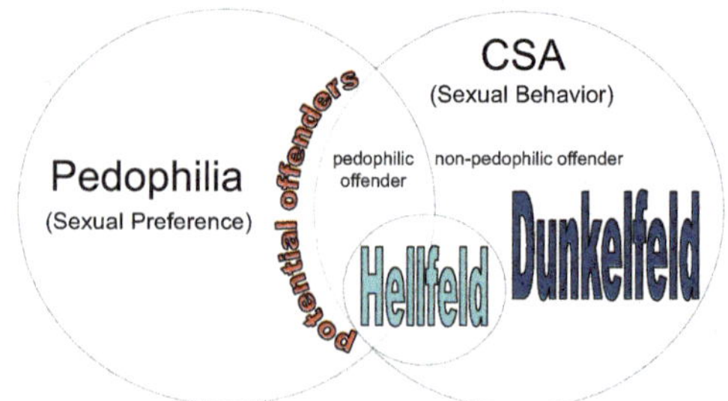

become an offender and not to traumatize children, not even in the internet by using child abuse images. Furthermore, it is necessary to consider that most sexual assaults happen in the "Dunkelfeld" (whereas "Hellfeld" cases are reflected by official statistics).

Several typologies of not sexually motivated online offenders have been suggested in the literature. For example, it is suggested that some online offenders access child abuse images out of curiosity, by accident, or in order to shock people, without a specific sexual arousal function. Others create and distribute CAI solely for financial gain (Krone 2004; Lanning 2001).

Finally, because most research on pedophilia is based on forensic mental health or correctional samples of sex offenders, little is known about pedophiles who are not formally involved with the criminal justice system, and even less is known about the factors that distinguish those who act upon their sexual interest in prepubescent or early pubescent children from those who do not.

However, as pedophiles have been found to have a greater risk to recommit CSA or to use CAI, particularly at an early age (Eke et al. 2010), it must be assumed that these individuals also have a greater life-time risk for initial offending, and therefore they are considered to be an important target group for prevention approaches.

The relevance of a sexual preference for children regarding sexual offending behavior is all the more worrying considering data from the general population, which revealed that one fifth of university males reported some sexual attraction to small children, and one tenth had fantasized about having sex with children (Briere and Runtz 1989). Using phallometry, researchers have found that non-pedophilic men also show penile response to pictures of early pubescent and prepubescent images of children (Quinsey et al. 1975). Over a quarter of community participants in another study indicated pedophilic interests via self-reporting or phallometric response (Hall et al. 1995). Lykins and colleagues studied sexual arousal in a clinical and forensic sample of 214 men sexually attracted to females. Participants (no child sexual abuse and/or "child pornography offenders") showed physiological arousal to early pubescent and prepubescent girls, as measured by phallometric testing. Arousal to prepubescent girls was greater than to neutral stimuli (Lykins et al. 2010).

Many, but not all, child sexual offenses were committed by pedophiles. Phallometric research revealed that about half of first-time child sex offenders were not pedophilic (Blanchard et al. 2001). This underlines the importance of a reliable assessment of sexual orientation in child sex offenders, given that treatment strategies for child sex offenders depend on the offenders' sexual preferences. Assessment of sexual preferences in child sex offenders is also important for the prediction of recidivism, because the probability of re-offending is much higher in pedophilic child sex offenders than in non-pedophilic child sex offenders (Hanson and Bussière 1998; Hanson and Morton-Bourgon 2005).

Recent research has shown that pedophilic interests can be assessed using specific brain response measurement to visual sexual stimuli (Ponseti et al. 2012). Thus, automatic pattern classification of MRI scans could be a promising advance in the objective measurement of pedophilia.

Recent epidemiological data state that the prevalence of a pedophilic inclination is between 0.37 % and 6 % of the male population (Ahlers et al. 2009). In comparison: 1 % is the prevalence of Parkinson's disease in the German male population. While many people may know someone who is suffering from Parkinson's disease, only few will be consciously aware of knowing a pedophilic person: pedophilia cannot be (visibly) identified and those affected do not admit to it for fear of social discrimination; not even when they have never offended against children.

It is important to acknowledge that no one can "choose" his or her sexual preference—it is a matter of "fate, not choice"—, which is why it would be wrong to pass moral judgement on it. Moral judgement is only permitted—and then by all means—when someone acts on his or her sexual interest in children, thereby damaging the individuality and integrity of a child. Moreover, clinical experience suggests that sexual age and gender preference manifests itself at a young age as part of sexual identity and remains unchanged over the lifespan (APA 2000; Beier 1998; Wille 1968).

Thus, from their late teens or early twenties on, individuals sexually interested in children have to cope with the ramifications of their unusual sexual preference (Schaefer et al. 2010). Facing these challenges time and time again, the development of clinically significant distress at some point would not be surprising. Thus, non-offending pedophiles and pedophilic offenders in the "Dunkelfeld" appear to be ideal target groups for the prevention of sexual offending against children: they are at-risk individuals, some of whom are motivated for treatment due to distress and therefore reachable (Beier, Ahlers et al. 2009; Schaefer et al. 2010).

4 Dynamic Risk Factors and Treatment

Dynamic risk factors (DRF) have been described to be associated with the likelihood of re-offending and potentially responsive to interventions. A number of meta-analyses have shown the importance of addressing DRF in the treatment of

sexual offenders (Hanson and Bussière 1998; Hanson and Morton-Bourgon 2005; Mann et al. 2010).

DRF are included in contemporary theories of sexual offending against children or pathological internet use, and are considered to be important treatment targets within prevention approaches aiming at detected sex offenders (Davis 2001; Ward and Beech 2006; Quayle and Taylor 2003). In past research on CSA offenders, a set of DRF has been identified (Hanson and Harris 2000; Hanson et al. 2007). It was suggested that sexual reoffending is predicted by three major types of dynamic risk factors: (1) emotional or intimacy deficits; (2) offense-supportive cognitions such as the belief that children benefit from sex with adults; and (3) problems with sexual and general self-regulation (e.g., sexual preoccupation, poor cognitive problem-solving skills, impulsivity) (Hanson et al. 2007). However, the extent to which identified recidivism risk factors are applicable to pedophiles at risk to initially offend or to undetected pedophile offenders has not yet been established (Duff and Willis 2006). Other factors such as denial, minimization, poor victim empathy, or low self-esteem could not be empirically supported, although clinicians deem them to be core elements of sex offender treatment. These factors might enhance treatment responsivity through motivation for treatment and help to constitute therapeutic alliance (Marshall et al. 2006).

5 Primary and Secondary Prevention Efforts

Conventionally, primary prevention efforts focus on children, families, teachers, youth welfare and social service workers, and others who may be in a position to intervene. Educational programs have been most successfully delivered through schools and have recently also been adopted by other organizations (Finkelhor 2009). The main goal is to teach the difference between acceptable and unacceptable touching and how to disclose to a trusted adult if sexual touching occurs. Evaluation data suggest that school-based programs increase knowledge about sexual abuse and protection strategies, and participants are more likely to report experiencing sexual abuse (Gibson and Leitenberg 2000; Rispens et al. 1997). A more recent meta-analysis on studies evaluating school-based programs in North America found improvements in knowledge and protective behaviors in simulated at-risk situations among children asked a short time after participating, but also revealed increased anxiety (Zwi et al. 2007). Regarding prevention of the use of CAI or additional online offenses against children (e.g., grooming), approaches such as the ThinkUKnow (TUK) program provide internet safety advice to children aged between 5 and 16 years, parents, and professionals. However, first evaluation data on a non-stratified sample of 1,718 children (aged 11–16) do not suggest a decrease in risk-taking internet behavior after participating in TUK (e.g., interaction and sharing personal information with strangers). Also, more than half of the program participants report difficulties to recall the safety messages well or over time, and even if they do, they do not always act on the advice

(Davidson et al. 2009). Thus, educational approaches addressing the prevention of internet offenses need to be expanded with an appropriate quality management including evaluation.

Primary prevention can also be focused on at-risk individuals, including persons who are pedophilically or hebephilically inclined and who have not yet sexually offended against children. That is why the general idea of primary prevention is to prevent the offense itself, no matter how. Therefore, targeting pedophiles at risk to commit initial offenses could also be seen as a proactive primary prevention approach, given that strategies provide successful preventive treatment to these individuals (Beier, Neutze et al. 2009; Beier and Neutze 2012). There are few clinical data suggesting that men sexually interested in children may be reached for prevention offers before initial child sexual offending behavior occurs. For example, a Canadian outpatient clinic for men with paraphilic sexual disorders was contacted by 26 non-offending and self-referred pedophiles (Fedoroff et al. 2001). It is a fact that these patients, as well as some self-referred patients in another study (Bogaert et al. 1997), sought professional help because they experienced distress related to their sexual preference for minors. Regardless of whether these patients were distressed out of fear of society, or out of a sense of being sick or dangerous to society, their distress was clearly related to their sexual preference (Schaefer et al. 2010).

Despite this, some authors have defined preventive work with at-risk (not yet offending) individuals as secondary (Seto 2008). This does not hold true, because secondary prevention is called for to prevent a relapse if an offense has already occurred—even if it has not been detected and took place in the "Dunkelfeld". One approach dealing with at-risk individuals in a primary and a secondary preventive way is the "Stop It Now!" campaign that uses social marketing strategies to reach persons who are at risk of committing sexual offenses against children in order to convince them to seek treatment and to encourage non-offending adults to intervene if they suspect that child sexual abuse may take place. With numbers of up to 1,960 self-identified potential (n = 313) or "Dunkelfeld" (n = 249) offenders voluntarily contacting the campaign office within a four-year period, and 34 % of all calls addressing the use of CAI or other internet offenses, the results of the "Stop it Now!" campaign indicate a similar demand for comparable prevention approaches (Stop it Now 2009).

Other strategies try to mobilize third parties (family members, friends, and colleagues of either victims or offenders) to detect situations where abuse is actually or potentially occurring and to intervene or report the situation. Some surveys have shown that overall community knowledge and attitudes about sexual abuse can shift in the wake of advertising campaigns (Chasan-Taber and Tabachnick 1999).

However, a fundamental problem with the hot line and self-referral strategy for potential offenders is that, given the current statutory and retributive environment of most countries, it is difficult to promise or persuade an offender that he will receive confidential help.

6 Legal Framework Conditions in Germany

In Germany, all those working in community-based treatment programs are subject to the requirement of confidentiality (section 203 of the Criminal Code: "Violation of private secrets"—imprisonment for not more than 1 year or a fine), which also includes information regarding sexual abuse (the only explicit exception is the treatment of previously convicted offenders in the context of so-called supervision of conduct, section 68a (8) of the Criminal Code).

The requirement of confidentiality also applies to possible future child sexual abuse, since it is not listed in section 138 of the Criminal Code ("Failure to report planned crimes")—in contrast to, among others, serious trafficking in human beings, murder, manslaughter or other crimes against personal liberty (in which case the failure to report would constitute a punishable offense).

However, with reference to section 34 of the Criminal Code ("Necessity as justification"), medical confidentiality can be broken and the case reported to the police if the therapist is convinced, in the context of a community-based treatment relationship, that a patient will commit a sex offense. The clinician can then invoke the fact that, upon weighing the conflicting interests, the protected interest that is in danger (abuse of a child) substantially outweighs the one interfered with (the requirement of confidentiality). Nevertheless, under the Criminal Code this only applies to the extent that reporting the matter "is a proportionate means to avert the danger". That is questionable, since the person reported will deny any motivation whatsoever to commit the offense when official investigations are instituted, and permanent deprivation of liberty cannot be justified on this basis. In addition, one must remember in the context of self-referred pedophiles who seek self-motivated professional help, that these individuals want to prevent anything from happening, which is the experience taken from the PPD (see below): A conflict could only arise if different assessments were made of the risk that the impulse can no longer be controlled and the participant does not act on the means of averting the danger recommended by the therapist. But even in such a case (which, to date, has never occurred in the PPD), the participant would not reveal his inner life to the authorities if he were reported, and he would no longer be accessible for interventions.

For that reason, the legal situation in Germany must be regarded as an extremely favorable starting point for prevention work in this field, because it enables a protective framework which leads to potential offenders or real undetected offenders being prepared to accept help in the first place. Since, however, these offenders certainly do exist and the probability that they would commit their first or further sexual offenses or use of CAI would be much greater if they did not accept help, it is definitely better to have the opportunity to begin an intervention than not to gain any access to this target group at all.

With regard to prevention work, Germany is in a privileged position compared to other countries, since in other countries therapists working in community projects are subject to the requirement of disclosure if they become aware of acts of child sexual abuse or the use of CAI, or if they have reason for suspecting their patient to commit such acts. An ethical debate on this matter would raise the question of whether utilitarian principles (choice of the lesser evil) in view of the benefit achieved (being able to prevent offenses against sexual self-determination) permit a procedure obligated more to protecting children than a strictly normative orientation (duty to report cases on account of the interest being in danger), which is also linked to the restriction of civil liberties (lifting of requirement of confidentiality).

The ethical dilemma is therefore not about the question of whether or not a therapist reports one single individual to the authorities in order to try to protect one single child. The ethical dilemma is about the question whether a society creates or obstructs circumstances which allow a higher number of individuals to face their problems, giving professionals the opportunity of protecting a greater number of children.

7 The Prevention Project Dunkelfeld (PPD)

In 2005, the PPD was launched as an approach for the therapeutic prevention of sexual offenses against children. At the beginning, it was supported by the foundation "Volkswagen Stiftung", the child protection organization "Hänsel und Gretel", and the advertising agency "Scholz and Friends". Since 2008, it is funded by the German government.

Through a media campaign, self-identified, judicially unknown pedophiles and hebephiles were encouraged to seek professional help to avoid committing CSA and using CAI (Beier, Ahlers et al. 2009). The media campaign encouraged the necessity of an empathic, non-judgemental, non-discriminating, non-pathologizing, non-criminalizing approach, assuring anonymity and resulting in the following message: "You are not guilty because of your sexual desire, but you are responsible for your sexual behavior. There is help! Do not become an offender!" (see Fig. 3).

Individuals are screened by trained interviewers with respect to basic sociodemographic data, sexual interests, criminal history, use of sexually non-explicit and explicit materials for sexual arousal, and data on current and lifetime involvement with the authorities related to sexual offending behavior (Beier, Ahlers et al. 2009). Also, appointments for information on the treatment and further assessments are offered. The clinical interview serves primarily to assess aspects of psychosexual development, criminological data to verify the presence of pedophilia or hebephilia, and to verify the absence of the treatment exclusion criteria (see below).

Questionnaires are administered in order to assess previously identified risk factors including offense-supportive attitudes, empathy deficits, loneliness, intimacy deficits, coping strategies, sexual and general self-regulation, personality measures, self-reported psychopathy, perceived self-efficacy to control problematic

Fig. 3 Image from the Berlin Prevention Project Dunkelfeld's media campaign. Text translates as: "Do you like children in ways you should not? There is help free of charge and confidential. Charité—Institute of Sexology and Sexual Medicine". The TV spot is available under www.dont-offend.org

behavior, and attitudes towards the use of CAI (Neutze et al. 2010). In addition, questionnaires are administered to investigate the individual's motivation for starting treatment and to establish the preconditions for an evaluation of the treatment results.

Finally, decisions regarding the inclusion of an individual into the treatment evaluation study are made following a clinical case conference. Individuals with acute drug or alcohol problems, psychotic disorders, or developmental disabilities are excluded from the treatment program, as resources for appropriate treatment or management of their special needs are not available. Volunteers who had currently been involved with the legal authorities (e.g., being investigated for sexual crime, being under parole) are also excluded.

A treatment program was developed, the *Berlin Dissexuality Therapy* (BEDIT 2013). According to the integrated theory of sexual offending, the group-based treatment program using a broad cognitive-behavioral approach was developed as a multimodal program comprising pharmacological (particularly androgene deprivation treatment), psychotherapeutical, and sexological intervention strategies to prevent child sexual offending behavior in pedophiles and hebephiles (Ward and Beech 2006; Beier and Loewit 2013). Cognitive-behavioral interventions include aspects of the relapse prevention, the self-regulation, and the good-lives model (Pithers 1990; Ward and Gannon 2006; Ward and Hudson 1998, 2000). Treatment targets comprise motivation for change, self-efficacy, self-monitoring (including sexual fantasies and interests), sexualized versus adequate coping strategies, emotional and sexual self-regulation, social functioning, attachment and sexuality, offense-supportive attitudes, empathy with children involved in CSA or the use of CAI, and relapse prevention strategies and goals. The written manual provides strategies to deal with threats of contact child sexual abuse during therapy.

The BEDIT is a treatment approach in line with current practice in the United States of America and Canada, where most treatment providers for detected sex offenders identify themselves with a broader cognitive-behavioral approach (McGrath et al. 2010). However, adaptations of previously existing treatment approaches were required in order to meet basic assumptions derived from years of clinical experience gained at the Berlin outpatient clinic with individual treatment of clients suffering from sexual preference disorders. These basic assumptions are (Beier et al. 2005; Beier and Loewit 2013):

1. The sexual (body) age and gender preference, and additional paraphilia-associated sexual arousal patterns are unchangeable components of an individual's personality. An individual is not responsible for their existence, but for behavioral consequences thereof. Thus, dealing with inappropriate sexual impulses directed at prepubescent or early pubescent children is linked to lifelong demands regarding sexual self-regulation and behavioral control.
2. Because sexual fantasies are genuinely integrated into an individual's personality structure, sexually deviant fantasies can undermine self-esteem and lead to personal devaluation, which, in turn, impedes the development of a socially adequate coping strategy for dealing with one's sexual impulses.
3. Based on a multi-dimensional understanding of sexuality (three dimensions: desire, reproduction and attachment), it needs to be taken into account that pedophilically inclined individuals try to achieve fulfilment within the dimension of attachment (focusing on the bio-psycho-social needs for acceptance, security and warmth) with a child as a partner. Therefore, it is necessary to establish other relationships in order to receive these emotionally stabilizing factors, even if those persons are not attractive on the level of sexual desire according to the sexual preference structure.

In summary, the treatment program BEDIT is based on three pillars that represent the bio-psycho-social nature of the preventive approach: sexological interventions help participants to accept their sexual interest by integrating their fantasies into their self-concept in order to assume responsibility for sexual behaviors; cognitive-behavioral therapy improves the participants' general and sexual self-regulation by restructuring attitudes toward sexuality and increasing coping and social skills; with the aid of pharmacotherapy, sexual impulses and fantasies can additionally be reduced (Beier et al. 2010; Amelung et al. 2012).

8 First Results from the Prevention Project Dunkelfeld (PPD)

Between June 2005 and March 2015, on average 15–20 individuals contacted the research office in Berlin per month, resulting in 2,181 applications, 906 assessments and treatment offers to 459 individuals. The decrease was mainly due to geographic distances.

The applicants came from all over Germany. As expected, the vast majority were either pedophiles or hebephiles. Half of them had already committed CSA, and three quarters admitted to the use of CAI in the "Dunkelfeld".

The men seeking help were on average 38 years old. They belonged to all levels of society, most of them were single at the time of questioning, one third had children of their own. They have all become aware of their pedophilia at an average age of 22 years.

In a pilot study within a sample of self-identified help-seeking pedophiles and hebephiles from the community participating voluntarily in the PPD, the effects of a one-year group treatment program were examined. Applying a non-randomized waiting list control design, a treatment group and control group were assessed before and after a twelve-month treatment/waiting period, respectively. Within-group and between-groups comparisons were conducted to evaluate treatment change (Beier et al. 2015).

Analyses of pre-treatment dropouts indicated no selection bias for the observed sample and distance to the location of the program as a major obstacle for participation. Characteristics of dropouts from treatment pointed at problems including men with additional paraphilias, and a selection bias towards better-educated participants. Treated individuals showed multiple changes on dynamic risk factors in the desired direction.

After treatment, participants reported less loneliness, less emotion-oriented coping, less emotional victim empathy deficits, less CSA-supportive attitudes, less coping self-efficacy deficits, and less sexual preoccupation compared to their pre-treatment scores. Treatment change was distributed differentially over lifetime offender groups. Lifetime mixed offenders seemed to have benefited the most. In contrast to the hypotheses, self-esteem deficits, cognitive victim empathy deficits, and sexualized coping did not improve significantly over treatment.

Relapse occurred for both CSA and the use of CAI with rates in the treated group of 20 % and 91 %, respectively. No initial offending occurred for CSA. However, 24 % of men with no history of the use of CAI reported the first-time consumption of these materials over treatment. Single item analyses showed a trend towards a reduction of severity of persistent CSA behaviors for treated individuals.

Regarding the sample composition, most outstanding was the absence of women applying for the project. Given the focus on sexual preference disorder rather than sexual behavior, this finding might underline an assumed difference between male and female sexual offenders. On the other hand, female pedophiles may not have felt addressed by the media campaign depicting a man feeling aroused by children.

The psychometric results are in line with previous research on modulation of dynamic risk factors through therapy in sexual offenders (Beggs and Grace 2011; Wischka 2013; Edwards et al. 2012; O'Reilly et al. 2010). With lifetime mixed offenders, a high risk group showed the greatest benefit from the program. This finding may point at differential needs in pedophiles and hebephiles in the "Dunkelfeld".

Given that the treatment manual was based on manuals for convicted sex offenders, it appears reasonable that this high-risk group's needs were best addressed. The seeming loss of self-esteem in the overall treatment group represents a change towards normative scores and is thus difficult to interpret. Whether on a behavioral level the numbers represent a "change for the better" remains unanswered. Strikingly, only cognitive empathy with child sexual abuse victims before treatment differentiated persisters. The phenomenon is not new. Barnett et al. (2012) found only weak relationships between psychological markers and recidivism, and pre-treatment more helpful than post-treatment scores.

Regarding the use of CAI, approx. 90 % of the sample reported further consumption of child abuse images and were therefore classified as persisters. Of further concern are men taking up the consumption of these materials. This obvious lack of effect on child abuse image use may result from an iatrogenic effect, e.g., that non-offenders learned how to offend online when participating in group treatment with real offenders. This cannot be ruled out, as the original design did not provide for a differentiation of group participants according to their offense history.

Given the small sample at hand and short observation period, it would be premature to draw any firm conclusions. Furthermore, the relation between self-reported behaviors and recidivism in detected offenders is complex. Concerning recidivism in terms of offenses known to the legal authorities, the recidivism rate within the PPD was 0 % for CSA and for the use of CAI, as none of the self-reported offenses during the course of treatment was detected or reported. This finding underlines the significance of the "Dunkelfeld" for both research on child abusive behaviors and the sexual traumatization of children.

However, the German primary prevention approach shows that it is possible to reach pedophiles and hebephiles from the community and it is widely accepted by the public. Since July 2012 with the help of Google AdWords, potential consumers of child abuse images are guided to the therapeutic offer of the PPD by typical search keywords. Since the beginning of the project in 2012 until the year 2015, there have been more than 20 million Ad Impressions and more than 240,000 clicks on the website (www.dont-offend.org).

Currently, the PPD is being expanded. In addition to the one in Berlin, nine further contact points in other German states have been successfully established. One of the exclusion criteria of the PPD was the age limit of over 18 years. This—as well as the success of the PPD—has encouraged the launching of a further project at the Institute of Sexology and Sexual Medicine of the Charité in Berlin (Germany) in November 2014: the Prevention Project for Juveniles (PPJ). The project aims at this target group with the help of a media campaign and with the same proactive prevention approach in mind, but focusing on the special particularities of adolescents (Beier et al. 2016). This new project will also be funded by the German government.

9 Outlook and New Challenges

It is commonly known that there are cultures in which girls get married before being at the developmental stage of an adult woman (although it is not a hallmark of most cultures; see Buss 1989). However, this should be no reason not to differentiate between a sexually erotic responsiveness toward the body of a child (in the sense of pedophilia) as a motivational reason for sexual contact to minors, and social traditions, in which men who marry their wives as a child are not automatically responsive toward the body of a child. In the latter case, their sexual interest in the partner usually awakens when she develops the body scheme of an adult woman.

Rather, the aim and intention must be to reveal the pedophilic inclination in the person concerned in order to ensure that this preference toward children is not acted out on the behavioral level. In this sense, it is necessary to relieve the individual by making it easier for them to come forward and take responsibility by learning to reliably control their behavior, if necessary–and in most cases called for–with therapeutic support. Yet, one can only expect pedophilic individuals to take this step, if the underlying social and legal framework allows for such an opening, i.e. if fear of social stigmatization is minimized.

Conversely, those social stratifications need to be considered, which promote the realization of sexual contact to children by pedophiles. To give an example, the caste system in India reduces the likelihood of victims of sexual assault or abuse (in particular if they belong to a lower caste than the offenders) to come forward and confide in law enforcement authorities, because their trust in these institutions is low and they feel that they can hardly hope for support (Harendra de Silva 2007).

Further obstacles for this are the lacking (health) structures of supply that could help victims to get over their experienced traumatization. This is all the more to be deplored, given that study results concerning psychological consequences of trauma strongly indicate that neurobiological changes in brain structure might (negatively) influence the future lives of the victims. This involves, for instance, measurable cortical thickness in the somato-sensorical cortex exactly in those areas responsible for the sensitive interconnection within the genitals (Heim et al. 2013).

The comparatively riskless viewing of child abuse images due to the various opportunities offered by the internet will in the near future lead to a situation where, at an early stage (i.e. during adolescence) practically every pedophile and hebephile will have been exposed to the temptation of using these images and will be a more or less experienced consumer. This makes the consumption of CAI a crucial target for primary prevention, especially because the group of "child pornography offenders" will then be likely to already include those later committing contact offenses. There should be no contradiction between law enforcement and the promotion of preventive strategies, and detected "child pornography offenders" should regularly be assessed to secure prevention on a reliable basis to avoid crossover (hands-on) offenses.

The fact that a certain social framework is basically in a position of promoting sexual violence, which does not only involve danger and harm for children, but also for women, can currently very impressively be seen from the example set in India, where a number of rape cases of women (partly by groups of men, and some with lethal outcome) have become public and, as a result, have led to massive protests within the community. It is most likely that rapes such as those have taken place in the past, but were not made public. There are possibly very different reasons from the point of view of the rapists for their actions and these should and could be very carefully analyzed. From a sexological point of view, it is to be assumed that the offenders experience sexual arousal by acting out coercion and violence, and by experiencing power, this being a characteristic of their sexual preference structure. Other elements of these crimes are circumstantially related to a depreciatory perception of women, indicating insecure male identities in an ever changing world in which, in reality, there are even societies distinguishing themselves by their endeavours to obtain gender equality.

The availability of information via new media and internet technologies, particularly in a country like India, also encompasses the availability of pornographic contents and, along with that, contrasting role images of men and women, which are highly focused on sexual interaction and depict (by film) the consumatory aspect of other human beings obviously being degraded and treated as mere objects. The fact that all this reaches a young, maturing generation having access to all this film and image material on the internet, is a huge challenge for the next decade. There is no way of stopping technological development, so it should be the aim to steer it in a reasonable direction by implementing well-conceived and effective counter measures for the benefit of society.

There can definitively be no doubt that the prevention of sexual violence against children and women is a global health issue and should be regarded as such.

10 Conclusions

The importance of the first results from the Berlin Prevention Project Dunkelfeld (PPD) for current policy is highlighted in the following:

1. A significant number of pedophiles and hebephiles from the community are not known to the justice system and have no contact with preventive services. These pedophilic and hebephilic men are either potential offenders or real offenders. However, they remain undetected in the "Dunkelfeld".
2. Many pedophiles and hebephiles who are not known to the justice system would be willing to participate in a treatment program aiming to prevent child sexual

abuse and the use of child abuse images, provided they know how to access it and feel they can trust on anonymity and the pledge of confidentiality by experts specialized in assessment and therapy of their disorder.
3. A media campaign is able to communicate these goals.
4. The legislation in Germany regarding the reporting of child sexual abuse and the use of child abuse images is an advantage for the success of this preventive program: According to German law, it is considered a breach of confidentiality for the treating therapist to report either committed or planned child sexual abuse or use of child abuse images.
5. The current situation in countries with mandatory reporting laws concerning CSA and the use of CAI would allow at least to focus on potential offenders, and, in those countries with mandatory reporting laws only concerning CSA (but not the use of CAI), in addition even on real users of child abuse images in the "Dunkelfeld" for preventive purposes. The use of child abuse images is an indicator for a pedophilic inclination and therefore the user is an important target for prevention. The PPD shows that it is possible to reach pedophiles/hebephiles from the community and to encourage these men to change their habit of using child abuse images. Furthermore, it indicates the probability of preventing crossover to child sexual abuse—which would be a promising primary prevention approach for this cause. It will work, if trust is achieved, i.e., by ensuring anonymous and confidential access to prevention offers.

Five Questions

1. Pedophilia is a sexual preference disorder according to the ICD-10 of the World Health Organization. Why is it socially stigmatized, even if the person has never acted out his sexual impulses towards children?
2. Which obstacles need to be overcome in other countries in order to establish the German primary prevention approach there?
3. Why do victim-based and offender-based prevention measures often seem contradictory?
4. How is it possible to involve all social forces in the fight against sexual exploitation, regarding it as a serious public health problem in societies all over the world?
5. Why is it so difficult to effectively stop the worldwide distribution of sexually abusive images depicting minors, including posing material?

References

Ahlers, C. J., Schaefer, G. A., Mundt, I. A., Roll, S., Englert, H., Willich, S., et al. (2009). How unusual are the contents of paraphilias – Prevalence of paraphilia-associated sexual arousal patterns (PASAPs) in a community-based sample of men. *Journal of Sexual Medicine, 8*, 1362–1370. doi:10.1111/j.1743-6109.2009.01597.

Amelung, T., Kuhle, L. F., Konrad, A., Pauls, A., & Beier, K. M. (2012). Androgen deprivation therapy of self-identifying, help-seeking pedophiles in the Dunkelfeld. *International Journal of Law and Psychiatry, 35*, 176–184.

American Psychiatric Association APA (2000). *Diagnostic and statistical manual of mental disorders* (4th ed., text rev.). Arlington VA: American Psychiatric Association.

American Psychiatric Association APA. (2013). *Diagnostic and statistical manual of mental disorders DSM-5*. Washington, D.C.: American Psychiatric Association.

Bailey, J. M. (2014). A failure to demonstrate changes in sexual interest in pedophilic men: Comment on Müller et al. (2014). *Archives of sexual behavior, 44*, 249–252.

Banse, R., Schmidt, A. F., & Clarbour, J. (2010). Indirect measures of sexual interest in child sex offenders a multimethod approach. *Criminal Justice and Behavior, 37*, 319–335.

Barnett, G. D., Wakeling, H. C., Mandeville-Norden, R., & Rakestrow, J. (2012). How useful are psychometric scores in predicting recidivism for treated sex offenders? *International Journal of Offender Therapy and Comparative Criminology, 56*, 420–446.

BEDIT. (2013). *The Berlin dissexuality therapy program*. Weimar: Gutenberg Druckerei GmbH.

Beggs, S. M., & Grace, R. C. (2011). Treatment gain for sexual offenders against children predicts reduced recidivism: A comparative validity study. *Journal of Consulting and Clinical Psychology, 79*, 182–192.

Beier, K. M. (1998). Differential typology and prognosis for dissexual behaviour - a follow-up study of previously expert-appraised child molesters. *International Journal of Legal Medicine, 111*, 133–141.

Beier, K. M., Ahlers, C. J., Goecker, D., Neutze, J., Mundt, I. A., Hupp, E., et al. (2009). Can pedophiles be reached for primary prevention of child sexual abuse? First results of the Berlin Prevention Project Dunkelfeld (PPD). *Journal of Forensic Psychiatry and Psychology, 20*, 51–67.

Beier, K. M., Amelung, T., Kuhle, L., Grundmann, D., Scherner, G., & Neutze, J. (2013). Hebephilie als sexuelle Störung. [Hebephilia as sexual disorder.] *Fortschritte der Neurologie Psychiatrie, 81*, 128–137.

Beier, K. M., Amelung, T., & Pauls, A. (2010). Antiandrogene Therapie als Teil der Prävention von sexuellem Kindesmissbrauch im Dunkelfeld. [Antiandrogen therapy as a part of the prevention of child sexual abuse in the "Dunkelfeld".] *Forensische Psychiatrie, Psychologie, Kriminologie, 4*, 49–57.

Beier, K. M., Bosinski, H. A. G., & Loewit, K. (2005). *Sexualmedizin* (2nd ed.). [Sexual Medicine.] München: Elsevier Urban & Fischer.

Beier, K. M., & Loewit, K. (2013). *Sexual medicine in clinical practice*. New York: Springer.

Beier, K. M., Grundmann, D., Kuhle, L. F., Scherner, G., Konrad, A., & Amelung, T. (2015). The German Dunkelfeld Project. A pilot study to prevent child sexual abuse and the use of child abusive images. *Journal of Sexual Medicine, 12*, 529–542.

Beier, K. M., & Neutze, J. (2012). Proactive strategies to prevent the use of child abusive images – The Dunkelfeld project. In E. Quayle & K. M. Ribisl (Eds.), *Understanding and preventing online sexual exploitation of children* (pp. 204–227). New York: Routledge.

Beier, K. M., Neutze, J., Mundt, I. A., Ahlers, C. J., Goecker, D., & Konrad, A. (2009). Encouraging self-identified pedophiles and hebephiles to seek professional help: First results of the Berlin Prevention Project Dunkelfeld (PPD). *Child Abuse & Neglect, 33*, 545–549.

Beier, K. M., Oezdemir, U. C., Schlinzig, E., Groll, A., Hupp, E., & Hellenschmidt, T. (2016). Just dreaming of them: The Berlin project for primary prevention of child sexual abuse by juveniles (PPJ). *Child Abuse & Neglect, 52*, 1–10.

Blanchard, R. (2010). The DSM diagnostic criteria for pedophilia. *Archives of Sexual Behavior, 39*, 304–316.

Blanchard, R., Barbaree, H. E., Bogaert, A. F., Dickey, R., Klassen, P., Kuban, M. E., et al. (2000). Fraternal birth order and sexual orientation in pedophiles. *Archives of Sexual Behavior, 29*, 463–478.

Blanchard, R., Klassen, P., Dickey, R., Kuban, M. E., & Blak, T. (2001). Sensitivity and specificity of the phallometric test for pedophilia in nonadmitting sex offenders. *Psychological Assessment, 13*, 118–126.

Blanchard, R., Kuban, M. E., Blak, T., Cantor, J. M., Klassen, P., & Dickey, R. (2006). Phallometric comparison of pedophilic interest in nonadmitting sexual offenders against stepdaughters, biological daughters, other biologically related girls, and unrelated girls. *Sexual Abuse: Journal of Research and Treatment, 18*(1), 1–14.

Blanchard, R., Lykins, A. D., Wherrett, D., Kuban, M. E., Cantor, J. M., Blak, T., et al. (2009). Pedophilia, hebephilia, and the DSM-V. *Archives of Sexual Behavior, 38*, 335–350.

Bogaert, A. F., Bezeau, S., Kuban, M., & Blanchard, R. (1997). Pedophilia, sexual orientation, and birth order. *Journal of Abnormal Psychology, 106*(2), 331–335.

Briere, J., & Runtz, M. (1989). University males' sexual interest in children: predicting potential indices of "pedophilia" in a nonforensic sample. *Child Abuse & Neglect, 113*, 65–75.

Buss, D. M. (1989). Sex differences in human mate preferences: Evolutionary hypotheses tested in 37 culture. *Behavioral and Brain Sciences, 12*, 1–49.

Cantor, J. M. (2014). Purported changes in pedophilia as statistical artefacts: Comment on Müller et al. (2014). *Archives of Sexual Behavior, 44*, 253–254.

Chasan-Taber, L., & Tabachnick, J. (1999). Evaluation of a child sexual abuse prevention program. *Sexual Abuse: A Journal of Research & Treatment, 11*, 279–292.

Davidson, J., Martellozzo, E., & Lorent, M. (2009). Evaluation of CEOP ThinkuKnow Internet Safety Programme and Exploration of Young People's Internet Safety Knowledge. Retrieved April 4, 2011 from: http://www.cats-rp.org.uk/pdf%20files/Internet%20safety%20report%204-2010.pdf.

Davis, R. A. (2001). A cognitive-behavioral model of pathological Internet use. *Computers in Human Behavior, 17*, 187–195.

Duff, S., & Willis, A. (2006). At the precipice: Assessing a non-offending client's potential to sexually offend. *Journal of Sexual Aggression: An international, interdisciplinary forum for research, theory and practice, 12*, 43–51.

Edwards, R., Whittaker, M. K., Beckett, R., Bishopp, D., & Bates, A. (2012). Adolescents who have sexually harmed: An evaluation of a specialist treatment programme. *Journal of Sexual Aggression, 18*, 91–111.

Eke, A. W., Seto, M. C., & Williams, J. (2010). Examining the criminal history and future offending of child pornography offenders: An extended prospective follow-up study. *Law and Human Behavior, 35*(6), 466–478.

Fedoroff, J. P., Smolewska, K., Selhi, Z., Ng, E., & Bradford, J. M. W. (2001). Victimless Pedophiles. *Paper presented at the Annual Meeting of the International Academy of Sex Research (IASR)*, July 11–14. Montreal, Quebec, Canada.

Finkelhor, D. (2009). The prevention of childhood sexual abuse. *The Future of Children, 19*, 169–194.

Finkelhor, D., Ormrod, R., Turner, H., & Hamby, S. L. (2005). The victimization of children and youth: A comprehensive, national survey. *Child Maltreat, 10*, 5–25.

Freund, K., McKnight, C. K., Langevin, R., & Cibiri, S. (1972). The female child as a surrogate object. *Archives of Sexual Behavior, 2*, 119–133.

Gibson, L. E., & Leitenberg, H. (2000). Child sexual abuse prevention programs: Do they decrease the occurrence of child sexual abuse? *Child Abuse and Neglect, 24*, 115–125.

Glueck, B. C. (1955). Final report: Research project for the study and treatment of persons convicted of crimes involving sexual aberrations. June 1952 to June 1955. New York: New York State Department of Mental Hygiene.

Grundmann, D., Krupp, J., Scherner, G., Amelung, T., & Beier, K. M. (2016). Stability of self-reported arousal to sexual fantasies involving children in a clinical sample of pedophiles and hebephiles. *Archives of Sexual Behavior* (accepted for publication).

Hall, G. C. N., Hirschman, R., & Oliver, L. L. (1995). Sexual arousal and arousability to pedophilic stimuli in a community sample of normal men. *Behavior Therapy, 26*, 681–694.

Hanson, R. K., & Bussière, M. T. (1998). Predicting relapse: A meta-analysis of sexual offender recidivism studies. *Journal of Consulting and Clinical Psychology, 66*, 348–362.

Hanson, R. K., & Harris, A. J. R. (2000). Where should we intervene? Dynamic predictors of sexual offense recidivism. *Criminal Justice and Behavior, 27*, 6–35.

Hanson, R. K., Harris, A. J., Scott, T., & Helmus, L. (2007). *Assessing the risk of sexual offenders on community supervision: The dynamic supervision project*. Ottawa: Public Safety Canada.

Hanson, R. K., & Morton-Bourgon, K. E. (2005). The characteristics of persistent sexual offenders: A meta-analysis of recidivism studies. *Journal of Consulting and Clinical Psychology, 73*, 1154–1163.

Harendra de Silva, D. G. (2007). Children needing protection: experience from South Asia. *Archives of Disease in Childhood, 92*(10), 931–934.

Heim, C. M., Mayberg, H. S., Mletzko, T., Nemeroff, C. B., & Pruessner, J. C. (2013). Decreased cortical representation of genital somatosensory field after childhood sexual abuse. *American Journal of Psychiatry, 170*, 616–623.

Henry, F., McMahon, P. M. (2000). What survivors of child sexual abuse told us about the people who abused them. Paper presented at the National Sexual Violence Prevention Conference, Dallas, Texas.

Hirschfeld, M. (1906). *Vom Wesen der Liebe: Zugleich ein Beitrag zur Lösung der Frage der Bisexualität.* [*On the essence of love: Simultaneously a contribution to the question of bisexuality.*] Leipzig: Max Spohr.

Kahl, H., & Schaffrath Rosario, A. (2007). Pubertät im Wandel - wohin geht der Trend? Sexuelle Reifeentwicklung von Kindern und Jugendlichen in Deutschland. [Puberty in change - which direction is it taking? Sexual maturation of children and adolescents in Germany.] *BZgA Forum, 3*, 19–25.

Krafft-Ebing, R. (1912). *Psychopathia sexualis – mit besonderer Berücksichtigung der konträren Sexualempfindung. Eine medizinisch-gerichtliche Studie für Ärzte und Juristen.* [*Psychopathia sexualis - with special reference to contrary sexual instinct. A medico-judicial study for physicians and lawyers.*] Stuttgart: Enke.

Krone, T. (2004). Typology of online child pornography offending. *Trends and Issues in Crime and Criminal Justice, 279*, 1–6.

Lalumière, M. L. (2014). The lability of pedophilic interests as measured by phallometry. *Archives of Sexual Behavior, 44*, 255–258.

Lanning, K. V. (2001). Child molesters: A behavioral analysis. Retrieved October 10, 2011 from http://www.missingkids.com/en_US/publications/NC70.pdf.

Lykins, A. D., Cantor, J. M., Kuban, M. E., Blak, T., Dickey, E., Klassen, P. E., et al. (2010). Sexual arousal to female children in gynephilic men. *Sexual Abuse: Journal of Research and Treatment, 22*, 279–289.

Mann, R. E., Hanson, R. K., & Thornton, D. (2010). Assessing risk for sexual recidivism: Some proposals on the nature of psychologically meaningful risk factors. *Sexual Abuse: A Journal of Research and Treatment, 22*, 191–217.

Marshall, W. L., Marshall, L. E., & Serran, G. A. (2006). Strategies in the treatment of paraphilias: A critical review. *Annual review of sex research, 17*, 162–182.

McGrath, R., Cumming, G., Burchard, B., Zeoli, S., & Ellerby, L. (2010). *Current practices and emerging trends in sexual abuser management: The Safer Society 2009 North American Survey*. Brandon, VT: Safer Society Press.

Müller, K., Curry, S., Ranger, R., Briken, P., Bradford, J., & Fedoroff, J. P. (2014). Changes in sexual arousal as measured by penile plethysmography in men with pedophilic sexual interest. *The Journal of Sexual Medicine, 11*(5), 1221–1229.

National Sex Offender Public Website (2012). URL: http://www.nsopr.gov/.

Neutze, J., Seto, M., Schaefer, G. A., & Beier, K. M. (2010). Predictors of child pornography offenses and child sexual abuse in a community sample of pedophiles and hebephiles. *Sexual Abuse: A Journal of Research and Treatment, 22*, 1–31. doi:10.1177/1079063210382043.

O'Reilly, G., Carr, A., Murphy, P., & Cotter, A. (2010). A controlled evaluation of a prison-based sexual offender intervention program. *Sexual Abuse A Journal of Research and Treatment, 22*, 95–111.

Pereda, N., Guilera, G., Forns, M., & Gómez-Benito, J. (2009). The prevalence of child sexual abuse in community and student samples: A meta-analysis. *Clinical Psychology Review, 29*, 328–338.

Pithers, W. D. (1990). Relapse prevention with sexual aggressors: A method of maintaining therapeutic gain and enhancing external supervision. In W. L. Marshall, D. R. Laws, & H. E. Barbaree (Eds.), *Handbook of sexual assault: Issues, theories and treatment of the offender* (pp. 343–361). New York: Plenum.

Ponseti, J., Granert, O., Jansen, O., Wolff, S., Beier, K., Neutze, J., et al. (2012). Assessment of pedophilia using hemodynamic brain response to sexual stimuli. *Archives of General Psychiatry, 69*(2), 187–194.

Quayle, E., & Taylor, M. (2002). Paedophiles, pornography and the internet: Assessment issues. *British Journal of Social Work, 32*, 863–875.

Quayle, E., & Taylor, M. (2003). Model of problematic Internet use in people with a sexual interest in children. *Cyber Psychology and Behavior, 6*, 93–106.

Quinsey, V. L., Steinman, C. M., Bergersen, S. G., & Holmes, T. F. (1975). Penile circumference, skin conductance, and ranking responses of child molesters and "normals" to sexual and nonsexual visual stimuli. *Behavioral Therapy, 6*, 213–216.

Riegel, D. L. (2004). Effects on boy-attracted pedosexual males of viewing boy erotica [Letter to the editor]. *Archives of Sexual Behavior, 33*, 321–323.

Rispens, J., Aleman, A., & Goudena, P. P. (1997). Prevention of child sexual abuse victimization: A meta-analysis of school programs. *Child Abuse & Neglect, 21*, 975–987.

Schaefer, G. A., Mundt, I. A., Feelgood, S., Hupp, E., Neutze, J., Ahlers, C. J., et al. (2010). Potential and Dunkelfeld offenders: Two neglected target groups for prevention of child sexual abuse. *International Journal of Law and Psychiatry, 33*(3), 154–163.

Seto, M. C. (2008). *Pedophilia and sexual offending against children: Theory, assessment, and intervention.* Washington, DC, USA: American Psychological Association.

Seto, M. C. (2012). Is pedophilia a sexual orientation? *Archives of Sexual Behavior, 41*, 231–236.

Seto, M. C., Cantor, J. M., & Blanchard, R. (2006). Child pornography offenses are a valid diagnostic indicator of pedophilia. *Journal of Abnormal Psychology, 115*, 610–615.

Spitzer, R. L. (2012). Spitzer reassesses his 2003 study of reparative therapy of homosexuality. *Archives of Sexual Behavior, 41*, 757.

Stoltenborgh, M., Ijzendoorn, M. H., Euser, E. M., & Bakermans-Kranenburg, M. J. (2011). A global perspective on child sexual abuse: Meta-analysis of prevalence around the world. *Child Maltreat, 16*, 79–101.

Stop it Now! (2009). Helpline Report 2005 – 2009. Retrieved March 26, 2011 from http://www.stopitnow.org.uk/Helpline%20Report.pdf.

Tanner, J. M. (1962). *Growth at adolescence*. 2nd Ed. Oxford: Blackwell.

United Nations, General Assembly A/55/297; Promotion and protection of the rights of children: Sale of children, child prostitution and child pornography, 10 August 2000.

Ward, T., & Beech, A. (2006). An integrated theory of sexual offending. *Aggression and Violent Behavior, 11*, 44–63.

Ward, T., & Gannon, T. A. (2006). Rehabilitation, etiology, and self-regulation: The good lives model of sexual offender treatment. *Aggression and Violent Behavior, 11*, 77–94.

Ward, T., & Hudson, S. M. (1998). A self-regulation model of the relapse process in sexual offenders. *Journal of Interpersonal Violence, 13*, 700–725.

Ward, T., & Hudson, S. M. (2000). A Self-regulation model of relapse prevention. In D. R. Laws, S. M. Hudson, & T. Ward (Eds.), *Remaking relapse prevention with sex offenders: A sourcebook* (pp. 79–101). Thousand Oaks, CA: Sage.

Wetzels, P. (1997). Prävalenz und familiäre Hintergründe sexuellen Kindesmißbrauchs in Deutschland: Ergebnisse einer repräsentativen Befragung. [Prevalence and family backgrounds of child sexual abuse in Germany: Results from a representative survey.] *Sexuologie, 4*(2), 89–107.

Whitaker, D. J., Le, B., Karl Hanson, R., Baker, C. K., McMahon, P. M., Ryan, G., et al. (2008). Risk factors for the perpetration of child sexual abuse: A review and meta-analysis. *Child Abuse & Neglect, 32*, 529–548.

Wille, R. (1968). Die forensisch-psychopathologische Beurteilung der Exhibitionisten, Pädophilen, Inzest- und Notzuchttäter. [The forensic-psychopathological assessment of exhibitionists, pedophiles, incest and rape offenders.] Postdoctorial thesis, Universität Kiel.

Wischka, B. (2013). Das Behandlungsprogramm für Sexualstraftäter. [The treatment program for sexual offenders.] *Recht und Psychiatrie, 31*, 138–145.

World Health Organization (1993). The ICD-10 Classification of mental and behavioural Disorders. World Health Organization.

Zwi, K., Woolfenden, S., Wheeler, D. M., O'Brien, T., Tait, P., & Williams, K. J. (2007). School-based education programmes for the prevention of child sexual abuse. *Cochrane Database of Systematic Reviews, 3*, 1–36.

Women and Children as Victims of Sex Offenses: Crime Prevention by Treating the Offenders?

Gunda Wößner

Abstract In the context of crime, women and children are very often discussed as victims of sex crimes such as rape or sexual abuse. This chapter provides an overview of the number of sex crimes in comparison to other crimes, the problem of the dark figure, and discusses how valid these data are. As a measure of victim protection, one of the most important aspects of offender treatment is crime prevention. Sex crimes can have long-lasting negative effects. What can be done to reduce this damage? Does it help to treat the offender, and what are the effects of these treatment programs? Does offender treatment facilitate a reduction in the number of sex crimes or should sex offenders be incarcerated for longer periods, perhaps even for the rest of their lives? How can we predict a sex offender's potential "dangerousness" after release in these cases?

1 Introduction

In the last decades, sexual violence against women and children has become the focus of political and public concern in numerous countries. First and foremost, the United States of America, where by 1996 all states and the District of Columbia had introduced some kind of sex offender registration statute and public notification system (Silverman 2011), deserve particular mention. In Europe, England and Wales tightened its sentencing policy (Harrison 2014), France and Germany introduced, at least and partly temporarily, mandatory treatment for incarcerated sex offenders and follow-up measures to better monitor released sex offenders (see Haverkamp and Wößner 2014; Hirschelmann 2014). Other countries still embrace surgical castration, defying objections raised by the European Committee for the Prevention of Torture and Inhuman or Degrading Treatment or Punishment (CPT, see Škvain 2014). As can be seen, different countries have tried to find answers to

G. Wößner (✉)
University of Applied Police Sciences Baden-Wuerttemberg, Villingen-Schwenningen, Germany
e-mail: gundawoessner@hfpol-bw.de; g.woessner@mpicc.de

H. Kury et al. (eds.), *Women and Children as Victims and Offenders: Background, Prevention, Reintegration*, DOI 10.1007/978-3-319-28424-8_20

sexual offending in order to protect the public from these crimes. But are harsh sentencing practices and control measures an appropriate answer? Is offender treatment an effective means of victim protection in the field of sex offenses or does it embody mere social romanticism that runs contrary to victims' needs?

Given the tremendous traumatizing effects sexual victimization can have on victims, it is undoubtedly justified to do as much as possible to prevent sexual crimes and to respond to sexual violence appropriately. Victims of sexual violence frequently develop posttraumatic stress disorder (PTSD), a mental health disorder that is defined by three clusters of symptoms: extreme fear, helplessness, or horror resulting from a serious threat of injury. The symptoms include recurrent and intrusive recollections and dreams of the incident, hyperarousal, such as an increased startle reaction, sleep and/or concentration difficulties, and trying to firmly avoid cues or reminders of the trauma. Avoidance symptoms may also encompass emotional numbness, i.e., the inability to feel any positive emotions such as love, satisfaction, or happiness (Keane et al. 2009).

In addition to this general concept of trauma, Burgess and Holmstrom (1974) identified a specific *rape trauma syndrome* that usually implies a two-phase reaction: the acute phase of disorganization with a wide range of expressive emotions such as shock, disbelief, fear, and anger (demonstrated by sobbing, crying, restlessness, and smiling) which might alternate with a controlled behavior right after the rape occurred, and the second, long-term phase "when the woman begins to reorganize her lifestyle" (p. 982). The consequences of sexual victimization are not only restricted to severe affective disorders such as PTSD, anxiety, depression, or substance (ab)use: They may also encompass reproductive and physical health problems, chronic pain, gastrointestinal and gynecological complications as well as sexually transmitted diseases. Other possible long-term effects are financial loss and economic hardship (Dignan 2005; Zinsstag 2014). Such long-term effects are also found in victims of child sexual abuse (for further details see Shirwadkar in this volume).

Specific negative effects of sexual violence victimization arise for victims of armed conflicts (see Nikolic-Ristanovic and Stevkovic in this volume). Not all individuals who experienced sexual victimization will develop the described disorders. Psychological strain as a result of sexual violence depends on the severity and frequency of the assault(s) as well as on the victim's individual disposition of resilience and coping with the crime (Fischer and Riedesser 1998; Putnam 2003). Particularly important protective factors are the support of significant others, especially close emotional support, attachment, and satisfaction (Thornberry et al. 2013). It is also important that the victim's experiences with the criminal justice system are not re-traumatizing.

There is a widespread assumption that sex offenders—especially those who have abused children—exhibit a particularly high risk of reoffending (Hood et al. 2002) and this assumption might be one of the driving forces for the continuous attention to sex offenders and the upsurge of punitive actions against them. This increase of measures of control and retribution has been critically discussed among scholars.

But is sex offender treatment an appropriate response to sex offenders and does offender treatment really impact victim protection?

2 The Extent of Sexual Violence

Sexual violence is a ubiquitous phenomenon in all societies through all social classes. It can be assumed that every third woman worldwide has experienced some form of sexual violence in her life (Willman and Corman 2013, p. 5). The extent of sexual violence, however, can only approximately be determined since collecting data on sexual violence faces different issues. Data sources can encompass official police records, victim surveys, self-reports on delinquency, and incarceration rates. Survey rates on sexual violence largely depend on the willingness to report such crimes (thus, depending on the method of the survey) and the definition of the crime. Official data focus on a very specific number (such as reported sex crimes, the number of suspects, the number of incarcerated sex offenders). Nonetheless, some consistent trends from a number of national and international crime surveys have regularly indicated that—looking at lifetime prevalence—up to half of the female population of Western societies has experienced sexual victimization of some kind (Kury et al. 2004a). According to Heiskanen (2010, p. 24), Southern Africa, Oceania, and North America exhibit the highest recorded rape rates with a large variability between different states.

In 2006, rapes accounted for 0.8 % of the *police recorded crimes* in the United States. In Sweden, 1.2 % of the police recorded offenses were sexual assaults (Kristensen et al. 2011). In France, this number amounted to 1.5 % in 2010 (Ministère de la Justice et des Libertés 2012). In England and Wales as well as in Germany similar numbers (i.e., 1 %) are reported (Grubin and Thornton 1994; Bundesministerium des Innern 2014). Reported sex crimes per 100,000 inhabitants differ from country to country: In 2006, Denmark reported 60 sex crimes per 100,000 inhabitants (rape: 12, see Kristensen et al. 2011, p. 252). Equivalent rape rates for other countries are 3 for China (2000) and Russia (2012), 17 for France (2004), and 92 for Australia (2003, Australian Bureau of Statistics 2003).[1]

Victim surveys usually provide higher numbers: The average 1 year prevalence victimization rate (being a victim of any kind of crime in the last year before the survey) for 30 countries was 16 % according to the *International Crime Victim Survey* (ICVS) 04/05 (van Dijk et al. 2007). Almost 2 % of the surveyed women reported having experienced sexual assault, 0.5 % of the surveyed men did too. This means that 10.6 % of all female victimizations concerned sexual assault, but only 3 % of male victimizations. However, the survey only covered subjects aged 16 or older and referred to the previous year only. The ICVS applies the same questionnaire in different countries, thus facilitating the comparison of the numbers. The

[1] Statistical analyses based on miscellaneous sources, e.g., www.nationmaster.com.

number of women aged 16 and older who reported having been sexually assaulted in the previous 5 years in a survey period between 1992 and 1997 yielded—not surprisingly—very different prevalence rates. In Africa, 4.5 % of Ugandan but only 0.8 % of Batswana women reported that they had been a victim of sexual assault in the previous 5 years. In South America, prevalence rates ranged between 1.4 % in Bolivia and 8 % in Brazil. In Asia, the percentage of women reporting sexual violence ranged from 0.3 % in the Philippines to 2.7 % in Indonesia. Finally, the reported frequency of having been a victim of sexual violence in Europe varied from 2 % in Hungary to 6 % in Albania (Jewkes et al. 2002, p. 151). However, in general victim surveys, items referring to sexual victimization are embedded in an array of questions on all kinds of victimization and attitudes toward crime. Victim surveys regularly yield smaller prevalence rates of sexual victimization than studies with more sophisticated methods (see Kury et al. 2003; Young et al. 2009). Prevalence rates for sexual assault vary greatly, not only between different nations but also within nations. In the USA, for instance, between 17 % and 25 % of women reported a life time prevalence of rape (see Campbell 2008); in Germany between 3 % and 16 % reported attempted or completed rape (see Kury et al. 2004a).

Concerning *child sexual abuse*, a meta-analysis including studies from 22 countries showed that about 19 % of the female population and about 7 % of the male population experienced some form of child sexual abuse (Pereda et al. 2009). Prevalence rates for both sexes differed substantially between continents: Africa: 34.4 %, America 15.8 %, Asia 10.1 %, Europe 9.2 %, and Oceania 23.9 % (Pereda et al. 2009). Due to methodological, cultural, and definitional differences, direct comparisons should, however, only be drawn cautiously. In China, for instance, incest is a taboo (Lung and Huang 2004, p. 557). Consequently, it comes as no surprise that in Taiwan only about 10 % of all sex offenses were child sexual abuse cases compared to approximately 80 % rape cases in the years from 1999 to 2001 (Lung et al. 2007). Methodological problems arise from the retrospective character of most findings or the selection of the sample. When using a clinical as opposed to a nonclinical sample, for instance, it is very likely that male subjects (boys and men) are underrepresented (Putnam 2003). In a German study, the range of child sexual abuse varied between 2 % for boys and 20 % for girls (Kury et al. 2004b). A recent German study on sexual abuse victimization with a representative sample of subjects between the age of 16 and 40 years examined the prevalence of sexual abuse during childhood and adolescence (i.e., before the age of 16, Bieneck et al. 2011). Between 1 % and 4 % of the participants reported having been sexually abused, depending on the type of inquired incident (exhibitionism, touching, penetration). In a longitudinal comparison of the numbers of reported child sexual abuse victimization that included several studies, Casey and Nurius (2006) found divergent trends. Some studies yielded a decline in the prevalence rates (e.g., Dunne et al. 2003), others an increase within the period under scrutiny between the 1980s and 1990s or from the beginning to the end of the 1990s.

Prevalence rates of sexual violence pose a particular problem in regions were the *indigenous population* has been displaced by immigrants (Native Americans in the USA, Inuit in Canada, Maori in New Zealand, or Indigenous Australians, and finally, in South Africa). In Canada, for instance, First Peoples represent over 19 % of the incarcerated male population but only 3.7 % of the adult male population (Helmus et al. 2012, p. 857). Cossins (2006, p. 320), with reference to the Australian Institute of Health and Welfare, reports of a higher incidence of child sexual abuse in Indigenous Australian communities compared to the non-Aboriginal population. Dysfunctional family structures, drug, alcohol and other substance abuse, experiences of parental separation, and inappropriate sexual behavior seem to promote a milieu conducive to abuse and neglect (Ellerby and MacPherson 2002).

Likewise, *countries in war and conflict* exhibit particularly high rates of sexual victimization unsheathing the full dimension of this heinous crime (see Nikolic-Ristanovic and Stevkovic in this volume). In the civil-war like conditions of the 1980s, 70 % of the Ugandan women in Luwero District fell victim to rape (UN Secretary General 2006).

In general, the extent of sexual offenses in comparison to other crimes is very low and amounts to approximately 1 % in police records. Survey data provide higher rates. Especially with regard to sexual victimization, it is common criminological knowledge that the dark figure is even higher (see van Dijk as well as Schröttle and Vogt in this volume).

Turning to the *incarceration rates of sexual offenders*, again figures vary enormously between different countries. In Germany, in 2012 only 7 % (Statistisches Bundesamt 2012) of the prison inmates were convicted of sexual offenses. Lower rates can be found in Turkey (1 %, Turkish Statistical Institute 2011) or Denmark and Finland (3–5 %, Kristoffersen 2010, p. 24), whereas in the vast majority of prisons worldwide sex offenders have a higher share in the population of incarcerated offenders: Almost 8 % in Chile referring to 2001 (Jiménez 2009), 15 % in England and Wales (Berman and Dar 2013, p. 21), 16 % in Iceland (Kristoffersen 2010, p. 24). According to Hirschelmann (2014), France exhibits a comparatively high rate with 22 %. Incarceration rates in the USA vary strongly between states with Utah exhibiting the nation's highest percentage of incarcerated sex offenders with 33 % (Bench and Allen 2013, p. 411). In California, in 2010, only 9 % (2012: 10 %) of the inmates were sentenced for sex offenses (Carson and Golinelli 2013, p. 5). Different rates of incarcerated sexual offenders can be partly traced back to different prevalence rates of sexual offenses, but other important factors contribute too, such as definitional and legal differences and of course differences in the total incarceration rate.

Of particular interest is the group of adolescent sexual offenders. In 2008, 36 % of the police recorded sexual offenses in 34 states of the United States were committed by juvenile sex offenders (Finkelhor and Shattuck 2012); in France almost 13 % of all sentenced sex offenders in 2010 were under the age of 16. The majority of adolescent sex offenders stop sexual offending in their 20s. However, there is evidence that about half of all adult sex offenders already committed a sex crime (not always detected) during their youth (Chu and Thomas 2010).

3 Treatment Programs for Sexual Offenders

Nowadays, sex offender therapy is a constant for managing sex offenders in many countries worldwide. Yet, having said this, a good number of countries have not integrated sex offender treatment. Since sex offender therapy was introduced, it "has changed and improved with new research and information" (Mann and Fernandez 2006, p. 155). Some of the current strategies are based on paradigms that are well-established in other therapies. In its early days, literature on sex offender therapy had more of an anecdotal character (Mann and Fernandez 2006), yet in recent years, it has become virtually impossible to keep track of the numerous publications that deal with sex offender treatment.

3.1 The Advent and Development of the Treatment Notion

In its early days, sex offender therapy relied mainly on a psychoanalytic approach. The focus was on working on and resolving the inner conflicts of the offender (see Mann and Fernandez 2006). Especially in Europe, i.e., in Belgium, the Netherlands, and England and Wales, the psychodynamic model was endorsed (van Beek and Mulder 1992, p. 155; Palmucci 2006, p. 382). The emphasis was put on the personality of the offender (van Beek and Mulder 1992, p. 155). After a controversial discourse about the benefits of psychoanalytic therapy (see García García and Sancha Mata 1985, p. 149), the focus soon shifted to behavioral approaches, since evaluation research could not substantiate the proper effectiveness of psychoanalysis with sex offenders. Though in Germany, until the 1990s (Rüther 1998) and in France (Hirschelmann 2014) and parts of Switzerland (Endrass et al. 2012) still today, psychoanalytic one-on-one therapy has still been and is currently endorsed; as a matter of fact, treatment of sex offenders in French prisons draws largely upon psychodynamic approaches (Hirschelmann 2014). Other European countries have had a long tradition in psychodynamic approaches, too, such as Austria, Italy, Spain, and Scandinavia (Frenken 1999). The shift to behavioral approaches initially happened with very limited notions of how to treat sex offenders. It was hypothesized that deviant masturbatory fantasies affect the development and maintenance of sexual deviation (Evans 1968; McGuire et al. 1965). Consequently, *aversion therapy* was the first choice of sex offender therapy (Marshall 1973; Quinsey and Earls 1990).

In 1990, Quinsey and Earls in the Handbook of Sexual Assault (Marshall et al. 1990) provided an overview of interventions that aimed to reduce and modify inappropriate sexual preferences. Usually, an electric shock was delivered during the presence of paraphilic stimuli (i.e., slides of a nude female child). Quinsey and Earls (1990) conclude that there are "variations in the effectiveness of these methods of changing erectile patterns" (p. 284) and that "[o]ne of the disturbing aspects of the literature on electrical aversion is that the literature itself appears to have dried up" (p. 285). *Covert sensitization*, a method where an imagined aversive event is simultaneously linked with the paraphilic stimulus, is another technique that was popular in the 1980s. Evidence of effectiveness, however, has remained unimpressive (Quinsey and Earls 1990). Finally, *satiation* was used as a typical practice of behavior therapy in the 1970s using, i.e., the excessive fantasizing about sexually inappropriate stimuli while masturbating to orgasm (see Quinsey and Earls 1990).

3.2 The Rationale of Sex Offender Treatment

Over the years, sex offender treatment therapy has become more and more comprehensive. The behavioral approach was gradually extended by cognitive building blocks. Gene Abel and colleagues as well as William Marshall and colleagues are the pioneers of comprehensive sex offender treatment programs (see Mann and Fernandez 2006). Over time, criminological research contributed to the further development of sex offender treatment. The identification of core treatment targets largely relied on retrospective recidivism studies that had identified risk factors for reoffending (e.g., Andrews et al. 1990; Gendreau et al. 1996). There are risk factors that are (sex) *offense-specific* (deviant sexual interests in the case of sexual recidivism) and risk factors that are *offense-unspecific* (prior criminal history, young age, negative peer associations, substance abuse, and antisocial personality, respectively antisocial attitudes, Hanson and Morton-Bourgon 2004). Therapy for sexual offenders should target *dynamic* risk factors that are associated with the risk of reoffending and that are amenable to change (Andrews et al. 1990); *static* risk factors such as early onset of criminal behavior, prior criminal history, or features of past victims are not modifiable. Thus, dynamic risk factors are risk factors that are amenable to change. With regard to general offending, Andrews and Bonta (2010) identified eight key dynamic risk factors: antisocial personality pattern, procriminal attitudes, procriminal associates, work/school problems, family/marital problems, poor use of leisure/recreation time, and substance abuse. Hanson and Harris (2001) refined this approach and identified the following dynamic risk factors that should be addressed in sex offender treatment: 1. sexual self-regulation, 2. general self-regulation, 3. intimacy deficits, 4. compliance and understanding for the need of treatment and control, 5. existence of supportive significant others, and 6. distorted attitudes or attitudes tolerant to sexual violence. Particularly important dynamic risk factors for sex offenders include sexual deviant interests, sexual preoccupations, emotional congruence with children, and intimacy deficits (Hanson and Morton-Bourgon 2005; Mann et al. 2010). These dynamic risk factors are defined as *stable dynamic* risk factors and can be tested with the instrument Stable-2000 and its advanced version, Stable-2007. Stable dynamic risk factors "are relatively persistent characteristics of the offender, which are subject to change" (Craig et al. 2005, p. 65). In addition, scholars discern *acute dynamic* risk factors: dynamic factors that are less persistent and can rapidly change, such as substance abuse, isolation, or negative emotional states (Craig et al. 2005; Hanson and Harris 2000). The specific dynamic of acute risk factors is that they "can signal the onset of offending" (Ward and Maruna 2007, p. 46).

The most prominent model of sex offender treatment is the *Risk-Need-Responsivity* (RNR) model of offender treatment (Andrews and Bonta 2010; Andrews et al. 1990). What works in (sex) offender treatment, according to the authors, are interventions that reflect key psychological principles: 1. treatment should be aimed at higher risk offenders, 2. treatment should target criminogenic needs, and 3. treatment styles and modes should match the clients' learning styles. Andrews and Bonta (2010) identified the above-mentioned "Big-Eight" covariates of criminal conduct that are also considered as criminogenic needs (antisocial personality pattern, procriminal attitudes, procriminal associates, employment/education problems, family/marital dysfunctions, poor use of leisure/recreation time, and substance abuse). Even though the authors state that personal strengths and resilience (e.g., intelligence, supportive relationships) are important factors to reduce recidivism (Andrews and Bonta 2010), the RNR-model very much focuses on risk-factors—a fact that has increasingly been criticized.

A more recent model on the other hand, is closely linked to this perspective of stressing the importance of protective factors in the dynamics of reducing recidivism. The authors of the *Good Lives Model* (GLM) theorize that the promotion of specific goods and goals will automatically eliminate or modify commonly targeted dynamic risk factors (Ward and Brown 2004; Ward and Marshall 2007; Ward and Maruna 2007). It is a strengths-based approach grounded on the theoretical assumptions that offenders—as all other human beings—strive for primary goods, that motivation to change is facilitated by focusing on benefits (primary goods) rather than criminogenic needs, and that interventions that pursue positive goals will help to protect offenders from risk factors (Ward and Maruna 2007, p. 108). Thus, sex offender therapy should be aimed at the primary human goods of: 1. life (healthy living, physical functioning, and sexual satisfaction), 2. knowledge, 3. excellence in play and work, 4. excellence in agency (autonomy and self-directedness), 5. inner peace (freedom from emotional stress and turmoil), 6. relatedness and community (intimate and family relations), 7. spirituality, 8. happiness, and 9. creativity. To date, little is known about the concrete implementation of GLM concepts in practice (Willis et al. 2014, p. 59). Motivational interviewing with sex offenders is one approach to bring about the motivation for personal change (see Prescott 2009). It should be noted that some authors emphasize the complementarity of the two theoretical approaches (e.g., Wilson and Yates 2009). In sum, both theories relate to the rehabilitation of offenders as opposed to the reintegrative aspects of correctional interventions. Rehabilitation focuses on changing an offender's personality or habits in order to prevent him/her from recommitting a crime whereas the opportunities to participate in social life and the enhancement of a prisoner's ability to return and "function" in civil society are key to the notion of reintegration (see van Zyl Smit and Snacken 2009, pp. 83, 106; compare with the resettlement concept, Maguire and Raynor 2006).

3.3 Established Treatment Approaches

Over the last decades, several sex offender treatment programs have evolved following the RNR rationale that treatment targets should be defined by dynamic criminogenic factors, i.e., those factors that are amenable to change and have been empirically linked to the risk of recidivism (Mann and Fernandez 2006). Mann and Fernandez (2006, p. 158) criticize this approach as atheoretical since this rationale may result in the treatment of several therapeutic goals that, however, lack a "unifying underlying theory of sexual offending". Ward and Maruna (2007, p. 27) also complain that "for much of its history the practice of rehabilitation has taken place within a theoretical vacuum." The authors miss clear explanations of how the process of change works.

As key issues for sex offender treatment, the following subjects have been identified (see Mann and Fernandez 2006):

Sexual arousal factors

Especially paraphilic[2] child molesters (i.e., persons who present with the mental disorder of pedophilia, a sustained sexual orientation toward children) are only sexually aroused by children, in most cases preferably boys.

Dysfunctional attitudes related to sexual assaults

So-called rape myths, negative views of women, sexual entitlement, or dysfunctional cognitive distortions related with sex with children in the case of child abusers.

Interpersonal deficits

Low self-esteem in sex offenders may foster beliefs about negative expectancies of themselves and others, under-assertiveness, emotional loneliness, attachment and intimacy deficits.

Self-regulation deficits

Poor self-regulation is a critical risk factor in criminal behavior in general, and as such also for sex offenders: Lack of emotion regulation, lifestyle impulsiveness, and poor problem-solving are relevant factors and thus treatment targets.

Singular treatment approaches that have attracted widespread attention are the *Reasoning and Rehabilitation Program* (R&R), *Relapse Prevention*, and the *Sex Offender Treatment Program* (SOTP).

Ross et al. (1988, p. 30) found that many offenders are not skilled in anticipating the consequences of their behavior and in reasoning how to achieve their goals. They tend to impulsive, action-oriented, egocentric, and non-reflective problem-

[2] Paraphilias are mental disorders including recurrent, intense sexually arousing fantasies, sexual urges, or behaviors that are targeted toward nonhuman objects, the suffering or humiliation of a person involved, or children respectively other non-consenting individuals (e.g., exhibitionism, pedophilia, voyeurism, sadism). The diagnosis requires personal distress about the person's interest, another person's psychological distress, injury, or death, or a desire for sexual behaviors involving unwilling persons or persons unable to give legal consent. It is important to note that not every unusual sexual behavior is a paraphilia.

solving. Based on the identification of these deficits, Ross and associates developed the *Reasoning and Rehabilitation Program* (R&R) consisting of nine interrelated modules (Ross and Ross 1995, p. 93): problem solving, values enhancement, social skills, critical reasoning, negotiation skills, skills in review, creative thinking, cognitive exercises, and the management of emotions. Even though the use of social skills training not only in general offender therapy but in the treatment of sex offenders is appealing, a number of authors have criticized the lack of theoretical foundation. To date, it has not been substantiated that sex offenders lack social skills in general (even though some authors found evidence for social skills problems in sex offenders, see, in sum, Robertiello and Terry 2007). Mann et al. (2010) conclude that the social skills deficits of sexual offenders are more "specifically related to intimacy deficits and hostile attitudes toward women, rather than to poor dating skills or problems negotiating routine social situations" (Mann et al. 2010, p. 208).

The *Relapse Prevention* (RP) approach is originally a method to maintain therapeutic gains of substance abusers. It was described by Marlatt and colleagues in the late 1970s and early 1980s to increase self-control among substance abusers and was later extended to the work with sex offenders (see Pithers et al. 1983). The core ideas that were transferred to the RP approach with sex offenders are the identification of crucial situations and decisions preceding a relapse and the development of strategies to avoid or cope with these problematic issues. Thus, RP is a highly individualized approach requiring thorough assessment to determine the central issues for an offender (Pithers 1990, p. 349). Therapy consists of the identification of a sex offender's high-risk situation, including seemingly irrelevant decisions in constructing these situations, the specification of his/her skills to cope with these situations, and the precursors of the sex crime. Based on these analyses, strategies to avoid further reoffending are worked out (i.e., stimulus control procedures, avoidance strategies, coping responses, escape strategies, coping with urges, skills-building interventions, cognitive restructuring, contracting, see Pithers 1990, p. 352). In sum, RP is a self-management approach that is meant to improve an offender's self-control.

In England and Wales, the *Sex Offender Treatment Program* (SOTP, see Grubin and Thornton 1994; Mann and Thornton 1998) focuses on a cognitive-behavioral approach. The cognitive aspects include exploring and reframing the offender's distorted thinking patterns and attitudes toward sexually deviant behavior (sexual entitlement, rape myths, abuse myths). The program also seeks to determine on how these issues are related to the sex offenders' self-esteem. A key aspect is the identification of the thoughts and beliefs precedent to the offending behavior similar to RP. Other central elements are (victim) empathy, social functioning, and sexual preferences. The offender is to understand that his behavior has consequences. In this sense, in most SOTPs offenders discuss their crimes, what led to the crimes, what the consequences were, and what their thoughts and attitudes with regard to the crimes are (Brown 2010). Methods include role-play, modeling, and disputing irrational thoughts. SOTP was introduced in 1991 into the English prison system (Mann and Thornton 1998). It covers a Core Program (for repeat sex offender), an Extended Program (providing special needs interventions), and a Booster Program (delivered prior to release, focusing on RP). Allocation to treatment is based on the diagnostic assessment of risk of reoffending and seriousness of the offense (Grubin and Thornton 1994). A special feature of SOTP is that it was developed right from the start to be delivered by trained lay personnel. Since prison officers have the advantage of observing and interacting with the offenders between treatment sessions they can more easily verify whether treatment contents are transferred; they also serve as role-models on a daily basis (Grubin and Thornton 1994).

Most cognitive-behavioral programs are "delivered in a group format" (Mann and Fernandez 2006, p. 157) even though only few scholars have attended to the question whether group therapy prevails over individual therapy.

Next to this general sex offender treatment programs, specific treatment approaches have evolved during the last decades. Juvenile offenders, for instance, pose a particular focus group with age specific needs and concerns (e.g., Letourneau et al. 2009). However, it remains largely unclear, to which degree treatment approaches developed for adult offenders can be transferred to adolescent offenders without knowing whether they are effective for a younger focus group. After child sexual abuse in the Catholic Church has emerged as a virulent problem, it has been discussed by a few authors how clergy offenders may be reached and may benefit from treatment (Kelly 1998; Keenan 2012; Rossetti and Müller 1996). This overview should not hide the fact that, even though there are general trends and programs that are geographically spreading out, sex offender treatment approaches are eclectic and very often run on a small scale. Likewise, there cannot be any doubt that there is diversity in interpretation of treatment approaches that bear the same name.

3.4 Treatment of Mentally Ill Sex Offenders

Many countries favor a twin-track system, i.e., sanction systems that provide measures of prevention and correction as one pillar and penalties as the second pillar. Thus, next to the penitentiary treatment of sex offenders, a mental hospital order is possible for mentally ill sex offenders or—to be more precise—sex offenders whose criminal responsibility was diminished or non-existent at the time of the offense.

A specialized measure of prevention and correction is preventive detention. The focus of preventive detention and comparable measures is to protect society from dangerous offenders. It is important to note that according to the ECtHR it is unlawful to retroactively apply preventive detention (Haverkamp and Wößner 2014). In addition, there has to be a "distance" between the living conditions of prisoners and preventive detainees. The distance requirement is based on the fundamentally different objectives and legal grounds for both sanctions and demands a manifest difference between the execution of imprisonment and the conditions of preventive detention (Haverkamp and Wößner 2014, p. 34). The Netherlands has been at the vanguard of humane long-term treatment of dangerous offenders. "Ter Beschikking Stelling" (TBS) is a measure for offenders who committed a certain violent crime and who were suffering from a mental illness at the time of the crime while a causal context between the illness and the crime is not a necessary prerequisite for the application of the underlying law "Beginselenwet Verpleging TBS-gestelden (BVT)" (Braun 2013). The objectives of this TBS-measure are the protection of the public at large, the reduction of reoffending, and the resocialization into an autonomous situation. Pharmacotherapy, psychotherapy (mainly cognitive-behavioral), sociotherapy, creative therapy, behavioral training, and work therapy are the main building blocks of forensic treatment in the TBS-setting. The Netherlands has additionally established long-term forensic care for dangerous offenders who exhibit 6 years of unsuccessful treatment with regard to reducing the risk of reoffending, who were treated in at least two different clinics, and who are not expected to change. These prerequisites have to be established by the clinic and an independent committee (Braun 2013). The Longterm Forensic Psychiatric Care (TBS-LFPC) focuses on the security of society, the stabilization of the psychiatric and clinical situation of the inhabitant (this is the term used for individuals who live in TBS-LFPC), and the optimization of life including slow preparation for further possibilities (Braun 2013, see also de Jonge 2012).

While the Dutch longterm forensic care is a very innovative approach, forensic psychiatric treatment of mentally ill offenders in general is widespread and can be found all over the world (e.g., Palmucci 2006, p. 218). During the past decades, an increasing awareness of the special needs of sex offenders with intellectual disabilities has developed (see e.g., Murphy and Sinclair 2009). Interventions for this focus group adapt key features of cognitive-behavioral therapy and psychoeducation to the intellectual capabilities of these offenders. Treatment facilitators need to be specially trained when working with these offenders.

3.5 A Global Perspective of Sex Offender Treatment

As can be seen, Anglo-American players have been the motor of sex offender treatment and the programs have spread from there to countries that were also inclined to facilitate offender treatment as a means of realizing the sentencing objective of offender reintegration. In Europe, in addition to England and Wales, initiatives from the Nordic countries have influenced the discourse of offender treatment (Palmucci 2006; Stürup 1960; van Beek and Mulder 1992; Wößner 2014). The vast majority of sex offender treatment literature has always originated from English-speaking countries, first and foremost the USA, followed by Canada, the UK, Australia, and New Zealand. Ross and Ross (1995), for instance, estimated that "by the end of 1994, R&R had been delivered to more than eight thousand offenders world-wide" (p. 3). The information what sex offender treatment looks like in other countries on different continents is rather rudimentary. A general review of the literature suggests that most of the countries worldwide, for which offender treatment has become an important means of victim protection and offender reintegration and rehabilitation, endorse some kind of variation of the aforementioned English language concepts of the so-called Western World. R&R is applied in Western European countries such as Spain (Redondo et al. 2012) or Germany (Haverkamp and Wößner 2014). An overview of general correctional treatment approaches that are not specifically aimed at sex offenders in the Ibero-American regions of the world also suggests that R&R is known, at least partly, in the Spanish-speaking areas of the world (Rodriguez Mesa 2012). With regard to sex offenders, Terol Levy (2009) also relies on programs that have worked in other countries and, in doing so, refers exclusively to Anglo-American programs and literature to infer interventions for sex offenders in Spain (see also Garrido Genovés 1993, p. 234). Still, in the 1970s and 1980s there were only isolated interventions in single prisons using specific approaches such as psychodrama or non-directive therapy combined with relaxation techniques (García García and Sancha Mata 1985, p. 148). Subsequently, these initiatives were replaced by Anglo-American treatment approaches. In 1987 and 1988, some correctional facilities implemented for the first time cognitive and skills programs (aimed at juvenile delinquents, see Garrido and Sanchis 1991, p. 111).

Italy, however, seems to have refrained from adopting treatment approaches from Canada and the USA (Gulotta 2011, p. 389) even though equivalent approaches are discussed and correspondent psychometric measures are endorsed (Gulotta 2011; Palmucci 2006). France favors and applies a clinical and psychodynamic approach for sex offender treatment administered in a one-on-one setting (Hirschelmann 2014, p. 26). Additional psychotherapeutic tools are used; they were developed in single penitentiaries and combine mindfulness, psychodynamic, and cognitive-behavioral techniques on a group level (Hirschelmann 2014, p. 26). The Netherlands has also developed special approaches (e.g. van Beek and Mulder 1992, see also above: TBS). In Germany, sex offender treatment primarily takes place in so-called social therapeutic facilities, independent prison units or separate prison wards; the interventions are mainly based on cognitive-behavioral therapy, include (social) work and leisure time measures, and are realized in a social-therapeutic milieu, a key element in the logic of this treatment approach. More and more general correctional treatment approaches have been adapted to fit sex offenders, with most of these approaches stemming from English speaking countries as well (Haverkamp and Wößner 2014, p. 35). After the German government (temporarily) introduced the mandatory treatment of certain sex offenders in social-therapeutic facilities that were initially not meant to focus on sex offenders, practitioners gratefully assimilated these treatment approaches originating from the UK, Canada, and the USA.

Fifteen years after Frenken (1999, p. 87) stated that "[p]ublications in international journals about sexual offender treatment efforts in European countries are scarce", this is still today's status quo. This makes it difficult to draw a comprehensive picture of sex offender treatment. This is especially true for former socialist countries in which women's rights movements, which led to the advent of sex offender treatment, were absent (Frenken 1999, p. 90). Still today, little is known and probably little is done with regard to modern correctional treatment in former socialist countries, especially in the case of sex offenders (Parti et al. 2014; Safin and Salagev 2014). Doubts against more "lenient and humanitarian means and measures" seem to prevail in these countries (e.g., Zalewski 2014, p. 51). Thus, it comes as no surprise that some authorities such as lawmakers in the Czech Republic advocate testicular pulpectomy or bilateral orchidectomy (known as physical castration) as a useful sex offender treatment approach—even against the Committee for the Prevention of Torture's objections (Škvain 2014). Androgen Deprivation Therapy (ADT, i.e., chemical castration)—the less intrusive measure in trying to lower testosterone levels of men—is more widespread e.g., in Poland (Zalewski 2014). In 2005, the Croatian Prison System introduced sex offender treatment as a pilot project in two Croatian penitentiaries. The program incorporated Dutch approaches and includes relapse prevention, learning social skills, empathy training, psychosexual education with the focus on cognitive-behavioral approaches (Muzinic and Vukota 2011).

Looking at Asia, the knowledge about treatment approaches is even less detailed. After several heinous group rapes shattered Indian society recently, India has also started to discuss the introduction of chemical castration (Gill and Harrison 2013). In recent years, China has also started to offer special care for sex offenders, even though little is known about the structure and content of the measures (Lung and Huang 2004, p. 557).[3] The Criminal Code of Taiwan mandates the completion of treatment programs for all incarcerated sex offenders before being paroled or released from prison (Lung et al. 2007). According to a survey conducted by Lung and colleagues (2007), the Taiwanese treatment method focuses on the prevention of sexual recidivism, i.e., it aims at "learning to control their behavior to decrease the risk of recidivism" (p. 344). The survey also showed that sex offender treatment in Taiwanese prisons is still in its infancy.

According to Carranza (2012), Latin American and the Caribbean Countries have faced increasing prison overpopulation over the last two decades. The author argues that both rising crime rates and punitive law reforms have contributed to this development (adding to the particular problem of incarcerated persons without conviction). There is a need for very basic reforms of the penitentiary system in these countries (Carranza 2012), and the necessity of implementing offender treatment, and especially sex offender treatment, is not of first priority. At the same time, some scholars in these countries have recognized the importance of correctional interventions for sex offenders to decrease the risk of reoffending (such as Chile, see Jiménez 2009).

As mentioned above, indigenous sex offenders present a virulent problem in societies where white settlers have immigrated to. Some of these nations, such as

---

[3] http://www.chinapost.com.tw/taiwan/national/national-news/2012/06/15/344424/Protests-halt.htm, accessed 1 July 2014.

Canada (which has always been at the forefront of developing sex offender treatment programs), have also developed programs for this special target group. Single research results substantiate the notion that programs that give special attention to the cultural background of these target groups are more effective than mainstream sex offender treatment programs. Stewart et al. (2015) demonstrated that a culturally specific treatment program for Canadian First Peoples including both cognitive-behavioral methods and traditional Inuit healing knowledge was more effective in reducing recidivism than the alternative programs or no treatment at all. The program also takes into account further related issues such as family violence or substance abuse. Such results point to the importance of an appropriate cultural embedment of treatment; it can prevent treatment attrition and thus improve sex offender treatment outcome (see e.g., Olver et al. 2011).

There surely is a vast array of different treatment programs and treatment approaches for sex offenders all over the world. This overview makes no claim to be complete. Its aim was to show the different levels at which different countries operate in treating sex offenders and the influence that Western stakeholders have in this field.

4 Sex Offender Treatment and Recidivism?

4.1 Recidivism Rates of Sex Offenders

It is a particularly difficult challenge to produce recidivism rates of sex offenders. Being aware of the problem of the dark figure of sex crimes (see above and Selmini in this volume), it is common knowledge among criminologists that the reoffending rate of sex offenders is relatively low, in fact for both sexual and non-sexual offenses (e.g. Hood et al. 2002). Another aspect that has to be considered is the distinctive feature that the recidivism rate of sex offenses increases with a longer follow-up period. While non-sex offenders usually reoffend in the first months or 1–2 years after release, the risk of sex offenders committing another sex crime is more elevated *after* this time frame (e.g., Hood et al. 2002, p. 375).

The standard that is applied to the effectiveness of sex offender treatment is whether these interventions are associated with reduced rates of reoffending. Much attention has been given to the meta-analytical study of Hanson and Bussière (1998), who found an overall sex offense recidivism rate of 13 % within an average follow-up period of 4–5 years. The general recidivism rate for violent offenses was 12 %. For both sex offense recidivism and violence offense recidivism the reoffense rate varied between rapists and child molesters: The sex offense recidivism rate for rapists was 19 %, that of child molesters was 13 %; the reoffense rates for violent offenses were 22 % for rapists, and 10 % for child molesters. With regard to any reoffense as the crucial indicator for recidivism, 36 % of the total sample recidivated, 46 % of the rapists, and 37 % of the child molesters. Even though the most common measures of recidivism were officially registered reconvictions, the meta-analysis included studies that used other indicators such as self-reports, parole violations, indexes, or did not provide the source of the data on recidivism. An overview including more recent studies, however, shows that reoffense rates do not only vary significantly *between* offense types but also *within* offense types. Vess and Skelton (2010, p. 543) cite studies with a range of recidivism rates for rapists between 5 % and 35 % and for child abusers between 3 % and 43 %. The authors themselves conducted a 15-year follow-up study and found the lowest overall reoffense rate for offenders with child victims (11 %, compared to 13.5 % for offenders with adult victims and 17.7 % for offenders with mixed victims). There was a rapid linear increase as the level of actuarial risk increased with the high-risk offenders showing reoffense rates of 35–39 % in the three offense type categories (p. 546).

As mentioned above, reoffense rates very much depend on the considered follow-up period. Studies that use shorter follow-up time frames usually yield smaller recidivism rates. In a study by Hood et al. (2002) only 1.1 % of released sex offenders were imprisoned for a new sex offense 2 years after release, 4.3 % after 4, and 8.5 % (which amounts to 1 in 12 cases) after 6 years. However, 18.1 % were reconvicted and imprisoned for another offense (all in all, 30.9 % of the follow-up sample were reconvicted at some time but without a custodial sentence). However, a comparable ratio of a 5 % reconviction rate with sex offenses was found by Friendship and Thornton (2001) in a 4-year follow-up period. In an earlier study by Marshall (1994), 7 % of 402 sex offenders recidivated with a sex offense 4 years after prison release. The same author detected a sex offense related reconviction rate of 10 % in a follow-up study analyzing a 5-year post-release period (Marshall 1997). All things considered, it is impossible to find a valid and condensed reoffense rate for sex offenders since its calculation depends on many parameters that vary between studies. In borrowing a sentence from a Norwegian recidivism study, it can thus be concluded that sex offense related recidivism is quite low and "can often be viewed as part of a criminal career which includes multiple kinds of crimes" (Weihe 1998, p. 138).

4.2 *Does Sex Offender Treatment Have an Impact on Recidivism?*

The difficult question, though, remains whether sex offender treatment reduces the risk of reoffending after the sex offenders' release from prison. As shown above, the risk of committing a new sex offense is relatively small and varies for different offenders. It is important to have these small base rates in mind when discussing the success of interventions based on recidivism rates. Various research results as to whether sex offender treatment has proven to be effective or not have been controversially discussed. Meta-analyses tend to show a treatment effect. In general, i.e., not only sex offender specific, the most effective treatment programs are cognitive-behavioral models that are well structured and theoretically-based (see Rodriguez Mesa 2012).

In Schmucker and Lösel's (2005, p. 225) meta-analysis, studies with the best internal validity exhibited the lowest differences in reoffense rates between treated and untreated sex offenders. The authors thus conclude—on the basis of the only few experimental studies—that no unambiguous conclusions about the effectiveness of sex offender treatment can be drawn. The authors established the greatest effectiveness for cognitive-behavioral programs that are specifically targeted toward sex offenders (Schmucker and Lösel 2008): 11 % of treated and 17.5 % of untreated control subjects reoffended, which amounts to a sex offense specific re-offense rate difference of 37 %. But even though there is a small overall positive effect to be detected, due to the heterogeneity of the study outcomes Schmucker (2004, p. 259) warns against exaggerated optimism. Rice and Harris (2013) as well as Eher and Pfäfflin (2011) are even more cautious. They arrive at the conclusion that there is no treatment effect left, once all confounding variables are taken into consideration. Factors influencing the outcome of the results include an array of factors such as: authors' affiliation to the treatment program, offense type, voluntariness of treatment participation, treatment termination or drop-out, sample size, control group formation, source of recidivism data, treatment approach, treatment setting (only outpatient treatment was effective), publication status (published versus unpublished), and design quality (Schmucker and Lösel 2008). Likewise, Hanson et al. (2009) did not infer any treatment effect. Marques et al. (2005), who conducted one of the few "Gold Standard" RCT studies, also failed to provide evidence for sex offender treatment effectiveness. It has to be kept in mind that the gauge for effectiveness is always the reduction of reoffense rates. With regard to this measure, a stable and robust effect of sex offender treatment can only be claimed very cautiously.

Only recently, scholars have turned their attention to the relationship between treatment change and recidivism. Beggs (2010) conducted a review of publications on within-treatment outcomes among sexual offenders from 1994 to 2007 and found that the majority of the included studies resulted in prosocial treatment change. Only three of the included studies analyzed the relationship between therapeutic change and recidivism. In these studies, only single effects between prosocial change and reduced recidivism could be found; thus, there was no overall relationship between therapeutic change and reduced recidivism. The studies that have—since then—addressed this issue produced inconclusive findings as well. Some researchers found individual treatment changes of the measures under scrutiny but no relationship with recidivism (Beggs and Grace 2011; Woessner and Schwedler 2014). Barnett and colleagues (Barnett et al. 2012, 2013) analyzed the treatment outcome of 3402 sex offenders who had been treated in a community program with regard to recidivism. According to their first study, a few single test scores at pre- or posttest level correlated with recidivism. Their second study yielded comparable recidivism rates for sex offenders who showed a clinically significant or reliable change and those who did not show such meaningful improvements on the various psychometric measures. In addition, recidivism could not be predicted after the single scale measures were combined into domains.

For the sake of completeness, we need to briefly discuss whether Androgen Deprivation Therapy (ADT; chemical castration or pharmacotherapy) produces the intended effects. It has been argued that ADT is only designed to treat pedophiles. Sexual arousal plays a crucial role for offender types with a preferential paraphilia, e.g., pedophilia. In such cases it might be useful to deplete the sexual arousal for children. In contrast, rapes involving adult victims are only very rarely based on sexual arousal per se, they are most likely associated with anger, power, or a lack of emotional coping and problem solving skills, and cognitive distortions (see Gill and Harrison 2013, p. 171). Thus it is crucial to identify whether the sex offender indeed presents with a problem that can be treated with sex drive depressant pharmaceuticals (Gnoth and Borchard 2012, p. 370).

In closing, we will draw our attention to specific features that scholars found to be associated or not to be associated with treatment and its benefit for recidivism. Hood et al. 2002 (p. 387) found that denial of treatment is not associated with increased reoffense rates. Recidivism rates vary depending on the type of offense. Sex offenders who offend against boys, for instance, exhibit a particularly high reconviction rate, sex offenders who offended against a child in their family a particularly low reconviction rate (e.g. Hood et al. 2002; Vess and Skelton 2010). Paraphilic offenders, not only including pedophiles but also offenders who present a sexual sadistic disorder, are in general difficult to treat (Garrido Genovés 1993). It has also been a long-term discussion that offenders with personality disorders are a particular challenge for correctional treatment.

In sum, only a few studies have investigated whether therapeutic change is indeed related to recidivism. This may surprise, since the logical fundament of most offender treatment programs is the supposition that correctional treatment should improve dynamic (changeable) criminogenic risk factors and thus lead to reduced recidivism. At the same time, there is solid empirical evidence that dynamic risk factors are associated with reoffending. Albeit the heterogeneity of the results, something works with regard to the effects sex offender treatment exerts on reducing reoffending even though the effects are small. It is important to note "that it is still difficult to draw firm conclusions about the efficacy of these programmes [...] and [...] that it is unlikely that firm conclusions can be easily drawn in the future given the wide range of methodological issues that make evaluating the programmes problematic" (Brown 2010, p. 100). Differences in control and comparison groups are an important issue that may account for the small outcome effects. In addition, appropriate evaluation research should—in theory—distinguish between different types of sex offenders in order to detect the "real" effectiveness for more homogeneous subgroups: A demand that fails because subsamples will become so small that statistical analyses and conclusions become very difficult. However, trying to detect a treatment effect for such a heterogeneous group as sex offenders is almost impossible. Finally, researchers can only determine what really is hidden behind sex offender treatment when a clear cut manualized treatment program is delivered—which hardly ever is the case—and it is very unlikely that these are the programs that sex offenders benefit the most from. No matter if a manualized or more comprehensive intervention is delivered, most of the evaluation studies solely focus on the relationship between whether an intervention took place and its effects on reoffense rates.

Rarely does any study look into the quality of treatment delivery. After all, discouraging therapy effects may also result from weak treatment delivery, a high personnel fluctuation, and many other aspects that are closely linked with what is "inside" the treatment box. Lastly, a particular group of sex offenders that exhibits high-risk and high-needs is thus, at the same time, a group that is the least likely to complete treatment (Olver et al. 2011). It is a specific challenge for this high-risk and high-needs group to benefit from treatment and to be able to transfer the acquired competencies to real-life even years after prison release. Summing up, sex offender treatment approaches that have yielded the largest effects with regard to reducing recidivism comply with the Risk-Need-Responsivity principle by Andrews and Bonta (2010) and endorse cognitive-behavioral treatment.[4] More recent approaches such as the GLM have—to date—not been satisfactorily tested (see Willis et al. 2014). Each sex crime that can be prevented by treating an offender is an asset, thus practitioners and researchers alike should not stop trying to improve our knowledge on what works in sex offender treatment and how it actually works.

5 The Dangerousness of Sexual Offenders

According to the basic assumptions of the RNR-model, sex offender treatment should be directed at the risk-level of offenders. Therapy aims to reduce the dangerousness of sex offenders. Thus, once a sex offender is to be released, it is equally important to determine the risk of reoffending. Sex offenders in general have become the "folk devils" of society (Cohen 2002). They are perceived as omnipresent perpetrators (McAlinden 2010, p. 381), who are ready to lunge out at any time. This general public attitude has impeded the rehabilitation of released sex offenders, as the release of sex offenders into a community sparks fear and opposition. The realities of sexual violence are vastly biased to a large degree due to the media's constant trend of recent years to sensationalize sex offenses (Della Giustina 2009). Thus, since the 1990s the risk management approach has boomed (Golding 2010). Excessive and preventative sentencing, multi-agency public protection programs, sex offender notification and registration laws, and electronic monitoring of released sex offenders have mushroomed (Golding 2010; Harrison 2014; Haverkamp and Wößner 2014; Thomas 2005). Gradually, the punitive turn has spilled over from the US to Western Europe, first to the UK but also to other countries, such as France and Germany, albeit to a different extent. This

[4] However, the abovementioned evaluation biases have to be kept in mind, that is, that authors who are affiliated to treatment programs tend to yield more positive findings.

development has entailed the need for risk assessment in order to identify dangerous offenders. There are several tools that assist the diagnostician in so doing. These tools represent the wish to manage this crucial and difficult assessment of whether a given sex offender is still dangerous or not.

The assessment of dangerousness is mainly concerned with the question whether released sex offenders will commit future sex or violent offenses. There are a number of risk assessment instruments to measure this, most of which focus on *static* risk factors (remember, these are historical factors that are no longer changeable, see Sect. 3.2 in this chapter). Actuarial risk assessment tools use statistical results in order to predict the likelihood of future behavior. Crucial items, established to be associated with recidivism, are scored (mostly in "absent" or "present" items), summed up, and result in a determined risk-level (e.g., low, medium, high; Craig et al. 2009). Some of the most prominent actuarial risk assessment tools are the *Rapid Risk Assessment for Sexual Offense Recidivism* (RRASOR, Hanson 1997), the *Static-99* and its successor *Static-2002* (Hanson and Thornton 2000, 2003), the *Sex Offense Risk Appraisal Guide* (SORAG, Quinsey et al. 1998), or the *Sexual Violence Risk-20*[5] (SVR-20, Boer et al. 1997). Actuarial risk assessment tools are quite popular since they are very effective in predicting sexual reconviction (Hanson and Morton-Bourgon 2005). Dynamic assessment instruments measure stable and acute factors that can be modified. The *STABLE-2007* (Hanson and Harris 2007a) covers six stable dynamic dimensions (social influences, intimacy deficits, attitudes supportive to sex crimes, cooperation with supervision, sexual self-regulation, and general self-regulation). The *ACUTE-2007* (Hanson and Harris 2007b) is an instrument that measures acute risk factors (e.g., emotional distress, substance abuse, and sexual preoccupations). Most of these tools aim at adult offenders, thus, youth-specific instruments were accessorily developed such as *the Juvenile Sex Offender Assessment Protocol-II* (J-SOAP-II, Prentky and Righthand 2003) or the *Estimate of Risk of Adolescent Sexual Offense Recidivism* (ERASOR, Worling and Curwen 2001; Hoge and Andrews 2006).

Similar to sex offender treatment, risk assessment tools stemming mainly from Canada, the US, and England and Wales have since been used in other countries (and continents), too. This gives rise to the question whether these instruments are still valid in other cultural settings. In a study on the suitability of the widely used STABLE-2007, Helmus et al. (2012) showed that some of the Stable-2007 items, an updated version of its original predecessor STABLE-2000, are not predictive for Canadian First Peoples sex offenders (a subgroup of sex offenders who is overrepresented in Canadian prisons). Especially the items aiming at antisocial personality traits were less predictive for First Peoples. This result substantiates that we should transfer such assessment tools with caution to any other cultural setting.

[5] The SVR-20 is not a true actuarial tool since it allows for the assessment of three acute dynamic risk factors and does not use a final score to determine the risk-level.

New Zealand researchers also stress the cultural insensitivity of risk assessment instruments (Tamatea et al. 2011, p. 313).

France has developed its "own" assessment tools and hardly uses actuarial instruments (Hirschelmann 2014, p. 25). A Dutch research team developed a structured assessment tool to measure protective factors for violence risk which may add to the risk assessment of sex offenders (SAPROF, de Vogel et al. 2007). Research on the implementation of sex offender risk assessment has indicated that these measures are not always properly administered (Lanterman et al. 2014). Given the tremendous consequences false applications can have, it is important to warn against misuse and inadequate use of risk assessment instruments. The risk assessment tools are not theory-based. Some of them suggest a simple but undue sum-up of scores. In addition, it is difficult to discern in which cases a prognostic criterion has a stark impact or not. Finally, the application of risk assessment tools is associated with running the risk of disregarding other factors that might be additionally important to predict sex offenders' probability to reoffend. Scoones et al. (2012) showed, for instance, that proper and comprehensive release planning is associated with a decreased rate of recidivism.

6 Some Concluding Reflections: Where Do We Stand and Where Are We Going?

In the last decades, managing sexual offenders has emerged as a crucial issue of criminal policy in many countries. Among both the public at large and politicians an increased punitive trend has evolved, accompanied by the call for harsher sanctioning, i.e., longer or lifelong sentences or even the death penalty. However, those demands are short-sighted. It has to be kept in mind that long-term detention in a total institution such as a correctional facility is inevitably associated with major side-effects that are not conducive to offender rehabilitation. Long-term incarceration in general "raise existential problems of coping" (van Zyl Smit and Snacken 2009, p. 50). That said, it is important to note that the impact long-term imprisonment has on an inmate is influenced by both the prisoner's individual characteristics and the prison's and society's characteristic (van Zyl Smit and Snacken 2009, p. 50). But still, long-term detention has detrimental effects: psychological regression toward childlike behavior and dependence on staff, emotional regression and instability, passivity and apathy, psychosomatic symptoms, and fear of release (van Zyl Smit and Snacken 2009, p. 51). However, there are also studies suggesting that long-term imprisonment does not have detrimental psychological effects (see, in sum, van Zyl Smit and Snacken 2009, p. 52). Since sexual offending is to a great extent associated with a dysfunctional coping style, one can imagine that long-term incarceration does not work against but for the risk of reoffending. The same applies to the fact that long-term incarceration can lead to decreased self-esteem or increased acting-out: low self-esteem might increase the risk of child abuse; hostile thinking patterns are likely to be a prerequisite of sexual aggressive behavior. Incarcerated sex offenders in particular are very likely to start masturbating to fantasies surrounding the offense that led to their conviction; a problem that is discussed by several authors (see Epps 1994; Marshall 1989). Such mechanisms are very likely to reinforce deviant and/or violent sexual behavior. Long-term incarceration may—especially for sex offenders—have a detrimental effect on their ability to relate to others, to develop intimate relationship skills, and to develop a healthy sexuality. Thus, a long incarceration will not contribute to healing the intimacy or attachment deficits some sex offenders exhibit (see Epps 1994; Marshall 1989). Thus, a longer period of incarceration as an alternative to correctional treatment does not present an alternative and is out of the question with regard to the rule of law, even though qualitative research has shown that imprisonment may elicit a positive personal change preventing some sex offenders from continued offending and forcing them to reflect about themselves and their behavior (Elisha et al. 2012). While noting the pitfalls of long-term imprisonment, this is not a plea for the release of all sexual offenders. Some sex offenders clearly present a real danger and our knowledge on how to distinguish sex offenders who present a continuous risk for women and children has to be steadily improved to decrease both false negative but also false positive prognoses. However, given the comparably low numbers of sex crimes, the relatively small recidivism rates, and the fact that the majority of sex crimes are committed in the direct vicinity of the offender, it is desirable that the discussion about incapacitation, treatment, and dangerousness of sex offenders should experience a *rational* rather than a *punitive* turn.

The history of correction has seen different phases from "nothing works" (Martinson 1974) to "something works" (Ross and Gendreau 1980). Although skepticism as to whether sex offender treatment is effective remains, it can be concluded that the "negative effect of punishment has in fact overpowered its positive effects" (Sarangi 2000, p. 96). Punishment alone usually removes the punished behavior only as long as punishment occurs. However, how do we reach a balance between punishing criminal behavior and resocializing the offender? A basic rationale of correctional intervention is the idea that prisoners—after their release from prison—will only be able to desist from reoffending if they are permitted to reassimilate and reintegrate into the community and find their place and way in "mainstream" society (see van Zyl Smit and Snacken 2009, p. 106).

The strong urge for public protection has led to measures that interfere with rehabilitative objectives. Sex offender residence restrictions, for instance, have devastating effects on rehabilitation, virtually precluding reintegration due to housing instabilities, limited accessibility to employment opportunities, and severed social support (Levenson and Hern 2007).

So, with this plea in mind, what will future sex offender treatment entail? Spirituality as an important building block for a new life without delinquency has been recently detected by Ward and colleagues (GLM, see above). Sarangi (2000, p. 97) also emphasizes that different meditational and yoga techniques have been introduced to Indian prisons in order to help prisoners maintain their psychophysical homeostasis. The author argues that especially the ancient meditation technique "Vipassana" ("insight") has "much potential for reforming criminal behavior". The inmates are encouraged to analyze and observe themselves in order to realize "negative dimensions of their personalities". But not only is the inner analysis of negative aspects of importance. It might also be promising to increase the motivation to change since it brings a sense of wellbeing and a notion of what kind of person the prisoner wants to be into the life of the inmate. Sarangi (2000, p. 98) argues that "Vipassana" reduces hostility and helplessness. In some parts of India, it is believed that "Vipassana" has a "tremendous impact in changing the lifestyle [...] of the prisoners in a positive way" (Sarangi 2000, p. 98). Beech and Gillespie (2014) emphasize that the problematic attachment and further formative developmental experiences in sex offenders lead to neurobiological impairment and that these conditions should be taken into account when treating these offenders especially with regard to the emotion regulation skills. The authors propose adding mindfulness and breathing therapy to classic cognitive-behavioral treatment since the physiological underpinnings of emotion regulation and controlled breathing suggest a benefit for prefrontal neurobiological conditions of emotion regulation. It is all but impossible to keep track of further alternative approaches that have doubtlessly been established all over the world. Interestingly, although meta-analyses support—however with small effect sizes only—cognitive-behavioral approaches, singular interventions stemming from a different therapeutic discipline have been adopted, i.e., attachment-based psychodynamic psychotherapy (Haley 2010) or systemic psychotherapy (Shelton 2010).

It should be welcomed that stakeholders constantly try to improve interventions that aim to prevent further sex crimes. Further discussions may profit from the criticism of the treatment models, for instance that the RNR-model stresses the "negative", i.e., risk factors of individuals. Even though traits such as self-control, agreeableness, or extraversion play a central role in the measurement of risk, need, and responsivity (Ward and Maruna 2007, p. 84), a person and his/her motivation to change cannot be reduced to these traits. More novel approaches take the personality as a whole into account, thus stressing the role of the narrative identity. Self-narratives are expected to shape and guide a person's behavior, as persons act in ways that agree with the stories or myths they have created about themselves (Ward and Maruna 2007, p. 85). The narrative identity is an active information processing structure including sets of cognitive schemas that evolve over time on the grounds of the experiences a person makes and the people a person deals with. Sex offender therapy—as opined by Maruna (2001)—may benefit from including this approach into treatment in that it helps offenders develop a more adaptive self-narrative and "change their habitual ways of understanding their life" (Ward and Maruna 2007, p. 86). At most, it is an important concept in understanding desistance from crime and for opening up to innovative approaches to sex offenders (e.g., restorative justice (see Kury in this volume).

Sexual violence against women and children not only affects the victim and the offender. Sexual violence may also have a bearing at an institutional or community level. Communities and society at large respond to sex crimes, as can be shown more in the form of punitive and disintegrating reactions. Sex offender treatment and rehabilitation and reintegration efforts are deeply linked to this community level. There is universal reluctance of some professionals to treat sex offenders (Frenken 1999) thus impeding the treatment of sex offenders in the community. This is astounding since outpatient treatment proved to be the most efficient therapeutic approach to sex offenders. In addition, outpatient treatment may serve as a preventive measure before a crime occurs. Furthermore, it may take a while for societies with prevailing patriarchal values to introduce and realize sex offender treatments that work with rape myths, or a gender balanced attitude toward women—key issues in the interventions that address cognitive distortions and belief systems of offenders and change coping patterns. Finally, sex offender treatment approaches have for the most part been developed for and applied to ethnic majorities, not minorities.

In closing, it has to be emphasized that sex offender treatment is an important means of crime prevention even though research regularly yields finite results. Too little is known as to the question how programs actually work. There is a tremendous need to increase this knowledge since offender treatment is an important fundamental aspect of a humane society—and incarceration increases the likelihood of reoffending (see Soyer 2014, p. 91). The expectations of bringing about changes to individuals in a total institution (prison) should not be too high. The base rate of sex offender recidivism is comparatively small—even though this statement should not hide the fact that the implications sexual victimization have can be devastating. However, long-term imprisonment or lifelong detention can only present an alternative for the most dangerous offenders. We have to make sure those mistakes with regard to the identification of high-risk offenders and with regard to the treatment and management of sex offenders are constantly reduced. In order to do so, it helps to take a differentiated look at sex offending, sex offenders, and treatment and incarceration effects to improve offender reintegration prospects and at the same time victim protection.

Five Questions

1. How can sex offender treatment be improved in order to increase victim protection and which contents and methods should future sex offender treatment entail?
2. What are the actual mechanisms of treatment change and its transfer to post-release desistance?
3. What are appropriate measures of successful interventions for sex offenders to evaluate the benefits of sex offender treatment and by means of which methodological approaches can we improve the evaluation of sex offender treatment and prognosis?
4. Do sex offenders need specific therapeutic attention and what are the key treatment targets for different subgroups of sex offenders? Is it justified to transfer treatment programs from one cultural setting to another or from adults to adolescent?
5. What is the link between sex offender therapy and theoretical knowledge about sex offending?

References

Andrews, D. A., & Bonta, J. (2010). *The psychology of criminal conduct* (5th ed.). Newark, NJ: LexisNexus/Anderson.

Andrews, D. A., Zinger, I., Hoge, R. D., Bonta, J., Gendreau, P., & Cullen, F. T. (1990). Does correctional treatment work? A clinically relevant and psychologically informed meta-analysis. *Criminology, 28*, 369–404.

Australian Bureau of Statistics. (2003). *Prisoners in Australia 2003*. Canberra: ABS. http://www.abs.gov.au/ausstats/abs@.nsf/mf/4517.0. Accessed 13 June 2014.

Barnett, G. D., Wakeling, H., Mandeville-Norden, R., & Rakestrow, J. (2012). How useful are psychometric scores in predicting recidivism for treated sex offenders? *International Journal of Offender Therapy and Comparative Criminology, 56*(3), 420–446.

Barnett, G. D., Wakeling, H., Mandeville-Norden, R., & Rakestrow, J. (2013). Does change in psychometric test scores tell us anything about risk of reconviction in sexual offenders? *Psychology, Crime and Law, 19*(1), 85–110.

Beech, A. R., & Gillespie, S. M. (2014). The understanding and treatment of sexual offenders in the 21st century. *Monatsschrift für Kriminologie und Strafrechtsreform, 97*(1), 78–84.

Beggs, S. M. (2010). Within-treatment outcome among sexual offenders: A review. *Aggression and Violent Behavior, 15*, 369–379.

Beggs, S. M., & Grace, R. C. (2011). Treatment gain for sexual offenders against children predicts reduced recidivism: A comparative validity study. *Journal of Consulting and Clinical Psychology, 79*(2), 182–192.

Bench, L. L., & Allen, T. D. (2013). Assessing sex offender recidivism using multiple measures: A longitudinal analysis. *The Prison Journal, 93*(4), 411–428.

Berman, G., & Dar, A. (2013). *Prison population statistics*. London: Library House of Commons.

Bieneck, S., Stadler, L., & Pfeiffer, C. (2011). *Erster Forschungsbericht zur Repräsentativbefragung Sexualler Missbrauch 2011*. Hannover: Kriminologisches Forschungsinstitut Niedersachsen.

Boer, D. P., Hart, S. D., Kropp, P. R., & Webster, C. D. (1997). *Manual for the Sexual Violence Risk – 20. Professional guidelines for assessing risk of sexual violence*. Burnaby, BC: Simon Fraser University, Mental Health, Law, and Policy Institute.

Braun, P. (2013). *The Longstay concept for dangerous offenders in the Netherlands*. Lecture held at the expert meeting "The development of sexual offender laws and treatment in Europe", Max Planck Institute for Foreign and International Criminal Law, Freiburg i.Br., 17 May 2013.

Brown, S. (2010). An introduction to sex offender treatment programmes and their risk reduction efficacy. In K. Harrison (Ed.), *Managing high-risk sex offenders in the community. Risk management, treatment and social responsibility* (pp. 81–104). Cullompton: Willan Publishing.

Bundesministerium des Innern. (2014). *Polizeiliche Kriminalstatistik PKS 2013*. Berlin: Bundesministerium des Innern.

Burgess, A. W., & Holmstrom, L. L. (1974). Rape trauma syndrome. *The American Journal of Psychiatry, 9*, 981–986.

Campbell, R. (2008). The psychological impact of rape victims' experiences with the legal, medical, and mental health systems. *American Psychologist, 68*, 702–717.

Carranza, E. (2012). Situación penitenciaria en América Latina y el Caribe ¿Qué hacer? *Anuario De Derechos Humanos, 8*, 31–66.

Carson, E. A., & Golinelli, D. (2013). *Prisoners in 2012 - Advance Counts*. U.S. Department of Justice, Office of Justice Programs, Bureau of Justice Statistics.

Casey, E. A., & Nurius, P. S. (2006). Trends in the prevalence and characteristics of sexual violence: A cohort analysis. *Violence and Victims, 21*(5), 629–644.

Chu, M. C., & Thomas, S. D. M. (2010). Adolescent sexual offenders: The relationship between typology and recidivism. *Sexual Abuse: A Journal of Research and Treatment, 22*(2), 218–233.

Cohen, S. (2002). *Folk devils and moral panic* (4th ed.). London and New York: Routledge.

Cossins, A. (2006). Prosecuting child sexual assault cases: To specialize or not, that is the question. *Current Issues in Criminal Justice, 18*(2), 318–341.

Craig, L. A., Beech, A. R., & Harkins, L. (2009). The predictive accuracy of risk factors and frameworks. In A. R. Beech, L. A. Craig, & K. D. Browne (Eds.), *Assessment and treatment of sex offenders: A handbook* (pp. 53–74). Chichester: John Wiley and Sons.

Craig, L. A., Browne, K. D., Stringer, I., & Beech, A. (2005). Sexual recidivism: A review of static, dynamic and actuarial predictors. *Journal of Sexual Aggression, 11*(1), 65–84.

de Jonge, G. (2012). *Unterbringung gefährlicher Täter in den Niederlanden.* 38. Arbeits- und Fortbildungstagung der Bundesvereinigung der Anstaltsleiter und Anstaltsleiterinnen im Justizvollzug e.V., Lingen, 7–11 May 2012.

de Vogel, V., de Ruiter, C., Bouman, Y. H. A., & de Vries Robbé, M. (2007). *SAPROF. Richtlijnen voor het beoordelen van beschermende factoren voor gewelddadig gedrag.* Utrecht: Forum Educatief.

Della Giustina, J.-A. (2009). Sexual violence and restorative justice. In R. G. Wright (Ed.), *Sex offender laws: Failed policies, new directions* (pp. 449–469). New York, NY, US: Springer.

Dignan, J. (2005). *Understanding victims and restorative justice.* Maidenhead: Open University Press.

Dunne, M. P., Purdie, D. M., Cook, M. D., Boyle, F. M., & Najman, J. M. (2003). Is child sexual abuse declining? Evidence from a population-based survey of men and women in Australia. *Child Abuse and Neglect, 27*(2), 141–152.

Eher, R., & Pfäfflin, F. (2011). Adult sexual offender treatment – Is it effective? In D. P. Boer, R. Eher, L. A. Craig, M. H. Miner, & F. Pfäfflin (Eds.), *International perspectives on the assessment and treatment of sexual offenders: Theory, practice, and research* (pp. 3–12). Chichester, UK: Wiley-Blackwell.

Elisha, E., Idisis, Y., & Ronel, N. (2012). Window of opportunity: Social acceptance and life transformation in the rehabilitation of imprisoned sex offenders. *Aggression and Violent Behavior, 17*, 323–332.

Ellerby, L. A., & MacPherson, P. (2002). *Contrasting aboriginal and non-aboriginal sexual offenders to determine unique client characteristics and potential implications for sex offender assessment and treatment strategies* (research report no. R-122). Ottawa, ON: Correctional Service of Canada. http://www.csc-scc.gc.ca/research/r122-eng.shtml. Accessed 20 June 2014.

Endrass, J., Müller-Pozzi, H., & Rossegger, A. (2012). Deliktpräventive Therapie aus der Perspektive der Psychoanalyse. In J. Endrass, A. Rossegger, F. Urbaniok, & B. Borchard (Eds.), *Interventionen bei Gewalt-und Sexualstraftätern* (pp. 142–163). Berlin: MWV.

Epps, K. J. (1994). Treating adolescent sex offenders in secure conditions: The experience at Glenthorne Centre. *Journal of Adolescence, 17*(2), 105–122.

Evans, D. R. (1968). Masturbatory fantasy and sexual deviation. *Behaviour Research and Therapy, 6*, 17–19.

Finkelhor, D., & Shattuck, A. (2012). *Characteristics of crimes against juveniles.* Durham, NH: Crimes against Children Research Center. (CV26R).

Fischer, G., & Riedesser, P. (1998). *Lehrbuch der Psychotraumatologie.* München: Ernst Reinhardt.

Frenken, J. (1999). Sexual offender treatment in Europe: An impression of cross-cultural differences. *Sexual Abuse: A Journal of Research and Treatment, 11*(1), 87–93.

Friendship, C., & Thornton, D. (2001). Sexual reconviction for sexual offenders discharged from prison in England and Wales. *British Journal of Criminology, 41*(2), 285–292.

García García, J., & Sancha Mata, V. (1985). *Psicologia penitenciaria (areas de intervencion terapeutica).* Madrid: UNED.

Garrido Genovés, V. (1993). *Técnicas de tratamiento para delincuentes.* Madrid: Editorial Centro de Estudios Ramon Areces.

Garrido, V., & Sanchis, J. R. (1991). The cognitive model in the treatment of Spanish offenders: Theory and practice. *Journal of Correctional Education, 42*(2), 111–118.

Gendreau, P., Little, T., & Goggin, C. (1996). A meta-analysis of the predictors of adult offender recidivism: What works! *Criminology, 34*(4), 575–607.
Gill, A. K., & Harrison, K. (2013). Sentencing sex offenders in India: Retributive justice versus sex-offender treatment programmes and restorative justice approaches. *International Journal of Criminal Justice Sciences, 8*(2), 166–181.
Gnoth, A., & Borchard, B. (2012). Gesamtbehandlungsplan in der medikamentösen Behandlung von Sexualstraftätern. In J. Endrass, A. Rossegger, F. Urbaniok, & B. Borchard (Eds.), *Interventionen bei Gewalt-und Sexualstraftätern* (pp. 368–380). Berlin: MWV.
Golding, B. (2010). Sex offender management in the community: Who are the victims? In M. Nash, & A. Williams (Eds.), *Handbook of public protection* (pp. 234–250). Abingdon: Willan Publishing.
Grubin, D., & Thornton, D. (1994). A national program for the assessment and treatment of sex offenders in the English prison system. *Criminal Justice and Behavior, 21*(1), 55–71.
Gulotta, G. (2011). *Compendio di psicologia giuridico-forense, criminale e investigativa*. Milano: Giuffrè Editore.
Haley, M. (2010). Attachment-based psychodynamic psychotherapy. In J. Harvey, & K. Smedley (Eds.), *Psychological therapy in prisons and other secure settings* (pp. 48–70). Cullompton: Willan Publishing.
Hanson, R. K. (1997). *The development of a brief actuarial risk scale for sexual offense recidivism* (User Report No. 1997-04). Ottawa: Department of the Solicitor General of Canada.
Hanson, R. K., Bourgon, G., Helmus, L., & Hodgson, S. (2009). The principles of effective correctional treatment also apply to sexual offenders: A meta-analysis. *Criminal Justice and Behavior, 36*(9), 865–891.
Hanson, R. K., & Bussière, M. T. (1998). Predicting relapse: A meta-analysis of sexual offender recidivism studies. *Journal of Consulting and Clinical Psychology, 66*(2), 348–362.
Hanson, R. K., & Harris, A. J. (2000). Where should we intervene? Dynamic predictors of sexual offense recidivism. *Criminal Justice and Behavior, 27*(1), 6–35.
Hanson, R. K., & Harris, A. J. (2001). A structured approach to evaluating change among sexual offenders. *Sex Abuse, 13*, 105–122.
Hanson, R. K., & Harris, A. J. (2007a). *Stable-2007 master coding guide*. Ottawa: Public Safety and Emergency Preparedness Canada.
Hanson, R. K., & Harris, A. J. (2007b). *Acute-2007 scoring guide*. Ottawa: Public Safety and Emergency Preparedness Canada.
Hanson, R. K., & Morton-Bourgon, K. (2004). *Predictors of sexual recidivism: An updated meta-analysis* (Research Rep. No. 2004-02). Ottawa: Public Safety and Emergency Preparedness Canada.
Hanson, R. K., & Morton-Bourgon, K. (2005). The characteristics of persistent sexual offenders: A meta-analysis of recidivism studies. *Journal of Consulting and Clinical Psychology, 73*(6), 1154–1163.
Hanson, R. K., & Thornton, D. (2000). Improving risk assessment for sex offenders: A comparison of three actuarial scales. *Law and Human Behavior, 24*, 119–136.
Hanson, R. K., & Thornton, D. (2003). *Notes on the development of Static-2002* (User Report 2003-01). Ottawa: Department of the Solicitor General of Canada.
Harrison, K. (2014). Governing serious offenders: Developments in legislation in England and Wales. *Monatsschrift für Kriminologie und Strafrechtsreform, 97*(1), 10–18.
Haverkamp, R., & Wößner, G. (2014). New responses to sexual offenders: Recent developments in legislation and treatment in Germany. *Monatsschrift für Kriminologie und Strafrechtsreform, 97*(1), 31–39.
Heiskanen, M. (2010). Trends in police-recorded crime. In S. Harrendorf, M. Heiskanen, & S. Malby (Eds.), *International statistics on crime and justice, HEUNI Publication Series No. 64* (pp. 21–47). Helsinki: European Institute for Crime Prevention and Control.
Helmus, L., Babchishin, K. M., & Blais, J. (2012). Predictive accuracy of dynamic risk factors for Aboriginal and Non-Aboriginal sex offenders: An exploratory comparison using STABLE-

2007. *International Journal of Offender Therapy and Comparative Criminology, 56*(6), 856–876.

Hirschelmann, A. (2014). Some new penal and therapeutic tendencies in France in the trade-off between treating sexual offenders and protecting society. *Monatsschrift für Kriminologie und Strafrechtsreform, 97*(1), 19–30.

Hoge, R. D., & Andrews, D. A. (2006). *Youth Level of Service/Case Management Inventory (YLS/CMI). User's manual*. Toronto: Multi-Health Systems.

Hood, R., Shute, S., Feilzer, M., & Wilcox, A. (2002). Sex offenders emerging from long-term imprisonment. *British Journal of Criminology, 42*, 371–394.

Jewkes, R., Sen, P., & Garcia-Moreno, C. (2002). Sexual violence. In E. G. Krug, L. L. Dahlberg, J. A. Mercy, A. B. Zwi, & R. Lozano (Eds.), *World report on violence and health* (pp. 147–182). Geneva: World Health Organization.

Jiménez, P. (2009). Caracterización psicológica de un grupo de delincuentes sexuales Chilenos a través del test de Rorschach. *Psykhe, 18*(1), 27–38.

Keane, T. M., Marx, B. P., & Sloan, D. M. (2009). Post-traumatic stress disorder: Definition, prevalence, and risk factors. In J. E. LeDoux, T. Keane, & P. Shiromani (Eds.), *Post-traumatic stress disorder. Basic science and clinical practice* (pp. 1–19). Totowa, NJ: Humana Press.

Keenan, M. (2012). *Child sexual abuse and the Catholic church. Gender, power, and organizational culture*. New York: Oxford University Press.

Kelly, A. F. (1998). Clergy offenders. In W. L. Marshall, Y. M. Fernandez, S. M. Hudson, & T. Ward (Eds.), *Sourcebook of treatment programs for sexual offenders* (pp. 303–318). New York: Plenum Press.

Kristensen, E., Fristed, P., Fuglestved, M., Grahn, E., Larsen, M., Lillebaek, T., et al. (2011). The Danish Sexual Offender Treatment and Research Program (DASOP). In D. P. Boer, R. Eher, L. A. Craig, M. H. Miner, & F. Pfäfflin (Eds.), *International perspectives on the assessment and treatment of sexual offenders: Theory, practice, and research* (pp. 251–262). Chichester, UK: Wiley-Blackwell.

Kristoffersen, R. (2010). *Correctional Statistics of Denmark, Finland, Iceland, Norway and Sweden 2004–2008*. Correctional Service of Norway Staff Academy.

Kury, H., Chouaf, S., Obergfell-Fuchs, J., & Woessner, G. (2004a). The scope of sexual victimization in Germany. *Journal of Interpersonal Violence, 19*(5), 589–602.

Kury, H., Obergfell-Fuchs, J., Kloppenburg, V., & Woessner, G. (2003). New approaches to preventing sexual crimes in Germany. In H. Kury, & J. Obergfell-Fuchs (Eds.), *Crime prevention. New approaches* (pp. 277–320). Mainz: Weisser Ring.

Kury, H., Obergfell-Fuchs, J., & Woessner, G. (2004b). The extent of family violence in Europe. *Violence against Women, 10*(7), 749–769.

Lanterman, J. L., Boyle, D. J., & Ragusa-Salerno, L. M. (2014). Sex offender risk assessment, sources of variation, and the implications of misuse. *Criminal Justice and Behavior, 41*(7), 822–843.

Letourneau, E. J., Borduin, C. M., & Schaeffer, C. M. (2009). Multisystemic therapy for youth with problem sexual behaviors. In A. R. Beech, L. A. Craig, & K. D. Browne (Eds.), *Assessment and treatment of sex offenders: A handbook* (pp. 453–472). Chichester: John Wiley and Sons.

Levenson, J. S., & Hern, A. L. (2007). Sex offender residence restrictions: Unintended consequences and community reentry. *Justice Research and Policy, 9*(1), 59–73.

Lung, F.-W., Chou, F. H.-C., Lu, Y.-C., Wen, J.-K., Yen, Y.-C., & Kao, C.-Y. (2007). In-prison treatment for sexual offenders in Taiwan. *International Journal of Offender Therapy and Comparative Criminology, 51*(3), 340–347.

Lung, F.-W., & Huang, S.-F. (2004). Psychosocial characteristics of criminals committing incest and other sex offenses: A survey in a Taiwanese prison. *International Journal of Offender Therapy and Comparative Criminology, 48*(5), 554–560.

Maguire, M., & Raynor, P. (2006). How the resettlement of prisoners promotes desistance from crime. *Criminology and Criminal Justice, 6*(1), 19–38.

Mann, R. E., & Fernandez, Y. M. (2006). Sex offender programmes: Concept, theory, and practice. In C. R. Hollin, & E. J. Palmer (Eds.), *Offending behaviour programmes. Development, application, and controversies* (pp. 155–177). Chichester, UK: John Wiley and Sons.

Mann, R. E., Hanson, R. K., & Thornton, D. (2010). Assessing risk for sexual recidivism: Some proposals on the nature of psychologically meaningful risk factors. *Sexual Abuse: A Journal of Research and Treatment, 22*(2), 191–217.

Mann, R. E., & Thornton, D. (1998). The evolution of a multisite sexual offender treatment program. In W. L. Marshall, Y. M. Fernandez, S. M. Hudson, & T. Ward (Eds.), *Sourcebook of treatment programs for sexual offenders* (pp. 47–57). New York, London: Plenum Press.

Marques, J. K., Wiederanders, M., Day, D. M., Nelson, C., & van Ommeren, A. (2005). Effects of a relapse prevention program on sexual recidivism: Final results from California's sex offender treatment and evaluation project (SOTEP). *Sexual Abuse: A Journal of Research and Treatment, 17*(1), 79–107.

Marshall, P. (1994). Reconviction of imprisoned sexual offenders. *Home Office Research Bulletin, 36*, 23–29.

Marshall, P. (1997). The prevalence of convictions for sexual offending. In *Home Office Research Findings* (Vol. 55). London: Home Office.

Marshall, W. L. (1973). The modification of sexual fantasies: A combined treatment approach to the reduction of deviant sexual behavior. *Behaviour Research and Therapy, 11*, 557–564.

Marshall, W. L. (1989). Intimacy, loneliness, and sexual offenders. *Behaviour Research and Therapy, 27*, 491–503.

Marshall, W. L., Laws, D. R., & Barbaree, H. E. (1990). *Handbook of sexual assault. Issues, theories, and treatment of the offender*. New York: Plenum Press.

Martinson, R. (1974). What works? – Questions and answers about prison reform. *The Public Interest, 35*, 22–54.

Maruna, S. (2001). *Making good: How ex-convicts reform and rebuild their lives*. Washington, DC: American Psychological Association.

McAlinden, A.-M. (2010). Punitive policies on sexual offending: From public shaming to public protection. In M. Nash, & A. Williams (Eds.), *Handbook of public protection* (pp. 380–398). Abingdon: Willan Publishing.

McGuire, R. J., Carlisle, J. M., & Young, B. G. (1965). Sexual deviations as conditioned behaviour: A hypothesis. *Behaviour Research and Therapy, 2*, 185–190.

Ministère de la Justice et des Libertés. (2012). *Annuaire statistique de la Justice - Édition 2011–2012*. Paris: La Documentation française.

Murphy, G., & Sinclair, N. (2009). Treatment for men with intellectual disabilities and sexually abusive behaviour. In A. R. Beech, L. A. Craig, & K. D. Browne (Eds.), *Assessment and treatment of sex offenders: A handbook* (pp. 369–392). Chichester: John Wiley and Sons.

Muzinic, L., & Vukota, L. (2011). Book review: Therapy of sex offenders and protection of Community in Croatia. *Sexual Offender Treatment, 6*(1), 1–7.

Olver, M. E., Stockdale, K. C., & Wormith, J. S. (2011). A meta-analysis of predictors of offender treatment attrition and its relationship to recidivism. *Journal of Consulting and Clinical Psychology, 79*(1), 6–21.

Palmucci, V. (2006). La presa in carico del delinquent sessuale: Caratteristiche e finalità del principali modelli utilizzati nel panoram mondiale. In S. Ciappi, V. Palmucci, P. Scala, & I. Toccafondi (Eds.), *Aggressori sessuali. Dal carcere alla società: Ipotesi e strategie dei trattamento* (pp. 191–223). Milano: Giuffrè Editore.

Parti, K., Szabó, J., & Virág, G. (2014). Sex offenders in Hungary. Law, treatment, and statistics. *Monatsschrift für Kriminologie und Strafrechtsreform, 97*(1), 57–69.

Pereda, N., Guilera, G., Forns, M., & Gómez-Benito, J. (2009). The prevalence of child sexual abuse in community and student samples: A meta-analysis. *Clinical Psychology Review, 29*(4), 328–338.

Pithers, W. D. (1990). Relapse prevention with sexual aggressors: A method for maintaining therapeutic gain and enhancing external supervision. In W. L. Marshall, D. R. Laws, & H. E. Barbaree (Eds.), *Handbook of sexual assault* (pp. 343–361). New York, NY: Plenum Press.

Pithers, W. D., Marques, J. K., Gibat, C. C., & Marlatt, G. A. (1983). Relapse prevention: A self-control model of treatment and maintenance of change for sexual aggressives. In J. Greer, & I. Stuart (Eds.), *The sexual aggressor*. New York: Van Nostrand Reinhold.

Prentky, R., & Righthand, S. (2003). *Juvenile sex offender assessment protocol-II (J-SOAP-II) Manual*. Washington, DC: Office of Juvenile Justice and Delinquency Prevention.

Prescott, D. S. (2009). *Building motivation for change in sexual offenders*. Brandon, VT.

Putnam, F. W. (2003). Ten-year research update review: Child sexual abuse. *Journal of the American Academy of Child and Adolescent Psychiatry, 42*(3), 269–278.

Quinsey, V. L., & Earls, C. M. (1990). The modification of sexual preferences. In W. L. Marshall, D. R. Laws, & H. E. Barbaree (Eds.), *Handbook of sexual assault. Issues, theories, and treatment of the offender* (pp. 279–295). New York: Plenum Press.

Quinsey, V. L., Harris, G. T., Rice, M. E., & Cormier, C. A. (1998). *Violent offenders: Appraising and managing risk*. Washington, DC: American Psychological Association.

Redondo, S., Martínez-Catena, A., & Andrés-Pueyo, A. (2012). Therapeutic effects of a cognitive-behavioural treatment with juvenile offenders. *The European Journal of Psychology Applied to Legal Context, 4*(2), 159–178.

Rice, M. E., & Harris, G. T. (2013). Treatment for adult sex offenders. In K. Harrison, & B. Rainey (Eds.), *The Wiley-Blackwell handbook of legal and ethical aspects of sex offender treatment and management* (pp. 219–235). Chichester, UK: John Wiley and Sons.

Robertiello, G., & Terry, K. J. (2007). Can we profile sex offenders? A review of sex offender typologies. *Aggression and Violent Behavior, 12*, 508–518.

Rodriguez Mesa, L. S. (2012). *Características de los programas de tratamiento para delincuentes basados en la terapia cognitivo-conductual*. Asociacón Iberoamericana de Psicología Jurídica. http://aipj.co/index.php/publicaciones/func-startdown/26/. Accessed 26 June 2014.

Ross, R. R., Fabiano, E., & Ewles, C. D. (1988). Reasoning and rehabilitation. *International Journal of Offender Therapy and Comparative Criminology, 32*, 29–36.

Ross, R. R., & Gendreau, P. (1980). *Effective correctional treatment*. Toronto: Butterworth.

Ross, R. R., & Ross, R. D. (1995). *Thinking straight. The reasoning and rehabilitation program for delinquency prevention and offender rehabilitation*. Ottawa: Air Training and Publications.

Rossetti, S. J., & Müller, W. (1996). *Sexueller Missbrauch Minderjähriger in der Kirche: psychologische, seelsorgliche und institutionelle Aspekte*. Mainz: Grünewald.

Rüther, W. (1998). Internationale Erfahrungen bei der Behandlung von Sexualstraftätern. *Monatsschrift für Kriminologie und Strafrechtsreform, 81*, 246–262.

Safin, R., & Salagev, A. (2014). Treatment of sexual offenders in Russia: Recent developments in legislation and implementation of practices. *Monatsschrift für Kriminologie und Strafrechtsreform, 97*(1), 70–77.

Sarangi, S. (2000). Reality and reform in Tihar Central Jail. In R. D. Shankardass (Ed.), *Punishment and the prison. Indian and international perspectives* (pp. 87–111). New Dehli: Sage.

Schmucker, M., & Lösel, F. (2005). Die Wirksamkeit von Behandlung bei Sexualstraftätern: Nationale und internationale Befunde. In K. P. Dahle, & R. Volbert (Eds.), *Entwicklungspsychologische Aspekte der Rechtspsychologie* (pp. 221–238). Göttingen: Hogrefe.

Schmucker, M., & Lösel, F. (2008). Does sexual offender treatment work? A systematic review of outcome evaluations. *Psicothema, 20*(1), 10–19.

Schmucker, S. (2004). *Kann Therapie Rückfälle verhindern?* Herbolzheim: Centaurus.

Scoones, C. D., Willis, G. M., & Grace, R. C. (2012). Beyond static and dynamic risk factors: The incremental validity of release and planning for predicting sex offender recidivism. *Journal of Interpersonal Violence, 27*, 222–238.

Shelton, D. (2010). Systemic psychotherapy in prison. In J. Harvey, & K. Smedley (Eds.), *Psychological therapy in prisons and other secure settings* (pp. 130–149). Cullompton: Willan Publishing.

Silverman, E. (2011). United States of America. In H.-G. Koch (Ed.), *Wegsperren? Freiheitsentziehende Maßnahmen gegen gefährliche, strafrechtlich verantwortliche (Rückfall-)Täter* (pp. 365–430). Berlin: Duncker and Humblot.

Škvain, P. (2014). Physical (surgical) castration as treatment of male sex offenders? Recent developments in legislation in the Czech Republic. *Monatsschrift für Kriminologie und Strafrechtsreform, 97*(1), 40–47.

Soyer, M. (2014). The imagination of desistance – A juxtaposition of the construction of incarceration as a turning point and the reality of recidivism. *British Journal of Criminology, 54*, 91–108.

Statistisches Bundesamt. (2012). *Rechtspflege: Strafvollzug – Demographische und kriminologische Merkmale der Strafgefangenen zum Stichtag 31.3., Fachserie 10/Reihe 4.1.* Wiesbaden: Statistisches Bundesamt.

Stewart, L. A., Hamilton, E., Wilton, G., Cousineau, C., & Varrette, S. K. (2015). The effectiveness of the Tupiq program for Inuit sex offenders. *International Journal of Offender Therapy and Comparative Criminology, 59*(12), 1338–1357.

Stürup, G. K. (1960). Sex offenses: The Scandinavian experience. *Law and Contemporary Problems, 25*(2), 361–375.

Tamatea, A. J., Webb, M., & Boer, D. P. (2011). The role of culture in sexual offender rehabilitation: A New Zealand perspective. In D. P. Boer, R. Eher, L. A. Craig, M. H. Miner, & F. Pfäfflin (Eds.), *International perspectives on the assessment and treatment of sexual offenders: Theory, practice, and research* (pp. 313–329). Chichester, UK: Wiley-Blackwell.

Terol Levy, O. (2009). Medidas de seguridad con agresores sexuales. In A. García-Pablos de Molina (Ed.), *Víctima, prevención del delito y tratamiento del delincuente* (pp. 223–260). Granada: Comares.

Thomas, T. (2005). *Sex crime: Sex offending and society* (2nd ed.). Cullompton, UK and Portland, OR: Willan.

Thornberry, T. P., Henry, K. L., Smith, C. A., Ireland, T. O., Greenman, S. J., & Lee, R. D. (2013). Breaking the cycle of maltreatment: The role of safe, stable, and nurturing relationships. *Journal of Adolescent Health, 53*, S25–S31.

Turkish Statistical Institute. (2011). *Prison Statistics 2011.* http://www.turkstat.gov.tr. Accessed 13 June 2014.

UN Secretary General. (2006). *Ending violence against women - From words to action.* United Nations Publication.

van Beek, D. J., & Mulder, J. R. (1992). The offense script: A motivational tool and treatment method for sex offenders in a Dutch forensic clinic. *International Journal of Offender Therapy and Comparative Criminology, 36*(2), 155–167.

van Dijk, J., van Kesteren, J., & Smit, P. (2007). *Criminal victimisation in international perspective. Key findings from the 2004–2005 ICVS and EU ICS.* Den Haag: WODC.

van Zyl Smit, D., & Snacken, S. (2009). *Principles of European prison law and policy.* Oxford: University Press.

Vess, J., & Skelton, A. (2010). Sexual and violent recidivism by offender type and actuarial risk: Reoffending rates for rapists, child molesters and mixed-victim offenders. *Psychology, Crime and Law, 16*(7), 541–554.

Ward, T., & Brown, M. (2004). The good lives model and conceptual issues in offender rehabilitation. *Psychology, Crime and Law, 10*(3), 243–257.

Ward, T., & Marshall, B. (2007). Narrative identity and offender rehabilitation. *International Journal of Offender Therapy and Comparative Criminology, 51*(3), 279–297.

Ward, T., & Maruna, S. (2007). *Rehabilitation. Beyond the risk paradigm.* London: Routledge.

Weihe, H.-J. W. (1998). Sexual offence in Norway and the need for treatment programs for sexual offenders. *International Journal of Offender Therapy and Comparative Criminology, 32*, 135–141.

Willis, G. M., Ward, T., & Levenson, J. S. (2014). The Good Lives Model (GLM): An evaluation of GLM operationalization in North American treatment programs. *Sexual Abuse: A Journal of Research and Treatment, 26*(1), 58–81.

Willman, A. M., & Corman, C. (2013). *Sexual and gender-based violence: What is the World Bank doing and what have we learned? A strategic review*. Washington: World Bank.

Wilson, R. J., & Yates, P. M. (2009). Effective interventions and the Good Lives Model: Maximizing treatment gains for sexual offenders. *Aggression and Violent Behavior, 14*(3), 157–161.

Woessner, G., & Schwedler, A. (2014). Correctional treatment of sexual and violent offenders: Therapeutic change, prison climate, and recidivism. *Criminal Justice and Behavior, 41*(7), 862–879.

Worling, J. R., & Curwen, T. (2001). Estimate of risk of adolescent sexual offense recidivism (Version 2.0: The "ERASOR"). In M. C. Calder (Ed.), *Juveniles and children who sexually abuse: Frameworks for assessment* (2nd revised ed., pp. 372–397). Lyme Regis: Russel House Publishing.

Wößner, G. (2014). Foreword. *Monatsschrift für Kriminologie und Strafrechtsreform, 97*(1), 1–2.

Young, A., Grey, M., & Boyd, C. (2009). Adolescents' experiences of sexual assault by peers: Prevalence and nature of victimization occurring within and outside of school. *Journal of Youth and Adolescence, 38*(8), 1072–1083.

Zalewski, W. (2014). Therapeutic and legislative approaches to sex offenders in Poland. *Monatsschrift für Kriminologie und Strafrechtsreform, 97*(1), 48–56.

Zinsstag, E. (2014). *Sexual violence against women in armed conflicts: Towards a transitional justice perspective*. Cambridge: Intersentia.

Women and Children at the Centre of Preventing Organised Crime

Bojan Dobovšek and Boštjan Slak

Abstract There are constant debates about what organised crime is and how to define it, and this despite the fact that organised crime has accompanied humanity from the beginning of early civilisations. The development has seemed to be more affecting the role of women in organised crime groups then the behavioural aspects of the criminal activities in which organised crime groups engage in; technological advances have affected the modus operandi, yet the core activities of smuggling, white slavery, forced prostitution and other acts have remained the same. This can also be stated for children that were always exploited by organised (crime) groups. On the other hand, evolution and an ever-changing degree of female emancipation in legal spheres of societies are reflected in criminal activities undertaken by women. The more active the roles that women have, which can be achieved legitimately in society, the more power they can also achieve in the hierarchy of organised crime. However, organised crime can also give strength to women in societies that hamper the formal acquisition of power for women, therefore making organised crime an attractive alternative. Egalitarian societies have provided possibilities for women to engage in business or politics and this has translated into possibilities for them to also be engaged in organised white-collar crime. Victims of white-collar crime are not gender specific, but children probably are affected most since their health and future is more fragile. Yet, ironically, it is the moral quality and knowledge of future generations that can change society for the better. We see education and knowledge as the most important factor for prevention. Yet in the end, it all depends on the integrity of policy makers.

B. Dobovšek (✉) • B. Slak
University of Maribor, Maribor, Slovenia
e-mail: Bojan.Dobovsek@fvv.uni-mb.si; bostjan.slak@gmail.com

H. Kury et al. (eds.), *Women and Children as Victims and Offenders: Background, Prevention, Reintegration*, DOI 10.1007/978-3-319-28424-8_21

1 Introduction

Due to the many attempts by scholars, preventive and investigative practitioners and international organisations to coin a valuable and useful definition of organised crime (see e.g. United Nations Convention against Transnational Organized Crime and the Protocols Thereto 2004; see also von Lampe 2014) it has become somewhat crucial to first note its deliberate absence in this chapter. This chapter includes the old historical accounts, decades of ideas, notations and views of scholars and societies on the phenomena of organised crime, a definition that would suit or be equal to the picture of organized crime that was in the minds of scholars when they write about organised crime cannot be given. We did however strive to maintain coherence by acknowledging the time period, behavioural aspects of organised crime described/included crimes and insights from works that are not cited here but are part of the opus of authors that were used as references. We also allowed ourselves to do this because firstly, the aim of the chapter is to present a general overview, hence a detail description of standpoints and views, and mostly because every single prevention focused approach or idea listed here could take up numbers and volumes by itself. Secondly, because the lack of a unified and worldwide accepted definition of organised crime has never hindered the research or investigation of organised crime to a great degree until now.

Throughout the chapter, we use the terms *classic organised crime* and *white-collar organised crime*. The first we use to label and include behaviours that are "typically" ascribed to organised crime. These are crimes such as drug, weapon or human trafficking, racketeering, usury etc. We use the term *white-collar organised crime* when speaking of deviant acts that are done by a respected or influential member of society. This is somewhat similar to the view held by researchers that use the term *organised crime of the elites*, *elite organised crime* or *elite deviance* when describing these acts. There are some socio-psychological differences among such organised crimes and more "classic" organised crime, which impinge on our point of interest, which is the position and role of women and children, and should be kept in mind.

Both organised crimes and gender/sex defined roles are complex issues and much researched subjects but also strongly influenced by stereotypes and (mis) perceptions due to various factors. The perception of *what is organised crime* is heavily influenced by popular culture and media mis-representation (Allum and Siebert 2003; Kanduč 2006; Finckenauer 2007; Clinard and Meier 2011). It is stereotyped or associated to a Mafia-like structure that deals with drugs, arms and human trafficking and often excluding economic or corporate crimes (Woodiwiss 2003; van Duyne 2010). At the same time, the gender and sex based roles are dominated by socio-cultural characteristics of society itself or as Ritter and Terndrup (2002) note, by acknowledging the views, opinions, rhetoric and empirical finding of many scholars, the fact that most men or women are classified on the basis of physiological characteristics and then linked to the role that is expected in the society is undeniable.

Both primary and secondary socialization educates individuals on the basis of the social construction of gender roles, which defines the socially acceptable behaviour of men and women. However, in the process of socialization, ethnic origin, culture, religion, education, etc. also contribute a large part. Consequently, this does not just affect how we as member(s) of the social community behave or are expected to behave but also influences the (mis)perceptions of who victims or perpetrators *should be* instead of seeing *who* they actually *are*. This in turn also affects the gender based differences and actual usage of defence and justification mechanisms of crime commission (Steffensmeier et al. 2013). When we speak of "longer lasting" cycles of crimes the evolvement or mimicking of criminal/ victimisation behaviour can appear. This is most evidenced in cases when children from abusive or violent families become family abusers (or victims) themselves. That children model and interiorise the behaviour of members of their primary family and society or even the media is often used to explain this cycle behaviour and is based on Bandura's idea of modelling and social learning (Jasinski 2001).

Organised crime can also be one of longer lasting or recurring types of crimes and here the "evolution" of the roles occurs most often when victims of traffickers become recruiters of future victims. In white-collar organised crime, facilitation factors such as a corporation setting or informal rules are at play. While only adult men and women can fall under the spell of facilitating factors of organised white-collar crime, classic organised crime engages and (ab)uses children in a variety of roles.

1.1 Children and Organised Crime

Children are either seen as victims of organised crimes groups or victims of circumstance (e.g. they "help" organised crime groups due to the catastrophic socioeconomic state in which they live) and this "help" role of children in organised crime is diverse. They are being exploited in the informal economy in sweatshops or other labour tasks. They are frequent victims of human trafficking (including for illegal organ harvesting) and sexual exploitation. In some tragic cases children are hurt or even lose their lives as collateral damage to turf wars, intimidation or disposal of witnesses, or just because they were in the wrong place at the wrong time (e.g. see entries on Coll, Vincent "Mad Dog"; Colombian Mafia and "Cuban Mafia" in Sifakis 2005). They are also often used as drug (or weapons) mules and for corner street dealing and the fact that they are children it will be considered a mitigating circumstance in potential trials. Children and especially young boys are easily convinced to participate in such activities because of the prestige, power and impression of wealth surrounding organised crime members (Kanduč 2006; D'Andria 2011). Also economic or sociological benefits that are derived from being part of a group (see e.g. Logonder 2013) are great motivational factors. Additional motivations such as beautiful women that accompany organised crime members (Kanduč 2006; Finckenauer 2007) are particularly attractive for adolescent boys.

Not many (if any at all) countries are immune to the exploitation and recruitment of children by organised crime. Even in highly developed western democracies street gangs appear and exploit children in different manners. DeVito (2005) for instance writes that the age of the BLOODs and Crips (United States) street gang member rang(ed) from 8 to 35, and the 8–18 year olds were the most violent since they strive(ed) to impress older members. These are strong and long-lasting gangs, in contrast to the majority of those discussed in Weerman et al. (2015), who report that the majority of current gang membership is short-lived., also because they actually allow members to leave the gang. However, in both cases there are strong (mainly negative) social and psychological dynamics that are present in these gang groups that affect the larger social life and future of not just the gang members themselves but also their parents, friends, teachers and potential victims.

1.2 Women, Organised Crimes and White-Collar Crimes

When considering the roles of women in classic organised crime the recognised perception is that they are either victims, wives[1] or just "*appendixes to their male counterparts, as their mistresses, as sex objects, or as femmes fatales*" (Arsovska and Begum 2014 p. 91).[2] However, is this really the case? Historic research and probing into various sub-activities and behaviours, that are today hastily and non-critically ascribed to organised crime has shown us that the roles of women in either traditional-classic or modern white-collar organised crime forms and activities are far more complex as they may first seem. This is best illustrated in the case of prostitution.[3]

---

[1] Whose primal role was and is to take care of children and to educate them about the informal (social) laws, while the marriage itself in some cases serves as a tool for creating partnership, alliances or strengthen comradeship (Siegel 2014). However, van San (2011) on observing Curaçao women who are in relationships with criminal men, makes another observation very important for prevention purposes: that such women will with great possibility raise their sons to become dangerous men involved in crime, who once again will attract women that like (or perhaps even believe that they need) such men. Thus, a vicious circle takes place.

[2] And van San (2011) shows that this attraction of danger, power and possibility of financial safety that surrounds organized crime group member and attracts women into their arms, is as much present today in the Netherlands and Curaçao as it was in the 1940s in America.

[3] We agree that perhaps the synonym *sex worker* would be less stigmatising; unfortunately the term *prostitution* is more recognised and focused on one type of sex work. The sex industry also includes stripping, pornography, hotlines etc., and men and women employed in such industries are actually all sex workers (see Ditmore 2006), and though organised crime can be (and almost always was) involved in all these activities (ibid.), discussing its role in proper details is by far too comprehensive a task for this chapter.

Prostitution, which is believed to be one of the oldest professions, is usually seen as a female occupation (Ditmore 2006). Moreover, it is seen as the main activity of organised crime or as crime in general in many countries. However, that was not always the case. In the nineteenth century prostitution took place in brothels in the U.S.A., which were "*largely owned and operated by women and were one of the few means by which women could attain wealth independently of men. In the latter half of the 19th century, control began to shift away from female brothel owners to male vice entrepreneurs, particularly ones who had strong connections to law enforcement, politicians, and other vice industries (such as gambling, rum-running, and narcotics*" (Ditmore 2006, p. 339). Even before that the picture was different from today's perception, as we can read in Newton's chronology of organised crime: "*In c. 594 B.C.E., the Greek statesman Solon (638 B.C.E. – 558 B. C.E.) establishes publicly funded brothels in Athens to "democratize" the availability of sexual pleasure. Greek literature describes three classes of prostitutes: slaves (pornai), freeborn streetwalkers and educated prostitute-entertainers (hetaera). The first two classes included both males and females, while the third was strictly female.*" (Newton 2011, p. 10). Firstly, this shows that there are constant diverse evolutions of geopolitical attitudes towards prostitution taking place and secondly, that there have always been different types of prostitution and therefore different types of victims or even absence of victimisation. Admittedly, here one collides with the theories that freewill prostitutes are in reality victims of certain socio-economic factors and that is the reason that they do not actually recognize themselves as victims. Today, when economic factors play even a stronger role, there are many reports of women that voluntarily travel abroad even though knowing full well of the type of work they will have to engage in (Weitzer and Ditmore 2010). This demonstrates that prostitution is by far too complex an issue and cannot be resolved with ad hoc repression based approaches inspired by a lack of knowledge and insight.

Prostitution that was taken from the management of women and given into hands of men presented one of the main sources of income for organised crime groups in the U.S.A. in the "golden era of organised crime" (Ditmore 2006), that is in the 1920s and 1930s, the times when the Italian mafia emerged as an archetype of organised crime. At that time, among their ranks, women were also engaged in assistant roles (not greatly punishable by law)[4] (Arsovska and Begum 2014).

Yet this is not typical just for organised crime since the use of female attractiveness for diversion or the exploitation of the perception of women being less dangerous or suspicious is recognised beyond the organised crime sphere and was always frequently used in other criminal activities (Steffensmeier 1983). The development and evolution of the emancipation of women and/or social roles of

[4] For instance they were used as "bagmen"—persons that used to carry (usually) large amounts of money from and to a certain person/place. Probably the best known woman in that role was Virginia Hill, who was involved with numerous mafia-related people and later questioned in front of the Kefauver Committee (Sifakis 2005).

women in society is reflected in the type and frequency of occurrences of women as organised crime member(s). For instance, street gangs in the USA that have appeared in the 1970s and onwards quite often include female members and there were even all-female fractions (DeVito 2005).

Even in Argentina some all-women thief groups or groups lead by a women appeared (Rossi 2007). Institutions and scholars (e.g. Arsovska and Begum 2014) noticed that since 1990 women became even more engaged in organised criminal behaviour, especially in regard to human trafficking, showing the same or even more viciousness as male recruiters and conductors of these sorts of activities.

Cases of Svetlana (Ceca) Raznatovic,[5] Maria Licciardi[6] and others[7] show the development and the highest degree of female involvement in organised crime matters. However in patriarchal societies, the women remain mostly in the background of criminal activity (Beare 2010). This continues to be the case in Albanian organised crime (Arsovska and Begum 2014) or in the case of modern-day[8] Yakuza. Even though Japanese women are a very active and emancipated part of society (Otomo 2007), wives of Yakuza members play more psychological but very important financial and other strong support roles by managing family matters while their male partners engage in criminal matters (Otomo 2007; Alkemade 2013).[9]

Somewhat similar is the picture of women and white-collar crimes. Here the victimisation is not gender specific, however among perpetrators, official or research statistics state that men usually dominate, and this is noticed even in egalitarian countries (e.g. for some insights in gender/women and white-collar crime in Norway see Gottschalk and Glasø (2013); for the USA see Steffensmeier

[5] Svetlana (Ceca) Raznatovic took over one of most notorious and successful Serbian organised crime group after her husband, Zeljko Raznatovic-Arkan, (war criminal, paramilitary leader and politician) was killed. During a house search of her premises numerous illegal weapons and information on economic crimes related to the football club they owned were found. Later on she was only convicted to a few months of house arrest and a fine of EUR 1.5 million (Logonder 2013; Arsovska and Begum 2014). Arsovska and Begum (2014) also (in our view justifiably) see Ceca's husband's godmother, Stanislava Cocorovska-Poletan as a women strongly involved in organised crime in the Balkan region.

[6] Who was once on the list of the 30 most wanted Italians. She successfully took over the leadership of a Camora clan after all of the high position males were arrested and/or killed in the war among clans. She also expanded the criminal activities of her clan from the drug trade to include prostitution as well. She was arrested in 2001 (DeVito 2005).

[7] For some historical as well as contemporary examples of positions, roles and attitudes of different organised crime groups towards women see van San (2011), Siegel (2014) and (Fiandaca 2007).

[8] This must be emphasized because from the description of (Otomo 2007) it, it becomes obvious that in the not too distant Yakuza history there were several significant and important women in more leading roles.

[9] However, it would be foolish to think that these women do not know in detail about their husband's or partners' affairs, especially if they are in a relationship with a more higher ranking member of the organisation, and this is true for Yakuza or other Mafia type organisations (Alkemade 2013; Arsovska and Begum 2014; Siegel 2014). In addition, in lower ranks and less organised groups such support and the absence of discouragement or disacceptance in a way reinforces and supports the criminal behaviour to a higher degree than perhaps first perceived (van San 2011).

et al. (2013) and, on a somewhat different note, about politically successful Argentinian women that have turned to crime see (Rossi 2007)).[10]

The reasons of "male dominance" can be partly ascribed to the inability of women to actually occupy positions that would enable them to perform white-collar criminal acts and also, because there are socio-psychological (ethics) differences in female leadership and management[11] (Steffensmeier et al. 2013). Gottschalk and Glasø (2013, p. 30) summarize this well:. "*When addressing the low fraction of female white-collar criminals (a mere 9 percent) to qualified audiences, the following reasons are typically mentioned: Women have less opportunity to commit white-collar crime. Women are less opportunistic as they are more committed to relationships and rules. It is more seldom that women are invited by criminals to participate in crime. For example, a criminal will prefer to bribe a man rather than a woman. Women have a greater sense of risk aversion, rather than risk willingness. Companies are typically registered in the name of the husband, rather than the wife. Women are more readily perceived as victims of crime rather than perpetrators. Female criminal acts tend to carry lesser legal penalties. Women are not as efficient as men are in terms of successfully applying neutralization techniques. It is commonly recognized that women's career prospects are worse than those of men.*" A closer look into the white-collar cases where women were one of the significant offender(s) shows that there are not many differences after all in the form of damages and the actual carrying out of the criminal activity, yet one must keep in mind the problems of researching white-collar crime (see footnote 10) and the low number of white-collar cases with female leaders (or significant involvement) (Dodge 2007).[12]

---

[10] It is to be agreed with Steffensmeier et al (2013), that the problem of *what is white-collar* crime and *what types* of crimes or *what sorts of offenders* to include in statistics or sample heavily affects the picture(s).

[11] There is a recurring empirically based notion that there is less corruption in environments where there are more women in leading roles (Dollar et al. 2001), but there are always certain sociological and cultural predispositions that have to be considered (Swamy et al. 2001; Esarey and Chirillo 2013). From a preventive perspective the idea/question is well exposed by Steffensmeier et al.: "*Would more women in positions of corporate leadership and power reduce corporate fraud?*" (Steffensmeier et al. 2013 p. 471). The authors believe that there is good reason for a positive answer. However, indoctrination into a (criminogenic) corporate or business culture must also be considered (Koehn 2005; Davis and Rothstein 2006; Thoms 2008) as well as general social norms. The latter because as Rafidah Aziz (Malaysia's trade minister from 1987 to 2008) quoted in Morrison (2001, p. 67) eloquently said: "*What is corruption to one person, may be the norm for the other.*" It is known that in some countries cheating and bribing is (or worse, it is starting to) becoming a normal social norm. This is worrisome because damage of corruption is not short reached and also affects future generations because—and here we agree with (Lambsdorff 2007)—profit-oriented behaviour could have an influence on the future education of young people, who instead of studying engineering and similar trades, would prefer disciplines such as law, as it equips them better for working in profit-oriented societies willing to exploit legal loopholes.

[12] A thought occurs if perhaps the characteristic of female management and approach to business (less risk prone, more detailed approach, strategic exploitation of femininity etc.) doesn't reflects also in the (better) *modus operandi* for the commission of crimes, and the low number of discovered cases is the result of the fact that women are just better criminals.

In sum, women in organised crime do not always take over just passive or victim-like roles, but can also be very active leaders and organisers. They engage in organised crime because of poverty or other economic factors, substance abuse, desire of gaining informal power or simply because they "need to step in" when the male perpetrators are somehow absent (Otomo 2007; Rossi 2007; Beare 2010; van San 2011; Alkemade 2013; Gottschalk and Glasø 2013; Arsovska and Begum 2014). Yet involvement in organised crime is more likely to occur if society in general enables them to do so (e.g. see Arsovska and Begum 2014). If society gives women a chance to engage in all forms of legal businesses, economic and social activities, this usually also reflects in their engagement in illegal activities as well. This all shows that it is to be agreed with Steffensmeier (1983, p. 1016) that: "*… sex-segregation in the underworld is variable, being more prevalent in some crime groups and in some kinds of criminal enterprise than in others*".

2 Prevention of Organised Crime with a Focus on Women and Children

The preventive measures described in more detail in the following pages are roughly based on the three staged preventive approach proposed by Brantingham and Faust (as quoted in Fisher and Lab 2010) and to some level modified by van Dijk and de Waard (1991), i.e. primary, secondary and tertiary prevention.

We focus more on the elements that we see as the most important in the prevention of organised crime, but it must be said that prevention that aims to decrease or remove facilitating factors in other crimes must also be considered and acknowledged (see Levi and Maguire 2004). These measures affect the sub-activity of organised crime or prevent organised crime from later engaging in other activities, to relocate to a different/new area, or hamper its development capacity.

2.1 Primary Prevention

In the primary prevention stage, the identification, search and possible removal of crime facilitating factors takes place. This can only be done with (more or less scientific) research. In case of women for instance, researchers should investigate why [women] "commit crimes and seek leading positions on the criminal ladder" (Siegel 2014, p. 46), or to investigate how different dynamics of exploitation truly work; or why women do not identify themselves as victims of human trafficking or forced prostitution; or even why later on, they help recruit future victims. Here criminology, but more victimology and its theories can shed some light (Mandisa and Lanier 2012). Those who are involved in prevention and giving support to victims of such cases should be equipped with knowledge from victimization studies, criminology, psychology and other sciences. Granted, some NGO workers who are first "at the scene" develop some common sense insights, yet is this enough? Or worse, there is also the danger that they are not listened to by academics or bureaucrats who are engaged or tasked on these matters, but only from theoretical and distant sterile positions. In addition, properly designed and practice driven research is not just preventive but also useful in investigations, even in the investigation of organised crime. (van Duyne 2000) for instance, offers some good insights into the usefulness of behavioural scientists not just in academic prevention development but also in real-time (organised crime) investigations.

Research on these matters should later facilitate proper legislative and economic responses by policy makers. History has shown that this is usually a utopian idea but which we must nevertheless strive for. Secondly, the empirically based insights should also facilitate the amendments of curriculums or actually enable new provisions for education, since the starting point of every (in)desirable social attitude and/or behavioural pattern is upbringing[13] and (usually lack of) education. Education reveals itself as perhaps as an even far more complex issue than (organised white-collar) crime (see e.g. Powell and Barber 2006).

At one time, education was reserved for the privileged or the right gendered, but even now some of the most developed societies suffer from unequal or low-quality education in slums and ghettoes (see also discussions in Powell and Barber 2006). Even on the "upper" sides there are, due to permissive education, problems concerning the quality of education or better said the moral quality of future generations. It is not just that the pupils are coming to classes with a different view on morals, ethics and (lack of respect for) authority. Permissive education is especially seen as the main culprit for the improper attitude schooling youth has towards its teachers (and poorer academic success). Anecdotal and public discussions (see e.g. Woods 2014) are often confirmative on this and are not without academic support (Masud et al. 2014; Seth and Asudani 2013), yet the link is not easily empirically confirmed (see e.g. Heaven and Ciarrochi 2008). The schools themselves are continuing to be "*laboratories for social change and control*" (Powell and Barber 2006 p. 46).[14] The tertiary educators (receiving already "tainted

---

[13] Here we mainly consider parenting and family structure; Posick and Rocque (2015) and Bertok et al. (2014), provide some insights and research suggestion on this. Also (van San 2011) research in Curaçao on family dynamics of families engages in crime shows well how norms and behaviours transfer from parents to children. Therefore she suggests the development of proper intervention programs that consider and influence economic, social, educational, and other facilitating factors, in order to counter such circles.

[14] Both scientific research and primary and secondary education (as well as the majority of all other prevention initiatives) are heavily dependent on state funding and economic predisposition of the state or sub-region. Economic crises and blind austerity usually heavily affect this, as myopic

animals") (ibid.) have also have taken on different roles. The roles vary on the location, the subject matter and the moral standpoint of the tutors and professors.

Lately, this has been most notably seen in economic science, which believes that objective mathematical models can be used to predict economic human behaviour, to minimise risk and so forth. The economic crisis has proved them wrong and (Ferguson 2010) the documentary *Inside Job* shows the connection between the involvement of the most distinguished economic schools and the collapse of various state economies well.[15] Critical sociologists, criminologists and even a few (critical) economists are becoming very worried about the neoliberal path on which we are travelling. Nevertheless, even though these academic "internal disputes" are strong, education remains the main tool (or weapon) to fight against crime, even as complex as terrorism.[16] Here, IT should not be forgotten as it can be used to show such stories, spread knowledge or just simply make teaching easier by making subject matters more fun and interactive. IT can also be in various ways used to improve awareness and help in prevention (see Fisher and Lab 2010).

However, educational curricula should be more critical (at least at the higher levels), conscious, and especially the economic sciences or political sciences should make greater use of the knowledge base of psychology, sociology, criminology, biology and history (Drew and Drew 2012; Kotios and Galanos 2012) as these sciences reveal more about human nature than economics alone can. They portray the picture of the human animal, showing the irrationality of the human species that seems to be forgotten in economics or politics.

It is for this and other reasons why governments should consider the advice given by Geis (Geis 2011), who suggests that policy-makers should include criminologists, fraud experts and other social scientists on their staff. However, we must not forget that such knowledge about the factors that trigger certain human behavioural patterns can also be exploited for economic or political gains. So the

policymakers do not realise that such an approach (of taking much needed funds from science, education and other social programs and giving it to bankrupted banks or ill-managed firms) prolongs the economic crises, worsens the social environment and even causes deviant behaviour (Alderslade et al. 2006; DeKeseredy 2011). Repression often used and regarded as the main tool in crime prevention, does not remove the white-collar factors that brought on the crisis. Furthermore, the political PR demand to bring justice for the guilty of the crises not just burdens the law-enforcement that has to tackle problems that could be tackled by financial and economic institutions far better it also demotivates investigators and the (demoralises) public because such investigations are not always successful in the view of restorative justice (e.g. see (Kirk 2012) or successful in amending the problematic legislation (Rajan and Zingales 2004; Freeman 2010; Tomasic 2011). However, this is a usual response to an outraged public who—not without cause—(see Calavita et al. 1997; Pontell 2005; Brown et al. 2010; Hetzer 2012) believes that there are crimes behind economic crises and this is contrary to the views of politicians or economists who see various crises as a "natural" economic event (Hetzer 2012).

[15] See also the discussion in Drew and Drew (2012) about the roles of financial schools on these matters.

[16] Education is strongly seen as a key factor in much publicized story of Malala Yousafzai. One must agree with Ban Ki-moon when he said that what terrorists fear most is a girl with a book (Walsh 2014).

question is how to convince policy makers that natural and social sciences should be more acknowledged in economics and politics, but not to be abused? We can only provide one answer and that is integrity (see Morrison 2001; Koehn 2005; Davis and Rothstein 2006; Thoms 2008). Only integrity in leaders and policy makers will make sure that those in power shall not abuse their knowledge and power too much.[17] However, zero abuse of power is not to be expected at the current stage of human and social development.

In the development, adjustment and/or implementation of many prevention programs the role of Non-Government Organisations (NGOs) is very important. NGOs are becoming a vital part of human society; they are becoming the reflection of society itself and a critical watchdog. However, this can be precisely the reason why they are feared by the top echelon of societies,[18] which in turn can affect NGO legislation and funding. NGO's are also those who are heavily involved with those who already show signs of offending or are already imprisoned.

2.2 Secondary Prevention

Secondary prevention targets people that already show signs of offending or victimisation or are at greater risk in eventually engaging in such behaviour or becoming victims themselves.

Women who come from countries where they are oppressed or unable to provide for their families are an easy prey for traffickers, especially if there is a history of abuse or other trauma. This can be seen in the frequent involvement of the recruitment of potential victims by women who were trafficked at one time (Mandisa and Lanier 2012). Proper economic and socio-psychological help must be provided in order to identify victims of trafficking. Women that are mainly victims of trafficking for future sexual exploitation can be to some degree easier protected if decriminalisation and legalisation of prostitution occurs. Though legalisation has some strong positive effects (taxation of services is a benefit for the state budget and the health and social protection of prostitutes etc.) such an

---

[17] We suggest the application of integrity tests (Slak and Lesjak 2013) in public and private spheres in as broad a scope as possible. Entry level public administration workers, notaries, tax administrators, inspection service workers and all who give out licenses and perform administrative screening are the crucial starting point where people with a higher level of integrity must be employed if we want to suppress the problems in the bud. Not to be neglected is the fact that a lot of "administrative desk clerk" positions are filled by women, and these "clerks" are those that give permission for entry into states, work permits for foreign women that latter engage in prostitution under work permits for erotic dancers, "massage therapists" etc. There are also those who technically perform financial transactions, manage accounting books etc.

[18] Sometimes the work of a critical NGO is indirectly affected by actions of more powerful/ connected interest and/or activist groups. Weitzer and Ditmore (2010) note that activists in the U.S.A. have successfully influenced the creation of a policy where funding can only be given to NGO's whose views of which are against the legalisation of prostitution.

approach can only be applied where the proper social and cultural settings are present (mainly the absence of moral crusaders, acceptance of the sex industry, proper administrative screening and/or proper legislative framework) (see Weitzer and Ditmore 2010). The question though arises if a potential legitimation would perhaps "(re)enforce" the development of such settings, if society would see that prostitution is not the root of evil? There are also other options to be considered, like the Swedish approach, where only clients and not prostitutes are penalised and—as some believe—thus eliminates or at least weakens the main motivational and facilitating factor behind human trafficking (Ekberg 2004).[19] Yet such an approach also demands proper socio-cultural support and must include the development and implementation of additional intervention and support programs.

Similarly, in order to refocus youthful energy programs must be developed for juveniles that show signs of delinquency as they can be more easily motivated to join gangs or entry level organised crime groups.

2.3 Tertiary Prevention

Sentencing (and so removing) offenders is the last measure used for prevention. The investigation that accumulates evidence and is later used in court is the backbone of this process. However, when the offenders are women or children some obstacles hinder the investigation process. At first, usually it is the (mis)perception of adult male offenders. Such (mis)perception can even be a tool used deliberately by female perpetrators in order to misguide the investigators, for instance, the use of the spouse's name when registering questionable business in white-collar crimes (Gottschalk and Glasø 2013) or using pregnancy as a mitigating circumstance. Research undertaken by Meško et al. (2014) also shows that compliance with laws, especially by juveniles and younger population is also affected by how legitimate police behaviour is seen. This perception in turn is based on personal experience with police officers and police procedures. The more objectively and positively these procedures were carried out, the more police and certain legislation is seen as legitimate. Therefore, the basic aspect of police behaviour and activities must be considered and always strive to improve their quality.

The main problem of tertiary prevention is that while it does remove offenders from the streets, it sends them to the best criminal school, the prisons (or juvenile homes). Here, first, he/she receives (or must request in order to ensure his/hers physical integrity) the support of a certain group in prison or the juvenile home. Therefore, this also expands his/her social network, which in turn presents

[19] Indeed, the paper argues well that the approach is successful in decreasing the number of domestic and foreign women involved in prostitution (Ekberg 2004), especially because it extends its reach on Swedish males to foreign territories, for instance in the case of Swedish solders on missions (ibid.).

additional tools for a crime commission (access to funding, fencing networks, accomplices) and also additional knowledge (discussing what was done wrong and caused their capture is the best of trial-and-error approach). Secondly, stereotyping and labelling a person as *being an ex- prisoner* heavily affects the possibilities of accessing legitimate means of earning a living for those that wish to leave the criminal lifestyle. Thirdly, there is the whole problem of private prisons that are becoming a good business and prisoners are seen as a source of income. In order to increase profits the volume of therapeutic, re-socialisation etc. programs is decreased. Fourthly, the proceeds of crimes, if well hidden and not taken away, will motivate offenders to sit out the penalties or even to engage in other crimes. Here female partners are (un)knowingly involved because the assets are written in their names.

This is a worldwide practice as can be seen in the case of Yakuzas (Otomo 2007) or many other criminal groups (see other chapters in (Fiandaca 2007). Therefore, in case of organised crime, especially of white-collar crime, imprisonment should also be accompanied by foreclosure of assets or heavy taxation and in cases of low ranking organised crime members, proper therapeutic support is essential. However, the latter still needs some extensive research in order to develop approaches that would be of equal interest to offenders as was the fast-lane, adrenalin filled and easy money life (or just its perception) of organised crime.

3 Conclusion

It seems that the existence of (mis)perceptions of organised crime fuelled by the media or exaggerated autobiographies and narrations (Logonder 2013) is one of the few facts in which almost all organised crime scholars agree on. In addition, it is the key notion to be addressed in organised crime prevention. This must be done in order to eliminate the allure of romanticism, fast-and-easy profit and the overall attraction of organised crime that serves as a recruitment tool. In this down-to-earth category of organised crime, white-collar crimes must be included as there is no setback in doing so (Levi 2008) and thus to show that white-collar crimes should be considered as (or far more) damaging as classic organised crimes.

However, all this demands time and the policy makers' support for research, which are usually dependent on funding and the latter on economic factors and the economic state of the country. This in turn is influenced by the extent and degree of white-collar crime, yet this time on a global scale. Socio-economic factors are also crucial since organised crime competes with the state in provision of services (jobs, loans) and goods to the public and as such receives public support. If organised crime will better promote the emancipation of women and take better "care" of children (of the street) then again they will gain support.

These actions of organised crime are not to be seen as acts of altruism but as well delivered self-serving, financial and empowering means to gain profit. On this, the general worldwide approach of causing panic and exaggerated fear of organised crime may not be the correct approach. The repression approach does not tackle the reasons why people engage in organised crime and why the broader public uses its services. The manner of using the services of organised crime changes when the users of services and goods fear police repercussions. Organised criminals only change their *modus operandi*, if they do not seriously fear the state, because if they did they would not be engaged in (organised) crime. If we wish to properly tackle organised crime we must remove all factors and means that make organised crime the better provider than the state and thus to make sure that offers that cannot be refused, just cannot be given.

Five Questions

1. Why does a repression driven approach continue to be the approach primarily used?
2. What are the policy measures that may help to demystify organised crime?
3. What is to be the future of prostitution prevention: the legalisation of prostitution or the criminalisation of customers?
4. Why do the policy makers not apply or use empirically based findings in their work and how can we correct this?
5. How can we increase proper and unbiased funding for NGOs?

References

Alderslade, J., Talmadge, J., & Freeman, Y. (2006). *Measuring the informal economy: One neighborhood at a time*. Washington, DC: Brookings Institution, Metropolitan Policy Program.

Alkemade, R. (2013). Outsiders amongst outsiders': A cultural criminological perspective on the sub-subcultural world of women in the Yakuza underworld. In GlobalCriminology.com. http://www.globalcriminology.com/main/criminology-articles/organised-crime/52-outsiders-amongst-outsiders-a-cultural-criminological-perspective-on-the-sub-subcultural-world-of-women-in-the-yakuza-underworld-by-rie-alkemade.

Allum, F., & Siebert, R. (2003). Organized crime: A threat to democracy? In F. Allum & R. Siebert (Eds.), *Organized crime challenge democracy* (pp. 1–22). London, New York: Routledge.

Arsovska, J., & Begum, P. (2014). From West Africa to the Balkans: Exploring women's roles in transnational organized crime. *Trends in Organized Crime, 17*, 89–109. doi:10.1007/s12117-013-9209-1.

Beare, M. (2010). *Women and Organized Crime*, Report No. 013. Research and National Coordination Organized Crime Division Law Enforcement and Policy Branch Public Safety Canada

Bertok, E., Wikstroem, P. O., Hardie, B., & Meško, G. (2014). Starševski nadzor nad najstniki v osnovni in srednji šoli ter s tem povezana odklonskost [Parental control of teenagers in primary and high school and related deviance]. *Rev Za Kriminalistiko Kriminol J Crim Criminol, 63*, 311–320.

Brown, S. E., Esbensen, F. -A., & Geis, G. (2010). *Criminology: Explaining crime and its context* (7th ed.). New Providence, NJ: LexisNexis/Anderson

Calavita, K., Tillman, R., & Pontell, H. N. (1997). The savings and Loan Debacle, financial crime, and the state. *Annual Review of Sociology, 231997*, 19–38.

Clinard, M. B., & Meier, R. F. (2011) *Sociology of deviant behavior* (14th ed). Australia; Belmont, CA: Wadsworth Cengage Learning

D' Andria, D. (2011). Investment strategies of criminal organisations. *Policy Studies, 32*, 1–19. doi: 10.1080/01442872.2010.520558

Davis, A. L., & Rothstein, H. R. (2006). The effects of the perceived behavioral integrity of managers on employee attitudes: A meta-analysis. *Journal of Business Ethics, 67*, 407–419. doi:10.1007/s10551-006-9034-4.

DeKeseredy, W. S. (2011). *Contemporary critical criminology*. New York: Routledge.

DeVito, C. (2005). *The encyclopedia of international organized crime*. New York, NY: Facts on File.

Ditmore, M. H. (Ed.). (2006). *Encyclopedia of prostitution and sex work*. Westport, Conn: Greenwood Press.

Dodge, M. (2007). From pink to white with various shades of embezzlement: Women who commit white-collar crimes. In H. N. Pontell & G. Geis (Eds.), *The International Handbook of White-Collar and Corporate Crime* (pp. 379–404). Boston, MA: Springer US.

Dollar, D., Fisman, R., & Gatti, R. (2001). Are women really the "fairer" sex? Corruption and women in government. *Journal of Economic Behavior, 46*, 423–429. doi:10.1016/S0167-2681 (01)00169-X.

Drew, J. M., & Drew, M. E. (2012). Who was swimming naked when the tide went out? Introducing criminology to the finance curriculum. *Journal of Business Ethics Education, 9*, 63–76.

Ekberg, G. (2004). The Swedish Law that prohibits the purchase of sexual services: Best practices for prevention of prostitution and trafficking in human beings. *Violence Women, 10*, 1187–1218. doi:10.1177/1077801204268647.

Esarey, J., & Chirillo, G. (2013). "Fairer sex" or purity myth? Corruption, gender, and institutional context. *Politics & Gender, 9*, 361–389. doi:10.1017/S1743923X13000378.

Ferguson, C. (2010). Inside job [Film]. New York: Sony Pictures Classics.

Fiandaca, G. (Ed.). (2007). *Women and the mafia*. New York, NY: Springer.

Finckenauer, J. O. (2007). *The mafia and organized crime: A beginner's guide*. Oxford: Oneworld Publications.

Fisher, B., & Lab, S. P. (Eds.). (2010). *Encyclopedia of victimology and crime prevention*. Thousand Oaks, California: SAGE Publications.

Freeman, R. B. (2010). Financial crime, near crime, and chicanery in the wall street meltdown. *Journal of Policy Modeling, 32*, 690–701.

Geis, G. (2011). *White-collar and corporate crime a documentary and reference guide*. Santa Barbara, California: Greenwood.

Gottschalk, P., & Glasø, L. (2013). Gender in white-collar crime: An empirical study of pink-collar criminals. *International Letters of Social and Humanistic Sciences, 4*, 22–34.

Heaven, P. C. L., & Ciarrochi, J. (2008). Parental styles, conscientiousness, and academic performance in high school: A three-wave longitudinal study. *Personality and Social Psychology Bulletin, 34*, 451–461. doi:10.1177/0146167207311909.

Hetzer, W. (2012). *Financial crisis or financial crime? Competence and corruption* (pp. 217–269). Boca Raton: Financial Crimes: A Threat to Global Security.

Jasinski, J. L. (2001). Theoretical explanations for violence against women. In C. M. Renzetti, J. L. Edleson, & R. K. Bergen (Eds.), *Sourceb. Violence women* (pp. 5–21). Thousand Oaks, California: Sage Publications.

Kanduč, Z. (2006). Mafijsko načelo, kriminalna podjetja in zakonito "organizirani kriminal" [Mafia principle, criminal enterprise and lawfully "organised crime"]. *Rev Za Kriminalistiko Kriminol J Crim Criminol, 57*, 42–56.

Kirk, D. (2012). Criminalising bad bankers. *Journal of Criminal Law, 766*, 439–441.

Koehn, D. (2005). Integrity as a business asset. *Journal of Business Ethics, 58*, 125–136. doi:10.1007/s10551-005-1391-x.

Kotios, A., & Galanos, G. (2012). The international economic crisis and the crisis of economics. *World Economics, 35*, 869–885. doi:10.1111/j.1467-9701.2012.01468.x.

Lambsdorff, J. (2007). *The institutional economics of corruption and reform theory, evidence, and policy*. Cambridge, New York: Cambridge University Press.

Levi, M. (2008). White-collar, organised and cyber crimes in the media: Some contrasts and similarities. *Crime, Law and Social Change, 49*, 365–377. doi:10.1007/s10611-008-9111-y.

Levi, M., & Maguire, M. (2004). Reducing and preventing organised crime: An evidence-based critique. *Crime, Law and Social Change, 41*, 397–469. doi:10.1023/B:CRIS.0000039600.88691.af.

Logonder, A. (2013). Kriminološka analiza notranjih in zunanjih odnosov članov organiziranih kriminalnih skupin iz Srbije: (doktorska disertacija). Univerza v Ljubljani, Pravna fakulteta

Mandisa, T., & Lanier, M. (2012). An integrated theoretical framework to describe human trafficking of young women and girls for involuntary prostitution. In J, Maddock (Ed.), *Public health - Social and behavioral health* (pp. 555–570). Rijeka, Croatia; Shanghai, China: InTech

Masud, H., Thurasamy, R., Ahmad, & M. S. (2014). Parenting styles and academic achievement of young adolescents: A systematic literature review. *Quality & Quantity*. doi: 10.1007/s11135-014-0120-x

Meško, G., Tankebe, J., Jere, M., et al. (2014). Vpliv postopkovne pravičnosti in legitimnosti policijske dejavnosti na spoštovanje zakonov pri slovenskih mladostnikih [Impact of Procedural Justice and Police Legitimacy on Compliance with Law among Slovenian Adolescents]. *Rev Za Kriminalistiko Kriminol J Crim Criminol, 65*, 35–47.

Morrison, A. (2001). Integrity and global leadership. *Journal of Business Ethics, 31*, 65–76.

Newton, M. (2011). Chronology of organized crime worldwide, 6000 B.C.E. to 2010. McFarland & Co, Jefferson, N.C

Otomo, R. (2007). Women in organized Crime in Japan. In G. Fiandaca (Ed.), *Women mafia* (pp. 205–217). New York, NY: Springer.

Pontell, H. (2005). White-collar crime or just risky business? The role of fraud in major financial debacles. *Crime, Law and Social Change, 42*, 309–324.

Posick, C., & Rocque, M. (2015). Family matters: A cross-national examination of family bonding and victimization. *The European Journal of Criminology, 12*, 51–69. doi:10.1177/1477370814538777.

Powell, L. C., & Barber, M. E. (2006). Savage inequalities indeed: Irrationality and urban school reform. In G. M. Boldt & P. M. Salvio (Eds.), *Love's return: Psychoanalytic essays on childhood, teaching, and learning* (pp. 33–60). New York: Routledge.

Rajan, R. G., & Zingales, L. (2004). Capitalism for everyone. The National Interest, *74*, 133–141.

Ritter, K., & Terndrup, A. I. (2002). *Handbook of affirmative psychotherapy with lesbians and gay men*. New York: Guilford Press.

Rossi, A. (2007). Women in organized crime in Argentina. In G. Fiandaca (Ed.), *Women mafia* (pp. 149–179). New York, NY: Springer.

Seth, M. R., & Asudani, V. H. (2013). The impact of indulgent parenting style on educational performance of learners at high school level. *International Journal of Research & education, 2*, 56–64.

Siegel, D. (2014). Women in transnational organized crime. *Trends in Organized Crime, 17*, 52–65. doi:10.1007/s12117-013-9206-4.

Sifakis, C. (2005). *The mafia encyclopedia* (3rd ed.). New York: Facts On File.

Slak, B., & Lesjak, R. (2013). Integrity test - A neglected tool or object of ridicule. In G. Meško, A. Sotlar, & J. R. Greene (Eds.), *Criminal justice and security – Contemporary criminal justice practice and research conference proceedings* (pp. 329–346). Ljubljana: Faculty of Criminal Justice and Security.

Steffensmeier, D. J. (1983). Organization properties and sex-segregation in the underworld: Building a sociological theory of sex differences in crime. *Social Forces, 61*, 1010–1032. doi:10.1093/sf/61.4.1010.

Steffensmeier, D. J., Schwartz, J., & Roche, M. (2013). Gender and twenty-first-century corporate crime: Female involvement and the gender gap in Enron-Era corporate frauds. *American Sociological Review, 78*, 448–476. doi:10.1177/0003122413484150.

Swamy, A., Knack, S., Lee, Y., & Azfar, O. (2001). Gender and corruption. *Journal of Development Economics, 64*, 25–55. doi:10.1016/S0304-3878(00)00123-1.

Thoms, J. C. (2008). Ethical integrity in leadership and organizational moral culture. *Leadership, 4*, 419–442. doi:10.1177/1742715008095189.

Tomasic, R. (2011). The financial crisis and the haphazard pursuit of financial crime. *Journal of Financial Crime, 18*, 7–31.

United Nations Convention against Transnational Organized Crime and the Protocols Thereto (2004). Vienna International Ctr & Austria: United Nations Office on Drugs and Crime.

Van Dijk, J. J. M., & de Waard, J. (1991). A two-dimensional typology of crime prevention projects: With a bibliography. *Criminal Justice Abstracts, 483–503.*

Van Duyne, P. C. (2000). Mobsters are human too: Behavioural science and organized crime investigation. *Crime, Law and Social Change, 34*, 369–390.

Van Duyne, P. C. (2010). Organised crime (threat) as a policy challenge: A tautology. *Varstvoslovje, 12*, 355–366.

Van San, M. (2011). The appeal of "dangerous" men. On the role of women in organized crime. *Trends in Organized Crime, 14*, 281–297. doi:10.1007/s12117-011-9128-y.

Von Lampe, K. (2014). Definitions of organized crime. www.organized-crime.de/organizedcrimedefinitions.htm

Walsh, D. (2014). Two champions of children are given nobel peace prize. http://www.nytimes.com/2014/10/11/world/europe/kailashsatyarthi-and-malala-yousafzai-are-awarded-nobel-peace-prize.html?_r=0

Weerman, F. M., Lovegrove, P. J., & Thornberry, T. (2015). Gang membership transitions and its consequences: Exploring changes related to joining and leaving gangs in two countries. *European Journal of Criminology, 12*, 70–91. doi:10.1177/1477370814539070.

Weitzer, R., & Ditmore, M. (2010). Sex trafficking: Facts and fictions. In R. J. Weitzer (Ed.), *Sex for sale: Prostitution, pornography and the sex industry* (2nd ed.) (pp, 325–351). Routledge: New York

Woodiwiss, M. (2003). Transnational organized crime: The strange career of an American concept. In M. E. Beare (Ed.), *Critical reflections on transnational organized crime, money laundering, and corruption* (pp. 3–34). Toronto, Ontario: University of Toronto Press.

Woods, J. (2014). Have Sweden's permissive parents given birth to a generation of monsters? http://www.telegraph.co.uk/women/mother-tongue/10636279/Have-Swedens-permissive-parents-given-birth-to-a-generation-of-monsters.html.

Systemic Vulnerabilities on the Internet and the Exploitation of Women and Girls: Challenges and Prospects for Global Regulation

Simon Howell

Abstract The Internet, as a global phenomenon, has increasingly become host to pervasive forms of cybercrime, ranging from financial fraud to sexual abuse. Often as a result of underlying socio-economic and political disparities, women and girls may be more vulnerable to many of these forms of cybercrime. This is especially true in least-developed countries, some of which have seen a dramatic rise in Internet usage not matched by educational campaigns.. Using examples drawn from Africa, the chapter argues that global regulation is both urgent and needed, but that the development of such a framework will continue to be fraught with difficulties. In thinking beyond these difficulties, it is argued that the development of any regulatory framework will need to be contextually and strategically specific to the areas and places in which it is applied. As such these responses, whether domestic or international, will need to draw on the intellectual capital and resources of multiple state and non-state actors, ranging from local police forces to transnational regulatory agencies such as the United Nations Office on Drugs and Crime (UNODC).

1 Introduction

The Internet has fundamentally altered the means by which ideas and information are communicated and shared. Whether as an educational tool, a facilitator of business, a conduit for the transfer of data, or as a mechanism of surveillance and manipulation, its use has become increasingly entrenched in a diverse range of contexts. Moreover, while the Internet was first developed as a tool to facilitate the communication and sharing of research data (Glowniak 1998, pp. 135–144), its dynamic nature and reach has led to various parties adopting it as a *strategic* instrument by which information can be shared, whether legitimate or criminal.

S. Howell (✉)
University of Cape Town, Cape Town, South Africa
e-mail: Simon.Howell@uct.ac.za

H. Kury et al. (eds.), *Women and Children as Victims and Offenders: Background, Prevention, Reintegration*, DOI 10.1007/978-3-319-28424-8_22

Consequently, while there are innumerable instances of the positive use of the Internet, it has also been used as a powerful weapon with which to extend criminal networks and facilitate a multiplicity of nefarious activities, from the sharing of operational plans to the trading of illegal forms of pornography (Gogolin 2010, pp. 3–8). Although its design includes protocols that enable the tracking and tracing of individual nodes and users—through standard IP (Internet Protocol) and MAC (Media Access Protocol) addresses for instance—the development of various forms of software and extremely covert peer-to-peer networks have led to the expansion of what has become colloquially known as the "dark web" (Bradbury 2014, pp. 14–17). Because these networks employ mechanisms that prevent the traditional tracing of electronic signatures, they have found extensive use in the sharing of secretive information, whether that be bomb-making instructions or explicit images of underage children. The Internet and its derivatives then, much like any tool, can be manipulated and used for a variety of ends. Importantly though, the system itself does not exist outside the ambit of the human potential for good and bad—however so defined—but is rather a product of them.

As a function of the Internet being global in its design and use, and because it can be easily used to facilitate criminal activity, its use (and what constitutes the illegal use of it) has predominantly been governed at the state level, the individual frameworks of which are further facilitated through inclusion in supranational regulatory frameworks. It has however become increasingly apparent that such frameworks lack the adapatibility and speed needed to respond to online threats, and often struggle to account for the ethereal nature of digital communication technology. The Westphalian regulatory frameworks remain then largely reactive, while the prescriptive transnational regulatory frameworks that have been suggested have attracted significant criticism. As is document below, this has led to an ineffectual regulatory environment that is increasingly making vulnerable not just individuals, but entire groups of people. Indeed, at the time of writing there is no single or substantive global regulatory framework to control the multiple forms of cybercrime, despite its increasing cost and danger. However, this does not mean that local, specific, and important regulatory statutes and operational protocols cannot be developed, especially those that utilise existing data on vulnerabilities and problems found more broadly.

In the spirit of working towards such a framework, this chapter's purpose is to specifically focus on women and children in the developing world in relation to those forms of cybercrime that impact them the most. It is argued that the vulnerabilities that are created by the Internet are not unique or isolated, but often serve to further magnify existing socio-economic, political, and cultural disparities. The result, inevitably, is that those that are already more vulnerable will become likely targets of cybercrime. Importantly, though, counter-measures and responses cannot be generic but must take into account the cultural specificities and concerns from which victims' very vulnerability first arose. Their pre-existing vulnerability can be understood through numerous lenses, with disease prevalence and susceptibility, criminal exploitation (such as through sex work or child slavery), and economic exclusion (such as through forced marriage) perhaps being the most prominent. As is documented, the Internet has become a convenient and powerful weapon by which these groups may be further exploited and coerced. Taking the embedded nature of these differences and vulnerabilities seriously, some of the specific issues that any regulatory body will need to be adept at engaging with are highlighted, so as that they can be drawn upon in making regulatory frameworks substantively effective. While there is a growing body of work documenting these vulnerabilities, attention is also directed towards the manner in which women and children can be empowered by the Internet, and how some have also began to exploit the Internet for their own ends. By documenting these opposing dynamics, it is hoped that a more balanced overview of the particular issues at play are presented. Before doing so, an outline of why regulatory attempts will need to be global in nature and yet local in focus, and in illustrating the scale of the concerns with which this chapter deals, a brief overview of the Internet's dimension and operational nature is illustrative.

2 The Internet as a Global Phenomenon

The Internet has grown at such a rapid pace, and is so dynamic in nature, that its contemporary size and reach can be difficult to accurately conceptualise. Moreover, because the system is fundamentally open and largely unregulated, it has continually expanded in a myriad of ways, whether be it through the adding of a new server to the "cloud" or the development of kitchen appliances that are integrated into home networks (Gershenfeld and Vasseur 2014, pp. 60–62). As a consequence it is simply not possible to offer stable and consistently accurate measurements of its present size, reach, entrenchment, and total users. Minimally, it expands at the rate of gigabytes per second. What is presented is here at best a brief snapshot of a particular time and place.

In spite of this, the Internet is both enabled and constrained by the broader parameters that constitute different societies and the international state system as a whole. While one may not be able to provide a definitive overview of the Internet, it can be broadly understood in terms of the pre-existing social, political, and economic arrangements that structure the social world. For instance, there are at present approximately 2.8 to 3 billion Internet users, which equates to just over a third of the current global population.[1] Moreover, its total size grew at the rate of 675–678 % in 2013.[2] In short, the Internet doubled in size every 2 months. More men use the Internet than women—in 2013, 41 % of users were male, while 39 % were female.[3] This may seem a relatively small difference, but considering the total number of Internet users even one percentile is equal to many millions of people. The lack of accurate data can also easily be seen at this juncture; the percentages

[1] Internet World Database, a highly cited website, as accessed in November 2014.

[2] Ibid.

[3] Ibid.

Table 1 Age distribution of Internet users—June 2014

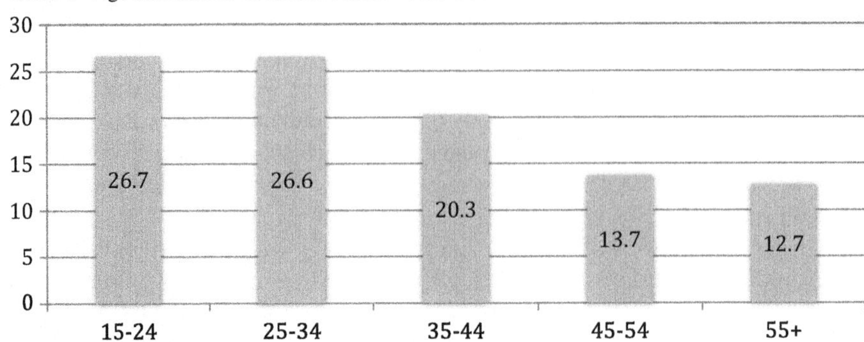

mentioned above only equate to 80 % of the total, with the remaining 20 % of Internet users remaining unidentifiable, as a result of research difficulties and the popularisation of tools that hide any trace of identity. This equates, directly, to a simple result: at least 20 % of Internet users—some 140 million users using the lowest estimate of total users—are either not being surveyed or are successfully hiding their identity to such an extent that previous research has been unable to determine the gender of the person behind the screen. Table 1 provides a breakdown of global Internet users by age. These divisions may however greatly differ in individual countries.

It has been widely recognised that the Internet, including the many anonymous networks and the "dark web", are now a conduit for numerous forms of violence, manipulation, intimidation, and abuse. Indeed, the global cost of cybercrime is estimated to exceed US $ 100 billion per year, with over 556 million people falling victim to various Internet-related crimes per year (Anderson et al. 2013, pp. 265–300). This equates to some eighteen per second. Specifically, for instance, over 600,000 Facebook accounts are compromised every single day.[4] While it is very difficult to garner accurate data, it is estimated that over a lifetime of usage 71 % of male and 63 % of female Internet users will fall victim to some form of cybercrime.[5] As shown in Table 2 below, while this difference may exist at the global level, there are significant variations at the regional level, which are especially applicable when focussing on vulnerable groups.

Moreover, there are also vast disparities in the depth and rates of use between different population groups. For instance, for those of whom the Internet has become an indispensible tool for business and finance, and who use Internet-based services every day, forms of cybercrime may have a profound impact on their daily lives. Deeply embedded users may also become more substantively vulnerable, with criminals exploiting the many connections that make services

[4] See the Techcrunch report 2014.

[5] Ipsos MORI (2011), p. 11.

Table 2 Internet user gender distribution by economic development

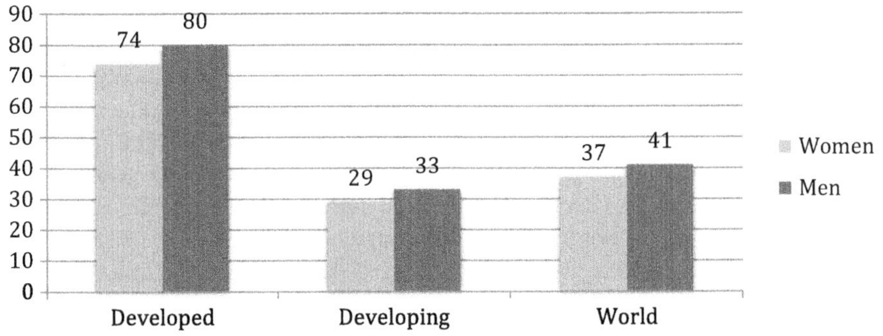

convenient as conduits for crimes, ranging from the theft of financial information to personal details and contacts. Indeed, for those who have been socialised with the Internet, it may be argued that forms of cybercrime can be as impactful as traditional forms of violence and intimidation.

Specific examples are more easily and accurately attainable at the level of individual countries, and by making reference to specific forms of abuse. For instance, in the United States, 25.8 % of adolescent female Internet users fall victim to some form of cyberbullying (with 16 % of adolescent males experiencing similar crimes).[6] Importantly, in the same cohort, 21.1 % of females report these abuses, while a lesser percentage (18.3 %) of males take action.[7] Again, while these statistical differences may not seem large, it must be remembered that each percentile is equal to many hundred of thousand of users. Various awareness campaigns have been launched in response, from community-led initiatives to those run by the global corporations such as Google and Facebook. Overall awareness levels of the vulnerabilities do however seem to track national economic development levels. For instance, in India, only 38 % of parents were sufficiently aware and informed of the various types of cyber crime and bullying, while in Sweden this number stands at 65 %. As is shown below, this is again statistically and operationally important in formulating an adaptive regulatory framework.

Furthermore, the statistical congruency between an awareness of the various forms of Internet crime and economic development are especially important to this chapter. While the Internet's overall level of penetration in North America may be 84.9 %, its growth between 2000 and 2014 was relatively low at 177.8 %. In Africa however, while the penetration level may only stand at 21.3 %, growth of the Internet on the continent over the same time period stands at a significant 5219.6 %.[8] It may thus be argued that while the Internet is reaching levels of

---

[6] Ibid.

[7] Ibid.

[8] Internet World Data 2014, as cited above.

saturation in developed nations, the developing world is becoming an increasingly important destination and market for users and Internet-based companies, corporations, and industries. Moreover, more African nationals are gaining access to rapidly increasing levels of bandwidth with the development of a number of high-speed fibre optic undersea cables directly linking the continent to Europe and India. As such, with increased bandwidth comes the *potential* for more substantive forms of exploitation. Concomitant to this, with increasing bandwidth more users may rely on more Internet-based tools, making them more vulnerable to various forms of cybercrime should they not be educated and regulatory efforts not be effective.

Indeed, and in spite of rapidly increasing penetration levels, few awareness campaigns and information drives have been conducted. As a result, new users in the developing world have become especially vulnerable to established forms of cybercrime and bullying, even though many of these strategies are no longer effective in more developed and security conscious nations (for further information, see Goodman and Harris 2010, pp. 24–27). In short, developing nations—as a result of the relative inexperience and lack of awareness of Internet-based forms of abuse and crime—have become new destinations for criminals, sexual offenders, and traffickers. These vulnerabilities, as is shown below, are magnified by pre-existing differences—many of which are symptomatic of differences in gender and age—and thus of particular concern.

Utilising the above data as a departure point, this chapter interrogates five interrelated cyber security issues. In the first, the objectives and key concerns of the contemporary international regulatory framework that is slowly emerging in response to these abuses are highlighted. Secondly, some of the new vulnerabilities and sites of resilience that have emerged in contemporary Internet usage patterns are explored. Here the concern is with understanding what drivers create or magnify vulnerabilities for individuals, institutions, and countries. In drawing specific attention to the development and deployment of various new technologies, their relevance for an effective international regulatory framework is documented. Following this, thirdly, the role of the "dark web", and its implications for effective legislation, is highlighted. In the fourth, a discussion of how "old" crimes—such as the creation and sharing of illegal forms of pornography—is provided, showing how these have expanded and targeted many more individuals. Here the particular focus concerns how these technologies, and the Internet as a whole, have become complicit in preying on new markets, many of which are now found in developing nations. Again, these concerns are of systematic importance to the development of regulatory frameworks, which may ultimately act as a guide for local legislation and policing. Finally, an area of cyber crime often missed or left unattended is engaged with, perhaps as a result of its political sensitivity—that of women and young people as offenders themselves. As noted above, overall Internet penetration levels are higher among younger people, many of whom possess (through a lifetime of computer use) the knowledge and skill sets needed to commit these crimes.

3 The Emerging Regulatory Paradigm

Two prominent international bodies, the UN (United Nations) and the CoE (Council of Europe), have been the key facilitators in the formulation of a substantive international regulatory framework in which to both understand and control cybercrime. The UN has, at the time of writing, yet to adopt a significant or coherent framework, with previous efforts having attracted strong objections and criticism.[9] The CoE has however both formulated and implemented the 2004 Convention on Cybercrime (which is at times referred to the Budapest Convention on Cybercrime).[10] Each of these efforts will be individually outlined, as the challenges met by the former and the successes of the latter are both useful indicators of the requirements of, and reveal some of the potential problems to be encountered by, an international regulatory framework specifically targeted at the various forms of cybercrime.

The UN Department of Economic and Social Affairs (DESA), which has played a central role in driving the development of an UN-based regulatory framework, argued that "cybersecurity is a complex transactional issue that requires global cooperation for ensuring a safe Internet".[11] The various issues and concerns relating to cybercrime were engaged with in detail, for instance, at a special UN event, "Cybercrime and Development", held on the 9th of December 2011, in New York. The resulting discussions highlighted three overarching themes that required immediate attention. These are (1), the need to "build awareness at the international policy level", that (2) this required the identification of "a range of best practice policies and initiatives in place around the world to build a culture of cybersecurity", and (3) to "explore options for a global response to rising cybercrime".[12] While integrative responses by a number of regulatory and policing bodies were acknowledged as important, so too was the continued salience of economic discrepancies and difference between countries, areas, and populations the world over. Indeed, it was noted that

> ... the role of economic disparities between nations and the fact that developing countries do not have sufficient capacity to combat cyber attacks and cybercrime, and its global threat to cyberpeace. The lack of partnership between developed and developing countries could generate 'safe havens', where cyber criminals can make use of the legal loopholes, and the lack of strong security measures present sometimes in developing countries to perpetrate cybercrimes.[13]

As is argued below, these economic differences have played a significant role in the growth and penetration of the Internet in less- and least-developed countries. This is a product of its growth being driven, in part, by private companies seeking

[9] Council of Europe Cybercrime Convention 2001.

[10] Ibid.

[11] ECOSOC 2014.

[12] Ibid.

[13] Ibid.

both new markets and customers. Problematically however local legislative frameworks, strategies, and protocols have not kept pace with this growth (Jewkes 2013, pp. 4–5). The result is that large areas and many millions of people are gaining access to the Internet for the first time, with little knowledge of, or protection from, the various potential forms of threat, abuse, and criminal activity that are enabled by its spread, development, and entrenchment (Touray et al. 2014, pp. 1–17).

While the aforementioned efforts show sustained resolve, continued disagreements over how such a structure would be practically implemented have prevented the formulation of a concrete framework. Indeed, many of the concerns and issues that were raised at this and other UN-led meetings focussed on the proposed harnessing of the CoE's Convention of Cybercrime as a broader multilateral model. These worries have focussed particularly on the Convention's implicit prioritisation of at least some European considerations.[14] In 2010, for instance, Russia opposed the Convention's recommendation of the expansion of police powers to access restricted data, especially that gathered information using state resources. In turn, Russia's proposals have been rejected by the US and EU, primarily because representatives feel that the proposed measures would infringe on their respective privacy protection laws.[15] In the same year, a competing cyberspace treaty outlining regulatory conventions and protocols was presented to the Twelfth UN Congress on Crime Prevention and Criminal Justice, for further action by the Commission on Crime Prevention and Criminal Justice.[16] While the treaty was debated at length, and while the Congress agreed on the importance of regulation in some form, continued disagreements and concerns prevented its implementation in any operative form. As a consequence, no firm resolutions have been passed as yet, and the framework remains tentative at the time of writing.

Such debate should be expected, as it must be remembered that the regulation of cybercrime ultimately entails the control, in a substantive form, of the Internet itself. As the Internet becomes more deeply entrenched in modern forms of governance, and indeed as a key tool, questions of sovereignty and security become pivotal and play a key role in preventing the realistic adoption of a global security framework.

The Council of Europe's Convention on Cybercrime—which came into effect on the 1st of July 2004 after having been adopted at the Council's 109th session on the 8th of November 2001—is however far more substantive in both its form and recommendations.[17] The Convention covers a broad spectrum of potential risks, offences, and threats. These include, but are not limited to, confidentiality/copyright/privacy concerns, the facilitation of criminal offences and activity through the

[14] Council of Europe Cybercrime Convention 2001.

[15] Ibid.

[16] United Nations DESA report 2013.

[17] Council of Europe Cybercrime Convention 2001.

use of the Internet or its associated structures, accessing and storing data (including the collection and/or seizure of data by enforcement agencies), and the production and dissemination of dangerous, damaging, or abusive data/information.[18] From a legislative and policing perspective, the Convention's primary purposes are (1) to harmonise the various domestic frameworks in use by member countries, ensuring legal consistency and effective transnational policing measures, (2) empower domestic enforcement agencies to effectively police the Convention's various concerns by providing support, pooling resources, and ensuring effective communication, and (3) the facilitation of an environment in which effective and dynamic transnational cooperation can be achieved and sustained. An additional protocol, ratified on the 1st of March 2006, further criminalised the online proliferation of racist and xenophobic materials.[19] Finally the convention has also been adopted (controversially) by the US, with further signatories including Canada, South Africa, Japan, Australia, Panama, Mauritius and the Dominican Republic.[20] As is argued below, while the Convention is a useful starting point and resource, it has been designed with the policing capacities and knowledge economies of developed nations in mind. It may therefore not be effective if simply adopted wholesale by those who have significantly different or weaker policing structures, and yet are experiencing the highest growth rates in Internet usage and penetration. These countries are primarily found in the developing world.

The currently emerging policing paradigm is thus caught in a tension between the acknowledgment of the need to create an effective regulatory framework which specifically targets cybercrime, and continuing disagreements between individuals and governments concerning access to private content, data, and the possibility of utilising the framework as a tool by which to access restricted information. As a result, while the CoE Convention may serve as foundation for a more broadly-accepted framework, numerous diplomatic, political, and cooperative hurdles will need to be overcome. Moreover, critical attention will need to be paid to its utility and use if it is to be implemented in structural conditions for which it was not designed—the economic, political, and social structures of developing nations are typically far more heterogeneous and less well resourced (Wallsten 2005, pp. 502–503), both of which severely impact the levels and manner in which such frameworks can be deployed and policed (Wallsten 2005, p. 502).

With this in mind, the chapter now explores what new vulnerabilities, threats and risks such a framework would need to be able to both understand and regulate. In so doing, the vulnerabilities and threats that have emerged in the developing world are further examined, by documenting what impact they may have and what factors will need to be considered in formulating an effective and resilient regulatory framework.

---

[18] Ibid.

[19] Ibid.

[20] Ibid.

4 New Vulnerabilities, New Dynamics

In seeking to understand the context in which cybercrime has become a threat to people, one that invariably relies on entrenched political, economic, and social vulnerabilities (as a function, for instance, of a lack of experience, knowledge, and a regulatory framework itself), there are two useful examples that illustrate the often subtle dynamics at play. They are also useful in illustrating the manner in which individuals can become vulnerable to, and exploited by, Internet users many thousand of miles away.

A number of South African schools have now begun to seek permission from their pupils' guardians before posting any pictures of them on their websites or social media accounts.[21] Indeed, some have also begun to password-protect this information, in an attempt to ensure that only authorised members of the community can access them. While this may have been done to protect private and copyrighted material in the past, these regulatory and restrictive protocols are increasingly finding use in efforts to protect the identities of the pupils, in an attempt to prevent the pictures from being utilised for any purpose other than the original one. A simple picture of a school netball or cricket team may seem innocent enough, yet for some these images are material for very different ends, and may be shared to a number of individuals utilising covert networks and conduits. The pictures can be further used in identifying vulnerable children, or those that can be easily abducted for a variety of purposes, such as child slavery or as hostages with which to elicit monetary ransoms—in South Africa for instance, the use of websites are normally the preserve of private schools attracting parents from higher income brackets. Consequently, the protection of what may seem like innocent sites and pictures becomes important in preventing far more serious crimes, and in preventing children from falling victim to organised criminal strategies and tactics. These preventative strategies are however not often conceptualised in a risk-limitation paradigm, especially considering the ease by which visual materials, such as pictures, can be so easily created, posted, and disseminated through social media networks.

Drawing on a more regional example, in 2012 Boko Haram—an Al-Qaida linked transnational terrorist organisation blacklisted by the UN—was purported to have infiltrated the database containing the personnel records of employees of the Nigerian State Security Services (see Oluwaremi et al. 2013, pp. 103–109). While the information acquired as a result of the cyber attack was not explicitly used for criminal purposes, it was publicly released. As a consequence, the names, addresses, bank account information and close family members of past and present employees became easily accessible, undermining the Service's ability to effectively fulfil its operational mandates (Oluwaremi et al. 2013, pp. 103–104). Beyond this, the cyberattack demonstrated how vulnerable many of weakly secured some of

[21] See, for instance, Rustenburg Girls High School 2014.

African countries Internet-based structures and databases are—even those that are by their very nature supposed to be protected from such attacks.

Minimally, gaining access to much of this information could be strategically used as a potent bargaining tool by recognisable terrorist groups. The release of this information thus not only undermined the service, but also endangered a number of employees' lives. An increase in cyberattacks and hacking attempts have been reported across the continent, with the two strongest economies—Nigeria and South Africa—experiencing pervasive and systematic attempts to acquire information as varied as banking details, government contact details, and medical records (Grobler et al. 2013, pp. 32–41). Again, the release of this information may make vulnerable people and groups who are completely unaware that the data has been compromised, further susceptible to methods of exploitation, harassment, and manipulation. Not knowing that this information has been compromised, in short, prevents people from taking mitigating action. How might we understand these two examples in the context of the emerging regulatory framework explored above? While specific concerns would be contextually unique, there are a number of broader structural conditions that are of particular relevance to the effective implementation of a transnational regulatory framework.

As was noted by the UN, a key challenge to the development and effective implementation of a regulatory framework stems from pre-existing macro-economic disparities.[22] This challenge has three facets. The first, as touched upon, is that the Convention was designed for, and implemented by, the European Union. The vast majority of EU member states are considered developed, well policed and are relatively well resourced. This stands in direct contrast to many less- or least-developed countries. Second, and as a function of their economic status, many developing countries lack the extensive policing networks (not to mention policing resources) possessed by signatories to the Convention (Touray et al. 2014, pp. 1–6). Third, with particular reference to women and children, it must be remembered that many developing nations are highly unequal, and it is often women and children who experience the brunt of this inequality (Dalton 2013, pp. 1107–1112). Indeed, and as has been extensively noted in contemporary academic and research literature, structural inequalities impact on the lives of women and children in a myriad of ways, including making them vulnerable to sexual exploitation, slavery, sexual violence and rape (for a paradigmatic overview of these many issues, see Lombard and McMillan 2013).

A key driver of these problems and the resulting forms of violence is economic—even in countries that have experienced sustained economic growth and development, women and children continue to be the most vulnerable and exploited members of many society (Madon 2000, pp. 85–101).

Economic disparities play a further role in preventing members of individual societies from accessing social services and policing agencies. Any regulatory framework would not only have to make these services easily available, but make

[22] United Nations DESA 2013.

them accessible even for those that *do not* have access to the Internet. As Susan Kreston has noted, for instance (Kreston 2007, p. 40), women and girls are frequently trafficked from East Africa through a network that is facilitated by the use of the Internet and mobile technology. A regulatory framework would remain ineffective if it were to solely concentrate on responses to these crimes while not providing the means and mechanisms whereby potential victims can alert authorities to their vulnerability. Thus while Internet-based technologies facilitate these criminal networks, they may also offer the tools needed in their prevention, a theme that is explored in more detail below.

In congruence with these economic concerns, perhaps expectantly, many political challenges can be found. The EU Convention was formulated in an environment in which there are high levels of economic interdependence, an already-existing co-operative political community, and numerous interdependent policing and regulatory bodies. Even in using the example of Southern Africa, one of the more economically integrated regions in the developing world, the political climate in individual countries can be vastly different.

While the region has an economic union, SADC (Southern African Development Community), less substantive *social* integration exists—the frequent outbreaks of xenophobic violence being an example of this. Moreover, it has been widely noted that policing bodies have been manipulated to perform functions ultimately concerned with state sovereignty rather than effective governance (Saurombe 2009, pp. 100–104). These concerns are especially relevant in the regulation and policing of the Internet, which by its structural design and nature is transnational, pays no heed to traditional borders or policing jurisdictions. Again, specific attention should be drawn to the vulnerability of women and children in these contexts; the political disenfranchisement and exclusion of women remains a continuing concern in a number of developing countries (Wurtele et al. 2014, pp. 546–568).

Contemporarily, many of these concerns have themselves become political tools in the strategic development of competing concepts of nationhood (Carpenter 2006, pp. 25–53). One need only point to the conflicting understandings and views of female circumcision to understand this; the practice has increasingly become a strategic flag-bearer for the construction of competing ontological definitions of statehood, citizenship and femininity (Ibid). As a result, international legislation outlawing the practice has been interpreted as another form of "Western" political and moral intervention and dominance.

Whether correct or not, any international regulatory framework that is understood to be a tool for strategies of foreign imposition will not be seen as legitimate and thus unlikely to find cohesive traction and adoption. As noted above, Russia's concern with the deployment of the CoE convention further afield was ultimately underpinned by a concern with sovereignty. These national disagreements can have global ramifications, as any area or state that excludes itself from the agreements will become a haven for the hosting of servers and tools used in conducting cybercrime. As a result, an international regulatory framework will need to be as inclusive and dynamic as possible, while also requiring that it be seen as legitimate and actionable to the broadest range of stakeholders. This will, unfortunately, be especially difficult as a result of the unfettered and unregulated expansion/growth of the Internet and the continuing salience of sovereignty and state-led concerns with self-determination and privacy.

While the hardware and machines on which the Internet relies can easily be seen as artefacts external to social configurations and human relationships, it must be remembered that the Internet is increasingly becoming a social experience in and of itself (Chayko 2014, pp. 976–991). While the rise of social media platforms such as Facebook may be an obvious example, the myriad of channels of communication and methods of sharing personal experiences have served to embed online forms of technology into the very way in which the social has come to be constituted. While this effect may be felt far more in developed countries, as shown by the penetration figures above, the Internet is rapidly expanding in the developing world and is becoming ever more integrated into peoples' lives. The cumulative effect may often be positive—allowing individuals to share information more effectively and more widely—yet it also create opportunities for forms of crime that can harness peoples' very identity as a form of leverage (Chayko 2014, p. 978).

Regulation is thus also made more difficult—limiting the possibility of an Internet-based tool or conduit from being used for criminal purposes often involves limiting other (legitimate) users' experience of that tool. When those tools have become socially embedded and personally important to users, limitations may be seen as a personal imposition if enforced, while unlikely to be followed if merely made optional.

Facebook is (again) a useful example. Responding to sustained criticism, the company has made available a whole host of options and tools with which users can safeguard their privacy and limit access to their account.[23] Yet, and as noted above, 600,000 Facebook accounts continue to be compromised every day. If these very well publicised and easy-to-use tools remain unutilised, how might a regulatory framework find implementation in a broader environment?

Such a regulatory framework will not only have to account for criminal intention, but for potential victims to be unwilling to make themselves less vulnerable. Limiting experiences that have become fundamental to peoples' daily lives is, as Facebook has found out, a very hard sell. This will only become more difficult as more of the basic appliances and tools found in daily use are brought online. With the development of the "internet of things" as such, so too do the possibilities for abuse expand. It has been shown, for instance, that "smart" cars can be remotely hijacked and driven.[24] As a consequence, any regulatory framework will need to be highly adaptive and flexible in order to take into account these rapid changes and developments.

---

[23] See Facebook's current privacy document, cited here in late 2014.

[24] See, for instance, Forbes' 'Hackers reveal nasty new car attacks with me behind the wheel', 2013.

Concomitant to this structural quagmire is a further dynamic—societies in developing countries are often highly unequal, with gender disparities frequently exasperated by unquestioned patriarchal norms (Carpenter 2005, pp. 295–334). Resultantly, it is again women and children that may feel the effect of these disparities the most, at times being left powerless and vulnerable to exploitation and abuse (ibid). As a result, an effective regulatory framework with which to prevent the many forms of cybercrime cannot simply be limited to the criminal acts themselves, but will need to be integrated into broader frameworks that speak to concerns with inequality, gender, violence, trafficking, and abuse. This is not however a limitation—many of these frameworks have already been in existence for some time, with at least some proving themselves successful (Ali 2011, pp. 185–193). Cybercrime regulation can thus be seen as another weapon in a broader arsenal of defences against organised criminal activity.

Many of these structural concerns, and indeed much of the CoE's Convention, is reactive. While necessary, the limitation of vulnerabilities (especially with regard to women and children) needs to prescriptive and proactive. As in many other areas, education and information are the most important preventative tools that can be made available to new and vulnerable Internet users. Indeed, it is precisely because campaigns and educational drives in countries that have higher levels of Internet penetration (and which have had to respond to the associate crimes and forms of abuse for much longer) have been effective in limiting cybercrime that new regions and more vulnerable users are now being targeted (Chin and Fairlie 2010, pp. 153–167).

The deployment of educational strategies and tools cannot however be the sole responsibility of governments. The expansion of the Internet is frequently driven by private investment concerns, and as a consequence a regulatory framework would do well to harness the private sector in ensuring that the tools, services, and channels they offer to users are secure, transparent, and that potential users are made aware of the associate risks (Chin and Fairlie 2010, pp. 155–157). Coupled with broader campaigns and the dissemination of simple "best practice" guidelines (with regards to password protection methods, privacy settings, and so forth), both governments and private institutions may be able to limit much of the "softer" forms of cybercrime, as it is often these easily accessible "trapdoors" that serve as the springboard for more complex and persuasive forms of abuse (Chin and Fairlie 2010, pp. 157–159).

Indeed, it is to these more persuasive and problematic forms of cybercrime that the chapter now turns. As law-enforcement authorities have begun to discover, criminal and illegal uses of the Internet are often well hidden behind a myriad of security "walls", preventing ease of access while also allowing their specific interests to continue unabated. Many of these have now been classified as forming part of the "dark web". However problematic the term, many of these P2P (peer-to-peer) networks are not only hidden in themselves, but users "hide" themselves behind tools that make them further "invisible". In such an open system as the Internet, in truly Foucauldian fashion, the possibility for identification is frequently the only limit preventing further abuses. With this in place, the chapter now highlights how "old" or traditional crimes and criminal strategies have found a new lease on life in utilising the Internet. Finally, it seeks to provide an overview of how the Internet has been used by women and children to commit criminal offenses. While not often discussed, this politically sensitive area of criminal activity cannot be ignored, especially as younger people grow up with Internet access and learn to exploit the system for their own ends.

4.1 Development and the Dark Web

In both the media and academic literature, the abuse of women and children by Internet users is invariably mentioned in relation to the "dark web". Beyond the academic literature, however, the "dark web" is frequently undefined, or in a manner that is incorrect. As such, it is important to understand *what* the "dark web" is, and what specific aspects of it need regulation. Indeed, the "dark web" is somewhat of a misnomer and not particularly accurate. There are, analytically, three different forms or "dark" areas of the Internet, the "dark internet", "deep web" and "darknet". As they are frequently confused, especially by sensationalist media reports and exposés,[25] an overview of their differences serves as a useful means by which to focus attention on the specific implications that these networks have for a developmental agenda and regulatory framework, not to mention documenting how they may be used for criminal purposes.

The "dark internet" has existed since the creation of ARPANET (the Advanced Research Projects Agency Network), the Internet's precursor. The "dark" Internet is simply those addresses and networks that cannot be reached by anyone online—they are, in other words, completely offline. As such, the actual machines cannot be used to share information or data directly, but can be used for purposes of storage or computation. Thus, for instance, an isolated computer could be used to store illegal pornography, but for that data to be shared it would first have to be manually transferred to a computer with access to the wider Internet. While this would physically limit the possibility of sharing information, it does also make the remote access of the information impossible without physical interventions; it is for this reason that the dark Internet has found military application. These machines, in short, are beyond the "light" of the Internet.

The "deep web" is any part of the Internet not indexed by standard search agents (with Google, Bing, and Yahoo having the largest market share). Using a frequently used metaphor, in acquiring data search engines drag a net across the surface of the Internet. While much may be caught in the net, there remains a massive amount of data below the surface that is not captured or indexed. Indeed, while it is not possible to accurately define the size of the "deep web", as a function of it not being possible to capture all of the information, it is often thought of as being

[25] See, for instance, USA Today 2014.

several times larger than the surface—a well-known yet now dated paper estimated that the "deep web" consists of 7,5 petabytes of data (Cassim 2011, pp. 123–138). While a small portion of the "deep web" may be used for nefarious purposes, as explained below, most of it is constituted by content that is used daily, but is simply not accessible to search engines. The most common resources include dynamic content, such as forms and pages that require user-based input, content that is not linked to other pages (the links of which are utilised by search engines to identify individual pages), private content that requires login details, contextual content which has dynamic navigation sequences (the data used by mapping websites to allow users to browse areas, for instance), limited access content such as those used by websites that require user-interpreted data (such as sites protected by dynamic CAPTCHA (an acronym for "Completely Automated Public Turing test to tell Computers and Humans Apart" processes to prevent robotic exploitation)), and scripted content as used by Java and Flash, and content that is not handled by search engines (such as some forms of multimedia)(Salifu 2008, pp. 432–443). The vast majority of Internet users thus access the "deep web", in some form or another, typically at points where their input is required. Simply logging into a company website or university intranet is to technically access the "deep web". The major difference between the "deep web" and the "darknet" is that websites constituting the former do not explicitly attempt to hide their identity or IP addresses, but are typically not "seen" by search engines, as they do not have access to them. The latter, however, are usually *intentionally* hidden.

The "darknet", which by definition forms a small part of the "deep web", is constituted by networks that are severely and purposefully restricted—connections are only made between trusted addresses and peers (Schell et al. 2007, pp. 45–63). These "friends" use non-standard protocols and ports, further limiting access and the ability to monitor their activity. While similar to more widely used peer-to-peer networks, these F2F (friend-to-friend) networks require various levels of user-authorisation. Thus while torrent sites allow all users to connect to one another (known as "seeding"), a F2F network will require the individual authorisation of all the possible connections (Schell et al. 2007, p. 45). This prevents permanent links between individual nodes from being established (thus preventing indexing) with the networks requiring levels of authorisation that allow only trusted users access. Their utilisation of non-standard protocols and ports further discourages easy access or surveillance, and prevents standard means and mechanisms from being effective in the identification and tracking of users and machines. The networks are usually also decentralised, preventing their reliance on a single machine or node, and can often only be accessed using specialised software (Schell et al. 2007, pp. 47–49).

The "darknet" may not necessarily be used for nefarious or criminal purposes, with many governmental and corporate bodies relying on them for specific transactions. The networks' purpose, ultimately, is to safeguard information and ensure the highest levels of privacy possible on the Internet. However, because they are designed to prevent the identification of users and facilitate the secret sharing of information, they have been utilised by those who wish to share data that may attract sanctions or reprisal, in disseminating data protected by copyright laws for instance, and by those wishing to share content that is illegal, harmful, or viewed as problematic by the societies in which individual users live (Schell et al. 2007, p. 48). It must be remembered that cybercrime is not necessarily limited to the use of these networks, with the vast majority of crimes utilising the ordinary, "visible" web. Moreover, while much has been made of these networks in recent years, they represent a very small proportion of the "dark web" and are utilised by comparatively few people. While they have been used to share very different forms of data—ranging from pornography to state secrets—they are by their nature limited. Newer, and perhaps larger, criminal uses of the Internet exploit its common features, through which far more users and machines can be accessed (Grobler and Jansen van Vuuren 2010). As is highlighted below, this is especially true in developing nations that are rapidly increasing Internet access with comparatively few safeguards and precautionary measures finding congruent implementation.

As a whole, thus, the Internet can be a powerful tool with which to further enhance the economic, political, and social development of individual countries. The Internet is now a necessary tool for communication, and is needed in order to facilitate the expansion of trade and commerce, having been used in such diverse applications as policing, emergency response coordination, and the tracking of deliveries. Moreover, its use is pivotal in maintaining both local and national security regimens. As such,

> A major component of information and infrastructure security is a nation's ability to deter, detect, investigate, and prosecute cyber criminal activities. Weaknesses in any of these areas can compromise security not only in that country, but also around the globe (Salifu 2008, p. 432).

The overall development of a country cannot substantively occur without the utilisation of the various resources and tools offered by the Internet. In regions that are undergoing rapid urbanisation, or in those nations that seek to further integrate their markets into the world economy, the development and expansion of their online capabilities is extremely important. The laying of numerous high-capacity fibre cables, which now circumvent the African continent, is testament to how important the entrenchment of Internet capabilities are to many nations (Grobler and Jansen van Vuuren 2010, pp. 3–5).

The deployment and expansion of these networks is however a "double-edged sword" (Chawki and Wahab 2013, pp. 1–33). On the one hand, they are pivotal to the further development of trade and economic integration. On the other, the increasing of capabilities increases the possibility and potential of utilising the resulting networks for exploitative and criminal activities. Furthermore, the development of IT capabilities and services are not divorced from the development trajectory of individual countries themselves, the frequent result of which is unequal penetration levels that follow pre-existing socio-economic distribution patterns (Ibid). In South Africa, for instance, 31 % of citizens have access to the Internet, but the vast majority of this access is concentrated in well-resourced areas (Chawki and Wahab 2013, p. 1). When Internet access does penetrate less-resourced areas, its use is often unregulated and users uneducated, further increasing the ease by which they can be exploited. Thus, in those countries in which women and children are already marginalised, the Internet can increase their chances of exploitation simply by being users, notwithstanding further political concerns with equality and individual rights. If the development of specifically tailored security and protection measures does not keep pace with the expansion of the Internet into new regions and areas, then the *likelihood* of these new nodes being targeted by experienced users elsewhere also increases. As is documented in the next section, this has repeatedly occurred in a number of African countries, many of which have become seen as the "new frontier" for the expansion and growth of the Internet and e-commerce. So too have these regions become the new frontier for exploitative practices and strategies, some of which prey on those who do not have direct access to the Internet (Chawki and Wahab 2013, p. 3).

As a result, the development of an effective regulatory paradigm must be cognisant of at least four fundamental areas of concern:

1. The Internet is a global phenomenon, with global reach. Any regulatory framework must then, in its very design, be global in nature and reach. It must not only be cognisant of what occurs online, but the *results* of this online activity. Regulation must therefore extend to the offline domain as well.[26] Should there be even one isolated or excluded area, whether geographic or electronic, it will be used to further facilitate a vast plethora of criminal and exploitative practices.
2. The Internet is an extremely fluid and highly dynamic decentralised network that is adaptable and resilient. Communication and cooperation between various regulatory bodies, security agencies, and government departments will be required to implement and respond to any occurrence. Again, should even one area be overlooked, it will severely weaken broader attempts at regulation.
3. The implementation of effective and practical security measures must occur in conjunction with the increasing expansion of the Internet. These measures may range from international regulatory frameworks to ensuring that new users install anti-virus software on their personal machines. The dissemination of information and practical guidelines that are easily understandable will be pivotal in limiting the risks that individual users may expose themselves to.
4. Those members of society who are already vulnerable—women and children perhaps being the most common—need to be protected by specific laws and regulations. These efforts should however not simply be protective, but should be empowering, allowing vulnerable people to utilise the Internet effectively and as a means of further developing themselves.

With the above concerns in mind, specific examples of how the Internet has been used to facilitate criminal activities in developing nations are now highlighted, showing how important the congruent expansion of safety measures are in the limitation of exploitative and manipulative strategies, often perpetuated by far more experienced users and syndicates in the developed world.

---

[26] For specificities, see the UNODC Comprehensive Study on Cybercrime, 2013, p. 256.

5 Old Crimes, New Targets: The African Example

Much has been made of the increasing prevalence of groups and syndicates that use the "dark web" to share problematic data, such as pornographic images of children. Highly publicised raids and arrests have revealed to the public that the nefarious use of the Internet is not limited to those people and places traditionally thought of as criminal, but have implicated a number of established journalists, lawyers, teachers, politicians, and celebrities.[27]

There are numerous forms of cybercrime that have been found to have originated from or target African countries and/or nationals. Amongst these are all of the "traditional" cybercrimes, which include but are not limited to: the theft of information, the facilitation of criminal organisations, the manipulation of Internet users in general or specific targets (ranging from individuals to governments and multinational conglomerates), identity theft, defamation, the unauthorised acquisition of personal data, copyright infringement activities, and the use of the Internet to further or achieve exploitative crimes (such as the sharing of pornographic images of people, or the facilitation/organisation of activities supporting prostitution, abuse, child slavery/labour, and hostage-related/ransom related concerns)(see Cassim 2011, pp. 125–127). Indeed, many of these crimes specifically rely on Internet-based tools and information conduits, many of which are entirely open and well known, such as Facebook, although some use F2F networks found in the "deep web".

There are also a number of "new" targets and forms of exploitation that have emerged as a direct consequence of dynamics related specifically to the African continent. In highlighting these, thus, it should be noted that any analysis or practical attempt at regulation *must* be cognisant of local dynamics and factors that may further facilitate direct forms of cybercrime. In following Grobler and Jansen van Vuuren's analysis (2010, pp. 1–8) new forms of cybercrime on the continent are made possible by a serious lack of IT education and understanding, with very few users having received formal training or guidance. Many forms of cybercrime are opportunistic, and thus this lack of structured guidance has contributed to the creation of a highly vulnerable cohort of users, many of which fall prey to forms of cybercrime that would no longer be successful in countries with substantive education policies, or in which Internet safety protocols have become entrenched in the daily practices of users (see Cassim 2011, pp. 125–127). In tandem with this, few operating system manufacturers offer their products in African languages, and very few Internet sites and portals utilise these languages. As a result,

> Many African computer users do not necessarily understand error messages or warnings about cyber fraud that are not presented in their mother tongue. As a result, the absence of

[27] See, for instance, the Daily Mail's report on the police search of Sir Elton John's personal computer, 2013.

> African languages in cyber space poses a serious threat to cyber space fraud and vulnerability to cyber space fraud (Cassim 2011, p. 126).

There is, furthermore, a lack of standardisation and communication between local regulatory bodies, preventing interstate investigations and regulatory attempts from effectively protecting users or investigating instances of criminal behaviour (Ibid). This weakness is especially important to any international regulatory framework, as the meaningful cooperation of all signatories will be a prerequisite of effective control, as touched upon above. Finally, many African users utilise older technology and software, making them more vulnerable to contemporary forms of cybercrime. MS Windows is the most used operating system, and is by far the most frequently exploited system in the perpetuation of cybercrime (Ibid). The bandwidth available to individual users, while increasing, is also comparatively low by global standards, often preventing or standing in obstruction to the regular updating of system security software and preventative programmes. This is often the result of security updates not being seen as a priority by users, who prefer to dedicate the limited bandwidth to personal pursuits.

These structural concerns have created an environment in which users are especially vulnerable (as a result of a lack of training and information), policing is weak and unsystematic, and personal computers and machines are vulnerable to exploitation. The opportunities offered by forms of cybercrime are furthermore often made more desirable as a result of the socio-economic and political conditions found in many countries on the continent, increasing the likelihood of otherwise law-abiding citizens turning to easily committed forms of cybercrime to supplement their income, committed in climates in which the fear of reprisal is relatively low and/or stunted by high levels of corruption and lacklustre policing measures (Beech et al. 2008, pp. 216–228).

All of these factors can be seen in operation in Uganda, for instance. In a web-based survey it was found that some 92 % of respondents had been victim to at least one form of cybercrime (Tushabe and Baryamureeba 2005). Of these 53 % of respondents never told anyone, with only 34 % reporting the incidents. Contradistinctively, from the same sample, 25 % of respondents reported that they had "planned and successfully implemented" at least one form of cybercrime. "SPAM spreaders, intellectual property infringers and hackers are the most rampant". The study also found that only 60 % of users new how to detect common cybercrime threats, with 30 % of users not utilising any protective software. From the perspective of policing itself, "[m]ost perpetrators said that they find it easy to commit these acts because they are protected by a feeling of invisibility while online, the acts are relatively simply to conduct and also for adventure" (Beech et al. 2008, pp. 216–228).

In another example, there have been a number of arrests following an investigation by the South African Police Service into the proliferation and dissemination of pornographic images of adolescents. It was found that perpetrators were befriending young people using phone-based chat services, often pretending to be from the same age and area. Ultimately, they would convince the users—who were mostly young girls—to share pornographic images and "selfies" with them, which they would then further disseminate and/or use as bargaining tool with which to further extort additional images, money, or information from their victims. Such examples could have been easily prevented had sustained education campaigns been implemented and found traction with the users of these services. Fortunately, in South Africa, there are specific laws under which these actions can be charged, but this is not true for many other countries on the continent.

These are but two examples of an ever-broadening criminal arena, ranging from the targeting of large banks to individuals and children. Many of these crimes are opportunistic and rely on the pervasive lack of information, education, and guidance that can be found or that is offered in African countries. With the continent experiencing massive increases both in the number and quality of connections to the Internet, and with access to the Internet becoming ever more easy through the use of "smart" and "feature" phones, a overarching regulatory framework is needed. Such a framework cannot simply be responsive however, but must aim to empower individual users to protect themselves from many of these forms of cybercrime through education campaigns and strategies that are specifically tailored to the local contexts and conditions in which they are deployed. An effective regulatory framework will require the cooperation of numerous stakeholders, but it will also require that individual users are empowered to protect themselves from many of the most common forms of cybercrime. As a result such a framework cannot be deployed in isolation, but will form part of a larger structure of efforts specifically aimed at the development of those who are already vulnerable and easily exploited.

5.1 Women and Children as Offenders: An Uncomfortable Truth

While there is a rapidly expanding literature on women and children as victims of various forms of cybercrime, from cyberbullying and stalking to child slavery, there is comparatively little on women and children as offenders themselves (Seto 2002, pp. 67–75). While it remains true, both statistically and historically, that the vast majority of cybercrimes have been committed by men, there are also a number of documented instances of women and children committing cybercrimes. Often, however, the crimes committed are "softer" in nature, more pernicious, less shocking, and therefore less newsworthy (Cassim 2011, pp. 128–131). Reports of the police searching prominent male musicians' houses for child pornography, for instance, generate far greater media coverage than systematic yet subtle forms of cyberbullying, such as "fat shaming" by adolescents of their peers. While perhaps not as immediately "brutal" these passive-aggressive campaigns can continue for many years, preventing targets from accessing many of the resources—the educational aspects of which are increasingly important in contemporary schooling systems—and social networks offered by the medium (Salifu 2008, pp. 432–443).

They may also stunt development, enforce forms of self-hatred, and be pivotal in the development of lifelong psychological states that may severely limit the quality of life of victims (Seto 2002, pp. 67–72).

Research done on forms of cybercrime perpetuated by women and children is based on two important measurements. The first is that, at a global level, the largest percentage of Internet users are between the ages of 15 and 24 and 25 and 34 (both approximately 27 %) (Beech et al. 2008, pp. 222–227). Over half of the Internet's users are then below the age of 34, with an increasing majority having grown up with access to, and knowledge of the Internet and associated tools and technology. Minimally, this means that younger users will often be more proficient at the use of the technology, and will be far more adapt at integrating the use of the technology into their daily lives. Secondly, the data that has been acquired has pointed to women and children being far more likely to commit "softer" forms of cybercrime, such as cyberbullying, and that these forms of cybercrime are linked to Internet penetration levels (themselves, as explained above, linked to socio-economic development levels). The data that has thus been acquired points to cybercrimes perpetuated by women and children as far more likely to occur in more developed nations, although there may be an implicit bias in the data in that far fewer studies focussing on this topic have been undertaken elsewhere (Chen et al. 2004, pp. 50–56). Minimally, the data points to cybercrime by women and children as only becoming prominent in those nations in which the Internet and related technology has become deeply entrenched in the lives of users, and in which these forms of technology have become pivotal to the development and sustaining of relationships. In those places where penetration levels are not as high or as fundamental, cybercrimes such as online bullying are not as developed or as pertinent (Seto 2002, pp. 67–76). However, considering the very high expansion rate of the Internet in many developing nations, the lessons learnt by those studies already conducted need to be taken seriously, in an attempt to proactively limit these forms of cybercrime, which will be felt even more keenly should they be perpetuated against people who are already far more marginal or more easily abused.

Of those studies that have been conducted, the on-going "Halt Abuse" campaign has generated very detailed data, over a period of some 14 years.[28] As a case study, the data points to a number of interesting trends that have implications for policy and should be carefully considered in the formulation of a coherent and applicable regulatory framework. Perhaps the most prominent concern is the sheer scale of cybercrime, even in nations with high levels of Internet penetration, education, and safety. In the US, for instance, 71 % of male Internet users, and 63 % of female Internet users, have fallen victim to at least one form of cybercrime over the course of their online lives. Specifically focussing on cyberbullying, which includes forms of harassment, shaming, identity theft, manipulation, extortion, and the threatening

[28] For the original data, see the Halt Abuse website, 2014. All data quoted below drawn directly from the website.

of specific users, 25.8 % of adolescent females have reported being subject to at least one of these activities. Interestingly, some 16 % of adolescent males also reported having experienced at least one of these forms of cyberbullying, which implicitly brings into question the gender bias found in both the academic and grey literature. Adolescent females were also more likely to report these occurrences (21.1 % for adolescent females versus 18.3 % for adolescent males). Importantly, the on-going studies have also found that in a number of instances, more adolescent females have reported other forms of cyberbullying, including the unsolicited posting of media online without permission, and were slightly more likely to continue to harass the victim beyond online media and interactions.

Such data presents a complicated picture, but one that ultimately points to the importance of understanding online phenomena as embedded within pre-existing social, political, and economic structures. Much like other more "traditional" forms of crime, serious forms of cybercrime are committed by a very small percentage of the population in developed nations, with the perpetrators predominantly being male. However, less serious forms of cybercrime, such as cyberbullying, are committed by a far greater percentage of the population, with the ratio of female-to-male perpetrators within 10 % of each other. Of course, these ratios may not translate into conviction or incarceration ratios, but for a variety of reasons they still point to a serious problem. From a legislative perspective, moreover, they are important; legislation and regulation cannot simply target serious forms of cybercrime, but should seek to establish an enabling online environment in which users can safely interact with others, and in which reporting structures are easily accessible and anonymous. Much like the reporting of sexual crimes, the lower likelihood of adolescent men reporting forms of cyberbullying may be the result of the fear of stigma and shame, as these actions may be seen as an acknowledgement of weakness (Brenner 2007, pp. 12–28). This is especially pertinent in societies in which patriarchal norms and prescriptions have implicitly informed understandings of gender and identity, and will remain pertinent and powerful in an environment in which many online identities are also very public forms of identity.

As has been noted, the formulation of an adaptable regulatory framework must aim to create an infrastructure that is not only concerned with the limitation of certain activities, but the enabling of a safe environment. There is a broad ambit of cybercrimes, and to attempt to simply restrict the possibility of their occurrence may ultimately serve to limit the potential of the Internet. Moreover, while a globally applicable framework is needed, minimally to prevent isolated areas from becoming sites of reprieve for criminal activities, such a framework must also be cognisant of the many nuances and local differences that define individual nations and societies. Cyberbullying, for instance, may be an increasingly prominent phenomenon in developed countries, but may not be applicable to parts of the world in which Internet penetration levels are much lower, and in which pre-existing inequalities create ideal conditions for the substantive abuse of vulnerable people.

6 Conclusion

There have thus far been a number of commendable efforts to initiate and construct an international regulatory framework with which define the legitimate—and illegitimate—uses of the Internet and associated technology. However, concerns with privacy, security, and the use of the Internet as a means of surveillance continue to worry a number of governments and individuals. Moreover, such a regulatory framework would need to be highly adaptable and yet also resilient, in order to continue to remain effective as the Internet expands and changes. Indeed, adaptability is especially pertinent considering that the Internet is increasingly being used in places and for purposes not envisioned just 5 years ago—biometric data is now collected by phones, cars are "smart", and household appliances can be remotely controlled. All of these developments may be seen as advances. Yet they may also offer new opportunities and conduits for malicious and criminal activity.

The Internet's "new frontier" is the developing world, where its growth has been extraordinary. Again, this development has greatly aided a myriad of sectors and services, from banking to healthcare and policing. Increasingly however the Internet is becoming a conduit for a variety of crimes, many of which are driven by opportunism, itself often driven by and yet also reliant on deeper socio-economic and political inequalities. Consequently, the Internet tends to magnify those problems and differences that are already manifest within individual societies. The result is that those who are already vulnerable or weak become an easy prey for more experienced users and syndicates.

From a regulatory perspective, there are thus two important considerations that will need to be taken into account. In the first instance, policing measures will only be effective in a climate of cooperation and integration. The Internet is a global phenomenon and effective responses will also have to be global in nature. Secondly, while reactive measures will be needed to control criminal activities, preventive measures and policies are elemental in producing an environment in which cybercrimes becomes more difficult to perpetuate. Thus, for instance, educational strategies and programmes are desperately needed in those countries and regions experiencing very high increases in Internet growth and penetration. These campaigns would do well to be integrated into pre-existing structures and strategies, the development of which can take much longer in isolated communities.

In the instances of women and children, they are often the victims of various forms of cybercrime, ranging from child prostitution to cyberbullying. As noted above, in regions where, by virtue of law or culture, there are gender discrepancies and inadequate education these two cohorts may become easy targets for international forms of organised crime. These criminal networks often rely heavily on the Internet in order to facilitate and coordinate their activities. In developed nations, or in those areas of the world where the use of the Internet has become ubiquitous, young users make up the largest number of users. These young people have grown up with the Internet, and have integrated the technology into their daily lives in very deep ways, through which they often define themselves to varying degrees. Indeed, the use of the Internet is often fundamental to the very way in which they articulate and project their identity to the rest of the world. As such, subtle and nefarious forms of cyberbullying, often by their peers, create a detrimental environment that cannot simply be "switched off". A regulatory framework will need to account for these two poles, and everything in between. It is for this reason that a future regulatory framework will need to be integrative, responsive, and pragmatic.

While a global regulatory framework will remain unlikely, considered and specific responses by both state and non-state actors can still be effective. These responses will however have to be conscious of the contexts in which they are deployed, and cannot operate in isolation from the deeper socio-economic and political environments in which they are formulated.

Five Questions

1. What role can transnational regulatory bodies—such as the UN and CoE—play in the development of an effective regulatory paradigm aimed at mitigating forms of cybercrime?
2. What obstacles stand in the path of the formulation of a mutually agreeable and beneficial transnational regulatory paradigm?
3. What pre-existing bodies and structures, whether regional or global, can be utilised in the development and deployment of a realisable regulatory framework?
4. How can regulatory policies and programmes aimed at cybercrime complement pre-existing strategies aimed at ensuring the safety and development of marginalised countries, peoples, and individuals?
5. What underlying socio-economic and political phenomena drive cybercrime, and how can these be undermined or eliminated?

References

Ali, A. (2011). The power of social media in developing nations: New tools for closing the global digital divide and beyond. *Harvard Human Rights Journal, 24*, 185–193.

Anderson, R., Barton, C., Boehme, R., Clayton, R., van Eeten, M. J. G., Levi, M., et al. (2013). Measuring the cost of cybercrime. In R. Böhme (Ed.), *The economics of information security and privacy* (pp. 265–300). Berlin: Springer.

Beech, A. R., Birgden, A., Elliott, I. A., & Findlater, D. (2008). The Internet and child sexual offending: A criminological review. *Aggression and Violent Behavior, 13*, 216–228.

Bradbury, D. (2014). Unveiling the dark web. *International Journal of Network Security, 1*(4), 14–17.

Brenner, S. (2007). Cybercrime: Re-thinking crime control strategies. In Y. Jewkes (Ed.), *Crime online*. London: Routledge.

Carpenter, C. (2005). Women, children, and other vulnerable groups: Gender, strategic frames and the protection of civilians as a transnational issue. *International Studies Quarterly, 49*(2), 295–334.

Carpenter, R. (2006). *Innocent women and children: Gender, norms, and the protection of civilians*. London: Ashgate Publishing.

Cassim, F. (2011). Addressing the growing spectre of cyber crime in Africa: Evaluating measures adopted by South Africa and other regional role players. *Comparative and International Law Journal of Southern Africa, 5*(1), 123–138.

Chawki, M., & Wahab, M. (2013). Technology is a double-edged sword: Illegal human trafficking in the information age. Special report for *Droit*, 1–33.

Chayko, M. (2014). Techno-social life: The internet, digital technology, and social connectedness. *Social Compass, 8*(7), 976–991.

Chen, H., Chung, W., Jie Xu, J., & Yi Qin, G. (2004). Crime data mining: A general framework and some examples. *Computer Journal, 18*(9), 50–56.

Chin, M., & Fairlie, R. (2010). ICT use in the developing world: An analysis of differences in computer and Internet penetration. *Review of International Economics, 18*(1), 153–167.

Dalton, R. (2013). Abolishing child sex trafficking online: Imposing criminal culpability on digital facilitators. *University of Memphis Law Review, 43*(1), 1107–1112.

Gershenfeld, N., & Vasseur, J. (2014). As objects go online: The promise (and pitfalls) of the internet of things. *Foreign Affairs, 93*(2), 60–62.

Glowniak, J. (1998). History, structure, and function of the internet. *Seminars in Nuclear Medicine, 28*(2), 135–144.

Gogolin, G. (2010). The digital crime tsunami. *Digital Investigations, 7*(1), 3–8.

Goodman, S., & Harris, A. (2010). The coming African tsunami of information insecurity. *Communications of the ACM, 53*(12), 24–27.

Grobler, M., Jansen van Vuuren, J., & Zaaiman, J. (2013). Preparing South Africa for cyber crime and cyber defense. *Journal of Systemics, Cybernetics and Informatics, 11*(7), 32–41.

Grobler, M., & Jansen van Vuuren, J. (2010). Broadband broadens scope for cyber crime in Africa. In *Proceedings from the 2010 ISS Conference*.

Ipsos MORI. (2011). Cyberbullying: A total global perspective. Special Report, p. 11

Jewkes, Y. (2013). Killed by the internet: Cyber homocides, cyber suicides and cyber sex crimes. In Y. Jewkes (Ed.), *Crime online* (pp. 4–5). London: Routledge.

Kreston, S. (2007). Trafficking in children in South Africa: An analysis of pending legislation. *Child Abuse Research in South Africa, 8*(1), 40.

Lombard, N., & McMillan, L. (2013). *Violence against women: Current theory and practice in domestic abuse, sexual violence and exploitation*. London: Jessica Kingsley Publishers.

Madon, S. (2000). The Internet and socio-economic development: Exploring the interaction. *Information Technology and People, 13*(2), 85–101.

Oluwaremi, O., Adesuyi, F., & Abdulhamid, S. (2013). Combating terrorism with cybersecurity: The Nigerian perspective. *World Journal of Computer Application and Technology, 1*(4), 103–109.

Salifu, A. (2008). The impact of Internet crime on development. *Journal of Financial Crime, 15* (4), 432–443.

Saurombe, A. (2009). Regional integration agenda for SADC: Caught in the winders of change problems and prospects. *Journal of International Commercial Law and Technology, 4*(2), 100–104.

Schell, B. H., Vargas Martin, M., Hung, P., & Rueda, L. (2007). Cyber child pornography: A review paper of the social and legal issues and remedies – and a proposed technological solution. *Aggression and Violent Behavior, 12*(1), 45–63.

Seto, K. (2002). How should legislation deal with children as the victims and perpetrators of cyberstalking? *Cardozo Women's Law Journal, 9*(1), 67–75.

Touray, A., Salminen, A., & Mursu, A. (2014). ICT barriers and critical success factors in developing countries. *Electronic Journal of Information Systems in Developing Countries, 56*(1), 1–17.

Tushabe, F., & Baryamureeba, V. (2005). Cyber crime in Uganda: Myth or reality. *World Academy of Science, Engineering and Technology, 8*(1), 1–13.

Wallsten, S. (2005). Regulation and Internet use in developing countries. *Economic Development and Cultural Change, 53*(2), 502–503.

Wurtele, S., Simons, D., & Moreno, T. (2014). Sexual interests in children among an online sample of men and women: Prevalence and correlates. *Sex Abuse, 26*(6), 546–568.

Online documents

Computer Weekly (2014) UN rejects international cybercrime treaty. http://www.computerweekly.com/news/1280092617/UN-rejects-international-cybercrime-treaty

Council of Europe (2001) Convention on cybercrime. http://conventions.coe.int/Treaty/en/Treaties/html/185.htm

Daily Mail (2013). Elton John defends photograph seized in 'child porn' art raid. http://www.dailymail.co.uk/news/article-483748/Elton-John-defends-photograph-seized-child-porn-art-raid.html

Facebook (2014) Privacy policy. https://www.facebook.com/fbprivacy

Forbes (2013) Hackers reveal nasty new car attacks with me behind the wheel. http://www.forbes.com/sites/andygreenberg/2013/07/24/hackers-reveal-nasty-new-car-attacks-with-me-behind-the-wheel-video/

Halt Abuse (2014). http://www.haltabuse.org

Internet World Data (2014). http://www.internetworlddata.com

Pure Insight (2014) Online report. https://www.pureinsight.com/images/resourceCenter/5462-lg.jpg

Rustenburg Girls High School (2014). http://www.rghs.org.za

Techcruch (2014) Facebook sees 600,000 compromised logins per day. http://techcrunch.com/2011/10/28/facebook-sees-600000-comprised-logins-per-day/

United Nations (2013) 12TH Congress on crime prevention and criminal justice press release. https://www.unodc.org/documents/crime-congress/12th-Crime-Congress/Documents/A_CONF.213_18/V1053828e.pdf

United Nations Department for Economic and Social Affairs (2014) Cybersecurity: A global issue demanding a global approach. http://www.un.org/en/development/desa/news/ecosoc/cybersecurity-demands-global-approach.html

United Nations Office on Drugs and Crime (2013) Comprehensive study on cybercrime (Draft). http://www.unodc.org/documents/organized-crime/UNODC_CCPCJ_EG.4_2013/CYBERCRIME_STUDY_210213.pdf

USA Today (2014) Police take down Dark Web markets around the globe. http://www.usatoday.com/story/news/world/2014/11/07/police-knock-dark-web-markets-offline/18622501/

Protecting Children and Women Against Online Dangers

Gerald Quirchmayr, Barbara Buchegger, and Sandra Gerö

Abstract This chapter argues for increasing the efforts to protect children from online dangers in a rapidly changing technology-driven world. After briefly describing the current situation and identifying the resulting challenges for educational efforts, the contribution introduces one of the leading European-based computer networks dedicated to this task and looks at efforts aimed at online protection of female users. It finishes with arguments for a truly international solution.

1 Introduction

The problem of children and women being exposed to a multitude of dangers on the Internet has long been recognized by experts in the field (see e.g. Oswell 1999; Stanley 2001) as one of the darkest sides of this technology. Statistics recently published by UNODC (UNODC 2013, pp. 26–27) do again document the extent of the current threat against children and women and show very worrying trends. Starting from these highly critical facts, this contribution provides a more detailed look at current forms of cybercrime that are mainly targeted against children and women and then gives some examples of efforts to develop educational countermeasures. It closes with providing arguments why only a truly international approach can lead to an ultimately satisfactory solution of the current problem.

G. Quirchmayr (✉)
University of Vienna, Vienna, Austria
e-mail: gerald.quirchmayr@univie.ac.at

B. Buchegger
Saferinternet, Vienna, Austria
e-mail: buchegger@oiat.at

S. Gerö
Office of Ombudsman for Victims of Violence and Abuse in the Catholic Church, Vienna, Austria
e-mail: office@geroe.com

H. Kury et al. (eds.), *Women and Children as Victims and Offenders: Background, Prevention, Reintegration*, DOI 10.1007/978-3-319-28424-8_23

2 Changing Technology and the Networked Youth

The rapid development of technology, especially in the field of Internet-based communication and online social networks has dramatically changed the way in which especially young people live and communicate. Always being online has become part of their daily life, with all positive and negative side effects. Being able to use this technology has significantly changed communication patterns and has also lead to new problems, such as Internet addiction. While mobile equipment, from tablets to smart-phones is already ubiquitous in industrialized countries, this is still to come for other parts of the world. For some youths however, the technology has already become a status symbol and life without a smart-phone unthinkable. Young people and increasingly also children belong to this fully networked generation with the expression “digital natives” being a commonly used term for them. Online storage and cloud-based applications especially, are changing the control over personal data. While in the time of desktops and notebooks the user was in control of the stored data, it now often sits on the servers of “cloud” storage providers.

With cloud computing technology starting to profoundly affect professional and personal life and data often being referred to as “oil of the digital age,” the pressure on privacy is growing enormously. The consumer being the main target of data collections for marketing purposes, young people and even children are primarily viewed as consumers and as potential customers. This development leads to data hungry systems that try to best profile a consumer to offer targeted products and services. That is where providers such as Google, Apple and Facebook are in a very strong position, because they know their users very well through the analysis of their data. Personal interests and activities documented in Facebook entries are only one of the many examples of data that is extremely valuable for marketing purposes. In this context it is an almost irresistible temptation to use this data for offering targeted products and services. The data of young people and children may all too easily be used in this context. As a society we still need to develop the right models for a responsible use of the new smart technology. The best example is that industry efforts to limit the use of technology below a certain age are often undermined by well-meaning parents who for the sake of their child’s future make the latest technological toys available to children, and even set up Facebook accounts for their babies, sometimes containing highly personal information. The next problem is the inability of many users to envisage the legal and practical consequences of publishing highly personal information. The current privacy debate is amongst others highlighted by the website of Europe vs. Facebook (Europe vs. Facebook 2014).

3 Online Dangers

While opportunities provided by the technology are huge, it is not without problems, as described in the introduction. The negative aspects are however not limited to purely commercial misuse and the loss of privacy. It is well known that the dangers especially for young people and children are constantly growing through the abuse of the technology by criminals who can because of the global nature of the network operate from a far distance and are often outside the jurisdiction of their victims. Other problems range from social isolation to full Internet addiction. In isolated cases this has already led to children severely damaging themselves. The major dangers we see today can be grouped around several areas of criminal activity, the most atrocious form certainly being the exploitation of children through online channels. Different forms of identity theft, phishing attacks and online scams are targeted at audiences who can be manipulated by appealing to instincts such as fear or greed. Offering the possibility of winning nice technology toys, e.g. the latest smart-phone or computer games can easily lead to children revealing substantial personal data. Criminals can then use this data for all sorts of dark activities.

A relatively new problem is cyber-mobbing. While traditional forms of mobbing only have a limited reach, cyber-mobbing has a potentially unlimited space and time. In some schools this problem has already escalated to a degree where police support was necessary to bring the situation back under control. In very isolated and rare cases, cyber-mobbing has led to suicide, and Internet addiction has resulted in violent crime. The ubiquitous character of smart-phones and tablets and the general availability of wireless networks, many of them still unprotected, especially the ones offered as services in public spaces, led to a partial and even full loss of parental control over a child's activities on the Internet. Legal perspectives on the issue were given as early as the dangers developed into materialized threats (Gillespie 2002). While legislation in most industrialized countries is adequate, enforcement still is a major challenge.

When the access to technology could still be controlled through technical means via firewalls, parental control software and other protective mechanisms on a personal computer, a sort of safety perimeter could fairly easily be established around children. With smart-phones and tablets this possibility is now eroding quickly. Adding to the problem is the fact that children as "digital natives" are often more technology savvy than their parents and can easily outsmart the controls their parents install on their devices.

As this at least partial loss of control is a fact that cannot be changed, the best way of protecting children against harming themselves on the Internet is education, or as Safer Internet calls it, an educational "vaccination".

According to a list of dangers children are exposed to when active in social media networks and on the Internet in general, these threats are today manifold (Safer Internet 2014). Starting with more commercially oriented threats, such as spam, phishing, the collection of personal data and illegal activities, hacking and the violation of intellectual property rights, the list moves on to aggressive forms of behavior, namely the promotion of violence, the admiration of racist attitudes, mobbing and stalking. The next section of this list is extremely worrying, pointing to the different dangers of sexual exploitation children can be threatened by. The last section on values and attitudes contains forms of self-harming that criminals might lure children into. This includes attempts to convince them to commit suicide. Another chart published by the same organization is aimed at informing schools what they need to teach children in order to keep them safe on the Internet. This includes the dangers of spreading of dangerous, e.g. racist material, the violation of intellectual property rights, grooming, sexting and blackmailing, cyber-mobbing, and Internet scams. It closes with the necessity of teaching measures for keeping the devices used by children secure (Shariff 2009).

Given this situation, especially the long list of issues identified by the Safer Internet initiative, the need for immediate and comprehensive action becomes obvious. The challenges this situation causes for an already hard-pressed educational sector are discussed in the following section.

4 Challenges for Education and Awareness Programs

The major challenge for education is that only a holistic approach will produce the desired results. Families, schools and crime prevention specialists have to work hand in hand to equip children not only with the necessary knowledge, but also with the right attitude towards dangers on the Internet. Sometimes the biggest problem is the parents who are completely unaware of the dangers. They need to be educated as well as their children. Crime prevention experts and teachers also need to link up to deliver the right information to children and parents. Where such an integrated approach is implemented, it is usually also very successful. The main objective is to empower children, parents and teachers to recognize the dangers and to react adequately. Today parents confronted with nasty issues such as cyber-stalking, cyber-mobbing or cyber-grooming often do not know where to get help. This can quickly be improved through schools distributing contact points to parents. The strategy can be extremely efficient when crime prevention officers are included in these awareness efforts.

The other challenge is to ensure the availability of suitable educational material. While industrialized nations and supranational organizations, often in partnership with leading industry players, are making available an abundance of general computer security information and tutorials, it is only a few years ago that programs targeted at the protection of children were established. Especially European and North American networks are now beginning to have a significant impact on improving the online safety of children. What is needed at this stage are networks that reach out beyond national and regional borders and supply materials in local languages and adapted to local contexts. Synchronizing such efforts however is a laborious task, which nonetheless needs to be undertaken if the successful move of criminal operations from one country to another is to be prevented. This needs a concerted joint effort of educational institutions and crime prevention experts. Especially in Europe, there is plenty of ongoing activity to make children safer on the Internet.[1]

The leading example, also primarily based in Europe, but developing partnerships outside Europe too, is the Insafe network, which is described in the following section of this chapter.

4.1 The Insafe Network as Example for a Successful International European-Driven Approach

In 1999 the European Commission launched the new Safer Internet Programme and follow-up Programme: European Strategy for a Better Internet for Children,[2] in order to find appropriate answers to these challenges. A few countries started their efforts, and over the years a strong network of safer internet centres could be created. In 2014, 31 countries are members of the Insafe network,[3] which is coordinated by the European Schoolnet in Brussels.[4] This network is highly important for the work on an operational national level, since it enables the quick exchange of information among the network and makes it possible to learn from each other.

The goal of the network is summarized in the mission statement: "The mission of the Insafe cooperation network is to empower children and young people to use the internet, as well as other online and mobile technologies, positively, safely and effectively. The network calls for shared responsibility for the protection of the rights and needs of citizens, in particular children and youths, by government, educators, parents, media, industry and all other relevant actors. Insafe partners work closely together to share best practice, information and resources. The network interacts with industry, schools and families in the aim of empowering people to bridge the digital divide between home and school and between generations."[5]

---

[1] See e.g. saferinternet.org, safesocialmedia.org.

[2] http://ec.europa.eu/digital-agenda/en/european-strategy-deliver-better-internet-our-children.

[3] www.saferinternet.org.

[4] www.eun.org. The following text is written by a member of the network, who is active in a national awareness centre. It does not represent the official view of Insafe, but is an individual point of view.

[5] www.saferinternet.org/about.

4.2 Safer Internet Centres

In each participating country a Safer Internet Centre consists of three parts[6]:

a) **Awareness centre**: The goal is to conduct awareness campaigns, implement trainings, develop and implement new awareness raising tools. The Safer Internet Awareness Centre also evaluates new emerging trends among children and young people and their caretakers in order to develop new tools. In different countries the organization of these centres are quite different, depending on their hosting organization. Some centres have a strong focus within the schools, e.g. because they are situated within the ministry of education (e.g. Finland, Estonia, Portugal, Luxembourg). Other centres are hosted by non-governmental organizations and are focusing more on awareness campaigns and media campaigns. This focus also derives from the local situation, such as possibilities to reach as many children and young people as possible. A collaboration either with ministries or industry is essential in order to reach this goal.[7]
b) **Helpline**: Goal of the helpline is to offer children and young people a place to get help for their individual problems or find an answer for their questions. Some helplines are "general helplines", which means they are helplines for all topics concerning the life of children and young people. Internet is only one part (e.g. Sweden, Austria, etc.). In other countries, the safer Interne helpline is specifically focusing only on Internet-related topics (e.g. Romania, Luxembourg, Spain, etc.). Questions and problems raised by young people within the work of the helpline is a vital part for the work of the awareness centres, if the collaboration is working well. It provides the possibility to get insights of new trends and emerging new topics. For example the trend of "Sextorsion" (blackmailing young male adults for their sex videos, which they produced online due to an internet-fraud) was first seen by helplines through Europe. This meant that Awareness Centres could include this new trend in their material and in their training.
c) **Hotlines**: This is a possibility to report illegal content via Internet.[8] In each country the main goal of all hotlines are to fight illegal child sexual abuse imagery. Due to the fact that hotlines collaborate with law enforcement on an international level, means that such content can be taken down within short time. Some countries also include in their work other content, such as general youth protection (e.g. Germany), xenophobia or racist content (e.g. Czech Republic, Germany, Austria), terrorism (e.g. Luxembourg), child sex tourism (e.g. the Netherlands), suicide (e.g. Russia) or self-harm and eating disorders (e.g. Spain).

---

[6] An overview over all centres can be found on www.saferinternet.org/countries.

[7] An overview of awareness materials for schools can be found here: http://lreforschools.eun.org/web/guest/insafe.

[8] Network of European-Hotlines: www.inhope.org.

4.3 *Safer Internet Day: Highlight of the Year*

Every second Tuesday of February a special day is celebrated: Safer Internet Day. In 2014, already 107 countries throughout the world participated. Every year has its own motto and is always celebrated on the national level as an event. Safer Internet Day is a good vehicle in order to establish successful media campaigns and raise the topic of Internet safety and positive online experiences for children and young people. Although the topic itself is always being considered as "highly important", a special day, such as Safer Internet Day makes it more likely that media covers it broadly. It is a possibility of being covered in mass media on a prominent place.

5 Local Trainings and Awareness Raising

One of the tasks of local Safer Internet Centres is to provide training or material for trainings, which then is conducted by different stakeholders (training organizations, individual trainers, training networks or school teachers). Providing training for such fast changing topics makes it necessary to have a very effective way for training the trainers themselves. How can you relate to changes? How can you make sure that all trainers have similar knowledge? Several ways are taken in order to achieve this goal:

a) *Centralized approach*: The Safer Internet Awareness Centre prepares the training (course outline, content of training and presentation for training). All trainers are obliged to use these materials and conduct the training in exactly the same way. By this one can ensure similar input throughout the country, but does not enable trainers to focus on their personal strengths or react fast on new emerging trends. A powerful awareness centre with enough resources and functioning quality control is necessary to follow this approach;
b) *Trainer Network*: The Safer Internet Centre provides a framework for training sessions (e.g., presentations, content), but all trainers set their own focus based on the target group, their knowledge or strengths and new emerging trends. This makes it possible to react much more quickly to new topics or local necessities, but does not ensure the same quality throughout the country. A good relationship and willingness to share experiences is necessary in order to follow this approach.

6 Changes of Topics Over the Years

Awareness raising in this field has changed over the years quite dramatically: In the early years of the century the focus was set on technical solutions. It was assumed that technology provides solutions in order to protect children from harmful content online. Children and young people were seen as consumers that had to be protected from evil online. Over the years the focus has changed more into the direction of empowering children and young people to use the Internet safely. It is furthermore assumed that it is not possible to protect children effectively, since they have so many possibilities to get in contact with harmful situations. They need—so it is assumed—to know, what to do in difficult situations or how to behave in order not to damage other children and young people on purpose ("risk competence"). Since children and young people are heavy users of digital technologies in Europe, this change of focus is necessary.

6.1 A Good Online Experience Needs Good and Safe Online Tools

Awareness raising and education itself will not be able to offer the only solution in order to make it possible that children and young people have a truly positive online experience. Technology and industry has to do their part in order to achieve this. This can mean usability, but also to offer tools that value legal standards, such as European Data protection. The "CEO Coalition"—a coalition of CEOs of important technology companies in the field[9] is a start in order to obtain this goal. Further efforts have to be taken in order to not let industry forget their shared responsibility for keeping children and young people online safe.

Having so far focused on the protection of children, this contribution now moves on to dangers a second group of potential victims is exposed to. Like children, women are also suffering from increasing abuse and threats.

7 Dangers Women Are Exposed to on the Internet and What Can be Done to Protect Them

Women are affected by dangers through digital media in a new way, though the background doesn't change: domestic and sexual violence against women is a worldwide problem, violence by an intimate partner and family member being the most common form (WHO 2010).

Digital media comes into play when the perpetrator, who can be an intimate partner or a stranger, starts stalking his victim using the Internet or mobile phone. This form of stalking is called cyber-stalking and signifies the misuse of digital media to harass, intimidate and threaten a person. Cyber-stalking includes unwanted contact by e-mail, phone, instant messenger or a social media platform, which can also be established under false pretense of a fake personality. Apart from

---

[9] http://ec.europa.eu/digital-agenda/en/self-regulation-better-internet-kids.

sending harassing or threatening messages, the perpetrator wants to control and intimidate his victim by collecting data and using it against her, for instance by tracing her steps, posting private pictures or videos to public sex-sites ("revenge-porn"), causing damage to her accounts and software and involving her family, friends and workmates online. One form of abuse is to impersonate the victim ("identity theft") and cause damage in her name.

Unlike in the early days of the Internet, cyber-stalkers don't need to have special computers skills anymore; with social media and content sharing platforms everyone can publish worldwide, so it is no wonder the number of reported cases of cyber-stalking is steadily increasing. Perpetrators are often former or current partners, and domestic violence victims are especially vulnerable to cyber-stalking (Moore 2014).

Example cases (names changed):

Case 1 Vera gave her consent when her boyfriend wanted to record their sexual acts for personal use. A year later, after he became more and more jealous and controlling, Vera wanted to end the relationship, but he started blackmailing her by threatening to publish the videos and pictures. Vera, who is a public official, is afraid to lose her reputation and her job, and remains in the abusive relationship.

Case 2 When Martina met and fell in love with her husband-to-be, he convinced her that it was a matter of love and trust to tell him her password, which she used for several of her logins. During their marriage he took control over her money and beat her repeatedly. After many years of struggling, finally Martina got a divorce. After their separation he hacked one of her e-mail accounts and sent a message to his own address impersonating her. The e-mail said she would kill him if he ever came near the house or wished to see his daughter again. He reported her to the police and she is facing a criminal charge.

Case 3 Gaby was shocked when a man she knew from a business meeting started to send her naked pictures. She confronted him, and he told her he has been answering to messages with a similar content that he had received from her. It turned out that an unknown person had put up a fake profile on Facebook and contacted men she had in her contact list by sending them obscene messages and pictures of naked body parts the receivers assumed were hers.

As presented in the examples above, the risk to be cyber-stalked and manipulated online increases when the victim gives away important personal data. The mixture of unawareness concerning possible threats and a lack of knowledge about self-protective measures constitute the main risk factors. A significant part of the vulnerability of women in this context is grounded in the socialization of women in society. Gender stereotypes include the common attitude that the use and knowledge about technical equipment is only suited for boys and men. Thus, women are often lacking the necessary skills to protect themselves efficiently online.

The use of digital media by women is still lower than that of men, and while this "digital divide" is becoming smaller every year, it still exists. In almost all European countries, men use the Internet more frequently than women, the differences going up to 10 % (Italy, Austria). In non-European countries, where Internet usage is altogether lower, the differences between women and man reach up to 20 % in Turkey and 25 % in Morocco (ITU 2010–2012).

The differences between the sexes concerning Internet use show even more clearly in the context of factors such as income, ethnicity, age, and educational level. In Germany, between men and women over 50 the differences are rising with age and reach up to 20 % ((N)ONLINER Atlas 2007).

Differences between men and women concerning Internet use are also reported in developing countries (UNCTAD 2014). Women and girls encounter barriers such as literacy, education, language, time, cost, geographical location and social and cultural norms and skills. Also the already mentioned general attitude that computers and technology are a male domain stands in their way (Hafkin and Taggart 2001).

But women not only use the Internet less frequently, they also lack appropriate competencies. In Europe surveys show that women in comparison to men tend to have lower level digital skills. Although the difference has been decreasing over the past years, the percentage of men appearing to have high computer skills is by 14 points higher than the percentage of women (Digital Agenda Scoreboard 2012).

A big German study describes different user types, and while the skeptics and non-regular Internet-users are described as "mostly female", the more competent and frequent Internet users with good media skills are mostly male, well-educated and pursue their careers (D21-Digital-Index 2013).

Another vulnerability factor can be found in typically romantic behavior. Even in a violent relationship there was a beginning phase in which the partners engaged in trust-building activities, and girls and women are often too confiding and ready to share very private information and recordings like passwords, intimate pictures and videos. These can later easily be used against them, to hack their accounts, fake their identities, and expose them publicly or to blackmail them. When this happens, the victim is additionally blamed for her behavior by society, which sees it as "her own fault" for having exposed herself to harassment.

Not always has a woman to use the Internet herself to become a victim of misuse of digital media. Also, good Internet and software skills are no warrant for a 100 % online safety. We see that illustrated in the case of Victoria Schwartz, who became a victim of the digital media despite of being a very skilled user herself.

Victoria Schwartz, who had published her story online,[10] started in 2011 a Twitter-conversation with an interesting stranger, who would eventually turned out to be a "Catfish", a fake. Soon their online communication grew more and more intense and interesting, they fell in love online and planned to meet, but since he lived on another continent, it took months before a meeting could be arranged. Meanwhile, he sent her more than a thousand pictures of himself, also presents, and she got to know many of his friends and family members—of course just online. It wasn't until almost a year later that she found out that he was a fake and everything

[10] http://victoriahamburg.wordpress.com/2013/06/29/fake-englishversion/.

including his family and friends was made up. The case was no "Love Scam", meaning she never was asked for money, so the police couldn't help, though the emotional exploit was huge. Victoria published her story in her blog that went viral. Surprisingly, she got hundreds of e-mails from women who had fallen for a fake too. Meanwhile she has turned her experience into a resource for prevention.[11]

Any victim of cyber-stalking should seek advice from a professional women-counseling center such as are provided by many countries worldwide. These should be able to empower the victims in the safe use of technology and give information on how to proceed best concerning the respective legal possibilities.

The network WAVE (Women Against Violence Europe) gathers and systematically evaluates information on women's support services in Europe.[12] In the US, the NNEDV (National Network To End Domestic Violence) provides nation-wide information about women's hotlines and shelters and also offers information on technology safety, online content consideration and general privacy tips.[13]

Most safety plans include:

a) Technology measures: using a safe computer and phone, setting up anti-virus software and firewall, checking passwords, security and privacy settings of phone and computer, etc.;
b) Practice tips: carefulness with sharing information online, limiting contact to strangers, gender- and age neutral screen names, closing of accounts, etc.
c) Social measures: telling friends, family and workmates to help preserve one's privacy etc.;
d) Legal measures: collecting evidence, contacting Internet service providers and platform owners, seeking legal advice, etc.

When it comes to counseling, legal knowledge is essential. Countries deal differently with stalkers and cyber criminals, and often the misuse of technical possibilities is way ahead of necessary legal regulations.

The challenges for protection of women from dangers online are to ensure well-equipped and competent counseling services for victims seeking help. Above their general counseling competencies they need solid technology skills and up-to-date knowledge of Internet trends and dangers as well as the ability to provide victims with information on safety measures and the legal background.

8 The Need for a Truly International Solution

While the introductory chapters were focused on the perspective of industrialized regions of the world and a more detailed description was given of a very successful and primarily European-based network, a truly global solution developed from such

[11] http://realfakes.wordpress.com/.

[12] http://www.wave-network.org/country-info.

[13] http://nnedv.org/resources/safetynetdocs.html.

pioneering activities is ultimately needed if criminal activity is to be stopped effectively and not only in limited regions. Possible experienced organizations able to lead the coordination of worldwide efforts are in place and some of them, such as the United Nations Office on Drug and Crime (UNODC), have shown their effectiveness in a worldwide approach to combating different types of crime. Their educational efforts, when backed by the necessary financial means can once more pave the way towards successful international cooperation. With Asian countries strongly joining such UN efforts, and African nations usually getting involved too, a worldwide outreach is possible. Translating currently leading North American, European and Asian educational approaches for less developed countries becomes more urgent as the new technologies are being used in these countries too. The probably only way to deliver educational material in a cost-efficient way is via Internet-based platforms. As today cloud storage is already very cheap and even applications can be offered at a low cost, this becomes doable also for less wealthy countries.

Another possibility is to team up with leading industry players in whose best interest it is to provide a safe environment for the use of their products. Online learning platforms and learning management systems are today available for free, content is supplied by educational institutions and industry. The major challenge for a truly international program will however be the adaptation of the learning materials to different regions, languages and ultimately different cultural environments.

9 Outlook

Given the rising awareness about the problem, a significant increase in activities to keep children safe on the Internet can be expected. Leading industry players and governments of industrialized countries have understood the urgency of the situation and have started to act. Supranational organizations such as the European Union and the United Nations have long been arguing for measures to increase the online safety of children with especially the European Union helping to develop networks, programs and tools. Thus a worldwide movement in the right direction has started and is showing significant improvements. In this situation it is important to use free or industry-supported technology to assure that there is no second digital divide in the sense of safe and unsafe areas. Less developed countries not being able to afford the necessary solutions will certainly backfire on industrialized countries, because the old wisdom that as long as there are safe havens for crime nobody can be safe, definitely holds true for the tightly networked world we live in today.

10 Core Issues from an International Perspective

In all societies the awareness for the problem is growing, but so is its size. The most pressing question to be answered however is how a truly international solution can be developed that leaves no one behind. While, as shown in this contribution, industrialized regions have the necessary resources and the knowledge to implement measures, other parts of the world are again facing the threat of being left behind with their children and women remaining unprotected against a criminal danger that is even causing stress for highly developed law enforcement agencies and legal systems. The worst case scenario would, like in several areas of crime, be a situation where whole countries are undermined by criminals, unable to defend themselves against criminal networks and becoming safe havens for criminal activities launched on a worldwide scale. While criminals usually have to make considerable efforts in the real world, the Internet, as we have seen with so many cases already, is a prime platform for such types of activity at a comparatively low cost. That is why it is so important to transfer knowledge and solutions developed in industrialized countries to poorer regions of the world now. Once the cybercrime wave against children and women fully hits them, it will be too late. The nature of cybercrime as transnational crime is again underlined by a UNODC cybercrime report (see UNODC 2013, p. 183 ff.). So it is not only a matter of helping poorer regions, it is also in the best interest of industrialized regions of the world to prevent criminals from getting a foothold in poorer countries and launching worldwide attacks from there.

Five Questions

1. How can the problem of cyber crime against women and children be addressed more effectively on a global scale?
2. How can we best learn from exiting national and international efforts and implement the lessons learned in a global context?
3. Which new educational and awareness programs can we put in place based on already existing efforts?
4. How can educational efforts best benefit from the use of expert and organizational knowledge in truly international organizations, such as UNODC?
5. What needs to be done to put the necessary technical infrastructure and organizational frameworks in place for developing a truly international response?

References

D21-Digital-Index. (2013). Auf dem Weg in ein digitales Deutschland?! Eine Studie der Initiative D21, durchgeführt von TNS Infratest, 2013 (http://www.initiatived21.de/wp-content/uploads/2013/04/digitalindex.pdf, retrieved on 21-07-2014).

Digital Agenda Scoreboard. (2012). Eurostat's Community Survey on ICT Usage in Households and by Individuals, European Commission, 2012 (http://ec.europa.eu/digital-agenda/sites/digital-agenda/files/scoreboard_digital_skills.pdf, retrieved 21-07-2014).

Europe vs Facebook. (2014). http://www.europe-v-facebook.org/.

Gillespie, A. A. (2002). Child protection on the Internet - challenges for criminal law. *Child and Family Law Quarterly, 14*, 411.

Hafkin, N. J., & Taggart, N. (2001). *Gender, information technology and developing countries: An analytic study*. Washington, DC: United States Agency for International Development (USAID).

ITU. (2010–2012). Percentage of Internet users by gender, ITU Data and Statistics (http://www.itu.int/ITU-D/ict/statistics/Gender, retrieved 21-07-2014).

Moore, A. A. (2014). Cyberstalking and Women - Facts and Statistics. About.com June 12, 2014 (http://womensissues.about.com/od/violenceagainstwomen/a/CyberstalkingFS.htm, retrieved 24-07-2014).

(N)ONLINER Atlas. (2007). Internetnutzung von Frauen und Männern in Deutschland, Sonderauswertung Gender & Diversity des (N)ONLINER Atlas 2007. Hg. Vom Kompetenzzentrum Technik-Diversity-Chancengleichheit e.V., Bielefeld 2007 (http://www.initiatived21.de/wp-content/uploads/alt/NOA_Umzug/Sonderauswertungen/H5_Nonliner_Sonderauswertung_2007.pdf, retrieved 21-07-2014).

Oswell, D. (1999). The dark side of cyberspace internet content regulation and child protection. *Convergence, 5*(4), 42–62. doi:10.1177/135485659900500404.

Safe Social Media. (2013). www.safesocialmedia.org.

Safer Internet. (2014). www.saferinternet.org.

Shariff, S. (2009, May). *Confronting cyber-bullying: What schools need to know to control misconduct and avoid legal consequences*. Cambridge University Press, ISBN 9780521700795.

Stanley, J. (2001). Child Abuse and the Internet, Issues vol. 15/2001. Australian Institute of Family Studies.

UNCTAD. (2014). Measuring ICT and gender: An assessment. *United Nations Conference on Trade and Development*. UN, New York and Geneva, 2014 (http://unctad.org/en/PublicationsLibrary/webdtlstict2014d1_en.pdf).

UNODC. (2013). Comprehensive Study on Cybercrime Draft - February 2013. UNITED NATIONS, New York.

WHO. (2010). *Preventing intimate partner and sexual violence against women: Taking action and generating evidence*. Geneva: World Health Organization/London School of Hygiene and Tropical Medicine.

Part VI
Final Discussion

The United Nations, Equal and Inclusive Society and Crime Prevention: Chinese Philosophical Contributions to the Idea of Sustainable Development for Women and Children, and the Current Practice in China

Zhang Ying Jun

Abstract The difference between Chinese and Western legal thought in terms of concepts and methods into the question of crime prevention for women and children is very substantial. In Western criminology very little is known in this regard. The intersection of legal thoughts between one and the other world of science takes place more readily in environmental justice, among other social science fields. But in China's 42-century long and reclusive history among many feudalization and patriarchal policies, the treatment of women, regarded as inferior to men, has been one of the recurrent governance leitmotifs. More than twenty centuries ago, the idea of equal education and women's rights had emerged in Chinese traditional philosophy, especially through the "Hundred Schools of Thought" during the period of Spring and Autumn and the Warrior States pre-Qin dynasty. But, to some extent, the ruling class distorted the philosophical claims of that time, including Confucianism, which has been set up as the only one national philosophy since the other schools of thought had been abolished in the West Han dynasty, thirty centuries ago. The United Nations post-2015 sustainable development agenda strongly emphasizes that education for all and promoting an equal and inclusive society would contribute to reducing crime. Against the historical and United Nations background, this chapter highlights the relevant connotations of sustainable development in traditional Chinese philosophy and reinvigorates them in the interest of attaining some elements of the envisioned peaceful and inclusive societies in a culture-sensitive manner, with particular reference to crime prevention for women and children, and the respective legal domestic regulation.

Zhang Y.J. (✉)
School of Law, South-Central University for Nationalities, Wuhan, P. R. China
e-mail: zyj2161@sina.com

H. Kury et al. (eds.), *Women and Children as Victims and Offenders: Background, Prevention, Reintegration*, DOI 10.1007/978-3-319-28424-8_24

1 Introduction

Crime prevention is not only an art, but also science (Sherman et al. 1998, pp. 2–3). Its aim is to promote social stability and the security of people's lives and property. However, in the history of human civilizations, even the most rigorous "law and order" policy that pursued the above aim could not fully and truly eliminate crime and prevent it in the future (Waller 2011, p. 14). Future generations should learn from the mistakes of the previous ones, so as to not worsen their lot. Indeed, the moral obligation of our generation is to contribute to the prosperity of the succeeding generation as much as we care now about ourselves, if not more.

Sustainable development originally refers to "development that meets the needs of the present without compromising the ability of future generations to meet their own needs" (A/RES/42/187, para. 28).

Currently, this concept extends to a self-generating, creative, albeit also conflicting, mechanism for renewing socio-economic and other resources. It is geared toward their multiplication and, generally, the broadening of human intergenerational capital in any creative areas of mankind, including science and education—the necessary doorway to a change in mindset and behavior. A change in behavior by every instance concerned (citizens, companies, local and regional authorities, governments and international institutions) counter the threats looming over our planet (climate change, loss of biodiversity; industrial, health and security risks; excessive but preventable economic and social inequality, likewise crime and victimization levels) (Redo 2012, p. 237).

The UN Open Working Group (OWG) on Sustainable Development Goals proposed for the years 2016–2030 new sustainable development goals, all pointing to one overriding objective: the amelioration of poverty (A/68/970). Achieving this necessitates actions in state governance and government management.

In the ongoing international discussion on how to build an equal and inclusive society through poverty reduction and sustainable development, it may be important to note that several of the current aspects of it (including crime prevention) were already tackled a long time ago. In the *Gabčíkovo-Nagymaros* case at the International Court of Justice, Justice Weeremantery in his opinion noted that sustainable development is one of the oldest ideas in human heritage (ICJ Reports 1997, p.110). Traditional Chinese culture is known for its profundity and long history, as represented by the prosperity of "Hundred Schools of Thought" in the pre-Qin Dynasty (c. 551–233 B.C.E). Nowadays, many scholars can only be specialized in one school of thought because of the richness of philosophy in this period.

This chapter highlights the relevant connotations of sustainable development in traditional Chinese philosophy and reinvigorates them in the interest of a culture-sensitive attaining of some elements of the envisioned peaceful and inclusive societies, with particular reference to women and children. Their richness interplays with many ideas on inclusive and equitable education and gender equality, conveyed by the OWG on Sustainable Development Goals (A/68/970, paras. 4–5; A/69/700).

This chapter first looks into these old ideas of the Chinese imperial society, known for its feudal hierarchy that lasted more than 2000 years.

2 Historical Background

Although the origin of Chinese civilization is still a topic of much debate, it is generally agreed that 42000 years ago the Xia Dynasty (c. 2205–1766 B.C.E.) had been the first one in China's history (Mote 1971, p. 9). Before, it was a period of a primitive commune in the history of China, which dates back to remote antiquity and is said to have been governed by the ancestors of the Chinese people and their descendants, the most important of them being the *yellow emperor* (黄帝) (Fan 2010, pp. 7–20).[1] Next came the Shang Dynasty (with the capital founded in Yin, c. 1766–1122 B.C.E.) (Bo 2012, pp. 10–16). Its territory was confined to the alluvial plain in the middle reach of the Yellow River, which was considered as the hinterland of ancient China. The last emperor of the Shang Dynasty, King Zhou, was a cruel and incompetent ruler. The Shang Dynasty was overthrown by Zhou, one of its vassal states. Later, Zhou became the third dynasty in Chinese history. It wanted to be acknowledged as the legitimate successor of the respectable Shang Dynasty rather than of those who took it over by military force. This shows that the royal class strove to develop Chinese culture and establish its legitimacy. Zhou finally achieved this goal by adopting the feudal system of enfeoffment that had a European counterpart many centuries later (Mote 1971, pp.9–13).

The king of the Zhou Dynasty rearranged more than 70 vassal states along the lines of patriarchal clans and relatives bonded by marriage as well as the allies during battles and the descendants of the Shang Dynasty. Besides, the Zhou Dynasty had over two hundred local lords within their own territories. By the eighth century B.C.E., those territories comprised about 150 vassal states, but of their history is very little known, except for some 25 of them. By the fourth century B.C.E., most of the vassal states were merged into seven larger vassal states and a number of less powerful small states, all of which coexisted with the faltering royal class of the Zhou Dynasty. The royal class barely maintained military deterrence in only 1/4 of the period of its reign (Mote 1971, p.12).

[1] To be exact, they were not real emperors but the heads of primitive tribes at that time. According to folk tales, the Yellow Emperor was the head of the Hua ethnic group (华族), which is said to be the earliest ancestor of the Chinese people. He and his descendants gradually took control of most of the land which was mainly located in the north-west of Henan province and the north-east of Shanxi province, near Yin, which was always the capital city of the Shang Dynasty and is at present called Anyang city, located in the north of Henan Province, about 500 km south-west off present-day Beijing (Fan 2010, pp. 7–15).

After 770 B.C.E., the military power possessed by the king of the Zhou Dynasty was so weak that the capital was dislocated to Luoyang city.[2] However, the royal class of the Zhou Dynasty was still the nominal overlord and continued the reign for more than 500 years. In 256 B.C.E., the Qin State, one of the most powerful vassal states, abolished the position of the king of the Zhou Dynasty as overlord. From 230 B.C.E. to 220 B.C.E., the Qin State launched numerous battles and finally united China. This was the beginning of the age of the empire of China (Mote 1971, p. 12).

Before the Chinese empire was born, the last years of the Zhou Dynasty witnessed the golden days of thoughts in China's history. Within the period of three or four centuries, from the days of Confucius to the unification of China by the Qin Dynasty, the basis of Chinese thought was laid (Mote 1971, p.13). This period is also called the Spring and Autumn Period (c.770–476 B.C.E.) and the Warring States Period (c.476–221 B.C.E.) (Xu et al. 2004, p. 574)

As the royal class of the Zhou Dynasty lost its power, the officials working at the governmental department also lost their positions and moved to different regions. Those officials began to teach specialized knowledge as private tutors (Fung 2013, p. 34). This may be considered as the origin of the "Hundred Schools of Thought"(诸子百家)(Cai Ed. 2006, p. 1).There were ten major schools, namely the School of Yin-Yang (阴阳家), Confucianism (儒家), Mohism (墨家), The School of Names[3] (名家), Legalism (法家), Taoism (道家), the School of Diplomacy (纵横家), the Miscellaneous School (杂家), the School of Agronomists[4](农家), and the School of "Minor-talks"(小说家).[5] These schools "focused on different

[2] Because the rebels weakened the governance, the Zhou Dynasty was forced to abandon the original capital and move eastward, to Luoyang city, south-west of Henan Province, some 800 km south-west off current Beijing. See: Xu et al. 2004, p. 249.

[3] Also known as Logicians, in Chinese Pinyin *Míngjiā*; *Ming-chia*. The Logicians or School of Names grew out of Mohism during the Warring States period. It is also sometimes called the School of Forms and Names (Chinese: 形名家; *pinyin*: *Xíngmíngjiā*; Wade-Giles: *Hsing-ming-chia*). The term "Logicians" is used only to emphasize their intellectual character. Actually, they neither created syllogism nor discovered any law of thought (Chan 1963, p. 232).

[4] Also known as Agriculturalism, the School of Agrarianism, the School of Tillers, known in Chinese as the *Nongjia* (農家/农家), was an early agrarian Chinese philosophy that advocated peasant utopian communalism and egalitarianism. For the interpretation in English, please see Deutsch, Eliot; Ronald Bontekoei (1999). A Companion to World Philosophies. Wiley Blackwell. p. 183, reprinted from http://en.wikipedia.org/wiki/School_of_Agrarianism#cite_note-wp-1, accessed 10 December 2014.

[5] The first known classification comes from the historian Sima Tan (?—110 B.C.E.). He divided the philosophers who lived several centuries ago into six main genres, i.e., Yin-Yang School, Confucianism, Mohism, Logicians, Legalism, Taoism. Later another historian Liu Xin (46B.C.-A. D. 23) divided the Hundred Schools of Thought into ten genres: School of Diplomacy, Miscellaneous, Agriculturalism and School of "Minor-talks" in addition to Sima Tan. So did the Eastern Han Dynasty historian Ban Gu. But this classification did not include the Military Strategist, who was famous for the book of The Art of War, which has been influential up to now, and unfailing (the end of this sentence is not clear, could you please go over it). See: Fung 2013, pp. 33–35; Ruan 1998, p. 3.

aspects of the world, advocated different principles and tried their best to propagate their thoughts" (Ruan 1998, p. 3).

The present work mainly focuses on the philosophy of Taoism, Mohism and Confucianism, especially on their ideas on crime prevention and the treatment of women and children. Other schools may be mentioned but not discussed.

3 Crime Prevention and Sustainable Development Goals in Chinese Legal Thought

More than 2000 years ago, Guanzhong (管仲),[6] one of China's well-known thinkers from the "Hundred Schools of Thought", clearly emphasized that:

> Whether a state is in order or in chaos rests upon three factors,[7] and death and other penalties are not enough to safeguard the order of a nation. Whether a state is safe or in danger is based on four factors, and firm protective walls and dangerous geographical conditions are not enough to defend it. Whether a state is wealthy or poor rests upon five factors, and measures such as levying light taxes and collecting a few things from the people cannot be resorted to exclusively. Putting a state in order should resort to San Ben (三本, which means three essentials in governing a state), safeguarding a state should resort to Si Gu (四固,[8] which means the four most important measures for safeguarding a state), and enriching a state should resort to Wu Shi (五事).[9] (Guanzi 2005, Vol. 1, p. 53).

---

[6] Also known as Guanzi (管子, ?- 645 B.C.E.). See further: Chi 2004, p. 16; Liu and Li 2003, p. 1.

[7] San Ben in Chinese *pinyin*, means the three essentials in governing a state. As explained in the Work of Guanzi, "A sovereign should be prudent with three things: The first is that the virtues of court officials do not match their powers; the second is that the achievements of court officials do not match their salaries; the third is that the abilities of court officials do not match their positions. These three most important factors are the innermost causes leading to order or chaos of a state." See: The Work of Guanzi 2005, Vol. 1, p. 53.

[8] Si Gu, in Chinese *pinyin*, means the four most important measures for safeguarding a state. As explained in the Work of Guanzi, "A sovereign must be aware of four factors: The first is that people with distinguished virtues but who do not really behave benevolently should not be conferred with the authority of governing the state; the second is that people unwilling to retire and give room to better ones should not be conferred with honorable ranks; the third is that people not punishing their relatives and absolving the powerful one should not be appointed to leading the army; the fourth is that people not attaching importance to farming, not making good use of favorable geographical conditions or levying taxes and collecting things willingly should not be conferred with fiefs. These four most important measures for safeguarding the nation are the roots for safety of a state." See: The Work of Guanzi 2005, Vol. 1, p. 57.

[9] Means the five most important things required of a sovereign. As explained in the Work of Guanzi: "A sovereign must pay attention to five things: The first, if measures for fire prevention are not taken in mountainous and swampy areas and therefore plants cannot grow there, it will lead to poverty of the state; the second, if conduits are not well dredged and therefore waters break the watercourses, it will lead to poverty of the state; the third, if silkworm thorns and hemp plants are not planted in the fields, and all kinds of crops are not inseminated in the suitable fields, it will lead to poverty of the state; the fourth, if all kinds of livestock are not raised at home, and things such as melons, gourds, vegetables and various fruit are not well prepared, it will lead to poverty of the

Chinese philosophers were probably the first ones who claimed that to successfully prevent crime we have to "look into" the offender's heart to understand the reason why it came to crime. This is perhaps the most effective way to counter crime. Just like L.W. Sherman said, "The major strength of scientific evaluations is that rules of science provide a consistent and reasonably objective way to draw conclusions about cause and effect" (Sherman et al. 1998, p. 2).

A scientific way in crime prevention is to build a society of sustainable development. In contrast to rigorous laws and punitivity, found to be an ineffective penal policy, as most recently internationally reviewed by Helmut Kury and Evelyn Shea (2011), this alternative approach stresses the reorganization of society by the rule of law, democracy, and the human rights doctrine. This approach promotes good governance, in which human dignity and freedom are respected, and poverty and inequality is ameliorated. Compared with punitivity, this way mainly concerns the human being itself (Kury and Shea 2011)—this has been likewise very much emphasized by the United Nations Secretary-General in his recent report "The Road to dignity by 2030: Ending poverty, transforming all lives" (A/69/700).

Traditional Chinese philosophy dealt with these issues thousands of years ago. Various schools of thought carried out in-depth discussions and came up with diversified propositions. In the Work of Guanzi, published more than 2000 years ago, is written that "Regarding governing a state, the most important is to enrich the common people. If the people are wealthy, they can be easily administered. If they are destitute, it will be very difficult to administer them... Hence, states in order are usually rich and those in disorder are normally destitute. So, a sovereign good at governing the state should enrich his people first, and then he can manage to administer them and put them in order." (Guanzi 2005, Vol. 3, p. 974).

Mencius (c. 372–289 B.C.E), a well-known Confucian philosopher, gave the following brilliant answer when asked how to govern a state: "Institute a government whose action shall be benevolent (仁政). That is to say, the interests of the people should be the top priority, and the people's living standard shall be elevated by institutional design" (Mencius 2011, p. 21). Mencius said further, that "when people no longer worry about their livelihood, and their income is sufficient to support their own life, their parents and their brothers and sisters, the government can then educate them and improve their spiritual state. If the government presses too hard, the people will do anything to earn a living at the risk of violating rigorous law and penalty" (ibid, p. 22).

Mencius also used the phrase "entrapping the people" when he discussed the topic of state governance. He said, "It is only men of educations, who, without a certain livelihood, are able to maintain a fixed heart. As to the people, if they don't have a certain livelihood, it follows that they will not have a fixed heart. And if they

state; the fifth, if craftsmen are competing with each other on working with great care on their products, and female workers are focused on complicated patterns of the needlework, it will lead to poverty of the state." See: The Work of Guanzi 2005, Vol. 1, pp. 60–61.

do not have a fixed heart, there is nothing, which they will not do, in the way of self-abandonment, of moral deflection, of depravity, and of wild license. When they thus have been involved in crime, to catch them and to punish them, this to entrap the people. How can such a thing as entrapping the people be done under the rule of a benevolent man?"[10] That means the state not executing benevolent administration does injustice to the people and goes contrary to the goal of building a good social order. This well may be the first-ever definition of sustainable development that coincides strongly with the concept of sustainable development pursued by the UN.

4 Inclusive and Equitable Education: Equality in Receiving Education Regardless of Gender and Qualification in the Claims of Mohism and Taoism

The UN report referred to previously proposed in aim 4 to "Ensure inclusive and equitable quality education and promote lifelong learning opportunities for all" (A/68/970, para 13). Almost the same ideas can be found in Chinese traditional philosophy, especially represented by Mohism and Taoism.

Laozi, (ca. 571 BC–ca. 531 BC) the founder of Taoism, believed that there is no person that cannot be educated. What is important is whether the educator is good at educating. He said, "That is why the sage is always good at saving people and abandoning no one; that is why the sage is always good at saving things and abandoning nothing. That is called the intrinsic wisdom. Thus the good man is the bad man's teacher; the bad man is the material from which the good draws lessons" (Lao Tzu 2007, pp. 75–77).

This reflects Laozi's views on education, that is, the educator should teach by personal example as well as verbal instruction without making exceptions. As long as the educator has both virtue and capacity, he can set an example for others. That is what he means by saying that "there is no man that cannot be educated".

Mozi (ca. 470 BC–ca. 391 BC) the founder of Mohism, a pragmatic and utilitarian school of thought, also attached great importance to education. Mozi fully acknowledged the limitation of personal power, so he considered education as an important means to realize his social ideals. He emphasized that "enlightened persons should teach others diligently." He did not require any material stipulation and never refused anyone who wanted to learn, thus truly embodying the thought of equal opportunity education. For those who did not want to improve, Mozi still took

[10] Mencius advised King Hui of Liang that "an intelligent ruler will regulate the livelihood of the people, so as to make sure that, for those above them, they shall have sufficient wherewith to serve their parents, and for those below them, sufficient wherewith to support their wives and children; that in good years they shall always be abundantly satisfied, and that in bad years they shall escape the danger of perishing. After that, educate them, he may urge them, and they will proceed to what is good, for in this case the people will follow after it with ease." See: Mencius 2011, p. 22.

the initiative in enlightening and encouraging them to study (Zheng and Zhang 2010, pp. 127–129). As for the moral education of students, Mozi felt that a truly worthy man, in addition to being "discerning in speech, and erudite in the techniques of the way," also had to be "good at moral conduct" (Tan and Sun 2012, p. 36). This coincides with the modern practice of sustainable crime prevention that enhances education for the whole society, particularly children and youth, as well as pursuing reintegration for those in conflict with criminal law.

5 Gender Equality and Children's Right in Traditional Chinese Philosophy

For most Western readers the ancient Chinese culture is about the hierarchies, the patriarchal system that stressed male superiority and the paternal intervention in children's life. These understandings are partial due to the lack of insufficient cross-fertilization of ideas between China and the Western world.

A closer scrutiny of traditional Chinese philosophy, however, makes it easier to see that most schools of thought did not make a distinction between different social classes, compared to what we see in China today with a growing middle class. The ideas in traditional Chinese philosophy rather reflect the goal envisioned in the UN OWG report on sustainable development goals to "achieve gender equality and empower all women and girls" (A/68/970, para. 14).

During the time of the "Hundred Schools of Thought", some schools even held very open views that were ahead of their times. For example, Taoism highly valued maternity. Other schools did not put a particular value on female or male, and they did not stress gender difference and the difference between father and son in social status when talking about the issue of rights. However, these claims of equality and coequality were not upheld by the despotic rule of ancient China. As the Qin Dynasty adopted the strategy of "abolishing Hundreds of Schools and respecting only Confucianism", these schools were massively attacked as heterodoxies (Jin and Hu 2009, p. 3). For this reason, the ancient wisdom of Hundreds of Schools was unknown to the world or even to the common Chinese people over the long course of that despotic rule.

5.1 The Claims of Taoism

Taoism highly valued maternity. The core of Taoism's theory is "the Way of Heaven"[11] a cosmic concept. Tao Te Ching, as the representative work of this school, is divided into two parts, Scripture of the Way of Heaven and the Scripture

[11] This is the world view that refers to the Cosmos.

of Virtue. So what is "the Way of Heaven"? In Chapter 25 of Tao Te Ching, he claimed, "There is a thing integratively formed and born earlier than Heaven and Earth. Silent and empty, /it relies on nothing, /Moving around forever. We may regard it as the mother of all things. I don't know its name, /so I name it as Tao, / And further name it as Great." (Lao Tzu 2007, pp. 68–71). According to this interpretation, "the Way of Heaven (Tao)" is the source of all things. It comes into being at the same time as nature is created and develops along with nature. "The Way of Heaven" is the highest law and the natural rule governing nature and human society.[12] This understanding is confirmed by Laozi's definition. He said at first in the Book of Tao and Teh, that, "The word Nothingness may be used to designate the beginning of Heaven and Earth; The word of Existence (Being) may be used to designate the mother of all things. Hence one should gain an insight into the subtlety of Tao by observing Nothingness, and should gain an insight into the beginning of Tao by observing Existence (Being)" (Lao Tzu 2007, pp. 2–3).

Moreover, Laozi believed that the virtue of "Tao" corresponds to the low profile and softness of maternity, which is underpinned by firmness. That is why Laozi highly valued maternity and softness in his life philosophy. Laozi is known for the claim of "the great Tao is like water" and "the highest good is like that of the water" because he thinks "Nothing in the world is more supple than water, yet nothing is more powerful than water in attacking the hard and stone" (Lao Tzu 2007, p. 220). Water is as soft as maternity but can contain everything and change even the hardest rock with its soft but enduring power. When it comes to the issue of dealing with family relationship, interpersonal relationship, international relationship and interethnic relationship, Laozi also favored the soft way mentioned above, that is: "The female always conquers the male by motionlessness, because the motionless female always takes the lower position" (Lao Tzu 2007, p.177). Laozi's viewpoint is not to push the maternal society to its extreme, but to arrive at the most fundamental law by observing the real world.

Although we cannot arrive at the conclusion that Laozi advocated a society dominated by females, it is certain that Taoism does not disparage females. If fact, we can hardly find a single sentence in support of gender discrimination and a hierarchical society in Taoism. Instead, it advocates to accept nature rather than to conquer it (Mote 1971, p. 62).

[12] This opinion is based on my understanding of the conception and nature of "Tao" explained in the Book of Tao and Teh (Jin and Hu 2009, p. 3). Because that short Book (5000 words) is written in very simple ancient Chinese, it is difficult to identify the exact meaning of "Tao". Hence, there are many translations and annotations on it, some of them contentious.

5.2 The Eminent Example: The Mother of Mencius

As an eminent woman, the mother of Mencius devoted herself to contribute to the greatness of Mencius. As a well-known Confucian philosopher, Mencius was left fatherless at a young age, and his mother played a great role in raising him. The popular Confucian teachings primer for children, in existence for over 700 years—*The Three Characters Scriptures* (三字经)—tells stories about her (Qian 2009, p. 17) and provides standard examples of maternal ideals (Stearns 2008, p. 53), as she knew well how to be a good mother.

In order to find the right place for bring up her son, she moved three times from the house near a cemetery to the marketplace and then finally near the school. She knew about the right influences from outside for her sons (Qian 2009, p. 17).

As a mother, she understood the way of motherhood. When she found that Mencius was away from school one day at a young age, she took a knife and cut the finished cloth on her loom. She said to Mencius, "Your neglecting your studies is very much like my cutting the cloth. The superior person studies to establish a reputation and gain wide knowledge. He is calm and poised and tries to do no wrong. If you do not study now, you will surely end up as a menial servant and will never be free from troubles. It would be just like a woman who supports herself by weaving to give it up. How long could such a person depend on her husband and son to stave off hunger? If a woman neglects her work or a man gives up the cultivation of his character, they may end up as common thieves if not slaves!" (Stearns 2008, p. 54). Shaken, from then on Mencius studied hard from morning to night. He studied the philosophy of the master and eventually became a famous Confucian scholar (Qian 2009, p. 17).

The mother of Mencius understood also the way to be a mother-in-law. One day as Mencius was going into his private quarters, he encountered his wife not fully dressed. Displeased, Mencius stopped going into his wife's room and treated her like a stranger, because he thought she broke the etiquette between a man and a woman. She then went to his mother, begged to be sent back to her parents.

Mencius's mother called him to her and said, "It is polite to inquire before you enter a room. You should make some loud noise to warn anyone inside, and as you enter, you should keep your eyes low so that you will not embarrass anyone. Now, you have not behaved properly, yet you are quick to blame others for their impropriety. Isn't that going a little too far?" Mencius apologized and took back his wife (Stearns 2008, pp. 54–55).

When Mencius felt very depressed because his ideas were not being used in one state and planned to go somewhere else, but was worried that his mother was getting too old to travel, his mother answered: "A woman's duties are to cook the five grains, heat the wine, look after her parents-in-law, make clothes, and that is all! Therefore, she cultivates the skills required in the women's quarters and has no ambition to manage affairs outside of the house." (Stearns 2008, p. 55). As a mother and elder, she knew how to release and encourage her children.

The story of the mother of Mencius is well known in Chinese society. She has been appreciated highly as an admirable Chinese woman. In Chinese traditional philosophy, the mother has always been regarded as playing the most important role for the cultivation of their children although they didn't obtain enough education generally at that time (Qian 2009, p. 18).

5.3 System of Rites in Confucianism and the Building of China's Feudal Hierarchies: Against the Rights of People, Women and Children

Confucius, as the founder of Confucianism, mentioned the hierarchical system composed of king, courtiers, fathers and sons that are supposed to play their assigned roles. Rites and filial piety should be respected without exception, and an exquisite set of rites was designed to ensure obedience. The original intention of Confucius in setting up such a hierarchical system was to instruct people how to conduct themselves properly and to show filial piety and courtesy according to their social status. In short, this hierarchical system was initially a set of standards for a person to elevate himself in moral attainment (Gu 2008, p. 35). The hierarchical structure of Confucius, Mohists, Legalists and the like was still the same: Teachers on the top—businessmen (a part of contemporary "middle class" in China) at the bottom (The Work of Mozi, vol. II. p. 441).

When the centralized feudal monarchy was founded by Qin, generations of emperors made good use of the theories in traditional Chinese philosophy that could help them sustain their autocracy. At that time, the scholars and philosophers had to depend on the ruling class to make a living. In order to cater to the different taste of different emperors, they had proposed different ways to find the right claims from their theories to serve them as the doctrinal basis of their governance (Fan 2010, p. 98). They exaggerated the aspects, to some extent, in favor of their rule and intensively popularized these theories. In the late years of the Warring States Period, especially after the Qin Dynasty united China, the emperors wished to consolidate their feudal rule after long years of disintegration. For this reason, in order to establish an autocratic monarchy and the legitimacy of sovereignty, they generally adopted obscurantism, "abolishing Hundreds of Schools and respecting only Confucianism" since the West Han Dynasty[13] (Bo 2012, p. 241).

The evolution of the tradition of sacrifice seems to be a good example as evidence for the argument above. In the Chapter of Book I of Analects, Zeng Zi said: "Conduct the funeral of your parents with meticulous care and let not

[13] Some scholars argue that the exact time when Confucianism was adopted as the national philosophy was around the period of the King of Wu in the west Han dynasty, who had been in place from 140 to 88 B.C.E. See: Lv 2012, pp. 72–73.

sacrifices to your remote ancestors be forgotten, and the virtue of the common people will incline towards fullness." (The Analects of Confucius 2008, p. 7).

Although there are many different interpretations for different interests, originally, it is the way to teach people to show filial piety to their parents and then to train the moral attainment of people because conduct like this would make the people become pure and honest (Chen 2014). However, from the interest of the state, the pure and honest people only could contribute to the stability of society especially in that agrarian era, which was not enough to unify the mind of people to maintain its monarchy. In order to conquer the people spiritually, the feudal emperors need philosophical support. As a result, many scholars who served the emperors or the state took this responsibility. One of them was Dr. Kong An-guo.[14] Belonging to the 21th generation after Confucius and being the most famous Confucian scholar in the West Han dynasty, he knew well the importance of a national memorial service (or sacrifice offering) in maintaining the authority of emperors (Chen 2014).

In order to find the precedent where the state was entitled to take charge of a national memorial service, except for launching a war, both of which were regarded as the two most important matters for the state, he researched past history and found that the emperor of Zhuan Xu 颛顼, (c.2514–2437 B.C.E.[15] had appointed an officer responsible for the national memorial service for the first time, taking charge of the national memorial service officially to stop the civil society from taking it in their hands (Zuo 2005, p. 275).[16] Although the truth of this event still needs to be confirmed, it had exerted a very strong influence so that it was recorded repeatedly in the books concerning pre-Qin history. Hence, Dr. Kong An-guo advised the emperor he served that the state could take charge of the national memorial service strictly in line with the orthodox doctrine of Confucianism and precedents, and then provided the philosophical evidence for the ruling class to make use of the memorial service (Stearns 2008, pp. 54–55) in order to make people loyal to the emperors (Chen 2014).

Furthermore, from the Confucian doctrines and precedents, a set of complicate rites of sacrifice was developed, calling every country to "sacrifice to their ancestors" (事其先主). After, it evolved for three dynasties into the System of Patriarchal Clan (宗法制) which prevented the young generation from going beyond the rules

[14] His name in Chinese is 孔安国. The exact period of his life has not been confirmed yet. He was famous for the in-depth study of Shang Shu, one of the most important works of Confucianism, and worked as a high-ranking officer responsible for the national academy, especially the research on Shang Shu. He also was a very famous bibliophile in Chinese history. See: Li and Huang (2005), pp. 8–9.

[15] It is said that he is one of the grandsons of the Yellow Emperor. See: Fan 2010, p. 13.

[16] The book of Discourse of State, also named Kuo Yu, the Conversation of State, in Chinese *pinyin*: 国语, records this event for the first time (Chen 2014). The Discourse of State is the first history book of its kind in China, which records the stories and discourses of the historical figures of the eight states of the Zhou Dynasty and covers a span of 515 years, from 967 to 453 BC. It provides much important material about the pre-Qin dynasty (The Discourse of State 2012, p. 27).

set by their ancestors and then served as the main content of feudal hierarchy for a long time (Chen 2014).

On the other hand, Confucianism, as the only school respected since the West Han Dynasty (mentioned above), in its core thought originally emphasized harmony among humankind and social order (Chan 1967). Confucius advocated five basic relationships: ruler/subject, father/son, husband/wife, older brother/younger brother, and friends (Reagan 2012). Filial piety (*xiao,*孝), then, emerges from this relational structure. Mencius defined further how to teach these relations of humanity: "how, between father and son, there should be affection; between sovereign and minister, righteousness; between husband and wife, attention to their separate functions; between old and young, a proper order; and between friends, fidelity"[17] (The Work of Mencius 2011, p. 99). From this interpretation, it can be seen that he did not intend to design the hierarchy by this five relations but to emphasize the harmony. This could be the code of good conduct. In conclusion, *xiao* denotes reciprocity that secures mutual care in a dependent arrangement (Westbrook 2012, p. 143).

However, this relational structure was interpreted and popularized in later days in a distorted way that helped sustain sovereignty, and feudal hierarchies were then established with the domination of imperial power and patriarchy. Under this system of ignorance, backwardness and despotism, people had no rights; the "officials had no choice but to die if it was the wish of the emperor." Under the "Three Obediences[18] and Four Virtues"(三从四德) (Zhang 2014, p. 224) evolved from this structure, women were inferior to men (Stearns 2008, p. 52).

Completely subjected to them as men's property, their right to dignity was inexistent. The contemporary concept of "domestic violence", including rape, other sexual or physical abuses or victimization had no place in the realm of ancient households. As the property of their husbands, women had no control over their marriage, let alone participating in the social and political life as husbands did. For example, a husband could marry more than one woman legally at that time while a woman could only marry one man. Moreover, it was the exclusive right of the husband to ask for a divorce. It was the highest punishment for a wife to be divorced by her husband and returned to her parent's home (Shan 1987, p. 3). It was hard for her to live after a divorce because of being dishonored.

Under the system of strict filial piety, the son had no right to determine his own life and career, but had to follow the arrangement of his father, including marriage. As the core value of Confucianism, filial piety is regarded as the very foundation of all virtues and the main duty which the child should have. *DiziGui (*弟子规 or *Dos and Don'ts for Children*, one of the most popular textbooks in feudal China, written

[17] This is claimed in original Chinese that, "父子有亲,君臣有义,夫妻有别,长幼有序,朋友有信". See: The Work of Mencius 2011, p. 99.

[18] Also known as Three Submissions which refers to that when a woman is young, she must submit to her parents. After her marriage, she must submit to her husband. When she is widowed, she must submit to her son. These are the rules of propriety which the woman must follow. From this, we can judge that a woman's duty was not to control or to take charge in the old time in China. See: Stearns 2008, p. 55.

especially for private primary school pupils or children, contained the sayings of Confucius and conveyed the instruction for children throughout the ages. According to it, first, children should be dutiful to parents (filial piety) and fraternal to brothers, and then be strict with themselves and honest to others. Furthermore, they should befriend all the people around them, but stay close to those with virtue. If children have done these and have spare time, it is good for them to search for knowledge (Gu 2010, p. 125). The instruction aimed to teach children how to be a well-educated person instead of depriving them of their freedom and basic rights, although the filial piety of Confucianism has many profound explanations.

In sum, the fact that China's feudal hierarchical system could continue so long in this philosophical framework can be explained as follows:

First, Confucianism was used by the ruling class for its domination.

Second, the ruling class one-sidedly emphasized the feudal etiquette and divided the social hierarchy. This resulted in an unequal status that man is superior to woman, and that the monarch-servant and father-son status cannot be questioned.

Third, such a rigid hierarchy and feudal etiquette deprived women, children and people in destitute situations of their basic rights to participate in social and political life. This strengthened the dominance of the patriarchal society and consolidated the emperor's domination.

As a result, the feudal ethics were the bondage on people's mind. It deprived them of their basic human rights and freedom and restricted social development and ideological progress in ancient China. It was the major reason that ancient China lagged behind the trend of the world after the long reign of feudalism.

6 The Practice for Gender Equality and the Rights of the Child in Modern China

China, the Host of the Fourth World Conference on Women (1995), has been actively pursuing gender equality and children's rights. In the year of the fiftieth anniversary of the founding of the United Nations that Conference adopted the following Declaration:

(a) It "recognized that the status of women has advanced in some important respects in the past decade but that progress has been uneven, inequalities between women and men have persisted and major obstacles remain, with serious consequences for the well-being of all people";
(b) It also "recognized that this situation is exacerbated by the increasing poverty that is affecting the lives of the majority of the world's people, in particular women and children, with origins in both the national and international domains"; and it

(c) reaffirmed "the equal rights and inherent human dignity of women and men and other purposes and principles enshrined in the Charter of the United Nations, the Universal Declaration of Human Rights and other international human rights instruments, in particular the Convention on the Elimination of All Forms of Discrimination against Women and the Convention on the Rights of the Child, as well as the Declaration on the Elimination of Violence against Women and the Declaration on the Right to Development" (A/CONF.177/20/Rev.1, PP1).

In line with China's commitment to the Beijing Declaration and the implementation of the Convention on the Elimination of All Forms of Discrimination against Women (1249UNTS13), China's Law on the Protection of the Rights and Interests of Women stipulates that "domestic violence against women is prohibited. The State takes measures to prevent and stop domestic violence" (CEDAW/C/CHN/7-8, para 88).

The same national report from which the above was quoted, informs in Annex 37 (p. 74) of the numbers of cases solved in the years 2006–2009 involving rape, trafficking in women and children, organizing, forcing, seducing, sheltering or introducing women to engage in prostitution, and last, but not least of women and children victims of trafficking that were rescued. This data suggests that countering domestic violence is quite a challenge (Zhang 2014).

Similarly, concerning the Convention on the Rights of the Child (1577UNTS3), in 2010 China reported to the UN Committee on the Rights of the Child, that "from 2002 to 2008, courts nationwide convicted a total of 72,527 people for crimes involving violent interference in marital freedom, illegal detention, extortion of confessions through torture, violent extraction of evidence, maltreatment of detainees, organizing disabled and child beggars, and employing child laborers to engage in dangerous or heavy labor. The above data include circumstances in which adults are the victims of such crimes" (CRC/C/CHN/3-4, para 81).

Both national reports document the seriousness and openness with which since the time of China's new Constitution of 1947 the authorities confront the problems involved in the advancement of women and the protection of children. Criminological research in this area confirms that.

The Constitution specifies, that "all citizens... are equal before the law. The state respects and guarantees human rights." The Constitution clearly provides the basis to abolish feudal patriarchy and hierarchy and the negative aspects in Chinese traditional culture, such as the male superiority and a son's obedience to his father's wish. Article 48 of the Constitution says, that "the women of the People's Republic of China enjoy equal rights in politics, economics, culture, social life and family life as men." The state protects the rights and interests of women, implements the policy of equal pay for equal work and trains and selects female cadre (The Constitution of P. R. China, Article 33, 48).

As to the protection of women and children's rights, Article 49 of the Constitution says, that "the state protects marriage, family, mothers and children. Parents have the obligations of rearing their children not having reached adulthood;

children having already reached adulthood have the obligations of supporting and providing for their parents. The violations of freedom of marriage and the abuse of the aged, women and children are forbidden." On the first day of May 1950, the Marriage Law of the People's Republic of China was adopted, which stipulated gender equality in marriage and applied monogyny. It was replaced by a new Marriage Law on 10th September 1980.

It shifted the focus from reforming the unequal feudal marriage system where women were inferior to men to maintaining stable family relations and constructing the current legal system for marriage. It was like a breath of fresh air especially during a time when mainland China had just survived the Cultural Revolution, which had caused much damage to political, legislative and private affairs. However, it was insufficient to protect both sides in marriage, especially women, because it was too simple a legislation to deal with the complicate problems emerging from family life. For example, it did not elaborate clear rules on how to divide the family property in case of divorce and said nothing about domestic violence. As a consequence, it was amended by the National Congress of China on 28th April 2001 to respond to the challenges in the field of family matters emerging in this new era. This is the so-called Marriage Law of China 2001, which now applies in Mainland China. It includes domestic violence and provides that, "Divorce shall be granted if mediation fails under any of the following circumstances: ... (2) Domestic violence or maltreatment and desertion of one family member by another" (Marriage Law of China 2001, Article 32). This law is hopefully more effective in protecting women's rights in marriage than before.

In order to clarify some of the issues, the Supreme People's Court of China adopted the *Interpretation of a Number of Issues on the Application of the Marriage Law* which defines domestic violence as battery, the tying up of a person, mutilation, or restriction of personal freedom or other means leading to injury of family members, both in body and spirit (Zhang 2014, p. 227).

In 1992, the Law of P. R. China on the Protection of the Rights and Interests of Women and Children was adopted. It was amended in 2005 and aimed specifically at protecting the rights and interests of women and children (Law of the P. R. China on the Protection of Rights and Interests of Women 2005).

Now the Chinese Government empowers women to fully participate on the basis of equality in all spheres of society, and to develop the fullest potential of girls and women of all ages. A case in point is a basic state policy of China, according to which women enjoy equal rights with men when it comes to the signing of contracts, property management, litigations, the freedom of movement, and the freedom to choose residence (CEDAW/C/CHN/7-8, para 218).

Despite the adoption of legislation concerning the protection of women and children's rights, the discrimination against girls still exist in Chinese society, especially in the rural areas due to the traditional sense of "men being superior to women", rooted in traditional stereotyping. In order to eliminate this kind of gender discrimination, the 25th Meeting of the Standing Committee of the Ninth National People's Congress adopted The Population and Family Planning Law of P. R. China on 29 December 2001. It provides that "Use of ultrasonography or other techniques to identify the sex of a fetus for non-medical purposes is strictly prohibited. Sex-selective pregnancy termination for non-medical purposes is strictly prohibited." Furthermore, it stipulates the corresponding penalties in the next clause (The Population and Family Planning Law 2002, Article 35 and 36). Finally, in response to the recommendations No. 31 and No. 32 of the Committee on the Elimination of Discrimination against Women, the Chinese Government has further strengthened publicity, education and training, in order to enhance the awareness of citizens about gender and gender equality. In reforming the curriculum at the stage of compulsory education, the Chinese Government has increased the gender equality content in the curriculum and teaching materials, so as to guide students towards a better understanding of the fact that gender inequality still exists in Chinese society and of the harm it does, with an emphasis on the elimination of social stereotypes and prejudices regarding the roles of men and women, highlighting the important role and contribution of women in human progress. It has also added women's studies courses to the curriculum in universities and colleges, in an effort to strengthen women's studies.

The current Chinese government attaches great importance to the essence of traditional Chinese culture, proposing the "core values of socialism" and the principle of rule of law. The "concluding observations" and other recommendations of the United Nations expert treaty bodies are given serious consideration as well as appropriate follow-up action in the context of national sovereignty and the legal culture of China, the beginnings of which started forty-two centuries ago.

On November 8, 2012, the Chinese Communist Party released a report at the 18th Party Congress, which defined the core values of socialism: prosperity, democracy, civility, harmony, freedom, equality, justice, rule of law, patriotism, devotion to work, integrity and amicability. It was stressed that the core values of socialism should be cultivated and practiced (Hu 2012, p. 37). These core values correspond to a large degree to traditional values of Chinese culture, such as equality, harmony, amicability, justice, freedom and rule of law. They are also the key aspects of sustainable development in modern times. They represent the progress of the concept of good governance in China.

In order to facilitate the construction of a socialist country ruled by law, the new leaders of the central government have carried out a discussion on the key issues concerning the governance of state by law at the fourth plenary session of the 18th Communist Party of China. The Decisions over the Key Issues on Comprehensive Promotion of Rule of Law by the Central Committee of the Communist Party of China was published in 2014 (The Decision of CPC 2014, p. 1). In order to realize the protection of the interests and benefits of women and children, the emphasis should be placed on "reinforcing and standardizing public services according to the law, perfecting education, employment, income distribution, social security, medical care and sanitation, food security, poverty relief, charity, social relief, and the protection on the interests and benefits of the aged, women, children and the disabled" (The Decision of CPC 2014, p. 14).

All the strategies above reflect the emphasis placed by the central government on the promotion of the essence of traditional Chinese culture. President Xi Jinping reiterated that the excellent traditional Chinese culture is the most profound spiritual pursuit of the Chinese nation and the most fundamental gene. It is the soft power by which the Chinese nation can establish itself in the tide of the world's culture. The Ministry of Education of the People's Republic of China released the "Guidelines for Perfecting the Education on Excellent Traditional Chinese Culture" in April 2014 (Guangming Daily 2014, April 28). It aimed to promote the integration of traditional Chinese cultural education in primary schools, secondary schools and colleges and universities. The teaching materials of primary schools, secondary schools and colleges and universities are revised with the purpose of promoting traditional Chinese culture based on the core values of socialism (Guangming Daily 2014, April 28).

7 Conclusion

Ideas of inclusiveness and equality in education and women's rights in China are by no means recent, having emerged already thousands of years ago in traditional Chinese philosophy. They are as important today as they were then, as is manifest in the actual Chinese legal doctrine and recent reports by the UN Secretary-General.

The recently published Secretary-General's "Synthesis Report on the Post-2015 Agenda—The Road to Dignity by 2030: Ending Poverty, Transforming All Lives and Protecting the Planet", highlights that the future we want should be peaceful, inclusive, equitable and prosperous (A/69/700). This is not only in line with Chinese philosophy but also with the overall idea of sustainable development, which—in the opinion of the International Court of Justice—is one of the oldest in human heritage.

However, one more common way manifests itself throughout the UN and the current dominant legal philosophies and practice in China: that of equitable treatment of women and children.

The UN Secretary-General reminds us in the report referred to above that:

> Seventy years ago, in adopting the Organization's founding Charter, the nations of the world made a solemn commitment: "to save succeeding generations from the scourge of war, to reaffirm faith in fundamental human rights, in the dignity and worth of the human person, in the equal rights of men and women and of nations large and small, to establish conditions under which justice and respect for international law can be maintained, and to promote social progress and better standards of life in larger freedom (A/69/700, para 6).

In the above context it may be opportune to remember likewise what Lao Tzu said was in his view the archetypal sense of international equality:

> A large state should play the role of the female,
> Just like the lowest reaches of a river,
> Where all the other streams meet.
> The female always conquers the male by motionlessness,
> Because the motionless female always takes the lower position.
> Hence the large state can annex the small one;

> The small state can gain the trust of the large one by taking the lower position,
> The case being either the former or vice versa.
> The large state wants to put the small one under its protection,
> The small state wants to be shielded by the large one.
> Thus both can satisfy their own wishes.
> After all, the large state should be more willing to take the lower position
> (Lao Tzu 2007, pp. 176–177).

This is a kind of international equality of complementarity or correlation, which sounds fine in theory but not in practice, whether international or domestic (d'Auvergne n.d.). These two worlds (UN and Taoism) are far apart. In fact, the feudal hierarchy considered for more than 1000 years women inferior to men, and only a few rulers pursued benevolence (or good governance in contemporary sense) in practice, and even fewer managed to address that kind of equality well, also in economic terms. And the same applies to children—passive members of the family. This is not the full meaning of traditional Chinese culture, and certainly not what China nowadays is looking for, both in terms of empowering women and giving children viable chances in life, and in terms of its international role.

After the founding of the People's Republic of China, it strongly advocated rejecting the negative and assimilating the fine essence of Chinese traditional culture, and this has become the driving force of promoting sustainable development and practicing the socialist core value system of contemporary government. Chinese traditional culture will not only be conducive to the better exploration and research of advanced ideas in ancient Chinese philosophy and the construction of sustainable development of Chinese characteristics but also to crime prevention. In this way, people can live with more dignity (A/69/700). Crime prevention will once more be seen not only as a science, but also as an art of living together in peaceful and more inclusive societies.

Five Questions

1. What is the core of Mencius' statement on sustainable development?
2. How does the Work of Guanzi explain the idea of good governance to prevent crime?
3. By what means does Mohism claim to achieve inclusiveness in education?
4. What is the feature of the claims of Taoism for gender equality?
5. What does Confucian filial piety mean for children?

References

A/68/970, "Report of the Open Working Group on Sustainable Development Goals", General Assembly, United Nation, 12 August, 2014, http://www.un.org/ga/search/view_doc.asp?symbol=A/68/970&Lang=E, last accessed Nov. 8, 2014.

A/69/700, UN Synthesis Report of the Secretary-General on the Post-2015 Sustainable Development Agenda, The Road to Dignity by 2030: ending poverty, transforming all lives and protecting the planet, 4 December 2014.

A/CONF.177/20/Rev.1.Report of the Fourth World Conference on Women, 4-15September1995, http://www.un.org/womenwatch/daw/beijing/official.htm, Last accessed December 13, 2014.

Bo Y. (2012), *The historical chronology of China (First Volume).* Beijing: People's Literature Publishing House (柏杨. 中国历史年表 [上].北京:人民文学出版社.2012).

Cai, X. Q. (Ed.). (2006). *Laozi Says, the wise man talking series, Chinese-English* (Q. Wang & F. Z. Jiang, Trans.). Preface. Beijing:Sinolingua Press(蔡希勤编注.老子说.老人家说系列.汉英对照.王琴、姜防震译.序言.北京:华语教育出版社.2006).

CEDAW/C/CHN/7-8, Combined Seventh and Eighth Periodic Report by People's Republic of China on the implementation of the Convention on the Elimination of All Forms of Discrimination against Women,20 January 2012.

Chan, W.-T. (1967). The story of Chinese philosophy, In: *The Chinese mind: Essentials of Chinese philosophy and culture* (Ch. A. Moore Trans.). Honolulu: East–west Center Press.

Chan, W.-T. trans. and comp. (1963). *A source book in Chinese philosophy.* Princeton, NJ: Princeton University Press.

Chen, Z. G. (2014). Finding the final home for souls through worshipping parents' funerals and ancestors' commemorations. *Wuhan University Journal (Philosophy & Social Sciences), 67* (5), 123–127 (陈仲庚.慎终追远与国人之灵魂归宿.武汉大学学报{哲学社会科学版}.2014年第5期,总第67卷,第123-127页).

Chi, W. X. (2004). *Research on the work of Guanzi*. Beijing: Higher Education Press (池万兴.管子研究.北京:高等教育出版社,2004).

CRC/C/CHN/3-4, People's Republic of China third and fourth combined report on the implementation of the Convention on the Rights of the Child, May 2010.

D'Tamara d'Auvergne (n.d). Femininity and Women in Early Chinese Philosophy, http://www.academia.edu/2296381/Feminity_and_Women_inEarly_Chinese_Philosophy. Accessed December 26 2014.

Fan, W. L. (2010). *The concise edition of general history of China (First Volume).* Beijing: The Commercial Press (范文澜.中国通史简编(上册).北京:商务印书馆。2010年).

Fung, Y. L. (2013). *A short history of Chinese philosophy* (T. U. You-guang Trans.). Beijing: Peking University Press (冯友兰.中国哲学简史.涂又光译.北京:北京大学出版社,2013).

Gu, H. M. (2008). Research on the ConfucianismI. In: *The comments of Gu Hong-ming on Chinese traditional philosophy* (Chinese). Shenyang: Jilin People's Publishing House (辜鸿铭.孔教研究之一.载:辜鸿铭讲国学.沈阳:吉林人民出版社.2008).

Gu, D. K. (Trans.) (2010). The Book of Filial Piety• Twenty-four Stories of *Filial Piety• Di zi Gui: Dos and Don'ts for Children*, Chinese-English, Beijing: China Translation Press Company (顾丹柯.孝经•二十四孝•弟子规.汉英对照. 北京:中国对外翻译出版公司.2010).

Guangming Daily (2014). Enhance the education concerning Chinese Good Traditional Culture, http://www.bjwmb.gov.cn/zxfw/wmwx/wskt/t20140428_570716.htm, accessed Nov.11, 2014 (加强中华优秀传统文化教育,来源:光明日报,时间:2014-04-28. http://www.bjwmb.gov.cn/zxfw/wmwx/wskt/t20140428_570716.htm, 2014年11月11日访问).

Guanzi (2005). The Work of Guanzi (Vol. 1 and3), Library of Chinese Classics, Chinese-English, English and Modern Chinese translation by Zhai Jiang-yue, Guilin: Guangxi Normal University Press (管子.大中华文库.汉英对照.第一卷.翟江月译.桂林:广西师范大学出版社,2005).

Hu, J. T. (2012). Report at 18th Party Congress of Chinese Communist Party, Beijing: People's Press. The English translation can be available at http://news.xinhuanet.com/english/special/18cpcnc/2012-11/17/c_131981259_14.htm#,last accessed December 16, 2014.(胡锦涛:《坚定不移沿着中国特色社会主义道路前进为全面建成小康社会而奋斗——在中国共产党第十八次全国代表大会上的报告》,北京:人民出版社•英文版参见http://news.xinhuanet.com/english/special/18cpcnc/2012-11/17/c_131981259_14.htm#, 2014年12月16日访问).

I.C.J Reports. (1997). *Case concerning the Gabcikovo-Nagymaros Project (Hungary v. Slovakia),* Seperate Opinion of Vice-President Weeramantry.

Jin, Y., & Hu, X. R. (2009). *The modern Chinese translation and annotation on the Work of Laozi.* Wuhan: Chongwen Publishing House (靳永、胡晓锐译注.老子.武汉:崇文书局.2009).

Kury, H., & Shea, E. (2011). *Punitivity. International developments, Vol. 1: Punitiveness – a global Phenomenon?* Bochum: Universitätsverlag Dr, N. Brockmeyer.

Law of the P. R. China on the Protection of Rights and Interests of Women (2005). from: official website of the Central People's Government of P.R. China, http://www.gov.cn/flfg/2005-08/29/content_27174.htm, last accessed Dec.13, 2014(中华人民共和国妇女权益保障法(全文).来自:中国中央政府官方网站,2014年12月13日最后访问).

Li, Y. A., & Huang, Z. Y. (Ed.) (2005). *The general dictionary of Chinese bibliophiles*. Hong Kong: China International Culture Press (李玉安、黄正雨编著.中国藏书家通典.香港:中国国际文化出版社.2005)

Liu, K., & Li, K. H. (2003). *The translation and annotation on the work of Guanzi*. Harbin: Heilongjiang Publishing Group (刘柯、李克和.管子译注.哈尔滨:黑龙江人民出版社,2003).

Lv, S. M. (2012). *The grand history of Han Dynasty*. Beijing: Beijing United Publishing Company (吕思勉.汉朝大历史.北京:北京联合出版公司.2012).

Mencius (2011). In: Z. Z. Sun (Ed.), *The works of Mencius*. Chinese-English. English translation by James Legge. Hangzhou: Zhejiang University Press (孙芝斋编注.孟子今译.汉英对照.杭州:浙江大学出版社.2011).

Mote, F. W. (1971). *Intellectual Foundations of China* (2nd edition). The McGraw-Hill Companies, Inc. Chinese edition: Frederick W. Mote (2009).中国思想之渊源. (Trans: WANG Li-gang). Beijing: Peking University Press (【美】牟复礼.中国思想之渊源, 王立刚 译.北京:北京大学出版社。,2009).

Mozi, (2006). *The work of Mozi (vol. II),* Library of Chinese Classics, Chinese-English. Modern Chinese translation by Zhou Cai-zhu, Qi Rui-rui, English translation by Wang Rong-pei, Wang Hong. Changsha: Hunan People's Press (墨子.大中华文库.汉英对照.第二卷.周才珠、齐瑞瑞今译,汪榕培、王宏英译.长沙:湖南人民出版社.2006).

Qian, W. Z. (2009). *The interpretation on three character scriptures (First Volume)*. Beijing: China Publishing Group (钱文忠.钱文忠解读〈三字经〉(上册).北京:中国民主法制出版社.2009).

Reagan (2012), Non-Western Educational Traditions: Indigenous Approaches to Educational Thought and Practice, 140. T. P. Westbrook (2012), Journal for the Study of Religions and Ideologies, vol. 11, issue 33:143.

Redo, S. M. (2012). *Blue criminology-The power of United Nations ideas to counter crime globally: A monographic study*. Helsinki: European Institute for Crime Prevention and Control. http://issuu.com/slawomirredo/docs/redo_blue_criminology.

Ruan, Z. (1998). The *preface for the series of Chinese strategies*. In: C. Long-hai (Ed.) *The strategy of school of legalism* (pp. 1–6). Wuhan: Wuhan Technology University of Surveying and Mapping Press (阮忠.中国智谋丛书.总序.载:陈龙海.法家智谋.武汉:武汉测绘科技大学出版社, 1998年. 第1-6页).

Shan, C. L. (1987). *The history of Chinese women* (Japanese originally) (G. Da-lun,& F. Yong). Xi'an: Sanqin Publishing House (【日】山川丽.中国女性史.高大伦、范勇译.西安:三秦出版社,1987).

Sherman, L. W., Gottfredson, D., Mackenzie, D., Eck, J., Reuter, P., & Bushway, S. (1998). Preventing Crime: What Works, What Doesn't, What's Promising-A Report to the United States Congress, prepared for the National Institute of Justice. U.S. Department of Justice, Office of Justice Programs, Research in Brief, July 1998.

Stearns, P. N. (2008). *World history in documents: A comparative reader* (2nd ed.). New York/London: New York University Press.

Tan, J.J., & Sun, Z. Y. (2012). *The translation and annotation on the work of Mozi*. Beijing: The Commercial Press (谭家健.孙中原.墨子今注今译.北京:商务印书馆.2012).

The Analects of Confucius (2008). Chinese- English. Modern Chinese translation by Yang Bo-jun, English translation by D. C. Lau. Beijing: Zhonghua Book Company (论语.汉英对照. 杨伯峻今译,刘殿爵英译.北京:中华书局.2008).

The Constitution of P. R. China (2004). from the official website of the Central People's Government of P. R. China, http://www.gov.cn/gongbao/content/2004/content_62714.htm, last accessed Dec. 14, 2014 (中华人民共和国宪法(全文),来自:中国中央政府官方网站, http://www.gov.cn/gongbao/content/2004/content_62714.htm, 2014年12月14日访问).

The Decision of CPC (2014). The Decisions over the Key Issues on Comprehensive Promotion of Rule of Law adopted by Central Committee of the Communist Party of China at the Fourth Plenary Session of the 18th C PC, Beijing: People's Press (中共中央关于全面推进依法治国若干重大问题的决定(全文).北京:•人民出版社).

The Discourse of State (2012). The Library of Chinese Classics. Chinese-English. Translated by Shang Xue-feng and Xia De-kao (Modern Chinese), Wang Hong and Zhao Zheng (English). Changsha: Hunan Peoples Publishing Group (国语,大中华文库,汉英对照.尚学峰、夏德靠今译,王宏、赵峥英译.长沙:湖南人民出版社.2012).

The Marriage Law of P. R. China (2001). from: official website of The Central Government of P. R. China, http://www.gov.cn/banshi/2005-05/25/content_847.htm, last accessed December 14, 2014 (中华人民共和国婚姻法(全文).来自:中国中央政府官方网站. http://www.gov.cn/gongbao/content/2004/content_62714.htm, 2014年12月14日访问).

The Population and Family Planning Law of P. R. China (2002). from: official website of the Central People's Government of P. R. China, http://www.gov.cn/banshi/2005-05/25/content_878.htm, last accessed December 13, 2014 (中华人民共和国人口与计划生育法.来自:中国中央政府官方网站,2014年12月13日最后访问).

The Work of Mencius (2011). Chinese-English, English translation by James Legge. Beijing: Foreign Language Research Publishing House (孟子, 汉英对照,【英】James Legge译.北京:外语教学与研究出版社.2011).

Tzu, L. (2007). *The Book of Tao and Teh, Chinese-English* (G. Zheng-kun, Trans.). Beijing: China Translation Press Company (【春秋】老子.道德经.辜正坤英译.北京:•中国对外翻译出版公司.2007).

Waller, I. (2011). Less law, more order (Chinese translation). Translated by Jiang Wen-jun. Checked: Mei Jian-ming, Beijing: Chinese People's Public Security University Press (【加拿大】欧文·沃勒.有效的犯罪预防:公共安全战略的科学设计.蒋文军译.梅建明译校,北京:中国人民大学出版社,2011年).

Westbrook, T. P. (2012). An Investigation into the effects of Confucian filial piety in the intercultural Christian education experience. *Journal for the Study of Religions and Ideologies, 11*(33), 137–163.

Xu, X. C., Si, W. Z., & Yang Z. (Ed.). (2004). The general history of China (Vol. 3). In: S. Y. Bai, et al. (Eds.), *The Series of The General History of China* (Vol. 12). Shanghai: Shanghai People Publishing House(徐喜辰、斯维至、杨钊主编:《中国通史》第三卷。白寿彝主编:《中国通史》,12卷本。上海:上海人民出版社,2004).

Zhang, H. W. (2014). Domestic violence and its official reactions in China. In L. Cao, I. Y. Sun, & B. Hebenton, et al. (Eds.), *The Routledge handbook of Chinese criminology*. London: Routledge.

Zheng, J.W., & Zhang, Q. (Ed.) (2010), *Mozi: Collection of critical biographies of Chinese thinke*r (Concise Edition). Chinese-English, English translation by David B. Honey, Nanjing: Nanjing University Press (郑杰文.张倘编著.墨子.中国思想家评传系列.汉英对照.David B. Honey 英译,南京:南京大学出版社,2010).

Zuo, Q. M. (2005). *The discourse of state*, collated by Bao Si-tao, Jinan: Shandong Press (左丘明.国语.鲍思陶点校.济南:齐鲁书社.2005).

The Right to a Safe City for Women and Girls

Michael Platzer

Abstract Currently two billion women live in cities. Youth under 25 amount to three billion people. By 2050, 70 % of human beings will be city dwellers. Logically, therefore, city managers should focus on the young female. But the world often looks different from the viewpoint of a male urban planner or police chief than that of an adolescent girl. UNESCO and UN-Habitat propagate "a right to city" which includes participatory, integrated, and sustainable human settlement planning to ensure inclusive and sustainable urbanization. This means the provision of adequate, safe, and affordable housing and infrastructure, but more than that, access to good education, health, transport, human development, social and recreational services. But most importantly it provides urban safety—for the individual to go about her/his business without fear and risk of being assaulted. This is the major United Nations message of the Sustainable Development Goals (2016–2030). This chapter shows, how urban governance puts adolescent girls at the centre of transforming cities to become places of inclusion, tolerance, and opportunity for everyone. By bringing city officials and adolescent girls together, there is a real opportunity to create sustainable economic and social change within these societies that will benefit all.

1 Introduction

The vulnerability of women and girls in cities around the world, from gang rapes in India to the murder of "streetwalkers" in the Americas and the kidnapping, trafficking, and enslavement of girls in Africa and the Middle East, has received prominent coverage in the media. The phenomenon of violence against women in cities is brutal and increasing. In the last decade and a half, although various governmental and nongovernmental organizations have emphasized the right of women to walk safely in their towns without the fear of death or injury, more needs

M. Platzer (✉)
Academic Council on the United Nations System/ACUNS, Liaison Office, Vienna, Austria
e-mail: michaelkplatzer@yahoo.com

H. Kury et al. (eds.), *Women and Children as Victims and Offenders: Background, Prevention, Reintegration*, DOI 10.1007/978-3-319-28424-8_25

to be done. The United Nations is dealing with the issue in the Sustainable Development Goal 11.7 "by 2030, [to]provide universal access to safe, inclusive and accessible, green and public spaces, particularly for women and children, older persons and persons with disabilities" (A/68/970, pp. 18/24). Nevertheless, the rights of women and girls to cities have been painfully slow to be recognized, and unless approaches are unified and intensified, crisis proportions will be soon reached.

2 The Right to the City

Today over 4 billion people live in cites, half of them women. By 2030 there will be 5 billion or 60 % of the world's population living in cities. By 2050 that figure will be 70 % (UNDESA 2008). Many cities will become megalopolises, incorporating the semi-rural areas around and between them. The challenges of achieving peaceful, sustainable societies with good governance will be greater than ever before because of population pressures, social conflicts, migration, growing inequalities, and lack of economic opportunities.

As Shelley Buckingham and David Harvey argue "the right to the city is a collective right for all people who inhabit, access, and use the city. It entails not only the right to use what already exists in urban spaces, but also to define and create what should exist in order to meet the human needs to live a decent life in urban environments." (http://www.hic-net.org/articles.php?pid=3390). In short, it includes the right to use the city and to participate in its creation or re-creation. Moreover, no single "identity" exists in any given society; thus, cultural, gender, and other differences must be included in the city's development. Not taking account of these differences in the past has led to the inequalities we see today in our cities: inequalities that are set to worsen without major policy interventions to make cities safer and more sustainable.

The history of the "right to the city" goes back to the early twentieth century. It was as a result of fieldwork conducted in the 1920s and 1930s by the Chicago School of urban sociologists that the concept of the city emerged as more than a conglomeration of large numbers of individuals and abundance of facilities such as hospitals, schools, parks, police stations, court houses, shops, theatres, highways, and other social infrastructure that form and shape the actions and attitudes of a city's inhabitants (e.g. Park et al. 1921). According to these findings, each city has a distinct urban culture, a state of mind, a body of customs, and traditions. Indeed, cities have attracted "world changers" in science, medicine, music, literature, engineering, and enlightened policies.

> Throughout history, towns and cities have been the main sites of human diversity, where people of different geographical background and culture came together and lived side by side. They are places where goods and ideas are exchanged, and this has always been the main motor of human economic and cultural progress (Council of Europe 2011, in part two, B.7).

However, the city also has more crime than rural communities and often more pockets of persistent poverty and delinquency. Park and Burgess (1925) contributed to the Chicago School's social disorganization theory, linking crime to place-based characteristics, namely, that the different ecological environments in a city could have effects on human behaviours. Shaw and McKay (1942) further linked social disorganization in the form of immigrant delinquency rates to the urban environment where the arriving poor were most likely to settle in the hope of gaining a livelihood. Newcomers can quickly assume both positive and negative attributes.

The notion of the "right to the city," was expanded by Lefebvre (1996 [1968], p. 179) who argued for the right to "urban life, to renewed centrality, to places of encounter and exchange, to life rhythms and time uses, enabling the full and complete usage of ... moments and places..." Harvey (2003, p. 939) argued that Lefebvre's concept was "not merely a right to access what already exists [in the city], but a right to change it after our heart's desire." A World Charter for the Right to the City movement started in 1992, originating from grassroots initiatives rather than a regional or governmental organization (Brown and Kristiansen 2009). In 2004, UNESCO and UN-HABITAT were among those elaborating the "World Charter for the Right to the City" in Quito, Ecuador. This has been ratified by over 350 cities in 21 countries.

The **European Charter for the Safeguarding of Human Rights in the City** (2000) is the result of the Conference "Cities for Human Rights" in Barcelona in 1998 held to commemorate the 50th Anniversary of the Universal Declaration of Human Rights. Every 2 years a conference has been organized to exchange information about progress made in the signatory cities, they are now more then 400.

Since 2005 UNESCO and UN-HABITAT have undertaken a series of actions on the question of urban citizenship and the right to the city. In 2005 the organizations initiated a project on "Urban Policies and the Right to the City: Rights, Responsibilities and Citizenship" (Brown and Kristiansen 2009). The UN-HABITAT (2010) report on the state of the world's cities stresses the importance of taking forward the right to the city as a vehicle for social inclusion.

The Commonwealth Principles on Good Practice for Local Democracy and Good Governance, (elaborated in 2005) set standards for the 53 Commonwealth nations (http://www.clgf.org.uk/userfiles/1/file/AberdeenAgendaleaflet8pp.pdf).

3 The Right to the City from a Gender Perspective

The recognition of the rights of women to have (safe) use of the city has been long in coming, with a patchy literature mainly emerging this century. According to Harvey (2003), human rights, although derived from basic human needs, for example, food, water and shelter, also comprise notions of equality based upon different identities including gender, race, and religion. Including a gender dimension in the right to the city debate is essential. In 2006 the Council of European

Municipalities and Regions launched the "European Charter for Equality of Women and Men in Local Life". More than 1400 local and regional governments have signed the Charter. An Observatory was launched in 2012 to support the signatories.

Buckingham (2010, p. 61) eloquently argues that the right to the city has to be expressed in terms of the plurality of identities living in a particular urban environment. All stakeholders need to be included, as different groups will contribute to a comprehensive understanding and practice of the right to the city.

> It is absolutely essential to understand that there exists no one identity in any given society and as such, difference must be included in the development of the right to the city so as to avoid the same hegemonic power dynamics which have contributed to the massive inequalities that exist in contemporary cities. Gender roles must be challenged so as to break down these power dynamics, which relate directly to the social construction of space and have negative impacts on realizing women's rights to the city. Further, women must be included in the participatory planning processes, which shape debates around the right to the city, as they represent an overarching group of intersecting identities, which experience the city in different ways.

Among the major criteria affecting women's equal use of the city are: their safety in urban environments; public infrastructure and transportation; security of land tenure; access to employment; access to community facilities and services; and ensuring a connection to reproductive responsibilities (hospitals or clinics). For those reasons, it is "absolutely vital that women are involved in urban planning, local governance and decision-making processes related to their urban environments" (Buckingham 2010, pp. 60–61).

According to Urban Gateway for the International Urban Development Community,[1] women amount to more than half of the world's urban population of 4 billion. The dramatically evolving urban landscape poses tremendous qualitative and quantitative challenges for women and society.[2] Since the first observance of International Women's Day by the United Nations, the world has seen many positive changes for women. For instance, programs have been developed to improve maternal and child health; there has been expanded provision of educational, occupational, and leadership opportunities. However, for millions of women worldwide much more remains to be done to bring them out of poverty and to provide them and their families with clean water, sustainable forms of energy, better nutrition, and other essential aspects of an equitable and sustainable life. Women face ever-more complex challenges as urbanization takes hold; new opportunities frequently involve the acquisition of new skills against the background of a rapidly changing global economy; family support, especially to help with child care while mothers earn a living, can be lacking in the urban context, especially where new migrants are concerned.

---

[1] www.urbangateway.org.

[2] http://www.urbangateway.org/document/creating-safe-spaces-cities-women.

The United Nations formulated 17 Sustainable Development Goals (SDGs) for the "post-2015 agenda" which should remain valid until the year 2030. Goal number 11 is to "make cities and human settlements inclusive, safe, resilient, and sustainable", with 11.7 specifically related to the needs of women and children. By 2030 all persons should have access to "adequate, safe, and affordable housing and basic services" and all slums are to be upgraded (11.1); in addition they should have "access to safe, affordable, accessible and sustainable transport systems" (11.2). Perhaps most importantly, there should be "participatory, integrated and sustainable human settlement planning" to ensure "inclusive and sustainable urbanization" (11.3). By 2030, there should be "universal access to safe, inclusive and accessible green and public spaces, particularly for women and children, older persons and persons with disabilities" (11.7). There should also be regional planning linking "urban, peri-urban and rural areas" (11.a) and holistic disaster risk management as well as integrated mitigation and adaptation policies in relation to climate change (11.b).

4 Migrant Women and Cities

The number of women migrating is increasing. Today women account for half the international migrant population, reaching 70–80 % in some countries, and they suffer a higher exposure to exploitation and abuse in the form of human trafficking (UNDP 2014, p. 76). For young women and girls, the reasons to migrate to cities vary from escaping the boredom of village life, the narrow-mindedness of the village elders, the tedium of agricultural work, the prospects of forced marriage, family obligations, and continued grinding poverty to obtaining better employment prospects, higher education, personal development, and independence.

In fact, more girls migrate to urban areas than boys, to work as domestic servants and in textile factories. While most young women find their new lives in the city satisfactory and return to their jobs year after year, many suffer long hours and low pay in often unsafe and unsanitary conditions. Others are physically abused and sexually harassed in households. All are vulnerable to assault and violence in unfamiliar environments. Some are forced into prostitution because they cannot find regular jobs—often girls must sell their bodies to pay for their transportation to the receiving country or their first month's rent. Others enter into a contractual arrangement with an intermediary to obtain transport and a "good job" in the city but only find out on arrival that it is sex work that is required of them. Some accept their lot because it is better-paying than household or factory work; others are "enslaved" literally or by debt bondage and having their documents taken from them.

Nonetheless, for the majority it is a better life they have in the city: independence, being able to continue their education (villages only have primary schools), having the opportunity to find a greater range of possible marriage partners, and controlling their fertility. They can also send money back to their families, which helps to offset parental embarrassment at having their daughter living alone in the urban environment.

A growing phenomenon is the international migration of girls and young women. Most go to places where members of their community already reside. This has the advantage that they find a support system to help them get jobs, apartments, even husbands. However, it may also delay their integration into mainstream society.

One of the biggest challenges is the inclusion of the internal and external migrants in the prosperous mainstream of urban society (UNESCO/UN-Habitat 2010). While migrants provide a low-cost flexible workforce for the urban informal economy and contribute directly to the construction of the modern city, they often work in poor conditions, without social security and health benefits, and without legal protection. UNESCO and UN-Habitat stress a right to the city that "encompasses access to food, housing, education, health, work and local democracy" and that these rights should also be enjoyed by migrants. Urban planners and policymakers in all these fields, including the police, should devise creative ways of including new migrants in the city, recognize their contribution, and help reverse the negative portrayal of immigrants that currently exists.

To foster tolerance, mitigate ethnic, cultural and religious tensions and conflicts of interest, fight against discrimination, celebrate cultural diversity and foster social cohesion, UNESCO and UN-HABITAT recommend careful analyses and the evaluation of detailed information about the various communities' problems, conflicts, and needs in each neighbourhood as well as establishing cooperation with the stakeholders through partnerships (UNDESA 2007).

The Council of Europe has issued a "European Manifesto for Multiple Cultural Affiliation" to facilitate peaceful coexistence and mutual understanding between cultural groups with a view to resolution and prevention of conflicts. The most important concern is to provide access to services (housing, education, health care, welfare, and recreation) and equal employment opportunities for all; this may necessitate the recruitment of bilingual and bi-cultural staff and the production of information materials in many languages. Underlying all these provisions of services is the protection of the "rights of migrants", that their voices be heard and their participation in decision-making assured through representation and direct citizen involvement in democratic institutions (Creating Better Cities for Migrants).

UN-Habitat is promoting the theme of inclusive cities through its Global Campaign on Urban Governance and the Urban Governance Index. It has found that few cities promote the inclusion of migrants. The right to the city encompasses rights to basic services. In cities throughout the world it is mainly the women who live in abject poverty with their children. The empowerment of women in political, social, and economic life is central to eradicating poverty and creating sustainable human settlements. The increasing multiculturalism of cities has heightened tensions between newcomers and those who had previously settled in urban areas and this is expressed in racism and ethnic or religious discrimination.[3] "All migrants must be able to exercise their fundamental rights. Local governments should not only protect and promote migrants' rights but also inform migrant communities properly on their rights and responsibilities. Migrants have to be enabled and encouraged to exercise their rights and become active citizens."[4]

Migrants are often viewed with suspicion by other members of society and can be subject to populist and xenophobic campaigns in politics or media. Intolerance, racism, and discrimination continue to threaten the development of individuals and the coexistence of different communities (UNESCO/UN-HABITAT 2010).

From the existing identified case studies and research, "eight key principles for success" have been identified by UNESCO and UN-HABITAT with respect to migrants[5]:

1. Protect and promote the rights of migrants;
2. Provide access to services and ensure equal opportunities for all;
3. Promote representative democracy through the participation of all communities;
4. Celebrate cultural diversity as a source of exchange and dialogue;
5. Foster tolerance and fight against discrimination and racism;
6. Mitigate ethnic, cultural and religious tensions and conflicts of interest within urban communities;
7. Foster social cohesion and shared belonging;
8. Urban planning towards cities as common goods;

5 Migration of Women and Girls to the Cities

"Migration is transforming our world: by the end of this decade, most developing countries will have more people living in cities than in rural areas. Adolescent girls in developing countries are an overlooked population, but they are a group that is migrating to urban areas in ever greater numbers. Girls are on the move because they lack opportunity in their rural hometowns and want to work, learn, and gain skills and resources. They also move to escape hardship: poverty, war, or early marriage. While migration can carry risks, for many girls moving can unlock opportunity, autonomy, and the chance for prosperity" (Temin et al. 2013, p. XV).

---

[3] UN 2006, http://unesdoc.unesco.org/images/0017/001780/178090e.pdf.

[4] http://www.logiqo.com/easycontact/ec/british/opencities/jul10/creating_better_cities_for_migrants.pdf, p. 8.

[5] http://www.logiqo.com/easycontact/ec/british/opencities/jul10/creating_better_cities_for_migrants.pdf, p. 7.

5.1 *Marriage*

Often girls are brought to foreign countries to marry their countrymen and are in effect confined in their homes and ghettos and abused and exploited by their older husbands. Many migrant married women are dependent on their husband's immigration status and are afraid of reporting violence to the police because of deportation or losing their children (Temin et al. 2013).

"One in three girls in low and middle-income countries (excluding China) will marry before the age of 18. One in nine girls will marry before their fifteenth birthday. In the least developed countries the prevalence of child marriage is even higher – nearly one in two" (Loaiza 2014, p. 10).

5.2 *Sexual Exploitation*

Research on adolescent girls' migration and commercial sexual exploitation is limited, but existing evidence indicates that the two intersect in critical ways. A large study of the sex trade in Ethiopian cities found that just under 90 % of sexually exploited 15–19 year olds were migrants from rural areas or small towns (Girma and Erulkar 2009). Migrants comprised a third of sexually exploited young people studied in Ghana and half in the Philippines and Ecuador (ILO 2004). In towns and cities, factors such as low wages, the difficulty of gaining decent paid employment, and the failure of some employers to pay for work push migrant girls into commercial sexual exploitation." (Temin et al. 2013, p. 58)

5.3 *Sexual Harassment*

One of the major concerns for women and girls in cities is physical safety in public spaces. Fear of violence in urban areas restricts women's and girls' freedom of movement as well as their access to essential services and therefore impacts their health and wellbeing.

"Sexual harassment [touching, cat calls, ogling, rude comments, stalking or following] and other forms of sexual violence occur every day for women and girls globally. It happens on streets, in and around schools and workplaces, in parks, in public sanitation facilities, and in neighborhoods. Violence and sexual harassment in public spaces restrict women's freedom of movement, reduces their access to essential services, and negatively impacts their health and wellbeing."[6]

[6] http://www.urbangateway.org/document/creating-safe-spaces-cities-wo.

6 Slum Communities and Challenges for Women and Girls

The Center on Housing Rights and Evictions COHRE, has issued a report,[7] which has examined the situation of women and girls in Bangladesh and Kenya as well as in 20 other countries and found a predominance of violence against women in slum communities.

As pointed out in an article by Urban Gateway for the International Urban Development Community, 76 per cent of the 4500 women respondents in the slums of Dhaka, Bangladesh "had endured physical or sexual abuse during the past 12 months with 43 per cent having suffered both physical and sexual abuse."[8]). Kibera in Kenya, the second largest slum in Africa, was one of the hotspots for violence against women and mass rapes during the country's civil riots in 2008.

"What is most disturbing about these figures is that many women migrate to cities in order to escape from domestic violence and health-damaging cultural practices, yet these threats persist in cities or women may experience a complex set of new challenges including a lack of access to services, housing insecurity, and employment discrimination" (ibid.)

7 UN Women's Safe Cities Global Initiative

"Several important steps need to be taken to combat violence against women in urban areas worldwide. A fundamental step is to accurately identify the prevalence and nature of the problem. The UN Women's Safe Cities Global Initiative is developing and implementing models to reduce and prevent sexual violence against women and girls in public spaces. The initiative first administered surveys to assess the specific concerns of women in the communities of participating cities. In New Delhi, India, a 2012 study found that 92 per cent of women had experienced sexual violence in public spaces, and that 88 per cent of women had experienced sexual harassment in their lifetime. In Quito, Ecuador, a 2011 study reported that 68 per cent of women had experienced sexual harassment or sexual violence in the previous year. In Port Moresby, Papua New Guinea, a 2011 survey revealed that 55 per cent of women experienced sexual violence while visiting marketplaces in the previous year."[9]

Men and women often experience the same urban space in different ways, as women usually do the shopping and escort their children to and from school (in India, middle-class men take the car to the office while their women must use public transport). In many countries, women walking on the street suffer cat calls,

---

[7] http://globalinitiative-escr.org/wp-content/uploads/2013/05/women_slums_and_urbanisation_may_2008.pdf.

[8] http://www.urbangateway.org/document/creating-safe-spaces-cities-women.

[9] http://www.urbangateway.org/document/creating-safe-spaces-cities-women.

sexual harassment, and groping in crowded buses—even assault. In one study covering four cities in 4 continents, 60 % of women felt unsafe in urban areas ("Learning from Women to Create Gender Inclusive Cities", Women in Cities International). The time of day is also experienced differently, after dark with poor street lighting, empty streets, but also crowded, jammed streets. Broken pavements, graffiti, idle young men on street corners, dirty or non-existent toilet facilities, or the absence of shops or policemen (or noisy pubs and corrupt police) can make women nervous.

Particular groups of women are also more vulnerable than others—street vendors, the homeless, sex workers, domestic workers (often young themselves) running errands, shopping or returning after dropping children off at their school, factory workers or office workers returning home in the evening. The worst is that their complaints of sexual harassment are not taken seriously by the police and no one is ever arrested—arrests for such offences are almost non-existent.

UN Women has declared that a safe city for women and girls is "a city where women and girls can enjoy public spaces and public life without fear of being assaulted; where violence is not exercised against women and girls in either the home or the street; a city where the state and local government take actions to provide attention, prevention, and punishment for violence against women and girls; where the state and local government guarantee women's and girls' access to justice; where women and girls participate in making decisions that affect the community in which they live; where women are not discriminated against and where their economic, political and cultural rights are guaranteed; where the state guarantees the human rights of all people without excluding women and girls."[10]

8 New Technologies Available

Local authorities are partnering with women and girls in their communities to map with mobile phones safety risks such as defective infrastructure, obscured walking routes, and deficient lighting. By improving infrastructure including transportation services, the city can better protect the safety and wellbeing of its vulnerable population. The city of Vienna, Austria has been a pioneer in its efforts to make urban planning more gender-inclusive. Improvements range from additional installed lighting and safer underground car parking to more sport-specific public parks and an innovative apartment complex—"Women-Work-City"—built to target to the unique needs of working women by providing services and shops all in one place.[11]

[10] http://www.endvawnow.org/en/articles/237-what-are-safe-cities-and-communities-for-women-and-girls-.html.

[11] http://www.urbangateway.org/document/creating-safe-spaces-cities-women.

9 Addressing Women's Urban Safety Through the Right to the City

"Threats of crime and violence are highest in cities, particularly among groups of women, and increasing incidents in urban public spaces are becoming of greater concern, especially when considering the rapid expanse of urbanization which has been occurring around the world for decades. This phenomenon has progressed to the point where over half of the world's population currently lives in cities, thus shedding light on the pertinent importance of addressing women's safety in the city."[12]

"If violence occurs in large part in the city, then action needs to be taken not only in the city, but through the creation of the city itself. While urban designs and planning do not directly create violence, they facilitate environments that can present greater or lesser opportunities for assault. Therefore, urban designs and plans must be examined in order to fully understand why women experience threats and actual incidences of violence. By understanding these threats, steps may then be taken to change the way women experience and live in the city without the threat of violence. All women have this right to the city, which must be understood as their collective right to safety and security in the spaces they inhabit."[13]

10 Adolescent Girls' Views on Safety in Cities

UN-Habitat has pioneered the use of rapid situational assessments (RSAs) to provide snapshots of the situation of the most vulnerable group in a city, adolescent girls, in order to inform future programming. RSAs identify the key opportunities and challenges in each city, and how girls perceive their city in terms of its safety and inclusivity. Girls are asked to show the spaces they use, the routes they take, and how they feel along the way (e.g. a girl may say that she "never" feels safe when using public transport). The girls identify the priority issues they would like to see addressed and offer recommendations for making their communities safer and more inclusive. It was interesting that the results of surveys were remarkably similar in terms of experiences of insecurity, sexual harassment, and feelings of exclusion. The issue of street lighting was an important factor in how safe girls feel (they usually avoided unlit streets at night and areas where gangs congregated). Sometimes, the social use of public parks changes in a 24-hour day. Public transportation in all cities was a large concern for all the girls in the survey. Sexual harassment, groping and theft were common complaints, as was the general inaction of other passengers who witnessed such acts. Moreover, the girls felt that the

[12] http://hic-gs.org/articles.php?pid=3496.

[13] http://hic-gs.org/articles.php?pid=3496.

police were also unresponsive to their problems, untrustworthy or located too far away to respond in a timely manner. Girls stressed that toilets were scarce or poorly maintained, forcing them to use open spaces, putting them at risk of sexual harassment and assault. Lack of signage, poor drainage systems, and piles of garbage in the street also hindered their walking direct routes.

These young women had very clear ideas of what "their right to a city" or an ideal city should look like: access to emergency services, hospitals, health centres/clinics, including reproductive health services, good security in the area, many police stations, and female police officers. Next, public toilets, clean water, waste baskets at every street corner and access to basic services like electricity. Spaces for play and leisure, playground areas with flower gardens and trees, grass and benches were also considered important. Sidewalks for pedestrians (free of vendors and loiterers), zebra crossings, traffic lights, wide roads, and well maintained road infrastructure (so accidents could be avoided) were mentioned as well as clean markets and shopping areas (with reasonable prices for the poor) and transit routes and bus stations in their community. Housing with planned roads and proper lighting, schools nearby for all levels, as well as religious institutions (temples, mosques, churches) were considered important. Most people would agree to such a vision, but more important is the participation of all stakeholders in budgeting and deciding where particular facilities should be located.

In the end, it is the government that has the responsibility to make commuting on public transport safe for women (monitoring and policing systems, authorized stops, certifying drivers and buses). Campaigns should be launched to raise awareness about the prevalence of sexual harassment and encourage bystander interventions if any form of harassment is witnessed. In cities where it is not deemed appropriate for girls to be alone in public spaces, information campaigns should be developed to promote girls' freedom to move through the city unaccompanied. In other words, putting the perspective of girls/women at the centre of transforming cities to become places of inclusion, tolerance and opportunity for everyone. "By bringing city officials and adolescent girls together there is a real opportunity to create sustainable economic and social change within these societies that will benefit all citizens."[14]

This aligns well with Sustainable Development Goal No. 5 to achieve gender equality and empower all women and girls. Goal 5.2 is to "eliminate all forms of violence against women and girls in public and private spheres"…. Goal 5.3 is to "eliminate all harmful practices, such as child-, early and forced marriage and female genital mutilations". Goal 5.5 wants "to ensure women's full and effective participation and equal opportunities for leadership at all levels of decision-making in political, economic and public life" and 5.c to "adopt and strengthen sound policies and enforceable legislation for the promotion of gender equality and the empowerment of all women and girls at all levels".

[14] www.plan-international.org/girls/reports-and publications.

Goal 16 of the post-2015 Agenda is "to promote peaceful and inclusive societies for sustainable development, provide access for all and build effective, accountable and inclusive institutions at all levels." The first target is "significantly to reduce all forms of violence and related death rates everywhere." This target is measurable, as death statistics are available in each country. However, the killing of a woman or girl, because she is a woman is more difficult to determine. Violence is defined differently in each society; nonetheless measures to prevent violence against women can be put into place and their effectiveness measured. The second target is to end all forms of violence, torture and abuse of children, including exploitation and trafficking. Unfortunately, underage children are still exploited in the mining, agricultural and manufacturing businesses in many parts of the world. Others are trafficked and forced into prostitution, begging and stealing. Again, these horrendous practices can be estimated, measured and combated.

Other targets of Goal 16 "to promote the rule of law. . .significantly reduce illicit financial and arms flows. . . combat all forms of organized crime. . . .substantially reduce corruption and bribery. . . .develop effective, accountable and transparent institutions at all levels. . .ensure responsive inclusive, participatory and representative decision-making at all levels. . . .and to ensure public access to information and protect fundamental freedoms" are more difficult to measure. In fact, no target dates are mentioned for the post-2015 Agenda.

On the other hand, indicators for the first two targets—reducing violence against women and abuse of children—have been well developed by numerous reputable institutions. Recent media accounts have described the horrible sexual attacks on women on public transport in India (India present reports), the murder of women by narco-gangs just to show that they controlled a specific area of the city (UNODC), the use of women as drug couriers, and the violence against injecting drug users, lesbians (South Africa—Corrective Rape), and "transgender" persons or just demonstrating that men have power of superiority over women (Vasant 2015, p. 126ff).

11 What Does an Ideal City Look Like?

The most commonly recurring elements taken from a women's survey carried out in Cairo, Delhi, Hanoi, Kampala, and Lima are:

1. Emergency Services: hospitals, health centres and clinics, security in the area; many police stations, female police officers;
2. Basic Services; public toilets, clean water made available through public taps, water tanks;
3. Spaces for Play and Leisure; clean parks with trees, flower gardens, playgrounds;
4. Grass, Benches, Cultural Spaces; libraries, movie theatres, bookstores, swimming pools;

5. Road Infrastructure-traffic lights, uncluttered sidewalks, zebra crossings, flyovers;
6. Markets and Shopping areas; reasonable prices for poor people; big malls;
7. Schools; a school system for all levels in their area;
8. Transit Routes—bus stations in their communities;
9. Cleanliness—clean public areas, parks, streets; waste baskets at every corner;
10. Housing: organized with planned roads, proper lighting; green areas;
11. Religious Institutions; temples, mosques, and churches (UN-Habitat 2014).

In addition to the necessary infrastructure and services to be provided, significant attitudinal and behavioural changes are needed on the part of men and boys. Boys must be sensitized in schools, police and first responders given special sensitization training, and the general public in media campaigns and strong messages by political, religious, and cultural leaders must be told clearly that certain types of behaviour is not to be tolerated and that men should always be respectful of women and girls.

In November 2014, an open-ended Intergovernmental Expert Group on Gender Related Killing of Women and Girls took place in Bangkok organized by the UN Office of Drugs and Crime. The group underlined, as part of a broader effort to create a culture of lawfulness, the importance of preventive policies and pro-active measures, which are regularly monitored. It was recommended to review, evaluate and update relevant criminal and civil laws in order to ensure that all forms of violence against women are penalized. It was recognized that investigations and prosecutions are hampered by factors such as negative gender stereotypes, secondary victimization, corruption, impunity and a lack of confidence in the criminal justice system. The meeting recognized the right of victims to be treated with dignity, especially elderly women, indigenous women, foreign women, immigrant women in irregular situations, women with disabilities, and women victims of human trafficking. Girls are to be treated in line with the Convention on the Rights of the Child in a child-sensitive manner. The welfare of "street children" or youth in conflict with the law must be considered foremost in any juvenile justice proceeding. Runaways, girls without parental supervision, underage females living on their own in precarious situations are particularly vulnerable to sexual exploitation, drugs, and gangs. Special programmes need to be established for girls living on the streets (Report of the Secretary-General during the 24th Session of the Commission on Crime Prevention and Criminal Justice on the Outcome of the Open-Ended Intergovernmental Expert Group on Gender Related Killing of Women and Girls, Platzer and Fillip 2015).

12 UN Secretary-General's Report

In 2006, the UN Secretary-General issued a study "Ending violence against women: From words to action" (United Nations 2006)[15] in which the various manifestations of femicide, the murder of women because they are women, are described: intimate partner violence, stalking and stranger violence, targeting women in war, but also crimes committed in the name of honour, acid attacks, and dowry disputes. The latter illustrate the interrelationship between cultural norms and the use of violence in the subordination of women. Some of these acts of violence have a collective dimension with family or the community wishing to control women's choices not only in the area of sexuality but also other aspects of behaviour, such as freedom of movement. In other cultural contexts, female sexuality is promoted in the media, advertising, and social pressure.

Femicide occurs everywhere, but the scale of the murder of women within a community context—for example in Ciudad Juarez, Mexico, and India—has drawn attention to this growing phenomenon. Although the media has highlighted these killings, the data on the domestic disputes and deaths (crimes of passion or jealousy, dowry murders, honour killings, foeticide, neglect of infant girls) are underreported. Other crimes committed in times of war, gang wars, violence against certain ethnic minorities, migrant and undocumented women are "invisible", as these murders are either unreported or considered part of the general violence and not disaggregated. If one considers traditional harmful practices (genital mutilation), forced marriages, child marriages, and rape within marriages as extreme forms of violence which are illegal but accepted in many communities the number of unreported acts of violence increases substantially. Of course, "safe inclusive cities" should have programmes to prevent both the individual acts but also the structural violence, including sexual and economic exploitation. In addition to shelters and protection schemes, the municipal judicial and police authorities must actively investigate and prosecute domestic cases as well as combat patterns of violence.

The Human Rights Council has appointed a Special Rapporteur Rashida Manjoo on violence against women, its causes and consequences. The Rapporteur submits both country reports as well as thematic reports. In 2012 Ms Manjoo addressed the topic of gender-related killings of women whether they occur in the family or community or are perpetrated or condoned by the State (A/HRC/20/16). In addition to focusing on the above-mentioned forms of femicide, she described the killings of women due to accusations of sorcery/witchcraft, the killings of aboriginal/indigenous people and killings as a result of sexual orientation and gender identity. The Rapporteur listed the human rights treaties that place a duty on States to prevent, punish and provide compensation for all acts of violence.

The Commission on the Status of Women (2013) urged countries to strengthen national legislation to punish violent gender related killings of women and girls and

[15] http://www.un.org/womenwatch/daw/public/VAWStudy/VAWstudyE.pdf.

integrate specific mechanisms or policies to prevent, investigate, and eradicate such deplorable forms of gender based violence (E/CN.6/2013/L.5). It also recommended the establishment of comprehensive, co-ordinated, inter-disciplinary, accessible and sustained multisectoral services for all victims and survivors of violence (health care services, 24 hour hotlines, social aid services, one stop crisis centres, child services, public housing). The Commission emphasized that ending violence against women must be a priority in the post-2015 development agenda.

In December 2013, the General Assembly adopted a resolution "Taking Action Against Gender related killing of women and girls" initiated by the UN Commission on Crime Prevention and Criminal Justice, stressing that States have the obligation to prevent and investigate acts of violence against women and girls, punish perpetrators, eliminate impunity and provide protection to the victims. It urged Member States to adopt preventive measures including enactment of legislation, strengthen the criminal justice response, end impunity by ensuring accountability, and address the problem of underreporting. It recommended reparation and compensation to the victims and their families in accordance with the Declaration of Basic Principles of Justice for Victims of Crime and Abuse of Power and to give due consideration to the Updated Model Strategies and Practical Measures on the Elimination of Violence Against Women in the Field of Crime Prevention and Criminal Justice. The General Assembly viewed with appreciation the considerable input of the many civil society organizations, as well as academia, in addressing the different forms of violence against women, through research and direct Action (A/RES/68/191).

In November 2012, the Academic Council on the United Nations System (ACUNS Vienna) organized a symposium on Femicide which called for the creation of a platform where advocates, judges, prosecutors, law enforcement officials, academics, feminists, non-governmental organizations, UN organizations, intergovernmental and national institutions, and other relevant actors could share their expertise and good practices, in order to transfer knowledge across regions. Since that symposium organized on the International Day for the Elimination of Violence Against Women, ACUNS has published three volumes of "Femicide: A global issue that demands action" (ACUNS 2013, 2014, 2015) and held numerous symposia, side events at UN meetings, and lectures to raise awareness to the issue. ACUNS has promoted both the Istanbul Convention on Preventing and Combating Violence Against Women and the Panama Protocol for the Investigation of Femicide. Special topics of concern have been female infanticide and gender based sex selective foeticide, killing of women in the name of honour, dowry related femicide, witchcraft, female genital mutilation, child marriages, violence against migrant women, organized-crime-related femicide and the targeted killing of women in war. ACUNS representatives have attended the General Assembly, sessions of the Human Rights Council, the Commission on the Status of Women, UN Congress on Crime Prevention and Treatment of Offenders and published relevant documents from these bodies as a resource handbook for diplomats and practitioners. ACUNS has republished the Secretary-General's report on conflict related sexual violence, Security Council resolutions and President's statements, and statements of UN Special Representative Margot Wallstrom, the High Commissioner for Human Rights, and the Special Representative on Sexual Violence in Conflict. Ms Zainab Hawa Bangura has thanked "the research institutions, individual scholars and practitioners who are members of the Academic Council on the United Nations System for their dedication. The insights of scholars are invaluable to our continued efforts".

Mrs. Ban Soon-Taek has stated in an ACUNS sponsored High Level event "Every woman and girl has the fundamental right to live free from violence. Yet violence against women is one of the world's most pervasive human rights violations. Wherever this violence happens, it is unacceptable and should shock us all."

13 Conclusion

It is a good time to advance the cause of women to live safely in large cities. City planners have long promoted the "Right to the City"; more and more cities are declaring themselves "Safe Cities" and "Human Rights Cities". Cities are implementing better services and providing safe spaces for women and children. Feminist movements in developing countries are demanding such services, safe transport, more women in the police force—which are now supported by large numbers of the populace. Finally, huge demonstrations now take place when women are gang-raped in buses or public spaces. Impunity is no longer accepted and it is expected that perpetrators are brought to justice.

The United Nations is no longer timid about femicide, acid attacks, honour killings, traditional harmful practices, sexual harassment and other forms of violence previously considered acceptable among families. Starting with the Beijing Declaration, the Secretary-General has issued strong statements against violence against women. Within UN agencies such as UNICEF, HABITAT, UNFPA, UN Women, UNDP and UNODC active programs to change laws, train police and judiciary and assist women and girls directly have been established.

Governments and civil society are now ready to honestly deal with the problems women and girls are facing in the city and to make the "Right to the City" a real thing. It is wonderful to see that girls are participating in the transformation of urban spaces to suit their own needs.

Five Questions

1. Why do young women come to the city?
2. How can they help to design better cities?
3. What are the special dangers they face in cities?
4. What are the international initiatives (or in your community) to empower women and girls?
5. How can discriminatory cultural practices and male attitudes against women be changed?

References

A/68/970 Report of the Open Working Group of the General Assembly on Sustainable Development Goals, 12 August 2014.

Brown, A., & Kristiansen, A. (2009). *Urban policies and the right to the city: Rights, responsibilities and citizenship*. MOST-2 Policy Papers Series UNESCO-UN-HABITAT, Paris.

Buckingham, S. (2010). Examining the right to the city from a gender perspective. In A. Sugranes & C. Mathivet (Eds.), *Cities for all. Proposals and experiences towards the right to the city* (pp. 57–63). Habitat International Coalition (HIC).

Council of Europe. (2011). *Living together. Combining diversity and freedom in 21st-century Europe*. Report of the Group of Eminent Persons of the Council of Europe.

Girma, W., & Erulkar, A. (2009). *Commercial sex workers in five Ethiopian cities: A baseline survey for USAID targeted HIV prevention program for most-at-risk populations*. Addis Ababa: Population Council.

Harvey, D. (2003). The right to the city. *International Journal of Urban and Regional Research, 27*(4), 939–941.

ILO. (2004). *Girl child labour in agriculture, domestic work and sexual exploitation: Rapid assessments on the cases of the Philippines, Ghana and Ecuador* (Girl child labour studies, Vol. 1). ISBN 92-2-115291-X.

Lefebvre, H. ("The Right to the City" in Writings on Cities, Oxford, Blackwell, 1996. Originally published as Le droit à la ville, Paris, Anthropos, 1968).

Loaiza, E. (2014). Child marriage: A violation of human rights & deterrent to development. In M. Platzer & S. Domazeposka (Eds.), *Femicide. A global issue that demands action*. Vienna: ACUNS.

Park, R., & Burgess, E. W. (1925). *Introduction to the science of sociology*. Chicago: University of Chicago Press (3rd revised edition, 1969). ISBN 0-226-64604-1.

Park, R., Miller, H. A., & Thompson, K. (1921). *Old world traits transplanted: The early sociology of culture*. New York: Harper & Brothers.

Platzer, M., & Domazeposka, S. (2014). *Femicide. A global issue that demands action* (Vol. 2). ACUNS.

Platzer, M., & Fillip, A. (2015). *Femicide. A global issue that demands action* (Vol. 3). Vienna: ACUNS.

Platzer, M., Laurent, C., & Idomir, M. (2013). *Femicide. A global issue that demands action*. Vienna: ACUNS.

Shaw, C. R., & McKay, H. D. (1942). *Juvenile delinquency in urban areas*. Chicago: University of Chicago Press.

Temin, M., Montgomery, M. R., Engebretsen, S., & Barker, K. M. (2013). *Girls on the move: Adolescent girls & migration in the developing world*. The Population Council.

UNDESA. (2006). *Compendium of recommendations on international migration and development*. United Nations. Department of Economic and Social Affairs, Population Division.

UNDESA. (2007). Final Report of Expert Group Meeting "Creating an inclusive society: Practical strategies to promote social integration". Department of Economic and Social Affairs, Population Division.

UNDESA. (2008). *World Urbanization Prospects* (http://esa.un.org/unpd/wup/default.aspx).

UNDP. (2014). *Sustaining human progress: Reducing vulnerabilities and building resilience*. United Nations Development Programme, Human Development Report.

UNESCO/Habitat. (2010). *Creating better cities for migrants: Urban policies and practices to build more inclusive cities*.

UN-Habitat. (2013). *State of the world's cities 2010/2011 bridging the urban divide*. London, UK: Earthscan.

UN Habitat. (2014). Plan international. "Adolescent Girls" views on safety in cities. In M. Platzer & S. Domazeposka (Eds.), *Femicide: A global issue that demands action* (pp. 35–41).

UNODC. (2014). *Handbook on effective prosecution responses to violence against women and girls*. Asylum and the right to the city: Lessons from Turkey's Syrian guests and other urban refugees. http://www.rsc.ox.ac.uk/publications/civitas-polis-and-urbs-reimagining-the-refugee-camp-as-the-city.

Vasant, K. (2015). "He said I needed to stop being a lesbian". The unpunished crime of corrective rape in South Africa. In M. Platzer & A. Fillip (Eds.), *Femicide, A global issue that demands action* (Vol. 3). Vienna: ACUNS.

Women as Actors in Community Safety: Taking Action Worldwide

Margaret Shaw

Abstract It has been customary to refer to women's involvement in the criminal justice system and in the field of crime prevention as either victims or offenders, or sometimes as professionals. It is much less common to think of the role which women—and girls—themselves play in actively promoting safer cities or preventing the violence and crime which affects them because of their gender. This chapter looks at the growth of women's participatory approaches in crime prevention, and how they are helping to increase the role of women and girls in decision-making, especially at the local level. It tracks the expansion of participatory approaches globally, and the importance of this movement in helping to change policies, attitudes and behaviours towards women and girls in both public and private spaces. Some examples of current or recent comparative projects illustrate the expansion of what is now a global movement. The final section of the chapter reflects on the ways in which the Doha Declaration of the Thirteenth United Nations Congress on Crime Prevention and Criminal Justice (Doha, Quatar, 12–19 April 2015) aims to strengthen and support this work.

1 Introduction

In 2015 UN Women published a report setting out a new policy agenda for the post 2015 development era, aiming to "transform economies and make women's rights a reality". The report, *Progress of the World's Women 2015–2016: Transforming Economies, Realizing Rights* (UN Women 2015), focuses on increasing women's social and economic rights, and establishes ten priorities for action. These include creating more and better jobs for women, reducing occupational separation and pay gaps, and strengthening their income security throughout their lives. Yet for women in many countries around the world, their ability to travel to and from work on a daily basis and to participate fully in city life without fear for their safety and

M. Shaw (✉)
Crime and Social Policy Consulting, Montreal, QC, Canada
e-mail: mjshaw9@gmail.com

H. Kury et al. (eds.), *Women and Children as Victims and Offenders: Background, Prevention, Reintegration*, DOI 10.1007/978-3-319-28424-8_26

security is severely limited. It often places them at personal risk of harassment and violence, because of their gender. As an earlier report has stressed (UN Women 2013), for women to achieve gender equality, realize their full human rights and be empowered to take part in decisions and policy making, they need to have freedom from violence.

Over the past 30 years, as this book underlines, violence against women (VAW) has become widely recognized as a public policy issue, and considerable strides have been made, especially in relation to intimate partner violence (ICPC 2014a). The violence which women experience in their homes at the hands of intimate partners or family members is now widely seen as a breach of criminal law. It is no longer considered a minor or private social issue, and women in many countries are now more willing to report such violence. While homicide rates for men are much higher than for women, the majority of female homicides are at the hands of intimate male partners, or less often, close relatives (Racovita 2015; UNODC 2014a; Shaw 2013).

At the international level, the United Nations Office on Drugs and Crime (UNODC) among other UN bodies has been instrumental in promoting norms and standards, helping countries to eliminate violence against women, to develop legislative frameworks, improve justice system responses, and to provide services such as shelters for victims (UNODC 2014b). There is now far more data and information about the incidence and patterns of violence against women globally, and on the attitudes of men to the use of such violence (PAHO 2012; FRA 2014; Barker et al. 2011; Manjoo 2012; Fulu et al. 2013). In over 90 countries victimization surveys on VAW have been undertaken at the national level, or in regions or cities, although the majority have focused on intimate personal violence (IPV) rather than non-intimate sexual violence (Johnson 2013). There is guidance on how countries can develop appropriate and disaggregated statistical data on VAW (UNSD 2013). In terms of knowledge, as Barberet (2014, p. 91) has put it "since the 1980's there has been an explosion of research on violence against women."

Yet as suggested above, much of the focus has been on intimate personal violence which occurs in private settings, especially the home (see Box 1 for definitions). Less well understood is the issue of women's safety in public spaces, a phenomenon for which women themselves have often been blamed as having "brought it on themselves". In the 1980s and 1990s governments tended to put the burden of responsibility to avoid the risk of violence on women themselves, in terms of how they dressed, where they went, and at what hours (Stanko 1996). The disappearance of women and girls from public places has also been ignored or downplayed, especially those who are poor and disadvantaged as in the case of indigenous women in Canada, or migrant women in Cuidad Juarez, Mexico or in Guatemala (NWAC 2010; RCMP 2014; Shaw et al. 2013; Beltran and Freeman 2007; Racovita 2015).[1]

[1] Between 1980 and 2012 a total of 1017 Aboriginal women were murdered, and 164 reported missing in Canada—figures well over representative of the population of Aboriginal women in the country.

Again it is women who disproportionately experience sexual violence in public spaces because of their gender, ranging from sexual harassment and stalking to rape, as well as during war and conflict (UNGA 2012). Some specific and horrific instances of rape and sexual assault in public spaces do receive attention and lead to some action. This has been the case of the young woman raped on a bus in Delhi in December 2012 (Natarajan 2013), or some cases of sexual assault on university campuses. But the prevention of violence against women in public spaces is less often seen as a public responsibility or necessity than in the case of IPV. The importance of taking account of the differences between men and women's experiences of living in the city tends to be unexamined or ignored.

This chapter focuses on the growth of action around on women's safety in urban settings, and the role which women and girls, and local governments, have been playing in public awareness and policy development at the local level, especially through the use of participatory approaches. It highlights the role of women as actors in promoting their own safety, rather than as victims.

2 Women Experiencing the City

However we dress, wherever we go, Yes means Yes and No means No![2]

How are the experiences of men and women in public urban settings different? It has long been known that women express more insecurity and fear of crime than men, but they also experience different behaviours. Far from being "irrational" as many early explanations of the high fear levels of women suggested, they are based on their day-to-day experiences as women. Numerous studies have shown that women experience sexual harassment of various kinds from men in public settings. In India, sexual harassment, known as "eve teasing", is a very common experience for women and girls. In a recent four country study 80 % of women interviewed in Delhi reported sexual harassment in the daytime, 50 % in Petrozavodsk, Russia, 40 % in Dar el Salaam, Tanzania, and 35 % in Rosario, Argentina (Viswanath 2013). The same study also found that women voluntarily restrict their daily routines and travel outside the home.

Public infrastructure is often not adapted to the needs of women. In Mumbai, for example, it was found that the main train station had 24 men's urinals but only two toilets for women (Padke 2010). Access to water and sanitation is a major issue in low income communities in some countries, where households do not have private toilets, and where it is women and girls who have to fetch water, wash clothing, or dispose of rubbish. In so doing they put themselves at risk of harassment and violence on a daily, and nightly, basis (WICI and Jagori 2011). In many counties, women tend to use public transport more than men, yet experience more insecurity

[2] One of the chants used by women during "Take Back the Night" marches in the 1970s.

and sexual harassment (Whitzman 2013). In New York, for example, a survey of 2000 subway users found that two-thirds of women reported past experience of sexual harassment (Loukaitou-Sideris et al. 2008).

The daily lives of women are, therefore, often constrained by lack of access to safe transport, or by cultural norms which restrict their ability to travel freely. They may limit their travel outside the house after dark for safety reasons. Their routines often differ from those of men. They have greater responsibility for child care and household tasks, and less access to private transport. In the case of poor women and migrant women, they often have to work at unsocial hours and travel long distances to access poorly paid work (Ortiz Escalante and Sweet 2013). In observing women in public spaces in Mumbai, one writer described women's behaviour as exhibiting a "tyranny of purpose" with women on their own:

> Carrying something, shopping, heading towards bus-stops or railway stations, but rarely, if ever, loitering around, sitting in a park or *maidan* [public square] or standing at a street corner smoking or simply watching the world go by as one is wont to see men doing. (Padke 2010, p. 5 quoted in Whitzman 2013, p. 41).

It is these gendered differences which have motivated many women to consider the possibilities of safer cities for women that do not rely on them alone to restrict their movements or change their habits.

3 Women Working with the City

Over the past 30 years or more, the movement to increase the safety of women in cities has spread across many regions of the world. Combining notions of the importance of participatory action and personal experience—women as experts on their own safety—with empowerment of citizens to take an active part in local decision-making—this movement has expanded to encompass a wide range of issues around safety and personal autonomy, and the rights of citizens, especially for women and girls in urban spaces. From the early 1970s when "Take back the night" marches began to be organized in European and North American cities, women's groups and academics and researchers began critiquing the inequalities women experienced in terms of their ability to take part in city life in the same ways as men, and their lack of voice in urban decisions.

In a number of Canadian cities in the 1980s, for example, inspired in part by calls to "take back the night", there was a growth of activity among local community organizations, academics and local governments to increase women's safety (Shaw and Andrews 2005). In Toronto in 1982, following a series of sexual assaults and murders of women, groups of women lobbied the city and local police, which led for the first time to the establishment of a task force on public violence against women. The report of the task force resulted in the creation of the multi-partner *Metropolitan Action Committee on Public Violence against Women and Children* (METRAC) in 1984, to implement the recommendations of the task force.[3] Among the innovative tools developed by METRAC, in collaboration with the Toronto Transit Commission, was what became known as women's "safety walks" or safety audits (METRAC 1992; Whitzman 2013).

Essentially drawing on theories of situational crime prevention, the safety audit tool involves groups of women walking systematically around their local communities, and in parks and public spaces, at different times of the day or night, using a checklist. They identify areas where they feel unsafe. This might be because they cannot see well in the absence of good lighting at night, because of the presence of blind corners, of trees and other vegetation obscuring good visibility, or the absence of signs etc. The second step involves developing a series of recommendations which are then discussed with local governments, asking for action. In a number of cases local city administrators or personnel will be invited to take part in the walk. Thus the safety audit is both an analytical tool for gathering information and data, *and* a tool for empowering women.

The use of safety audits led to a number of changes in the administration and design of urban infrastructure in Toronto, such as the establishment of designated waiting areas and requests stops for women on the transport system at night, better lighting in parking garages, and improvements to safety in public housing areas, and assault prevention campaigns on university campuses. In 1991 the city published *Take Back Toronto: A Guide to Preventing Violence Against Women in Your Community* (Gilmore 1991), and in 1997 a handbook *Toronto Safer City Guidelines* (Whitzman and Wekerle 1997).

In part inspired by Toronto and METRAC's work, women in a number of other Canadian cities began to demand similar action from city administrators, and municipal departments concerned with women's safety were established. The city of Montreal, for example, established the *Women in the City* programme in 1990, following requests from local women's groups. From 1992 they worked in partnership with community groups and others in a cross-sector committee set up to ensure full community participation and consultation, the *Comité action femmes et sécurité urbaine* (CAFSU). A number of initiatives promoting women's safety in the city were set up, tailored to local needs and concerns. These ranged from forums for public discussion; community-city-transport consultations on changes to the urban landscape around Metro stations; a *Between Two Stops* initiative enabling women to get off city buses between stops at night, in order to be closer to their homes; and training programmes and tools such as a toolkit on *Women's Safety: From Independence to Autonomy* published in 2001 (FCM and City of Montreal 2004).

Other Canadian cities such as Ottawa, Edmonton and Cowichan Valley in British Columbia, established comparable initiatives, while the Federation of Canadian Municipalities, and the National Crime Prevention Centre provided support at the federal level. In all cases the focus was on participatory approaches which listened to women's concerns, and collaborative partnerships between municipal administrators, services, women's groups and local communities.

[3] This section draws from METRAC's website www.metrac.org.

Interest in women's safety was growing in a number of countries, and since that time many organizations and cites have developed initiatives promoting the safety of women in cities, often at the instigation of women's groups, and using participatory tools such as the women's safety audit. Thus in addition to advocating for change, or establishing community-based services to respond to unmet needs, as is often the case when NGOs are concerned about social issues, the movement to improve women's safety recognized the necessity of working *with* cities to effect change, and empowering women to take an active part in shaping solutions.

The movement has become a global one in which international conferences, networking and research have all played an important part. It has also been interdisciplinary, combining theories and concepts in which gender is a key construct, and drawing from the disciplines of criminology and crime prevention, political science and governance, urban planning and design, and social change and community development.

4 The Development of an International Movement

> Making progress in confronting these complex realities [violence against women in cities] means analysis and proposals that are more comprehensive and innovative, negotiation mechanisms, collaboration and solidarity. It also implies conceptual and theoretical developments, as well as learning from concrete experiences. (Falu (2008) in Falu and Segovia (Ed.), p. 9–10).

In 2002, the first international conference on women's safety "Making the Links" took place in Montreal, Canada, and brought together a wide range of participants from 33 countries, including 55 cities and municipalities, and produced a manifesto setting out its conclusions. The conference also led to the creation of the NGO *Women in Cities International* (WICI), based in Montreal.[4] It was founded by a group of city practitioners and academics to act as an international network and undertake action research on women's safety. When WICI organized the first Women's Safety Awards in 2004 it received 96 applications from 28 countries again illustrating the extent of interest and activity (WICI 2004).

In the United Kingdom, for example, the Women's Design Service, founded in 1987 to ensure that the build environment met the needs of women, began developing a number of projects in different communities using safety audits from 2002 onwards.[5] In Sweden, the planning department of the City of Goteborg developed a handbook on Safer Cities (Goteborg 2002), which focused on women's access to city spaces. A large number of initiatives have been developed in Latin America.

---

[4] The Montreal Manifesto and other WICI publications can be accessed at www.femmesetvilles.org.

[5] See the website www.wds.org.uk The London-based Women's Design Service was wound up in 2012.

They included the extensive work initiated by a group of non-government organizations, notably the Red Mujer y HABITAT de America Latina (Women and HABITAT Network of Latin America), the Centre for Exchange and Services of the Southern Cone Argentina (CISCA), and the Centre for Peruvian Women Flora Tristan in Peru. Apart from developing women's safety initiatives with cities in their countries of location, these organizations all played a major role in the UNIFEM[6] Regional Programme on *Cities Without Violence against Women, Safe Cities for All* in the 2000s (Falu and Segovia 2008).

At the international level, organizations such as the HUAIROU Commission which coordinates networks of grassroots women's organizations, and United Cities and Local Governments have campaigned for women's participation in local governance, and UNIFEM and UN HABITAT among others both played a significant role in promoting women's safety at the local level and promoting participatory processes and partnerships with women on the ground. UNIFEM's Regional Programme was initiated in 2006 and built on the experiences of an earlier women's safety project in 2004 in Argentina and Peru. The Programme was implemented in the cities of Rosario, Argentina, Santiago, Chile, Bogota, Colombia, and Recife, Brazil, engaging local governments, non-government and community based organizations (Falu and Segovia 2008; Falu 2010; Vargas 2007). Cities in Guatemala and El Salvador joined the Programme in 2008.

UN HABITAT's Safer Cities Programme, established in 1996 at the request of a number of African mayors, recognized the significance of safety issues for women in urban settings from the start. Having initiated a number of victimization surveys in African cities, and with a major focus on inclusion and vulnerable urban populations, they funded a number of programmes to improve women's safety in public settings and strengthen their role in urban governance (UN-HABITAT 2001). This includes projects in Dar el Salaam, Tanzania, for example, where women's safety audits were used as one tool to assess women's safety in markets, streets and other public settings, resulting in a number of changes to the urban environment by the city. They have also funded reviews and evaluations of the use of women's safety audits across different regions (WICI et al. 2008a, b).

Inevitably, when action research is funded by governments or organizations, one of the challenges is to be able to establish that real changes have taken place as a result of interventions. One early assessment the use of the women's safety audit methodology, as a tool for both analysis and empowerment, concluded:

> Through this study of six women's safety audit initiatives in three continents, we have shown that this tool can be effective in validating local women's experiences, developing partnerships with local governments and other key urban decision-makers, creating the impetus for spill-over effects such as women's employment programmes, or training for architects and planners, and making small but concrete improvements to places. The question of whether these improved built, social, and policy environments have, in turn, led to behavioural changes amongst women and other vulnerable groups, still remains

[6] UNIFEM (UN Development Fund for Women) was one of the four predecessor entities, which became UN WOMEN in 2010.

under researched. Women's safety audits can thus be conceptualized as a promising tool not only in reducing violence and insecurity in public space, but as a mechanism for increased gender equality in urban planning, design, and governance. (Whitzman et al. 2009).

In 2004 the second international conference on safer cities for women took place in Bogota, Colombia, with representatives from civil society, academics, urban planners, NGOs, police forces, national and municipal governments and international women's networks, as well as UN-HABITAT, the United Nations Development Programme, and UNIFEM.

By 2010, the third international conference held in Delhi, India included some 240 participants from 40 countries, primarily from the global South. The Delhi conference highlighted the urgency of the situation for women and girls in terms of the impacts of globalization. The majority of the world's population is now urban, and cities are growing at an exponential rate. In addition to urbanization, some of it affected by climate change, environmental disasters and conflict, there is increasing movement of people across borders, as well as human trafficking and smuggling (ICPC 2014b).[7] The proportion of women and girls in migrant and refugee populations has been increasing markedly in recent years while women and girls are also the primary targets of trafficking for the purposes of sexual exploitation (UNODC 2012; ICPC 2014b).

In the case of each international conference on women's safety a consortium of non-government organizations, municipalities, national governments and international organizations have provided support and resources, illustrating the cross-sector and collaborative nature of turning advocacy and research into concrete action and policy change.

5 Developing Methodologies and Comparing Experiences Between Cities and Countries

One of the important contributions of action research is its flexibility and ability to adapt to local social, cultural and economic circumstances, as well as the possibilities for sharing information and learning from the experiences of others (Whitzman 2008). This was evident from the UNIFEM Regional Programme in Latin America, as well as those developed by WICI, for example.

A three year project, coordinated by WICI and funded by Status of Women Canada from 2007 to 2010, worked with women's groups in four different Canadian cities, in each case focusing on women who in various ways were marginalized

[7] ICPC's *4th International Report on Crime Prevention and Community Safety* was launched in November 2014 in Palermo, Sicily. This edition focuses on the movement of people—especially migration, human trafficking and indigenous populations migrating to urban areas—and the impacts on those individuals, including women and girls, and receiving communities and on local governments. The report can be found at www.cipc-icpc.org.

or vulnerable. They included Aboriginal women in Regina, Saskatchewan, disabled women in Montreal, elderly women in Gatineau, and women from immigrant and visible minority backgrounds in Peel, Ontario (WICI 2010). In addition to initial training on the methodology and use of safety audits for the four women's organizations implementing the projects on the ground, representatives from each site met together on several occasions to exchange experiences and discuss the challenges they faced in implementing the project: how they had created partnerships across the city, how they accessed media support, who they talked to among city administrators and services, and some of the innovative ways they had adapted the safety audit to their environment and concerns. At the end of the project it was concluded that:

> The diverse makeup of each of the groups, and between the groups, is the real richness of this project. Differences among participants' first languages, ages, ethnic identities, places of residence, and abilities provided the basis for unique and touching stories of ideas and experiences of women's safety in Canada. Most of the women had never before taken part in activities linked to women's safety. The awareness that similar work was being done simultaneously in four cities across Canada helped to validate the experiences of each and gave them courage and drive to confront challenges head on. Safety concerns facing each of the groups and in each of the cities were extremely diverse, but underlying all of them was the drive to make their city safer for the women and girls who live there, and the rest of the community. (WICI 2010, p. 53).

The experiences drawn from that project were in turn valuable in the development of an international comparative action project, the *Gender Inclusive Cities Project* (GICP). Funded by the UN Trust Fund from 2009 to 2011, this three-year project involved non-government women's organizations in the four cities of Dar el Salaam, Tanzania, Delhi, India, Rosario, Argentina, and Petrozavodsk in Russia (Viswanath 2013). The local organizations had all had some, although varying, experience of working on women's safety issues. The NGO Jagori in Delhi, a feminist organization established in 1984, for example, has a long history of working on issues of justice for women, and had developed the *Safe Delhi Campaign* which undertook to a series of safety audits in 17 different areas in Delhi, essentially mapping the city from the perspective of women and girls (Jagori 2007). They had established a good partnership with the police and transport authority to educate and train staff on women's safety issues, undertaken public awareness campaigns and worked with young men and women on gender issues in public space.

One of the "defining features" of the GICP project, illustrating the evolution of work on women's safety, was the range of research tools used (WICI 2012; Viswanath 2013).[8] In each city, both qualitative and quantitative methodologies were used to provide base-line information on local and national policies affecting women's safety issues, including legislation and regulations, city plans, budgets and services. Key stakeholders were identified and interviewed, and information on

[8] A number of publications report the outcomes of the GICP and be accessed at www.femmeseetvilles.org.

women's safety experiences and concerns collected through street surveys and women's safety audits in a variety of public sites commonly used by women in their daily lives. A series of focus groups was also conducted. An external evaluator worked with the project from the beginning to establish outcome indicators and enable comparison of the baseline findings, and output and outcome results across cities.

Not surprisingly, the outcomes varied across the cities, reflecting cultural differences among other factors. Women in Petrozavodsk, for example, were more reticent than those in other cities in talking about their personal concerns, and while they were able to create partnerships with the police and municipality, the implementation of recommendations proved to be less easy than elsewhere.

As Viswanath (2013), p. 80) concludes in summing up the outcomes of the GICP:

> Early work on creating safer cities was largely focused on developed nations (the United Kingdom, Canada, Australia), and the emphasis was largely on physical design and urban planning. . .The GICP recognizes that the growth of cities, especially in the developing world, is a story of the marginalization of the poor and vulnerable. . .Thus the range of issues that came to the forefront included poverty, drugs, lack of faith in the police and deep-seated patriarchal attitudes as playing a role in creating unsafe and exclusive cities.

6 Marginalized Groups and New Challenges

In a separate action research project, also undertaken in Delhi, the focus was on access to essential services, in this case public toilets and community water taps (WICI and Jagori 2010; Jagori 2010). The project focused on residents in two poor relocation or resettlement communities, many of them slum dwellers who had been evicted or relocated for the purposes of urban upgrading and development (Menon-Sen and Bhan 2007). Funded by the International Development Research Centre in Canada, the project used safety audits to enable women and girls to map their concerns around safety. Many of their concerns about safety and sexual harrassment were associated with accessing community toilets, water standpipes and sewage disposal. In the resettlement communities, houses were built without running water or toilets in favour of shared community facilities (Khosla and Djar 2013). Access to community toilet complexes was limited at certain times of the day and they were closed at night, they were very poorly maintained, yet users had to pay a fee for their use, as well as for bathing and washing clothes. As a consequence many women and girls used open areas of public land, and often at night.

Access to water was similarly very limited, and it was often the role of women and girls to queue at taps for several hours each day or to transport water from work places. In all cases women and girls said they were very vulnerable to sexual harassment and abuse. One innovative aspect of the project was a gender responsive budget study to measure the opportunity costs of the time spent by women accessing water in terms of lost wages, as well as the opportunity costs of the sanitation and water policies of the city in relation to resettlement communities. This gave them additional tools in their approach to local government.

7 A Broader Understanding of the Gendered Nature of Safety

7.1 Safer and Inclusive Cities for Women and Men and the Right to the City

The arguments for changing cities and public spaces to create safer places for women and girls have always stressed that those places are also going to be safer for everyone. What is evident is the evolution from the 1970s and 1980s from talking about the concept of women's safety in public space, to the more ambitious notion of safer cities for women and all citizens (Falu 2010). There is now an emphasis not only on how the urban infrastructure can be changed to improve safety, but also how laws, regulations and policies governing city life can help to promote greater safety for women, and the important of public education and awareness of the issues.

It is now more widely accepted that men and boys must also be part of the solution, so that many initiatives now specifically engage with men and boys to raise awareness of the gendered nature of safety, and help promote safer cities (Barker 2005; Barker et al. 2007; EMERGE 2015). Attention has also turned more recently to the plight of young women and girls, rather than focusing on adult women alone. In turn the concept of safety has expanded from concerns about being safe from sexual harassment or assault in public spaces, to being empowered to move about freely and access the city as a right.

One of the outcomes of the Delhi international conference on women's safety in 2010 was the publication of a book on the range of themes which have emerged as the women's safety movement has gained momentum. *Building Inclusive Cities, Women's Safety and the Right to the City* (Whitzman et al. 2013) assesses the progress which has been made, as well as the new challenges emerging for women and girls in cities. It looks at such issues of safety on public transport, migrant women, issues of the intersection between gender, race, class and poverty, the use of partnerships, at emerging tools such as social media and cultural and artistic interventions for public awareness, advocacy and empowerment, and at the evaluation of action research in women's safety.

The concept of women's safety now includes not just freedom from fear and violence, and exclusion from decision-making, but freedom from poverty, and financial and housing insecurity. It is also closely linked to the concept of the "right to the city", the freedom to enjoy the benefits of living in a city with access to transport, work, leisure and education (Brown and Kristiansen 2009). The concept of the right to the city is discussed in more detail in this volume by Platzer.

Currently, at the international level, the broader vision of safe cities for women is well illustrated in UN Women's flagship programme the *Global Programme on Safe Cities Free of Violence Against Women and Girls.* The programme was launched in Delhi in 2010 at the women's safety conference. It grew out of, and expands on, the work of UNIFEM and Red Mujer y HABITAT in Latin America, and draws from the experience and lessons of UN HABITAT's Safer Cities Programme on the use of women's safety audits in cities, and the *Gender Inclusive Cities Project* coordinated by WICI. The initial programme is working in local communities in five cities: Quito, Ecuador, Cairo, Egypt, New Delhi, India, Port Moresby, Papua New Guinea, and Kigali, Rwanda, undertaking baseline assessments and research and evaluation of policies to prevent sexual harassment and violence against women and girls. The project's *Impact Evaluation Strategy* is flexible using a "theory of change" model, and sensitive to the challenges of comparing cities and countries with very different experiences and capacities. Overall, the strategy aims to:

- measure the impact of the intervention model(s);
- assess which strategies have been successful and which have not;
- show how the results were achieved;
- assess the circumstances or conditions which helped determine their effectiveness.

A second UN WOMEN initiative, *Safe and Sustainable Cities for All,* is a joint programme launched in 2011 with UN-HABITAT and UNICEF. This programme is working in collaboration with the cities of Rio de Janeiro, Brazil; San José, Costa Rica; Tegucigalpa, Honduras; Nairobi, Kenya; Beirut, Lebanon; Marrakesh, Morocco; Manila, Philippines; and Dushanbe, Tajikistan.[9]

8 Promoting the Safety of Girls in Cities

A further evolution is the shift from a focus on violence against adult women in public space to include girls and young women (Plan International 2010). A number of recent projects illustrate this trend in addition to UN WOMEN's Global Programme. A three year project in Montreal, Canada, *My City, My Safety!* worked with young women using participatory tools to increase personal and public awareness of violence, and empower the participants (WICI 2013). Funded by Status of Women, Canada, the project was part of a federal "Blueprint" programme on "Engaging Youth: Preventing Violence Against Girls and Women". It involved young women aged 13–17 from three secondary schools in three different and diverse communities, and used a variety of tools and activities to engage young

[9] See http://www.unwomen.org/en/what-we-do/ending-violence-against-women/creating-safe-public-spaces#sthash.1H9Lx8UW.dpuf.

people, including workshops, theatre, safety walks, media and social networking, and facilitation and leadership training.

At the global level, the *Because I am a Girl Urban Programme* is a joint international project jointly organized by Plan International, WICI and UN-HABITAT. The overall aims of the programme are to increase the girls' safety and access to public places, increase their participation in urban development and governance, and to increase their autonomous mobility in the city. The initial phase involves the five cities of Cairo, Delhi, Hanoi, Kampala and Lima. In each case baseline studies using participatory tools have been undertaken to understand the issues faced by adolescent girls from different communities, as they move about the city (Plan International 2013, 2015). This has include mapping existing stakeholders, programmes and policies; key informant interviews to assess the safety issues affecting adolescent girls; social cartography exercises enabling both girls and boys to map their use of space and their ideal vision of their city; girls' assessments of the elements that make cities safe and inclusive; and a series of girls' safety walks. In each case girls, governments and community members have been involved in the assessments and consultations, and the results discussed at consultative meetings. A series of training curricula has been developed for adolescent girls, government stakeholders and transport authorities and staff.

9 The Importance of the Role of Civil Society in Engendering Crime Prevention

The action research projects discussed above illustrate the importance of what are variously referred to as community-based organizations, women's groups and grassroots organizations, in changing norms and advancing policy change. In all cases they have worked to engage with local authorities and services in shaping policies and initiatives.

A strong case has been made for the importance of civil society in promoting progressive policy change (Htun and Weldon 2012). Taking the example of feminist women's groups advocating for change in policies on violence against women, the authors examined national policies over four decades in 70 countries. They concluded that civil society pressure by women's organizations—what they term a "strong autonomous feminist movement"—has been more important in effecting changes in government policies and improving responses to VAW, than a number of other factors. They outweighed the contributions of such factors as the presence of women in government, left-leaning political parties, or levels of national wealth, which are more usually thought to be critical factors influencing public policy change.

Since the time of "take back the night" marches, pressure on governments to act to increase women's safety has often followed a tragic event such as the assault or murder of a women in a public setting. This was the case in India after the horrendous gang rape of the 23 year old young woman on a bus in Delhi in December 2012, who subsequently died from her injuries. Delhi has long been known as the rape capital of the country (Jagori 2007; Sen 2013). In that case a huge national and international public outcry resulted in the appointment by the government of the Verma Committee. It was chaired by former Chief Justice Verma, and given a month to make recommendations on changes to the much out-dated criminal law.[10] Parts of the Criminal Code dated back to the nineteenth century, exempted marital rape, and described verbal sexual assault as "an insult to a women's modesty". The committee received over 80,000 responses from the general public, women's groups, victims and lawyers. The report published on 23 January 2013 made some major recommendations on laws relating to rape, sexual harassment, trafficking, child sexual abuse, domestic workers, and medical examinations of victims, as well as police, electoral and educational reforms. The latter extends down to sexual education in schools. While not all of the recommendations were seen as going far enough and have neither so far been acted on by the government, the report was called "insightful and ground-breaking". It was hoped that it would have far-reaching repercussions in changing the debate and attitudes towards violence against women in India.[11] This had not stopped the continuing sexual violence against women and girls in cities or in rural areas in India, but they appear to receive far greater attention in the media than in the recent past.

As has been noted, and underlined by Michael Platzer in his chapter, the movement, which resulted in the development of the *World Charter on the Right to the City* was itself initiated by grassroots organizations, not by governments (Brown and Kristiansen 2009). In the case of the women's safety movement, therefore, it would seem that women's groups have often been the catalysts for change in persuading local governments to establish committees and forums, and engage in multi-sector partnerships with civil society and non-government organizations to promote women's safety.

There comes a point, as Michael Platzer's chapter well underlines, when the actions of national and regional governments take on a momentum which results in changes to international norms and standards. This was also evident in the study by Htun and Weldon (2012). They found that when international agreements and declarations begin to incorporate policy changes relating to VAW, then the influence of civil society groups declined relatively. Once there is movement at the government and international level, they argue, the catalytic role of civil society groups becomes less evident.

[10] *Report of the Committee on Amendments to Criminal Law*, Justice J.S. Verma, Justice Leila Seth and Gopal Subramanium January 23 2013.

[11] Kalpana Kannabiran "A moment of triumph for women", *The Hindu*, January 25, 2013; Brinda Karat "Insightful and path-breaking", *The Hindu,* January 28, 2013, http://www.thehindu.com.

10 Conclusion: Policy Travels, International Norms and Doha and Beyond

The transfer or replication of crime prevention policy from one setting to another is always a complex process (Crawford 2009). Especially when policies travel across borders, there is a need for adaptation to specific country, city and neighbourhood situations. Many attempts to transplant prevention programmes to other settings have not been successful because of major social, cultural or economic differences, or political histories. Nor is policy change necessarily always a progressive process. Policies can be influenced by changes in government, where new incumbents choose new priorities, or seek to dissociate themselves with the initiatives of predecessor governments. Yet what has been interesting about the women's safety and the safe city movement, has been that many of the action research projects, while small in themselves in terms of their geographic coverage, or time-limited, have by nature been flexible and adaptable. They have provided tools enabling women's groups with relatively few resources to develop their expertise and successfully engage with urban governments.

Many cities in developing and developed countries have accepted that specifically promoting their cities as safe places for women and girls *is* part of their responsibility, and have invested in safety initiatives and continued to sustain them. As suggested at the beginning of this chapter, there are very strong cultural links between private and public violence against women, and this represents an important step towards eliminating such violence in urban life. At the international level, norms and standards focus more explicitly on the safety of women and girls than in the recent past. Yet there is no room for complacency, violence against women in public and in private spaces, still occurs on a daily basis, and it is evident that the role of civil society organizations is not over.

Development, globalization, and migration are all major factors which will continue to affect the lives of women and girls and men and boys in cities in quite different ways, and require the tailoring of policies, services and prevention programmes appropriately. As with many other issues, continuing improvements in data collection and in the monitoring and evaluation of those policy and programmes are essential for assessing their impacts, as are public awareness and increasing gender-mainstreaming and budgeting at the city level.

For UNODC, security and justice are fundamental components for the UN Post-2015 Sustainable Development Goals (UNODC 2013). The 1995 and 2002 ECOSOC guidelines on the prevention of crime and of urban crime both underline the role of local governments—and the responsibility of national governments to facilitate and support action at the local level. A report on 100 promising practices on safer cities released in 2014 marks some of the progress made in recent years (ICPC, EFUS and UN HABITAT 2014). Currently, proposed new UN guidelines on Safer Cities are being developed by UN HABITAT in consultation with UNODC and other entities and organizations. The aim is to develop international norms which complement the existing guidelines on crime prevention, with more detailed guidance on how cities can implant stronger policies and programmes to promote safety, including for women and girls, and boys and men.

The Doha Declaration of the Thirteenth United Nations Congress on Crime Prevention and Criminal Justice (Doha, Qatar, 12–19 April 2015) reinforces many of these trends. It has emphasized "the importance of promoting peaceful, corruption-free and inclusive societies for sustainable development, with a focus on a people-centred approach..." (A/CONF.222/L.6; UN 2015, para. 4). It commits to "mainstream a gender perspective into our criminal justice systems by developing and implementing national strategies and plans to promote the full protection of women and girls from all acts of violence, including gender-related killing of women and girls..." and in support of international obligations relating to the elimination of VAW (para. 5(f)). The Declaration also underlines its commitment "to consultative and participatory processes in crime prevention and criminal justice in order to engage all members of society, including those at risk of crime and victimization, to make our prevention efforts more effective and to galvanize public trust and confidence..." (para. 10).

Box 1 Defining Violence against Women, Intimate Partner Violence & Women's Safety

Article I of the "Declaration on the Elimination of Violence Against Women" defines VAW as follows:

'Violence against women means any act of gender-based violence that results in, or is likely to result in, physical, sexual or psychological harm or suffering to women, including threats of such acts, coercion or arbitrary deprivation of liberty, whether occurring in public or in private life.' (UNGA 1993).

Many terms have been used to describe VAW occurring in intimate relationships, including intimate personal violence, family violence, spousal violence, and most commonly, domestic violence. Domestic violence is still the preferred term in some countries, although the distinction between domestic and family violence, which includes victims of all ages and relationships to the perpetrator (i.e. partners, children, other family members and domestic workers) is not always clear. More recently, intimate personal violence, or IPV, has become the preferred term internationally. It refers to any behaviour that causes physical, psychological or sexual harm expressly within an intimate relationship (WHO and PAHO 2012). It may involve current or former spouses, partners or dating relationships. While the majority of IPV is perpetrated by men against women, it also includes violence by women against men and between same-sex partners.

Violence against women in public—non-intimate settings—includes verbal, physical and emotional harassment, flashing, stalking, sexual assault and

(continued)

Box 1 (continued)

rape. It is sometimes referred to as sexual violence. The concept of women's safety has been defined as involving 'strategies, practices and policies with the goal of reducing gender-based violence and women's fear or insecurity of violence'. It acknowledges that there is a continuum between private and public violence which requires us to work on both.

Sources: UNGA (1993), WHO & PAHO (2012) and Shaw et al. (2013).

Five Questions

1. In what ways do the daily lives of girls and women in urban settings differ from those of boys and men.
2. In what ways is violence against women by intimate partners in private, linked to violence against women in public spaces?
3. Why is it important that women and girls should have a voice in local government decision-making, such as the design and planning of urban environments and transport?
4. How have women's community-based organizations helped to shape national and international norms about safer cities for women and girls?
5. Why are men and boys important components in preventing violence against women and the creation of safe cities for all?

References

A/CONF.222/L.6. *Draft Doha Declaration on integrating crime prevention and criminal justice into the wider United Nations agenda to address social and economic challenges and to promote the rule of law at the national and international levels, and public participation.* Thirteenth UN Congress on Crime Prevention and Criminal Justice, Doha, 12–19 April 2015.

A/RES/48/104. Declaration on the Elimination of Violence against Women, 20 December 1993.

Barberet, R. (2014). *Women, crime and criminal justice: A global inquiry*. Abingdon: Routledge.

Barker, G. (2005). *Dying to be men: Youth, masculinity and social exclusion*. London: Routledge.

Barker, G., Ricardo, C., & Nascimento, M. (2007). *Engaging men and boys in changing gender-based inequity in health*. Geneva: WHO.

Barker, G., Contreras, J. M., Heilman, B., Singh, A. K., Verma, R. K., & Nascimento, M. (2011). *Evolving men: Initial results from the International Men and Gender Equality Survey (IMAGES)*. Washington, DC/Rio de Janeiro: International Centre for Research on Women and Instituto Promundo.

Beltran, A., & Freeman, L. (2007). *Hidden in plain sight: Violence against women in Mexico and Guatemala* (WOLA Special Report). Washington, DC: Washington Office on Latin America.

Brown, A., & Kristiansen, A. (2009). *Urban policies and the right to the city: Rights, responsibilities and citizenship* (MOST Policy Paper No. 2). Paris/Nairobi: UNESCO/UN-HABITAT.

Crawford, A. (Ed.) (2009). *Crime prevention in comparative perspective*. Cullompton, Devon: Willan Publishing.

EMERGE. (2015). *Engaging men: A collaborative review of evidence on men and boys in social change and gender equality* (Summary of Evidence Report). Rio de Janeiro: Instituto Promundo. www.promundoglobal.org

Falu, A. (2010). *Women in the city: On violence and rights.* Santiago da Chile: Red Mujer y HABITAT de America Latina, Editions Sur.

Falu, A., & Segovia, O. (Eds.) (2008). *Living together: Cities free of violence against women.* Santiago da Chile: Red Mujer y HABITAT de America Latina, Editions Sur.

FCM and City of Montreal. (2004). *A city tailored to women: The role of municipal governments in achieving gender equality.* Ottawa/Montreal: Federation of Canadian Municipalities and Femme et ville programme, City of Montreal.

FRA. (2014). *Violence against women: An EU-wide survey. Main results.* Vienna: European Union Agency for Fundamental Rights.

Fulu, E., Warner, X., Miedema, S., Jewkes, R., Roselli, T., & Lang, J. (2013). *Why do some men use violence against women and how can we prevent it? Quantitative findings from the United Nations multi-country study on men and violence in Asia and the Pacific.* Bangkok: UNDP, UNFPA, UN Women and UNV.

Gilmore, M. (1991). *Take back Toronto: A guide to preventing violence against women in your community.* Toronto: City of Toronto Safe City Committee.

Goteborg. (2002). *Safer cities: Is it possible to change the places which generate fear?* Goteborg: City Planning Authority

Htun, M., & Weldon, S. L. (2012). The civic origins of progressive policy change: Combatting violence against women in global perspective. *American Political Science Review, 106*(3), 548–569.

ICPC. (2014a). Intimate partner violence against women. *Fourth international report on crime prevention and community safety: Trends and perspectives* (pp. 150–177). Montreal: International Centre for the Prevention of Crime.

ICPC. (2014b). *Fourth international report on crime prevention and community safety: Trends and perspectives.* Montreal: International Centre for the Prevention of Crime.

ICPC, EFUS, UN-Habitat. (2014). *Work in progress. 100 promising practices on safer cities.* Montreal/Paris/Nairobi: The Global Network on Safer Cities.

Jagori. (2007). *Is this our city? Mapping safety for women in Delhi.* New Delhi: Jagori.

Jagori. (2010). *A handbook on women's safety audits in low-income urban neighbourhoods: A focus on essential services.* New Delhi: Jagori.

Johnson, H. (2013). The gendered nature of violence: An international focus. In C. M. Renzetti, S. L. Miller, & A. R. Gover (Eds.), *Routledge international handbook of crime and gender studies* (pp. 91–114). Oxon: Routledge.

Khosla, P., & Dhar, S. (2013). Safe access to basic infrastructure: More than pipes and taps. In C. Whitzman, C. Legacy, C. Andrew, F. Kladowsky, M. Shaw, & K. Viswanath (Eds.), *Building inclusive cities: Women's safety and the right to the city* (pp. 117–139). Abington/New York: Earthscan Routledge.

Loukaitou-Sideris, A., Bornstein, A., Fink, C., Samuels, L., & Gerami, S. (2008). *How to ease women's fear in transportation environments: Case studies and best practices.* Los Angeles: Mineta Transportation Institute & University of California Transportation Centre.

Manjoo, R. (2012). A/HRC/20/6. *Report of the Special Rapporteur on violence against women, its causes and consequences, Rashida Manjoo.*

Menon-Sen, K., & Bhan, G. (2007). *Swept off the map: Surviving eviction and resettlement in Delhi.* Delhi: Yoda Press.

METRAC. (1992). *Women's safety audit guide.* Toronto: METRAC.

Natarajan, M. (2013). The Delhi "Rape Crisis". In *Inter-News*, Newsletter of the Division of International Criminology of the American Society of Criminology, 35, Spring 2013.

NWAC. (2010). *What their stories tell us: Research findings from the sisters in spirit initiative.* Ottawa: Native Women's Association of Canada. http://www.nwac.ca/sites/default/files/reports/2010_NWAC_SIS_Report_EN.pdf>.

Ortiz Escalante, S., & Sweet, E. L. (2013). Migrant women's safety: Framing policies and practices. In C. Whitzman, C. Legacy, C. Andrew, F. Kladowsky, M. Shaw, & K. Viswanath (Eds.), *Building inclusive cities: Women's safety and the right to the city* (pp. 53–71). Abingdon/New York: Earthscan Routledge.

Padke, S. (2010). *Gendered usage of public spaces: A case study of Mumbai* (Background Report for "Addressing Gender-Based Violence in Public Spaces" Project). Centre for Equality and Inclusion India.

PAHO. (2012). *Violence against women in Latin America and the Caribbean: A comparative analysis of population-based data from 12 countries*. Washington, DC: PAHO.

Plan International. (2015). *Because I am a girl: Global analysis*. London/Montreal/Nairobi: Plan International/WICI/UN-HABITAT.

Plan International. (2013). *Adolescent girls views on safety in cities: Findings from the because I am a girl urban programme study in Cairo, Delhi, Hanoi, Kampala, and Lima*. London/Montreal/Nairobi: Plan International/WICI/UN-HABITAT.

Plan International. (2010). *Because I'm a girl. The state of the world's girls 2010. Digital and urban frontiers: Girls in a changing landscape*. London: Plan International.

Racovita, M. (2015). Lethal violence against women and girls. In G. McDonald, E. Le Brun, A. Alvazzi del Frate, E.G. Berman, & K. Krause (Eds.), *Global burden of armed violence 2015: Every body counts* (pp. 87–120). Cambridge: Cambridge University Press.

RCMP. (2014). *Missing and murdered aboriginal women: An operational overview*. Ottawa: Royal Canadian Mounted Police.

Sen, A. (2013). India's women: The mixed truth. *New York Review of Books*, October 10, pp. 24–27.

Shaw, M. (2013). Too close to home: Guns and intimate partner violence. In E. Le Brun, G. McDonald, A. Alvazzi del Frate, E.G. Berman, & K. Krause (Eds.), *Small Arms Survey 2013: Everyday dangers* (pp. 17–45). Cambridge: Cambridge University Press.

Shaw, M., & Andrews, C. (2005). Engendering crime prevention: International developments and the Canadian experience. *Canadian Journal of Criminology and Criminal Justice, 47*(2), 293–316.

Shaw, M., Andrew, C., Whitzman C., Klodawsky, F., Viswanath, K., & Legavy, C. (2013). Introduction. In C. Whitzman, C. Legacy, C. Andrew, F. Kladowsky, M. Shaw, & K. Viswanath (Eds.) *Building inclusive cities: Women's safety and the right to the city* (pp. 1–16). Abington/New York: Earthscan Routledge.

Stanko, E. (1996). Warnings to women: Police advice and women's safety in Britain. *Violence Against Women, 2*(1), 5–24.

UNGA. (1993). *Declaration on the elimination of violence against women*. A/RES/48/104 (1993).

UNGA. (2012). *Report of the Special Rapporteur on violence against women, its causes and consequences, Raschida Manjoo*. A/HRC/20/6 (2012).

UN-HABITAT. (2001). *Women and urban governance* (Policy Dialogue Series No. 1). Nairobi: UN-HABITAT.

UNODC. (2012). *Global report on trafficking in persons*. Vienna: UNODC.

UNODC. (2013). *Accounting for security and justice in the post-2015 development agenda*. Vienna: UNODC.

UNODC. (2014a). *Global study on homicide 2013*. Vienna: UNODC.

UNODC. (2014b). *Strengthening crime prevention and criminal justice responses to violence against women*. Vienna: UNODC.

UN. (2015). *Draft Doha Declaration on integrating crime prevention and criminal justice into the wider United Nations agenda to address social and economic challenges and to promote the rule of law at the national and international levels, and public participation*. Thirteenth UN Congress on Crime Prevention and Criminal Justice, Doha 12–19 April 2015. A/CONF.222/L.6.

UNSD. (2013). *Guidelines for producing statistics on violence against women: Statistical surveys*. New York, NJ: UNSD.

UN Women. (2013). *A transformative stand-alone goal on achieving gender equality. Women's rights and women's empowerment: Imperatives and key components*. New York: UN Women.
UN Women. (2015). *Progress of the world's women 2015–2016: Transforming economies, realizing rights*. New York: UN Women.
Vargas, V. (2007). Public spaces, citizen safety and gender based violence. Reflections emerging from debate in Latin America in 2006–2007. *Regional programme cities without violence against women, safe cities for all. Cuadernos de Dialagos*. Brazil and Southern Cone: UNIFEM.
Viswanath, K. (2013). Gender inclusive city programme. In C. Whitzman, C. Legacy, C. Andrew, F. Kladowsky, M. Shaw, & K. Viswanath (Eds.), *Building inclusive cities: Women's safety and the right to the city* (pp. 75–89). Abingdon/New York: Earthscan Routledge.
Whitzman, C. (2013). Women's safety and everyday mobility. In C. Whitzman, C. Legacy, C. Andrew, F. Kladowsky, M. Shaw, & K. Viswanath (Eds.), *Building inclusive cities: Women's safety and the right to the city* (pp. 1–16). Abington/New York: Earthscan Routledge.
Whitzman, C., & Wekerle, G. R. (1997). *Toronto safer city guidelines*. Toronto: City of Toronto Safe City Committee.
Whitzman, C. (2008). *The handbook on community safety, gender and violence prevention: Practical planning tools*. London: Earthscan.
Whitzman, C., Andrew, C., Shaw, M., & Travers, K. (2009). The effectiveness of women's safety audits. *Security Journal, 22*(3), 205–218.
Whitzman, C., Legacy, C., Andrew, C., Kladowsky, F., Shaw, M., & Viswanath, K. (Eds.). (2013). *Building inclusive cities: Women's safety and the right to the city*. Abingdon/New York: Earthscan Routledge.
WHO & PAHO. (2012). *Understanding violence against women: Intimate partner violence*. Geneva: WHO.
WICI. (2004). *Women's Safety Awards 2004: A compendium of good practice*. Montreal: Women in Cities International.
WICI et al. (2008a). *Global assessment of women's safety*. Montreal/New York/Cordoba/Nairobi/Stockholm: WICI/HUAIROU/Red Mujer y HABITAT de America Latina/UN-HABITAT/SIDA.
WICI et al. (2008b). *Women's safety audits: What works and where?* Montreal/Nairobi/Stockholm: WICI/UN-HABITAT/SIDA.
WICI. (2010). *Together for women's safety: Creating safer communities for marginalized women and everyone*. Montreal: Women in Cities International.
WICI. (2012). *Tackling gender exclusion: Experiences from the gender inclusive cities project*. Montreal: Women in Cities International.
WICI. (2013). *My city, my safety*. Montreal: Women in Cities International.
WICI and Jagori. (2011). *Gender and essential services in low income communities*. Montreal/New Delhi: Women in Cities International and Jagori.

Juvenile Justice and Human Rights: European Perspectives

Frieder Dünkel

Abstract International human rights standards and in particular the Convention of the Rights of the Child (CRC) have had a major impact on juvenile justice reforms in Europe during the last 25 years. The general orientation towards the ideal of education has been further developed in Europe. The development of human rights standards has played a major role in this context. The United Nations Standard Minimum Rules for the Administration of Juvenile Justice ("The Beijing Rules") of 1985 and the more binding CRC of 1989 have been mark-stones in the juvenile justice human rights movement. In Europe, the Council of Europe's Recommendations of 2003 and 2008 have kept the general orientation towards diversion, minimum intervention, education, restorative justice and other constructive measures, even for more serious young offenders. After a period of strengthening the punitive approach in some European countries such as England/Wales (UK) and France (as in the US), a revitalization of the traditional perspectives of education and rehabilitation of offenders can be observed. Most European countries have experienced a reduction in juvenile delinquency as well as in youth imprisonment rates. Juvenile crime policy furthermore tends to expand the scope of juvenile justice to the age group of young adults (18–21 year olds) and even beyond as the new Dutch Juvenile Justice Act of 2014 demonstrates (up to 23 years). Furthermore the children's rights movement has increasingly led to a full integration of legal guarantees in juvenile justice proceedings in order to prevent disadvantages for minor offenders.

The present chapter is an extended and updated version of the chapter in the 2013 edited book on *European Penology* (see Dünkel 2013), and inspired by the discussion on "new punitiveness" (Pratt et al. 2005) and so-called neo-liberal orientations which can be observed in some European and in particular Anglo-Saxon jurisdictions (see amongst others Tonry 2004) in contrary to Scandinavian countries that are characterized under the label of "penal exceptionalism", see Pratt 2008a, b and Lappi-Seppälä 2007. The present chapter will show that not only Scandinavian countries, but a lot of others, and in particular juvenile justice systems succeeded in 'resisting punitiveness in Europe'(Snacken and Dumortier 2012). A further extension of earlier papers are the reflections on human rights standards as pointed out under Sect. 2, see for this Dünkel 2009.

F. Dünkel (✉)
University of Greifswald, Greifswald, Germany
e-mail: duenkel@uni-greifswald.de

H. Kury et al. (eds.), *Women and Children as Victims and Offenders: Background, Prevention, Reintegration*, DOI 10.1007/978-3-319-28424-8_27

1 Introduction

In the last 25 years, youth justice[1] systems in Europe have undergone considerable changes, particularly in the former socialist countries of Central and Eastern Europe. However, differing and sometimes contradictory youth justice policies have also emerged in Western Europe. So-called neo-liberal[2] tendencies can be seen particularly in *England and Wales*, and also in *France* and the *Netherlands* (Cavadino and Dignan 2006, p. 215ff, 2007, p. 284ff; Goldson 2002, p. 392ff; Tonry 2004; Muncie and Goldson 2006; Bailleau and Cartuyvels 2007; Muncie 2008; Cimamonti et al. 2010). In other countries, such as *Germany* and *Switzerland*, a moderate system of minimum intervention with priority given to diversion and educational measures has been retained (Dünkel et al. 2011). In many countries, elements of restorative justice have been implemented (see in summary Dünkel et al. 2015a, b).

This chapter evaluates youth justice policies and practice in Europe from a comparative perspective.[3] The focus is on tendencies in youth justice legislation and on the sentencing practice of prosecutors and judges in youth courts. Attention is also paid to the traditional "welfare" and "justice" models of youth justice and how they have become intertwined in modern European practice. The claim that a "new punitiveness" is the prevailing strategy is questioned and attention is drawn to the practice of many youth justice systems, which seem to be fairly resistant to neo-liberal policies. Snacken (2012, p. 247ff) has recently sought to explain why continental European countries in general have succeeded in resisting "penal populism". In the conclusion this reasoning is applied to youth justice systems in particular.[4]

---

[1] A note on terminology: I have used the terms, youth and youth justice as well as juvenile justice in this contribution in the same sense. The term juvenile justice is in use in a number of international, European and national instruments, where it usually refers to persons under the age of 18 years. However, the Convention on the Rights of the Child uses the term, "child" to refer to anyone under the age of 18 years. I have not followed this usage of 'child', as it is not always appropriate in this context. Finally, I use the term, young adults, to refer to persons at the age of 18 until 21 who are treated as youths or juveniles as it is proposed by the European Rules for Juvenile Offenders Subject to Sanctions or Measures (Rec. (2008) 11), see Rule Nr. 17.

[2] The meaning of the term "neo-liberal", which derives from the concept of Garland's 'culture of control' contains different concepts and aspects that cannot be simply characterized by more repressive sanctions or sentencing: see Crawford and Lewis 2007: 30 ff. These include the criminalization of anti-social behaviour (ASBO's), increased use of youth custody, managerialism and the reduction of risk by social exclusion rather than by integrating vulnerable offender groups through specific programmes.

[3] The comparison is based largely on a survey of 34 countries conducted by the Criminology Department at the University of Greifswald: Dünkel et al. 2011. The project was funded by the European Union (AGIS-programme) and by the Ministry of Education of the Federal State of Mecklenburg-Western Pomerania in Germany.

[4] See also Snacken 2010 and the contributions in Snacken and Dumortier 2012.

2 International Human Rights Standards Concerning Juvenile Offenders

2.1 The Role of the UN: Standard Minimum Rules for the Administration of Juvenile Justice (Beijing-Rules) of 1985 and the Convention of the Rights of the Child of 1989

One of the first mark-stones in developing human rights standards concerning juvenile offenders were the United Nations Standard Minimum Rules for the Administration of Juvenile Justice ("*The Beijing Rules*"), which were adopted by the General Assembly as Resolution No. 40/33 of 29 November 1985 (A/RES 40/33, Annex). The major aim was to encourage the establishment of a separate juvenile justice system and juvenile courts in order "to further the well-being of the juvenile and her or his family" (see Fundamental Principle No. 1.1 and Rule No. 5). Rule No. 5 further specifies the aims of juvenile justice systems that shall ensure that any reaction to juvenile offenders shall always be in proportion to the circumstances of both the offenders and the offence (see also Rule 17.1 lit. a). Since then the principle of proportionality has become an essential part of juvenile justice legislation by also furthering the principles of diversion and minimum intervention and of education instead of punishment as expressed in Rules No. 11 (diversion) and 17 of the Beijing Rules and in the following years in the European recommendations described under Sect. 2.2. Of particular importance is Rule No. 17.1 lit. c which restricts juvenile imprisonment and deprivation of liberty in general to cases where juveniles are adjudicated of "a serious act involving violence against another person or of persistence in committing other serious offences and unless there is no other appropriate response".

Rule No. 17.1 lit. b further states that "restrictions on the personal liberty of the juvenile shall be imposed only after careful consideration and shall be limited to the possible minimum." All following international standards emphasize that the deprivation of liberty shall not only be a measure of last resort, but also be as short as possible in order to avoid long-term imprisonment as it is practised in many countries in particular for adult offenders.

The priority for alternative (community) sanctions is expressed by Rule No. 18.1, which requires the member states to provide for a large variety of disposition measures that "shall be made available to the competent authority, allowing for flexibility so as to avoid institutionalization to the greatest extent possible." As examples for community sanctions or measures are enumerated care, guidance and supervision orders, probation, community service orders, financial penalties, compensation and restitution, intermediate treatment and other treatment orders, orders to participate in group counselling and similar activities, and orders concerning foster care, living communities or other educational settings see Rule 18.1 lit. a-g).

Countries such as the USA and some Asian or Arabic countries for a long-time had difficulties to accept Rule No. 17.2, which stipulates that "capital punishment shall not be imposed for any crime committed by juveniles." It was only in the year 2005 that the US-Supreme Court outlawed capital punishment for juvenile offenders in its decision *Roper v. Simmons* (No. 03-0633 of 1 March 2005).

The *Convention of the Rights of the Child* (CRC, 1577 UNTS 3) of 1989 is an even more powerful instrument of human rights standards as the countries that ratified this convention have a binding obligation to follow it. Only Somalia, South Sudan and the USA so far have not ratified the CRC yet. The CRC goes far beyond dealing with juvenile offending, most regulations concern general children's rights issues (see in detail Belser et al. 2009). In the context of the present chapter Art. 37 and 40 are of major importance.

Art. 37 deals with the prevention of torture and other cruel, inhuman or degrading treatment and arbitrary deprivation of liberty (Art. 37a and b CRC). Art. 37b further stipulates that deprivation of liberty must be "a measure of last resort and for the shortest appropriate period of time". Furthermore the preservation of the child's human dignity and respect for the needs of the child ('best interests') shall be observed, see Art. 37c. Art. 37d requires prompt access to legal and other appropriate assistance particularly to children deprived of their liberty.

Art. 40 CRC contains specific aspects of due process standards such as *nulla poena sine lege*, the presumption of innocence, the right to a defence council or other appropriate assistance, to bring the case to an appeal court, to have access to an interpreter etc. According to Art. 40.3 the States Parties are encouraged to promote the establishment of laws, procedures, authorities and institutions specifically applicable to juvenile offenders and in particular to define by law the minimum age of criminal responsibility. Under lit. b diversion is mentioned as a priority measure "whenever appropriate and desirable". Similar to Rule 18.1 of the Beijing Rules Art. 40.4 of the CRC requires a "variety of dispositions" and "alternatives to institutional care", emphasizing the principles of proportionality of well-being of the juvenile offender.

As can be shown, these principles of the CRC and the Beijing Rules had a major impact on the development of juvenile justice in Europe. Many of these rules and standards have been taken over and further developed by the Council of Europe (see Sects. 2.2 and 2.3) and often also by national legislation.

2.2 The Recommendation on "New Ways of Dealing with Juvenile Delinquency and the Role of Juvenile Justice"

The Recommendation of the Council of Europe on "*New Ways of Dealing with Juvenile Delinquency and the Role of Juvenile Justice*" (see Council of Europe 2003 and the texts of Council of Europe Recommendations under www.coe.int) of the year 2003 pursues the following paramount goals:

1. The prevention of offending and re-offending,
2. the rehabilitation and reintegration of offenders, and
3. regard for the needs and interests of victims of crime.

The strategic approach incorporates the following perspectives:

The juvenile justice system has to be treated as a component of a wider community-based strategy for the prevention of juvenile delinquency that takes account of the wider family, school, neighbourhood and peer group context within which offending occurs (No. 2 of the Recommendation). Resources should in particular be targeted towards addressing serious, violent, persistent and drug- and alcohol-related offending where possible (No. 3). There is a need for the development of more suitable and effective measures of prevention and reintegration that are tailored to young migrants, groups of juveniles, young girls, and children and young people under the age of criminal responsibility (No. 4).

Sanctions should—as far as possible—be based on scientific results of what works, with whom and under which circumstances (No. 5).

The consequences for ethnic minorities require particular policy attention. Therefore, the persons in charge are to be obliged to compile so called *impact statements* (No. 6).

The Recommendation proposes the following 'new responses':

The expansion of the range of suitable alternatives to formal prosecution should continue. The principle of proportionality is to be upheld, and the voluntariness of the offender must be regarded (No. 7). Regarding serious, violent and persistent juvenile crime, (proportional) community sanctions should be further developed (this can also imply the inclusion of the parents into the criminal responsibility of their children, so long as this is not counter-productive), especially such measures that incorporate elements of reparation and restoration to the victim (Nos. 8, 10).

The recommendation to expand community sanctions in cases of serious crime is remarkable in that emphasis is usually placed on the necessity of imprisonment in this context. However, experiences with suspended sentences as well as with community education-/treatment programmes within the framework of the probation or youth welfare services have shown that positive results can be achieved with repeat and/or violent offenders or groups of offenders. Insofar, juveniles who were viewed as the traditional clientele of the juvenile prison system 20 or 30 years ago can now be successfully supervised in the community.

With regard to the extended phases of (school and vocational) education and transition into adulthood, the sanctions of juvenile criminal law should be applicable to young adults according to their degree of maturity and development (No. 11). This matches the stated positive experiences that have been made in Germany, and mirrors contemporary legal reform in, for example, Lithuania, Spain and Austria (see above).

Incidentally, the recommendations repeatedly emphasise the need for "risk assessment, evidence based interventions and empirical evaluation". Although aspects of neo-correctionalist" thinking (for example regarding parental liability) can also be observed, the Recommendation Rec (2003) 20 remains adherent to the tradition of a moderate justice system that prioritizes education (key term: "minimum intervention") and that emphasises community based interventions also in cases of more serious offending. This should serve as a mental note for counter-reforms in a more repressive direction.

The implementation of the 2003 Recommendation is to be executed in close collaboration with the local prevention and intervention agencies and should take quality standards into account. Continuous "*monitoring*" and the *dissemination* of good practices also belong to the recommended strategies.

It remains to be seen to what extent the Recommendation shall influence the reforms in Europe, especially in the central and eastern European countries. Unfortunately, one can assume that there shall be problems with the funding of scientific evaluations. The importance of evidence based criminal justice policy can, however, not be valued highly enough.

2.3 The European Rules for Juvenile Offenders Subject to Sanctions and Measures of 2008

In January 2006 the Committee of Ministers of the Council of Europe adopted the new *European Prison Rules* (EPR). At the same time the *Committee on Crime Problems* (CDPC) set up a further expert group which was to draft European Rules for juveniles under community sanctions and measures and deprived of their liberty. The terms of reference explicitly referred to community sanctions and sanctions with deprivation of liberty and thus went beyond the scope of the EPR. But also with regards to deprivation of liberty the new Rules are more comprehensive than the EPR as they cover all forms of deprivation of liberty such as pre-trial detention, detention in (closed) welfare institutions, youth imprisonment and psychiatric juvenile facilities (see for the text and a commentary Council of Europe 2009).

The Rules have been drafted until April 2008, and the CDPC in first session from June 2008 has accepted them (with minor changes), and on 5 November 2008 the Committee of Ministers of the Council of Europe has passed the Rec. CM/Rec (2008) 11 on "*European Rules for Juveniles Subject to Sanctions and Measures*".

The Rules are structured in eight Parts. In the same way as the EPR they start with "Basic Principles" which concern the imposition and execution of community sanctions and all forms of deprivation of liberty. Rules on the scope of application and definitions also belong to Part I. The most important issue in that respect is that the scope of application is extended to young adults of 18–21 years of age (as far as national law provides the application of juvenile law or sanctions or special rules for the execution of sanctions or measures for this age group). The second Part deals with community sanctions and measures, while Part III covers issues regarding the deprivation of liberty. Part IV concerns "legal advice and assistance" and Part V is dedicated to "complaints procedures, inspection and monitoring". Questions related to staffing are dealt with in Part VI, those related to evaluation and research as well as to work with the media and the public are contained in Part VII. The closing Rule 142 requires the Rules to be regularly updated.

The preamble formulates the following general directive: "*The aim of the present Rules is to uphold the rights and safety of juvenile offenders subject to sanctions or measures and to promote their physical, mental and social well-being when subjected to community sanctions and measures or any form of deprivation of liberty. Nothing in these Rules ought to be interpreted as precluding the application of other relevant international human rights instruments and standards that are more conducive to ensuring the rights, care and protection of juveniles. In particular, the provisions of Recommendation Rec(2006)2 on the European Prison Rules and of Recommendation R (92) 16 on the European Rules on Community Sanctions and Measures shall be applied to the benefit of juvenile offenders in as far as they are not in conflict with these Rules.*"

This statement makes it clear that the present Rules do not go beyond the guarantees formulated in earlier Recommendations and Rules concerning the human rights of offenders. This must be interpreted as a formal prohibition of any discrimination or restriction of rights and legal guarantees for juveniles, for example with regard to educational needs. Basic Principle 13 requires in the same way: "Juveniles shall not have fewer legal rights and safeguards than those provided to adult offenders by the general rules of criminal procedure."

The 20 "Basic Principles" are as follows (see Council of Europe 2009: 7f):

1. *Juvenile offenders subject to sanctions or measures shall be treated with respect for their human rights.*
2. *The sanctions or measures that may be imposed on juveniles as well as the manner of their implementation shall be specified by law and based on the principles of social integration and education and on the prevention of re-offending.*
3. *Sanctions and measures shall be imposed by a court or, if imposed by another legally recognised authority, they shall be subject to prompt judicial review. They shall be determinate and imposed for the minimum necessary period and only for a legitimate purpose.*
4. *The minimum age for the imposition of sanctions or measures as a result of the commission of an offence shall not be too low and shall be determined by law.*
5. *The imposition and implementation of sanctions or measures shall be based on the best interests of the juvenile offenders, limited by the gravity of the offences committed (principle of proportionality) and take account of their age, physical and mental well-being, development, capacities and personal circumstances (principle of individualisation) as ascertained when necessary by psychological, psychiatric or social inquiry reports.*
6. *In order to adapt the implementation of sanctions and measures to the particular circumstances of each case the authorities responsible for the implementation shall have a sufficient degree of discretion without leading to serious inequality of treatment.*

7. *Sanctions or measures shall not humiliate or degrade the juveniles subject to them.*
8. *Sanctions or measures shall not be implemented in a manner that aggravates their afflictive character or poses an undue risk of physical or mental harm.*
9. *Sanctions or measures shall be implemented without undue delay and only to the extent and for the period strictly necessary (principle of minimum intervention).*
10. *Deprivation of liberty of a juvenile shall be a measure of last resort and imposed and implemented for the shortest period possible. Special efforts must be undertaken to avoid pre-trial detention.*
11. *Sanctions or measures shall be imposed and implemented without discrimination on any ground such as sex, race, colour, language, religion, sexual orientation, political or other opinion, national or social origin, association with a national minority, property, birth or other status (principle of non-discrimination).*
12. *Mediation or other restorative measures shall be encouraged at all stages of dealing with juveniles.*
13. *Any justice system dealing with juveniles shall ensure their effective participation in the proceedings concerning the imposition as well as the implementation of sanctions or measures. Juveniles shall not have fewer legal rights and safeguards than those provided to adult offenders by the general rules of criminal procedure.*
14. *Any justice system dealing with juveniles shall take due account of the rights and responsibilities of the parents and legal guardians and shall as far as possible involve them in the proceedings and the execution of sanctions or measures, except if this is not in the best interests of the juvenile. Where the offender is over the age of majority the participation of parents and legal guardians is not compulsory. Members of the juveniles' extended families and the wider community may also be associated with the proceedings where it is appropriate to do so.*
15. *Any justice system dealing with juveniles shall follow a multi-disciplinary and multi-agency approach and be integrated with wider social initiatives for juveniles in order to ensure an holistic approach to and continuity of the care of such juveniles (principles of community involvement and continuous care).*
16. *The juvenile's right to privacy shall be fully respected at all stages of the proceedings. The identity of juveniles and confidential information about them and their families shall not be conveyed to anyone who is not authorised by law to receive it.*
17. *Young adult offenders may, where appropriate, be regarded as juveniles and dealt with accordingly.*
18. *All staff working with juveniles perform an important public service. Their recruitment, special training and conditions of work shall ensure that they are able to provide the appropriate standard of care to meet the distinctive needs of juveniles and provide positive role models for them.*

19. *Sufficient resources and staffing shall be provided to ensure that interventions in the lives of juveniles are meaningful. Lack of resources shall never justify the infringement of the human rights of juveniles.*
20. *The execution of any sanction or measure shall be subjected to regular government inspection and independent monitoring.*

The following comments are largely based on the commentary to the Rules which have been drafted by the experts of the Council of Europe since 2007 (see Dünkel 2008, 2011a, b).

Rule 1 corresponds to Rule 1 of the EPR. As stated in the Preamble, the European Rules on Community Sanctions and Measures of 1992 are of particular relevance as well. Human rights issues arise not only when deprivation of liberty is used, but also when community sanctions and measures are applied. Both full-scale deprivation of liberty and lesser restrictions of liberty can be intrusive and may violate human rights if the principle of proportionality contained in Rule 5 is not applied. It is a basic standard of all international instruments that the human rights of juveniles have to be protected in the same way as it is the case for adults. The United Nations Convention on the Rights of the Child as well as the recommendations of the Council of Europe in the field of juvenile justice emphasise this issue. It should be noted that Rule 1 refers to protecting not only human dignity, but all human rights of juvenile offenders both deprived of their liberty or under community sanctions and measures. It should be clear that, in addition, other international instruments such as the United Nations Rules for the Protection of Juveniles Deprived of their Liberty of 14 December 1990 (the so-called Havana Rules) have also played an important part in the development of these Rules.

Rule 2 refers to the fact that all juvenile justice and welfare systems are based on the principles of social integration and education with regards to imposing and executing community sanctions and measures and sanctions of deprivation of liberty. This leaves much less space, and in some countries no space at all, for the principle of general deterrence or other (more punitive) aims that are a feature of the criminal justice system for adults.

In the field of juvenile justice it is recognised that the personalities of juveniles are still developing and open to positive influences. Emphasis must be placed on the possibility of re-integrating young persons. This may be achieved in some cases only by intensive educational or therapeutic efforts. The rule on social integration would therefore not allow long-term security measures or life sentences that aim solely at protecting society from juvenile offenders and do not give them the prospect of release within a reasonable period. (See in this respect the case law of the European Court of Human Rights: *T. v. the United Kingdom* [GC], no. 24724/94, 16 December 1999*; V. v. the United Kingdom* [GC], no. 24888/94, ECHR 1999-IXT*)*.

The emphasis that is placed on the major aim of education for the prevention of re-offending is important. In most international instruments education is not clearly defined. This is problematic as the term "education" may be misused as can be seen by repressive forms of authoritarian education, for example military style detention regimes that do not correspond to the European concept of human rights and dignity. On the one hand, the aim of preventing re-offending is modest, for it does not seek to achieve more than law-abiding integration into society. On the other hand, it is ambitious, for it is connected to the term social integration and therefore aims at promoting the juveniles' personal and wider social development, and their taking responsibility for their behaviour. Education therefore should be understood as including measures such as enhancing their communication skills or requiring them to make reparations, for instance writing appropriate letters of apology. Equally, society has to enable these changes to take place. It is important that the opportunities for learning and the interventions chosen to achieve these goals should be evidence-based and should contribute to the development and differentiation of the capacities of perception, interpretation, decision-making and responsible action.

The restriction of the power to impose sanctions and measures to a court or to another legally recognised authority—as stipulated in *Rule 3*—enshrines the principle of legality. Prompt judicial review where the imposition is decided by another authority is a further guarantee in this regard. Detention only for a legitimate purpose follows the requirements set by the European Court of Human Rights in its interpretation of Article 5 of the ECHR. It further relates to Rule 2, which emphasizes the primary goals of any sanction or measure imposed on juvenile offenders.

It is important that all sanctions and measures imposed on juveniles be of determinate duration because of the need for legal certainty and realistic prospects for reintegration into society. Where the sanctions or measures are open-ended this can be achieved by making them subject to regular review. The principle of proportionality applies both to the imposition and to the implementation of sanctions and measures. This principle should be applied at every stage of the procedure, so that juveniles are not subject to unnecessary restrictions.

The principle of minimum intervention in Rule 3 refers to the sentencing stage. Sanctions and measures should be imposed "*for the minimum necessary period*". Rule 9 contains the same idea but for the level of the execution of sanctions and measures, and Rule 10 emphasises this idea with regards to deprivation of liberty (see below).

Rule 4 stipulates that the law should set a minimum age for any type of intervention resulting from an offence. This includes the determination of the age of criminal responsibility as well as the age from which more punitive penal measures can be taken. It follows directly from the universally recognised principle of legality: the condition for any criminal liability is that the criminalized behaviour and the possible offender must be described by law. The principle of legality applies in the same way to other types of intervention.

The age of criminal responsibility has to correspond to "an internationally acceptable age" *(see United Nations, Committee of the Rights of the Child, General Comment No. 10 (2007), para. 32 (CRC/C/GC/10)*. Although it might be difficult to find a general European consensus, such a minimum age should not be too low and should be related to the age at which juveniles assume civil responsibilities in other spheres such as marriage, end of compulsory schooling and employment. The majority of countries have fixed the minimum age between 14 and 15 years and this standard should be followed in Europe. Criminal responsibility for juveniles of less than 12 years exists only in a few countries such as England and Wales (UK) and Switzerland (see Table 1).

In any case, very young offenders who are formally criminally liable should not be admitted to juvenile penitentiary institutions. In some countries the age for admission to such institutions is 15 (as in Switzerland) or 16, whereas the general age of criminal responsibility might be lower, usually between 12 and 14 years.

Rule 5 provides that all sanctions and measures must be subject to what is in the best interests of the juvenile, and this needs to be established in every individual case. This implies regular assessments by social workers, psychologists, psychiatrists or other professionals. On the other hand, the best interests of the juvenile should not be an excuse for excessive or disproportionate interventions. Measures that promote social integration are generally in the best interests of the juvenile.

This Rule contains two further interrelated principles. The principle of individualization is inherent in traditional juvenile justice. When a sanction or a measure is imposed, the age, physical and mental well-being, development, capacities and personal circumstances of the offender shall be taken into consideration. Information about these individual circumstances of the juvenile will usually be obtained from psychological, psychiatric or social inquiry reports and therefore a multi-agency approach as indicated in Rule 15 is necessary. The principle of proportionality serves as a corrective to avoid extended educational sanctions or measures that cannot be justified in terms of the gravity of the offence. The principle of individualisation should, therefore *not* be used to justify interventions that are disproportionately severe with respect to the offence.

Rule 6 stipulates that in the implementation of sanctions and measures a certain degree of discretion must be given to the implementing authorities in order to meet the individual circumstances of each case. This should, however, not lead to serious inequality of treatment. There should be careful documentation of the sentencing practice as well as of the implementation of sanctions and measures. In order to avoid discrimination particular attention must be paid to identifying local, cultural, ethnic and other differences and determining whether a different treatment would be justified in order to achieve the same results of social reintegration, education and prevention of re-offending.

Rule 7 prohibits any violation of human dignity. Overcrowding in institutions and harsh, military-type regimes, solitary confinement, depriving juveniles of social contacts are examples of what should be avoided. Equally, some forms of community work can also stigmatise juvenile offenders and would not be consistent with this rule (special uniforms which identify them as offenders, etc.).

Rule 8 corresponds to Rule 102.2 of the EPR. There should be no forms of implementation of sanctions or measures that aggravate their afflictive character, for example by hard and degrading work either in prisons or as a form of community service. Therefore, different regimes in juvenile penitentiary institutions which are (for punitive reasons) related to the gravity of the offence are not allowed.

Table 1 Comparison of the age of criminal responsibility and age ranges for youth imprisonment

Country	Minimum age for educational measures of the family/youth court (juvenile welfare law)	Age of criminal responsibility (juvenile criminal law)	Full criminal responsibility (adult criminal law can/must be applied; juvenile law or sanctions of the juvenile law can be applied)	Age range for youth imprisonment/custody or similar forms of deprivation of liberty
Austria		14	18/21	14–27
Belgium		18	16[a]/18	Only welfare institutions
Belarus		14[b]/16	14/16	14–21
Bulgaria		14	18	14–21
Croatia		14/16[c]	18/21	14–21
Cyprus		14	16/18/21	14–21
Czech Republic		15	18/18 + (mitigated sentences)	15–19
Denmark[d]		15	15/18/21	15–23
England/Wales		10/12/15[c]	18	10/15–21
Estonia		14	18	14–21
Finland[d]		15	15/18	15–21
France	10	13	18	13–18 + 6 m./23
Germany		14	18/21	14–24
Greece	8	15	18/21	15–21/25
Hungary		12[b]/14	18	14–24
Ireland		10/12/16[c]	18	10/12/16–18/21
Italy		14	18/21	14–21
Kosovo		14	18/21	16–23
Latvia		14	18	14–21
Lithuania		14[b]/16	18/21	14–21
Macedonia		14[b]/16	14/16	14–21
Moldova		14[b]/16	14/16	14–21
Montenegro		14/16[c]	18/21	16–23

Netherlands		12	16/23	15–24
Northern Ireland		10	17/18/21	10–16/17–21
Norway[d]		15	18	15–21
Poland	13		15/17/18	13–18/15–21
Portugal	12		16/21	12/16–21
Romania		14/16	18/(20)	14–21
Russia		14[b]/16	18/21	14–21
Scotland	8[e]	12[e]/16	16/21	16–21
Serbia		14/16[c]	18/21	14–23
Slovakia		14/15	18/21	14–18
Slovenia		14/16[c]	18/21	14–23
Spain		14	18	14–21
Sweden[d]		15	15/18/21	15–21[f]
Switzerland		10/15[c]	18[g]	10/15–22
Turkey		12	15/18	12–18/21
Ukraine		14[b]/16	18	14–22

[a]Only for traffic offences and exceptionally for very serious offences
[b]Only for serious offences
[c]Criminal responsibility resulting in juvenile detention (youth imprisonment or similar custodial sanctions under the regime of the Ministry of Justice)
[d]Only mitigation of sentencing without separate youth justice legislation
[e]The age of criminal prosecution is 12, but for children from 8 up to the age of 16 the children's hearings system applies, thus preventing more formal criminal procedures
[f]Youth custody. There are also special departments for young offenders in the general prison system (for young adults until about 25 years of age)
[g]Article 61 of the Swiss Criminal Code for adults provides for a special form of detention, a prison sentence for 18–25 years old young adult offenders who are placed in separate institutions for young adults, where they can stay there until they reach the age of 30

Overcrowding is one of the well-known circumstances that can endanger the well-being and physical or mental integrity of detained juveniles. An undue risk of physical or mental harm can be caused by exposing detained juveniles to other detainees who are dangerous or violent. Conditions of detention that are not sufficiently stimulating and social or sensory deprivation of any kind are prohibited by Rule 8. As far as community sanctions are concerned, special emphasis should be given to avoiding stigmatizing or humiliating conditions (see also Rule 7 above).

Rule 9 refers to the principle of the speedy implementation of sanctions and measures. Undue delay is undesirable also because it undermines the effectiveness of the interventions. Rule 9 relates to Rule 5 and limits community sanctions or measures as well as deprivation of liberty to the minimum necessary. Therefore, review schemes must be provided by law that can shorten the execution of a sentence where continued enforcement does not seem to be necessary for the social integration of the juvenile offender. All countries have introduced early release schemes concerning imprisonment. Community sanctions and measures can also be adjusted in order to lessen their negative impact, or their duration may be reduced. The principle of minimum intervention also better protects human rights and preserves social ties while not increasing the risks posed to society.

Rule 10 reflects No. 37 of the UN Convention on the Rights of the Child, Rule 17 of the Beijing Rules and the Council of Europe's Recommendation N° R (87) 20 concerning "Social Reactions to Juvenile Delinquency" as well as Recommendation Rec (2003) 20 on "New Ways of Dealing with Juvenile Delinquency and the Role of Juvenile Justice". It follows from Rule 9 on minimum intervention and emphasizes that deprivation of liberty should only be a measure of last resort: normally other, less intrusive sanctions should have been tried first. The Beijing Rules give examples of what is meant by the provision that deprivation of liberty shall be limited to "exceptional cases": Deprivation of liberty shall be restricted to older juveniles involved in violent or persistent serious offending. Many national legislations have responded to this idea by raising the age for being sentenced to youth custody or youth imprisonment to a minimum of 15 or 16 years, whereas the general age of criminal responsibility might be lower (see Table 1 and the commentary to Rule 4 above).

Furthermore, deprivation of liberty is also to be restricted to the minimum necessary period. This is important as it prevents detention from being unnecessarily prolonged, for instance in order to complete educational and treatment programmes or other forms of interventions. Instead, there should be provisions so that juvenile offenders who have been released early can complete such programmes outside of the institution. Even where the initial deprivation of liberty is also linked to other goals, for instance retribution, it must be clear that preparing the juvenile for re-integration into society becomes increasingly important as the implementation of the sanction progresses ("progressive principle"). The final decision remains with the judicial authority that has the legal power to order the deprivation of liberty.

The problem of pre-trial detention is already extensively addressed by Rules 16–18 of the Recommendation Rec (2003) 20. It reflects the empirical evidence that pre-trial detention is used extensively in many countries, for longer than justified and for purposes that are not provided by law; for example, as a form of crisis intervention or for reducing public concern. Therefore, Rule 16 of Rec (2003) 20 states: "When, as a last resort, juvenile suspects are remanded in custody, this should not be for longer than six months before the commencement of the trial." In addition, Rule 17 of the above Recommendation clearly outlines that "where possible, alternatives to remand in custody should be used for juvenile suspects, such as placements with relatives, foster families or other forms of supported accommodation. Custodial remand should never be used as a punishment or form of intimidation or as a substitute for child protection or mental health measures." The present Rules incorporate these restrictions on pre-trial detention by requiring that "special efforts must be undertaken to avoid pre-trial detention."

The principle of non-discrimination laid out in *Rule 11* is a basic principle in all human rights instruments of the Council of Europe and the United Nations (see, for example, Art 14 of the ECHR and Rule 13 of the EPR). It does not mean that formal equality should be the ideal if it would result in substantive inequality. Protection of vulnerable groups is not discrimination, nor is treatment that is tailored to the special needs of individual juvenile offenders. Therefore, this principle is not infringed by special positive measures aimed at addressing juvenile offenders or groups of juvenile offenders with specific needs.

Rule 12 emphasises mediation and other restorative justice measures that have become important forms of intervention in juvenile welfare and justice systems. In many countries recent national legislation gives priority to mediation and restorative justice as methods of diversion from formal proceedings at various stages in the juvenile justice process. These strategies should be considered at all stages of dealing with juveniles and be given priority because of their special preventive advantages for the juvenile offenders as well as for the victims and the community.

Rule 13 includes the right to be informed, to have access to legal remedies, to legal assistance, complaints procedures and other procedural rights and safeguards (see also Rule 15, Recommendation Rec (2003) 20). The principle of effective participation in this case refers to the stage of imposition as well as of execution of sanctions and measures. Independently of which specific model of criminal investigation and procedure is followed, the juveniles and their parents or legal guardians must be informed about the offence or offences the juveniles are alleged to have committed and the evidence against them. The juveniles have the right to legal defence counsel also in purely welfare proceedings. In cases where deprivation of liberty is possible, a legal defence counsel must be allocated to the juveniles from the outset of the procedure. The Rule makes it clear that there is no justification for giving juveniles lesser rights than adults. Therefore regulations that restrict the right to appeal or complaints procedures with arguments of education cannot be justified. Other examples refer to issues of data protection: The more comprehensive social inquiry reports and case records within the juvenile justice and welfare system should not be transferred to criminal records that could possibly disadvantage juvenile offenders in their later adult life. Juvenile criminal records should include only serious sanctions and interventions in order to prevent stigmatisation as far as possible.

Rule 14 emphasizes the rights and responsibilities of parents and legal guardians to participate at all stages of investigations and proceedings. This is already inherent in the general principle of effective participation. However, it is important to stress the parents' or legal guardians' individual rights of participation. Nevertheless, these rights can be restricted if parents or guardians act against the best interests of the juvenile. The need for such restrictions should be assessed by psychologists or other professional staff of the juvenile welfare authorities and formally decided by the judicial authorities. While the participation of parents or legal guardians of juveniles is generally mandatory, this is not the case for young adults who have reached the age of civil majority. Nevertheless, their participation may still be desirable, especially if the young adults still live with them. Even if the juveniles' parents and guardians live abroad, attempts should be made to contact them. Where these parents and guardians cannot participate, their place should be taken where appropriate by an appointed representative. Restrictions may also be imposed where required by ongoing criminal investigations, but only for the period for which it is strictly necessary.

Proceedings against juveniles and the execution of resulting sanctions and measures take place in a wider context in which family members and the wider community may have a role to play where this is applicable and can have a positive impact on the juvenile and society. One example of such community involvement is the execution of a community sanction or measure where the local community is by definition involved. Reintegration after deprivation of liberty also necessarily supposes acceptance by and interaction with the local community. This too is subject to the principle that such involvement must be in the best interests of the juvenile. The corollary of Rule 14 is that juveniles have a right to have contact with the members of their family.

The characteristics of juveniles require a specific multi-disciplinary and multi-agency approach. This is emphasised by *Rule 15*. The key disciplines to be included are psychology, social work and education. The multi-agency approach is a normal form of co-operation between youth welfare and justice agencies in many countries. Social workers, the police, school and vocational training authorities, prosecutors and juvenile judges as well as lay organisations of juvenile welfare should work closely together in order to act in the best interests of the juvenile. The multi-agency approach should involve as fully as possible agencies and organisations outside the justice system, for they may be socially and environmentally closer to the juvenile. In this context the principle of through care is of major importance. The principle of "end to end" offender management where a community based social worker or probation officer maintains contact with the offender throughout the sentence is of particular value in providing continuity of care. Discharge arrangements should be planned carefully so that continuity of care is ensured. Institutions for the deprivation of liberty must work closely together with aftercare services and other relevant welfare agencies. However, data protection concerns must be borne in mind when cooperating in this way.

Rule 16 emphasises the rights to privacy and data protection. Juvenile offenders and their families have specific rights to privacy to protect them from negative stigmatisation. This recognises the need to help juveniles in their development to adulthood. Rule 16 places a duty on the state to provide the necessary protection for juvenile offenders and their families. In particular, the identity of juveniles and their families should not be communicated to anyone who is not legally authorised to be informed thereof.

Legal authorisation to receive information must be limited strictly to persons and institutions that require particular information related to a specific case. This should not lead to the public disclosure of entire lists of names of specific juvenile offenders. It follows too that only information that is necessary for this purpose should be collected in the first place.

Rule 17 deals with young adult offenders. Recommendation Rec (2003) 20 states in Rule 11 that "reflecting the extended transition to adulthood, it should be possible for young adults under the age of 21 to be treated in a way comparable to juveniles and to be subject to the same interventions, when the judge is of the opinion that they are not as mature and responsible for their actions as full adults." Similarly, Rule 3.3 of the Beijing Rules states: "Efforts shall also be made to extend the principles embodied in the Rules to young adult offenders." Rule 17 continues in the same vein. Young adults in general are in a transitional stage of life, which can justify their being dealt with by the juvenile justice agencies and juvenile courts. Particularly in the past 15 years, many countries have taken into consideration this extended period of transition by either providing the possibility of applying educational measures to young adult offenders or at least by providing for special mitigation of their sentences (see for a summary Pruin 2007; Dünkel and Pruin 2012; Pruin and Dünkel 2014). Applying sanctions or measures provided under the juvenile criminal law does not automatically mean that young adults will receive milder sanctions than adults over the age of 21; but where appropriate, they should benefit from the variety of educational sanctions and measures that are provided for juvenile offenders. It is an evidence-based policy to encourage legislators to extend the scope of juvenile justice to the age group of young adults. Processes of education and integration into the social life of adults have been prolonged and more appropriate constructive reactions with regard to the particular developmental problems of young adults can often be found in juvenile justice legislation (see for example the special emphasis given to mediation, and family conferencing in many new juvenile justice laws).

Rule 18 corresponds to Rule 8 of the EPR and places the staff of juvenile welfare and justice agencies or institutions at the centre of caring for juvenile offenders as they need special and intensive assistance. Rule 18 is strongly related to Rule 15 emphasizing the co-operation of different agencies involved (multi-agency approach). All staff in the field of juvenile welfare and justice must be suitable for working with juveniles and be specially trained or experienced in developmental and educational matters. Regular in-service training and supervision should be provided. Positive role models are particularly important, as in many instances staff has to play the role, which is normally taken by members of the juvenile's family.

The standards of care and accountability apply not only when staff are employed on a permanent basis but also when execution is delegated to, or commissioned from other agencies.

Rule 19 is related to Rule 18 and is designed to clarify that juvenile welfare and justice agencies must receive the necessary funding in order to achieve the required educational and social integration goals. The different agencies must be equipped in a way that enables them to provide the appropriate standard of care to meet the distinctive needs of juveniles. This can also mean that services are allocated according to different needs and risks posed by offenders. The rule corresponds to Rule 4 of the EPR. It conveys the message that lack of resources can never justify the infringement of human rights of juveniles. By imposing sanctions or measures on juvenile offenders the state intervenes at an age where normally the family is responsible for the juvenile's upbringing. If the state partially replaces the parents it must guarantee that its interventions are meaningful, positive and effective.

Rule 20 reflects the necessity of regular government inspection as well as of independent monitoring. This Rule corresponds to Rule 9 of the EPR. Independent monitoring by persons or institutions that are not controlled by state agencies is an essential and important element of democratic control as it may guarantee effective supervision of the general juvenile justice system that is independent from individual complaints procedures. The Rule envisages monitoring by recognised bodies such as boards of visitors or accredited NGOs, ombudsmen and other similar agencies. An effective individual complaints procedure available to juveniles concerning the imposition and execution of sanctions and measures complements the inspection and monitoring mechanisms.

3 Contemporary Trends in Youth Justice Policy

Across Europe, policies based on the notions of subsidiarity and proportionality of state interventions against juvenile offenders have remained in force or emerged afresh in most, if not all, countries. Recently however, we have also witnessed developments that adopt a contrary approach in several European countries. These developments intensify youth justice interventions by raising maximum sentences for youth detention and by introducing additional forms of secure accommodation. Youth justice reforms in the *Netherlands* in 1995 and in some respects in *France* in 1996, 2002 and 2007 should be mentioned in this context, as should the reforms in *England and Wales* in 1994 and 1998 (Albrecht and Kilchling 2002; Cavadino and Dignan 2007, p. 284ff., 2006, p. 215ff.; Junger-Tas and Decker 2006; Bailleau and Cartuyvels 2007; Crawford and Lewis 2007; Hartjen 2008; Hazel 2008; Junger-Tas and Dünkel 2009; Dünkel et al. 2011). The causes of the more repressive or "neo-liberal" approach in some countries are manifold. It is likely that the punitive trend in the USA, with its emphasis on retribution and deterrence, was not without considerable impact in some European countries, particularly in *England and Wales*.

These developments at the national level, which are the primary focus of this chapter, have to be understood against the background of international and regional instruments that set standards for juvenile justice. Most important in this regard is the 1989 UN Convention on the Rights of the Child, a binding international treaty that all European states have ratified. It makes clear that the common and principal aim of youth justice should be to act in the 'best interests of the child'—"child" defined for the purpose of this Convention as a person under the age of 18 years—and to provide education, support and integration into society for such children. These ideas are developed further in the 1985 UN Standard Minimum Rules for the Administration of Juvenile Justice and at the European level in the recommendations of the Council of Europe, in particular the 2003 Recommendation regarding new ways of dealing with juvenile offending (Rec [2003]20) and the 2008 Rules for juvenile offenders subject to sanctions or measures (Rec [2008]11; Dünkel 2009; Dünkel et al. 2011, p. 1861ff).

In the last few years a remarkable shift towards the educational ideal of juvenile justice can be observed in countries, such as England and Wales (see Smith 2010; for a critical comment Goldson 2011), and the Netherlands, which claimed to be driven by neo-liberal ideas in the 1990s and 2000s. From outside Europe a comparable revival of traditional youth justice ideas can be observed in the US as well (see Dünkel 2014; Bishop and Feld 2012).

3.1 Responsibilisation and Neo-Liberalism

In *England and Wales*, and to some extent elsewhere, the concept of responsibilisation has become a pivotal category of youth justice.[5] Responsibilisation is not just limited to young offenders, but also includes parents who are increasingly being held criminally responsible for the conduct of their children.[6] Making parents more responsible may have a positive impact. There is empirical evidence that parental training, combined with child support at an early stage may have positive preventive effects. However, it is not necessary to criminalise parents, because parents who have neglected their parental duties will be better assisted by the welfare rather than the criminal justice system.[7] Ideally, parental training should be offered by welfare agencies (as is the case in *Germany* and the Scandinavian countries) instead of being enforced by penal sanctions (Junger-Tas and Dünkel 2009: 225f.).

---

[5] See critically, Crawford and Lewis 2007, p. 27, and Cavadino and Dignan 2006, p. 68 ff. with regards to the "managerial" and the "getting tough" approach.

[6] See, for example, the so-called parenting order in *England* and *Wales* or similar measures in *Belgium*, *Bulgaria*, *France*, *Greece*, *Ireland* or *Scotland*: Pruin 2011, p. 1559ff.

[7] Punitive sanctions for parents, such as fines or prison sentences, are counterproductive, as parents are often unable to afford to pay fines, and incarceration takes them away from their children.

A positive aspect of making young offenders take responsibility for their actions is that it has contributed to the expansion of victim-offender-reconciliation (*Täter-Opfer-Ausgleich*), mediation and reparation. In the English context, however, it is more problematic as it has been accompanied by the abolition of the previously rebuttable presumption that 10- to 14-year olds may lack criminal capacity. Although in practice the presumption had been relatively easily to rebut, its formal abolition in 1998 was indicative of determination to hold even very young offenders responsible for their actions. The tendencies in English youth justice may be regarded as symptoms of neo-liberalism, characterised by four key terms: responsibility, restitution (reparation), restorative justice and (occasionally openly publicised) retribution. These "4 Rs" have replaced the "4 Ds" (diversion, decriminalization, deinstitutionalization and due process) that shaped the debates of the 1960s and 1970s (Dünkel 2008). The retributive character of the new discourse is exemplified by the requirement that community interventions be "tough" and "credible". For example, the "community treatment" of the 1960s was replaced by "community punishment" in the 1980s and 1990s. Cavadino and Dignan attribute these changes to the so-called "neo-correctionalist model" that has come to dominate official English penology (Cavadino and Dignan 2006: 210ff.; Bailleau and Cartuyvels 2007; Muncie 2008).

A number of authors have established that there are many reasons for the increase in neo-liberal tendencies (Garland 2001a, b; Roberts and Hough 2002; Tonry 2004; Pratt et al. 2005; Muncie 2008). These include the renewed emphasis on penal philosophies such as retribution and incapacitation, and related sentencing policies that demonise youth violence, often by means of indeterminate sentences. There are also underlying socio-economic reasons. More repressive policies have gained importance in countries that face particular problems with young migrants or members of ethnic minorities, and that have problems integrating young persons into the labour market, particularly where a growing number of them live in segregated and declining city areas. They often have no real possibility of escaping life as members of the "underclass", a phenomenon that undermines "society's stability and social cohesion and create mechanisms of social exclusion" (Junger-Tas 2006, p. 522f., 524). They are at risk of being marginalised and eventually criminalized. In this context recidivist offending is of major concern. Therefore many of the more punitive changes to the law are restricted to recidivist offenders in *England* and *Wales*, *France*, and *Slovakia*.

It should be emphasised, however, that most continental European countries have not regressed to the classical penal objectives and perceptions of the eighteenth and nineteenth centuries. Instead, the idea of "education" (rehabilitation) has been maintained, even though "justice" elements have also been reinforced. The tension between education and punishment remains evident. The reform laws adopted in *Germany* in 1990, the *Netherlands* in 1995, *Spain* in 2000 and 2006, *Portugal* in 2001, *France* and *Northern Ireland* in 2002, *Lithuania* in 2001, the *Czech Republic* in 2003 and *Serbia* in 2006 are examples of this dual approach. The reforms in *Northern Ireland* in 2002 and *Belgium* in 2006 are of particular interest, as they strengthened restorative elements in youth justice, including the concept of family conferencing, and thus arguably contributed to responsibilisation without necessarily being "neo-liberal" in their fundamental orientation (Christiaens et al. in Dünkel et al. 2011; O'Mahony and Campbell 2006; Doak and O'Mahony 2011).

It must be recognized, however, that, even in countries with a moderate and stable youth justice practice, the rhetoric in political debates is sometimes dominated by penal populism with distinctly neo-liberal undertones. Nevertheless, this does not necessarily result in change, as can be demonstrated by a German example. At the end of 2007 several violent crimes in subways (filmed by automatic cameras) led to a heated public debate about the necessity to increase the sanctions provided by the Juvenile Justice Act. The leader of the Christian Democratic Party (CDU) of the federal state of Hesse, Roland Koch, made this a core element of his electoral campaign by proposing the use of boot camps and other more severe punishments for juvenile violent offenders. He also made several xenophobic statements against young immigrant offenders. Within a few days almost a thousand criminal justice practitioners and academics signed a resolution against such penal populism, and in January 2008 the CDU lost the elections. Since then penal populism has not been made a major issue in electoral campaigns again. The CDU had gone too far. Muncie (2008, p. 109) refers to this debate in Germany and interprets it as an indicator for increased punitiveness. Yet, youth justice practice in *Germany* has remained stable and sentencing levels relatively moderate (Heinz 2009).

3.2 Diversion, Minimum Intervention and Community Sanctions

Research related to disposals that are made applicable to young offenders has shown a clear expansion of the available means of diversion. However, this is often linked to educational measures or just warnings. Such warnings are not real sanctions, but they make it clear to the young offender that he has done wrong and that if he continues to commit crimes, more severe reactions will follow (Dünkel et al. 2011). Sometimes, however, the concern for minimum intervention still means that diversion from prosecution leads to no further steps being taken at all.

In most countries the deprivation of liberty is generally used as a measure of last resort. In practice, the concept of "last resort" varies across time and in cross-national comparison. *England* and *Wales*, for example, experienced sharp increases in the juvenile prison population from the 1990s to the mid-2000s, but the reduction of unconditional youth imprisonment by 45 % from 2007 to 2012 demonstrates a shift in the sentencing policy, as demographic changes were only of minor importance in regard to this reduction (Horsfield 2015). *Spain* and a few other countries showed an increase in the use of youth custody in previous years, but recent developments have reversed this trend. This is also true for Central and Eastern European countries. *Croatia*, the *Czech Republic*, *Hungary*, *Latvia*, *Romania* and

Slovenia, and recently *Russia* have achieved higher levels of diversion and community sanctions and lower levels of custodial sanctions that remain characteristic of continental Western European and Scandinavian countries. However, *Lithuania* and *Slovakia* still use deprivation of liberty more often, albeit not as frequently as in Soviet times.

With the exception of some serious offences, the vast majority of youth offending in Europe is dealt with out of court by means of informal diversionary measures: for example, in *Belgium* about 80 %, and in *Germany* about 70 % of youth offending is dealt with in this way (Dünkel et al. 2011, p. 1684ff.). In some countries, such as *Croatia*, *France*, the *Netherlands*, *Serbia* and *Slovenia*, this is a direct consequence of the long recognised principle of allowing the prosecution and even the police a wide degree of discretion—the so-called expediency principle. On the other hand, while Central and Eastern European countries do not allow for such prosecutorial discretion, a majority of youth offending is still dealt with out of court as offences that cause minimal damage are not treated as statutory criminal offences. *Italy* provides for a judicial pardon, which is similar to diversionary exemptions from punishment, but awarded by the youth court judge (see for the moderate Italian style of sentencing with particularly low juvenile incarceration rates Nelken 2009, 2010). Thus, a large variety of forms of non-intervention or minor (informal or formal) sanctions can be seen across Europe.

Constructive measures, such as social training courses (*Germany*) and labour and learning sanctions or projects (*The Netherlands*), have also been successfully implemented as part of a strategy of diversion. Many countries explicitly follow the ideal of education (*Portugal*), while at the same time emphasising prevention of re-offending, that is, special prevention (as suggested by the Council of Europe's 2003 Recommendation on new ways of dealing with juvenile delinquency and the role of juvenile justice).

3.3 Restorative Justice

One development that appears to be common to Central, Eastern and Western European countries is the application of restorative justice policies (see in summary Dünkel et al. 2015a, b). Victim-offender-reconciliation, mediation, or sanctions that require reparation or apology to the victim have played an important role in all legislative reforms undertaken in the last 15 years. Pilot mediation projects were established in the 1990s in Central and Eastern European countries such as *Poland*, *Slovenia* and the *Czech Republic*.

In some countries, legislation provides for elements of restorative justice to be used as independent sanctions by youth courts. In *England* and *Wales*, for example, this is done by means of reparation or restitution orders, and in *Germany* by ordering victim-offender-reconciliation as an educational directive (*Wiedergutmachungsauflage)* (see §§ 10 and 15 of the Juvenile Justice Act). In 2006, family group conferences—originally introduced and applied in New Zealand—were introduced in *Belgium*. These conferences are forms of mediation that take into account and seek to activate the social family networks of both the offender and the victim. Even before the Belgian reform project, youth justice reform in *Northern Ireland* had introduced youth conferences, which have been running as pilot projects since 2003. In addition Northern Ireland, made provisions for reparation orders: an idea that had been introduced in *England* and *Wales* in 1998 (O'Mahony and Campbell 2006; O'Mahony and Doak 2009; Doak and O'Mahony 2011).

Whether these restorative elements actually influence sentencing practice or are merely a 'fig-leaf' seeking to disguise a more repressive youth justice system can only be determined by taking into account the different backgrounds and traditions in each country. Victim-offender-reconciliation has attained great quantitative significance in the sanctioning practices of both the *Austrian* and the *German* youth courts.[8] If one also takes community service into account as a restorative sanction in the broader sense, the proportion of all juvenile and young adult offenders who are dealt with by such—ideally educational—constructive alternatives increases to more than one third (Heinz 2012).

In *Italy* procedural rules for youth justice introduced in 1988 have led to a move away from a purely rehabilitative and punitive perspective to a new conception of penal procedure. Restorative justice measures have gained much more attention and victim-offender mediation can be applied at different stages of the procedure: during preliminary investigations and the preliminary hearing when considering "the extinction of a sentence because of the irrelevance of the offence" or in combination with the suspension of the procedure with supervision by the probation service (*Sospensione del processo e messa alla prova*).

In general one can summarize that the idea of restorative justice has been successfully implemented all over Europe, but numbers remain moderate. Mediation, reparation and restitution orders quantitatively cover only a small part, regularly less than 10 % of all informal (juvenile prosecutor) and formal (juvenile court) reactions of the juvenile justice system (see Dünkel et al. 2015a, b).

4 Youth Justice Models

If one compares youth justice systems from a perspective of classifying them according to typologies, the "classical" orientations of both the justice and the welfare models can still be differentiated (Doob and Tonry 2004, p.1ff.; Pruin 2011). However, one rarely, if ever, encounters the ideal types of welfare or justice models in their pure form. Rather, there are several examples of mixed systems, for instance within German and other continental European youth justice legislation.

[8] Roughly 8 % of all sanctions imposed on juveniles, see Dünkel in Dünkel et al. 2011: 587; for *Austria* see Bruckmüller 2006. In summary for 36 European countries, see Dünkel et al. 2015a, b.

Youth justice policy in recent decades has demonstrated a tendency to strengthen the justice model by establishing or extending procedural safeguards, and providing welfare measures. This tendency also includes a strict emphasis on the principle of proportionality, thereby moving away from sentences and educational measures that are disproportionately harsh.

An emphasis on the justice model also denotes a clear differentiation of the kind of misbehaviour that is subject to juvenile justice interventions. Most European juvenile justice laws rely on criminal behaviour defined by the general criminal law, whereas other forms of problematic behaviour which could endanger the juvenile and its future development are dealt with by separate welfare or family laws. A unified welfare and justice approach (as in the classic welfare model) in Europe is only to be found in Belgium, Scotland and Poland.

Recently other states have passed legislation related to certain misbehaviour ("anti-social" behaviour), which is addressed by civil law, but with a "hidden" form of criminalisation in case of civil law order violations (Bulgaria, England and Wales, Ireland, and Northern Ireland). For instance, a violation of Anti-Social-Behaviour-Orders constitutes a criminal offence, and therefore a young person may be subject to criminal punishment even if he has only violated a civil law obligation. In contrast, status offences such as truancy or running away from home in the continental European juvenile justice systems are dealt with in separate civil or welfare laws, and therefore cannot be "punished" by youth courts (see in summary Pruin 2011: 1553ff.). On the other hand, restorative justice and minimum intervention policies, as well as "neo-liberal" tendencies towards harsher sentences and "getting tough" on youth crime are not necessarily based squarely on "justice" or "welfare", and can be viewed as independent models of youth justice (Albrecht and Kilchling 2002; Tonry and Doob 2004; Jensen and Jepsen 2006; Junger-Tas and Decker 2006; Bailleau and Cartuyvels 2007; Ciappi 2007; Patané 2007; Cimamonti et al. 2010; Pruin 2011). Cavadino and Dignan (2006, p. 210ff.) identify not only a "minimum intervention model" (including diversion and community sanctions) and a "restorative justice model" (including restorative/reparative reactions), but also a "neo-correctionalist model", which, as mentioned previously, is particularly characteristic of contemporary trends and developments in England and Wales.

Here, too, there are no clear boundaries, for the majority of continental European youth justice systems incorporate not only elements of welfare and justice philosophies, but also minimum intervention (as is especially the case in Germany, see Dünkel 2006, 2011a, b), restorative justice and elements of neo-correctionalism (for example, increased "responsibilisation" of the offenders and their parents, tougher penalties for recidivists and secure accommodation for children). The differences are more evident in the degree of orientation towards restorative or punitive elements. In general, one can conclude that European juvenile justice is moving towards mixed systems that combine welfare and justice elements, which are further shaped by the trends mentioned above.

5 Reform Strategies

Against this background of a range of old and newly prominent ideas combined with somewhat fractured models, one can identify a number of reform strategies.

In many Western European countries, such strategies seem to have been relatively well-planned. In Austria, Germany and the Netherlands, the community sanctions and restorative justice elements that were introduced by reforms in 1988, 1990 and 1995 respectively were systematically and extensively piloted. Nationwide implementation of the reform programmes was dependent on prior empirical verification of the projects' practicability and acceptance. The process of testing and generating acceptance—especially among judges and the prosecution service—takes time. Continuous supplementary and further training is required, which is difficult to guarantee in times of social change, as has been the case in Central and Eastern Europe. Yet, reform of youth justice through practice (as developed in Germany in the 1980s) appears preferable to a reform "from above", which often fails to provide the appropriate infrastructure.

As a result of major political changes at the end of the 1980s, drastic reform was required in the Central and Eastern European countries. The situation as it existed at the time was not uniform across the region but differed amongst groups of countries. One group comprised of the Soviet republics, Bulgaria, Romania and to some degree the German Democratic Republic (East Germany) and Czechoslovakia. These countries had developed a more punitively oriented youth justice policy and practice. The other group comprised of Hungary, Poland and Yugoslavia, which had rather moderate youth justice policies with many educational elements.

Across Central and Eastern Europe developments since the early 1990s have been characterised by a clear increase in the levels of officially recorded youth crime. The need for youth justice reform, a widely accepted notion in all of these countries, stemmed from the need to replace old (often Soviet or Soviet-influenced) law with (Western) European standards as contained in the principles of the Council of Europe and the United Nations. This process has, however, produced somewhat different trends in criminal policy.

Since the early 1990s, there has been a dynamic reform movement both in law and in practice. It is exemplified in numerous projects, including in the creation of law reform commissions and also in the adoption of reform legislation especially in Estonia, Lithuania, Serbia, Slovenia and the Czech Republic.

The development of an independent youth justice system has been a prominent feature of these reforms: as seen in the Baltic States, Croatia, the Czech Republic, Romania, Russia, Serbia, Slovakia, and Turkey. These countries have recognised the importance of procedural safeguards and entitlements that also take the special educational needs of young offenders into account. However, while Russia and Romania have succeeded in setting up their first model youth courts, independent youth courts in the Baltic States remain to be seen. It is also important to note that in general, the required infrastructure for the introduction of modern, social-pedagogical approaches to youth justice and welfare is widely lacking.

In order to deter recidivists and violent young offenders in particular, some of this new legislation not only involves new community sanctions and possibilities of diversion, but also retains tough custodial sentences. The absence of appropriate infrastructure and of widespread acceptance of community sanctions still results in frequent prison sentences. However, developments in Russia, for example, show that a return to past sanctioning patterns, where roughly 50 % of all young offenders were sentenced to imprisonment has not occurred. Instead, forms of probation are now quantitatively more common, and more frequently used than sentences of imprisonment.

What is becoming clear in all Central and Eastern European countries is that the principle of imprisonment as a last resort (ultima ratio) is being taken more seriously and the number of custodial sanctions have been reduced. However, it has to be noted that youth imprisonment or similar sanctions in the ex-Yugoslavian republics and to a lesser extent also in Hungary and Poland had already been restricted to a small minority of cases during the period before the political changes at the beginning of the 1990s.

Regarding community sanctions, the difficulties of establishing the necessary infrastructure are clear. Initially, the greatest problem in this respect was the lack of qualified social workers and teachers. This has remained a problem as to a great extent the appropriate training courses have not yet been fully introduced and developed (Dünkel et al. 2011). Again one has to differentiate as there are exceptions: Poland has a long tradition in social work. Also in the former Yugoslavia social workers were trained, following the introduction of "strict supervision" as a special sanction in 1960.

The concept of "conditional" criminal responsibility (related to the ability of discernment and the capability to act according to this discernment) found in German and Italian law—has recently been adopted in Estonia (2002), the Czech Republic (2003) and Slovakia (for 14 year olds, see Pruin 2011, p. 1566ff.). This is an interesting development, as it reflects another instance where reforms in Central and Eastern European countries have been influenced by Austrian and German youth justice law as well as by international standards. Despite obvious and undeniable national particularities, there is a recognisable degree of convergence among the systems in Western, Central and Eastern Europe.

6 The Scope of Juvenile Justice

On the basis of comparative research one may speak, albeit cautiously, of an emerging European philosophy of juvenile justice, which includes elements of education and rehabilitation (apparent in, for example, the recommendations of the Council of Europe), the consideration of victims through mediation and restoration, and the observance of legal procedural safeguards. However, there are some issues on which such a development is not as clear. In this regard we consider the age of criminal responsibility and its corollary, the age at which offenders cease to be regarded as juveniles and are treated as adults. The latter issue also raises the question of whether there should be some mechanism for the converse, namely, allowing juveniles to be tried in adult courts.

6.1 Age of Criminal Responsibility

In spite of the common "European philosophy" of juvenile justice mentioned above, the minimum ages of criminal responsibility differ vastly across the European continent. Indeed, the 2008 European rules for juvenile offenders subject to sanctions or measures recommend no particular age, specifying only that some age should be specified by law and that it "shall not be too low"(Rule 4).

The minimum age of criminal responsibility in Europe varies between 10 (England and Wales, Northern Ireland, and Switzerland), 12 (Netherlands, Scotland, and Turkey), 13 (France), 14 (Austria, Germany, Italy, Spain and numerous Central and Eastern European countries), 15 (Greece and the Scandinavian countries) and even 16 (for specific offences in Russia and other Eastern European countries) or 18 (Belgium). After the recent reforms in Central and Eastern Europe, the most common age of criminal responsibility is 14 (see Table 1).

While England and Wales can be criticized for their low age of criminal responsibility, in many countries only educational sanctions imposed by the family and youth courts are applicable at an earlier age (for example, France and Greece). Also in Switzerland, the youth court judge can only impose educational measures on 10–14 year olds (who are, however, seen as criminally responsible), whereas juvenile prison sentences are restricted to those aged at least 15. The same is the case in the ex-Yugoslavian republics of Croatia, Kosovo, Serbia and Slovenia for 14 and 15 year old offenders. Further still, some countries, such as Lithuania and Russia, employ a graduated scale of criminal responsibility, according to which only more serious and grave offences can be prosecuted from the age of 14, while the general minimum age of criminal responsibility lies at 16 (for a summary, see also Pruin 2011). This graduated scale of criminal responsibility must be criticized as it contradicts the basic philosophy of juvenile justice, according to which sanctions must be decided in relation to individual development of maturity or other personality concepts rather than the seriousness of the offence (see also the criticism under Sect. 6.3).

Whether these notable differences can in fact be correlated to variations in sentencing is not entirely apparent. Even within systems based solely on education, under certain circumstances the possibility of being accommodated as a last resort in a home or in residential care (particularly in the form of closed or secure centres as in England and Wales and France) can be just as intensive and of an equal or even longer duration than a sentence of juvenile imprisonment. Furthermore, the legal levels of criminal responsibility do not necessarily give any indication of whether a youth justice or welfare approach is more or less punitive in practice. What happens in reality often differs considerably from the language used in reform debates

(Doob and Tonry 2004: 16ff.). Legal changes that make a regime more intensive not only contribute to changes in practice, but may also be the result of changes in practice. The effect of these changes varies, too. Despite the dramatization of events by the mass media that sometimes leads to changes in the law, there is often, in Germany for instance, a remarkable continuity and a degree of stability in youth justice practice (Dünkel 2006; Dünkel in Dünkel et al. 2011).

6.2 Young Adults

There are also interesting developments in the upper age limits of criminal responsibility (the maximum age to which juvenile criminal law or juvenile sanctions can be applied). The central issue in this regard is the extension of the applicability of juvenile criminal law—or at least its educational measures—to young adults between the ages of 18–20, as occurred in Germany as early as in 1953 (see also the recent reforms in Austria, Croatia, Lithuania and the Netherlands; Pruin 2007; Dünkel and Pruin 2011, 2012).

This tendency is rooted in a criminological understanding of the transitional phases of personal and social development from adolescence to adulthood and a recognition that such transitions are taking longer. Over the last 50 years, the phases of education and of integration into work and family life (the establishment of one's "own family") have been prolonged well beyond the age of 20. Many young people experience developmental-psychological crises and difficulties in the transition to adult life, and increasingly such difficulties continue to occur into their mid-twenties (Pruin 2007; Dünkel and Pruin 2011, 2012; Pruin and Dünkel 2014). Furthermore, new neuro-scientific evidence indicates that maturity and psycho-social abilities are fully developed only in the third decade of life (Weijers and Grisso 2009, p. 63ff.; Bonnie et al. 2012, chapters 4 and 5; Loeber et al. 2012 p. 336ff.), which would justify a juvenile justice system up to the age of 21 or even 24. The Dutch government has recently extended the scope of juvenile justice until the age of 23 (see for the respective reform proposals Loeber et al. 2012 pp. 368ff., 394ff.; Dünkel 2014).

An increasing number of states have statutory provisions for imposing educational and other sanctions of the youth justice law on young adults. Historically however, such laws have not always had the same impact in practice. While in Germany the laws applicable to juveniles are applied in more than 90 % of the cases concerning young adults who commit serious crimes (overall average: more than 60 %; see Dünkel in Dünkel et al. 2011), in most other countries this has remained the exception. One reason is that in Germany the jurisdiction of the juvenile court has been extended to young adults, whereas in other countries the criminal court for adults is responsible for this age group. However, adult criminal courts can impose some of the measures otherwise reserved for juveniles (for example, in the former Yugoslavia, which introduced this possibility in 1960: Gensing 2011, 2014).

The Yugoslavian experience is a good example of how substantive and procedural laws have been harmonized in order to prevent counterproductive effects of such provisions. There was therefore good reason in 1998 for Croatia and Serbia, former Yugoslavian states, to transfer the jurisdiction of young adults to juvenile courts. Austria took the same step in 2001.

In other instances keeping young adults fully in the adult framework does not mean that they cannot be treated like juveniles in practice. In the Netherlands, for example, the general criminal law provides for a plethora of alternative sanctions, which can be seen as educational or rehabilitative (for example, community service) and which are not provided for in the German criminal law for adults.

The Council of Europe has taken these new considerations about the prolongation of the transitional phase of young adults into account in its 2003 Recommendation on "New ways of dealing with juvenile offenders and the role of juvenile justice" (Rec. (2003) 20) and in the "European Rules for Juvenile Offenders Subject to Sanctions or Measures" (ERJOSSM) passed in 2008 (Rec. (2008) 11). Rule 11 of the 2003 Recommendation reads as follows: "Reflecting the extended transition to adulthood, it should be possible for young adults under the age of 21 to be treated in a way comparable to juveniles and to be subject to the same interventions, when the judge is of the opinion that they are not as mature and responsible for their actions as full adults."

In September 2004 the International Association of Penal Law (AIDP) held its World Congress in Beijing, China. The final Resolution of the Congress emphasizes "that the state of adolescence can be prolonged into young adulthood (25 years) and that, as a consequence, legislation needs to be adapted for young adults in a similar way as it is done for minors." The age of criminal majority should be set at 18 years, and the minimum age not lower than 14 years (see No. 2 of the Resolution). Under No. 6., the Resolution states: "Concerning crimes committed by persons over 18 years of age, the applicability of the special provisions for minors may be extended up to the age of 25."

Also, Rule 17 of ERJOSSM states that "young adult offenders may, where appropriate, be regarded as juveniles and dealt with accordingly". The commentary to this rule states that "it is an evidence-based policy to encourage legislators to extend the scope of juvenile justice to the age group of young adults. Processes of education and integration into social life of adults have been prolonged and more appropriate constructive reactions with regard to the particular developmental problems of young adults can often be found in juvenile justice legislation" (Council of Europe 2009, p. 42).

This inclusion of young adults (defined by the age between 18 and 21) in juvenile justice legislation is being seen increasingly across Europe, and especially in the 2014 reform of the Dutch Juvenile Justice system that extended the scope of juvenile justice even up to the age of 23.

The United Nations' recommendations until recently did not reflect this issue by just defining the scope of juvenile justice for "children", i. e. the age group below 18 years of age (see e.g. No. 4 of the so-called Beijing-Rules of 1985). However, in its recent proposal for a Model Law on Juvenile Justice of 2013 the authors make an interesting statement: "States should note that a majority of European States have extended the applicability *ratione personae* of their juvenile justice laws to the age of 21 as neuro-scientific evidence and brain development studies have indicated that it is difficult to distinguish between the brain of an older child and that of a young adult." (United Nations Office of Drug and Crime 2013: 57). The Model Law opens the floor to states who wish to do so to extend the scope also for the age group of young adults. Indeed, there exist a few examples concerning the scope of juvenile justice in Non-European countries in that way, as e. g. in Japan or in Brazil and Uruguay (see Castro Morales 2015: 18ff.).

6.3 Transfer to Adult Criminal Courts or Jurisdiction (Waiver Procedures)

While an extension of juvenile justice law to young adults may be seen as a way of imposing more appropriate sentences on immature young adults, there is also an opposite trend, most prominent in the USA (Stump 2003; Bishop 2009) but also found in many European countries (Pruin 2011), of referring children for trial in adult courts. Such referrals have a distinctively punitive purpose.

In some European countries, such as Scotland and Portugal, juvenile offenders as young as age sixteen can be dealt with in the adult criminal justice system. Beyond that, in a few other countries, specific juvenile offenders can be transferred from youth court to adult court, where waiver or transfer laws provide for the application of adult criminal law to certain offences (Stump 2003; Bishop 2009; Weijers et al. 2009; Beaulieu 1994, p. 329ff.; Goldson and Muncie 2006, p. 91ff.; Keiser 2008). This is in fact a qualified limitation of the scope of juvenile justice (Hazel 2008: 35) and a lowering of the minimum age for the full application of adult criminal law.

Some countries, such as Belgium, provide for the application of adult criminal law to juveniles aged 16 or 17 that commit serious offences including rape, aggravated assault, aggravated sexual assault, aggravated theft, (attempted) murder and (attempted) homicide. The reforms that took place in 2006 allowed for the jurisdiction of Extended Juvenile Courts to conduct such trials. Prior to this reform juveniles were tried by adult courts. In the Netherlands the youth court remains competent as well, but the general criminal law can be applied to 16 and 17 year-old juveniles. In 1995 the requirements were relaxed. The seriousness of the criminal offence, the personality of the young offender, or the circumstances under which the offence is committed can lead to the application of adult criminal law. The law provides the judge with a great deal of discretion. In most cases, in practice it is the seriousness of the offence that leads to the application of adult criminal law. In England and Wales, juveniles, even at the age of 10, can be transferred to the adult criminal court (Crown Court) if charged with an exceptionally serious offence (including murder and crimes that would in the case of adult offenders carry a maximum term of imprisonment of more than 14 years). The Crown Court has to apply slightly different rules for the protection of juveniles in this case. The number of juvenile offenders who are sent to the Crown Court has fluctuated over the last 25 years without any indication of a clear-cut trend in either direction.

In Serbia and in Northern Ireland, transfers are limited to juveniles who have been charged with homicide or who are co-accused with adult offenders. In the latter case, there is an interesting alternative as well: the juvenile has to be referred back to the youth court for sentencing following a finding of guilt (O'Mahony in Dünkel et al. 2011). In Ireland, in exceptional cases like treason or crimes against the peace of nations, murder and manslaughter, juveniles are tried by the Central Criminal Court before a judge and jury.

In France, in contrast, less serious offences, rather classed as misdemeanours, are brought before an adult court. Since 1945 in cases of misdemeanours (contraventions des quatre premières classes) juvenile offenders are judged by the Police Court which can issue reprimands or fines. Since 2002, the competences of the Police Court have been conferred on a specific 'proximity judge', who is neither a lawyer nor a youth justice specialist, but has the competence to 'punish' juveniles up to a certain level (Castaignède and Pignoux in Dünkel et al. 2011).

In Scotland there are no waivers or transfer laws, but the same effect can be achieved in another way. In most severe cases the juvenile offender will not be transferred to the children's hearings system. Formally, this is not a transfer to the adult criminal court, because the criminal court has original competence to try all cases, even if in practice the vast majority is transferred to the children's hearings system. However, Scotland shares the idea that in very serious cases the offenders should not be dealt by the juvenile criminal system but in the adult criminal system.

Countries, like those in Scandinavia that do not have specialised juvenile jurisdictions, thus (naturally) do not have provision for transfers either. It should be emphasized though, that, in general, in the Scandinavian countries the same regulations apply in cases of "aggravated" as well as "normal" offences.

The application of adult law to juveniles through waivers or transfer laws can be regarded as a systemic weakness in those jurisdictions that allow it (Stump 2003). Whereas normally the application of (juvenile) law depends on the age of the offender, transfer laws or waivers rely on the type or seriousness of the committed offence. The justification for special treatment of juvenile offenders (as an inherent principle of youth justice) is challenged by such provisions (Keiser 2008, p. 38). The fundamental idea is to react differently to offences that are committed by offenders up to a certain age, based on their level of maturity or on their ability of discernment. Waivers or transfer laws question this idea for serious offences. On the one hand, the maximum age of criminal responsibility signifies—independently from the type of offence—from which age on a young person is deemed "mature enough" to receive (adult) criminal punishment. On the other hand, however, the introduction of "transfer laws" makes exactly those offenders fully responsible who often lack the (social) maturity to abstain from crime or even differentiate right from wrong. Furthermore, it is hard to imagine that the same juvenile would be regarded as not fully mature when charged with a "normal" offence, but fully criminally responsible for a serious offence. As Weijers and Grisso (2009, p. 67) have put it: "An adolescent has the same degree of capacity to form criminal intent, no matter what crime he commits." A systematic approach would treat all offences equally.

States with transfer laws or waivers often argue that these laws are justified by the alleged deterrent effect of more severe sanctions on juvenile offenders. Additionally, they claim that waivers are needed as a "safety valve" (Weijers et al. 2009) for the juvenile courts because juvenile law does not provide adequate or suitable options for severe cases. However, so far criminological research has not found evidence for positive effects of transfers or waivers. In fact, research has suggested that transferring juveniles to adult courts has negative effects on preventing offending, including increased recidivism.

The second argument misses the point as well: Does adult criminal law provide adequate or suitable options for reacting to severe criminality? How do we measure effectiveness? If we look at recidivism rates, then long prison sentences—the typical reaction by adult criminal law to serious offending—are relatively ineffective in preventing further crimes (Killias and Villettaz 2007, p. 213). Furthermore, research shows that a lenient, minimum-interventionist juvenile justice system does not produce any more juvenile offenders than an active and punitive one (Smith 2005, p. 192ff.).

In practice, transfers may be of declining significance in Europe. In the Netherlands the number of transfers to the adult court has been reduced considerably: Whereas in 1995, 16 % of all cases were dealt with by the adult criminal court, it was only 1.2 % in 2004 (Weijers et al. 2009, p. 110). In Belgium the use of transfers is very limited as well: transfer decisions amount to 3 % of all judgments (Weijers et al. 2009, p. 118 with references to regional differences). In Ireland, adult criminal courts are competent in less than 5 % of all cases against juveniles. In Poland, from 1999 to 2004 the number of cases transferred to public prosecutors swung between 242 and 309, which is 0.2–0.3 % of all cases tried by the courts (Stańdo-Kawecka in Dünkel et al. 2011).

Even if waivers and transfer laws are of little significance in practice in most countries, they are nonetheless systemic flaws that ultimately undermine the special regulations for juvenile offenders. Additional safeguards in adult courts are unable to compensate for them (Keiser 2008: 38). Therefore the UN Committee on the Rights of the Child recommends abolishing all provisions that allow offenders under the age of 18 to be treated as adults, in order to achieve full and non-discriminatory implementation of the special rules of youth justice to all juveniles under the age of 18 years (Committee on the Rights of the Child 2007, paras. 34, 36, 37 and 38; Doek 2009, p. 23).

7 Summary and Conclusion

Juvenile justice systems in Europe have developed in various forms and with different orientations. Looking at sanctions and measures, the general trend reveals the expansion of diversion, combined in some countries with educational or other measures that aim to improve compliance with law (Normverdeutlichung). Mediation, victim-offender reconciliation or family group conferences are good examples of such diversionary strategies. On the other hand, from an international comparative perspective, systems based solely on child and youth welfare are on the retreat. This is not so evident in Europe where more or less "pure" welfare oriented approaches exist only in Belgium and Poland as in, for instance, Latin American countries, which traditionally were oriented to the classic welfare approach (Tiffer-Sotomayor 2000; Tiffer-Sotomayor et al. 2002; Gutbrodt 2010).

Across Europe elements of restorative justice have been implemented, both in countries that to some extent adopt neo-liberal or neo-correctional approaches, and in those with a relatively strong welfare orientation. In addition, educational and other measures, such as social training courses and cognitive-behavioural training and therapy, have been developed more widely. These developments are in line with international juvenile justice standards. The 2003 Recommendation of the Council of Europe on new ways of dealing with juvenile delinquency clearly emphasizes the development of new, and more constructive community sanctions for recidivist and other problematic offender groups. This maintains the traditional idea of juvenile justice as a purely, special "educational" system of intervention designed to prevent the individual from re-offending.

Although the ideal of using deprivation of liberty only as a measure of last resort for juveniles has been hailed as desirable across Europe, it cannot be denied that in some countries "neo-liberal" orientations have influenced juvenile justice policy and, to a varying extent, also practice (see Muncie 2008 with further references). The widening of the scope for youth detention in England and Wales, France and the Netherlands may be interpreted as a "punitive turn". And indeed the youth prison population in these countries did increase considerably in the 1990s, a trend that has been reversed in the last few years. Muncie (2008, p. 110) refers to public debates and statements of academics in other (including Scandinavian) countries and comes to the conclusion that "such commentaries clearly suggest that not only in the USA and England and Wales but throughout much of Western Europe, punitive values associated with retribution, incapacitation, individual responsibility and offender accountability have achieved a political legitimacy to the detriment of traditional principles of juvenile protection and support."

This conclusion reflects only a facet of the full reality. A different reality emerges, however, when one considers the practice of juvenile prosecutors, courts, social workers and youth welfare agencies and projects such as mediation schemes. These continue to operate in a reasonably moderate way and thus resist penal populism. Deprivation of liberty remains the truly last resort in Scandinavia and indeed most other regions and countries (von Hofer 2004; Storgaard 2004;

Haverkamp 2007). This differentiated picture of a "new complexity" (Habermas 1985) is the main message of the research presented by the major comparative study on juvenile justice legislation and sentencing practice in Europe (Dünkel et al. 2011) on which this chapter is largely based (see in detail Dünkel et al. 2011; Dünkel et al. 2011).

Sonja Snacken has sought to explain why many European countries have resisted penal populism and punitiveness (Snacken 2010, 2012; Snacken and Dumortier 2012). She has emphasized that European states are constitutional democracies strongly oriented towards the welfare state, democracy and human rights. These fundamental orientations, which can be found most clearly in many continental Western European states, and particularly in Scandinavian states (Lappi-Seppälä 2007, 2010), serve as "protective factors" against penal populism (see also Pratt 2008a, b).

It is undoubtedly true that penal populism does not halt at the gates of youth justice (Pratt et al. 2005; Ciappi 2007; see also Garland 2001a, b; Roberts and Hough 2002; Tonry 2004; Muncie 2008). Generally speaking however, the same factors that have allowed such punitiveness to be resisted in many European countries apply even more strongly to youth justice. Moreover, juvenile offending is different from that of adults. Its episodic nature allows for more tolerance and moderate reactions.

The relative invulnerability of youth justice to punitive tendencies is reinforced by the strong framework of international and European human rights standards that apply to it, courtesy of the 1989 UN Convention on the Rights of the Child and the other instruments mentioned above. More specifically, these instruments also emphasise the expansion of procedural safeguards, on the one hand, and the limitation or reduction of the intensity of sentencing interventions, on the other hand.

Clearly more needs to be done, and this chapter has highlighted three areas in which policies are still unresolved, at the international and European level.

- One step forward would be to raise the age of criminal responsibility to at least the European average of 14 or 15.
- A second step would be to build on interesting initiatives to increase the maximum age at which young offenders can be treated as if they were juveniles. This could do much to protect a potentially vulnerable group and to divert them from a career of adult crime. The recent reform of April 2014 in the Netherlands increasing the scope of juvenile justice up to the age of 23 may be seen as the forerunner in juvenile justice reform in this respect.
- Thirdly, the tendency towards trying juveniles as adults should be resisted. Only a small minority of European countries provides such a waiver procedure, but it must be clear that this is not only doctrinally dubious, as explained above, but also holds the risk of increasing the impact of the worst features of the adult criminal justice system on young offenders.

In sum, youth justice policy as reflected in legislation and practice in the majority of European countries has successfully resisted a punitive turn. While there is more work to be done in areas where policy is not yet clear, it is realistic to hope that neo-liberal approaches will be moderated. Important signs in this direction can be observed in England and Wales (see Smith 2010; Horsfield 2015; Dünkel 2014) or the Netherlands (see Loeber et al. 2012), where such approaches have been rhetorically prominent in the past decades. Therefore there is some important evidence that the ideal of social inclusion and reintegration will be the *Leitmotiv* for juvenile justice reforms of the twenty-first century in Europe and other continents as well.

Five Questions

1. What has been the role of international human rights standards in the development of juvenile justice policy in Europe?
2. Why has the "punitive turn" in juvenile justice policy been rather moderate or even non-existent in many European countries?
3. What would be the ideal scope of juvenile justice according to new evidence in developmental psychology, sociology and neurosciences?
4. What kind of reactions seem to be most effective in reducing re-offending and at the same time in preserving a humane juvenile justice approach and what could be the role of restorative justice measures in this context?
5. Which procedural and other principles should be guaranteed in order to establish a rational and humane juvenile justice system?

References

A/RES 40/33. United Nations Standard Minimum Rules for the Administration of Juvenile Justice ("The Beijing Rules", Annex), 29 November 1985.

Albrecht, H.-J., & Kilchling, M. (Eds.) (2002). Jugendstrafrecht in Europa, Freiburg i. Br., Max-Planck-Institut für ausländisches und internationales Strafrecht.

Beaulieu, L. A. (1994). Youth offences – Adult consequences. *Canadian Journal of Criminology, 36*, 329–341.

Bailleau, F., & Cartuyvels, Y. (Eds.). (2007). *La Justice Pénale des Mineurs en Europe—Entre modèle Welfare et infléxions néo-libérales*. Paris: L'Harmattan.

Belser, E. M., Hanson, K., & Hut, A. (2009). *Sourcebook on international children rights*. Bern: Staempfli.

Bishop, D. M. (2009). Juvenile transfer in the United States. In J. Junger-Tas & F. Dünkel (Eds.), *Reforming juvenile justice* (pp. 85–104). Dordrecht: Springer.

Bishop, D. M., & Feld, B. C. (2012). Trends in juvenile justice policy and practice. In B. C. Feld & D. M. Bishop (Eds.), *The Oxford handbook of juvenile crime and juvenile justice* (pp. 898–926). New York: Oxford University Press.

Bonnie, R. J., Chemers, B. M., & Schuck, J. (Eds.). (2012). *Reforming juvenile justice: A developmental approach*. Washington, DC: National Research Council of the National Academies.

Bruckmüller, K. (2006). Austria: A protection model. In J. Junger-Tas & S. H. Decker (Eds.), *International handbook of juvenile justice* (pp. 263–294). Dordrecht: Springer.

Castro Morales, A. (2015). *Jugendstrafvollzug und Jugendstrafrecht in Chile, Peru und Bolivien unter besonderer Berücksichtigung von nationalen und internationalen Kontrollmechanismen.*

Rechtliche Regelungen, Praxis, Reformen und Perspektiven. Mönchengladbach: Forum Verlag Godesberg.

Cavadino, M., & Dignan, J. (2007). *The penal system: An introduction* (4th ed.). London: Sage.

Cavadino, M., Dignan, J. (2006). *Penal systems: A comparative approach*. London/Thousand Oaks/New Delhi: Sage.

Ciappi, S. (2007). *La nuova punitività—Gestione dei conflitti e governo dell'insicurezza*. Soverina Mannelli: Università Rubbettino.

Cimamonti, S., di Marino, G., & Zappalà, E. (Eds.). (2010). *Où va la justice des mineurs? (Allemagne, Espagne, France, Italie, Russie)*. Torino: G. Ciappichelli Editore.

Convention on the Rights of the Child. (1989). 1577 UNTS 3.

Council of Europe. (2003). Recommendation Rec 20, New Ways of Dealing with Juvenile Delinquency and the Role of Juvenile Justice, 24 September 2003.

Council of Europe. (2008). Recommendation Rec 11, European Rules for Juveniles Subject to Sanctions and Measures, 5 November 2008.

Council of Europe. (Ed.). (2009). *European rules for juvenile offenders subject to sanctions or measures*. Strasbourg: Council of Europe Publishing.

Crawford, A., & Lewis, S. (2007). Évolutions mondiales, orientations nationales et justice locale: les effets du néo-liberalisme sur la justice des mineurs en Angleterre et au Pays de Galles. In F. Bailleau & Y. Cartuyvels (Eds.), *La justice pénale des mineurs en Europe—Entre modèle welfare et infléxions néo-libérales* (pp. 23–43). Paris: L'Harmattan.

CRC/C/GC/10. Committee of the rights of the Child, General Comment No. +0 (2007, para. 32, 25 April 2007.

Doek, J. (2009). The UN convention of the rights of the child. In J. Junger-Tas & F. Dünkel (Eds.), *Reforming juvenile justice* (pp. 19–31). Dordrecht: Springer.

Doak, J., & O'Mahony, D. (2011). Developing mediation and restorative justice for young offenders across Europe. In F. Dünkel, J. Grzywa, P. Horsfield, & I. Pruin (Eds.), *Juvenile justice systems in Europe—Current situation and reform developments* (2nd ed.) (pp. 1717–1746). Mönchengladbach: Forum Verlag Godesberg.

Doob, A. N., & Tonry, M. (2004). Varieties of youth justice. In M. Tonry, & A. N. Doob (Eds.), *Youth crime and justice* (pp. 1–20). Chicago/London: University of Chicago Press (Crime and Justice, Vol. 31).

Dünkel, F. (2006). Juvenile justice in Germany—Between welfare and justice. In J. Junger-Tas & S. H. Decker (Eds.), *International handbook of juvenile justice* (pp. 225–262). Dordrecht: Springer.

Dünkel, F. (2008). Jugendstrafrecht im europäischen Vergleich im Licht aktueller Empfehlungen des Europarats. *Neue Kriminalpolitik, 20*, 102–114.

Dünkel, F. (2009). Young people's rights: The role of the Council of Europe. In J. Junger-Tas, & F. Dünkel (Eds.), *Reforming juvenile justice* (pp. 33–44). Dordrecht: Springer.

Dünkel, F. (2011a). Werden Strafen immer härter? Anmerkungen zur strafrechtlichen Sanktionspraxis und zur Punitivität. In B. Bannenberg, & J.-M. Jehle (Eds.), *Gewaltdelinquenz. Lange Freiheitsentziehung. Delinquenzverläufe* (pp. 209–243). Mönchengladbach: Forum Verlag Godesberg.

Dünkel, F. (2011b). Die Europäischen Grundsätze für die von Sanktionen oder Maßnahmen betroffenen jugendlichen Straftäter und Straftäterinnen ('European Rules for Juvenile Offenders Subject to Sanctions or Measures', ERJOSSM). *Zeitschrift für Jugendkriminalrecht und Jugendhilfe, 22*, 140–154.

Dünkel, F. (2013). Youth justice policy in Europe – Between minimum intervention, welfare and new punitiveness. In T. Daems, D. van Zyl Smit, & S. Snacken (Eds.), *European penology?* (pp. 145–170). Oxford/Portland: Hart Publishing.

Dünkel, F. (2014). Jugendkriminalpolitik in Europa und den USA: Von Erziehung zu Strafe und zurück? In DVJJ (Hrsg.), *Jugend ohne Rettungsschirm? Dokumentation des 29. Deutschen Jugendgerichtstags* (pp. 506–544). Mönchengladbach: Forum Verlag Godesberg.

Dünkel, F., & Pruin, I. (2011). Young adult offenders in the criminal justice systems of European countries. In F. Dünkel, J. Grzywa, P. Horsfield, & I. Pruin (Eds.), *Juvenile justice systems in Europe—Current situation and reform developments* (2nd ed., pp. 1583–1606). Mönchengladbach: Forum Verlag Godesberg.

Dünkel, F., & Pruin, I. (2012). Young adult offenders in the criminal justice systems of European countries. In F. Lösel, A. Bottoms, & D. Farrington (Eds.), *Young adult offenders lost in transition?* (pp. 11–38). London/New York: Routledge.

Dünkel, F., Grzywa, J., Pruin, I., & Šelih, A. (2011). Juvenile justice in Europe—Legal aspects, policy trends and perspectives in the light of human rights standards. In F. Dünkel, J. Grzywa, P. Horsfield, & I. Pruin (Eds.), *Juvenile justice systems in Europe—Current situation and reform developments* (2nd ed., pp. 1839–1898). Mönchengladbach: Forum Verlag Godesberg.

Dünkel, F., Pruin, I., & Grzywa, J. (2011). Sanctions systems and trends in the development of sentencing practices. In F. Dünkel, J. Grzywa, P. Horsfield, & I. Pruin (Eds.), *Juvenile justice systems in Europe—Current situation and reform developments* (2nd ed., pp. 1649–1716). Mönchengladbach: Forum Verlag Godesberg.

Dünkel, F., Horsfield, P., & Grzywa, J. (Eds.). (2015a). *Restorative justice and mediation in penal matters in Europe – A stock-taking of legal issues, implementation strategies and outcomes in 36 European countries*. Mönchengladbach, Germany: Forum Verlag Godesberg.

Dünkel, F., Horsfield, P., & Păroşanu, A. (Eds.). (2015b). *European research on restorative juvenile justice. Volume 1: Research and selection of the most effective juvenile restorative justice practices in Europe: Snapshots from 28 EU member states*. Brussels: International Juvenile Justice Observatory.

ECHR (European Court of Human Rights), T. v. the United Kingdom [GC], no. 24724/94, 16 December 1999; V.v. the United Kingdom [GC], no. 24888/94, ECHR 1999-IXT).

Garland, D. (2001a). *The culture of control: Crime and social order in contemporary society*. Chicago: The University of Chicago Press.

Garland, D. (Ed.). (2001b). *Mass imprisonment: Social causes and consequences*. London: Sage.

Gensing, A. (2011). Jurisdiction and characteristics of juvenile criminal procedure in Europe. In F. Dünkel, J. Grzywa, P. Horsfield, & I. Pruin (Eds.), *Juvenile justice systems in Europe—Current situation and reform developments* (2nd ed., pp. 1607–1648). Mönchengladbach: Forum Verlag Godesberg.

Gensing, A. (2014). *Jugendgerichtsbarkeit und Jugendstrafverfahren im europäischen Vergleich*. Mönchengladbach: Forum Verlag Godesberg.

Goldson, B. (2002). New punitiveness: The politics of child incarceration. In J. Muncie, G. Hughes, & E. McLaughlin (Eds.), *Youth justice: Critical readings* (pp. 386–400). London/Thousand Oaks/New Delhi: Sage.

Goldson, B. (2011). 'Time for a Fresh Start', but is this it? A critical assessment of the Report of the Independent Commission on Youth Crime and Antisocial Behaviour. *Youth Justice, 11*, 3–27.

Goldson, B., & Muncie, J. (2006). *Youth, crime and justice*. London/Thousand Oaks/New Delhi: Sage.

Gutbrodt, T. (2010). *Jugendstrafrecht in Kolumbien*. Mönchengladbach: Forum Verlag Godesberg.

Habermas, J. (1985). *Die neue Unübersichtlichkeit*. Frankfurt/Main: Suhrkamp.

Hartjen, C. A. (2008). *Youth, crime and justice: A global inquiry*. New Brunswick, NJ/London: Rutgers University Press.

Haverkamp, R. (2007). Neuere Entwicklungen im Jugendstrafrecht in Schweden und Finnland. *Recht der Jugend und des Bildungswesens, 55*, 167–190.

Hazel, N. (2008). Cross-national comparison of youth justice. Youth Justice Board. Internet-publication: http://www.yjb.gov.uk/publications/Resources/Downloads/Cross_national_final.pdf

Heinz, W. (2012). Das strafrechtliche Sanktionensystem und die Sanktionierungspraxis in Deutschland 1882–2010 (Stand: Berichtsjahr 2010) Version: 1/2012. Internet-Publication http://www.uni-konstanz.de/rtf/kis/sanks12.pdf

Heinz, W. (2009). Zunehmende Punitivität in der Praxis des Jugendkriminalrechts? Analysen aufgrund von Daten der Strafrechtspflegestatistiken. In Bundesministerium der Justiz (Ed.), *Das Jugendkriminalrecht vor neuen Herausforderungen? Jenaer Symposium* (pp. 29–80). Mönchengladbach: Forum Verlag Godesberg.

Horsfield, P. (2015). *Jugendkriminalität in England und Wales – Entwicklungsgeschichte, aktuelle Rechtslage und jüngste Reformen*. Mönchengladbach: Forum Verlag Godesberg.

Jensen, E. L., & Jepsen, J. (Eds.). (2006). *Juvenile law violators, human rights, and the development of new juvenile justice systems*. Oxford/Portland/Oregon: Hart Publishing.

Junger-Tas, J. (2006). Trends in international juvenile justice—What conclusions can be drawn? In J. Junger-Tas & S. H. Decker (Eds.), *International handbook of juvenile justice* (pp. 505–532). Dordrecht: Springer.

Junger-Tas, J., & Decker, S. H. (Eds.). (2006). *International handbook of juvenile justice*. Dordrecht: Springer.

Junger-Tas, J., & Dünkel, F. (Eds.). (2009). *Reforming juvenile justice*. Dordrecht: Springer.

Keiser, C. (2008). Jugendliche Täter als strafrechtlich Erwachsene? Das Phänomen der 'Adulteration" im Lichte internationaler Menschenrechte. *Zeitschrift für die gesamte Strafrechtswissenschaft, 120*, 25–67.

Killias, M., & Villettaz, P. (2007). Rückfall nach Freiheits- und Alternativstrafen: Lehren aus einer systematischen Literaturübersicht. In F. Lösel, D. Bender, & J. M. Jehle (Eds.), *Kriminologie und wissensbasierte Kriminalpolitik* (pp. 207–225). Mönchengladbach: Forum Verlag Godesberg.

Lappi-Seppälä, T. (2007). Penal policy in Scandinavia. In M. Tonry (Ed.), Crime, punishment, and politics in comparative perspective: Crime and justice (Vol. 36, pp. 217–295). Chicago/London: The University of Chicago Press.

Lappi-Seppälä, T. (2010). Vertrauen, Wohlfahrt und politikwissenschaftliche Aspekte— International vergleichende Perspektiven zur Punitivität. In F. Dünkel, T. Lappi-Seppälä, C. Morgenstern, & D. van Zyl Smit (Eds.), *Kriminalität, Kriminalpolitik, strafrechtliche Sanktionspraxis und Gefangenenraten im europäischen Vergleich* (pp. 937–996). Mönchengladbach: Forum Verlag Godesberg.

Loeber, R., Hoeve, M., Farrington, D. P., Howell, J. C., Slot, W., van der Laan, P. H. (2012). Overview, conclusions, and policy and research recommendations. In: R. Loeber, M. Hoeve, W. Slot, P. H. van der Laan (Eds.), *Persisters and desisters in crime from adolescence into adulthood: Explanation, prevention and punishment* (pp. 335–412). Farnham, Surrey/Ashgate.

Muncie, J. (2008). The 'Punitive Turn' in juvenile justice: Cultures of control and rights compliance in Western Europe and in the USA. *Youth Justice, 8*, 107–121.

Muncie, J., Goldson, B. (Eds.) (2006). Comparative youth justice. London/Thousand Oaks/ New Delhi: Sage.

Nelken, D. (2009). Comparative criminal justice: Beyond ethnocentrism and relativism. *European Journal of Criminology, 6*, 291–311.

Nelken, D. (2010). *Comparative criminal justice—Making sense of difference*. Los Angeles: Sage.

O'Mahony, D., & Campbell, C. (2006). Mainstreaming restorative justice for young offenders through youth conferencing: The experience in Northern Ireland. In J. Junger-Tas & S. H. Decker (Eds.), *International handbook of juvenile justice* (pp. 93–115). Dordrecht: Springer.

O'Mahony, D., & Doak, J. (2009). Restorative justice and youth justice: Bringing theory and practice closer together in Europe. In J. Junger-Tas & F. Dünkel (Eds.), *Reforming criminal justice* (pp. 165–182). Berlin/New York: Springer.

Patané, V. (Ed.). (2007). *European juvenile justice systems* (Vol. 1). Milano: Giuffrè Editore.

Pratt, J. (2008a). Scandinavian exceptionalism in an era of penal excess. Part I: The nature and roots of Scandinavian exceptionalism. *British Journal of Criminology, 48*, 119–137.

Pratt, J. (2008b). Scandinavian exceptionalism in an era of penal excess. Part II: Does Scandinavian exceptionalism have a future? *British Journal of Criminology, 48*, 275–292.

Pratt, J., et al. (Eds.). (2005). *The new punitiveness: Trends, theories, perspectives*. Cullompton: Willan Publishing.

Pruin, I. (2007). Die Heranwachsendenregelung im deutschen Jugendstrafrecht. Jugendkrimi¬nologische, entwicklungspsychologische, jugendsoziologische und rechtsvergleichende Aspekte. Mönchengladbach: Forum Verlag Godesberg.

Pruin, I. (2011). The scope of juvenile justice systems in Europe. In F. Dünkel, J. Grzywa, P. Horsfield, & I. Pruin (Eds.), *Juvenile justice systems in Europe—Current situation and reform developments* (2nd ed., pp. 1539–1582). Mönchengladbach: Forum-Verlag.

Pruin, I., & Dünkel, F. (2014). *Young adult offenders in Europe: Interdisciplinary research results and legal practices*. Greifswald: Department of Criminology, Expertise for the Cadbury Trust.

Roberts, J., & Hough, M. (Eds.). (2002). *Changing attitudes to punishment: Public opinion, crime and justice*. Cullompton: Willan Publishing.

Smith, D. J. (2005). The effectiveness of the juvenile justice system. *Criminal Justice, 5*, 181–195.

Smith, D. J. (Ed.). (2010). *A new response to youth crime*. Cullompton: Willan Publishing.

Snacken, S. (2010). Resisting punitiveness in Europe? *Theoretical Criminology, 14*, 273–292.

Snacken, S. (2012). Conclusion: Why and how to resist punitiveness in Europe? In S. Snacken & E. Dumortier (Eds.), *Resisting punitiveness in Europe? Welfare, human rights and democracy* (pp. 247–260). London/New York: Routledge.

Snacken, S., & Dumortier, E. (Eds.). (2012). *Resisting punitiveness in Europe? Welfare, human rights and democracy*. London/New York: Routledge.

Storgaard, A. (2004). Juvenile justice in Scandinavia. *Journal of Scandinavian Studies in Criminology and Crime Prevention, 5*, 188–204.

Stump, B. (2003). *Adult time for adult crime—Jugendliche zwischen Jugend- und Erwachsenenstrafrecht*. Mönchengladbach: Forum Verlag Godesberg.

Tiffer-Sotomayor, C. (2000). *Jugendstrafrecht in Lateinamerika unter besonderer Berücksichtigung des Jugendstrafrechts in Costa Rica*. Mönchengladbach: Forum Verlag Godesberg.

Tiffer-Sotomayor, C., Llobet Rodríguez, J., & Dünkel, F. (2002). *Derecho penal juvenil*. San José/Costa Rica: DAAD.

Tonry, M. (2004). *Punishment and politics*. Cullompton: Willan Publishing.

Tonry, M., & Doob, A. N. (Eds.) (2004). *Youth crime and justice*. Chicago/London: University of Chicago Press (Crime and Justice, Vol. 31).

United Nations Office on Drugs and Crime. (2013). *Justice matters involving children in conflict with the law. Model law on juvenile justice and related commentary*. New York: United Nations.

von Hofer, H. (2004). Crime and reactions to crime in Scandinavia. *Journal of Scandinavian Studies in Criminology and Crime Prevention, 5*, 148–166.

Weijers, I., & Grisso, T. (2009). Criminal responsibility of adolescents: Youth as junior citizenship. In J. Junger-Tas & F. Dünkel (Eds.), *Reforming juvenile justice* (pp. 45–67). Dordrecht: Springer.

Weijers, I., Nuytiens, A., & Christiaens, J. (2009). Transfer of minors to the criminal court in Europe: Belgium and the Netherlands. In J. Junger-Tas & F. Dünkel (Eds.), *Reforming juvenile justice* (pp. 105–124). Dordrecht: Springer.

Intergenerational Practice: An Approach to Implementing Sustainable Development and Environmental Justice

Tamara Mitrofanenko

Abstract "Sustainable development"—the concept hardly pursued in non-environmental Criminal Justice, still nascent in Crime Prevention, especially with respect to the role of women and children—is strongly linked to the concept of Environmental Justice, including via the nexus of social, economic and environmental dimensions, as well as the intergenerational context and the role of public participation in both notions. This chapter introduces an idea of Intergenerational Practice as a way to operationalize sustainable development and environmental justice principles on the local level. The importance of involving younger and older generations in communities and in sustainable development has been recognized on the international level. Intergenerational practice has been shown to enhance community cohesion, improve understanding among the younger and older population, increase participation in community development by the elderly persons, children and youth, and diminish the fear of crime in communities. Although not an explicit goal, such initiatives also offer equal opportunities to engage for younger and older women. Accordingly, this chapter provides generic clues for projecting the precepts of intergenerational learning and practice in Environmental Justice into Crime Prevention.

1 Sustainable Development and Environmental Justice

Sustainable Development is a well-familiar concept today, embraced on the international level, by the United Nations, by national and regional authorities and governmental and non-governmental organizations, and by a growing number of individuals, while its definition, scope and effectiveness continue to be debated and

T. Mitrofanenko (✉)
United Nations Environment Programme, Vienna Office - Secretariat of the Carpathian Convention, Vienna, Austria

University of Natural Resources and Life Sciences, Vienna (BOKU), Institute of Landscape Development, Recreation and Conservation Planning, Vienna, Austria
e-mail: tomamit@gmail.com; Tamara.Mitrofanenko@unvienna.org

H. Kury et al. (eds.), *Women and Children as Victims and Offenders: Background, Prevention, Reintegration*, DOI 10.1007/978-3-319-28424-8_28

reinterpreted by scholars and practitioners (e.g. Magee et al. 2013). The generally accepted definition is that of the 1987 Brundtland report ("Our Common Future") issued by the United Nations World Commission on Environment and Development (WCED), which defines sustainable development as "development that meets the needs of the present without compromising the ability of future generations to meet their own needs" (WCED 1987, para. 27). The three recognized "pillars" of sustainable development are social, economic and environmental, as expressed in the paragraph 6 of the 1995 Copenhagen Declaration on Social Development[1] (UN 1995), although it has been argued that "cultural" development should also be considered in this respect (Hawkes 2001, Magee et al. 2013).

Environmental Justice "refers to the right of current and future generations to a clean, healthy, and safe environment" (Hawkins 2010, p. 74). A comprehensive definition is provided by the United States Environmental Protection Agency (US EPA) as "the fair treatment and meaningful involvement of all people regardless of race, color, national origin, or income with respect to the development, implementation, and enforcement of environmental laws, regulations, and policies. [...] It will be achieved when everyone enjoys the same degree of protection from environmental and health hazards and equal access to the decision-making process to have a healthy environment in which to live, learn, and work" (US EPA 2013).

Many works trace the emergence of environmental justice ideas to the practice of disproportional citing of polluting industries in the areas with predominantly racial minority populations, and the response thereto (Fisher 2003, Sandler and Pezzullo 2007). However, to-date the concept has broadened to include other disadvantaged groups "deprived of environmental rights, such as women, children and the poor" (Cutter 1995 and Agyeman 2000 in Agyeman et al. 2002). In fact, the same principles are reflected in the United Nations Guidelines for the Prevention of Crime (ESOSOC resolution 2002/13, Annex), which stated that "[p]articular emphasis should be placed on communities, families, children and youth at risk" (UN 2002, sec. 8.3). Moreover, the concept reached a particularly important international dimension, due to exporting of industrial production and waste to developing countries. A well-known example is the disastrous gas leak in the facilities of a multinational corporation in Bhopal, India, which resulted in death of thousands of locals; a more contemporary present issue—the threat of the Small Island States disappearing because of the sea level rise, due partly to the global climate change, exacerbated by the industrial countries' greenhouse gas emissions (Roberts 2007). In addition, environmental justice is not only focused on preventing environmental burdens, but also on promoting just access to environmental amenities (Agyeman et al. 2002).

The link between the concepts of sustainable development and environmental justice is evident already in the origins of the sustainable development discussion

[1] "We are deeply convinced that economic development, social development and environmental protection are interdependent and mutually reinforcing components of sustainable development, which is the framework for our efforts to achieve a higher quality of life for all people [...]" (UN 1995, para 6).

on the international level, at the United Nations Conference on the Human Environment held in Stockholm in 1972, which declared that "environment [...is...] essential to the enjoyment of basic human rights" (UN 1972, p. 3). Further elaboration and recognition of sustainable development on the international level continued to include references to ideas of justice: such as the assertion that nature conservation "cannot be achieved without development to alleviate poverty" by the World Conservation Strategy (WCS) in 1980 (IUCN 1980), the prioritization of essential needs of the world's poor by the Brundtland report (WCED 1987), the recognition of the nations' rights "to pursue social and economic progress," and the acknowledgement of the rights to participation of the major groups, including women and youth, by the UN Conference on Environment and Development (UNCED, also known as the Earth Summit, UN 1992a, b).

More recently, the United Nations Conference on Sustainable Development took place in Brazil in 2012, 20 years after the 1992 Earth Summit (end hence referred to as Rio + 20), with a goal to renew commitments of the international community to sustainable development. The outcome document "The Future We Want" encourages "action at regional, national, sub-national, and local levels to promote access to information, public participation, and access to justice in environmental matters, as appropriate" (UN 2012, para 99), and stresses the importance of "fostering [...] social justice and cohesion" (para 156). The document also refers to Sustainable Development Goals as a blueprint to steer the development agenda of the global community after 2015 (UN 2012, para 246).

Principles of environmental justice, adopted by the First National People of Color Environmental Leadership Summit in 1991, also refer to a link with sustainable development: "Environmental Justice mandates the right to ethical, balanced and responsible uses of land and renewable resources in the interest of a sustainable planet for humans and other living things" (People of Color Environmental Justice Summit 1991 in Agyeman et al. 2002 and CIEL 2002).

Several researchers have addressed the "nexus" of sustainability and environmental justice in various contexts (Agyeman et al. 2002; Fisher 2003; Ikeme 2003; Okereke 2006; Hawkins 2010). Some even agreeing that "sustainable development may well be seen as the next phase of the environmental justice movement". (Goldman 1993 in Agyeman et al. 2002).

An example of the "nexus" on the international/intergovernmental level, is the recent symposium of the United Nations Environment Assembly—*Environmental Justice and Sustainable Development*, which approached environmental justice as the Rule of Law, following the Decision 27/9 on Advancing Justice, Governance of Law for Environmental Sustainability (UNEA 2014a). The symposium aimed at discussing "ways and means by which the further development and implementation of environmental rule of law can help ensure just and sustainable developmental outcomes" (UNEA 2014a, p. 1). The elements of environmental rule of law include "adequate and implementable laws, access to justice and information, public participation, accountability, transparency, liability for environmental damage, fair and just enforcement, and human rights" (UNEA 2014b, p.1).

"Co-activism of sustainability and environmental justice" on a local community scale is evident from the origins of the environmental justice movement (Agyeman et al. 2002, Sandler and Pezzullo 2007). Agyeman et al. (2002) lists other examples, such as efforts to develop sustainable communities and cities (Roseland 1998; Rees 1995; Haughton, 1999 in Agyeman et al 2002.), and argues that environmental justice brings a more local and accessible dimension to the concept of sustainability.

The paper by the Center for International Environmental Law (CIEL) "One Species, One Planet: Environmental Justice and Sustainable Development" explores the legal relationship between sustainable development and environmental justice, and highlights three areas relevant for the nexus between them: (1) the right to life, including the right to a healthy environment; (2) the traditional and customary property rights of indigenous and other local communities, especially those in the Global South[2]; and (3) participatory and procedural rights (CIEL 2002).

2 Participation

One of the underlying principles of sustainability/justice nexus is that of public participation. According to Principle 10 of the Rio Declaration "Environmental issues are best handled with the participation of all concerned citizens, at the relevant level. At the national level, each individual shall have appropriate access to information concerning the environment that is held by public authorities, including information on hazardous materials and activities in their communities, and the opportunity to participate in decision-making processes. States shall facilitate and encourage public awareness and participation by making information widely available. Effective access to judicial and administrative proceedings, including redress and remedy, shall be provided" (UN 1992a, b, Principle 10).

Participation has been extensively discussed in both academic literature and in practice. Several degrees of participation are recognized, such as: awareness-raising and providing information to the public, consultation—receiving inputs of knowledge and skills from the public, cooperation through joint work, and collective decision-making (Rowe and Frewer 2005; Reed 2008). The original typology—Ladder of Participation—was proposed by Sherry Arnstein in 1969 and was based on the degree of empowerment of the public (Arnstein 1969). This highlights the eventual goal of the participation process—in addition to achieving sustainable results, it should also lead to the empowerment of the population (Bass et al. 1995; Reed 2008; Baral and Stern 2010).

Public participation in general, as well as participation of specific groups, such as women, children and youth, indigenous populations, etc. is often referred to in sustainable development agreements on the international level, such as Agenda 21 (UN 2002) and "The Future we Want" (UN 2012). Moreover, it is the focus of the Aarhus Convention on "Access to Information, Public Participation in Environmental Decision-Making and Access to Justice in Environmental Matters" of the

[2] The Global South generally refers to Africa, Latin America, and developing Asia.

United Nations Economic Commission for Europe (UNECE 1998). This intergovernmental agreement aims at ensuring the "right of every person of present and future generations to live in an environment adequate to his or her health and well-being, [...] the rights of access to information, public participation in decision making, and access to justice in environmental matters" (UNECE 1998, Article 1).

In order to support participation on the national and local level, guidelines exist of how to implement participatory development initiatives (e.g. Geilfus 2008). Many initiatives are focused on one or another group, whose lack of engagement is recognized, because of historic, economic or political reasons, which excluded them from the participation process. This is often the case with women, racial minorities, as well as the elderly, youth and children. At the same time, especially on the community level, participation of these groups is often crucial not only for justice and equity reasons, but also because it is essential to the long-term success and sustainability of development initiatives (for example, because women are often more likely to pass the knowledge and skills to their children, and, respectively, to the next generation) (World 1994, 2012).

3 Intergenerational Solidarity in Action

The intergenerational context is another essential component of both *Environmental Justice and Sustainable Development* concepts. For example, Hawkins (2010) describes environmental justice as "the right of the current and future generations to a clean, healthy and safe environment" (p. 74), which makes a clear reference to both the present and the future generations, just as the Brundtland definition of sustainable development. And "intergenerational justice" is a concept widely discussed in relation to the sustainability debate (Tremmel 2006).

Some authors distinguish among the *intergenerational approach* of sustainability, (which they perceive as the relation between the currently living generation to the future, i.e. currently not yet existing people) and *intergenerational focus* of environmental justice, which concerns equity in sharing the resources among the presently living groups of population, indicating this divergence as one of the differences among the two concepts (Beckerman 2006; Lumer 2006; Tremmel 2006). However, an alternative understanding of *intergenerational* is that among the living people of the older and the younger generations, which makes much sense for the implementation of sustainable development: younger people living today are the link between the current and the future society. At the same time, different generations living today do not always enjoy equitable access to resources and opportunities to engage in the development process.

The Rio + 20 outcome document bridges the "*inter-*" and "*intra*generational" approaches, by making references to youth and older persons, referring to "the need for promoting intergenerational solidarity for the achievement of sustainable development" and requesting the Secretary General to provide a report on this matter (UN 2012, para 86). The report of the Secretary General defines intergenerational solidarity as "social cohesion between generations", and, notably, while addressing the rights of the future generations, it acknowledges the importance of social participation of elderly people and children in communities and in implementation of sustainable development (UN 2013, para. 6).

Interaction and learning among generations has become of growing interest to the research community, due to the demographic changes, such as ageing (Bloom et al. 2011; UNDESA 2013), as well as economic and social processes, which reportedly have contributed to segregation among the older and younger generations (Hatton-Yeo and Ohsako 2000 in Buffel et al. 2014). While intergenerational communication has for centuries provided an informal way of transferring "knowledge, skills, competencies, norms and values" within families (Newman and Hatton-Yeo 2008, p. 31), interactions between the generations are not as prevalent in contemporary society as before (Buffel et al. 2014). Arguably, this is especially relevant in the economically stagnating regions, such as rural areas, where the younger people are moving away, due to the lack of opportunities, and the remaining older population has fewer opportunities to participate in the development process (Fischer et al. 2014). This further exacerbates the development and infrastructure challenges, the digital divide (i.e. inequalities in access to, use of, or knowledge of Information and Communication Technologies (ICTs)),[3] and the loss of knowledge, culture, and traditions (see "The main drivers for intergenerational policy and practice" in the Annex (1)).

The latter might have an effect on social behavior and the culture of lawfulness among the younger population, which has fewer opportunities (and potentially also less desire) to spend time with their older counterparts (Redo 2013). Moreover, the lack of interaction among generations may lead to mutual mistrust and misunderstanding. In some areas, such as deprived urban neighborhoods, intergenerational conflicts can be especially intense (Pain 2005 in Buffel et al. 2014).

In view of the above processes, intergenerational interaction has today become more relevant in a broader "extra-familial" social context (Boström 2003; Newman and Hatton-Yeo 2008), and has been the focus of a number of initiatives, such as the Centre for intergenerational Practice (CIP) of the Beth Johnson Foundation,[4] the European Map of Intergenerational Learning (EMIL),[5] the Intergenerational Partnership for Sustainability of the World Conservation Union (IUCN),[6] and the Intergenerational Foundation in the United Kingdom[7] (Mitrofanenko et al. 2013). Among the prevalent terms to describe intergenerational interaction are Intergenerational Learning and Intergenerational Practice.

[3] The definition by OECD is the gap between individuals, households, businesses and geographic areas at different socio-economic levels with regard both to their opportunities to access Information and Communication Technologies (ICTs) and to their use of the Internet for a wide variety of activities (OECD 2001, p. 5).

[4] http://www.centreforip.org.uk/.

[5] http://www.emil-network.eu/.

[6] http://www.iucn.org/about/union/commissions/cec/cec_how_we_work/youth___ips/.

[7] http://www.if.org.uk/.

Intergenerational learning (IL) is a process, through which individuals of all generations acquire and share skills and knowledge, but also attitudes, and values, via participation in purposeful, mutually beneficial activities (Fischer et al. 2014). A number of intergenerational learning principles and aspects have been elaborated. Some of them are included in the Annex to this chapter. IL is a component/result of Intergenerational practice (IP), which "aims to bring people together in purposeful, mutually beneficial activities, which promote greater understanding and respect between generations and may contribute to building more cohesive communities" (EAGLE 2008, p. 5). In other terms, "IPs are vehicles for the purposeful and *ongoing exchange of resources and learning* among older and younger generations" (Hatton-Yeo and Ohsako 2000 in Buffel et al. 2014, p. 1786). IP appears to be more encompassing, implying the opportunity of both individual and a wider community benefit.

As a response to the rapid demographic change and a perception of growing distance between the generations and changing family structure in Europe, 1993 was declared the European Year of Solidarity between Generations. Throughout the decade, the IP broadened in scope to facilitate community revitalization, integration of immigrants, active ageing (such as volunteering programmes for seniors) and social inclusion, and a number of intergenerational networks has developed in several countries (Hatton-Yeo 2014a). The year 2012 was devoted by the European Union to promoting active ageing as a basis for solidarity between generations. The issues of (re-)connecting generations have been tackled not only in Europe, but also in North America and throughout the globe, leading to the foundation of the International Consortium for Intergenerational Programmes (ICIP) in 2000 (Hatton-Yeo 2014a).

Despite recognition on the national, regional and international scales, according to the experts in the field, intergenerational work is rather promoted and steered from the bottom up, grass root initiatives (Hatton-Yeo 2014b). "It starts locally, is embedded, learner centered and is driven by [...] engaged citizens. Those initiatives are the 'source' or 'seed' to construct national programmes [...] Nevertheless scaling-up (not mainstreaming) of "top-down" programmes is limited and often falls back to local actors" (Fischer 2014). The latter implies substantial citizen interest in intergenerational initiatives, which must be strong enough to support the growing movement, both on the local action- and national/international policy level.

4 Intergenerational Practice in the Economic, Social and Environmental Context

The bottom-up interest and citizen engagement is critical to the success of sustainable development initiatives, evident in the widely known as "think globally, act locally" motto. In this respect, bridging sustainability with intergenerational practice might provide a way to motivate citizens to become involved in local sustainable development actions. In fact, intergenerational practice could provide economic, social, and environmental benefits to communities, thus it can indeed be useful in operationalizing the three pillars of sustainable development.

4.1 Economic

According to Buffel et al. (2014), research, discussion and policies have tended to emphasize the economic dimension of intergenerational exchange, due to the concerns about the challenges of the growing ageing population for the future labor force and public welfare systems. While in this context the older population is rather considered a burden, the seniors could on the contrary be viewed as valuable contributors to economic development, for example, via sharing their knowledge and skills with the younger generations (Newman and Hatton-Yeo 2008). In this respect, IP can facilitate combining traditional knowledge and practices of the older population with new approaches and communication media, which might encourage innovative marketable ideas. An example is the recognized role of IP in organizational learning (Orzea and Bratianu 2012): knowledge and skills of older professionals should be kept before they retire, while new visions and approaches can be introduced by younger, newly educated employees. Likewise, IP could contribute to increasing the employability skills of young people by helping them develop interpersonal and communication skills. Finally, engagement with older people can help young people to consider future career options in health and social care, which may be increasingly needed considering the growing older population (Hatton-Yeo 2014a, b).

4.2 Social

Researchers and practitioners refer to a range of social policy agendas, to which IP could contribute: improved community cohesion, the potential to address other community related policy areas, the diversification of volunteering, educational institutions becoming more involved in their communities (Springate et al. 2008), promoting active citizenship and engagement for both the young and old, promoting healthier more active lifestyle, and enabling older people to remain engaged longer (Hatton-Yeo 2014a, b), sharing societal and professional resources, tacit and explicit knowledge among generations, supporting lifelong and life-wide learning, maintaining and building human and social capital, and balancing the need for preservation and transformation in today's society (Fischer et al. 2014).

One way IP contributes to community cohesion is by challenging the age stereotypes, which can decrease both the negative approach to the elderly, and the fear of crime in communities (Hatton-Yeo 2014a, b). In the first case, older people are viewed only as service 'recipients', 'victims' rather than as 'active participants' in community regeneration programmes (Simpson 2010 in Buffel et al. 2014); in the second, youth "has been portrayed only in problematic terms in community safety" (Pain 2005 in Buffel et al. 2014, p. 1788). In addition, IPs can lead to reduced crime (Sanchez et al. 2008).

An example of an intergenerational learning project, which tackled the above issues, is "A Partnership of Trust. Young Offenders supporting older people in care settings. An example of social inclusion through intergenerational practice," which successfully brought together young offenders and elderly inhabitants of care facilities, including elders with dementia, and resulted in benefits for both generations. For the young offenders this provided an opportunity to gain professional experience, to receive positive feedback, to raise self-esteem; for the elderly—positive energy, attention, support in daily routine; and for both generations—an opportunity to shed stereotypes and form personal bonds with representatives of another generation (Granville and Laidlaw 2000).

With respect to young people, IPs can help children and youth especially in immigrant communities to understand their history and culture through intergenerational oral history and related projects, thus providing young people with a sense of place and an understanding of their roots (Hatton-Yeo 2014a, b). Moreover, intergenerational programmes can give both older and younger participants the opportunity to make a positive contribution to their communities, and support their integration, such as through various forms of volunteering and service: older people teaching in schools, or helping students with their homework, supporting integration of immigrant children, or younger people helping the older population with various needs. Intergenerational Practice can also address the problem of the digital divide for the elderly—as children and youth often eagerly teach their older counterparts how to use modern Information and Communication Technology (Mitrofanenko et al. 2013). Some examples of the IPs with social impact include: *Youth With Impact*—a community participation program in Switzerland, aiming at a better inclusion of young people in community development (Almeida Pinto 2009, p. 9); *Strategies Towards Active Citizenship (STAC)*, which brought together various IPs concerned with active citizenship of seniors in European context (Almeida Pinto 2009, p. 17); *Shared Places and Shared Spaces* program in Manchester, in which engagement in IPs facilitated involvement of older and younger people and collective community development action (Buffel et al. 2014, p. 1789); the project *"Fifty – Fifty" Junior and Senior Citizens discovering Social Europe through International Voluntary Service* (Almeida Pinto 2009, p. 13).

4.3 Environmental

Some studies suggest potential impacts of Intergenerational Practices on environmental activities (Sanchez et al. 2008; Springate et al. 2008; Buffel et al. 2014). For example, traditional land use practices of the older generations could be beneficial for conservation, and should be maintained, such as traditional farming (Kochler et al. 2008) or medicinal plant cultivation (Silori and Badola 2000). Buffel et al. (2014) discusses the potential of IP in developing sustainable communities and mentions the potential of engagement in environmental policy and planning by young and older people to improve the environmental quality. Mitrofanenko et al. (2015) propose IP as an approach to improve participatory protected area management.

In practice, several environmental organizations actively use intergenerational practice in their efforts of safeguarding the environment, such as the US Environmental Protection Agency via its Aging Initiative (US EPA 2013), the World Conservation Union (IUCN) via its Intergenerational Partnership (Hesselink and Stucker 2008) or the WILD foundation (WILD Foundation 2014).

Representatives of the older generation may have both professional and lay[8] knowledge of the local environment, its historical condition and process of landscape changes, traditional land use practices, local plant and animal species. The younger generation often learns new ecological paradigms in schools, which may be new to other members of the community, and may promote environmentally friendly practices, such as recycling (Maddox et al. 2011). Exchange of knowledge and ideas about the natural resources and the surrounding landscape can both lead to better understanding and appreciation of the local area, and could have economic benefits, such as by making improvements in agriculture, or attracting nature tourism (Mitrofanenko et al. 2015).

The project *Big Foot. Crossing Generations, Crossing Mountains (Big Foot)*, focused on intergenerational learning approaches to support sustainable development in rural mountainous communities, and tested them in Berkovitsa (Bulgaria), Trikala (Greece) and Gubbio (Italy). The older residents of each community, some professional naturalists and others nature connoisseurs and lovers, led the children and youth to explore the natural beauty surrounding their communities and the cultural heritage linked with it, discussed and demonstrated potentials of sustainable livelihoods using local products. (Mitrofanenko et al. 2013; Mitrofanenko et al. 2015).

[8] Non-professional.

5 Intergenerational Practice and Justice: In the Context of Community Participation

The above examples can also be viewed in the context of environmental justice: both the access of older and younger people to environmental amenities, and the protection from environmental hazards, as well as their right to participation in development initiatives. Buffel et al. (2014) refer to “institutional ageism” when discussing that youth and elderly persons are often excluded from participation in societal processes, for example, in neighborhood renewal (Pain 2005 in Buffel et al. 2014). The authors suggest that instead of perceiving the elderly as burden or victims, and youth as a threat to community safety, both of these age groups “can be ‘active participants’ who can help to transform the communities in which they live” (Buffel et al. 2014, p. 1788). Below some examples are provided of intergenerational practice application in the context of rural and urban communities.

Making urban and rural communities more age-friendly and including the engagement of younger and older residents in their development is the way towards ensuring that communal living spaces are accessible to people of different ages and physical abilities, and at the same time, provide a pleasant and healthy living environment (Buffel et al. 2014). In the urban context, this may involve constructing playgrounds, benches or other resting areas, sports facilities, bike lanes, sufficient lighting, green spaces, such as flowerbeds and community gardens, and safe and sufficient pedestrian spaces. In some projects, in addition to the cooperative process, where both older and younger people participated, the result was also intergenerational—reconstructed joint spaces for older and younger people (Buffel et al. 2014).

In rural communities, which are often situated in natural environments, intergenerational learning and practice can support preservation of the local cultural landscape and biological diversity, to ensure that residents of all ages and the future generations can enjoy access to them, for example, by transmitting traditional land use practices and values of respect for the local environment from the older to the younger generation (Mitrofanenko et al. 2015). During the intergenerational excursion of *Big Foot* in Berkovitsa (Bulgaria) when the elderly nature lovers organized a nature and culture hike for the local students, the younger population became aware of and concerned about the deforestation in the vicinity of their municipality (Mitrofanenko et al. 2013).

6 Gender Equality in Intergenerational Practice

Gender equality and participation of women remain a concern for sustainable development and environmental justice efforts, and a focus of debates to-date (e.g. Lubitow and Zarza 2013; Hunt 2014). Gender mainstreaming into policies and practice has brought attention to gender issues in connection with various fields, from environmental education (Sakellari and Skanavis 2013) to sustainable tourism (Skanavis and Sakellari 2008). At the same time, some find that the state of international commitment to women's rights, as expressed in the Rio + 20 outcome, is still weak (Ratha and Mahapatra 2014).

Mellor (2000) argues that the understanding of the gendered nature of society is important for addressing the human-nature relationship, which implies its relevance for approaching sustainable development. Mallory (2013) explores linkages between Ecofeminism and Environmental Justice, and argues that all systems of injustice are "interconnected and mutually reinforcing" (p. 251). This view suggests that gender and inter/intragenerational equality also share similar characteristics, and should be considered concurrently in order to be addressed successfully.

While gender equality is not the central focus of intergenerational initiatives, they could support participation of both older and younger women in various ways:

- Equal engagement of women and girls in intergenerational practice projects can be ensured (as compared to male participants);
- Engagement in community activities can encourage girls and women, who might not have been able to do so previously (e.g. with immigrant background), to become more active, confident, and integrated into the community;
- Elderly people can provide child care services for mothers, enabling them to work (Sandler Morrill and Morrill 2013; Arpino et al. 2014);
- In patriarchal societies, it is possible to introduce ideas of gender equality via the younger generations, who could be more open to accepting it, and affecting their older counterparts.

In fact, a number of intergenerational initiatives and projects in Europe have targeted women, aiming at enhancing their participation. Examples include: Project *CROSSTALK: Moving stories from across borders, cultures and generations*—providing training in story-telling and digital technology skills for women of different ages, social and cultural backgrounds from several European countries (EC EACEA 2012, p.11); Project *OWLE50+—Older Women Learning and Enterprise*—addressing employability and entrepreneurship and later life skills for Women aged 50+ from Italy, Sweden, and UK (EC EACEA 2012, p.20); *Literacy, sewing, computer, and driving training* for young immigrant and ethnic minority women by the senior volunteers in the UK (Sanchez et al. 2008, p.120). These examples can provide ideas for further activities, targeting women participation, and with a greater focus on sustainable development.

7 Conclusion: Intergenerational Practice Towards Sustainable Present and Future

The aim of the above discussion was to point out the potential contribution of intergenerational practice to the implementation of sustainable development, and to demonstrate its relevance both on the local community level, including in the environmental justice context, and to the global sustainable development agenda. The post-2015 agenda has been defined through the Sustainable Development Goals (SDGs), proposed by the Open Working Group of the General Assembly (OWG SDGs 2014) and adopted by the United Nations General Assembly in September 2015 (UN 2015b). In order to ensure implementation of the SDGs after their final elaboration, the recent Synthesis Report of the Secretary-General on the post-2015 sustainable development agenda proposed 6 essential elements: (1) Dignity: to end poverty and fight inequalities; (2) People: to ensure healthy lives, knowledge and the inclusion of women and children; (3) Prosperity: to grow a strong, inclusive and transformative economy; (4) Planet: to protect our ecosystems for all societies and our children; (5) Justice: to promote safe and peaceful societies and strong institutions; (6) Partnership: to catalyze global solidarity for sustainable development (UN 2014, p. 16). "Dignity" and "Justice" have been combined by the UN General Assembly into one "Peace" in its draft outcome document for the adoption of the post-2015 development agenda (see Table 1) (UN 2015a, p. 2)—altogether five essential elements.

A comprehensive discussion on the potential facilitating factors and barriers for the implementation of the SDGs (such as the underlying social, economic and political processes and paradigms) is beyond the scope of this chapter. However, its aim is to demonstrate that intergenerational practice can be an approach particularly useful to enhancing participation in the sustainable development process, by the inclusion of children, youth, elderly, and women of all ages. Table 1 proposes some examples of how IP could be applicable to the essential elements to ensure implementation of the SDGs, as they are presented in the draft outcome document of the UN General Assembly (UN 2015a, p. 2). In some areas IP can be more directly applicable than others, but in all cases it can provide the means of involving women and men of all ages in the planning and implementation of initiatives, and in building inclusive, cohesive, safe and sustainable communities for all; and it can facilitate equitable sharing of the benefits of sustainable development.

Table 1 Potential application of intergenerational practice (IP) to the sustainable development agenda

Elements for delivering on the SDGs	Potential application of intergenerational practice (IP)
People: to end poverty and hunger, in all their forms and dimensions, and to ensure that all human beings can fulfil their potential in dignity and equality and in a healthy environment	• It is possible to introduce and reinforce ideas of gender equality in patriarchal societies via the younger generations • IP can directly contribute to all-inclusive awareness-raising and education, as well as exchange of knowledge between the generations IP can support: • participation of children, youth and elderly in the sustainable development processes, and their involvement in the workforce • entrepreneurial initiatives by combining traditional knowledge and innovation • preserving traditional agricultural approaches, subsistence—based practices, and supporting introduction of new sustainable agriculture techniques
Planet: to protect the planet from degradation, including through sustainable consumption and production, sustainably managing its natural resources and taking urgent action on climate change, so that it can support the needs of the present and future generations	IP can support: • sustainable, participatory, community natural resource management • professional training of young women and men in research and development in various aspects of conservation and sustainable development • transfer and use of traditional sustainable lifestyles, knowledge, skills, attitudes and values, from the older generations to the younger • introducing new sustainable approaches via the younger generations to the older
Prosperity: to ensure that all human beings can enjoy prosperous and fulfilling lives and that economic, social and technological progress occurs in harmony with nature	IP can support: • involvement of younger and older women and men in the work force • professional training of young women and men in research and development • entrepreneurial initiatives by combining traditional knowledge and innovation, such as tourism development, etc. • transfer and reinterpretation of the societal values with respect to economic well-being and development
Peace: to foster peaceful, just and inclusive societies, which are free from fear and violence	• IP enhances community cohesion • IP can facilitate revitalized and inclusive neighborhoods • IP can lead to reduced crime • IP can support all-inclusive education and participation

(continued)

Table 1 (continued)

Elements for delivering on the SDGs	Potential application of intergenerational practice (IP)
Partnership: to mobilize the means required to implement this Agenda through a revitalized Global Partnership for Sustainable Development, based on a spirit of strengthened global solidarity, focused in particular on the needs of the poorest and most vulnerable and with the participation of all countries, all stakeholders and all people	• Children and youth are open to global solidarity, exchange and cooperation, and these ideas and practices can be facilitated by IP IP can support: • participation and involvement by the women and men of all ages incl. children and elderly in the local, national and international sustainable development processes • cooperation and exchange among the older professionals and active youth on an international level

Five Questions

1. What similarities exist between intragenerational equality and gender equality?
2. How can equal participation of older women and girls be ensured in intergenerational practice?
3. What can elderly women and men teach the children about environmental justice? About sustainable development?
4. What can the older generation learn from children about sustainable development?
5. Which aspects of Sustainable Development can be linked to crime prevention? How can intergenerational practice be useful to prevent crime in this respect?

Annex: Intergenerational Learning

1. The main drivers;
2. Principles;
3. Building blocks;
4. Benefits;
5. Practice ideas; and
6. Project examples

The Main Drivers for Intergenerational Policy and Practice (Adopted from Fischer 2013, p. 5)

- Demographic change, longevity, ageing society and workforce;
- Changing economic, insurance and welfare patterns;
- Increasing economic disparities;

- Shift from full- to part-time employment; economic need for mobility and flexibility;
- Shift from a industrial to a Knowledge Society;
- Individualised/atomised societies, flexible lifestyles;
- Dissolving traditional family structures, single households, social isolation of the elderly;
- Urbanization;
- Globalization, migration and ethnic diversity.

Eight Core Principles: Qualities of Intergenerational Approaches (Adopted from Almeida Pinto 2009, p. 20)

- Mutual and reciprocal benefits;
- Participation;
- Asset based;
- Thorough planning;
- Culturally grounded;
- Strengthening of community bonds and promoting active citizenship;
- Challenge to ageism;
- Cross-disciplinarity.

The Intergenerational Learning Building Blocks (Adopted from Kolland 2008, p. 7)

- Relation to interdependence and reciprocity;
- Importance of pursuing common activities and growing together—a relationship is more than a mere interaction;
- Explicitly addressing the different experiences of the different age groups or generations;
- Orientation towards the exchange of experience, use of the skills specific to each generation;
- Design fostering critical thinking about:
  - stereotypes
  - individual differences between people
  - inaccuracy of generalizations;
- Aim of counteracting a negative stereotype of ageing
- Taking into account the level of competence of the elderly and its relevance in the education of younger people.
- Intergenerational learning has the task of developing understanding of the attitudes of other age groups and correcting these as required.

Societal Benefits from Intergenerational Learning (Adopted from EAGLE 2008, p. 6)

- Uniting segregated generations and building better understanding between generations;
- Encouraging active citizenship and social participation;
- Encouraging cross-generational working;
- Sharing societal and professional resources, tacit and explicit knowledge among generations;
- Challenging social problems cross-generationally;
- Addressing different social & e-Inclusion objectives and competence areas simultaneously;
- Supporting Lifelong and Life-wide Learning;
- Maintaining & building human and social capital simultaneously.

Typology of Intergenerational Practice ideas (Adopted from EAGLE 2008, p. 15)

- Community development, living and safety, including intergenerational living and meeting places;
- Education, training and learning, including general education and training, Lifelong Learning, language learning, literacy, numeracy, digital literacy, senior universities, knowledge exchange, hobbies;
- Mentoring i.e. intergenerational support, services and consultancy;
- Mediation, such as problem/conflict solving, prevention of violent behaviour
- Media education, such as Information and Communication Technologies (ICTs);
- Social inclusion/participation, active citizenship;
- Employability;
- History and reminiscence, such as oral history, preserving cultural heritage, work with contemporary witnesses;
- Health;
- Arts, including culture, theatre, play, music;
- Environment and environmental protection;
- Grandparents and grandchildren and older kin;
- Travel, excursions and leisure time.

Examples of Intergenerational Projects (Adopted from EAGLE 2008, p. 18)

- Older and younger people coming together to share learning experiences and gain a better insight about each other;
- Older volunteers mentoring pupils in school;
- Skills and competence sharing;
- Young volunteers providing services and support to older people—helping them go to the shops, reading to them, visiting, running errands;
- Older volunteers supporting young parents;
- Toddlers visiting people with dementia in residential settings;
- Older people working with pupils on a project to promote cultural exchange using oral history or the arts;
- People of all ages working together to improve their community.
- People from different generations working together to transform a waste area into a neighborhood park;

References

Agyeman, J. (2000). *Environmental justice: From the margins to the mainstream?* London: Town and Country Planning Association.

Agyeman, J., Bullard, R. D., & Evans, B. (2002). Exploring the Nexus: Bringing together sustainability, environmental justice and equity. *Space and Polity, 6*, 77–90. doi:10.1080/13562570220137907.

Almeida Pinto, T. (Ed.) (2009). Guide of Ideas for Planning and Implementing Intergenerational Projects. Together: yesterday, today and tomorrow. Association VIDA.. http://files.eric.ed.gov/fulltext/ED507349.pdf. Accessed 23 Jan 2015.

Arnstein, S. R. (1969). A ladder of citizen participation. *Journal of the American Institute of Planners, 35*, 216–224.

Arpino, B., Pronzato, C.D., Tavares, L.P. (2014). The effect of grandparental support on mothers' labour market participation: An instrumental variable approach. *European Journal of Population, 30*(4), 369–390.

Baral, N., & Stern, M. J. (2010). Looking back and looking ahead: Local empowerment and governance in the Annapurna Conservation Area. *Nepal Environment Conservation, 37*, 54–63.

Bass, S., Dalal-Clayton, B., Pretty, J. (1995). Participation in strategies for sustainable development. *Environmental Planning* Issues 7. London, UK: Environmental Planning Group. http://pubs.iied.org/pdfs/7754IIED.pdf. Accessed 27 Feb 2016.

Beckerman, W. (2006). The impossibility of a theory of intergenerational justice. In J. C. Tremmel (Ed.), *Handbook of intergenerational justice 1970 II series* (pp. 53–71). Cheltenham, UK/Northampton, MA: Edward Elgar Publishing Limited.

Bloom, D. E., Boersch - Supan, A., McGee, P., Seike, A. (2011). Population Aging: Facts, Challenges, and Responses (Working Paper No. 7). Program on The Global Demography of Aging, Harvard Initiative for Global Health. http://www.hsph.harvard.edu/pgda/working.htm. Accessed 23 Oct 2014.

Boström, A. K. (2003). *Lifelong learning, intergenerational learning, and social capital*. Stockholm: Stockholm University, Institute of International Education.

Buffel, T., De Backer, F., Peeters, J., et al. (2014). Promoting sustainable communities through intergenerational practice. *Social and behavioral sciences, 116*, 1785–1791.

CIEL [Center for International Environmental Law] (2002). One Species, One Planet: Environmental Justice and Sustainable Development. Wachington DC, USA.

Cutter, S. (1995). Race, class and environmental justice. *Progress in Geography, 19*, 111–112.

EAGLE Project (2008). Intergenerational Learning in Europe. Policies, Programmes and Practical Guidance, European Approaches To Inter-Generational Lifelong Learning. FIM-NewLearning, University of Erlangen-Nürnberg, Erlangen, Germany.

EC EACEA [European Commission. The Education, Audiovisual & Culture Executive Agency] (2012). ICT For Seniors' and Intergenerational Learning. http://eacea.ec.europa.eu/llp/results_projects/documents/publi/ict_intergenerational_learning.pdf. Accessed 24 Oct. 2014.

Fischer, T. (2013). Intergenerational Approach Handbook. Project "Big Foot. Crossing Generations, Crossing Mountains". MENON Network EEIG, Brussels, Belgium.

Fischer, T. (2014). The origin of Intergenerational Practice - top-down or bottom-up? Correspondence via e-mail with Thomas Fischer, expert at MENON Network EEIG, Belgium and Greece, author of the Handbook of Intergenerational Learning (Fischer 2013), received on 15 October 2014.

Fischer, T., Di Pietro, B., Stoyanova, V., Thymiakou, G., Strapatsa, C., & Mitrofanenko, T. (2014). Big foot: Sustainable regional development through intergenerational learning. *Journal of Intergenerational Relationships, 12*, 75–80. doi:10.1080/15350770.2014.868780.

Fisher, E. (2003). Sustainable development and environmental justice same planet, different worlds? *Environs: Environmental Law and Policy Journal, 26*, 201–2017.

Geilfus F (2008). 80 Tools for Participatory Development: Appraisal, Planning, Follow-up and Evaluation. Inter-American Institute for Cooperation on Agriculture (IICA).. http://www.iica.int/Esp/regiones/central/cr/Publicaciones%20Oficina%20Costa%20Rica/80tools.pdf. Accessed 23 Jan. 2015.

Goldman, B. A. (1993). *Not just prosperity. Achieving sustainability with environmental justice*. Washington, DC, USA: National Wildlife Federation, Corporate Conservation Council.

Granville, G., & Laidlaw, J. (2000). *A partnership of trust. Young offenders supporting older people in care settings. An example of social inclusion through intergenerational practice*. London, UK: Beth Johnson Foundation.

Hatton-Yeo, A. (2014a) Perspectives on Intergenerational practice, in: Mitrofanenko T (ed), Intergenerational Learning and Innovation for Sustainable Development. Proceedings of the Final Conference of the Project "Big Foot: Crossing Generations, Crossing Mountains". UNEP Vienna - SCC, Vienna, Austria. http://www.bigfoot-project.eu/final-conference-proceedings.html. Accessed 2 Nov. 2014.

Hatton-Yeo, A. (2014b) The origin of Intergenerational Practice - top-down or bottom-up? Correspondence via e-mail with Alan Hatton-Yeo, the former CEO of the Beth-Johnson-Foundation, UK and Coordinator of the European Map of Intergenerational Learning, received on 11 October 2014.

Hatton-Yeo, A., Ohsako, T. (Eds.) (2000). *Intergenerational programmes: Public policy and research implications. An international perspective*. The UNESCO Institute of Education, The Beth Johnson Foundation. http://www.unesco.org/education/uie/publications/uiestud24.shtml. Accessed 9 Aug. 2014.

Haughton, G. (1999). Environmental justice and the sustainable city. In D. Satterthwaite (Ed.), *The Earthscan reader in sustainable cities* (pp. 62–79). London, UK: Earthscan.

Hawkes, J. (2001). *The fourth pillar of sustainability. Culture's essential role in public planning*. Melbourne: Common Ground P/L.

Hawkins, C. A. (2010), Sustainability, human rights, and environmental justice: Critical connections for contemporary social work. *Critical Social Work, 11*(3).

Hesselink, F., & Stucker, D. (2008). Buddy Experiment. Report on experiment with Intergenerational Partnership through pairing of different generations. IUCN Commission on

Education and Communication. http://www.earthcharterinaction.org/invent/images/uploads/Buddy_Experiment_Report,_Final,_19%5B1%5D.12.08.pdf. Accessed 23 Jan. 2015.

Hunt, K. P. (2014). "It's more than planting trees, it's planting ideas": Ecofeminist Praxis in the Green Belt movement. *Southern Communication Journal, 79*, 235–249.

Ikeme, J. (2003). Equity, environmental justice and sustainability: Incomplete approaches. *Climate Change Politics, 13*, 195–206. doi:10.1016/S0959-3780(03)00047-5.

IUCN [International Union for Conservation of Nature and Natural Resources] (1980). World Conservation Strategy. Living Resource Conservation for Sustainable Development. http://cisdl.org/natural-resources/public/docs/wcs.pdf. Accessed 23 Oct. 2014.

Kochler, Y., Plassmann, G., Ullrich, A., et al. (2008). Establishing ecological networks throughout the European Alps. *Mountain Research and Development, 28*, 168–172.

Kolland, F. (2008). What is inter-generational learning in a higher education setting? In: Waxenegger, A. on behalf of the Adding Quality to Life through Inter-Generational Learning via Universities (ADD LIFE) Consortium (ed), The ADD LIFE European Tool Kit for Developing Inter-generational Learning in Higher Education, Graz. http://add-life.uni-graz.at/cms/files/EN_SHEETSinclCOVER_ADTK_WEB080905.pdf. Accessed 02 Dec. 2014.

Lubitow, A., & Zarza, J. (2013). Gendering social sustainability: Barriers to women's inclusion in sustainable solution development International. *Journal of Social Sustainability in Economic, Social and Cultural Context, 8*, 73–86.

Lumer, C. (2006). Principles of generational justice, In: Tremmel, J.C. (ed.), Handbook of intergenerational justice (pp. 39–52). Cheltenham, UK/Northampton, MA, USA: Edward Elgar Publishing Limited.

Maddox, P., Doran, C., Williams, I. D., & Kus, M. (2011). The role of intergenerational influence in waste education programmes: The THAW project. *Waste Management, 31*, 2590–2600. doi:10.1016/j.wasman.2011.07.023.

Magee, L., Scerri, A., James, P., et al. (2013). Reframing social sustainability reporting: Towards an engaged approach. *Environment, Development and Sustainability, 15*, 225–243. doi:10.1007/s10668-012-9384-2.

Mallory, C. (2013). Environmental justice, ecofeminism, and power. In: R. Rozzi, S. T. Pickett, C. Palmer, J. J. Armesto, & B. Callicott (Eds.), *Linking ecology and ethics for a changing world, values, philosophy, and action, ecology and ethics*, (pp. 251–258). Springer Netherlands.

Mellor, M. (2000). Feminism and environmental ethics: A materialist Mary Mellor perspective. *Ethics and the Environment, 5*, 107–123.

Mitrofanenko, T., Di Pietro, B., Sannipoli, M., Stoyanova, V., & Strapatsa, C. (2013) Transferability Tool Kit. Big Foot. Crossing Generations, Crossing Mountains. Project "Big Foot. Crossing Generations, Crossing Mountains," UNEP Vienna - SCC, Vienna, Austria. http://www.bigfoot-project.eu/transferability-tool-kit.html. Accessed 9 Aug. 2014.

Mitrofanenko, T., Muhar, A., & Penker, M. (2015). Potential for applying intergenerational practice to protected area management in mountainous regions. *Mountain Research and Development, 35*(1), 27–38.

Newman, S., & Hatton-Yeo, A. (2008). Intergenerational learning and the contributions of older people. *Ageing Horizons, 8*, 31–39.

OECD [Organization for Economic Co-operation and Development] (2001). Understanding the digital divide. Organization for Economic Co-operation and Development. http://www.oecd.org/internet/ieconomy/1888451.pdf. Accessed 27 Oct. 2014.

OWG SDGs [Open Working Group of the General Assembly, on Sustainable Development Goals] (2014). Open Working Group proposal for Sustainable Development Goals. Full report of the Open Working Group of the General Assembly on Sustainable Development Goals (No. A/68/970). United Nations General Assembly. http://sustainabledevelopment.un.org/content/documents/1579SDGs%20Proposal.pdf. Accessed 26 Oct. 2014.

Okereke, C. (2006). Global environmental sustainability: Intragenerational equity and conceptions of justice in multilateral environmental regimes. *Geoforum, 37*, 725–738. doi:10.1016/j.geoforum.2005.10.005.

Orzea, I., Bratianu, C. (2012). Intergenerational Learning in Ageing Societies. In: Proceedings of the 9th International Conference on Intellectual Capital, Knowledge Management and Organizational Learning-ICICKM2012, Universidad Del Rosario and Universidad Jorge Tadeo Lozano, Bogota, Columbia,. Presented at the 9th International Conference on Intellectual Capital, Knowledge Management and Organizational Learning-ICICKM2012, Academic Publishing International, Reading, UK, pp. 193–2000.

Pain, R. (2005). Intergenerational relations and practice in the development of sustainable communities. Durham University. Intergenerational centre for regional regeneration & development studies. http://www.centreforip.org.uk/res/documents/publication/ODPM%20intergenerational%20report.pdf. Accessed 27 Oct. 2014.

People of Color Environmental Justice Summit (1991). Principles of Environmental Justice, Proceedings of the First National People of Color Environmental Leadership Summit. http://www.ejrc.cau.edu/princej.html. Accessed 23 Oct. 2014.

Ratha, K. C., & Mahapatra, S. K. (2014). Rio + 20: A missed opportunity. *Mediterranean Journal of Social Sciences, 5*, 438–445.

Redo, S. (2013). Linking Intergenerational Learning with Fostering a Culture of Lawfulness, Integration, and Retaining the Values of Ethnic Minorities. In: Mitrofanenko, (ed), Intergenerational Learning and Innovation for Sustainable Development. Proceedings of the Final Conference of the Project "Big Foot. Crossing Generations, Crossing Mountains," Vienna, Austria. http://www.bigfoot-project.eu/final-conference-proceedings.html. Accessed 2 Nov. 2014.

Reed, M. S. (2008). Stakeholder participation for environmental management: A literature review. *Biological Conservation, 144*, 2417–2431.

Rees, W. E. (1995). Achieving sustainability: Reform or transformation? *Journal of Planning Literature, 9*, 343–361.

Roberts, T. J. (2007). Globalizing environmental justice. In: Sandler R., Pezzullo P. C. (Eds.), Environmental *Justice and environmentalism. The social justice challenge to the environmental movement* (pp. 285–308). Cambridge, Massachusetts/London, England: The MIT Press.

Roseland, M. (1998). *Toward sustainable communities: Resources for citizens and their governments*. Gabriola Island, BC, Canada: New Society Publishers.

Rowe, G., & Frewer, L. J. (2005). A typology of public engagement mechanisms. *Science, Technology, & Human Values, 20*, 251–290.

Sakellari, M., & Skanavis, C. (2013). Environmental behavior and gender: An emerging area of concern for environmental education research. *Applied Environmental Education and Communication, 12*, 77–87.

Sanchez, M., Hatton-Yeo, A., Henkin, N. A., et al. (2008). Intergenerational programmes: Towards a society for all ages. *Journal of Intergenerational Relationships, 6*, 485–487.

Sandler, R., Pezzullo, P. C. (2007). *Environmental justice and environmentalism. The social justice challenge to the environmental movement*. Cambridge, Massachusetts/London, England: The MIT Press.

Sandler Morrill, M., & Morrill, T. (2013). Intergenerational links in female labor force participation. *Labour Economics, 20*, 38–47.

Silori, C. S., & Badola, R. (2000). Medicinal plant cultivation and sustainable development. *Mountain Research and Development, 20*, 272–279.

Simpson, C. M. (2010). *Older people and engagement in neighbourhood renewal: A qualitative study of Stoke-on-Trent*. Keele: Keele University.

Skanavis, C., & Sakellari, M. (2008). Gender and sustainable tourism: Women's participation in the environmental decision-making process. *European Journal of Tourism Research, 1*, 78–93.

Springate, I., Atkinson, M., Martin, K. (2008). Intergenerational Practice: A Review of the Literature. (LGA Research Report No. F/SR262). National Foundation for Educational

Research (NFER), Slough, Berkshire, England. http://www.nfer.ac.uk/publications/LIG01/LIG01.pdf. Accessed 08 Aug. 2014.

Tremmel, J. C. (2006). *Handbook of intergenerational justice*. Cheltenham, UK: Edward Elgar Publishing Limited.

UNDESA [United Nations, Department of Economic and Social Affairs, Population Division] (2013). World Population Ageing 2013 (No. ST/SEA/SER.A/348). United Nations, Department of Economic and Social Affairs, Population Division. http://www.un.org/en/development/desa/population/publications/pdf/ageing/WorldPopulationAgeing2013.pdf. Accessed 27 Oct. 2014.

UNEA [United Nations Environment Assembly] (2014a). Environmental Justice and Sustainable Development - A Global Symposium on Environmental Rule of Law. Summary and key messages. (No. UNEP /EA.1/CRP.1). http://www.unep.org/unea/docs/erl/unep-EA1-CRP1-en.pdf. Accessed 23 Jan. 2015.

UNEA [United Nations Environment Assembly] (2014b). Environmental Justice and Sustainable Development - A Global Symposium on Environmental Rule of Law. On the occasion of the 1st Session of the UNited Nations Environment Assembly (UNEA). Preliminary Background Note - Version of 3 June 2014. http://www.unep.org/unea/docs/background_note_erol.pdf. Accessed 23 Jan. 2015.

UNECE [United Nations Economic Commission for Europe] (1998) Convention On Access To Information, Public Participation In Decision-Making And Access To Justice In Environmental Matters. 2161 UNTS 447. http://www.unece.org/env/pp/documents/cep43e.pdf. Accessed 26 Oct 2014.

UN [United Nations] (1972). Report of the United Nations Conference on the Human Environment (No. A/COMF.48/14/Rev.1). Stockholm: United Nations.

UN [United Nations] (1992a). Agenda 21. Programme of Action for Sustainable Development. United Nations Conference for Environment and Development. http://sustainabledevelopment.un.org/content/documents/Agenda21.pdf. Accessed 23 Oct 2014.

UN [United Nations] (1992b). Report of the United Nations Conference on Environment and Development (No. A/CONF.151/26 (Vol. I)).

UN [United Nations] (1995). Copenhagen Declaration, World Summit on Social Development, 1995. http://www.un-documents.net/cope-dec.htm. Accessed 23 Oct 2014.

UN [United Nations] (2002). Guidelines for the Prevention of Crime (ESOSOC resolution 2002/13, Annex, 24 July 2002). https://www.unodc.org/documents/justice-and-prison-reform/crimeprevention/resolution_2002-13.pdf. Accessed 23 Jan. 2015.

UN [United Nations] (2012). Resolution adopted by the General Assembly on 27 July 2012. Agenda Item 19. 66/288 The Future We Want. http://unstats.un.org/unsd/broaderprogress/pdf/GA%20Resolution%20-%20The%20future%20we%20want.pdf. Accessed 21 September 2014.

UN [United Nations] (2013). Intergenerational solidarity and the needs of future generations. Report of the Secretary-General (No. A/68/100). United Nations General Assembly. http://sustainabledevelopment.un.org/content/documents/2006future.pdf. Accessed 21 September 2014.

UN [United Nations] (2014). The road to dignity by 2030: ending poverty, transforming all lives and protecting the planet. Synthesis report of the Secretary-General on the post-2015 sustainable development agenda. (No. A/69/700). http://www.un.org/ga/search/view_doc.asp?symbol=A/69/700&Lang=E. Accessed 13 Jan. 2015.

UN [United Nations] (2015a). Draft outcome document of the United Nations summit for the adoption of the post-2015 development agenda. Draft resolution submitted by the President of the General Assembly (No. A/69/L.85) http://daccess-dds-ny.un.org/doc/UNDOC/GEN/N15/253/34/PDF/N1525334.pdf?OpenElement. Accessed 26 Sept. 2015.

UN [United Nations]. (2015b). Resolution adopted by the General Assembly on 25 September 2015 (A/RES/70/1). Transforming our world: The 2030 Agenda for Sustainable Development.

United Nations General Assembly. http://www.un.org/ga/search/view_doc.asp?symbol=A/RES/70/1&Lang=E. Accessed 27 Feb 2016.
UN WCED [The United Nations World Commission on Environment and Development] (1987). Our Common Future. Chapter 2: Towards Sustainable Development http://www.un-documents.net/our-common-future.pdf. Accessed 21 April 2014.
US EPA [United States Environmental Protection Agency] (2013). Intergenerational Activities [WWW Document]. URL http://www.epa.gov/aging/inter-gen-examples.htm. Accessed 21 April 2014.
Wild Foundation (2014). Intergenerational Collaboration [WWW Document]. URL http://www.wild.org/main/how-wild-works/intergenerational/. Accessed 21 April 2014.
World Bank (1994). Enhancing women's participation in economic development. A World Bank policy paper. http://www-wds.worldbank.org/external/default/WDSContentServer/WDSP/IB/1994/07/01/000009265_3970702134900/Rendered/PDF/multi0page.pdf. Accessed 27 Oct. 2014.
World Bank (2012). World Development Report 2012: Gender Equality and Development. World Bank. http://econ.worldbank.org/WBSITE/EXTERNAL/EXTDEC/EXTRESEARCH/EXTWDRS/EXTWDR2012/0,,contentMDK:22999750~menuPK:8154981~pagePK:64167689~piPK:64167673~theSitePK:7778063,00.html. Accessed 24 Oct. 2014.

Biopolitics, Ethics and the Culture of Lawfulness. Implications for the Next Generation?

Anetta Breczko and Sławomir Oliwniak

Abstract Europe is ageing faster than any other continent. The demographic crisis and the possibility of replacement of generations are currently among the problems most frequently discussed. The form of specific legal regulations depends on the axiological foundations accepted in a given system of law. This chapter describes the process of the formation of pastoral biopower (Foucault's concept of biopolitics) within the framework of the European culture of lawfulness. From the late nineteenth century, states became more and more interested in controlling the population. Foucault's analyses need to be supplemented by an indication of how contemporary bioethics determines a way of understanding the essence of the human being and his or her rights, and/or duties, in the sphere of procreation. The chapter shows how the schools of pronatalism, antinatalism and environmental ethics have shaped the policies of European countries with regard to procreation, as well as people's behaviours in that area. It also describes how demographic policy has evolved under the influence of progress in biotechnology.

1 Introduction

The axiology of law is the set of values that the law expresses. A particular set of values becomes incorporated into it through the processes of rationalization, legitimization and the creation of legal instruments. Axiological foundations for Western legal civilization were laid down by legal positivism, aiming to realize the ideals of Enlightenment philosophy, in particular the Kantian idea of an autonomous human being, capable of self-determination. Positive law was intended to protect those rights. The state was to be law-governed. Positive law became the basis for the functioning of public authorities and social institutions (the principle of legalism). The end of the eighteenth and start of the nineteenth century saw the beginning of the development in continental Europe of the doctrine of the

A. Breczko (✉) • S. Oliwniak
University of Białystok, Białystok, Poland
e-mail: anettabreczko@onet.eu; oliwniak@uwb.edu.pl

H. Kury et al. (eds.), *Women and Children as Victims and Offenders: Background, Prevention, Reintegration*, DOI 10.1007/978-3-319-28424-8_29

Rechtsstaat, based on recognition of the innate and natural rights of the individual, which may be restricted by the authorities only in especially justified cases. This concept, developed by German lawyers (Johann Wilhelm Placidus, Carl von Rotteck, Robert Mohl), emphasized the need for human freedom to be recognized across as broad a scope as possible, and for it to be defended against excessive interference and appropriation by the state. This material understanding of the *Rechtsstaat* was close to the Anglo-Saxon concept of the rule of law (Unger 1977, pp. 52–54 and 185–187, 273–274; MacCormick 2008, pp. 181–189 and 254–256; Bingham 2011). At the end of the nineteenth century the concept underwent formalization. The law gradually lost its dimension of *ius*, leaving only *lex*. The *Rechtsstaat* turned into a *Gesetzesstaat*—a state based on statutes. Positive law became separated from morality. Habermas referred to this process as juridification—a colonization of the lifeworld (Habermas 1975, pp. 1–8; idem 1989, pp. 355–357 and 367–373; 391–396).

Jurisprudence in the nineteenth century and the first half of the twentieth was dominated by the legal positivist paradigm. This was the age of modernism, which was supposed to free people from magical, transcendentally entangled thinking about the world—it was to "break the spell" that the world was under. A sovereign state creates positive law as necessary for the exercise of its increasingly numerous functions. To a greater and greater extent, the law becomes a social technique, or even embodies the concept of "social engineering through law". However, as Western societies evolved from the industrial to the post-industrial stage, the existing way of understanding the law proved to be inadequate, or even anachronistic.

A turn away from positivism in jurisprudence (recognition of the necessary relations between law and morality) was initiated by the work of Gustav Radbruch, Lon L. Fuller and Herbert Hart (Lyons 1984, pp. 71–75; Kelly 1992, pp. 415–421). We can also observe a trend towards communicative ideas (as put forward by J. Habermas and R. Alexy). On the other hand, there sprang up various schools of law described as postmodernist: Law and Economics, Critical Legal Studies, Feminist Legal Theory, Law and Literature (Minda 1995, pp. 83–167; Litowitz 1997, pp. 7–19; Balkin 1994, pp. 370–374; Morawski 2005, pp. 48–80). Postmodernism heralded the end of the Enlightenment project (Carty 1990, p. 1) and of the "grand narratives"—the traditional classical paradigms of learning, including those of law (Lyotard 1984).

In contemporary times, the belief in a need to respect natural and innate rights as fundamental rights of the individual, in particular the autonomy of the individual, the right to liberty and the right to defend one's property, as the basis for justice and the rule of law, is known as the Culture of Lawfulness.

Analyses of the juridical model of law characteristic of modernism are not the only ones possible. Another model of analysis of the changes in ways of understanding power, the law and its subjects can be found in the work of Michel Foucault. *"The analysis does not revolve around the general principle of Law or the myth of Power, but concerns itself with the complex and multiple practices of a 'governmentality' which presupposes, on the one hand, rational forms, technical procedures, instrumentations through which to operate and, on the other hand, strategic games which subject the power relations they are supposed to guarantee to instability and reversal"* (Foucault 1984, pp. 337–338; Golder and Fitzpatrick 2009, pp. 29–35; Hunt and Wickham 1998, pp. 52–55).

The rule of law is generally seen as an indispensable element of the liberal model of the state. In Foucault's view, there is no necessary connection between liberalism, the rule of law and representative democracy. *"Liberalism sought that regulation in 'the law', not through a legalism that would be natural to it but because the law defines forms of general intervention excluding particular, individual, or exceptional measures; and because the participation of the governed in the formulation of the law, in a parliamentary system, constitutes the most effective system of governmental economy. The 'state of right', the Rechtsstaat, the rule of law, the organization of a 'truly representative' parliamentary system was, therefore, during the whole beginning of the nineteenth century, closely connected with liberalism, but just as political economy"* (Foucault 1997, pp. 76–77). Power (in his later work Foucault uses the term "power relations") has more than one face: there is juridical-discursive sovereign power, disciplinary power (discipline), governmentality, and biopower.

Foucault described extensively and in detail the evolution of disciplinary power, born in the second half of the eighteenth century, into biopower, which began at the end of the nineteenth. Biopower is a form of realization of biopolitics. Earlier, however, the human being had been made subject to an objectifying discourse.

2 The Discourse of Disciplinary Power Involves a Code of Normalization. An Introduction to Biopower and Biopolitics

To begin with, Foucault was interested in the archaeology of discourse. He deals with this subject in works published in the later 1960s and early 1970s: *The Order of Things: An Archaeology of the Human Sciences* (1966), *The Archaeology of Knowledge* and *The Discourse on Language* (1969, 1971). A problem is posed by the ambiguity of the term "discourse" as he uses it. On the one hand, discourses are autonomous systems of rules, which constitute objects, concepts, subjects and strategies. On the other hand, from an analytic point of view, discourses are something other than social practices, institutions and techniques (Howarth 2000, pp. 80–82). In the aforementioned books, written using the archaeological method, Foucault is concerned primarily with linguistic (discursive) practices, the manner of their emergence in the modern episteme. The relations between them were of a discontinuous nature, and transition from one to another took place by way of a severance (Gutting 1989, pp. 181–260). In his later works, Foucault is more interested in vertical relationships. These exist between empirical practices, such as the foundation of hospitals, psychiatric institutions or prisons, and a specific type of discourse—medical, psychiatric, legal (Foucault 2001c, pp. 542–546). Unfortunately, the term "discursive ensembles" as used by Foucault also lacks an unambiguous definition. In *The Order of Things* these are sometimes descriptions of regularity in discursive systems, sometimes rules laying down the scope of permissible statements in discourse, and sometimes causes of the formation of discursive orders. Foucault is concerned above all with the institutionalization of discourse (Foucault 1998, p. 309).

In *The Discourse on Language*, He referred directly to the control, selection, delimitation and redistribution of the production of discourse in society by specified procedures. *"There are many systems for the control and the delimitation of discourse, (...) they function as systems of exclusion. (...) Disciplines constitute a system of control in the production of discourse, fixing its limits through the action of an identity taking the form of a permanent reactivation of the rules"* (Foucault 1972, p. 220).

Following his analyses of the coming into being of various types of discourse—psychopathology (*Madness and Civilization: A History of Insanity in the Age of Reason*), medicine (*The Birth of the Clinic: An Archaeology of Medical Perception*), grammar, political economy (*The Order of Things. An Archaeology of the Human Sciences*)—he begins to criticize them. The archaeological method of analysis is replaced by the genealogy of knowledge-power (savoir-pouvoir). *"Indeed, it is in discourse that power and knowledge are joined together. (...) Discourse transmits and produces power"* (Foucault 1978, pp. 100–101).

Questions concerning knowledge have an important connection with those concerning power. The possession of knowledge enables domination and provides the power to subjugate. Foucault speaks of disciplinarization, normalization, appropriation of the social world by disciplines, a new type of law. Contemporary power is a disciplining power. This does not mean that "law fades into the background or that the institutions of justice tend to disappear, but rather that the law operates more and more as a norm, and that the judicial institution is increasingly incorporated into a continuum of apparatuses (medical, administrative, and so on) whose functions are for the most part regulatory" (Foucault 1978, p. 144).

Sovereign power was superseded in the eighteenth century by another type of power, namely the new technology. In *Abnormal. Lectures at the Collège de France 1974–1975*, Foucault referred to *"a new economy of the mechanisms of power: a set of procedures and analyses that enabled the effects of power to be increased, the costs of its exercise reduced and its exercise integrated in mechanisms of production. By increasing the effects of power I mean that there was the discovery in the eighteenth century of a number of means by which, or at least, the principle in accordance with which power could be exercised in a continuous manner, rather than in the ritual, ceremonial, discontinuous way it was exercised under feudalism and continued to be exercised in the absolute monarchies. That is to say, it is no longer exercised through ritual, but through permanent mechanisms of surveillance and control"* (Foucault 2003a, p. 87).

There is a constant increase in the number of "disciplinary mechanisms", mechanisms for controlling people and making use of them. In the classical episteme, psychiatric, medical and legal discourse provided a method for separating the normal and abnormal, healthy and sick, insiders and outsiders, prisoners. Now, discursive practices have been replaced by subtle methods for normalization and the localization of people in a defined space. In guiding individuals to strive for optimum performance relative to some norm, discipline does not have a sense of coercion. In *Discipline and Punish*, Foucault gave the following definition: "*the mechanisms of the disciplinary establishments have a certain tendency to become 'de-institutionalized', to emerge from the closed fortresses in which they once functioned and to circulate in a 'free' state; the massive, compact disciplines are broken down into flexible methods of control, which may be transferred and adapted*" (Foucault 1979, pp. 181–182; 211). There is a change in the scale of control of the body (every gesture, movement, speed) and in the object of that control (it concerns the economy, or effectiveness, of movements of the body). There is created a "political economy of the body"; the body is blocked by relations of power and dominance, and is conflated in a system of subjugation. State authorities organize the micro-physics of power. Penitentiary systems become part of the political economy of the body, where the body as a productive force is blocked by power and dominance relations. There is created a political technology of the body, which is not manifested in concrete institutions or procedures. "Disciplines" appear, as universal forms of dominance. These are methods of minute control of bodily actions, based on the criterion of the body's usefulness or manipulability.

The object of disciplinary power is a human body that is named, described, and placed in an appropriate space—an objectified, subjugated body. Foucault uses the term *assujetissement*. This has been translated as "subjectivation" (in Foucault's writings on sexuality and ethics) or as "subjugation" (in his writings concerning power). In *The Subject and Power* he explains: "*This form of power that applies itself to immediate everyday life categorizes the individual, marks him by his own individuality, attaches him to his own identity, imposes a law of truth on him that he must recognize and others have to recognize in him. It is a form of power that makes individuals subjects. There are two meanings of the word "subject": subject to someone else by control and dependence, and tied to his own identity by a conscience or self-knowledge. Both meanings suggest a form of power that subjugates and makes subject to*" (Foucault 2000b, p. 331). He also writes: "*Discipline 'makes' individuals; it is the specific technique of a power that regards individuals both as objects and as instruments of its exercise*" (Foucault 1979, p. 170; Dreyfus and Rabinow 1983, pp. 153–160). Discipline is the mode of subjection (Simmons 1995, p. 31).

Foucault often uses the terms "power" and "power relations" interchangeably. Power relations lead to objectification of the subject *(assujetissement)*—its location in specified places. Those who cannot or do not wish to fit into their assigned social roles (the insane, vagrants, criminals, soldiers, pupils) are excluded. New, previously unknown, institutions of individual control come into being: psychiatric institutions, penal colonies, juvenile detention centres, hospitals, prisons, schools, barracks. Some of these operate on the basis of a binary division (the insane—later called mentally ill—versus the sane; normal versus abnormal). Others serve to train individuals, make them uniform and normalize through differentiating repartition and subjection to constant surveillance (Ransom 1997).

The most perfect method of subjugation is the placement of the human being (his or her body) within the authority's field of vision, and the most perfect device making it possible to see those placed in spatially separate places (cells) is the Panopticon—the ideal prison (Schwan and Shapiro 2011, pp. 127–139). The Panopticon is not just an ideal prison, it is the principle of a system (Foucault 2001b, p. 466; Foucault 2001e, pp. 1474–1477; Gros 1998, pp. 73–74). It may be used to supervise prisoners, but also to treat the sick, educate pupils, or oversee workers. *"And indeed what Bentham proposed to the doctors, penologists, industrialists and educators was just what they had been looking for. He invented a technology of power designed to solve the problems of surveillance"* (Foucault 1979, pp. 195–209; Foucault 1980a, p. 148). In *Discipline and Punish* Foucault stated that discipline was liberalism's not-so-silver lining. In *Security, Territory, Population* he writes: *"I believe that I was wrong"* (Foucault 2007, p. 50). Rather, under biopower, liberty becomes a prerequisite, a necessary condition for the exercise of governmental authority (Behrent 2009, p. 22).

The eighteenth century brought changes both in the scale of control (every aspect of bodily functioning, movements, gestures, postures), in the object of control (the economy of bodily movements), and in its modality. There is a constant coercion imposing a defined process of action in accordance with codes and rules, which parcel up time, space and gestures. *"The human body was entering a machinery of power that explores it, breaks it down and rearranges it. It defined how one may have a hold over others' bodies, not only so that they may do what one wishes, but so they may operate as one wishes, with the techniques, the speed and the efficiency that one determines. Thus discipline produces subjected and practiced bodies, 'docile bodies'"* (Foucault 1978, p. 138; see also Rouse 1994, pp. 92–111). The law, to a greater and greater extent, performs regulative functions, and the role of normalization increases at the cost of the juridical system of law.

Hierarchical observation is the first instrument used to discipline. Disciplining becomes a method of exercising power, which provides procedures for the education and training of individuals and society. Other "disciplining technologies of power" include examination and the passing of normalizing judgments (punishment). Disciplinary devices have changed the nature of punishment—they have introduced penalization based on a norm. This new kind of penalization penetrates all places, controls all instances of disciplinary institutions, and then compares, differentiates, hierarchizes, homogenizes and excludes human bodies. It serves to normalize (Foucault 1979, pp. 183–84). Thanks to discipline, the power of the Norm appears. Together with surveillance, it became one of the basic instruments of power at the end of the classical age. Normalizing power compels homogenization, even though—by making it possible to measure deviations from the norm, by defining levels, determining specialities and exploiting differences by matching them—it also individualizes (Ewald 1992, pp. 201–221). Power is no longer repressive, but productive. Normalization proceeds by way of confession rather than repression (Caputo and Yount 1993, p. 6).

By "norm", Foucault did not mean "rule" or "principle". He consistently counterposed his use of the term "norm" to these legal meanings (Foucault 2003a, p. 50; Foucault 2007, p. 56). Foucault gives the term a meaning close to that of the previously used concept of "discipline". A norm is a natural rule appearing in the discourse created by disciplines. Norms should be identified with standards. A set of standards or norms, understood in this way, in a given system of law at a given time might be called not a discursive formation, but a normative formation (Ewald 1991, pp. 38–61). Disciplines create their own discourse, separate from that of law. The legal discourse, and the associated concept of rule of law, are a product of the will of the sovereign or his representatives. Disciplines create a network of compulsions which bind the social body together. A power game is played out between law and disciplines, although disciplines are different from legal rules. The law operates by means of prohibition and punishment.

In disciplinary practices, the main role is played by norms and standards of proper behaviour. What can be defined as "normal" behaviour comes into being through the repetition of normalizing requirements. Disciplines are a kind of infra-law, transferring general legal norms to the level of individual behaviour—they are an element of the micro-physics of power (Foucault 1979, p. 222; Rouse 1994, pp. 93–99). Foucault writes of the "colonization" of the discourse of universal law and of the abstract juridical subject by the technologies and procedures of normalization (Foucault 1980c, p. 107).

Disciplinary power rapidly, and as early as the second half of the eighteenth century, took on a different character. Foucault concludes that a new, non-disciplinary, technology of power appeared at that time. Making use of the moulded, disciplined, subjugated human body, it transfers its action to another plane. Its object is now the human being as a biological entity. It wishes to supervise, control and exploit the multiplicity of individuals, the mass, the population. Its action encompasses the population, and within it, the birth, sexuality, productivity and death of beings who had previously been individualized, but are now massified.

The period from the latter half of the eighteenth century saw the development of state policy in relation to birth control and rate of birth. Other fields of intervention associated with biopolitics included a range of phenomena associated with old age and infirmities. Biopolitical government included various forms of control over the environment: water, swamps, conditions of urban life. Biopower intervenes in *"the birth rate, the mortality rate, various biological disabilities, and the effects of the environment"* (Foucault 2003b, pp. 245–247).

Disciplinary power transforms into biopower. While the object of sovereign power was the individual and a society created by a social contract between such individuals, and the object of disciplinary power is the individual and his or her body, the field of operation of biopower is the population. Within the population, serial processes of events take place. Hence biopower introduces new mechanisms of power, different from those which were employed by disciplinary power. They will include statistical estimation and forecasting, techniques to reduce human mortality, increase lifespan and stimulate reproduction, and for the regulation and optimization of life (Foucault 1980b, p. 125).

3 Foucault's Biopolitics

The central point of philosophical considerations concerning politics in the seventeenth and eighteenth centuries was the concept of sovereignty, the origin of power, the rights enjoyed by the king as sovereign. Foucault recalls, however, that the political philosophy of that period also discussed human life, above all as the object of the sovereign's power. The right of life and death belonged to the sovereign. One of the most important political changes in the nineteenth century was a change in the existing formula of the rights of life and death and their relationship with the power of the sovereign. *"It is the power to 'make' live and 'let' die. The right of sovereignty was the right to take life or let live. And then this new right is established: the right to make live and to let die"* (Foucault 2003b, p. 241).

Foucault's conception of power is concerned above all with its effects, with the repressive function of the law in societies governed by Western liberalism, and with the relations of power and knowledge. Foucault wrote about "modern states". He means the populations that are assigned to the territorial unities of liberal-democratic states in Europe and North America. As Michael Dean says *"He was Eurocentric"* (Dean 2001a, pp. 41–64). The study of colonial power relations and colonial bodies is largely absent from Foucault's studies of discipline and sexuality (Stoler 1995). In India, the post-liberalization era initiated in 1991. This attention to the welfare of the population was a form of biopower, one of the hallmarks of Foucault's governmentality (Gupta 2001, pp. 65–94). In China this was the official state politic of one child (Greenhalgh and Winckler 2005).

Importance is attached to the techniques and rationality of government, and methods of directing people and the state. There is a need to depart from the juridical-discursive presentation of power, and to concentrate on analysing transformations of the forms and techniques of power: from the appearance of disciplinary power at the end of the seventeenth century, up to the emergence of a different, non-disciplinary technology of power—biopower—in the second half of the eighteenth.

The term "biopolitics" has different meanings, depending on who is using it and in what context (Lemke 2011). Giorgio Agamben (1998, pp. 6, 19 & 122, 172–174; 2005, p. 1) and Roberto Esposito (2008, pp. 13–44) define biopolitics as the process of incorporating *bios* (bare life) into cultural, political and legal discourse (politicization). An authority (the sovereign) has the power to decide whose life is worthy of protection, and who can be killed with impunity *(homo sacer)*. The camp becomes a paradigm: toward a paradigm of the extinguishing of differences. The state of exception becomes the norm; the norm becomes the state of exception (Norris 2005, pp. 2–8; Patton 2007, pp. 203–228).

The term "biopolitics" as used in Foucault's work is also ambiguous. Its meaning changes and evolves in successive texts. The determination of a uniform meaning for the term is further hindered by the fact that Foucault also writes about biopower, and does not make any explicit distinction between the two concepts (Bertani 2000; Revel 2002; Colucci 2005).

Biopolitics is, first, a certain new type of power and of technology of power which, in a historical sense, supersedes sovereign power. Using the term in this meaning, Foucault is able to trace the transition from sovereign power in the classical episteme to biopower in the modern episteme *(Society Must Be Defended. Lectures at the Collège de France 1975–1976).*

Secondly, biopolitics was the reason for the birth of modern racism, and at the same time a form of politics of the population *(Society Must Be Defended).*

Thirdly, it is a technology of power characteristic of the development of liberalism *(Security, Territory, Population: Lectures at the Collège de France 1977–1978; The Birth of Biopolitics: Lectures at the Collège de France 1978–1979; The History of Sexuality vol. I: An Introduction 1978)* (Lemke 2011, pp. 33–35; Tepper 2010, pp. 78–82; Karskens 2009, pp. 122–127).

For Foucault, biopolitics is another name for the technology of power, biopower, which needs to be distinguished from the mechanisms of discipline that emerged at the end of the eighteenth century. This new configuration of power aims to take *"control of life and the biological processes of man as species and of ensuring that they are not disciplined but regularized"* (Foucault 2003b, p. 246). Biopolitics is juxtaposed in Foucault's analysis with the power of sovereignty, leading to an important distinction between them. He writes: *"Biopower is the power to make live. Sovereignty took life and let live. And now we have the emergence of power that I would could call the power of regularization, and it, in contrast, consists in making live and letting die"* (ibid., p. 247; Dean 2013, pp. 36–37). The nature and form of the new disciplinary and biopolitical modes of power are largely incompatible with the old forms of law and sovereignty. But sovereignty has not vanished, of course. It has been reactivated in the service of political regulation and security (Foucault 2007, pp. 8–10; Jaeger 2010, pp. 54–57).

For Foucault, biopower constituted nothing less than the entry of life into the order of politics—the emergence of a *"society in which political power had assigned itself the task of administering life"* (Foucault 1978, p. 137; Golder and Fitzpatrick 2009, pp. 20–22).

Biopolitics does not invalidate or annihilate the technology of disciplinary power. Biopower transfers the problem of the human body, which was the object of disciplinary power, to a higher level. It directs the processes of human life, controlling and modifying them. From now on a person is not exclusively a legal subject, but a living being which will be subject to the influences of biopower at the level of life itself. The basic targets of biopolitical control come to be the processes of birth, mortality, longevity, ratio of births to deaths, rate of reproduction, the fertility of a given population, and the like. The first statistical measurements of these phenomena and processes are introduced. Scientific demographics comes into being. *"We see the beginning of a natalist policy, plans to intervene in all phenomena relating to the birth rate"* (Foucault 2003b, p. 243).

Foucault links the birth of biopolitics and biopower with the evolution of liberalism at the end of the nineteenth century and the appearance of ordoliberalism in the 1920s and 1930s. In his lectures given at the Collège de France between January 10 and April 4, 1979, titled *Naissance de la biopolitique* (The Birth of Biopolitics), Foucault made a precise and profound analysis of the birth and development of economic and social liberalism, as well as the relations between liberalism and legal theory. Only by describing the changes in the way of treating the human body, subjugated by disciplinary and normalizing power, controlled and subjected to coercive, totalizing socialization carried out in social institutions for the management of individuals (the family, schools, psychiatric hospitals, prisons, the armed forces, the police, collective administration, individual medicine, etc.), does it become possible to understand the process of the emergence in the late nineteenth century of a new technology of power: biopower (Foucault 2008, p. 22). However, the biopolitics of population was a technology of power that was assimilated and creatively exploited by totalitarian states as well. Both Nazism and socialism carried out a generalization of biopower. The Nazi state bound the biopolitics of the population with racism. It raised the organization, control and protection of the biological nature of the population to an absolute level. At the same time a modification was made to the sovereign right to kill—to kill anyone, Germans as well as those "whose life was not worth living". Both socialist and capitalist states are tainted with racism. In the case of the socialist state, this is not purely ethnic racism, but rather racism of an evolutionistic type, a biological racism (ibid., pp. 254–263; Lemke 2011, pp. 40–42). Biopolitics and biological factors play a role in the analysis of other fields of social and political behaviour: education (Pierce 2013), bureaucracy (Flohr 1986), and criminology (Murray and Herrstein 1996; Rushton 1998).

Another field in which biopolitics operates involves issues relating to the unfitness or worthlessness of certain individuals for work—their neutralization. From the start of the nineteenth century this would involve cases of disability, accidents at work, or old age. *"This biopolitics will establish not only charitable institutions (...) but also much more subtle mechanisms that were much more economically rational than an indiscriminate charity. (...) We see the introduction of more subtle, more rational mechanisms: insurance, individual and collective savings, safety measures, and so on"* (Foucault 2003b, p. 244). Biopolitics is not just a technology of power whose object is the individual human body and control of the individual's life processes. The fundamental level on which biopolitics operates is the global level—that of the population. It is necessary to reduce the randomness associated with the life of the population. The objective is the optimization of life—bioregulation by the state. *"There is absolutely no question relating to an individual body, in the way that discipline does. It is therefore not a matter of taking the individual at the level of individuality, but, on the contrary, of using overall mechanisms and acting in such a way as to achieve overall states of equilibration or regularity; it is, in a word, a matter of taking control of life and the biological processes of man-as-species and of ensuring that they are not disciplined, but regularized"* (ibid., pp. 246–247). Biopower becomes a pastoral power (Foucault 2000a, p. 307; Dean 2001b, pp. 73–97).

Since the start of the eighteenth century, society has been subject to an increasing degree of medicalization. The medical technologies of government change across time, they tend to cohere around security problematics posed to, and by, the vitality, fecundity and productivity of the population (Foucault 2003c, pp. 320–322). Around the mid-eighteenth century there emerged and developed a biopolitics of the population dealing with the regulation of population processes (problems of natural population growth, human longevity, urbanization and processes of migration). It was the subjugated, trained and comprehensively normalized human body, a creation of disciplinary power and the power of the Norm, that was the social foundation on which the biopolitics of the population grew. The human body was to meet the requirements of reproduction of capitalist relations (political economy of the body). After individual bodies had been subjugated by the general application of techniques of disciplinary power in schools, colleges, barracks and prisons, from the mid-eighteenth century the era of biopower begins, an era of controlled regulation of bodies as a species (Foucault 1978, pp. 139–140). Foucault states that the emergence of biopower, as a modern form of power, was a necessary element in the development of capitalism. Capitalism adapted population phenomena to economic processes; however, it required new tools and techniques for exercising power. It became necessary to combine the accumulation of population with the accumulation of capital. People had to become more and more obedient and productive; they needed to work efficiently.

It was not by chance that at the end of the nineteenth century the first social laws were introduced. State authorities and other social organizations were interested in new methods of influencing the population's health, vitality and fertility. The life of humans as a species was made subject to knowledge and power. New methods and techniques of power (biopower) direct processes of life, subjecting them to classification, control and modification. *"One would have to speak of biopower to designate what brought life and its mechanisms into the realm of explicit calculation and made knowledge-power an agent of transformation of human life"* (ibid., p. 143). Biopower used two main techniques for managing individuals. Earlier there appeared an anatomo-political power over the body, whose goal was to integrate the forces of the human body with systems of effective economic control. *"The new technology that is being established is addressed to a multiplicity of men, not to the extent that they are nothing more than their individual bodies, but to the extent that they form, on the contrary, a global mass that is affected by overall processes characteristic of birth, death, production, illness, and so on. (...) After the anatomo-politics of the human body established in the course of the eighteenth century, we have, at the end of that century, the emergence of something that is no longer an anatomo-politics of the human body, but what I would call a '**biopolitics**' of the human race"* (Foucault 2003b, pp. 242–243). In the eighteenth century, these two techniques were still separated—there had not yet been shaped a single discourse that combined them. The nineteenth century, however, saw the constitution of a further, coherent technology of power, which Foucault called the *dispositif de sexualité*.

The binding together of power, knowledge, and the sexuality of both the individual and the population is a third area of interest of biopolitics. Biopolitics refers not only—or even most prevalently—to the way in which politics is captured by life, but also and above all by the way in which politics penetrates life. Foucault concludes: *"If one can apply the term bio-history to the pressures through which the movements of life and processes of history interfere with one another, one would have to speak of bio-power to designate what brought life and its mechanisms into the realm of explicit calculation and made knowledge-power an agent of transformation of human life"* (Foucault 2001a, pp. 95–97).

In *The History of Sexuality*, Foucault analyses the way in which modern biopower has induced people to submit to its mechanisms (subjugation, *assujetissement*) using specific confessional techniques and ethical identity-related practices (Dreyfus and Rabinow 1983, pp. 126–127). At the beginning of the first volume of *The History of Sexuality* Foucault set out a conception of the relations between knowledge, power, sexuality and the body. He called this the repressive hypothesis.

The repressive hypothesis is immanently connected with the characteristic Western "juridical-discursive" concept of power. Reference to this concept of power, and the stressing of its sovereign nature and the legality of actions, makes it more difficult to analyse the actions of other forms of power, which occur simultaneously with it and in whose description Foucault was primarily interested. It was the subjugated, trained and comprehensively normalized human body, a creation of disciplinary power and the power of the Norm, that was the social foundation on which the biopolitics of the population grew (Muble 2014, pp. 78–80). The human body was to meet the requirements of reproduction of capitalist relations (political economy of the body). After individual bodies had been subjugated by the general application of techniques of disciplinary power in schools, colleges, barracks and prisons, from the mid-eighteenth century the era of biopower begins, an era of controlled regulation of bodies as a species (Foucault 1978, pp. 139–140).

The repressive hypothesis explains the change in the attitude taken by the authorities towards sexuality: from the treatment of sex, in the classical age, as a part of human nature, (*"The scheme for transforming sex into discourse had been devised long before in an ascetic and monastic setting. The seventeenth century made it into a rule for everyone"*—Foucault 1978, p. 20), to the treatment of sex that does not serve procreation as a sin and an object of confession (Catholic doctrine), increasing repressiveness (from the seventeenth century onwards—ibid., p. 15) and the continuous proliferation of discourse concerning sex in the eighteenth and nineteenth centuries. *"Sex was not something one simply judged; it was a thing one administered. It was in the nature of public potential; it called for management procedures; it had to be taken charge of by analytical discourse. In the eighteenth century, sex became a 'police matter' – in the full and strict sense given the term at the time: not the repression of disorder, but an ordered maximization of collective and individual forces"* (ibid., pp. 24–25). Liberation was brought only by a new discourse on sexuality in the post-modern age.

The fundamental change which took place in the eighteenth century was the recognition of the population as an economic and political problem. The object of government is not people, only the population: *"population as wealth, population as manpower or labor capacity, population balanced between its own growth and the resources it commanded (...) population with its specific phenomena and its peculiar variables: birth and death rates, life expectancy, fertility, state of health, frequency of illnesses, patterns of diet and habitation."* However, the most important problem of the population is sex. *"It was necessary to analyze the birthrate, the age of marriage, the legitimate and illegitimate births, the precocity and frequency of sexual relations, the way of making them fertile or sterile, the effects of unmarried life or the prohibitions, the impact of contraceptive practices"* (ibid., pp. 25–26).

Sex becomes the basic object of interest of the authorities and the state. Sex is to serve the goal of procreation. The state analyses the sexual behaviours of individuals, their determinants and consequences. It does not stop at just observation and analysis—the state wishes to oversee and to plan these behaviours. Sex is not only a biological question, but an economic one: a new domain for the political economy of the body. The state, apart from its traditional means—moral and religious dictates and prohibitions, tax burdens (higher taxes on the income of unmarried and childless men)—creates new mechanisms for stimulating procreative behaviours in the population: advertising campaigns promoting the family, control of fertility through legal prohibition of abortion, control of sex education and of the availability of contraceptives. It supports the traditional, Catholic model of the family: the man works professionally, while the woman looks after the home and children. It reinforces standards and norms of sexual, marital and family life. It defines the proper social roles of individuals. Sex is no longer just a part of people's private, intimate lives. It is the subject of manifold discourses and of scientific knowledge (McNay 1994, p. 96). *"From the singular imperialism that compels everyone to transform their sexuality into a perpetual discourse, to the manifold mechanisms which, in the areas of economy, pedagogy, medicine, and justice, incite, extract, distribute, and institutionalize the sexual discourse"* (Foucault 1978, p. 33).

4 Ethical Aspects of Human Procreation: On the Need for a New Definition of Morality Arising Out of Neo-Naturalist Environmental Ethics

Biotechnological progress in the field of medicine gives rise to many ethical problems whose resolution is of immeasurable importance, not just from the perspective of the individual, but also in the context of population policy and the operational techniques of biopower. One of the areas at issue is human procreation. Dilemmas relating to that area have become especially apparent in the globalized world. They cannot be considered in isolation from cultural determinants.

From the perspective of the culture of lawfulness, a fundamental role is played—as has been mentioned previously—by the conviction that it is necessary to protect innate individual rights, in particular the right to freedom. Human procreation is one of the fundamental rights, being linked to the concept of human dignity and the right to self-determination. Decisions in the area of procreation are of a dual nature. They concern on the one hand the right to have children, and on the other—the right not to have them.

The right to have children is expressed in, among other things, the ability of potential parents—exercising the liberty that the law guarantees—to realize their procreative plans autonomously by striving to give birth to a child. In case of problems with getting pregnant, modern medicine provides them with the possibility of fertility treatment, using methods of artificial insemination and *in vitro* fertilization. In some countries, there is also legal access to pre-implantation diagnosis and surrogate motherhood services. The parental instinct can also be satisfied through adoption. The right not to have children, on the other hand, is linked to the possibility of using methods to prevent reproduction (usually in the form of contraceptives, and more rarely through sterilization), but also to the ability to take a decision to terminate a pregnancy.

Issues relating to procreation are among the fundamental problems of modern ethics, and in particular of that branch which goes by the name "bioethics". Because of the possibilities that modern medicine offers, there is a broadening of the range of problems relating to human procreation considered in the context of demographic (population) policy. It also comes to include questions concerning the possibility of "creating" future generations, for instance by the use of pre-implantation diagnostic techniques to impart desired features to children who are yet to be born. This will have an influence on the quality of the population and of future generations.

There is currently a noticeable fascination in bioethics with futuristic visions of a "bionic" human being (*homo bionicus*), or one who is everlasting (*homo continuus*), and thus of a person who is to live for as long and in as good a condition as possible. In view of the possibilities offered by medicine, some foresee that in the near future there will exist a practically immortal human being: genetically improved, reproducing by cloning, resistant to cancers, making use of gene therapy, using the potential of stem cells to grow replacement tissues and organs, etc. Naturally some of these visions still lie within the domain of science fiction, but many of them have become realistic thanks to biotechnological progress. Medicine is able to make real (at least partially) ideas that until recently would have been considered entirely utopian. Numerous questions nonetheless need to be answered. Is it right that doctors should make use of existing technologies and carry out all possible forms of interference with the human body, even if this leads to an increase in the fertility rate? Is the fact that the expected result of actions may prove favourable for society as a whole a sufficient argument for the legitimacy of those actions? How are we to determine the legal limits of medical (and in particular genetic) experiments carried out on humans?

The eternal dilemma between the law of nature and enacted law (between *ius* and *lex*) takes on a new importance. The chief cause of moral and legal controversy is that biotechnology has now encroached on the "sanctuary of the secret of life", while mankind is preparing to carry out processes in which it itself will be the object of transformation. With the development of genetics, there is now a blurring of the boundary between nature and organic equipment, between subject and object, between the natural and the artificial (Ostasz 1994).

The logic of technical progress apparently forces the assumption that medicine (and genetics) will continue to develop. These fields will also certainly exert a growing influence on the life of individuals and of society. Considering the inevitability of this process, modern states ought to prepare for the elimination of potential threats: to ensure that the achievements of science are made to serve the common good. Properly constructed laws should be an instrument for attaining that goal.

A fundamental issue in bioethics is the dispute over the permissibility of medical intervention relating to human procreation, as well as related controversies concerning the essence of humanity. These controversies have an undoubted impact on specific decisions concerning the directions of demographic policy, whose purpose is also to shape population relations in such a way as to produce a desirable population in terms of numbers and structure. Two basic approaches can be distinguished in this area of policy: the pronatalist one, where the state acts to increase the fertility rate, particularly in the context of the projected sub-replacement rates in highly developed European countries; and the antinatalist one, where the aim is to decrease this rate, usually due to concerns relating to projected overpopulation in certain parts of the world (such as China and India).

The dispute over the definition of a human being is connected with, among other things, the fact that in the twenty-first century there is a visible friction between traditional culture and the "fluid" culture of the modern world. Traditional values have proved incongruent with the pluralist, global reality, based on individualism, pluralism and rationalism. At the same time, the modern philosophy of optimistic pragmatism appears to be lacking a "transcendental extension". The primary challenge comes to be the utilitarian balance sheet, belief in success and potential benefits, which are available to every individual, on condition that he or she is sufficiently dynamic, strongly motivated, healthy and efficient. Such an individual should have—as has already been mentioned—a legally guaranteed autonomy, including in the area of procreation. Usefulness, rationality, economy and ecology take precedence over the domain of morals and philosophy. New approaches to the eternal problem of human procreation are therefore a consequence of the appearance of new value systems.

There is currently a growth in the popularity of ideas which oppose the traditional positivist and natural-law approaches. A revaluation of issues relating to the essence of humanity is proposed by what is called "environmental ethics". This addresses existential, morally important matters, being the result of the problems of mankind (society, globalized humanity) with the natural environment. The sphere of philosophical inquiry is the totality of interdependencies and mutual interactions between people and nature, and their interpretation from the point of view of the well-being of humans and of the biosphere.

Environmental ethics was founded in the late 1970s and early 1980s. The fundamental object of its considerations came to be *bios* (life), seen chiefly from the perspective of relations between species. Environmental ethics leads to the formulation of moral principles concerning the co-existence of *Homo sapiens* with its natural surroundings. Specific issues are resolved based on the conclusions of evolutionary axiology. Moral patronage of the founding of environmental ethics can be considered to belong to the voluntaristic "ethics of reverence for life" of Albert Schweitzer (Schweitzer 1966). The idea that concern for the future of humanity is the overriding duty of people in our modern technical civilization, while metaphysical responsibility goes beyond the individual fate of *Homo sapiens* and begins to concern the rest of the living world, was promulgated thanks to Hans Jonas (Jonas 1996). A need was perceived for a redefinition of the category of nature, in accordance with the ideological matrix of sustainable development and taking account also of nonhuman interests (Bińczyk 2012, p. 170).

As environmental ethics has evolved, various options have developed within it. One of these is known as "ethical humanism". This is an application of traditional humanist ethics (anthropocentrism) to moral issues relating to aspects of protection of the natural environment. It should be noted that environmental ethics seen from this perspective does not in fact require either a new definition of morality, or a departure from the intellectual tradition of the Mediterranean cultural area (the European-American model of utilitarian culture). The target of regulatory measures is the human being, while the protection of nature is an instrument serving to provide humanity—as the master species—with general well-being.

In considerations concerning biotechnological progress, a particular role is played today by what is called *neo-naturalist environmental ethics*, which puts forward new proposals for defining morality, these being of particular significance in connection with the technological capabilities offered by modern medicine (and by genetics in particular). This ethics attempts to determine methods for resolving the moral and legal dilemmas arising from such progress. It includes a set of individualistic ethics known as humane moralism or biocentrism. This school has given the whole of counter-anthropocentric environmental ethics a decidedly anti-Cartesian character. Living organisms of all species are treated here as sensitive—and above all sentient—individual beings. The result is the postulate that we should respect the sensitivity and the ability to distinguish good and bad experiences—particularly as regards pleasure (happiness) and pain (suffering)—exhibited by what are called nonhuman animals. The humanist axiology is therefore extended to cover sentient beings which are not human, but are in biological terms fundamentally similar. A key issue addressed by the originators and theoreticians of this approach (such as Peter Singer, Paul W. Taylor, Tom Regan and Robin Attfield) is the identification of an evolutionarily determined threshold for being considered a morally and legally relevant object (Wawrzyniak 2000, pp. 49–50).

In considering environmental ethics, one should not neglect the importance of what is known as biomedical ethics. This has been developing intensively since the mid twentieth century. It is stimulated by the new capabilities and conflict situations created by rapid scientific and technical advances in diagnostics and therapy, while legal regulation in this area remains stagnant and inadequate. *"The fundamental values (...): life (biological survival), health and freedom from pain, as assigned to specific people, are as a rule not realized simultaneously in situations of danger, and medical actions remain inherently characterized by a dual effect (the effects inevitably accompanying therapeutic and care procedures, and the expected but undesirable biologically destructive consequences of those procedures)"* (ibid., p. 64).

Answers to questions concerning the essence of humanity, which are essential from the standpoint of biomedical ethics, are clearly affected by cultural factors. An enormous influence is exerted by the Judeo-Christian roots of European culture, and in particular by Catholic doctrine.

Deriving from classical ethical concepts, a dispute came to light at the end of the twentieth century between competing visions relating to the problem of human life. The traditional, abstract and not totally coherent—grounded in the Judeo-Christian cultural model—ethics of the "sanctity of life" (bound up in the paradox of the axiological absolutization of the physiological layer of life, and then only in relation to the species *Homo sapiens*) began gradually to be displaced by the realist ethics of the "quality of life" (understood as respect for personal life which has a defined value; for conscious life). This new view of human life—treated as an object of moral evaluation—is undoubtedly a consequence of medical progress. The fact that the quality of a person's life is determined not only by the body, but above all by the human capacity for autonomous action, has been confirmed by a large number of court judgements relating to, among other things, issues of procreation. The view has become more and more common that autonomy or its potential attainability is a necessary condition for someone's life to deserve fully to be called a human life. At the same time, increased social acceptance for the ethics of "quality of life" has been (and continues to be) accompanied by the question of how to measure that quality (Chańska 2009, p. 108).

In considerations concerning the ethics of life, there are at present two fundamental ways of defining the essence of humanity: the metaphysical and the descriptive.

According to the metaphysical (axiological) view, a person is a particular being, different from other beings, at least because of its specific genotype. It is a "pre-value", subject to legal protection irrespective of its phase of development, without regard to any incidental circumstances or features (such as psychophysical state). Such a view of the essence of humanity is based on the monistic definition of the human being, formulated classically by the Roman philosopher and theologian Boethius. According to this definition, a person is a substantial unity of soul and body. This unity lasts from the moment of conception and does not end at the time of death. An embryo or foetus is a "potential human", and thus from the beginning is entitled to human dignity (Boethius 1990, p. 24). Views of this kind were later put forward by Saint Augustine, Thomas Aquinas and the proponents of Christian personalism. In contemporary times this approach retains a consolidated position in Christian countries, and particularly those (such as Poland) in which Catholic ethics are dominant.

Besides the metaphysical approach just described, increasing popularity is being acquired by the descriptive approach, which is particularly important from the standpoint of neo-naturalist environmental ethics. It is based on an attempt to find other defining features of humanity, other than the specific human genome, which can distinguish the human being from other living beings. Science has already forced a re-evaluation of many of the features traditionally associated with the essence of humanity, such as ability to feel pain and suffering, consciousness, ability to rationalize, memory of the past, and ability to plan. Qualitatively, a person does not differ very much from animals.

At the roots of descriptive approaches to the essence of humanity lies the dualist definition of the human being, due to Descartes. This is based on a new way of understanding carnality. It is assumed that the body is an autonomous entity with respect to the soul, and does not co-create humanity. The body is a system of parts—a material object which decomposes at death. Its actions can be described in the categories of mechanics. A human being, however, is a mind or soul. Its essence is that it alone, of all living species, is aware that it exists (Descartes 1989, p. 3). Neo-naturalist environmental bioethics has re-evaluated these theses, raising the status of other nonhuman beings capable of feeling pain and suffering and having a certain level of consciousness (certain mammals and birds). By the same token there arises the question of the status of the human embryo, which according to neo-naturalist environmental ethics is accorded a status equal to that of other nonhuman animals. It has been proposed that "potential life" (an embryo or foetus) should not be considered equal to life "already in existence". The difference between potentiality and actuality is well summed up in the statement that eggs are not omelettes, acorns are not oak trees (Stanton and Harris 2005, p. 222). Indeed, even after a person is born, it is becoming considered more and more legitimate to make differentiations or gradations of quality of life (the quality of the life of someone in a permanent vegetative state not being comparable to that of a healthy person).

Medical progress has made it possible to observe the development of a human being from the very start. This provides a basis for precise planning of the moment of conception and selection of appropriate gametes, and for creating life in entirely artificial conditions. The conception of a child need not involve even casual intimate relations between two people. It may take the form of a medical service using gametes from the future parents or from anonymous donors, or it may be made the subject of a surrogate motherhood agreement. The technicalization of human procreation thus entails a difficult encounter between *Homo sapiens* and *homo technicus*. Natural conception has been replaced by artificial fertilization, which may occur inside a woman's body, but may also take place outside it. The foetus need not necessarily develop in a woman's womb—that of either the genetic or the surrogate mother. Proponents of ectogenesis research point out that when an artificial womb is created, an age will begin which will either bring a definitive end to natural motherhood, or will provide the possibility of choice between types of motherhood—natural or artificial. The new medical possibilities are intended to help, among others, women who see maternity as a "biological yoke", and the experience of pregnancy as a kind of slavery.

In the context of ethical discussion concerning the status of the human embryo, attempts have been made in the bioethical literature to determine the moment at which someone begins to be a human being. This is particularly important with regard to the legal consequences of the recognition of a given being as a legal subject. Apart from the genetic criterion, defining a human as an entity with a specific genotype (corresponding to the metaphysical viewpoint), other criteria have also been offered. Of particular significance are the legal criterion (which makes someone a natural person from the time of birth until death), and the related obstetric criterion (where the beginnings of a human being are linked with the start of the labour process, including as a result of caesarean section). An increasing role is played, however, by "developmental" criteria, which include the neurological criterion (according to which one starts to become a human being when brain activity begins, namely around the eighth week of prenatal life), the criterion of animation (the start of human life takes place when the foetus moves in the womb, at around 13–20 weeks), and the criterion of viability (where what matters is the capacity for independent life outside the mother's body, at around 24 weeks).

The most controversial is the psychological criterion. Here, an attempt is made to identify the start of one's becoming a human being as the time at which the human organism acquires awareness of its own existence. It has been proposed that human rights should be attributed only to self-aware beings. Suggestions of this type are found in the works of Peter Singer (Singer 1980, 2009), Derek Parfit (Parfit 1984), Hugo T. Engelhardt (Engelhardt 1996, pp. 135–138) and Michael Tooley (Tooley 2010). A degree of outrage was provoked by the proposal of the Italian bioethicists Alberto Giubilini and Francesca Minerva, who attempt to give legal and moral justification for so-called "postnatal abortion" (Giubilini and Minerva 2013). The starting point for those authors' considerations was the abovementioned psychological criterion, along with scientific findings that an infant acquires awareness only some time after birth. "Postnatal abortion" would become an expression of the procreative autonomy of the parents, who ought to be given time to decide whether they wish to be parents or not.

The development of genetics gives rise to new debates concerning the essence of humanity, particularly with regard to genetic manipulations (instrumental and anthropological), linked to technological possibilities of creating hybrids and chimeras. This problem was raised by Francis Fukuyama (Fukuyama 2004). The author is concerned that the "posthuman future" may be a world in which the concept of humanity loses its meaning, if only because human genes become mixed with the genes of so many species that it will no longer be entirely clear who or what is a human (ibid., p. 286).

Questions concerning the essence of humanity are made all the more relevant by the current biotechnological experiments which lead (by way of genetic manipulation) to the production of various types of "transgenic" beings that cannot be unambiguously classified. One might recall the work titled *Edunia*, created by the artist Eduardo Kac, a representative of the bio-art movement. The work is a central element of the project *Natural History of the Enigma*, and was first exhibited at the Weisman Art Museum in Minneapolis in 2009. The artist has incorporated his own DNA into a genetically modified petunia flower. The title of the work alludes to the attempt to merge together two entities, "Eduardo" and "petunia", into a single one, called by the name "Edunia". This new form of life is described as a *plantimal* (a cross between plant and animal). Critics have described the work as a *"strange and radical form of humanization of a nonhuman other"* (Gajewska 2012, pp. 105–114). This transgenic hybrid appears on the surface to serve as a symbolic and physical missing link, expressing the closeness of human and nonhuman species, but ultimately it becomes an attack on the traditional view of man as a being that is hierarchically superior to all other entities. It leads to a levelling of the distinction between human and nonhuman beings (DeGrazia 2002; McMahan 2003; Chamayou 2012, p. 68).

The problem of defining the essence of humanity is also complicated by the development of information technologies, robotics and mechanics. Advanced work is being done which aims to construct machines and computer programs capable of performing selected functions of the mind and the human senses. The euphoria associated with predictions that the near future will see the creation of artificial intelligence (and possibilities of using "thinking" machines in the service of people) is accompanied by fears as to whether such an "electronic person" can be made to fit into a system of humanist values. Who will such an entity be in relation to human beings? Is it to be given the protection of the law? In view of its self-awareness, should a machine be accorded the dignity characterizing a human being (Braidotti 2013; Sedlak 1980)?

The examples given above indicate that increasing molecular biological and genetic knowledge, and the technological practices based thereon, erase the traditional lines separating nature and culture, biology and society: *"In this way, recourse to a pre- or extrapolitical nature is blocked, and biology cannot be separated from political and moral questions"* (Lemke 2010, p. 100). Modern technologies enable the disassembly and recombination of the body, which Foucault did not foresee when he linked biopolitics with an integral body (ibid., p. 94). Thanks to the possibilities afforded by modern medicine, a person who dies is never in fact entirely dead. Human material is no longer tied to the same biological rhythms as the organic body. Parts of a dead person, his or her cells or organs, blood, bone marrow, etc. can continue to exist in the bodies of other people, improving the quality of their life or delaying the time of death. Human material can be stored as information, held in databases or grown in stem cell lines (ibid., p. 95).

Ethical problems relating to human procreation are bound up with cultural contexts (particularly religious ones), which condition the axiological evaluation of particular actions. Environmental ethics affirms the internal diversity of being, regarding culture as neither bad nor good in itself, nor as constituting a rule structure which might replace organic evolution and change the principles of coexistence of various forms of organization of life. Culture has the status of a naturally selected manner of existence for the species *Homo sapiens*. It ought to be understood as a kind of adaptive system: as a multidimensional ecological niche for mankind. According to this view it is a nomological locality in the biosphere, similar to the spectra of particular ecotypes of other species. The very existence of a cultural niche, of its internal regularity (and particularly of the conscious purposefulness of human actions) is subject to the macro-rules of natural being. Failure to respect these rules leads to the self-elimination of the human species from the biosphere, which has already begun. This is revealed by statistical data indicating low birth rates in modern states that subscribe to the culture of lawfulness.

It should be noted that environmental ethics not only reaches basic ontological, axiological and meta-ethical conclusions concerning human existence (in relation to, among other things, human procreation). It also formulates specific prescriptive proposals. Its assumptions are based on the thesis that prescriptivism does not exist extra-empirically. Only that which is empirical can become prescriptive. Being a value is a certain manner of existence of an empirical fact, namely a fact, which can be described and explained by scientific methods. The "factualization" of values from a realistic-empirical perspective enables a better justification of the moral obligations of *Homo sapiens* in the biosphere. The empirical recognition of reality and the constitution of prescriptions on that basis is made possible by references to the complex of socio-natural disciplines: biology, evolutionary philosophy, genetics, ecology, comparative ethology, sociobiology, evolutionary epistemology, cognitive science, comparative zoopsychology, linguistic philosophy, and so on. These disciplines supply detailed data and theoretical generalizations, which can be used to re-equip the human being with a full biocultural dimension from an anthropological-philosophical perspective.

From the standpoint of environmental ethics, Foucault's proposed concept of "biopolitics" seems somewhat constricted. It does not enable one to grasp fully how ecological management and discourses on protection of the environment interfere with the (re)production of the human species. It is consequently proposed to extend the semantic field so as to apply the concept of biopolitics in relation to the management and control of the conditions of life in their entirety (Rutherford 1999). The anthropocentric simplification of biopolitics as found in Foucault (who remained influenced by the view that the ability to act is a human feature) is being more and more frequently criticized. In the light of the new anthropology (reflective and symmetric anthropology) the following question recurs every so often: empirically, who can be included in the set of "social persons"? According to neo-naturalist environmental ethics, subjects capable of action include humans as well as nonhuman animals (Lemke 2010, p. 96). At the same time, not every human being has such a capability. It cannot be ascribed to a person in the phase of prenatal life (a human embryo or foetus). People in permanent vegetative state also lack the ability to act. The question therefore arises as to whether they are to be treated by the law as "persons" or as "human beings". If the second option is taken, their legal status ought to be equal to that of nonhuman animals. Conclusions as to what entities (and in what conditions) can be members of a society are extremely important from the standpoint of population policy.

It should be borne in mind that international (including European) standards relating to human procreation lay down only minimum requirements for the protection of human rights and the protection of a child following conception. Prescriptive formulas set a course for the interpretation of particular regulations. The overriding interpretative directive should be considered to be the duty to protect human dignity and to place the good of a human being above the interests of society or of science. Fundamentally important from a European perspective is the *Convention for the Protection of Human Rights and Dignity of the Human Being with regard to the Application of Biology and Medicine*. This document leaves the definition of a "person" as a matter for national law. However, it provides for different degrees of legal protection. Every "human being", irrespective of his or her personal status, is subject to protection at least as regards dignity and identity, but guarantees of integrity and other basic rights and freedoms are applied only to a "person" (*Bioethics Convention* 1997).

Perhaps human procreation ought to be viewed from a broader perspective today than in the past, taking account of theoretical findings other than those formed within Judeo-Christian culture, which might prove significant for the resolution of legal questions. The solutions proposed by Christianity (and Catholicism in particular) do not fit the contemporary world. They entail the sanctification of the traditional family, treating sexuality as a social taboo. According to the teaching of the Catholic Church, one of the chief aims of marriage is to pass on life, subject to invariable and inviolable divine laws. Any interference in procreation is therefore considered a sin. The basic principles regulating family planning involve the rejection of abortion, prohibition of artificial fertilization and embryo manipulation, and respect for human life from the moment of conception (*Donum Vitae* 1987).

From the perspective of neo-naturalist environmental ethics, it may be of interest to consider other religions, particularly those of the East. Buddhism has proved to be particularly attractive, particularly in connection with the vanishing of the religious and spiritual dimension of Christianity (Churchland 2013, p. 311). Perhaps Buddhist spirituality and wisdom will be able at least partially to fill that vacuum, offering the principles of *ahinsa* (refraining from doing harm) and liberation from suffering. These principles also relate to the sphere of human sexuality, being manifest in, among other things, the treatment of sex between two loving people as a value in itself (irrespective of whether or not the partners are married). Buddhist doctrine, treating marriage and procreation as private matters, is becoming more and more popular within the juridified culture of lawfulness (Clarke 2003).

Neo-naturalist environmental ethics often alludes to feminist doctrine, emphasizing autonomy in the area of procreation, manifest chiefly in a woman's freedom to decide about her own body. The scope of such freedom includes, among other things, conscious motherhood, birth control, abortion, surrogacy and sexual freedom. Since the problem of relations between the sexes concerns the whole of humanity, the global reach of the ideology of feminism should come as no surprise.

According to the radical feminist viewpoint, new technologies relating to fertility and reproduction are the product of a battle fought by men for control over women's bodies and procreation. It is presumed that such motives have played an important role in the history of medicine. Some express fears that these technologies may be used to strengthen the position of a specific race and privileged classes, and may serve to eliminate competition in the labour market (Sawicki 1999, pp. 190–203).

5 The Problem of the Replacement of Generations as a Challenge for the Culture of Lawfulness

The highest statistical fertility rates are recorded in certain African countries (as high as 7.03 in Niger, and over 6 in such countries as Mali, Somalia and Uganda). At the same time, African countries also record the highest rates of mortality, disease, poverty, armed conflict, religious fundamentalism, etc. (https://www.cia.gov/library/publications/the-word-factbook/rankorder/2127rank.htm).

Analysis of the statistics for countries that embrace the culture of lawfulness may incline one to the conclusion that their societies are dying out. There is a failure of replacement of generations—successive generations are found to be less populous than the preceding ones. It is generally accepted that, to ensure such replacement, the total fertility rate (the number of children per woman of childbearing age, that is, aged between 16 and 49) should be at least somewhere between 2.10 and 2.15.

In most highly industrialized countries, particularly in Europe, fertility rates have been decreasing constantly since the mid 1960s. The warnings of experts who predict a radical reduction in demographic growth over the next two decades are causing concern among governments, which are thus attempting to implement pronatal policies.

It is not possible to grasp the essence of this social phenomenon without making reference to people's procreative plans and decisions. These should be viewed from a broad perspective, determined by a defined sociocultural space.

One of the reasons for the population decline is the increased popularity of the "modern lifestyle" (including the acceptance of women performing professional work). This has had a negative effect on the procreative behaviours of modern societies. Some importance also attaches to the ongoing deinstitutionalization of the family. Procreation has become separated from marriage, and the importance of the marriage contract for forming a relationship has declined. Attention is drawn to the destabilization of the family, visible particularly through the growing number of divorces, as well as the growth in non-marital relationships. It is also evident that in modern society the decision to start a family often comes later than was previously the case—the average age of a woman giving birth to her first child is now between 25 and 30 (Titkow and Duch-Krzystoszek 2009).

The maintenance of a low fertility rate speeds up the process of population ageing, and exacerbates unfavourable changes in the age structure. For example, according to a projection from the Polish Central Statistical Office, by 2035 the number of persons of post-productive age will have risen to 9.6 million (an increase of 3.5 million), while the number of persons of productive age will have fallen to 20.7 million (a decrease of 3.8 million). Data for 2013 show that, statistically, the average Polish woman gives birth to 1.32 children. This is one of the worst results in Europe.

In Poland, under the influence of the dominant Catholic faith, instead of the implementation of pro-family policies, there is debate about the inviolability of the traditional family and the sanctity of human life. Sex that does not serve the purpose of procreation is still sometimes regarded as a matter for confession. Paradoxically, however, the actual number of traditional families is steadily decreasing. There is a marked decrease in the number of marriages (although the percentage of people who are married, 63.9 %, is still relatively high in comparison with other European countries). Regardless of religious influences, many women are deciding to live in informal relationships (5.1 %), and many are choosing single motherhood (one in five Polish children are born outside marriage). In spite of the prohibition on abortion, there is a thriving backstreet abortion sector. The facts therefore show that the ideal model of Christian morality is not realized in practice.

The particular character of the Polish family, different from that of families in other countries subscribing to the culture of lawfulness, is undoubtedly a consequence of the conservatism of Polish society. It is still strongly influenced by ideas of moral nature and cultural norms, which in turn are shaped by Catholicism. Of course, this is only one of the factors. Economic issues also appear to be important: these include the low level of wealth in Polish society, as well as housing problems. Also of some significance are the legal measures, which offer only fictional state assistance to families, and give preference to formal relationships. As has already been mentioned, government policy in matters of procreation is highly ideologized, oriented towards moral edification rather than the solution of real problems. At the same time it can be noticed that Polish women living abroad (particularly in the United Kingdom) are giving birth to increasing numbers of children.

Among European countries, only France is capable of achieving full replacement of generations. In 2013 the total fertility rate in that country reached 2.08, the highest figure among members of the European Union. Other leaders in terms of birth numbers include Ireland (2.01), the UK (1.90) and Iceland (1.80). Moderately high rates are recorded in the Netherlands (1.78), Finland (1.73), Denmark (1.73), Sweden (1.67) and Belgium (1.65). It would appear to be a matter of concern that in all of these countries the fertility rates are below the level required to ensure the replacement of generations.

It should be noted that France and the Scandinavian countries have been implementing procreation policies with great determination for many years, and the effects are now beginning to become visible. All kinds of mechanisms—the tax system, organization of childcare and the education system, the health service and the labour market—favour the "production" of children, who will later work to pay for the pensions of the ageing society. Such high fertility rates may be surprising, however, in view of the fact that the position of marriage-based families in those countries is relatively the weakest. It might be thought that this would deter people from deciding to have children. At the same time, however, single-parenthood is becoming the standard—in Sweden, for example, one half of all mothers choose that model (http://epp.eurostat.ec.europa.eu/portal/page/portal/population).

Analysis of the facts tends to indicate that the most important role is indeed played by active policy supporting women in motherhood, including such things as a guarantee of appropriate medical care during pregnancy and childbirth, and the ability to take leave and holidays from work for childcare purposes (including for fathers). Of great importance is the shaping of a labour market, which is friendly to those bringing up children, as well as the availability and quality of care-giving institutions. An appropriately constructed system of financial and legal support is undoubtedly the most important stimulus favouring procreative decisions. The role of sex education must also not be overlooked.

Attempts to stimulate procreative behaviours among the population through appropriate government policy do not always produce the intended result, namely increased fertility rates. In some countries (such as Germany), in spite of favourable economic conditions and the authorities' pronatal initiatives, the fertility rate remains at a shockingly low level (1.43). It turns out that the number of children born in a given society is also affected by mental factors, resulting from, for example, a fashion for not having children. Such a trend has come about in Germany undoubtedly under the influence of stereotypes of deprecated women acting purely as homemakers. The slogan *Kinder, Küche, Kirche*, referring to the traditional role of the woman in society, has over time, under the influence of the feminist movement, come to be replaced by *Kinder, Küche, Karriere*, and the desire for self-realization has made a major contribution to the fall in the fertility rate.

6 Human Procreation in the Context of Medical Progress: Ethical and Legal Problems

Demographic policy evolves under the influence of progress in biotechnology. Apart from the now classical problem of abortion, the development of medicine has brought with it new problems of an ethical and legal nature, resulting from new technical capabilities such as *in vitro* fertilization and pre-implantation diagnosis. Procedures of this type intensify the controversy regarding the definition of a human being and the status of the human embryo. Attempts are made to determine whether (and to what extent) the legal regulation of abortion, artificial procreation, surrogate motherhood and genetic selection may affect fertility rates. Do restrictions on access to contraception and on prenatal and pre-implantation diagnosis, and restrictive abortion laws, lead to higher numbers of births?

The problem of where the threshold lies for an entity to be a legally relevant subject is particularly visible in the context of the abortion debate. The directions of the discourse indicate an evolution involving changes in perceptions of the essence of humanity. The fundamental question of when the life of a human begins has given way to the question: from what point in time does a human foetus acquire the status of a legal subject? Analysis of theoretical viewpoints as well as practically implemented legal measures supports to an ever greater degree the arguments in favour of the permissibility of abortion and the gradation of legal protection afforded to the foetus. Justification for the moral acceptance of termination of pregnancy is provided by the developmental criteria, and recently more and more often by the psychological criterion. It is pointed out that, since a human embryo does not yet have consciousness, which is the decisive factor in identifying someone as a subject, decisions about its identity should be made by a defined community. It has been proposed that "human persons" should be taken to include only conscious and rational beings (Singer 1997, p. 41). Degrees of acquisition of personality are at the same time degrees of the evil which can be done to a developing human body by terminating its existence: from the negligible evil represented by destruction of an embryo, to the serious evil associated with the liquidation of a self-aware person (Parfit 1984). The life of a foetus or of a severely disabled child may be of little qualitative value. The taking of a decision to terminate a pregnancy may be seen as an expression of parental responsibility. People should refrain from giving birth to children if it can be foreseen that the quality of their life will not come up to even the minimum standards (Tooley 1983; Steinbock and McClamrock 1994).

Theoretical viewpoints contribute to the predominance, in countries embracing the culture of lawfulness, of the "abortion on demand" model or a model in which the permissibility of abortion is dependent on defined indications. Both models offer reproductive autonomy, though to differing extents. They are reflected in existing legal regulations. The on-demand model is realized most fully in the United States, where legal judgments have in practice created a right to abortion, based on the constitutional right to privacy (Breczko and Radwanowicz-Wanczewska 2013).

The laws of most European Union countries, and European court judgments, are based on the indications model, which enables a compromise solution to the conflict of interests of a pregnant woman and the embryo. European laws provide freedom to terminate a pregnancy within a particular length of time (usually up to the twelfth, sometimes even the twenty-fourth, week), thus becoming close to the on-demand model. The possibility of carrying out abortion is generally made dependent on the satisfaction of specified requirements (these are usually medical, legal or eugenic indications, and sometimes also include material, social and personal factors). The most liberal abortion laws in the European Union are currently those of the UK, which are strongly influenced by American case law. The legal measures in force there are closest to the on-demand model. Countries with easy access to abortion include France, the Scandinavian countries, the Czech Republic, Lithuania, Latvia, Slovakia and Slovenia. The greatest restrictions on the possibility of terminating pregnancy are found in the laws of Germany and Austria (ibid., pp. 364–382).

The legality of abortion has become seen as a reflection of the right of a woman to determine her own procreative wishes and to control her own body. It is emphasized that it is the woman—as an autonomous subject—who ought to have the power to decide about the fate of the foetus, whose subjectivity has a much more limited scope and is conditional. A mother should therefore be guaranteed the freedom to decide about herself and her child. Protection of not only her life, but also her physical and mental health, becomes a moral and legal priority. Only a few European countries embracing the culture of lawfulness have implemented a model in which abortion is prohibited; these are Ireland, Malta and Poland. Such a model is founded on a constitutional right to life, which applies also to the prenatal stage.

It can be observed how social views and legal and deontological assessments have changed over a period of several decades in relation to another significant ethical and legal issue: that of artificial procreation. An evolution has taken place from absolute prohibition towards increasing tolerance and assent. The philosophical debate *"(...) on the permissibility of research using embryos and of pre-implantation diagnosis has so far proceeded along the path marked out by the discussion over abortion"* (Habermas 2003, p. 37). The controversies concern chiefly the differences in definition of the value of a "potential human life". Every *in vitro* fertilization treatment gives rise to the problem of spare embryos, which are not implanted. Serious dilemmas consequently arise in relation to their selection, storage, destruction and so on.

There is no single "rational" template for the regulation of artificial procreation. Significant differences exist between the laws of various European countries. A common feature is the absence of any explicit prohibition of *in vitro* fertilization (Bosek 2010, pp. 155–174). The differences are a result of differing constitutional traditions and socio-axiological determinants. From a European Union perspective, there are two models that play an important role, based respectively on the concepts of autonomy and dignity.

The autonomy model provides basically for the legalization of intervention in the nature of human procreation, subject to government oversight and the consent of the person involved. This model has been implemented in practice in the UK, as a result of the Human Fertilisation and Embryology Act. It is also reflected at least partially in the laws of France, Belgium, the Netherlands and Spain. In no European country has it been implemented explicitly, if only because of inconsistencies with the Bioethics Convention, which the UK has not signed. However, similar solutions are adopted in certain US states (including California).

The dignity model protects human embryos and human genetic integrity. Such a model functions in Germany, where the measures contained in the laws *On the protection of embryos* and *On the prohibition of trade in children and surrogate motherhood* reflect the precedence accorded to the dignity of the human being from the moment of conception. This is also reflected in the view of the legal status of the embryo as a legal subject, comparable to a "human person". The position is similar in Switzerland and Italy.

Closely connected with issues of artificial procreation is the idea of surrogate motherhood. This is a particularly controversial expression of procreative autonomy, primarily because the natural parental urge collides somewhat with the laws of economics and the "production process" of a human being in a "hired womb". Some see it as a dehumanization of human procreation, pointing to the instrumental treatment of women as incubators, and of children as the subject matter of a contract.

The spectrum of legal approaches to this issue ranges from prohibition and punishment for surrogacy agreements (as in certain US states, France, the Netherlands, Germany, Sweden and Switzerland) up to their legalization (as in Belgium, the UK, Israel, Hungary, Australia, and other US states).

Once again the development of medicine has shown how the law fails to keep pace with social reality, and many legal definitions are now out of date. This applies at least to such concepts as family, motherhood and fatherhood. With the increased use of *in vitro* fertilization, doubts have begun to appear concerning terminology. The practice of medically assisted procreation has challenged the legal understanding of family relationships that has developed over the centuries.

For example, in matters of surrogate motherhood, the courts need to determine who is the child's legal mother: the surrogate, biological mother (the woman who gave birth to the child), the client mother (the woman whose mind produced the idea of bringing the child into the world), or else the genetic mother (the donor of the genetic material). The rich body of court judgments also illustrates other dangers relating to surrogacy agreements, such as problems of the commercialization of reproduction, exploitation of mothers, unwanted defective children, and so-called "nobody's babies" (Soniewicka 2010, pp. 82–112).

The development of medicine constantly brings up new dilemmas relating to parenthood. Further experiments are being carried out which in practice cause still greater instability in the concepts of motherhood and fatherhood. For example, in 2012, ova from two women were combined into one, which was then successfully fertilized. This pioneering experiment was performed so that in the future it would be possible to avoid congenital defects. In this situation the child would come into being not from the combination of one woman's ovum and one man's sperm (as in the case of surrogacy arrangements), but with the involvement of one person more. This case shows that the mixing of genes from multiple persons has already begun in practice. This can undoubtedly be considered a serious interference with the law of nature. The question then arises as to the status of the donor—will she be a second mother? A substitute mother? A second-class mother (in view of her smaller contribution to the child's DNA)?

Many ethical controversies are triggered by pre-implantation genetic diagnosis. The laws of most modern countries that embrace the culture of lawfulness (including Germany, Italy, Austria and Switzerland) explicitly prohibit the use of this technique. It is nonetheless legally applied in many places in the world, including the United States, the UK, Sweden, France and Australia. Embryonic selection, made possible by the development of genetics, usually involves choosing those embryos, which do not have mutations or chromosomal anomalies, and transferring them to the woman's body. Pre-implantation diagnosis is therefore used mainly to eliminate diseases, particularly in the case of families with a history of genetic disorders. It is also becoming increasingly common to allow such selection as to produce a child having compatible tissue with a family member already suffering from a disease, so that the "designed" human being might in the future become a donor of bone marrow or stem cells. A new category has thus been created—that of a "saviour sibling". Such children are being born in many countries, chiefly in places where the law permits procedures of this type, but also in countries (including Poland) where the law takes an indifferent attitude.

Particularly controversial are attempts to extend pre-implantation diagnosis so as to create a child with specified defects. More and more often, courts have to deal with cases in which potential parents demand that doctors use pre-implantation diagnosis to enable them to give birth to, for example, a deaf child or one with dwarfism. Such situations have occurred in countries including Canada and the United States. These cases show clearly how difficult and complex have become the issues concerning the limits of eugenic activity, and how blurred and ambiguous have become typical eugenics-related concepts such as health, disease, improvement and correction (Sandel 2014).

A possible manifestation of the right to autonomy in decisions about procreation is the claims made for "prenatal injuries", identified with doctors' civil liability for damage done to a child between conception and birth. Such liability has for a long time been generally accepted in many systems of law. It most often results from unwanted or unplanned conception ("wrongful conception"). It may be related to complaints from children who feel that their life does not come up to the minimum standards of quality and that it would have been better for them not to have been born at all ("wrongful life"). Sometimes it results from claims by parents against a doctor who failed to diagnose damage to the foetus and thus prevented the possibility of abortion ("wrongful birth"). Together with biotechnological progress in the field of medicine, there has appeared over time, alongside prenatal injuries, the even more controversial concept of "pre-conception injuries"—done to someone who has not yet even been conceived.

7 Implications for the Next Generation and Conclusion

The law is only one component of a whole battery of means used by modern governments to regulate people's behaviour. It produces an ever increasing number of regulatory norms, remaining the primary system of prescription in democratic societies.

Countries, which subscribe to the culture of lawfulness apply various totalizing techniques (Foucault 2001d, pp. 1645–1646; 2000b, p. 341). These relate to many different spheres of life, both public and private. The scale of modern surveillance practices is well illustrated by the actions of the National Security Agency in the United States. The techniques used by the authorities are now coming to include surveillance using industrial camera systems (e.g. Echelon, Impast, Carnivore). These are linked to the use of programs to aggregate data about the activity of network users and the information placed on social websites. They entail the design of public buildings and structures in such a way as to enable monitoring by ensuring visibility. More and more frequent use is also made of biometric applications and devices: sensors recording body movements (XOEye, LumoBack, Robin), or intelligent headbands, which monitor users' brainwaves (Melon). Alluding to Foucault's concepts of biopolitics and biopower, we can therefore speak today of the new fields of infopolitics and infopower. Another developing area is physiopolitics, which involves the integration of intelligent accessories for data analysis (for example, for the purpose of tracking employees) (Koopman 2014, pp. 105–106). This makes it possible not only to oversee the activities of individual human bodies and population behaviours, but also to monitor thoughts. The scope and scale of control of the behaviours of network users and the aggregation of data about them (carried out by various government and corporate agencies) mark this as one of the most serious threats to the rights of the individual and the culture of lawfulness at the present time.

Totalizing techniques are also used in population policy, chiefly through the juridification of sexuality and the existing possibilities for designing a body which is still to be created. At the same time, scientists are focusing efforts on creating a "spiritual dimension" for the future human being. A practical expression of the eternal human striving to create such an ideal is the making of deposits in sperm banks by a number of Nobel prize winners, in the hope that at some time, thanks to *in vitro* methods, children will be born who are similarly capable of earning that prestigious prize. Modern medicine offers not only abortion, artificial insemination, *in vitro* fertilization, prenatal testing and surrogate motherhood, but also genetic selection of embryos, reproductive cloning and various "intelligent accessories" which might contribute to the attainment of that eugenic goal.

The moral aspects of artificial procreation cannot remain outside the scope of rational social debate. Ethical discourse on these subjects should be cleansed of the ideological element—of taboos, myths, mental shortcuts, stereotypes, and allusions to Nazi practices. It must not serve the specific interests of particular social groups and political parties. The use of a single type of argumentation based on the assumptions of Catholic doctrine avoids the essence of the problem, and is not the right way for the bioethical debate to be conducted in a pluralist society.

It is therefore also necessary to underline the huge role played by the education of society, including sex education, taking place free of religious influences. It is this which enables rationalization of the discourse, ensuring that it is based on empirical facts, which as an end result become a basis for regulatory measures. Statistics show that in those countries, which provide rational sex education (such as France and Sweden) the fertility rate is increasing. Appropriate education can lead to changes in consciousness, which in turn have an impact on procreative plans and decisions (Michałowska and Turek 2013).

Understandably, society fears the negative consequences of artificial procreation. This problem poses a huge challenge for lawmakers, who have the task of designing regulations in the area of population policy taking account not only of the replacement of generations, but also—as a priority value—the good of humanity, in a broad cultural context. Technological capabilities incline one to consider the possible effects of medical interventions from the perspective of future generations.

It can be claimed that humanity today finds itself in a state of "moral weightlessness". It lacks certainty as to the legitimacy and the consequences of the actions that are made possible by modern medicine (Dworkin 2002). In this situation, it is not entirely clear whether the dignity of human life can allow conditional procreation at all (Habermas 2003, p. 27). The social effects of the creation of a "modelled" human being, and in the near future possibly also a "duplicated" one, cannot be fully foreseen. It may turn out that this new creation will be deprived of humanity, as the power of medicine leads to the disappearance of the variety of the human species, loss of people's integrity and identity. It is not certain whether a liberal eugenics is even possible within the standards of democracy. One thing is certain—the era of genetic innocence has ended, and progress in medicine and genetics may prove either to offer a chance to improve the world, or to be the proverbial Pandora's box.

It should be considered whether it is appropriate to maintain restrictive laws against abortion, if only because of the vast backstreet abortion industry and the ineffectiveness of bans on termination of pregnancy given the open borders of the European Union. Strict laws undoubtedly have an effect on the number of procedures officially performed, but do not, as it turns out, have a direct effect on the number of births. This was noted in Poland following the tightening of the anti-abortion law in 1997 (following a verdict of the Constitutional Court). Instead of rising in line with earlier forecasts, the number of births declined significantly. It would appear that the prohibition on abortion is not of great significance in terms of procreative plans and decisions. It is certainly not causing a national demographic renewal. It should be noted that the highest fertility rates are recorded in countries in which abortion is legal (France, the United Kingdom). A basis for the legalization of abortion in Poland might be the differentiation, promulgated by environmental ethics, between persons and nonhuman animals, with human embryos being classed together with the latter group (as human beings, but not as persons).

The possibility of giving birth is undoubtedly favoured by the general availability of *in vitro* methods. In Poland such procedures have been carried out since 1987, and although they are not approved by the Church, they are accepted by the greater part of society (as many as 60 % of survey respondents) (Titkow and Duch-Krzystoszek 2009, p. 93). These data should be used as a basis for the rapid legal regulation of *in vitro* fertilization, in accordance with the standards widely applied within the European Union. Taking account of religious factors, the most realistic direction to be taken in Poland's case is adoption of the German model. General access to methods of artificial fertilization may prove a powerful stimulant for reproduction and an opportunity for many childless couples to realize their dream of becoming parents.

A policy of restricting access to prenatal tests can also hardly be considered a factor that would favour an increase in the birth rate. The availability of such tests undoubtedly makes it easier for a woman to take a decision to have a child. According to research carried out in Poland, as many as 810 out of 1124 surveyed women who had had prenatal tests stated that without the availability of prenatal diagnosis they would have given up their reproductive plans entirely. Improved access to tests of this type is particularly important, if only because women are now having children increasingly late in life. The unavailability of tests may cause such women to give up the idea of having children, due to the risk of birth defects (Nowicka 2007; http://resmedica.pl/archiwum/ffxraport1299.html).

Society fears that genetic selection may deprive future generations of a way to self-determination. The decisive argument in this case is that everyone has the right to an open, unprogrammed and undetermined future (Feinberg 1992, pp. 76–97). It would appear that fears of manipulation of this type are a consequence of certain taboos. Rationalization of the discourse shows that in most cases there are no significant moral differences between interference with genes (such as those responsible for vision) and traditional methods for repairing dysfunctions (such as the use of glasses or contact lenses). Modern embryonic selection has nothing to do with the practices of the Nazis, or the forced procreation and sterilization that took place in that era. It can take place only with the consent and at the request of the future parents, given in most cases out of concern for the health of their child. This is an expression of conscious and responsible procreative decisions. We should note that the selection of features of one's future offspring is in fact something that is done every day—through choice of partner, diet, avoidance of alcohol, giving up of medicines, postponement of conception, etc.—and this does not arouse any social or moral controversy. The choice of a particular lifestyle so as to achieve desired characteristics for one's child (and to eliminate undesirable ones) is considered a sign of the responsibility of the future parents (Parfit 1984).

It is true that negative selection (screening out) involves a choice between embryos that have already been created, taking account of genetic defects, but this can be morally justified by rational premises: the argument from the moral principle of not doing harm, the argument from the prohibition of causing suffering, and the argument based on the concept of "wrongful life".

The diminishment or even loss of the formative role of religion in modern secularized countries subscribing to the culture of lawfulness has become a social fact. Even in countries such as Poland, a gradual deinstitutionalization and destabilization of the family can be observed. The actual state of society, social expectations, and the good of the population and of subsequent generations require that the law stop giving preference to the traditional family, understood as a formalized relationship between a woman and a man jointly bringing up children. Such a definition does not fit contemporary reality. It is necessary also to give legal protection to informal partnerships, and this may additionally lead to an increase in the fertility rate (evidence that this may be the case is provided by the Scandinavian countries).

To conclude, lawmakers are faced with a difficult and responsible task. Considering all of the dangers associated with biotechnological progress in the field of medicine, they have the task of laying down the moral and legal boundaries of artificial human procreation in such a way as to ensure not only that improving interventions lead to a stimulation of reproduction (to guarantee the replacement of generations), but at the same time that there is no violation of basic legal paradigms in the form of human dignity, freedom, equality and justice.

Five Questions

1. What does biopolitics really mean? Is it an idea, an ideology, a concept or a technology of power?
2. Can a culture of lawfulness be the guarantee of human rights in the postmodern world?
3. How does contemporary bioethics determine a way of understanding the essence of the human being and his or her rights, and/or duties, in the sphere of procreation?
4. Is the wrongful life becoming a new bare life concept?
5. Do women have the right to self-determination in the area of procreation or are they subject to legal regulation?

References

Agamben, G. (1998, 2005). *Homo sacer: Sovereign power and bare life*. Stanford, CA: Stanford University Press.

Balkin, J. M. (1994). What is a postmodern constitutionalism? In D. Patterson (Ed.), *Postmodernism and law*. Aldershot.

Behrent, M. C. (2009). A seventies thing: On the limits of Foucault's neoliberalism course for understanding the present. In S. Binkley & J. Capetillo (Eds.), *A Foucault for the 21st century governmentality, biopolitics and discipline in the new millennium*. Cambridge Scholars Publishing.

Bertani, M. (2000). Sur la généalogie du bio-pouvoir. In *Lectures de Michel Foucault. A propos de "Il faut defender la société"* (Vol. 1, pp. 15–36). Lyon: ENS Editions.

Bińczyk, E. (2012). *Technonauka w społeczeństwie ryzyka. Filozofia wobec niepożądanych następstw praktycznego sukcesu nauki*. Toruń: Wydawnictwo Naukowe Uniwersytetu Mikołaja Kopernika.

Bingham, T. (2011). *The rule of law*. Penguin Books.

Bioethics Convention. (1997). http://193.205.211.30/lawtech/images/lawtech/law/convenzioneoviedo.pdf.

Boethius. (1990). *O dobru najwyższym czyli o życiu filozofa*. Warsaw: Państwowe Wydawnictwo Naukowe.

Bosek, L. (2010). Modele regulacyjne wspomaganej prokreacji w świetle standardów konstytucyjnych. In L. Bosek & M. Królikowski (Eds.), *Współczesne wyzwania bioetyczne* (pp. 155–174). Warsaw: C.H. BECK.

Braidotti, R. (2013). *The Posthuman*. Cambridge: Polity Press Ltd.

Breczko, A., & Radwanowicz-Wanczewska, J. (2013). Legal models of artificial procreation in Europe and Polish law. In B. Sitek, J. J. Szczerbowski, & A. W. Bauknecht (Eds.), *Comparative law in Eastern and Central Europe*. Cambridge Scholars Publishing.

Caputo, J., & Yount, M. (1993). *Foucault and the critique of institutions*. The Pennsylvania State University Press.

Carty, A. (1990). *Post-modern law. Enlightenment, revolution and the death of man*. Edinburgh University Press.

Chamayou, G. (2012). *Podłe ciała. Eksperymenty na ludziach w XVIII I XIX w.* (J. Bodzińska & K. Thiel-Jańczuk, Trans.). Gdańsk: Słowo/obraz terytoria.

Chańska, W. (2009). *Nieszczęsny dar życia. Filozofia i etyka jakości życia w medycynie współczesnej*. Wrocław: Wydawnictwo Uniwersytetu Wrocławskiego.

Churchland, P. S. (2013). *Moralność mózgu. Co neuronauka mówi o moralności* (M. Hohol & N. Marek, Trans.). Cracow: Copernikus Center Press.

Clarke, J. J. (2003). *Oriental enlightenment. The encounter between Asian and Western thought*. Taylor & Francise e-Library.

Colucci, M. (2005). De la psychiatrie à la biopolitique, ou la naissance de l'état bio-sécuritaire. In A. Beaulieu (Ed.), *Michel Foucault et le contrôle social* (pp. 91–124). Les Presses de l'Université Laval.

Dean, M. (2001a). "DEMONIC SOCIETES". Liberalism, biopolitics, and sovereignty. In Th. Blom Hansen & F. Steputat (Eds.), *States of imagination. Ethnographic explorations of the postcolonial state*. Duke University Press.

Dean, M. (2001b). *Governmentality. Power and rule in modern society*. London: Sage Publications.

Dean, M. (2013). *The signature of power. Sovereignty, governmentality and biopolitics*. Sage.

DeGrazia, D. (2002). *Animal rights. A very short introduction*. Oxford: Oxford University Press.

Descartes, R. (1989). *Człowiek. Opis ciała ludzkiego* (A. Bednarczyk, Trans.). Warsaw: Państwowe Wydawnictwo Naukowe.

Dreyfus, H. L., & Rabinow, P. (1983). *Michel Foucault: Beyond structuralism and hermeneutics* (2nd ed.). The University of Chicago Press.

Dworkin, R. (2002). *Sovereign virtue. The theory and practice of equality*. Harvard University Press.

Engelhardt, H. T. (1996). *The foundations of bioethics*. New York: Oxford University Press.

Esposito, R. (2008). *BIOS. Biopolitics and philosophy*. Minneapolis: University of Minnesota Press.

Ewald, F. (1991). Norms, discipline and the law. In R. Post (Ed.), *Law and the order of culture*. Berkeley: University of California Press.

Ewald, F. (1992). Michel Foucault et la norme. In *Michel Foucault, lire l'oeuvre sous la direction de L. Giard*. Grenoble: Jerome Millon.

Feinberg, J. (1992). *Freedom and fulfillment. Philosophical essays*. Princeton, NJ: Princeton University Press.

Flohr, H. (1986). Bureaucracy and its clients: Exploring a biosocial perspective. In E. White & J. Losco (Eds.), *Biology and bureaucracy* (pp. 57–116). Lanham, MD: University Press of America.

Foucault, M. (1972). *The archaeology of knowledge and the discourse on language* (A. M. Sheridan Smith, Trans.). Tavistock Publication Limited.

Foucault, M. (1978). *The history of sexuality, vol. 1: An introduction* (R. Hurley, Trans.). New York Vintage: Random House Inc.

Foucault, M. (1979). *Discipline and punish. The birth of the prison* (A. Sheridan, Trans.). New York Vintage: Random House Inc.

Foucault, M. (1980a). The eye of power. In C. Gordon (Ed.), *M. Foucault, power/knowledge: selected interviews and other writings 1972–1977*. New York: Pantheon Books.

Foucault, M. (1980b). Truth and power. In C. Gordon (Ed.), *M. Foucault, power/knowledge: selected interviews and other writings 1972–1977*. New York: Pantheon Books.

Foucault, M. (1980c). Two lectures. In C. Gordon (Ed.), *M. Foucault, power/knowledge: selected interviews and other writings 1972–1977*. New York: Pantheon Books.

Foucault, M. (1984). Preface to the history of sexuality, volume II. In P. Rabinow (Ed.), *The Foucault Reader*. New York: Pantheon.

Foucault, M. (1997). The birth of biopolitics. In P. Rabinow (Ed.), *M. Foucault, ethics, subjectivity and truth. Essential works of Foucault 1954–1984* (Vol. 1). New York: The New Press.

Foucault, M. (1998). On the archeology of the sciences: Response to the epistemology circle. In J. D. Faubion (Ed.), *M. Foucault, aesthetics, method and epistemology. Essential works of Foucault 1954–1984* (Vol. 2). New York: The New Press.
Foucault, M. (2000a). Omnes et singulatim: Toward a critique of political reason. In J. D. Faubion (Ed.), *M. Foucault, essential works of Foucault 1954–1984, vol. 3: Power*. New York: The New Press.
Foucault, M. (2000b). The subject and power. In J. D. Faubion (Ed.), *M. Foucault, essential works of Foucault 1954–1984, vol. 3: Power*. The New Press.
Foucault, M. (2001a). Bio-histoire et bio-politique. In *Michel Foucault, Dits et ecrits II, 1976–1988*. Paris: Quarto Gallimard.
Foucault, M. (2001b). Dialogue sur le pouvoir. In *Michel Foucault, Dits et ecrits II, 1976–1988*. Paris: Quarto Gallimard.
Foucault, M. (2001c). Entretien avec M. Chapsal. In *Michel Foucault, Dits et ecrits I, 1954–1975*. Paris: Quarto Gallimard.
Foucault, M. (2001d). La technologie politique des individus. In *Michel Foucault, Dits et ecrits II, 1976–1988*. Paris: Quarto Gallimard.
Foucault, M. (2001e). La vérité et les formes juridiques. In *Michel Foucault, Dits et ecrits II, 1976–1988*. Paris: Quarto Gallimard.
Foucault, M. (2003a). *Abnormal. Lectures at the Collège de France 1974–1975* (G. Burchell, Trans.). New York: Picador.
Foucault, M. (2003b). *Society must be defended. Lectures at the Collège de France 1975–1976* (D. Macey, Trans.). New York: Picador.
Foucault, M. (2003c). The birth of social medicine. In P. Rabinow & N. Rose (Eds.), *The essential Foucault*. New York: The New Press.
Foucault, M. (2007). *Security, territory, population: Lectures at the Collège de France 1977–1978* (G. Burchell, Trans.). New York: Palgrave Macmillan.
Foucault, M. (2008). *The birth of biopolitics. Lectures at the Collège de France 1978–1979* (G. Burchell, Trans.). New York: Palgrave Macmillan.
Fukuyama, F. (2004). *Koniec człowieka. Konsekwencje rewolucji biotechnologicznej* (B. Pietrzyk, Trans.). Cracow: Znak.
Gajewska, G. (2012). Przyroda (i) kultura w epoce antropocenu. In *Przestrzenie Teorii* (Vol. 17). Poznań: Adam Mickiewicz University Press.
Giubilini, A., & Minerva, F. (2013). After-birth abortion: Why should the baby live? *Journal of Medical Ethics, 39*.
Golder, B., & Fitzpatrick, P. (2009). *Foucault's law*. New York: Routledge.
Greenhalgh, S., & Winckler, E. A. (2005). *Governing China's population: From Leninist to neoliberal biopolitics*. Stanford University Press.
Gros, F. (1998). *Michel Foucault*. Paris: Presses Universitaires de France.
Gupta, A. (2001). GOVERNING POPULATION. The Integrated Child Development Services Program in India. In Th. Blom Hansen & F. Steputat (Eds.), *States of imagination. Ethnographic explorations of the postcolonial state*. Duke University Press.
Gutting, G. (1989). *Michel Foucault's archaeology of scientific reason*. Cambridge University Press.
Habermas, J. (1975). *Legitimation crisis* (Th. McCartthy, Trans.). Boston: BEACON PRESS.
Habermas, J. (1989). *The theory of communicative action, vol. 2: Lifeworld and system: A critique of functionalist reason* (Th. McCarthy, Trans.). Boston: Beacon Paperback.
Habermas, J. (2003). *Przyszłość natury ludzkiej. Czy zmierzamy do eugeniki liberalnej?* (M. Łukasiewicz, Trans.). Warsaw: Scholar.
Howarth, D. (2000). *Discourse*. Buckingham, Philadelphia: Open University Press.
Hunt, A., & Wickham, G. (1998). *Foucault and law. Towards a sociology of law as governance*. Chicago: Pluto Press.
Jaeger, H.-M. (2010). UN reform, biopolitics, and global governmentality. In *International Theory* (Vol. 2(1)). Cambridge University Press.

Jonas, H. (1996). *Zasada odpowiedzialności. Etyka dla cywilizacji technologicznej*. Cracow: Platan.
Karskens, M. (2009). Biopower – A slip of the polemical mind. In S. Binkley & J. Capetillo (Eds.), *A Foucault for the 21st century: Governmentality, biopolitics and discipline in the new millennium*. Cambridge Scholars Publishing.
Kelly, J. M. (1992). *A short history of western legal theory*. Oxford University Press.
Koopman, C. (2014). Michel Foucault's critical empiricism today: Concepts and analytics in the critique of biopower and infopower. In J. D. Fubion (Ed.), *Foucault now. Current perspectives in Foucault studies*. Polity Press.
Lemke, T. (2010). *Biopolitics. An advanced introduction*. New York University Press.
Lemke, T. H. (2011). *BIO-POLITICS. An advanced introduction*. New York: New York University Press.
Litowitz, D. E. (1997). *Postmodern philosophy and law*. University Press of Kansas.
Lyons, D. (1984), *Ethics and the rule of law*. Cambridge University Press.
Lyotard, J. F. (1984). *The postmodern condition. A report on knowledge* (G. Bennington & B. Massumi, Trans.). University of Minnesota Press.
MacCormick, N. (2008). *Institutions of law. An essay in legal theory*. Oxford University Press.
McMahan, J. (2003). *The ethics of killing: Problems at the margins of life*. Oxford: Oxford University Press.
McNay, L. (1994). *Foucault: A critical introduction*. Cambridge: Polity Press.
Michałowska, M., & Turek, J. (2013). *Czy jest coś złego w diagnostyce preimplantacyjnej? Głos w dyskusji wokół Stanowiska Komitetu Bioetyki przy Prezydium PAN w sprawie preimplantacyjnej diagnostyki genetycznej*; www.ptb.org.pl.
Minda, G. (1995). *Postmodern legal movements. Law and jurisprudence at century's end*. New York University Press.
Morawski, L. (2005). *Główne problemy współczesnej filozofii prawa. Prawo w toku przemian* (4th ed.). Warsaw: LexisNexis.
Muble, M. (2014). A genealogy of biopolitics: The notion of life in Canguilhem and Foucault. In V. Lemm & M. Vatter (Eds.), *The government of life. Foucault, biopolitics, and neoliberalism*. New York: Fordham University Press.
Murray, C., & Herrstein, R. (1996). *The bell curve: Intelligence and class structure in American life*. New York: Free Press Paper Books.
Norris, A. (2005). *Politics, metaphysics, and death. Essays on Giorgiio Agamben's Homo Sacer*. Durham: Duke University Press.
Nowicka, W. (2007). *Prawa reprodukcyjne w Polsce. Skutki ustawy antyaborcyjnej. Raport*. Warsaw: Federacja na rzecz Kobiet i Planowania rodziny.
Ostasz, L. (1994). *Rozumienie człowieka. Antropologia filozoficzna*. Cracow: Tasso.
Parfit, D. (1984). *Reasons and persons*. Oxford: Clarendon Press.
Patton, P. (2007). Agamben and Foucault on biopower and biopolitics. In M. Calarco & S. DeCarole (Eds.), *Giorgio Agamben. Sovereignty & life*. Stanford, CA: Stanford University Press.
Pierce, C. (2013). *Education in the age of biocapitalism. Optimizing educational life for a flat world*. Palgrave Macmillan.
Ransom, J. S. (1997). *Foucault's discipline. The politics of subjectivity*. Durham and London: Duke University Press.
Revel, J. (2002). *Le vocabulaire de Foucault* (pp. 13–15). Paris: Ellipses.
Rouse, J. (1994). Power/Knowledge. In G. Gutting (Ed.), *The Cambridge Companion to Foucault*. Cambridge University Press.
Rushton, J. P. (1998). Race differences: A global perspective. In A. Somit & S. A. Peterson (Eds.), *Research in biopolitics* (pp. 119–136). Stanford, CT: JAI Press.
Rutherford, P. (1999). The entry of life into history. In E. Darier (Ed.), *Discourses of environment* (pp. 37–62). Oxford: Blackwell Publishers.

Sandel, M. J. (2014). *Przeciwko udoskonalaniu człowieka. Etyka w czasach inżynierii genetycznej* (O. Siara, Trans.). Warsaw: KURHAUS.

Sawicki, J. (1999). Disciplining mothers: Feminism and the new reproductive technologies. In J. Price & M. Shildrick (Eds.), *Feminist theory and the body* (pp. 190–203).

Schwan, A., & Shapiro, S. (2011). *How to read Foucault's discipline and punish*. Pluto Press.

Schweitzer, A. (1966). *Die Ehrfurcht vor dem Leben*. München: CH. Beck.

Sedlak, W. (1980). *Homo electronicus*. Warsaw: Państwowy Instytut Wydawniczy.

Simmons, J. (1995). *Foucault and the political*. London and New York: Routledge.

Singer, P. (1980). *Practical ethics*. Cambridge University Press.

Singer, P. (1997). *O życiu i śmierci. Upadek etyki tradycyjnej* (A. Alichniewicz & A. Szczęsna, Trans.). Warsaw: Państwowy Instytut Wydawniczy.

Singer, P. (2009). *Animal liberation: The definitive classic of the animal movement*. New York: Harper Perennial.

Soniewicka, M. (2010). Prokreacja medycznie wspomagana. In J. Stelmach, B. Brożek, M. Soniewicka, & W. Załuski (Eds.), *Paradoksy bioetyki prawniczej* (pp. 82–112). Warsaw: Wolters Kluwer Business.

Stanton, C., & Harris, J. (2005). The moral status of the embryo post-Dolly. *Journal of Medical Ethics, 31*(4).

Steinbock, B., & McClamrock, R. (1994). When is birth unfair to the child. *Hastings Center Report, 24*(6).

Stoler, A. L. (1995). *Race and the education of desire: Foucault's history of sexuality and the colonial order of things*. Duke University Press.

Tepper, R. (2010). *Michel Foucault: Toward a philosophy and politics of the event. Continuity in discontinuity*. LAP Lambert Academic Publishing.

Titkow, A., & Duch-Krzystoszek, D. (2009). Intencje i decyzje prokreacyjne w społeczeństwie polskim a polityka przyjazna prokreacji. *Studia Demograficzne, 1*(155).

Tooley, M. (1983). *Abortion and infanticide*. Oxford: Clarendon Press.

Tooley, M. (2010). Aborcja i zabijanie noworodków (W. Galewicz, Trans.). In W. Galewicz (Ed.), *Początki ludzkiego życia. Antologia bioetyki* (Vol. 2). Cracow: Universitas.

Unger, R. M. (1977). *Law in modern society. Toward a criticism of social theory*. New York: The Free Press.

Wawrzyniak, J. (2000). *Teoretyczne podstawy neonaturalistycznej bioetyki środowiskowej*. Poznań: Wydawnictwo Naukowe Instytutu Filozofii.

Comparing and Delivering Juvenile Justice Across the World

Philip Reichel and Jay Albanese

Abstract There are both assumptions and evidence that undergird the official response to juvenile delinquency in different countries. The similarities and differences among these approaches are evaluated to assess their contribution to fairness, justice, crime control, and delinquency prevention. A brief historical review of the recognition of childhood innocence is followed by the nature of formal procedures for handling juvenile offenders, and specific governmental and multilateral responses to juvenile delinquency that form the basis for greater consistency in dealing with juveniles in the justice process.

1 Introduction

This chapter considers the variation in attitudes and approaches used over time and place when governments respond to misbehaving young people. It aims to make clear the assumptions and evidence that undergird the official response to juvenile delinquency in different countries. The similarities and differences among these approaches are evaluated to assess their contribution to fairness, justice, crime control, and delinquency prevention. After reviewing the historical recognition of childhood innocence, we review the introduction of formal procedures for handling juvenile offenders then proceed through specific governmental and multilateral responses to juvenile delinquency.

P. Reichel (✉)
University of Northern Colorado, Greeley, CO, USA

University of New Hampshire School of Law, Concord, NH, USA
e-mail: p_reichel@yahoo.com

J. Albanese
Virginia Commonwealth University, Richmond, VA, USA
e-mail: jsalbanese@vcu.edu

H. Kury et al. (eds.), *Women and Children as Victims and Offenders: Background, Prevention, Reintegration*, DOI 10.1007/978-3-319-28424-8_30

1.1 The Discovery of Childhood

The terms juvenile and delinquency are fairly new, but the people and the behavior are not. Ariès (1962) reminds us that during the Middle Ages and well into the seventeenth and eighteenth centuries, many Western civilizations did not have words to distinguish babies from bigger children. The concept of "adolescence" was not formed until 1890. Even the term childhood is recent; apparently, first being used during the thirteenth century. Before that time, the child was seen as no more than a miniature adult.

Ariès (1962) sees the seventeenth century as a turning point in the conception of childhood. It was then that we begin to find a vocabulary relating to infancy and the idea of childhood innocence began to develop. Before this time, all types of language and behavior were permitted in front of children, since there was no idea of an *innocence* to be violated. By the end of the sixteenth and the start of the seventeenth century, Protestants and Catholics in France and England began regulating access of children to certain books. Although Christianity had implied childhood innocence centuries earlier (e.g., Christ advising people to "become as little children"), the idea did not have much impact until the 1500s and 1600s.

After the discovery of childhood, and the attaching of special meaning to it, society was forced to show how the ideal child might be produced and how the undesirable one might be prevented from developing—or controlled if one did develop. But describing just what was undesirable was still in the developmental stage. Just as society has always had children, whether identified as such or not, those children have always been rather consistent in their behavior. Consider, for example, three current areas of concern linked to juveniles: use of weapons, sexual misbehavior, and alcohol/drug abuse. In fact, juveniles have been engaging in these types of activities for centuries. As late as the seventeenth and eighteenth centuries, European children continued the medieval practice of wearing and using arms. The schools of seventeenth-century France had so many duels, mutinies, brawls, and beating of teachers that the result was regulations requiring that students store their weapons outside the school (Ariès 1962).

Sexual practices, portrayals, and references, which many may consider inappropriate if not obscene today, were often the norm in medieval times. That indulgence regarding sex carried over into later centuries. By 1760, Englishman Samuel Foote commented that public schoolboys practiced more vices by the age of 16 than anyone else would have by 60 (Ariès 1962, p. 324). Finally, the young people of the Middle Ages were heavy drinkers of alcohol. After regulations forbade it in school, they simply went to nearby taverns where it was not prohibited (Alarid and Reichel 2008, pp. 459–460).

This concept of childhood innocence began influencing how society perceived a child's ability to form criminal intent. By the time Blackstone's *Commentaries on the Laws of England*, was published in the late 1760s, common law had established age seven as the point at which one could understand their own actions and therefore be able to form criminal intent. Prior to that age, people were incapable—under common law—of committing a crime. This principle of *doli incapax* (inability to do wrong) gave immunity from criminal prosecution to children under age seven and those between ages seven and fourteen were presumed incapable of doing wrong unless there was evidence to the contrary. Persons over age 14 continued to be tried as adults. We return to this topic of age and criminal responsibility later in the chapter, but first we take time to review some of the initial steps toward a formal response to children and young people who engage in criminal acts and other mischief.

1.2 Formal Responses to Misbehaving Youth

Whether credit for establishing the world's first juvenile court lies with South Australia in 1890 (Sarri and Bradley 1980, p. 46) or Cook County (Chicago), Illinois in 1899 (Platt 1969), we can agree that a formal response to juvenile offenders began taking hold in the late nineteenth and early twentieth centuries. We also know that both South Australia and Chicago, Illinois operated under a legal system that was heavily influenced by British values. Especially important among such values was the concept of *parens patriae* wherein the court (as the agent of the state) is viewed as having ultimate responsibility for junior citizens.

Because of the *parens patriae* doctrine, the initial approach of the juvenile court was non-adversarial and based on a philosophy that assumed that all court personnel were interested in the child's welfare and best interests. The result was a statutory court, rather than criminal court, with jurisdiction over offenses committed by juveniles that would be a crime if committed by an adult. Also, since everyone involved was looking out for the rights and interests of the juvenile, there was no need to be overly concerned with due process issues. Why clog things up with procedural trappings, the attitude seemed to be, since there would be only rehabilitative consequences rather than penal.

The initial juvenile court model based on the child's welfare and treatment was copied, with modification of course, throughout much of the world. Mehlbye and Walgrave (1998) and McHardy (1998) explain that within the first 25 years of the twentieth century, separate jurisdictions, penal laws, or courts for children had been created in Argentina, Austria, Belgium, Brazil, Canada, France, Germany, Great Britain, Hungary, and the Netherlands. Typically, the laws and special courts followed a welfare model as the basic approach toward child offenders. Through the remainder of the twentieth century and into the twenty-first, nations continue to determine the most appropriate way for them to respond to juveniles in conflict with the law. In some places the welfare/treatment approach continues to be preferred, but in other jurisdictions modified approaches are holding sway. To best appreciate that diversity and to understand why a standard approach is unlikely to be taken, we first consider the diversity in the broader legal traditions within which the juvenile justice systems must operate.

2 Legal Systems and Legal Traditions

There are many legal systems in the world, but they can be grouped into several types. Comparative criminal justice scholars distinguish between these functional and conceptual aspects of justice by referring to the legal system (the functional aspect) operating in a state, province, or country, as distinct from a jurisdiction's legal tradition (the conceptual aspect).

Whereas legal systems depend on the nation-state for their specifics (e.g., how to structure police agencies and organize courts), legal traditions are more cultural than political. The term legal tradition refers to attitudes, values, and norms regarding the nature and role of law. It is a broad concept that implies a deeply rooted and historically based heritage. Legal systems, on the other hand, direct attention to the specific organization and procedures a political entity sets forth to carry out the ideas of a legal tradition. Of particular concern in this chapter is the concept of legal tradition—especially as it applies to the attitudes, values, and norms influencing and directing a country's response to misbehaving youth.

Broad descriptions of legal traditions are best accomplished by identifying only a few categories in which many countries can be placed. While legal systems can be described according to how they accomplish policing, adjudication, and sanctioning, legal traditions are typically categorized as falling into one of several legal families. Comparative legal scholars do not agree on how many legal traditions, or families, exist today. Depicting legal families requires the drawing of rather random lines. There is an arbitrary aspect to the delineation, but the resulting picture should make enough sense to people that it is reasonable if not precise.

The decision to group legal systems into legal traditions is easier than deciding what criteria to use for the categories and determining how many such categories to use. Bracey (2006) argues for concentrating on three legal traditions based on the perceived source of law. Glenn (2010) uses seven categories but suggests that even more exist. Reichel (2013) highlights four legal traditions (common, civil, Islamic, and Eastern Asia). Dammer and Albanese (2014) also recognize four legal traditions but identify them as common, civil, socialist, and sacred.

A key point upon which all those scholars agree is that any categorization of legal traditions is more provisional than conclusive. As Bracey (2006) puts it, any attempt at grouping legal systems into broader categories of legal traditions results in something reflecting the designer's goals more than any agreed-upon reality. So, why do it? Because doing so provides some clarity to a very complex situation. For our purposes, that attempt at clarity will follow the lead of Reichel, Dammer, and Albanese, and use a four-category scheme. The resulting legal traditions or families are referred to as common, civil, Islamic, and mixed. A brief description of each will provide a base from which we can discuss variations in how juvenile justice is conceived and implemented around the world.

2.1 The Common Legal Tradition

Because common law developed in England and influenced the law's application in the British colonies, Australia, Canada, India, New Zealand, the United States, and former British colonies in Africa, joined the United Kingdom in having legal systems counted among those of the common legal tradition.

Several things distinguish common law from the other legal traditions (Dammer and Albanese 2014; Reichel 2013), but the key feature is the belief that custom provides the primary source of law. The idea is that traditional, consistent, and reasonable ways of deciding disputes provides the appropriate source of law. Determining whether something was "customary" fell to members of the community who sat as a jury of peers.

Countries differ in the specific structure and procedures established for their legal system, but if they maintain that law originates in custom they are included among those countries following the Common legal tradition (Dammer, Reichel, & He, 2014). Identifying those countries where law is based on custom is often accomplished by reference to the use of precedent or *stare decisis*. Following this principle, decisions in current cases are guided by decisions made on similar points in earlier cases. The rationale for this practice was originally an understanding that earlier court decisions were evidence of custom. Judges were expected to follow legal custom by abiding by prior decisions in similar cases. In this manner, custom could be identified by reliance on the people and through reference to several cases.

Because the traditional way of identifying custom was through the court rather than legislative process, judges came to play a pivotal role in common law. A decision by a judge was accepted as legal recognition of a custom. It is important to note, however, that the case was not referred to as the source of law; it merely provided proof that a legal principle (i.e., a custom) was once applied. Eventually prior cases were used less to prove custom and more to reference authority—typically a higher court (Reichel 2010).

2.2 The Civil Legal Tradition

The civil legal tradition, which is also called the Roman or Romano-Germanic legal tradition, is the oldest and most widespread of contemporary legal traditions. Originating in the codes of Roman law (e.g., the *Corpus Juris Civilis*), the civil legal tradition views law as resulting from written codes provided by a political authority. When laws are put in writing, or codified, they are believed to provide a clear statement to citizens regarding their rights and obligations. In addition, written laws allow judges to easily determine if a crime has occurred and to set the appropriate punishment. In this way, law is made by legislators (or other political authorities) and the courts simply enforce the law rather than interpret it or make new laws (Reichel 2002).

Contemporary countries identified as falling in the civil legal family were most likely inspired by the civil codes of France or Germany. The French Code Napoléon (1804) was especially influential in continental Europe and Latin America. It was developed to be an easily read and understood handbook that would allow citizens to figure out for themselves (rather than relying on a lawyer) their legal rights and obligations. Like their French contemporaries, nineteenth-century Germans believed codification of law could help pull together a new nation. However, unlike the French, the Germans did not believe it was either desirable or possible to remove lawyers from the legal system. The German Civil Code of 1896 was a historically oriented, scientific, and professional document that assumed lawyers would be needed to interpret and apply the law (Merryman 1985; Reichel 2002).

Despite some dissimilarity between the French and Germany codes, both incorporated a sharp separation of powers in which the legislator makes law and the judge does not. Instead of offering direct and specific solutions to particular problems, codes supply general principles from which logical deduction provides a resolution in each case (Sereni 1956). In this manner, civil judges need only identify the applicable code principle to decide a particular case. The solution is expected to be reached through an independent process of legal reasoning that the judge can identify and explain. This process allows the judge to apply, not make, law. Therefore, under the civil legal tradition, the solution to each case is to be found in the provisions of the written law, and the judge must show that the decision is based on those provisions.

2.3 The Islamic Legal Tradition

Legal traditions based on religious principles have included such important examples as the Hindu and Judaic ones. The primary contemporary example, however, is Islamic law.

The Islamic legal tradition is unique among legal families in its view of law's source as being sacred rather than secular. The other legal traditions, especially civil and common, have religious links, but they remain distinct and separate from religion. The Islamic legal tradition, on the other hand, is completely reliant on religion.

Islamic law is called the Shari'a (the path to follow). Its primary sources, the Qur'an (Islam's holy book) and the Sunna (the statements and deeds of the Prophet Muhammad), specify the legal principles linked to right and wrong behavior. The Qur'an and Sunna identify both crimes and punishments but they provide little information regarding the legal process by which offenders are brought to justice.

Because Islamic law is presumed to be of divine origin, its authority is based on God's commands instead of long-held traditions (as in common law) or directives by state power (as in civil law). In fact, the divine nature of Shari'a means that no worldly authority can change it, let alone supplement it. So, like civil law judges, Islamic *qadi* (i.e., judges) must turn to written documents for solutions to disputes.

Also like their civil counterparts, *qadi* cannot do more than identify the correct principle for use in a particular case. The difference lies in the source of that principle—the code, for civil law judges, and the Qur'an and Sunna for *qadi*.

2.4 The Mixed Legal Tradition

Countries included in the mixed legal tradition are those that incorporate elements from several of the traditions. Also called hybrid systems, the countries in this grouping include those where components of one legal tradition have combined with components from another legal tradition to form a mixed or hybrid system (Dammer, Reichel, & He, 2014).

Palmer (2008) and Castellucci (2008), suggest that countries in this category will clearly have elements of two or more traditions. Using a family-tree approach, Castellucci describes a forest of legal system family trees wherein the branches and foliage of each tree (each legal system) intertwines with others. Such a forest/family tree model would allow, for example, the existence of a Chinese legal system coming from a mixture of civil law and socialist law. That "tree" intertwines with, for example, Hong Kong's Chinese-common law mix and with a Chinese-customary mix that may describe the North Korea legal system (Dammer et al. 2014).

Scholarship on mixed jurisdictions has a rich history but became more focused with the work of Palmer (2001), who argued that some mixed jurisdictions were so alike as to be considered a separate legal tradition. In 2002, the World Society of Mixed Jurisdiction Jurists[1] was organized to unite jurists and comparatists around the globe in the study and advancement of mixed jurisdictions. The initial focus was on "classical" mixed jurisdictions (those combining common and civil law) such as Israel, Louisiana, the Philippines, Puerto Rico, Quebec, Scotland, and South Africa. More recent interest has included Cyprus, Hong Kong and Macau, Malta, and Nepal (Donlan 2012).

2.5 Legal Traditions and Juvenile Justice

It is reasonable to expect that each legal tradition will give rise to a particular type of juvenile justice system just as it does to a criminal justice system. As explained in Sect. 4 below, that is not necessarily the case. However, it is still instructive to review the four major legal traditions because doing so highlights the diversity found in how social order is accomplished and reminds us of the role played by a country's values and norms—both indigenous and imposed. Values, norms, and a

[1] http://www.mixedjurisdiction.org/.

region's history also influence how a country responds to troubled and misbehaving young people. But, children and youths present problems and opportunities that are different from those presented by adult offenders. The next section highlights some of those differences before we move to a review of juvenile justice models.

3 Children as Different

Nations around the world have drawn an arbitrary line to distinguish juvenile delinquents from adult criminals in the eyes of the law. If a criminal act is committed by a person under the legal age established by the government, the act is considered delinquency. The same illegal act committed by someone who has reached this age threshold is considered to have committed a crime. Therefore, delinquency is distinguished from crime not by the behaviors engaged in, but by the age of the offender.

3.1 Differences in Definitions of Delinquency Globally

In the United States, a person becomes an adult in legal terms at age 18. Unlike most other countries, the United States empowers individual states with unique legal authority, so in three U.S. states a person legally becomes an adult at age 16, in seven states the legal age is 17, and in one state the legal age is 19. In most states, however, the age that distinguishes juvenile delinquency from adult crime is age 18.

Around the world, there is similar variation among nations in establishing the threshold age at which an act of juvenile delinquency becomes an adult crime. An analysis of 22 countries found that the age of criminal responsibility ranged from 7 to 21 years of age (Meuwese 2003). United Nations agreements (discussed below) indicate that age 18 is the most universally accepted age of adult criminal responsibility. In most countries, including the United States, there is also a certain age below which a child cannot be held legally responsible for any law violation. In the United States, that age of minimum responsibility is usually 7 years old, but it ranges from ages 6 to 16 in different countries. The reason for establishing such a minimum age is that small children are not seen as not being old enough to fully understand the consequences of their actions, and so they cannot be adjudicated as either a juvenile delinquent or an adult criminal. Therefore, juvenile delinquency is confined, in general terms, to the law violations of young people between the ages of 7 and 18.

Some nations add a middle category for which there is no criminal liability; often this category includes children from 7 to 12 years of age, but children may still be subject to child welfare interventions. This keeps young juveniles out of the adjudication process, but permits governments to intervene in their lives due to misbehavior.

One factor in defining delinquency is the existence of status offenses, acts for which only juveniles can be held liable. Status offenses do not involve violations of the criminal law but are undesirable behaviors designed to thwart more serious delinquent behavior. Examples of status offenses include habitual truancy, curfew violations, repeated running away, disobeying the reasonable requests of parents, and, in some countries, begging and suspected gang membership. Noncriminal offenses such as these are especially common in industrialized countries, where younger children are not expected to participate in the workforce. In England, for example, children under age 10 are not held criminally liable, but those between ages 10 and 18 are heard in Youth Court and are subject to special laws and procedures. Nevertheless, countries like Canada and Germany do not have status offenses.

3.2 Use of Age Limits in Other Settings

It is clear that the selection of any precise age to distinguish delinquency from crime is arbitrary, yet age limits continues to be used throughout the world. In fact, age is used as an arbitrary demarcation in many ways in society. For example, a person must be 25 to be elected a representative in the U.S. Congress, 30 to be a U.S. Senator, and 35 to be President of the United States. In England no one can be elected a Member of Parliament until he or she is 21 years old. There are similar wide variations around the world (and within the United States) in the ages at which people can have consensual sex, marry, join the military, drive an automobile, vote, and otherwise participate fully in civil life. It should be seen that age is merely an administrative convenience that is used as an arbitrary marker for "maturity" in the broadest sense.

An alternative to using age to distinguish delinquents from criminals might be to use the adjudication process solely as a fact-finding hearing to determine whether the suspect did indeed commit the offense alleged. If proof beyond a reasonable doubt could be established in a given case, then the offender would face a disposition hearing at which a judge would impose some kind of punishment, treatment, or both, after an investigation into the offender's background, experiences, needs, and maturity to determine an appropriate disposition (Albanese, 2008). This would be one way to avoid the arbitrary age cut-offs that cause problems in trying to answer difficult questions of the appropriate disposition when young persons commit very serious crimes, or commit very minor offenses.

4 Juvenile Justice Models

As explained earlier in this chapter at Sect. 2.5, four legal traditions were presented as one way to view the variation in how nations seek to establish a system of social order. Unfortunately, those traditions cannot easily be used to categorize juvenile justice systems. Certainly there are norms, values, and beliefs associated with each legal tradition that influence the philosophy and procedures of a country's juvenile justice system; but not with a consistency that results in one tradition producing a particular response to misbehaving youth. Instead, descriptions of youth justice have most often been linked with adherence to, and variation from, the welfare approach that was taken by those first jurisdictions to established separate laws, procedures, and courts for children and young people.

4.1 An Underlying Philosophies Model

As explained earlier in this chapter at Sect. 1.2, the first juvenile justice systems followed a welfare approach built on the *parens patriae* model. Delinquency was a symptom of underlying family and community problems requiring treatment to improve the welfare of children. The emphasis of the justice process was changed from the adjudication of guilt to diagnosis of a condition to be corrected through rehabilitative treatment of the juvenile, not punishment.

The evolution of juvenile justice in Western Europe followed a similar path with initial emphasis on the child's welfare and treatment. However, by the mid-twentieth century, there was disillusionment with the rehabilitative philosophy of juvenile justice, stemming from the government's poor record in trying to act as a surrogate parent. There were numerous instances of child maltreatment and neglect while children were in state custody leading to cynicism about the rehabilitative ideal. The result was a shift toward a system of juvenile justice that ensured a young person's legal rights were scrupulously regarded, so that their legal rights as citizens were protected. This model took hold during the 1950s through the 1970s, and it focused on ensuring justice for juveniles by providing them **due process** rights under law, ensuring fair and equitable hearing procedures.

Finally, beginning in the 1980s, a third shift occurred during a general rise in the crime rate in many countries (Dambach 2007; French 1999; Pfeiffer 1998). This rise in the overall crime rate (although rates of juvenile delinquency actually declined in many countries), combined with disillusionment from the poor success of many rehabilitation efforts, led to the emergence of punishment as a primary objective of juvenile justice. The result was changes in attitude, law, and policy, reflecting the view that the public safety was more important than the welfare of the child. The possibility of crime and victimization came to be viewed as more important than any underlying problems a juvenile might have. The outcome was a juvenile justice system that treated juveniles similarly to adults, much in the way it was in the nineteenth century. The difference, of course, is the existence of many more legal protections in the adjudication process, but these protections increasingly treat juveniles and adults alike—resulting in a juvenile justice system that looks more and more like the adult criminal justice system (Albanese 2013; Bala et al. 2002; Urbina and White 2009).

Table 1 Three underlying philosophies of juvenile justice

Primary thrust of adjudication	Underlying philosophy	Adjudication outcome
Rehabilitative (Welfare of child)	Serve best interests of *child* by changing juvenile's ability to lead a life that conforms with the law.	Rehabilitative treatment of juvenile.
Due process (Legal rights)	Serve best interests of *justice* by ensuring a fair and equitable proceeding.	In accord with the rule of law (process more important than outcome).
Punitive (Crime control)	Serve best interests of *public* by making sure that public safety is not put in jeopardy.	Punishment to ensure public safety.

These three basic philosophies are summarized in Table 1 and they serve to remind us of important issues that essentially all juvenile justice systems hope to attain. That is, a desirable response to misbehaving youth would be one that holds young people accountable for their acts (crime control) in a manner that protects their interests and provides opportunities for their betterment (rehabilitative) while protecting the person's rights throughout the process (due process). Not surprisingly, balancing these is more problematic than is first apparent. Attempts to find the right balance must take into consideration such things as a jurisdiction's overall legal tradition, culture, institutional capacity, public perception of justice agencies and agents, crime rate, and many other matters. An example of one attempt to describe a suitable balance is found in the work of the United Nations.

5 The United Nations and Juvenile Justice

The United Nations is a voluntary organization comprised of nearly all the countries in the world. Its charter states that its mission is, in part, "to reaffirm faith in fundamental human rights, in the dignity and worth of the human person, in the equal rights of men and women and of nations large and small, and to establish conditions under which justice and respect for the obligations arising from treaties and other sources of international law can be maintained, and to promote social progress and better standards of life in larger freedom" (United Nations 2004). Juvenile justice is clearly part of the UN's mission in its efforts to promote human rights, worth of the human person, equal rights, respect for law, social progress, and better standards of living.

The United Nations attempts to achieve these goals by developing rules, guidelines, standards, principles, and conventions by consensus among member nations. These tools are used to promote most desired practices on a worldwide scale in fulfillment of the UN charter. "Conventions" are more significant than "rules," principles," or "guidelines" because they are binding in nature, requiring ratifying nations to abide by their provisions or else face sanctions. In the area of juvenile justice, there have been four major United Nations efforts to develop international standards relating to juvenile delinquency.

- Convention on the Rights of the Child (Adopted by General Assembly resolution 44/25 of 20 November 1989)
- Standard Minimum Rules for the Administration of Juvenile Justice ("Beijing rules," Adopted by General Assembly resolution 40/33 of 29 November 1985)
- Rules for the Protection of Juveniles Deprived of Their Liberty ("Havana Rules," Adopted by General Assembly resolution 45/113 of 14 December 1990)
- Guidelines for the Prevention of Juvenile Delinquency ("Riyadh Rules," Adopted by General Assembly resolution 45/112 of 14 December 1990)

The **Convention on the Rights of the Child** entered into force in 1990, and it has since been ratified by nearly all UN member countries. No other international agreement relating to justice has such universal support. It defines a child as a person under 18 years of age, and established many protections, such as protection against cruel, inhuman, and capital punishment. It states that arrest, detention, or imprisonment of a child shall be in conformity with the law, that every child deprived of his or her liberty shall have the right to prompt access to legal and other appropriate assistance, and that children accused of law violations shall be treated in a manner consistent with the promotion of the child's dignity and worth. It also states the desirability of promoting the child's reintegration and resumption of a constructive role in society. Furthermore, the Convention states that children are presumed innocent until proven guilty according to law, should have appropriate assistance in the preparation and presentation of his or her defense, and must not be compelled to give testimony or to confess guilt; it also describes related legal protections (United Nations 1989).

The Standard **Minimum Rules for the Administration of Juvenile Justice** were adopted in 1985 at the United Nations meeting in China (and thus are sometimes called the Beijing Rules). The Beijing Rules are historic in that they constitute the first international legal instrument to detail comprehensive rules for the administration of juvenile justice with a child rights and child development approach. The Beijing Rules predate the binding Convention on the Rights of the Child; they provided earlier guidance for countries on protecting children's rights and observing their needs in separate juvenile justice systems. Many of the Beijing Rules were later incorporated into the Convention on the Rights of the Child. The Beijing Rules encouraged fair and humane treatment of juveniles, emphasizing their well-being and the importance of rehabilitation for young people (United Nations 1985).

The **Rules for the Protection of Juveniles Deprived of Their Liberty** (sometimes called the "Havana Rules"), adopted in 1990, are standards for the treatment of persons under age 18 when confined to any institution or facility by the order of a court or similar body. These Rules set forth principles to universally define the circumstances under which children can be deprived of their liberty, emphasizing that deprivation of liberty must be a last resort, for the shortest possible period of time, and limited to exceptional cases. Rules are also included for the training of juvenile justice personnel and the inspection of juvenile facilities (United Nations 1990b).

The **Guidelines for the Prevention of Juvenile Delinquency** (called the Riyadh Guidelines) were also adopted in 1990. They represent a proactive approach to delinquency prevention involving the roles of the family, the school, the community, the media, social policy, legislation, and juvenile justice administration. Prevention should involve "efforts by the entire society to ensure the harmonious development of adolescents." Countries are encouraged to develop community-based interventions to prevent children from coming into conflict with the law, and to use legal systems only as a last resort in addressing juvenile delinquency. The Riyadh Guidelines also call for the decriminalization of status offenses (United Nations 1990a).

The Convention of the Rights of the Child, like all U.N. conventions, is a binding document that requires all signing countries to abide by its standards in its national laws, procedures, and policies. It has become the most universally approved treaty in the world, with only two countries—Somalia and the United States—refusing to ratify it. The U.S. Senate has not, and presumably will not, ratify the convention because some individuals and groups believe the convention will interfere with parents' ability to raise and discipline their children, and could even elevate the rights of children above the rights of parents.

When agreeing to the CRC, countries are allowed to note reservations they have regarding any of the provisions. This procedure provides countries an opportunity to avoid abiding by certain provisions as long as a majority of the other signing nations make no objection to the reservations. For example, Australia, Canada, and several other countries registered reservations regarding separation of detained children from adults. Those countries generally accept the principle involved but maintain there are situations when separation is not feasible or could even be inappropriate. Several countries following Islamic law have made reservations regarding the application of the CRC when its articles conflict with the provisions of Shari'a. Germany and the Netherlands noted that minor offenses could be tried without legal assistance (International Child Development Centre 1998). Despite the occasional reservation, however, the CRC stands as an important international document that provides minimum standards for handling young offenders and has encouraged countries around the world to recognize and respect the rights of children.

5.1 Summary of International Agreements Related to Juvenile Justice

These four international agreements demonstrate an evolving international consensus regarding the appropriate response to juvenile delinquency. The combined substance of these agreements is summarized below.

- All children should be respected as fully fledged members of society, with the right to participate in decisions about their own futures, including in official proceedings, without discrimination of any kind.
- Children have the same rights to all aspects of due process as those accorded to adults, as well as specific rights due to their special status as children.

- Children should be diverted from the formal system of justice wherever appropriate and specifically to avoid being labeled as criminals.
- There is a set of minimum standards that should be provided to all juveniles in custody.
- Custodial sentences should be used as a last resort, for the shortest possible time, and limited to exceptional cases.
- A variety of noncustodial sentences should be made available, including care, guidance and supervision orders, counseling, probation, foster care, education, and vocational training programs.
- Capital and corporal punishment of children should be abolished.
- There should be specialized training for personnel involved in the administration of juvenile justice.
- Children have the right to be released from custody unless there are specified reasons why a release should not be granted.
- Children have the right to measures to promote recovery and reintegration for victims of neglect, exploitation, abuse (including torture and ill-treatment), and armed conflict.
- States are obliged to establish a minimum age of criminal responsibility that is not set too low but reflects children's capacity to reason and understand their own actions.
- States should invest in a comprehensive set of welfare provisions to contribute to preventing juvenile crime (International Human Rights, 2004).

These rules and guidelines set minimum standards for juvenile justice by providing fair trial guarantees and basic procedural safeguards (for example, presumption of innocence, right to notification of charges, right to legal representation) and by promoting the desirability for rehabilitation and reintegration of the young person. Unfortunately successful implementation of the standards into some national legal and judicial systems has not been fully achieved, but progress is apparent.

6 Implementing the Standards

6.1 Indicators

The implementation of international standards occurs at the national and subnational level. Experts under the auspices of the United Nations have been gathered to develop indicators, or common measures, to assess compliance with international standards set by the conventions. The United Nations introduced 15 indicators it believed that all countries should use to gauge their juvenile justice efforts (United Nations 2007, p. 5). These indicators are shown in Table 2.

As the table shows, the proposed indicators are rudimentary, but important to document the experience of juveniles in the justice process. Some countries now collect these data, but many do not. In some cases, the lack of data reflects a more

Table 2 The UN's fifteen juvenile justice indicators

Indicator		Definition
Quantitative indicators		
1	Children in conflict with the law	Number of children arrested during a 12 month period per 100,000 child population
2	Children in detention (CORE)	Number of children in detention per 100,000 child population
3	Children in pre-sentence detention (CORE)	Number of children in pre-sentence detention per 100,000 child population
4	Duration of pre-sentence detention	Time spent in detention by children before sentencing
5	Duration of sentenced detention	Time spent in detention by children after sentencing
6	Child deaths in detention	Number of child deaths in detention during a 12 month period, per 1000 children detained
7	Separation from adults	Percentage of children in detention not wholly separated from adults
8	Contact with parents and family	Percentage of children in detention who have been visited by, or visited, parents, guardian or an adult family member in the last 3 months
9	Custodial sentencing (CORE)	Percentage of children sentenced receiving a custodial sentence
10	Pre-sentence diversion (CORE)	Percentage of children diverted or sentenced who enter a pre-sentence diversion scheme
11	Aftercare	Percentage of children released from detention receiving aftercare
Policy indicators		
12	Regular independent inspections	Existence of a system guaranteeing regular independent inspection of places of detention Percentage of places of detention that have received an independent inspection visit in the last 12 months
13	Complaints mechanism	Existence of a complaints system for children in detention Percentage of places of detention operating a complaints system
14	Specialised juvenile justice system (CORE)	Existence of a specialised juvenile justice system
15	Prevention	Existence of a national plan for the prevention of child involvement in crime

general inattention across a particular country. In others, it reflects a lack of priority placed on the treatment of juveniles in the justice process.

6.2 Trends

The actual implementation of international standards has not been universal or uniform. An assessment of the experience in 15 countries found that "the global progress made in terms of juvenile justice has been very uneven" (Defence for Children International 2007). The problem of most concern was the over-use of pre-trial detention and the conditions under which children were often held (including non-segregation of children and adults, poor hygiene, and lengthy pre-trial detention periods).

Also, there was found to be a lack of government data and statistics on the lengths of imprisonment and pre-trial detention imposed. Many countries did not track how long children actually remained in custody, and there was limited data regarding the extent to which alternatives to detention were employed.

Violence against children was reported to occur in juvenile justice systems in all the countries surveyed. Finally, there was a distinct lack of resources devoted toward implementing better juvenile justice practices, even when the rhetoric appeared to show a commitment to do so.

The report made a series of recommendations both for government and for civil society (Defence for Children International 2007, p. 56):

Governments should undertake the following actions:

- Monitor more closely the conditions and length of pre-trial detention in accordance with international standards;
- Establish effective complaints mechanisms within juvenile justice systems and conduct exit interviews with children to gauge the upholding of the rights of children deprived of their liberty; and commit to investigating and sanctioning those responsible for violations.
- Develop diversionary practices and alternatives to the deprivation of liberty; and, monitor their use and effectiveness;
- Develop programmes for the prevention of juvenile delinquency which do not stigmatise certain groups or children and young people in general;
- Establish a national action plan on juvenile justice if one is not already in place;
- Collaborate with NGOs throughout the development and implementation of all strategies for juvenile justice;
- Collaborate meaningfully with children throughout the development and implementation of all strategies for juvenile justice

Civil society should undertake the following actions:

- Lobby their governments to uphold the rights of children in juvenile justice systems by raising awareness about General Comment No 10 on "Children's Rights in Juvenile Justice" of the UN Committee on the Rights of the Child (2007);
- Monitor the conditions of detention centres and remand homes and report on abuses where possible; where not possible, create a visible presence and pressure nonetheless;
- Talk with children and young people; record their stories and make their voices heard;
- Educate and inform children of their rights in juvenile justice systems; provide them with a place to turn when their rights are violated;
- Work to change negative public perceptions about children and young people;
- Educate and train prison staff, police officers and judges on violence against children in juvenile justice systems and alternative forms of discipline

A recent follow-up to the DCI report was undertaken by the International NGO Council on Violence Against Children, which was established to work with NGOs and member states to ensure that the recommendations from the UN Study on Violence against Children are effectively implemented. The International NGO Council includes representatives from nine international NGOs, including major human rights and humanitarian agencies, as well as nine representatives selected from their regions. Their 2013 report (The International NGO Council on Violence Against Children 2013) found many instances of needless arrests, brutal interrogations, conviction without cause, and lengthy incarceration. It concluded that:

> although there has been ample time, guidance and encouragement to address this growing crisis, distinct juvenile justice systems remain underdeveloped, underutilized, underresourced and underappreciated. All too often, promises of positive, healing interventions into children's lives have collapsed into inevitable violations of their rights. (p. 43)

The report found many instances of violations of international principles in the treatment of juveniles that continue today, despite the conventions, earlier surveys of compliance, and attention given to the situation. The 2013 report made recommendations for change, which include many that have been made before:

- *A Distinct Juvenile Justice*: Operate a separate justice system for children accused of being in conflict with the law that is firmly grounded in the rehabilitative ideal and fully recognises children's unique rights and vulnerability.
- *Reach and Jurisdiction*: Ensure that all and only children accused of being conflict with the law are processed through the juvenile justice system, meaning that no child is tried in adult criminal court and that any child in contact with the law not suspected of committing an offence is handled through a suitable alternate channel.
- *Minimum Age*: Prevent the criminalisation of children by raising the minimum age of criminal responsibility to match the internationally accepted age at which children attain majority.

- *Staffing*: Screen and hire qualified professionals, treat all juvenile justice personnel with suitable respect and appreciation, and offer staff continued training and education on children's rights, non-violent interaction, and other pertinent topics.
- *Prevention*: Adopt a preventive focus as a front-line strategy, respecting children's rights from birth and providing the familial, educational, social and financial support necessary to help every child grow, develop and reach his or her full potential.
- *Diversion and Non-Custodial Measures*: Promote diversion and non-custodial measures, recognising both that children in conflict with the law are better rehabilitated in the community and that children may only be lawfully detained as a matter of last resort and for the shortest possible period of time.
- *Restorative Justice*: Building on traditional notions of justice, adopt community-based, restorative solutions that help children to take responsibility for their actions outside the formal justice system.
- *Data Collection*: Systematically collect data on juvenile justice indicators to determine the extent of violence against children in conflict with the law and aid in the analysis and evaluation of relevant laws, policies and practices.
- *Research*: Encourage and fund research studies in the area of juvenile justice with a view to improving the effectiveness of non-violent interventions.
- *Public Support*: Raise awareness of children's rights and the non-violent juvenile justice imperative, enhancing public support and respect for children in conflict with the law.

It should be noted that many of these observations in 2013 reflect the concerns that brought about the international standards, including the Convention on the Rights of the Child (1990), Minimum Rules for the Administration of Juvenile Justice ("Beijing Rules," 1985), Rules for the Protection of Juveniles Deprived of Their Liberty (1990), and Guidelines for the Prevention of Juvenile Delinquency ("Riyadh Rules," 1990). Therefore, it is clear that greater vigilance, oversight, and priority are needed to ensure that the needs and rights of juveniles are respected and acted upon across the world.

7 Conclusion

It must be concluded that the promise of justice for juveniles has not yet been met. Despite international consensus being reached and codified in important and universally acclaimed international agreements, the implementation of indicators and procedures to ensure justice for juveniles has lagged. Clearly, greater priority and resources are required (internationally, nationally, and subnationally). Vigilance is required to keep attention focused on the problem, so the world is not left to reacting to horrifying incidents, violence, and crises in juvenile justice.

The Interagency Panel on Juvenile Justice (IPJJ) was created to provide technical assistance in juvenile justice and help States comply with their obligations under the international standards adopted for juvenile justice. The IPJJ is composed of 13 United Nations agencies and non-governmental organizations actively involved in juvenile justice, and it works on the development and dissemination of implementation tools and good practices. It is only through the ongoing work of NGOs like IPJJ, together with governments, academics, and civil society (see Fritz 2011; Hamilton and Harvey 2004), that the objectives of juvenile justice will be realized in practice.

Five Questions

1. The idea of children as "different" certainly includes the concept of age as a social status, but it may also include topics related to physical, social, and psychological development. To what extent should a juvenile justice system take psychological development into consideration when determining such things as criminal responsibility and appropriate sanctions for misbehavior? How about physical and social development?
2. What do you see as the most important underlying philosophy of juvenile justice? In what way should this philosophy drive the operations of the juvenile justice process?
3. The treatment of juveniles under law, historically, has been susceptible to change, based on crime rates, school discipline problems, and other kinds of contemporary social problems. Should the treatment of juveniles change in this way, or should it be consistent over time?
4. In order to manage juvenile courts, detention facilities, and prevention programs on the national and subnational levels, local conditions must be accounted for. How should local conditions be permitted to impact compliance with international standards?
5. Review the summary of international agreements related to juvenile justice (Sect. 5.1). Do you find any of those listed to be inappropriate or unreasonable? Why? Are there other concerns that should be addressed in the list that are missing? Which ones?

References

Alarid, L. F., & Reichel, P. L. (2008). *Corrections: A contemporary introduction*. Boston, MA: Pearson Allyn & Bacon.

Albanese, J. S. (2013). *Criminal justice* (5th ed.). Boston: Pearson.

Ariès, P. (1962). In R. Baldick (Trans.) *Centuries of childhood: A social history of family life*. New York, NY: Vintage Books.

Bala, N., Hornick, J. P., Snyder, H. N., & Paetsch, J. J. (Eds.). (2002). *Juvenile justice systems: An international comparison of problems and solutions*. Toronto: Thompson.

Bracey, D. H. (2006). *Exploring law and culture*. Long Grove, IL: Waveland Press.

Castellucci, I. (2008). How mixed must a mixed system be? *Electronic Journal of Comparative Law, 12*, 1. http://www.ejcl.org/121/art121-4.pdf.

Dambach, M. (2007). *Shifting paradigms towards a culture of control within juvenile justice in New South Wales, Australia*. Paper presented at the Law & Society, Annual Meeting

Dammer, H. R., & Albanese, J. S. (2014). *Comparative criminal justice systems* (5th ed.). Belmont, CA: Wadsworth Cengage Learning.

Dammer, H. R., Reichel, P. L., & He, N. (2014). Comparing crime and justice. In P. Reichel & J. Albanese (Eds.), *Handbook of transnational crime and justice* (2nd ed., pp. 23–46). Los Angeles, CA: Sage Publications.

Defence for Children International. (2007). From legislation to action? Trends in juvenile justice systems across 15 countries. Retrieved May 3, 2014, from https://www.defenceforchildren.org/files/DCI-JJ-Report-2007-FINAL-VERSION-with-cover.pdf

Donlan, S. P. (2012). Mixed and mixing systems worldwide: A preface. *Potchefstroom Electronic Law Journal, 15*(3). Retrieved from African Journals Online website: http://dx.doi.org/10.4314/pelj.v15i3.1

French, H. W. (1999, October 12). Japan's troubling trend: Rising teen-age crime. New York Times, A6. Retrieved May 29, 2014 from http://www.nytimes.com/1999/10/12/world/japan-s-troubling-trend-rising-teen-age-crime.html

Fritz, D. (2011). Child pirates from Somalia: A call for the international community to support the further development of Juvenile justice systems in Puntland and Somaliland. *Case Western Reserve Journal of International Law, 44*, 891–919.

Glenn, H. P. (2010). *Legal traditions of the world: Sustainable diversity in law* (4th ed.). New York, NY: Oxford University Press.

Hamilton, C., & Harvey, R. (2004). The role of public opinion in the implementation of international juvenile justice standards. *International Journal of Children s Rights, 11*(4), 369–390.

International Child Development Centre. (1998). Juvenile justice. *Innocenti Digest, 3*. http://www.unicef-irc.org/publications/105

McHardy, L. W. (1998). Preface. *Juvenile and Family Court Journal, 49*(4), i. doi: 10.1111/j.1755-6988.1998.tb00783.x

Mehlbye, J., & Walgrave, L. (Eds.). (1998). *Confronting youth in Europe: Juvenile crime and juvenile justice*. Copenhagen, Denmark: AKF Forlaget.

Merryman, J. H. (1985). *The civil law tradition* (2nd ed.). Stanford, CA: Stanford University Press.

Meuwese, S. (Ed.). (2003). *Kids behind bars*. Amsterdam, The Netherlands: Defense for Children International.

Palmer, V. V. (2001). *Mixed jurisdictions worldwide: The third legal family*. Cambridge, UK: Cambridge University Press.

Palmer, V. V. (2008). Two rival theories of mixed legal systems. *Electronic Journal of Comparative Law, 12*(1). http://www.ejcl.org/121/art121-16.pdf.

Pfeiffer, C. (1998). *Trends in juvenile violence in European countries*. Washington, DC: US Department of Justice, Office of Justice Programs, National Institute of Justice.

Platt, A. M. (1969). *The child savers: The invention of delinquency*. Chicago, IL: University of Chicago Press.

Reichel, P. L. (2002). Civil law legal traditions. In D. Levinson (Ed.), *Encyclopedia of crime and punishment* (Vol. 1, pp. 231–236). Thousand Oaks, CA: Sage.

Reichel, P. L. (2010). Justice systems in selected countries. In S. Kethineni (Ed.), *Comparative and international policing, justice, and transnational crime* (pp. 79–104). Durham, NC: Carolina Academic Press.

Reichel, P. L. (2013). *Comparative criminal justice systems: A topical approach* (6th ed.). Boston, MA: Pearson.

Sarri, R., & Bradley, P. W. (1980). Juvenile aid panels: An alternative to juvenile court processing in South Australia. *Crime & Delinquency, 26*(1), 42–62. doi:10.1177/001112878002600105.

Sereni, A. P. (1956). The code and the case law. In B. Schwartz (Ed.), *The code Napoleon and the common-law world* (pp. 55–79). Westport, CT: Greenwood Press.

The International NGO Council on Violence Against Children. (2013). Creating a non-violent juvenile justice system. Retrieved May 29, 2014, from http://www.crin.org/docs/InCo_Report_2013.pdf

United Nations, (1985). Standard minimum rules for the administration of juvenile justice. Retrieved July 23, 2014 from http://www.unodc.org/pdf/criminal_justice/UN_Standard_Minimum_Rules_for_the_Admin_of_Juvenile_Justice_Beijing_Rules.pdf

United Nations. (1989). Convention on the rights of the child. Retrieved July 23, 2014, from http://www.unodc.org/pdf/criminal_justice/UN_Convention_on_the_Rights_of_the_Child.pdf

United Nations. (1990a). Guidelines for the prevention of juvenile delinquency. Retrieved July 23, 2014 from http://www.unodc.org/pdf/criminal_justice/UN_Guidelines_for_the_Prevention_of_Juvenile_Delinquency_Riyadh_Guidelines.pdf

United Nations. (1990b). Rules for the protection of juveniles deprived of their liberty. Retrieved July 23, 2014 from http://www.unodc.org/pdf/criminal_justice/United_Nations_Rules_for_the_Protection_of_Juveniles_Deprived_of_their_Liberty.pdf

United Nations. (2004). Charter of the United Nations. Retrieved May 29, 2014, from http://www.un.org/en/documents/charter/index.shtml

United Nations. (2007). Committee on the rights of the Child. UN convention of the rights of the child. Forty-fourth session. Geneva, 15 January-2 February. General Comment No. 10: Children's rights in juvenile justice. Retrieved July 23, 2014 from http://www2.ohchr.org/english/bodies/crc/docs/CRC.C.GC.10.pdf

Urbina, M. G., & White, W. S. (2009). Waiving juveniles to criminal court: Court officials express their thoughts. *Social Justice, 36*, 122–139.

Epilogue

I have recently attended the United Nations Congress on Crime Prevention and Criminal Justice in Doha, Qatar, where Member States adopted the "Doha Declaration on integrating crime prevention and criminal justice into the wider United Nations agenda to address social and economic challenges and to promote the rule of law at the national and international levels, and public participation".

This wider United Nations agenda involves the United Nations sustainable development goals for the period 2016–2030.

My own international law education and one and a half year involvement as the President of the Economic and Social Council, the United Nations' principal organ for coordination and policy guidance with regard to its development agenda, prompts me to contribute a few reflections on the meaning of justice which is necessary to end poverty and fight inequalities, promote safe and peaceful societies and strong institutions.

This book addresses the impact of socio-economic inequality in countering crime and victimization of women and children. Building a safe and peaceful future for women and children—the "succeeding generations"—is the leitmotif of all its contributors.

This very focused call in the name of justice to end absolute poverty—the root cause of crime—should be an invitation for all the United Nations entities to "deliver as one" in achieving the agreed goals of sustainable development. Partnerships of all kinds will become ever more important involving government agencies, the private sector, civil society, academia, philanthropic foundations and faith-based organizations. This collaboration will prove critical for the implementation of the new development agenda.

The Thirteenth UN Congress on Crime Prevention and Criminal Justice stressed the need to integrate crime prevention, criminal justice and other rule-of-law aspects into the domestic educational systems. It called for awareness-raising programmes that convey key values based on the rule of law, to be accompanied by economic and social policies promoting equality, solidarity and justice, and reaching out to young people, as agents of positive change. The Congress

H. Kury et al. (eds.), *Women and Children as Victims and Offenders: Background, Prevention, Reintegration*, DOI 10.1007/978-3-319-28424-8

emphasized that education for all young people, including the eradication of illiteracy, is fundamental for the prevention of crime and corruption. Equally, the promotion of a culture of lawfulness that supports the rule of law and human rights while respecting cultural identities is important. In this regard, the Congress also pointed at the fundamental role of youth participation in crime prevention efforts. The Congress emphasized the need to create a safe, positive and secure learning environment in schools, as well as protecting children from all forms of violence, harassment, bullying, sexual abuse and drug abuse. Educators and practitioners from many countries contributed to this book with different perspectives, hopefully broadening our understanding of conditions around the world.

I hope that the book's gender and age-specific research will contribute to policy recommendations regarding women and youth to be more fully inscribed into the wider post-2015 United Nations development agenda.

Finally, I hope that readers may be stimulated to contribute their own ideas and energies to the sustainable development goals, in multi-stakeholder partnerships, for the benefit of peace and the succeeding generations.

Ambassador Martin Sajdik
70th President of the Economic and Social Council
Former Permanent Representative of Austria to the United Nations in New York
Doha, Qatar/Vienna, Austria/New York, NY, USA
2015

Post Scriptum

The United Nations Post-2015 Sustainable Development Agenda and Education in a Culture of Lawfulness

When the editors of these two volumes planed this publication they did not yet fully realise the enormity of the global refugee crisis and the problems the steady stream of asylum seekers into Western Europe would present. What we experience today is not new: the first victims of violent conflicts are always the weakest groups in society—women and children. Among the refugees who have reached in the past weeks and months Western Europe are many women and children, and many of these children have been separated from their parents and are thus even more helpless and vulnerable. Given the large numbers, aid organisations are stretched to their limits and cannot always give even the basic support the refugees would need (Kurz-Adam 2015).

In armed conflicts today the majority of victims are usually women and children. Sometimes the crimes against them have a (wrongly interpreted) religious base; religious traditions may also elevate men to a privileged position. Apart from cases of severe domestic violence, the development potentialities of women are also frequently blocked through a lack of access to education and jobs. Several chapters in the two volumes provide well-documented examples of this phenomenon (see in particular the chapters by Mehrdad and Byouki or by Pakzad and Alipour). It would however be wrong to think in this context only of developing countries, even if in some of them the situation is particularly serious. Industrialized countries too have not achieved complete equality of the sexes, for instance as far as salaries are concerned, or in the treatment of men and women by political institutions (Kury 2015). The serious victimisation of children and women often leads to their life-long traumatisation. This in turn generates considerable costs for society, not to speak of the ethical implications. As Zedner (2002, p. 429) points out: "Personal crimes such as physical and sexual assault commonly entail longer-term effects", and she adds: "General feelings of vulnerability among women, ethnic minorities,

H. Kury et al. (eds.), *Women and Children as Victims and Offenders: Background, Prevention, Reintegration*, DOI 10.1007/978-3-319-28424-8

and the poor also increase the impact of crime" (ibid., p. 429ff.). Similarly, Skogan (1986) identified four key factors that increase the level of traumatisation: isolation, lack of resources, vulnerability and previous experience. Female refugees are in this context particularly vulnerable.

Compared to their victimisation rates, the role played by women and children as actual delinquents appears rather secondary. If we take Germany as an example of an industrialised society, the proportion of women suspected of having committed an offence registered by the police was 25.7 % in 2013. As far as children were concerned (under 14 years of age) their share was only 3.3 %, for youths (14 to and including 17 years old) it was 9.1 %, and for young adults (18 to below 21 years) 9.0 %. In other words, 78.6 % of all registered offences were committed by adults (21 years and older) (Bundeskriminalamt 2014). It should be added that women and children as a rule also commit less serious offences than older youth and men. Furthermore, we must keep in mind that the age of criminal responsibility is not the same in all countries, and sometimes it is lower for women than for men (see for example Pakzad and Alipour in these volumes).

A feminist criminology, dealing particularly with such questions, has only been developed in Western industrialised countries in the 1970s and 1980s (see Hartmann and Sundt 2011; Schneider 2014, p. 443ff.). Formerly, female offenders had been often considered as suffering from a personality disorder, and the "male part" of their deviant behaviour was usually overlooked (see Lombroso and Ferrero 2004). Social causes of female delinquency were rarely taken into account, but this was also the case for male delinquent behaviour. In public discussion and in media reporting the offender is often presented as he is "now" and what counts is what he has done "now" (see for instance the chapter by Hestermann in these volumes). The question why he became an offender is rarely asked. Politicians and the public tend to content themselves with the "classical" notion that all that is needed is harsher punishment to solve "the problem" (see the chapters of Hermann and Dölling or Zapatero in these volumes, also Kury and Shea 2011; Kury 2015). Collateral damages caused by incarceration for the offender and his family are rarely taken into account (see Beichner and Hagemann, Robertson et al., or Allen in these volumes). Even if alternatives to imprisonment have been rediscovered in many countries, traditional sentences are still the norm (see the chapters of Dandurand, Hamilton and Yarrow, Ehret et al. or Kury in these volumes).

Over the last few decades, criminological research has increasingly stressed the importance of (unfavourable) conditions of early socialisation for the emergence of deviant or delinquent behaviour (see Farrington, Nores und Barnett or Marshall in these volumes). The psychological damage that children and young people experience, who have to flee their home country may have a negative impact on their socialisation that may later result in deviant behaviour. Much depends on how well the host country is able to integrate them and in particular give them access to education and professional training, in order to enable them to find satisfying jobs and a sufficient income for their needs (see in particular Barberet in these volumes).

In the book "Revisiting Keynes. Economic Possibilities for our Grandchildren", one of its authors reminded us how naïvely Keynes assumed the total eradication of poverty in today's world (Baumol 2010, p. 203). When the United Nations were established in 1945 this naïve assumption still prevailed. At the time of the adoption of the UN Charter, its stipulation to promote higher standards of living, full employment, and conditions of economic and social progress and development, and the solutions of international economic, social, health, and related problems and international cultural and educational cooperation (art. 55) implied a nearly linear progression from poverty to affluence. In fact, only sixty years later, at the end of the First United Nations Decade for the Eradication of Poverty (1997–2006), according to the World Bank's analysis the total number of people in the world living on less than US$1.25 a day has begun to decrease sharply (Chen and Ravallion 2008). Not the immediate post-Second World War generation, but the likewise impoverished people succeeding it could start experiencing substantial improvements in the quality of life. If this trend continues, from the current one billion poorest people, by 2030 there may be none left—a very hopeful and inspiring vision for the United Nations post-2015 sustainable development agenda. We should however also take note that at the same time in industrialised countries, in Germany for instance, the gap between rich and poor is growing: whereas the middle class is shrinking the number of the very rich and very poor—the latter especially among the elderly—is growing.

The post-2015 agenda envisions also a substantial reduction in various forms of crime, in particular of organised crime and corruption. Here too, we should not lose sight of the fact that closer international ties, the opening of borders, for instance in the European Union, or new technologies such as the internet create new opportunities for criminal activities, many aimed at women and children, such as trafficking in persons, (child-)pornography and sexual exploitation (see e.g. the chapters by Kangaspunta et al., Howell, or Quirchmayr et al. in these volumes).

Poverty eradication is certainly an important step in the fight against crime, but it is not enough. Below are seven general suggestions for succeeding generations, suggestions, which must go beyond the confines of economic arguments.

First, because economic inequality or poverty (to use this more colloquial term) as a "root cause" of crime, even if totally eradicated will not put an end to crime. "Causes", "factors" or "motives" are by far more intricate drivers of human nature and crime than is the fixed, compelling and elaborate UN rationale to end absolute poverty by 2030. There is no society without crime, and it can therefore not be the aim to completely wipe out crime but to deal with it more effectively.

The views of two Nobel Prize winners in economics and two winners of the Stockholm Prize in Criminology (contributors to this publication) will be for us a departure point to deliver our final words in these volumes about "Women and Children as Victims and Offenders".

Gary Becker, the first of the two afore mentioned Nobel Prize winners in economics (1992) together with Luis Rayo observed that human nature is insatiable. This is because in nature there is no "absolute" of any kind, as the needs are relative. In a classically utilitarian fashion Becker argues that "as individuals strive to do better, they partly but never fully succeed since their reference points continue to rise along their earning power" (Becker and Rayo 2010, p. 181). And, indeed, the

UN analysis suggests that individuals or groups are most likely to engage in crime if they perceive a gap between what they have and what they believe they were deprived of (UN Habitat 2006/2007, pp. 143–144). Here, education and public attitudes play an important role in what the media present as a desirable aim, as "success" in life.

The UN analysis outlined above inscribes itself into a broader observation about the criminogenic role of relative deprivation. It alerts us to the need for preventive education and clear policy decisions that take to a greater extent into account sustainable development goals (SDGs) than is the case now.

Moreover, material and time deprivation do condition each other. "[T]hose who are present-oriented are swept into the future that others have laid out for them" (Rifkin 1995, p. 166). Regarding children, if inattentive parents do not prepare them for mainstream culture's daily routines that ordain kids' lives, their idle time activities may involve drugs and delinquency (Levine 1997, p. 189).

As of 1987 (the year of the first UN definition of sustainable development (SD) by the World Commission on Environment and Development), SD has been understood as "development which meets the needs of the present without compromising the ability of future generations to meet their own needs" (A/42/187, Annex, para. 2). In 2002, UNESCO, in addition, defined the meaning of education in SD. It made SD "a dynamic concept that encompasses a new vision of education that seeks to empower people of all ages to assume responsibility for creating and enjoying a sustainable future" (UNESCO 2002, p. 1).

UNESCO projected into this concept of education key SD issues for teaching and learning, "for example, climate change, disaster risk reduction, biodiversity, poverty reduction, and sustainable consumption". SD "also requires participatory teaching and learning methods that motivate and empower learners to change their behaviour and take action for sustainable development. Education for Sustainable Development consequently promotes competencies like critical thinking, imagining future scenarios and making decisions in a collaborative way" (ibidem).

One author of these volumes (Mitrofanenko) documented this more advanced sense of SD as the intergenerational learning process. This is a welcome orientation that may be helpful in extending this process to other walks of life. However, among one of the complexities of sustainable development in general is that the future Environmental Justice—in societies hopefully more affluent than now, and with generations of people living even longer than now—may be confronted with a far more health-endangering environment than we have now, if it is true that affluence and environmental diseases go hand in hand (Landes 1998, p. 11). In the light of this claim, the United Nations sustainable development agenda 2016–2030 may have to be critically analysed by all concerned.

In his Presidential Address to the American Society of Criminology, Laub (2004) noted that criminology has a developmental life course with specific turning points that allow for innovations in how we understand and respond to crime. The UN sustainable development agenda has now five such essential interlocked elements: "Planet", "People", "Prosperity", "Peace", and "Partnership" (A/69/L.85).

They may help to project into the post-2015 education (and the crime prevention education for succeeding generations relevant to these volumes) the concepts, methods, and—eventually—mandates and policies that will genuinely and effectively alter the rather superficial ways of dealing with sustainable development in general. Criminology and other disciplines may be helpful if they draw more often and more comprehensively on SD as a fundamental "unit of analysis" for charting social progress. In academic discussions the content of that unit varies more in terms of close ups than generically (Weisburd 2015). The UN generic focus on SD should motivate both academics and field practitioners to invest more in it.

Second, aware of the very energetic and recent review by the United Nations of its sustainable development agenda, we now would like to advance further the SD concept relevant to women and children as offenders and victims of crime. As pointed out in these volumes by Jan Van Dijk, winner of the Stockholm Prize in Criminology (2012), violence by intimates is most prevalent in countries where gender inequality is greatest. We therefore propose that the academic and policy-making world should more incisively and comprehensively include in it gender- and age-sensitive crime prevention as a balancing force for countering the criminogenic potential of relative deprivation.

In our view, SD includes a self-generating, creative, albeit also conflicting mechanism for renewing socio-economic and other resources. SD is geared toward their multiplication and, generally, the broadening of human intergenerational capital in any creative area of humankind, including science and education—the necessary doorway to a change in mind-set and behaviour. To live in and pursue a culture of lawfulness necessitates a change in behaviour by everyone. Citizens, companies, local and regional authorities, governments and international institutions are called to counter the threats looming over our planet (climate change, loss of biodiversity; industrial, health and security risks; excessive but preventable economic and social inequality, likewise crime and victimization levels, and so on), in the SD gender and age-sensitive crime prevention manner. This includes new paradigms, such as Restorative Justice (see the relevant chapters in volume 2), but should also include more incisively innovative anti-corruption policies.

In support of this proposal, we would like to recall what James J. Heckman, winner of the Nobel Prize in economics (2000) and David Farrington, winner of the Stockholm Prize in Criminology (2013) and many other distinguished researchers have been communicating to the world. They all emphasize that the sooner children, their parents and other educators engage in the prevention of conflict with the law, the better returns this yields for the law-abiding conduct of the children later (Heckman 2008; Farrington in these volumes). At the same time, the important role of just and visible social policies has to be stressed.

Third, the (un)successful intergenerational transmission of values is relevant to the broad interpretation of sustainable development outlined above. For instance, if one agrees that it is very difficult to alter the personal dispositions of criminals, would this not be a strong reason to modify their behaviour by changing social and situational risk factors and their perceptions of those factors (social and situational crime prevention)? Can this be done by assisting communities in developing and pursuing legitimate ownership of certain crime prevention activities, so they themselves facilitate an investment climate to prosper in the future? If such communities fail, what else can be done to prevent humanely and effectively crime?

Fourth, both questions suggest the need of a critical and multidimensional analysis of the relevance of criminological theories from their aetiological and preventive side to see whether or not they account for SD. SD is a global and universal idea of such a high rank that it breaks all intellectual clichés. It opens a path to a broader reconceptualization and verification of the suitability of criminological ideas, especially the older ones. Some of them could stand the test, others not. Basically, several sociological theories, most particularly those belonging to social learning theories, would initially qualify for their reinterpretation and verification, if and when they emphasize the importance of equal life chances in making a rational choice of behaviour ("rational choice theory", balance of chances). But also the aetiological theory of relative deprivation would retain its scientific and practical relevance at the present stage of global socio-economic development because its imbalances (sharp inequalities) undermine sustainable development.

Fifth, the concept of sustainable development may be instrumentalized and operationalized in terms of countering particular forms of crime. So far, only the sister term of "alternative development" has practically been applied to counteract one form of organized crime in developing countries—illicit drug cultivation. For the 2016–2030 SDGs, this goes not far enough.

Sixth, critical as this practical application is for countering narcotic drug addiction that "constitutes a serious evil and is fraught with social and economic danger to mankind" (Single Convention on Narcotic Drugs, 520 UNTS 151), these volumes took an interdisciplinary view of sustainable development (see also the experiences with less punitive forms of reacting to illegal drug misuse in Portugal, Kury and Quintas 2010a, b; Hughes and Stevens 2010, 2012). By if we emphasize that the treatment of women and children is even more fundamental to the future of humankind than the battle against drug addiction (i.e. SDG 3.5). This is because against the historical background of the concept of sustainable development we have to recognise a more basic evil that threatens them—slavery (Landes 1998, ch. 5; Redo 2015, p. 71).

Those deliberating universal moral values wonder whether slavery is an evil that is merely prohibited or *mala in se*. Reportedly, economists claim that the eventual prohibition of slavery was the result of its diminishing exploitation profits, and not the recognition of its inhuman nature (Landes 1998, p. 119). Rather than continuing these endless deliberations, Leszek Kołakowski (1927–2009), a Polish moral philosopher, cut them off. He pointed out that: "When one attempts to derive human rights from historical or anthropological material, these will always be the laws of particular groups, races, classes, nations that on the strength of those laws are free to eliminate or enslave other groups. Humankind is a moral concept, and if we do not accept it, we have neither a good basis to question slavery nor its ideology" (Kołakowski 1990, p. 87).

Eradication of slavery as a universally laudable moral objective is the core ideology of sustainable development, as the UN puts it (SDGs 5.2 and 16.2). To understand this objective's essential role, it must be recalled that the UN origin of sustainable development dates back to the right to self-determination of the post-colonial era. That latter right, in turn, coincides with the UN origin of human rights. It precedes the right to development of countries where that development was earlier debilitated by slavery (Landes 1998, p. 122; Redo 2012, p. 79).

The UN concept of sustainable development can thus only be understood fully when one sees that it intertwines the right to self-determination and the right to development. Internationally, the latter entails not only the compensation for earlier economic exploitation through slavery, but also the shared responsibility of countries and civil societies for the international and intercultural countering of "uncivil societies" implicated in sustainable development problems (A/51/950), whereby slavery/trafficking in people is merely one of them. "Shared responsibility" implies technical assistance in every aspect of sustainable development. For the donor countries, assisting in national capacity building in developing countries to make them more self-sustaining will be a major challenge in the years to come. If that challenge is surmountable, in 2030 sustainable development goals may be met.

Last but not least, and probably most importantly, the United Nations sustainable development agenda 2016–2030 has therefore a stimulating and transformative character. Not only are its goals progressive in the way outlined above, but they also aim at equalizing the life chances with gender mainstreaming that meets the needs of succeeding generations—all this in the name of peaceful, just and inclusive societies.

To this end the UN seeks to advance normatively the rules of our life by contributing to free societies from fear and violence. In this context, the Organization resolved "to protect human rights and promote gender equality and the empowerment of women and girls" (A/69/L.85, pp. 2/35 and 3/35). Surely, in both cases, social justice and other improvements are possible—indeed, for all children and both sexes. Therefore educationists, educators, academics, students, practitioners and others interested in gender mainstreaming, crime prevention and criminal justice reform, and all interested in any of the other sustainable development reforms according to the United Nations agenda, should begin looking into the SDGs soon.

These SDGs will advance the sustainable livelihood of succeeding generations. They also may enrich the academic science with new interdisciplinary background, facts and figures relevant to women and children. They finally can lead to the further evidence-based prevention, reintegration of women and children as offenders and victims of crime and, generally, to further social progress in the world.

A few years ago, a scholar of Polish-German Second World War history and of the difficult time of post-war reconciliation wondered:

> When you look back in history, you cannot but question, what would be today's world like, if all energy, resources and intellectual potential that were dedicated by empires and dictatorships to build ideologies against other nations were spent on universities, schools and common meeting places (Wolff-Powęska 2011).

Let us hope that our successors will find a positive response for the future we want for all.

Freiburg im Breisgau, Germany
Wien, Austria
Zürich, Switzerland
October 2015

Helmut Kury
Sławomir Redo
Evelyn Shea

References

A/42/187. (1987, August 2). Annex, The World Commission on Environment and Development, Our Common Future.

A/51/950 (1997, July 1997). Renewing the United Nations—A Programme for Reform, Report of the Secretary-General.

A/69/L.85. (2015, August 12). Draft outcome document of the United Nations summit for the adoption of the post-2015 development agenda.

Baumol, W. J. (2010). The microtheory of innovative entrepreneurship. In L. Pecchi & G Pigo, (Ed.) MIT Press: Cambridge, MA.

Becker, G. S., & Rayo, L. (2010). Why Keynes underestimated consumption and overestimated leisure for the long run. In L. Pecchi & G. Piga (Eds.), *Revisiting Keynes. Economic possibilities for our grandchildren* (pp. 179–184). Cambridge, MA/London, England: The MIT Press.

Bundeskriminalamt. (2014). *Polizeiliche Kriminalstatistik Bundesrepublik Deutschland. Berichtsjahr 2013*. Wiesbaden: Bundeskriminalamt. http://www.bka.de/DE/Publikationen/PolizeilicheKriminalstatistik/pks__node.html?__nnn=true.

Chen, S., & Ravallion, M. (2008). *The developing world is poorer than we thought, but no less successful in the fight against poverty*. Policy Research Working Paper. World Bank. http://econ.worldbank.org/docsearch

Hartmann, J. L., & Sundt, J. L. (2011) The rise of feminist criminology: Freda Adler. In F. T. Cullen, C. L. Johnson, A. J. Myer, & F. Adler (Eds.), *The origins of american criminology. Advances in criminological theory* (Vol. 16, pp. 205–220). New Brunswick, USA/London, UK.

Heckman, J. J. (2008). The case of investing in disadvantaged young children. In *Big ideas for children: Investing in our nation's future, first focus* (pp. 49–58). Washington, DC.

Hughes, C. E., & Stevens, A. (2010). What can we learn from the Portuguese decriminalization of illicit drugs? *British Journal of Criminology, 50*, 999–1022.

Hughes, C. E., & Stevens, A. (2012). A resounding success or a disastrous failure: Re-examining the interpretation of evidence on the Portuguese decriminalisation of illicit drugs. *Drug and Alcohol Review, 31*, 101–113.

Kołakowski, L. (1990). *Cywilzacja na ławie oskarżonych (Civilization on the defendant's bench)*. Warszawa: Res Publica.

Kury, H., & Quintas, J. (2010a). Zur Wirkung von Sanktionen bei Drogenabhängigen – Argumente für eine rationale Drogenpolitik. *Polizei und Wissenschaft, 1*, 32–56.

Kury, H., & Quintas, J. (2010b). Sanktionen oder Hilfe? Einstellungen zu Drogentätern – Ergebnisse aus Portugal. *Kriminalistik, 64*, 403–409.

Kury, H., & Shea, E. (Eds.). (2011). *Punitivity. international developments* (3 Vols.). Bochum/Germany: Universitätsverlag Dr. Brockmeyer.

Kury, H. (2015). *Punitivity and punishment. Results from different countries*. Bochum/Germany: Universitätsverlag Dr. Brockmeyer.

Kurz-Adam, M. (2015). Jugendhilfe ohne Grenzen? Anmerkungen zur Zukunft der Arbeit mit unbegleiteten minderjährigen Flüchtlingen in der Kinder- und Jugendhilfe. *Zeitschrift für Jugendkriminalrecht und Jugendhilfe, 26*, 272–276.

Landes, D. S. (1998). *The wealth and poverty of nations. Why some are so rich and some so poor.* New York/London: W.W. Norton & Company.

Laub, S. (2004). The life course of criminology in the United States: The American Society of Criminology 2003 presidential address. *Criminology, 42*(1), 1–26.

Levine, R. (1997). *A geography of time. The temporal misadventures of a social psychologist, or how every culture keeps time just a little bit differently.* Oxford: One World.

Lombroso, C., & Ferrero, G. (2004). *Criminal women, the prostitute, and the normal woman.* Durham/London.

Redo, S. (2012). *Blue criminology. The power of United Nations ideas to counter crime globally. A monographic study.* Helsinki: European Institute for Crime Prevention and Control, affiliated with the United Nations.

Redo, S. (2015). The UN criminal justice system in the suppression of transnational crime. In N. Boister & R. Currie (Eds.), *The Routledge handbook of transnational criminal law* (pp. 57–72). Abingdon, Oxon: Routledge.

Rifkin, J. (1995). *The end of work: The decline of the global labor force and the dawn of the post-market era.* New York: Putnam Publishing Group.

Schneider, H. J. (2014). *Kriminologie. Ein internationales Handbuch. Band 1: Grundlagen.* Berlin: De Gruyter.

Single Convention on Narcotic Drugs, 520 UNTS 151

Skogan, W. (1986). The impact of victimization on fear. *Crime and Delinquency, 33*, 135–154.

UN-Habitat. (2006). *State of the world's cities.* London: Earthscan.

UNESCO. (2002). *Education for sustainability - from Rio to Johannesburg: Lessons learnt from a decade of commitment.* Paris: UNESCO.

Weisburd, D. (2015). The 2014 Sutherland address. The law of crime concentration and the criminology of place. *Criminology, 53*(2), 133–157.

Wolff-Powęska, A. (2011, July 16). *Interview: Nienawidze, podziwiam, boje_się (I hate, admire and fear).* Gazeta Wyborcza. http://wyborcza.pl/1,76498,9953968,Nienawidze_podziwiam_boje_sie.html?as=4&startsz=x#ixzz1Ta0zalek

Zedner, L. (2002). Victims. In M. Maguire, R. Morgan, & R. Reiner (Eds.), *The Oxford handbook of criminology* (pp. 419–456). Oxford: Oxford University Press.

Index[1]

[1] Note: Page numbers in Roman indicate volume 1 and in *Italics* indicate volume 2

H. Kury et al. (eds.), *Women and Children as Victims and Offenders: Background, Prevention, Reintegration*, DOI 10.1007/978-3-319-28424-8

D

F

G

N

P

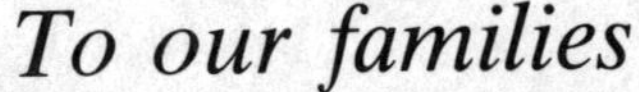

To our families

First published 1985 in the United Kingdom by
Mansell Publishing Limited (A subsidiary of The H. W. Wilson Company)
6 All Saints Street, London N1 9RL, England

First published 1985 in the United States of America by
St. Martin's Press, Inc., 175 Fifth Avenue, New York, New York 10010

British Library Cataloguing in Publication Data

Cunningham, Stephen

Fisheries economics.
1. Fisheries management
2. Fisheries—Economic aspects
I. Title II. Dunn, Michael R. III. Whitmarsh, David
338.3′727 SH328

ISBN 0-7201-1702-X

Library of Congress Cataloging in Publication Data

Cunningham, Stephen
Fisheries economics.

Bibliography: p.
Includes index.
1. Fisheries—Economic aspects. 2. Fish trade.
3. Fishery policy. I. Dunn, Michael R. II. Whitmarsh, David.
III Title.
HD9450.5.C86 1985 338.3′727 84–12577
ISBN 0-312-29406-9

Typeset by Spire Print Services Ltd, Salisbury, Wilts.
Printed in Great Britain by
Whitstable Litho Ltd., Whitstable, Kent

Fisheries Economics

An Introduction

Stephen Cunningham, Michael R. Dunn and
David Whitmarsh

Mansell Publishing Limited *London*
St. Martin's Press *New York*

Contents

List of acronyms

AC	average cost
AFC	average fixed costs
AR	average revenue
ATC	average total costs
AVC	average variable costs
BOSY	biological optimum sustainable yield
BWU	blue whale unit
CFP	Common Fisheries Policy (of the EEC)
CPUE	catch per unit of effort
CR	consumer rent; conversion ratio
CS	coastal state
CSA	closed-season allocation
CYRA	(Inter American Tropical Tuna) Commission's Yellowfin Regulatory Area
DMEY	dynamic maximum economic yield
DWS	distant-water-fishing state
ECC	environmental carrying capacity
EEC	European Economic Community
EEZ	exclusive economic zone
FAO	Food and Agriculture Organization (of the United Nations)
FCZ	Fishery Conservation Zone (U.S.)
FEOGA	Fonds Européen d'Orientation et Garantie Agricole
FMP	fishery management plan
GDP	gross domestic product
GDS	geographically disadvantaged state
GER	gross energy requirement
GRT	gross registered tonnage
GS	Gordon–Schaefer (fishery model)

HIB	Herring Industry Board
HPF	household production function
IATTC	Inter American Tropical Tuna Commission
ICCAT	International Commission for the Conservation of Atlantic Tunas
ICES	International Council for the Exploration of the Sea
ICNAF	International Commission for Northwest Atlantic Fisheries
IFQ	individual fish quota
IJV	international joint venture
IPHC	International Pacific Halibut Commission
IWC	International Whaling Commission
LDC	less developed country
LLS	land-locked state
LRAC	long-run average cost
LRMC	long-run marginal cost
LRTC	long-run total cost
MAFF	Ministry of Agriculture, Fisheries and Food (U.K.)
MC	marginal cost
MCF	marine commercial fishery
MES	minimum efficient scale
MR	marginal revenue
MRF	marine recreational fishery
MSC	maximum standing crop
MSY	maximum sustainable yield
NAFO	Northwest Atlantic Fisheries Organization
NEAFC	North East Atlantic Fisheries Commission
NMFS	National Marine Fisheries Service (U.S.)
NOAA	National Oceanographic and Atmospheric Administration (U.S.)
NSB	net social benefit
oa	open access
OECD	Organization for Economic Co-operation and Development
OMB	Office of Management and Budget (U.S.)
OSY	optimum sustainable yield
OY	optimum yield
PAQ	partially allocated quota (system)
PO	producer organization
PR	producer rent
QC	quota certificate (system)
RAN	resource-adjacent nation
R&D	research and development
RFMC	Regional Fishery Management Council (U.S.)
RR	resource rent
SCP	single-cell protein
SFIA	Sea Fish Industry Authority
SI	Statutory Instrument

SMEY	static maximum economic yield
SOC	social opportunity cost
SRAC	short-run average cost
SRMC	short-run marginal cost
SRTC	short-run total cost
SRY	short-run yield
TAC	total allowable catch
TC	total costs
TP	total profit
TR	total revenue
UN	United Nations
UNCLOS	United Nations Conference on the Law of the Sea
WFA	White Fish Authority
WSB	worker satisfaction bonus
WTP	willingness to pay
WTS	willingness to surrender

Introduction

It seems to have become customary in many recently published books to commence with a justification for adding to the existing literature on the subject. Sometimes this justification has undertones that approach being apologetic. Such an apology is not needed for this book, for the minor explosion in the literature concerned with the subject over the last decade has been very largely restricted to journal papers, reports and research monographs, with only a handful of textbooks. This expanding literature has in addition been diffuse and frequently inaccessible to students and administrators, not least, from the point of view of Europeans, because so much of it has been published in North America. This difficulty of access is a pity, because interest in the study of fisheries, and of fisheries economics, has expanded along with the literature. There have been a number of developments associated with this expansion over the past decade, including the initiation of a range of courses at various levels dealing with fisheries management and development, within which economics has an important role. There has also been a recognition that the subject area 'agricultural economics' properly should include the analysis of fishing (and forestry) as well as agriculture (Hill and Ingersent, 1982, p. 1). Together with this has been the greater awareness on a much broader front of the need to identify optimal utilization patterns for the world's natural resources. This awareness has been heightened by the visible conflicts in resource use of which we are constantly reminded, and the only too obvious and painful failures within fisheries management itself. Finally, since the mid 1970s there has been a transition away from regarding commercial fishing as a hunting activity based on a resource that belongs to no one towards thinking of it as a management activity based on a resource owned by individuals or nations. As fisheries have the dangerous property of being biologically renewable but destructible, it is vitally important that the right answers emerge whenever conflict occurs or management objectives are being decided.

One might however still ask why any book on fisheries should be restricted solely to 'the economics' of the activity. Certainly it is obvious that fish, unlike the raw materials used in producing cars or videos, have biological patterns of birth, growth and death, influenced by environmental features, and that these can undermine all our best endeavours as fishermen. Yet fishing and fish production is important just because it *is* an economic activity. It involves the application of inputs of resources such as human beings and capital that from society's point of view could be employed elsewhere—possibly in some better alternative use. In addition, it is carried out by agents who respond to economic stimuli, making decisions that are intended to fulfil their economic objectives, although that is not to say that these agents might not have non-economic objectives also. Since resource use and decision-making are the very subject matter of economics, it follows that there is a very important position for the economist in fisheries studies. Indeed, it is evident that economists have begun to play an increasingly important role in fisheries during the past fifteen or so years.

This is not to deny in any way the importance of recognizing that fish are a natural resource, and though the quantities of man-made inputs into the fishing process can be known with certainty, one can never be entirely sure what the outcome of these will be in terms of production. Fish stocks will always fluctuate naturally, some greatly, and so will catches, although management may well seek to reduce the amount of variation. In contrast, in the production of cars and videos we can identify a fairly reliable relationship between inputs and outputs; that is, we have a reasonably quantifiable production function. In fishing, the production function is identifiable but much less stable and hence less predictable. Thus in a renewable-resource-based industry, one cannot understand what is happening without some appreciation of the relevant biology. In the case of fisheries economics, the link to fisheries biology is so strong that separation would be unacceptable. This does not however imply that a profound knowledge of biology is required, and this book includes a vital but limited discussion of elements of the biological model of fisheries as a sufficient base for more extensively developed economic modelling. For those readers with some background in biology, we can state that we have followed common practice in fisheries economics by generally adopting the logistic growth model, which assumes the growth of a fish stock to be some function of its size in weight; it is recognized that some might claim this to be a restrictive basis, but it is sufficiently pervasive for us to feel that departing significantly from it in an introductory text would be unwise.

At this point, a rather different issue presents itself. One might be interested in fisheries simply for 'academic' reasons. However, economists believe that they can make a useful contribution to solving the problems that arise in fisheries rather than merely conceptualizing them. Thus in practice, economists often feel impelled to make a prescriptive contribution to fisheries management and development plans. This contribution, which may or may not be requested in the first place or listened to in the second, is important because the conclusions and recommendations that economists reach are not necessarily those of fisheries biologists or non-economist fisheries administrators. This is not of course to claim that the advice of economists is alone sufficient to solve the problems, but it is a potentially vital input. What really matters is that fisheries economists and other specialists should work jointly, with a full understanding of each other's techniques and objectives. As Butlin (1974, p. 64) argues, 'Without fisheries biology, fisheries management is not possible. Without fisheries economics in collaboration with biology, fisheries management has been shown to be at best only partly successful and at worst self-defeating.'

Notwithstanding what we have said so far, it is not immediately obvious what should or should not be included in any book seeking to cover the subject matter of fisheries economics adequately. Those books already in the field have taken quite differing approaches, and topics such as, for example, fisheries policies, recreational fishing and aquaculture are not always included, especially where the main emphasis is upon fisheries management. This book is intended as an introduction, and as such we have tried to combine elements of both depth and breadth, no doubt at some cost to both. In order to compensate for losses in depth especially, each chapter has a tailpiece called 'bibliographic notes', which directs the reader to the more important sources of further information on topics raised in the chapter. Losses in breadth tend to be referred to with regret in the text itself. We have tried to make the book essentially self-contained, but we are of course conscious that some readers will be approaching the book with very little prior knowledge of fishing, fisheries biology, or perhaps even of economics. Consequently, to make the work as widely accessible as possible, the attempt is made to explain each new idea as and when it occurs as the argument develops. There is however a limit to the extent to which this can be done, and those who would wish to read more widely, in both fisheries biology and economics, may be directed towards textbooks on these subjects: Pitcher and Hart (1982), Hardy (1959), Open University (1978), Samuelson (1982) and Mishan (1981) might be a suitable cross-section.

The structure of the book is for the most part deliberately linear, to achieve progression of argument and linkage of ideas. Such an approach has its strengths, but also weaknesses, and we shall say in a moment something of what is *not* here. In Chapter 1 the notion of fish production as an economic activity is covered, and this chapter outlines what is involved in converting inputs (which have valuable alternative uses) into output in a production function. The same chapter also considers the objectives of the decision-taking units involved in fisheries and the economic environment within which they operate. Chapter 2 develops a model (or stylized picture) of commercial fishing, in which both biological and economic factors are considered. The biological dimension shows that a fish stock will be capable of producing a surplus each year that is sustainable indefinitely if a catch of this amount is taken. The economic dimension reveals that, in the absence of regulation, a fishery will end up being overexploited (as defined). Chapters 3 and 4 then show how this analytical model can be usefully applied. Chapter 3 shows the impact of technological change on the fishery and reveals that such change may well not produce the benefits that we are accustomed to anticipate. Chapter 4 demonstrates with the model that fisheries management is required for both biological and economic reasons. It then continues to analyse the fundamental goals of management, bringing together both biological and economic dimensions of possible alternative objectives.

Having established a framework for identifying the nature of the problems of fisheries, we then look in turn at how fishermen themselves and outside management agencies might solve these problems. Chapter 5 examines the ways in which fishing firms have responded to the wide range of problems that they face. Although some of these strategies have not been without successes, it is argued that for as long as the natural resource base remains a common property, then actions by firms are likely to produce only transitory successes. Having thus reinforced the conclusion of Chapter 4 on the need for management, Chapter 6 considers the main methods of regulation available. These are divided into 'biological' and 'economic' methods, and the biological ones are shown not to be likely to alter the long-run economic situation in the fishery, although they may well have some beneficial effects. Economic methods are preferred, although of such methods it is only the allocation of some form of property rights to the fishermen that seems to solve the main problems.

Chapters 7 and 8 then look in some detail at how fisheries policies have in fact been conducted. Chapter 7 reviews international aspects of policy, and examines three main dimensions of these: management by international bodies, the move towards coastal-state management under the emerging regime of the Law of the Sea, and finally a brief case study of the Common Fisheries Policy of the European Economic Community. Chapter 8 reviews national fisheries policies, examining as examples the policies of Canada, the United States and the United Kingdom. At this point, we widen the study to respond to the increasing importance of non-food uses of fish stocks, and Chapter 9 reviews the many problems arising in attempts to analyse the economics of recreational fishing. Finally, it can be argued that fish farming overcomes many of the problems associated with commercial fishing in the same way that agriculture overcame the problems of food-gathering and hunting. In consideration of the fact that our primary aim must be to maximize the net benefits derived from the asset represented by the fish resource, Chapter 10 reviews some of the basic economics of aquaculture.

It is probably apparent even from this summary that our basic conclusion is that, as fisheries are an open-access common property resource, it is theoretically demonstrable and empirically verifiable that substantial economic and biological problems will emerge. Hence fisheries management is essential, for without it fisheries will not produce the great benefits of which they are capable. Sadly, so many mistakes have been made in management, and so many of the world's developed fisheries are in difficulty, that sorting out the problems of management and establishing suitable policies will not be easy, but it is clear that the ability to control one's fortunes and to learn from the past is essential. While there is no simple solution to all the problems, it would appear that the acquisition of property rights in some form offers the foundation on which individual countries might then develop policies best suited to their own particular circumstances. Systems of this kind will need to allow for the exchange of such rights, and payments for the benefits that they confer, much as property rights systems for land resources have done.

The linear thread of the main part of this book has, as we have said, caused us to neglect certain areas of interest, and this neglect has been compounded by the customary restraints on length. Although the last two chapters attempt to develop some ideas in two directions, there are others that receive regrettably scant justice here. We are conscious especially of not developing the industrial/onshore aspect of fisheries, including fish marketing, nor the issues that become important in considering the regional significance of fisheries. The issue of fisheries development is not pursued here as we have concentrated primarily on the economic problems that have emerged in mature commercial fisheries mainly in the northern hemisphere. It should be evident however that fisheries in developing countries have much to learn from these mature fisheries, in terms both of past difficulties and present policy responses. As economists we would have liked more space to develop some further analytical tools such as second-best theory, but any book is ultimately a compromise between the ideal and the feasible. Finally, space constraints have not permitted us to employ a case study approach, which might have been useful, but readers are directed towards relevant sources in the bibliographic notes.

It remains then to identify to whom this book may be of value. Over the past thirty years, which is roughly the life span of fisheries economics as a separate subject, people have tended to become interested in it from a diversity of directions. Economists, both professional and student, have moved into the topic from a surprising variety of initial interest areas, including agricultural economics, industrial economics, resource economics, welfare economics, regional economics and recreational economics. It is indeed interesting to see that this diversity is reflected in the contribution that academic economists have made to the fisheries literature. Secondly, biologists have developed in recent years an increasingly keen interest in and awareness of fisheries economics, as its subject area and implications have impinged upon their own. The same is true of oceanographers and environmental scientists—to a lesser extent perhaps. Finally, there is another, less specific group, particularly those responsible for managing and developing fisheries, who have also shown an increasing interest in what economists have been doing and saying. It is partly with this in mind that we have continued in the tradition of Gordon (1953) and Anderson (1977) in writing for a mixed audience, in the hope that our final product will be accessible to a range of interest groups.

This book is an introduction, not a research monograph, and as such it is set at a standard appropriate for undergraduates on relevant courses in economics, agricultural economics, geography and fisheries studies degree programmes. It may also serve as a short introduction to the topic for graduate students on courses in these areas. However the manner in which the book is written should make the contents accessible to others, including students on courses in marine biology, environmental studies, aquaculture and oceanography. While it is not intended primarily as a practical handbook, we hope that it will also be of use to those actively involved in fisheries as administrators and within the industry. It remains to say that we have attempted to avoid empirical material that will date too rapidly, although obviously some of the contents may do so, and readers may pursue the more descriptive aspects of fisheries in suitable books and particularly the industry press; the bibliographic notes give some guidance on sources.

Finally, it would be inappropriate to conclude without expressing our thanks to other people who have contributed directly or indirectly to this book. Much of the coverage and approach was developed on our undergraduate course in fisheries economics at Portsmouth Polytechnic, and students on that course have played a vital role in refining our appreciation of what is or is not required in the contents. Our colleagues within the Department have also helped greatly, and we would wish to single out Alan Radford and James Young for their valuable advice throughout, and Guy Judge and Dee Sathaye for their comments on Chapter 2. Our thanks go also to those involved in producing the original manuscript, particularly Ed Kopinski, who produced the diagrams, and Carol Lacey, who had the unenviable task of transferring our drafts into typescript. The errors that remain are of course attributable to us rather than any of these.

REFERENCES AND FURTHER READING

ANDERSON, L. G. (1977). *The economics of fisheries management*. Baltimore: Johns Hopkins Press.

BUTLIN, J. (1974). 'The role of economics in fisheries management research.' *Maritime Studies and Management* **2** : 56–65.

GORDON, H. S. (1953) 'An economic approach to the optimum utilization of fisheries resources.' *Journal of the Fisheries Research Board of Canada* **10** (17) : 442–57.

HARDY, A. C. (1959). *The open sea II: fish and fisheries*. London: Collins.

HILL, B. E. and K. A. INGERSENT (1982). *An economic analysis of agriculture*, 2nd ed. London: Heinemann Educational.

MISHAN, E. J. (1981). *Introduction to normative economics*. Oxford: Oxford University Press.

OPEN UNIVERSITY (1978). *Oceanography: biological elements*. Milton Keynes: Open University Press.

PITCHER, T. J. and P. J. B. HART (1982). *Fisheries ecology*. London: Croom Helm.

SAMUELSON, P. (1982). *Economics*, 11th ed. New York: McGraw-Hill.

CHAPTER 1

Fish and fishing: some fundamentals

1.1 INTRODUCTION

This chapter gives an overview of fish production as an economic activity. We look first at the 'output' side of this activity and address ourselves to the question of what it is that makes fish products and fishing valuable to society, what causes value to change and what the implications are of such changes. Attention is then given to the production system itself, in a section that discusses the input–output relationships, the agents responsible for production and the economic circumstances under which they operate.

1.2 THE PRODUCT

1.2.1 The problem of valuation

Fishing is a multi-product industry in the broadest sense of the term. It is important to understand that the output of a fishery may not necessarily be a physical commodity but may, in some cases, be a service. Thus while some fisheries are exploited mainly to obtain the fish themselves, others are exploited for recreational purposes. Within each of these broad categories of output there exists a diversity of products.

To gain an idea of the economic importance of these products some attempt must be made at valuation. Where output is bought and sold through a market then price can be used as a measure of unit value. In this way, for example, the relative economic importance of different species of food fish can be evaluated because the product is commercially marketed. This is not the case for all output, however. Recreational fishing is an outstanding example of a commodity that is not always bought and sold commercially and where no clear market price prevails. What complicates the issue further is the fact that the unit of output is difficult to identify. Output may not necessarily correspond to the quantity of fish caught by the sports fisherman, or even to the length of time he spends trying to catch fish. Sport fishing is merely part of total 'recreational activity'. These difficulties do not, of course, mean that recreational fishing is of no value to the recreator or to society; indeed, one fisheries economist is of the opinion that, in the United States at least, recreational fishing is a 'sleeping giant' in terms of economic importance (Bell, 1978, p. 239). They do imply, however, that unless we have some way of valuing output it becomes virtually impossible to make any kind of decision regarding the best use of resources.

Because this chapter is concerned to explain fundamental principles, the discussion will be centred mainly on fishing that is directed towards food production, which, as already suggested, is analytically less awkward than recreational fishing. The latter will be dealt with in Chapter 9.

1.2.2 Output values over time

For those commercial fisheries where reliable price data exist, it is possible to assess the trend in values over time. Throughout most of the period since the Second World War the tendency has been for the real value of output to rise. The generally accepted reason for this is that world demand for fish products has exceeded the supply potential of the production system. The dominant influences on the demand side have been population growth and rising incomes *per capita*, while supply constraints have arisen because of the limited biological potential of the natural resource. It is the latter problem, above all, that will concern us throughout much of the book.

The expectation of most commentators is that the future trend in the real value of fishery resources will continue upwards. Projections made by the United Nations' Food and Agriculture Organization (FAO) suggest that, if price relativities were to remain unchanged, global demand for fish up to the end of the century would increase at approximately 3.3% p.a. compared with an estimated growth in production of about 1% p.a. (Robinson, 1980). Population growth is expected to account for over half the increase in consumption. Though part of the supply and demand imbalance might be resolved by international trade it is clear that the constant-price assumption is untenable; it seems highly likely that the relative price of some fish products, notably those whose supply is most inelastic, will rise (Robinson, 1980).

It is much harder, however, to foresee the implications of these changes. Some writers have taken a pessimistic view and have argued that if prices do rise then supplies will tend to be diverted away from countries where the need for food is greatest and towards rich nations with the greatest purchasing power (Bell, 1978, p. 72; Krone, 1979, p. 259). Against that it can be argued that increasing demand, and the proliferation of so-called exclusive economic zones, may result in the creation of new fisheries in new areas, notably on the continental shelves of maritime developing countries. These countries could then enjoy the potential benefits associated with the ownership of, or preferred access to, an increasingly valuable resource. Even if this were to occur however, there is no certainty that consumption of fish in those countries would rise, since many developing countries might exchange their fish resources for foreign currency. Thus, while it may be possible to say something about the changing value of fish products, it becomes extremely speculative to try to say what effects these changing values will have.

1.2.3 Value differences between products

It is axiomatic that the existence of a multi-product industry will imply a diversity of values among the products. Differences in raw-material input, location of production, degree of processing and end use will inevitably result in differences in unit values. What is more surprising however is that if a comparison is made between fish species that are physically and biologically similar and have not undergone processing, then one still finds very great variations in unit values.

To illustrate the point let us consider the situation in the United Kingdom. In 1978 the landed value of molluscan shellfish ranged from £28 per tonne for cockles to £1514 per tonne for oysters; among crustaceans the range was between £338 per tonne for crabs and £5175 per tonne for lobsters; among demersal (i.e. bottom-swimming) species values ranged from £32 per tonne for Norway pout to £2285 per tonne for sole, while for pelagic species (i.e. those living at or near the surface) the range was from £49 per tonne for sprats to £677 per tonne for whitebait (Ministry of Agriculture, Fisheries and Food, 1979). The significance of this range of values is enhanced when we realize that many of the food fish sold for human consumption are very similar in nutritional composition. Indeed, many of the cheaper varieties tend to be of relatively high dietary quality. *Table 1.1* compares the calorific and protein content of some of the commoner demersal species landed in the United Kingdom with their marketed value. The evidence of this table leaves one in no doubt that nutritional composition has little or no influence on the value of fish varieties, relative to one another.

TABLE 1.1 Nutritional composition and values of major demersal fish species in the United Kingdom

Species	*Calorific content* (kilocalories per 100 g edible material)	*Protein content* (g per 100 g of edible material)	*Unit value in 1978* (£ per tonne)
Cod	78	17.6	535
Dogfish	156	17.6	247
Haddock	79	18.3	478
Pollack	95	20.4	475
Skate	98	21.5	397
Sole	79	16.7	2285
Whiting	105	18.3	291

Sources: Ministry of Agriculture, Fisheries and Food (1979); Pyke (1970).

A conceptual framework that helps explain why these differences in unit value exist is provided by Lancaster's theory of goods characteristics (Lancaster, 1969), which has been applied by economists to the analysis of demand in a number of industries and markets. Basically the theory suggests that goods are of value to the buyer because of the properties or characteristics they possess; the goods themselves are merely the vehicle for supplying these characteristics. As applied to fisheries it means that demand will be a function of how far a particular fish product supplies certain characteristics that are desirable to the purchaser. Now the point is this: fish products are likely to embody a number of sought-after characteristics and it is the combination of these within the one product that endows it with value. In the case of food fish these characteristics might include taste, texture, freshness, perishability, 'convenience', colour and nutritional quality. The theory is also applicable to recreational fisheries where, as Bell has stated, 'the consumer is willing to pay for many components other than fish for food' (Bell, 1978, p. 243). What makes sport fisheries valuable is that the recreator imputes a number of other characteristics to the activity of fishing (such as the pleasure of 'escapism' or 'being outdoors'). The fishery itself is perceived as playing an integral part in the supply of these characteristics.

The theory of goods characteristics provides a number of important insights. In particular it helps to explain why some products are never consumed at all. As far as fish products are concerned an example is the attempts made by international organizations such as the FAO to overcome malnutrition in developing countries. Synthetic fish-based food supplements, described by one expert as 'mysterious, gritty powders', have often turned out to be a complete failure in the sense that people will not consume them even if they are given away (Lucas, 1980). While these foods have certain characteristics, such as protein, that the benefactors think *ought* to make them desirable, they may lack other qualities, such as taste, that are actually sought by the recipients. When such deficiencies are rectified then the results are more encouraging.

1.2.4 Elasticities of demand

Let us consider how the demand for a particular fish product will change as economic conditions alter. In the first instance the total quantity purchased is likely to depend on the aggregate number of purchasing units. This is why population is believed to be so important in the growth of demand for fish products throughout the world. But individual consumer behaviour is itself not a constant. For example, we should anticipate that consumption of a certain commodity would be inversely related to the price of the commodity, positively related to the price of competing products and income *per capita*, as well as being affected by a plethora of influences that dictate the individual's preference for the product. If it were possible to estimate the relationship between changes in these factors and changes in the quantity of a product purchased, and if it could be assumed with reasonable certainty that these relationships would stay constant in the future, then it would be possible to foresee the circumstances likely to induce a change in demand for the commodity.

To help clarify these relationships let us formulate a *demand function* for a certain product. Symbolically, this can be expressed as

$$Q_X = f(N, p_X, Y/N, p_{S1} \ldots p_{Sn}, Z) \tag{1.1}$$

where Q_X is the total quantity of product X demanded, N is the total population of consumers, p_X is the price of product X, Y/N is income per head of population, $p_{S1} \ldots p_{Sn}$ are the prices of other products and Z is a residual factor representing the influence of personal tastes, lifestyle, advertising, and so on.

The concept of a *demand curve* is based on one aspect of the above relationship. It is necessary to explain this concept because it features in later chapters. An example of a demand curve for a particular product is depicted in *Figure 1.1* and shows how the quantity demanded, Q_X, varies inversely with the price of the product, p_X. In drawing the curve, the other factors that affect demand (i.e. N, Y/N, $p_{S1} \ldots p_{Sn}$ and Z) are treated as if

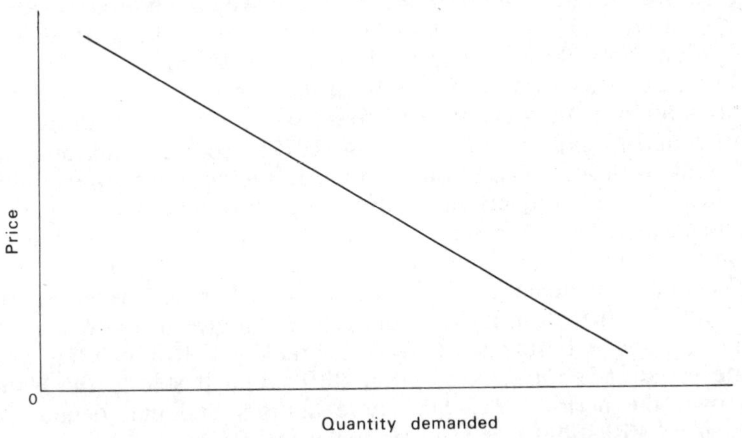

FIGURE 1.1 A demand curve.

they were constants and are said to be *parameters* of the demand curve. If any of the parameters should change, the demand curve shifts. For example, an increase in income *per capita* would be expected to shift the demand curve to the right. The reason for this is that at any given price, higher income enables a larger quantity of the product to be purchased than before. The demand curve would also be expected to move to the right if there were an increase in the total population of consumers, a rise in the price of substitutes, or an enhanced preference for the product. Parametric changes in the opposite direction to those suggested would obviously tend to shift the demand curve to the left.

Estimates have been made of the relationship between the demand for fish products and some of the independent variables mentioned above, namely the particular product's own price, the price of substitutes, and income *per capita*. These are termed *elasticities of demand*. Where a given change in the independent variable brings about a more than proportionate change in the quantity demanded, then demand is said to be *elastic* with respect to that variable. Where the change in quantity is less than proportionate, demand is said to be *inelastic*. For example, if a 1% increase in the price of a commodity induces a fall of 2% in the quantity demanded, then it follows that demand is elastic with respect to its own price. If an increase in income *per capita* of 10% brings about a rise in the quantity demanded of 5%, then demand for the product is inelastic with respect to income. Elasticities are normally expressed as the percentage change in the quantity demanded for every 1% change in the independent variable being considered. Thus, a price elasticity of demand of −3.0 means that for every 1% increase (decrease) in price, there follows a 3% decrease (increase) in quantity demanded.*

It is difficult to make generalizations about elasticities of demand for fish products, since results differ according to the time period covered, the country or region in which the products are marketed, and the estimating technique used. It is also not easy to compare the results of different investigations since the products involved are not identical. Nevertheless, virtually all studies carried out concur on the expected finding that price elasticities for fish products are negative (*see*, for example, Bell, 1978; Buchanan and Nicholson, 1977; Young, 1977; Tsoa, Schrank and Roy, 1982), while with some exceptions, income elasticities appear generally to be positive. Some products have also been shown to have a positive cross-price elasticity of demand with other fish or food items, meaning that demand is dependent upon the prices of these substitute goods.

A knowledge of demand elasticities is useful both in explaining past events and in anticipating those in the future. To give just one example, consider a study undertaken by Tsoa, Schrank and Roy (1982), which estimates elasticities for selected groundfish products sold in the United States over the period 1967–80. These authors find that demand for certain groundfish fillets tends to be inelastic with respect to price and elastic with respect to income. As regards the first finding, the implications are that a given change in price can be expected to bring about a disproportionately small change in the quantity demanded; or,

*The responsiveness of demand to changes in a product's own price is related to the *slope* of the demand curve for that product. Letting ε_d stand for the price elasticity of demand, then at any given point on the demand curve,

$$\varepsilon_d = \frac{P_X}{Q_X} \times \frac{dQ_X}{dP_X}$$

The greater the slope of the demand curve at the point corresponding to the particular values of P_X and Q_X, the less will dQ_X/dP_X be, and thus the lower the elasticity.

equivalently, that given changes in the quantity put on the market will induce relatively large changes in price (in the opposite direction). The second finding means that as real personal income rises by a given percentage amount, demand for these products will rise by a greater percentage amount. However the reverse is also true: falls in income will bring about falls in demand of a disproportionately greater amount. Now, recent developments in North America and elsewhere involving extended fisheries jurisdiction (to be discussed in Chapters 7 and 8) may well result in greater supplies coming on to the U.S. market from both the U.S. fishing industry and other countries. Tsoa, Schrank and Roy argue that if this happens then, given their findings, 'there will be a drastic reduction in the price of fish products unless U.S. income, and therefore demand, rise substantially' (p. 489). They conclude that the benefits of extra production may be lost unless existing marketing arrangements are changed.

A knowledge of demand parameters is important not just from the point of view of fish product marketing, however. As will be explained in later chapters, the assumptions made about price elasticity are crucial in analysing the effects of fishing on the natural resource itself.

1.3 THE PRODUCTION SYSTEM

1.3.1 Systems interactions

Fish production comes about by the interaction of two systems, one natural and the other man-made. The biological and other elements which comprise the first of these are, in varying degrees, under human control. The hunting of wild populations of fish represents a situation where people have only an indirect control over the aquatic environment, while fish farming illustrates an attempt to gain greater control of the natural resource base by deliberately creating an artificial environment. The man-made system can be thought of as comprising the instruments of harvesting (and, where relevant, those of processing) that are applied to the fish population.

Though the interaction between the natural and the man-made system is extremely complicated, it should be understood at the outset that the two are mutually interdependent; the activities of fish harvesting will affect the natural environment, and vice versa. In the remainder of this chapter we shall present a preliminary examination of the fish production system, leaving a more detailed analysis to Chapters 2 and 3.

1.3.2 The production function

The economist's usual starting point in any analysis of production is to hypothesize the existence of a *production function*, which can be defined as a technical relationship between physical output and the inputs needed to produce it. Often this relationship is expressed in mathematical form, represented by one or more equations. When one is discussing the output of a recreational fishery, a 'production function' may lose its meaning since, as we have already established, output is not a physical item. The concept does have some operational significance in the case of food fish since we can at least identify a physical end product.

For any given output there will be several inputs. In this context the inputs include the fish population available for exploitation, and the labour and capital applied to it. For the moment it will suffice to think of inputs under these broad headings. As we probe more deeply into the problems of fishing however, it may be necessary to consider more narrowly defined inputs. For example, one might need to have some knowledge of the structure of the fish population, details of the vessels that comprise the capital stock, and so on.

The level of output attained depends upon the quantities of inputs used, the proportions in which they are combined and the technology of production. To understand what happens when fishing takes place let us start by making the naïve assumption that the fish population remains constant, and that increasing quantities of labour and capital (e.g. vessels and their crews) are applied to it. The expectation is that output of fish will increase, but not in direct proportion to the increase in input. As more and more boats compete for a fixed stock of fish, it becomes progressively harder for each boat to maintain its catch rate. The relationship between output (fish) and variable inputs (labour and capital) is therefore likely to be non-linear owing to the fact that one of the inputs (the fish population) is assumed constant. This situation is familiar to economists and is one of *diminishing returns*. The model that is developed in Chapter 2 explicitly incorporates the assumption of diminishing returns.

The assumption of a constant fish population may be approximately valid in the short run but not in the long run. Fishing will tend to reduce the size of the population, which, even though it has the capacity to regenerate, is unlikely to restore itself to its original size. A higher level of fishing will be associated with a new (lower) population size. It now becomes somewhat more difficult to say how output will change as more labour and capital are applied to the fishery, because it is clear that in the long run there are opposing forces at work. Output will be affected *positively* by the increasing application of labour and capital, but *negatively* by the depletion of the natural resource. The notion that output is a function of input is therefore not wrong as such; it is merely incomplete, because as far as fish production is concerned it fails to explain how one input (the fish population) is determined. More importantly, it fails to explain how changes in one set of inputs (labour and capital) will be systematically related to changes in the other. In short, a more complex model is needed, showing not only how output depends on input but how the inputs themselves are functionally related. Such a model will be developed in the next chapter.

Finally, we need to introduce a term that is widely used in fisheries science and which will be employed throughout the book, namely 'fishing effort'. Two definitions of this term are possible. *Nominal fishing effort* refers to the volume of resources devoted to fishing, quantified either in monetary or physical units. It therefore corresponds to the concept of input used in the previous paragraphs. In practice nominal fishing effort may be represented by a single input such as time spent fishing, or as an amalgam of inputs that can include all the labour and capital used to exploit the fishery. The term *effective fishing effort* refers to fishing mortality, usually measured as the biomass of fish extracted by fishing, expressed as a proportion of the mean population. Both terms are measures of the amount of fishing, but whereas one attempts to quantify the factors that give rise to this activity, the other assesses it in terms of the impact that it has. To avoid ambiguity we shall make it clear throughout the book in what sense the term 'fishing effort' is being used.

1.3.3 Fishing methods and gear

The previous section introduced the term 'nominal fishing effort'. Because of its importance in later chapters the concept needs enlargement. For practical purposes nominal fishing effort is usually measured by reference to a particular method of fishing or type of gear used. The diversity of methods and gear that are employed in real life indicates the difficulty of arriving at a unified measure of effort, especially since they differ considerably in their fishing power.

Four main types of gear can be identified (after Sainsbury, 1971).

(a) *Encircling nets*, which, as their name suggests, surround shoals of fish. Purse seines, beach seines and Danish seines are examples.
(b) *Towed gear*, where a net or other device effectively 'sieves' the water. Notable here are trawls and dredges.
(c) *Static gear*, which is left in one position so that the fish become entangled, snared or trapped. Examples of this type include gill nets, long lines and pots.
(d) *Other mobile methods* such as harpooning, trolling, etc.

Fishing methods and gear differ not only in their mode of operation but also in their capital intensity, technological sophistication, the sea areas and conditions in which they can be operated, and the types of fish they can be used to catch. Some are long-established and traditional, others are of more recent origin. In many cases the effectiveness of a certain method of fishing is highly dependent on the existence of some other technology or item of capital equipment. For example, the use of steam and, later, diesel power in vessels enabled trawls to be towed at greater speed and did much to increase the efficiency of this type of gear.

Moreover one particular method may form the basis of a number of separate techniques. A trawl, for example, may be towed along the sea bed, kept on the bottom by means of a weighted footline. This enables demersal species such as cod and haddock to be caught. The trawler itself may be designed to launch and haul the net over the side of the ship, or down a ramp at the stern. Recent years however have seen the development of so-called pelagic trawling in which the trawl, instead of being towed along the sea bed as in conventional bottom trawling, is modified for use in mid-water so as to catch pelagic species such as mackerel. The precision of this technique has been enhanced by a number of technological developments, notably acoustic sonar devices, that allow the fish shoal to be detected and monitored. Likewise, encircling methods of fishing have been modified and developed in very distinct ways. The Danish seine, for example, is used to catch demersal fish while the purse seine is used mostly in the capture of shoaling pelagic species. The type of vessel involved, the accompanying equipment and the operating conditions also differ considerably between the two.

A point that needs to be emphasized is that different gear can be, and often is, used to exploit a single fish stock. So, for example, we find that in the central North Sea area in 1977, cod were caught using seines, trawls, gill nets, and hooks and lines. How then do we quantify the 'total' amount of fishing? Because gear is not standard we cannot simply add up the length of time for which each gear type was operating. One approach in theory is to derive an implied measure of total effort, using data on the total catch of a given species in a given area and the catch per unit of effort (CPUE) of a sample of vessels fishing for the species in that area. Total effort is then simply calculated by dividing total catch by CPUE. The derived quantity will be in 'equivalent effort' units; that is, in terms of the effort measure used for the standard sample (e.g. so many hours of fishing). The fact that the sample boats may be dissimilar to all other vessels in terms of technology and fishing power does not invalidate the essential logic of this procedure.

1.3.4 Costs

The production function, and the prices of factor inputs, will determine the costs incurred directly by the fishing enterprise. A shift in the production function or a change in factor prices will alter total costs. We can also distinguish *average cost* and *marginal cost*: the former is simply total costs divided by total output, the latter is the change in total cost consequent upon a change in output.

However, costs are more than merely accounting concepts. Their true significance lies in the fact that the inputs into a production system could be put to some alternative use, producing another good or service that is valued by society. The alternative-use value of an input is termed its *social opportunity cost* (SOC). Where input prices perfectly reflect SOC, then production costs may be taken to indicate the alternative-use value of the resources employed. In this situation, if a given quantity of fish costs £1 to produce, then by implication £1 worth of some other good or service has now been foregone. However it may be that the costs incurred by the fishing firm are different from the SOC of the resources actually employed. For example, a fishing firm may not find it worth while to employ crewmen at the going wage rate.* If, however, the men concerned have no alternative job opportunities, with the result that they would otherwise remain unemployed, then it may be to society's net benefit that they should be employed in fishing. At least they might then be producing something of value.

The concept of opportunity cost also has a time dimension, which is especially relevant in the present context. Time is, in a sense, an input into the production function since the harvesting of fish is time-dependent; that is to say, the biomass depends *inter alia* on the length of time it has been allowed to grow. It is usually possible within certain limits to vary the proportion in which time is 'combined' with other inputs. More importantly, time, like other inputs, also has an opportunity cost. To appreciate this statement we must realize that the fishery can be treated not only as a renewable resource that produces a stream of net benefits in perpetuity but as an item that can, in principle, be consumed instantly. To let the fish stock serve as a capital asset providing a flow of income over time is to forego the option of immediate consumption of the entire fish stock. In this sense time has an opportunity cost if consumption now is preferable to consumption in the future. In a more material sense the opportunity cost of time is likely to be reflected in the rate of return that the resources employed in fishing could earn in alternative occupations. It is quite conceivable that society might prefer to 'fish out' a stock completely rather than letting it provide a stream of net benefits *ad infinitum* if the discounted value of that stream is deemed to be insufficient.

Economic efficiency dictates that changes in relative input prices will alter the optimum input combination. If some degree of technical substitution between inputs is possible then it will pay to substitute cheaper inputs in place of more expensive ones. To achieve the least-cost combination of inputs necessary to produce a given level of output, inputs should be substituted up to the point where the cost saved by reducing the amount of one input is just equal to the extra cost of using more of another. If time is an input, then the same argument applies. Thus, if time becomes more valuable because society's preference for consumption now as opposed to in the future has increased, it pays to economize on time in the production function. Because of the time-dependent nature of production however, such a move may entail a different pattern of output than would otherwise have been the case. A limiting case of this kind of change in output pattern, as mentioned above, is for a zero input of time and complete cessation of production.

Before we leave this section it must be explained that fish production that is based on a common property resource involves external as well as internal costs. More precisely, the activities of one fishing enterprise have externalities, which will create costs for others, as can be illustrated by a hypothetical example. Consider a high-seas fishery exploited by a given number of standard vessels. If other vessels enter the fishery the

---

*The fact that labour employed in fishing is often paid on the basis of a share in the value of the catch, rather than a fixed wage, has not been overlooked. We consider the wage–labour situation merely in order to illustrate how private costs and social opportunity costs may diverge.

abundance of the fish stock will be reduced. But since the stock is common property, depletion will be manifested in a reduction in CPUE for all vessels. Now CPUE is, in effect, a measure of the productivity of the resources that comprise nominal effort; that is, it is a ratio of output per unit of input. Other things being equal, a fall in this ratio must necessarily result in higher average costs for all vessels. The externalities engendered by the exploitation of common property resources, of which the above is just one illustration, give rise to some of the central problems that will be discussed throughout the book.

1.3.5 The decision-making unit

Input–output connections do not simply 'happen' but are deliberately brought about by human agency. The individual decision-making units, the firms, will undertake fish production in pursuit of their own objectives. These objectives warrant closer examination.

Over the world as a whole, fish producers vary enormously in type, size and objectives. In socialist countries, as one would expect, ownership of the means of production is normally vested in the hands of the state, whereas in the Western world private enterprise sets the pattern. In the latter case we find a diversity of ownership types. The largest firms are public limited companies or corporations; the smaller ones are usually owned by a handful of individuals, either on the basis of partnership or as a private limited company; and the very smallest are sole proprietorships. These observations would appear to be valid not only for traditional fish catching but also for aquaculture. For recreational fisheries however, it is not so easy to generalize. In some instances a firm may, as well as undertaking commercial fishing for itself, also 'supply' sport fishing if the demand exists. In other instances the supplier may be a local authority, a government department, a company or an individual. Because of the complexity of analysing production decisions in recreational fishing the remainder of the chapter will be confined to non-recreational aspects.

It is commonly assumed in much of the fisheries economics literature that firms are profit-maximizers. How justified is this assumption? For fish producers in capitalist countries there are three main arguments or pieces of evidence that may be advanced to support it.

First, it is argued that competition gives firms very little option but to be profit-maximizers since a firm that attempts to be anything else will ultimately be forced out of business. This argument, in other words, suggests that a kind of 'natural selection' will operate in capitalist economies such that fish producers that consistently fail to maximize profits will be weeded out and eliminated. This argument is persuasive because competition among fish producers is typically very intense. However, as will be explained in the next section, competition is not 'perfect' in the neoclassical economic meaning of the term.

Secondly, it can be shown that in sea fisheries, input–output correlations are higher when output is measured in terms of value rather than physical weight (Carlson, 1975; Buchanan, 1978). Thus, fishing effort tends to be directed towards the grounds that generate the highest monetary return, not necessarily the greatest physical yield. While this observation indicates at the very least that fishing firms are not concerned with biomass for its own sake, it does not prove conclusively that they are profit-maximizers. The finding is also consistent with the hypothesis that firms may be attempting to maximize *revenue* (that is, gross income rather than net).

Thirdly, and perhaps most importantly, there is a great deal of evidence to suggest that the greater the commercial opportunities, the faster will fish producers respond. For example, it seems that the more profitable a fishery, the faster will new entry occur. Response to technical innovations is similar: generally, the greater the anticipated advantages, the quicker will they be adopted (Whitmarsh, 1977). Profit is thus an important stimulus. Moreover the fact that in real life firms may not respond immediately to profitable opportunities does not invalidate the argument. A firm cannot be certain *ex ante* that a new fishery or new technique will increase its profitability. Lack of relevant knowledge, or the high costs of obtaining that knowledge, may cause a profit-motivated firm to postpone its decision.

If these points are accepted then at the very least it seems that profits are an important consideration for fish producers under private enterprise. Even then however, the pursuit of profit will not be the only business motivation. For one thing, if maximizing behaviour is followed, it will be subject to a leisure constraint. That is to say, there is bound to be some minimum amount of leisure that producers will insist on taking. It may also be contended that firms will not be indifferent to risk and uncertainty; as we shall see in the next section, these are an important feature of the business environment. Profit-maximizing behaviour will certainly be compromised where firms are either risk-averters or risk-preferers. For example, faced with a choice of two fishing grounds, a firm that is risk-averse may choose to exploit the one where catches are relatively stable and predictable, even if on average it is known to yield lower returns than the other. Unfortunately the evidence on fishing firms' attitudes to risk and uncertainty is very sketchy and conflicting. The 'conventional wisdom' of economics suggests that firms will tend to be risk-averse. However it is not unknown for boats to enter a fishery in the hope of landing a single very large catch, and one observer (Acheson, 1975, p. 663) has remarked that 'there is good evidence that fishermen . . . have a very strong preference for occupations involving risk. Without the prospects of high risks and high payoffs, life seems dull, lifeless and painfully boring'. To add to the confusion, it has been shown that even within the same fishery motivational differences exist, such that one vessel captain will behave as a risk-preferer and another as a risk-averter (Cove, 1973). In the light of this evidence we have little choice but to assume that firms as a whole are not so strongly risk-biased as to depart from optimizing behaviour.

The profit-maximizing assumption is certainly weakened when we consider the state-owned enterprises of socialist countries. In such countries, fishing is often viewed as part of the national food production system in which the objective is to maximize edible protein supplies. On the face of it this statement might be taken to mean that the value of different species and the costs of fishing have no influence on production decisions. This is not altogether true for two reasons. The first is that fish products are often 'valued' in terms of nutritional and other characteristics, and resources allocated to their production accordingly. Thus, while market values are not necessarily a relevant decision variable, imputed values may be. It is also clear that in many socialist countries, such as the Soviet Union and Poland, costs are not ignored entirely. The low productivity of agriculture in the Soviet Union has meant that it is economically rational, given the national objective, to concentrate resources on fishing, where productivity is very much higher (Spangler, 1970). A similar emphasis on fishing has occurred in Poland since production costs per unit of animal protein have been much lower in that industry than in livestock production (Strak, 1969). While these remarks suggest that in a broad sense economic considerations are not ignored altogether, it is obvious that the pursuit of profit must be incompatible with the aim of maximizing protein supplies. As two Polish commentators have pointed out, in practice 'the enterprise has to continue fishing, even when operations become unprofitable during a period of reduced fishing yield' (Formela and Kazmierski, 1964, p. 180).

1.3.6 The decision environment

The objectives of fish producers, and the decisions they make, are conditioned to a large extent by the economic environment in which they operate. The forces that shape this environment will now be considered.

In the first place, producers will face competition in some form. Fishing firms exploiting a common property resource will face competition on the fishing grounds as well as in the market place. In other words, not only must they beware of losing potential customers to other, rival firms but they also run the risk of losing 'their' share of the common property resource. Fish farmers, on the other hand, are distinguished in that they do have sole ownership of the natural resource. Though to this extent they have eliminated 'resource' competition, fish farmers will usually have to face market competition, like their hunter–gatherer counterparts. For recreational fishing it is not easy to generalize about the nature of competition. Some sport fisheries are based on common property resources while others are not. Moreover the circumstances under which recreational fishing is supplied may vary from a situation in which there is only a single supplier (a monopoly) to one in which there are a very large number (atomistic competition).

The factors that affect price and product competition deserve some examination. In much of the literature on fisheries economics it is assumed that, as well as being profit-maximizers, firms have no market power. To justify this assumption it could be pointed out that in most capitalist countries fishing firms are numerous, that entry barriers into the industry are relatively low and that product differentiation at first-stage marketing is virtually non-existent.* Moreover the fact that the price of fish at first-hand sale can clearly be shown to alter in response to changing supply and demand conditions suggests that prices are set by the market and are not 'administered' by individual firms. Though it is generally true that prices are set by the market, two qualifying remarks need to be made.

To start with, the degree of price competition between fish processors and distributors is very much weaker than it is between fish catchers. Processing and distribution are often characterized by high concentration (that is, the sector may be dominated by a few large firms). There may also be barriers to entry and, especially for manufactured consumer products, significant product differentiation. Firms' discretion over price is usually substantial, and competitive responses take the form of either quantity adjustment or the creation of 'new' products, often aided by advertising.

The other qualification is that the conditions of entry and exit into and out of fishing are not symmetrical (Crutchfield, 1979). While there are relatively few impediments to setting up production on a small scale, and even fewer when it comes to moving from one fish stock or market segment to another, there are often circumstances that militate against a firm's leaving the industry altogether.

There are two possible explanations for this. The first is in terms of so-called fixed-asset theory. At its simplest this asserts that in fishing, as in other industries, there is a divergence between the acquisition cost of fixed assets and their salvage value. For example, it might cost £1 million to acquire a vessel but its sale value outside fishing may be only a fraction of this figure. The more specialized and unadaptable are fixed assets, the greater is the divergence in values likely to be. If salvage values are relatively low then it means that the earning power of assets can fall to an equivalently low level before it is worth disposing of them. Fixed-asset theory has been applied to the Pacific salmon fishery to explain why there was a net entry of resources following years of good catches, but no net exit following bad years (Stevens and Mattox, 1973). The second explanation is in terms of the share system of rewards that operates throughout many fishing industries. The system, under which the crew are paid a proportion of the value of the catch, effectively means that when total revenue falls, so does total labour cost. This reduction helps to cushion the impact of falling landings and prices, and may sustain marginal firms that might otherwise have been forced out of business. The result of this asymmetry between entry and exit is that labour and capital flow into the industry during the 'good times' but do not transfer out so easily during the 'bad times'.

*The term 'product differentiation' often causes confusion. It is used here to describe a situation in which the products of individual sellers within the group comprising the market are not regarded by the consumer as perfect substitutes; that is, each firm's product is to some extent unique in the eyes of the consumer. As a result the consumer may be willing to pay more for one firm's product than another's.

Risk and uncertainty also have an important bearing on the decision environment. We make the usual distinction between these two concepts, risk being defined as a situation where probabilities can be assigned to the range of possible outcomes that may flow from a particular course of action, and uncertainty as a situation where probabilities cannot be assigned. Of the various fish production systems, conventional fishing is undoubtedly the riskiest activity because of random variations in price and yield. In the latter case the 'risk' may take the form not merely of the boat returning empty, but of not returning at all. To the extent that fishermen have some notion, based on experience, of expected prices or CPUE, they may be said to be facing risk. There will be plenty of situations, however, where they face pure uncertainty: for example, the outcome of fishing for underutilized species whose stock abundance is unknown.

To conclude this section, let us briefly analyse the two components of risk. For the fishery as a whole, variations in yield may cause compensatory changes in price, and to this extent the two components offset one another. However, as Turvey has pointed out, for a single boat owner operating over one season the risk is much greater than that borne by the fleet as a whole since there is much less chance that the price will be high when his catch is low (Turvey and Wiseman, 1957). In capitalist countries it is what happens at 'boat' level that is important for decision-making, not only because of the preponderance of owner-operated vessels but also because of the system that operates in multi-vessel companies whereby each skipper is awarded substantial executive powers.

Fluctuations in the natural environment are the main source of yield variations. It must be stressed that some fish populations are very much more prone to environmental fluctuations than others. *Table 1.2* contrasts

TABLE 1.2 Yield variability in three U.S. fisheries

Fishery	*Av. landings, lbs/boat (11 years, 1959–69)*	*Standard deviation*	*Coefficient of variation (S.D. as % of mean)*
Blue crab	20081	784	3.9
Tuna	163999	27120	16.5
King crab	223500	186550	83.4

Source: Smith (1975).

three U.S. fisheries, where risk caused by yield variations is measured by the standard deviation of landings as a percentage of the mean.

Though yield variations can also be caused by changes in fishing effort, in practice effort does not fluctuate in the same unpredictable manner as ecological parameters do. Rather, the tendency is for effort to increase systematically over time so as to cause CPUE to fall monotonically.

The extent to which supply variations cause changes in price depends on the elasticity of demand for the product of the fishery. The lower the price elasticity of demand, the greater will be the price fluctuations brought about by a given change in supply, other things being equal. It should be clear, therefore, that some types of fishery will be especially risky because both yield and price will be particularly volatile. The rational decision-maker cannot afford to ignore either element.

1.4 SUMMARY

The fish production system creates a range of different goods and services. Assessing the economic significance of fish products is made more difficult by the fact that, in some cases, market prices are indeterminate, and that the unit of output is sometimes impossible to define. It seems however that the real value of fishery resources at a global level has risen, and is likely to continue doing so. Implicit in the diversity of products is a range of unit values. Where these can be measured it is found that very great differences exist, this being true even when products are narrowly defined. An explanation for this phenomenon is that products embody certain characteristics that are sought by the purchaser, and products differ in the quantity and combination of these characteristics. Empirical estimates of elasticities also aid our understanding of demand. Price elasticity, cross elasticity and income elasticity of demand help to explain past patterns of consumption and highlight possible future ones.

Fish production itself arises from the application of labour and capital to the natural resource. The concept of a production function is a useful first step to analysing this interaction, but a more complex model than that normally encountered in economics texts is required. Man-made inputs into the production function differ in their effectiveness and mode of operation, and this factor complicates the task of deriving a unified measure of fishing effort. To the extent that a production function for a fishery can be said to exist, then other things being equal it defines the direct costs of production. The input prices paid by the firm, however, may not necessarily equate with their social opportunity cost. External costs also have to be considered, since the activities of any one firm will impose costs on others. The firms themselves undertake production in pursuit of their own goals. In free-enterprise economies it can be argued that profits are a sufficiently important consideration, for most firms, to allow one to explain *aggregate* industrial behaviour using the profit-maximizing assumption. (For fishing enterprises in socialist countries however, the assumption is untenable.) The economic environment in which firms operate is strongly influenced by competition, risk and uncertainty, whose intensity is often such as to make fish production a unique kind of activity.

BIBLIOGRAPHIC NOTES

Since many of the themes and concepts introduced in this chapter are developed in greater depth elsewhere in the book, only a short bibliography is given here in order not to pre-empt what follows. The books and articles we recommend are, for the most part, of a fairly basic and general nature.

World supply and demand are discussed by Robinson (1980) and Krone (1979), and a short description of the global pattern of fishing in the post-war period is given in Pitcher and Hart (1982) and Nicholson (1978, Ch. 7). Bell (1978, Ch. 2) deals with a variety of basic themes relating to consumption, value and the nature of fish products, also from a world perspective. Those readers interested in knowing more about different species of fish should refer to Lythgoe and Lythgoe (1971), whose book is comprehensive and well illustrated. Descriptions of fishing methods and gear are given by Sainsbury (1971) and in the fourth edition of the World Fishing publication *The fisherman's manual*. Kaczynski (1977) provides a very readable account of how Western- and Eastern-bloc countries differ in their fishing objectives, and in their attitude to such issues as conservation and exploitation. Finally, two elementary economics texts that explain concepts of business behaviour and market power are those of Turvey (1971) and Reekie and Allen (1983).

REFERENCES AND FURTHER READING

ACHESON, J. (1975). 'Fisheries management and the social context: the case of the Maine lobster fishery.' *Transactions of the American Fisheries Society* **104** (4): 653–68.

BELL, F. (1978). *Food from the sea: the economics and politics of ocean fisheries*. Boulder, Colorado: Westview Press.

BUCHANAN, N. (1978). *The fishing power of Scottish inshore white fish vessels*. White Fish Authority. FERU Occasional Paper.

BUCHANAN, N. and NICHOLSON, M. (1977). 'Price/supply relationships for demersal fish in the U.K. 1956–65.' White Fish Authority. FERU Occasional Paper.

CARLSON, E. (1975). 'The measurement of relative fishing power using cross section production functions.' In J. Pope (Ed.), *Measurement of fishing effort*. (*Rapports et Procès-verbaux des Réunions du Conseil International pour l'Exploration de la Mer* **168**: 84–98.)

COVE, J. (1973). 'Hunters, trappers and gatherers of the sea: a comparative study of fishing strategies.' *Journal of the Fisheries Research Board of Canada* **30** (2): 249–59.

CRUTCHFIELD, J. A. (1979). 'Economic and social implications of the main policy alternatives for controlling fishing effort.' *Journal of the Fisheries Research Board of Canada* **36** (7): 742–52.

FORMELA, M. and KAZMIERSKI, K. (1964). 'Business decisions in Polish fishing fleet management.' In FAO Fisheries Report *Meeting on business decisions in fisheries industries*. R.22.2. Rome: FAO.

KACZYNSKI, V. (1977). 'Controversies in strategy of marine fisheries development between Eastern and Western countries.' *Ocean Development and International Law Journal* **4** (4): 399–407.

KRONE, W. (1979). 'Fish as food.' *Food Policy* **4** (4): 259–68.
LANCASTER, K. (1969). *Introduction to modern microeconomics*. Chicago: Rand McNally.
LUCAS, K. (1980). 'How changes in fish resources and in the regime of the sea are affecting management, development and utilization.' In J. Connell (Ed.), *Advances in Fish Science and Technology*. Farnham, Surrey: Fishing News Books.
LYTHGOE, J. and G. LYTHGOE (1971). *Fishes of the sea*. London: Blandford Press.
MINISTRY OF AGRICULTURE, FISHERIES AND FOOD (1979). *Sea fisheries statistical tables 1978*. London: HMSO.
NICHOLSON, J. (1978). *Food from the sea*. Farnham, Surrey: Fishing News Books.
PITCHER, T. and P. HART (1982). *Fisheries ecology*. London: Croom Helm.
PYKE, M. (1970). *Man and food*. London: Weidenfeld & Nicolson.
REEKIE, D. and D. ALLEN (1983). *The economics of modern business*. Oxford: Blackwell.
ROBINSON, M. (1980). 'World fisheries to 2000.' *Marine Policy* **4** (1): 19–32.
SAINSBURY, J. (1971). *Commercial fishing methods*. Farnham, Surrey: Fishing News Books.
SMITH, F. (1975). *The fisherman's business guide*. Ann Arbor, Michigan: UMI Publications Inc.
SPANGLER, M. (1970). *New technology and marine resource development*. New York: Praeger.
STEVENS, J. and B. MATTOX (1973). 'Augmentation of salmon stocks through artificial propagation: methods and implications.' In A. Sokoloski (Ed.), *Ocean fishery management: discussions and research*. NOAA Technical Report. NMFS Circ. 371.
STRAK, W. (1969). 'Programming of the development of the marine fishing industry in Poland.' In FAO Fisheries Report *International conference on investment in fisheries*. R.83.2. Rome: FAO.
TSOA, E., W. E. SCHRANK and N. ROY (1982). 'U.S. demand for selected groundfish products, 1967–80.' *American Journal of Agricultural Economics* **64** (3): 483–9.
TURVEY, R. (1971). *Demand and supply*. London: Allen & Unwin.
TURVEY, R. and J. WISEMAN (Eds) (1957). *The economics of fisheries*. Rome: FAO.
WHITMARSH, D. (1977). *Technological change in the U.K. fishing industry*. Unpublished M.A. Thesis, University of Exeter.
WORLD FISHING (1982). *The fisherman's manual*. Sutton, Surrey: IPC Business Press Ltd.
YOUNG, T. (1977). *A study of the demand for fish in the U.K.* University of Manchester, Department of Agricultural Economics.

CHAPTER 2

A bioeconomic model of the fishery

2.1 INTRODUCTION

In the previous chapter we stressed the need to develop a special kind of model for fisheries analysis to take account both of biological and of economic forces. If we do not do this, there is a danger that our analysis of fisheries will be at best misleading and at worst incorrect. To give one example, let us consider the elasticity of the supply of fish purely from the economic viewpoint. At any particular *moment*, the supply of fish will be perfectly inelastic (that is, given) and price therefore will be demand-determined. If the price so determined is high enough, skippers will be encouraged to fish longer and use their boats more intensively so that *short-run* supply will be elastic to some extent. While this conclusion appears to be perfectly valid, it might then be argued on economic grounds that if the price of fish remained high enough, new fishermen would be attracted to the fishery and the *long-run* supply of fish would be yet more elastic.

This latter result is not necessarily incorrect but it does depend on certain implicit assumptions. Possibly the simplest assumption that would justify it is that an extra unit of input into the fishery always results in an extra unit of fish output. Unfortunately such an assumption may well be unjustified in fishing because the limited biological productivity of the fish stock may mean that increases in input actually decrease output in the long run. Consequently, once the biological side of the model is included, a continuing high price of fish, far from resulting in ever-increasing supplies of fish, may well result in ever-decreasing supplies. It is one aim of this chapter to show how this may be so.

2.2 THE GORDON-SCHAEFER MODEL

A number of bioeconomic models have been developed over the years and the interested reader is referred to some of them in the bibliography.

However, perhaps the most straighforward and widely used, particularly by economists, is the so-called Gordon–Schaefer model, named after the economist, H. S. Gordon, and the biologist, M. B. Schaefer.

2.2.1 The basic biology of the model

The Gordon–Schaefer (GS) model considers a single fish stock in isolation and is concerned with the way in which the stock (as opposed to the individuals that comprise it) grows over time. It is based upon the *logistic* growth model.

Let us suppose that we have an area of sea where there are no fish and that we introduce a small fish population to it. The fundamental postulate underpinning the model is that the growth, G (in terms of weight), of the population P over a time period t will be a function of the initial size (in weight) of that population; that is,

$$\frac{dP}{dt} = G = f(P) \qquad (2.1)^*$$

Now, because our imaginary population is small relative to the area of sea, it appears reasonable to suppose that to begin with, population growth will be roughly proportional to the initial population; that is,

$$G = aP \qquad (2.2)$$

The constant a is called the *intrinsic growth rate*, and it represents the fastest growth rate ever attained by the fish stock.

However, since any given area of sea is, by definition, limited in size, there must be some maximum size of fish population that can be supported. This maximum is usually called the environmental carrying capacity (ECC) and is denoted by K. As the fish population size approaches the ECC so crowding of the sea area will increasingly become a problem. The growth rate, G, of the population may then be expected to fall, according to the degree of crowding. In the logistic model, it is postulated that, at any particular moment, the growth rate will be proportional to the difference between the ECC and the population at the time. This gives us the growth equation

$$\begin{aligned} G &= aP[(K - P)/K] \\ &= aP\left(1 - \frac{P}{K}\right) \qquad (2.3) \end{aligned}$$

This equation, then, describes the way in which the fish population will grow as a function of the existing population size. Setting it equal to zero,

*Strictly speaking dP/dt denotes an instantaneous growth rate. Usually however, we are interested in rates of growth over a discrete time period such as a year or a season. In the remainder of this chapter we shall therefore take our growth (G) function to indicate growth over time.

we see that, in the absence of fishing, the population size will be equal to the ECC. Once reached, the ECC will tend to be maintained indefinitely, although the population size may be expected to fluctuate around this value in response to changes in environmental parameters, such as water temperature. Equation 2.3 implicitly assumes such parameters to be fixed.

Differentiating equation 2.3 and setting it equal to zero, we may see that maximum growth of the fish stock occurs when the population size is half of the ECC; that is,

$$G' = a\left(1 - \frac{2P}{K}\right) = 0$$

Hence

$$P = K/2 \tag{2.4}$$

These conclusions are summarized in the biological productivity curve. While the precise shape of the curve will depend on the values assigned to the variables a and K, the general shape will be that depicted in *Figure 2.1*.

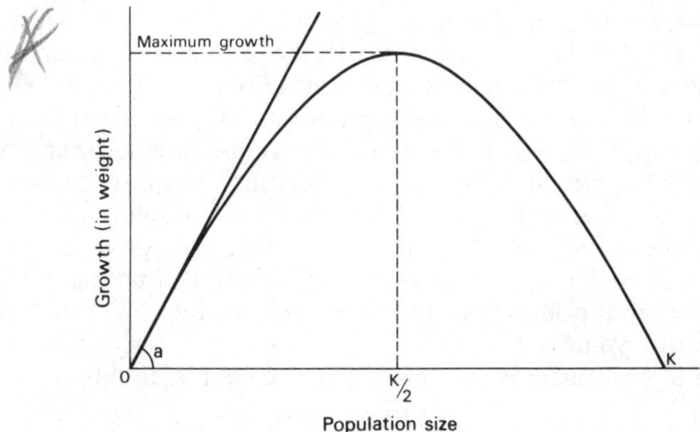

FIGURE 2.1 The biological productivity curve.

Many examples of empirical biological productivity functions are available. For instance, Radovich and MacCall (1979), investigating the Californian northern anchovy (*Engraulis mordax*) fishery, estimated the following growth equation:

$$G = 0.36P - 0.00000009\,P^2 \tag{2.5}$$

where a, the intrinsic growth rate, is 0.36 and K, the environmental carrying capacity, is 4 million tons of anchovy. Maximum growth of the stock occurs at a population size of 2 million tons (i.e. half of ECC) and, from equation 2.5, is equal to 360000 tons annually.

2.2.2 The effect of fishing: the short run

Having considered the biological characteristics of the unexploited fish stock, we now introduce fishing. In the model, it is postulated that the yield, Y, or catch in any period will depend on only two factors: the size of the fish population at the beginning of the period, and the amount of fishing effort, f; that is,

$$Y = y(P,f) \tag{2.6}$$

2.2.2.1 *Fishing effort*

Before we can analyse the way in which yield depends on population size and effort, we need further to consider what we mean by the term 'fishing effort', introduced in Chapter 1.

Economists think of effort in terms of the boats, men, gear and so on that are required for the fishing activity. This is usually termed *nominal* effort, f, and is calculated by using some standardized measure such as vessel-ton-days. Biologists, on the other hand, refer to *effective* fishing effort, F. This may be defined as 'the fraction of the average population taken by fishing' (Rothschild, 1977, p. 98). The measurement of F is achieved, however, by considering the proportion of the stock that survives fishing. Precisely, it is 'the negative of the natural logarithm of the proportion of fish surviving fishing in a year' (Pope, 1982, p. 5). Hence if fishing removed 60% of the average population, 40% would survive, giving an F value of −ln (0.4), which is 0.9163. It is argued further that doubling the level of fishing would result in a further 60% of the remaining 40% being captured, giving in F value of 1.8326 (which implies 16% survival overall). Notice however that this argument requires an implicit assumption of diminishing returns to nominal effort: a doubling of the fleet results in less than a doubling of the catch (*see* section 2.2.2.4 for further discussion of this point).

These two effort concepts are related by the simple equation

$$F = qf \tag{2.7}$$

where q is called the *catchability coefficient.* Clearly if q equals 1 then F and f are the same thing and the analysis of fishing will be the same whichever is used. Possibly for this reason, fisheries texts often make the assumption that q does equal 1 and then analyse fishing using effective effort. We shall not follow that approach here however, first because leaving q in the equation does not add greatly to the difficulty of the analysis and secondly, and more importantly, because changes in its value may have significant implications for the management of fisheries.

In effect, q represents the state of technical efficiency. Of course, the value of q will depend to an extent on the units assigned to nominal effort. In a given fishery, for instance, we should not expect q to be the same if we define nominal effort in terms of vessel-ton-days as if we define it in vessel-ton-years. Nonetheless, once the units of nominal effort are defined, q provides some indication of the technical efficiency of the fishing fleet.

In this chapter we shall use *nominal* effort, and our simple short-run yield equation becomes

$$Y = qfP \tag{2.8}$$

Let us now consider the way in which short-run yield will change in response to changes in effort and population size. We shall begin by assuming that the amount of nominal effort is given, and shall consider the effect of different population sizes.

2.2.2.2 *Population size*

The short-run yield equation, equation 2.8, states that for a given level of nominal effort, yield will vary linearly with population size: the greater is the population size, the greater will be the yield. This situation is depicted in *Figure 2.2*. The figure shows a family of short-run yield curves (SRY_{f1}, etc.)

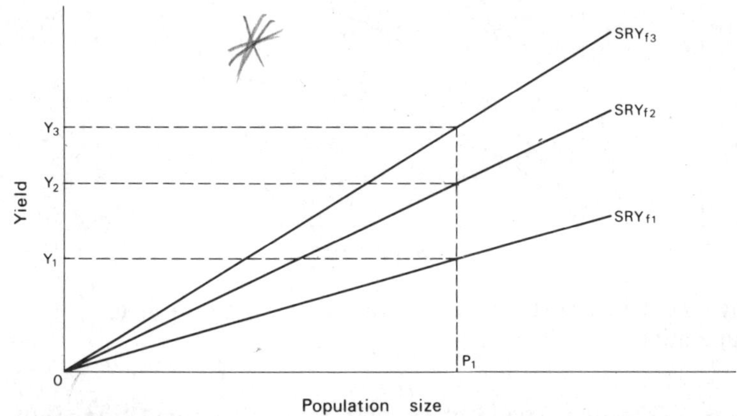

FIGURE 2.2 Short-run yield as a function of population size.

with each curve depending on the nominal effort level. As the level increases (from f_1 to f_2 to f_3) so the yield associated with a given population size (such as P_1) increases. Once the level of effort is specified (at, say, f_1), the simple linear relationship between short-run yield and population size is apparent. In the development of the model we shall use these short-run yield curves. Let us briefly however consider the implications of a non-linear relationship.

2.2.2.3 *Diminishing returns to population size—a digression*

This section is not essential to the development of the model and may be omitted without loss of continuity.

The linear relationship between yield and population depicted in *Figure 2.2* amounts to assuming no diminishing returns to population. That is, as population increases from, say, 10 to 20 to 30 to 40 thousand tons so yield increases proportionately, from say 3 to 6 to 9 to 12 thousand tons. In fact however, there are reasons for thinking that yield may rise less than proportionately, from say 3 to 5.5 to 7.5 to 9 thousand tons.

The principal reason for so thinking is that the amount of nominal effort is given. Therefore as the population size increases, this given amount of effort will be spread more and more thinly across the population. The ability of the fleet to catch and land the fish is likely therefore to be less than adequate to take advantage of the opportunities presented by the increased population size. We may expect, therefore, short-run yield to be a non-linear function of population size, as shown in *Figure 2.3*. Our short-run yield equation would then be modified to

$$Y = qfP^{\alpha} \tag{2.9}$$

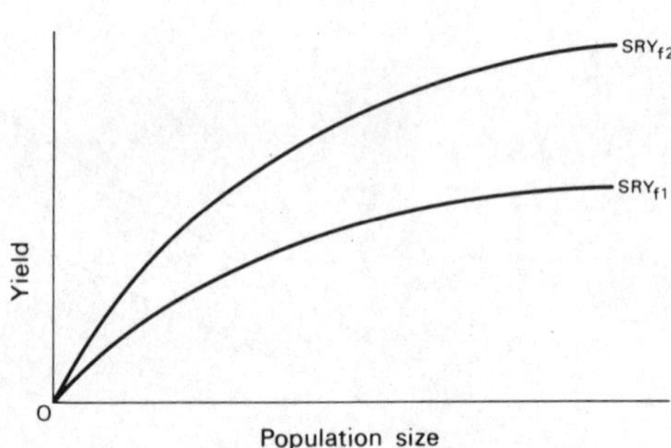

FIGURE 2.3 Short-run yield with diminishing returns to population.

where α reflects the degree of variable returns to population. Setting α equal to 1 corresponds to our original case of no diminishing returns. A value of α between 0 and 1 implies diminishing returns, and the lower is the value assigned to α, the more severe will they be. In terms of *Figure 2.3*, the more severe are the diminishing returns, the greater will be the degree of curvature of the yield lines.

From a fisheries management point of view, diminishing returns to population, if they exist, may be extremely important, particularly in the case where the population size is falling as a result of fishing. In this case, yield may hold up remarkably well for a period of time, but then suddenly decline. Such a situation is likely to lead to difficult biological and economic problems.

The expectation that such a situation may in fact materialize is reinforced in the case of pelagic species such as herring and anchovy by the fact of their schooling behaviour. It seems that the principal reason for this behaviour is to reduce the heavy predation to which such species are usually subject. Brock and Riffenburgh (1963) demonstrate that the rate of predation is a decreasing function of school size. If, therefore, heavy fishing pressure reduces significantly the size of schools, the fish stock may collapse because it is unable to withstand either even the usual level of predation, or any unfavourable environmental change. Hence in the case of pelagic species, yields may be maintained for a while in the face of heavy fishing, only to decline dramatically once a certain critical point is passed. This is one aspect of a *depensatory* growth curve and is discussed further by Clark (1974).

It seems reasonable to argue that diminishing returns to population may have played an important role in the spectacular collapses during the 1970s of the Peruvian anchoveta fisheries and the North Sea herring fisheries, among others.

However, while we may recognize the potential practical importance of diminishing returns to population, it is beyond the scope of this book to include them in a formal way in the development of our model. Consequently, although we may refer to such diminishing returns below, our formal analysis will be based on the assumption that they do not exist. Our short-run yield function will thus be of the form of equation 2.8; that is,

$$Y = qfP$$

2.2.2.4 *Diminishing returns to nominal effort*

From the point of view of nominal effort however, equation 2.8 is particularly unrealistic, because it implies that there are no diminishing returns to effort. If this were the case, it would mean that if effort were, say, doubled then yield would also double; and if effort were increased one millionfold so would be yield. This is clearly nonsense. In the short run, the population size is more or less given, so that there is an upper limit to yield.

It seems likely that the closer is actual yield to this maximum potential yield, so the smaller will be the increases in yield resulting from increases in effort. That is, as effort increases so does yield but at a *decreasing rate*. In other words, diminishing returns to nominal effort occur. One way to show this is to modify our short-run yield equation to

$$Y = qf^{\beta} P \tag{2.10}$$

where β represents variable returns to effort. Values of β between 0 and 1 imply diminishing returns and a value of 1 implies the absence of diminishing returns.

It is true that even with this yield equation, *predicted* short-run yield may exceed the maximum possible catch. Although if it does, this might be taken simply as an indication that excessive effort in the short run may result in the extinction of the species, it is sometimes perceived as a problem. One way to avoid it might be to specify a piecewise function of the form

$$Y = qf^{\beta} P \text{ for } 0 \leqslant f \leqslant f_{ymax} \qquad Y = Y_{max} \quad \text{for } f > f_{ymax}$$

(where f_{ymax} is the effort level required for extinction.) Alternatively, some researchers have used different specifications of the short-run yield equation, particularly the general form

$$Y = Y_{max}(1 - e^{-f}) \qquad (2.11)$$

where Y_{max} is the maximum short-run catch, e is the exponential constant and f is nominal effort. This equation predicts well in the sense that zero effort means zero yield while as effort tends to infinity so yield tends to Y_{max}. However it has the drawback that it cannot allow for extinction, save in the trivial case of infinite effort. It implies moreover that whatever the value of Y_{max}, yield still approaches it asymptotically. For these reasons and to avoid the complication of piecewise functions, we prefer to use equation 2.10 with the obvious caveat that its predictions are valueless beyond Y_{max}.

The diagrammatic form of equation 2.10 will be roughly that shown in *Figure 2.4*, although the precise shape will depend on the values assigned to the various parameters, particularly β. *Figure 2.4* shows only one short-run yield curve, but there will be a whole family of such curves—one

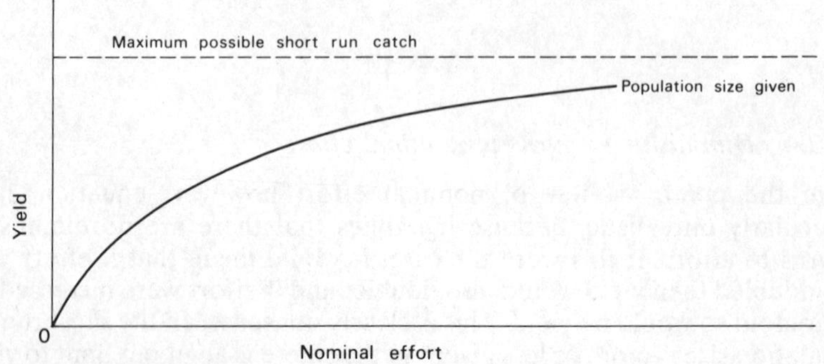

FIGURE 2.4 Short-run yield with diminishing returns to nominal effort.

for each and every population size. For the population size existing at the beginning of the period, the curve tells us the yield that will result from the application of any particular level of nominal effort. If at the end of the period the population size has not altered then the same short-run yield curve will be relevant for the next period. Otherwise, the fishery will be shifted to a new short-run yield curve defined with respect to the new population size. We shall have much more to say about this later.

2.2.3 The effect of fishing—the long run

Having considered the short-run impact of fishing we now consider the long-run aspects and in particular how an equilibrium is reached. To do this we must combine our biological production function (equation 2.3) with our yield function (equation 2.10):

$$G = aP\left(1 - \frac{P}{K}\right) \tag{2.3}$$

$$Y = qf^{\beta} P \tag{2.10}$$

Let us suppose that the population is initially in its unexploited state at ECC. We know from equation 2.3 that at this point growth of the stock is zero, and therefore the harvesting of any fish must decrease the population by that amount. Let us assume that a given effort level of f_1 is applied to the fishery and that this results in a yield of Y_1 units of fish. This situation is shown in *Figure 2.5*.

At the beginning of the second period therefore the population size must be ECC minus Y_1. If we assume that the effort level does not change, it is apparent from *Figure 2.5* that at this lower population level two things will happen. First, yield must be less, and secondly, growth of the fish stock must become positive. Consequently we may expect the population size to change less in the second period than it did in the first. In this way the fishery will gradually move to a stable equilibrium.

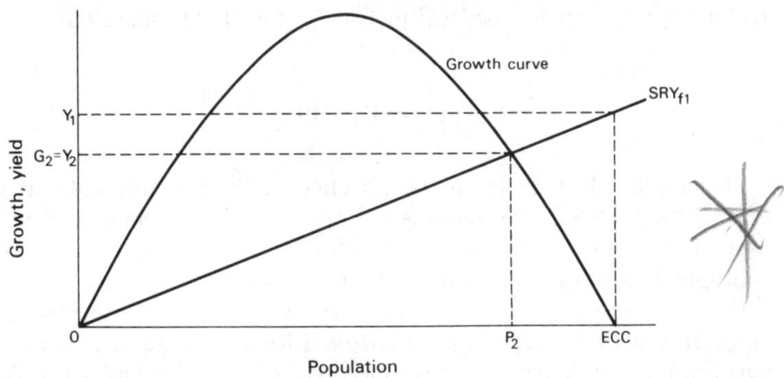

FIGURE 2.5 The impact of fishing on the population size.

Let us suppose that, quite fortuitously, the population size happens to be P_2 at the beginning of the second period. Yield from fishing, Y_2, will then be balanced by the growth of the stock, G_2, and there will be no reason for the population size to change further. Thus for an effort level of f_1, a population of P_2 and a yield of Y_2 may be sustained into the long run.

This move to the new equilibrium may be considered algebraically. Combining equations 2.3 and 2.10, we obtain

$$G = aP\left(1 - \frac{P}{K}\right) - qf^{\beta} P \tag{2.12}$$

Since, by hypothesis, we begin at ECC the above equation clearly does not equal zero, and the population will be in disequilibrium. To find the population size at which equilibrium is restored, we must set equation 2.12 equal to zero and solve for P, which gives

$$P = K\left(1 - \frac{qf^{\beta}}{a}\right) \tag{2.13}$$

as our new equilibrium population.

For our chosen effort level, equation 2.13 tells us the sustainable population, and once we know this it is relatively straightforward to calculate the sustainable yield. If the effort level changes then a different sustainable yield will emerge and thus by considering various effort levels we may establish a sustainable yield function. The equation of the function is easily derived. We know from equation 2.10 that, in general,

$$Y = qf^{\beta} P$$

and from equation (2.13) that, in equilibrium,

$$P = K\left(1 - \frac{qf^{\beta}}{a}\right)$$

By straightforward substitution for P, therefore, sustainable yield, Y_s, is given by

$$Y_s = Kqf^{\beta}\left(1 - \frac{qf^{\beta}}{a}\right) \tag{2.14}$$

If β equals 1 (that is, in the absence of diminishing returns to nominal effort) then sustainable yield is a simple quadratic function of effort. In this case, the sustainable yield curve will be simply the mirror image of the biological productivity curve. It is important, however, to notice the difference between the two: the former is defined with respect to *effort*, the latter with respect to *population*. More significantly, the *origin* of the sustainable yield curve corresponds to ECC on the biological productivity curve. An outward move along the effort axis thus implicitly indicates a fall in the size of the fish population.

If diminishing returns to effort are present (that is, β has a value between 0 and 1) then the sustainable yield curve takes longer to reach its maximum (maximum sustainable yield, MSY—an extremely important concept in fisheries management) and it declines more slowly beyond it. The greater are the diminishing returns (the lower is β) the more apparent will be this shape. The general relationship between the biological productivity curve and the sustainable yield curve for various values of β is shown in *Figure 2.6*.

It should perhaps be noted that in constructing *Figure 2.6* we are implicitly assuming that the value of q, the catchability coefficient, is less than half the value of a, the intrinsic growth rate. For most commercial fisheries this seems a perfectly valid assumption, so that the conclusions outlined above may be expected to hold in practice. If however this were not the case, then the effect of diminishing returns would be to shift the

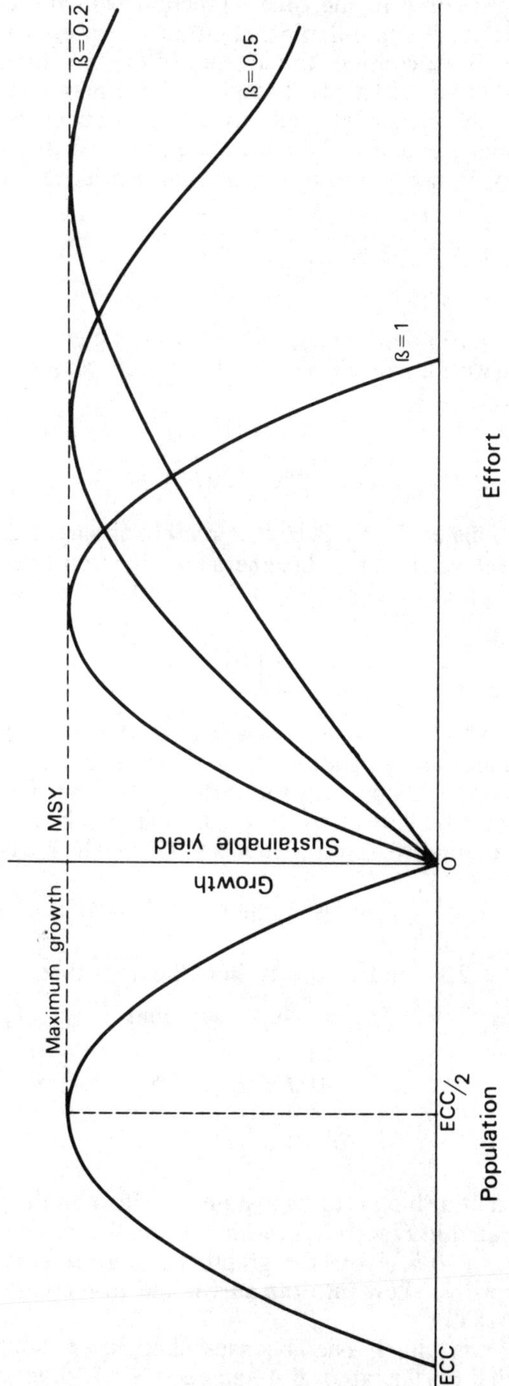

FIGURE 2.6 Sustainable yield curves.

sustainable yield curve in the other direction with respect to the curve corresponding to the non-diminishing-returns case. This will perhaps become clearer if we consider the algebra of the situation.

If we set equation 2.14 equal to zero then we may find the effort level required to reduce sustainable yield to zero (or equivalently to extinguish the stock). Solving equation 2.14 for f, we find that this value, which we shall call f_{max} even though this is a somewhat restrictive use of the term, is given by

$$f_{max} = \left(\frac{a}{q}\right)^{1/\beta} \tag{2.15}$$

If we next differentiate equation 2.14 with respect to effort and set it equal to zero, we may establish the effort level corresponding to MSY, which is

$$f_{msy} = \left(\frac{a}{2q}\right)^{1/\beta} \tag{2.16}$$

From equations 2.15 and 2.16 it is readily apparent that if $\beta = 1$, the MSY effort level is half of f_{max}. In general, the relationship between the two effort levels is given by the equation

$$f_{msy} = \left(\frac{1}{2}\right)^{1/\beta} f_{max} \tag{2.17}$$

From equation 2.17 it may be seen that as the value of β falls so f_{msy} becomes a smaller and smaller fraction of f_{max}, the total amount of effort that the fishery could support without the stock's being extinguished.

This result may be illustrated if we take a simple hypothetical example. Suppose that a equals 0.7 and q equals 0.07, in which case

$$\frac{a}{q} = 10 \quad \text{and} \quad \frac{a}{2q} = 5$$

From equations 2.15 and 2.16 it is then apparent that

if β equals	f_{max} equals	and	f_{msy} equals
1	10		5
$\frac{1}{2}$	100		25
$\frac{1}{3}$	1000		125
$\frac{1}{4}$	10000		625

This effect of diminishing returns to nominal effort on the sustainable yield curve is illustrated in *Figure 2.7a*, which shows the curve for the two cases of $\beta = 1$ and $\beta = 0.5$. From the graph, we can see that the effect is to introduce a positive skew into the curve, and to increase the effort level required for MSY.

Notice, however, that if a had been less than 2q we should have obtained different results. For instance, if q had equalled 1, then

$$\frac{a}{q} = 0.7 \qquad \frac{a}{2q} = 0.35$$

in which case

if β equals	f_{max} equals	and	f_{msy} equals
1	0.7		0.35
$\frac{1}{2}$	0.49		0.12
$\frac{1}{3}$	0.34		0.04
$\frac{1}{4}$	0.24		0.02

Here, while diminishing returns continue to give a positive skew to the sustainable yield curve, the effort level required to take MSY falls, rather than rises, as the value of β falls. In other words, the sustainable yield curve is moved in the opposite direction, as shown in *Figure 2.7b*. The reader might like to verify that if a equals 2q, the effort level required to take

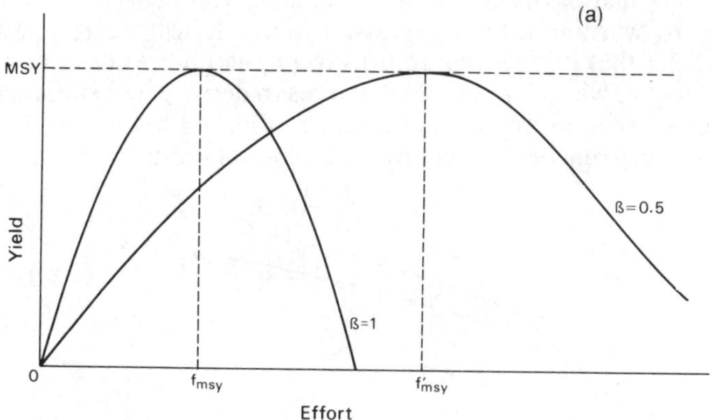

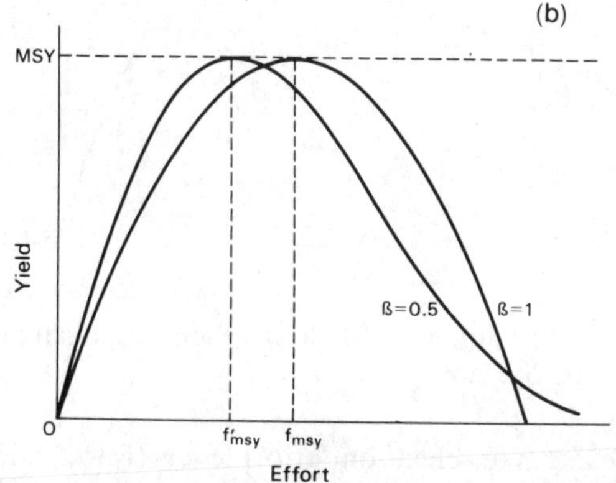

FIGURE 2.7(a), (b) Differing impacts of diminishing returns to nominal effort on sustainable yield.

MSY is not affected by diminishing returns although a positive skew continues to be introduced to the sustainable yield curve. Thus, the impact of diminishing returns depends to some extent on the particular values of a and q. As we have already said, for most commercial fisheries we should expect a to exceed 2q and hence *Figure 2.7a* to be the relevant one.

Before we leave this section, we must emphasize that the sustainable yield function shows the long-run effect of fishing, once the population has adjusted from its original equilibrium to its new one. In the short run, the yield that will result from the application of a particular level of effort is given by the short-run yield equation, equation 2.10.

2.2.3.1 *Diminishing returns to population and sustainable yield*

This section is not essential to the development of the model and may be omitted without loss of continuity.

Although we shall not model it formally, the effect of diminishing returns to the fish population itself on the sustainable yield curve is sufficiently interesting to warrant a brief digression here. It will be recalled from section 2.1.2.3 that diminishing returns to population result in non-linear short-run yield curves. If we use these curves to derive the sustainable yield curve then we obtain somewhat different results. As before, we begin by relating the short-run yield curves to the biological productivity curve. This

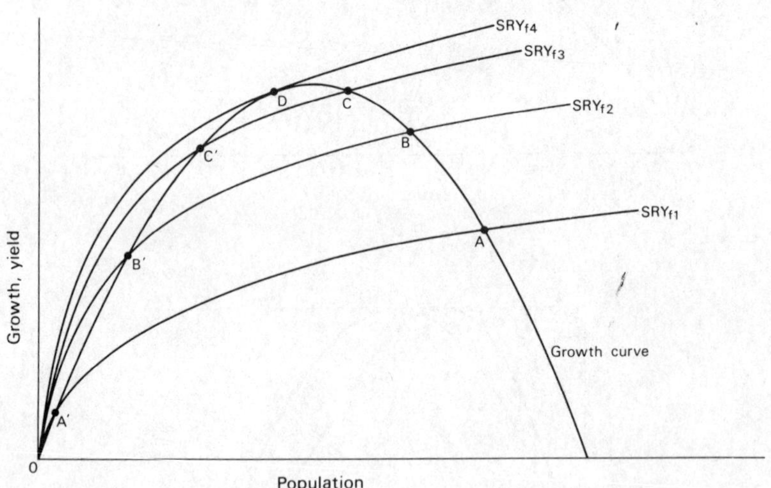

FIGURE 2.8 The impact of fishing when diminishing returns to population are present.

is done in *Figure 2.8*. We select four effort levels (f_1 to f_4). Except for f_4 the short-run yield curves corresponding to these effort levels intersect the biological productivity curve twice. However only the unprimed points represent stable equilibria. Each of the points A′, B′ and C′ is unstable in the sense that any move away from it is amplified. Thus for instance if the population increases from C′, growth of the stock exceeds yield and the population will continue to increase until C is reached, while a decrease from C′ results in a state where yield exceeds growth so that the population falls back to zero. Thus only states, A, B and C would persist into the long run. The point D is semi-stable in the sense that if the population were to decrease it would be taken away from D down to zero. The effort level f_4 is thus a critical effort level in that it is the greatest level for which a sustainable population (and therefore a sustainable yield) exists. Effort levels greater than this result in extinction of the stock.

The sustainable yield curve derived (in *Figure 2.9*) when there are diminishing returns to population will thus comprise two distinct sections, one corresponding to stable (solid line in *Figure 2.9*) and one to unstable (dashed line) biological equilibria. Looking purely from the biological side,

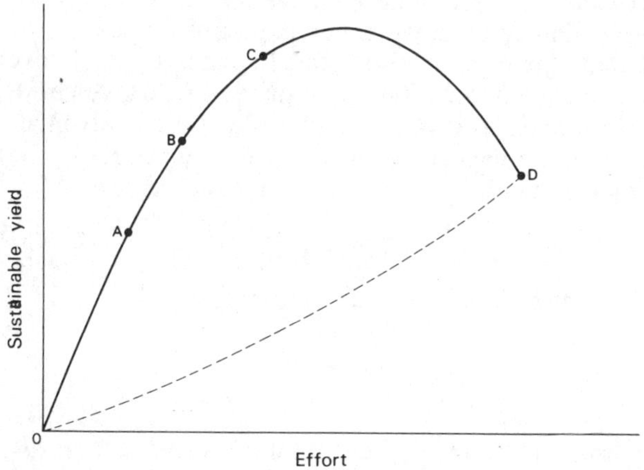

FIGURE 2.9 The sustainable yield curve when diminishing returns to population are present.

we should not expect an unstable equilibrium to be maintained for very long because given the effort level, any random fluctuation in population size would either boost the fishery up to a stable equilibrium or reduce it to nothing. However the problem is to decide what the effort level actually would be in practice.

For the moment, let us just note that the instability in the sustainable yield curve is here due solely to diminishing returns to population. A similar result may be achieved however if we allow for a minimum viable population in the biological productivity function. This gives what is called a *critical depensatory growth curve*, and we shall return to it in Chapter 4 (section 4.2.2).

2.2.4 The economics of fishing—revenue

Until now we have analysed the effects of fishing by simply assuming that a particular level of effort occurs. In practice however, the amount of fishing that is carried out will be determined (largely at least) by economic factors. Let us now introduce those factors into the model and consider their implications.

In the basic version of the GS model, the price of fish is taken to be a constant. Generally this is justified by assuming that the fishery being considered provides only a small part of the total supply of the particular species, and consequently variations in local supply would not be expected to affect price. At any particular time therefore the local price would be simply the prevailing world price and would be constant.

If we multiply the sustainable yield curve by this price, we derive a total revenue curve for the fishery as a whole. Since price is constant, the total revenue curve will have the same shape as the sustainable yield curve and will be simply scaled up or down depending on the actual price. It must be emphasized that this curve shows what happens to total revenue *in the long run*; that is, once population has adjusted to the given effort level and equilibrium has been restored. In the short run, revenue would be determined by multiplying the short-run yield by price.

We have then a simple long-run total revenue function:

$$TR_f = pY_s$$

which by substitution from equation (2.14) gives

$$TR_f = pKqf^{\beta}\left(1 - \frac{qf^{\beta}}{a}\right) \qquad (2.18)$$

It is very important to notice that our total revenue function TR_f is in terms of effort—that is, in terms of an input. Usually in economics, by contrast, revenue is related to output.

We may use the total revenue equation, 2.18, to derive the *average* and *marginal* relationships for the fishery. As always the difference between these two concepts is very important. Average revenue is simply total revenue divided by total effort, while marginal revenue shows the *change* in total revenue consequent upon a *change* in total effort. To take a simple example, suppose total revenue is initially £180 and that effort is 9 units, and that effort then increases to 10 units, raising total revenue to £190. Average revenue when effort is 9 units is then clearly £20 and at 10 units is £19. The marginal revenue resulting from the increase from 9 to 10 units is £10. If we make the effort changes smaller and smaller then we may obtain a better and better estimate for marginal revenue at a point. From this simple example, it will be apparent that average revenue is an arithmetic mean and marginal revenue is the first-order derivative of total revenue with respect to effort. Algebraically we have

$$AR_f = \frac{TR_f}{f} = pKqf^{\beta-1}\left(1 - \frac{qf^{\beta}}{a}\right) \tag{2.19}$$

and

$$MR_f = \frac{d(TR_f)}{df} = \beta pKqf^{\beta-1}\left(1 - \frac{2qf^{\beta}}{a}\right) \tag{2.20}$$

If we assume that $\beta = 1$ then these functions may be depicted diagrammatically as in *Figure 2.10*.

If diminishing returns to effort were present then the sustainable yield function would be 'stretched' as in *Figure 2.6*; this would stretch the total revenue curve (assuming a constant price of fish), which in turn would stretch the average and marginal curves.

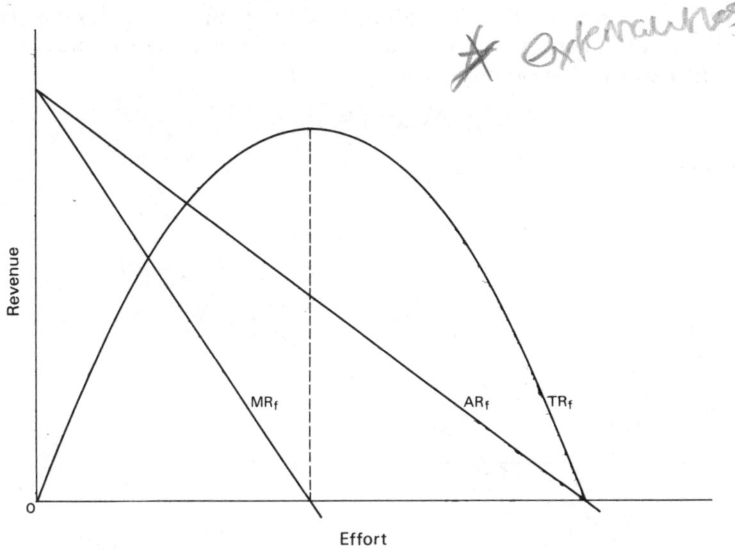

FIGURE 2.10 Revenue as a function of fishing effort.

Figure 2.10 will probably seem familiar to most students of economics. Unfortunately, this familiarity is often a source of confusion. It is important to notice the difference between this diagram and that which is typically encountered in economics. Usually, the average revenue curve slopes downwards because *price* is variable, whereas here price is assumed constant. The reason why the average revenue curve slopes downwards is the changing biological productivity of the fish stock as effort changes. Therefore the average revenue curve presented here does *not* show the price of fish *nor* is it a demand curve. Finally, it seems to have become traditional in fisheries economics to refer to the above curves as revenue curves. However, strictly speaking, since we are relating revenue to effort (an input), they should be called revenue product curves.

2.2.5 The economics of fishing cost

Finally, to complete the GS model, we need to consider the cost of fishing. Once more the analysis is in terms of effort and relates to the long run. It is postulated that, in the long run, effort will be expanded by the addition to the fishing fleet of new, optimally sized boats, rather than by an increase in effort on the part of existing boats. Consequently, the cost of effort will be a linear function of the amount of effort—each new unit of effort will add the same amount, c, to total cost TC. Thus we have

$$TC_f = cf \tag{2.21}$$

where c is a constant. The derivation of average and marginal cost (which are naturally analogous to average and marginal revenue) is then straightforward. It should be apparent that

$$AC_f = MC_f = c \tag{2.22}$$

as depicted in *Figure 2.11*.

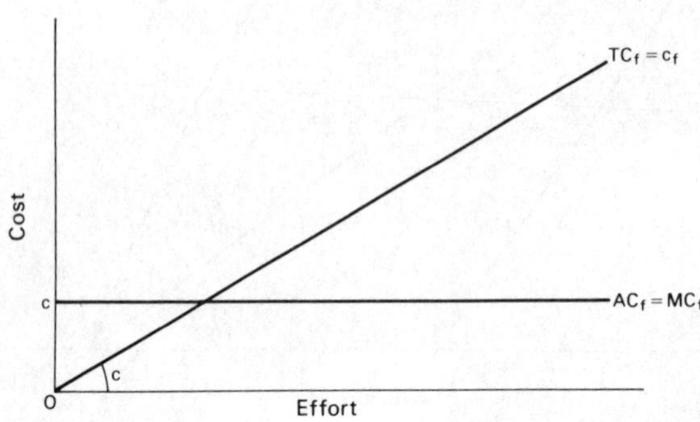

FIGURE 2.11 Cost as a function of fishing effort.

2.2.6 Bioeconomic equilibrium

The building of the Gordon–Schaefer bioeconomic model is now complete and if we put the elements together we can see how the bioeconomic equilibrium is established. We shall consider what is called an *'open-access'* (i.e. completely unregulated) fishery. In such a fishery it is argued that new fishermen will be attracted into the fishery so long as there is a profit to be made; that is, so long as total revenue exceeds total cost. If losses are being made some people will leave the fishery. In the long run therefore the fishery will end up at the effort level where total revenue equals total cost.

To the uninitiated this may seem somewhat strange since it implies that no profit is earned in the long run. However, economists define total (and therefore average) cost to include the return that must be earned by the owner of a business to stop him transferring his assets to some other line of operation. This amount (which is likely to vary from person to person and occupation to occupation) is called *normal profit*. Thus in fishing, in the long run it is argued that the marginal fisherman will be earning normal profit. Logically this must be the case—if he were earning less he would leave and if he were earning more some other fishermen would be attracted into the fishery. The term 'profit' in economics thus refers to a situation where more than normal profit is being earned. For clarification this type of profit is sometimes referred to as 'economic' or 'pure' profit, but perhaps unfortunately it is also referred to simply as profit. In any case, this discussion underlies the zero-profit bioeconomic equilibrium reached by the open-access fishery.

Diagrammatically this equilibrium is illustrated in *Figure 2.12*. Once

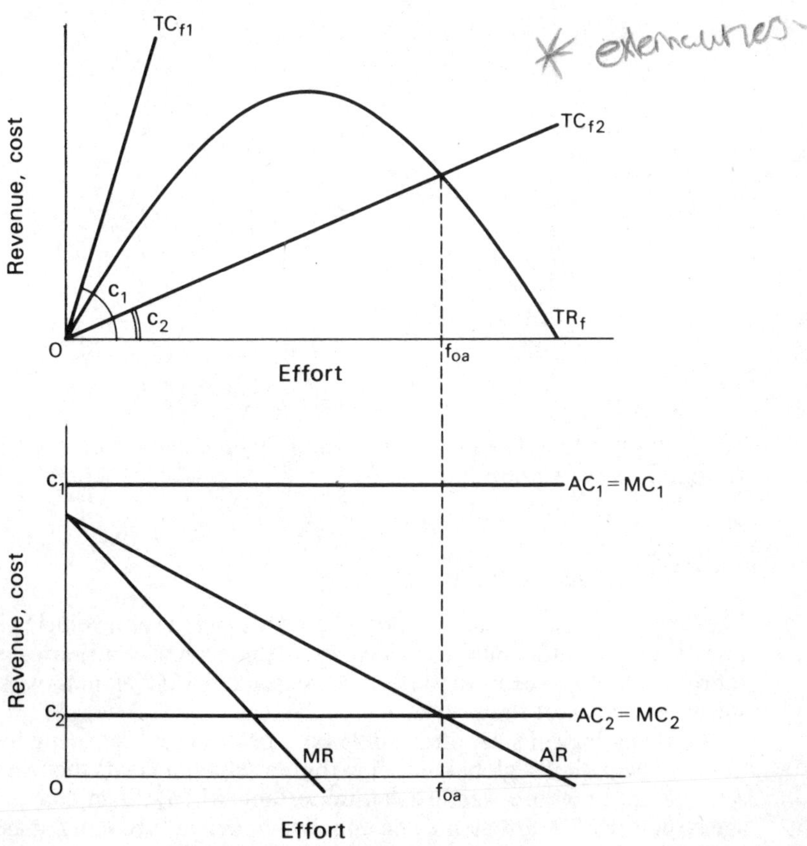

FIGURE 2.12 The open-access equilibrium.

again, for illustrative purposes, we shall assume that β is equal to 1. If the fishery faces a cost curve such as TC_{f1} then the fishery will not be exploited because, given the existing revenue structure, there is no effort level at which revenue is sufficient to cover costs. If however the cost curve were TC_{f2} then fishing would be profitable and an open-access equilibrium would be established at an effort level f_{oa}.

In itself this open-access equilibrium is stable. However there is some evidence, first that real fish prices are tending to increase over time and secondly that fishing technology is improving over time, thereby raising q, the catchability coefficient. Since we have developed our model in terms of nominal effort, both of these factors have the result of pulling the total revenue curve upwards (from say TR_{f1} to TR_{f2} in *Figure 2.13*). The effect of this change is to cause the open-access equilibrium level of effort to increase through time.

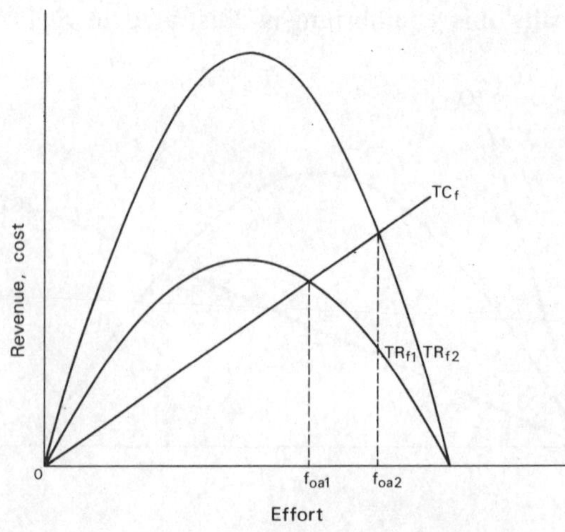

FIGURE 2.13 The effect of shifting revenue curves on the open-access equilibrium.

2.2.7 A critique of the model

The basic Gordon–Schaefer model is an extremely useful vehicle via which to explain the fundamental principles of bioeconomic fisheries analysis. Moreover it often seems to fit the facts reasonably well. Nonetheless, it does suffer a number of drawbacks.

On the biological side, the model might be criticized for being too naïve. To begin with, it is a global model in the sense that it treats the fish stock as a single entity whose weight is all-important, when in fact changes in the age structure of the stock may be equally important. Secondly, it assumes a stable marine environment, but in practice, changes in environmental parameters (such as water temperature) may have an extremely important bearing on the state of the stocks and therefore on our ability to exploit them. The recent history of the Peruvian anchovy fishery is ample evidence of this. Thirdly, the model is perhaps unrealistic in that extinction of a stock could occur only if the very last fish were caught, because for any stock size greater than zero (and less than the environmental carrying capacity), growth of the stock is positive. As we have already mentioned, there may in practice be a minimum viable population.

On the economic side, the model is essentially long-run, but problematically so for at least three reasons. First, the concept of the long run (or more accurately, its obverse the short run) is a little misleading in fisheries, where the capital tends to have a very long working life, and where various institutional factors, such as the share system of crew payment, tend to cushion the return to capital, with the consequence that the adjustment period may be very long. Secondly, concentration on the long run may have misled some fisheries economists in their management prescriptions. Thirdly, in an open-access fishery, the fishermen themselves are not concerned about the long run; they are concerned to exploit the stock as it exists at a given time (that is, they are concerned with the short run). Thus although the model, correctly, characterizes open access as a situation where long-run total revenue equals long-run total cost (or equivalently, long-run average revenue equals long-run average cost), this is only part of the story, and probably the least interesting part at that.

A second economic problem with the model as a whole is that it is couched in terms of effort (that is, an input) rather than in terms of output, which is the more usual case in economics. As an unfortunate consequence, it is somewhat difficult to analyse what happens when the fishery faces a variable price of output (that is, a downward-sloping demand curve whereby the greater the quantity of fish that this fishery attempts to place on the market, the lower is the price received).

Having made these criticisms, let us go on to consider a second model that extends the basic GS model. In fact, this new model, which we shall call the backward-bending supply curve/variable price model, is purely an economic reformulation of the old one. The basic biology remains the same.

2.3 THE BACKWARD–BENDING SUPPLY CURVE/VARIABLE PRICE MODEL

The principal advantage of this reformulation of the model is that revenue and cost are related directly to output. Let us begin by considering the cost situation of the fishery.

2.3.1 Cost: a diagrammatic presentation

We are going to use the sustainable yield curve (which relates output to effort) and the total cost of effort curve so as to find the *total* cost of producing output. We do so by using a four-quadrant diagram as in *Figure*

2.14. We draw the sustainable yield curve in quadrant 1, the total cost of effort curve in quadrant 3 and thus we may derive the total cost of output curve in quadrant 4. The curve in quadrant 2 relating effort to effort is merely a construction enabling us to 'turn the corner', so to speak.

The actual mechanics of the derivation of the total cost of output curve are straightforward. We choose some level of effort, such as f_1, in quadrant 1 and we see that this results in an output of Y_1. From quadrant 3 we may see that this amount of effort costs TC_1 and thus in quadrant 4 we know that it costs TC_1 to produce an output of Y_1. The remaining points on the total cost of output curve may be derived similarly.

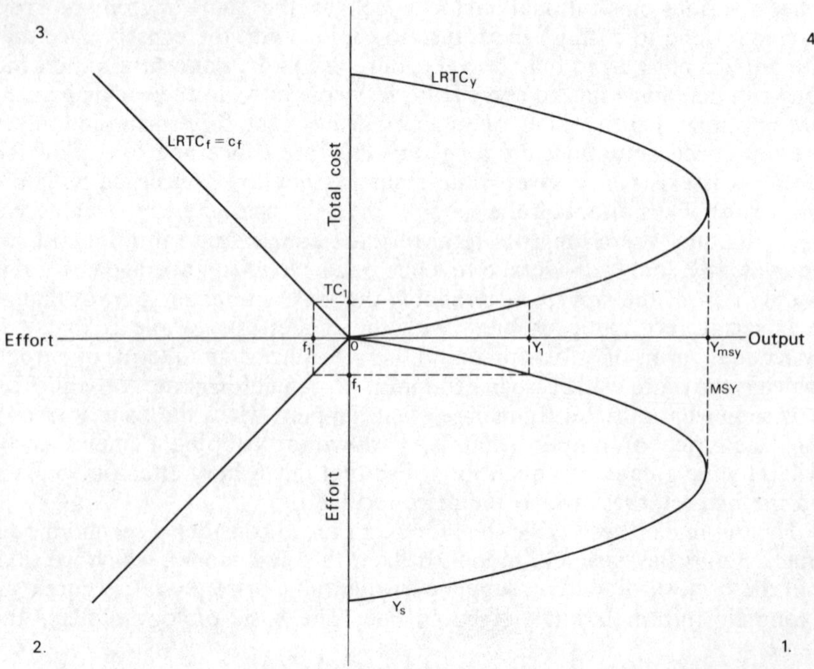

FIGURE 2.14 The derivation of the total cost of fish output curve.

Having derived the total cost of output curve, we may use it to derive the average and marginal cost curves, which are, in many ways, more useful than the total curve. The average cost of output is merely the total cost divided by the quantity produced. In other words, it is the cost per unit of output. It will be seen from quadrant 4 of *Figure 2.14* that as output increases up to maximum sustainable yield, so total cost increases *at an increasing rate*. Thus each successive unit of output produced is causing a larger increase in total cost than did the previous unit. Consequently, the cost per unit must be gradually increasing; that is, the average cost curve slopes upwards, as MSY is approached. Beyond MSY, output actually begins to fall, but total cost continues to rise, so that the average cost curve will *bend back* upon itself and begin to increase rather quickly.

The general form of the average cost curve is shown in *Figure 2.15*. The marginal cost of output shows the change in total cost resulting from a change in output. Since total cost increases at an increasing rate as output expands, marginal cost will be increasing. At the point of maximum sustainable yield, output changes from increasing to decreasing and the change in output must therefore be zero. Hence marginal cost becomes indeterminate here. For the backward-bending portion of total cost,

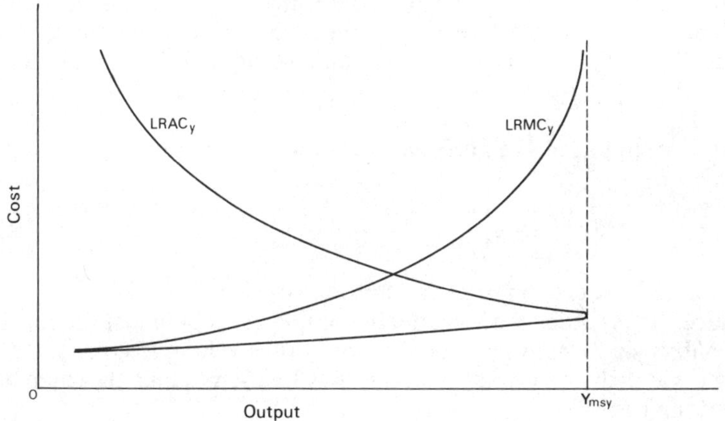

FIGURE 2.15 The long-run average and marginal cost of fish output curves.

marginal cost does not have any economic meaning. Thus in *Figure 2.15* only the marginal cost curve up to maximum sustainable yield is shown. One final point to note about these cost curves is that they are all long-run curves.

So far in this diagrammatic presentation of the cost situation we have again made the implicit assumption that $\beta = 1$. If we were to allow for diminishing returns to effort however, the total cost of output curve would come to resemble the long-run average cost curve shown in *Figure 2.15* and the already strange shape of the long-run average and marginal cost curves would be accentuated yet further.

2.3.2 Cost: an algebraic treatment

In this section we shall give formal expression to the relationships discussed intuitively in the last. We shall begin by deriving long-run total cost as a function of output. We do this simply by rearranging the sustainable yield equation, 2.14, so as to obtain an expression for effort as a function of output, and we then substitute for effort in the total cost of effort equation, 2.21.

Taking equation 2.14

$$Y_s = Kqf^{\beta}\left(1 - \frac{qf^{\beta}}{a}\right) \tag{2.14}$$

and rearranging and simplifying we obtain

$$f = \left(\frac{a}{2q} \pm \frac{a}{2q^2K}\sqrt{(qK)^2 - \frac{4q^2KY_s}{a}}\right)^{1/\beta} \tag{2.23}$$

Now that we have derived effort as a function of sustainable yield, it is an elementary task to derive the total, average and marginal costs of output. To begin with total cost, we take equation 2.21:

$$TC_f = cf \tag{2.21}$$

and substitute in for f as given in equation 2.23, so that

$$LRTC_y = c\left(\frac{a}{2q} \pm \frac{a}{2q^2K}\sqrt{(qK)^2 - \frac{4q^2KY_s}{a}}\right)^{1/\beta} \tag{2.24}$$

where $LRTC_y$ is the long-run total cost of output.

Notice that each level of sustainable output (except in fact the maximum sustainable yield) may be taken at two cost levels, reflecting, of course, the fact that high and low effort levels may be used to take the same output in the long run.

The long-run average cost of output, $LRAC_y$, is then simply total cost divided by output, giving

$$LRAC_y = \frac{c}{Y}\left(\frac{a}{2q} \pm \frac{a}{2q^2K}\sqrt{(qK)^2 - \frac{4q^2KY_s}{a}}\right)^{1/\beta} \tag{2.25}$$

Finally, let us consider the long-run marginal cost of output, $LRMC_y$ As we have already mentioned, long-run marginal cost has economic meaning only up to the point of maximum sustainable yield. It is thus relevant to the 'low' part of the total cost equation, 2.24. Differentiating this with respect to output we obtain the long-run marginal cost equation, which is

$$LRMC_y = \frac{c\left(\frac{a}{2q} - \frac{a}{2q^2K}\sqrt{(qK)^2 - \frac{4q^2KY_s}{a}}\right)^{(1/\beta)-1}}{\beta\sqrt{(qK)^2 - \frac{4q^2KY_s}{a}}} \tag{2.26}$$

2.3.3 Revenue

The introduction of revenue into the model is straightforward. We simply consider the revenue resulting from particular output levels. We have the choice either of keeping the assumption that the price of fish is constant or of allowing price to vary according to the quantity of fish available in the local market.

If we assume constant price, then total revenue is simply the output produced multiplied by this price; that is,

$$TR_y = pY \tag{2.27}$$

Average revenue (total revenue divided by output) and marginal revenue (the change in total revenue resulting from a unit change in output) will then both be equal to price; that is,

$$AR_y = TR_y/Y = p = MR_y = d(TR_y)/dY \tag{2.28}$$

If we assume a variable price of output then the price actually paid will depend upon the quantity produced. Usually it is expected that the greater is the output the lower will be the price. We shall suppose that there is some maximum price d that people would be prepared to pay for this particular fish species. The greater the output that producers wish to sell therefore, the lower will price have to be relative to this maximum. We shall assume that price declines linearly as output expands, so that we obtain the function

$$P = d - eY \tag{2.29}$$

where the values assigned to d and e will depend on the particular fishery being considered.

Now we know from equation 2.27 that in general, total revenue is simply price multiplied by quantity. However when we allow for variable price, price itself becomes a function of quantity so that substituting equation 2.29 into equation 2.27 gives a new quadratic total revenue function:

$$\begin{aligned} TR &= (d - eY)Y \\ &= dY - eY^2 \end{aligned} \tag{2.30}$$

Clearly, if we divide total revenue in equation 2.30 by output we derive equation 2.29, so that the terms 'price' and 'average revenue' are in fact synonymous.

Differentiating equation 2.30 with respect to output, we obtain marginal revenue, which is now given as

$$MR = d - 2eY \tag{2.31}$$

Comparing equations 2.31 and 2.29, it is apparent that marginal revenue will decline from d twice as fast as average revenue. Two other points may be made about the relationships developed here. First, when marginal revenue is zero, total revenue will be at a maximum. Secondly, when average revenue is zero, total revenue must also be zero. Diagrammatically we have the situation shown in *Figure 2.16*. Notice the (very misleading) similarity between *Figures 2.16b* and *2.10.* When we developed *Figure 2.10* we pointed out the problem of its similarity with the variable price situation, but the risk of confusion seems sufficient to warrant a further warning. In *Figure 2.16b* price is variable, so that the average revenue curve now is a *demand* curve. In *Figure 2.10* price is constant. Thus despite appearances, *Figure 2.10* in fact corresponds to *Figure 2.16a*.

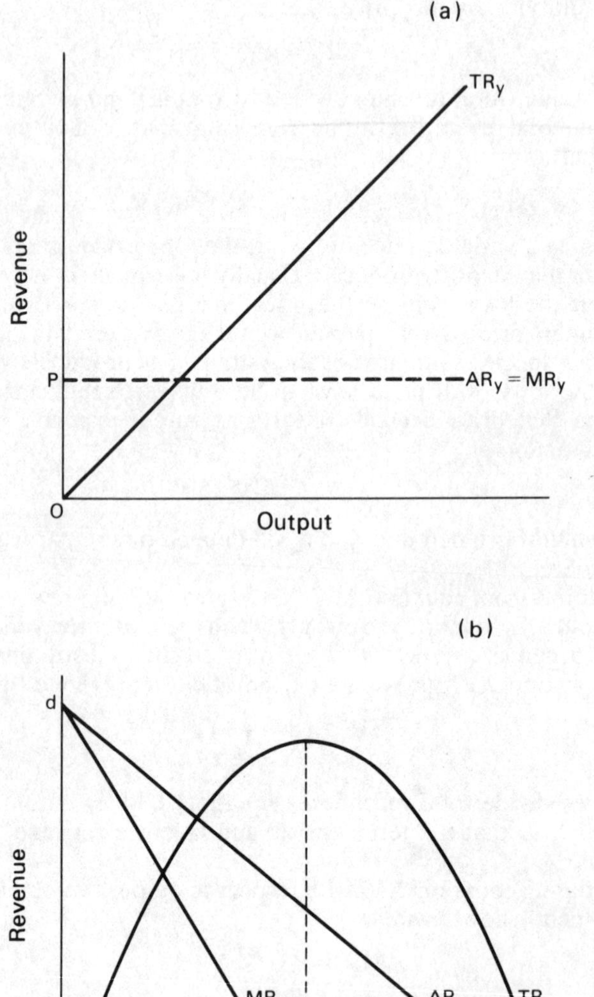

FIGURE 2.16 Revenue as a function of the output of fish.

2.3.4 Bioeconomic equilibrium

Now that we have derived the cost and revenue elements of the model, let us consider the bioeconomic equilibrium. We know that in the open-access fishery, equilibrium will occur when zero profits are earned; that is, when average cost equals average revenue. *Figure 2.17* depicts this equilibrium for both the constant and variable price cases. Open-access equilibrium occurs at an output Y_{oa} with an effort level f_{oa}. At lower effort levels such as f_2, supernormal profits will be earned, encouraging increases in effort, while at greater effort levels such as f_1, subnormal profits will cause decreased effort. To illustrate this, we have included in *Figure 2.17* quadrant 1 of our four-quadrant diagram (*Figure 2.14*) rather than simply concentrating on quadrant 4, which is what we shall usually do from now on.

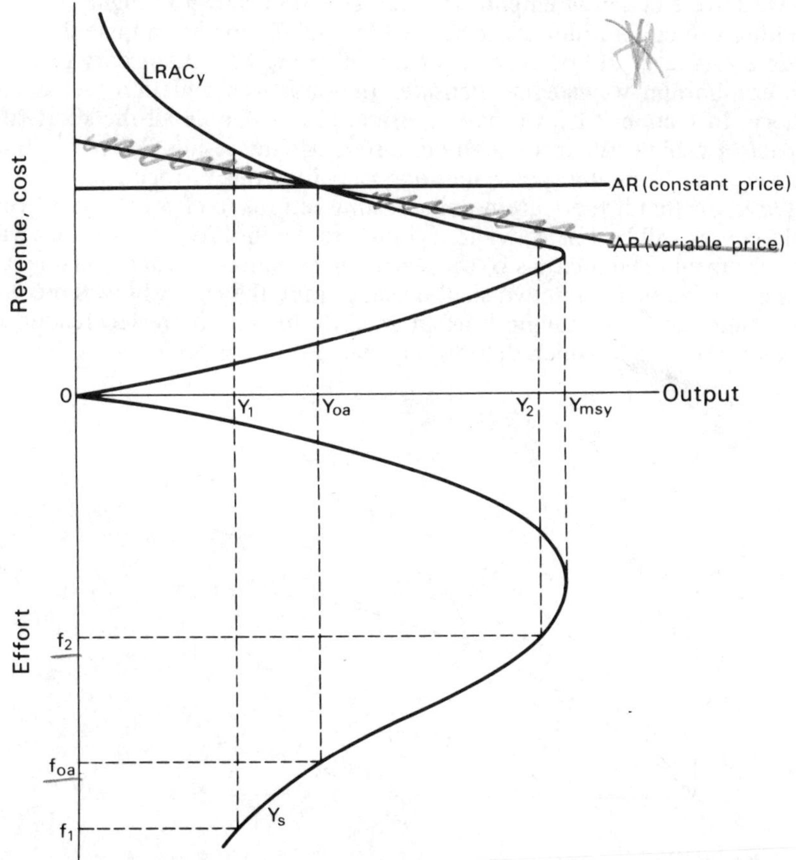

FIGURE 2.17 The open-access equilibrium reconsidered.

From *Figure 2.17* we see that there are two possible LRACs for each output level (save MSY) and two effort levels also. The high costs are associated, of course, with greater effort. Thus the output Y_{oa} being produced at the higher of the two costs must involve an effort level f_{oa}.

An increase in effort to f_1 results in a long-run decrease in yield to Y_1 and an increase in average cost, giving rise to subnormal profits, which drive the fishery back to Y_{oa}. A decrease in effort to f_2 increases yield in the long run to Y_2 and decreases average cost, resulting in supernormal profits, which drive the fishery back to Y_{oa}. Thus although effort is not explicitly mentioned in quadrant 4, we may characterize effort changes as movements along the average cost curve: an increase in effort is shown as a movement up the curve and a decrease, a movement down (in the long run).

2.3.5 The short-run situation

As we have frequently emphasized, the situation shown in *Figure 2.17* is the long-run equilibrium attained once the population has adjusted to the given effort level. If however we wish to discover how the fishery reaches this equilibrium we need to consider the short-run situation facing the fishery. In section 2.1.2 we have considered in some detail the short-run impact of fishing. What we shall do here is use the results derived in that section to see how the short- and long-run situations fit together.

We know that if there are no diminishing returns to effort the short-run yield curves will be linear, while if there are diminishing returns they will be non-linear. The analysis of the short-run situation is exactly analogous in the two cases, so here we shall consider only the case where there *are* diminishing returns, leaving it as an exercise for the interested reader to develop the case in which diminishing returns do not occur.

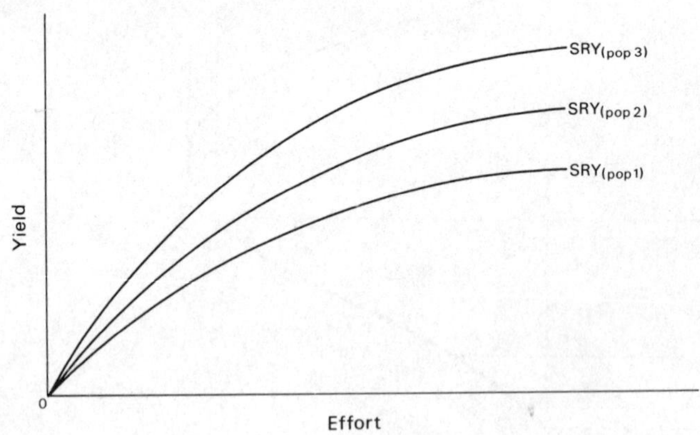

FIGURE 2.18 Short-run yield curves as a function of nominal effort.

We have then a family of short-run yield curves, each defined for a particular population size. These are shown in *Figure 2.18*. The greater is the population, the greater will be the yield resulting from a given level of effort. Thus, population 3 must exceed population 2, which exceeds population 1. Now, we may use these short-run yield curves to derive short-run total cost curves in precisely the same way in which we used the sustainable yield function to derive our long-run functions. If we continue to assume that the cost of providing effort increases linearly, then it may be verified that we obtain short-run total cost curves as in *Figure 2.19*. Our ranking of populations is now reversed, in the sense that the *smaller* is the population, the *more* must it cost to achieve any given yield.

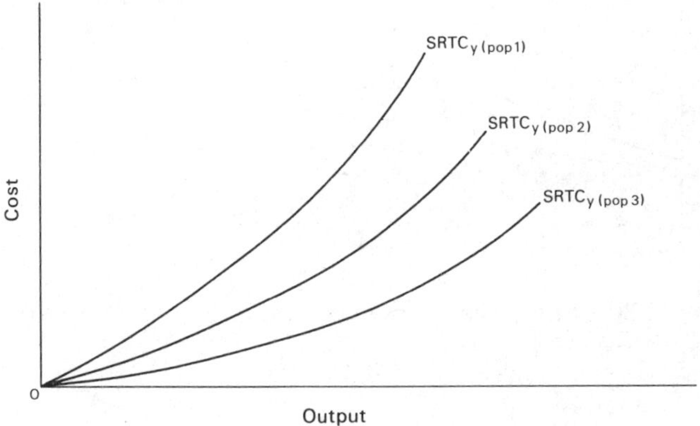

FIGURE 2.19 Short-run total cost as a function of fish output.

It is arguable that, in the short run, effort could be increased only at increasing marginal cost (because, for instance, existing boats were working much longer hours, or less suitable boats were being attracted from other fisheries). In this case, the total cost of *effort* function would be curved upwards rather than being linear. The effect of this however would be merely to make the short-run total cost of output curves rise even faster. For this reason we shall ignore this complication here.

Since our short-run total cost of output curve increases at an increasing rate from the beginning, both the short-run average and marginal cost curves must do likewise. Moreover they are divergent, and the marginal is above the average curve (*Figure 2.20*). The reasoning underlying this is simple. If the average is increasing then the addition to the total (i.e. the marginal) must have been greater than the previous average. The divergence of the average and marginal curves is entirely due to the assumption of diminishing returns to effort. As we shall see in a moment from the algebra of the situation, if there are no diminishing returns then the average and marginal curves will coincide.

Each set of short-run cost curves is defined for one population level only. Thus a change in the population size will shift the fishery to a new set of curves. A fall in the population will result in an upward shift of the curves while an increase will shift them downwards (that is, the greater is the population, the cheaper will it be to take any given output of fish). Consequently, only if the output produced in a period represents a

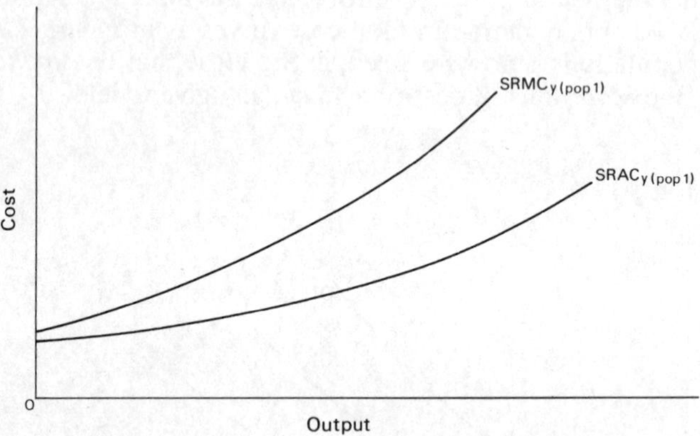

FIGURE 2.20 Short-run average and marginal cost of fish output curves.

sustainable yield will the cost curves continue to be relevant for the next period. On each short-run average cost curve therefore there will be only one point (that corresponding to sustainable yield) that could continue into the long run. The long-run average cost curve is then the locus of all such points. (Note that the same relationship does *not* exist between long- and short-run marginal cost curves.)

Let us now derive the equations underlying the curves. Once again we wish to derive cost curves in terms of output rather than in terms of effort. As we have already mentioned, the short-run yield is given by equation 2.10; that is,

$$Y = qf^{\beta} P \tag{2.10}$$

which on rearranging becomes

$$f = \left(\frac{Y}{qP}\right)^{1/\beta} \tag{2.32}$$

The short-run total cost of effort equation is, by assumption, the same as the long-run equation, 2.21; that is,

$$TC_f = cf \tag{2.21}$$

Thus combining equations 2.32 and 2.21, we obtain the short-run total cost of output ($SRTC_y$) equation, which is

$$SRTC_y = c\left(\frac{Y}{qP}\right)^{1/\beta} \tag{2.33}$$

Short-run average cost of output, $SRAC_y$, is then easily derived:

$$SRAC_y = \frac{c}{Y}\left(\frac{Y}{qP}\right)^{1/\beta} \tag{2.34}$$

Finally, if we differentiate equation 2.33 with respect to output we obtain the equation for short-run marginal cost, $SRMC_y$. This is

$$SRMC_y = \frac{c}{\beta qP}\left(\frac{Y}{qP}\right)^{(1/\beta)-1} \tag{2.35}$$

Notice that in the special case of β equal to 1, $SRAC_y$ and $SRMC_y$ will both equal c/qP and thus they will not depend on the output level. They will still however depend on the population size; as population falls, the curves will shift upwards, and as population rises, they will shift downwards. If β does not equal 1, then the two curves will diverge as in *Figure 2.20*.

2.3.6 The approach to equilibrium

Let us now consider the way in which the short-run and long-run elements of the model combine to move the fishery to a long-run equilibrium. In *Figure 2.21* the fishery faces an average revenue curve AR and a long-run average cost curve $LRAC_y$. We shall suppose that the population size is

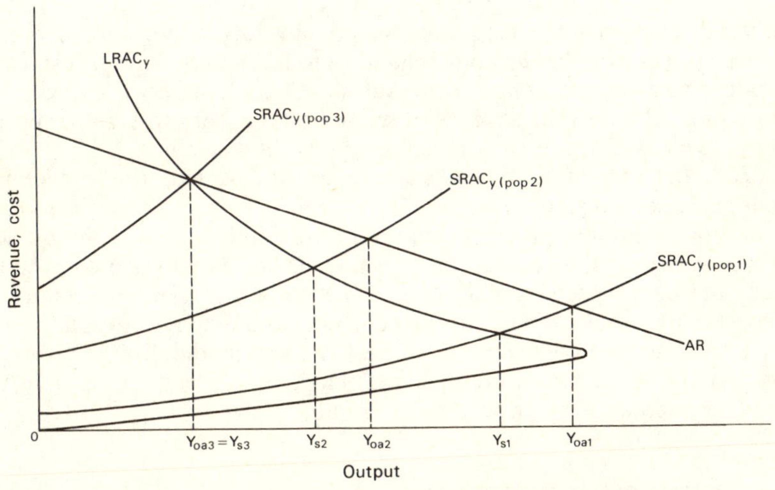

FIGURE 2.21 The derivation of the complete open-access equilibrium.

initially such that $SRAC_{y(pop.1)}$ is the relevant short-run average cost curve. Given our demand curve (AR), it will pay fishermen to increase output up to output Y_{oa1} (that is, where $SRAC_{y(pop.1)}$ equals AR). At any smaller output, average revenue exceeds short-run average cost so that fishermen will be encouraged to fish harder to increase output; while higher outputs involve subnormal profits which would tend to discourage fishing.

However, output Y_{oa1} does not correspond to a sustainable yield. Given the population size, sustainable output would be shown by the intersection of short- and long-run average cost; that is, output Y_{s1}. Since the output actually being taken exceeds sustainable yield, the population will fall, shifting the short-run average cost curve upwards. In the next period, we might have a short-run cost curve $SRAC_{y(pop.2)}$, which would give rise to an output Y_{oa2}. Although the output being taken has fallen, so has the sustainable yield (to Y_{s2}), so that once again population falls. Eventually (and in practice it may take many periods to achieve), short-run cost curve $SRAC_{y(pop.3)}$ will be established. This gives rise to an output Y_{oa3} which is not only a short-run equilibrium but also sustainable (Y_{s3}). This situation will therefore be maintained into the long run.

Thus an open-access fishery will be characterized by the fact that short-run average cost will be equal to average revenue. Its long-run equilibrium situation will have these two also equal to long-run average cost; that is,

$$AR = SRAC_y = LRAC_y$$

It is thus something of a simplification to argue that under open access LRAC equals AR.

2.4 SUMMARY

In this chapter we have been concerned to develop a bioeconomic model of a fishery. The simple Gordon–Schaefer model shows that a fish stock will produce a surplus each year that is sustainable indefinitely if a catch of this amount is taken. In the absence of regulation a fishery will end up producing at the point where total revenue equals total cost.

From the economic viewpoint, one drawback with this model is its assumption of constant fish price. We therefore reformulated the model to allow for a variable price of output. To this end we recast the model in terms of fish output rather than fishing effort. Finally we showed that complete open-access equilibrium, in the long run, involves equality between both long- and short-run average cost and average revenue.

In the following two chapters we shall use this model, first to investigate the problem of technical progress in fishing, and secondly to establish the need for, and aims of, fishery management.

2.5 BIBLIOGRAPHIC NOTES

The basic Gordon–Schaefer model is established in works by Gordon

(1953, 1954) and Schaefer (1954, 1957a, b, 1959). *See also* however Graham (1935, 1952). Good expositions of the biological side of the model (and its variations) are to be found in works by Gulland (1974, Ch. 4), Hannesson (1978, Ch. 7) and Pitcher and Hart (1982, Ch. 7). Interesting developments of the basic surplus yield model are those of Fox (1970), Horwood (1976), Pella and Tomlinson (1969), Schnute (1977, 1979) and Silliman (1971).

The more complex, so-called dynamic pool, model that considers individual year classes of fish rather than simply biomass was put forward by Beverton and Holt (1957), and there are good expositions by Hannesson (1978, Ch. 8) and Pitcher and Hart (1982, Ch. 8). The dynamics of the model are discussed by Clark, Edwards and Friedlander (1973).

Models containing a minimum viable population (critical depensation) are discussed by Clark (1976, Ch. 1). The relationship between schooling and depensation is considered by Clark (1974).

The definition and measurement of fishing effort is extremely difficult. For interesting discussions *see* Rothschild (1972, 1977), Pope (1982), and Hildebrandt (1975) and the papers following it.

There have been close examinations of the problem of uncertainty and random fluctuations in fish stock size. *See*, for instance, Beddington and May (1977), Lewis (1980), Ludwig (1980), May *et al.* (1978), Mendelssohn (1979) and Sissenwine (1977).

The backward-bending supply curve model seems to have been used first by Turvey (1957) and developed by Crutchfield and Zellner (1962) and Copes (1970). Anderson (1973) adds the downward-sloping demand curve to the model and compares this to the more traditional Gordon–Schaefer model.

Hannesson (1983) considers the bioeconomic production function under a variety of cost and demand conditions. Anderson (1982) considers specifically the problem of increasing effort cost.

REFERENCES AND FURTHER READING

ANDERSON, L. (1973). 'Optimum economic yield of a fishery given a variable price of output.' *Journal of the Fisheries Research Board of Canada* **30** : 509–18.

ANDERSON, L. (1982). 'Optimal utilization of fisheries with increasing costs of effort.' *Canadian Journal of Fisheries and Aquatic Sciences* **39** : 211–14.

BEDDINGTON, J. and R. MAY (1977). 'Harvesting natural populations in a randomly fluctuating environment.' *Science* **197** : 463–5.

BEVERTON, R. and S. HOLT (1957). *On the dynamics of exploited fish populations*. London: HMSO.

BROCK, V. and R. RIFFENBURGH (1963). 'Fish schooling: a possible factor in reducing predation.' *Journal du Conseil International pour l'Exploration de la Mer* **25** : 307–17.

CLARK, C. (1974). 'Possible effects of schooling on the dynamics of exploited fish populations.' *Journal du Conseil International pour l'Exploration de la Mer* **36** : 7–14.

CLARK, C. (1976). *Mathematical bioeconomics: the optimal management of renewable resources.* New York: Wiley Interscience.

CLARK, C., G. EDWARDS and M. FRIEDLANDER (1973). 'Beverton–Holt model of a commercial fishery: optimal dynamics.' *Journal of the Fisheries Research Board of Canada* **30** : 1629–40.

COPES, P. (1970). 'The backward-bending supply curve of the fishing industry.' *Scottish Journal of Poltical Economy* **17** : 69–77.

CRUTCHFIELD, J. A. and A. ZELLNER (1962). 'Economic aspects of the Pacific halibut fishery.' *Fishery Industrial Research* **1** : 1–173.

FOX, W., Jr (1970). 'An exponential surplus yield model for optimizing exploited fish populations.' *Transactions of the American Fisheries Society* **99** : 80–8.

GORDON, H. (1953). 'An economic approach to the optimum utilization of fishery resources.' *Journal of the Fisheries Research Board of Canada* **10** : 442–57.

GORDON, H. (1954). 'The economic theory of a common property resource: the fishery.' *Journal of Political Economy* **62** : 124–42.

GRAHAM, M. (1935). 'Modern theory of exploiting a fishery and application to North Sea trawling.' *Journal du Conseil International pour l'Exploration de la Mer* **10** : 264–74.

GRAHAM, M. (1952). 'Overfishing and optimum fishing.' *Rapports et Procès-verbaux des Réunions du Conseil International pour l'Exploration de la Mer* **132** : 72–8.

GULLAND, J. (1974). *The management of marine fisheries.* Bristol: Scientechnica.

HANNESSON, R. (1978). *Economics of fisheries.* Bergen: Universitetsforlaget.

HANNESSON, R. (1983). 'Bioeconomic production function in fisheries: theoretical and empirical analysis.' *Canadian Journal of Fisheries and Aquatic Sciences* **40** : 968–82.

HILDEBRANDT, A. (1975). 'A fishery economist's problems with fishing effort.' *Rapports et Procès-verbaux des Réunions du Conseil International pour l'Exploration de la Mer* **168** : 64–6.

HORWOOD, J. (1976). 'Interactive fisheries: a two species Schaefer model.' *International Commission for Northwest Atlantic Fisheries, Selected Papers* **1** : 151–5.

LEWIS, T. (1980). *Optimal resource management under conditions of uncertainty: the case of an ocean fishery.* Seattle: University of Washington Press.

LUDWIG, D. (1980). 'Harvesting strategies for a randomly fluctuating population.' *Journal du Conseil International pour l'Exploration de la Mer* **39** : 168–74.

MAY, R., J. BEDDINGTON, J. HORWOOD and J. SHEPHERD (1978). 'Exploiting natural populations in an uncertain world.' *Mathematical Biosciences* **42** : 219–52.

MENDELSSOHN, R. (1979). 'Determining the best trade-off between expected economic return and the risk of undesirable events when managing a randomly varying population.' *Journal of the Fisheries Research Board of Canada* **36** : 939–47.

PELLA, J. and P. TOMLINSON (1969). 'A generalized stock production model.' *Inter American Tropical Tuna Commission Bulletin* **13** : 421–58.

PITCHER, T. and P. HART (1982). *Fisheries ecology*. London: Croom Helm.

POPE, J. (1982). 'Background to scientific advice on fisheries management.' *MAFF Laboratory Leaflet* no. 54.

RADOVICH, J. and A. MACCALL (1979). 'A management model for the central stock of the northern anchovy.' *CAL Cofi Reports* **20** : 83–8.

ROTHSCHILD, B. (1972). 'An exposition on the definition of fishing effort.' *Fishery Bulletin* **70** : 671–80.

ROTHSCHILD, B. (1977). 'Fishing effort.' In J. Gulland (Ed.), *Fish population dynamics,* Chapter 5. London: Wiley Interscience.

SCHAEFER, M. (1954). 'Some aspects of the dynamics of population important to the management of the commercial marine fisheries.' *Inter American Tropical Tuna Commission Bulletin* **1** : 27–56.

SCHAEFER, M. (1957a). 'A study of the dynamics of the fishery for yellowfin tuna in the eastern tropical Pacific Ocean.' *Inter American Tropical Tuna Commission Bulletin* **2** : 247–85.

SCHAEFER, M. (1957b). 'Some considerations of population dynamics and economics in relation to the management of commercial marine fisheries.' *Journal of the Fisheries Research Board of Canada* **14** : 669–81.

SCHAEFER, M. (1959). 'Biological and economic aspects of the management of commercial marine fisheries.' *Transactions of the American Fisheries Society* **88** : 100–4.

SCHNUTE, J. (1977). 'Improved estimates from the Schaefer production model: theoretical considerations.' *Journal of the Fisheries Research Board of Canada* **34** : 583–603.

SCHNUTE, J. (1979). 'A revised Schaefer model.' *Investigacion Pesquera* **43** : 31–40.

SILLIMAN, R. (1971). 'Advantages and limitations of "simple" fishery models in light of laboratory experiments.' *Journal of the Fisheries Research Board of Canada* **28** : 1211–14.

SISSENWINE, M. (1977). 'The effect of random fluctuations on a hypothetical fishery.' *International Commission for Northwest Atlantic Fisheries, Selected Papers* **2** : 137–144.

TURVEY, R. (1957). 'Introduction.' In R. Turvey and J. Wiseman (Eds), *The economics of fisheries*. Rome: FAO.

CHAPTER 3

Technical progress: a positive application of the model

3.1 INTRODUCTION

The purpose of this chapter is to show how bioeconomic theory can provide an analytical framework for the phenomenon of technological change in fishing. After reviewing the empirical evidence we consider how technological change can be incorporated into the bioeconomic model developed in Chapter 2. The relevance of the model is then discussed.

The term 'positive' in the title of this chapter is used in contradistinction to the term 'normative' used in the next. Economists define positive propositions as those concerned with matters of fact, while normative propositions are those that depend upon the value judgements of the proponents. In the present context the aim is not to say whether technological change in fishing is in any sense 'good' or 'bad' but simply to analyse it as a phenomenon in its own right. The question of what ought to be done about technological change is a normative issue and one that is touched on elsewhere in the book.

3.2 THE EXPERIENCE OF TECHNOLOGICAL CHANGE

3.2.1 The creation and diffusion of new technology

The technology of fish harvesting has been continuously evolving and this evolution has been especially conspicuous since 1945. Over the past forty years there has been a tendency in many areas for fishing to become more capital-intensive. Of greater importance is that the technology itself has become more sophisticated, as reflected in the large number of innovations that have been made available to fishing firms, innovations affecting vessel construction and propulsion, gear handling, capture techniques and materials, navigation, communication and fish detection.

Manufacturing industry has played a major part in the creation of this new technology. A list of some of the more important manufactured items would include hydraulic transmission systems, synthetic ropes and nets, radio and radar equipment, marine autopilots, echo sounding and sonar devices, and fibreglass and ferrocement hulls. However, fishing industries themselves, or public bodies associated with them (such as the Sea Fish Industry Authority in the United Kingdom), have been responsible for some innovations, mostly those concerned with improvements in the technique of fishing, or attempts to find the optimum combination of gear, equipment and operating procedure. Stern trawling, a method by which the trawl is shot from the stern as opposed to the side of a vessel, is one of the more important concepts to be brought into use. The first stern trawler, the *Fairtry*, was developed by a British firm and went into service in 1954.

One of the outstanding innovations of the post-1945 period originated from the fishing and manufacturing sectors jointly. This is the Puretic power block, a hydraulically powered V-shaped pulley through which large nets can be hauled from the water. Invented by an American fisherman, Mario Puretic, the power block was developed by the Marine Construction and Design Co. of Seattle, which initially produced a unit for the salmon purse seine fleet of the Pacific north-west, and subsequently for many other fisheries.

As fishing firms have adopted innovations, so new technology has diffused throughout the industry. The diffusion of fish-catching innovations often appears to be a slow process, a fact that has led a number of commentators to criticize the industry for failing to take full advantage of best-practice production techniques. Miller and Norton (1967) claim that the reason why the number of U.S. fishermen declined during the 1950s and early 1960s was the lag in adopting fish harvesting technology. Their view is endorsed by Spangler (1970), who also claims that the United States has lost technological leadership to other fishing nations, notably the Soviet Union. To take another example, the British fishing industry has been severely criticized by Tunstall (1968), who has dubbed it 'Britain's most antiquated industry' (p. 1), adding that the industry's leaders have been 'excessively slow to follow others' leads' and have 'an extreme reverence for the past' (p. 11). Unfortunately these opinions give a somewhat misleading impression of the changes that have taken place in world fishing as a whole. Economists have long accepted that 'gaps' in technology exist in all industries in the sense that there will always be a productivity difference between average and best-practice techniques of production. Fishing is no exception. It is not difficult to find some firms whose capital stock is not of the most modern vintage; and, by extension, some countries will tend to lag behind others in the introduction of more modern productive capacity. Indeed, the whole question of 'backwardness' is essentially relative. As Scott (1962) has pointed out, the reason why some fishermen appear to be unprogressive with respect to technology is precisely because others are very progressive. This disparity then tends to colour one's impression of the industry as a whole.

While it is clear to all observers that most fishing firms do not respond immediately to the opportunities offered by science and technology, the important point to appreciate is that they do respond eventually. In the case of the British fishing industry, for example, it has been shown that a lag of at least ten years between the time when an innovation is made available to when the majority of the fleet start to use it is not untypical (Whitmarsh, 1977). However, the passage of time eventually witnesses the complete penetration of new technology into those sections of the fleet where it can be used to advantage. We have also to realize that where fishing firms have been confronted with a fairly large number of innovations from which to choose, then it may be impractical as well as irrational to adopt all at once. The greater the number of innovations, the lower is the probability that any one of them will be adopted by all firms simultaneously. In such a situation therefore, we should hardly expect the diffusion of any single innovation to be rapid. Now, the characteristic of Western fisheries since the Second World War is precisely that firms have been faced with a large 'menu' of innovations from which to choose. In the United Kingdom, it is possible to identify at least twenty which, by common consent, can be regarded as important. That it has generally taken several years for many of these to be fully adopted understates the totality of change. Reinforcing this argument is the fact that the innovations which have the greatest influence on firms' unit costs tend to be adopted preferentially, with the result that the technological developments which cause a substantial rise in the industry's efficiency are introduced *relatively* quickly. A clear illustration is the case of the Puretic power block. Though initially produced for a local salmon fleet, its very great potential was perceived by other fishermen throughout the United States and in other countries. Within twelve years over 7000 power blocks had been installed on fishing vessels throughout the world (Loftas, 1974), and in some areas its adoption was especially rapid. In the Norwegian purse seine herring fishery, for example, it was recognized as having such a major effect on profitability that it took only six years for it to be adopted by the entire fleet (Mietle, 1969).*

*The reader may wonder why we have made no attempt in this section at quantifying the overall rate of technical progress in fishing. The reason is as follows. The classic method used by economists to measure the rate of technical progress in the economy or in any of its component parts is to measure the trend in output per unit of labour and capital (i.e. productivity) over a period of time. Technical progress is thus quantified in terms of the effects that it has on the production system; a high growth in productivity signifies a rapid rate of technical progress, and vice versa. In fishing however, this approach is unreliable because productivity depends upon the natural resource as well as the quantity and quality of man-made inputs. Moreover, the natural resource is itself affected by the technology of fishing in a systematic way. Section 3.3 explains the interrelationship.

3.2.2 Impact

Many of the advances in marine science and technology that have been made available to the fishing industry are capable of bringing about substantial improvements in catch rates and profitability for those *individual* firms or vessels that take advantage of them. An OECD survey of marine electronics has testified to the very great importance of modern navigational, fish-finding and communication aids to fishing (OECD, 1967). In the field of capture techniques, stern trawling stands out as a major development whose productivity-raising effects, when compared with the conventional method of side trawling, have been estimated as approximately 29% for a sample of U.S. vessels (Bell, 1966) and as high as 40% for a sample of British vessels (Whitmarsh, 1978). The combined use of sonar, purse seining and hydraulic power blocks has proved spectacularly productive when used in pelagic fisheries. The echo-ranging sonar allows a shoal to be detected; the fish are encircled in the purse seine, a net that can extend to a depth of several hundred feet; and the entire net is then hauled up with the aid of the power block until it is sufficiently close to the vessel to allow the contents to be pumped aboard.

The superiority of modern fishing methods is well illustrated by a study of herring boats fishing the Minches from the late 1960s to the early 1970s (MacSween, 1973). The data for the years 1971–73 showed that the average purse seiner had a fishing power of seven and a half times that of the average drift netter. Now, it is true that purse seiners are generally larger than drift netters in terms of physical capacity and labour requirements, and so would be expected to achieve higher catch rates. But even allowing for the size difference it seems likely that the physical productivity of the newer technology is higher than that of the old. Using data supplied by the Department of Agriculture and Fisheries for Scotland for 1974, we have estimated that Scottish purse seiners had an average gross tonnage approximately two and a half times that of Scottish drifters, and the average crew number was approximately double. If the Minches study can be taken as a reasonable indication of the performance differential between these two vessel types, then it would seem that purse seiners still manage to achieve higher productivity even when allowance is made for their greater size.

When one is considering the aggregate effects of technological change however, the evidence seems ambiguous and contradictory. On the one hand it has been claimed that the increase in the total world catch of fish from an estimated 2 million tons a year in the mid nineteenth century to approximately 75 million tons a year in the early 1980s was made possible by the use of mechanical power and electronic aids to harvesting, processing and distribution (Eddie, 1980). Certainly in the United Kingdom's case there is little doubt that technological developments, notably steam power and trawling, were important contributory factors in the rise in productivity that occurred over the two decades up to 1914, during which period output doubled while the total number of vessels fell. And yet when we look more closely at the impact of new technology, especially in recent times, it appears that productivity does not always rise *pari passu* with increases in technical efficiency. An OECD survey of international fisheries in the mid 1960s estimated that over the period 1957–65 the harvesting capacity of the fleet in the North Atlantic rose by 40% compared with an increase in catch of 20% (OECD, 1966). The greater capacity was a consequence not just of an increase in the gross tonnage of the fleet but also of an improvement in the technical efficiency of vessels. The same survey also demonstrated an inverse relationship between aggregate fishing power and catch rates: in the North Atlantic the former had risen while the latter had declined. Similarly, the aggregate effect of technological change on profitability is often disappointing. In the British fishing industry between the world wars, firms made a number of improvements to gear and equipment. Kelsall (1948, p. 169) has argued however that 'though . . . there had been technical progress in many different ways, fishing was nevertheless less profitable than it had been before the new devices were introduced'.

Studies of individual fisheries likewise yield ambiguous results. The Peruvian anchoveta fishery, one of the most important sources of world protein, owed its initial development after the Second World War in large part to modern methods of fish capture (notably power block purse seining) and the use of synthetic nets. It has been shown however that throughout the 1960s, catch rates underwent a secular decline despite a statistically significant time trend of technological advance (Segura, 1973). Perhaps the most dramatic illustration of a case where improved technology has been accompanied by a reversal in economic performance is that of the herring fisheries of the North Sea and Scandinavia. Mietle (1969) describes how the introduction of the power block into the Norwegian purse seine fleet in the early 1960s marked an explosive development in the herring fishery. Subsequently however, catch rates and profitability both fell, and by 1968/9 the natural resource could no longer support the same number of vessels. A similar fate befell British vessels, except that here the demise came a few years later. The greater fishing power of vessels exploiting the Shetland and Minch herring fisheries resulted in higher catches in the late 1960s, but this increase was short-lived. A fall in catch rates and absolute landings occurred thereafter, despite the introduction of still more sophisticated gear and equipment. Finally, mention should be made of the Antarctic baleen whale, catches of which underwent a dramatic fall from 1937. Catches recovered after the Second World War but the early 1960s saw another sharp decline. An indication of the way in which the overall situation has changed is the fact that whereas in the early 1930s the total Antarctic pelagic catch of baleen whales at one time reached 30 000 BWU (blue whale units), in 1981 the stocks were so depleted that a moratorium had been imposed on pelagic whaling for all species other than minke whales. Again, this fall in the catch level took place in spite of major developments in whaling technology, both on the catching and the processing side (McHugh, 1977; Clark and Lamberson, 1982).

Though a cause-and-effect relationship cannot be shown conclusively, the evidence accords with the suggestion that technological change in fishing is a 'two-edged sword' (Bell, 1978, p. 371). That is to say, it may have a propitious or a deleterious effect on economic performance, depending on the circumstances, for reasons that should become apparent after the next section.

3.3 BIOECONOMIC THEORY AND TECHNOLOGICAL CHANGE

In this section we use the bioeconomic model developed in Chapter 2 to analyse the long-run effects of technological change. Accordingly, the basis of our analysis is the long-run production function and its associated cost curves. By largely ignoring the short-run analysis we are, of course, disregarding the approach path by which the long-run equilibrium is reached. This emphasis on the long-run situation is justified on the grounds that the diffusion of innovations is a fairly gradual process, and so it is unrealistic to think of technological change as occurring erratically. Were this not the case, then the neglect of the short-run analysis would be a serious omission, as Chapter 4 makes clear.

Technological change can be incorporated into the Gordon–Schaefer model by way of changes in the *catchability coefficient*, q. This approach is appropriate provided that we also define nominal fishing effort, f, in terms of an index of all factor inputs. The significance of this proviso will become clear in due course.

We shall consider the general case which allows for diminishing returns to effort, but restrict ourselves by assuming the absence of diminishing returns to population. The effects of relaxing this assumption will be considered later. The relevant short-run yield function is given by equation 2.10 in the previous chapter, viz.

$$Y = qf^{\beta} P$$

On our definition this shows that, if nominal fishing effort and fish population are constant, technological change (higher values of q) will result in higher yields. We know however that fishing causes biological adjustments to the fish population, and that the long-run situation is more complex. The relevant long-run production function is

$$Y = Kqf^{\beta}\left(1 - \frac{qf^{\beta}}{a}\right)$$

This is identical to equation 2.14.

The effect of increasing q is represented by *Figure 3.1*. The shape of the curves as drawn implies that there are no diminishing returns to effort; that is, $\beta = 1.0$. The presence or otherwise of diminishing returns does not affect the main point we are making, however, which is that increases in q shift the sustainable yield curve to the left. The simple reason for this is that technological change enables any given quantity of fish to be caught with fewer factor inputs. The shift in the curve gives us our first insight into why technological change may be a mixed blessing, because it is clear that at some points on the f axis, higher values of q imply *lower* catches. In other words, whether output goes up or goes down as a result of technological change depends on the level of exploitation of the fish stock.

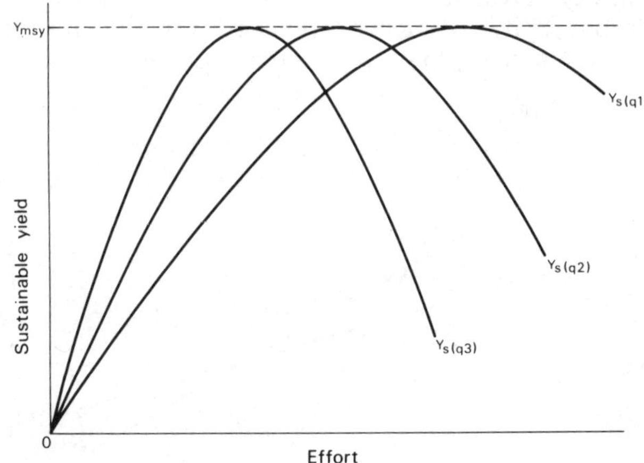

FIGURE 3.1 The effect of increases in the catchability coefficient on the sustainable yield curve.

The ambiguous nature of technological change can also be shown by deriving a function that relates *productivity* to technical efficiency. Economists are interested in productivity because it is a crucial determinant of other aspects of industrial performance, notably costs and prices, and ultimately the competitiveness of fishing vis-à-vis other food-producing sectors. Productivity is simply output per unit of input, and since input is just another term for nominal fishing effort, then productivity is measured as Y/f. Biologists will recognize this as catch per unit of effort (CPUE), though because of the way we have defined f, the ratio has rather a special meaning. Here, nominal fishing effort refers not simply to one particular input such as fishing time or number of vessels, but to all inputs used to exploit the fishery. Accordingly, Y/f must be conceived of as the ratio of output to total input. It is an example of what economists refer to as *total factor productivity*. The derivation of Y/f is straightforward: we divide the long-run production function (equation 2.14) through by f, giving

$$Y/f = Kqf^{\beta-1}\left(1 - \frac{qf^{\beta}}{a}\right)$$

We can appreciate the effects of technological change by seeing how different values of q affect the relationship between Y/f and f, as illustrated in *Figure 3.2*.

The assumption that $\beta = 1.0$ implies that the functions will be linear. Again however, the shape of the curves does not affect the essential point we are making, which is that increases in q alter the steepness of the curve. The result may come as a surprise to those economists who are brought up in the conventional wisdom that the effect of technological change is to raise productivity. It will be seen that at low levels of f, greater catchability does raise productivity. At higher levels however, the effect is reversed: increases in q may actually lower productivity. Let us just remind ourselves

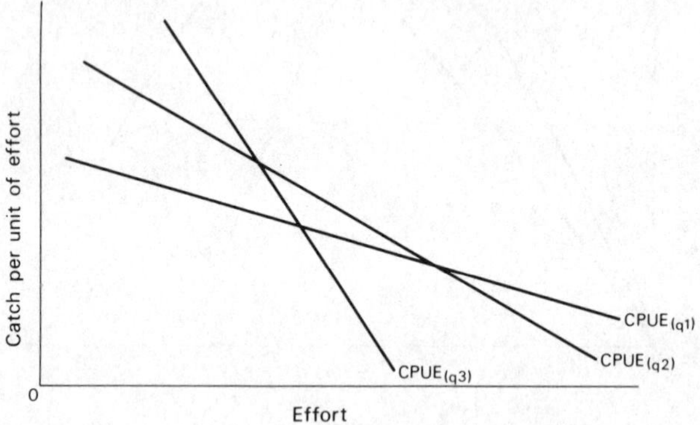

FIGURE 3.2 The effect of increases in the catchability coefficient on the CPUE curve.

why this paradoxical result occurs. Greater catchability implies, other things being equal, that effective fishing effort (F, defined in Chapter 2) increases. The result is that a higher proportion of the population is being extracted by fishing, which in turn causes the population to fall. Technological change thus sets up two opposing forces: in itself it will (by definition) raise the intrinsic productivity of the factors of production, but the concurrent depletion of the fish stock has the reverse effect. However, effective fishing effort is also determined by the volume of resources devoted to fishing (i.e. f), such that increases in f also tend to deplete the fish population. At low levels of f, stocks may still be sufficiently large that greater catchability may succeed in raising productivity. At high levels of f however, greater catchability may so reduce the population from its already small size that productivity falls.

The effect of technological change therefore depends upon the amount of fishing that is undertaken. In other words, whether technological change raises or lowers output and productivity depends, *inter alia*, on the level of nominal fishing effort. As was seen in Chapter 2, the effort level will be determined by economic as well as biological factors. To see the effect of technological change we therefore need to establish the economic equilibria that will obtain in the fishery. The most comprehensive way of doing this is to use the backward-bending supply curve model, which allows us to cope with the possibility of a variable price. The general equation for the long-run supply curve (equation 2.25) was

$$LRAC_y = \frac{c}{Y}\left[\frac{a}{2q} \pm \frac{a}{2q^2K}\sqrt{(qK)^2 - \frac{4q^2KY_s}{a}}\right]^{1/\beta}$$

For given values of c, a, β and K, increases in q have the effect of shifting the supply curve downwards, as illustrated in *Figure 3.3*.

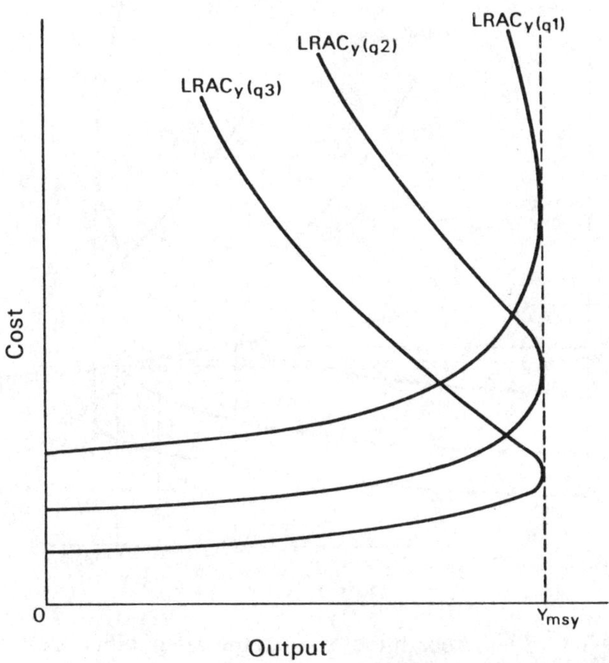

FIGURE 3.3 The effect of increases in the catchability coefficient on the LRAC curve.

The logic of this discussion is that technological improvement allows any given quantity of fish to be caught at lower unit cost. This conclusion is consistent with our explanation of the shift in the sustainable yield curve considered in *Figure 3.1*; that is, that technological change enables any quantity of fish to be caught using fewer total resources (such as men, boats and fuel). The open-access equilibrium associated with different states of technology can be determined by superimposing a demand curve. It makes a difference, however, whether demand is relatively elastic or inelastic with respect to price. We shall consider each case in turn.

3.3.1 Equilibrium when demand is elastic

The situation in the case when demand is elastic is depicted in *Figure 3.4*. Let us suppose that with the least efficient technology the relevant cost curve is $LRAC_{y(q1)}$. Open-access equilibrium will be at point a_1, where the demand curve intersects $LRAC_{y(q1)}$. The level of exploitation is sufficiently low that maximum sustainable yield (MSY) has not yet been attained.

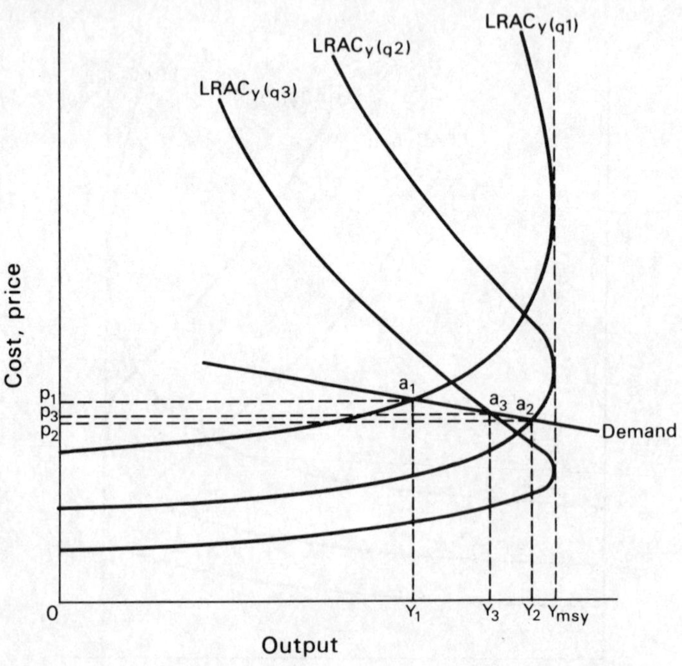

FIGURE 3.4 The effect of increases in the catchability coefficient on the open-access equilibrium, when the demand is elastic.

Technological change now occurs, increasing efficiency, lowering the cost curve to $LRAC_{y(q2)}$ and opening up profitable fishing opportunities. Firms respond to the incentive by applying more effort to the fishery and in the long run output rises from Y_1 to Y_2. Given the downward-sloping demand curve, this increase in output implies a fall in price (from p_1 to p_2).

Now, clearly there will be some state of technology that will make it profitable to produce an output corresponding exactly to MSY; that is, there must be a cost curve which intersects demand at MSY. We are, however, considering changes in technology rather than absolute levels. It should be apparent that continuous technological advance will lower the cost curve sufficiently that the equilibrium point will eventually 'turn the corner' represented by MSY. Consider the effect of a further advance in technology that shifts the cost curves from $LRAC_{y(q2)}$ to $LRAC_{y(q3)}$. Equilibrium moves to a_3, resulting in a *fall* in output and a *rise* in equilibrium price. Should technological change lower the cost curve again then output will fall further and price will be forced higher. It should also be noted that technological change does not make the fishery, or the individual fisherman, more profitable. This follows directly from the open-access assumption, under which effort is free to enter the fishery if profits are being made or leave it in the event of losses. Whatever the technology, therefore, resource adjustment will take place until price equals average cost.

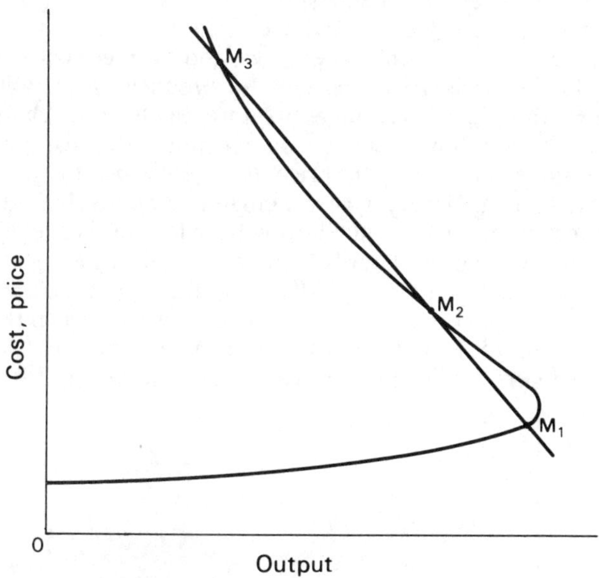

FIGURE 3.5 Multiple open-access equilibria (three intersections).

Implicit in the analysis are the changes that take place in other important variables. If the reader has understood the biological basis of the model, he or she should appreciate that an increase in the catchability coefficient and a higher level of exploitation will result in a falling fish population. We can also infer how productivity changes from the movements in the equilibrium level of unit costs. We saw how higher output caused price and average costs to fall as MSY was approached, but the fall in output thereafter caused price and average cost to rise. Now, it follows by definition that productivity will change in precisely the opposite direction. To understand why, we must recall that productivity is defined here as output divided by total input. But unit cost is simply a monetary measure of total input divided by output. Given constant input prices, higher productivity implies lower costs, and vice versa. It follows, then, that with a downward-sloping demand curve, technological change in the long run will cause productivity to rise until MSY is reached, whereafter it will fall.

3.3.2 Equilibrium when demand is inelastic

It is important to understand that when the demand curve is relatively inelastic it may cut the supply curve in three places. In *Figure 3.5*, only two of the three possible equilibrium positions are stable, namely M_1 and M_3. M_2 is unstable since a small change in output will force the fishery to move to either M_1 or M_3. For example, a decrease in effort permits sustainable yield to rise, and given the steepness of the demand curve, price falls below unit costs. Profitability declines and encourages a further exit of resources, and the process stabilizes only when price and average cost are in equality again (at M_1). Similarly an increase in effort reduces sustainable yield and, even though this reduction makes it more costly to catch fish, scarcity forces up the price sufficiently to encourage more effort to enter. Again the process continues until cost and price are equalized (at M_3).

Consider, then, a fishery where demand is relatively inelastic and is subject to technological change. Starting from low levels of exploitation the effect will initially be as described in the previous analysis: the LRAC curve shifts down, output rises to MSY, and the equilibrium levels of price and unit cost fall. A critical stage is reached, however, when the cost curve has shifted so that it is tangential to the demand curve near MSY (*Figure 3.6*). In this figure the demand curve is tangential to the LRAC curve at

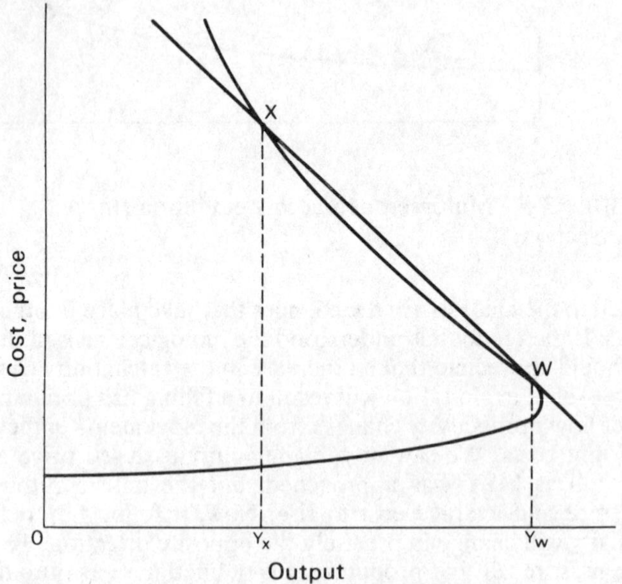

FIGURE 3.6 Multiple open-access equilibria (one intersection, one point of tangency).

point W, where output (Y_W) is just below MSY. Point W represents a semi-stable equilibrium. A decrease in effort raises output, but since between Y_W and MSY price is greater than average cost, resources would be encouraged into the fishery, reversing the process and forcing output back to Y_W. An increase in effort, however, is destabilizing. If output falls below Y_W, price exceeds average cost and further effort is encouraged into the fishery. This process will continue until output has fallen to a level where price equals average cost. This will be at Y_X, the output level corresponding to stable equilibrium point X.

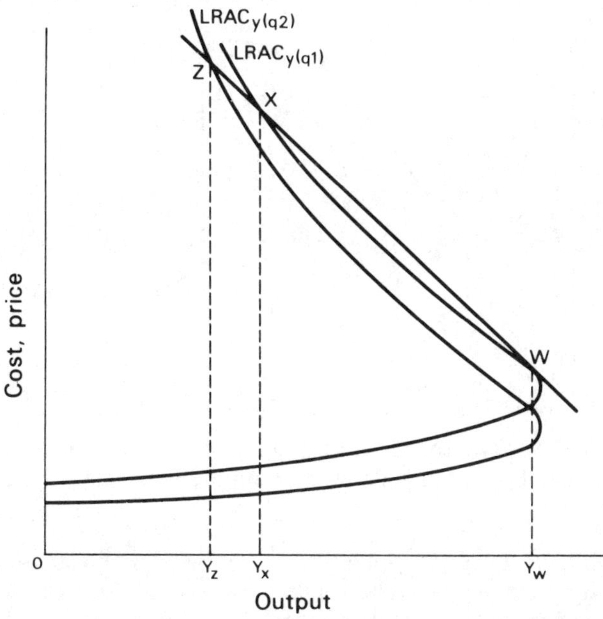

FIGURE 3.7 The effect of increases in the catchability coefficient on open-access equilibrium, when demand is inelastic.

If the fishery is at point W then it should be apparent that a slight downward shift in the cost curve will be destabilizing, as shown in *Figure 3.7*. A shift in the cost curve from $LRAC_{y(q1)}$ to $LRAC_{y(q2)}$ means that there is no longer any point of tangency between demand and LRAC at the higher output level. Price now exceeds average cost at all output levels between Y_Z and MSY. Effort accordingly enters the fishery, causing output to fall substantially until price and average cost are equalized at point Z, where output is Y_Z. The crucial point to understand however is that a slight change in one parameter (in this case the catchability coefficient) can cause a major change from one output level to another. The effect can be seen more clearly in *Figure 3.8*, which shows how the open-access level of output for a fishery changes in response to increases in q, assuming that demand is relatively inelastic.

Figure 3.8 does *not* assume that 'other things are equal'. Central to the analysis is that other variables will alter as higher values of q shift the open-access equilibrium. If output changes greatly, then we can expect these to do the same. For example, a large drop in output, given the inelastic demand, implies a large rise in equilibrium price and unit costs. Productivity, for the reasons explained above, will therefore move in the opposite direction as compared with price and costs. The transition from a relatively high to a low equilibrium level of output also entails a move from

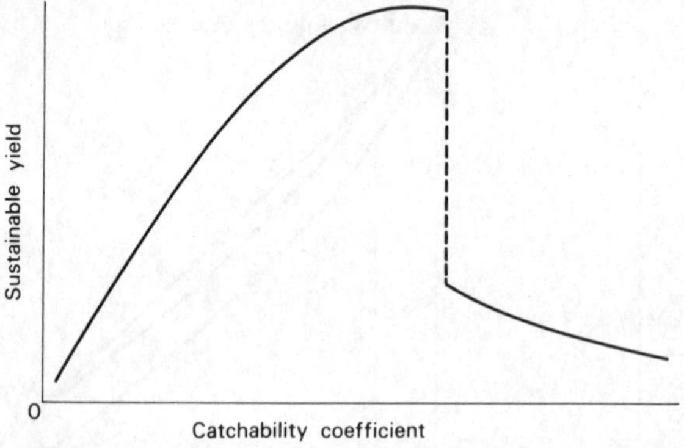

FIGURE 3.8 The response of equilibrium output to increases in the catchability coefficient, when demand is inelastic.

one sustainable level of population to another. It must be appreciated however that even though small changes in technology may be accompanied by much greater changes in other variables, equilibrium is eventually restored. Our theoretical predictions suggest that though output and population may 'collapse' under the effects of technical progress, the levels to which they fall will be sustainable. The fish may be less abundant, more costly to harvest and more expensive to buy, but at least it will still be possible to catch them on a long-term basis. This follows directly from the assumptions on which the Gordon–Schaefer model, represented by equation 2.26, is based. If we modify some of the assumptions, however, we may find that the effects of technological change are even more severe than our previous analysis suggests.

The two assumptions that are of most relevance in the present context are first, that growth of the fish stock is positive for all stock sizes between zero and environmental carrying capacity (ECC); secondly, that there are no diminishing returns to population. It was suggested in Chapter 2 however that in practice there may be a critical lower level to the population, greater than zero, below which the species cannot sustain itself. If, in such a situation, higher levels of effective fishing effort brought about by technological change were to reduce the equilibrium population to its minimum viable size, further technological advance would cause extinction of the stock, since below the minimum size growth is negative and fishing will no longer result in a sustained yield. Chapter 2 also suggested that extinction could result where the short-run production function displayed diminishing returns to population. The reason why this is the case was explained in section 2.2.2.3, but we shall now see how it relates to technological change. Diminishing returns to population imply that the short-run yield function is of the form $Y = qf^{\beta}P^{\alpha}$, where $\alpha < 1.0$, and a rise in the fish population of x%, other things being equal, causes yield to rise by less than x%. But the reverse is also true: a fall in population of x%, other things being equal, results in a fall in catch of less than x%. Now, the long-run effect of technological change is to deplete the fish stock in much the same way as an increase in nominal effort. However because of diminishing returns to population, yield in the short run may show less tendency to fall as population declines. Accordingly there may come a point where biological equilibrium will never be attained except at a population of zero. For both these reasons, then—the existence of a minimum viable population, and the possibility of short-run diminishing returns to population—the effects of new technology in fishing may be more serious than simpler versions of the Gordon–Schaefer model might imply.

3.4 THE RELEVANCE OF THE MODEL

3.4.1 Explaining the 'paradox' of technological change

The bioeconomic model helps us to resolve some of the ambiguities and contradictions surrounding technological change that were considered in section 3.2.2. We are now in a position to understand more clearly how the creation and use of modern fishing methods and equipment can be instrumental both in the rise and fall of such fisheries as the Peruvian anchoveta, the North Atlantic herring and the Antarctic whale. Similarly, the fact that an innovation may raise the profitability or catch rate of an *individual* firm that adopts it, but fail to do so in the long run when used by the fleet as a whole, can also be explained. The model showed that the bioeconomic effect of technical progress is a fall in stock abundance; for the innovator the effects are externalized, but are eventually experienced by non-innovators in terms of falling CPUE and rising costs.

Our previous analysis also sheds light on the wider aspects of industrial performance. Consider, for example, the growth of productivity in the U.S. fishing industry. Two American studies both concur on the finding that labour productivity in U.S. fishing grew more slowly than in agriculture, with the implication that fishing's competitive position vis-à-vis other food-producing industries had been jeopardized (Bell and Kinoshita, 1973; Miller and Norton, 1967). Now, one explanation for this relatively slow rise in productivity is that the underlying rate of technological change in fishing has also been relatively slow. That indeed is how some observers have interpreted such evidence, and have criticized the industry for being 'technologically backward'. But low growth in productivity is also consistent with there having been a positive rate of technological change offset by a fall in the abundance of the stocks on which the industry is based. Stock abundance could have fallen for many reasons, but if the Gordon–Schaefer model is to be believed then technological change would have been one of the contributory factors. Given that major advances in marine science and technology undeniably have taken place, then it could be argued that the latter explanation is at least as convincing as the former.

3.4.2 Foreseeing the implications of future technological change

The bioeconomic model has highlighted the circumstances that will cause the 'two-edged sword' of technological change to cut in one direction rather than another. As such it allows us to foresee the effects that the creation and application of fishing technology are capable of having in the long run. It is therefore an essential basis for policy formulation, considered in later chapters.

The first point to appreciate is that, so long as a fishery remains unregulated, then in the long run technological change will not succeed in increasing the profitability of the fishery as a whole or the income of the 'average' fisherman. This is not to deny, of course, that the adoption of new technology will be a perfectly sensible strategy for the individual firm. Indeed, such action may be forced upon it either by falling catch per unit effort or falling price. To the extent that the aggregate effect of this response is to deplete fish stocks still further, and thus to coerce fishermen into seeking still greater improvements in their efficiency, then technological change may become a 'treadmill' as far as the average fisherman is concerned. (The dynamics of this process will be examined more fully in Chapter 5.) The same argument applies to the single fishing nation in rivalry with others in international waters; competition for shares of the common property resource will put a premium on technological leadership. Nevertheless so long as a 'free-for-all' situation obtains, then for the fishery as a whole greater technical efficiency can never overcome the tendency for price and average cost to be brought into equality.

Secondly, the sustainable yield of a fishery can be expected to increase as a result of technological change until MSY is reached. After that, further technological improvement will result in overexploitation and cause sustainable yield to fall. Quite literally, therefore, new fishing technology may in the long run be counterproductive. Moreover, in the absence of regulation this effect is not self-correcting. Even if a stock is severely depleted and output is below its maximum, individual firms and fishing nations may still find it worth while to carry on applying the results of science and technology. The adverse consequences of so doing are, as mentioned above, externalized.

The final, and possibly the most important implication of the model is that technological change may result in what might be termed 'catastrophes'. It will be recalled that events of this kind can occur, according to the model, where demand is relatively inelastic, where there is a minimum viable stock size or where the short-run yield function exhibits diminishing returns to population. The latter two circumstances are potentially more serious since they may give rise to total extinction of the fishery. The relevant question now becomes: can these circumstances be identified in practice so that such a situation may be foreseen? The answer is that in principle they can be, but to do so requires fairly detailed economic and biological investigations into the fishery concerned. Thus economic information on the price elasticity of demand for the product of the fishery will be needed. Other things being equal, species with a relatively low elasticity of demand will be more vulnerable to technological change than others whose demand is more elastic. On the biological side there is now a growing body of evidence concerning the factors that may predispose a fishery to 'collapsing'. Pelagic stocks seem particularly prone, either because they have a minimum viable population size or because of their very tight shoaling behaviour, which makes them especially vulnerable to modern fishing methods. It is its shoaling behaviour that seems to have contributed to the collapse of the Peruvian anchoveta in 1973. Apparently, as the population declined, because of fishing and also because of the oceanic disturbance called 'El Niño', the remaining fish confined themselves to a smaller sea area. They thus remained just as susceptible to capture or became even more so, giving rise to further stock depletion and eventual collapse (Saville, 1980, p. 514). Species that are as yet underexploited but which are subject to a high degree of aggregation may therefore be more likely to experience fishing 'catastrophes' in future if techniques of capture continue to improve.

3.5 SUMMARY

Fishing has become technologically more sophisticated over the past forty years, owing to the large number of innovations that have originated from the manufacturing sector and from the industry itself. The spread of new technology is a gradual process because fishing firms do not respond instantaneously, but experience shows that innovations are eventually adopted by all firms that can expect to benefit from their use in terms of higher catches or profits. While these expectations are often amply fulfilled at the level of the individual boat or firm, the aggregate effects are equivocal. That is to say, technological change does not always result in higher output or profitability for groups of firms exploiting the same resource.

Bioeconomic modelling allows us to analyse the long-run effects of new technology in a more precise way. If technological change is represented by increases in the catchability coefficient, q, then it can be shown that an increase in q will shift the sustainable yield/effort function and the CPUE/effort function. These shifts in turn alter the relationship between LRAC and output: specifically, an increase in q shifts the LRAC curve downwards. Given the demand function for the fishery, the open-access equilibrium position can be shown to change. When demand is relatively elastic, continuous technological change causes output to rise and price to fall, until MSY is reached, after which technological change has the reverse effect. There is an important difference, however, where demand is relatively inelastic; in this situation technological change may cause a relatively sharp fall in landings and an equivalently sudden rise in price. Other circumstances that may cause fishing 'catastrophes' of even greater potential seriousness are the existence of a minimum viable stock size below which the fish population cannot sustain itself, and the possibility of short-run diminishing returns to population.

The bioeconomic model is relevant in two respects. First, it helps to explain why technological change has often been a mixed blessing for firms exploiting an open-access fishery; innovation by each individual firm creates external effects, which are eventually reflected in the performance of the fleet as a whole. Secondly, the model allows us to foresee what the implications of future technological change in fishing might be. In an open-access fishery it seems unlikely that the use of new technology will cause any lasting improvement in profitability. Technological change may be expected to cause sustainable yield from a fishery to increase while the stock is underexploited, but continued technical advance will eventually cause output to fall from its MSY level. Moreover, the fall may be severe if any of the theoretical conditions mentioned above occurs in practice, but identifying these conditions is an empirical problem.

If technological change can be likened to a 'two-edged sword' it would therefore appear that one side may be sharper than the other.

3.6 BIBLIOGRAPHIC NOTES

An overview of technological change in fishing, including an account of the major innovations, is given by Loftas (1974). The origin and use of one particularly important development (power block purse seining) is described by Mietle (1969) and Browning (1981). On the factors affecting technological change, and its effects, *see* Scott (1962, 1964), Christy and Scott (1965, Ch. 2), Anderson (1977, pp. 47–50) and Bell (1978, Ch. 9). Two important empirical studies are those of Bell (1969) and Bell and Kinoshita (1973).

REFERENCES AND FURTHER READING

ANDERSON, L. G. (1977). *The economics of fisheries management.* Baltimore: Johns Hopkins Press.

BELL, F. (1966). 'The economics of the New England fishing industry: the role of technological change and government aid.' *Federal Reserve Bank Research Report* No. 31.

BELL, F. (1969). 'The future role of investment and technological change in the world tuna fisheries'. In FAO Fisheries Report *International conference on investment in fisheries*. R.83.2. Rome: FAO.

BELL, F. (1978). *Food from the sea: the economics and politics of ocean fisheries*. Boulder, Colorado: Westview Press.

BELL, F. and R. KINOSHITA (1973). 'Productivity gains in U.S. fisheries.' *Fishery Bulletin* **71** (4) : 911–19.

BROWNING, B. (1981). 'The Puretic block: salvation of the tuna industry.' *Fishing Gazette* **98** (9) : 24–32.

CHRISTY, F and A. SCOTT (1965). *The common wealth in ocean fisheries*. Baltimore: Johns Hopkins Press.

CLARK, C. and R. LAMBERSON (1982). 'An economic history and analysis of pelagic whaling.' *Marine Policy* **6** (2) : 103–20.

EDDIE, G. (1980). 'Technology and fisheries development.' Paper given at Conference on *Technology and the Challenges of the World's New Fisheries Regime*. London: Society for Underwater Technology.

KELSALL, R. (1948). 'The white fish industry.' In M. Fogarty (Ed.), *Further studies in industrial organisation*. London: Methuen.

LOFTAS, T. (1974). 'Fisheries technology.' in E. de Bono (Ed.), *Eureka! how and why the greatest inventions were made*. London: Thames & Hudson.

MCHUGH, T. (1977). 'Rise and fall of world whaling: the tragedy of the commons illustrated.' *Journal of International Affairs* **31** (1) : 23–33.

MACSWEEN, I. (1973). 'The measurement of fishing power.' White Fish Authority. FERU Occasional Paper.

MIETLE, P. (1969). 'Developments and investments in recent years in Norwegian purse seine fisheries for herring, capelin and mackerel.' In FAO Fisheries Report *International conference on investment in fisheries*. R.83.2. Rome: FAO.

MILLER, M. and V. NORTON (1967). 'The fishing labour force: scarcity or surplus.' In F. Bell and J. Hazleton (Eds), *Recent developments and research in fisheries economics*. New York: Oceana Publications.

OECD (1966). *Fishery policies and economies*. Paris: OECD.

OECD (1967). *Impact of electronics on fishing*. Paris: OECD.

SAVILLE, A. (Ed.) (1980). 'The assessment and management of pelagic fish stocks.' *Rapports et Procès-verbaux des Réunions du Conseil International pour l'Exploration de la Mer* 177.

SCOTT, A. (1962). 'The economics of regulating fisheries.' In R. Hamlisch (Ed.), *Economic effects of fishing regulation*. Rome: FAO.

SCOTT, A. (1964). 'Food and the world fisheries situation.' In M. Clawson (Ed.), *Natural resources and international development*. Baltimore: Johns Hopkins Press.

SEGURA, E. (1973). 'Optimal fishing effort in the Peruvian anchoveta fishery.' In A. Sokoloski (Ed.), *Ocean fishery management: discussion and research*. NOAA Tech. Rep. 371.

SPANGLER, M. (1970). *New technology and marine resource development*. New York: Praeger.

TUNSTALL, J. (1968). *Fish: an antiquated industry*. Fabian Society, tract 380.

WHITMARSH, D. (1977). *Technological change in the U.K. fishing industry*. Unpublished M.A. Thesis, University of Exeter.

WHITMARSH, D. (1978). 'Stern trawling: a case study in technological change.' MRRU Research Paper No. 5, Portsmouth Polytechnic.

CHAPTER 4

Fisheries management: a normative application of the model

4.1 INTRODUCTION

In Chapter 2, we developed a bioeconomic fishery model which we then used to investigate briefly the situation likely to be reached by an open-access fishery. In this chapter, we shall begin by looking rather more closely at the nature of the open-access equilibrium so as to determine why management of commercial fisheries may be required. We shall then consider some of the objectives that such management might have.

Let us note at the outset, however, that we use the term 'objectives' in a somewhat restrictive way. Specifically, accepting that the open-access equilibrium is, in some sense, suboptimal, we are interested in determining what is the optimal level of fishing. Thus, by 'objective', we mean the target level of fishing that the management authority is attempting to achieve. We shall outline what appear to be the four major possibilities: namely, maximum sustainable yield (MSY), static maximum economic yield (SMEY), biological optimum sustainable yield (BOSY), and dynamic maximum economic yield (DMEY). Of course, what often happens in practice is that the management authority chooses one of the four targets (usually MSY or BOSY) as the basis of its management plan, and then modifies this, to some extent, in the light of prevailing biological, economic or social factors. Somewhat confusingly, the resultant target is frequently called optimum yield or optimum sustainable yield, but such a target is distinct from the four aims which we have listed above.

Many objectives other than MSY, SMEY, BOSY and DMEY are obviously possible and indeed are frequently specified as part of management plans. For the most part however we shall not discuss such goals in this book, principally because they appear to be qualitatively different from those mentioned above. Each of the four goals (MSY, etc.) may be used to define a *level of fishing*. Generally speaking, other aims of management plans are not like this, but instead require that the fishery be managed in a particular way, rather than at a particular level. For instance, an objective often found in management programmes is to improve the incomes of fishermen. Regardless of the level of fishing, such an aim will be achieved on a long-term basis only if the number of fishermen is controlled. If not, any improvement in incomes will attract new fishermen to the fishery, thereby depressing incomes all round. Success thus depends on *how* the fishery is managed, not the level at which it is managed. (*See* Chapter 6 for further discussion of this point.) To summarize, we shall be concerned here only with those objectives relating to what the management authority perceives to be the correct level of fishing activity.

4.2 WHY MANAGE COMMERCIAL FISHERIES?

We saw in Chapter 2 that an open-access fishery will reach a long-run equilibrium at an output where average revenue equals short-run average cost equals long-run average cost. There are a number of problems with such an equilibrium which mean that management is generally considered desirable.

4.2.1 Problems with open access

To begin with, let us envisage a situation common to many mature commercial fisheries; that is, one where the demand for fish is great relative to the potential supply. A situation such as this is shown in *Figure 4.1*, where the demand curve AR is at a level sufficient to warrant an

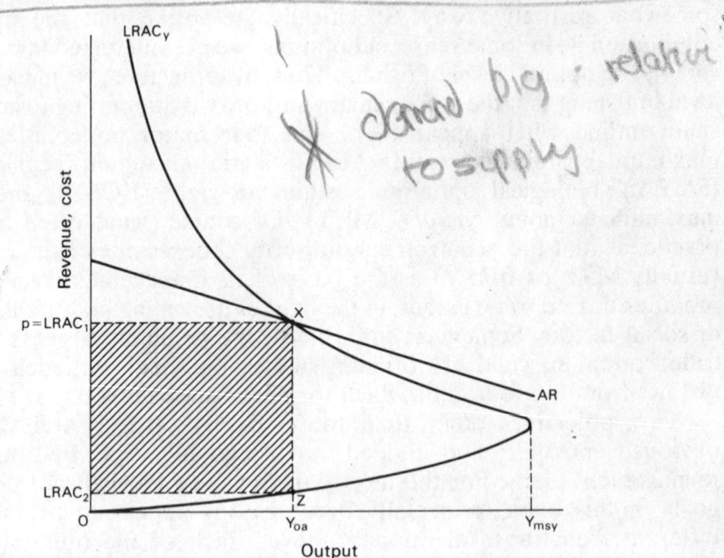

FIGURE 4.1 Open-access equilibrium in a mature commercial fishery.

expansion of effort, in the open-access fishery, to well beyond the level corresponding to maximum sustainable yield Y_{msy}. The result is that the output actually being produced, Y_{oa}, is much less than Y_{msy}.

The first problem with such a fishery is indeed its exploitation beyond the point of MSY, since most, if not all, biologists would consider this to constitute biological overfishing. A related problem is that the given output of fish, Y_{oa}, is being taken at the higher of the two possible long-run average costs (that is, $LRAC_1$ rather than $LRAC_2$). By implication, therefore, the amount of effort being used to take the output is much greater than that required.

For these reasons, the introduction of a management scheme simply to move the fishery from $LRAC_1$ to $LRAC_2$ is frequently seen as being desirable. A number of benefits would certainly result. First, we could clearly have the same output, Y_{oa}, at much lower cost. Secondly, although cost would be reduced, price would remain the same so that the shaded rectangle ($LRAC_1$-X-Z-$LRAC_2$) would come to represent profit rather than cost. Depending on the precise nature of the management regime, fishermen's incomes could then be improved and/or government revenue increased. Thirdly, by implication, the fish population is greater at $LRAC_2$ than at $LRAC_1$ and it may be expected, therefore, to be more resilient to environmental fluctuations. These benefits are not achieved costlessly however. It must not be forgotten that both $LRAC_1$ and $LRAC_2$ are points of long-run equilibrium. What must be considered (and what often seems to be overlooked) is the short-run sacrifice that may be required in order to achieve these long-run gains.

In *Figures 4.2a* and *4.2b* we reconsider the move from $LRAC_1$ to $LRAC_2$ in rather greater detail, paying particular attention to the short-run aspects. We shall assume that, to begin with, we have a complete open-access equilibrium at output Y_{oa}, so that price, p_1, equals $LRAC_1$ equals $SRAC_1$. This corresponds in *Figure 4.2b* to an effort level of f_1 units where the short-run yield curve for population size 1 ($SRY_{(pop.1)}$) intersects the long-run (sustainable) yield (Y_s) curve. We now suppose that the management authority wishes to move the fishery to $LRAC_2$. The first thing to notice is that, given the present population size (as implied by $SRY_{(pop.1)}$), $SRAC_{y(pop.1)}$ is the relevant short-run average cost curve, and with this curve $LRAC_2$ is simply not attainable. In other words, the fish population is so small that to achieve an output of Y_{oa} requires a lot of fishing effort, and is therefore expensive (relatively). Quite clearly, the population size must be increased so as to shift the short-run average cost curve downwards if we are ever to attain $LRAC_2$. This is evident if we recall the yield curve (equation 2.10); that is,

$$Y = qPf^{\beta}$$

If the management authority wishes to reduce the amount of effort involved in the fishery (which is what a reduction in cost implies), then either q or P must be increased (if yield is to remain the same). In the short run, increasing q is likely to be outside of the control of the management authority (although as we shall see in Chapter 6, *decreasing* it is not) and hence increasing population remains the only alternative.

Since Y_{oa} represents a sustainable yield, the fish population will increase only if the current yield is decreased. Let us suppose that the management

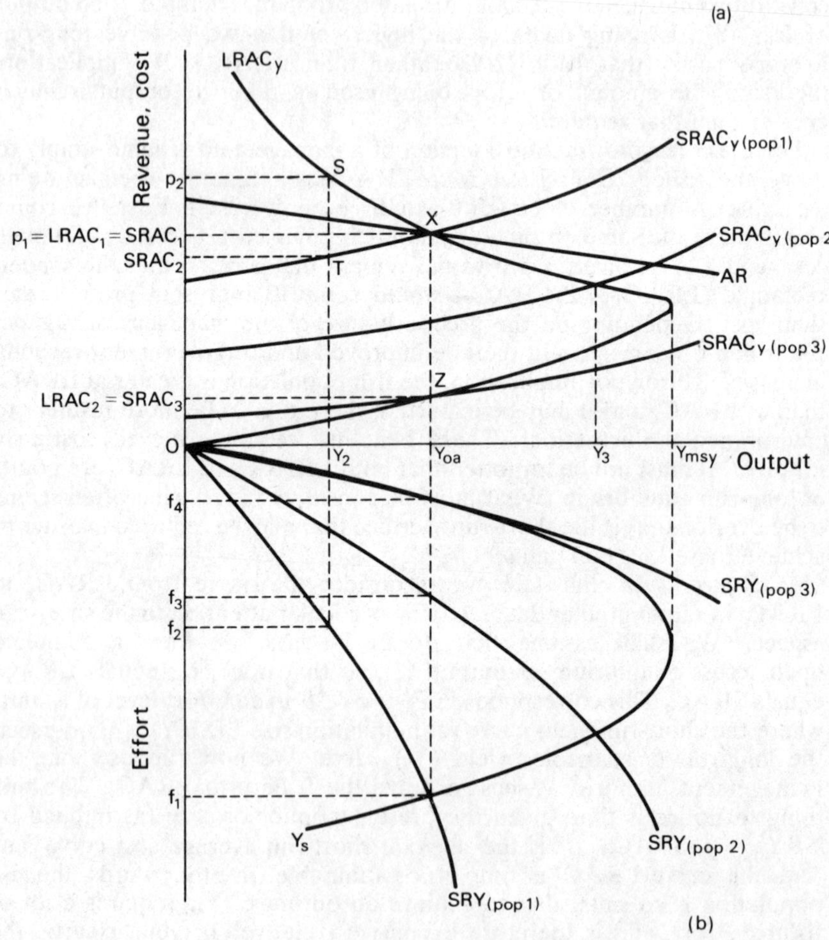

FIGURE 4.2 Management at the open-access output level.

authority decides to reduce catch to Y_2. Consumers of fish are now clearly worse off since they have a smaller output of fish available (Y_2 instead of Y_{oa}) at a higher price (p_2 rather than p_1). Fishermen may show some gain however, because first, they receive the higher price, and secondly, at this output the average cost of catching fish is less, given by the short-run average cost curve as $SRAC_2$. This latter is because, as is shown by *Figure*

4.2b, the effort level required to achieve output Y_2 is substantially less (f_2 rather than f_1). The area p_2-S-T-$SRAC_2$ therefore represents profit. Usually, of course, in an open-access fishery we should expect this profit to attract increased fishing effort, pushing up costs until the zero-profit equilibrium re-emerges. We shall make the heroic assumption however that fishing effort is under strict control (how, is considered in Chapter 6), so that as much effort is used as is required to achieve the target catch, and no more.

As Y_2 is less than the sustainable yield Y_{oa}, the size of the fish population will increase. Let us suppose that the short-run curves associated with this new population (population level 2) are $SRY_{(pop.2)}$ in *Figure 4.2b* and $SRAC_{y(pop.2)}$ in *Figure 4.2a*. Sustainable yield has therefore increased to Y_3. The management authority is now in the happy position of being able to allow catch to increase back to its original level Y_{oa}. The fish population will continue to increase in size because Y_{oa} is less than sustainable yield Y_3. It should be noted that although this position is reached in only one period here, in practice many years may elapse before the original catch is again attained. To cite a particularly extreme example, the North Sea herring fishery was closed in 1977 and did remain closed more or less continuously for six years. In the interim, adverse side effects of the closure have become apparent, such as a seemingly substantial loss of consumer interest in the product.

At output Y_{oa}, consumers are, of course, back where they began. From *Figure 4.2b* however, it is apparent that fishing effort must be reduced yet further. With population at size level 2, only f_3 units of effort are needed to achieve a catch of Y_{oa}. Notice however that while it must be the case that f_3 is less than f_1, it might have been greater than f_2 had the short-run curves been drawn differently. Whether it is less or greater makes no substantial difference to the analysis.

Eventually, population level 3 will be attained, when $SRY_{(pop.3)}$ and $SRAC_{y(pop.3)}$ will be the relevant short-run curves. The aim of the management scheme will now have been achieved, in that the fishery will be producing output Y_{oa} on a sustainable basis at the lower of the two possible long-run costs. Clearly, consumers of fish will have gained nothing directly from this since price remains at p_1, and indeed actually increased during the short run. The effort level involved in the fishery has been reduced substantially so that now only f_4 units are required. Depending largely on the actual management regime, this reduction may give rise to a number of problems, although of course it is precisely because effort has been reduced that fishing costs have been lowered. As an aside, we might note that in practice most of the economic benefits of fisheries management are likely to come from cost reductions.

In our example, one possibility is that f_4 units of effort represent a small number of optimally sized boats operating efficiently throughout the natural fishing season. This solution is probably the one that would most appeal to economists. The problem with it, if there is one, is usually to be found in social considerations. Clearly the move from f_1 to f_4 units of effort implies the displacement of a substantial proportion of the original amount of effort. Economic theory tends to make the implicit (or sometimes explicit) assumption that alternative uses may be found for the resources (mainly labour, gear and capital) no longer required in the fishery. However, given the regional character of many fisheries, alternative occupations may be few and far between so that, in some cases, it may make good social, and indeed economic, sense to use more resources in a fishery than are strictly required. It is precisely on such grounds that Crutchfield and Pontecorvo's (1969) book *The Pacific salmon fisheries: a study of irrational conservation* was criticized, especially with regard to the Alaskan salmon fishery. On the other hand, a policy of employment maximization is not without its problems.

A second interpretation of the move from f_1 to f_4 units of effort, and one that perhaps corresponds more closely with fisheries management practice, is that the catching capacity of the fishing fleet has remained roughly the same, but is being used only for a fraction of the natural season. The most outstanding example of this kind of situation is the Canadian Pacific herring roe fishery, where catching capacity is so great relative to the target catch that the *annual* seine season for each individual fishery is of the order of a couple of *hours*, and sometimes as little as fifteen *minutes* (Hourston, 1980). Needless to say, the fishery is naturally highly seasonal, since fishing has to take place during a relatively short period between the time that the roe content is best and the fish spawn. Nonetheless, the situation seems rather incredible. Another fishery with similar, if less extreme, problems is the Alaskan salmon fishery, where the capacity of the fleet is great enough that as the target catch level draws near, the boats that are still fishing often have the ability to exceed the target many times over. The management authority then has great difficulty in deciding precisely when to close the season.

Quite clearly, the biggest problem with such a situation is that it may become extremely difficult to control the actual catch in a precise way. Moreover any mistake in the setting of the length of the season may have important implications for the fish stock itself, if catching capacity is very great. Other things being equal, therefore, it would seem desirable to attempt to move the catching ability of the fleet into line with the catch actually available. (For more on the precise nature of regulation, *see* Chapter 6.)

What then should we conclude about the need for management in the simple case that we have considered, where the open-access level of exploitation is beyond MSY? As we have seen, many benefits do follow if we move the fishery from the high to the low long-run average cost (that is, $LRAC_1$ to $LRAC_2$), but this is not the whole story. Thus, although *in practice* we may well conclude that management is desirable, we cannot *a priori* make the assertion of its necessity, which many people seem prone to do.

Let us move on to consider the need for management in a slightly different case, that of a fishery which reaches an open-access equilibrium before the point of MSY is reached. Such a case is depicted in *Figure 4.3*, where it is apparent that the open-access output, Y_{oa}, is being taken at the lower of the two long-run average costs, and so our previous justification for management has disappeared.

The problem with this open-access output level (and indeed with *any* open-access output level) is that the price of fish, p_1, is less than the long-run marginal cost, $LRMC_1$, of catching them. If we consider in more

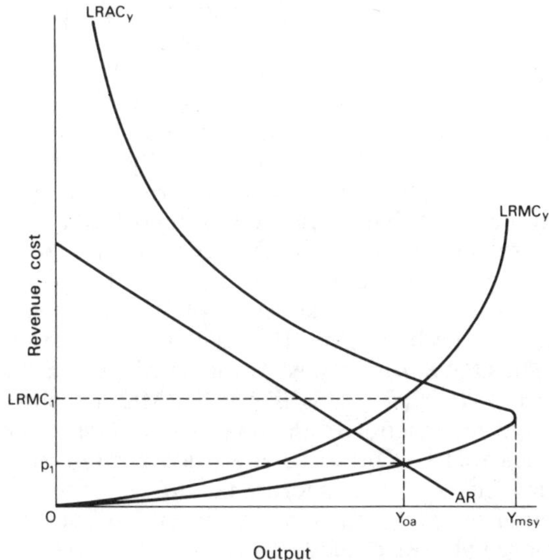

FIGURE 4.3 Open-access equilibrium attained before MSY.

detail the information given to us by the demand (that is, AR) and $LRMC_y$ curves, we shall be able to see that from society's viewpoint open access implies overexploitation. The demand curve shows the price that people are willing (and able) to pay for particular outputs of fish. If we make the undoubtedly heroic assumption that the income distribution is socially optimal, then the price paid gives us an indication of the value that society places on a given output of fish. The marginal cost curve shows the addition to total cost resulting from each increase in output. Therefore, at any point it shows (roughly) the cost of producing the last unit of output.

From *Figure 4.3*, it is apparent that the last unit of fish caught cost $LRMC_1$, but was worth to society only p_1. Hence, society would have gained had this final unit not been produced, and in this sense the open-access output level involves economic overexploitation. As the long-run marginal cost curve always lies above the long-run average cost curve, and as the open-access output occurs at the point where price equals long-run average cost, open-access exploitation must always imply economic overfishing. It should be noted however that the usual caveat applies, to the effect that we are dealing with the long run here. The introduction of the short run does modify things, but our conclusion that open access implies economic overexploitation remains valid except for very special circumstances. (*See* section 4.6 on dynamic maximum economic yield.) A definition of the economically optimal level of fishing should now be apparent (if it is not, *see* section 4.4 on static maximum economic yield).

The open-access fishery reaches this economic suboptimum principally because of what is called a 'congestion externality'. As successive fishing boats come to exploit the fishery so the grounds become increasingly congested. This increase in the number of boats tends to depress the catch per boat, raising the average cost of catching a unit of fish. For example, let us assume that initially the average cost is £50 per unit of fish and that there are 100 boats operating. Let us suppose that a new boat then enters the fishery with the result that average cost is increased to, say, £51. To the individual boat owner, entry to the fishery will have been worth while provided that the price of fish is at least £51. For the fishery as a whole, however, and to society, the introduction of the new boat has increased costs by £1 per existing boat (i.e. £100) plus the £51 for the new boat; a total of £151. Thus the *marginal* cost of the new boat is £151 even though the average cost is only £51. This is why LRMC lies above LRAC. To society, therefore, introduction of the new boat will be worth while only if the price is at least £151. But at such a price a profit emerges and this would attract new boats. Hence, because no individual boat can control the number of boats fishing, an open-access fishery will always operate at a point where marginal cost exceeds price. The only way to stop it from doing so would be to manage the fishery.

In *Figures 4.1–4.3*, we have drawn the AR and LRAC curves such that they intersect once only. As we saw in Chapter 3 however, if the demand curve is sufficiently inelastic, the two curves may intersect in three places, giving rise to the phenomenon of multiple open-access equilibria. This may provide some justification, within the context of overexploitation, for fisheries management, but in any case it seems a sufficiently interesting topic to warrant some discussion here. In *Figure 4.4*, we begin with a demand curve AR_1, which intersects LRAC once only giving rise to a unique and stable open-access equilibrium output, Y_1. This equilibrium is stable in the sense that any move away from it sets into motion forces to restore it. For instance, if output were to increase for some reason, cost would exceed price, resulting in losses which would encourage a contraction of effort and thus a reduction of output back to Y_1.

Now suppose that real incomes increase, shifting the demand curve to AR_2. Three equilibrium outputs (Y_2, Y_3 and Y_4) are now possible. However, of these Y_3 is unstable and could not be expected to be a long-run equilibrium although it may represent a transitory one. *A priori*, we cannot say whether the fishery will be at Y_2 or Y_4 (both of which are stable); it will depend, largely at least, on the way in which the fishery develops over time in response to shifts in the demand curve. Let us assume however that the fishery develops gradually so that it moves from Y_1 to Y_2 in the long run.

Suppose that real incomes now increase again so that the demand curve shifts to AR_3. Only one long-run equilibrium now exists (at output Y_5), and this occurs on the high, or backward-bending, part of the LRAC curve. Thus because of the relationship between the relatively inelastic demand curve, and the LRAC curve, a quite small shift of the demand curve may have major implications for the long-run exploitation level of the fishery.

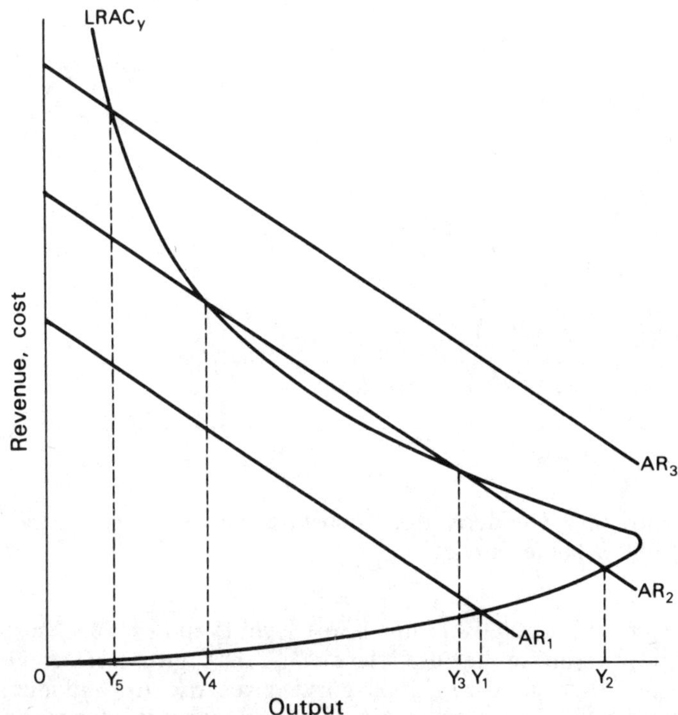

FIGURE 4.4 Multiple open-access equilibria.

Most of the problems associated with an equilibrium such as Y_5 have been discussed in Chapter 2. In particular, because the effort level is so great, the population is, by implication, reduced to very low levels so that environmental fluctuations may result in stock collapses. This danger is not brought out by the simple Gordon–Schaefer model, because that model implies that a unique stable equilibrium is associated with each effort level. Let us now go on to consider how instability in the sustainable yield curve may imply a need for management.

4.2.2 The problem of instability in the sustainable yield curve

We shall start here by briefly reviewing the derivation of the sustainable yield curve within the elementary Gordon–Schaefer model to see in what ways we may make this more realistic. The derivation of the (theoretical) curve is quite straightforward: we simply postulate different effort levels, observe the equilibrium yields established, and plot the resulting sustainable yield curve, as in *Figures 4.5a* and *4.5b*.

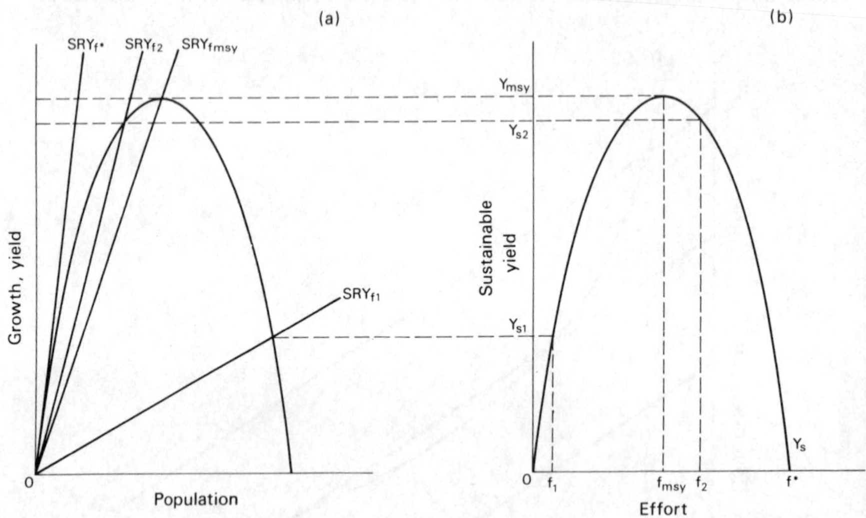

FIGURE 4.5 The derivation of sustainable yield curve in the Gordon–Schaefer model.

We begin with a relatively low effort level f_1 and establish sustainable yield Y_{s1}; f_{msy} results in the output level Y_{msy}, and f_2 gives a sustainable yield Y_{s2}. Hence, each short-run yield curve gives rise to a unique, stable equilibrium point. The effort level f^* is critical in that it is tangential to the population growth curve at zero in *Figure 4.5a*. Thus the equilibrium yield and population associated with this effort level will be zero, that is, it is the effort level required to extinguish the stock. If we differentiate the growth equation

$$G = aP\left(1 - \frac{P}{K}\right)$$

giving

$$G' = a\left(1 - \frac{2P}{K}\right)$$

and solve for $P = 0$, it is apparent that this critical effort level (f^*) corresponds to the intrinsic growth rate, a. That is, a sustained effort level at or beyond the intrinsic growth rate eliminates the stock, in the long run.

(Note that in this particular case, we make the assumption that $q = 1$. Strictly speaking, f^* must be greater than a/q.)

However, while the model is realistic enough to allow for extinction in this way, two things must be noted. First, f^* here represents a relatively great effort level. Secondly, if effort has been greater than f^* for some time but the population has not yet fallen to zero, then the model predicts that a reduction of effort below f^* will enable the establishment of a new stable equilibrium yield and a new stable population. In other words, the model implicitly assumes that, provided the population has not actually been extinguished, the effects of overexploitation are easily reversible. However the empirical evidence tends to indicate that this prediction is rather optimistic; some of the effects of overexploitation may be reversible only with great difficulty and over a long period of time, others may not be reversible at all.

A possibly more realistic model may be derived by including the idea that there is a minimum viable population; that is, a population size below which the stock is unable to regenerate itself and hence below which the effects of overexploitation clearly are not reversible. It is difficult to say precisely how great this critical population size is, and in any case it must vary from species to species. However, taking the well-known example of the Antarctic blue whale, the evidence tends to suggest that, in fact, the minimum viable population may be a rather small proportion of the environmental carrying capacity. For blue whales, the ECC has been estimated at between 150000 and 200000 individuals. By 1965, the population had been reduced to a very low level, certainly to less than 10000 individuals, perhaps to 4000 or even lower. Some scientists apparently thought that the minimum viable population had been passed, but happily this appears not to have been the case in that the blue whale stock is slowly recovering. The point, however, is that given the rather solitary lifestyle of blue whales, the vast oceans in which they live and the relatively slow growth rate of whale stocks, we might perhaps have expected the minimum viable population to be a reasonably large proportion of the environmental carrying capacity, but this does not seem to be the case.

Notwithstanding such reservations, logically it seems that, for many species at least, there must be some minimum viable population below which the net growth of the stock becomes negative. The biological productivity curve corresponding to this situation is shown in *Figure 4.6a*. Each short-run yield curve (with the exception of that corresponding to effort level f^*) now intersects the biological productivity curve in two places, so that the sustainable yield curve derived in *Figure 4.6b* has a different shape. In particular, each effort level up to f^* is now associated with two equilibria. The sustainable yield curve may be divided into two sections. The solid line up to f^*, which corresponds to the more traditional sustainable yield curve, shows equilibria that are biologically stable, in the sense that any move away from them sets in motion forces to restore them. For instance, in *Figure 4.6a* suppose that the fishery is initially in equilibrium with an effort level f_1 and a population size P_1. If for some reason population were then to increase, with effort unchanged, catch would exceed growth and the equilibrium would tend to be restored. Similarly, a slight decrease in population would cause growth to exceed catch and again equilibrium would re-established.The backward-bending, dashed-line part of the sustainable yield curve, on the other hand, shows equilibria that are biologically unstable. For instance, if the fishery is initially in equilibrium with effort level f_1 and population P_2, then any change in the population size with effort unaltered will be amplified. An

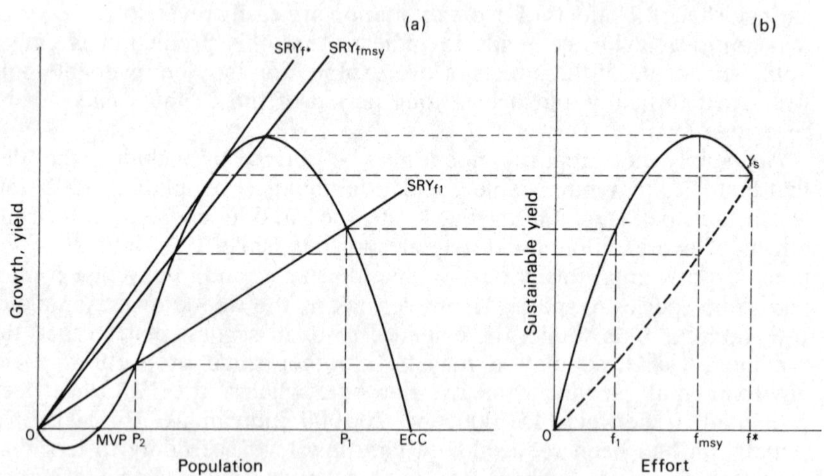

FIGURE 4.6 Sustainable yield with a minimum viable population (MVP).

increase in population will cause growth to exceed catch and a new equilibrium will eventually be established with population P_1. A decrease in population would leave catch greater than growth and would result in the long-run extinction of the stock if the effort level remained the same. Looking at matters purely from the biological point of view, therefore, a large part of the sustainable yield curve is unstable and we could not expect long-run equilibria to be established in this part of the curve. However, notice that in the above discussion we assume that the effort level remains given. To discover whether a *bioeconomic* equilibrium is possible in the backward-bending part of the sustainable yield curve, we must consider the way in which effort reacts to changes in population size.

To do this, we construct our bioeconomic model in the usual way. To derive a long-run total revenue curve we multiply the sustainable yield curve in *Figure 4.6b* by the price of fish (assumed constant). We introduce the total cost of effort in the usual manner. We also need curves showing short-run yield (and revenue, since price is constant) and in the drawing of these we shall assume that there are diminishing returns to effort. If we do not make this assumption, the short-run revenue curves overlie the total cost curve, making the establishment of an equilibrium a rather haphazard process.

In *Figure 4.7* we begin from a situation where an equilibrium has been established in the backward-bending part of the sustainable revenue curve.

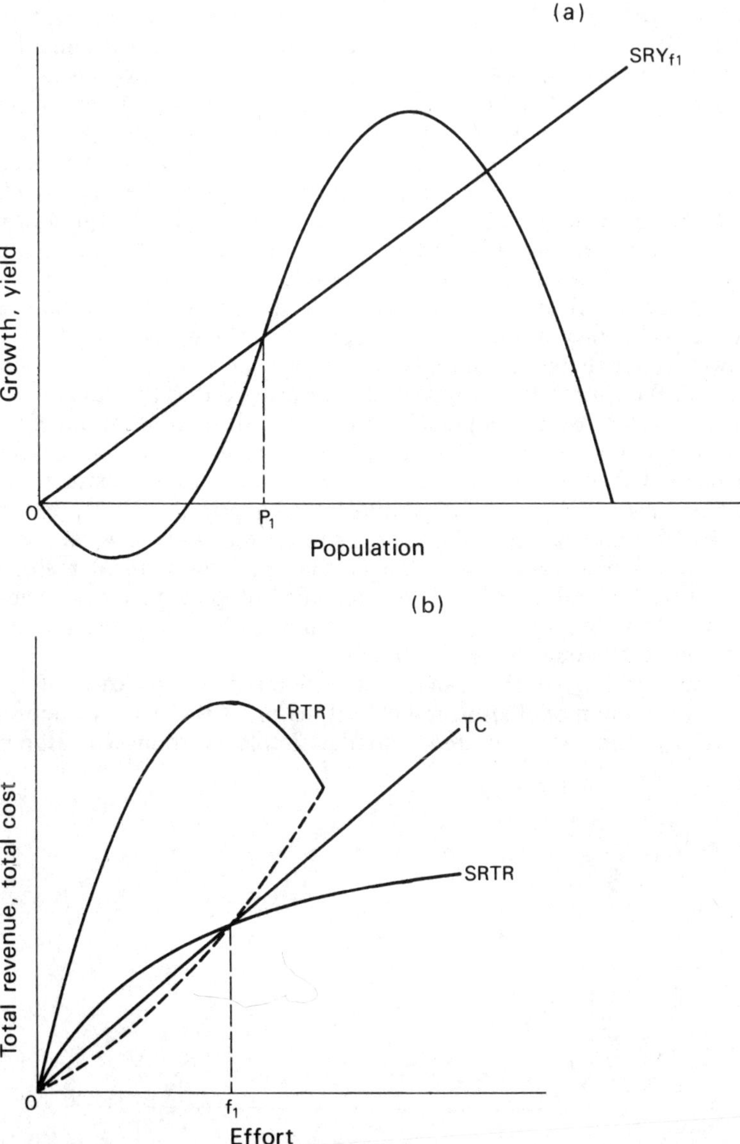

FIGURE 4.7 Open-access equilibrium with a minimum viable population.

From *Figure 4.7b* it may be seen that this involves an effort level f_1, which corresponds in *Figure 4.7a* to a population P_1. We have now to decide whether this equilibrium is stable or not. Let us begin by supposing that the fish population size increases slightly for some reason. We have already seen that because P_1 is biologically unstable, growth would exceed catch if effort remained unchanged. However the increase in population will have the effect of shifting the short-run revenue curve upwards so that the effort level will increase. Short-run yield will now exceed the sustainable yield, putting downward pressure on the population. In this way the equilibrium population, P_1, will tend to be restored. Hence, in the case where the population increases from its equilibrium we may be reasonably confident that equilibrium will eventually be restored, although this may take some time to achieve. In the short run, and depending on the relative changes induced in growth rates, effort levels and catch size, the disequilibrium may become more serious. Nonetheless, in the long run, economic factors will restore the fishery to the equilibrium population.

The same may not be true however if initially the population size decreases for some reason. As this happens, catch will become greater than growth, other things remaining equal. However, the decline in population will shift the short-run yield curve downwards so that the effort level falls, tending to increase the population back towards its equilibrium level. This also may take some time however. If in the meantime the population size has been pushed below the minimum viable level, clearly extinction of the species must result. Again, whether this happens will depend on the relative size and speed of the changes in growth and catch rates, and the effort level. Nonetheless the danger that extinction might result surely provides justification for the management of such fisheries. The more variable is the population size, the greater must be this danger, and the more justified would be management.

Quite apart from the danger of extinction in this case of variable population, the model also predicts extinction as the result of open access at positive cost, as compared with the simple Gordon–Schaefer model,

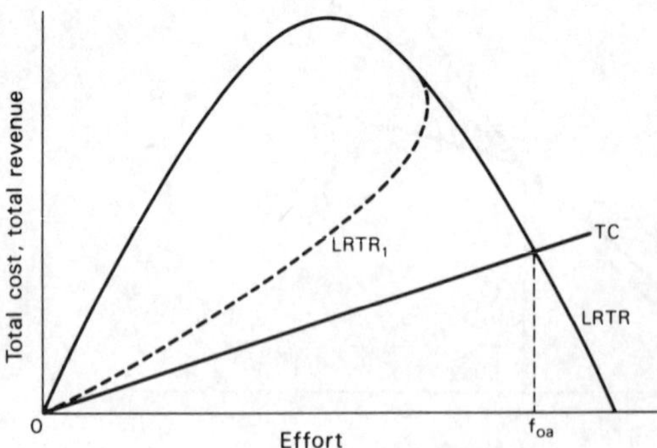

FIGURE 4.8 A comparison of open access with and without a minimum viable population.

which predicts extinction only at zero cost. This prediction may easily be demonstrated (*Figure 4.8*). The curve LRTR is the long-run total revenue curve based upon the simple model. This predicts an open-access equilibrium at an effort level f_{oa}. However the more complex curve, $LRTR_1$, based on the model that assumes a minimum viable population, has an equilibrium only at zero effort, corresponding to zero population. In other words, in such a fishery, with a cost level of TC it would be profitable to fish out the stock, as would presumably be done in the absence of management.

Which of the models is more relevant to a particular fishery must obviously be an empirical matter. Nonetheless an increasing number of the world's fisheries seem to confirm the rather pessimistic predictions of the model with a minimum viable population, in that many populations have been reduced to very low levels if not actually made extinct.

4.2.3 The problem of overcapitalization

A final justification for management is to avoid overcapitalization. In many open-access fisheries an excessive and increasing amount of capital becomes tied up (although it is fair to note that some management schemes may actually worsen this problem—*see* Chapter 6 on regulation). Given that capital is scarce in most, if not all, economies, and especially in developing countries, it seems desirable that excess capital be transferred out of the fishery, wherever possible, or better still prevented from entering the fishery in the first place.

Most of the gains from fisheries management come from the control of overcapitalization. Usually in open-access fisheries, there is little scope for increasing output, but much scope for decreasing input. Henderson and Tugwell (1979), for instance, estimate that the optimal management of two lobster areas in Canada would result in resource savings equivalent to about 60% of the value of the optimal catch.

We may distinguish two kinds of overcapitalization, although they are closely related. First, there is that associated with the open-access equilibrium itself. This is economically suboptimal because too many resources are being devoted to fishing. Secondly, there is some danger that the fishery may overshoot the open-access equilibrium, so that the actual level of exploitation is greater than that which might have been expected simply on the basis of average revenue being equal to long-run average cost.

The principal reason for this second kind of overcapitalization is the high profitability that seems typical of many fisheries in the early stages of development. This results in effort being attracted to the fishery not in a smooth, continuous fashion, but rather in a lump. Generally speaking, this initial rush is uncontrolled so that the build-up of fishing effort can occur extremely quickly. The problem is compounded, moreover, when *new* vessels are involved because of the time lag between their being ordered and operated. Thus current profitability (and expectations based upon it) may bear little relation to the profitability that actually occurs after a few years, but it may well continue to attract fishermen.

Of course if long-run average cost is greater than average revenue, then less than normal profits will be being earned and we might expect some people to leave the fishery. In practice however there are a number of reasons why this may not happen, or at least may happen only very slowly. To begin with, fishing vessels are very durable and tend to be fairly specific as to usage, so that it may take a long time for the long-run equilibrium to assert itself. Secondly, for what seem to be mainly sociopolitical reasons, many fishing nations subsidize their fishing fleets. This has the, perhaps unintended, result of maintaining a fishing capacity beyond even the level required for open access. There are some signs that this situation may change with the advent of 200-mile fishing limits, but within the EEC for instance it remains a major problem. Without fisheries management there seems little hope of avoiding competitive subsidization, since what one country's fleet gains another's loses. Consequently subsidies are often related to the general level of subsidy, and are frequently used to modernize the fishing fleet in some way. Often the result is simply to increase the catching capacity of the fleet without greatly affecting catch, and perhaps even decreasing it in the long run.

If the full benefits of the world's fisheries are to be realized management to avoid overcapitalization certainly seems to be required. Some overcapacity may be acceptable if a fishery is being used to create employment in a particular region, but this is clearly not an argument in favour of generalized overcapitalization.

4.3 MAXIMUM SUSTAINABLE YIELD

Having considered various reasons why management of commercial fisheries may be required, we shall now proceed to analyse the major goals that such management might have. We begin by looking at the aim that has been the most important of all in practice; that is, maximum sustainable yield (MSY). For many years, MSY was almost the only goal sought in fisheries management. As we shall see however, a number of drawbacks with it have become apparent over the years, so that other objectives have tended to take its place. Nonetheless it remains of major importance, particularly in the early stages of a management regime; and even in more mature schemes, MSY often provides the benchmark for management. For instance, under the American Fishery Conservation and Management Act, the goal of management is to achieve MSY as modified by social, economic and other factors (*see* Chapter 8 for further discussion of U.S. fisheries policy).

Doubtless one reason for the dominance of fisheries management by MSY is that it is relatively straightforward to obtain an estimate of its size. Since it is a purely physical concept, the amount of information required to be able to estimate it is much less than is the case with economically based objectives. This abstraction from economic factors also makes MSY very useful in reaching agreement on international fisheries management, since the problem that different countries tend to value fisheries in different ways is avoided.

A second reason for the popularity of MSY is perhaps the dominance of fisheries research by biologists (at least historically). Notwithstanding Burkenroad's (1953) comment that management of fish is intended for the benefit of man, not fish, many biologists seem to place the fish first in their management prescriptions. Since, for a long time, biological overfishing was considered to comprise exploitation beyond the MSY level, MSY was the obvious goal if the underlying aim was to avoid overfishing. Equally, it might be argued that MSY was in fact a misspecified economic objective in that according to Larkin (1977, p. 1), admittedly writing in a light-hearted vein, the MSY effort level was considered optimal because 'to use more is wasteful of effort, to use less wasteful of food'.

A third reason for the practical importance of MSY may also be that in many cases it was the only goal upon which agreement could be reached. As we have already mentioned, MSY was very useful for international fisheries management. Even in domestic fisheries MSY was useful because the underlying concepts are straightforward and appealing so that the support of the fishermen for a management scheme with such an aim could often be obtained. As their support is generally considered essential for successful management, MSY was a very important first step in that it enabled the move to be made from open access to management. This aspect of MSY is of more importance historically than at present however, first because of the widespread adoption of 200-mile fishing limits, which has greatly reduced the scope of international fishery bodies (*see* Chapter 7), and secondly because many fishermen now accept the need for some kind of management and they therefore ought to be persuaded that other goals are available. To a large extent this is happening in practice, in that in many fishery management programmes MSY remains as the basis but is modified according to what are perceived to be relevant factors. Whether in fact these move us very far from MSY management is much more debatable. (For further discussion *see* section 4.5 of this chapter, and Chapters 7 and 8 on international and national policy.)

The reason why MSY has been modified in practice, and why alternatives to it have been suggested, is that numerous drawbacks with it have become apparent. To begin with, no account is taken of either the value of the catch or the cost of catching it. Hence, if the open-access level of exploitation were less than MSY, management would presumably have as its aim increasing the level of effort, which is clearly nonsense. Rather more importantly from the practical viewpoint, if MSY is the goal of fisheries management, the clear implication is that management is not required if the open-access exploitation level is below MSY. Thus the espousal of MSY as the principal management goal may help to explain why in most cases management was not introduced until a fishery was in serious difficulty.

MSY, at least when based on the simpler biological models, also has deficiencies on the biological side. First, the Gordon–Schaefer model implicitly assumes a stable marine environment. In practice, however, changes in environmental conditions and year class strength (i.e. the number of fish in each cohort) are likely to make the relationship between sustainable yield and effort variable. Hence, if the management authority attempts to specify the MSY effort level and manage the fishery to this, the consequence is likely to be underexploitation in good years and over-exploitation in poor ones. There is even a possibility that in times of poor year class strength, attempting to take MSY might result in a collapse of the stock.

A second and related problem is that MSY ignores the existence of sub-stocks of a species. If within a particular fishery there are genetically different sub-stocks, then the attempt to take the MSY of the species as a whole may result in the overexploitation and possible extinction of the less productive sub-stocks. The best-known example of this phenomenon seems to be the Pacific salmon fishery. Because it is difficult to predict the strength of the salmon run, the fishery is managed by opening and closing the fishery in short bursts in an attempt to achieve the optimal escapement level. The need to do this arises principally because the fishery is vastly overcapitalized. It now appears however that sub-stocks may pass through the fishing grounds *in succession* with the result that whereas some have been very heavily fished, almost certainly to extinction, others have hardly been fished at all. It has been suggested therefore that if genetic variability is considered desirable MSY may have to be modified. It might be noted however that these problems appear to have arisen as much from the way that MSY has been sought as from the actual seeking of it. Thus, in this case, improving the techniques of management may be as much the answer as altering the objective.

To conclude, MSY has been, and to a lesser extent continues to be, very important as the basis for fisheries management. Its problems are such however that a number of alternatives to it have been suggested, and to some degree these have been adopted. Let us then go on to consider these alternatives, beginning with the goal of static maximum economic yield, which differs from MSY principally in that specific account is taken of revenue and costs.

4.4 STATIC MAXIMUM ECONOMIC YIELD

In *Figure 4.9* the open-access equilibrium is reached when average revenue equals long-run average cost with output Y_{oa} and price p_{oa}. As has already been argued, open access is suboptimal economically, because long-run marginal cost exceeds price so that the last unit produced cost society more than it was worth (on the, perhaps naïve, assumption that private and social values coincide). The optimal point would thus be where long-run marginal cost equals price, with output Y_{smey} and price p_{smey}. This position cannot be improved, since any increase in output results in a greater increase in costs than value, while any decrease causes a greater fall in value than in costs. This point is called *static maximum economic yield* (SMEY), although this terminology is perhaps a little misleading in that it is a *social* optimum. Society is making the best economic use of its resources at this point. The reason for the term 'static' will become apparent later.

Given then that Y_{smey} is the optimal output, the shaded area a-b-c represents the cost to society of overexploiting the fishery to the open-access level. Notice that this area is measurable only if the open-access equilibrium occurs with an output less than MSY. Beyond this

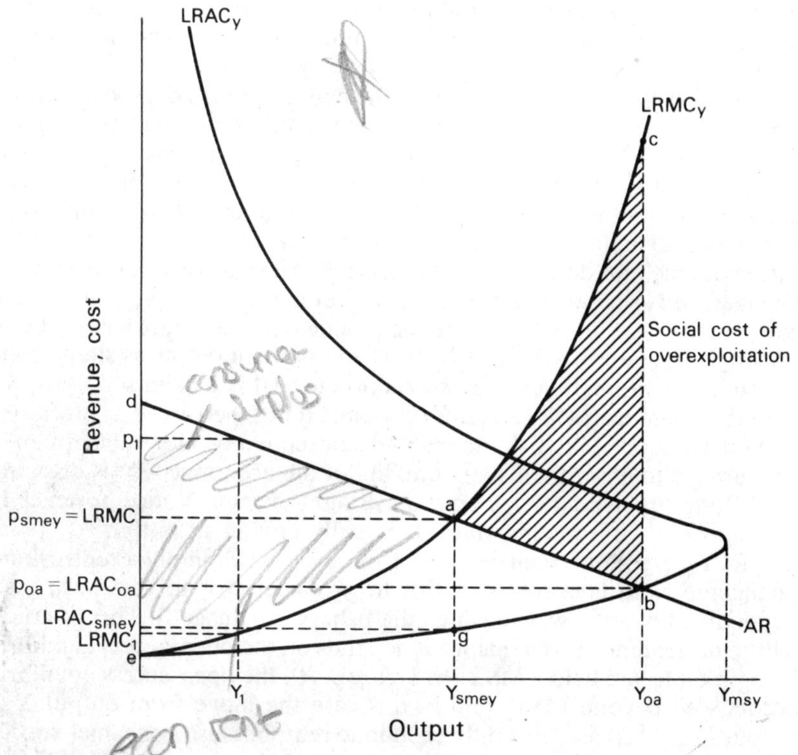

FIGURE 4.9 The static maximum economic yield and open-access equilibria.

point long-run marginal cost becomes negative and hence has no economic meaning. Notice also that because the long-run marginal cost curve is asymptotic to MSY, this latter could never be the social optimum. The model implies therefore that SMEY will always lie within the MSY level.

So far we have argued that Y_{smey} is the optimal output because it is the point at which long-run marginal cost equals price. Equivalently we might argue that it is the optimal output because the sum of *consumer surplus* and *economic rent* is maximized. The two are equivalent definitions of socially optimal resource use. Consumer surplus may be defined as the value derived by consumers from a product *in excess* of the price paid for that product. If we refer back to *Figure 4.9*, we can see that at the socially optimal output Y_{smey}, the price is p_{smey}. This is the price paid by all consumers, but some of them would have been willing to pay a higher price in order to consume the product. This is shown by the demand curve (AR). Thus if the price were to rise to, say, p_1, demand would not fall to zero but would be for an output of Y_1. The fact that consumers may have this output for p_{smey} instead of p_1 indicates that they receive a consumer's surplus of p_1 minus p_{smey}. The same is true for all other outputs up to Y_{smey}. Thus the area between the demand curve and the market price shows the consumer surplus; that is, area d-a-p_{smey}.

As well as there being this gain on the consumption side, society makes a similar gain on the production side. Once again, the market clearing price is p_{smey}. However, to produce an output of, for example, Y_1 requires resources with a marginal cost of $LRMC_1$. Society therefore receives an economic rent of p_{smey} minus $LRMC_1$ on this unit of output. A similar gain is made on all units of output up to Y_{smey}. The area of e-a-p_{smey} thus measures the economic rent derived from the fishery. Alternatively this amount may be measured as the difference between average revenue, p_{smey}, and average cost, $LRAC_{smey}$, in which case economic rent is represented by the rectangle p_{smey}-a-g-$LRAC_{smey}$. The socially optimal output is simply where the sum of consumer surplus and economic rent is maximized.

In the open-access fishery, this economic rent is perceived as profit being earned by individual fishermen, and consequently more fishermen are encouraged to enter the fishery until all of the economic rent is dissipated, when long-run average cost equals average revenue. Notice however that in *Figure 4.9* consumer surplus is actually greater at output Y_{oa} than at output Y_{smey}, so that management of the fishery will imply a redistribution of income from consumers of fish to producers (or to the government, depending upon the way in which the fishery is managed). This situation is a little misleading however since it depends on the open-access equilibrium being established below MSY. In *Figure 4.10*, the open-access equilibrium occurs well beyond MSY, and in this case the move from output Y_{oa} to output Y_{smey} increases not only economic rent, but also consumer surplus.

Much of the analysis of fisheries economics has been conducted under the assumption of a constant price of fish. In this case, there is no consumer surplus because consumers will pay the same price whatever the output, and the socially optimal output becomes simply the one that maximizes economic rent. This is where the terminology 'maximum economic yield' originates.

The traditional Gordon–Schaefer model has been widely used to explain static MEY. Because of this, and because the model often seems to result in some confusion, it may be worth briefly outlining it here. It will be recalled from section 2.2.6 that an open-access fishery is in long-run equilibrium when long-run total revenue equals total cost, at which point average revenue also equals average cost. Economic rent—the difference between total revenue and total cost—is zero. The greatest difference between total revenue and total cost occurs at the point where marginal revenue equals marginal cost, and this is therefore the point of maximum economic rent (f_{smey}). This discussion is all summarized in *Figure 4.11 a–c*. The confusion, if any, caused by this diagram generally results from its similarity to the profit-maximizing monopoly situation. As has already been pointed out (section 2.2.4), this similarity is misleading. It is true that the monopolist would produce at the point where marginal revenue equals

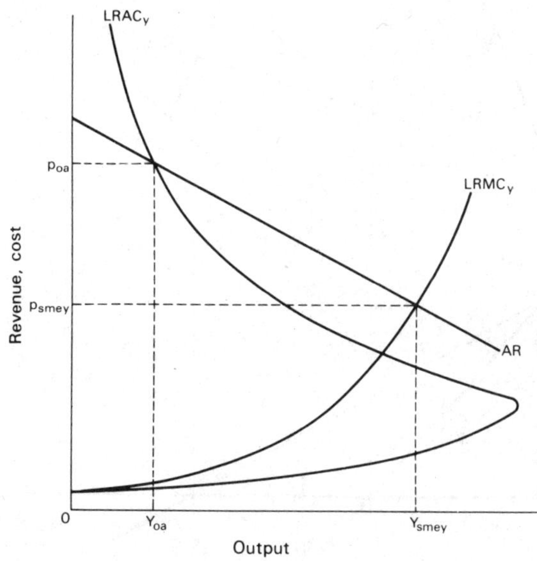

FIGURE 4.10 Static maximum economic yield.

marginal cost. Usually, such an output is suboptimal because price exceeds marginal cost so that society would gain from increased output. However in *Figure 4.11* the average revenue curve is not a demand curve and thus it does not show price. In fact, price is constant by assumption and the average revenue curve slopes downwards, owing to the diminishing biological productivity of the fish stock as fishing effort increases. Because of this diminishing productivity the socially optimal output occurs when marginal revenue equals marginal cost. If exploitation is pushed beyond this point, the decline in productivity leaves society worse off. Thus in this case we reach the paradoxical conclusion that competition is suboptimal and that a monopolist would operate at the socially optimal level. This is true however only in the particular case of a constant price of fish. If price is variable, the typical monopoly solution of insufficient output is reached, as is best demonstrated by returning to our backward-bending long-run average cost curve model.

In *Figure 4.12* we begin by assuming that the price of fish is a constant, p_1. In this case, average and marginal revenue coincide

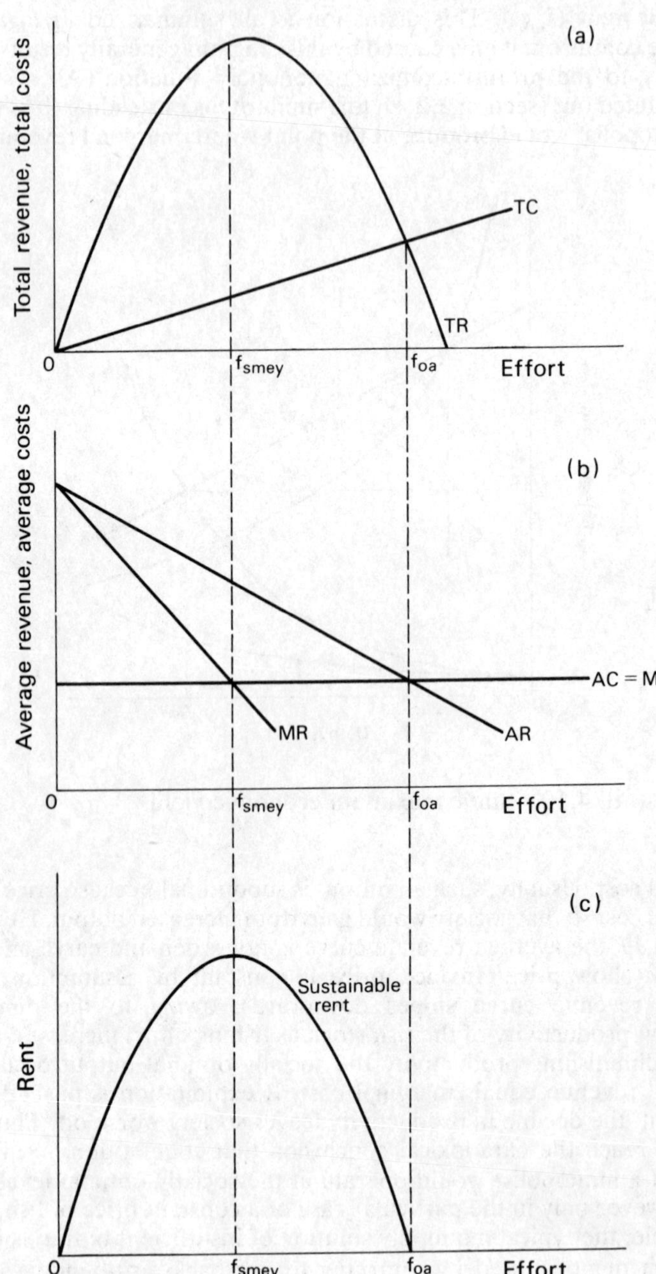

FIGURE 4.11 Open access and static maximum economic yield in the basic Gordon–Schaefer model.

($AR_1 = MR_1 = p_1$), and so therefore will the output levels corresponding to SMEY and monopoly. If however the demand curve is downward-sloping, like AR_2, then average and marginal revenue, MR_2, diverge. The socially optimal output remains at Y_{smey}, where the sum of consumer surplus and economic rent is maximized. The monopolist, however, is not concerned with consumer surplus, but simply wishes to maximize economic rent, and thus he will produce an output Y_m, where

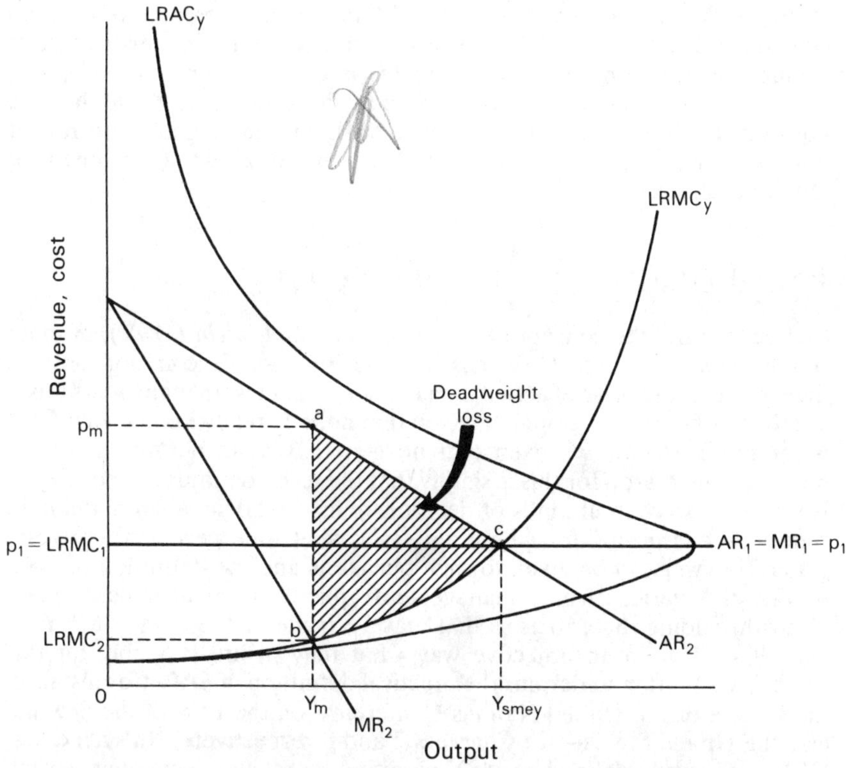

FIGURE 4.12 Monopoly and static maximum economic yield with constant and variable fish price.

marginal revenue equals long-run marginal cost, and he will charge a price p_m. As a result of his search for profit, society loses the area a-b-c. In keeping with our earlier terminology this might be called the social cost of underexploitation, although traditionally it is known as deadweight loss. Our conclusion that a monopolist will produce the socially optimal output is therefore true only under the, possibly restrictive, assumption of a constant fish price.

The principle underlying the concept of SMEY is to provide the best use of the fish stock for society. From the early 1950s to the early 1970s, this aim was consistently advocated by fisheries economists, but, to the best of our knowledge, it was not adopted in any practical management situation. A fundamental reason for this failure to adopt the SMEY concept was that during that period many of the world's more important fisheries were international in character, so that agreement on the appropriate management regime had to be reached between a number of countries. While agreement could usually be reached on the goal of MSY, it could not on appropriate economic management. As it turns out however, the failure to adopt SMEY may have been no bad thing. Recent research in fisheries economics has shown SMEY to be a special, and rather unrealistic, case of a more general concept, called *dynamic maximum economic yield*, and about which we shall have much more to say in section 4.6. As we shall see however, the fundamental problem with SMEY is that it ignores the role of time—a crucial omission in the case of fish, where growth over time is of such importance.

4.5 OPTIMUM SUSTAINABLE YIELD

In recent years, the concept of *optimum sustainable yield* (OSY), or more simply *optimum yield* (OY), has become increasingly common both in theory and as the basis of actual management schemes. In many ways this is a rather surprising development given that nobody really knows what OSY is, or more accurately, given that no generally valid definition of it is possible. The reason for this is simply that the term 'optimum' is hopelessly value-laden so that all kinds of decisions must be taken when defining it, especially concerning for whom and over what time period. Clearly, no general answer can be given to such questions and the definition of OSY necessarily varies from management plan to management plan. Notwithstanding the criticisms that may be made of MSY and SMEY, at least it is clear in an objective way what they mean. Probably for this reason, MSY often underpins the practical definition of OSY (for instance, in the case of the United Nations Conference on the Law of the Sea and also the United States—*see* Chapters 7 and 8 respectively). In such cases, OSY is generally defined as MSY modified by relevant economic, social, environmental and other factors. The crucial issue is then to decide which factors are relevant, to what extent and in what direction. The answers given to such questions are likely to vary not only from place to place, but also from time to time, in response to changes in variables such as the price of fish, the cost of fishing, unemployment among fishermen, recruitment and so on. Furthermore, although the term OSY may give the impression of being some long-run goal to be attained and maintained on a continuing basis, in fact the optimum yield may have to be less than sustainable in some years and more in others, if full use is to be made of a stock.

Probably the biggest drawback of using the concept of OSY as discussed above is that, because it is so imprecise, it may be invoked to justify virtually any level of fishing. Running a stock down, for instance, might be justified by an appeal to social factors. On the other hand, biologists may find it tempting to be rather conservative in their management prescriptions so as to minimize the risks of stock depletion. The idea of OSY as the striking of a balance between various factors is likely quickly to be lost. In practice, biological considerations tend to dominate in that, as we have said, the purely biological goal of MSY is usually specified and then modified to some extent according to relevant factors. Many fisheries biologists, perhaps not surprisingly, seem to think that this is the best general approach, even if they disagree on the detail. Larkin (1977, p. 10) states 'My personal preference is . . . fish first . . . economics second . . . and social problems a distant third.' Pitcher and Hart (1982, p. 366) claim that 'The best policy [is] to produce sound purely biological recommendations, decide what regulations might achieve them, and then bring in economic and other considerations as a way of choosing between alternative strategies of gaining the *optimal* biology, which may of course include conservation aspects as well as fish yields' (emphasis in original). We disagree with the thrust of both these statements, that it is the fish biology which is, or should be, the foremost element of management. We can see no reason why, in principle, fisheries management should not proceed by first identifying the economic optimum and then modifying it according to relevant social and biological factors (in that order). The correct way to interpret biological considerations is as a constraint on our ability to achieve the best socioeconomic situation.

What the above discussion really demonstrates is how difficult, if not impossible, it is to obtain agreement on what OSY is. As economists, we tend to put economics first; biologists put biology first. Doubtless sociologists would emphasize social factors. When interpreted in this way, OSY becomes little more than a tautology: optimum is what optimum does. However, recently a rather more concrete definition of OSY has emerged, which to distinguish it from our earlier discussion we shall call biological optimum sustainable yield (BOSY). The main aim of this concept is to deal with one drawback of MSY, namely that, at least as interpreted from simple models, it assumes a stable marine environment. In practice, environmental fluctuations may have a significant impact on population size, and hence on the available sustainable yield. Quite clearly, in the presence of such fluctuations it will not be possible simultaneously to stabilize population and catch. If population is stabilized, catch will be variable and vice versa. Controlling effective effort results in an intermediate outcome with some (smaller) variability in both population and catch. If however the effective effort level corresponding to MSY is chosen, then in the presence of unfavourable environmental fluctuations, there is a risk of stock depletion. As might be expected, the greater the degree of fluctuation the more serious are the problems posed. It has been suggested, therefore, that BOSY may be somewhat less than MSY, with a greater population size. One suggestion (Doubleday, 1976) is that population should be two-thirds of the environmental carrying capacity rather than half, as with MSY, but this level is clearly arbitrary. Generally speaking, the greater are the environmental fluctuations, the greater should be the difference between BOSY and MSY. A number of advantages are claimed for BOSY, as compared with MSY. First, the risk of stock depletion is reduced. Secondly, catch rates are increased (that is, catch per unit of effort is greater). Thirdly, fluctuations in total allowable catch (TAC) will be less from year to year.

At least some of the studies on which the above conclusions are based appear to suffer significant drawbacks. One important deficiency is that they tend to ignore the role of economics in determining the desired operating point (as opposed to the management goal). The typical approach seems to be to consider what happens if the effective effort level corresponding to MSY is applied to the fishery for a number of years. The models predict a risk of stock collapse. The question is however whether such an outcome is likely in practice. Unfortunately, it does not seem possible to give a general answer to this question—it all depends on the economic situation facing the particular fishery, coupled with certain biological factors. Of course, some stocks have collapsed (such as anchovy off Peru, and herring in the North Sea) so the debate is not empty, but at the same time many stocks exploited beyond MSY have not collapsed; for instance, the International Council for the Exploration of the Sea (1977, p. 8) estimated that almost all stocks in the North-East Atlantic Fisheries Convention region were 'overexploited' (i.e. beyond MSY).

In *Figure 4.13*, we depict a fishery being regulated to the MSY output level, which, for the sake of simplicity, is taken to coincide with the open-access equilibrium. Now suppose that an unfavourable environmental fluctuation reduces the population. This will shift the short-run cost curve upwards (from $SRAC_{y(pop.0)}$ to $SRAC_{y(pop.1)}$), reducing the desired output to Y_1. If the fall in the population size is very severe, $SRAC_{y(pop.2)}$ may become the relevant cost curve and no fishing will occur because no output exists at which demand is sufficient to cover costs. The steeper the demand curve, the greater would have to be the rise in costs for this to occur, but the crucial point is that, in the presence of environmental fluctuations, economic factors may be expected to have at least a mitigating effect and possibly even a countervailing one. Their importance is hidden however if we simply assume that effective effort is at the MSY level for a number of years.

However, stock collapses do occur, so that plainly these stabilizing forces do not always operate. It is now thought that for some species, notably shoaling pelagics like anchovy and herring, the value of the catchability coefficient may be inversely related to the stock size (e.g. Ulltang, 1980). Other things being equal, a rise in the catchability coefficient shifts the short-run cost curve downwards and this shift offsets the rise that would otherwise occur when the population falls. In the case of such species, effective effort may remain at high levels even as the population size is falling, and the risk of stock depletion is therefore likely to be much greater. The creation of a buffer stock may be required if stock collapse is to be avoided.

Overall therefore, some stocks clearly do face a significant threat of collapse given a management goal of MSY, but this seems true only of a minority. For many species, at least given current demand and cost levels, economic factors may be expected to counterbalance biological instability at least to some extent. Certainly, in our view, the need for the *general* adoption of a much more conservative strategy is not proven.

Avoiding stock depletion is not the only claim made for BOSY, however. Let us look more closely at the issue of stabilizing catch rates. The situation depicted in *Figure 4.14* is the same as that in *Figure 4.13*,

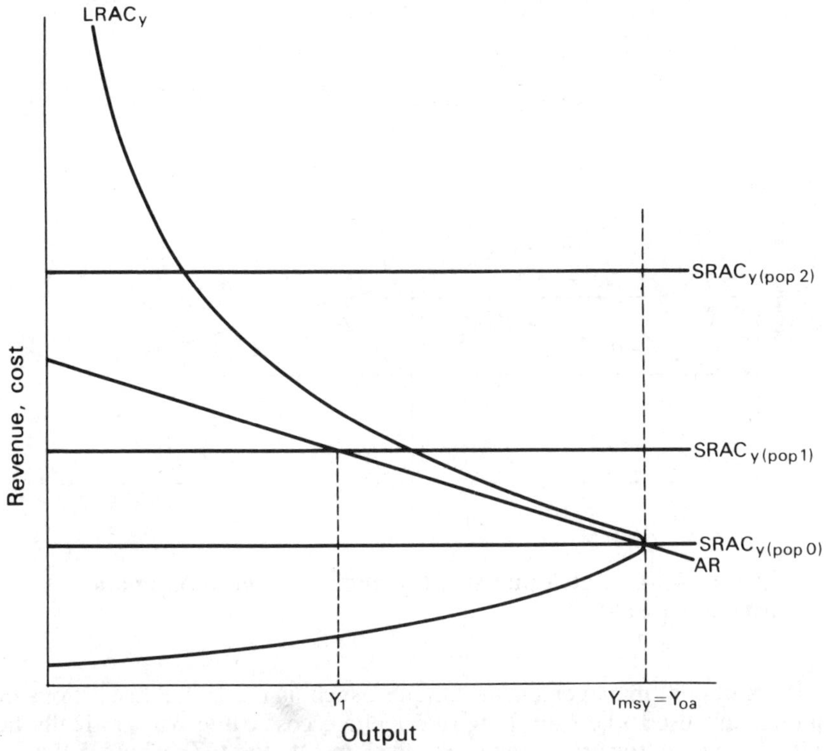

FIGURE 4.13 The effect of environmental fluctuations on the desired output level.

except that we now assume that the TAC has been established at Y_1, some way below MSY. Let us suppose initially that SRAC$_{y(pop.1)}$ becomes the relevant short-run cost curve. In this situation, there is indeed scope for stabilizing the TAC in the face of environmental fluctuations provided that these are not too great. As we have already argued, for most stocks an unfavourable environmental change will reduce the population size and shift the short-run cost curve upwards. Within the range XZ, the *desired* operating point will always lie to the right of Y_1 so that maintaining the TAC at this level will be a feasible solution. If, however, the environmental change is very severe and pushes the short-run cost curve above Z, then the desired operating point will be less than Y_1 and, *ipso facto*, catches will become variable. The question is whether the range XZ will actually exist. Once again it appears that no general answer exists. The situation depends crucially on the way in which the fishery is actually being managed. (For a full discussion of various methods of regulation, *see* Chapter 6.)

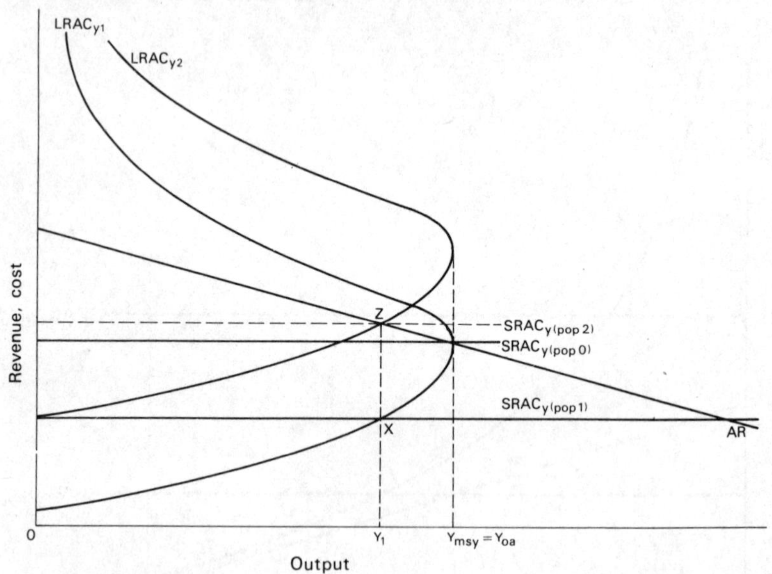

FIGURE 4.14 Catch rate stability under biological optimum sustainable yield.

If traditional management techniques, such as mesh size restrictions or quotas, are used, then the long-run average cost curve will gradually be shifted upward towards a new equilibrium, at point Z, where $LRAC_{y2}$ equals AR. Once this position is reached, any unfavourable environmental change will again be reflected in catches—because any increase in the short-run cost curve above $SRAC_{y(pop.2)}$ will decrease the *desired* output level. Only if a management regime is instituted wherein $LRAC_{y1}$ equals $SRAC_{y(pop.1)}$ represents an equilibrium situation (which in practice means an economic regulatory framework) will it be true that there is some leeway available to respond to stock size variations. Hence, the contention that BOSY will stabilize TACs appears to depend on an implicit assumption that such a regime is instituted.

Finally, let us consider the third advantage of BOSY, that catch per unit of effort is increased. This is perfectly true, but the problem is that the analysis of BOSY is generally conducted in terms of *effective* effort. By itself, this tells us very little, unless we assume that *nominal* effort declines proportionately. Again, the realism of this assumption depends on the management regime adopted. The empirical evidence (*see* Chapters 6–8) appears to indicate that nominal effort will decline only if a proper economic regulatory framework is instituted, so that once more the validity of BOSY as a goal for management depends on an implicit assumption as to the nature of this management.

In the end, therefore, we must conclude that of the three main advantages claimed for BOSY, two in fact depend on the way in which the fishery is managed rather than the output (or effort) level to which it is managed; while the other, the reduced risk of stock collapse, is much more important for some species than others. Without doubt, environmental fluctuations constitute a serious difficulty for fisheries management, but if we really do want such management to be 'optimal', we must beware of adopting unnecessarily conservative rules.

Before leaving this section let us briefly make two other points. First, BOSY appears to share with MSY the defect that it may imply that where the open-access exploitation level is below it, no management is required. In fact however, there are persuasive reasons why management should be introduced as soon as possible. Secondly, notwithstanding the clear limitations of MSY as a management goal, in most practical situations where it has been tried and failed, the blame can usually be laid squarely on the management techniques that have been used. For instance, the widespread use of quotas led, in many fisheries, to a gradual shortening of the fishing season and build-up of fishing capacity. This would have happened, however, whatever the management goal being pursued. We must be careful therefore not to alter our aims when it is our management methods that are lacking.

4.6 DYNAMIC MAXIMUM ECONOMIC YIELD

Perhaps the most serious deficiency of the objectives discussed above is their concentration essentially on the long-run situation. Implicitly if not explicitly, they consider what is happening now and over the whole adjustment period to be irrelevant provided that the appropriate long-run equilibrium is finally attained. In practice however, short-run considerations are certainly not without importance. The reason why is contained in Keynes' famous dictum, 'In the long run, we are all dead.' Dynamic maximum economic yield (DMEY) attempts to balance short- and long-term factors.

The method by which the analysis proceeds is to regard the fish stock as a capital asset, similar to a machine, that is capable of producing interest, in the form of fish, in the future. The problem is then to determine how society can best exploit this asset. Three basic strategies suggest themselves. The first strategy is that the asset should be 'cashed in'; that is, that the stock should be fished to extinction. Such a policy is most likely to appear optimal in the case of slow-growing species, such as whales. Thus, it might be argued that one of the problems in international whale management has been that the whalers themselves have had no incentive to conserve their resource base. Note however that the theory concerns itself only with the economics of the situation. Almost certainly, there will be many reasons why extinction should be avoided. A second possible strategy would be to live on the interest; that is, maintain a given size of fish stock and merely take the sustainable yield each year. Thirdly, the interest could be allowed to accumulate; that is, no fish taken at present so that a greater or more certain catch might be taken in the future. The analogy of a capital asset is less appropriate in this instance however, because as the fish population approaches the environmental carrying capacity so sustainable yield approaches zero. Of course, combinations of the three basic strategies are possible: for instance, we might take some but not all of the interest; or all of the interest, plus a little of the stock. The problem, in any case, is to decide the socially optimal strategy.

Arriving at a solution to this problem is not easy. The formal analysis is rather complex, and is well beyond the scope of an introductory text, as the reader may easily verify by following up some of the references to this section given at the end of the chapter. We shall attempt therefore merely to use the model developed earlier to indicate the major issues involved. However it must be noted that the model is essentially a static equilibrium one and is not especially well suited to explaining what is basically a dynamic disequilibrium analysis!

Let us begin by noting that society generally exhibits time preference, which simply means that any given sum of money (say, £100) will be preferred now rather than later. The difficulty is to determine how strong this preference is. What must be discovered is the amount of money that must be offered in the future so as to leave society indifferent between having that amount and having the £100 today. This will tell us the *social rate of discount*.

Suppose that we have £100 today and we invest it for one year at 15% per annum. Clearly in one year's time we shall have £115. Hence, £115 represents the future value of £100 invested today at 15% p.a. And if we were indifferent between having £115 in one year's time and £100 today, then we would be discounting the future at 15% per annum. Thus the discount rate is a kind of inverse interest rate. The £100 is said to be the *present value* of £115 available in one year's time and discounted at a rate of 15%.

If the discount rate were zero, then a given sum, again of say £100, to be received at any date in the future would have precisely the same present value as £100 available today. At the other extreme, if the discount rate were infinity then no matter how great the sum on offer in the future, its present value would always be zero. Just to emphasize how unlikely each of these extreme values is, note that a zero discount rate would imply that £101 to be received in 10000 years' time would be preferred to £100 today; while an infinite rate would imply that £100 now was preferable to £10 million to be received in two minutes' time. Fairly evidently therefore, social (and private) discount rates must be somewhere between zero and infinity, but these limits are nonetheless analytically useful for defining relevant ranges.

Let us proceed to consider the way in which DMEY uses these concepts to determine the socially optimal exploitation rate for a fishery. Let us suppose that our fishery is initially being managed at the output Y_{smey}, and is in equilibrium. This situation is shown in *Figure 4.15*. As we know, SMEY represents a social optimum in the sense that the sum of consumer surplus and economic rent is maximized. This however is a *long-run* equilibrium; it is the maximum sum available on a *sustainable basis*. SMEY does not indicate the maximum available in any one period.

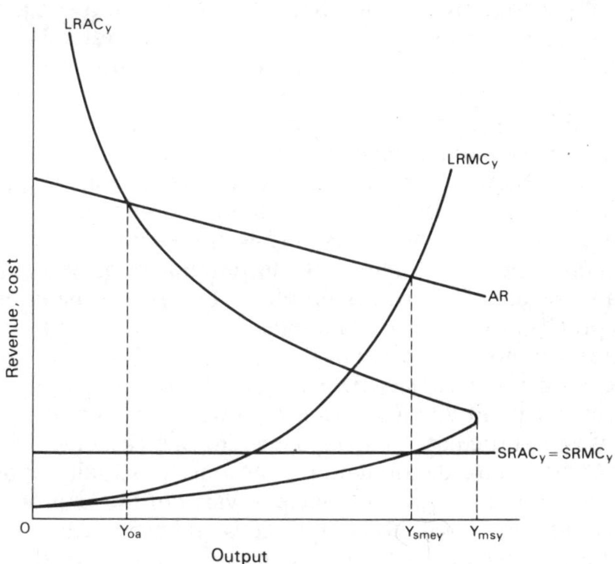

FIGURE 4.15 Static maximum economic yield.

From *Figure 4.15* it is apparent that at output Y_{smey} short-run marginal cost does not equal price. In this particular period therefore, because it is the short-run cost curves that are relevant, society can increase its welfare by increasing output up to the point where price and short-run marginal cost are équalized (output at this point being that which maximizes the sum of consumer surplus and economic rent in any one period—although because of the implicit assumption of no diminishing returns there is no economic rent). The drawback is that this output is greater than the sustainable one, and population will therefore fall, shifting the short-run cost curve upwards.The equality between *long-run* marginal cost and price will then have been lost, and consequently in future periods the sum of consumer surplus and economic rent will necessarily be at less than its potential maximum. Society must therefore counterbalance a short-run gain with a long-run loss, which of course is where the social discount rate has a vital role to play. Under DMEY it is argued that provided the value of the gain is greater than the discounted present value of the loss, then it will be worth while to increase output in the short run.

It may well be clear already that SMEY must correspond to a social discount rate of zero. If this is not apparent, consider again the move away from SMEY. Effectively, what SMEY implies is that it does not matter how great is the short-run gain; the move is not worth making because in the long run the sustainable sum of consumer surplus and economic rent will be less than its maximum. Intuitively this does not seem correct. Most people if offered the choice between £1 million today or £1 per year forever, would choose the former. SMEY however chooses the latter. The only logical basis for doing so is a zero discount rate. Here, because the £1 must be given up for each and every future period, and—crucially—because it is not discounted, the total loss must eventually exceed £1 million (or any other figure). Quite clearly therefore, SMEY represents a special, and unrealistic, case of DMEY.

Turning to the other extreme, let us consider the implications of an infinite discount rate. In this case, society would ignore the future completely in making its decisions, and would simply do the best that it could in each period. It is here that the limitations of our simple model become most severe. The principal problem however is the interpretation, and conceptualization, of what is implied by an infinite rate of discount. Such a rate does not simply mean that the future is of little importance; strictly speaking, it means that the next instant is of *no* importance. Thus, if society truly had an infinite discount rate, it would optimize from instant to instant. It is very difficult to imagine the circumstances under which society might have an infinite discount rate. The only possibility appears to be something like imminent, certain nuclear war; but the sense in which any decisions could then be said to be optimal is, at best, unclear. Obviously it is very difficult to incorporate such a concept into our model. Perhaps the closest that we can come is to consider the effect of a strategy of setting price equal to short-run marginal cost.

In *Figure 4.16* we adopt this strategy. Beginning from an equilibrium situation at Y_{smey}, our new strategy will result in an output of Y_1 being produced in the first period. Since this exceeds the sustainable yield, the fish population will fall, pushing up the short-run cost curve to, say, $SRAC_{y(pop.2)}$. The result is output Y_2, which is again greater than sustainable. Eventually, short-run cost curve $SRAC_{y(pop.3)}$ will be established, where the short-run output is sustainable. Obviously this occurs at the open-access output level, and thus an infinite rate of discount will push the fishery to this point. The range of outputs corresponding to DMEY is thus bounded by SMEY, for a zero discount rate, and open access, for an infinite rate. For normal rates, DMEY will lie between these extremes.

Possibly the most important thing to notice about DMEY is that it may be socially optimal to operate the fishery at the higher of the two long-run average costs, beyond the MSY output level. The reason why this is so is simply that if the discount rate is high enough, a short-run gain may be preferred to a long-run loss. Thus under certain conditions the move from

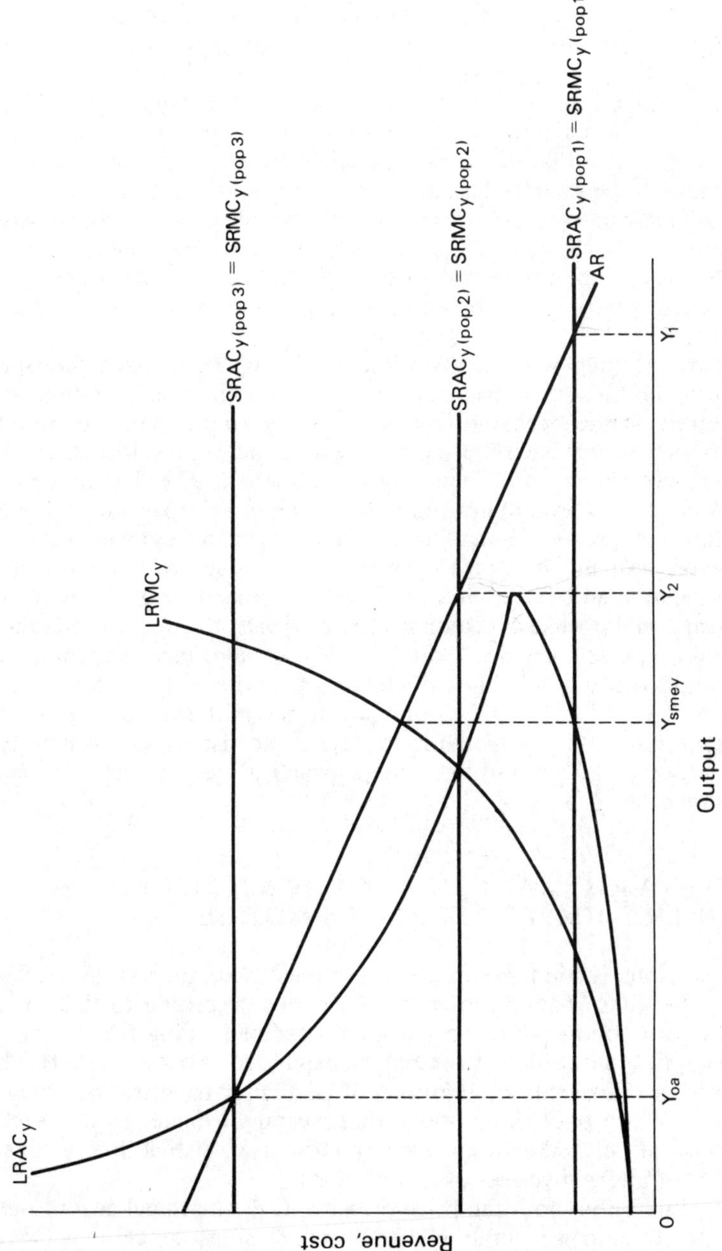

FIGURE 4.16 Dynamic maximum economic yield.

the high to the low long-run average costs that we considered at the beginning of this chapter would not be optimal.

The development of DMEY clearly represents a major theoretical advance for fisheries analysis in a number of areas. Probably its greatest contribution however has been the apparently simple one of making us aware of the crucial importance of trade-offs between the short run and the long run. This awareness has dispelled a number of myths, including the idea of the economic optimality of SMEY. One hopes that it has also laid to rest the problem that the sustainable yield curve and its cost counterpart have tended to be regarded as 'approach' curves, when they actually show points of long-run equilibrium. The classic example of this problem was the argument that MSY was suboptimal because as effort increased towards the MSY level, so output increased only at a very slow rate. Such a conclusion depends, of course, entirely on ignoring the short-run aspects of the situation.

Perhaps the biggest difficulty with DMEY concerns its practicability. Depending on the actual discount rate finally adopted, information would be required on the probable course of supply and demand for the next thirty to forty years. Clearly, we can have only the vaguest idea of what the actual figures will be. Consequently Crutchfield (1979) has argued that DMEY assumes 'a level of information on a forecast basis which is not only unavailable at present, but almost certainly will be unavailable at any conceivable cost in the future'. While there is much to this view, it is a criticism that might be applied with equal force to a great many very important social projects, including, *par excellence*, the decision whether or not to adopt nuclear energy. Crutchfield's argument merely demonstrates the great difficulty of making such decisions. In the end, it seems that one has to agree with Clark (1977b) when he argues that 'the static approach is seriously deficient . . . a dynamic theory of the fishery is not merely an academic exercise but rather a basic practical requirement in fishery management'.

4.7 DYNAMIC MAXIMUM ECONOMIC YIELD IN THE SIMPLE FISHERIES MODEL

In the previous section, we made the implicit assumptions, as shown by *Figure 4.16*, first, that the price of fish varies according to the quantity landed and secondly, that the marginal cost of landing fish is constant (which implies that fishing effort may be expanded at constant cost). These may well be reasonable descriptions of particular fisheries, but they are certainly not the only assumptions that we might make. In this section, which may be omitted without loss of continuity, we shall briefly consider the effect of alternative sets of assumptions.

If we assume that both the price of fish and the marginal cost of output are constant, then we obtain the same conclusions concerning DMEY: namely, that a zero discount rate corresponds to SMEY and an infinite one to open access. Notice however that the short-run situation is different, in that the model predicts that output will be infinite if price exceeds marginal cost and zero if vice versa (assuming an infinite discount rate). Although these assumptions are clearly too extreme, they may in fact give a reasonable description of the situation faced by a fishery where effort may easily be diverted to and from alternative fisheries. The Georges Bank haddock fishery (discussed in detail in Chapter 8) is a good example.

A more intriguing situation arises if we assume that there are diminishing returns to nominal effort so that the short-run marginal cost curve slopes upwards and diverges from short-run average cost, as in *Figure 4.17* (curves $SRMC_{y(pop.1)}$ and $SRAC_{y(pop.1)}$). Since the demand situation is not relevant, we assume constant fish price for simplicity. Again

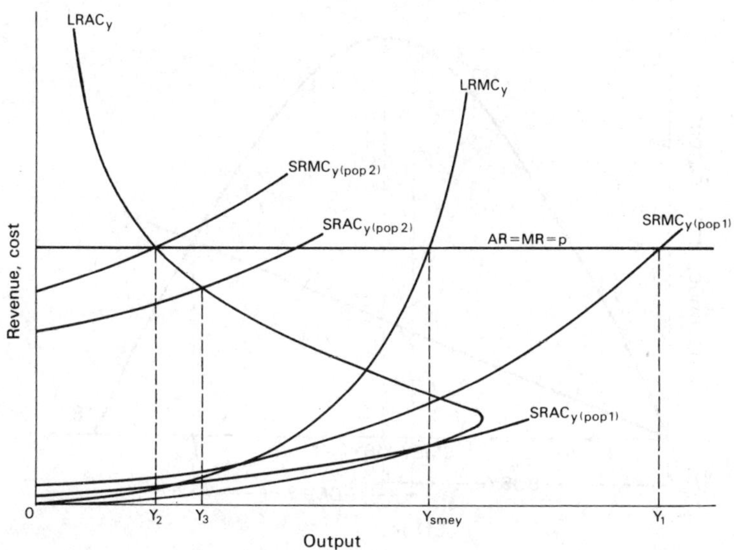

FIGURE 4.17 Dynamic maximum economic yield reconsidered.

let us assume that we begin from output Y_{smey} and, assuming an infinite rate of discount, let price equal short-run marginal cost. The socially optimal output is again greater in the first period, being Y_1. Since this exceeds the sustainable yield (Y_{smey}), the stock size must decline, shifting the cost curves upwards. It is tempting to argue that, as in the previous section, the equilibrium situation must be at the open-access level with LRAC equal to price equal to $SRMC_2$. However, this argument appears to be incorrect since the sustainable yield, Y_3 (indicated by the equality of LRAC and $SRAC_{y(pop.2)}$), exceeds Y_2. Hence the stock size must increase, shifting the cost curves downwards. The simple fisheries model appears to predict, therefore, that where there are diminishing returns to nominal effort,

DMEY with an infinite discount rate will be somewhere between SMEY and open access.

4.8 THE INTERRELATIONSHIP BETWEEN THE VARIOUS OBJECTIVES

In this section, we shall briefly indicate the relationship between the various aims. The easiest way to do this seems to be using the simple version of the Gordon–Schaefer model as shown in *Figure 4.18*. We begin by establishing the unique effort levels corresponding to MSY and

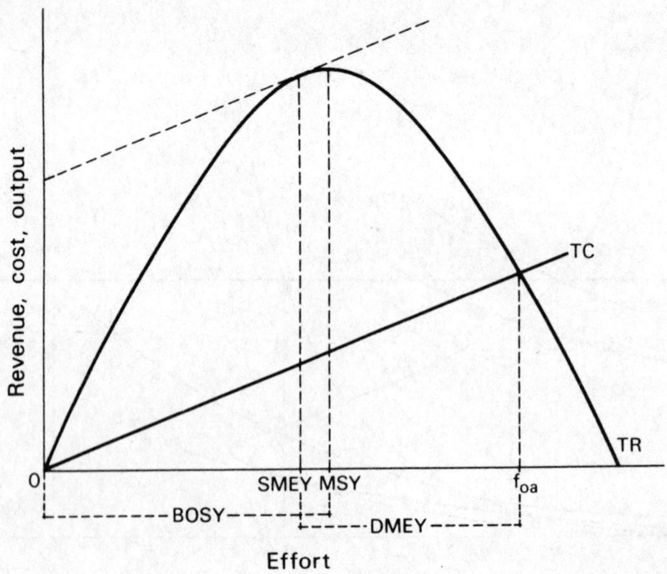

FIGURE 4.18 The interrelationship between the various objectives.

SMEY, and we then use these to define the ranges corresponding to BOSY and DMEY. There is some argument that BOSY might be continued beyond MSY, for instance in the case of the least preferred stock in a mixed fishery where taking the MSY of a preferred stock might result in overexploitation of the others. However, at least in the case of a single stock, *Figure 4.18* seems a reasonable representation of the way the objectives relate to one another.

4.9 SUMMARY

In this chapter we have analysed the fundamental goals of fisheries management. We began however by considering in some detail why such management may be required at all. Unmanaged fisheries are seen to result certainly in economic and often in biological overexploitation. As fishing technology has improved over time, there has been an increasing risk that certain stocks will suffer economic and even biological extinction in the absence of controls. This danger is heightened when there is a minimum viable population since the biological productivity curve exhibits a certain instability.

The most important goal of management is maximum sustainable yield, MSY. This has been extremely useful in the past, but, although it remains of importance, its limitations have become increasingly evident. Its major drawback seems to be that it has no economic rationale—why maximize fish production? Economists first proposed static maximum economic yield, SMEY, as an objective, but this too has drawbacks, principally its failure to take into account the importance of time.

Recently there has been a shift in opinion towards adopting optimum sustainable yield (OSY). We have argued that this concept is not definable in general terms and must necessarily vary from situation to situation. A particular version of it—biological OSY (BOSY)—seems to be of rather limited value, notwithstanding its widespread practical use, mainly because the advantages claimed for it in fact depend on a particular management course being adopted. The most important theoretical advance has been the development of dynamic maximum economic yield (DMEY). Here, the fish stock is treated as a capital asset to be exploited optimally over time.

Overall, despite the widespread debate over the goals of management, the way in which the problems of fishing are tackled is probably of more immediate importance for establishing successful fisheries in the future. It is to that issue that we next turn, looking first at the way that fishermen may solve their own problems and secondly at the ways in which management agencies may proceed.

4.10 BIBLIOGRAPHIC NOTES

For a general review of the need for and aims of management, *see* Anderson (1977, *passim*), Bell (1978, Ch. 4), Cunningham (1981) and Gulland (1974, Ch. 5).

Most papers referred to here include some discussion of the problems of not managing natural resources. Probably the best-known analysis is Hardin (1968), although as Dasgupta (1982, Ch. 2) argues, this tends to overstate the case rather. On overcapitalization *see* Clark (1977a).

MSY was long felt to be such an obvious goal for management that justifications of it are hard to find; *see*, however, Burkenroad (1953). Criticisms of the concept are much easier to come by, for example those of Larkin (1977) and Sissenwine (1978). Christy and Scott (1965, Ch. 12) compare MSY and SMEY.

SMEY is discussed by many authors. The fundamental ideas are usually attributed to Gordon (1953, 1954) and Scott (1955). Discussion and extensions of the basic theory may be found in works by Anderson (1973, 1975a–c, 1977 *passim*, 1982), Copes (1972), Crutchfield (1965, 1967, 1973) and Gates (1974). A more recent empirical application is that of Kim (1983).

The general concept of OSY is discussed by Roedel (1975). On BOSY *see* Doubleday (1976) and ICES (1977) as well as many of the references under random variations in Chapter 2.

The dynamic aspects of fisheries management, including DMEY, are discussed fully by Clark (1976) (*see also* Quirk and Smith, 1970; Sancho and Mitchell, 1975, though the following are rather more straightforward introductions to the ideas: Clark and Munro (1975), Clark (1977b), Morey (1980) and Peterson and Fisher (1977). For some criticism of the concepts *see* Bishop (1977), Crutchfield (1979) and Rettig (1973). Empirical application is rather more difficult, but *see* Henderson and Tugwell (1979).

Social factors in management are debated by Acheson (1975) and Arnold and Bromley (1970). Silvert (1978), following Walters and Hilborn (1976), considers the idea that management policy should be formulated to yield improved knowledge of the fishery so enabling better management in the future.

REFERENCES AND FURTHER READING

ACHESON, J. (1975). 'Fisheries management and the social context: the case of the Maine lobster fishery.' *Transactions of the American Fisheries Society* **104** (4): 653–68.

ANDERSON, L. (1973). 'Optimum economic yield of a fishery given a variable price of output.' *Journal of the Fisheries Research Board of Canada* **30** : 509–18.

ANDERSON, L. (1975a). 'Analysis of open-access commercial exploitation and maximum economic yield in biological and technologically interdependent fisheries.' *Journal of the Fisheries Research Board of Canada* **32** : 1825–42.

ANDERSON, L. (1975b). 'Optimum economic yield of an internationally utilized common property resource.' *Fishery Bulletin* **73** (1) : 51–66.

ANDERSON, L. (1975c). 'Criteria for maximizing the economic yield of an internationally exploited fishery.' In H. Knight (Ed.), *The future of international fisheries management*. St Paul, Minnesota; West Publishing.

ANDERSON, L. (1977). *The economics of fisheries management*. Baltimore: Johns Hopkins Press.

ANDERSON, L. (1982). 'Necessary components of economic surplus in fisheries economics.' *Canadian Journal of Fisheries and Aquatic Sciences* **37** (5) : 858–70.

ARNOLD, V. and D. BROMLEY (1970). 'Social goals, problem perception and public intervention: the fishery.' *San Diego Law Review* **7** (3) : 469–87.

BELL, F. (1978). *Food from the sea: the economics and politics of ocean fisheries.* Boulder, Colorado: Westview Press.

BISHOP, R. (1977). 'Review of "Mathematical Bioeconomics".' *Transactions of the American Fisheries Society* **106** (5): 500–1.

BURKENROAD, M. (1953). 'Theory and practice of marine fishery management.' *Journal du Conseil International pour l'Exploration de la Mer* **18** (3): 300–10.

CHRISTY, F. and A. SCOTT (1965). *The common wealth in ocean fisheries: some problems of growth and economic allocation.* Baltimore: Johns Hopkins Press.

CLARK, C. (1976). *Mathematical bioeconomics: the optimal management of renewable resources.* New York: Wiley Interscience.

CLARK, C. (1977a). 'Overcapitalization in commercial fisheries: symptoms, causes and cures.' *Environmental Biology of Fishes* **2** (1): 3–5.

CLARK, C. (1977b). 'Control theory in fisheries economics: frill or fundamental?' In L. G. Anderson (Ed.), *Economic impacts of extended fisheries jurisdiction.* Ann Arbor, Michigan: Ann Arbor Science Publishers.

CLARK, C. and G. MUNRO (1975). 'The economics of fishing and modern capital theory: a simplified approach.' *Journal of Environmental Economics and Management* **2** : 92–106.

COPES, P. (1972). 'Factor rents, sole ownership and the optimum level of fisheries exploitation.' *Manchester School of Economic and Social Studies* **40** (2): 145–163.

CRUTCHFIELD, J. (1965). 'Economic objectives of fishery management.' In J. A. Crutchfield (Ed.), *The fisheries: problems in resource management.* Seattle: University of Washington Press.

CRUTCHFIELD, J. (1967). 'Management of the North Pacific fisheries: economic objectives and issues.' *Washington Law Review* **43** : 283–307.

CRUTCHFIELD, J. (1973). 'Economic and political objectives in fishery management.' *Transactions of the American Fisheries Society* **102** (2): 481–91.

CRUTCHFIELD, J. (1979). 'Economic and social implications of the main policy alternatives for controlling fishing effort.' *Journal of the Fisheries Research Board of Canada* **36** (7): 742–52.

CRUTCHFIELD, J. and G. PONTECORVO (1969). *The Pacific salmon fisheries: a study of irrational conservation.* Baltimore: Johns Hopkins Press (for Resources for the Future).

CUNNINGHAM, S. (1981). 'The evolution of the objectives of fisheries management during the 1970s.' *Ocean Management* **6** (4) : 251–78.

DASGUPTA, P. (1982). *The control of resources*. Oxford: Basil Blackwell.

DOUBLEDAY, W. (1976). 'Environmental fluctuations and fisheries management.' *International Commission for Northwest Atlantic Fisheries, Selected Papers* **1** : 141–50.

GATES, J. (1974). 'Demand price, fish size and the price of fish.' *Canadian Journal of Agricultural Economics* **22** (3) : 1–12.

GORDON, H. (1953). 'An economic approach to the optimum utilization of fishery resources.' *Journal of the Fisheries Research Board of Canada* **10** (7) : 442–57.

GORDON, H. (1954). 'The economic theory of a common property resource: the fishery.' *Journal of Political Economy* **62** (2) : 124–42.

GULLAND, J. (1974). *The management of marine fisheries*. Bristol: Scientechnica.

HARDIN, G. (1968). 'The tragedy of the commons.' *Science* **162** : 1243–8.

HENDERSON, J. and M. TUGWELL (1979). 'Exploitation of the lobster fishery: some empirical results.' *Journal of Environmental Economics and Management* **6** : 287–96.

HOURSTON, A. (1980). 'The decline and recovery of Canada's Pacific herring stocks.' *Rapports et Procès-verbaux des Réunions du Conseil International pour l'Exploration de la Mer* **177** : 143–53.

INTERNATIONAL COUNCIL FOR THE EXPLORATION OF THE SEA (ICES) (1977). 'Report of the ad-hoc meeting on the provision of advice on the biological basis for fisheries management.' *Co-operative Research Report* No. 62.

KIM, C. (1983). 'Optimal management of multi-species North Sea fishery resources.' *Weltwirtschaftliches Archiv* **119** (1) : 138–51.

LARKIN, P. (1977). 'An epitaph for the concept of maximum sustained yield.' *Transactions of the American Fisheries Society* **106** (1) : 1–11.

MOREY, E. (1980). 'Fishery economics: an introduction and review.' *Natural Resources Journal* **20** : 827–51.

PETERSON, F. and A. FISHER (1977). 'The exploitation of extractive resources: a survey.' *Economic Journal* **87** : 681–721.

PITCHER, T. and P. HART (1982). *Fisheries ecology*. London: Croom Helm.

QUIRK, J. and V. SMITH (1970). 'Dynamic economic models of fishing.' In A. Scott (Ed.), *Economics of fisheries management, a symposium.* MacMillan Lectures, University of British Columbia.

RETTIG, R. (1973). 'Multiple objectives for marine resource management.' In A. Sokoloski (Ed.), *Ocean fishery management: discussions and research.* NOAA Technical Report, NMFS Circular 371.

ROEDEL, P. (1975). *Optimum sustainable yield as a concept in fisheries management.* American Fisheries Society, Special Publication No. 9.

SANCHO, N. and C. MITCHELL (1975). 'Economic optimization in controlled fisheries.' *Mathematical Biosciences* **27** : 1–7.

SCOTT, A. (1955). 'The fishery: the objectives of sole ownership.' *Journal of Political Economy* **63** (2) : 116–4.

SILVERT, W. (1978). 'The price of knowledge: fisheries management as a research tool.' *Journal of the Fisheries Research Board of Canada* **35** : 208–12.

SISSENWINE, M. (1978). 'Is MSY an adequate foundation for optimum yield?' *Fisheries* **3** (6) : 22–4; 37–42.

ULLTANG, O. (1980). 'Factors affecting the reaction of pelagic fish stocks to exploitation and requiring a new approach to assessment and management.' *Rapports et Procès-verbaux des Réunions du Conseil International pour l'Exploration de la Mer* **177** : 489–504.

WALTERS, C. and R. HILBORN (1976). 'Adaptive control of fishing systems.' *Journal of the Fisheries Research Board of Canada* **33** : 145–59.

CHAPTER 5

Response by firms to the problems of fishing

5.1 INTRODUCTION

In previous chapters we have considered the way in which fishing affects certain biological and economic variables. Theory and empirical evidence have been used to show that in open-access fisheries resources are likely to be misallocated. As such this misallocation is a social problem, since it is society that loses out in terms of foregone output, whether it be of fish or some other commodity. It should nonetheless be apparent that the situation described may also be a problem to the industry itself. In this chapter therefore consideration will be given to the problems as they may be perceived by individual firms, and the way firms have responded to them.

5.2 THE NATURE AND CAUSE OF THE PROBLEMS

Anything that makes it harder for a commercial firm to achieve its objective will be seen as a problem. This definition would therefore apply to whatever jeopardizes profitability, if one accepts the arguments of Chapter 1 that commercial firms are profit-orientated. In the case of firms with other objectives, then factors affecting these could also be defined as problematical.

Problems are classified into three main groups. Their selection is based not on the multitude of things that *could* make commercial life more difficult for a firm but on the events and circumstances that *have* been witnessed in fishing at various times and places. The list, in other words, is an empirical one.

In the first group are included those characteristics of fishing which are, so to speak, a fact of life for those involved. Catch per unit of effort (CPUE) varies in the short term with changes in the natural environment, and this variation in turn causes price movements. The combined effect is to cause *fluctuations in income*. The reason why these may be a problem for the individual firm is that first, they constitute risk to which the firm may be averse, and secondly, they may be embarrassing to a firm that needs a reasonably steady cash flow to cover variable costs. Another problem which can be included here is that of *perishability* of the raw material. This, of course, is a purely biological characteristic, and one that is common to all species without exception. What mitigates the severity of these problems is that, provided firms have reasonable knowledge of their magnitude, then when choosing whether or not to enter a fishery they at least have some idea of the difficulties they may face. Many firms would no doubt prefer not to have to cope with them, but so long as income fluctuations or perishability do not worsen over time, then they represent merely an 'occupational hazard' rather than an ever-growing threat to commercial viability.

The same cannot be said for the problems in the second group. To start with one can point to the *downward trend in CPUE* that occurs as stocks are depleted, owing to increasing exploitation over time. The theory of why this occurs has been explained in Chapter 2, and actual instances of it are given throughout the book. As we have argued in Chapter 1, a fall in CPUE implies an increase in unit costs for the individual firm.

Falling CPUE and rising unit costs may be perceived as problems in themselves, but their significance goes further. Specifically, they will affect fishing's competitive position vis-à-vis other food industries—all the more severely where the productivity of competitor industries has been rising relatively rapidly. This appears, in fact, to have been the case in the United States, with adverse consequences for the demand for fish products (Bell and Kinoshita, 1973). However what sets these apart from the other problems mentioned above is that, so long as they persist, they constitute a worsening problem for the fishing industry. This is made all the more serious by the failure of many firms to foresee accurately that the time path of CPUE may well continue downwards into the future. Problems in this category are thus inherently more pernicious than those in the first.

The third category comprises those events which are wholly exogenous; that is, they stem from outside the industry. Such events may be non-recurring but their severity is often magnified by their being unforeseen. A once-and-for-all *rise in the cost of key inputs*, such as occurred in the case of fuel oil in 1973–74, is an example. Here the rise was greater than the underlying rate of inflation, and was unexpected. Though the effects of the oil price rise were eventually dissipated, the immediate impact on the fishing industry was a reduction in profitability. Also within this category one can include *catch and effort restrictions* imposed by national and supra-national authorities. Details of some of these will be given in the next chapter. What must be understood now is that though these restrictions may be designed to solve some of the problems of open-access fisheries, the short-run effect on individual firms may be one of severe hardship. Moreover the contention that 'in the long run' such restrictions may well improve the financial performance of fishing firms overlooks the concept of time preference; a given sum of money now is always to be preferred to the same sum received in the future. In any case, such an argument presupposes that catch and effort restrictions will be successful in the long run. Past experience shows this is not always so.

5.3 POSSIBLE RESPONSES BY FIRMS

In this section we shall review the range of options that are open to a firm seeking a solution to any of the problems identified above. There are numerous ways of classifying these responses, and the approach taken requires some explanation.

A conceptual distinction often made by economists is between 'targets', which are the variables that the decision-maker wishes to change, and 'instruments', which are the variables that the decision-maker is able to change. If there is a link between them then it is via certain intermediate variables; these, however, cannot be manipulated directly by the decision-maker. Nevertheless, possessing the instruments and knowing the links clearly gives the decision-maker a course of action.

The decision-maker in this context is the individual firm, and the possible responses listed below are in the nature of instruments. The targets are those variables which give rise to the problems. An alternative approach would have been to list intermediate variables, but this would have suffered the drawback that it would not make clear exactly what the firm was expected to do to affect these variables. For example, if profitability is the target variable then one can hypothesize that it would be affected by, among other things, the level of demand. Merely to state that 'raising demand' is a possible response by a firm suffering from low profitability is oversimplistic. It immediately invokes the question: 'but how?'. Accordingly, we have tried to identify the courses of action that are under the firm's control and which, on the basis of links that may exist *a priori*, could ameliorate the problems they face.

The catalogue of possible responses that we are about to list is limited in two respects. First, it focuses only upon the *active* behaviour of firms. That is to say, it illustrates the ways in which fishing firms actively attempt to modify or remove the constraints under which they have to operate. These constraints are set by the natural and human environment, and determine the shape and position of the demand and cost curves which the firm has to face at any point in time. We do not consider *passive* behaviour, which involves the acceptance of constraints by the firm and the attempt to reach its objective within them. Such behaviour would include, for example, price and output adjustments by a firm in response to changes in demand, or shutdown and withdrawal from the industry if market price fell below a firm's average variable cost. Unlike active behaviour therefore, passive behaviour is essentially non-discretionary; a firm that wishes to maximize profit has little choice but to 'move with the market' or, in the limiting case, cease trading completely (so as to minimize loss). As an analytical framework for studying business behaviour, the distinction between active and passive does have considerable merit (Hay and Morris, 1979, p. 29). Its application in the present context would appear to be valid, though one should be mindful of the fact that some of the constraints under which fishing firms have to operate are peculiar to the industry.

The discussion is also limited to the non-political behaviour of fishing firms. Such courses of action as representations to government, or negotiations with public authorities, are therefore excluded. Though these may have important implications for the industry or society, we feel that economics can offer only a partial explanation for their occurrence.

The possible responses we have identified are as follows:

(1) *Shift to different fishing grounds or stock*—perhaps by hunting for the same species but on grounds where stock abundance is higher, or which are not subject to restriction, or where CPUE is less prone to fluctuations. An alternative would be to search for different varieties of fish, either in the same or another area. The first option offers a possible way of overcoming the effects of falling and/or variable CPUE; the second gives the firm a chance to exploit potentially better market opportunities for the species being sought; for example, the new species may have a higher income elasticity of demand than the original one, and thus a greater future earnings potential.

(2) *Transform the product*. The options here are either the transformation of the raw material into another standardized product such as fishmeal, fillets, fish oil, etc., or into a 'unique', that is, a differentiated, product. Both are ways in which the firm may increase value added by its activities, and hence the amount of money available for wages and profits. Income elasticity of demand may also be positively affected. Another advantage is that depending on how it is carried out, transformation of the raw material can help to overcome the perishability problem, especially if the product is a dried one such as fishmeal.

(3) *Restructure the firm or its fleet*. There are a number of organizational changes that can be made. To start with, the firm may modify its ownership status, perhaps by changing from a sole proprietorship or partnership into a limited company. Changes of this kind may enable it to take advantage of greater security and/or tax benefits attaching to one legal entity rather than another. Then there are the opportunities offered by integration.* Horizontal integration is in theory a way in which a firm can achieve the benefits that often accompany large size: specifically, by being able to exploit economies of scale or by obtaining some degree of market power. Vertical integration allows the firm to increase its involvement in processing and marketing (in the case of a fishing firm that is integrating 'forwards') or in fish catching (in the case of a processing firm that is integrating 'backwards'). The benefits here would be in terms of reduced

*A firm may integrate its activities either 'horizontally' or 'vertically'. Horizontal integration refers to the undertaking by a single firm of one distinct stage in the production of a good or service. Vertical integration refers to the undertaking by a single firm of successive stages in the production of a good or service.

risks, cost savings, greater opportunities for changing the nature of the product, or greater control over the natural resource (depending upon the direction in which the integration takes place). Diversification into other products and activities similarly helps reduce risks as well as being a way of moving into areas with greater growth potential. Finally, a firm may develop more flexible production capacity (e.g. multipurpose vessels), in order for it to be able to adapt relatively swiftly to changes in resource availability and market circumstances.

(4) *Increase efficiency*. The options for increased efficiency are as follows. First, by withdrawing the least efficient vessels the firm can raise the efficiency of the fleet as a whole. The margin of efficiency can also be extended at the other end, so to speak, by adopting any available technical innovations or by adding to the fleet vessels large enough to exploit economies of size. Even within the confines of a given technology however, it may be possible to economize on the more expensive inputs and in effect to substitute others in their place; for example, to carry out fishing in such a way as to minimize the use of higher-priced fuel.

(5) *Undertake research and development*. The main areas for R & D as far as commercial fishing firms are concerned relate to the production system (including aquaculture), processing techniques and the products themselves. For example, a firm may experiment with alternative methods of search and capture, new ways of gutting and filleting the raw material, or new consumer fish preparations. The common element in all these is that the firm is trying to generate technical know-how which did not previously exist. If successful, the firm then has the option of applying the results either to production (in terms of lower costs) or to the product (in terms of quality, market potential or price). If the latter, some accompanying market research may be needed. It should be apparent that options (2) and (4) listed above are to some extent facilitated by the knowledge generated by R & D.

(6) *Cooperate with other fishing firms*. There are four main areas for cooperation. First, there is the regulation of fish supplies to the market so as to raise average returns. Cooperation may be extended to other stages in the marketing chain, especially if processing is undertaken. Generic advertising and other promotional techniques may also be tried, the aim here being to increase the quantity bought at any given price. The second area for cooperation is in procurement, the intention being that group purchasing may secure cheaper inputs to member firms. The third area concerns the production process itself and involves the limitation of fishing effort, the rationale being that in the short run this may restrict output and raise price, and in the long run permit recovery of stocks and an increase in CPUE. Finally, there is cooperative R & D. The scope and rationale would be the same as for an individual firm's R & D (discussed under heading 5), though cooperation makes it possible to carry out R & D on a larger scale.

Like the limitation of fishing effort however, cooperative R & D is essentially a long-run attempt to solve a firm's problems.

5.4 ACTUAL RESPONSES

We shall now consider the way in which firms have actually responded to economic problems in practice, The headings below do not correspond precisely to those used in describing the possible responses by firms, one reason being that some types of response have not been extensively practised and accordingly we shall discuss them together under a single heading. Another reason is that one of the more important developments of recent years—international joint ventures—does not fall neatly into any one of the previous categories and therefore deserves to be treated separately.

5.4.1 Effort relocation

Until comparatively recently, firms were able to transfer catching capacity from one sea area or fish stock to another in an almost unimpeded fashion. In fact the relocation of fishing effort, both geographically and biologically, is one of the classic ways in which firms have responded to economic problems.

The development of the British fishing industry provides a useful case study to illustrate how the area fished gradually extended during the nineteenth and twentieth centuries (Oddy, 1971). Before 1840 fishing was mainly coastal. In 1891, trawling off Iceland by British vessels commenced. By 1905 trawlers had begun visiting the Barents Sea, and by 1914 fishing grounds extended from Bear Island, Spitzbergen and the White Sea in the north to the Moroccan coast in the south. The period between the world wars witnessed a continuation of the process. Falling CPUE on near and middle-water grounds goaded many firms into searching for fish in more distant waters where stock abundance was higher. Admittedly, not all firms responded in this way. While Hull trawlermen concentrated increasingly on distant-water exploitation, skippers in other ports aimed to secure a limited quantity of high-quality, high-unit-value species from waters nearer to home (Kelsall, 1948). Though in retrospect it would appear that Hull made the 'correct' decision, to judge by the fact that the profitability of distant-water fishing was nearly three times that of near and middle-water fishing (Kelsall, p. 104), the correct course of action at the time was not an obvious one. What seems to have been common to all ports however was the belief that a possible solution to economic problems could be found by changing the resource base of the industry, either in terms of geographical location or raw material input.

This kind of response was facilitated in the United Kingdom's case by a number of factors. The application of steam and (later) diesel power in vessels, and the use of preservation techniques (initially ice and later on-board freezing), made it possible to extend the area fished while still retaining reasonable standards of product quality. Market acceptance did not seem to present many difficulties since the species offered to the consumers were familiar to them. Moreover, access to distant waters remained virtually unhindered until the 1970s.

However, the political events of that decade have reversed the earlier historical trend. Exclusion from Iceland's 200-mile Exclusive Economic Zone in the late 1970s forced the United Kingdom's distant-water operators to take greater advantage of alternative catching opportunities to the north of Norway in the Barents Sea. When Norway in turn extended her limits the fleet was forced back onto waters nearer home (Select Committee on the European Communities, 1980, p. 36). Whereas in 1968 over one-third of all fish landed by weight in the United Kingdom by British vessels came from the main distant-water grounds of Iceland, Norway and the Barents Sea, by 1978 the proportion was down to less than 5%. Concomitantly, landings from the near and middle-water grounds of the North Sea and English Channel rose over the same period from 37% to nearly 70%. Unfortunately for many firms however, the comparative ease with which the area of exploitation had been extended in the past did not hold in reverse. Generally, distant-water vessels found the stock abundance of near and middle-water grounds insufficient to support viable operations. In this situation, many firms responded by either laying up vessels, scrapping them or selling out.

The British experience appears to be fairly typical. Dr Kenneth Lucas of the FAO sees the shift of effort to less heavily exploited stocks as the 'traditional reaction' by fishing firms to reductions in the availability of raw materials (Lucas, 1980, p. 3). Supporting evidence comes from other writers. For example, Cary (1979) describes how U.S. tuna fishermen responded to the imposition of management measures by fishing outside the regulatory area after the season closed, which brought them towards the central Pacific and close to the African coast. McHugh (1972), discussing the marine fisheries of New York State, shows how over a ninety-year period landings were maintained by 'constantly shifting from one resource to another as the stocks of each have declined in turn' (p. 585). Driscoll and McKellar (1979) draw attention to the movement of fishing effort from successive stocks in the north-east Atlantic and give two examples. One is the increasing exploitation of the western mackerel stock by several countries in response to the reduced availability of herring, caused by stock depletion as well as catch restrictions. Another is the movement of the Norwegian purse seine fleet from the Atlanto–Scandian herring stock, which became depleted during the period 1955–70, to the North Sea herring, to mackerel and then to capelin. The economic history of pelagic whaling is likewise characterized by a relocation of fishing effort, away from stocks of blue whale and towards those of other species. The sequence of exploitation appears to have been blue whales, fin whales, sei whales, and most recently, minke whales (Clark and Lamberson, 1982, pp. 105–6).

Now that many distant-water grounds have been closed or have had access restricted by extended fisheries jurisdiction, and grounds nearer home have become more heavily exploited and subject to greater regulation, so the freedom of action by individual firms to catch what they like and where they like has been impaired. It has been claimed that the Antarctic is virtually the only region where this option of transferring effort from one area to another still exists, and that even the Antarctic would be fished much more than it is if species such as krill could be converted into a more marketable product (Lucas, 1980, p. 3). If it is true that firms will find it harder in future to make this kind of 'supply-orientated' response, then they may be obliged to take fuller advantage of some of the other options.

5.4.2 Restructuring

As indicated in Chapter 1, the ownership pattern in most fishing industries is extremely diverse. Though it might be expected *a priori* that firms would consider changing their ownership status as economic circumstances alter, it is hard to demonstrate empirically that they do so. Broad historical trends are, however, discernible. In the United Kingdom's case, the adoption of limited-liability status can be traced back to the nineteenth century and at present a multi-vessel British firm is more than likely to be run as a limited company. However, such firms even now are in the minority, and though they tend to be the larger ones on average, in the early 1980s they still accounted for less than half the total catching capacity of the British fleet. The rest comprises vessels run on a sole-proprietorship or partnership basis. Moreover, one fact is clear: once a fishing firm has taken on a certain legal form it does not alter it very readily. That this should be the case despite the ups and downs of commercial life suggests that firms do not regard ownership status as a variable that can be adjusted to cope with these changing fortunes, except perhaps where sustained long-term economic pressure forces it upon them.

Horizontal integration, which was also mentioned as a possible structural response, does not appear to have taken place to any great extent. More especially, there is no clear evidence that fishing firms have pursued horizontal growth as a deliberate way of capitalizing on economies of scale or greater market power. Part of the reason could be that in fishing, economies of scale may be non-existent or relatively unimportant; another is that the majority of firms are so small relative to the size of the market that any thoughts of achieving dominance individually are pure delusion. One exception to these remarks concerns the proposed merger in 1966 between the two large British fishing firms, Ross Group Ltd and Associated Fisheries Ltd, which was investigated by the Monopolies Commission and subsequently vetoed (Monopolies Commission, 1966). The justification for the merger—which would have given the combined firm a fleet of about 150 large vessels as well as substantial onshore facilities—was that economies in trawling could be obtained which, it was estimated, would raise the rate of return on capital by approximately $1\frac{1}{2}$%. The two firms denied any possibility of being able to restrict supplies of fish and to regulate the price, though this was the reason why the Monopolies Commission in the end disallowed the merger. Whether the Commission's decision was correct is not, however, the point at issue. The point is that the firms clearly believed that benefits (to them) would accrue from the merger—presumably some combination of 'genuine' cost savings as well as market power—and they tried to take advantage of them. It is doubtful however whether such benefits could have materialized if the two firms concerned had not already been large; indeed, they were at the time the largest in the British industry. The vast majority of firms were, then as now, small one-vessel enterprises. It is difficult to envisage any benefits accruing from an amalgamation between two such firms, other than perhaps slightly greater financial stability. In any event, there was no obvious 'merger mania' apparent in the British fishing industry in the mid to late 1960s (as there was in other sectors of the economy), despite the onset of fairly severe economic difficulties towards the end of the decade. To the extent that the fishing industries of other Western countries are similarly characterized by large numbers of small decision-making units, then these observations may have some general validity.

In a similar way, the majority of fishing firms have shown no propensity to integrate forwards into processing, marketing and distribution. Where forward integration has occurred it is invariably the larger fishing firms that have been responsible. However, processors and manufacturers have shown a far greater willingness to integrate backwards into fishing, as can be illustrated by the Peruvian anchoveta fishery. During the 1950s and 1960s most of the seiners in this fishery soon became owned by the fishmeal companies, who found supplies delivered by the independent operators too irregular (Coull, 1974). U.S. tuna processors have also bought up vessels with the result that in the 1970s approximately 25% of the U.S. tropical tuna fleet was 'cannery-owned' (King, 1978). Additionally, the processors may either provide financial backing to independent skippers who buy new vessels, or help with the sale of older vessels, in return for a contract with the skipper over the sale of his catch (King, 1978, 1979). Atlantic menhaden is another product for which vertical links have been established by the processors, most of whom own or control fishing vessels (Penn, 1977).

But if processors have responded in this way, why not the primary producers themselves? There are four possible explanations. The first is that fishing firms, being small, may find it insuperably difficult to acquire the capital necessary to establish processing and distribution facilities at a technically efficient scale. A second explanation, offered by Nicholls (1978), is that in fishing the time horizon between the commitment of variable inputs and the attainment of output is relatively short—basically, the length of a fishing trip. This in itself makes for planning flexibility. In agriculture, by contrast, the farmer has to commit resources well in advance of the harvest, and at a time when future market conditions are uncertain. Accordingly, there may be less incentive for fishermen to try to ensure themselves a price or a market in advance by integrating forwards. The third reason is that the 'opportunist' nature of some types of fishing (that is, catching what is available rather than directing effort at a target species) does not lend itself to processing, which normally requires a degree of uniformity in size and type of fish. Thus a fishing firm that wished to set up processing facilities would also need to reorientate its strategy to one of 'directed' rather than 'opportunist' fishing. Lastly, those firms that do direct their effort to a target species can hardly be oblivious of the possibility that the fishery they are currently exploiting may not last forever and that they may have to seek another in due course. If they were vertically integrated then this change of fishery would probably entail modification of their processing facilities to cope with any new species. The recognition that such an adjustment would be expensive would detract from the benefits of forward integration.

Though fishing firms do not seem to have responded by vertical integration, there are signs that they have been prepared to diversify away from commercial fishing in certain circumstances. The evidence is somewhat anecdotal, and the response seems to vary from country to country. As far as the United Kingdom is concerned, some firms have become involved in sport fishing. Vessel owners in the south-west, for example, have taken advantage of the growth in tourism in that region since the Second World War by offering summer angling trips to holidaymakers. At the other end of the country some firms have abandoned fishing, partly or wholly, in favour of offshore installation servicing, an example being the provision of standby vessels for oil rigs in the North Sea. This switch from fishing occurred noticeably in the 1970s, a time when the economic conditions in the oil industry contrasted sharply with those in fishing. Other firms have gone into the oil business directly. In March 1980 the Fishermens Petroleum Company was set up to drill in the North Sea. Another direction in which diversification has taken place is into general food manufacturing, though as we might imagine this type of diversification has been limited to the few large fishing firms that already have processing facilities. Elsewhere the picture is less clear. One documented case of firms trying to reduce their dependence on fishing is in the Atlantic ground fishery. MacKenzie (1979) reports that in the early 1970s, Canadian fishermen as a whole derived only 50% of their income from fishing, the rest coming from other sources. MacKenzie argues that this diversification has been a response to the depressed state of the industry.

The logic of diversification clearly applies to the development of more flexible production capacity. Multipurpose vessels (ones capable of exploiting several discrete fisheries) are an example of such a development. Huppert (1979, p. 852) has likened them to a diversified investment portfolio, since they are less exposed to financial risk. Though it has been argued that the technologically advanced nations have increased their multipurpose harvesting capability during the 1960s and 1970s (McDiarmid, 1980), the statistical evidence is not very convincing. Figures published by the FAO suggest that, of the developed countries, the United States had the greatest proportion of multipurpose vessels in her fleet; in 1975, 27.5% of the total gross registered tonnage of fishing vessels consisted of multipurpose vessels (FAO, 1981). For Canada the equivalent figure was 12.5%. Many countries made little or no use of such boats. Also of significance is the fact that in the United States the reliance on multipurpose vessels has not altered very rapidly; even in 1970, 25% of the fleet's total tonnage consisted of multipurpose vessels. What these figures suggest is that globally, firms have not made very strong moves in the direction of greater harvesting flexibility; and in the United States, where some degree of flexibility is in evidence, recent years have not witnessed any great increase.

5.4.3 Research and development, and product transformation

Research and development and product transformation are two aspects of business behaviour that can be dealt with together, since in practice we find that they are not perceived by many fishing firms as a feasible solution to economic problems. Most fishing firms are too small even to countenance the idea of R & D. Even if size were not a constraint it is questionable whether firms would regard R & D as the complete answer; the outcome is long-term and uncertain, and if firms embark on a costly solution to their problems then they wish to be reasonably certain that the remedy will work, and without too much delay. The small minority of firms that undertake R & D concentrate on those areas where the economic ramifications are clearest. In practice they have carried out R & D concerned with the development of vessels, equipment and methods, experimental fishing and the investigation of underutilized species, and aquaculture. Some fishing firms undertake R & D into improved processing methods and new product development, though invariably the few firms concerned are all large, vertically integrated or diversified.

The fact that the fishing industries of Western countries consist of many small, specialized firms is also a reason why product transformation is not extensively practised by firms whose principal activity is on the catching side. Product transformation, and the advertising that may need to accompany it, is really the prerogative of firms which not only catch fish but which have forward linkages into processing, marketing and distribution. Such vertically integrated firms are, as we have already seen, in the minority. This is not to say that the raw material remains unchanged. Transformation does take place, but the agents responsible for it are, typically, firms whose main activities are onshore. By the same token, where brand labelling and advertising take place, it is usually the processors and distributors who do it. Besides, if fish processors are engaged in other functions it may not necessarily be in fish catching; it is just as likely to be in the manufacture of other foodstuffs such as meat and vegetables.

It would seem therefore that the reason why R & D and product transformation are not commonly undertaken by fishing firms is to be found in the structure of the industry itself. Because large, multifunction firms are in the minority, the preconditions for these two types of conduct are lacking.

5.4.4 Efficiency improvement

We indicated earlier that one of the ways in which a fishing firm can increase its overall efficiency is by withdrawing its less efficient vessels from service. In practice it is clear that firms do respond in this way if economic conditions are severe enough. We can illustrate the point by observing what happened in the British fishing industry during the mid 1970s. The period was a bad one for the profitability of the deep-sea fleet, as shown by the data in *Table 5.1*. Gross profitability, which was already negative in 1973, deteriorated drastically over the following three years.

TABLE 5.1 Gross annual profitability of British deep-sea vessels 1973–76

Length	*1973*	*1974*	*1975*	*1976*
80–110 ft	–26.3	–42.4	–67.9	–72.2
110–140 ft	–34.6	–53.5	–94.3	–97.4
140 ft and over (wet fish)	–87.1	–108.6	–191.6	–221.2
Freezer vessels	–143.9	–157.6	–309.4	–235.7

Figures are given in thousands of pounds sterling per vessel, with depreciation. (1 ft = 0.305 m.)
Source: McKellar and Steel (1980, p. 16).

This was accompanied by a shakeout of vessels at a much faster rate than previously. In the four years 1969–72 inclusive, boats were withdrawn from the deep-sea fleet at an average rate of 20 per year. In the four years 1973–76 the rate more than doubled to 48 vessels p.a. The average number of vessels per firm in the offshore sector fell from over 9 in 1973 to less than 8 in 1976, suggesting that firms reacted to the problem by cutting back on catching capacity, starting with the least profitable in the fleet. While some of the vessels that were withdrawn were transferred by their owners to other maritime activities, and as such represented an act of diversification by the firm, it is known that a large number were simply scrapped or mothballed. The effect of this was to allow fishing firms to consolidate their activities on the basis of fewer, more profitable and more efficient vessels.

An interesting case study of the response by one firm to the economic difficulties of the 1970s is that of Associated Fisheries PLC, the largest firm in the British fishing industry. The net profits of the company were on a rising trend up to the early 1970s, reaching a peak of £5.9 million in 1974. The following year however, the company made a loss of over £2 million, and since that date every recovery has been followed by further losses. The onshore activities of the company have generally proved more profitable than its fishing operations, a fact that has stimulated a restructuring of the company away from catching as well as an attempt to increase the efficiency of its fleet. In the early 1970s the company had over 140 vessels; by 1982 the figure was down to 31. Contractions in the size of the fleet occurred on each occasion in which there was a reversal in economic performance. One such contraction took place in 1975; despite the granting of a temporary government subsidy on 1 January of that year, by the following December the fleet had been reduced by 24. Of this number, 19 were scrapped, 4 were sold abroad and 1 was lost at sea.

Another option open to firms that wish to improve their efficiency is a technological one, and the opportunities here have been substantial. As described in Chapter 3, the number and variety of technical innovations made available to fishing firms since 1945 has been great. It was also explained in that chapter that the response by fishing firms to these opportunities has been positive, even though the rate at which new technology spreads throughout the industry often appears slow.

Nevertheless, proving that technological responses are conditioned by the problems of the industry is not so easy. It may well be argued that in theory, deteriorating economic conditions discourage the adoption of new technology, since reduced profitability lowers the capacity for investment. This argument assumes however that investment in new technology is financed out of retained earnings, which is not necessarily the case. For example, power block purse seining proved so profitable in the Norwegian fleet that owners found little difficulty in raising the capital needed to invest in the innovation (Mietle, 1969). Nonetheless it does seem to be the case that new vessel construction slows down following a period of low profitability in the industry, and to the extent that some changes are embodied in new vessels (rather than being 'appendages' to old ones), then it follows that depressed economic conditions may impede technical progress.

Perhaps the strongest argument in support of the view that the adoption of new technology is favoured by depressed economic conditions is that fishing firms are forced to respond in this way in order to restore profitability to acceptable levels or to stave off possible annihilation. This appears to have happened in the British fishing industry between the two world wars, where declining CPUE forced trawler owners to improve the efficiency of their gear, as well as resorting to more distant grounds (Kelsall, 1948). It has also been suggested that technological change, by the use of purse seining, was one of the ways in which the U.S. tropical tuna fishermen responded to the threat posed by Japanese competition (Cary, 1979). The most elaborate variation on this argument asserts that fishermen are forced to improve their techniques in order to offset the effects of stock depletion *which has itself been worsened by innovation*. Technical progress then interacts with falling CPUE to set up a self-sustaining momentum, so that the fishermen 'will always remain on a treadmill—attempting to balance changes in technology against the finite productivity of the resource' (Bell, 1978, p. 333). An instance of where this has happened is in the Western Australia lobster fishery where, according to Meany (1979, p. 792), an important factor making for a more technically sophisticated fleet was the need for non-innovators to match the technology of the innovators in order to remain competitive.

Since there is no way of establishing which of the above arguments is the stronger, we cannot easily decide how far the underlying economic conditions of the industry will impinge on innovation. However, the significance of innovation in this context should not be underestimated. The point is this: to the extent that fishing firms exploit new technology in pursuit of the higher profits that it may offer, and do so successfully, they will improve their overall economic performance (in the short term). In itself this improvement will mitigate some of the economic problems that the firm may be encountering or might otherwise have encountered in the course of time. The need to act directly so as to solve these problems is thus deferred.

We indicated earlier that input substitution is one way in which firms may respond to the problem of a large and unexpected rise in the price of one input. Such a problem confronted the fishing industry in 1974 and again in the late 1970s when fuel oil prices rose sharply. In practice however, it is far from simple to substitute cheaper inputs in place of more expensive ones since fishing vessels are designed around a given set of technical relationships that cannot easily be altered in the short run. Many European vessels now in use, for example, were built before 1974 at a time when fuel was relatively cheap. There are limits to how far they can be operated so as to economize on fuel without impairing performance. Not surprisingly therefore, firms have responded to this problem indirectly. We have in effect already discussed some of the indirect responses. These were essentially reactions to the low profitability of fishing (to which the oil price rise contributed) rather than to the high price of fuel oil as such. The way firms have tackled this aspect has been to look toward less energy-intensive methods of fishing. McDiarmid (1980) reports that there is a renewed interest in passive fishing methods such as gill netting, trap fishing and long lining. Pair trawling, which economizes on fuel because of reduced friction and the ability to operate efficiently at low engine speeds, has regained popularity with many fishermen. In Scotland, for example, demersal pair trawling by the inshore fleet increased through the 1970s, and in fact doubled between 1978 and 1979 (Oakeshott, 1980). Thus, the way in which fishing firms have circumvented the problem of higher-priced inputs such as fuel has not been to economize on the use of fuel within the parameters of a given technology but to seek out alternative technologies that indirectly permit economy. As such the response is a technological one, similar to those we have discussed above.

5.4.5 Cooperation

It is often said that individualism and independence are the hallmarks of commercial fishing. While this is largely true, it remains a fact that firms do cooperate in a number of important areas. Over the past half century, cooperative structures have come to play an increasingly important role in the fishing industries of most Western countries, but particularly in Europe.

In the EEC at the present time there are two main types of cooperative structure. To start with there are the fishermen's cooperatives as such, and they share the following characteristics. Typically, they are voluntary associations whose objective is to obtain a number of services for members and to increase their profitability. Profits are distributed to each member in proportion to his share in the turnover of the cooperative and not on the basis of shareholding. Not all profits are distributed and a substantial proportion of profit is likely to be retained. Democratic control is on a 'one man, one vote' basis, irrespective of the number of shares held by each member. Cooperatives generally have limited-liability status and, depending upon the country, there may be legislation specific to them. In the United Kingdom, for example, all trading cooperatives have to be registered under the Industrial and Provident Societies Acts.

The other type of cooperative structure involved in the European fishing industry is termed a *producer organization* (PO). Though the concept of the PO owes its origins to the EEC, the actual establishment of producer organizations is left to the initiative of the producers themselves. Their purpose is to 'ensure that fishing is carried out along rational lines and that conditions for the sale of their produce is improved' (Mourier, 1976, p. 36). POs are permitted to withdraw produce from the market in the event of market saturation. EEC measures, however, fix minimum withdrawal prices for species. Like cooperatives, POs generally have limited-liability status. Their precise constitution varies. In the United Kingdom, POs may either be registered under the Industrial and Provident Societies Acts (and thereby embody the characteristics of cooperatives) or registered under the Companies Acts.

Under EEC regulations the activities of POs are fairly tightly defined. They do not interfere with marketing outlets unless these conflict with the 'orderly' marketing of fish. Essentially their function is to regulate fish supplies within their operational area and thereby gain some control over price. The activities of cooperatives however are less circumscribed. In some cases a cooperative may take on several functions. For example, the Fishermen's Mutual Association (Eyemouth) Ltd, which is one of the largest cooperatives in Scotland, undertakes the following: marketing fish on behalf of members, selling gear and equipment, providing a management service to fishermen, operating a market intelligence system on prices in other ports, and investing in vessels on a part-ownership basis. It also runs a processing yard, chill store and deep freeze.

Few European cooperatives are as comprehensive as the one at Eyemouth, and in general most concentrate simply on marketing their members' produce. Promotion of auctions, creation of onshore infrastructures for landing and handling, preparation of fish for the market, concentration of supply, transport and distribution, are the kinds of activity typically undertaken. Provision of supplies is of secondary importance. In some countries, cooperatives are involved in specialist processing activities. In Denmark, for example, in 1976 there were six cooperative factories in the major ports, producing fishmeal, oil and glue. Together they accounted for almost 70% of Danish production of fish by-products (Mourier, 1976, p. 13). With this notable exception however, it seems to be the case that most fishermen's cooperatives do not involve themselves in activities beyond first-stage marketing, except to the extent that they may engage in fillet production. It is possibly for this reason that cooperative advertising is also uncommon. Likewise, fishing firms do not appear to undertake cooperative R & D.

Concerted action by European firms to control fishing directly has not been extensively practised in the past. In the mid 1970s very few cooperatives were involved at the production stage. One exception to this generalization is to be found in the United Kingdom, where one of the cooperatives active in the Solent oyster fishery, Stanswood Bay Oystermen Ltd, manages production and prepares production forecasts. It is empowered to do this by an Act of Parliament that gives it exclusive rights to the oyster beds and in effect enables the fishermen to restrict access. Another instance of where fishermen in the United Kingdom have voluntarily agreed to limit effort is in the Fal River oyster fishery. According to Cove (1973), the fishermen believed that the fishery would die out before too long since younger men were no longer attracted into it. Their objective was thus to preserve the oyster beds for as long as possible. Group norms were against working too hard, and two newcomers who did so were obliged to leave the river. 'Going out late, returning early and skipping Saturday were normal patterns' (p. 258). The attitude to innovation was similarly conservationist, and the fishermen deliberately used gear that was known to be inefficient.

What made this voluntary limitation possible, it seems, was that the numbers concerned were relatively few and a set of group norms helped enforcement. Moreover, and this obviously applies to the Solent oyster fishery as well, the fact that exploitation was of a sedentary species in a relatively small geographical area helped the fishermen to regulate production more effectively. The advent of POs in the United Kingdom and other EEC countries may witness the start of more widespread attempts at controlling fishing effort on a cooperative basis. An indication of this trend was the Scottish PO's recommendation to its members in January 1982 that there be a voluntary quota on haddock landings.

Cooperation among fishermen can, in a number of instances, be shown to be a direct response to economic pressures. In Ireland, for example, it has been argued that: 'The main influence behind the development of cooperatives was the high proportion of wholesale fish products on the Dublin Central Market. Transport and storage costs, agents' commissions and poor handling of produce have prompted fishermen to set up cooperatives, primarily in order to reduce marketing costs . . .' (Mourier, 1976, p. 17). The largest cooperative in the United Kingdom, Brixham and Torbay Fish Ltd, was established in 1965 in an attempt to reverse the decline in commercial fishing that had occurred over several years at the port of Brixham in south-west England. In Denmark, the involvement of cooperatives in by-product processing occurred not so much in response to a problem but as an attempt to take advantage of the profitable and expanding European livestock breeding market.

Possibly the best example of concerted action by firms in the face of economic difficulties is one that took place before the time when cooperatives as such were common. In the mid 1930s the international whaling companies made a number of agreements to restrict catches from the Antarctic area. The stimulus for these production agreements came in the first instance from the collapse of the whale oil market in 1931 and later from a realization of the need to conserve stocks (Clark and

Lamberson, 1982; Elliot, 1979). This response was the forerunner of a number of important policy developments that are dealt with in Chapter 7.

5.4.6 International joint ventures

One of the most important phenomena of the 1970s and early 1980s has been the advent of so-called *joint ventures* in world fisheries. As the term suggests, they involve cooperation, and as such could have been discussed in the previous section. However, because they encompass a number of new dimensions not previously considered, we have decided to classify them separately.

One major review describes joint ventures as partnerships that 'typically involve private or government interests of a host country (usually where the base of operations is located) and a foreign partner. In most instances, the host partner is the one with the resource, while the foreign partner is likely to be a long-range or other fishing nation with an established or technologically advanced fishing industry' (Kaczynski and Le Vieil, 1980, p. 2). A joint venture may be a short-term contractual arrangement, such as a survey project, or an equity arrangement in which a jointly owned company is created. The latter type is more common. By 1980 there were approximately 500 joint ventures in world fisheries (Kaczynski and Le Vieil, p. 3).

The arrangements vary in complexity, in 'who does what' and in the share-out of risks and benefits. Joint ventures are particularly concentrated around the central and south Atlantic, though the Middle East and Australasia are also important host areas. Of the joint ventures surveyed by Kaczynski and Le Vieil, 287 were established in 'less developed countries', whilst the vast majority of foreign partners were from developed countries and the Eastern bloc. The country with the greatest number of foreign partnerships was Japan. Groundfish, tuna, shrimp and squid were the commonest target species.

The problems encountered by many fishing firms in the 1970s gave a major impetus to the establishment of joint ventures. Probably the biggest single factor was the declaration of 'exclusive economic zones' by large numbers of coastal states, and the effect which that had on distant-water fleets—which had previously enjoyed unimpeded access to the fish resources throughout the world. To nations such as Japan, the Soviet Union, Poland, Bulgaria, France and Spain, whose vessels had lost their traditional distant-water grounds, joint ventures were a logical response. An accommodation could be reached between the foreign partner and the host country in which both might gain. Because potential benefits could accrue to the nations as a whole as well as the private interests involved, it is understandable that governments as well as firms should have taken a hand in the establishment and regulation of many joint ventures.

5.5 AN OVERALL ASSESSMENT

The crucial question that must now be asked is: does self-help solve any of the firms' problems? The answer is that it can do, but the solution may be only temporary or partial.

This is conspicuously the case with efficiency improvement and effort relocation. Firms that have responded to problems by adopting new technology may benefit greatly in the short run, but when all firms respond in the same way then the overall benefits may be dissipated as the common property resource becomes depleted. Similarly, some fishermen may earn high rewards by being quick to move in on a new fishery, but in an open-access situation this state of affairs will last only for as long as it takes the remaining firms to respond. Ironically, the short-lived benefits from adopting this kind of response hasten the requirement to follow the same pattern again. The 'treadmill' ensures that firms are always under pressure to improve efficiency, and in so doing bring about the demise of the fishery. This then becomes the signal to exploit another, where the story is repeated. In this way fishing firms may get locked into a pattern of behaviour that puts the emphasis on catching, even though other types of response might in theory have been more successful. As we have seen however, circumstances may militate against certain kinds of response; for example, industrial structure may not be conducive to second-stage marketing.

Some of the other strategies followed by fishing firms may offer more promise. For example, cooperation has been shown to produce positive results in a number of instances. The growth of the Danish fishing industry since the Second World War up to the mid 1970s owes a great deal to the development of an extensive and tightly organized cooperative movement in Denmark (Mourier, 1976). In the United Kingdom, the largest fishermen's cooperative (Brixham and Torbay Fish Ltd) is regarded by its members as having been successful, and it does seem to have succeeded in raising the level of landings and average values.

Cooperation between the larger British fishing firms has also met with some success. The best example of this is the Distant Water Vessels Development Scheme run by the (then) British Trawlers Federation until 1973, and whose participants included the distant-water operators at the Humber ports and Fleetwood. The scheme, which aimed to maintain minimum reserve prices at first-hand auctions for four major varieties of fish, did succeed in raising the prices of these varieties above their free-market level but, more importantly, had a wider impact on other prices. One expert states quite emphatically that even though it covered only three ports and four varieties, the scheme 'had a pervasive and marked influence on the prices obtained by all the U.K. fishermen for their produce' (Barback, 1976). International joint ventures, which represent a special type of cooperative response by firms, are a relatively new phenomenon and so far there is insufficient evidence on which to judge their effectiveness.

Some types of self-help may be more likely to succeed than others. Effort relocation and efficiency improvement are likely to be unsuccessful in the long run since in either case increases in profitability will be transitory, or else are achieved only by creating external costs (in the form of stock depletion). The cause of the difficulty is the open-access nature of the resource and its limited biological productivity. The fact that cooperative responses appear to be successful in some cases may be because they tend to concentrate on marketing. It may be easier to restrict entry into a market and prevent profit from being competed away than it is to restrict entry to a fishery. Moreover, marketing does not engender technological externalities.

Though some strategies may be more successful than others, it is doubtful whether action taken by firms individually or collectively can, on its own, solve the fundamental problems of fishing. The moribund state of some of the fishing fleets of Western Europe is testimony enough. We would argue that a governmental response is required to tackle the root of the fisheries problem, which is the absence of property rights to the natural resource. In short, the need is for fisheries regulation. This is not to say that industrial self-help does not have a role; our view is that action by the firms themselves can do much to improve economic performance but that such action can only be successfully conducted within a regulatory framework.

5.6 SUMMARY

The problems encountered by fishing firms are numerous. They include fluctuations in income, perishability, falling CPUE, static or falling demand, unforeseen increases in the cost of key inputs, and catch and effort restrictions. In theory a number of 'instruments' are available to firms to help them to reach their 'target' of overcoming particular problems. The active responses which a firm can make include: shifting to different grounds or fish stocks; transforming the product; restructuring the firm or its fleet; increasing efficiency; undertaking R & D; and cooperating with other fishing firms.

In practice some response patterns are more common than others. Biological and geographical relocation of fishing effort represents the classic response to economic problems, though the future scope for this kind of strategy may be constrained. Restructuring, mainly in the form of diversification, does occur to a limited extent in some circumstances. The potential benefits to be gained from R & D and product transformation do not seem to be taken advantage of, and the reason for this can be traced back to the structure of the industry. Ways of reducing the costs of fishing do seem to have been actively pursued, and have been facilitated by the technological opportunities open to fishing firms in recent years. Concerted action by firms, most noticeably at the first marketing stage, has also been a common occurrence. As a special case of cooperation, international joint ventures have been created as a direct response to the problems of access faced by distant-water fleets.

Industrial self-help may offer only a temporary or partial solution to economic problems. Though some strategies may be more effective and durable than others it is clear that they cannot be a panacea. So long as the natural resource remains unmanaged common property, then any success brought about by firms' actions is likely to be fragile. Self-help in combination with a government policy of fisheries regulation offers greater promise.

5.7 BIBLIOGRAPHIC NOTES

The behaviour of fishing firms has received relatively scant attention in the academic literature, though some aspects are explored by Bell (1978, Ch. 9) and Anderson (1977a, Ch. 3). The importance of developing a behavioural theory of fisheries economics is emphasized by Wilen (1979), who also discusses this in the context of regulation. Two FAO Fisheries Reports contain some interesting papers on decision-making and business strategy (FAO, 1965, 1969). In the one, Crutchfield (1965) examines the significance of the industrial structure of fishing, and in the other, Hovart (1969) discusses R & D and the spread of information. A recent in-depth survey of decision-making and management practices amongst British fishing firms is made by Oliver (1982). The fishing press is a good source of information on current problems and how fishermen try to overcome them, but for a more systematic analysis in the context of fisheries policy, Anderson (1977b) should be consulted. The motivation of individual fishermen, their differing strategies and attitudes to risk and innovation, is studied in detail by Cove (1973). Papers by Kaczynski (1979a) and Lucas (1980) are worth reading because they deal *inter alia* with effort relocation and other responses by firms to changing fishing opportunities, whilst international joint ventures specifically are examined by Kaczynski (1979b) and Kaczynski and Le Vieil (1980). Some aspects of industrial structure, especially cooperatives, have received very much more attention than others. A very comprehensive source of information on the development of cooperatives and other forms of concerted action in Europe is Mourier (1976).

REFERENCES AND FURTHER READING

ANDERSON, L. G. (1977a). *The economics of fisheries management*. Baltimore: Johns Hopkins Press.

ANDERSON, L. G. (1977b). 'A classification of fishery management problems to aid in the analysis and proper formulation of management.' *Ocean Development and International Law Journal* **4** (2) : 113–20.

BARBACK, R. (1976). 'United Kingdom.' In G. Mourier (Ed.), *Forms of co-operation in the fishing industry*. Luxembourg: Commission of the European Communities.

BELL, F. (1978). *Food from the sea: the economics and politics of ocean fisheries*. Boulder, Colorado: Westview Press.

BELL, F. and R. KINOSHITA (1973). 'Productivity gains in U.S. fisheries.' *Fishery Bulletin* **71** (4) : 911–19.

CARY, H. (1979). 'The fishing industry's response to the porpoise problem.' In V. Flagg (Ed.), *Transient Tropical Tuna (Proceedings)*. San Diego: San Diego State University.

CLARK, C. and R. LAMBERSON (1982). 'An economic history and analysis of pelagic whaling.' *Marine Policy* **6** (2) : 103–20.

COULL, J. (1974). 'The development of the fishing industry in Peru.' *Geography* **59** (4) : 322–32.

COVE, J. (1973). 'Hunters, trappers and gatherers of the sea: a comparative study of fishing strategies.' *Journal of the Fisheries Research Board of Canada* **30** (2) : 249–59.

CRUTCHFIELD, J. A. (1965). 'Horizontal and vertical integration in the fishing industry.' In FAO Fisheries Report No. 22, Vol. 3, *Meeting on business decisions in fishery industries*. Rome: FAO.

DRISCOLL, D. and N. MCKELLAR (1979). 'The changing regime in North Sea fisheries.' In C. Mason (Ed.), *The effective management of resources: the international politics of the North Sea*. London: Frances Pinter.

ELLIOTT, G. (1979). 'The failure of the IWC, 1946–1966.' *Marine Policy* **3** (2) : 149–55.

FAO (1965). FAO Fisheries Report *Meeting on business decisions in fishery industries*. Fisheries Report No. 22. Rome: FAO.

FAO (1969). FAO Fisheries Report *International conference on investment in fisheries*. R.83.2. Rome: FAO.

FAO (1981). *Fishery fleets statistics 1970–1978*. Fisheries Circular No. 731. Rome: FAO.

HAY, D. and D. MORRIS (1979). *Industrial economics: theory and evidence*. Oxford: Oxford University Press.

HOVART, P. (1969). 'Investment in human capital in the fishing industry.' In FAO Fisheries Report *International conference on investment in fisheries*. R.83.2. Rome: FAO.

HUPPERT, D. (1979). 'Implications of multipurpose fleets and mixed stocks for control policies.' *Journal of the Fisheries Research Board of Canada* **36** (7) : 845–54.

KACZYNSKI, W. (1979a). 'Responses and adjustments of foreign fleets to controls imposed by coastal nations.' *Journal of the Fisheries Research Board of Canada* **36** (7) : 800–10.

KACZYNSKI, W. (1979b). 'Joint ventures in fisheries between distant-water and developed coastal nations: an economic view.' *Ocean Management* **5** (1) : 39–48.

KACZYNSKI, W. and D. LE VIEIL (1980). 'International joint ventures in world fisheries.' *WSG Technical Report* (80.2).

KELSALL, R. (1948). 'The white fish industry.' In M. Fogarty (Ed.), *Further studies in industrial organisation*. London: Methuen.

KING, D. (1978). 'Measuring the economic value of the eastern tropical Pacific tuna fishery.' In *Proceedings of the 1978 Western Division Meeting of the American Fisheries Society*, San Diego.

KING, D. (1979). 'The economic theory of the fisheries applied to the tuna industry.' In V. Flagg (Ed.), *Transient Tropical Tuna (Proceedings)*. San Diego: San Diego State University.

LUCAS, K. (1980). 'How changes in fish resources and in the regime of the sea are affecting management, development and utilization.' In J. Connell (Ed.), *Advances in fish science and technology*. Farnham, Surrey: Fishing News Books.

MCDIARMID, H. (1980). 'International developments in catching and gear handling methods.' Paper given at Conference on *Technology and the Challenges of the World's New Fisheries' Regime*. London: Society for Underwater Technology.

MCHUGH, H. (1972). 'Marine fisheries of New York State.' *Fishery Bulletin* **70** (3) : 585–610.

MCKELLAR, N. and D. STEEL (1980). *The catching sector of the fishing industry: a case for aid*. White Fish Authority.

MACKENZIE, W. (1979). 'Rational fishery management in a depressed region: the Atlantic groundfishery.' *Journal of the Fisheries Research Board of Canada* **36** (7) : 811–26.

MEANY, F. (1979). 'Limited entry in the Western Australian rock lobster and prawn fisheries: an economic evaluation.' *Journal of the Fisheries Research Board of Canada* **36** (7) : 789–98.

MIETLE, P. (1969). 'Developments and investments in recent years in Norwegian purse seine fisheries for herring, capelin and mackerel.' In FAO Fisheries Report *International conference on investment in fisheries*. R.83.2. Rome: FAO.

MONOPOLIES COMMISSION (1966). *Ross Group and Associated Fisheries Ltd. Report on the proposed merger*. Report No. 42. London: HMSO.

MOURIER, G. (Ed.) (1976). *Forms of co-operation in the fishing industry*. Luxembourg: Commission of the European Communities.

NICHOLLS, J. (1978). 'Marketing orders: potential application to the marketing problems of the seafood industry.' Washington, D.C.: U.S. Dept. of Commerce, NOAA, NMFS, Off. Fish. Dev. Econ. Analysis Group.

OAKESHOTT, E. (1980). 'Possible responses by fish catchers to increases in relative fuel costs'. *Fisheries Economics Newsletter* No. 10 (Nov.).

ODDY, D. (1971). 'The changing techniques and structure of the fishing industry.' In T. Barker and J. Yudkin (Eds), *Fish in Britain: trends in its supply, distribution and consumption during the past two centuries*. London: University of London.

OLIVER, T. (1982). *The management and organisation of the fish catching industry on the north east coast of England*. Humberside College of Higher Education, Centre for Fisheries Studies.

PENN, E. (1977). 'Economic impact of the Atlantic menhaden fishery.' Washington, D.C.: U.S. Dept. of Commerce, NOAA, NMFS, Scient. and Techn. Services Discussion Paper.

SELECT COMMITTEE ON THE EUROPEAN COMMUNITIES (1980). *EEC fisheries policy*. H.L. 351. London: HMSO.

WILEN, J. (1979). 'Fisherman behaviour and the design of efficient fisheries regulation programmes.' *Journal of the Fisheries Research Board of Canada* **36** (7) : 855–8.

CHAPTER 6

The regulation of commercial fisheries

6.1 INTRODUCTION

In this chapter we analyse the principal methods via which commercial marine fisheries have been or might be regulated. Regulatory techniques are often classified according to whether they affect mainly the composition of the catch or the total amount of fishing effort. However, because many techniques affect both of these things, it seems to us that the distinction is not as analytically useful as it might be, and accordingly a slightly different split will be used here.

We have seen frequently in earlier chapters that open access is the fundamental cause of many fisheries problems. By itself, it is sufficient always to result in economic overfishing (except in the limiting case of an infinite social discount rate), and when coupled with the limited long-run productivity of fish resources, rising real fish prices and advances in fishing technology, it tends to result also in biological overfishing (however that may be defined). Hence a mature, open-access commercial fishery is likely to be plagued with both biological and economic problems.

Reducing things to their simplest level, the manager of a fishery may adopt regulations that deal either with open access, or with the problems resulting from it, and we propose to follow this kind of split in our analysis of fisheries regulations. At the risk of being somewhat pejorative, one might call the former set of regulations 'economic', since they tend to be concerned principally with the economic situation of the fishery, and the latter 'biological', since they tend to be concerned principally with the health of the fish stock. It should be noted however that the term 'economic' is used here in the neoclassical sense of resource allocation. We have mentioned before in this book that where fishing is regionally important it may be socially desirable to have high employment levels. As will soon become apparent, such an aim, which might be broadly considered 'economic', will probably be best achieved by the use of 'biological'-type regulations.

6.2 REGULATIONS THAT DO NOT RESTRICT ACCESS

The regulations discussed in this section have been, and continue to be, widely used in fisheries management. The common drawback of such measures is that because none of them deals with the problem of open access, none of them is able to improve the long-term economic position of the fishery. Certainly, the equilibrium fish population, output and employment levels may be altered by the regulation, but in the end the fishery will continue to operate at an essentially open-access equilibrium, where average revenue equals average cost. The economic (i.e. resource allocative) problems with such an equilibrium have been discussed in Chapters 2 and 4, but may be summarized in the fact that marginal cost exceeds price.

Despite this drawback, such regulations are not without use. Their principal beneficial impact is likely to be on the fish stock itself, in that by lessening the fishing pressure they usually enable even severely depleted stocks to recover. Of course, this is probably to the advantage of everyone since greater and continuing yields may then be possible. However the failure to deal with open access will have consequences which, although some of them—such as higher employment—may be favourably received, are likely to undermine the management scheme. This point is best illustrated if we consider the impact of the most important technique in this section, the setting of quotas.

6.2.1 Quotas

The setting of an overall quota for a fishery is a management technique that has been used frequently. One reason for this is doubtless the simplicity of the technique, in that the management authority merely announces the quota and, once this has been taken, the fishery is closed for the remainder of the season. The management of a fishery by a quota may be analysed using the bioeconomic model that we outlined in Chapter 2. As our example, we shall consider an open-access fishery initially in equilibrium at an output Y_{oa} (in *Figure 6.1*), which is being taken at the higher of the two possible long-run average costs. Let us then suppose that the management authority decides to move the fishery to the effort and output levels corresponding to maximum sustainable yield (MSY). We choose this kind of fishery and this aim simply because they appear to represent best the practical situations where quotas have been used. It might be noted however that the analysis to follow does not depend on either of these assumptions. For the sake of simplicity we shall assume also that there are *no* diminishing returns to nominal effort (which means first that the sustainable yield curve is parabolic and secondly that the short-run average and marginal cost curves coincide).

In *Figure 6.1* we begin from a situation where output Y_{oa} is being produced at a cost of $LRAC_1$ and with an effort level f_1. This represents the sustainable open-access equilibrium. We now suppose that the management authority wishes to move the fishery to Y_{msy} by the use of a quota. Since Y_{oa} is a sustainable yield, it should be apparent that Y_{msy} is attainable only if the population size is increased. In the first few periods of management therefore, catch will have to be less than Y_{oa}. This catch reduction will increase the population size, thereby turning the short-run yield curve up and around the sustainable yield curve until it reaches $SRY_{(pop.2)}$, and lowering the short-run average cost of output curve until it reaches $SRAC_{y(pop.2)}$. At this point, a quota of Y_{msy} is biologically sustainable.

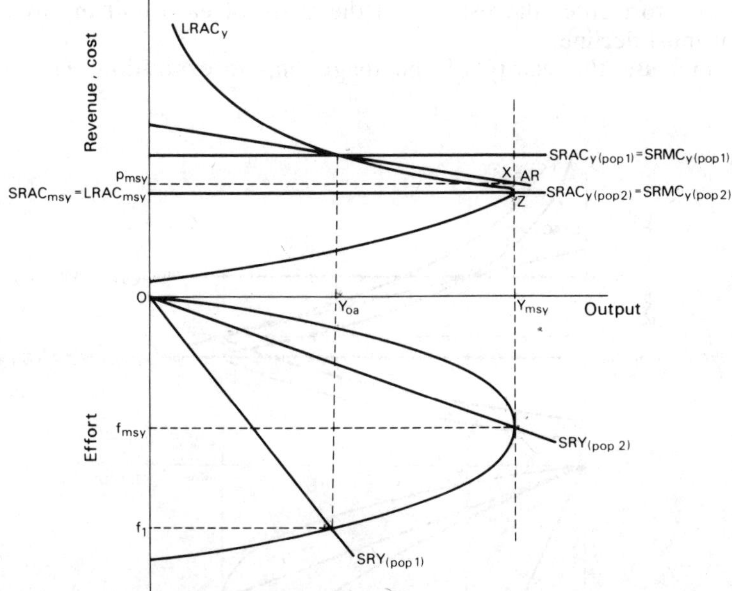

FIGURE 6.1 Management by a quota—a first view.

However this is not the end of the story. While the MSY output is biologically sustainable, it is apparent from *Figure 6.1* that economically it is not. At that output, the price of fish is p_{msy} but the catching cost is only $LRAC_{msy}$, giving rise to a profit per unit equal to the difference between the two. Total profit in the fishery is then shown by the rectangle p_{msy}-X-Z-$LRAC_{msy}$. The problem is that the only control being placed on the fishery is on total output. In all other aspects it remains open-access. Hence the presence of these profits will attract extra units of nominal effort to the fishery.

The consequence of this extra effort is best considered by recalling from Chapter 2 that

$$Y = qfP$$

that is, yield depends on the population size, the amount of effort and the 'catchability' coefficient. In our hypothetical fishery however, output is being held constant at the MSY level (by the quota) and moreover since this output is sustainable, the population size also must be constant. The short-run yield equation thus becomes

$$\bar{Y} = qf\bar{P}$$

where the bars denote constant terms. Quite clearly, in this situation any increase in the amount of effort must imply a fall in the value of the catchability coefficient. The underlying logic is evident: as more and more units of effort enter the fishery, so the share of each unit in any *given* output must decline.*

To increase the clarity of the diagrammatic exposition, *Figure 6.2*

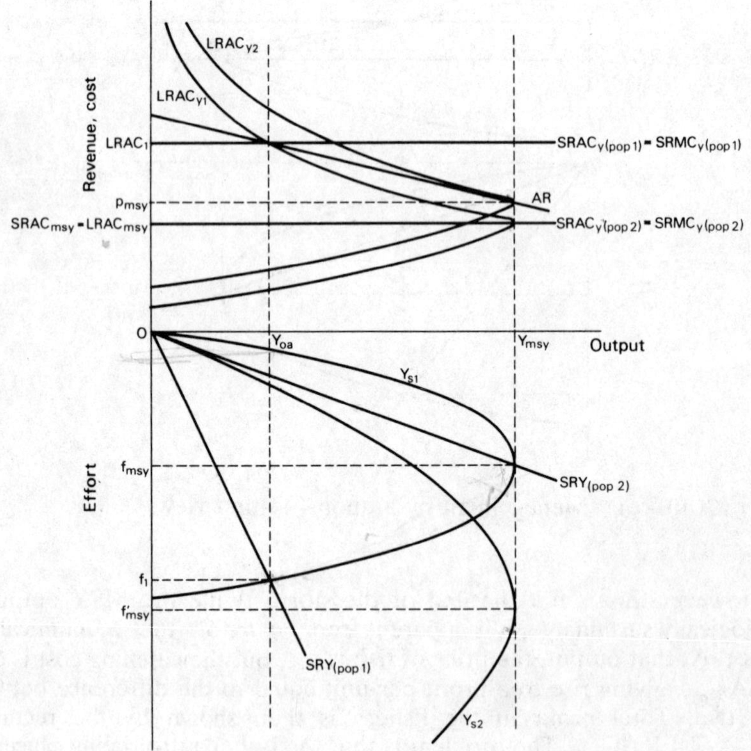

FIGURE 6.2 Management by a quota—the complete picture.

*Notice that the value of q can no longer be taken as an indicator of the technical efficiency of the fleet.

repeats *Figure 6.1* and then adds the final pieces of analysis to it. The effect of the fall in the catchability coefficient is to shift the long-run average cost curve upwards (from $LRAC_{y1}$ to $LRAC_{y2}$) and to expand (so to speak) the sustainable yield curve from Y_{s1} to Y_{s2}. The short-run curves are also moved, of course, but their movement is not shown, to avoid making the diagram unintelligible. Full bioeconomic equilibrium will be restored when the catchability coefficient has fallen sufficiently for long-run average cost and average revenue to be equated at the MSY output level. Notice that the equilibrium reached is essentially one of open access. The quota means that output is (or at least should be) under control, but effort clearly is not. In *Figure 6.2* the final effort level, f'_{msy}, actually exceeds the initial level, f_1. In practice it might have been less, but it will certainly be greater than the effort level originally needed to take MSY (f_{msy}). Thus the quota works essentially by making the fishery artificially inefficient, thereby raising costs and altering the output level at which fishermen wish to operate.

Nonetheless, clearly some gains result from the quota. To begin with, output has been increased and the price of fish has been lowered. Also, by implication, the fish population has been increased in size, thereby probably increasing its resilience to environmental fluctuations. It might be argued that economic inefficiency is a price worth paying to achieve such gains. Such a view is a little naïve however. It is probably true that management by a quota is worth while for a limited period of time. If however we attempt to manage a fishery solely by the imposition of a quota over an extended period of time, the results are likely to be undesirable economically. This is because over time for most, if not all, fisheries there is a tendency for real fish prices to increase and real fishing costs to decrease. Each time one or other (or both) of these events happens a profit will emerge in the fishery. This will attract extra units of effort to the fishery and the available quota will be taken in an even shorter period. Thus, in a fishery managed purely by a quota, the fishing season may be expected to become progressively shorter and the amount of effort involved in the fishery progressively greater.

A number of consequences may follow. First, the amount of effort will become excessive, and if capital is in short supply in an economy it may be desirable to avoid this overcapitalization. On the other hand however, in an economy (or part of an economy) where unemployment is a serious problem, it may be the best social and/or political course to encourage overemployment in fishing. Secondly, as the season becomes shorter, so quite clearly any shore-based processing industry dependent on the fishery will have to expand its capacity to be able to deal with the greater amount of fish available during the open season. If this extra capacity has no alternative use during the closed season, then it is clearly wasteful. Thirdly, the period during which fresh fish is available will correspond roughly to the open season, which will be declining. For some species an increasing proportion of the catch will have to be frozen, which may result in decreased consumer satisfaction and increased processing costs. For species that do not freeze well the effects may be more drastic, in that an increasing proportion of the catch may have to be used for meal or oil, where it would previously have been available for direct human consumption. It is somewhat difficult to generalize on this particular issue since it very much depends on the species under consideration, but the kinds of problem involved should be apparent.

A quota, then, may be of some use as a short-run management measure and even more useful as the basis of a management plan, but prolonged use of it as the *only* measure is likely to lead to difficult problems. It appears therefore that alternative, or at least supplementary, management techniques must be considered.

6.2.2 Gear restrictions

A second common method of regulating commercial fisheries is by gear restrictions. Certain kinds of fishing equipment are either banned outright or circumscribed in their use. Such restrictions might include limitations on engine size, boat length, number of hooks per line, net size, dredge size and beam width; they could even go so far as to ban the use of motorized vessels (in the Chesapeake Bay oyster fishery, for example).

Although there are many reasons why gear restrictions may be introduced (over-wide beam trawls, for instance, may damage the sea bed), the principal rationale for such measures is to reduce the catchability coefficient—which is why it is generally the technically more efficient kinds of gear that are controlled. Gear restrictions have precisely the same result (although it is achieved more directly) as a quota, that of raising the average cost of catching fish. In this way, the fishery may be moved to the desired output level (whatever that may be), but essentially of course it will remain in open-access equilibrium. As with a quota, any gains are likely to be made at the expense of economic efficiency.

However, a case might be made for gear restrictions where one kind of gear is exceptionally efficient technically. In such a situation, *if* for whatever reason fishing effort is not controllable, limiting or even banning the use of the gear may be the only way to ensure survival of the fishery and indeed of the fish species itself. The best-known example of this predicament is the Pacific salmon fishery. In its early years, traps were set across river mouths. These proved so efficient technically that, at the time, outlawing their use appeared to be the only way of safeguarding the future of the fishery.

6.2.2.1 *Mesh size limitations and eumetric yield*

The particular gear restriction of mesh size limitation is worthy of separate discussion, principally because of its relationship with the famous concept of *eumetric yield*. The argument in favour of restrictions is relevant to those cases where the fish population exhibits a distinct age structure (in terms of year classes or *cohorts*) and where the fishing gear is selective (that is, by altering the gear we may determine the age at which fish first become liable to capture, or are *recruited* to the fishery). In fact, various kinds of restriction might be used to control the size (and hence age) at first capture, including for example sizes of the hooks, or size limits for the fish themselves. By far the best-known and most widely used method is by adjusting the size of the mesh in trawl fisheries, and that example will be used here.

Since the simple Gordon–Schaefer model developed in Chapter 2 specifically abstracts from the age structure of the population, the more complex model due to Beverton and Holt (1957) must be used to analyse this problem. The model is based upon the growth pattern of the typical member of the year class, which is then multiplied by the number of fish in the class. It is postulated that individual fish will grow according to a von Bertalanffy weight function, which gives a sigmoid growth curve as shown in *Figure 6.3a*. The typical fish initially grows exponentially, reaching a maximum rate of growth at the point of inflection on the curve. Thereafter it grows only at a slower rate. This growth pattern will be repeated for all members of the year class.

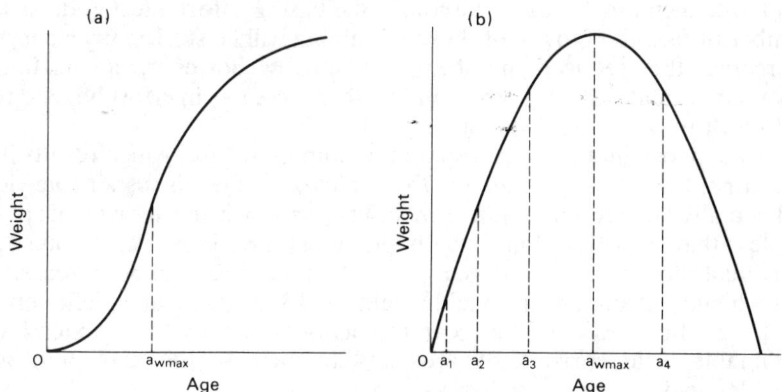

FIGURE 6.3 Growth related to age in the Beverton–Holt model.

At any moment, the total weight of the class will depend on the weights of the individuals that comprise it multiplied by their number; and this latter will itself depend on the natural mortality rate affecting the population. In the early stages of a year class it is postulated that growth of the individuals will outweigh (literally) the effects of mortality so that weight will be increasing. At a certain age, a_{wmax}, the weight of the class will reach a maximum, and thereafter mortality will dominate. Thus for an unexploited fishery, the curve relating weight to age of the class will be as shown in *Figure 6.3b*.

Now assume that fishing commences. Let us suppose that the gear being used is absolutely selective, in the sense that all fish above a critical age are caught and all below it escape. This is not, of course, a particularly realistic assumption. Usually in practice, there will be an age above which fish certainly will be caught, if they come into contact with the gear, and a lower age below which they will escape. In between there will be a range of ages where they may or may not be captured. Moreover the size of this range will vary from species to species and gear to gear depending on how good the particular species of fish is at escaping from the particular type of gear. This effect might be modelled by, for instance, introducing a probability function into the yield equation. However the assumption of what Clark (1976, p. 271) calls 'knife-edge' selectivity does not appear to alter greatly the results, and for simplicity it is made here.

By controlling the mesh size (or other gear) we are in a position to determine the age at which fish will be recruited to the fishery. As we shall see, the consequence of so doing is that there will be a *separate* sustainable yield curve corresponding to each age of first capture. To begin with however, let us suppose that *no* gear controls are imposed and hence all fish in the population are liable to capture. In this case, the sustainable yield curve will be similar to that which we derived using the Gordon–Schaefer model. As effort increases from zero, so sustainable yield will increase because, although increasing effort must reduce the number of fish, the growth of those remaining will be sufficiently strong to overcome the reduced numbers. Eventually however, a maximum sustainable yield will be reached and further increases in effort beyond this will result in declining sustainable yield.

Now suppose that we establish a minimum mesh size, which results in a recruitment age of a_1 (in *Figure 6.3b*). At low effort levels sustainable yield will actually be less than in the unrestricted case because individuals of an age less than a_1 will no longer be liable to capture. However, because all individuals do attain at least age a_1, growth of the stock will be increased so that a higher maximum sustainable yield will be available at a higher effort level. The first effect of the gear restriction will thus be to extend the sustainable yield curve rightwards and to increase the maximum sustainable yield.

A second important effect also occurs. Because there is now a minimum age at which fish are recruited to the fishery, the right-hand side of the sustainable yield curve (i.e. that part beyond MSY) can no longer fall to zero. To understand why, let us suppose that effort were *infinite*. This would mean that as soon as a fish reached the minimum age it would be harvested. Total yield from the year class would then equal the weight of each fish at the minimum age multiplied by the number of fish. The effect, therefore, of introducing a minimum age of first capture is to introduce a *minimum* sustainable yield, at high effort levels. (The term 'minimum sustainable yield' may be misleading unless it is recalled that it applies only to the right-hand side of the sustainable yield curve. It will still be the case, of course, that as effort falls to zero so will sustainable yield.)

Effort, however, certainly will be less than infinite. At lower effort levels, not all fish will be harvested the instant that they attain the minimum age, and thus some ageing beyond a_1 will occur. The lower is the effort level, the greater will be the amount of extra ageing. Up to the age a_{wmax} this results in a net increase in the weight of the year class, and hence increases the potential sustainable yield. Beyond a_{wmax} however, natural mortality dominates so that sustainable yield declines. Thus it is expected that the sustainable yield curve will increase with effort up to some maximum, beyond which further increases in effort result in falls in the sustainable yield curve, asymptotically approaching the minimum sustainable yield corresponding to a_1 as effort tends to infinity (*Figure 6.4*). As the age of fish capture is increased to, say, a_2 and then a_3 (in *Figure 6.3b*), so the sustainable yield curve will be extended further and further to the right and so the minimum and maximum sustainable yields will be increased (as shown in *Figure 6.4*).

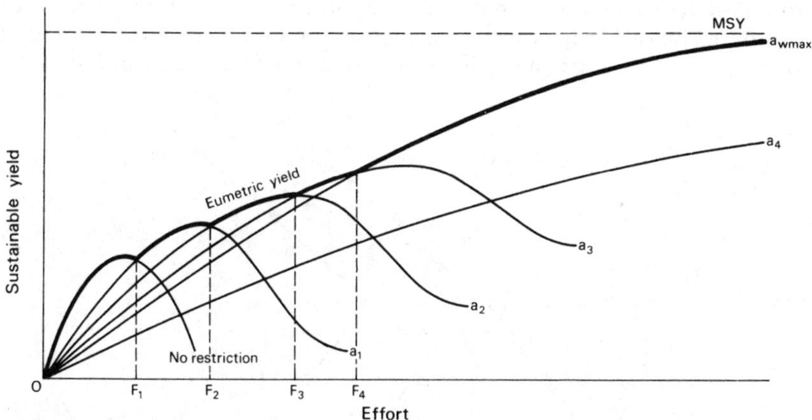

FIGURE 6.4 The eumetric yield curve.

The age a_{wmax} represents a watershed however, because it corresponds to the maximum possible sustainable biomass. Consequently, the sustainable yield curve corresponding to an age of first capture of a_{wmax} will not have a downward-sloping segment. Instead, as effort tends to infinity so catch will tend to MSY. The reasoning is similar to that above. An infinite effort level implies that the instant fish reach age a_{wmax} they are captured. If effort is less than infinite, not all fish are captured immediately and some ageing beyond a_{wmax} must occur. However since a_{wmax} corresponds to the maximum weight, extra ageing results in falling sustainable yield because natural mortality outweighs individual growth. Thus as effort approaches infinity, so sustainable yield will approach MSY; at lower effort levels, sustainable yield will be less than MSY.

If the age of fish capture is increased beyond a_{wmax} (say to a_4 in *Figure 6.3b*), then the sustainable yield curve will be extended to the right yet again. However, since a_{wmax} has been passed, the level which the curve approaches as effort tends to infinity must be less than MSY corresponding to age a_{wmax}. Thus at *any* effort level, sustainable yield could be increased by decreasing the age of first capture (and the same is true for any age beyond a_{wmax}). *Figure 6.4* depicts the various sustainable yield curves discussed above.

If we draw the envelope curve of the sustainable yield curves up to and including a_{wmax}, then we obtain a global curve which shows the greatest sustainable yield that may be taken at each effort level, once the age at first capture has been adjusted. This curve is called the *eumetric* ('well-proportioned') *yield* curve. In *Figure 6.4* the eumetric yield curve is 'lumpy', which indicates that age at first capture cannot be varied continuously but rather that the options are no restriction, a_1, a_2, a_3 and a_{wmax}. In this case, it makes most sense to have no restriction for levels up to F_1, a_1 for effort levels F_1–F_2, a_2 for F_2–F_3, a_3 for F_3–F_4, and a_{wmax} for F_4 onwards. Generally however, the eumetric yield curve is drawn as a smooth curve, implying that the age of first capture may be varied continuously. In a fishery where mesh size is under control this may not be an unreasonable assumption. The smooth curve is adopted in *Figure 6.5*.

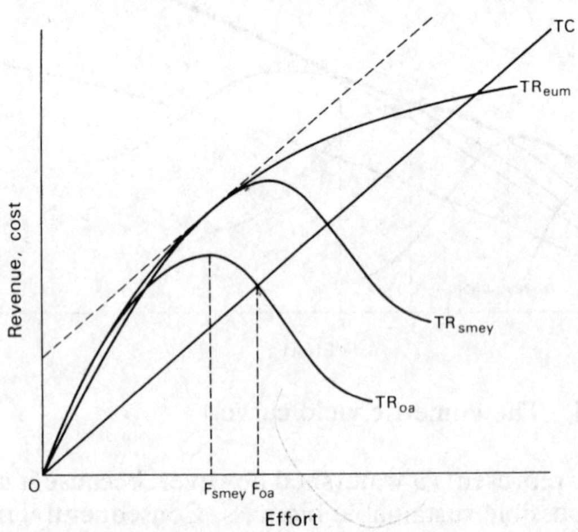

FIGURE 6.5 Maximum economic yield and open-access equilibria with the eumetric yield curve.

The eumetric yield curve is important because it indicates that an open-access fishery may reach a suboptimum not only because fishing effort is excessive, but also because the age at first capture will probably be too low. To see why, let us introduce the economic aspects of the model. If we assume that the price of fish is constant and we multiply the eumetric yield curve by this price, we derive what might be called the 'best-practice' long-run total revenue curve. We shall assume also that total cost is a linear function of the amount of effort. These curves are shown in *Figure 6.5* as TR_{eum} and TC.

In an unregulated fishery however, fishermen may be expected to attempt to capture any fish of a marketable size and thus the relevant sustainable yield curve for them will be the one corresponding to the lowest marketable age, a_m. Multiplying this curve by the price of fish gives the open-access total revenue curve (TR_{oa}, in *Figure 6.5*). The open-access fishery will reach its usual equilibrium where TR_{oa} equals TC. It can be seen from *Figure 6.5* that this equilibrium is associated with two problems. First, for the given age at first capture (a_m) and hence the given total revenue curve (TR_{oa}), fishing effort is excessive in that all economic rent has been dissipated. Secondly, for the given level of fishing effort (F_{oa}), the age at first capture is too low. By increasing the age at first capture, the fishery might be moved onto the eumetric total revenue curve, thereby establishing an economic rent equivalent to the difference between this curve and the total cost curve at effort level F_{oa}.

Since open access is associated with these two suboptima it is frequently asserted that both must be regulated if the fishery is to be moved to the optimum position. This however is not necessarily the case. Depending on the *way* in which effort is regulated, such regulation may be sufficient on its own.

To begin with however, it should be fairly clear that mesh size restrictions (or other controls on age at first capture) on their own will be insufficient to improve the economic wellbeing of the fishery. For instance, increasing the mesh size may result in greater sustainable yield in the long run, thus creating an economic rent, but then more fishermen will be attracted, thereby eroding any gain. The situation is thus analogous to that discussed earlier in connection with quotas: if effort is not controlled, any economic gains will be short-lived. This is not to say that mesh size limitations are of no use. They may well improve the biological health of a fishery, and indeed it seems that they are usually introduced for this reason. Economically however they are not sufficient.

As we have already mentioned, whether they are in fact necessary depends on the way in which effort is regulated. The various techniques for regulating effort are discussed more fully throughout this chapter. The three most important 'economic' techniques are licensing (of the boat, say), taxation and individual fish quotas (i.e. licences to land certain quantities of fish). Of these three it seems that only licensing requires mesh size regulations to support it; the other two seem capable of managing the fishery optimally without such support.

Briefly, the problem with licensing in a fishery where there is a distinct age structure is that there is no control over what happens at the boat level. The total number of boats participating in the fishery is controlled, but those boats are free to fish as they like. Suppose that the management authority were to regulate the fishery to the SMEY effort level (in *Figure 6.5*). Ideally the minimum age at first capture should be a_{smey}, which results in (sustainable yield curve and hence) total revenue curve TR_{smey}. However we already know that the minimum marketable age is a_m, which must clearly be less than a_{smey}. If there is no control on the age at first capture, then it will pay each fisherman within the licensing scheme to attempt to capture any fish of at least marketable size. This is because within the scheme the situation remains similar to that under open access. If any fisherman leaves fish to grow on, the chances of his catching those fish later are minimal because other fishermen will be free to take them. Therefore, instead of being on curve TR_{smey} at the point where it is tangential to TR_{eum}, the fishery will be pushed on to the curve TR_{oa}. This will reduce economic rent by the difference between TR_{eum} and TR_{oa} at the SMEY effort level. An economic rent of TR_{oa} minus TC is still produced (and it will not be eroded because effort is being controlled),* but the rent is less than it might have been. The greater is the difference between the optimum age at first capture and the minimum marketable age the greater will be the rent loss. The only way to prevent this loss would be to control the mesh size as well as controlling effort.

Regulation by taxation will be sufficient on its own to move the fishery to the desired level, because taxation works simply by changing the open-access position where the fishermen find it profitable to fish. For instance, by a combination of tax on catch and tax on effort it is possible to make the *perceived* total revenue and total cost curves intersect at the SMEY effort level. However, as we shall see below, taxation is a rarely used management technique.

Finally, if he is given an individual fish quota, the skipper of each boat knows the quantity of fish that he is allowed to land. Whatever the level of effort that the management authority chooses, it would appear to be in the fishermen's interest to be on the eumetric total revenue curve, because profit will then be maximized. The case is different from that of licensing, because here it will be worth each fisherman's while to wait until the age of fish is optimal, knowing the amount of fish that he may land.

It would appear therefore that, while mesh size limitations by themselves will always be insufficient, effort limitation may be all that is required, depending on how it is operated.

Two other drawbacks of mesh size regulation also limit its usefulness. First, most trawl fisheries aim for more than one species at a time, and the optimum size for each species will almost certainly be different. Secondly, although nets of different sizes all cost much the same to make and operate, once a fisherman has bought a net of a particular size, changes in mesh size regulations will be expensive for him. Thus the best that mesh size control may reasonably be expected to achieve is to point the fishery in the correct direction. Certainly, close short-term control of the fishery cannot be achieved using this method alone.

The biggest single criticism that may be made of the analysis of eumetric yield developed above is that it is entirely static. Points on the eumetric yield curve are implied to be optimal in some sense. However, because it must take time for the population to adjust to changes in mesh size, it may well be that some points off the eumetric curve will be socially preferred to those on it. Unfortunately the dynamic analysis of the Beverton–Holt model is complex and well beyond the scope of this book. The interested reader is referred to the bibliography.

*Notice that to say effort is being controlled may in fact impute too much power to a licensing scheme; it may turn out that licensing is unable to control effort adequately. *See* section 6.3.2 on licensing for further discussion of this point.

6.2.3 Closed seasons

A closed season is simply a period of time during which fishing may not take place. There are a number of reasons why one may be introduced. For instance, one problem with an open-access fishery is that fishermen may carry on fishing even though the *quality* of the fish is poor. It makes sense for them to do so provided that they earn a return on their catch at least sufficient to cover their running costs. From society's viewpoint however, it may well be worth waiting until the condition of the fish improves before attempting to catch them. As usual, under open access the individual fisherman will not find it profitable to make this investment in the fish stock because he has no way of ensuring that he reaps the benefit of his patience. In such a situation, imposing a closed season when the fish are in poor physical condition is likely to result in an increase in the value (suitably discounted) of the catch that exceeds the temporary sacrifice. Note however that the regulation attacks the symptom, rather than the problem itself (which once again is open access).

Frequently however, the purpose of the closed season is simply to reduce or at least to control total catch. In this respect, closed seasons are of course very similar to quotas. A quota limits total catch directly; a closed season limits the period during which fishing may be undertaken (the expectation being that only a certain catch may be taken during the open season). If the fish are equally vulnerable to fishing at all times, a closed season is not likely to be very successful. Fishing effort will probably be transferred from one time to another so that the overall level of effort changes little, if at all.

In cases where the stock is particularly vulnerable at certain times, a closed season during these periods may be an effective way of reducing catch, and in practice it is generally at such times that closures are implemented. The drawback with closures of this kind is that usually the periods of vulnerability are the best time to fish, from an economic viewpoint, because the fish are easy and hence cheap to catch. To the extent therefore that a closed season brings a fishery under control, it will do so by making it more expensive to fish, thereby altering the open-access equilibrium. The *biological* condition of a fishery may well improve following the introduction of a closed season, but the *economic* condition will not. If there is no other way to control fishing effort, then a closed season may make sense in order to ensure the survival of the fishery. Where alternative management techniques are available, it probably makes good sense to use them.

It may be concluded therefore that a closed season *by itself* is unlikely to result in optimal management of the fishery. Closed seasons are nevertheless of great use in fisheries management. Their strength is that they are so easy to implement and enforce. For this reason they are likely to have a vital back-up role in any fisheries management plan, the idea being that they are introduced as a short-term measure, if and when things do not work as planned. To anticipate a little: if, in a licensed fishery, it became apparent during the season that too many boats were operating, it might well prove easier simply to close the fishery rather than attempt to adjust the number of licences immediately. The adjustment would then be made at a later date.

Thus while closed seasons are of limited value as the sole regulatory technique of a management programme, they have a very important role to play as a safety valve for more complex methods.

6.2.4 Closed areas

A closed area is merely an area of sea within which fishing may not take place. The area may be closed for part or all of the season, and is generally introduced to protect either young or spawning fish. Since, as we have seen, fishermen in an open-access fishery will tend to capture fish at too early an age, the introduction of a nursery area may be expected to increase the weight of the sustainable catch. The best results will be achieved in a fishery where the immature fish are spatially separated from the mature ones. The greater the degree of mixing of fish of different ages, the more expensive will be a nursery area in terms of the weight of mature fish that must be given up in order to protect the immature. Clearly, at a certain level what is being given up will exceed what is being gained. It will be an empirical matter to decide whether a nursery area is justified or not. One important use of nursery areas may be to protect the immature fish of one species that are being taken as a by-catch of a fishery directed at a second species. This is the case, for instance, in the Norway pout box in the North Sea, where immature haddock and whiting are protected from the industrial fishery directed at Norway pout.

Spawning areas are usually introduced *not* for the explicit purpose of ensuring a sufficient spawning stock (the high fecundity of most fish species makes this inessential), but because the congregation of fish stocks during spawning renders them particularly vulnerable to fishing. If fishing effort is not controlled, the stock might well be obliterated at this time. Historically, because fishing effort has generally not been under control, spawning areas have been used as one means of ensuring the future of the fishery. Their biggest drawback is that, economically, the spawning period is probably the best time to fish, first because any given catch may be taken at low cost and secondly because usually the fish themselves are in their best condition. Thus a spawning area controls effort essentially by increasing cost. Once again the fundamental problem of open access is left, so that little, if any, long-run improvement in the economic condition of the fishery is to be expected.

6.2.5 Conclusions

Whilst this section of the chapter is certainly not exhaustive on regulations that do not deal with open access, we have discussed the principal alternatives. It is apparent that the major drawback of all of the regulations is their failure to combat open access. Judged on their own terms, they are usually fairly successful, ensuring the future of fisheries and enabling even severely depleted stocks to recover. With hindsight however, it has become fairly clear that most of the benefits obtained by the methods discussed above may be achieved by altering the competitive environment within which the fishermen operate, so as to make it worth their while to conserve fish stocks. This is what the regulations to be discussed in the next section attempt to achieve.

6.3 REGULATIONS THAT DO DEAL WITH OPEN ACCESS

In this part of the chapter we shall analyse the three most important types of regulations that attempt to resolve the open-access problem. The first technique—the use of taxation—is included for the sake of completeness because it has been so frequently advocated, particularly by economists. However for reasons that will become apparent later, no fishery has been managed solely by taxation, although there is some reason to believe that the recent trend towards 200-mile fishing limits may increase its importance. The second method discussed—licensing—has been widely used. In the 1960s and early 1970s it appeared that licensing was going to be very much a 'magic wand' so far as fisheries management was concerned, but unfortunately things have not worked out like this in practice. Finally, we look at individual fish quotas (that is, property rights to catch a certain amount of the total available catch) and we conclude that these appear to offer the best hope for management in the future.

6.3.1 Taxation

As we have already seen, an open-access fishery will operate at output and effort levels that are economically suboptimal. It is important to note however that the open-access equilibrium is suboptimal only in the sense that too many resources are attracted to the fishery. In other ways, competition in the fishery brings results that are usually considered desirable (at least in the context of other industries). For instance, each fishing firm will be forced to adopt the best available technology (assuming no gear restrictions, of course!), because if it does not, its operating costs will exceed those of other firms and it will probably be forced out of the fishery, at least in the long run. The price paid for fish by consumers will also be as low as possible given the output being produced. That is to say, there is no monopoly power amongst producers and the marginal fisherman earns only normal profit. The open-access problem is simply that because the fishery is a scarce resource, the marginal cost of catching fish always exceeds the average cost so that an economic rent emerges at the socially optimal output level. In the absence of regulation, fishermen perceive this rent as profit and consequently too many of them are attracted to the fishery.

Since taxation is able to correct the open-access suboptimality without affecting what are seen as the desirable effects of competition, its use as a means of regulating commercial fisheries has often been proposed by fisheries economists. A tax would be imposed such that fishermen simply found it unprofitable to operate at the original open-access level. Depending on the magnitude of the tax imposed, they might be made to move to whatever level is considered optimal.

Theoretically, it makes no difference whether the tax is imposed on catch or effort. *Figures 6.6* and *6.7* illustrate the way in which a tax on catch and effort respectively might be used to move a fishery from its original

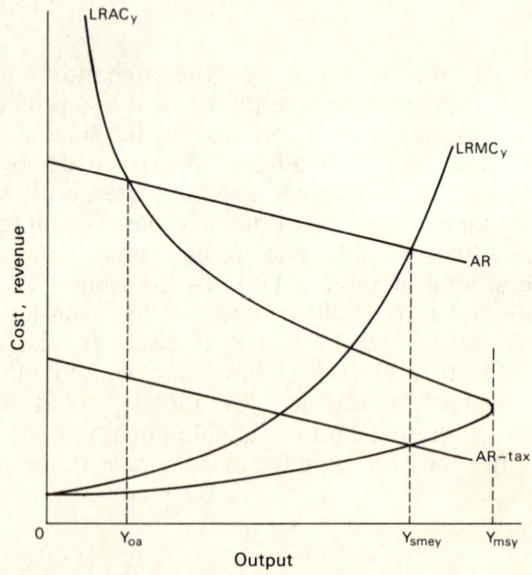

FIGURE 6.6 A tax on catch.

open-access level (output Y_{oa}) to the static maximum economic yield level (output Y_{smey}). It may be seen that the tax on catch results simply in a fall in *perceived* revenue while a tax on effort results in an increase in *perceived* cost. It is apparent from these two diagrams that, in essence, the fishery does in fact remain open-access. The imposition of the tax has meant however that the level at which fishermen wish to operate has been changed from Y_{oa} to Y_{smey}. It may seem that this situation is the same as those discussed in section 6.2 above, as in the case of quotas, for example. However, while they are similar, the crucial difference is that with taxation the economic rent existing at the SMEY level has been captured by the regulating authority. It will not serve therefore to attract extra units of effort into the fishery, and the long-run average cost of catching fish will not be pushed up. This is clear from *Figure 6.6*. In *Figure 6.7*, where the regulation shifts the cost curve upwards, the curve $LRAC_y$ continues to show catching costs. The tax is of course a cost to the fishermen, but it is not a cost to society; that is, it does not represent the cost of resources required to catch fish. Instead, it represents the economic rent being gained by society. Moreover this rent will be captured on a sustainable basis.

Although in theory it does not appear to matter whether the tax is imposed on catch or effort, in practice it is likely to be much simpler to tax the catch. To begin with, it is obvious what the catch is, whereas it is usually extremely difficult to obtain a very good definition of effort. Moreover even if we had perfect knowledge of the factors of production comprising fishing effort, we should require a separate tax on each factor. Otherwise,

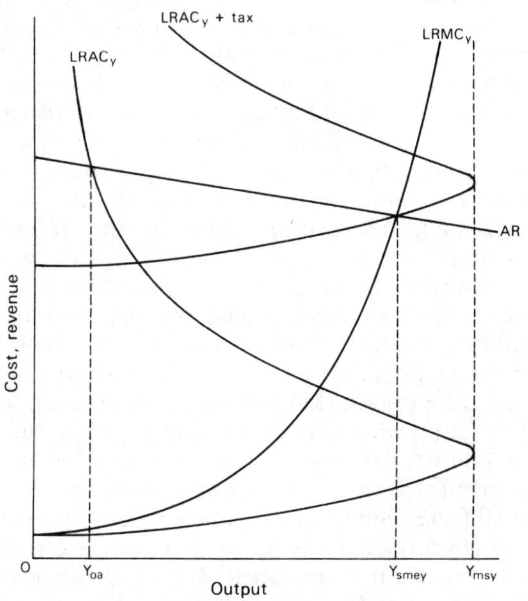

FIGURE 6.7 A tax on effort.

fishermen would be encouraged to substitute one factor for another in the production of effort and thus the regulation scheme would have the undesirable consequence of making it profitable to use less than the best factor combination. It is also a possibility that even if optimal taxes were imposed on each factor of production *presently* utilized, fishermen might then find it profitable to introduce a previously unprofitable factor. For all these reasons, it will be generally more straightforward to tax the catch.

Taxation suffers however from a number of drawbacks that have severely limited its usefulness as a major weapon of fisheries management. Depending on the opportunities available in other fisheries or occupations, the use of taxation may well prove to be an extremely painful way of reducing effort. In *Figures 6.6* and *6.7*, the most painful alternative of all is illustrated, since effectively the rent per unit available at Y_{smey} is calculated and a tax equal to this then imposed. The fishing fleet is simply left to adjust to the tax. In practice it would be possible to move more gradually. However it must be the case that at some point the fishing fleet as a whole is unable to cover all of its costs and those least able to withstand such a squeeze will be forced out of the fishery.

In theory those who leave the fishery first should be either those who are potentially very good at some alternative occupation, so that just a small fall in income is sufficient to encourage them to leave the fishery, or those who are very bad at fishing so that financially they simply cannot stand even a small reduction in income. Looking at things purely from the viewpoint of resource allocation in the economy as a whole, it makes no difference which leave, because these two groups would comprise those for whom fishing has a high opportunity cost; that is to say, in order to have their production from fishing, society must give up relatively much in terms of what these people (and capital) might have produced in their next best occupation. Once sufficient numbers have left the fishery, the marginal fisherman will once again be earning normal profits and the exit process will cease. Since it will have been the high-opportunity-cost fishermen who have left the fishery, the given output of fish will then be produced at the lowest possible opportunity cost—which is the definition of optimal resource allocation.

At the end of the transition period, all fishermen will have lost in the short run; some will have been priced out permanently; and since the regulating authority captures all of the sustained economic rent, even those remaining will be no better off in the long run. Indeed it may be argued, on quite plausible assumptions, that fishermen who remain in the fishery will be worse off under taxation than they would have been under open access. The logic is as follows. In open-access equilibrium, the marginal fisherman earns normal profit, which means that he just covers his opportunity cost. However not all fishermen have the same opportunity cost, either because they are better fishermen or because they are less good at alternative occupations. Let us assume that each successive fisherman has a slightly greater opportunity cost. The normal profit of the marginal fisherman will then be above normal for all remaining fishermen; that is, it more than covers their opportunity costs. This extra payment is called an intra-marginal rent, and on our assumptions it will be received to some degree by all fishermen except the marginal one. Now suppose that taxation is introduced. Some fishermen earn less than their opportunity cost and leave the fishery. Equilibrium is restored when the marginal fisherman again earns normal profit. However the identity of the marginal fisherman is no longer the same. Since there are now fewer fishermen, the new marginal fisherman must be someone who was previously receiving an intra-marginal rent. The level of normal profit must also have declined therefore, and so must all other intra-marginal rents. Thus the consequence is that regulation by taxation makes even those who remain in the fishery worse off to the extent that intra-marginal rents are eroded.

Taxation thus enables the economic rent from the fishery to be captured only at the expense of making the fishermen worse off. Since most fisheries management programmes include the aim of improving fishermen's incomes (often as the way of enlisting their support for the management measures), it is not really very surprising that taxation has not been seen as the best way of managing fisheries by those actually in charge of such management. And it is even less surprising when it is noted that many countries actually *subsidize* their fishermen.

A further practical problem with using taxation as the main regulatory device is its inflexibility. Institutional factors tend to make it difficult to alter tax rates (at least quickly), so that taxation cannot really be used as a means of achieving close short-term control of a fishery. Probably the best that might reasonably be expected is to move the fishery in the correct direction regarding output and effort. Supplementary management techniques would then be required to deal with urgent short-term problems.

Thus we may conclude that, mainly for political reasons, taxation has only a limited role to play in the management of domestic fishing fleets. However it is possible that the advent of 200-mile fishing limits may increase its importance in the management of foreign fleets, simply because foreign vessels operating within a coastal state's limit do not usually have any political power in that state. It will, therefore, be in the state's interest to attempt to tax away as much economic rent as possible from the foreign fleet (except, of course, where it is concerned for its own distant-water fleet). Thus, for example, foreign vessels fishing in U.S. waters must pay not only an annual permit fee, but also various taxes on their catch (*see* Chapter 8, section 8.3).

6.3.2 Licensing

Taxation works by making it unprofitable for some fishermen to take part in the fishery, hence bringing fishing effort under control. In contrast, licensing works by seeking to regulate directly who may and who may not participate in the fishery. Only those with a licence may take part.

In the establishment of any licensing scheme, the first problem to be resolved is precisely what is to be licensed. Occasionally it is the fishing gear itself. More frequently, it is the fisherman. This is the case, for instance, in the Alaskan salmon fishery, where the regulatory authority was attempting to give the fishermen some leverage vis-à-vis the processing companies. Usually, however, it is the boat that is licensed. Whichever the alternative chosen, it is effectively being used as a proxy for effort. The aim of the licensing scheme is to bring effort under control by licensing, say, the boat. As we shall see however, since neither men, gear nor boat is a perfect proxy for effort, problems can arise, particularly concerning the substitution of inputs.

Once a decision has been taken as to what to license, the management authority must then decide how to issue the licences. Because the support of the fishermen is usually seen as being essential to the success of any management programme, licences are often simply given away on the basis of past involvement in the fishery. More often than not, a minimum landings requirement during a reference period is also established. Thus, for example, the scheme might allocate a licence to everyone who caught more than the minimum amount in the previous season. One drawback with such an approach is that it may end up excluding part-timers or fishermen who exploit many species consecutively during the year. Since these may, in fact, be very efficient fishermen, their exclusion is often considered undesirable (although not necessarily by so-called 'full-time' fishermen). The problem can, however, be dealt with by the establishment of a special hearings board. Such a board is likely to be required, in any case, to deal with the hard-luck stories that are almost certain to arise at the beginning of any licensing scheme. For instance, in the establishment of the Solent oyster fishery licensing scheme, allowance had to be made for a fisherman who had always taken part in the fishery but whose boat had sunk immediately prior to the reference period; and for a fisherman whose boat had needed a major overhaul and who had found it cheaper to take a season off fishing to carry out the work himself.

Another problem (although not from the fisherman's point of view) with giving away licences is that whatever value they may acquire will represent a windfall gain to the fishermen. While it may be desirable to improve the lot of fishermen, it might also be argued that a fishery is a social resource and hence should benefit the whole of society. This problem seems more interesting when it is noted that the economic rent potential of U.S. fisheries, for example, has been estimated to be in excess of $300 million annually (Christy, 1977). A way around this particular problem would be to charge a licence fee such that society leaves the fisherman with whatever share of the rent is considered equitable.

One final problem with giving away licences, particularly on the basis of a historical-involvement criterion, is that the number of fishermen engaged in the fishery is likely to be too great (because the scheme will approximate to open access). In such a case, either the management authority will have to use some other management measures to support the licensing scheme, or it will have to buy back immediately some of the licences that it has just issued. This latter alternative may seem a little strange, but in fact it may be the best, or at least the easiest, way of proceeding. Fishermen will not be forced to leave the fishery but will do so voluntarily, provided they are offered sufficient inducement. It is to be expected that those with the greatest opportunity cost will leave first so that, as with taxation, the optimal output (whatever that may be) will be taken at the lowest opportunity cost. In contrast to taxation however, the buy-back scheme will be painless. Unfortunately, it is also likely to prove expensive in that fishermen may require a substantial inducement to encourage them to leave the fishery, and the initial reduction in effort required may be rather large. Moreover, technical progress over time will tend to result in fewer and fewer units of nominal effort being required, so that continuing disbursements of funds may be expected. If the licensing scheme does result, as is often hoped, in the emergence of important economic rents, then the management authority may be in a position to charge a licence fee so as to recover the cost of the initial buy-back programme. Such costs might then be regarded as a loan by society to be recouped (in part or in total) against the future economic rents that the fishery is expected to yield.

However, as we shall argue below, large-scale economic rents may not materialize under a licensing scheme.

A cheap alternative to the buy-back scheme would be to auction the optimal number of licences in the first place. Each fisherman will find it profitable to bid for a licence up to what he considers to be the discounted present value of the economic rent which he expects from the fishery. Thus it should be those fishermen with the lowest opportunity costs who bid successfully for licences, because they should be the ones who anticipate the most rent—on the possibly heroic assumption that expectations are, shall we say, rational. The stumbling block with this approach is that clearly the licensing authority captures the capitalized (i.e. discounted net present) value of the economic rent expected from the fishery. The support of most fishermen cannot realistically be expected for such a scheme, and since their support is generally considered indispensable, so far as we know the auctioning of licences has yet to be attempted.

Although obviously crucial for deciding who receives the economic rent from the fishery, the way in which licences are initially distributed should be irrelevant from the viewpoint of optimal resource allocation *provided* they are transferable. This is because transferability should cause high-opportunity-cost holders of licences to sell them to low-opportunity-cost buyers. Since the mechanism via which this redistribution happens is discussed in some detail in the next section for the analogous case of individual fish quotas, it will not be discussed here.

Sometimes however, licences are issued that are not transferable. Generally what happens is that the licensing authority issues a licence on the proviso that if it is not worked (say, for longer than a complete season) then it reverts to the authority. A decision is then made whether to kill the licence or reissue it either to the original holder or to somebody new. Unfortunately, non-transferability usually results in the ossification of the fishery. Most fishermen find it worth while to fish at least for any qualifying period so as not to lose their licences. It is also likely to be more difficult for them to leave the fishery even if they want to because the, possibly substantial, addition to capital made by the sale of a transferable licence is not available. Moreover the situation may be made worse in that frequently the fishermen themselves have a say in who their successor should be if they do leave. For these reasons it is probable that few licences will in fact revert to the authority, and since this latter will usually be attempting to control effort, even fewer will become available for fishermen new to the fishery. Optimal resource allocation seems most unlikely in such a situation. In fact both society and the fishermen themselves seem to have everything to gain from transferable licences.

The biggest disadvantage with licensing is that, although strict control may be exercised over some part of fishing effort (be it the number of fishermen, the amount of gear, or the number or gross tonnage of vessels), because not all elements of effort are under control, fishermen are likely to find it profitable to substitute uncontrolled inputs for controlled ones. Since licensing most frequently applies to the boat, this phenomenon has become known as 'capital stuffing'. Let us suppose that it is gross tonnage that is under control and that the licensing scheme is working well with economic rents emerging. Individual fishermen will then find that the price of fish is greater, perhaps much greater, than the average cost of catching it. They will therefore find it attractive to attempt to increase their catch and thereby increase their profits. Since gross tonnage is controlled, they will attempt to do this by using more efficient inputs in the boat itself; for instance, they may fit a bigger engine, or acquire more powerful hauling gear so as to be able to use larger nets. The end result will be that the catching ability of the licensed vessel will be greater than previously.

The problem is that all fishermen will react in roughly the same manner, so that the catching ability of the whole fleet may be expected to increase. The licensing authority may react in a number of ways to this development. First, it may try to hold catch at the original level by means of a quota or closed season. To do so will clearly result in the erosion of economic rents because costs have increased but catch will not change. Secondly, it may do nothing. In this case, catch will probably increase in the short run so that extra investment will pay off to some extent. However, this increased catch is unlikely to be sustainable in the long run so that eventually catch will probably fall back to, or perhaps below, its original level. Thus in the longer run the extra catching capacity will probably result in a smaller catch (depending on the position from which we begin). Once again therefore economic rents will be eroded. The third option for the licensing authority is to attempt to maintain economic rents by buying back licences corresponding to the excess catching capacity of the fleet. In this case, the extra investment will be profitable for those fishermen left in the fleet, but socially the extra cost has been incurred for nothing. The existence of the licensing scheme artificially makes it profitable to use a combination of inputs that otherwise would not be so. Moreover so long as the economic rents exist, fishermen within the scheme will find it worth while to attempt to increase their share of the catch. Thus unless the licensing authority always stays one jump ahead of the game, economic rents must eventually be eroded.

It might be argued that the reason why licensing brings this result is the way that it has been operated; in particular, because only one element of effort is controlled. Thus operating a successful licensing scheme, in this view, would just be a question of pushing licensing far enough; that is, simply licensing enough components of effort to bring it under control. There are a number of problems with this viewpoint. First, effort itself is difficult to define adequately. Secondly, even if effort is adequately defined to begin with, the emergence of rents may well make it profitable to use previously unprofitable inputs. Thirdly, the more inputs that have to be controlled, the more bureaucratic and costly the administrative machinery will become and the more difficult it will be to predict accurately the likely impact of further restrictions. In practice, therefore, licensing schemes have stuck to trying to control just one or two elements of effort.

It may be that there are other ways to solve the problems of licensing, but investing a great deal of time in trying to find them does not appear to be worth while because the next management measure to be discussed—individual fish quotas—in fact appears to deal with the major difficulties.

6.3.3 Individual fish quotas

Essentially, individual fish quotas (IFQs) are licences that grant the right not merely to participate in a fishery but also to catch, or more accurately, to land, a specified amount of fish. That is, each licensed individual fisherman, or boat (depending on the licensing unit), is permitted to take a certain quota of fish, hence the terminology 'individual fish quota'. Although this system is clearly related to the licensing schemes discussed in the previous section, the allocation of rights in terms of a specific quantity of fish leads to important differences which appear to make the IFQ system preferable.

IFQs may be denominated either as simple quantities such as tons of fish or as percentages of the total allowable catch (TAC). Each system has its merits and demerits, and we shall consider these more fully below. On the whole however, the quantity-denominated scheme seems to be the more advantageous and we shall therefore use it to illustrate the principles of an IFQ management regime.

The TAC is decided by the management authority and is then divided into many 'small' IFQs. These are allocated to the fishing fleet in some way. The choice will be similar to that with licences. IFQs may be either given away or sold, a choice that will have some bearing on the distribution of rent from the fishery. As with licences however, charging the appropriate fee for IFQs can ensure an equitable rent distribution. Despite such similarities, IFQs offer much greater flexibility than licences. For example, the problem of part-time fishermen may be solved simply by allocating IFQs in proportion to historic catch, although the relevant reference period may still be difficult to determine. IFQs also offer the management authority more flexibility in the achievement of subsidiary aims. For instance, in the distribution of IFQs it would be straightforward to favour a region particularly dependent on the fishery.

Moreover, while the management authority is given flexibility in their initial distribution, IFQs should result eventually in an optimal allocation of resources to the fishery provided that they are made transferable. The combination of many, low-denomination IFQs and transferability should ensure that a market for them develops. If it should be the case that the distribution of IFQs has been economically suboptimal, then it is to be expected that high-opportunity-cost fishermen will sell their rights to low-opportunity-cost ones.

To illustrate the way in which a fishery might be managed using IFQs, let us imagine an open-access fishery initially in equilibrium at an output Y_{oa} and with an effort level f_1, as shown in *Figure 6.8*. As we know, at this point the marginal fisherman will just be covering his opportunity cost. Now suppose that the management authority decides to implement an IFQ system and, as a way of enlisting the fishermen's support for the scheme, simply allocates rights according to the existing open-access situation.

Clearly, the TAC will then be equal to Y_{oa} and little will have changed in the fishery.

It may seem tempting to argue that because an open-access fishery is usually overcapitalized, the fishermen themselves will have an incentive to rationalize fishing effort. The problem is that while it is true that the fishery is overcapitalized in the sense that effort level f_1 is being used where effort level f_3 would suffice, this represents a long-run view. In the short run, an

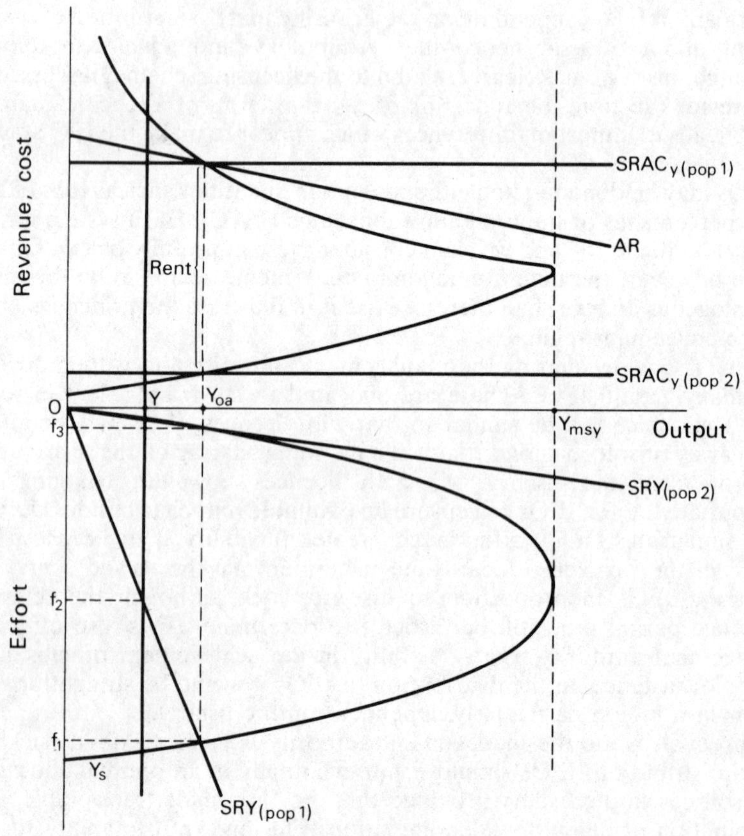

FIGURE 6.8 Management by IFQs.

effort level of f_1 is the only way to achieve an output of Y_{oa} because the fish population has been reduced to such a small size. Only if the population is allowed to recover will f_3 units of effort result in a catch of Y_{oa}. It is difficult to see scope, therefore, for a large-scale rationalization of effort in the fishery. IFQs may take on some value, for instance, because of speculation, or because some fishermen do find it worth while to purchase rights, but on the whole allocation of IFQs in accordance with open access is not likely to change the fishery very much.

Let us assume then that the management authority adopts the aim of moving the fishery from the high LRAC to the low LRAC at the open-access output level. Quite clearly the first thing that must be done is to reduce catch below Y_{oa} (the sustainable yield) so as to enable the fish stock to recover. The authority therefore enters the market and purchases some rights so that the total allowable catch falls from Y_{oa} to Y, say. At this output, only f_2 units of effort are required and a profit equal to average revenue minus short-run average cost will materialize. The emergence of this profit will make the fishery more attractive and fishermen are likely to want to increase their catch. To do so however, they must acquire IFQs from other fishermen and the price of such rights will begin to increase.

The value that the IFQs take on, while clearly representing a windfall gain to those fishermen given them, will represent an opportunity cost in the sense that they may be sold and the proceeds reinvested. Fishermen will therefore, implicitly at least, have to take account of two opportunity costs: first, that of being a fisherman at all in relation to their next best occupation, and secondly, that of holding fishing rights. Different fishermen may be expected to have different alternatives for each of these; that is, they will not all have the same alternative occupation available, and they will not all have the same opportunities for using funds raised from the sale of IFQs.Their overall decision on whether to stay in the fishery or not will depend, largely at least, on the combined effect of these two opportunity costs.

If a fisherman has an alternative occupation that is almost the equivalent to him of fishing, and he also has a very profitable use to which to put any funds he may raise, the price at which he will find it profitable to sell his IFQs and leave fishing will be lower than for the fisherman who has only poor alternatives available. At the limit, the fisherman who is not interested in any other occupation and has no alternative use for funds will not find it profitable to sell his rights at any price. This is to be expected since his combined opportunity cost will be zero. Such a case is of course unlikely, but in general the lower is the combined opportunity cost of fishing facing a particular fisherman, the greater will have to be the price of IFQs to make it worth his while to sell. As the price of IFQs rises therefore, it will be the higher-opportunity-cost fishermen who find it worth while to sell their rights to the management authority or to other fishermen. The chosen output of fish will then be being taken at the lowest possible opportunity cost, which—to emphasize once more—implies that resource allocation is optimal.

The point at which the price of IFQs stops increasing will depend, *inter alia*, on the time period for which rights have been granted. If they are for one year only then the price will reach equilibrium when the rent produced by the fishery is equivalent to the annual return available in the next best alternative to the marginal fisherman. If IFQs are granted in perpetuity then obviously we should expect prices to be higher, and in fact the price of IFQs will represent the discounted present value of the expected future rent from operating them. In either case, equilibrium is effectively established when the marginal fisherman just covers his combined opportunity cost. It is simply that the longer is the period of rights, the greater will be this opportunity cost—for all fishermen.

In *Figure 6.8*, as the fish stock recovers, the short-run yield curve turns upwards towards $SRY_{(pop.2)}$ and the short-run average cost curve shifts downwards towards $SRAC_{y(pop.2)}$. Economic rent will be increasing and so therefore will the price of IFQs. Given the management goal of output Y_{oa}, at some point the rights which the authority has bought will have to be resold (or at least reissued in some way). Since the price of IFQs will have increased, the management authority will actually be in the position to make money from the situation! Such is not necessarily the case however. In general it depends on the relationship between the initial and target levels of catch. If for instance the aim had been to reduce catch from Y_{oa} to Y on a long-run basis, the money that the authority paid for the rights would not have been recoverable directly. However, because IFQs operate on catch, they have a significant advantage over licences which, since they must operate on effort, will always result in the long-run disbursement of large amounts of money in the attempt to reduce fishing effort.

The aim of the management plan will have been achieved, and equilibrium will have been restored, when the short-run yield curve is given as $SRY_{(pop.2)}$, implying an effort level f_3 and short-run average cost curve $SRAC_{y(pop.2)}$. Economic rent will then be given as the difference between AR and $SRAC_{y(pop.2)}$ at output Y_{oa}. Although such rent will still be attractive to fishermen, its attraction will be reflected in the price of IFQs so that excessive entry and overcapitalization will not occur. Instead, the price of fishing rights will come to represent the capitalized value of the rent expected from the fishery over the time period of the rights.

This is the way in which the management authority might use IFQs to achieve its aims for the fishery. Effectively it undertakes open-market operations in rights much in the same way as a central bank does in treasury bills. Notice that the adjustment process is essentially painless. Fishermen leave the fishery only if they find it profitable to sell their rights. Otherwise they are free to carry on fishing with, moreover, a more or less guaranteed catch, thereby enabling them to plan their operations much better than previously.

The alternative proposed to the simple quantity IFQ scheme is to have IFQs denominated as percentages of the total allowable catch. With this approach the management authority merely announces the new lower total catch and all percentage shares are simply worth less than before. It is then left to the fishing industry to reorganize itself. The reduction in catch all round may well leave all fishermen in the position where they cannot manage. The adjustment process is likely to be much more painful than with the quantity scheme.

The principal advantage of a percentage-based scheme is that no government finance is required. In cases where the management authority is short of funds this may be the only approach possible. Alternatively some hybrid may be feasible whereby IFQs are denominated as percentages but the management authority buys back rights to the extent of funds before simply imposing the lower total allowable catch. It is important however not to overemphasize the funding problem. As we have already mentioned, in cases where the target level of catch exceeds the initial level, a quantity-denominated scheme may even be profitable; and whatever the situation, IFQs will not prove a continuous drain on resources in the way that licences might.

The major problem with any IFQ scheme lies in its enforcement. As may be seen from *Figure 6.8*, the scheme is likely to result in the emergence of significant economic rents, so that individual fishermen will have an incentive to exceed their quota if possible. Illegal landing and marketing may therefore become a problem. However it is equally true that those fishermen not exceeding their quota will have every incentive to report transgressors, so that the fishing fleet may well become its own police force—to an important extent at least. Perhaps a more pervasive and potentially more difficult problem will be that of *upgrading*. Fishermen may be expected to attempt to land fish of the greatest individual value and, so far as possible, will attempt to sort their catch. The likely result is that effective effort in the fishery will be greater than indicated by landed catch. A further problem is that total allowable catch is unlikely to remain constant from year to year but will instead vary with strength of the year class. For those species where variability is very great, IFQs may not be very practicable and may simply become, in effect, licences to participate in the fishery. The difficulty is to decide how variable TAC must be before IFQs are unworkable.

In cases where the TAC must be varied within an IFQ scheme, the management authority simply intervenes to sell or buy rights. The problem is, however, that the fishing fleet cannot vary its capacity on an annual basis so that there will be overcapacity some years and undercapacity others. Presumably harvesting capacity will settle at the level appropriate to the expected average catch, although the degree of dispersion of total catch around the average and the relative opportunity costs of being under- and overcapitalized are likely to influence the capacity level adopted.This problem of TAC variability is not unique to the IFQ system however, but results from the inherent biological variability of the fish stock, and thus afflicts all management schemes to an extent. Dismissing the IFQ system as not workable just because of this drawback would certainly be unwarranted.

A particular practical problem with IFQ-based management is that often data on which to base the initial allocation of rights are inadequate or unavailable. In such cases, it is vitally important to avoid a situation where the fishermen feel obliged to go out and make as large a catch as possible so as to qualify for a greater amount of rights in the eventual share-out. To do so is easier said than done however. One possible approach is simply to ask the fishermen what their catch has been over some reference period in the hope that the tendency to overreport to obtain more IFQs will be balanced by a tendency to underreport to the tax authorities. Such an approach is hardly likely to be very popular with the fishermen however, and is probably unreliable. The alternatives seem to be either to institute some form of logbook and await adequate data, or adopt some arbitrary allocation criterion (e.g. X tonnes per boat) and then allow the market for rights to resolve any problems. Neither of these approaches is particularly satisfactory. The former obviously takes a rather long time and runs the risk mentioned above of encouraging overfishing; the latter is probably even more arbitrary than simply asking the fishermen. Overall however, the conclusion seems inescapable that where management has previously been very inadequate, it may prove very difficult to move directly to a management scheme based on property rights.

It would clearly be simplistic to claim that IFQs are sufficient to resolve all fishery management problems. At the very least, they have to be supported by the ability to close the fishery early in response to, for example, any unanticipated environmental disaster. On the other hand, IFQ-based management does appear to offer significant advantages over the other management alternatives available. It is also true that the problems facing the scheme, notably enforcement, biological variability and data adequacy, affect all management schemes. The problem of enforcement may seem worse with IFQs but to a large extent this is simply because the system will actually work, in the sense that large resource rents may well materialize.

6.4 SUMMARY

In this chapter we consider the principal regulatory methods available in fisheries management. We divide these into what we call 'biological' and 'economic' methods. In the first group, we discuss the use of quotas, gear restrictions, closed seasons and closed areas, and show that because none of these methods deals with the open-access problem, none of them will significantly alter the long-run economic situation of the fishery. However, this is not to say that such regulations are of no use. First, they may well be adequate for the fulfilment of broadly biological goals such as increasing the fish population size. Secondly, they may also be positively required for the achievement of certain socioeconomic goals in fishing, such as the maximization of employment. Thirdly, they may have an important role to play in supporting more complex, but consequently less flexible methods.

The second group of methods, the economic ones, comprises taxation, licensing, and individual fish quotas (IFQs). The use of taxation is not likely to become important as a major fisheries management weapon, essentially because it works by impoverishing the fishermen (at least in the short run). Licensing and individual fish quotas are quite similar in many ways, but the former is denominated in terms of effort, the latter in terms of catch. As is often the case, the method denominated in terms of catch appears preferable. Perhaps the most telling argument in favour of IFQs is that over time in a well-managed fishery the effect of technological advance will be to lessen the amount of fishing effort required to take the target catch. This latter will however remain more or less constant (at least on the long-run average). Hence licensing is likely to involve the management authority in increasing disbursements of money over time to buy back excess licences, whereas IFQs will require very little, if any, additional finance.

6.5 BIBLIOGRAPHIC NOTES

Discussions and critiques of what we have termed 'biological' management methods may be found in works by Bevan (1965), Crutchfield (1961), Dickie (1962), Scott (1962) and Tester (1948). The concept of eumetric fishing is considered by Hannesson (1978, Ch. 8). The dynamics of the Beverton–Holt model are discussed by Clark, Edwards and Friedlander (1973).

General reviews of the economic methods of management have been published by Clark (1980), Crutchfield (1979), Cunningham (1983), Scott (1979) and Stokes (1979). The desirability or otherwise of limited-entry schemes is debated by Bishop (1973, 1975), Wilson and Olson (1975), and Owers (1975). There are reviews of limited-entry systems by Cicin-Sain, Moore and Wyner (1978) and McKellar (1977).

On property rights the best introduction is that of Moloney and Pearse (1979), although *see also* Christy (1980) and Moloney and Pearse (1980). The general ideas are also discussed by Christy (1969, 1973) and Pearse (1981). For a consideration of property rights in oyster fisheries *see* the series of papers by Agnello and Donnelley (1975a,b, 1976).

An interesting paper that considers the data requirements of different management regimes is that of Hilborn (1979).

Many studies exist of practical management schemes; *see* for example Adasiak (1979) and Rogers (1979) on Alaskan salmon, Asada (1973) and Keen (1973) on Japan, Campbell (1973) and Fraser (1979) on British Columbia salmon, Fraser (1980) on British Columbia roe herring, Gates and Norton (1974) on New England yellow tail flounder, Gertenbach (1973) on South Africa, and Meany (1979, 1980) on Australia.

REFERENCES AND FURTHER READING

ADASIAK, A. (1979). 'Alaska's experience with limited entry.' *Journal of the Fisheries Research Board of Canada* **36** (7) : 770–82.

AGNELLO, R. and L. DONNELLEY (1975a). 'Property rights and efficiency in the U.S. oyster industry.' *Journal of Law and Economics* **18** : 521–33.

AGNELLO, R. and L. DONNELLEY (1975b). 'Prices and property rights in the fisheries.' *Southern Economic Journal* **42** : 253–62.

AGNELLO, R. and L. DONNELLEY (1976). 'Externalities and property rights in the fisheries.' *Land Economics* **52** (4) : 518–29.

ASADA, Y. (1973). 'Licence limitation regulations: the Japanese system.' *Journal of the Fisheries Research Board of Canada* **30** : 2085–95.

BEVAN, D. (1965). 'Methods of fishery regulation.' In J. A. Crutchfield (Ed.), *The fisheries: problems in resource management,* pp. 25–40. Seattle: University of Washington Press.

BEVERTON, R. and S. HOLT (1957). *On the dynamics of exploited fish populations*. London: HMSO.

BISHOP, R. (1973). 'Limitation of entry in the United States fishing industry: an economic appraisal of a proposed policy.' *Land Economics* **49** : 381–90.

BISHOP, R. (1975). 'Limitation of entry in the United States fishing industry: a reply.' *Land Economics* **51** : 182–5.

CAMPBELL, B. (1973). 'Licence limitation regulations: Canada's experience.' *Journal of the Fisheries Research Board of Canada* **30** : 2070–6.

CHRISTY, F., Jr (1969). 'Fisheries goals and the rights of property.' *Transactions of the American Fisheries Society* **98** : 369–78.

CHRISTY, F., Jr (1973). 'Fisherman catch quotas.' University of Rhode Island, Law of the Sea Institute, Occasional Paper 19.

CHRISTY, F., Jr (1977). 'Limited access systems under the Fishery Conservation and Management Act of 1976.' In L. G. Anderson (Ed.), *Economic impacts of extended fisheries jurisdiction,* pp. 141–56. Ann Arbor, Michigan: Ann Arbor Science Publishers.

CHRISTY, F., Jr (1980). 'Comment on quantitative rights as an instrument for regulating commercial fisheries.' *Canadian Journal of Fisheries and Aquatic Sciences* **37** (5) : 902–3.

CICIN-SAIN, B., J. MOORE and A. WYNER (1978). 'Limiting entry to commercial fisheries: some world wide comparisons.' *Ocean Management* **4** (1) : 21–49.

CLARK, C. (1976). *Mathematical bioeconomics*. New York: Wiley Interscience.

CLARK, C. (1980). 'Towards a predictive model for the economic regulation of commercial fisheries.' *Canadian Journal of Fisheries and Aquatic Sciences* **37** (7) : 1111–29.

CLARK, C., G. EDWARDS and M. FRIEDLANDER (1973). 'Beverton–Holt model of a commercial fishery: optimal dynamics.' *Journal of the Fisheries Research Board of Canada* **30** : 1629–40.

CRUTCHFIELD, J. A. (1961). 'An economic evaluation of alternative methods of fishery regulation.' *Journal of Law and Economics* **4** : 131–43.

CRUTCHFIELD, J. A. (1979). 'Economic and social implications of the main policy alternatives for controlling fishing effort.' *Journal of the Fisheries Research Board of Canada* **36** (7) : 742–52.

CUNNINGHAM, S. (1983). 'The increasing importance of economics in fisheries regulation.' *Journal of Agricultural Economics* **34** (1) : 69–78.

DICKIE, L. (1962). 'Effects of fishery regulations on the catch of fish.' In R. Hamlisch (Ed.), *Economic effects of fishery regulation*. FAO Fishery Report No. 5.

FRASER, G. (1979). 'Limited entry: experience of the British Columbia salmon fishery.' *Journal of the Fisheries Research Board of Canada* **36** (7) : 754–63.

FRASER, G. (1980). 'Licence limitation in the British Columbia roe herring fishery: an evaluation.' University of British Columbia, mimeo.

GATES, J. and V. NORTON (1974). 'The benefits of fishery regulation: a case study of the New England yellowtail flounder fishery.' University of Rhode Island, Marine Technology Report No. 21.

GERTENBACH, L. (1973). 'Licence limitation regulations: the South African system.' *Journal of the Fisheries Research Board of Canada* **30** : 2077–84.

HANNESSON, R. (1978). *Economics of fisheries*. Oslo: Universitetsforlaget.

HILBORN, R. (1979). 'Comparison of fisheries control systems that utilize catch and effort data.' *Journal of the Fisheries Research Board of Canada* **36** : 1477–89.

KEEN, E. (1973). 'Limited entry: the case of the Japanese tuna fishery.' In A. Sokoloski (Ed.), *Ocean fishery management: Discussions and research*, pp. 146–58. NOAA Technical Report, NMFS Circular 371.

MCKELLAR, N. (1977). 'Restrictive licensing as a fisheries management tool.' WFA, FERU Occasional Paper No. 6.

MEANY, T. (1979). 'Limited entry in the Western Australian rock lobster and prawn fisheries: an economic viewpoint.' *Journal of the Fisheries Research Board of Canada* **36** (7): 789–98.

MEANY, T. (1980). 'The nature and adequacy of property rights in Australian fisheries.' Paper presented at a seminar on Economic Aspects of Limited Entry, Melbourne, February 1980.

MOLONEY, D. and P. PEARSE (1979). 'Quantitative rights as an instrument for regulating commercial fisheries.' *Journal of the Fisheries Research Board of Canada* **36** (7) : 859–66.

MOLONEY, D. and P. PEARSE (1980). 'Quantitative rights—a reply.' *Canadian Journal of Fisheries and Aquatic Sciences* **37** : 903–4.

OWERS, J. (1975). 'Limitation of entry in the United States fishing industry: a comment.' *Land Economics* **51** (2) : 177–8.

PEARSE, P. (1981). 'Fishing rights, regulations and revenues.' *Marine Policy* **5** (2) : 135–46.

ROGERS, G. (1979). 'Alaska's limited entry program: another view.' *Journal of the Fisheries Research Board of Canada* **36** (7) : 783–8.

SCOTT, A. (1962). 'The economics of regulating fisheries.' In R. Hamlisch (Ed.), *Economic effects of fishery regulation*, pp. 21–96. FAO Fishery Report No. 5.

SCOTT, A. (1979). 'Development of economic theory on fisheries regulation.' *Journal of the Fisheries Research Board of Canada* **36** (7): 725–41.

STOKES, R. (1979). 'Limitation of fishing effort—an economic analysis of options.' *Marine Policy* **3** (4) : 289–301.

TESTER, A. (1948). 'The efficacy of catch limitations in regulating the British Columbia herring fishery.' *Transactions of the Royal Society of*

Canada **42** : 135–63.
WILSON, J. and F. OLSON (1975). 'Limitation of entry in the United States fishing industry: a second comment.' *Land Economics* **51** (2) : 179–81.

CHAPTER 7

Fisheries policy at the international level

7.1 INTRODUCTION

There are essentially two ways in which satisfactory fisheries management regimes might evolve: either by international agreement and cooperation, or under the extended fisheries jurisdiction of individual nation states. In this chapter, we consider the way in which international management of fisheries has worked, and in the next we look at management at the national level.

We begin this chapter by reviewing, via four case studies, the historical performance of international bodies, which have for many years been the main agents of fisheries management. As we shall see, despite a long history, the facts suggest that their performance has not always been good and has at times been conspicuously poor, primarily because of the related problems of voluntary membership and 'free riders'. In such situations, it becomes almost impossible to enforce unpopular decisions. Partly because of the inadequate performance of international management and partly thanks to an increasingly acquisitive attitude towards marine resources, a widespread move towards 200-mile limits followed, emerging from within the United Nations Conference on the Law of the Sea (UNCLOS) from the 1950s to the mid 1970s and confirmed by that Convention in 1982. In the final section of the chapter, we consider the Common Fisheries Policy of the European Economic Community, which is the latest, and possibly the last, great international management regime. We shall argue that, unhappily, it retains almost all the defects of international management that led to the emergent regime of coastal state management based on exclusive economic zones.

7.2 INTERNATIONAL FISHERIES ORGANIZATIONS

7.2.1 Introduction

There are, of course, a great many international fishery organizations, and there is simply not the space to discuss them all here. Instead, we have chosen to look briefly at the work of four bodies, covering somewhat different aspects of international management. The first two, the North-East Atlantic Fisheries Commission (NEAFC) and the Northwest Atlantic Fisheries Organization (NAFO), are illustrative of the kind of international management body that emerged in the post-1945 period and dominated fisheries management until the move towards 200-mile limits after 1976. Both these bodies developed from the work of the International Council for the Exploration of the Sea (ICES), established in 1902 primarily as a forum for the exchange of scientific ideas between biologists. Based on the work by ICES, the Baltic Convention was signed in 1933 for the protection of plaice and flounder in the Baltic areas fished by five countries. NEAFC and NAFO then emerged, after the Second World War, as the basis for international management on a much wider scale in the North Atlantic.

Notwithstanding the advent of 200-mile limits, some international bodies remain vitally important, notably in the management of wide-ranging species. We consider here the international management of two such species: first the International Whaling Commission (IWC) for whales, which are nowadays of interest principally because of their role in the vanguard of the conservation movement; and secondly the management of tuna, a species of considerable commercial interest, especially to many less developed countries, and one that raises some particularly awkward issues relating to the management of a migratory fish stock.

7.2.2 The North-East Atlantic Fisheries Commission

7.2.2.1 *The background*

The problem of overfishing had been recognized and widely discussed between the two world wars, and was felt by most experts principally to affect demersal fish species. Russell (1942, pp. 10–11), for instance, said: '. . . the English sea fisheries [are of] two main kinds—that for the fish that swim near the surface, and that for fish living on or near the bottom. The principal fish in the first category are the herring and the mackerel . . . we shall not deal with this form of fishery at all, important though it is, for the problem of depletion seems hardly to arise with it, so huge are the stocks.' Thus it was that when the Atlantic fishing nations met at the end of the Second World War and negotiated the Overfishing Convention, it applied only to *demersal* species. As its name indicates, the purpose of the convention was to prevent the overfishing of such stocks, essentially in the sense of the capture of immature fish. The main regulatory methods to be used were minimum mesh and landing sizes.

During the eight years that it took for the convention to be ratified, it became apparent that it was inadequate, particularly because of its failure to include pelagic species, and consequently negotiations began almost immediately on a new convention. The North-East Atlantic Fisheries Convention was eventually signed early in 1959, entering into force some four years later. (*See Figure 7.1*.) In addition to mesh and landing size restrictions, the new North-East Atlantic Fisheries Commission (NEAFC) could recommend closed seasons and areas, gear restrictions, and total allowable catches (TACs). Regrettably, as it turned out, the implementation of TACs was made rather difficult; for instance, a two-thirds majority was required

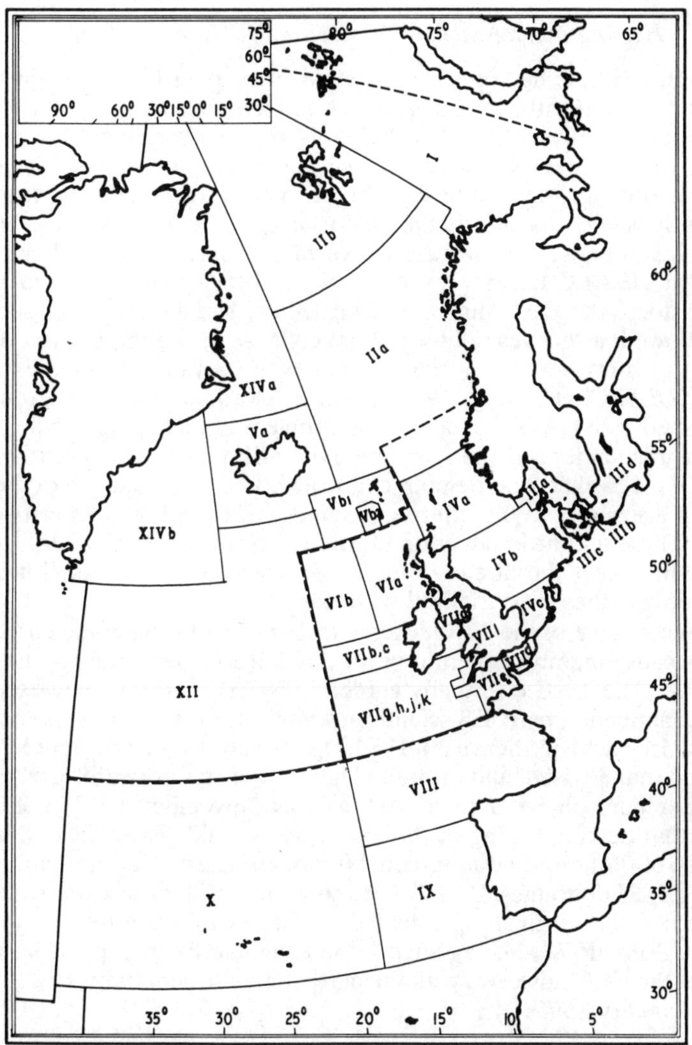

FIGURE 7.1 ICES Fishing Areas. Adapted from *Bulletin Statistique des Pêches Maritimes*, 1980, p. 103.

and the objection of a single state was sufficient to render the agreed TAC inapplicable. This had the, perhaps predictable, result that member nations were unable to agree on the need for TACs until the condition of a stock became serious, and even then there was a tendency to set such TACs at too high a level. This led McKellar (1980, p. 1) to conclude that NEAFC '. . . has been characterized by its failures rather than its successes'.

7.2.2.2 *Herring management—NEAFC in action or inaction?*

Although NEAFC had and has much wider responsibilities, its history is intimately bound with, and its problems and weaknesses are well illustrated by, the management of the North Sea herring stocks. Since the time that Russell wrote, a number of technological advances, particularly the advent of purse seining, have radically altered matters so that it is now most frequently *pelagic* species that are associated with overfishing and particularly stock collapse. In the case of North Sea herring, things began very badly for NEAFC because by the time (*c*. 1964) that it took control of pelagic stocks the East Anglian herring fishery had already collapsed. This was followed, a few years later, by the collapse of the important Atlanto-Scandian fishery—an event that did not even warrant a formal discussion within NEAFC! (Cushing, 1977, p. 232). Eventually a study group was established by NEAFC to look at the problem of managing herring stocks and this recommended the implementation of a TAC scheme. It was not until 1974 however that member countries could be persuaded of the need for such a scheme. In the interim, a number of closed seasons were established. These had little effect on mortality however, initially because they tended to reflect the already established seasonal pattern of fishing and later because they were riddled with exemptions.

The acceptance of the TAC scheme in 1974 was far from the end of the story, because members then found it difficult to agree on what the TAC should be. The TAC eventually agreed in NEAFC consistently exceeded that recommended by ICES scientists, whose task it was to advise on such matters. In each of the years 1974, 1975 and 1976, the agreed TAC exceeded that advised, and even the higher total was not enforced because some members objected to it. As early as November 1975, ICES had argued that herring fishing in the North Sea should cease, yet a TAC for 1976 of 160000 tonnes was agreed, but not enforced, with the actual catch reaching 183000 tonnes. By 1977 the condition of the stock was so serious that members were finally persuaded of the need for a total ban and this began in April 1977. Management of herring had by then passed into the hands of the EEC however, with the extension of fishery limits to 200 miles from 1 January 1977.

7.2.2.3 *Why did NEAFC fail?*

It is possibly a little harsh to argue that NEAFC was a complete failure, but from the management point of view it was certainly close to it. Probably the fish stocks would have been in an even worse condition had NEAFC not existed, but it is difficult to see how they could have been *much* worse; the herring stock collapsed, and almost every species was exploited beyond the point of maximum sustainable yield (MSY), up to what was probably close to the open-access level (ICES, 1977, p. 8).

There are doubtless many reasons for the failure of the NEAFC regime. International management of fisheries is complex and it is extremely difficult to persuade different countries to agree on appropriate measures. At the simplest level however, NEAFC failed because the fisheries under its jurisdiction remained essentially open-access—not perhaps in the classic sense of fishermen competing for their share of the catch, but at the national level where governments, despite meeting to discuss regulation, apparently did not perceive it to be worth while to reduce fishing effort, presumably because the future gains from such a course of action were insufficient. A contributory factor may have been the failure of some scientists at least to present their case in a sufficiently powerful way; but for the most part governments appear simply to have used genuine scientific doubt as a justification for their preferred course.

Fishing the herring stock out, and fishing beyond MSY in general, are quite possibly optimal strategies in the sense of dynamic maximum economic yield discussed in Chapter 4. However, we can be almost certain that it is not on such grounds that the levels of fishing effort used in the north-east Atlantic have been determined. Rather, one factor that seems to enter into government welfare functions is political kudos, and some at least of the governments involved in the NEAFC were not willing to be seen to be making political compromises, apparently preferring instead to see fish stocks run down. In other words, what seems to have happened is that the political gains involved in not compromising on fisheries management have exceeded the perceived biological, economic and social losses. The optimality, or otherwise, of such a strategy depends, as always, upon one's definition of 'optimal'.

7.2.2.4 *The future*

The widespread adoption of 200-mile limits has greatly reduced the importance of NEAFC, and a new convention has had to be drafted. This, the Convention on Future Multilateral Co-operation in North-East Atlantic Fisheries, was opened for signature in November 1980 and was ratified by sufficient signatories to enter into force on 17 March 1982. The first annual meeting of the new NEAFC took place in London on 22–25 November 1982.

The aims of the new NEAFC are to promote the conservation and (the undefined) optimum utilization of the fishery resources of the north-east Atlantic area within a framework appropriate to the regime of extended coastal state jurisdiction over fisheries, and to encourage international cooperation and consultation with respect to these resources. Advice on the biological basis of fisheries management will continue to be provided by ICES. The jurisdiction of NEAFC will now be limited to areas beyond national 200-mile limits but NEAFC will continue to play an advisory role within such limits, with coastal states free to accept or reject recommendations made (*see* section 7.3.2).

7.2.3 North-west Atlantic fisheries management

7.2.3.1 *The background*

International fisheries management in the north-west Atlantic is presently the responsibility of the Northwest Atlantic Fisheries Organization (NAFO), which assumed control of the fish stocks in its region (*see Figure 7.2*) on 1 January 1979. NAFO however is the successor to the International Commission for Northwest Atlantic Fisheries (ICNAF) and its roots are to be found here.

ICNAF entered into force in July 1950, its role in the north-west Atlantic being similar to that played by NEAFC in the north-east. In contrast to NEAFC however, ICNAF was responsible not only for providing advice on fisheries regulation but also for organizing research, via its Standing Committee on Research and Statistics—a role played by ICES in the NEAFC system.

Initially ICNAF attempted to achieve the maximum sustainable yield in the fisheries that it managed, primarily by the use of mesh size restrictions. Success was somewhat limited however, and overfishing (on the MSY definition) affected many stocks. Though there may have been many reasons for such overfishing, essentially the problems were similar to those faced by NEAFC, particularly the lack of control over fishing effort. In an attempt to combat this problem, ICNAF's regulatory framework was developed quite substantially from the late 1960s onwards.

First, following NEAFC, the enforcement of regulations was placed on an international footing, with the inspector of any member state being able to board and inspect the fishing vessels of any other member. All infractions were reported to ICNAF. The great weakness of the system was that the punishment of offenders remained the responsibility of home states (i.e. those in which the vessel was registered). This led to some bad feeling between, for instance, North American inspectors and East European fishermen, the former believing that infractions committed by the latter were going unpunished.

Secondly, a system of TACs and national catch quotas was instituted. Quotas were based on a mixture of historical performance and coastal preference, with some attention being paid to regional needs. By 1975, ICNAF had fifty-five stocks under the TAC system (Cushing, 1977, p. 234).

Laudable however as these developments were, they failed to deal adequately with the related weaknesses of international management: open access and inadequate enforcement. Possibly, in the longer term, the member states might have been prepared to grant to ICNAF sovereign rights over their fishing vessels, although such a state of affairs always appeared most unlikely, but in the event the solution of extended coastal state jurisdiction was adopted in the north-west Atlantic as elsewhere.

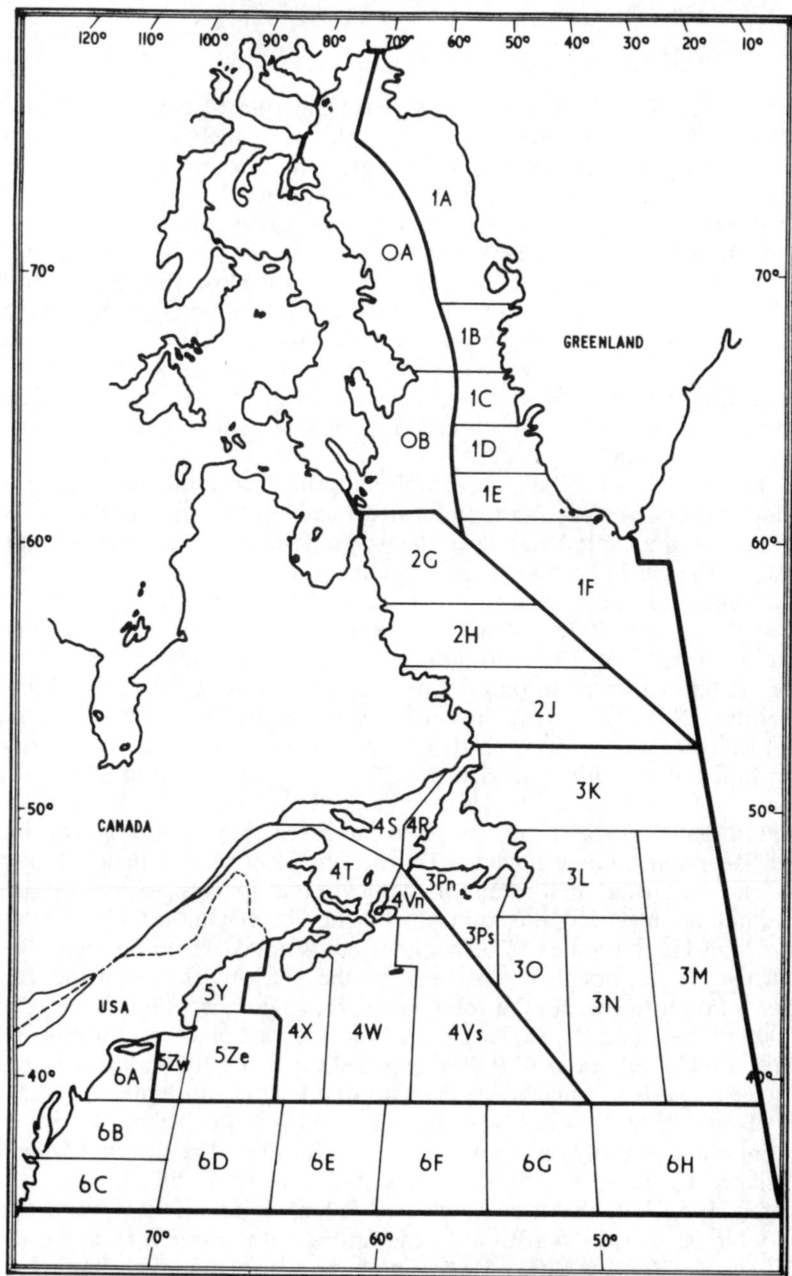

FIGURE 7.2 NAFO Fishing Areas. Adapted from *NAFO Annual Report* **1**, 1979, p. 4.

7.2.3.2 *The Georges Bank haddock fishery*

The Georges Bank haddock fishery plays the role of *bête noire* in the north-west Atlantic, a role similar to that played by the North Sea herring fishery in the north-east. A number of important lessons for fisheries management may be deduced from the management of the Georges Bank fishery and a discussion of it seems, therefore, to be worth while.

Until about 1960, the fishery was exploited almost solely by the United States and most of the time the annual catch was close to the estimated MSY of 50 000 tonnes. Nonetheless, in 1929, following an exceptionally good year class, some 130 000 tonnes of haddock was landed. When the following year the catch dropped to 60 000 tonnes, fears were expressed for the future of the fishery and a study group was established. This recommended a minimum mesh size, although implementation was voluntary on the fishermen's part.

By the time that ICNAF was established, therefore, the Georges Bank haddock fishery had been fairly intensively studied for a number of years. Moreover, as the United States was the only nation involved, it was straightforward to reach international agreement on management of the fishery and a minimum mesh size was introduced. This seemed to work well so long as the United States remained the only nation exploiting the fishery. However, from about 1960 onwards, Canadian and European, particularly Soviet, fishermen came to play a more important role in the fishery. Consequently, in the early 1960s the catch began slightly to exceed the MSY.

Ironically however, disaster struck the fishery only when favourable environmental conditions caused the 1962 and especially the 1963 year classes to be exceptionally large. When these haddock attained the minimum legal size in 1965, so numerous were they on the banks that those fishermen, mainly Soviet, who had previously taken haddock as a by-catch now turned their attention wholly to that species. As a result, the total catch attained 155 000 tonnes, with the Soviet Union taking 82 000 tonnes, the United States 57 000 tonnes and Canada 15 000 tonnes. The following year, although it was clear by the end of the season that the stocks were on the wane, the total catch was again exceptionally large at 127 000 tonnes, with the Soviet Union now in second place catching 48 000 tonnes, the United States 57 000 tonnes and Canada 19 000 tonnes. Needless to say, haddock catches declined substantially in subsequent years. A total of only 25 000 tonnes was taken in 1969, by which time the Soviet fishermen had withdrawn from the fishery. In 1972, the directed fishery was closed by ICNAF although some haddock were still allowed as a by-catch. By 1974, the total catch had fallen to just 4000 tonnes, and fishery biologists were fearful as to the future of the fishery. Happily, the 1975 and 1976 year classes were both reasonable and permitted an increase in landings back to the 15 000–20 000-tonne mark. However, recent year classes have been poor and the future of the fishery again looks rather bleak.

In 1977, with the enactment of the U.S. Fishery Management and Conservation Act (*see* section 8.3 in the next chapter), control of the haddock fishery passed from ICNAF to the United States. The management of the fishery remains extremely difficult however. Most fishery biologists would like to protect the next good year class to try to boost the fishery back toward its MSY level. Unfortunately, to do so is less straightforward than it may appear because of the significant intermingling of haddock, cod and flounder stocks. Hence, protection of the haddock stock almost certainly imposes a reduction of cod catches. According to Douglas Marshall, the executive director of the New England Fisheries Management Council, the trade-off is unlikely to be made. If this is the case, it is difficult to see the Georges Bank haddock fishery as anything more than a fishery that will have, after each good year class, a couple of good years followed by a number of poor ones awaiting the next good class. Possibly, given the present state of the stocks, this is the best approach to the management of the fishery—although we rather doubt it. *A priori*, it would appear preferable to try to increase the stock size, but further study is required on this issue.

The history of the Georges Bank haddock fishery offers a number of lessons for fisheries management. First, distant-water fleets may easily fish out a stock that has long supported a local fishery. Secondly, international fisheries management is inadequate. These two lessons have been well learned the world over, and in large part explain the move to 200-mile fishing limits (discussed later in this chapter). Thirdly, mesh size restriction on its own is clearly inadequate. Fourth, while a good year class may occur even if the spawning stock is very small (e.g. as in 1975), it is much more likely to occur if the spawning stock is large. Other things being equal, therefore, a larger spawning stock is preferable. However the problem is that to attain the increase in stock size, current catches must usually be reduced, and the question arises, how much current catch should be sacrificed for a larger spawning stock? Fifth, where different stocks intermingle, management is much more complicated, and once one of the stocks has collapsed it may prove extremely difficult to allow it to recover, since recovery will require not only the foregoing of current catches of that species, but also the foregoing of current catches of interrelated species. Sixth (related to both the previous comments), where there is a need to make a trade-off, it is essential to define precisely what the management regime is intended to achieve, otherwise there is clearly no way in which to decide whether the trade-off is worth making or not. The result is that many management programmes end up protecting the status quo because they are unable to determine when to undertake a trade-off and when not.

In the case of the Georges Bank haddock fishery, it would appear desirable, the next time a good year class occurs, to reduce the amount of fishing so as to enable the stock to rebuild. Fishermen should then be compensated for any loss they suffer from a government-financed fund. In the long run, assuming that the plan works and greater sustainable yields are available, a tax should be imposed so that the fund may be reconstituted. Such a plan, presented here in the barest of outlines, requires a number of preconditions to be met: for example, it requires a strong management authority, good scientific advice, and most of all a clear statement of what the plan is intended to achieve. Nonetheless, this is the kind of direction in which fishery management must move if it is to become something more than simply deciding total allowable catches of the available stock. The Georges Bank haddock fishery is presently interesting as an example of all that can go wrong in fishery management; one hopes that in the future it will be seen as an example of the way in which good management can enable a fish stock to recover and achieve its full potential in the fishing industry.

7.2.3.3 *NAFO and the future*

As with NEAFC, the development of 200-mile fishing limits implied great changes for ICNAF and the need to negotiate a new convention became evident. Accordingly the Convention on Future Multilateral Cooperation in the Northwest Atlantic Fisheries was opened for signature in October 1978 and entered into force on 1 January 1979. Under this, members agreed to establish and maintain the Northwest Atlantic Fisheries Organization (NAFO).

Under the convention, NAFO is responsible for all fish species in its regulatory area except for sedentary species, highly migratory ones (such as tuna) and cetacean stocks under the control of the IWC. The aim of management measures is now to achieve 'optimum utilization' rather than the maximum sustainable yield of ICNAF, although it looks as if 'optimum' is going to be defined on an ad-hoc, empirical basis. The regulatory framework remains much as it was with ICNAF—that is, a reliance on TACs and national quotas—and the allocation of quotas is similar, although possibly greater emphasis is placed on regional needs.

The system of joint international enforcement continues, and in an attempt to increase its impact, Article XVII of the Convention requires that members take *effective* action (including the imposition of adequate penalties) to ensure that NAFO regulations are respected, and annual returns of such action must be submitted.

Quite apart from any difficulties concerning the TAC, or its apportionment or enforcement, one of the biggest problems faced by NAFO is fishing by non-member states. Since the fishing capacity of member states is more than adequate to make full use of the fish resources in the NAFO area, the extra effort of non-members threatens the effective management of such fish stocks. Moreover, it has been argued by NAFO (NAFO Annual Report, I, 1979, p. 61) that, to some extent, non-members are simply being used as a flag of convenience to circumvent NAFO regulations: '. . . at least some of these vessels are owned either wholly or in part by fishing interests in Member Countries, and . . . at least some of the catch of these vessels is landed in Member Countries.' There is little that NAFO can do to prevent such action however, other than asking members to try to prevent the use of vessels of non-members, and to indicate to the governments of non-member countries the problems caused by fishing vessels flying their flag. This problem shows another drawback with international agreements on the high seas—the lack of any enforceable boundary—and demonstrates yet further why the move to extended coastal state jurisdiction was almost inevitable.

7.2.4 The International Whaling Commission

The International Convention for the Regulation of Whaling was signed late in 1946, and entered into force two years later. It established the International Whaling Commission (IWC), which since its inception has been concerned principally with the problem of the overexploitation of whale stocks. By the time that the IWC was established, large-scale exploitation of whales had been occurring for more than twenty years. Previously there had been very little in the way of conservation measures, and nothing of any lasting value to limit total catch. Hence by the end of the 1930s, although the blue whale remained the most highly valued species, its numbers had already been so reduced that whalers were beginning to direct their efforts principally towards the fin whales, whose greater abundance more than made up for their smaller size.

One innovation of the years between the two world wars that became an important element of post-war management was the idea of the 'blue whale unit' (BWU). In the 1931 season, such a vast catch of whales, particularly blue whales, was made that the markets for whale oil collapsed. In an attempt to prevent the recurrence of such a problem, the whaling companies (then principally Norwegian and British) agreed between themselves to try to regulate total catch. This was to be done in terms of the BWU, whereby one blue whale was equivalent to two fin or six sei—this equivalence representing approximately the oil yield.

During the Second World War a number of conferences concerning post-war whale management were held, and finally in 1944 it was proposed that total Antarctic whale catches should not exceed 16000 BWUs. Following its formation in 1946, the IWC adopted this amount as the total allowable catch. Unfortunately, while this was certainly a step in the direction of conservation of whale stocks, it did not go quite far enough. This TAC turned out to be slightly above the sustainable yield of the whale stocks, with the consequence that they continued to decline. As would be expected, over time the gap between the sustainable yield and the TAC gradually widened so that the pace of decline accelerated. Regrettably the IWC found it practically impossible to negotiate an agreed reduction in the TAC, and it was not until the situation became truly desperate in the 1960s that any reduction was achieved.

Just after the Second World War, most of the decline was reflected in blue whale stocks. Catches of fin whales were for a while at or below the estimated MSY level of 20000 individuals. As blue whale stocks declined further however, whalers became increasingly reliant on the fin whales and even greater numbers of these had to be taken if the 16000 BWU TAC was to be achieved. In 1952 and 1953 around 22000 fin whales were taken, and from 1954 to 1962 in excess of 27000 were taken every year.

Quite clearly stocks of fin whales could not be expected to sustain this level of catch for long.

By 1963 the situation was extremely serious. The stock of blue whales had been reduced to something less than 10000 individuals, compared with an environmental carrying capacity estimated at around 200000; and fin whale stocks were facing a similar situation. The need for conservation measures had never been more apparent, yet the IWC still could not convince sufficient signatories of the Convention. Eventually in 1963, a TAC of 10000 BWU was agreed, but in the end the whalers could not manage to catch that amount. In 1964 no agreement was reached within the forum of the IWC and although the whalers agreed among themselves not to exceed 8000 BWU this also proved unobtainable. Effectively therefore no control at all was imposed on catching during 1963 or 1964.

The IWC finally managed to take a firmer line in 1965 when a moratorium on the catching of blue whales was introduced. For a while it appeared that this might have come too late to save the blue whale from extinction but happily this catastrophe appears to have been avoided. At the same time as the moratorium, substantial reductions in TACs were agreed. The pressure was also reduced on fin stocks to some extent, in that during the 1960s whalemeat overtook oil as the most valuable whale product. The whalers, therefore, turned their attention somewhat to the higher meat-yielding sei whales.

During the period from its founding to the middle 1960s, the IWC presided over the decline of the whaling industry and the whale stocks. Although it is possible to be highly critical of the IWC for this it might also be argued that, to an extent at least, the IWC was simply unlucky in that the initial, and as it turned out unalterable, TAC was set at slightly too high a level. The IWC's principal defect was that it possessed no adequate mechanism for changing the TAC as the sustainable yield declined. It is interesting to speculate as to what might have happened if the initial TAC had been set at or below sustainable yield. It is possible that whaling nations might then have left the IWC and operated outside its ambit. It is equally possible however that whale stocks might have been maintained at roughly their 1945 levels and that the world would still have a viable whaling industry. Of course if this scenario had emerged, the other defects of the IWC would probably have become more apparent—particularly its inability to control effort. However, the symptoms of this problem—shortening season and overcapitalization—did emerge to some extent in the 1950s and were dealt with by agreements outside of the IWC to allocate quotas to each nation. There is some reason to believe therefore that such problems could have been resolved. The principal disaster afflicting the whalers was simply the failure to conserve their resource base.

Whether it would have been optimal in any sense to have maintained whale stocks at their 1945 level is much more debatable. There is now a well-developed literature demonstrating that in the case of slow-growing species such as whales it may be profitable to 'cash in' the capital asset (i.e. stock) and reinvest the proceeds in outlets offering greater returns (e.g. Fife, 1971; Clark, 1973). Thus it may be argued that the whaling nations themselves had no incentive to conserve the resource base and that running it down was in fact the best policy from their point of view. On the other hand, there is some, rather casual, evidence to indicate that the principal problem afflicting whale stocks may simply have been open access to the resource. As we have mentioned, during the early 1930s when the industry was dominated by the United Kingdom and Norway, agreement was reached on limiting total catch, mainly to prevent a collapse of markets for oil but to an extent to preserve stocks (or at least this would have been a side effect of the first aim). When Japan and Germany began large-scale whaling in the late 1930s however, this agreement had to be abandoned and a free-for-all situation re-emerged. We may also quote from Elliott (1979, p. 153), the managing director of an ex-whaling company, who blames Soviet whalers for ignoring whaling agreements in the 1950s and says: 'The Soviet government's failure to observe the agreement . . . considerably affected the attitude of the whaling companies. Why should they cut their catches in the interests of conservation when the whales they preserved would be taken by Soviet expeditions flouting the whaling agreements? . . . They might just as well press for the maximum catch while there were still whales to be caught.' This is a rather good description of the open-access problem, but it is, of course, an *ex-post* perception of the situation and does not of itself provide incontrovertible evidence that open access was the whaling problem.

However we may finally point to the experience of other international fisheries management agreements. These also have generally failed to conserve their resource base, but the reason is palpably open-access problems. Indeed the principal reason for the advent of 200-mile 'exclusive economic zones' seems to have been the failure of international agreements to function effectively in the area of fisheries management.

From 1965 onwards, the IWC managed to push through a much more effective line on conservation. One after another species of whale was protected so that eventually moratoria were in force not only for blue whales, but also fin, sei and sperm. By 1980 almost the whole of the world catch comprised minke whales, and even there conservation was the key. For instance, in 1981, the IWC allowed a quota for the Southern Hemisphere of only 8102 individuals despite a recommendation from its scientific committee that a yield of 10 000 was sustainable. This quota was further reduced to 7072 individuals for the 1982–83 season.

The historic decision to end commercial whaling completely came at the thirty-fourth meeting of the IWC, held in July 1982, when members voted 25 to 7 in favour of a ban from the 1985–86 season onwards. In an attempt to ensure the support of the seven remaining whaling nations (Japan, the Soviet Union, South Korea, Peru, Brazil, Iceland and Norway), the IWC allocated a quota of what would otherwise have been protected species; for instance, Japan was allowed to take 850 sperm whales over the next two years. Nonetheless, Norway, Japan, the Soviet Union and Peru took advantage of IWC rules that gave them ninety days to lodge an objection to the ban, following which they could continue whaling. Whether the whalers will actually defy the ban, after 1985, even if they object to it, is much more difficult to answer. Certainly if they did so they would have to expect to face sanctions of various kinds: for instance, fisheries legislation in the United States empowers the government to penalize countries that contravene international fisheries agreements. In the case of Japan, this might mean 50% of her fleet being excluded from the United States' 200-mile zone, as well as a ban on fish imports.

The ban is to be reviewed in 1990; whether it should continue beyond that date is a tricky issue. However it is difficult not to agree with Clark and Lamberson (1982, p. 116) when they argue that a complete ban on whaling (at least in the long run) is unlikely to 'meet the approval of a hungry world population—too much conservation might prove to be as unpalatable as too little'. The IWC must therefore consider very carefully which course to steer, otherwise there must be a real danger that large-scale whaling could resume outside the IWC's scope and the gains to date might easily be lost.

7.2.5 The international management of tuna

7.2.5.1 *The background*

Historically, international agreement has always been necessary for the effective management of tuna because of their highly migratory behaviour. Atlantic bluefin, for instance, move between the eastern coast of North America and the western coast of Europe, while southern bluefin appear to migrate from spawning areas around Australia to the Atlantic, Pacific and Indian Oceans (Saila and Norton, 1974, pp. 2–3). So pronounced is this migratory lifestyle that tuna management will almost certainly continue to require international agreement, notwithstanding the recent emergence of 200-mile fishing zones. However the advent of 200-mile limits has certainly had ramifications for the tuna industry. For instance, the recent move to such limits by many island states in the South Pacific has led to much conflict, principally because the U.S. government chooses not to recognize extended limits where tuna are concerned. Whatever the rights and wrongs of the situation, U.S. tuna seiners have been heavily fined for fishing in waters that are now claimed by the islands; their catch has been confiscated and threats have been made that boats also will be confiscated.

A number of international bodies have responsibility for tuna management in various parts of the world. In the Atlantic, the International Commission for the Conservation of Atlantic Tunas (ICCAT) was established in 1969. Unfortunately ICCAT suffers from a number of drawbacks that appear to have reduced its effectiveness. To begin with, it relies both for data collection and scientific study on member states and this reliance has led, as is the case for many international fishery commissions, to divergent opinions as to the need for management. It also suffers from the relatively more successful management regime in the eastern Pacific (*see* below), in that once the Pacific fishery is closed, many boats make their way to the Atlantic. There is clearly a need to bring catch and especially effort levels under control in the Atlantic. In the western Pacific, tuna is simply one species that comes under the aegis of the

Indo-Pacific Fisheries Council, which was established in 1948 within the FAO framework. A similar arrangement was agreed in 1967 with the establishment of the Indian Ocean Fishery Commission. Both of these bodies appear to suffer similar, and manifold, problems—principally relating to an inadequate data base, difficulties in obtaining agreement concerning the allocation of the catch, and inadequate enforcement of management measures adopted.

By far the best-known and best-documented body involved in tuna management is the Inter American Tropical Tuna Commission (IATTC), which was established in 1949 as a result of an agreement between the United States and Costa Rica concerning tuna in the eastern Pacific. Since then membership of the IATTC has increased, although it has varied over time. In 1979, its members included the United States, Canada, Japan, France, Panama and Nicaragua. The primary responsibilities of the IATTC are to investigate the eastern Pacific tuna stocks and, where appropriate, to make recommendations to maintain such stocks at the level corresponding to the maximum sustainable yield. A new convention is being discussed however, so that the situation may well change in the future.

To date, the IATTC has been concerned principally with the management of the yellowfin tuna stock in the eastern Pacific. The major regulatory method used in this management programme has been the

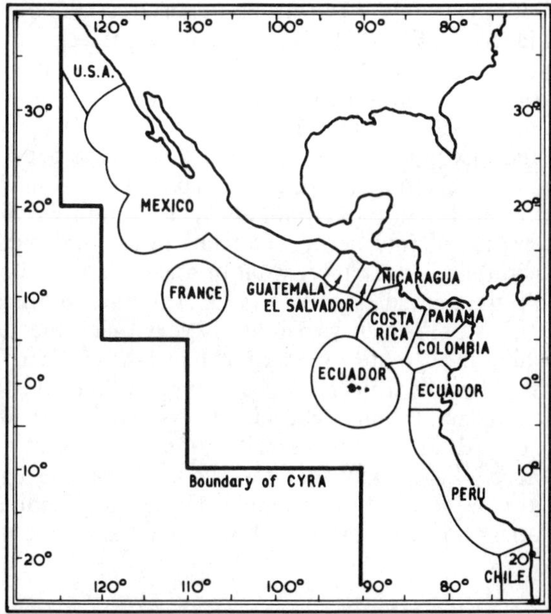

FIGURE 7.3 Boundary of CYRA and approximate 200-mile limits in the eastern Pacific. Adapted from Joseph and Greenough (1979), p. 28.

simple overall quota. This was first introduced in 1966 for a specified area of sea known as the Commission's Yellowfin Regulatory Area (CYRA), which at that time comprised the important fishing area for yellowfin (*see Figure 7.3*). This reliance on an overall quota, coupled with a failure to regulate effort, has led to the emergence of the kinds of problem that we indicated in Chapter 6. The fishing fleet has increased dramatically in size from a carrying capacity of 44 000 tons in 1967 to 183 000 tons in 1977, and in capital sophistication. The consequence of these two trends has been an ever-shortening open season. Needless to say, catch per unit of effort has also been declining, from 5 tons of tuna per ton of carrying capacity in 1967 to only 2.3 tons in 1975 (Joseph and Greenough, 1979, p. 32). Finally, an increasing amount of fishing has been taking place outside the CYRA.

One consequence of these problems has been that the poorer, less efficient fishermen have found it impossible to take their traditional catch during the ever-shortening open season. In response to this, in 1968, the IATTC introduced the concept of 'closed-season allocations' (CSAs), which were to be granted to the less efficient fishermen. In other words, those fishermen identified as being especially deserving would be granted a special allocation of tuna for which they would be able to fish in what was otherwise the closed season. By 1974, such CSAs accounted for around 30% of the total allowable catch in the CYRA.

The recent advent of 200-mile fishing limits has exacerbated the problems faced by the IATTC. It has caused a number of so-called Resource-Adjacent Nations (RANs) to claim a greater share of the tuna resource, which the non-RANs have been reluctant to concede. Within the IATTC, a short-term solution to the problem has been attempted by the allocation of extra CSAs; but this approach has clearly been less than satisfactory since Ecuador, Chile, Mexico and Costa Rica have already withdrawn from the Commission over the issue. In fact, a simple solution in terms of allocating CSAs looks unlikely to be found within the present IATTC framework, mainly because catches inside and outside 200-mile limits are so variable; for instance, what quota should be allocated to, say, Panama, where the annual catch within its 200-mile limit has varied from nothing to 29 000 tons? Such variability is very much the rule with tuna. Moreover, while the greater part of catches have been taken within 200-mile limits, there is little reason to suppose that non-RANs, if they were excluded from 200-mile coastal waters, could not intensify their high-seas efforts. Although this intensification might be at greater cost to themselves, there is little doubt that it would affect catches within 200-mile limits, and it would more than likely render any management plan ineffective. A negotiated revision of future tuna management thus appears required.

7.2.5.2 *Tuna management in the future*

A number of possible alternative management schemes have been proposed. Probably the best known is the 'partially allocated quota' (PAQ) system developed by IATTC scientists (Joseph, 1977; Joseph and Greenough, 1979). Under this plan, the total allowable catch (TAC) for each year would be decided by the IATTC. The fishing nations would then negotiate some percentage of this TAC which would be set aside for the RANs. Depending on the particular method adopted for deciding this percentage, Joseph and Greenough (1979, Ch. 8) estimate a minimum of about 11% and a maximum of around 58%, with the actual figure probably lying somewhere between these two extremes. Whatever the figure finally adopted, the remainder of the TAC would be available on a simple open-access basis, and fishermen would remain free to fish all areas. It is interesting to note that the fishery would continue to be managed essentially on an overall quota/closed-season basis; that is, once the TAC had been achieved, the season would end. This is likely to cause quite difficult problems in deciding when to close the season, and how to count the allocated portion of the TAC. Joseph and Greenough (1979, Appendix I) suggest two-tier RAN fleets; an 'allocation' fleet, and an 'open-season' fleet. The former would take the allocation and the latter would compete for the unallocated TAC. The season would be closed once the unallocated TAC had been reached, but the allocation fleet would be free to continue to fish until the allocated TAC had been achieved.

All countries operating in the fishery would pay a participation fee to the IATTC. Having made an appropriate deduction for management expenses, such as research costs, the IATTC would then redistribute such fees among countries, on the basis of resource contribution in the case of catches made in the waters of RANs, and on the basis of the catch itself in the case of catches made on the high seas. The fee would represent effectively a per unit landings tax, and would be negotiated by member countries. By way of illustration, Joseph and Greenough (1979, p. 79) assume a fee of $40 per ton, which they estimate to be 'close to the maximum that efficient harvesters could afford to pay under mid-1970s conditions of fleet size and resource availability'. Such a fee would have yielded a total revenue of about $10 million.

Within this system, a RAN would have essentially two options. Either it could harvest its tuna allocation and pay nothing (or at least receive back the fees that it has paid, net of management expenses), or it could decide not to participate in the fishery, in which case it would simply receive a payment from the IATTC. Intermediate positions would be possible, of course, with a RAN harvesting more or less of its allocation. If a RAN did not harvest its allocation, then this extra amount would be made available to the fleets of other members on an open-access basis; that is, the previously allocated catch would become part of the unallocated TAC. Hence, quotas would not be transferable, except in the most oblique sense, and their price would not be negotiable. Joseph and Greenough do occasionally consider the possibility of transfer, but they appear to see this as an adjunct to the PAQ system rather than as an integral part of it (*see* for example Joseph and Greenough, 1979, pp. 84–5).

King (1979) criticized, correctly in our view, the PAQ system both on the issue of non-transferability and on the issue of fixed price of rights. As he has said, it is difficult to see why prices need to be determined centrally. The major problem with such an approach is that it would probably mean that economically mutually advantageous trades in rights would not occur. For instance, a country might feel that it would not be worth selling, or rather giving up, rights at $40 per ton, where it would be with a fee of, say, $60 per ton. The country might then be persuaded to expand its fishing fleet, adding to the overcapacity problems already apparent in the fishery. The non-transferability provision would exacerbate the situation further since countries could not bid for rights, but instead would have to wait for countries to give them up and then attempt to increase their catch in the open-access mêlée. In this situation, most of the economic advantages of allocating quotas are likely to be lost the minute that the country to which they are allocated does not use them. King therefore proposes that allocated quotas should be freely transferable, a system that he calls the 'quota certificate' (QC) system, although in fact it appears to differ little from the PAQ system.

The major problem from an economic viewpoint with both systems, however, is that the allocated quotas themselves would represent a maximum of 60% of the catch. The remainder would continue to be taken on an open-access basis. In such a situation, the economic problems of the open-access part of the tuna fishery would be unlikely to be altered. Over-capitalization and a progressive shortening of the season would probably continue. In an ideal world it would perhaps be logical to extend the QC system to include all countries operating in the eastern Pacific. Member countries could negotiate a percentage allocation of the TAC, and such allocations would then be transferable. Countries wishing to build up their fleet would purchase rights from other countries. Thus we would have essentially a percentage IFQ system as discussed in Chapter 6.

It may be, however, that, because a large amount of the catch is taken outside 200-mile limits, the international legal ramifications would be too great to enable the development of an IFQ system. In that case, the QC system would probably be the best presently available, but it is not likely to be particularly satisfactory as regards the future economic health of the open-access part of the tuna fishery.

7.2.6 The move to national management

Given the problems that emerged in various ways within the international management bodies, it is not surprising that increasingly countries involved in these became dissatisfied with events. Not only was there a basic problem with the whole issue of appropriate management objectives, but in many cases it seemed to be impossible to obtain agreement on effective management even when everyone involved could see how badly it was needed. Allied to this dissatisfaction was a deeper and more powerful force: the drive to obtain rights of ownership over the increasingly valuable resources of the oceans, of which fish were just one dimension among many.

Unilateral declarations of extended limits of various kinds were made by a number of South American countries in the later 1940s, but were regarded as essentially idiosyncratic moves, running against the mainstream views of oceanic resources as either *res nullius*—the property of no one and available thus to anyone with the necessary capital and technology to exploit them—or as *res communes*—common property owned by everyone with the rights to exploit held in common. However, during the 1950s and 1960s the tide began to change, and by the 1970s was moving inexorably in the direction of private ownership for the coastal state. Thus, for example, Canada became increasingly convinced that management of fish stocks offshore of its east coast by ICNAF was not satisfactory, and moreover that extended limits and improved management regimes directed towards its own national and regional interests would have a substantial national impact—and events after its declaration of 200-mile limits in 1977 confirmed the correctness of this appreciation (*see* Chapter 8.2).

Thus we now turn our attention to the move away from international management. However, it is important to bear in mind that most of the international bodies have remained in existence, albeit with considerably modified roles, and continue to be the principal institutions for the management of fisheries outside the 200-mile zones and to offer important scientific advice on what should happen within the zones. We shall also return to the question of international management soon, when we look at management within the European Economic Community.

7.3 THE LAW OF THE SEA

7.3.1 Introduction

After nine years of protracted discussion and dispute, the 3rd United Nations Conference on the Law of the Sea (UNCLOS III) at last produced in April 1982 an agreed text for the Convention of the Law of the Sea, to become international law one year after at least sixty nations signed it. Although accepted, it was a reflection of the misgivings and hostility that some felt towards it that four nations voted against it (including the United States), with a further seventeen nations abstaining (including the Soviet Union, West Germany and the United Kingdom).* Nevertheless, it seems certain that the Convention will form the basis for international law from 1984 onwards, and many nations have already incorporated it into their legal structures. This is especially true of its provisions affecting fisheries, which, although comprising only a small part of the 320 Articles, nine

*The misgivings that caused these problems arose largely from deepsea ocean mining, with many developed countries being unwilling to share the right to this, and—more sensitive—their technical knowledge, with developing nations. *See* Treves (1983) for a detailed background.

Appendices and five Resolutions, have in fact been largely agreed since 1976. The Convention is thus immensely important for the future of the world's sea fisheries, setting the legal framework within which, for better or for worse, fisheries management will take place.

It has been variously estimated that as much as 99% of oceanic fish natural productivity lies in coastal waters, beyond which is a vast area, some 90% of which is almost a 'biological desert'. By the mid 1970s somewhere between 85 and 95% of the world's marine catch (estimates vary) of approaching 70 million tonnes was being taken within the putative 200-mile Exclusive Economic Zones (EEZs) that UNCLOS was beginning to support. Moreover, by the late 1970s at least 12 million tonnes of the catch was being caught and carried away from the grounds by non-coastal-state vessels (OECD, 1982). The new regime will thus not only affect virtually all the world's marine catch, but will have a substantial redistributive effect by turning historically common property resources into the 'sole ownership' rights of coastal nations.

In this section we review the basic provisions of UNCLOS and attempt to identify its most important economic consequences. For reasons of space, the process whereby UNCLOS arrived at its eventual Convention—referred to by one observer as 'an unseemly scramble' (Dasgupta, 1982)—and the legal aspects are excluded, but are referred to in the bibliographic notes.

7.3.2 UNCLOS III and fisheries

At the risk of oversimplification, we may identify six principles that underlie the provisions of the LOS Convention. At its core is the principle of extended fisheries jurisdiction by the coastal state (CS), within an EEZ of 200 miles (including a territorial limit of 12 miles), which confers on the CS the sovereign rights and jurisdiction for exploring and exploiting all living and non-living resources in the water and on and under the sea bed, and over all activities relating to them such as conservation and pollution (Article 56 of the Convention: A/Conf.62/122). Thus the CS has substantial rights, including especially that of determining 'the allowable catch of the living resources in its exclusive economic zone' (Article 61, para. 1), but also certain obligations, which extend to the 'proper conservation and management' of resources to prevent overexploitation (Article 61, para. 2).

Second, the basic principle on which living resources should be managed is an obligation on the CS (Article 61, para. 3) to: '. . . maintain or restore populations of harvested species at levels which can produce the maximum sustainable yield, as qualified by relevant environmental and economic factors, including the economic needs of coastal fishing communities and the special requirements of developing States, and taking into account fishing patterns, the interdependence of stocks and any generally recommended international minimum standards, whether subregional, regional or global'. Elsewhere (Article 62, para. 1) it is argued that the CS should also 'promote the objective of optimum utilization of the living resources

. . . without prejudice to Article 61'. This whole question of management objectives was one of the most contentious discussion areas, and the eventual Convention sees the CS as part owner, part beneficiary and part caretaker. Given all the conflicting interests represented at UNCLOS, it is hardly surprising that MSY was extensively discussed as the basis for formulating TACs, and embedded in Article 61. However, the idea of optimum sustainable yield (OSY) was discussed as early as UNCLOS I at Geneva in 1958, and the eventual package clearly has strong OSY dimensions. Although this OSY element leaves the position rather loose, the package was seen as preferable to setting no management goals whatsoever, for fear that the coastal state might then be entirely arbitrary in its management objectives, either from lack of knowledge or deliberately, both of which could result in inefficiency and/or wastage.

In fact, this principle was resisted by some developing states, partly to give themselves a freer hand in determining exploitation rates, but partly because it was closely linked to the third principle (Article 62, para. 2). This was that: 'The coastal State shall determine its capacity to harvest the living resources of the exclusive economic zone. Where the coastal State does not have the capacity to harvest the entire allowable catch, it shall, through agreements and other arrangement . . . give other States access to the surplus of the allowable catch, having particular regard to . . . land-locked States and geographically disadvantaged States . . . especially in relation to the developing States mentioned . . .' The 'access' principle was strongly supported by the global and regional distant-water-fishing states (DWSs), which sought preferential rights of access to such surpluses rather than conceding 'exclusivity' to the coastal state. Although finally it was this exclusivity that became the dominant doctrine, the idea of an obligation for mandatory sharing was forced into the Convention by a number of 'pressure groups'. These included countries with a widely varying set of interests and objectives: the DWSs, both Western developed and socialist, pushed for access as a 'right', usually based on claims to be traditional fishers of the waters. Developing countries such as Nigeria, Taiwan and Ghana, which had regional fishing fleets, sought access as of right for fear that exclusivity with licensed 'traditional fishing' access would result in their being excluded. Another grouping was those coastal states which saw themselves as neighbours to other states' fish resources, and who wanted first priority or reciprocal access on the grounds of proximity. Additionally, there were the geographically disadvantaged states (GDSs) and the land-locked states (LLSs) both keen to establish access rights as a matter of principle—and indeed both did achieve 'special consideration' under Article 62.2. Finally, there was a group of developing countries which, as coastal states, sought primarily to maximize their freedom to reach suitable bilateral or multilateral access arrangements on the most favourable terms.

It was quite impossible to satisfy everyone, and the Convention has left the CSs to set the TAC, with international advice from appropriate bodies where relevant, to decide upon any management measures, and then to determine the extent of access to any surplus, largely by licensed access or by joint ventures. However, much discretion remains: the CS, according to Article 62.3, '. . . shall take into account all relevant factors, including *inter alia* the significance of the living resources of the area to the economy of the coastal State concerned and its other national interests, the provisions of Articles 69 and 70 [on GDSs and LLSs], the requirements of developing States in the sub-region or region in harvesting part of the surplus and the need to minimize economic dislocation in States whose nationals have habitually fished in the zone or which have made substantial efforts in research and identification of stocks'. Since the CS can easily adjust TAC *downwards*, and/or access fees and barriers plus estimates of its own catching capacity *upwards*, the practical importance of the access provisions is debatable, especially where a CS may claim to be a developing state anyway.

This raises the fourth principle. While the CS determines the TAC, and may use a wide range of laws and regulations (outlined in Article 62), management may be bilateral or multilateral, and the CS is requested to cooperate with 'competent international organizations, whether subregional, regional or global' (Article 61, para. 2). The Convention seeks the exchange of relevant scientific information, catch and effort data through these regional organizations and between all fishing states. Quite how this interrelationship will develop in the long run remains to be seen, but at the present it seems that regional organizations such as NAFO will contribute data and guidelines but leave the details such as dividing up the TAC to others. Many developed nations would have liked a much more dominant, perhaps even overriding, role for the international bodies, hoping for better stock management on the basis of better data and scientific expertise, but in practice the ultimate decision and enforcement lies with the CS. Finally here, another conflict arose over this principle concerning who would have the right to belong to regional bodies, for there was a strong lobby at UNCLOS to restrict membership to relevant coastal states only, thus excluding the countries of origin of the DWS fleets and 'traditional access' countries. If such a principle does establish itself post-UNCLOS, this will involve a major reorganization of the international bodies.

The fifth principle was that the modified-MSY basis of management ought also to be extended to those stocks in the 'high seas' fisheries beyond the EEZs. Indeed, much the same wording is used in the relevant articles (Article 119, *et seq*.). However, this issue was rather neglected in the massive sharing-out at UNCLOS, and it is unlikely that the Convention will provide a viable long-run basis for managing these stocks. Very likely a new UNCLOS will have to look at the whole problem of these fisheries in due course.

Finally, it was accepted that there were special issues arising in the management of interdependent stocks, highly migratory species, and anadromous and catadromous species* that would make the management of

*Anadromous species are those that ascend rivers in order to spawn (e.g. salmon), while catadromous species are those that descend to lower rivers or the sea in order to spawn (e.g. eels).

these more difficult. The relevant sections of the Convention (Articles 63–67) stress the need for cooperation and multilateral and/or international management, but the 'primary interest in and responsibility' for the *states of origin* in the case of anadromous fish was clearly set out in Article 66. This interest includes the right to establish a TAC, as can the primary *coastal state* in the case of catadromous species. For migratory fish, especially tuna, the need for cooperation was stressed, to promote 'optimal utilization' both within and without the EEZs. The Convention was, however, distinctly vague in all these three areas, especially on enforcement.

7.3.3 The economic impact: the dimensions of benefit and loss

The moves towards extended fishing limits since 1976 and the likely general adoption of 200-mile EEZs have a wide-ranging set of economic impacts. These are both complex and multidimensional, and one must also recognize that in the dynamic world the effects of one action may be over- or underemphasized by non-associated changes, such as changes in the production function or market prices. Some of these effects are already apparent and the reader is directed in the bibliographic notes to general sources.

7.3.3.1 *Improved fisheries management*

The movement towards extended fisheries jurisdiction does not in itself improve the management of fisheries, nor does it solve the common-property problem. However it does provide a framework within which management schemes based on limited entry can develop to deal with the problems and within which enforcement can be made practicable for 90–99% of the world's fish catch. This is not to say that nationally based resource management will necessarily always be more successful (*see* for example McHugh, 1972; Cooper, 1975; Holt, 1978), nor indeed does the establishment of private property rights necessarily increase welfare (*see* for example Dasgupta, 1982, p. 29).

In the case of UNCLOS, this uncertainty is compounded by the adoption of the concept of using MSY with OSY dimensions. Apart from the theoretical reservations (*see* Chapter 4), it is also difficult to see how this concept will work in Southern Hemisphere fisheries, where multi-species catches are more normal and thus inter-species dimensions become crucial in framing practical management regulations. At best, it sets a common theoretical framework, but at worst it fails to establish a coherent practical basis (*see* Balasubramanian, 1981, 1982). Thus in establishing TACs, it is perfectly possible that adjacent coastal states using ostensibly the same framework will reach entirely different conclusions and therefore adopt conflicting policies. It was partly for these reasons that some observers, and nations, would have preferred a much narrower EEZ, with management taking place primarily at an international level. Nevertheless, there can be no doubt that with extended jurisdiction, improved management is possible and improvements in catches in countries such as Iceland and Canada already reflect this.

We must however recognize that there are several substantial problems associated with arguing that generally improved fisheries management will in fact result. There are doubts over the scientific capacity of every CS to achieve optimal management. There will almost certainly be differences in interpretation, particularly on the question of identifying 'surpluses' to which access must be allowed, which could produce underutilization via deliberately low TACs. Also differences in emphasis on the OSY dimensions will emerge. Clearly the management of interdependent and transboundary stocks will be difficult, and is likely to lead to disputes over boundaries and agreeing a joint TAC, made worse if the fish go outside EEZs and into the high-seas areas (e.g. not only salmon and tuna, but some demersal and pelagic stocks).

Finally, as the basis for management now becomes geographical rather than ecological, differential schemes will produce a patchy pattern of management, with some countries perhaps pursuing short-run objectives and others more long-run. Moreover, as more rational management often means reducing nominal effort, catching capacity may switch between areas, and in particular may direct towards the relatively 'unmanaged' stocks, which will be especially those partly or wholly in the high-seas areas such as tuna and oceanic squid. The prospects for managing these stocks are arguably worsened by EEZs.

Overall, the FAO has estimated that improved fisheries management within the EEZs could provide up to 20 million tonnes of extra landings, an important part of the 44 million tonnes of extra fish that the world will need by 2000. Others have suggested that the benefits will be taken more as lowered costs (via increased CPUE) than in increased catches (OECD, 1982).

7.3.3.2 *Increased production and consumption in coastal states*

An important implication of EEZs is that coastal states will have the opportunity to increase local fish landings, and hence possibly consumption. This increase may arise from improved resource management, or from insisting that DWS access is conditional on increased local landings, or simply by switching effort away from DWSs towards the CS's own inshore fleet. This increase should also then generate an increase in national income through landings, processing and marketing. Whether there will be effective demand locally is less clear, although the potential also exists to reduce the extent to which fish is used by DWSs for reduction to meal and oil and to direct fish into food consumption. The total amount of fish involved is difficult to estimate, but both the FAO (1979) and Holt (1978) suggest that in 1972 about one-quarter of total world landings of 56 million tonnes was taken by non-CS vessels, and of this at least 5 million tonnes (9–15%) was taken off developing countries, worth some $2 billion (OECD, 1982). The reservation of this fish for domestic fishermen represents a very substantial economic redistribution in their favour.

An active pursual of policies to develop CS fish resources, especially for consumption, is already evident in many countries, particularly in Latin America, where most DWSs are now effectively excluded. The FAO has developed programmes to assist CSs to make the best use of this potential, preferably as food fish for direct consumption. Additionally, many fisheries in the Southern Hemisphere have been developed since 1977 with the assistance of joint ventures with ex-DWSs such as West Germany and Japan, which provide consultancy, finance, vessels and equipment (Kaczynski and Le Vieil, 1980). Such help is vital, for otherwise CS fisheries may be trapped at the artisanal level by deficiencies in training, organization and credit.

An additional dimension of this potential gain is the ability of CSs to plan the future development of their fishing industries. This can now be done in a manner to suit local economic and social objectives, rather than suiting DWS requirements. That this is not easy however, is demonstrated by the United States, a major CS gainer with its huge EEZ resources. The United States has reduced foreign takings from 3.3 million tonnes in 1974 to an allocation of only 2.0 million tonnes in 1980 (with less actually taken than allocated). Yet even so the foreign fleets of the Soviet Union, Japan and European countries take fish that could be landed in the United States by local vessels, and some 57% of edible fish is still imported. This situation appears to be largely due to the inability of the U.S. inshore fleet to take up the opportunities that the EEZ offers, mainly because of problems with capital availability, processing capacity and in marketing 'new' species (such as Alaskan pollack, Pacific flounder, cod, squid and mullet), leading incidentally to demands for tax protection from cheap imports (*see* section 7.3.3.5).

7.3.3.3 *Improved welfare of coastal communities*

With the extended EEZ, the opportunity exists for the CS to adopt policies that positively discriminate in favour of coastal communities, which frequently suffer from low incomes, under- and unemployment, and lack of alternative occupations. They can benefit, for example, by active encouragement to fill the catching capacity 'gap' that may emerge as DWS vessels are excluded. Already such policies have been adopted in North America, for example on the east coast of Canada, where in Newfoundland the number of licensed local fishermen virtually doubled between 1976 and 1979 (*see* Chapter 8, section 8.2).

Despite its obvious benefits, such a policy runs risks. There may be a temptation to replace overfishing by DWSs with overfishing by the CS simply to prop up coastal communities: as Copes puts it, fisheries as 'employer of last resort and dispenser of social welfare' (Copes, 1981, p. 223). Moreover it is by no means clear that CS inshore fishing will be as efficient in exploiting the resource as the previous DWS fleets; in world terms, least-cost fleets may be excluded, and in the short run at least scarce resources may be wasted.

7.3.3.4 *Benefits from permitted access*

Both the CS and the DWSs can benefit indefinitely from permitting access to the EEZ, the CS in terms of access fees and arrangements, and the DWSs in terms of fish caught and disruption prevented (Munro, 1982). There will be a transfer of income from DWSs to CS, which may be particularly valuable to a developing country, especially where that country could not otherwise exploit the resource. In addition to any licence fees, the CS may gain in terms of foreign exchange, increased local landings, local fishery development by for example joint ventures, and the use of least-cost technology. It may even permit access only under some reciprocal-benefit arrangements, perhaps for its own vessels elsewhere or in non-fishery terms (such as credit or aid).

Some developing countries already have reached the conclusion that allowing access by licence has relatively little impact on their economic growth and development. One response has been to raise licence fees to the point of economic impracticability, forcing the participating companies to agree to joint ventures, perhaps on a fifty–fifty capital investment basis. Mauretania for example has done just this with French fishermen exploiting her langoustine fishery, presenting them with the choice of enduring increased costs or agreeing to joint ventures, especially when existing vessels need replacing (*see Fishing News International*, August 1982, p. 39). Worldwide, some 400 ventures were in operation by 1979, especially with Japan and the Comecon countries, and they seemed to offer the desired balance of access with local control.

We must note however that not only the CS benefits here; the system of access helps to ensure that fish stocks of little or no economic value to the CS are in fact utilized, quite probably using low-cost systems from DWSs. This may apply not only to locally unpopular fish species but also to stocks offshore of inhospitable land areas, such as Patagonia or Labrador, where locally based exploitation may be impracticable.

7.3.3.5 *Trade effects*

Probably one of the most significant impacts of the UNCLOS decisions will be in the area of trade, for the EEZ gives the CS the opportunity to increase its exports and reduce imports, while the ex-DWSs will have to increase imports and possibly increase overall trade as the opportunities for better management and eventually improved yields are taken up, making fish even more of an international commodity than at present.*

Precisely who will benefit and how, is not at all clear. We must initially bear it in mind that the EEZ will redistribute income, which will therefore affect demand in both CS and DWSs, which will itself affect not only

*World exports of fish in 1979 were worth $13 billion, three times their value in the early 1970s, and were increasing at a time when world catch was steady: by 1981 they had reached $15.5 billion.

resource use but trading patterns. The immediate implication is that the CS will see an improvement in its balance of trade, other things being equal, while ex-DWSs will face a decline. However it is the DWS that possesses the technology, expertise and capital equipment to carry out the fishing, and if it can obtain access elsewhere, then in any single CS, imports *from* the DWS might undercut and stifle the infant domestic industry. Partly for this reason UNCLOS has been accompanied by demands from CS local fishermen in some countries, such as the United States, for 'infant industry' protection, to include tariff protection and subsidies. Conversely, it is the DWSs that tend to have well-developed markets for the fish that they used to catch offshore of the CS, and they may then permit CS exports into this market only in exchange for certain benefits, such as access to the fishing for themselves (*see* the discussion of the Canada–EEC relationship, section 8.2). Thus the new trade flows may well be associated with access via licences or joint ventures between the CS and the DWS, and this would therefore generate capital flows as well, with an impact on the balance of payments of both.

The potential impact on trade has been studied by the OECD, without its reaching very clear conclusions (OECD, 1982). Although OECD countries represent 85% of the world's imports and 59% of its exports in terms of value of sea products, it is still not easy to determine the overall impact, not least because the price changes that could very well result will interact with non-fish food prices, with consequent leakages of demand for fish out of the present pattern. The main conclusion is that fish markets will become increasingly international, and that the relative price rise for fish that took place during the 1970s will probably continue, but as the impact of UNCLOS on prices, costs and total production is indeterminate, so then is the impact on trade. This internationalization of markets is already evident: thus the recession in the early 1980s caused the demand for cod in U.S. fast-food restaurants to decline at a time when better resource management was producing more cod from the EEZs of Canada and Iceland. The consequent price slump and increase in stocks of frozen cod affected other markets such as the United Kingdom, whose exclusion as a DWS from many EEZs might otherwise have been expected to cause domestic price to hold or rise; in fact prices fell. This fall held substantial implications for the development of the British inshore fleet, which ostensibly had no connection with demand for fish in U.S. restaurants.

7.3.3.6 *Economic disruption in distant-water states*

Notwithstanding the Convention's hopes on 'dislocation' (section 7.3.2), the rearrangement of resource ownership, management based on modified MSY, and CS (partial) exclusivity are all sources of considerable economic disruption to DWSs, whose distant-water fleets face exclusion or expensive entry to what were previously free-access resources. We can identify three aspects especially, the first being reductions in landings by the DWS fleets, causing a reduction in food supplies that will tend to raise domestic prices and deflect demand towards imports. Secondly, there is the certainty of disruptive industrial effects within the fishing and associated industries, concentrated at a port or regional level: specifically, the decline of the home ports of distant-water fleets. Thirdly, one may expect to find a rise in fishing activity within the DWS's own EEZ, with a changed structure of the domestic industry, including changing location of catching bases, processing and distribution systems. In the short period since EEZs have become general, indications already exist of this type of disruption. For example, Japan's distant-water catch fell from some 4 million tonnes in 1973 to 2 million tonnes in 1979 (partly because pollack resources were less abundant, too), and the proportion of that country's total catch that was taken from foreign EEZ areas fell from 40% in 1976 to 23% in 1979 (OECD, 1982). The Soviet Union has also faced a substantial decline in opportunities for its huge distant-water fleets,* the total catch declining from 10.1 million tonnes in 1976 to 8.9 million tonnes in 1978, recovering to 9.1 million tonnes in 1979. Accompanying this decline was a shift away from prized species such as cod, haddock and flatfish towards less desirable but accessible pollack, blue whiting, sardinellas and capelin (for meal).

To deal with the problem of exclusion, there are a number of strategies open to a DWS, not mutually exclusive. It may accept exclusion by the CSs, but shift its distant-water fleet to free-access stocks, either in the high seas, as Japan has done by exploiting skipjack tuna and cephalopod, or possibly within its own coastal areas. Of course, it may simply be possible for the DWS to seek access for as long as possible by purchasing annual licences, accepting that doing so will increase costs to the fleet and possibly necessitate subsidies. Otherwise, the DWS may be able to negotiate reciprocal access, even though this may inhibit the DWS's own coastal fleet development. Thus Japan allows the Soviet Union access to her sardine and mackerel stocks in exchange for access to the Soviet Union's Alaskan pollack, squid, and so on. A flexible alternative may lie in seeking medium- or long-run continued involvement by forming joint ventures with CS capital; these can take many forms, including simply the provision of mother ships to buy and process CS inshore catches of fish previously taken by the DWS's own vessels (for example, off Britain and Canada). In default of anything better, the DWS may consider renting out its idle fleet capacity to the CS, especially for experimental fishing; for example, Australia, Brazil and Vietnam have all leased ex-DWS vessels. Finally, when all else fails, then laying up, selling (but to whom?) or eventually scrapping of the distant-water vessels may be necessary, as has occurred on quite a large scale in, for example, the United Kingdom.

Each of these strategies has interesting implications; for example, shifting the distant-water fleet to one's own EEZ may be feasible, say if new stocks and species are being exploited, but in general such vessels are

*In 1980, the Soviet Union possessed 52% of the world's total tonnage of large fishing vessels (those of over 100 gross registered tons (GRT)), and within this, some 83% of the total of floating fish factories or carriers by tonnage (Jackson, 1982).

inappropriate and will inflict high costs on the fishery, which in turn may affect sales and trade prospects if these are reflected in higher prices.

Thus the DWS faces disruption and difficulties; yet there are some benefits. Even though its vessels may be displaced by CS vessels, the desirable fish stocks to which access has been lost may now be better managed, with improved yields and possibly increased CS catches. The DWS may then be able to buy from the CS at lower relative prices, as demonstrated by Hannesson (1978). If, as is typical, the DWS had already been subsidizing its own distant-water fleet because of problems associated with overfishing, then the overall gains to it might be significant, and subsidies could be removed or redirected towards developing indigenous resources.

One interesting area into which resources might be switched is aquaculture. Many nations, not just the major DWSs, are finding themselves excluded from adjacent fishing grounds, and this has given a major stimulus to aquaculture. In Egypt for example, initially the Aswan Dam rendered Nile Delta grounds less fertile, and then fishing vessels were excluded from the Moroccan fisheries, forcing the country to look closely at the prospects for integrated and polycultural fish farming (*see* Chapter 10). This has brought land and water unsuitable for other uses into productive operation to farm tilapia, carp and grey mullet (*see World Fishing*, October 1982, p. 17). Similarly, the Soviet Union has launched a major aquaculture programme on an industrial scale to farm carp, salmon trout and sturgeon (OECD, 1982).

7.3.3.7 *Efficiency, equity and conflict*

The balance between efficiency and equity under UNCLOS is complex: in simple terms fishing will tend to become less distant-water capital-intensive and more inshore, coastal-based. In the long run, the latter is probably more efficient: it removes the need to process and store at sea, and may well be less energy-intensive. In addition, it can be argued that a move away from fleets of very large, powerful and sophisticated long-range vessels is desirable, for the pressures on the operations of these vessels are so intense that they have to fish for longer periods and search more widely in order to find catch rates that will satisfy the servicing of their higher capital and running costs. Such vessels are by no means always more efficient than smaller vessels (although sometimes their extra power may be significant); rather, they have been built in capitalist systems by owners seeking greater mobility, flexibility and versatility as an insurance against failures in single stocks or grounds, and by socialist countries in order to gain access to underexploited sources of fish protein—their extra range and endurance by no means make them more profitable than smaller boats, only somewhat more dependable for profits. Smaller boats may be just as 'efficient', but will lack range and endurance, rendering them more vulnerable to fluctuations in individual stocks.

However, in the short run at least, many CSs will lack the technology, capital and expertise to develop their coastal fishing opportunities significantly, and so excluded distant-water fleets may be replaced (partially?) by high-cost artisanal fishing. Although from the point of view of the CS artisanal fishing may itself have a number of advantages in terms of greater employment and welfare of coastal communities, and may directly improve food supplies, these advantages may be at the cost of inflicting higher production costs on the fishery, thereby reducing the rent that is earned from it. Moreover, encouragement of the coastal communities to take up the opportunities may meet resistance if this, as is likely, will mean changes in traditional ways of life and methods of fishing.

The equity of this rearrangement is inevitably open to subjective interpretation. Some would argue that the concept of extended national sovereignty is regrettable in the oceans (e.g. Cooper, 1975, p. 369). However, many would agree that ownership rights are better allocated on a 'geographical proximity' basis than a 'past capital accumulation' (= DWS) basis, with the need for developing CSs to receive positive discrimination to reinforce the former. However such an arrangement lacks ecological sense, and opens up a substantial area of conflict. Not only may there be conflict over boundaries, over one state 'intercepting' another's migratory or trans-boundary fish, and over terms of access and so on, but elements of protectionism in terms of trade and subsidies may well creep in, and exclusivity in resource ownership can inflict a cost in terms of resources wasted.

It is difficult to quantify 'net benefits' and 'net losses' to the gainers and losers from this redistribution of the rights to the world's fish resources. Broadly speaking, it is the CSs, developed and developing, that have benefited most, and since the value of fish resources is likely to increase with the impact of further exploitation, this benefit will be enhanced. The advantages for developing countries will be considerable; they may gain almost exclusive access to nearly two-thirds of the world's potential fish catch (Bell, 1977).

Earlier estimations based upon 1972 data suggested that the gain might be of the order of 3–4 million tonnes for developing countries on the basis of that year's catch alone. Yet some developing countries (such as India, Somalia and Kenya) will gain only a little or not at all, and others (such as Cuba, Thailand and Taiwan) with distant-water interests may be net losers (Shyam, 1982). Obviously, the nature of the benefit varies with the location and coastal configuration of a country, as well as with its economic status and existing fishing structure. *Table 7.1* suggests that in fact, of the 'gainers' a somewhat higher proportion of developed countries make 'large' gains as against 'small or no gains': the principal gainers include the United States, Australia, Canada, the Soviet Union, Indonesia, New Zealand and Japan—in other words, mainly well-developed capitalist or socialist economies. Some will however be offsetting EEZ gains against exclusions elsewhere: thus Japan will in fact lose free access to as much as 45% of its traditional fishing grounds (Cooper, 1975). Overall, the 200-mile EEZs will mean that some fifteen nations will control 40% of the enclosed ocean resources, just ten will control 30%, and one alone, the

United States, will have control over 20% of the world's edible fish resources, although in the late 1970s the United States was producing only 5% of the world's landings. If we then bear in mind that the equity issue should include not only 'ownership' of resources but also consideration of processing, marketing, exports and consumption, then the overall impact on equity is indeed difficult to estimate.

TABLE 7.1 States gaining large areas* in EEZ

	Large gain	*Small or no gain*	*Total*
Developed states	12 (33%)	25 (67%)	37 (100%)
Developing states	30 (27%)	80 (73%)	110 (100%)

*Note: Coastal states gaining 'large areas' are taken as being those which gain more than the average or those whose gain in ocean space exceeds five times their land area.
Source: based on Shyam (1982).

Within UNCLOS III one may find the seeds of many disputes: the issue of satisfactory boundary definition is obvious, but becomes intractable when dealing with mobile, possibly migratory fish. What happens if one country 'intercepts' fish on their way to another EEZ? What about trans-boundary fish stocks? Although economic theory suggests that, if both 'owners' cooperate, a compromise optimal management programme may be agreed, even if both seek maximum shares and have different goals and interests (Munro, 1979), it is very easy for disagreement to emerge, with the re-establishment of common-property problems (Levhari and Mirman, 1980).

One final point: the creation of EEZs with arrangements for fee-paying access effectively produces a market in property rights in the resources. A market of this kind is in many ways desirable in efficiency terms, as we have seen, yet it may in its turn create a problem. Many DWS governments are sufficiently committed to their fleets as to consider subsidizing their bids for access, for such reasons as food supply or employment maintenance. Hence an open-market sale of access rights would still potentially help these countries to obtain access, as their willingness to pay may greatly exceed the fees required.

7.3.4 UNCLOS: a second-best compromise?

Whatever may be the defects of UNCLOS and the management systems that emerge from it, it is already clear at least that the widely held belief pre-UNCLOS III that such a system would produce a fall in the world catch has proved unfounded; in fact it rose somewhat from 71.2 million tonnes in 1977 to 73.7 million tonnes in 1981. However, landings in many developed Western countries and especially in socialist countries have declined as DWS fishing declines, but increased landings in developing coastal states have counterbalanced these falls, leaving the world catch in fact quite stable over 1979–81. Hence, UNCLOS has so far been associated more with shifts than decline, a reallocation of the ownership and exploitation bases. *Table 7.2* shows the location of fish catches in 1972; it suggests not only something of the potential for this shift from developed to developing countries, but also the substantial potential for rearrangement between developed countries. In practice, by 1979 the developing countries were already taking some 46.3% of the total catch (marine and freshwater fish), compared with only 39% in 1972.

TABLE 7.2 The location of marine catches in 1972

		Percentage of catch taken by location					
					of which		
Country category	*Percentage of world catch, 1972*	*Off own coast*	*Off other coasts*		*Off developed countries*		*Off developing countries*
Developed countries	61	58.3	41.7	=	31.0	+	10.8
Developing countries	39	95.1	4.9	=	2.7	+	2.3

Source: Holt (1978).
N.B. Figures may not add up owing to rounding of data.

What was, however, notable initially in the years following the multilateral declaration of 200-mile limits in the period around 1976 was the development of a mobile surplus of catching power, attacking relatively unprotected stocks, and especially a movement towards joint enterprises in the Southern Hemisphere. Also, there were clear signs of new stocks being investigated and developed, an example being blue whiting off Norway.

As we have suggested, it is fairly easy to be critical of the new regime, and some observers have attacked it on a wide front (e.g. Balasubramanian, 1982). Undoubtedly it is heavily loaded towards national sovereignty, disadvantageous to many developed countries but benefiting some others immensely, while not beneficial by any means to all developing countries. Possibly it makes management more difficult in some circumstances (trans-boundary stocks, migratory stocks, etc.) and almost certainly more piecemeal. As Cooper (1975) argued, some might have preferred much more international control of fish as a 'common heritage', with a body taking mandatory powers over all actual or potential participants, and able to act rationally to achieve some sort of global optimum strategy.

The record of most regional international management bodies is, however, poor, as suggested earlier in this chapter; beset by lack of authority, resources, data, flexibility, mangement systems and the essential difficulty of their task, they generally failed to prevent overfishing and overcapitalization. Maybe a new UNCLOS-backed system could have overcome these problems, but such a 'first-best' solution still contains the dangerous elements of the common property resource problem; fishing faces the basic difficulty that whereas undoubtedly all countries would come out better if they cooperated, each individual country has the incentive not to cooperate. Moreover, management systems based on a 'narrow EEZ plus large-scale international management' approach would be difficult to attain, complex, probably unenforceable, and certainly very expensive in operation. Hence the UNCLOS provisions, even with the loosely defined objectives and parameters for action, may be viewed, as Copes (1981) suggested, as an applaudable 'second best', although attempts to quantify or 'prove' this in welfare terms are difficult. Even Balasubramanian, after a comprehensive critique, concludes that the Convention provides 'a more than adequate legal basis for the world's marine fisheries' which will 'rescue 90% of the world's marine fisheries from the fate of overexploitation' (Balasubramanian, 1982, p. 42).

It is also interesting to note that UNCLOS still leaves some room for DWSs to continue their operations, albeit by courtesy of the CSs and possibly therefore with increased costs. That they can do so is confirmed by the fact that in 1979, three alone of the top five distant-water fishing nations—the Soviet Union, Japan and South Korea—took 31.6% of the world's marine catch, employing 7363 large vessels over 100 GRT. These figures represent 34.2% of the world total of such vessels by numbers and 63.2% by tonnage.

If we accept as a general premise that the world's fishing nations (especially DWSs) have in many cases in the past allocated excessive resources towards fishing in the pursuit of profits or foodstuffs, then UNCLOS offers an opportunity to reverse this misallocation within a coherent and enforceable framework. Whether the proud new owners, the coastal states, have the inclination, the skills, the resources and the capability to reach the right decisions is however rather a matter of chance.

7.4 THE COMMON FISHERIES POLICY OF THE EUROPEAN ECONOMIC COMMUNITY

7.4.1 Introduction

Notwithstanding developments at UNCLOS III, the fisheries under the control of the European Economic Community (EEC) continue to be managed essentially on an international basis. The actual, and the anticipated future, impact of 200-mile fishing limits has consequently been rather different in Europe than it has been in the rest of the world. Instead of placing fish resources under the control of a single country, in an attempt to facilitate improved future management, the extension of limits in Europe has placed a significant quantity of resources under the control of a cooperating group of ten, perhaps to become twelve, countries. The present situation in Europe corresponds therefore much more closely to that which prevailed under NEAFC and NAFO than it does to the situation existing in, say, the United States or Canada following fishing limit extension.

7.4.2 The original policy

The Common Fisheries Policy (CFP) was originally established by the six founder members of the EEC (France, West Germany, Belgium, the Netherlands, Italy and Luxembourg). In 1966, the EEC Commission produced a report on the fishing industry in member states and this served in 1968 as the basis for two proposed regulations concerning a common policy that eventually passed into Community law in 1970. At this time, twelve-mile fishing limits existed so that the scope of the policy was rather limited. Moreover, none of the Six had particularly important inshore fisheries so that they found it *relatively* easy to reach agreement on a common policy. The two regulations initiated the dichotomous approach that continues to characterize the CFP. The catching side of the fishing industry is dealt with by the 'structural policy' and the on-shore sector by the 'marketing policy'. In the subsequent development of the CFP, by far the most controversy has been associated with the structural policy and it is with this aspect that we shall be principally concerned in the remainder of this section.

The fundamentals of the structural policy were first spelled out by Regulation 2141/70 of 20 October 1970, and have changed little if at all since then. Indeed, Regulation 2141/70 was subsequently codified as Regulation 101/76 of 19 January 1976, and it is this latter that continues to provide the common structural policy for the fishing industry. This lack of progress in the policy is certainly one of the reasons why it continues to have a distinctly 1960s character. The most important provision of the policy is given in Article 2 of Regulation 101/76, which says: 'Member States shall ensure equal conditions of access to and use of [their] fishing grounds for all fishing vessels flying the flag of a Member State and registered in community Territory.' In addition to this quite practicable aim, the policy also had vaguer objectives including the 'rational use of the biological resources of the sea', the prevention of 'overfishing' and the prevention or reduction of 'overcapitalization'. Because of the rather general nature of these goals, their implementation as the policy has proceeded has required the more or less ad-hoc definition in terms such as 'rational'. For instance, it seems that rational use has come to be equated with biological optimum sustainable yield simply because allowable catches are based mainly on advice from ICES, which has that objective.

The above aims were to be achieved by the use of 'the necessary conservation measures . . . including restrictions relating to the catching of certain species, to areas, to fishing seasons, to methods of fishing and to fishing gear' (Article 4). These methods comprise largely what we termed in Chapter 6 'biological' regulatory techniques, in that while they may usually be expected to improve the condition of the fish stock itself, no lasting improvement in the economic health of the fishery is to be anticipated. Despite a large literature demonstrating the need to adopt economically based regulatory techniques, the EEC continues to rely on the same old techniques. Most recently, Regulation 171/83 of 25 January 1983 lays down five technical measures for the conservation and management of fish resources. These relate to mesh size restrictions, fish size restrictions, closed areas, closed seasons and gear restrictions.

7.4.3 The Act of Accession 1973

From 1970 onwards, indeed from the very time that the CFP was agreed, the United Kingdom, Eire, Denmark and Norway began negotiations to enter the EEC. Since all four applicant countries had important inshore fisheries and fishing grounds that were of considerable interest to the fishermen of the other six countries, there was much suspicion among the applicants that the Six had hastily agreed a CFP as favourable as possible to themselves, particularly concerning equal access. The Six, however, argue that they merely adopted a business-as-usual approach to affairs and it was entirely fortuitous that the CFP happened to be agreed just prior to the commencement of negotiations. Whatever the truth of the situation, it remains a fact that, on application to join the EEC, the four applicants were presented with an *acquis communautaire* that included a rather unfavourable CFP. Eventually, largely as a result of this, Norway opted not to join the EEC at all and the Faeroese sought only a limited association.

The three other countries did finally join the EEC on 1 January 1973, but they all wished to negotiate some changes in the CFP. Significant alterations were not to be had however, and in the Treaty of Accession the best that could be achieved was a ten-year transitional period lasting until 31 December 1982. Before that date, the whole policy was to be renegotiated, and during the transitional period a coastal belt of six, and in places twelve, miles' width was to be reserved for local fishermen, subject to the historic fishing rights of EEC fishermen.

7.4.4 Two-hundred-mile limits

In the end, a reconsideration of the CFP began as early as February 1976, mainly because, like many other states, the members of the EEC, in concert, extended their fishing limits to 200 miles from 1 January 1977. At once, the area of sea coming under the jurisdiction of the policy was increased enormously, as was the need to develop a much more coherent policy. For a while, there was some doubt as to whether the CFP should apply to the whole of the new area of sea, but statements made in the early 1970s make it clear that the policy was always intended to apply to any extension. For example, speaking in the House of Commons on 13

December 1971, Geoffrey Rippon (the British negotiator) said: 'We have sought and obtained a formal assurance from the Community that the legal application of the Common Fisheries Policy would not permit, either in form or in fact, any discrimination by a Member State *in waters beyond twelve miles over which it might exercise fishing jurisdiction* against the fishing vessels of other Member States operating in such waters' (880 H.C. weekly *Hansard*, col. 52, emphasis added). It thus appears that the principle of equal access was intended to apply in the case of extended limits.

It should be obvious that the Act of Accession did not alter the CFP; parts of it were simply left in abeyance for ten years. At first sight, it may appear somewhat strange that the applicant countries should have accepted a CFP with which they disagreed so strongly, but presumably they regarded it as part of the price that had to be paid for entry to what was, then at least, a very desirable club. Perhaps however, acceptance also reflected differing understandings of Community procedure. At the fisheries meeting held in Berlin in January 1978, Josef Ertl, the West German fisheries minister, said that if the British had wanted matters to be different, they should have negotiated differently their accession. Thus, for the Germans, signing the Treaty of Accession implied acceptance of the CFP subject only to a time lag. The British perceived things rather differently. All along they stressed that fishing was for them a 'vital national interest' and as such, any policy should require unanimous agreement. Thus for the United Kingdom the reconsideration of the policy promised under the Treaty of Accession was more important than the temporary derogations from the policy. Possibly these different interpretations of Community procedure are one reason why it took so long for the members of the EEC to reach agreement on a common policy.

Following the adoption of 200-mile limits, and in keeping with UNCLOS III, the EEC adopted the system of total allowable catches (TACs) whereby the EEC as 'coastal state' determines the quantity of fish that may be taken, with any surplus being allocated to third countries. In the case of the EEC, the capacity of the fishing fleet was sufficient to take all the available TAC so that third-country fleets were quickly excluded, except where the country concerned could offer fishing rights in exchange.

The introduction of 200-mile limits both by the EEC and other countries led to some difficult problems of renegotiation for the CFP. The major difficulties were that first, fish resources were not distributed equally between the fishing zones of the member states and secondly, member states suffered unequally in being excluded from third countries' waters. Owing to these inequalities, the division and allocation of TACs to member states became an exceedingly difficult affair, taking from 1976 to 1982 to resolve finally. The principal difficulty was that the criteria on which national quotas were to be based were subject to negotiation. Not surprisingly, each member state advocated those criteria which gave it the largest share. Thus the British, whose fishing zone contains around 60% of the total EEC catch, argued that quotas should be linked to the contribution made by each country to the total EEC resource base. For good measure, the

United Kingdom was also the main loser (in quantity and value terms) of access to distant-water fishing grounds, and the British government argued that such losses should also be taken into account. On the other hand, the continental members of the EEC, which of course make very much smaller contributions to the fish base, argued that historic fishing performance should be the main criterion used in determining quotas. It was probably never realistic to expect the British to achieve a great deal; simply through weight of numbers the continental view was almost bound to prevail. Eventually, the EEC Commission's quota figures were based fundamentally on historic fishing performance, with some consideration of regional dependence on fishing and distant-water losses.

The problem of how to divide up the TACs was finally resolved in January 1983. At that time, the member states of the EEC managed to agree on the share-out of the 1982 TACs, although only on the basis of cod-equivalents of the top seven food fish in European waters, namely cod, whiting, redfish, plaice, haddock, saithe and mackerel. In other words, the

TABLE 7.3 Member states' shares of EEC TACs for 1982

	Cod equivalent (tonnes)	*Percentage*
Belgium	28000	2.0
Denmark	345000	24.2
France	184000	12.9
West Germany	182000	12.8
Ireland	61000	4.3
Netherlands	111000	7.8
United Kingdom	510000	35.8
Total EEC	1424000*	99.8*

*Rounding error.
Source: Agra Europe, *Eurofish Report* No. 146, 26/1/83.

TACs are determined for these seven species. These TACs are then translated into cod-equivalent terms, and the total is then divided among the member states. The EEC has been reluctant to publish figures giving a national percentage share, but the figures given in *Table 7.3* are claimed by Agra Europe to have come from Community sources.

In addition to deciding the quota share-out, the EEC member states agreed that the six- to twelve-mile coastal belt established under the Act of Accession of 1972 would be continued until 31 December 1992, and would be standardized to twelve miles in all places.

However, notwithstanding such agreements, it is vastly overstating the case to call the new legislation a revision of the CFP. For all intents and purposes the policy continues to rely upon Regulation 101/76, and most of the problems facing it continue to exist. Unless these are dealt with it seems highly likely that yet more renegotiation of the policy will be required fairly shortly.

7.4.5 Future problems

The CFP faces a number of difficulties that must be resolved if much more progress is to be made. The first major problem is the inadequacy of the present regulatory framework. As we have already noted, great reliance is placed on biological regulatory techniques, but these will not improve the economic health of the fishery. Moreover the lack of any adequate mechanism for the control of excess fishing effort has tended to mean that regulations which have actually been introduced have had to be very severe. For instance, the North Sea herring fishery had to be closed completely, despite the serious economic and social implications this closure had, partly at least because the catching capacity of the fleet was so great that any mistakes as to the TAC might have resulted in the eradication of the stock. The EEC has made available some finance for the restructuring of fleets, but the effect this will have is rather doubtful. Fishing effort may well be potentially greater as a result. The major problem remains however that the fishermen themselves have no incentive to conserve their resource base, because the regime under which they operate remains essentially one of open access.

A second difficulty is that the marketing and structural policies conflict to some extent. The marketing policy provides price support to fishermen on the basis of the quantity of fish landed. Thus in the past the overexploitation that the structural policy is attempting to prevent has been supported by EEC funds under the marketing policy. The EEC has attempted to come to grips with this problem, but there seems little doubt that support available under the marketing policy has enabled the maintenance of a fishing fleet greater than required under the structural policy.

A third difficulty, and one that is potentially the most serious for the future of the CFP, concerns the anticipated entry into the EEC of Portugal and particularly Spain. In the negotiations that led to the agreed CFP in January 1983 no account was taken of Spain, and it is only since then that the EEC Commission has begun tackling the problem of future Spanish entry. The Spanish government has already indicated that the question of access to the European 'pond' will play a central role in fisheries talks in the context of Spanish accession to the EEC, but so far the Commission apparently has no plans for granting access to Spanish fishermen in either the North Sea or off north-west Scotland. At present, Spanish fishermen apparently do not see significant advantage in joining the EEC. There are two major difficulties. First, Spain has negotiated many bilateral deals, and presumably these would eventually be taken over by the EEC and opened out to all EEC fishermen. Secondly, access to the European market is of little interest to the Spanish fishermen as compared with the more

profitable Spanish market. Hence at present they understandably feel that joining the EEC is likely to be disadvantageous for them. Consequently, the Spanish government appears likely to have to negotiate a favourable deal on access to present EEC fishing grounds if Spanish fishermen are to be persuaded of the value of EEC membership. Moreover, the negotiating position of Spain is likely to be constrained by the local importance of fishing in the already troubled Basque region. The result of all this is that Spanish accession is likely to require a further renegotiation of the CFP and yet another transitional period, unless some fairly radical revision of the present policy is undertaken prior to Spanish entry.

7.4.6 The Common Fisheries Policy: a way forward?

It is interesting to reflect that, in this particular case of 'international' management at least, it seems possible to provide solutions to many of the problems that have arisen by changing the basis of management, in a switch towards the principles of ownership by the fishermen and towards the concept of individual fish quotas (*see* section 6.3.3 of the previous chapter).

We have already discussed in some detail in that chapter the general advantages and disadvantages of such a scheme, so we will indicate them only briefly here. First, IFQs give the management authority very tight control over the quantity of fish landed. Secondly, technological progress will no longer result in an unnecessary increase in fishing effort, thereby putting pressure on the fish stock, but will be reflected in the price of rights. Thirdly, the fishermen themselves will have every incentive to conserve their resource base, and can perhaps be expected to become their own police force to a significant extent. On the negative side, enforcement may be more difficult under this scheme—to a large extent simply because the scheme actually works and circumventing it therefore becomes very profitable. It may also require rather close study of the fish populations in mixed fisheries in order to determine the allocation of IFQs to directed and incidental fisheries.

In addition to the above advantages, IFQs appear to be especially useful for the EEC. First, fisheries are particularly important in certain regions, where there are often few alternative forms of economic activity. In such cases, it would be straightforward to favour the regions in the initial allocation of IFQs, thereby assuring their future. Secondly, the entry of new members into the EEC may be facilitated. For instance, in the case of Spain, Spanish fishermen may either buy or be allocated IFQs to participate in the European pond; and European fishermen may similarly acquire rights to participate in Spanish waters and bilateral deals. In both cases, any transfer of catch opportunities becomes a voluntary matter on the part of the fishermen, and more importantly, new entry is reflected in the price of IFQs. In this way it should be possible to avoid yet another wholesale renegotiation of the CFP. Thirdly, a successful IFQ scheme should result in dramatically improved incomes for fish producers, thereby reducing the need for the kind of price support marketing policy that presently exists. Funds allocated to the marketing policy might then be used in more productive ways such as developing the market for currently underutilized fish species.

Overall therefore, a radical revision of the CFP based on an IFQ scheme appears to offer significant advantages for fisheries management in the EEC.

7.4.7 Conclusion

The EEC faces a set of problems with its existing fisheries policy that are only too familiar in the history of international management. The problems revolve around the issues of poorly defined goals, inadequate regulatory techniques and unsatisfactory enforcement procedures. The reason why regimes with such important faults have so often been created and perpetuated, often in the face of mounting evidence of failure, is that agreement between the various countries that are party to such conventions has been almost impossible to obtain on anything other than the 'lowest common denominator' basis. At times this has resulted in countries agreeing to the mechanisms of biologically based management, without fully identifying the goals of management and without a real commitment even to the purposes of the agreed mechanisms. Unfortunately, in the recent past the EEC has often seemed to suffer from similar difficulties. However, at the beginning of 1983 the EEC fisheries ministers demonstrated that the political will to reach agreement on such controversial matters can be found. It now remains to extend the CFP so that fundamental progress on fisheries management may be made, and in particular a new regime moving towards the principles of IFQs might be implemented.

7.5 SUMMARY

In this chapter we have considered the international management of commercial fisheries. The relative lack of success of this kind of management historically is illustrated by a number of case studies. Both the North-east Atlantic Fisheries Commission and the Northwest Atlantic Fisheries Organization (which replaced the earlier International Commission for Northwest Atlantic Fisheries) have presided over the decline of a number of important fisheries, with the best-known examples being the North Sea herring and Georges Bank haddock fisheries. The major reason for the relative failure of both organizations is the great difficulty in reaching agreement on fisheries management between many member states. Similar problems affected the International Whaling Commission, which we discussed next. The relative importance of many fisheries organizations has recently been greatly reduced owing to the general shift to 200-mile fishing limits. However for migratory species, especially tuna, international management remains unavoidable. The great difficulties of reaching agreement on such management were considered.

Partly as a response to the unsatisfactory record of international management, UNCLOS III, which was finally concluded in 1982, embraced the principle of extended coastal state jurisdiction. The fundamental ideas underpinning UNCLOS III are the management of fish stocks on a modified-MSY basis, partial exclusivity for the coastal state but with arrangements for surpluses to be harvested, cooperation in management between countries and international bodies, and the tentative extension of its management principles into high-seas fisheries.

Despite the development of coastal state influence via UNCLOS, the Common Fisheries Policy of the EEC continues to be essentially an international regime. It is clear that the problems remain the same, namely that it is very difficult for many countries to agree on the basis for fisheries management. It appears that a quite radical revision of the CFP is required if the full potential benefits of 200-mile limits are to be realized in Europe.

7.6 BIBLIOGRAPHIC NOTES

International management

A good if dated general introduction to the subject of international fisheries management is that of Koers (1973), which considers many more organizations than we have here.

On management in the north-east Atlantic in particular the following are all useful: Cushing (1977), Brander (1978), Driscoll and McKellar (1979), McKellar (1980) and Underdal (1980). On north-west Atlantic management *see* Graham (1970), Pontecorvo, Johnston and Wilkinson (1977) and Clark, Overholtz and Hennemuth (1982). The annual reports of NEAFC and NAFO contain the primary information.

A great deal has been written on whale management. A good recent introduction is by Clark and Lamberson (1982). Also well worth consulting are Gambell (1977), Elliott (1979), McHugh (1977) and Scarff (1977).

On tuna management the best introduction is by Joseph and Greenough (1979). *See also* Joseph (1977), Flagg (1978) and King (1979).

The Law of the Sea

Much of the prolific literature on the Law of the Sea prior to 1975 is now primarily of background value only, and it is mainly post-1978 work that reflects what has in fact been happening rather than what might happen. Useful sources for general background to UNCLOS include Knight (1975, 1977), Johnson (1975), the Open University (1978) and the FAO (1979). There are some old general economic review papers of an essentially *ex ante* nature, among which those of Katz (1975), Huppert (1977), Cooper (1975) and Kent (1978) are still useful, the latter two casting some basic doubts over the emerging regime. There is a dearth of solid economic analysis in the area, though works by Wong (1976), Hannesson (1978), Levhari and Mirman (1980) and Stokes (1981) are notable exceptions.

There are however a number of useful recent general reviews that include coverage of the economic issues, and the major work by Anderson (1977) remains important. Three articles provide good coverage: the long paper by Copes (1981) concentrates on North America, while that of Shyam (1982) looks especially at developing countries' interests. The two-part paper by Balasubramanian (1981, 1982) contains a full background and concentrates on comparing the achievements of UNCLOS with the objectives. Jackson (1982) has contributed a broad review pamphlet, looking especially at coastal-state interests.

Most of the *ex post* work examining the impact of the new regime is from North America, and includes especially Crutchfield (1979), Copes (1979, 1980) and Munro (1982). Other country or area studies—some essentially *ex ante* though—include those of Pontecorvo (1974), Tussing, Hiebert and Sutinen (1974—part of a useful series), Kaczynski (1979) and Watt (1979). Kingham and McRae (1979) present a complex review of the role of international organizations under UNCLOS, Tomlinson and Vertinsky (1975) and Kaczynski and Le Vieil (1980) analyse the growth of joint ventures, and Carroz and Savini (1979) look in detail at the emerging bilateral agreements, all topics that are only hinted at here. The study by the OECD (1982) on the trade impact contains much interesting information.

The Common Fisheries Policy of the EEC

Comparatively little has been written on the EEC's Common Fisheries Policy, at least from an economic point of view. Probably the best introduction remains that of Birnie (1978) although this is now a little dated. A more recent paper looking at both structural and marketing aspects is by Cunningham and Young (1983). The following are also well worth reading: Churchill (1977, 1979), Driscoll and McKellar (1979), McKellar (1980), Cunningham (1980), Allen (1980) and Mackay (1981).

REFERENCES AND FURTHER READING

ALLEN, R. (1980). 'Fishing for a common policy.' *Journal of Common Market Studies* **19** (2) : 123–39.

ANDERSON, L. G. (Ed.) (1977). *Economic impacts of extended fisheries jurisdiction*. Ann Arbor, Michigan: Ann Arbor Science Publishers.

BALASUBRAMANIAN, S. (1981). 'Fishery provisions of the ICNT: Part I.' *Marine Policy* **5** (4) : 313–21.

BALASUBRAMANIAN, S. (1982). 'Fishery provisions of the ICNT: Part II.' *Marine Policy* **6** (1) : 27–42.

BELL, F. (1977). 'World-wide economic aspects of extended fishery jurisdiction management.' In L. G. Anderson (Ed.), *Economic impacts of extended fisheries jurisdiction.* Ann Arbor, Michigan: Ann Arbor Science Publishers.

BIRNIE, P. (1978). 'The history of the EEC Common Fisheries Policy.' In HMSO, *The fishing industry*, pp. 92–118. 5th Report from the Expenditure Committee.

BRANDER, K. (1978). 'The effect of 200 mile limits on fisheries management in the north-east Atlantic.' Fisheries Technical Paper No. 183. 19pp. Rome: FAO.

CARROZ, J. and M. SAVINI (1979). 'The new international law of fisheries emerging from bilateral agreements.' *Marine Policy* **3** (2) : 79–98.

CHAN, K. (1978). 'The economic consequences of the 200 mile seabed zone.' *Canadian Journal of Economics* **11** : 314–18.

CHURCHILL, R. (1977). 'The EEC Fisheries Policy—towards a revision.' *Marine Policy* **1** (1) : 26–36.

CHURCHILL, R. (1979). 'International aspects of the Common Fisheries Policy.' Paper presented at the European Study Conference, *Fishing in European Waters, London, 13 December 1979*.

CLARK, C. (1973). 'Profit maximization and the extinction of animal species.' *Journal of Political Economy* **81** : 950–61.

CLARK, C. and R. LAMBERSON (1982). 'An economic history and analysis of pelagic whaling.' *Marine Policy* **6** (2) : 103–20.

CLARK, S., W. OVERHOLTZ and R. HENNEMUTH (1982). 'Review and assessment of the Georges Bank and Gulf of Maine haddock fishery.' *Journal of Northwest Atlantic Fishery Science* **3** (1) : 1–27.

COLOMBOS, C. (1967). *The International Law of the Sea*, 6th edn. London: Longmans.

COOPER, R. (1975). 'An economist's view of the oceans.' *Journal of World Trade Law* **9** (4) : 357–77.

COPES, P. (1977). 'The Law of the Sea and management of anadromous fish stocks.' *Ocean Development and International Law Journal* **4** (3) : 233–59.

COPES, P. (1979). 'The economics of marine fisheries management in the era of extended jurisdiction: the Canadian perspective.' *American Economic Review* **69** (2) : 256–60.

COPES, P. (1980). 'The British Columbia fisheries and the 200 mile limit: perverse effects for the coastal state.' *Marine Policy* **4** (3) : 205–16

COPES, P. (1981). 'The impact of UNCLOS III on management of the world's fisheries.' *Marine Policy* **6** (3) : 217–28.

CRUTCHFIELD, J. (1979). 'Marine resources—the economics of U.S. ocean policy.' *American Economic Review* **69** (2) : 266–71.

CUNNINGHAM, S. (1980). 'EEC fisheries management: a critique of Common Fisheries Policy objectives.' *Marine Policy* **4** (3) : 229–35.

CUNNINGHAM, S. and J. YOUNG (1983). 'The EEC Common Fisheries Policy: retrospect and prospect.' *National Westminster Bank Quarterly Review*, May : 2–13.

CUSHING, D. (1977). 'The Atlantic fisheries commissions.' *Marine Policy* **1** (3) : 230–8.

DASGUPTA, P. (1982). *The Control of Resources*. Oxford: Basil Blackwell.

DRISCOLL, D. and N. MCKELLAR (1979). 'The changing regime of North Sea fisheries.' In C. Mason (Ed.), *The effective management of resources: the international politics of the North Sea*, pp. 125–67. London: Frances Pinter.

ELLIOTT, G. (1979). 'The failure of the IWC 1946–1966.' *Marine Policy* **3** (2) : 149–55.

FAO (1979). *World fisheries and the Law of the Sea*. Rome: FAO.

FIFE, D. (1971). 'Killing the goose.' *Environment* **13** (3) : 20–7.

FLAGG, V. (Ed.) (1978). *Transient tropical tuna.* San Diego: Center for Marine Studies, San Diego State University.

GAMBELL, R. (1977). 'Whale conservation—role of the International Whaling Commission.' *Marine Policy* **1** (4) : 301–10.

GILCHRIST, A. (1978). *Cod wars—and how to lose them*. Edinburgh: Q. Press.

GRAHAM, H. (1970). 'Management of the groundfish fisheries of the north-west Atlantic.' In N. Benson (Ed.), *A century of fisheries in North America*, pp. 249–61. Special Publication No. 7, American Fisheries Society, Washington, U.S.A.

GULLAND, J. (1979). 'Developing countries and the Law of the Sea.' *Oceanus* **22** (1) : 36–42.

HANNESSON, R. (1978). 'A note on the welfare economic consequences of extended fishing limits.' *Journal of Environmental Economics and Management* **5** : 187–97.

HOLT, S. (1978). 'Marine fisheries.' In *Ocean Yearbook.* Chicago: University of Chicago Press.

HUPPERT, D. (1977). 'Constraints to welfare gains under extended jurisdiction fisheries management.' *American Journal of Agricultural Economics* **59** (5) : 877–82.

ICES (International Council for the Exploration of the Sea) (1977). 'Report of the Ad Hoc Meeting on the Provision of Advice on the Biological Basis for Fisheries Management.' Co-operative Research Report No. 62.

JACKSON, R. (1982). 'Extended national fisheries jurisdiction: palliative or panacea?' Washington Sea Grant: McKerman Lecture, 1981.

JOHNSON, B. (1975). 'A review of fisheries proposals made at the Caracas session of UNCLOS III.' *Ocean Management* **2** : 285–314.

JOSEPH, J. (1977). 'The management of highly migratory species: some important concepts.' *Marine Policy* **1** (4) : 275–88.

JOSEPH, J. and J. GREENOUGH (1979). *International management of tuna, porpoise and billfish*. Seattle: University of Washington Press.

KACZYNSKI, V. (1979). 'The economics of the Eastern bloc ocean policy.' *American Economic Review* **69** (2) : 261–5.

KACZYNSKI, V. and D. LE VIEIL (1980). *International joint ventures in world fisheries: their distribution and development*. Washington Sea Grant Technical Report WSG 80.2.

KATZ, S. (1975). 'Consequences of the economic zone for catch opportunities of fishing nations.' *Maritime Studies and Management* **2** : 144–53.

KENT, G. (1978). 'Fisheries and the Law of the Sea: a common heritage approach.' *Ocean Management* **4** : 1–20.

KING, D. (1979). 'International management of highly migratory species—centralised versus decentralised economic decision-making.' *Marine Policy* **3** (4) : 264–77.

KINGHAM, J. and D. MCRAE (1979). 'Competent international organisations and the Law of the Sea.' *Marine Policy* **4** (2) : 106–32.

KNIGHT, J. (Ed.) (1975). *The future of international fisheries management*. St Paul, Minnesota: West Publishing Co.

KNIGHT, J. G. (1977). *Managing the seas' living resources*. Lexington, Massachusetts: Lexington Books.

KOERS, A. (1973). *International regulation of marine fisheries*. Farnham, Surrey: Fishing News Books.

LEVHARI, D. and L. MIRMAN (1980). 'The great fish war: an example using a dynamic Cournot–Nash solution.' *Bell Journal of Economics* **11** (1) : 322–34.

MCHUGH, J. (1972). 'Population dynamics and fisheries management.' In R. Thompson (Ed.), *Marine fishery resources*. Corvallis, Oregon: Oregon State University.

MCHUGH, J. (1977). 'The rise and fall of world whaling: the tragedy of the commons illustrated.' *Journal of International Affairs* **31** (1) : 23–33.

MACKAY, G. (1981). 'The U.K. fishing industry and EEC policy.' *Three Banks Review* No. 132, December, pp. 48–62.

MCKELLAR, N. (1980). 'The political economy of fisheries management in the north-east Atlantic.' Paper given at a seminar on economic aspects of limited entry and associated fisheries management measures, Melbourne, 6–8 February 1980.

MUNRO, G. (1979). 'The optimal management of transboundary renewable resources.' *Canadian Journal of Economics* **12** : 355–76.

MUNRO, G. (1982). 'Fisheries, extended jurisdiction and the economics of common property resources.' *Canadian Journal of Economics* **15** (3) : 405–25.

OECD (1982). *International trade in fish products: effects of the 200 mile limit*. Paris: OECD.

OPEN UNIVERSITY (1978). *Oceanography: law of the sea*. Milton Keynes: Open University. S334 Units 15 and 16.

PONTECORVO, G. (Ed.) (1974). *Fisheries conflicts in the North Atlantic: problems of management and jurisdiction*. Cambridge, Massachusetts: Ballinger Publishing Co.

PONTECORVO, G., D. JOHNSTON and M. WILKINSON (1977). 'Conditions for effective fisheries management in the north-west Atlantic.' In L. G. Anderson (Ed.), *Economic impacts of extended fisheries jurisdiction*, pp. 51–103. Ann Arbor, Michigan: Ann Arbor Science Publishers.

RUSSELL, E. (1942). *The overfishing problem*. London: Cambridge University Press.

SAILA, S. and V. NORTON (1974). *Tuna: status, trends and alternative management arrangements*. Washington D.C.: Resources for the Future.

SCARFF, J. (1977). 'The international management of whales, dolphins and porpoises: an interdisciplinary assessment.' *Ecology Law Quarterly*. Part I, **6** (2) : 323–427; Part II, **6** (3): 571–638.

SHYAM, M. (1982). 'The new international economic order and the new regime for fisheries management.' *Ocean Management* **8** : 51–64.

STOKES, R. (1981). 'The new approach to foreign fisheries allocation: an economic appraisal.' *Land Economics* **57** (4) : 568–82.

TOMLINSON, J. W. C. and J. VERTINSKY (1975). 'International joint ventures in fishing and 200 mile economic zones.' *Journal of the Fisheries Research Board of Canada* **32** : 2569–79.

TREVES, T. (1983). 'The adoption of the Law of the Sea Convention: prospects for seabed mining.' *Marine Policy* **7** (1) : 3–13.

TUSSING, A., R. HIEBERT and J. SUTINEN (1974). 'Fisheries of the Indian Ocean: issues of international management and law of the sea.' RFF/PISFA Paper 5: Resources for the Future, Washington.

UNDERDAL, A. (1980). *The politics of international fisheries management: the case of the north-east Atlantic*. Oslo: Universitetsforlaget.

UNITED NATIONS (1982). *United Nations Convention on the Law of the Sea*. A/Conf. 62/122.

WATT, D. C. (Ed.) (1979). *Britain and the sea: the 200 mile zone and its implications.* London: Institute of Marine Engineers.

WONG, E. (1976). 'Application of the economic club: an approach to the Law of the Sea.' *Maritime Studies and Management* **3** : 175–86.

CHAPTER 8

Fisheries policy at the national level

8.1 INTRODUCTION

In this chapter we examine national fisheries policy in Canada, the United States and the United Kingdom. These three countries have been selected to illustrate contrasting approaches to policy, particularly in the instruments used. We shall see that fisheries policy in North America has been identified very closely with resource management, whereas in the United Kingdom, at least until fairly recently, relatively more emphasis has been placed on measures to aid the fishing industry directly. Even within resource management itself there are national differences: the United States, for example, has developed a more comprehensive regulatory framework than the United Kingdom. Each of these countries is, of course, unique in terms of the problems with which policy has had to deal and in the way governments have responded to the problems in formulating policy, and the differences are reflected in the format of each section.

8.2 CANADA

Canada has a considerable abundance of fish resources, exceeding her own domestic needs, and has been the world's largest fish exporter since 1979. Although from an early stage the Canadian industry has been orientated towards exporting as well as meeting domestic demand, it remained small until the early 1960s, even though foreign fleets were already rapidly increasing their exploitation of offshore resources. Today, it is a reflection of the influence of fisheries management ideas that virtually every fishery has been removed from the common-property regime of open access and is available only to those willing and able to purchase licences for their vessels or themselves, and for access to each specific fishery. Yet the experience of limited-entry management has by no means been an unqualified success, owing to a considerable extent to the regional pressures operating within the industry.

To understand these, it is first necessary to appreciate something of the nature of the Canadian industry. Though fishing contributes less than 0.5% to Canadian GDP, it is of great importance to particular areas such as Newfoundland, the Maritimes and Quebec, where alternative job opportunities are limited. Economically, the Atlantic coast has the more important part of the industry, accounting for 92% by weight and 79% by value of total Canadian landings in 1981. The disparity between these two figures is due to the reliance of the Atlantic coast on species of an average lower unit value as compared with the Pacific coast, where the dominant fisheries are for salmon (77% by value of west-coast landings in 1981). On the eastern seaboard the majority of fishermen are employed in the inshore fishery, typified by small vessels operating on a seasonal basis. The main species caught, by value, are cod, lobster, scallop and crab. The offshore sector, whose fishing is principally for demersal species, consists of vessels mainly over 100 GRT operating from large ports with full-time crews. Most vessels have vertical links with large processing plants which, in the absence of public markets or auctions, can exert considerable buying power. A major feature of the industry is that many fishermen are engaged less than full time. This, as we shall see, is of particular importance to resource management.

8.2.1 Resource management

Despite an abundant resource base and proximity to huge American markets, Canadian fisheries passed through a difficult decade in the 1970s. Total landings declined from 1.45 million tonnes in 1968 to less than 1.0 million tonnes in 1974 and 1975. As during this period the Pacific coast landings increased somewhat, the decline was entirely due to a dramatic 38% decline in the weight of Atlantic coast landings (1968–74), yet with effort increasing all the time. There were two main reasons for this decline, the first being the free entry to most fisheries (except for salmon and lobsters), which resulted in excessive inputs of indigenous capital and labour. Secondly, the open-access regime existing offshore attracted a large amount of foreign distant-water fishing effort, and despite some efforts by ICNAF, overfishing was occurring.

This production crisis was worsened by market problems, as a sharp decline in demand in the United States after 1973, together with increasing competition there from imports from Japan and Korea, left the Canadian producers with unsold stocks of the fish that had been caught. To add to these problems, cost pressures from domestic inflation and the 1973 world oil price rise threatened to destroy the precarious viability of the Canadian industry.

Previously the Federal government had been relatively passively interested in fisheries, but this crisis forced it to become positively involved, and, as in almost all similar cases, this involvement initially took the form of financial assistance. Over the period 1975–77, some C$130 million of special aid was dispensed, in addition to the regular C$200 million spent each year on research and management. More important however was that the crisis produced a serious and radical re-examination in 1975 of the whole basis of Canadian fisheries, with particular reference to their management in future. Both biological and economic overfishing had been apparent for some time, and while overfishing was not too unusual elsewhere in the world, the difference was that a positive policy emerged in Canada. This included the introduction of licensing on a general scale and strong pressures to acquire and benefit from a 200-mile EEZ.

Against this general background, two other factors are worth noting. First, the regional significance of fishing became an increasingly pressing problem, particularly in the Atlantic provinces such as Newfoundland. Here low incomes and underemployment typified the inshore fisheries, yet with few alternative viable occupations and immense problems with resettlement policies, there was a strong temptation, not only for the local provincial administrators but also for the Federal government, to look upon inshore fishing, as did local men, as an 'employer of last resort'. This problem became even more intractable with general economic recession in the 1980s.

The other factor was the increasing disenchantment of Canada with the international fisheries management off her Atlantic coast operated by ICNAF. From 1949–70, ICNAF operated biologically based management via gear control, which manifestly failed to prevent overfishing, especially as more and more nations joined the fisheries.*

By 1970 it was clear that some form of catch or effort controls were needed, and a rapidly expanding coverage of TACs was introduced after 1971, with recommended national quotas. However, as we suggested in Chapter 7, controls of this kind fail to prevent not only economic overfishing but biological overfishing even, and by 1975 ICNAF was forced to set TACs below the MSY levels. This curtailed everyone's efforts, including those of Canada, but great damage had already been done, and Canada looked towards sole ownership and Canadian-orientated management regimes to improve the state of her fisheries.

8.2.2 The role of economics in Canadian fisheries management

The chronology of events after the early 1970s in Canada is extensively covered elsewhere, for the management of Canadian fisheries is probably the best documented of all fisheries throughout the world (*see* the bibliographic notes). Of particular importance as a foundation stone was the Fisheries and Marine Service policy document produced as *Policy for Canada's commercial fisheries* in 1976. This document, which arose from a series of studies of the problems of the mid 1970s, contained much of interest, but in particular (p. 61) a firm commitment to move away from open access towards limitation of entry: 'If Canadian society as a whole is to get the best combination of benefits from development of the fisheries,

*The Soviet Union, Poland, West Germany, Japan, East Germany, Bulgaria, Romania and Cuba all joined ICNAF alongside the United States, France, Portugal, Spain, Italy, Denmark, Norway, Iceland, the United Kingdom and Canada.

open access to resource use must be curtailed.' Clearly this commitment required, *inter alia*, the ability for Canada to prevent open access, and so the establishment of a 200-mile EEZ in 1977 was a necessary prerequisite for the policy. Also, the administration of fisheries was reorganized, with the new Department of Fisheries and Oceans taking virtually total control of Canadian fisheries after 1977, although not without some resistance at the level of the provinces.

The changes that have occurred in the fortunes of the Canadian industry since this policy reappraisal are dramatic, although the extent to which they can be attributed specifically to management is inevitably debatable. For although landings climbed back from 1.0 million tonnes to the 1968 level of 1.4 million tonnes by 1979, albeit checking thereafter to 1.26 million tonnes in 1981 and 1.28 million tonnes (preliminary) in 1982, much of this gain came simply from the replacement of foreign fishing effort excluded from the Canadian 200-mile zone after 1977. In fact, over the period 1975–76, Canada was able to take appreciably more of a TAC that was being gradually reduced for conservation reasons, and after 1976 its own coastal state jurisdiction emphasized this trend.* The numbers of foreign vessels operating offshore declined from some 1500 in 1976 to 250 in 1979, which is at the least indicative of the changing pattern, and Canada's share of the main east-coast demersal TACs increased from 52% to 73% in the same period. Within this increase, cod was especially significant, being the main inshore species (with Greenland halibut), and here a deliberate policy increased Canada's share of the catch from 22% in 1972 to 72% in 1978.

At UNCLOS, Canada was a strong proponent of coastal state management but accepted the obligation to permit access to surpluses over and above the proportion of the TAC that could be taken by domestic fishermen (*see* section 7.3.2 of the previous chapter). However, access is generally permitted only under stringent requirements: foreign vessels must submit fishing plans, which are checked against foreign access quotas, and licences may be granted which then give very detailed permission by specifying which species may be caught, when and where. Licences have in fact been granted to vessels from a wide variety of countries, including Japan, the Soviet Union, Portugal, Spain and the EEC, but foreign takings have been considerably reduced, and confined more to those species not sought after by Canadian vessels. The countries especially affected by this exclusion have been the Soviet Union, Spain and Portugal, although access has been allowed for species such as capelin, silver hake, grenadier and argentine (although capelin itself became overfished and all offshore fishing was banned in 1980). As Canadian efforts increase, even this access

*Canada as the prospective coastal state 'sole owner' was able to insist even as early as 1975 that, for 1976, the effort levels of all fleets except coastal states' should be reduced by 40% of their 1973 level. While such a large reduction in one year would normally be unacceptable, it was borne by the foreign fleets of West Germany, Spain, Portugal and France, which to some extent moved elsewhere (Cushing, 1977).

may be curtailed in future. The granting of access quotas to foreign fleets has, as we suggested in section 7.3.3.5, become increasingly an issue of reciprocal benefits, including access to foreign markets for the increased Canadian fish exports in the 1980s. In 1983 quotas were allocated on a 'past performance' basis—not fishing performance, but how much Canadian fish that country had imported in the previous year and any proposed tariffs. Not surprisingly, this type of bargaining is less than popular at the fisherman's level (*World Fishing*, July 1982).

The new UNCLOS regime, although offering substantial advantages, had certain drawbacks for Canada, analysed by Copes (1982) in detail for the west-coast fisheries. These included the pressures, more potential than actual, on salmon from west-coast rivers while migrating or feeding in the unregulated high-seas areas. Also there were problems with loss of access to stocks off the U.S. coast after the failure to reach reciprocal-access agreements, and interception effects, as fish (particularly salmon, and also herring, hake and albacore tuna) potentially available for Canadian fishermen were intercepted, especially by Americans, while in other waters. In addition, there was a potential trade diversion effect, as the U.S. industry built up its fisheries, benefiting from the United States's own 200-mile zone, thereby reducing the groundfish market for Canadian exports, this being especially important as Canada exports some 40% of her total fish production to America. Finally there was a period of disputes over boundaries with adjacent coastal states (the United States), during which fishing and trading were disrupted. (Disputes over boundaries occurred on the east coast too, and the dispute over the Georges Bank scallop fishery was still continuing in 1982–83.) Thus, as suggested in Chapter 7, the coastal state receives both benefits and costs from the regime that emerged under UNCLOS, and while Canada has clearly benefited greatly, there have been costs to set against these benefits.

The principal changes in fisheries management, other than extended jurisdiction, lie close to the core of fisheries economics as it developed (partly in Canada itself) in the 1960s and 1970s, when economics played a central part in policy formulation and in three areas in particular.

8.2.2.1 *The principle of 'best use'*

The idea that fisheries ought to be managed on a basis other than that of maximum sustainable yield had been explored within Canada prior to 1976, yet it was a brave decision to incorporate the concept of 'best use' as a practical management framework in the *Policy* of 1976. The concept, which owes a lot to the influence of Parzival Copes and other economists, is that fisheries management should maximize 'the sum of net social benefits (personal income, occupational opportunity, consumer satisfaction and so on) derived from the fisheries and the industries linked to them' (*Policy,* 176, p. 53) rather than the crop sustainable over time. The principle was strongly, and indeed inevitably, linked in the 1976 *Policy* document with the need for Federal government and industry to make joint decisions on fundamental issues of resource management and the development of industry and trade; traditional commercial freedom had to be curtailed if best use was to be achieved.

However, 'best use' in practice proved to be less easily grasped than in theory; theoretically, the Federal authority sets the TACs overall, allocates them between various Canadian fleets on the basis of capacity and coastal community needs, allocates the rest to foreign vessels, and then collects the revenues (rents) from the fleets (as licence fees). In practice, the best-use principle is effectively an OSY idea, with the level of effort used distinctly below that related to MSY, but influenced in a rather indeterminate way by social factors. Biologists establish the basic TAC figure for each stock,* which is then modified in the light of economic data on costs and revenues, and 'an elaborate definition of socioeconomic welfare functions', albeit with 'crude approximations' (Copes, 1982) if necessary. The intent has been to move towards some form of long-run position with levels of effort much lower than at MSY but with only a relatively small penalty in reduced catches, thereby having a durably beneficial impact on CPUE performance and overall economic returns in the fisheries (Mitchell, 1979).

To achieve best use, limitation of effort was obviously needed, both of foreign and domestic users. Thus a logical consequence of the principle was the need to restructure the Canadian industry, especially on the Atlantic coast, and to do this in the short run yet without hardship and excessive disruption.

8.2.2.2 *The principle of limited entry*

Licences were first introduced into east-coast lobster potting and west-coast salmon netting in 1969. However in general terms, new effort, whether foreign or domestic, could enter all Canadian fisheries freely until the mid 1970s. ICNAF's response to the evident overfishing was to increase the coverage and stringency of quotas, using TACs based on MSY. These adversely affected Canada herself as reduced quotas were applied to a domestic fleet and processing capacity that had increased substantially since the 1960s. The industry's crisis of 1973–74 brought matters to a head, and a simple licence scheme that froze vessel numbers at the 1974 level was generally acceptable. Not surprisingly this did not solve the problem, and after the period of propping-up assistance in 1974–76 (*see* Anon., 1976), the Federal government grasped the nettle and introduced licensing on a broad basis. The system that evolved became increasingly complex, though the running costs (C$1.3 million (1980)) were covered by the licence fees charged.

*A rule-of-thumb biological reference point is employed, referred to as $F_{0.1}$ or F_{opt}—defined as fishing mortality at which a marginal yield per recruit is equal to one-tenth of the original catch per recruit per unit effort in the very lightly exploited fishery (Gulland and Boerema, 1973). This is based on a different biological approach from that employed in this book, using a yield per recruit model. For an explanation of this approach, *see* for example Pitcher and Hart (1982, Chapter 8).

Initially, a key factor was that licences would be transferable, thereby creating a market. Almost every fishery was brought under control, and benefits were seen quite rapidly in terms of improved catches, especially of Atlantic-coast scallop, lobster, crab and shrimp (Mitchell, 1981). However problems emerged, and were examined especially for the important Pacific-coast salmon fishery* (and the post-1972 herring), where licensing was introduced in 1969 for both biological and economic reasons, supported by high fees, transferability and 'buy-backs'. Here, incomes and returns in the fishery improved (partly owing to improved market prices), but the licence scheme was by no means totally successful. Various studies identified a range of problems (Fraser, 1977; Sinclair, 1978; Pearse and Wilen, 1979; Pearse, 1981). Effort and catching power was not in fact reduced, and actually increased in herring fishing, for the licensing of vessels allowed them to be replaced with much more powerful larger vessels on a 'one-for-one' basis, and thus effort would effectively increase until a 'ton-for-ton' or similar rule was inserted. Similarly, overcapitalization was not reduced, with 'capital stuffing' being partly responsible as individual units became more and more powerful. In addition, the government was reaping only a minimal amount of rent from the fisheries via the licence fees, while fishermen with licences had improvements to their incomes. These profits not surprisingly encouraged the licensed fishermen to invest in large vessels and improved gear on existing vessels.

A broad review of licensing policies took place over the 1978–79 boom period, where displaced foreign effort allowed landings and incomes to rise, during which it was clear, as suggested in Chapter 6, that licences, even with high fees, did not reduce excessive levels of capital and labour. In fact, as the licences referred essentially to a single input, the vessel, fishing production functions were becoming visibly distorted by the nature of the access arrangements, as other inputs such as vessel size and equipment could be increased (Pearse and Wilen, 1979). Although it seemed that the position on all counts was somewhat worse in unlicensed fisheries, the conclusion began to emerge that effort control by restricted access, while a necessary condition, was not in itself a sufficient condition for economically viable fisheries.

In addition to this conclusion, which stimulated economists to develop more sophisticated schemes, there were other voices raised against licensing. These included the excluded fishermen and potential fishermen, some provincial politicians who resented Federal interference, and a range of non-economist academics, who became involved in lobbying and media campaigns to remove or severely impair the operation of licensing schemes. Thus Story and Alexander (1974) argued that, whilst licensing

*The Pacific salmon is the classic example of overcapitalization: it was once calculated that if unrestricted fishing were allowed, even if only for the existing numbers of boats, gear, etc., this would still be enough to take 98% of the run in just six days (Needler, 1979). The extraordinary nature of this fishery not surprisingly attracted economists 'like wasps to a picnic lunch' (Larkin, 1979).

might confer certain possible economic gains, there were substantial costs involved in the inherent risks of rural disruption, particularly in the disadvantaged east-coast provinces. Likewise, Nowak (1980) attacked licensing in Newfoundland as a devious scheme by Federal government to introduce labour resettlement by indirect methods, and objected to the entire basis of limited access; the criticism implied in his comment that '. . . because something belongs to all, the State will safeguard this by giving it to a few!!' comprised a basic attack on the entire arguments of fisheries management, and was rejected by, for example, Pearse (1981).

In fact, it has been argued that licensing was reasonably successful in offshore east-coast fisheries, but less successful in the inshore case (Copes, 1982). The main reason has been the intense pressure to use inshore fishing as the 'employer of last resort', and the limitation principle was eroded by substantial 'exceptional cases'. This erosion produced a somewhat ironic situation: the Federal administration found that in attempting to tighten up the whole licence system it was in conflict with provincial governments and the larger vertically integrated processors, but supported by the fishermen with licences, and by economists who wanted (essentially) to reduce the numbers of fishermen holding licences. The processors' objection arose from the Federal decision to try to favour the inshore rather than the offshore fishery in its TAC allocation after 1977, so as to confer positive benefits from the improved prospects for fishing within the EEZ to the less mobile and flexible coastal communities on the east coast.

8.2.2.3 *The principle of cost recovery*

The third specific contribution was that of encouraging a cost–benefit attitude towards fisheries enhancement programmes—and indeed towards fisheries management activities in general—with the specific objective of achieving the recovery of costs in any programme from those who benefited from it. The principle was clearly laid out in the 1976 *Policy* document, where the stated objective was to produce a vigorous and stable industry '. . . productive enough to share the financial burden of resource maintenance or other services provided by the State to users of fishery resources' (Anon., 1976, p. 54). Thus, in the case of the Salmon Enhancement Programme on the west coast, the costs of a programme aimed at doubling commercial salmon landings and trebling the sports fishery catches by the 1990s were to be borne initially by the government but with a clear understanding that the total costs, estimated at C$250–300 million (1976), would ultimately be recovered from the beneficiaries. Although this objective may not sound especially contentious, in fact the principle is by no means widely accepted, and would not be possible in, for example, the United States, where the domestic industry cannot be charged fees except to cover the costs of licences or permits and their issuing. It does however remain to be seen precisely how the costs will in fact be recovered in Canada (Mitchell, 1981).

8.2.3 The Pacific halibut

It would be inappropriate to discuss Canada without some consideration of one of the most famous fisheries in the development of fisheries management, that for the Pacific halibut off the west coast of Canada, the United States and Alaska. This fishery has been managed since 1923, when the International Pacific Halibut Commission (IPHC) was originally formed. With its strong biological leaning, the IPHC elected to control effort on the fishery initially by a closed winter season, and after 1930 by closing the fishery by area when a target catch had been reached. It also introduced some gear controls and non-restrictive licensing. Not surprisingly, the result was a classic illustration of economic inefficiency, as the season fell from over 250 days in the 1930s to about forty days in the mid 1950s, with consequential inefficiencies in the use of boats and processing plants and so on, and accompanied by relatively low ex-vessel prices; an analysis of this inefficiency is one of the seminal papers in fisheries economics (Crutchfield and Zellner, 1962). The management regime in fact became specifically MSY-orientated in 1953, and achieved some success in protecting the stocks, although net returns declined and capital and labour inefficiencies were visible. Debates over the regime started, and indeed continue (Bell, 1981, Chapter 8). For Canada, the problem worsened with increasing international competition in the fishery. From the mid 1960s, Canada's catch share declined in the face of effort from the United States, the Soviet Union and Japan (much as incidental by-catches in fact), and by 1974 her catch stood at only 20% of the 1964 level.

With the declaration of 200-mile EEZs in 1977, the fishery became split solely between Canada and the United States, with the latter having some 75–80% of the TAC in 1977, although taking only 50%. A gradual mutual exclusion, particularly of Canadian vessels off Alaska, which provided two-thirds of their catch, allied to a serious environmental decline, produced a dramatic further fall in Canada's catch of some 50% over 1973–79 (Copes and Cook, 1982). Meanwhile, economic disorder with low catches and increasing entry by uncontrolled small boats forced the Commission to revert in 1977 to plans, originally drawn up in 1953, for a multiple season, with a succession of openings and closings. For example, the 1983 joint TAC of 30.6 million pounds (13.9 million kilograms) was to be taken in up to five short 'seasons' in each of the nine areas, varying from five to thirteen days in length (*Western Fisheries*, March 1983).

The need for overall management of what was clearly a joint fish stock was however recognized, and the IPHC continued to set the TAC while the coastal states did the fishing. Canada took the opportunity to try to limit effort by restrictive licensing in 1979 while her share of the TAC was safe; transferable licences were introduced, and the Halibut Relocation Plan sought to reduce effort, especially of those vessels then being excluded from Alaska, in a variety of ways. These included 'buy-backs' or surrender arrangements for licences and halibut gear, grants for conversion to other fisheries (especially the underfished sablefish), and the denial of licences to part-timers, with compensation. Here again, as in the case of the Pacific salmon fishery (Fraser, 1977; Pearse and Wilen, 1979), buy-backs and exclusions largely failed, removing only 20% of the halibut capacity while fishing opportunities fell by 50%. In fact, after 1980, restrictions on licences were effectively relaxed (Pearse, 1981), and the fleet expanded such that by 1981 there were 422 vessels in the fishery, against less than 100 prior to 'limited entry'. As these vessels fished a Canadian quota in 1982 (5.4 million pounds weight, or 2.45 million kilograms) that was only 20% of the weight of landings a decade before, it is difficult to argue that management had achieved a great deal.

The problems with the fishery led to a number of investigations. In particular, Copes (1979–80) identified three problems with licensing. The first is an 'expectations trap', caused by the rise in value of the licences as expectations of future returns rise, making buy-backs very expensive (and causing their abandonment in the case of salmon). Secondly, a 'transitional gains' trap arises in that first-generation holders of licences gain the capital value of the fishery, whereas second generations have to buy and receive no net benefits: they may also be tempted to make excessive commitments by the apparent success of the first generation. Finally, 'capital stuffing', as identified by Fraser (1977) in salmon and earlier in this book, will mean that effective effort continues to rise. Such problems led Copes to agree with Sinclair (1978) that licences should not be transferable, but should expire on retirement, thus gradually reducing excess capacity. The validity of this conclusion is questionable, for non-transferability is likely to be the source of a different and probably worse set of problems, and certainly the later Pearse Commission was firmly in favour of transferability in this halibut fishery as well as others (Pearse, 1981).

More fundamentally, the visible failure of restrictive licensing in the halibut fishery, together with deteriorating economic prospects, produced a search for radical change. Taxation was considered but rejected as income-reducing and politically unpopular, and the discussion turned towards IFQs as property rights. The halibut seemed rather suitable for IFQs in fact: a potentially fairly steady catch, determinable in advance, and sold through limited channels, allowing any black markets to be identified. The IFQ system would avoid capital stuffing and possibly the expectations trap, but not however the transitional-gains trap, and would involve enforcement efforts (*see* Copes and Cook, 1982). In 1981, the Canadian government appointed the Pearse Commission on Pacific Fisheries Policy and its Final Report, *Turning the tide*, was forcefully in favour of the use of an IFQ system in the fishery. Pearse recommended that the existing licensing system be scrapped, and replaced by specific 'quantity licences', with explicit ten-year terms (Pearse, 1982, Chapter 10). A decision to implement these was announced in March 1982, and a Halibut Vessel Quota Implementation Committee was established to plan the introduction of the system. Events in 1983 however combined to delay its implementation (*see also* section 8.3.1).

8.2.4 Canadian fisheries: past lessons and new directions

One especially important lesson from the Canadian experience between 1976 and 1982 has been the recognition that sole ownership plus licensing does not in itself improve fisheries management substantially, maybe not at all. The fishing community found methods whereby, as individuals, they circumvented regulations even when they recognized that these were in everyone's best joint interests. After the declaration of 200-mile limits in 1977, a wave of optimism spread through Canadian fisheries, resulting in an overexpansion and overcapitalization of the fleet, permitted and even aided by Federal or provincial governments. As predicted earlier in this book, the conflict between private benefit and social cost was not removed simply by issuing licences, and economic rent was still eroded. Another problem identified was that, while it was often difficult to establish licensing in the face of opposition from fishermen, it became even more difficult to arrange for new entrants later when existing licence holders had realized the benefits of the system. Moreover, licensing did not solve the access allocation problem among competing domestic groups of users (for example, offshore versus inshore fleets). Finally, it was seen as producing a 'regulatory nightmare', with a myriad of regulations and administrators, and involving costs that fishermen perceived as largely 'waste'.

Yet probably the greatest single problem was, and remains, the issue of resolving operationally the conflicting biological, economic and social considerations in fisheries management. As outlined earlier, this problem has been epitomized in the case of one province in particular. Newfoundland has an important fishing industry, consisting mainly however of a vast fleet of small vessels, operated by summertime fishermen from coastal communities with low labour mobility and few occupational alternatives. With easy entry, effort has poured in, especially during times of overall economic hardship, for as Kirby (1983, p. 115) quotes from W. C. MacKenzie, 'fishermen are not poor because they are fishermen. They are fishermen because they are poor'. The fishermen's low incomes drew the provincial and Federal governments into subsidies, loans and grants to support the industry, thereby often compounding the problem in a vicious circle of decline. Moreover the processing plants based on the fleet are small, dispersed and inefficient, and little is spent on quality control in the industry, resulting in low prices for sales. No money is available for technological improvement or new product or marketing development.

The combination of these factors has proved almost insuperable, and despite the Fisheries minister's statement in 1981 that '. . . the fishery will never have the capacity to absorb Atlantic Canada's excess labour', labour absorption is a role in which it clearly has been used (Copes and Wood, 1982). Indeed, in the period *after* 1976 and the introduction of the new management regime, the numbers of licensed fishermen in Newfoundland increased from 15 300 to 35 000 in 1980 (about 95% inshore), and the numbers of processing plants increased from sixty-one in 1973 to 225 in

1981. Much of this increase was permitted or encouraged by the provincial government against the wishes of the Federal authorities, inshore fishermen being regarded as a 'special case', and the increase in plants was contrary to express Federal advice (*Fishing News International*, March 1981). Not surprisingly, CPUE and incomes have remained very low, producing a call by the province for higher prices, subsidized if necessary, possibly from offshore oil revenues. As Copes and Wood (1982, p. 229) commented, 'Open entry to the fishery has long been known to dissipate the rents that the industry could yield. In Newfoundland, the fishery may have the opportunity as well to dissipate the rents of the oil industry!'

Some ground was gained in 1980, when the Federal government by means of subsidies and grants supported a move out onto the now available offshore stocks and reached agreement on limiting entry. Yet the basic problems remained, and disputes between factions at all levels became worse. By late 1981, the east-coast industry was approaching a state of collapse, and rather than simply bale it out again as it had done in 1974–76, the Federal government elected to undertake a thorough review on lines similar to those of the Pearse Commission's work on the west coast.

The review was conducted by the Kirby Task Force with terms of reference 'to achieve and maintain a viable Atlantic fishing industry, with due consideration for the overall economic and social development of the Atlantic provinces' (Kirby, 1982). After much consultation the Task Force committed itself to a priority ranking that sought an economically viable industry first, employment maximization second, and 'Canadianization' of the entire industry as a third objective. Its coverage was very wide, and it made some fifty-seven separate recommendations. In broadest terms, its proposals involve using the level of Federal financial aid to force change on a conservative industry. These changes cover reduction of effort, improvement of incomes, reduction and reorganization of processing facilities, the introduction of an auction system to curb the power of some monopsonistic buyers, the encouragement of more cooperative marketing efforts and, in particular, a substantial drive to improve the quality of production throughout the whole fish industry.

Of particular interest here are the recommendations concerning management, which are related to the far-reaching recommendations of the earlier Pearse Commission (Pearse, 1981). Pearse strongly advocated an IFQ system, calling for 'quantity licensing' of fishermen (except for the salmon and herring-roe fisheries), with many of the features advocated earlier in this book. Indeed, Canadian economists had been proposing such systems for several years (*see* Moloney and Pearse, 1979; Pearse, 1980; Scott and Neher, 1982), although others had expressed misgivings (*see* Olson; comment on Mitchell, 1981). The Pearse plan included an initial allocation to established fishermen of rights to a proportion of the TAC, with a licence to last for ten years and to be transferable. One-tenth of the TAC would be available each year for new entrants on a competitive bidding basis, bid for in terms of dollars per unit of quota. Individuals might ultimately buy any total quantity of IFQs, up to 5% of the TAC in major fisheries and 15% in others. These arrangements would be backed up by a royalty system on each fisherman's licensed quota landings, set at about 5–10% of landed value. The system would be administered by a Pacific Fisheries Licensing Board. Although by the time Kirby reported, few if any of these recommendations had been brought into effect (*see* section 8.2.3 above), clearly the arguments had been convincing. Recommendation 7 of Kirby advocated the institution of a licence as a 'quasi-property right', called a 'quota licence' or 'enterprise allocation'. Like Pearse, the Task Force found the arguments in favour of these sufficiently compelling, Pearse having stressed an amalgam of the ability to limit overcapacity, control the total catch, and improve economic welfare and security for fishermen. These controls would be combined with a lesser regulatory framework involving mainly simple administrative tasks, and which would offer various opportunities to raise revenues and secure change without disruption (Pearse, 1981, Ch. 7). Likewise, the associated IFQ problems of generating the required quantity of information, establishing separate quotas for each fishery, and later adjusting of the quotas, seemed not insuperable. However, Kirby felt that its application to the inshore industry, with up to 8000 craft of under 35 ft (about 11 metres) in length, would be very difficult, although it should be possible for larger boats by 1984, and gradually be extended to the smaller ones in the mid 1980s. Kirby also digressed into arguing an alternative case for an 'effort-related' licence, effectively trying to control capacity rather than landings. In view of the obvious deficiencies of such a system—which Kirby itself identifies (Kirby, 1982, pp. 79–80)—this is perhaps surprising, although the report cites the success of such schemes in the lobster, crab and scallop fisheries. Perhaps the truth is that 'effort licensing', although a second-best approach, might be more feasible and acceptable in the short run than quota licensing. In any case, Kirby went along with Pearse in recommending transferability (but not between inshore and offshore sectors), with a 'quota exchange' in each port.

The Kirby Report, like Pearse, contains a very interesting review of the practical desirability and problems of an IFQ system (Ch. 10). However, its recommendations do not include two issues widely discussed elsewhere in Canada. First, the Levelton Study, apart from confirming the need for limited entry and gear control, advocated that resource users should have more voice in licensing matters, and that policies should discriminate positively in favour of full-time fishermen. While accepting the latter (Recommendation 6), the former is implicitly rejected by Kirby, for its 'Licensing Review Body' organizing the quota or effort licensing system would be staffed from outside the industry, albeit operating in public. Secondly, the Sinclair Report (1978) on the British Columbian fisheries and the subsequent Pearse Commission both advocated a royalty system to gain for the nation some part of the benefits of improved management; Pearse in fact suggested that such a scheme might yield a royalty of C$15 million annually out of a net economic annual gain overall of $100 million as fleet capacity was reduced. The Kirby Report makes no recommendations on royalties, perhaps having been influenced by the many criticisms made of the proposals: McGaw (1979) calculated that royalties would have to be so high they would be politically unacceptable, and others have continued to argue that resource rents should be enjoyed by resource users, rather than 'owners', either as profits or employment opportunities (e.g. *World Fishing,* April 1982).

To date, little of Pearse and none of Kirby has been implemented. Kirby in fact planned a programme over 1983–85 but foresaw the possibility of his Report being pigeon-holed, and in his final sections pointed out the foolishness of neglecting the real problems. Elsewhere there was even some talk of nationalization to enforce rationalization. It is also worth reflecting finally that Newfoundland's problems, specifically, may reflect a situation where the local definition of 'best use' has a very strong social input, and perhaps a viable case can be made for setting effort at a level higher than might otherwise be optimal, and taking at least some of the rent from the fishery as employment opportunities in fishing and associated industries. Overall, there can be no doubt that the future of Canadian fisheries management lies in the direction of property rights systems based on some form of IFQ. The introduction of these will not be easy, for not only are there political and legal barriers, but the Canadian fisheries are so diverse in the nature of their enterprises, vessels and fisheries that no quick panacea exists to solve all the problems simultaneously.

Since 1970, Canadian fisheries have passed through the initial phases of a period of remarkable transition, and although this is not yet complete, the main framework for the future is becoming apparent. The inputs to this have been biological, economic and social—and political too, as Scott and Neher (1982) gently remind the decision-takers in their 1982 Report: 'Efficient management will be not only its own reward to industry participants, but will be rewarded at the polls as the fishery switches from being a net burden to becoming a net contribution to the Canadian economy. Husbandry, not patronage, will command the political premium.' At present, the discussion and implementation of proposals in the Pearse Commission and Kirby Task Force Reports will take some time, and meanwhile the often painful and disputatious transition period continues.

8.3 UNITED STATES OF AMERICA

The principal feature of U.S. fisheries policy, certainly to 1966, probably to 1976 and perhaps beyond, has been the dominance of fisheries management by the coastal states. Until recently, the Federal government, via the Bureau of Fisheries in its various forms,* played essentially an

*The Bureau of Fisheries was originally established in 1871 as the Commission on Fish and Fisheries. In 1903 it was renamed the Bureau, and in 1940 became part of the Fish and Wildlife Service. In 1956, two separate bureaux were established within the FWS: the Bureau of Sport Fisheries and the Bureau of Commercial Fisheries. The last reorganization occurred in 1970 when the Bureau of Commercial Fisheries became part of the National Marine Fisheries Service.

advisory role. That there was a fishery management problem was recognized quite quickly; for instance, at least as early as 1921 the Bureau of Fisheries warned of the need for conservation and scientific studies, and of the dangers posed by pollution. For the most part however, coastal states appear to have found it politically advantageous to intervene in commercial fisheries as little as possible, which has often meant not at all. The Bureau ably fulfilled its principal task of studying fisheries and offering advice on their management, but on the whole this advice was ignored. In such a situation, the Bureau's second main function of restocking via the distribution of eggs, fry and adult fish could hardly have been expected to have much lasting impact.

In the international fisheries arena, by contrast, the United States was much more productive. To give but two examples, in 1911 she took part in the remarkable International Fur Seal Convention, whereby the United States and Russia persuaded Canada and Japan not to hunt seals at sea in return for a share of the harvest taken on American and Russian territory. In 1923, the United States and Canada reached agreement on the joint management of the Pacific halibut fishery. Whatever its shortcomings, it is fairly clear that this management prevented the obliteration of the fishery.

Although the Federal government was not directly involved in fisheries management, a number of relevant Federal Acts were nonetheless implemented. For instance, in 1936 the government launched the Fishing Vessel Obligation Guarantee Program, which aimed (and still aims) to provide long-term debt financing for fishermen, who because of the risky nature of their business would otherwise find it difficult (and/or expensive) to obtain long-term loans. Under the scheme, the Federal government underwrites fifteen- to twenty-five-year loans contracted in the private loan market and representing up to 87.5% of the cost of vessel construction. In 1981, around $27 million was so guaranteed, with the total outstanding then being approximately $200 million. In 1954, the Saltonstall–Kennedy Act was passed, which provided that 30% of customs duties collected on fisheries products should be used for research and marketing support of domestic fishermen.

In the period since the Second World War, developments outside the United States have been significant for U.S. fisheries policy. The most important has been the widespread adoption of extended fisheries limits. For many years, the United States was opposed to such an extension. In 1953, the Submerged Lands Act affirmed the fishery management rights of coastal states within three miles of the shore. However as more and more countries adopted twelve-mile limits, the United States was bound to do likewise and in 1966 passed the Exclusive Fisheries Zone Act. Importantly, under this Act the Federal government took responsibility for fisheries management within the three- to twelve-mile zone, a precedent that perhaps laid the path for the great increase in Federal influence that came in 1976 with the Fishery Conservation and Management Act. One point of interest is that while implicitly acknowledging the rights of other states to extended jurisdiction, the United States has steadfastly refused to accept that such extension applies to tuna, and indeed has encouraged

American fishermen to fish for tuna in disputed waters. Coastal states have responded by seizing U.S. fishing vessels, which led the Federal government to establish in 1969 the Fishermen's Guarantee Fund Program, whereby owners would be refunded the value of vessels seized and fines paid. In 1981, forty claims were paid, totalling around $2.3 million.

Of more importance for the long-term development of fisheries policy, in June 1966 the Stratton Commission was established to investigate, *inter alia*, U.S. fisheries management. This Commission was critical of fisheries mangement, not only for rather typical problems such as a lack of specific aims, a failure to deal with economic as well as biological problems and a need to reduce effort while modernizing the fishing fleet, but also for the relative failure to define Federal and state roles and develop programmes based on inter-state cooperation. The Commission argued that the Bureau of Commercial Fisheries should increase analytical studies of fisheries and take over the management of species that migrate inter-state. On the institutional side, the Commission recommended the establishment of the National Oceanographic and Atmospheric Administration (NOAA), incorporating the new National Marine Fisheries Service (NMFS), and these came into being in 1970. During the 1970s, as more and more countries demonstrated support for the idea of 200-mile EEZs, the United States was eventually forced to follow the same course, and in 1976 the Fishery Conservation and Mangement Act heralded the beginning of a new era in U.S. fisheries management.

Before discussing this Act in detail, we shall briefly consider the industrial context within which policy has been conducted. As with Canada, the west-coast fisheries are an important source of high-unit-value species, notably salmon, tuna and crab, while the east coast is dominated by industrial fisheries, especially menhaden. Though contributing only a small amount to GNP, the industry is very important to certain regions such as Alaska, where in 1980 it accounted for approximately 13% of gross product (Anderson, 1982, p. 150). The structure of both the catching and onshore sectors is highly fragmented and industrial concentration is low. It is reported that in 1974 there were 86000 U.S. boats engaged in fishing, 80% of which were individually owned; and of the 3534 processing and wholesaling establishments, 42% had annual sales of less than $1 million (Sullivan and Heggelund, 1979, p. 16). It is however the changes that have taken place within the industry that are of relevance in the present chapter. Over the period 1950–75, the total U.S. catch of fish and shellfish stayed fairly constant at an average annual level of about 5 billion pounds (2.27 billion kilograms) (Anderson, 1982, p. 151). The important development, though, was that up to the mid 1970s there was an expansion of foreign fishing effort off the U.S. coast and increased dependence of the domestic seafood industry on imported raw material, mainly from Japan and Canada. From 1975 to 1980 however, the domestic catch has increased by about one-third while the foreign catch in the area has fallen (Anderson, 1982). It is generally accepted that this trend reversal owes a great deal to the impact of the Fishery Conservation and Management Act, to which we shall now turn.

8.3.1 The Fishery Conservation and Management Act 1976

The Fishery Conservation and Management Act 1976 (Public Law 94–265) came into force on 1 March 1977. It established a U.S. 200-mile Fishery Conservation Zone (FCZ) within which the United States has exclusive jurisdiction over all fish stocks, with the specific exception of tuna, possibly in the hope of protecting U.S. tuna fishermen operating inside other countries' 200-mile limits. It might be noted however that the United States' continuing argument that tuna must be managed internationally has not stopped the government from enacting a seasonal ban (1 June to 30 November) on foreign long lining on the eastern coast. This ban is intended to protect U.S. commercial and recreational swordfish fishermen. An important effect however is to ban Japanese tuna long liners. Prior to the closed season, gear conflicts between U.S. and foreign fishermen had reached serious levels, with for example U.S. fishermen towing away Japanese gear.

The heart of the Fishery Conservation and Management Act is the goal of the optimum yield (OY), defined as that giving 'the greatest overall benefit to the nation with particular reference to food production and recreational opportunities', and based upon MSY 'as modified by any relevant economic, social or ecological factor'. While the Federal government, in the form of the Secretary of Commerce, takes overall control of fishery management within the FCZ, the Fishery Conservation and Management Act established eight Regional Fishery Management Councils (RFMCs) whose role is to propose and implement fishery management plans (FMPs) for their areas. (The eight RFMCs are: (i) New England, (ii) Mid-Atlantic, (iii) South Atlantic, (iv) Gulf, (v) Caribbean, (vi) Pacific, (vii) West Pacific and (viii) North Pacific.) Any plan developed by an RFMC must be submitted to the Secretary of Commerce for approval, partial approval, or disapproval, essentially on the basis of seven national standards for fisheries management laid down by the Fishery Conservation and Management Act. Guidelines for the operation of these standards are issued periodically by the Secretary of Commerce.

Standard 1 states that management shall prevent overfishing while achieving, on a continuing basis, the optimum yield from each fishery. As we have already seen, the definition of OY is rather vague, and in any case its interpretation is left to the RFMCs in their fishery management plans, subject to Secretary of Commerce approval. Notwithstanding this vagueness however, it seems clear that OY is intended to be sustainable. Also, since overfishing appears to be interpreted as that beyond MSY, and is specifically to be avoided, it seems that OY cannot be a quantity greater than MSY. Hence, dynamic maximum economic yield (*see* Chapter 4) looks unlikely to play an important role in U.S. fisheries management.

Standard 2 states that management must be based on the best scientific information available, Standard 3 that individual fish stocks should be managed as units, and Standard 4 that management measures must not discriminate between the residents of different states.

Standard 5 says that management should promote efficiency in the utilization of fishery resources, except that no measure shall have economic allocation as its sole purpose. This is a rather strange standard. Clearly, the promotion of efficiency is vitally important since it is widely accepted that most of the benefits of fisheries management occur in the form of resource savings, rather than increased fish output. However if we accept that the fundamental problem in unregulated fisheries is economic (viz. open access), it seems strange to require that no measure be solely economically orientated. This requirement appears to mean that other management problems, such as biological ones, must emerge before management may proceed, though this may be to misinterpret the standard.

Standard 6 requires that allowance be made for unpredictable events, such as environmental fluctuations; and Standard 7 that management measures must where possible minimize costs and unnecessary duplication.

Recently, the guidelines issued by the Secretary of Commerce for the operation of these standards have been updated. Some reconsideration was given to the definition of OY, the principal effect being to lengthen the list of factors that might be taken into account by an RFMC. The major changes refer to Standards 6 and 7. With respect to the former, it was found in practice that obtaining approval of and implementing fishery management plans was such a lengthy process that rapid alterations in response to, say, environmental fluctuations were ruled out. In an attempt to avoid this problem, 'framework FMPs' have been introduced wherein the Secretary of Commerce, generally represented by the Regional Director of NMFS, may make certain, defined changes to the FMP at short notice. Two basic types of change may be made. The first is 'field orders', which are changes to be implemented once a predefined state is reached; for example, the fishery may be closed once the TAC is taken. More important is the 'regulatory amendment', which may be used to respond to unforeseen events. Of course, any measures must conform to the Fishery Conservation and Management Act and the aims of the FMP.

The alterations made to the interpretation of Standard 7 arise from a change in philosophy associated with the Reagan administration. The concern now is to reduce Federal regulation as far as possible. A number of criteria have been proposed to decide whether management is required and to what extent. These include the importance of the fishery to the nation, the condition of the stocks, the economic condition of the fishery and the costs and benefits of an FMP. More importantly, in practice, all FMPs must now be cleared by the Federal Office of Management and Budget (OMB), which has to go over any proposed plans in detail to ensure that they are in the best interests of the private sector. Obtaining OMB clearance has not always proved straightforward. On the Atlantic coast, for instance, the OMB blocked the implementation of a new plan for the squid/mackerel/butterfish fisheries. The RFMCs involved argued that there was a clear need for an integrated plan since the fisheries were both biologically and economically interdependent. The foreign fishing nations interested in the fisheries objected however, and made representations to the OMB. These were successful because the OMB felt that the U.S. fleet could not take the catch allocated to it, and it did not want to be seen to establish trade barriers in a fishery with little domestic appeal.

The OMB was also active in the Pacific halibut fishery. The Pacific RFMC had voted in favour of a moratorium closing further entry into the fishery for a three-year period. This was seen as both a first step towards limited entry and a breathing space within which future management might be discussed. Fishermen were divided in their views on the need for the moratorium, but those against made forceful representations to the OMB. Eventually, two days before the season was due to open, the OMB blocked the moratorium on the grounds that it 'interferes with basic liberties, especially to the extent that the terms conflicted with the traditions and work patterns of individuals employed in the fishing business' (letter from the OMB to the National Oceanographic and Atmospheric Administration quoted in *National Fisherman*, August 1983, p. 12). The OMB further stated that it was not against limited entry, *per se*, but did not believe that the plan would 'resolve the excess investment problem without creating additional economic problems' (ibid.).

Needless to say, in both the above cases the RFMCs concerned feel that the OMB has exceeded its duty. More importantly, they feel that this kind of Federal intervention undermines the intention of the Fishery Conservation and Management Act, which was to give fishery management control to the RFMCs. It appears likely that some kind of congressional move will be undertaken in an attempt to reduce the influence of the OMB and to assert the authority of the RFMCs.

8.3.2 Regional Fishery Management Councils

RFMCs vary in size depending on the number of states that they represent, the smallest being the Caribbean with seven voting members and the largest the Mid-Atlantic with nineteen. On each RFMC the first voting member is the relevant Regional Director of the National Marine Fisheries Service. Secondly, the principal official with marine fisheries management responsibility and expertise from each state is a voting member. Thirdly, there is one so-called obligatory member per state, who is selected by the Secretary of Commerce from a list of 'qualified individuals' submitted by each state governor. Finally, there are so-called at-large members, selected in the same way as the obligatory members and equal in number, but who are not necessarily chosen on a one-per-state basis. A qualified individual is defined as one 'knowledgeable or experienced with regard to the management, conservation, or recreational or commercial harvest of the fishery resources of the geographical area concerned'.

Each RFMC is required to appoint a Scientific and Statistical Committee, and may appoint advisory panels to assist it in its fishery management duties. For self-evident reasons, such assistance is usually sought from as broad a variety of individuals as possible, representing such diverse areas as the industry, consumers, Federal and state government, and academic institutions. While such an approach has the benefit of obtaining a wide range of views, it is clearly at the potential cost of some degree of conflict. In any trade-offs that may then occur, the question must be asked in what sense the yield that emerges is 'optimal'. On the other hand, whether there is any better approach seems somewhat doubtful, and it is true that the Secretary of Commerce commands the right of veto over any proposed measures that he or she considers suboptimal.

The principal task of each RFMC is to develop FMPs for those fisheries identified as being in need of management. Each FMP proposed by a RFMC for approval by the Secretary of Commerce must contain a number of items. First, there must be a description of the fishery including such information as the number of vessels involved, the kinds and quantities of fishing gear used, the position of recreational fishermen and so on. Secondly there must be an assessment of the present and likely future condition of the fishery, including MSY and OY. Thirdly, proposed conservation and management measures applicable to both U.S. and foreign fishermen must be included. Finally, an assessment of the U.S. harvesting capacity must be made so as to determine the proportion of the OY that may be made available to foreign fishermen.

In addition to the above, the FMP may contain other provisions, such as the designation of closed seasons, catch quotas, the establishment of limited-access systems and a proposed schedule of fees. It should be noted however that RFMCs have no regulatory authority of their own. They merely propose regulations to the Secretary of Commerce, who approves them or not. Any enforcement is then undertaken by the coastguard. One hopes that the revised system of framework FMPs will prove flexible enough to allow for short-term management measures to be introduced should any fishery run into real difficulties. The RFMCs also have their hands tied in the fees that they can recommend for U.S. fishermen since the FCMA provides that domestic fees must not exceed the administrative costs of issuing permits. This provision means that effort regulation by economic disincentives, such as taxation, is ruled out. It also means that any economic rent produced by the management of a fishery will go to the fishermen themselves, which may or may not be optimal depending upon one's value judgements.

8.3.3 Foreign fishing after the Fishery Conservation and Management Act

The approach taken to foreign fishing has altered quite markedly over the relatively short life of the Fishery Conservation and Management Act. Initially, the policy was almost one of benevolence. In accordance with the principle laid down by UNCLOS III, any part of OY that could not be harvested by U.S. fishermen was made available to foreign fishermen. Fees were charged for fishing rights, but these were kept at quite low levels, being limited to a landings tax equivalent to $3\frac{1}{2}$% of the ex-vessel value of the catch, plus a nominal permit fee. The main reason for this approach to foreign fishing seems to have been a belief that U.S. fishermen would quickly displace foreigners in U.S. FCZs. In fact however, while they have done so on the eastern seaboard, the same thing has not happened on the west coast and Stokes (1981a) suggests that there is little possibility of its occurring under present economic conditions. Consequently Japanese and Eastern-bloc fishermen are likely to continue to play an important role in the exploitation of these fisheries.

Possibly as a result of this realization, U.S. fisheries policy with respect to foreign fishing has become much tougher. In 1979 a surcharge of up to 20% of each foreign nation's permit and poundage fee was introduced. The revenue has been used to capitalize a Fishing Vessel and Gear Damage Compensation Fund for U.S. fishermen operating in the U.S. FCZs whose vessels are lost or damaged as a result of the activities of foreign vessels; or whose fishing gear is damaged or lost because of domestic or foreign vessels or 'Acts of God'.

In 1980 the American Fisheries Promotion Act (Public Law 96–561) was passed. This amended the Fishery Conservation and Management Act in numerous ways, particularly regarding foreign fishing. A number of criteria were established for determining foreign allocations, including such factors as the elimination of tariff and non-tariff trade barriers; the increase in purchases of U.S. fish or fishery products; cooperation in enforcement and so on. The Act also amended the fee structure relating to foreign fishermen. The original method of calculating the poundage fee was abandoned, and instead the target fee total was determined as the fraction of the total catch made by foreigners multiplied by the cost to the U.S. government of administering the FCZ. For example, if foreigners caught half the total catch and total cost was $1000, then the target fee level would be $500. The vessel permit fee has been standardized at $50 per vessel. Foreign boat owners must also reimburse the U.S. government the full cost of employing observers. The total of the four types of fee has increased significantly, from $7.1 million to a target of at least $43 million in 1983.

More recently it has been decided that there should no longer be any requirement that fish resources not harvested by the United States must be allocated to foreign fishermen. Also, only 50% of the country's allocation is released at the beginning of the season. The remainder is made available only if the Secretary of State determines that the country is cooperating with U.S. fisheries policy. Finally, there are moves to try to eliminate all foreign fishing by 1985, but, as we mentioned above, they look extremely unlikely to succeed in the case of Pacific-coast fisheries, especially for Alaskan pollack, where foreign fishermen account for a large proportion of the catch.

8.3.4 The Gulf of Alaska groundfish fishery

This section, an example of the Fishery Conservation and Management Act in action, is based principally on work by Larkins (1980), who presents an excellent and detailed description of the process by which a fishery management plan is formulated.

At its first meeting late in 1976, the North Pacific RFMC decided that the Gulf of Alaska groundfish fishery was in need of management, and a plan development team was established with a view to producing a management plan for the 1978 season. The composition of the development team perhaps gave some indication of the kind of plan that was likely to emerge, comprising as it did four biologists, a fisheries administrator and an economist.

The fishery was, and is, dominated by foreign fishing interests, and given this domination the team felt that two alternative strategies were feasible under the Fishery Conservation and Management Act. Either management could be aimed at developing a significant U.S. groundfish fishery or it could be aimed at rebuilding the stocks of Pacific halibut. Pursuit of both aims simultaneously was not possible because the development of a U.S. groundfish fishery would almost certainly imply large by-catches of juvenile halibut, thereby keeping halibut stocks in their depressed state. In the end, the Council chose to attempt to rebuild halibut stocks first, although the actual management of such stocks remained under the control of the International Pacific Halibut Commission.

The first problem faced by the plan development team (PDT) was to determine the optimum yield for each of the nine species under management. Eventually, in an attempt to allow for environmental fluctuations, variations in year class strength and perceived data deficiencies, it was decided to set the acceptable biological catch at the low end of the MSY range for so-called healthy stocks (that is, those where the current population size was at or above that required for MSY), and at less than the current sustainable yield for 'depleted' stocks. This acceptable biological catch then had to be modified by socioeconomic factors to determine the optimum yield. The development team felt however that such modification was required for only three out of the nine species being managed. By implication therefore, it was felt that in six cases the biological optimum was, in fact, the *optimum optimorum*.

Even for the three species where some adjustment was made, the approach seems to have been rather arbitrary. In the case of the (depleted) Pacific Ocean perch fishery, OY was set midway between no catch and the current sustainable yield, in an attempt to balance the desirable rapid stock rebuilding with the undesirable dislocation of foreign fishing fleets. In the (depleted) sablefish fishery, it was felt that there was great potential for U.S. expansion and it was consequently decided to set the OY well below current sustainable yield so as to move the fishery to MSY as rapidly as possible. An additional consideration was that to do so would tend to raise the average size of fish caught, which was considered beneficial because of the large difference in ex-vessel prices realized by large and small fish. In the case of the (healthy) flounder stocks, it was decided to set OY at half MSY in an attempt to protect the halibut, which intermingle with the other species.

Having established the OY for each species, the PDT then had to decide how much of this would be taken by U.S. fishermen, any remainder then being available for foreign fishermen. The decision appears to have been a very difficult one. An upper catch limit was established by estimating the physical catching capacity of the U.S. fleet. It was thought unlikely however that the actual catch would be anything like as large. Consequently, the team decided to ask the processors what they intended to purchase during the year, on the grounds that fishermen would catch only what the processors were prepared to purchase. Presumably such an assumption is justified by local conditions. The method does seem somewhat limited, however, in that it appears to ignore the role of price as a market-clearer. Probably, the best that could be expected would be an indication of what processors would be prepared to purchase at a certain price (or prices). However since the supply of fish will interact with this in determining the actual price and the quantity bought and sold, it seems somewhat naïve simply to ask processors what they intend to buy. Certainly, the plan development team itself appears to have had little confidence in its estimate of U.S. capacity since it then went on to propose a reserve fund equivalent to 30% of the OY. Should the actual U.S. catch then have turned out to be greater than anticipated, the reserve fund (or part of it) would have been allocated to U.S. fishermen. Otherwise, once it became apparent that the U.S. allocation was sufficient, the reserve fund would have been allocated to foreign fishermen. Quite clearly however, the estimation of domestic capacity represents a very problematical area.

A number of more minor management measures were also proposed. Most of these had to do with avoiding incidental halibut catch, but a couple were of more general interest. First, foreign trawling was banned near major domestic ports to prevent conflicts between U.S. and foreign gear. Secondly, the TAC was apportioned into five management areas, so as to prevent localized depletion of fish stocks.

A fisheries management plan based on the above was then proposed to the Secretary of Commerce, and was reviewed. Two major alterations were made. First, because sablefish was very important to Japanese fishermen, the TAC was increased from 10 000 tonnes to 13 000 tonnes. Secondly, it was felt that the reserve fund was too great at 30% of OY and it was subsequently reduced to 20%.

The plan, as implemented, represented a brave attempt to deal with the severe problems of practical fisheries management. At the same time however, the flavour of the management regime remains distinctly biological. In these circumstances, it is difficult to disagree with Stokes (1981b, p. 284) when he complains that 'the multiple-objective framework has not yet significantly affected the thinking of . . . many council members and management biologists who have the authority to make real decisions'.

8.3.5 U.S. fisheries policy—the future

Since the advent of 200-mile limits, U.S. fisheries policy has probably become more dynamic than at any stage in its history. The philosophy of the Reagan administration is that government influence in the economy should be substantially reduced. Hence there is every reason to expect further changes in fisheries policy. The U.S. government attitude generally

…ry should stand on its own two feet, and proposals have … made that expenditure on fisheries management should be …ased. Assuming however that there is no prospect of returning … fisheries entirely to the *laissez-faire* arena, the institution of …f property right system appears to accord with both prevailing …l economic opinion. We would anticipate, therefore, that U.S. … …nagement policy will take this road in the fairly near future.

8.4 UNITED KINGDOM

The broad objective of British government fisheries policy has consistently been that of economic viability for its domestic fishing industry. Explicit statements of this aim have sometimes been qualified with remarks such as 'having regard to the requirements of consumers' (OECD, 1982) or 'while maintaining a balance between the level of fishing activity and the need for conservation of stocks' (OECD, 1983). Recent years have also seen a preoccupation with the problem of obtaining a satisfactory deal for the United Kingdom from the Common Fisheries Policy negotiations. Unfortunately the goal of economic viability for the industry has proved elusive, a fact that probably explains why successive administrations have persisted with the same objective for so long. In this section we shall look at the means by which fisheries policy has been pursued, how successful it has been and the direction in which policy is likely to be heading in future.

To set the scene however, an overview of policy development is called for. As a generalization it could be said that the targets of British fisheries policy have altered less than the instruments used to reach them, the reason being that since the Second World War the underlying causes of the problems facing the fishing industry have changed, and hence different remedies have been warranted. In the 1950s and 1960s the requirements were seen as improved industrial performance through the maintenance of a technically efficient fleet, backed up by appropriate research and development. The government's role in this was the provision of an appropriate institutional framework and, crucially, financial support. At a time when a higher proportion of the British fleet was operating in international waters, and stock depletion was in general less of a problem than it was eventually to become, it could be argued that the government had little reason to regard national conservation measures as essential to the economics of the British fishing industry. This attitude was to change, however, during the 1970s. Loss of access by British vessels to traditional distant-water grounds, and increased pressure on stocks nearer to home, forced the government to consider ways in which it could improve the fishing opportunities that its domestic fleet appeared to be rapidly losing. Accordingly, much greater emphasis was placed upon such issues as jurisdiction, conservation and regulation than there had previously been.

Before we look in detail at the main elements of policy, financial support and resource management, it is useful to sketch in the recent changes that have taken place in the British fishing industry in order to clarify some of the problems to which the government has tried to respond. Total landings in the United Kingdom of all fish caught by British vessels reached a peak of just over 1 million tonnes in 1973 but fell in the following two years, largely owing to the exclusion of British distant-water vessels from Icelandic waters. From 1975 to 1978 total landings showed a recovery thanks to a rise in the quantity of certain pelagic species, but have remained on a downward trend since. Within the total there has been an important change in species composition. Loss of access to distant waters has been accompanied by a severe absolute decline in landings in the United Kingdom of certain demersal species, notably cod and haddock, which had hitherto been of very great importance to both the catching and processing sectors. (To some extent the shortfall suffered by the onshore sector was made up by increased imports, especially after 1976.) The growing importance of pelagic species owes much to the development of the western mackerel fishery, the exploitation of which was partly brought about by those vessels which had previously fished in distant waters. In the late 1970s increased landings of mackerel easily offset the fall in landings of herring, which had traditionally been Britain's most important pelagic species. Since 1979 however, landings of mackerel by British boats have declined, and supplies of other species have not risen sufficiently to prevent a fall in total landings from 954 000 tonnes in 1979 to 775 000 in 1982.

These changes have brought about concomitant movements in the structure of the fleet, the relative importance of various fishing ports and the pattern of fish consumption. The necessary adjustments, by processors as well as catchers, have proved difficult. Government policy has to some extent been directed towards helping overcome these and other problems suffered by firms, such as fuel cost inflation. In addition however, the government has tried to anticipate the *potential* problems that the events of recent years still hold in store, as well as endeavouring to create what it considers to be a suitable environment in which fishing can be conducted.

8.4.1 Industrial performance and financial support

The British fishing industry has received financial support from the government for over thirty years. There have been three main forms of support: operating subsidies; aid to capital investment; and support for research and development. The relative importance of each of these has altered over the years, and a résumé is given below. It should also be mentioned that since joining the EEC the industry has received financial support from FEOGA (Fonds Européen d'Orientation et Garantie Agricole), notably in the form of payments to producer organizations for market regulation, grants for the construction and modernization of inshore vessels, and assistance towards the development of aquaculture and certain onshore projects.

The initial purpose of operating subsidies was to offset the persistent losses incurred by many fishing firms in the late 1940s, following a period of relative prosperity immediately after the Second World War. In 1950 the government offered a subsidy on white fish landed by the middle, near and inshore sections of the fleet. In 1957 the scheme was extended to the herring fleet and in 1962 to distant-water vessels, defined as those over 140 ft (43m) in length. When it became apparent that the subsidies had failed to restore the profitability of the industry, it was decided to continue with them for another ten years. To impress upon fishermen that the government did not intend to grant subsidies in perpetuity, the revised plan made it clear that they would be phased out over the ten-year period. By the early 1970s it seemed as though this aim was going to be fulfilled, and in 1974 operating subsidies were discontinued. (They were, in any event, contrary to the rules of the EEC, which the United Kingdom joined in 1973.) The year 1974 represents what might be termed the last financially 'good' year for the British fishing industry and, as explained in Chapter 5, economic conditions worsened thereafter. To help cope with the exceptional rise in oil costs, a temporary subsidy of £8.7 million was paid in 1975. In 1979 the government made another 'exceptional' payment to deep-sea operators to mitigate the effects of reduced fishing opportunities and rising costs, and in every year since then aid has been given. At the time of writing however, there is considerable pressure within the EEC on member countries to discontinue what are, in effect, operating subsidies, and it seems likely that after 1983 the British government will be severely limited in the ways in which it can support the industry.

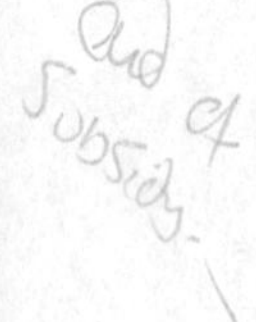

Aid for capital investment was started in the early 1950s by way of grants and loans for building new vessels. Initially these applied only to vessels of under 140 ft but were extended in 1962 to cover the distant-water fleet. Vessel improvement, harbour repair and the establishment of onshore installations also attracted financial support. The main purpose of grants and loans, at least originally, was not to enlarge overall tonnage of the fleet but to raise its efficiency through modernization. Grants and loans have been administered by the two statutory bodies, the White Fish Authority and the Herring Industry Board (now combined as the Sea Fish Industry Authority), and the Highlands and Islands Development Board.

Fisheries R & D has been conducted by several different bodies in the United Kingdom and has covered a wide area. Biological research such as stock assessment has been carried out by government fisheries laboratories, and in addition there has been research on underutilized species where consideration has been given to the problems of processing and product development, as well as raw-material availability. Other relevant areas have included marine fish farming, gear technology and fishing methods. The intended beneficiaries of this research effort, the fishing firms, have made an indirect contribution to its total cost through levies paid to the White Fish Authority and the Herring Industry Board which, along with the Ministries, have carried out much of the work. The bulk of R & D finance has been provided by the government however, and throughout the 1970s the amount of public money devoted to fisheries R & D has represented about 4–4½% of the gross value of fish landings (Fisheries Research and Development Board, 1978, p. 2).

Total aid given by the British government to the catching sector of the industry over the period 1978–81 has amounted to £89 million, with a steep escalation in support occurring during 1980 and 1981 (*Agra Europe*, 1981, p. 112). This, it should be stressed, is separate from any monies received from the EEC. Between 1971 and 1977, 240 individual projects in the United Kingdom received financial help from FEOGA, the total amount given being more than three times that given to any other EEC country's fishing industry (OECD, 1981, p. 159).*

8.4.2 Resource management

British laws on fisheries, and the changes in the law that have taken place over the past fifteen years or so, have reflected an increasing awareness by the government of the need to regulate fisheries. Since 1967 there have been four Acts of Parliament in particular which have had, and continue to have, an important influence on fishing. A brief summary of their main provisions is given below.

(a) The Sea Fish (Conservation) Act 1967 consolidates the existing law which provides for the regulation of sea fisheries, the landing and use of commercial fish, and the authorization of measures for the increase and improvement of fish stocks. Specifically it authorizes the issue of orders prohibiting the sale of undersized fish, prescribing minimum mesh sizes, prohibiting the landing of fish from certain sea areas, and regulating the landing of foreign-caught fish. It also makes provision for the implementation of internationally agreed measures for conserving stocks, and gives the relevant minister power to regulate salmon fishing at sea.

(b) The Sea Fisheries (Shellfish) Act 1967 also consolidates existing legislation, though as its title suggests, it deals specifically with shellfisheries. It provides for the establishment, improvement and management of crustacean and molluscan fisheries, and the control of depositing shellfish. One especially notable feature of the Act is that it empowers the minister to confer *several* rights.†

(c) The Fishery Limits Act 1976 provides for the extension of the United Kingdom's fishing limits to 200 miles, and the further regulation of sea fishing by foreign as well as British vessels.

*This should not be taken to mean that the British fishing industry is more heavily subsidized than others in the Common Market. Though the published figures do suggest that British fishermen receive relatively generous treatment from the national government and FEOGA, there is little doubt that some other EEC states give hidden aid to their own fishermen, notably in the form of fuel subsidies. It is therefore difficult to assess the true extent of subsidization.

†A several fishery is an exclusive right of fishing in a given place, either with or without the property in the seabed, which may be granted to one or more individuals. A several fishery is therefore a particular type of private fishery.

(d) The Fisheries Act 1981 provides for the replacement of the White Fish Authority (WFA) and the Herring Industry Board (HIB) by the Sea Fish Industry Authority (SFIA), which has the duty of promoting the efficiency of the sea fish industry in the United Kingdom. The Act reaffirms and extends the power to grant financial assistance to the industry, and also extends the minister's ability to regulate fishing by British and foreign vessels within the United Kingdom's 200-mile zone. Transhipment of sea fish is now brought specifically within the law. New provisions in relation to fish farming are made, and the law on whaling conservation is widened to protect all cetaceans.

It will be noticed that in many instances these Acts merely make *provision* for the introduction of regulations or changes of practice. Their actual implementation is via so-called Statutory Instruments or Orders. If, for example, a minister wishes to regulate fishing, then he may make an Order under a specified section of one of the Acts. The Order still has to go before Parliament to allow members of Parliament to object if they wish, after which it becomes law. As a legal device, Statutory Instruments have the merit that they overcome the problem of having to create a new Act every time the government wishes to legislate. It may be sufficient to supplement or extend an existing Act by one or a collection of Statutory Instruments. Indeed, that is what has happened in practice.

As well as laws made by Parliament there are also bye-laws, which may be made and enforced in England and Wales by local Sea Fisheries Committees (subject to ministerial approval). There are twelve districts covered by Sea Fisheries Committees and bye-laws are effective up to three miles from the coast.

The use of Statutory Instruments and bye-laws has allowed the law to be extended and amplified in a flexible manner, but at the same time has contributed to the piecemeal development of fisheries policy. Since the late 1960s a very large number of ad-hoc controls over fishing have come into being, together constituting a highly varied and eclectic assortment. Progress towards a unified and comprehensive framework of resource management, such as the one that operates in the United States, has been disappointingly slow. However, the signs are now a little more encouraging since, as will be explained shortly, there has recently been an attempt to reduce the plethora of licensing orders that came into being during the 1970s.

Prior to 1977, when international fisheries regulation within the European pond was taken over by the EEC, the British government passed a number of Orders implementing various conservation measures. In the majority of cases these were to enforce agreements made within the ICNAF (later NAFO) and NEAFC, though in a number of instances measures to deal with specific conservation problems were taken solely on the initiative of the government. All the controls were essentially biological, taking the form of closed areas and seasons, minimum mesh sizes and minimum landing sizes of fish, and gear controls. The species subject to most regulation was the herring, though controls were also imposed on other varieties, including cod, haddock and hake caught in the north-west Atlantic, and salmon and migratory trout in the NEAFC area.

From 1977 however the situation changed considerably. In the absence of an agreed CFP the British government continued to enact conservation measures operative within its newly declared 200-mile EEZ. In many cases these measures were designed to give direct effect to regulations approved at EEC level, such as the urgent package of conservation measures agreed by the Council of Ministers in February 1977, which included a temporary ban on herring fishing in the North Sea. In a number of instances the United Kingdom carried on with 'national' conservation measures after EEC regulations had expired, and with the approval of the Commission. However, there were other unilateral measures which were deemed by the EEC to be illegal and which remained in dispute until the final settlement of the CFP in January 1983. In 1978 the government passed Orders to extend the Norway pout 'box' east of the Shetlands, introduced a ban on herring fishing in two areas, and imposed a minimum mesh size for nephrops. Further controls were introduced the following year, and on both occasions incurred the disapproval of the Commission.

Licensing has become a pervasive feature of British fisheries regulation. With the exception of two fisheries, which are discussed below, the principal purpose of licensing before 1983 has *not* been to restrict entry. Rather, the aim has been to monitor the amount of effort expended and to provide an administrative framework within which to allocate and enforce quotas. As the number of TAC'd species has increased, so has the need for licensing. In June 1983 the Sea Fish Licensing Order was passed, extending licensing to all appropriate quota species and areas. At the same time seventeen previous Licensing Orders, dating from 1973, were revoked, an indication of the way in which policy had developed in piecemeal fashion. Licensing now applies not only to catching but also to transhipping. Under the Receiving of Transhipped Sea Fish (Licensing) Order 1982, all receiving vessels of whatever nationality need a licence if they wish to tranship any of the main pelagic species from British boats within British fishery limits.

Before 1983 there had been two exceptions to the normal system under which licences had been issued *ad lib*. The first was the Manx herring fishery where, in the 1977 season, only a limited number of licences were allocated (twenty-four to vessels from Eire, 100 to British vessels). How much good might have been done in terms of conservation will never be fully known since by 1980 the scheme had effectively been abandoned. What is certain is that a great deal of acrimony was generated as a result of licence refusals (*Fishing News*, 9 September 1977). Indeed, following a European Court ruling that the scheme was illegal, it was reported that the Irish Fisheries Organisation was to take advice on the question of compensation for the loss of fishing rights suffered by Irish fishermen who had been excluded under the scheme (*Fishing News*, 1 August 1980).

The second exception was to be found in the mackerel fishery. Licensing was first introduced in 1977 and, even though catch restrictions were imposed on all licence holders, until 1980 licences were freely available to all applicants. In that year however, the government took steps to limit the growth of catching capacity by refusing licences to those purse seiners and freezer vessels which had not previously participated in the fishery. In effect, therefore, a restraint was imposed on *new* entry. It should not go unrecorded, though, that the government's original intention was to introduce a proper system of restrictive licensing, but this was dropped in the face of 'deep opposition' from the industry (Buchanan-Smith, 1981).

At the end of 1983 a new move towards restrictive licensing was made, this time covering several species—including mackerel—where U.K. quotas were considered insufficient to allow unrestricted fishing ('pressure stocks', so-called). The measures were to take effect in February 1984, the element of restriction being the refusal to grant licences to British vessels of over 10 metres which did not have a record of fishing one or more of the 'pressure stocks'. In addition, transfers of licences from vessels which had received a (newly introduced) de-commissioning grant were disallowed. It is envisaged that these arrangements will apply for a three-year period in the first instance.

8.4.3 Assessment

Certain policy measures have been successful in achieving their specific aims, as is most clearly shown in the case of financial support. Operating subsidies given from 1950 to 1973, as well as the 'special' payments made in 1975 and in the years 1979–81, have probably sustained marginal firms and vessels that would otherwise have gone out of business. Investment incentives likewise appear to have had a positive impact. For example, in the six years prior to the introduction of the WFA Grant and Loan Scheme for the construction of vessels below 140 ft (43 m) in length, data published by the WFA in its Annual Reports show that the number of vessels in this category that were added to the fleet in England and Wales was twenty-nine. In the six years after the scheme was introduced, the number of such vessels built was 117. Clearly, then, the rate of investment increased after the incentives were offered. Support for fisheries R & D can also be shown to have had some positive effects to the extent that one can, for example, attribute the creation of specific advances in marine science and technology to the work of bodies which, in whole or in part, are publicly funded.

If we turn to the specific effects of measures concerned with resource management, the situation is more mixed. Arguably the one government action that produced positive benefits for the United Kingdom (and her EEC fishing partners) was the extension of U.K. fishery limits to 200 miles in January 1977. Within a short time most non-EEC vessels were evicted from the enlarged zone, except where reciprocal arrangements had been made. The extension of limits had a demonstrable effect on landings, especially marked in the case of mackerel. In the early 1970s the major contributors to the growth of effort in the western area were Eastern-bloc vessels. By 1978 however, their fishing activity had ceased, a cessation that opened up major catching opportunities of which British vessels were quick to avail themselves. By 1979 landings of mackerel in the United Kingdom were roughly what the Eastern bloc had been taking four years previously. In fact, the weight of mackerel landed in the United Kingdom by British vessels in 1979 accounted for over 40% of the weight of all fish landed.

However, the extension of her fishery limits did not fully compensate the United Kingdom for the loss of access to traditional distant-water areas. One reason for this is that cod, a species highly prized by fishermen, processors and consumers, was less abundant in the waters nearer the United Kingdom. Another reason is that, apart from a fairly narrow coastal belt and specific closed areas, fishing vessels of other EEC countries have had free access to stocks within the United Kingdom's EEZ. British vessels have thus continued to face competition for fish resources that would otherwise have been theirs alone.

Aside from the effects of extended fisheries jurisdiction, the impact of conservation measures *per se* does not appear to have been conspicuously successful. In the first instance, the British government has been able to exert only very limited control over non-British EEC fishing effort. Secondly, the restraints imposed on British vessels have tended on the whole to be in response to events rather than in anticipation of them. In the mackerel fishery, for example, stock depletion has necessitated a reduction in the TAC, which in turn has been translated into lower boat quotas and the imposition of other controls in the south-west region. In one sense therefore, these restrictions merely reflected the overfishing that had already occurred. In fairness however, it must be said that in a few cases severe controls have been imposed which could be crucial in determining whether a fishery has a future or not. This applies particularly to the North Sea herring ban in 1977 and the enlargement of the 'box' designed to protect immature mackerel in the south-west in September 1983.

Nevertheless, whatever may be decided about the impact of specific government measures, there is as yet no convincing evidence that the broad objective of fisheries policy—economic viability for the fishing industry—has been achieved. Subsidies have had to be reintroduced during the past decade and there has been a contraction in vessel tonnage and employment. Nevertheless there is plainly an imbalance between fleet capacity and fishing opportunities. The British government now recognizes this and has begun to take remedial action.

8.4.4 Fisheries policy—a new beginning?

The settlement of the CFP in January 1983 meant that the British fishing industry had a clearer notion of the longer-term fishing opportunities open to it, and the government had a more satisfactory framework within which to formulate national policy. In March of that year the Ministry of Agriculture, Fisheries and Food and the other Fisheries Departments circulated a consultation paper to relevant organizations in the industry, inviting their views on fleet restructuring and fisheries regulation (MAFF, 1983). Specific issues were raised, including the desirability or otherwise of restrictive licensing, the value of de-commissioning grants in helping adjustment, the degree of spare capacity in the fleet, the allocation of aid for vessel construction and modernization, and the precise way in which quotas should be managed. The question of fish marketing was also raised, but the document made it clear that the responsibility for marketing lay with the industry rather than the government.* The most important response to the Ministry document came from the SFIA, which put forward an IFQ scheme (*Fishing News,* 22 July 1983). The essentials of this, as reported in the fishing press, are that property rights would be assigned by way of transferable quota licences to fishermen, who would receive a share of the national quota applying to specific fisheries. The SFIA would undertake to administer the scheme, though enforcement would remain with the government.

The ideas and proposals for the future of fisheries policy that were circulated in 1983 reflected an increasing awareness of the problems that the fishing industry was likely to face in the future, and how they might be tackled. There was now an implicit recognition that subsidies did nothing to overcome the problem of overcapitalization, and that measures to improve industrial performance could not be separated from the issue of resource management. The licensing arrangements brought in at the end of 1983 were clearly conceived within this new understanding of the requirements of fisheries policy.

8.5 SUMMARY

Three countries—Canada, the United States and the United Kingdom—have been chosen to illustrate the way in which national governments have formulated fisheries policy. In Canada, the production crisis faced by the fishing industry after the late 1960s forced a re-examination of Canadian fisheries, the outcome of which was a positive policy based on economic as well as biological principles. Specifically, there was a commitment to the need for limited entry, and a move in that direction was taken in 1977 by the extension of Canada's 200-mile EEZ and greater centralized control of fisheries. Since the policy reappraisal the balance between Canadian and foreign fishing within the EEZ has changed to the benefit of the former. Needless to say, of course, the new regime has brought with it disadvantages as well as advantages. Resource management *per se* has been based on three main principles, namely 'best use', limited entry and cost recovery. Their implementation has proved awkward, and they have had to be modified in the light of experience. An interesting case study of the development of fisheries management is provided by the

*Notwithstanding what was said in this particular document, the promotion of marketing is now seen as part of fisheries policy. The SFIA has been charged with this task, and launched a fish marketing campaign in 1982. How far this will go towards solving the long-term problems of the industry is questionable, though in principle the promotion of underutilized species would appear beneficial.

Pacific halibut, which illustrates *inter alia* the problems associated with restrictive licensing. It is now recommended that restrictive licensing be replaced by an IFQ scheme. The Canadian experience of fisheries management demonstrates that no single regulatory technique can be a panacea for all dimensions of the 'fisheries problem'. Social as well as bioeconomic factors need to be taken into account, especially where regulation impinges on regions where fishing is locally important. Recent debates on the future of fisheries management in Canada have considered various options, though schemes based on property rights are likely to figure more prominently than in the past.

In the United States, at least up to 1976, the coastal states played the dominant role in fisheries management. The developments that led up to the great increase in Federal influence in that year were of international as well as domestic origin, including the general trend towards extended fisheries jurisdiction and an awareness that the U.S. fishing industry and fisheries policy were both in some disarray. A new era in U.S. fisheries policy was heralded by the Fishery Conservation and Management Act 1976, which established a 200-mile Fishery Conservation Zone around the United States, and eight Regional Fishery Management Councils. Their role is to implement fisheries management plans for their area, such plans having been vetted by the Secretary of Commerce on the basis of seven national standards. A major source of difficulty in implementing plans is the practical determination of 'optimum' yield, the central concept in the Fishery Conservation and Management Act. U.S. fisheries policy with respect to foreign fishing has become somewhat less benign than it was originally, the intention being to reduce even further the activities of foreign vessels in the FCZ. The process by which a Fishery Management Plan is formulated is well illustrated by the Gulf of Alaska groundfish fishery where, apart from the difficulty of determining the optimum yield of each of the different species, there was also the problem of deciding on the catch allocation between U.S. and foreign fishermen. While the plan is commendable for its attempt to deal with a practical problem, the approach is essentially biological.

The emphasis of fisheries policy in the United Kingdom has altered over the years as the circumstances facing the domestic fishing industry have changed. Before the 1970s the major requirement was seen as the improvement of industrial performance, a key element of which was financial support in some form. More recently greater weight has been given to resource management, as reflected in a variety of government Orders concerned with jurisdiction, conservation and regulation. Some of these, but by no means all, have had the approval of the EEC. Administrative licensing and quantitative restrictions have become the prevalent forms of management in the United Kingdom as the number of TAC'd species has grown. Though certain policy instruments can be shown to have achieved their specific aims, the broad objective of policy has proved elusive. There is still overcapacity in the fleet, a problem that requires remedial action. In recognition of this, the government has been reshaping fisheries policy so as to reconcile the requirements for technical efficiency, structural adjustment and resource management. Though it may be too early to say, there is at least the sign that fisheries policy may now be shifting to a more economically rational basis.

8.6 BIBLIOGRAPHIC NOTES

General and comparative sources

One of the best sources of factual information on fisheries policy in Canada, the United States and the United Kingdom, as well as other countries, is the *Review of fisheries in OECD member countries* (annual). Periodically, the OECD also surveys financial support given to fishing (*see*, for example, OECD, 1980). The development of fisheries policy up to the mid 1960s is examined in the report OECD (1970). All of these publications are especially useful for comparative studies of different countries. For up-to-date information on fishing industries and changes in policy, *Fishing News International* or *World Fishing* should be consulted (both monthly).

Canada

Canada not only has one of the best-documented fishing industries in the world, but also is the source of much of the more important theory and empirical research on fisheries management. Accordingly, the Canadian bibliography might be very long, but in fact from 1983 onwards there is a clear point of departure in any further reading, from the reports on the Pacific fisheries (Pearse, 1982) and the Atlantic fisheries (Kirby, 1982). It is important also to trace back the influence of certain academic writers, especially Copes, since the production of the key *Policy for Canada's commercial fisheries* (Anon., 1976). The papers by Larkin (1979) and Mitchell (1979) are especially interesting, and the Crutchfield and Zellner study (1962) is seminal.

United States

An interesting collection of papers considering the Fishery Conservation and Management Act from both theoretical and empirical (i.e. case study) points of view is contained in the book edited by Anderson (1981). All papers are useful. Quoted in the text are Siegel (1981) and Stokes (1981b). Useful introductory papers are those of Knight (1978), Kelly (1978), Mangone (1977, Ch. 4) and Anderson (1982). On foreign fishing under the Fishery Conservation and Management Act *see* Stokes (1981a), Sullivan and Heggelund (1979), Jelley (1983), Crutchfield (1983) and Meuriot and Gates (1982). For a political-science-orientated study *see* Young (1981, Ch. 4). Up-to-date information on management plans and the industry can be obtained from *National Fisherman* (monthly).

United Kingdom

Most of the written material on the United Kingdom's fisheries policy deals with it either in relation to the fishing industry or in the context of EEC fisheries policy. There are two descriptive but quite useful introductory papers (Mackay, 1981; Anon., 1980). For a deeper analysis of the problems of the industry, consult the Expenditure Committee Report (1978), MacSween (1980), McKellar and Steel (1980) and an updating paper (McKellar, Scott and Cormack, 1983). The European dimension is discussed in the Agra-Europe Report (1981) and in the report of the Select Committee on the European Communities (1980), while the competitive forces that lie behind national action are explored by Hood (1976). Finally, the Ministry consultation paper on restructuring and quota management provides a valuable insight into how the government perceives the problems of fishing and policy requirements in the future (MAFF, 1983).

REFERENCES AND FURTHER READING

AGRA-EUROPE (1981). *EEC fisheries: problems and prospects for a common policy.* Special Report No. 11.

ANDERSON, L. (Ed.) (1981). *Economic analysis for fisheries management plans.* Ann Arbor, Michigan: Ann Arbor Science Publishers.

ANDERSON, L. (1982). 'Marine fisheries.' In P. Portney (Ed.), *Current issues in natural resource policy.* Washington, D.C.: Resources for the Future.

ANON. (1976). *Policy for Canada's commercial fisheries.* Ottawa: Environment Canada.

ANON. (1980). *Resource prospects for Canada's Atlantic fisheries 1981–87.* Ottawa: Department of Fisheries and Oceans.

ANON. (1980). 'The U.K. fishing industry today.' *Midland Bank Review*, winter issue : 12–15.

BELL, F. (1981). *The Pacific halibut: the resource and its fishery.* Edmonds, Washington: Alaska Northwest Publishing.

BUCHANAN-SMITH, A. (1981). Debate on Fisheries Bill. *Hansard* 12 January 1981, p. 1214.

COPES, P. (1978). 'Canada's Atlantic coast fisheries: policy development and the impact of extended jurisdiction.' *Canadian Public Policy* **4** (2): 155–71.

COPES, P. (1979). 'The economics of marine fisheries management in the era of extended fisheries jurisdiction: the Canadian perspective.' *American Economic Review* **69** (2) : 256–60.

COPES, P. (1979–80). 'The evolution of marine fisheries policy in Canada.' *Business Administration* **11** : 125–48.

COPES, P. (1980). 'The British Columbia fisheries and the 200-mile limit: perverse effects for the coastal state.' *Marine Policy* **4** (3) : 205–16.

COPES, P. (1982). 'Implementing Canada's marine fisheries policy: objectives, hazards and constraints.' *Marine Policy* **6** (3) : 219–35.

COPES, P. and B. COOK (1982). 'Rationalization of Canada's Pacific halibut fishery.' *Ocean Management* **8** : 157–75.

CRUTCHFIELD, J. (1981). *The Pacific halibut fishery*. Case Study No. 2. Technical Report No. 17 of the Public Regulation of Commercial Fisheries in Canada. Economic Council of Canada.

CRUTCHFIELD, J. and A. ZELLNER (1962). 'Economic aspects of the Pacific halibut fishery.' *Fishery Industrial Research* **1** (1) : 1–173.

CRUTCHFIELD, S. (1983). 'Estimation of foreign willingness to pay for United States fishery resources: Japanese demand for Alaska pollock.' *Land Economics* **59** (1) : 16–23.

CUSHING, D. (1977). 'The Atlantic fisheries commissions.' *Marine Policy* **1** (3) : 230–8.

EXPENDITURE COMMITTEE (1978). *The fishing industry*. (5th Report). HC.356.HMSO.

FISHERIES RESEARCH AND DEVELOPMENT BOARD (1978). *Report 1976–77*. (3rd Report). London: HMSO.

FISHING NEWS (1977). 'Fury at Manx herring licensing system.' 9 September 1977, p. 5.

FISHING NEWS (1980). 'Advice on licences.' 1 August 1980, p. 21.

FISHING NEWS (1983). 'SFIA's plan for quota sharing.' 22 July 1983, p. 2.

FRASER, G. (1977). *Licence limitation in the British Columbia salmon fishery*. Environment Canada, Fish and Marine Service. Pac. Reg. Technical Report PAC/T–77–13.

GULLAND, J. and L. BOEREMA (1973). 'Scientific advice on catch levels.' *Fishery Bulletin* **71** (2) : 325–35.

HOOD, C. (1976). 'The politics of the biosphere: the dynamics of fishing policy.' In J. Rose (Ed.), *The dynamics of public policy*. London: Sage Publications.

IPHC (1978). *The Pacific halibut: biology, fishery and management.* Technical Report No. 16, IPHC, Seattle.

JELLEY, S. (1983). 'The price of fishing in American waters.' *Fishing News International* **22** (5): 8–9 (May).

KELLY, J. (1978). 'The Fishery Conservation and Management Act of 1976: organisational structure and framework.' *Marine Policy* **2** (1) : 30–6.

KIRBY, M. (1982). *Navigating troubled waters: a new policy for Atlantic fisheries.* Report of the Task Force on Atlantic Fisheries. Highlights and recommendations.

KNIGHT, H. (1978). 'Management procedures in the U.S. Fishery Conservation Zone.' *Marine Policy* **2** (1) : 22–9.

LARKIN, P. (1979). 'Maybe you can't get there from here: a foreshortened history of research in relation to management of Pacific salmon.' *Journal of the Fisheries Research Board of Canada* **36** : 98–106.

LARKINS, H. (1980). 'Management under FCMA—development of a fishery management plan.' *Marine Policy* **4** (3) : 170–82.

MCGAW, R. (1979). *Bioeconomic models of the Georges Bank scallop fishery.* Ottawa: Department of Fisheries and Oceans.

MACKAY, G. (1981). 'The U.K. fishing industry and EEC policy.' *Three Banks Review*, December 1981 : 48–62.

MCKELLAR, N., I. SCOTT and K. CORMACK (1983). *An update of the 'Case for aid' with a critique of alternative measures for fisheries management.* Sea Fish Industry Authority, Occasional Paper No. 4.

MCKELLAR, N. and D. STEEL (1980). *The catching sector of the fishing industry: a case for aid.* White Fish Authority.

MACSWEEN, I. (1980). 'The U.K. fishing industry in the eighties.' Paper at Conference *Technology and the Challenges of the World's New Fisheries Regime.* London: Society for Underwater Technology.

MAFF (1983). *Structure and management of the United Kingdom fishing fleet.* (Discussion Paper to the industry.)

MANGONE, G. (1977). *Marine policy for America.* Lexington, Massachusetts: Lexington Books, Heath & Co.

MEURIOT, E. and J. GATES (1982). *An economic evaluation of foreign fishing allocations.* University of Rhode Island Marine Technical Report No. 84.

MITCHELL, C. (1979). 'Bioeconomics of commercial fisheries management.' *Journal of the Fisheries Research Board of Canada* **36** : 699–704.

MITCHELL, C. (1981). 'Economic analysis and Canadian fisheries management.' In L. G. Anderson (Ed.), *Economic analysis for fisheries management plans.* Ann Arbor, Michigan: Ann Arbor Science Publishers.

MOLONEY, D. and P. PEARSE (1979). 'Quantitative rights as an instrument for regulating commercial fisheries.' *Journal of the Fisheries Research Board of Canada* **36** (7) : 857–66.

NEEDLER, A. (1979). 'Evolution of Canadian fisheries management towards economic rationalization.' *Journal of the Fisheries Research Board of Canada* **36** : 716–24.

NOWAK, W. (1980). *Some economic and geographical implications of the licensing policy in the Newfoundland fishery (Like it or not you will be resettled).* Hawk/Memorial University of Newfoundland.

OECD (1970). *Fishery policies and economics 1957—1966.* Paris: OECD.

OECD (1980). *Financial support to the fishing industry.* Paris: OECD.

OECD (1982). *Review of fisheries in OECD member countries 1981.* Paris: OECD.

OECD (1983). *Review of fisheries in OECD member countries 1982.* Paris: OECD.

PEARSE, P. (1980). *Regulating fishing effort.* FAO, Rome, Technical Paper No. 197.

PEARSE, P. (1981). *Conflict and opportunity: towards a new policy for Canada's Pacific fisheries.* Vancouver: Commission on Pacific Fisheries Policy.

PEARSE, P. (1982). *Turning the tide: a new policy for Canada's Pacific fisheries.* Vancouver: Commission on Pacific Fisheries Policy (Final Report).

PEARSE, P. and J. WILEN (1979). 'Impact of Canada's Pacific salmon fleet control program.' *Journal of the Fisheries Research Board of Canada* **7** : 764–9.

PITCHER, T. and P. HART (1982). *Fisheries ecology.* London: Croom Helm; Westport, Connecticut: AVI Publishing.

SCOTT, A. and P. NEHER (1982). *The public regulation of commercial fisheries in Canada.* Ottawa: Environmental Council of Canada.

SELECT COMMITTEE ON THE EUROPEAN COMMUNITIES (1980). *EEC fisheries policy*. H.L. 351. London: HMSO.

SIEGEL, R. (1981). 'Federal regulatory policy for marine fisheries.' In L. Anderson (Ed.), *Economic analysis for fisheries management plans*, pp. 23–40. Ann Arbor, Michigan: Ann Arbor Science Publishers.

SINCLAIR, S. (1978). *A licensing and fee system for the coastal fisheries of British Columbia.* Vancouver: Department of Fisheries and Oceans.

STOKES, R. (1981a). 'The new approach to foreign fisheries allocation: an economic appraisal.' *Land Economics* **57** (4) : 568–82.

STOKES, R. (1981b). 'Economics of development and management: the Alaskan groundfish case.' In L. Anderson (Ed.), *Economic analysis for fisheries management plans,* pp. 267–88. Ann Arbor, Michigan: Ann Arbor Science Publishers.

STORY, G. and D. ALEXANDER (Eds) (1974). *Report of the Committee of Federal Licensing Policy and its implications for the Newfoundland fisheries.* Memorial University of Newfoundland. 50 pp.

SULLIVAN, J. and P. HEGGELUND (1979). *Foreign investment in the U.S. fishing industry.* Lexington, Massachusetts: Lexington Books, Heath & Co.

VARIOUS (1978). *A review of the current Atlantic coast groundfish licensing policy.* Ottawa: Environment Canada.

YOUNG, O. (1981). *Natural resources and the state*. Berkeley, California: University of California Press.

CHAPTER 9

Fishing as recreation

9.1 INTRODUCTION

Throughout this book so far it has been assumed, either explicitly or implicitly, that all economic activity affecting fish stocks is commercial in nature, with the main objective of maximizing profits. It is no doubt already apparent that, even with this simplifying assumption, the economic analysis of fisheries can become somewhat complex. It is therefore with some reluctance that one further complicates the analysis, but it is increasingly unjustifiable in both theoretical and practical terms to omit recreational fishing from the overall discussion. Not only has economic theory itself gradually come to terms with the existence of recreational fisheries, but also their size and growth has reached such levels that the relationship between recreational and commercial fishing, and the management of these as a joint entity, is becoming an increasingly urgent problem facing fisheries administrators in several parts of the world. In contrast, there are still many areas of the world where recreational fishing is of negligible importance, and in many more areas relatively little is known about it in quantifiable terms.

As will soon be apparent, the economic analysis of recreational fishing throws forward a range of problems to which, as yet, there are no generally accepted solutions, and on which a lively debate has emerged. This book has been concerned almost entirely with marine commercial fishing (hereafter, MCF), and accordingly this chapter is directed mainly at marine recreational fishing (MRF). However a great deal of the relevant literature has been developed in the context of inland fishing or indeed in non-fishing recreation, so that inevitably the text will stray from strictly MRF-related issues from time to time.

9.2 THE OBJECTIVES OF FISHING: COMMERCIAL VERSUS RECREATION?

We have commenced by assuming that there is an identifiable activity labelled 'recreational fishing', undertaken by those who fish for recreation or home consumption. This immediately raises one difficulty, for fishing is an economic activity that has a range of dimensions, and specifically which types of fishing may be labelled 'commercial' or 'recreational' is not so evident as one might assume. Thus, while it is analytically perfectly defensible to make the customary assumption of profit-maximizing objectives for firms engaged in commercial fishing—that is, catching fish for sale—it is empirically evident that those people so engaged also receive a range of non-monetary satisfactions. Of course, the same is certainly true of many other occupations, but it has been suggested that non-monetary satisfactions are particularly strong in fishing (Smith, 1981) and of greater significance, for the presence of non-monetary objectives may have implications for the optimum level of effort in any management of fisheries.

The precise nature of these non-monetary benefits and their potential significance is beyond our present scope (*see* the bibliographic notes) but there is one aspect that is very pertinent. In his rigorous analysis of the components of economic surplus in fishing, Anderson (1980) argues that we should concern ourselves with something broader than Gordon's original concept of maximum profits (Gordon, 1953), not only with consumer surplus and factor input rents but also a more nebulous 'worker satisfaction bonus' or WSB. The principle that underlies the concept of WSB is that fishermen derive non-monetary satisfactions from being fishermen, and these arise from a wide variety of factors including independence, adventure, risk-taking, challenges with the outdoor elements, fellowship, physical and mental wellbeing, and links to a traditional way of life (*see*, for example, Poggie and Gersuny, 1974). Anderson looks at the implications that the presence of WSBs may have, bearing in mind that strictly one would need to evaluate WSB in fishing relative to other activities, and he concludes particularly that the MEY level of effort may not then be as low as would otherwise be the case, as the optimum labour force might be underestimated relative to other industries with low or zero WSB.

However of more direct concern here is that the proposal that fishermen enjoy WSBs of a non-monetary nature begins to blur the ostensibly clear distinction between those who fish for profit and those who do not. Indeed, the WSBs of commercial fishermen above sound uncomfortably like some of the main objectives one might expect of recreational fishermen. Perhaps, as Orbach (1979) suggested: 'What is often overlooked is that "commercial" fishermen value their fishing rights for exactly the same reasons [as "recreational" fishermen], albeit in somewhat different mixes . . .' The problem is complicated in that apparently 'recreational' fishermen may in fact value their catch for home food consumption, and may even dispose of part of it as a market good, perhaps by selling on a 'black market' to colleagues or local restaurants. This type of complication is well known to fisheries investigators, although not well documented, for it is quite common for fisheries policies to impinge on the question of MCF versus MRF in such matters as the distribution of licences (*see* section 9.6.2).

Nevertheless, quite often this complication is ignored, sometimes for lack of data or a lack of sympathy with recreational users of resources, but mainly because it is much easier to nominate just the two distinct groups, MRF and MCF. Yet there are certain circumstances where these overlapping features are ignored at peril, as Smith (1981) forcibly demonstrated in the case of the Pacific salmon fishery. Here, three resource user groups were identified: the commercial ocean *trollers* (hook and line), the inshore drift and set *gill netters*, and the rod-and-line *angling* fishery from charter and private boats, jetties, estuary shores and upstream banks. Using a cognitive approach to identify by social survey what phenomena are significant to people and how they organize these, Smith identified five broad groups of factors that influenced everyone taking part in the fishery (bracketed quotes are examples of the type of individual responses):

(a) Pleasure (fishing as 'a challenge', 'for pleasure', 'for freedom', etc.)
(b) Personal economic wellbeing ('reducing family expenses', 'providing some income', 'providing food', etc.)
(c) Identity ('way of life', 'pitting skills against others and elements', etc.).
(d) General economic wellbeing ('reducing imports', 'solve world food problems', etc.)
(e) Occupation ('making a living', 'my job', 'my profession', etc.)

When surveyed as to their positive or negative responses to each of the broad factors, fishermen did not divide neatly into two groups, although full-time commercial fishermen generally stressed positively factors (e), (d) and (c), with factor (b) rather weaker and factor (a) negative, while recreational fishermen stressed only factor (a) positively, with all the rest negative, especially factor (e). However, a third grouping emerged, who turned out to be those who undertook commercial trolling but with rather low catches as this was not their full-time occupation. This group exhibited a positive response to *all* the factors, with factor (b) stressed more strongly than for either of the other groups. This ostensibly 'commercial' group thus had strongly 'recreational' features, with the pleasure factor stimulating their fishing effort despite low or negative returns. Liao and Stevens (1977) indeed confirm that more than 50% of the Pacific salmon fishermen had 'gross returns less than "out-of-pocket" expenses (total costs less depreciation)'. If such a situation is durable—and Smith (1981) suggests that it is—then most of these salmon trollers supplement losses in fishing by means of other occupations.

Two points emerge: first, fishing effort of this type is less likely to respond predictably to 'normal' economic stimuli, and thus analyses of any such fisheries that ignore this element might be incomplete or even erroneous. Secondly, the commercial fishery, in which fishermen theoretically fish to generate all or most of their income, begins to take on features that one might more normally associate with recreational fishing. Hence, although we are about to do so, one should be cautious in dividing fishermen into two distinct groupings and talking about these as if their behaviour and responses were totally different. However we are not yet in a position to analyse fishing activities of all types under one analytical umbrella, and, at least at either end of the spectrum running from commercial to recreational fishing, important differences do exist.

9.3 RECREATION, AND FISHING AS RECREATION

Increasingly, leisure time is being used for outdoor recreational activities, and fishing is one of the principal forms of outdoor recreation. The factors that have produced this growth in recreation include especially the existence of more leisure time within the working week and year, the rise in personal disposable incomes, and the increased levels of mobility of the population, particularly associated with the growth of motor vehicle ownership. Other significant factors include the overall growth in population and its changing age structure, the concentration of the population into urban centres, a rising level of education, and a changing appreciation of the value of recreation, specifically in this context of recreation in a 'natural' setting.

The precise nature and definition of 'recreation' are not examined in depth here, and it is sufficient to borrow Simmons' (1975) definition of rural recreation as being leisure-time activities undertaken in relatively small groups (thereby excluding mass spectator recreations). Fishing is just one of many such activities, but it is an important one, and we can obtain some broad indication of this importance from *Table 9.1*. These data do not lend themselves to quantitative comparisons and are intended only to be illustrative. It is, however, reasonable to conclude that fishing is, in general terms, a significant form of outdoor recreation. Additionally, it is relevant to note that all studies of outdoor recreation have come to the conclusion that the amount of outdoor recreation taken has increased considerably and will continue to increase. Precisely how fast it will increase is not so clear; still less, how fast fishing itself will increase within this general growth.

Before proceeding any further, we must recognize an important issue. Fishing as recreation in the United Kingdom is usually considered in terms of angling with a rod and line, within which activity there are three distinct groupings (National Angling Survey, 1980): *sea angling* (fishing in the sea from either land, pier/jetty, or boat); *coarse angling* (fishing for 'coarse' fish inland in fresh water), and *game angling* (fishing for trout or salmon, in estuary or inland fresh waters). Theoretically any form of fishing could be recreational of course, and some potting, netting and shellfish raking certainly is; for our purposes, we shall limit recreational fishing nominally to angling. While there may be some rather awkward distinctions in practical terms to be made here and distinctions made in one country may not be entirely appropriate elsewhere, the important issue is that recreational fishing may interrelate with marine fisheries in two ways. First, in some instances MRF is in principle in direct competition with commercial fishing

TABLE 9.1 Recreational activities: illustrative participation rates and ranking of fishing as outdoor recreation

Country	*Year of data*	*Participation rate as % of population sampled**	*Ranking position of fishing within activities on popularity basis*†
U.S.A.	1960	30%	n.a.
	1965	29%	8th
Netherlands	1966	14%	6th
	1975	15%	n.a.
Sweden	1963	37%	5th
Canada	1966–67	26%	7th
Great Britain	1965	5%	2nd equal
	1980	8%‡	n.a.
France	1975	8%	n.a.

*Quite wide variations in the sample population taken and the methods employed existed; *see* sources for details.
†The rank quoted is only a broad indication as different studies used slightly different activities. Typically ranked *above* fishing were the activities swimming, walking for pleasure, driving, cycling, sightseeing and picnics.
‡The participation rate here was within the population of England, Scotland and Wales aged twelve or over.
Sources: Based on data of Simmons (1975), the National Angling Survey (1980) and Grover (1982).

in marine waters. Secondly, in the form of game angling when applied to anadromous fish, recreational fishing is based on the same fish stock as commercial fishing, but in a different place at a different time. Thus on Canada's west coast, something like 21% of the total Chinook salmon and 15% of the Coho salmon catches are taken by rod-and-line anglers (Pearse, 1982). Some wider indication of the relative importance of commercial and recreational catches based on the same fish stock is given in *Table 9.2*, although one must bear in mind here that the comparison is made only in terms of landed weights (and numbers in Scotland), which may prove to be a misleading indication of the relative economic importance of the recreational fishery.

In practice the position may be even more complex. For example, the data for Scotland in *Table 9.2b* reveal that the home-coming salmon faces a boat fishery, then a fixed-net estuary fishery, and then the rod-and-line

TABLE 9.2a Commercial and recreational catch shares in the United States for selected fish (1970)

Fish	*Commercial catch**	*Recreational catch**	*Recreational share of total catch*
Chinook salmon	14.37	6.88	32%
Atlantic cod	24.14	16.29	40%
Red snapper	4.15	7.86	65%
Bonitos	4.25	9.63	69%
Striped bass	5.07	38.00	88%
Atlantic mackerel	3.64	32.08	90%
Bluefish	3.27	54.80	94%
Spotted sea trout	2.78	48.26	95%
Red drum	0	30.16	100%
Catfishes	0	32.89	100%

*In thousands of tonnes.
Source: Rothschild *et al*. (1977) using Department of Commerce (1973) data.

TABLE 9.2b Commercial and recreational catch shares in Scotland for selected fish (1980)

	Commercial catch		*Recreational catch*		*Recreational share of total catch*	
Fish	*Weight* (tons)	*Numbers* (thousands)	*Weight* (tons)	*Numbers* (thousands)	*Weight*	*Numbers*
Grilse	202.6	88.0	27.0	10.3	13%	12%
Sea trout	129.6	113.7	29.5	34.1	23%	30%
Salmon	460.8	91.5	191.3	43.8	42%	48%

*In all three cases, the commercial catch is that taken by a combination of net and coble (boat) fishing and fixed engines (nets) in estuaries, and the recreational catch by rod and line.
Source: DAFS, *Fisheries of Scotland: Report for 1980*: HMSO, 1981; derived from Appendix II.

recreational river fishery—but in addition the fish may already have been the object of a different boat fishery while away on their feeding grounds in the North Atlantic, and may indeed also be the object of an illegal 'poaching' fishery (pseudo-commercial?) while passing upstream in the ostensibly recreational phase. Thus the single fish stock provides the basis for four (or five) separate fisheries, and there are strong interactions between them.

Fishing as recreation has shown very considerable growth in recent years, both in terms of participation and catch. In this chapter we are concerned primarily with rod-and-line MRF, to some extent with game fishing, but not greatly with freshwater coarse fishing. Unfortunately, data on recreational fisheries are most plentiful for the latter two, and very sparse on MRF, especially in Europe. Nevertheless, indications are that it is MRF that has grown fastest of the three over the last decades. In the United States, the long-term growth in the total numbers of habitual anglers was 3.15% p.a. over the period 1955–70, but the sea anglers increased in number even faster at an average rate of 5.0% p.a. By 1975, some 16.4 million sea anglers fished over 207 million days in the coastal streams, rivers, bays, estuaries and open ocean around America. Their expenditure had risen from $500 million in 1955 to $3.4 billion in 1975 (Schmied, 1982). In England and Wales, the National Angling Survey (1970) showed that in 1970 there were 2.79 million anglers of all types aged over twelve years and predicted a rise to 3.2 million by 1980; in fact, the number rose even faster to 3.38 million, an increase over the decade of 21%. Within this total, the numbers of sea anglers again rose fastest, rising 40% from 1.28 million to 1.79 million (National Angling Survey, 1980).

9.4 THE VALUATION OF MARINE RECREATIONAL FISHING

9.4.1 The need for valuation

There are a number of reasons why we shall want to establish the size and value of MRF. Where any fish stock is shared with MCF, so that there are interactions between the two, then the value of its use in MRF needs to be known, especially if there are any conflicts in resource use or where the question of allocating access rights arises. An obvious case is that of the salmon where, as noted above, the stock provides the basis for several fisheries and any failure to identify accurately its value in one use may have serious consequences for those users.

Secondly, valuation is essential where the fishery is under threat from non-fishing competing uses of the water resource, such as boating, pipelines and aquaculture. Thirdly, it will also be desirable or necessary to value the fishery when assessing any damage caused by environmental changes, such as threats to the fish habitat, and especially catastrophic events such as oil spills. Fourth, if it is to be attempted to make an investment appraisal of associated public or private sector investments, such as in fish hatcheries, then the value of the MRF will be required data.

Fifth—although this is of less relevance to MRF than to non-marine fishing recreation—it may be desirable for any private owner of a recreational fishing resource to establish an optimal access price for the provision of the good, and to do so may entail some assessment of the economic value of the associated fishery. For MRF, similar considerations might apply if the state wished to control access by user fees to what had hitherto been an open-access good.

Finally, there is a more specific need since the advent of 200-mile EEZs to value MRF within the EEZ, for, as stated in Chapter 7, the UNCLOS Convention requires coastal states to give other nations access to 'surplus' fish within the total allowable catch. Clearly, coastal states will increasingly wish to identify the size and value of MRF before defining what is 'surplus' and allowing such access.

There are therefore some compelling reasons for wishing to know the economic value of MRF. These are particularly strong given the trend towards the management of MCF, which will generally curtail effort and increase fish abundance, for such management will then very likely attract more MRF as catch rates rise; if MRF is open-access and MCF restricted-access, then the benefits of management may be transferred from commercial to recreational fishing in an unintentional manner, or possibly even dissipated by the MRF. This transfer might of course be beneficial, conceivably even optimal, but without valuations of MRF it would be impossible to judge.

Given the obvious needs, what then are the problems? Why can we not look to 'the market' to provide evidence of the value via the price created by the interaction of demand and supply, as with any other good?

9.4.2 Difficulties in valuation

To answer these questions we need first to recognize that the good 'recreational fishing' is not the same as the number of fish caught per period of time. Thus the MRF experience carries with it a wide variety of satisfactions apart from the prospect or reality of catching fish. These include the opportunity to relax, to 'escape' and perhaps gain some solitude, to be outdoors in a natural environment, and to explore new areas; an overall review paper studying motivational research in hunting and fishing identified sixteen different categories of satisfactions, drawn from fifty-six separate studies (*see* Dawson and Wilkins, 1980). These non-fish-related features have been very widely reported, and it is accepted that a high proportion of the motivation for recreational fishing is not associated with simply catching fish. However, clearly the prospect of a catch is a necessary condition for all recreationalists, and may approach being a sufficient condition for a minority primarily interested in the catch alone. Perversely, a very high stock density might well detract from the enjoyment of the fishing for others, as the elements of skill and challenge would be reduced. Generally, however, economists concerned with recreational fishing management issues are forced to assume that the value of the recreational fishing experience will *increase* with fish density over a relevant range; if it does not, then it is difficult to establish any rational basis for management of the fish resource.

One important factor concerns the extent of crowding on the recreational site. As the natural setting is clearly very significant, crowding will detract from enjoyment, and indeed may be more important as an influence on demand than the fish actually caught. This effect of crowding is a considerable complication, for later on we shall need to argue that consumer demand for MRF is likely to behave in the normal manner, increasing as access prices decline. Clearly when access price does decline—or stock density increases—total consumption may be expected to increase, but crowding then increases and this may well then in fact discourage the consumer from fishing at a given site (*see* section 9.6.1).

The output of MRF is thus not fish but recreation, and so we must discard simple valuation measures based on landed weight or sale value of the recreational catch for a serious study for any of the purposes outlined above. Confusingly, we must also bear in mind that some recreational fishermen not only value their catch as food but also may sell most or part of it for consumption by others, although they will still be defined as 'recreational' if their income from fishing is relatively insignificant (or, indeed, unrecorded!).*

Hence, while it is of interest to note that 54 million recreational fishermen landed 848 000 tonnes of fish, worth (as food) $2.5 billion, in the United States in 1975 (Grover, 1982, p. 614), and that anglers were responsible for 8% of Canada's total finfish landings by weight in 1975 (Grover, 1982, p. 539), neither statement really evaluates the relative importance of the recreational fisheries.

This issue leads to a very important dimension of the problem: the customary producer/consumer dichotomy that is central to much economic analysis of markets is no longer distinct. Recreationalists are both consumers of the good and participants in the production process; as consumers their fishing days and catch are part of their satisfactions (utility) derived from fishing, while as producers they have to make the necessary inputs of fishing days and gear to produce the recreation by applying them to the fish stock and making that catch. Thus 'fishing days' appears as part of both the production function *and* the consumption function, a not inconsiderable complication in the analysis.

However, why is it not possible to take the 'market price' for the good anyway, as one would for other marketed products? The immediate problem here is that a great deal of recreational fishing is a non-market good; that is, it is not bought and sold in the customary manner and has no conventional marketing system. MRF generally gives rise to no access prices as such, as it is customarily a common property resource. Much coarse angling is likewise, especially in the United States, where only 3.7% of inland waters are privately owned (Schmied, 1982). In contrast, game

*In the United States in 1978, consumption *per capita* of *recreationally* taken fish and shellfish was 4.67 kg per annum (liveweight)—over one quarter of *total* fish consumption (Grover, 1982, p. 615).

angling rights in the United Kingdom usually are privately owned, and access rights are bought and sold on short- and long-term bases in an identifiable market. Hence, while we may be able to discover market prices for some aspects of recreational fishing, for many others no market price exists, and so some form of proxy must of necessity be employed.

A rather different set of problems also revolves around the question of the characteristics of the good 'recreational fishing'. Recreation is now generally recognized as having five phases: planning, travel to the site, the recreational experience, travel back and recollection. All these may confer pleasure, to a greater or lesser extent. It is immediately obvious that the values of planning and recollection aspects are likely to be impossible to measure, but the travel and the activity itself reveal the preference of the consumer for this good by expenditures on goods and travel. Moreover these expenditures may have wider importance to others, such as in creating jobs. This leads us to an important distinction between first, the 'primary benefits' of the recreation, which accrue to those taking part in the activity and are reflected in the amount consumers spend on the good (more specifically, the consumers' surplus they derive from it), together with the economic rent any owners of rights may reap from it (e.g. salmon angling rights); and secondly the 'secondary benefits', which arise from the recreation for those not taking part themselves.

These secondary benefits may be divided into a number of classes, all of which may have some relevance if we wish to establish the value of the good in circumstances where, for example, the recreational fishery might cease to exist. First, the recreation may give rise to economic development in the area or locality around the site, based on the extra expenditure made on the activity and the multiplier effect of this. Fishing-based tourism would be a very important example. Studies of the resulting economic development would need to involve input–output modelling and the calculation of multiplier effects. Secondly, property rights in proximity to the site may be enhanced because of the existence of the recreation, thereby conferring benefits on the owners (e.g. salmon angling).

Thirdly, there is a group of non-consumptive benefits, as outlined by Krutilla (1967), where no direct expenditures are made and the persons benefiting may have no behaviour linked to the good at all. These benefits include the 'option value' that members of society derive from knowing that the recreational resource is available for optional future use. Option value may be especially relevant if the demand for, or especially the supply of, the good is uncertain, for the community may wish to insure itself against the possibility of future loss. There is an implication here that option value is always positive, but it has become more generally accepted that it may be either negative or positive (*see*, for example, R. J. Anderson, 1981). This view has simplified the acceptance of primary benefits as an adequate single-measure valuation, in that option value does not necessarily have to be notionally *added* to these to give a true total 'value'; however, it is an interpretation rejected by Bishop (1982), who treats option value as supply uncertainty, rather than demand uncertainty, in the future. There is also the 'existence value' received by persons who feel pleasure from knowing that an activity is being maintained and protected. They may then derive a measurable pleasure from its existence and enjoyment by others, but have no present or future use themselves. Likewise, there is the 'bequest value' in that users and non-users may benefit from the satisfaction of knowing that the resource will be available to future generations. Finally, society as a whole may be better off in terms of human welfare from the externalities of the recreation, particularly if it results in higher production or lower crime levels.

These non-consumptive secondary benefits will be very difficult to measure satisfactorily, as most persons will be free-riders on the benefit. In practice, some form of direct 'willingness to pay' enquiry represents a possible way forward, but such hypothetical questions tend to raise almost as many problems as they answer. It is also true that many other commercial goods have these characteristics, and one can argue that commercial fishing itself may have secondary benefits under each of the headings above. Hence, in practice, most investigations concentrate upon primary benefits as an initial synthesis of the value of recreational fishing, before possibly proceeding to other dimensions.

As a final complication, we must note that it was once suggested that the experience of recreation may be so personal and intangible that it cannot be measured in monetary terms (Trice and Wood, 1958). This idea is clearly erroneous in that the same is true of any good or service which confers a range of differing goods characteristics that vary from buyer to buyer; there is nothing unique about recreation in this respect. It has also been argued that the primary benefits reflected in people's willingness to pay may be misleading as they may not have enjoyed the good as much as expected or at all; again, given uncertainty, this is true of any good. It is however rather simplistic to dismiss these arguments, for there remains a strong body of opinion that has misgivings over estimates of the size and value of recreational fishing produced by the various techniques adopted from recreational economics, regarding these as hypothetical, tentative and of dubious validity. These doubts are especially pertinent where comparisons need to be made with the 'hard facts' of commercial fishing or non-fishing marine resource users (oil pipelines, marinas, etc.), where values may be estimated in more orthodox ways. It is, however, difficult to establish whether this rejection arises from an appreciation of the considerable methodological complexities or from a deep-felt mistrust of any recreational valuation.

To conclude then, recreational fishing and especially marine recreational fishing tend to be non-homogeneous, open-access, non-market goods. The complexities of establishing a value for this activity give rise to three main sources of concern. First, there will be a lack of comparability between data used in any comparison between recreational fishing and other commercial activities, especially commercial fishing. Secondly, there is a considerable risk that resources will be misallocated away from, or indeed towards, recreational fishing because of the problems of valuation. Valuation will be especially important in any conflict of usage where alternatives are to be compared. Finally, a loss of national welfare may be occurring because the valuation difficulties may cause recreational fishing to receive suboptimal treatment. It might be argued that recreational fishing is not unique in these respects; even so, these problems, combined with the considerable scarcity of quantitative data, especially on MRF, undoubtedly leave the overall position a source of considerable concern.

9.4.3 The basis of valuing primary benefits: consumers' surplus

We can argue that, in general terms, the economic value of a product is what people are willing to give up in order to obtain it. These values for an individual are the basis of his demand curve for the good in question, customarily relating quantity sought to prices charged. If we are interested in MRF, then the individual's demand curve for MRF opportunities may be expressed as in *Figure 9.1*. We are not however primarily concerned with the whole area beneath the hypothetical demand curve, but rather in the consumer surplus element, for this measures the *net* value of the good. In this context, consumer surplus is the difference between what consumers would be willing to pay for the good and what they actually pay for the quantity received. The same applies to any good, but in the case of MRF the good is not sold in any normal manner, therefore there is no market price for the quantity received by the individual. Here then, the consumer surplus *is* the entire area beneath the hypothetical demand curve; that is, the total willingness to pay (WTP).* In *Figure 9.1*, we consider the fisher-

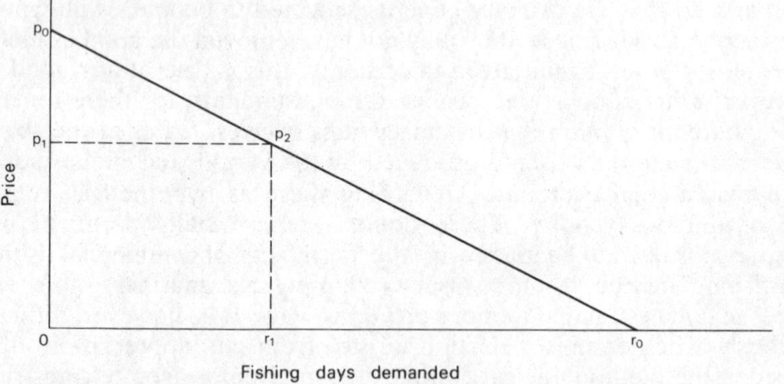

FIGURE 9.1 Individual demand curve for recreational fishing opportunities.

*Smith (1975) argues that the appropriate measure of value may not be the total area beneath the curve but the maximum revenue that could be obtained if prices were formed. Bowes and Loomis (1980) argue that consumer surplus calculated by the travel cost method (*see* section 9.5.3) has an exact theoretical equivalence to that measured using entry prices.

man as consumer alone, so fishing-days represents here a measure of the demand for the product. As can be seen, the curve suggests that the utility derived from the good is such that at price p_0, none is sought, whereas if the good is available freely a total of r_0 is sought. At intermediate prices, intermediate amounts are sought, such as p_1. However since there is no market price for the MRF and no restriction on access, in fact r_0 is enjoyed for free, and the consumer surplus is the total area of WTP beneath the curve.

If the recreational fishing in fact had a market price (perhaps in the case of a river game angling opportunity), then since the consumer receives no consumer surplus on the last angling access he (or she) is prepared to purchase on his demand curve, his surplus is the total area under the demand curve above the price level. If the access price were p_1, then total WTP is area O-p_0-p_2-r_1, the total actually paid is area O-p_1-p_2-r_1, and so consumer surplus is area p_0-p_1-p_2. Recently this area has often been referred to as *consumer rent* and this term is perhaps more useful here, as it has a certain comparability with other concepts of rent.

It is important to recognize that the fact that no money is exchanged in the open-access fishery (where consumer rent is O-p_0-r_0) does not make this rent value conceptually less significant: it merely raises the question of how to measure it satisfactorily.

MRF is not unique in that estimating an entire market demand curve for the good, such as the aggregate sum of all individuals' demand curves for MRF opportunities, is difficult. Here though, in the case of open access we shall not even be able to identify any coordinates such as p_1 r_1, and so alternative methods must be employed. Considering the demand curve for open-access MRF opportunities, one might attempt to establish it on some form of WTP basis. Conceptually, there are two basic approaches. We might employ the 'equivalent variation' measure, estimating in money terms the amount that anglers would be willing to pay so as to remain as well off with the fishery as they would be without it—that is, their preparedness to pay to forego the disappearance of the fishery. Alternatively, but not necessarily equivalently, we might employ a 'compensation variation' measure, estimating in money terms the amount that anglers would require as compensation to remain as well off without the fishery as they are with it—that is, their preparedness to surrender their rights to the fishery (willingness to surrender, WTS). Strictly speaking, the equivalent variation and the compensation variation are not necessarily the same as one another (obviously), nor the same as the area beneath a real market demand curve, but such differences are almost certainly swamped by the statistical inaccuracies of estimation techniques anyway (Willig, 1976). It is, however, important to recognize that consumer surplus or rent is a *net* economic yield from a recreational fishery. While it is true that, if any one fishery disappeared, anglers would switch their activities and expenditures to others and receive some rent, albeit less, from those, strictly this is not significant, because an angler's decision to partake in a certain fishery is made in his (or her) knowledge of possible rents from elsewhere, which therefore have determined his WTP for the chosen fishery. One must try to estimate either the equivalent variation or the compensation variation by trying to create a demand curve, which is difficult for any good, let alone for one for which no one pays any price.

9.5 THE TECHNIQUES OF VALUATION

It is not the intention of this chapter to undertake a complete review of the different methods suggested and employed for valuing recreational fishing activity. There are many such that have evolved, and continue to evolve, from within the field of what is properly recreation economics; some guidance is given in the bibliographic notes at the end of this chapter.

Instead, the intention is to examine key aspects of the three principal techniques that have been employed, in order to throw some light on the problems encountered. Although there are as yet relatively few empirical studies on MRF, especially outside North America, some emphasis on technique is justified in that the problems of valuation must be solved (or at least recognized explicitly) whenever any of those valuation-dependent decisions raised above are to be faced. Our emphasis is on primary benefits although there is increasing interest in secondary benefits: if anything, the problems with these are even greater.

9.5.1 User opinion surveys

Possibly the most obvious method by which to establish a hypothetical demand curve for MRF is to go out and ask questions about WTP or WTS. The sort of questions to be asked include how much participants would be prepared to pay for one day's access to a marine recreational fishery, over and above all associated expenditures (travel, equipment, etc.), given some assumptions about the aggregated usage levels (such as assuming that potential participants with higher evaluations are already participating). In practice, one would distinguish operationally between user surveys that posed open-ended questions such as 'what would it be worth to you . . .?', and more specific demand-orientated questions such as 'what quantity would you purchase if the price of access were . . .?', employing a range of price (or quality) situations.

Armed with the responses, one could then sum these to establish the aggregate demand curve and the total WTP. Such surveys tend to be fishery-specific and rather costly. However, carefully phrased questions can produce answers that allow one to estimate responses to marginal changes in the fishery (in quality, crowding, etc.), and also permit some element of dynamics in the study, both of which tend to be lacking in other techniques that have an 'all-or-nothing' nature.

The principal problem with user approaches lies not so much in the theoretical basis but in the essentially hypothetical valuation produced by the empirical estimation of the demand curve. This is especially so for open-access MRF with no other form of estimation used for any form of cross-check on the results. Respondents' answers to WTP questions are likely to be different from WTS answers, for responses to WTP are (logically) restrained by the real income or wealth of the respondent, whereas WTS answers are not.*

Although Willig (1976) argued that, for various reasons, there ought not to be more than a 5% difference in the valuations for normal goods, recreation researchers have found empirical variations in the range of a factor of between three and twenty! (Meyer, 1982). For example, one of the fairly rare studies of MRF was that by Smith, Conrad and Stone (1978) of recreational fishing for clams in Massachusetts in 1975, and they found that WTS was between six and seven times greater than WTP, even after initially rejecting 20% of the WTS responses as 'outliers' for being unacceptably high. It is of course possible that WTP responses are based on respondents' perception that they might indeed face a fee in future, whereas WTS responses are less biased. One might then wish to argue that the differences between the two are less than seem apparent, or possibly that WTS responses are less useful than WTP (as Smith *et al.* (1978) argue), but to do so is to miss the point that the divergence may be of interest in itself, and it is probably best to regard the two as different aspects of valuation.

Other problems lie in the questionnaire itself, in various respects. Specific phrasings of questions may be crucially important in determining the response received. Respondents may wish to please, or possibly annoy, the interviewer. Answers may be strategic responses: WTP assessed very high if possible loss of access is sensed, or low if a possible access fee is anticipated. Such gamesmanship would be difficult to eliminate. Finally, respondents may not understand the significance of the questions sufficiently to answer sensibly, and may give ill-considered or illogical answers.

Thus, while user opinion surveys are clearly linked to the basic idea of consumer rent and are usefully flexible, they suffer serious defects, sufficient to cause many observers to discount the technique. As Brown (1982, p. 147) summarizes: 'I would not recommend research involving WTP (WTS) techniques unless there are no alternative approaches.' Such valuations also attract a degree of scepticism amongst decision-makers, along the lines that 'hypothetical questions get hypothetical answers'.

9.5.2 Gross expenditure surveys

An alternative approach is to argue that if we cannot satisfactorily produce a demand curve from hypothetical values, we might be able to use the real expenditures that consumers make as some form of shadow valuation, employing as a surrogate the gross expenditures made by anglers in their pursuit of the recreational experience. Such an aggregation might then be

*Mishan (1975) argued that the WTP/WTS divergence arises more from the large differences in real income with and without access to the fishery, but it must be doubted that such differences are sufficiently powerful to change whole sets of preferences.

activity- or site-specific. Calculation of the gross expenditure would involve two main classes of costs: the travel or transfer costs (food, lodging, petrol, etc.), and the durable goods element (tackle, boats, etc.). To some extent these two classes would cover variable costs and fixed costs respectively, and thus allocating a share of the latter to each site/activity might become a problem familiar in production function analysis. It would remain open to debate whether or not to assess the time people spent, and the estimation of the value of time might be somewhat arbitrary (*see* section 9.5.3); it is not customarily assessed in such surveys.

The gross expenditure method has been quite a popular technique (especially in the United States), and there are several studies using versions of it. For example, in England and Wales the National Angling Survey (1980) estimated gross fishing expenditure per fishing trip (thus not site-specific) as an average of £8.25 for sea anglers and £9.37 for game anglers (£5.81 for coarse anglers). Such data can then be further aggregated, and the NAS estimated gross expenditure in England and Wales on sea angling in 1979 as £213 million and on game angling £120 million (with £300 million on coarse angling), while recognizing that some expenditures, such as lodgings, club memberships and annual permits, were not included. In Canada it was estimated that in 1975 6.5 million people spent C$900 million on food, lodging, transport and so on for some 75 million fishing days, while spending C$940 million on fixed assets such as gear and boats. The technique has also been applied to individual fisheries or sites, although not widely to sea angling (*see* for example Radford, 1980 on salmon angling on the River Wye in the United Kingdom*). Using a site-specific study technique, gross expenditures associated with the site can be estimated, although it must be recognized that the one element *not* included in the expenditure is for access to the activity itself (assuming free access), which casts an immediate doubt over the relevance of the estimation: one does not normally argue that the value of a market good such as commercially landed fish in the shops is reflected in expenditures made in travelling to the place of purchase and other expenditures while there.

The gross expenditure technique has four main merits: it is simple and easily comprehensible to those using it, it is fairly straightforward to obtain, it has some basis in opportunity costs in terms of money (actual expenditure is being measured, which is not the case for user opinion studies) and it produces impressively large figures, which pleases those who want to emphasize the value of recreational activity.† It can be argued also that the method has a valuable use in regional studies, where it may give some idea of the value of the activity to the region, such as in tourist expenditures.

However, the technique does have a number of rather significant defects. As we are primarily concerned here with a free-access good, then

*Radford estimated gross expenditure on the River Wye salmon fishery in 1977 by all anglers as £1.04 million, spent by 3800 anglers. As the study was not specifically designed as a gross expenditure survey, this figure excluded expenditure not linked to the fishing activity (food, drink, etc.).

all the expenditure measured of course concerns secondary benefits, as (usually) nothing is paid for the primary benefits of recreational fishing. In the extreme case, fishermen living adjacent to the site may be heavy users but spend very little (on travel, food, etc.), and as the method rates their valuation only by expenditures made, primary benefits are clearly not reflected. Generally, much of the gross expenditure would be incurred anyway, gives consumer utility in itself, and would be switched to other goods if the recreational fishery disappeared—all of which are grounds on which the method has been attacked as not measuring the *net* value and therefore as being of little use in decision-taking. There are problems too with the distinction between fixed and variable costs, for the division of the share of fixed costs between different sites and fisheries may well be arbitrary. It is also worth bearing in mind that the valuation of time would be extremely important, if used.

Nevertheless, a vigorous defence of the method when carefully employed has been made by Stabler (1982a), and many of its flaws are found in other techniques too. The data produced can be of considerable interest, especially at a regional or local impact level. They represent the minimum value of the fishery, if we assume that the expenditures recorded are made only if the utility that is derived is at least equal to this expenditure. At the very least, gross expenditure estimates provide a useful and comprehensible backup to other methods, and are of some use in reflecting the importance of recreational fishing in activity-specific studies.

9.5.3 The travel costs method

By far the most widely documented technique and one held in some acclaim until recent years is the travel costs method, which, like user opinion surveys, relies upon an indirect approach to estimating a demand curve and consumer rent. The technique is often named after the academics associated with its development, as the Clawson or Hotelling–Clawson method. The complexities of this widely reviewed and criticized technique can only be touched upon here (*see* for example Gibson, 1978; Baxter, 1979), but we can identify the basic principles and some of the problems.

Since people always travel to the recreational fishery, we can employ the travel expenditures that they incur as a form of 'price' they pay for enjoying the recreation. We may then employ the decisions of those living furthest away to visit a recreational fishery site despite facing higher supply costs as a reflection of what would happen to demand if those nearer the site faced access fees. Thus the participation rate of people living progressively further from the site in some ways shadows what the responses of people

---

†To illustrate this, a 1977 report on recreational fishing in the United States estimated that, in 1975, consumers purchased \$1840 million worth of goods and services at the retail level associated with MRF, and this generated \$700 million of value-added, \$343 million of wages and salaries, 50 580 person-years of employment, and \$53 million of capital expenditures in direct impact sectors (Grover, 1982, p. 614).

would be to higher access fees *if* these were charged. Given this, we have a surrogate demand curve based on implicit prices, and consumer rent can be estimated as in *Figure 9.1*.

The process of the method is briefly as follows: the area around the recreational fishery site is divided into zonal units, usually equidistant from it although data availability may require other zoning to be chosen. Surveys at the site or by post are then made of visitors to determine the visit rate from each zone, expressed as a visit rate *per capita*. Ideally such zones should have socioeconomic comparability such as similar income levels, although independent variables can account for variations. From this work, a curve such as that in *Figure 9.2a* can be constructed.

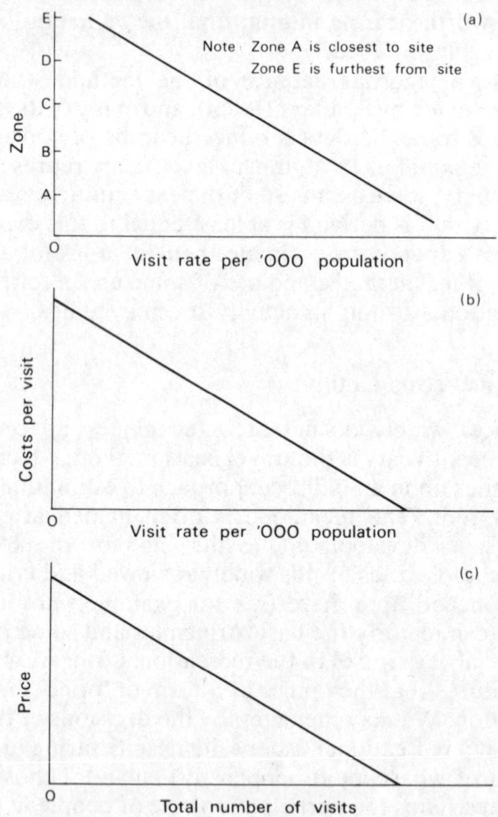

FIGURE 9.2 The travel cost method. (a) Visit rates per population. (b) Demand curve for the whole recreational experience. (c) Final demand curve for fishing at the site.

The next stage is to determine empirically the cost of using the site from each zone, especially the cost of travel, and this can then be used to translate the original curve into a demand curve (*see Figure 9.2b*). This function relates to the 'whole recreational experience', including all aspects of the recreational activity, yet it does give the basis on which to suggest an implied reaction by recreational fishermen to cost increases associated with *access*. This basis is thus the actual response to cost increases associated with *travel costs*, as reflected in the differing visit rates from each zone. The implied reaction allows us to derive consumption rates at various hypothetical access prices, employing demand reactions in terms of the numbers of people from each zone who would visit at the various possible access prices. These data can then be aggregated from all zones, and the process repeated for the range of costs. We then have a final demand curve (*Figure 9.2c*) this time a curve for fishing at the site, and we can employ this as suggested previously to quantify consumer rent as the total area beneath the curve.

As the technique is site-specific and may not be entirely relevant to linear sites, it appears to have been scarcely used in the case of sea angling, for example, but has had a wide application in coarse fishing and to some extent in game angling. Thus, in the previously cited study of salmon angling on the River Wye in the United Kingdom, Radford obtained a figure for consumers' surplus as approximately £5.25 per fishing trip, aggregating to a total of £365 000 for the river in 1977. This was then discounted at 8% over twenty years to give a capitalized value of consumers' surplus on the river of £3.6 million, 'probably an underestimate' (Radford, 1982) as travel time costs were not included.

The vital step in the travel cost technique is to employ the response of consumers to travel cost increases as a proxy for consumers' response to increased costs for access to the recreational fishing, thereby creating an implicit demand curve for as long as we can assume indifference between travel costs and real or hypothetical entry costs. This is a rather clever twist, but not without its problems, for it is probably immediately evident that the simplicity of the technique in both theoretical and empirical terms is both a strength and a weakness. For example, it can well be argued that the assumption of indifference between travel and access costs does not hold, or that the elasticities of demand for the two relationships are different (e.g. Harrison and Stabler, 1980). The technique in its most basic form also omits any consideration of alternative sites, even though it is evident that users in distant zones will almost certainly face a wider range of choice of sites, which will have a greater impact on their travel decisions. Omission of any consideration of alternative sites almost certainly produced overestimation of recreational values in early uses of the technique.

A difficult but now unavoidable problem arises over the question of time, both time spent at the site and time spent travelling, for recreational fishermen spend not only money but time on their activity. This time represents a significant cost of taking part in the activity and so ought to be included; unfortunately it is very difficult to reach agreement on how to value it, and travel cost estimates have proved to be unhappily sensitive to different values. Although there is no agreement on this problem of valuing time, Wilman (1980) suggested that time spent fishing (recreating) can be best measured by its *scarcity value* (that is, the next best alternative use), whereas time spent travelling is best measured by the 'value of time saved' (that is, the difference between scarcity value and *commodity value*, defined as its value in existing use). While until recently it has been fairly general not to include time spent recreating (e.g. Cesario, 1976), travel time seems a rather important element in any use of the travel cost method and has been more widely incorporated. Some studies recently have tended to suggest that such time may be costed at about 20% of household income or 25% of average earnings, but others have put it nearer to 50%, and Talhelm (1980) suggests that the relevant measure of the opportunity cost is the net wage rate. Obviously much depends on one's perception of opportunity cost as being related to alternative leisure and/or work usage. Even if quantifiable, the nature of travel remains a problem, for angling trips may very well be multipurpose or even multi-site (Cheshire and Stabler, 1976). A further complication is that some consumers may derive positive benefits from the travel. If, in any study, time is seen as having an opportunity cost but the time spent is not adequately valued, then it might be argued that the final demand curve is misplaced downwards and consumer rent undervalued.

A number of other problems must be mentioned. The question of the capacity of the fishery to absorb anglers, and the impact of any non-price rationing or congestion/crowding effects, is difficult to incorporate; the travel costs method may not measure consumer rent accurately if either is evident (McConnell and Duff, 1976; McConnell, 1977; *see also* the demand curve issue raised in section 9.6.1, later). The effect of quality changes, such as changes in the numbers, size and variety of fish and the natural setting, is not easily incorporated, yet it may be these dynamic changes that are at the centre of the purpose of an investigation. Obtaining data from many users can be expensive, but the use of sampling instead raises a whole set of problems with bias. In practice, it may prove difficult to justify the projected intersections of the demand curve for the whole recreational experience to both axes. The method's limitations in its naïve form as being site-specific and time-specific rather reduce its value in making anything other than limited statements about one fishery at one moment in time. This means that it cannot be used accurately to predict possible consumer rent under any but the existing resource use conditions, as for example in any consideration of potential benefits if there were a conflict concerning resource use, say between recreational and commercial fishing. Finally, as the method rests on estimating travel costs, problems with this process can be rather pervasive; how for example should less obvious aspects of car usage costs such as tyre wear be included? What happens if most of the users of a MRF live locally? Such a complication caused Smith, Conrad and Storey (1978) to abandon the travel cost method in their study of recreational clamming in Massachusetts.

Any technique such as the travel cost method that claims to derive the sought-after demand curve, and from it to calculate consumer rent, is also particularly sensitive to statistical problems, one of which is worthy of note here. This concerns the question of deciding upon the form of the demand function that the investigator fits to the available data. Economics provides little guidance as to the correct functional form, and there is a tradition, continued hereafter, of assuming a linear form. There are however at least two other strong claimants: a quadratic form, and a semilog form involving the natural logarithm of the dependent variable (quantity demanded). These three forms are represented in *Figure 9.3*, where all three curves terminate at the identified level of demand where free access obtains.

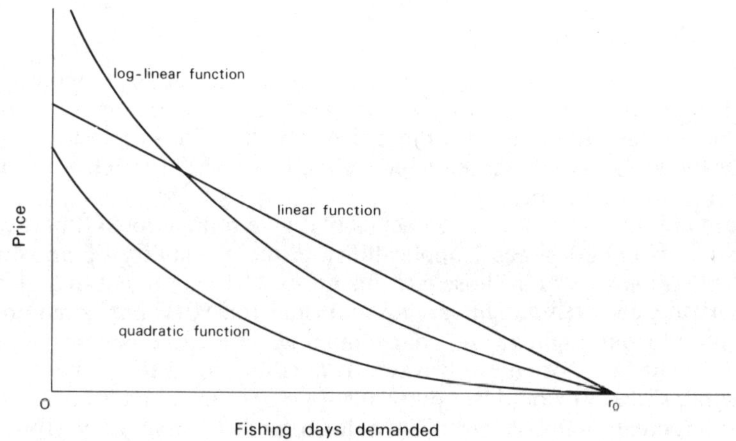

FIGURE 9.3 Individual demand curves for recreational fishing opportunities: functional forms.

While it is not relevant here to consider the statistical issues that might arise in practice, we should note that the consumer rent calculations are likely to be substantially affected by the functional form selected. For example, in their travel cost method study of the value of warm-water recreational fishing in Georgia, Ziemer, Musser and Carter Hill (1980) demonstrated that the linear functional form was not the most appropriate, and if used would have produced gross consumer rent (surplus) figures approximately four times larger than those given by the quadratic form and three times larger than for the semilog form. There are a number of techniques for testing the best choice of functional form; it is clearly important that they be used in any empirical studies.

The recognition of its deficiencies has led observers in recent years to become increasingly critical of the travel cost method (e.g. Brown, 1982; Stabler, 1982b). Yet it remains in use, and results obtained by its use are always studied with interest. Modern users have tried to meet as many of the emerging criticisms as possible, paying particular attention to the desirability of disaggregating to deal with the travel time problem and the inclusion of alternative sites. However, one must entertain grave reservations about its value when applied to open-access fisheries, where the entire valuation may rest on the single method; where other methods are also used or priced-access fisheries are studied, maybe the results have greater validity. Bishop and Haberlein (1979) argued that this method, and the other indirect type of evaluation obtained by user opinion surveys, are undermined by fairly large biases in their results. Stabler (1982b) went as far as to conclude that the method is, with exceptions, on its own theoretically unacceptable because of its basic simplicity, while also being empirically unworkable and operationally a failure.

9.5.4 Other methods

At this point the reader may well feel like joining other economists in despairing over the complexities of the measurement problem. One might even have some sympathy with those who revert to the simplest measures such as the weights and market values of the landed MRF catch—although not too much, one hopes.

There are however other approaches that give some hope. Of particular interest but limited general applicability is the possibility of measuring *economic resource rent* in those circumstances where a recreational fishery is in private ownership. This is most unusual for MRF but common for salmon and trout angling (and coarse angling) in Europe where river and estuary rights are often in private ownership; for MRF, the nearest applicable situation would be where just one or a few boats were licensed to take recreational fishermen to a location accessible only from the licence-granting base. Theoretically, economic resource rent is the return over and above that necessary to attract that factor input (the recreational resource) into the activity, which is the sum of opportunity costs and any costs involved in supplying the resource. As opportunity costs might often be considered as insignificant (Radford, 1982), the surplus of fishing rights owners' gross returns over their own costs plus the costs of any external body incurring relevant costs (for example, a water authority in river management) will then give us the economic resource rent. This we might calculate as the owners' net returns, minus the external bodies' costs; if we are then prepared to accept the proposition that the *capital value* of the fishery provides an indication of these owners' net returns (as in theory it is largely determined by them),* then all we have to do is determine the capital value of the fishery. Although such a determination is not always feasible, for some privately owned fisheries there is a fairly well established market in rights—at least in Europe, if less so elsewhere.

As an example, salmon fishing rights are sold in the United Kingdom via estate agencies. The latter employ a rule-of-thumb valuation for any one set of rights; essentially, the average annual catch taken over the previous five years is multiplied by a certain value per fish, this valuation being

*Capital value adjusts in a competitive market to ensure that the returns from owning the fishery are comparable to those from owning similar classes of assets; if they were more attractive, then their price would rise and net returns fall. Capital value is the present value of the future stream of income to be derived from owning the fishery, discounted to reflect the risk and uncertainty of ownership.

adjusted to reflect any specific advantages or disadvantages of the particular rights. To pursue again the Radford study already cited of salmon angling on the River Wye, here the mean value per salmon in 1977 was agreed by estate agencies at £1500 (although lower and much higher values were known). This was then multiplied by the Wye five-year average annual rod catch of 5525 fish, to give a discounted mean value of £8.3 million for the resource rent from the fishery. While of some interest in itself as a reflection of the worth of a fishery, this figure must of course then be *added* to any figure for consumer rent, for the total net yield or value of a recreational fishery is the sum of all yields to all those who benefit from its existence (minus any costs borne by others on their behalf, as for example by the water authorities). So, in the Radford study, resource rent (£8.3 million) was added to consumer rent (£3.6 million) to produce a final net value figure for the River Wye salmon fishery of £11.9 million (Radford, 1982).*

The resource rent dimension is however of limited applicability, for MRF especially, and other methods have been proposed. None of these is yet sufficiently widely tested empirically and operationally assessed to commmand general approval. One major step forward was developed by Talhelm (1972), who correctly considered that the main approaches were too concerned with demand, and instead stressed the angler as the producer, incorporating into his model a household production function approach and defining supply as the costs that anglers must meet in order to fish the site. Employing estimated demand and supply functions on a multi-site and multi-origin basis set within the resources of an area (defined by anglers' willingness to travel), Talhelm's approach offered a way forward that has not yet been fully explored empirically.

The *household production function* (HPF) approach has been used quite extensively in theoretical work in recent years, although often with little empirical estimation (e.g. Sutinen, 1982; Anderson, 1982). The strength of the approach is that we derive production functions based on the inputs that recreational anglers purchase in order to produce the desired good in a self-production function. They are seeking to maximize their utility from the purchases of inputs within an income restraint, or to minimize costs for a given level of utility. The costs of time can therefore be incorporated easily as one input, as can income foregone as an opportunity cost. This approach in particular allows for comparisons to be made on a similar marginal optimization basis between recreational fishing and other competing resource users, such as commercial firms, and can be used for assessing the impact of quality changes rather than the 'all-or-nothing' basis of many other approaches. While the technique is theoretically valuable, there are many problems in its use: one difficulty is that data requirements

*Radford (1982) in fact uses the broad term 'economic rent' for what is in this context resource rent. Strictly one should deduct from the total net value those relevant water authority costs; these can only be estimated arbitrarily, and Radford suggests that a net cost figure of £100,000 would, when also discounted, require some £1.1 million to be deducted from the £11.9 million.

are very demanding, and another problem revolves around the interdependence of the choice of quality and quantity, making the method almost impossible to use at times (Bockstael and McConnell, 1980). It seems likely that it will be some time before HPF-based valuations become operationally significant and usable for decision making.

A further possibility lies in the development of more sophisticated travel-cost-based techniques, including the so-called *hedonic travel cost* method favoured strongly by Brown (1982). This is derived from the work of Griliches, Lancaster and others, and is based on the proposition that the good purchased—a recreational fishing opportunity—has a multiplicity of pleasure characteristics. We can still take travel costs as one important cost component, but now use the argument that if people from one origin choose to travel further to a particular site rather than to a closer one, then the extra recreational pleasure characteristics that this site possesses must be worth the extra costs incurred. So, for every given origin, a hedonic price equation is estimated from travel costs regressed on observed sites characteristics. This yields the marginal value of the characteristic, which may or may not be constant. As people from different places face different opportunity sets—that is, they are in different markets—so we may expect price variation for each characteristic across markets. We may then determine demand for each characteristic using cross-sectional variations in hedonic prices across markets, observing the characteristics people choose and the relevant socioeconomic dimensions of the sample. The final step can be to estimate the number of trips of varying length that individuals take to one or more sites as a function of the price of the trip or other demand characteristics. If we have a demand curve for the quality of the recreational fishing from hedonic analysis, then the value of a hypothetical loss of one site characteristic, such as quality, can be approximated. The hedonic travel cost method was used by Brown and Mendelsohn (1981) in estimating the demand for steelhead stock density in Washington rivers.

Vaughan and Russell (1982) employed a *varying parameter travel cost* method in a study of freshwater fishing, allowing for differences in characteristics between a range of sites by including twelve site-characteristic variables and taking the visitation rate as a function of travel costs, zonal population and income *and* these characteristics, although not incorporating the cost of substitute sites. They were able to calculate specific values for the WTP of anglers for marginal changes in site characteristics, such as increases in mean catch per angler.

Finally, brief mention should be made of the *Delphi* technique, outlined by Zuboy (1982) and employed in his study of MRF for spiny lobsters in Florida. The technique is based on soliciting expert opinions on magnitudes, which are then systematically developed and refined into a consensus between the contributing experts by an iterative feedback process. It was employed by Zuboy to try to reach consensus only on the MRF quantity landed, but it might also have some application to valuations. The technique lacks any theoretical basis and may well not prove durable.

9.5.5 Can we do it?

It is clear from the above that, with the possible exception of privately owned recreational fisheries, the problem of producing acceptable measures of the value of recreational fishing has not yet been solved. This is a rather serious failing, for the decisions for which we need such data cannot be postponed until a method can be agreed. Thus, while none of the techniques is entirely acceptable, in default of anything better some must be used in decision-taking. In so doing, one must be very careful; in a comparison between MRF and MCF, for example on a particular fish stock with a view to possible restrictions on entry, would it be 'fair' to use the landed market value technique for MCF alongside the travel cost method for MRF? Some at least would argue that as the latter is based entirely on consumer rent while the former neglects it totally, to do so would produce a strange comparison. Such comparisons indeed often suggest that MRF is 'more valuable' than MCF, but the methodological problems in making such comparisons are very large. One overall review attempting to estimate the value of the sport fisheries of the United States for 1970–71 managed to find various estimates that ranged from $300 million (based on wholesale landed catch value) to $6800 million (total benefits), and resolved this ludicrous discrepancy by arguing that they were worth somewhere between $2 billion and $5 billion (North, 1976). As during this time the MRF catch accounted for 29% of the total landed weight of all finfish in the United States, the impossibility of evaluating the importance of this activity in meaningful terms is most regrettable for those involved.

It is also worth noting here that the nature of MRF is even more complex than we have allowed, for anglers not only may visit several sites on one trip, but while at each site may make use of what are, strictly, different fisheries by catching a variety of species of fish on site—a complexity that is possibly less pertinent in freshwater fishing. Moreover, the fish caught have a variety of relationships with one another: as competitors, as predator and prey, etc. How specific then are the MRF participants' intentions and/or fishing gear? Also, the intrinsic quality of the catch may be very important to an angler. Although we argue that stock density must be taken as the logical basis for analysis, in fact the angler may prefer the chance of one specimen-size fish to many smaller ones (and may throw these latter back). All such complexities are difficult to incorporate into simple models, and maybe, ultimately, simple models will not be enough.

Finally, where do we go from here? The answer depends on one's interpretation of the strengths and weaknesses of the available methods. Despite theoretical failings, gross-expenditure studies can have useful practical value, especially as decisions tend to be taken on the basis of total expenditures rather than on net-benefit grounds, whereas the theoretical strengths of the user opinion surveys are possibly overwhelmed by the empirical problems. Carefully used versions of the travel cost method show promise for future development, and household production function analysis seems especially useful theoretically in conflict situations. Even so, a recent reviewer (Brown, 1982, p. 152) put forward the view: 'I think there does not exist research on salt water fishing values and demand functions which [has] a theoretical framework and data of sufficient quality to warrant publication in a respectable professional economics journal.' Work continues in order to make good this deficiency, but decisions meanwhile have to be made.

9.6 CONFLICT, MANAGEMENT AND POLICY

There is no doubt that the primary purpose for which valuations of MRF are required is to resolve conflict, either with MCF or with non-fishing users of the water resource. The whole question of the scope of such conflicts is very large and not extensively pursued here, but we may note some of the potential conflicts as being between MRF and pipelines, oil wells, marinas, aquaculture, scuba diving, commercial shipping, other port facility users, as well as with MCF—and there may of course be conflict between different categories of MRF users of resources. If anything, an even wider range of sources of conflict applies to game and coarse fishing. However it is the conflict between MRF and MCF that has attracted most attention to date, with a particular emphasis on the problem of managing dual fisheries.

The question of competing usage and dual management has been subject to academic attention mainly since the late 1970s, principally in North America, where efforts are being made under the United States's Fishery Conservation and Management Act 1976 to develop management strategies towards recreational fisheries when these interact with commercial ones. In Europe, this aspect has been largely ignored, both theoretically and empirically. Not all of the studies are reconcilable for they tend to be constructed on differing assessments of the key factors and restraints. The basic approach below is taken from Copes and Knetsch (1981), with inputs from Anderson (1982). The central problem is to incorporate both commercial and recreational fishing within a common framework such as to give common criteria for optimization, while maintaining the linkages to the established bioeconomic analysis of commercial fishing and the value estimation models of recreational fishing. It is however immediately obvious that the essential common denominator is the fish that are caught, for there are both static interactions between the commercial and the recreational catcher, and also dynamic interactions between fish caught today and the fish that may be caught in future (by either group). However, since 'fish caught' is not identical with the 'output' of both activities, these interactions become especially complicated. Thus we find that much of the analysis of MRF uses 'fishing days' as the dependent variable, which leaves unclear the relationship between the value of the 'fishing day' and the marginal value of fish, for optimization in economic terms always revolves around marginal analysis.

Before proceeding to the analysis, we should note that the modelling of the bioeconomics of MRF is itself an area that has begun to attract an increasing number of studies. It is a complex area, and the alternative models proposed are not explored here for reasons of space and the lack as yet of any generally accepted model equivalent to the model of MCF employed in earlier chapters. However at this point the interested reader might well wish to examine the works of Anderson (1982), Bishop and Samples (1980), and McConnell and Sutinen (1979a), all of whom used models in which the anglers respond passively to changes in stock levels in the fishery to develop conditions for optimal management policy. None of these authors, however, incorporates the important features of stock externalities in terms of the demand curve for recreational fishing. McConnell and Sutinen (1979b) also went on to employ the household production function approach to permit anglers to vary their catch rates and the number of trips made.

9.6.1 Net social benefits in MRF and MCF management

We can establish some common ground between commercial and recreational fishing by considering the impact of any management intervention in terms of its effect on the aggregate net social benefits received by society from the fishery. We may suggest that the optimal allocation between MRF and MCF will be such as to maximize the present discounted values of net aggregate social benefits of the two combined, subject to a constraint concerning the biological growth of the fish stock. For both the commercial fishery and the recreational fishery, these net benefits theoretically have three component parts. First, there is a consumer rent (CR), as defined in section 9.4.3, enjoyed by consumers over and above what they have to pay for their consumption. Secondly, there is the producer rent (PR), specifically the difference between the producers' costs, including the opportunity cost of their effort, and their receipts.* We cannot easily identify this in MRF, where the definition of consumption and production is indistinct. Aggregate producer rent is then the sum of all the individual rents of participants in the fishery, no doubt varying widely with skills and costs, and one might have to include some valuation of WSB here for MCF. Finally, there is the resource rent (RR), which will tend to be eroded away in the open-access commercial fishery as demonstrated earlier, but which if the fishery were in sole ownership would be the owner's net returns. Thus a hypothetical (commercial) fishery in sole ownership, with the owner contracting fishermen to catch the fish and selling these to consumers, yields total net social benefits as the sum of the resource rent, producer rent and consumer rent respectively, i.e.

*Strictly PR is the sum of payments received by producers for the use of inputs they own or control above that necessary to prevent these inputs from being used for another purpose.

$$NSB = RR + PR + CR$$

Given these dimensions, how do the various management possibilities in fishing affect their magnitudes? First, in the case of commercial fishing we can identify the five possible situations reflected in *Table 9.3*. As we have already explored commercial fishing in depth, little needs to be said about these except to note particularly the following points. With free access and market, no benefits components are maximized, although some CR and PR may be earned: CR in the normal nature of the demand for goods, and PR by intramarginal (low-costs) fishermen. The main contrast can then be made to the situation where we hypothesize public MCF management with the objective of maximizing NSB as a combination of its component parts. We are not concerned here however with the distribution of these component parts, on the grounds that if unacceptable it can be corrected by redistributional policies. Here of course effort is restricted, and the combination of all elements is, by definition, optimized. The table also shows three other situations. The first is sole ownership by a profit-maximizer who will also restrict effort to maximize RR, but his high prices and low output will restrict PR and CR. Secondly, ownership of the fishery by a consumer cooperative (or the allocation of sole buying powers to one) will maximize the combined total of CR and RR. Finally, if the fishery is owned by a producers' cooperative, then the combined total of PR and RR will be maximized, but its higher prices will restrict CR. In each case, the interaction between the dimensions being jointly maximized is not specifiable.

We can now extend a similar view of management strategies to the recreational fishery, although here we shall not include PR for reasons stated. To understand and extend *Table 9.4*, examination of *Figure 9.4* will be helpful. In the figure, we consider a single recreational-only fishery

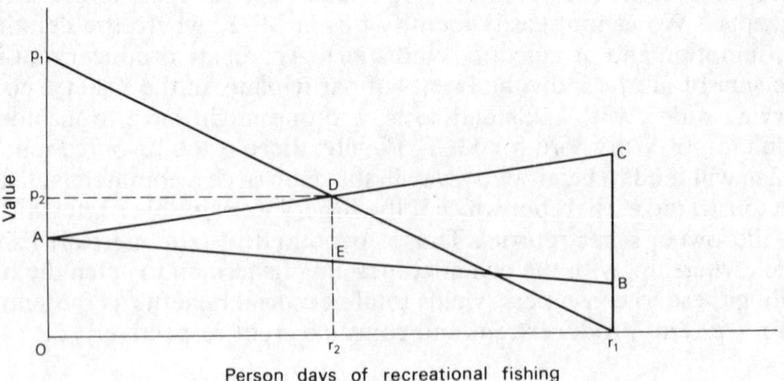

FIGURE 9.4 Free access and access fees in a marine recreational fishery: benefits and costs.

TABLE 9.3 Rents from alternative commercial fisheries management strategies at equilibrium levels of effort

Access management form	*Objective: social benefits maximized*	*Incidental: positive but non-maximized social benefits*	*Social benefits dissipated*	*Catch size*	*Effort level*	*Consumer prices*
				relative to socially optimal levels		
A. Free access and free market	–	CR and some PR	RR	Uncertain	Above	Uncertain
B. Public control to maximize NSB	CR + PR + RR	–	–	Optimum	Optimum	Optimum
C. Private sole ownership	RR	CR and PR (limited)	–	Below	Below	Above
D. Consumer monopsony	CR + RR	PR	–	Below	Below	Above
E. Producers' monopoly	PR + RR	CR	–	Below	Below	Above

Note: CR, consumer rent; PR, producer rent; RR, resource rent; NSB, total net social benefits.
Source: Based on Copes and Knetsch (1981).

TABLE 9.4 Rents from alternative recreational fisheries management strategies at equilibrium levels of effort

Access management form	*Objectives: social benefits maximized*	*Incidental: positive but non-maximized benefits*	*Social benefits dissipated*	*Catch size*	*Effort level*	*Access fees*
				relative to socially optimum levels		
A. Free access	–	CR	RR	Uncertain	Above	Below
B. Public control to maximize NSB	CR + RR	–	–	Optimal	Optimal	Optimal
C. Private owner: managed access	RR	CR	–	Uncertain	Uncertain	Uncertain

Note: CR, consumer rent; RR, resource rent; NSB, total net social benefits.
Source: Based on Copes and Knetsch (1981).

under public ownership and management. First consider free access: here anglers will enjoy r_1 days' fishing, and area O-p_1-r_1 represents their total consumer rent as evaluated when they entered the fishery. This representation, however, overvalues the fishery (whatever the technique we may choose to identify total CR empirically), for it fails to incorporate two elements of social costs that are relevant. First, as stated earlier, public authorities, such as water authorities or port authorities, may incur costs in providing access to and maintaining the recreational facility. These costs may be shown in the diagram as area O-A-B-r_1, and will decline per person-day because of scale economies. Secondly, there are two forms of externalities that are relevant in recreational fishing, for both 'crowding' externalities (congestion) and 'stock' externalities (as in MCF) are possible, and these are reflected here in the area A-B-C, increasing because each extra fisherman affects a gradually increasing number of existing fishermen. The curve AC represents average externality costs, aggregated vertically on top of AB.

Now if free entry is retained, private users will enjoy Or_1 person-days' fishing, but with a total social cost of O-A-C-r_1. Thus the fishery will be a net benefit to society to the extent that area O-p_1-r_1 exceeds area O-A-C-r_1, which is the equivalent of the difference between areas A-p_1-D and D-C-r_1. At a consumption level beyond r_2, the social costs per fisherman of providing a recreational fishery exceed private benefits per person-day (excluding though any secondary benefits), which we might consider to be 'overfishing' of the recreational resource, or a 'socially detrimental use of the resource' (Copes and Knetsch, 1981). Usage r_2 is, then, the socially optimal level of consumption, and might be achieved in theory by an access fee of p_2 (= Dr_2). If however free access is maintained, then the *net social* cost of permitting usage r_1 is the area D-C-r_1, although this is to overstate the loss somewhat in that practical restriction of access to the level r_2 would inflict enforcement costs on someone; if these costs actually exceed D-C-r_1, then it would be socially preferable to permit free access. Thus *Table 9.4* shows free access as not maximizing NSB and as dissipating the RR. However, any public authority associated with the fishery will still have costs O-A-B-r_1 though the fishermen enjoy CR as area O-p_1-r_1 minus area A-B-C (crowding and catch externality costs). The level of effort applied is above optimum, although the *catch* relative to a managed-access fishery cannot be determined as we do not know the impact of a discretely higher level of effort (as person-days of MRF) on the sustainable catch of fish.

With some form of public authority management aimed at maximizing NSB, an optimal outcome may be achieved. Ignoring enforcement costs, effort can be restricted to r_2 with an access fee p_2 charged, maximizing NSB. The public authority collects total revenue of O-p_2-D-r_2, offsetting expenses O-A-E-r_2, and this excess (A-p_2-D-E) is effectively a resource rent that can be passed into other fishing or non-fishing usages. Anglers reap net benefits (CR) of the area p_2-p_1-D *minus* area A-D-E, the latter subtracted as being a double cost to the participants, once as an access fee and once as a remaining loss from those externalities still arising despite restricted access.

As we have discarded the idea of 'producers' for the recreational fishery, there is no question of a producer cooperative or consumer monopsony here. However, one other situation remains, that of a profit-maximizing sole resource owner.* *Figure 9.5* reflects the position, and at the price charged the owner's marginal cost will be equal to MR. The owner's MR curve is determined by the demand curve p_1r_1 and is shown as p_1m_1; his MC curve (AB) shows the amounts he will have to spend in maintaining the

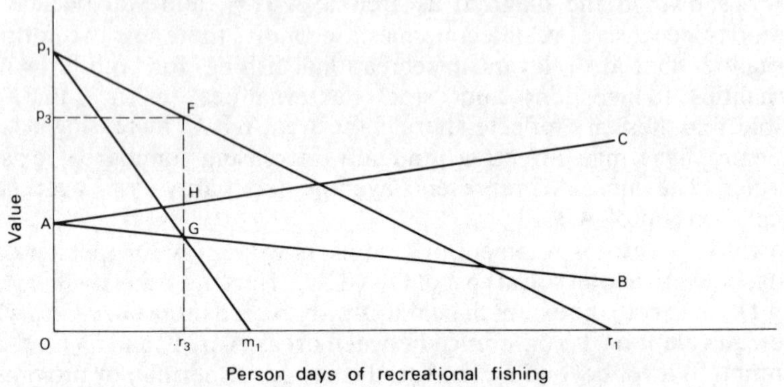

FIGURE 9.5 Privately owned marine recreational fishery: optimal access fees.

fishery at different usage levels. Thus, usage level r_3 at price p_3 is optimal (MC = MR), and he earns revenues O-p_3-F-r_3 less costs O-A-G-r_3. His maximum net RR is thus A-p_3-F-G. The anglers' CR is area p_3-p_1-F minus the externalities reflected in curve AC, which at usage r_3 are A-H-G. The levels of fees, effort and catches relative to public authority management cannot be easily determined, for while both have AB maintenance costs, the sole owner is relating to marginal revenue p_1m_1 while the public authority relates to demand p_1r_1. While the sole owner might set a high access price (p_3), he will not be internalizing social costs reflected in AC (unless he himself fishes), which might encourage the public authority that does so internalize to restrict entry even more than any sole owner.

The framework developed is analytically useful in clarifying the issues, but it does not overcome many of the problems involved in management decisions. One particular difficulty is in formalizing the relationship between the fishing experience and the stock of fish. Quite obviously there is some relationship: if maximization of fish caught were the angler's objective, then commercial and recreational fishing might conveniently be man-

*Copes and Knetsch extend the discussion to include a fishery owned and managed by a private club, but their analysis is not included here. The club effectively integrates maximization of RR and CR within the single objective, albeit seeking to restrict entry to minimize externalities (*see* Copes and Knetsch, 1981).

aged within the same bioeconomic framework. Alternatively, if it did not matter whether anything were caught and the prospect of catching nothing were immaterial, then it would not matter if no fish at all were provided for the recreational angler. As reality must lie between, we are again reminded that the recreational good has a variety of characteristics.

This difficulty does introduce an awkward complication, concerning demand and fishermen's expectations, reflected in *Figure 9.6*. Starting

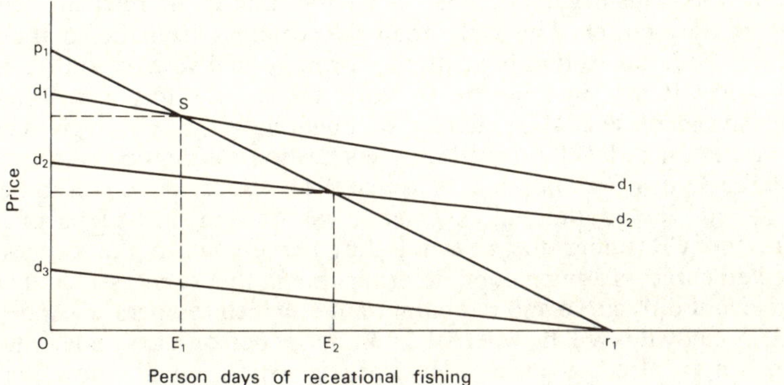

FIGURE 9.6 Congestion and the valuation of consumer rent in a recreational fishery.

from a set of individual demand curves, we might identify a combined market demand curve d_1d_1. This identification must be on the basis that each individual assumes total effort will in fact be at some *specific* level, say E_1, for only at this level are individuals' expectations concerning the congestion levels to be encountered determinable. In other words d_1d_1 is an aggregate market demand curve but for a given level of congestion; it is therefore this curve that the travel cost method quantifies. Thus if we change the anticipated level of congestion, we ought to have a new aggregate demand curve. This might be d_2d_2, if *everyone assumes* that effort will be at level E_2 (higher). There is thus a family of demand curves for different levels of congestion affecting the catch, from which we may establish another type of demand curve, p_1r_1; this is the locus of points of intersection between total effort used and the amount expected by individuals in formulating their individual demand curves (those that were aggregated to give d_1d_1, d_2d_2, etc.). This Wetzel (1977) called the *congestion-corrected* curve; it is the demand curve that would be observed if one could experiment to determine the number of days fished at various access fees per unit of recreational fishing effort, or in other words, it shows actual WTP that will arise as users adjust to changes in congestion arising from changes in the numbers of users. Wetzel argues that the area beneath this more inelastic curve is the correct measure of consumer rent. It would incidentally follow from this argument that the travel cost method, which identifies d_1d_1 curves, will underestimate consumer rent.

Anderson (1982) disputes this point however. He argues that the correct consumer rent at any usage level is that beneath the d_1d_1 curve, for the congestion-corrected curve is in fact not truly a demand curve, because it shows how demand will change with variations in price *and* congestion, and therefore breaches the customary economic assumption concerning demand curves that only the price may vary.* It is not appropriate for calculating consumer rent, since congestion levels vary as we move along the curve, and at any level such as E_1, consumer rent should not include the area d_1-p_1-S. This argument leads us to note that if the relevant demand curve is d_2d_2 rather than d_1d_1, then CR changes from being the area beneath the latter to that beneath the former—in *neither* case that below p_1r_1—and CR may increase or decrease; increased effort therefore does not always increase CR. Ultimately, we might have d_3r_1, which gives us the free-access usage level r_1 based on a congestion assumption of this level, and CR is O-d_3-r_1; at this point, marginal WTP is zero, and no further effort is attracted. The operationally efficient level of fishing is the level of effort where the CR under the relevant d_1d_1 curve, out to the congestion-corrected curve, is a maximum, determinable in theory by estimating both the relevant d_1d_1 curve and the point on it at which to operate (Anderson, 1983). Strictly this will be where the number of person-days under any d_1d_1 curve is maximized, given that level of congestion. Finally, note that the travel cost method will tend to overestimate the reduction in person-days of MRF if access fees are charged, because it ignores the positive impact of reduced congestion arising from the restricted access (*see* McConnell, 1980). Thus the method can present no valuations other than at the existing level of usage (i.e. on one single d_1d_1 curve).

9.6.2 MRF and MCF interaction and management

Various authors have tried to formalize the interaction between MRF and MCF, although most of the models that have emerged are too hedged about with assumptions or too removed from the essential theoretical foundations of the two activities to present a practical basis for empirical work. Indeed, there is a marked deficiency of substantial studies of this interaction on a combined basis of theory and empirical investigation. Anderson (1982) formalizes the relationships rather neatly; although the mathematical model fails to present ultimately useful predictions (Anderson, 1982, p. 25), the graphical model presented in *Figure 9.7* gives some insight into the issues that emerge. In order to make the analysis though, Anderson is forced, like other authors, into making several simplifying assumptions, including the taking of a very simple view of the relationship between effort (as 'fishing days' by both MCF and MRF) and fish caught,

*Formally, total person-days' effort is both the item being measured on the horizontal axis *and* a shift parameter of the individual curves. This is strictly a 'congestion' externality here as stated; if we considered the impact of higher use levels in terms of the sizes and numbers of fish caught, then this impact would be a 'stock externality', analogous to that in MCF.

and assuming that the value of the MRF can be related to certain components of the recreational activity such as catch per day and individual catch size. His analysis also implies that it is possible to measure the costs that one fishery will inflict upon another; in this context, it is interesting to note McConnell's point (1979) that one of the problems in joint fisheries management is that there tends to be a wish 'to do no direct harm', and as the costs of restricting the MCF are readily apparent whereas those of restricting MRF are much less so, managers might well tend to favour MCF just because the impact of this on MRF is in fact *not* readily measurable.

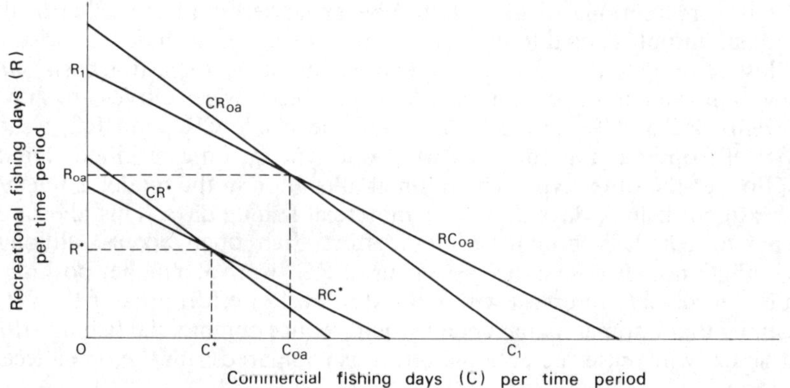

FIGURE 9.7 Optimal effort allocation in a joint recreational and commercial fishery.

The essence of the relationship is that an extra day of MCF will, in the long run, affect the catch per day or size of catch, and thus the value, of the MRF (and vice versa). The open-access equilibrium occurs when the open-access MCF has profits reduced to zero and simultaneously all those wishing to participate in the open-access MRF at zero price do so. The equilibrium level of each in a joint fishery is thus less than would occur in a solely commercial or recreational usage. In *Figure 9.7*, four lines are shown. The curve CR_{oa} (commercial open access) shows the amount of effort that will produce an equilibrium in the commercial fishery for various levels of effort in a competing recreational fishery. Curve RC_{oa} does the same for effort in the recreational fishery at various levels of effort in the competing commercial fishery. The intersection of these two curves is a general equilibrium for *both* in open access, as the efforts in each are in equilibrium (by definition) with efforts in the opposing fishery; the intersection gives an equilibrium combination of C_{oa} commercial fishing days and R_{oa} recreational fishing days. It is of course possible that the curves might not intersect in this quadrant of the model; if the intersect were in quadrant 2, then there would be no commercial fishery (that is, one would have the equivalent of R_1 recreational days), while if in quadrant 4, then no recreational fishery would exist (one would have the equivalent of C_1 commercial fishing days).

As previously established separately, in neither case however is open access optimal, although here an additional dimension is the impact that one fishery has on the other. In static terms, the economic optimal point is where the sum of the values generated by both uses is maximized: net profit in MCF and net value in MRF. This means that effort should be expanded in the commercial fishery until the value of the marginal output is equal to its total opportunity cost (defined now as goods and services given up in its production *plus* any decrease in the value of recreational fishing). Likewise, recreational fishing should be expanded until the value of the marginal output is equal to its total opportunity cost, which here consists of the loss in value to the previous recreational anglers (congestion costs) *plus* the loss in value in the commercial fishery. These revised curves are shown in *Figure 9.7* as CR^* and RC^* and both lie inside CR_{oa} and RC_{oa}; each shows the optimal amount of effort of one type, given a specified amount of effort of the other type. The optimal allocation in the model is thus R^* recreational fishing days and C^* commercial fishing days. This allocation seems to entail in both cases less effort than open access, although such might not always be the case. Thus, if RC^* were at a higher position it could conceivably intersect with CR^* at a level of effort greater than R_{oa}, meaning that optimal management would reduce commercial fishing effort but actually increase recreational effort as compared with the open-access position.

It is thus possible to reconcile theoretically, given a number of important simplifying assumptions, the conflict between different users of the fish stock. The modelling does not take us very much further than a fairly formal statement of what may be intuitively reasonable: that optimal regulation will always require a reduction in one of the two sectors using the fish stock, possibly both, possibly to the extent of prohibition of one. However, it does additionally reveal that an increase in one sector from the joint open-access level is not impossible. Ultimately it is the relative quantified values that determine the actual optimal effort levels, and thus we are back to the issue of estimating the value of MRF where the value of MCF is determinable in orthodox ways.

Finally, in discussing the interaction between MRF and MCF, we must recognize that the 'conflict' between the two takes on a vastly wider set of dimensions in practice than simply how much of the available catch each sector may take; friction includes such issues as the killing of small fish by MCF and the damage gear may do to spawning grounds. As Pownall (1979) reports in the case of Australia, such conflict is often based essentially on ignorance and envy, on both sides of the debate.

9.6.3 The management of MRF

The question of managing MRF is not, by and large, one that features prominently in countries' fisheries management priorities. Although a number of countries have developed policies towards MRF (*see* for example the excellent survey in Grover, 1982), most of these policies are conducted at a somewhat superficial level, and it is mainly in the context of competing usage with MCF that more specific policies are to be found. As this issue is itself confined for the most part to North America (and to some extent Europe) the most explicit discussion of MRF management has taken place there.

In section 9.6.2 we identified the economic conditions for the optimal management of a joint MRF/MCF fishery. It is worth noting that MRF participants are likely to favour management approaches in general—and especially if applied only to MCF—that are based on objectives other than MSY. In general terms, OSY-type strategies will produce more fish in the sea, and thus will favour MRF in broad terms if both types of fishing are being managed, and favour it even more if only MCF is being managed. It may not need repeating, but fisheries management policies that concern only MCF, where there is any significant MRF on the stock, will either transfer the benefits of management to MRF or permit these benefits to be dissipated.

In general terms, sport fishermen have themselves tended to recognize the case in favour of limited entry as a management tool (*see* for example McHugh, 1978). This recognition arises in part no doubt from self-interest by existing users, but the broader biological issues have been acknowledged, and also the point that open access will erode away the economic benefits from the fishery. Of course, most MRF participants will not be especially concerned with maximizing the economic benefits from the fishery, but will have some concept of their 'fair share' of the resource access. It is, however, generally accepted that MRF with open access will result in overfishing (McConnell and Sutinen, 1979a). Unfortunately the various mechanisms for restricting access that have been used in MCF are not particularly helpful in the case of MRF. One basic difficulty is that any system which prevents or inhibits entry to a recreational activity, often seen as a traditional right, will be unpopular and possibly even unacceptable. Politically these feelings may be of some consequence, as there may be more people who do, or might, take part in recreational fishing than are associated with commercial fishing.

Management has in practice tended to work on an ad-hoc basis, with the rather loose objective of preventing overfishing in the biological sense. The nearest approximation to the process in North America, in the 1970s at least, was typified by McHugh as being: take the TAC, deduct from it the known MRF catch, and allocate the rest to MCF. This approach might be inequitable, but there was no mechanism for assessing MRF claims other than known landings, and, in a rapidly growing activity, holding the MRF catch at its past level was contentious enough on its own. Not surprisingly, the need for valuations of MRF comparable to valuations of MCF before management can progress much further seems a necessary condition.

9.6.4 Marine recreational fisheries policies

Space restraints do not permit more than a brief mention of the movement towards specific policies for MRF, a development that has taken place largely in North America, where the conflict between MRF and MCF has been more pronounced than elsewhere. There, and indeed in all countries considering policy issues, the scarcity of data on MRF has been a major initial problem.

In the United States, fisheries management since the Fishery Conservation and Management Act 1976 has had to deal with MRF explicitly. Recreational fisheries are to be promoted 'under sound conservation and management principles', but nevertheless the first priority has still been given to MCF because of its importance and, moreover, the lack of any compensatory mechanisms were MCF to be disadvantaged in favour of MRF. However since the Act does not allow for user access fees, there has been a tendency to use other methods of restricting MRF access, especially quotas and closed seasons. The basic OSY objective of the Fishery Conservation and Management Act, designed so as to procure the greatest overall national benefit from fisheries in terms of food production and recreational opportunities (Public Law 94–265), is essentially favourable to MRF. Steps have been taken to implement these objectives (*see* Schmied, 1982), and a number of regional management plans have included specific allocations for MRF on species shared with MCF (including Pacific salmon, Atlantic mackerel, cod, haddock, yellowtail, flounder, shrimps, billfish and sharks). The period since 1976 has however been most distinctive for a burgeoning of literature in an attempt to improve the data base for eventual decision-taking and to draw up broad plans to implement the objectives (Stroud, Radonski and Martin, 1982). Broadly, the tendency has so far been to employ essentially physical regulations such as time and area closures, within a specific maximum MRF catch reflected in a daily catch (bag) limit.

In Canada, Pearse (1982) reported on the MRF issue on the Pacific coast, although Kirby (1982) did not cover it to any extent in the Atlantic coast report. On the Pacific coast, the Department of Fisheries and Oceans (Pacific Region) is responsible for managing sport fisheries, notably those for salmon and trout. As 1 million Coho and Chinook salmon were taken in 1980 in 2 million angler days (equal to 4% of the total salmon harvest), this task is of some importance. One reflection of the economic significance of MRF is that the capital value of the MRF fleet is equal to that of the MCF fleet (*c*. $850 million in 1980). Regulation in the past has been by a bag limit since 1951, decreasing over time, combined with a size limit, increasing over time. Non-restrictive licences were introduced in 1981, partly to gain information and partly to raise revenue from the activity for resource enhancement. Various closures have also been employed. The effectiveness of all these measures is most debatable however, as there has been no monitoring system and relatively little commitment officially to MRF.

The Pearse Commission recommended some changes to this attitude, based on the collection of more data and cautious movement towards a greater degree of management. The existing guidelines to the Department concerning MRF are unhelpfully vague: '. . . accommodate as far as possible the needs of the growing recreational fishery without major negative effects on the other user groups' (p. 190). Pearse suggests that the problem of how much fish to allocate to MRF should be dealt with by placing a ceiling on the total annual catch of MRF over the next five years (i.e. 1 million salmon) while further investigations take place. The associated question of who gets access to the fish is to be dealt with by issuing licences (partly in exchange for data) but at a doubled price, using income for stock enhancement as well as management. Historically, access has been permitted in Canada, as typically elsewhere in the world, on an unrestricted basis, allowing a lot of people access but to a gradually diminishing share of the available stock. Now Canada is moving in the direction of controlled access to produce an improved recreational experience; in other words, the emphasis is shifting away from open access towards preservation of the quality of the experience.

The question of exactly how to control MRF catches was analysed in theory by McConnell and Strand (1981a), who considered the three ways of restricting the recreational catch: reducing the catch per angler, the number of trips per angler, and the total number of anglers. Given their assumptions, they proved that it causes less welfare loss to reduce the number of trips per angler than the total number of anglers, but the choice between catch per angler (bag limits, etc.) and trips per angler depended upon the responsiveness of anglers to expected catch; broadly, the more responsive they are, then the more will welfare losses from catch-per-angler restrictions exceed losses from trip restrictions. These findings point in the direction of restricting trips, rather than angler numbers or even catch limits. Pearse *de facto* goes along with this tendency in recommending the controlling of effort rather than bag limits, although 'curtailing the rate of growth of sportfishing effort and maintaining average catches' (p. 192) could mean either that trips per angler or that the total number of anglers should be controlled. As however Pearse then recommends the doubling of licence fees *and* the maintenance of a bag limit on salmon catching per licence (thirty fish in fact), then to some extent all are controlled. It is worth noting that a licence with a bag limit, sold at a price and in the absence of restrictions on the numbers of licences any individual may hold, contains some of the central features of the IFQ system. Bag limits are, however, notoriously difficult to allocate, monitor and enforce, enforcement costs being especially high. Indeed, McHugh (1978) raised the issue of whether the overall costs of control of recreational fisheries may even be prohibitively high.

Policies in other countries have been reviewed by Grover (1982). Generally most such policies are in their infancy and tend not to have strong economic inputs.

9.7 SUMMARY

The recreational use of fish stocks has become an important consideration in the economic analysis of fisheries, having grown considerably over recent years to reach a level in some countries where the allocation of fishing rights between marine commercial fishing (MCF) and marine recreational fishing (MRF) has become a significant management problem. Valuations of MRF are needed for a number of pertinent reasons, especially concerning allocation of access rights and resources to MRF. Difficulties in valuations include the problem of defining 'the good', formulating any distinction between consumers and producers, and the typical absence of any market prices in what is customarily an open-access situation. Additionally, MRF must be recognized as having both primary and secondary benefits.

Consumer surplus or rent is seen as the principal dimension of primary benefits, but to quantify it involves estimating an entire demand curve in order to calculate the area beneath this. The main techniques of valuation in use are user opinion surveys, gross expenditure surveys and the travel costs method. While each has some important advantages, unfortunately each also carries with it a number of defects. Other methods have been suggested but are either limited in applicability or as yet essentially confined to theory.

When one is considering the need to manage MRF, especially in the context of any fishery that is also used for MCF, the dimensions of net social benefits need to be clearly established and related to alternative management strategies. These dimensions are consumer rent, producer rent and resource rent in the case of MCF, but the MRF will not contain identifiable elements of producer rent. Open access in the MRF will dissipate the resource rent in much the same manner as it was shown earlier to do in the MCF, although some consumer rent will probably remain. Restricted access can in theory maximize net social benefits, although to put it into operation may remain difficult. One particular problem with the demand function for MRF lies in that the individual will need to have some expectations concerning the level of congestion at the site before formulating his demand at various hypothetical access prices.

The interaction of MCF and MRF in a fishery, and an optimal joint management strategy, can be identified in a theoretical model, but the necessary assumptions and the amount of data that would be required to do so in practice mean that much management is practised on a rule-of-thumb basis. Except in North America and some European countries, fisheries policies aimed directly at MRF are as yet generally in their infancy, and even in North America they are only now being developed.

9.8 BIBLIOGRAPHIC NOTES

The main problem with the literature on marine recreational fishing is that it not only overlaps extensively with non-marine fishing, but that it quickly incorporates most of what has been written in the field of recreational economics on the issue of valuation. As recreational economics is a rapidly expanding topic in its own right, this literature is thus growing fast. For a general review on recreation, there are several books: that of Simmons (1975) is a comprehensive review on outdoor recreation. Probably the best single source on recreational fishing is Grover (1982), incorporating the Proceedings of the Consultation on the Allocation of Fishery Resources, held at Vichy in France in 1980; Gaudet (1981) provides an official report on this conference. Grover's book contains many excellent papers, and Part II is the only comprehensive description of recreational fishing on an international level. For fairly short papers that take an overview of the topic, *see* Stabler (1982b), Cauvin (1980) and Brown (1982). Clepper (1977) has edited another book containing useful papers.

The social aspects of fisheries and fishing motivations can be pursued in Bryan (1974), L. G. Anderson (1980), Dawson and Wilkins (1980) and Smith (1981). Option value has attracted some attention recently: *see* R. J. Anderson (1981), Greenley, Walsh and Young (1981) and Bishop (1982). The travel cost method is well reviewed by Gibson (1978) and Baxter (1979), who both suggest the need to develop other methods or refinements; for one of these applied to MRF *see* Vaughan and Russell (1982). The HPF approach is dealt with notably by Bockstael and McConnell (1980), and McConnell (1979) uses it and the travel cost method together.

The issue of congestion is especially pertinent to recreational fishing, and can be followed through Wetzel (1977) and McConnell (1980) to L. G. Anderson (1983). Another unsolved problem relates to the valuation of recreational time: *see* Cesario (1976), Wilman (1980) and McConnell and Strand (1981b).

The analysis of the interaction between MRF and MCF is dealt with in several papers, but *see* especially McConnell and Sutinen (1979a,b), Sutinen (1982), Bishop and Samples (1980) and L. G. Anderson (1982). Joint management issues were discussed in this chapter along the lines of Copes and Knetsch (1981); *see also* McConnell and Strand (1981a). Empirical estimations of the values of recreational fishing that are worth specific study include those of Daniel (1974), Smith, Conrad and Storey (1978), MacCall, Stauffer and Troadec (1976), McHugh (1978), Brown and Mendelsohn (1981) and Radford (1982), together with Grover (1982). Policy issues are covered by Grover (1982) and Clepper (1977), but *see also* McConnell and Strand (1981a) and Pearse (1982).

REFERENCES AND FURTHER READING

ANDERSON, L. G. (1980). 'Necessary components of economic surplus in fisheries economics.' *Canadian Journal of Fisheries and Aquatic Science*. **37** : 858–70.

ANDERSON, L. G. (1982). 'An economic analysis of joint recreational and commercial fisheries.' In J. H. Grover (Ed.), *Allocation of fishery resources. Proceedings of the Technical Consultation, Vichy, France, 1980*, pp. 16–26. FAO/AFS.

ANDERSON, L. G. (1983). 'The demand curve for recreational fishing with an application to stock enhancement activities.' *Land Economics* **59** (3) : 279–86.

ANDERSON, R. J. (1981). 'A note on option value and the expected value of the consumer's surplus.' *Journal of Environmental Economics and Management* **8** : 187–91.

BAXTER, M. J. (1979). *Measuring the benefits of recreational site provision: a review of techniques related to the Clawson method*. London: Sports Council.

BISHOP, R. C. (1982). 'Option value: an exposition and extension.' *Land Economics* **58** (1) : 1–15.

BISHOP, R. C. and T. A. HABERLEIN (1979). 'Measuring values of extra market goods: are direct measures biased?' Pullman, Washington. *Annual Meeting of the American Agricultural Economics Association*.

BISHOP, R. C. and K. C. SAMPLES (1980). 'Sport and commercial fishing conflicts: a theoretical analysis.' *Journal of Environmental Economics and Management* **7** : 220–33.

BOCKSTAEL, N. E. and K. E. MCCONNELL (1980). *Estimating and using the household production function for wildlife recreation*. University of Rhode Island. Department of Resource Economics. Staff Paper No. 14.

BOWES, M. D. and J. B. LOOMIS (1980). 'A note on the use of travel cost models with unequal zonal populations.' *Land Economics* **56** : 465–70.

BROWN, G. M. (1982). 'Recreation.' In G. M. Brown and J. A. Crutchfield (Eds), *Economics of ocean resources*, pp. 144–63. Seattle: University of Washington Press.

BROWN, G. M. and R. MENDELSOHN (1981). *The hedonic travel cost method*. Department of Economics, University of Washington.

BRYAN, R. C. (1974). *The dimensions of a salt water fishing trip*. Environment Canada: Southern Operations Branch Pacific Region. PAC/T-74-1.

CAUVIN, D. M. (1978). 'The allocation of resources in fisheries: an economic problem.' *American Fisheries Society Special Publication* **11** : 361–70.

CAUVIN, D. M. (1980). 'The valuation of recreational fisheries.' *Canadian Journal of Fisheries and Aquatic Science* **37** (8) : 1321–7.

CESARIO, F. J. (1976). 'Value of time in recreation benefit studies.' *Land Economics* **52** : 32–41.

CHESHIRE, P. C. and M. H. STABLER (1976). 'Joint consumption benefits in recreational site surplus: an empirical estimate.' *Regional Studies* **10** : 343–52.

CLEPPER, H. (Ed.) (1977). *Marine Recreational Fisheries 2*. Washington, D.C.: Sport Fishing Institute.

COPES, P. and J. L. KNETSCH (1981). 'Recreational fisheries analysis: management modes and benefit implications.' *Canadian Journal of Fisheries and Aquatic Science* **338** : 559–70.

DANIEL, D. L. (1974). *A survey of sport related expenditures in a selected portion of the Mississippi Gulf Coast*. University of Southern Mississippi. MASGP-74-19.

DAWSON, C. P. and B. T. WILKINS (1980). 'Social considerations associated with marine recreational fishing under FCMA.' *Marine Fisheries Review*, December 1980, 12–17.

DWYER, J. F. and M. D. BOWES (1978). 'Concepts of value for marine recreational fishing.' *American Journal of Agricultural Economics* **60** : 1008–12.

GAUDET, J-L. (Ed.) (1981). *Report of the technical consultation on the allocation of fishery resources at Vichy, France, 1980*. EIFAC Technical Paper 38.

GIBSON, J. G. (1978). 'Recreation and land use.' In D. W. Pearce (Ed.), *The valuation of social cost*, pp. 68–96. London: Allen & Unwin.

GORDON, H. S. (1953). 'An economic approach to the optimum utilisation of fishery resources.' *Journal of the Fisheries Research Board of Canada* **10** (7) : 442–57.

GREENLEY, D. A., R. G. WALSH and R. A. YOUNG (1981). 'Option value: empirical evidence from a case study of recreation and water quality.' *Quarterly Journal of Economics* **96** (4) : 657–73.

GROVER, J. H. (Ed.) (1982). *Allocation of fishery resources. Proceedings of the Technical Consultation, Vichy, France, 1980*. FAO/AFS.

HARRISON, A. and M. H. STABLER (1980). *The effect of income on travel to canal recreation sites*. Reading University. Mimeo.

HENRY, C. (1974). 'Option values in the economics of irreplaceable assets.' *Review of Economic Studies Symposium*, pp. 89–104.

KIRBY, M. J. L. (1982). *Navigating troubled waters*. Task Force on Atlantic Fisheries, Canada.

KRUTILLA, J. V. (1967). 'Conservation reconsidered.' *American Economic Review* **57** : 777–87.

LIAO, D. S. and J. B. STEVENS (1977). 'The economic performance of Oregon's commercial fishermen in 1972.' *Marine Fisheries Review* **39** (8) : 17–22.

MACCALL A. D., G. D. STAUFFER and J-P. TROADEC (1976). 'Southern California recreational and commercial marine fisheries.' *Marine Fisheries Review* **38** (1) : MFR Paper 1173.

MCCONNELL, K. E. (1979). 'Values of marine recreational fishing: measurement and impact of measurement.' *American Journal of Agricultural Economics* December 1979, pp. 922–50.

MCCONNELL, K. E. (1980). 'Valuing congested recreation sites.' *Journal of Environmental Economics and Management* **7** : 389–94.

MCCONNELL, K. E. and I. E. STRAND (1981a). 'Some economic aspects of managing marine recreational fishing.' In L. G. Anderson (Ed.), *Economic analysis for fisheries management plans*, Ch. 11. Ann Arbor, Michigan: Ann Arbor Science Publishers.

MCCONNELL, K. E. and I. E. STRAND (1981b). 'Measuring the cost of time in recreation demand analysis: an application to sport fishing.' *American Journal of Agricultural Economics* **63** (1) : 153–6.

MCCONNELL, K. E. and J. G. SUTINEN (1979a). 'Bioeconomic models of marine recreational fishing.' *Journal of Environmental Economics and Management* **6** : 127–39.

MCCONNELL, K. E. and J. G. SUTINEN (1979b). 'Using the household production function in bioeconomic models.' *Conference on the Economics of Renewable Resources, Brown University, Rhode Island*. No. 42.

MCHUGH, J. L. (1978). 'Limited entry as a conservation method.' In R. B. Rettig and J. C. Ginter (Eds), *Limited entry as a fishery management tool*, pp. 175–87. Seattle and London: University of Washington Press.

MEYER, P. A. (1982). 'Recreational fishing values at risk: recent developments in compensatory methodology in the United States and Canada'. In J. H. Grover (Ed.) (1982), *Allocation of fishery resources. Proceedings of the Technical Consultation, Vichy, France, 1980*, pp. 274–85. FAO/AFS.

MISHAN, E. J. (1975). *Cost benefit analysis*, 2nd edn. London: George Allen & Unwin.

NATIONAL ANGLING SURVEY (1980). *National angling survey*. Water Research Council/National Opinion Polls Ltd.

NORTH, R. M. (1976). 'Economic values for marine recreational fisheries.' In R. H. Stroud and H. Clepper (Eds), *Marine recreational fisheries,* pp. 3–52, First Annual Marine Recreational Fisheries Symposium. Washington, D.C.: Sport Fishing Institute.

PEARSE, P. H. (1982). *Turning the tide: a new policy for Canada's Pacific fisheries*. Commission on Pacific Fisheries Policy, Canada.

POGGIE, J. J. and C. GERSUNY (1974). *Fishermen of Galilee.* University of Rhode Island. Marine Bulletin Series No. 17.

POWNALL, P. (1979). *Fisheries of Australia.* Farnham, Surrey: Fishing News Books.

RADFORD, A. F. (1980). *Economic survey of the River Wye recreational salmon fishery*. Portsmouth Polytechnic, Marine Resources Research Unit, Research Paper No. 20.

RADFORD, A. F. (1982). *Estimating the net economic value of a recreational salmon fishery: a case study of the River Wye*. Portsmouth Polytechnic, Marine Resources Research Unit, Research Paper No. 33.

ROTHSCHILD, B., J. M. GATES and A. M. CARLSON (1977). 'Management of marine recreational fisheries.' In H. Clepper (Ed.), *Marine Recreational Fisheries 2*, pp. 149–72. Washington, D.C.: Sport Fishing Institute.

SCHMIED, R. L. (1982). 'Development of marine recreational fisheries in the southeastern United States: problems and some solutions.' In J. H. Grover (Ed.) (1982), *Allocation of fishery resources. Proceedings of the Technical Consultation, Vichy, France, 1980,* pp. 333–45. FAO/AFS.

SIMMONS, I. G. (1975). *Rural recreation in the industrial world*. London: Edward Arnold.

SMITH, C. L. (1981). 'Satisfaction bonus from salmon fishing: implications for economic evaluation.' *Land Economics* **57** (2) : 181–94.

SMITH, R. G. (1975). 'Problems of interpreting recreation benefits from a recreation demand curve.' In G. A. C. Searle (Ed.), *Recreational Analysis and Economics*, pp. 62–74. London: Longman.

SMITH, R. W., J. M. CONRAD and D. A. STOREY (1978). 'An economic valuation of recreational clamming in Massachusetts.' *Massachusetts Agricultural Experimental Station Research Bulletin*, No. 654.

STABLER, M. (1982a). 'Estimation of the benefits of fishing on U.K. canals: some problems of method.' In J. H. Grover (Ed.) (1982),

Allocation of fishery resources. Proceedings of the Technical Consultation, Vichy, France, 1980, pp. 346–55. FAO/AFS.

STABLER, M. (1982b). 'Estimation of the economic benefits of fishing: a review note.' In J. H. Grover (Ed.) (1982), *Allocation of fishery resources. Proceedings of the Technical Consultation, Vichy, France, 1980*, pp. 356–65. FAO/AFS.

STROUD, R. H., G. C. RADONSKI and R. G. MARTIN (1982). 'Evolving efforts in best-use allocations of fishery resources.' In J. H. Grover (Ed.) (1982), *Allocation of fishery resources. Proceedings of the Technical Consultation, Vichy, France, 1980*, pp. 346–55. FAO/AFS.

SUTINEN, J. G. (1982). 'Economic principles of allocation in recreational and commercial fisheries.' In J. H. Grover (Ed.) (1982), *Allocation of fishery resources. Proceedings of the Technical Consultation, Vichy, France, 1980,* pp. 432–42. FAO/AFS.

TALHELM, D. R. (1972). *Analytical economics of outdoor recreation: a case study of the Southern Appalachian trout fishery*. Ph.D. dissertation, North Carolina State University.

TALHELM, D. R. (1982). 'Defining angling supply: the key to recreational resource evaluation.' In J. H. Grover (Ed.) (1982), *Allocation of fishery resources. Proceedings of the Technical Consultation, Vichy, France, 1980*, pp. 443–51. FAO/AFS.

TRICE, A. H. and S. E. WOOD (1958). 'Measurement of recreation benefits.' *Land Economics* **34** (3) : 195–207.

VAUGHAN, W. J. and C. S. RUSSELL (1982). 'Valuing a fishing day: an application of a systematic varying parameter model.' *Land Economics* **58** (4) : 450–63.

WETZEL, J. N. (1977). 'Estimating the benefits of recreation under conditions of congestion.' *Journal of Environmental Economics and Management* **4** (3) : 239–46.

WILLIG, R. D. (1976). 'Consumers surplus without apology.' *American Economic Review* **66** : 589–97.

WILMAN, E. A. (1980). 'The value of time in recreation benefit studies.' *Journal of Environmental Economics and Management* **7** : 272–86.

ZIEMER, R., W. N. MUSSER and R. CARTER HILL (1980). 'Recreational demand equations: functional form and consumer surplus.' *American Journal of Agricultural Economics* **60** : 136–41.

ZUBOY, J. R. (1980). 'The Delphi technique: a potential methodology for evaluating recreational fisheries.' In J. H. Grover (Ed.) (1982), *Allocation of fisheries resources. Proceedings of the Technical Consultation, Vichy, France, 1980,* pp. 519–29. FAO/AFS.

CHAPTER 10

Economic aspects of aquaculture

10.1 INTRODUCTION

While the forecasting of future trends is notoriously prone to error, it has nevertheless become widely accepted that the world demand for food fish, which stood at just over 50 million tonnes in the late 1970s, is likely to increase to 70 million tonnes by the mid 1980s and to perhaps 110 million tonnes by 2000 (FAO, 1979a). These figures assume that the relative price of fish remains unchanged, and that over half the increase would be associated with a projected world population increase from some 4 billion in 1979 to 7 billion in 2000. To meet this, world landings of fish for food and non-food use, which increased at an average rate of 5% p.a. during 1950–70, were increasing during the 1970s at only 1–2% p.a. to reach 74.76 million tonnes in 1982. Some 70% of the total catch is used for direct food consumption, and most of the rest reduced to fishmeal.

Given the likely increase in demand, what then can be done to expand fish production even to approach 110 million tonnes? Four main strategies have emerged:

(a) Increased fishing effort on *underutilized stocks*
(b) *Improved management* of existing stocks
(c) The development of *aquaculture* as an additional source of supplies
(d) *Improved utilization* of supplies from all three sources (a), (b) and (c).

The extent to which strategies (a) and (b) can fulfil the latent requirements is debatable. Clearly, the extent of knowledge concerning the potential of presently underutilized stocks is limited; while reasonable estimates may be made for conventional species (e.g. tuna, pelagic species), major problems arise with unconventional species such as krill, the cephalopods such as squid, and the mesopelagic fishes. Not only are predicted production costs and prices extremely tentative, but even the basic biological data are sketchy. In addition, although 200-mile EEZs offer scope for improved management if we can overcome the many practical difficulties, optimal management under strategy (b) might well still entail a reduction of catches from MSY levels. Overall, the FAO estimated in 1979 that a combination of increased effort and improved management would have the potential shown in *Table 10.1*. The data concerning unconventional species must be regarded as highly speculative.

TABLE 10.1 Potential for increase in world fish catches over actual 1977 landings (thousand tonnes)

	Potential world catch	*Actual catch, 1977*	*Increase to be derived from:*	
			improved management	*increased effort*
Conventional marine resources				
Salmon	650	480	170	–
Flounder and cod	6700	3800	2500	400
Herring, anchovy, etc.	15600	1800	13800	–
Shrimp and lobster	1670 ?	1540	25–30	100
Tuna	2260	1590	100	550
Other demersal	37100	17100	4000	16000
Other pelagic	40200	28700	3000	8500
Unconventional marine species				
Cephalopods	50000 ?	1170	–	50000 ?
Other molluscs	unknown	3000	–	large ?
Krill	50000 ?	100	–	50000 ?
Mesopelagic fish	50000 ?	–	–	50000 ?

Source: FAO (1979).

Important gains can also be made under strategy (d). At present, only some 70% of the world catch is used for human consumption, the rest being mainly reduced to fish meal, which is used then to feed livestock (and other fish in aquaculture). This latter portion might be used directly, although many of the species so used are fragile, difficult to handle and spoil rapidly. In addition, improved preservation and protection of the landings would help; for example, over 10 million tonnes p.a. are lost through spoilage and pest attacks, mainly in developing countries. Finally, by-catches that are often discarded might also be utilized: in 1976 some 6.5 million tonnes of fish were estimated to have been destroyed in the catching of the world's shrimp landings of 1.3 million tonnes. Overall the FAO has estimated that 25–35 million tonnes of small pelagic fish could be added to human consumption, together with over 15 million tonnes presently wasted through spoilage or by-catch.

Hence, by these three strategies we might well be able to add to our existing fish supplies some 23–25 million tonnes by improved management, plus some 25–37 million tonnes from increased effort, giving a total variously estimated at about 100 million tonnes (Ryther, 1975) or 120 million tonnes (FAO, 1979)—and this could suffer less wastage and spoilage than is the case at present. More tentatively, we might also eventually add up to 100–150 million tonnes if we can develop systems to utilize the unconventional species commercially. However, although these figures look encouraging, the extent to which such landings might fill the 'protein gap' is debatable; the costs of exploitation would be much higher than at present, with higher costs in processing, preservation and distribution. Moreover such fishing will be particularly susceptible to increases in the price of fossil fuels.

Hence, much attention has been paid over the past decade to the contribution that aquaculture might make towards filling the gap. In the context of the FAO data already cited (FAO, 1979), the estimated potential of aquaculture was to increase from the 6 million tonnes in 1975 to some 20–40 million tonnes. Given the great uncertainties over any use of unconventional species, such an increase could take farmed fish from its present approximate level of 10% of world fish landings to perhaps 25–30%, and it has been suggested elsewhere that by 2080, farmed fish could well match capture fish in world landings (Bardach, Ryther and McLarney, 1972). Moiseev (1977) and others have predicted that ultimately aquaculture will replace capture fisheries.

This chapter attempts to introduce some basic economic aspects of aquaculture and is therefore essentially different from the rest of the book in that the approach now moves away from the bioeconomic model. Here, we are more squarely in the area of production economics, for now the production function becomes much more stable and predictable, as in agriculture. Here too, the tools of industrial economics might be used. Unfortunately however, the infancy of the industry and the dearth of economic analysis of this very diverse activity means that no sophisticated economic appraisal can be made of either production or industrial economics. Instead we have concentrated on introducing the basic production ideas, together with some background to the industry in general terms. As such, this chapter can be only a summary and a relatively long bibliography is presented to assist further enquiries. There is only one book on the topic (Shang, 1981), although no doubt others will soon be written.

One final point needs to be made: aquaculture is here used as an all-embracing term, referring to the husbandry of fish under controlled conditions, in marine, brackish and fresh water, but as the rest of the book is restricted in the main to marine fisheries, perhaps one might argue that this section should concentrate on 'mariculture'. We have taken the view that the distinction is not worth while. Admittedly marine aquaculture faces some particular versions of the general problems we mention—property rights being a prime example—but there are so many production and demand similarities that a pedantic restriction would be unproductive.

10.1.1 Why aquaculture: problems in commercial fishing

The artificial culturing of fish has a very long history, originating in Asia some 4000 years ago, and the first text on culture was written by Fan-Li around 500 BC, by which time oysters and mullet were important crops in China. However the recent rise of interest derives from more modern pressures, falling into two basic groups.

We have already suggested that the recent level of catches in many conventional fish stocks comprises not only economic overfishing but also biological overfishing. As well as the evidence of overcapitalization, there is the real fear of stock collapse. However while it is one matter to agree that management is necessary, it is quite another to agree on which objectives to pursue and by which means; progress on these matters has not been good.

Likewise, whilst we also suggested earlier that the catches from unconventional species could be as large as 150 million tonnes, the exploitation of these will face substantial problems in technology, production and marketing. Additionally, fishing for both conventional and unconventional species has faced substantial relative cost increases, arising especially from fossil fuel price increases.

An extra dimension is that many countries which have been involved in distant-water fishing have now found themselves excluded from their traditional grounds by the move towards 200-mile limits by coastal states (*see* Chapter 7). Such countries have been thrown back to the need to develop their indigenous resources, including any potential for aquaculture. A further impetus comes from the threat to capture fisheries arising from marine pollution and competing alternative uses of water resources. Finally we must not lose sight of the basic truth that, despite changing technological sophistication, fishing remains a hunting operation, whether it be of open access or managed stocks, with all the associated uncertainties and risks.

10.1.2 Advantages of aquacultural production

In contrast, the principal advantage of aquaculture lies in that it shifts fish production from the realm of hunting to that of agricultural production. Thus the overexploitation problems of the common property resource disappear and are replaced by the benefits of sole ownership and the externalities of production are reduced to much lower levels. Risk and uncertainty are by no means removed, but are reduced.

Moreover in comparison with agriculture itself, aquaculture has certain intrinsic advantages: production takes place in the vertical water column, facilitating high stocking rates per square metre of surface area. While a well managed cattle farm might produce 0.5–1.0 tonnes/hectare liveweight, a figure of 3–5 tonnes/ha is perfectly feasible in fish farming (although any such data must be treated with care because of the great variety of production systems both for land animals and fish—*see* section 10.2.1).

Additionally, as fish float, they tend to use less energy input for producing motion and skeletal material than land animals. Being cold-blooded, they use less input to maintain body temperature. Partly for these reasons, the rate at which fish convert food intake to flesh is generally superior to that of land animals, being perhaps twice as high as for cattle and sheep, and one and a half times the rate for pigs and chickens. Such advantages are likely to gain increasing significance as energy-cost elements in feedstuff production costs rise (*see* section 10.4.4).

Aquaculture also has advantages in its flexibility of approach. Systems in use vary from totally artificial, controlled systems through to slight modifications to natural systems. Moreover a very wide range of environments can be used, from tropical to subarctic. Freshwater culture can often be part of a multiple-usage resource system, including for example rice-and-tilapia farming, or food-and-recreation trout production.

Usefully, aquaculture often lends itself to the utilization of land and water areas such as mangrove swamps and fjords, which have few or low-value alternative uses; that is, areas with low social opportunity costs (*see* section 1.3.4). The FAO has estimated that of the 30 million hectares which could be suitable for aquaculture, only 10% were in use in 1980.

In comparison with capture fisheries, culture uses fewer resources in search efforts, and sensible production management can produce regular outputs of controlled quantity at predictable intervals, together with a greater degree of standardization of the final product, all of which are important commercial advantages. These tend to encourage investment, cost monitoring and control, and sales promotion expenditure, which jointly all lead towards lower production costs and encourage consumer demand.

A potentially important advantage lies in the scope for scientific improvement of output. Modern agriculture is vastly different from that of a century ago, and while aquaculture will not catch up immediately, the application of new technologies associated with biotechnology and microprocessors in the infant industry could have immense significance. Simple genetic selection, let alone genetic engineering, has scarcely begun in aquaculture, and there is great scope for the application of modern science to food production and water systems—and there are many species with which to experiment.

Aquaculture also has important advantages in that it has greatest potential and viability under tropical and subtropical conditions, where the need for food, and protein especially, is greatest. Hence production may be deliberately located close to latent demand, which reduces processing, transport and distribution costs as well as waste, and results in more being consumed directly; such deliberate location decisions are reported in centrally planned economies, for example in the Soviet Union (Sysoev, 1974, p. 102), and for 'city-farms' in China (*Fish Farming International*, Sept. 82).

While we noted pollution as threatening capture fisheries, some aquaculture has been stimulated by the waste warm water from industrial processes. There were eighty-eight such farms in the world in 1981, mainly based on power stations (*FFI*, April 1982), but water quality is important and by no means all waste warm water is suitable. The fish farms remain sensitive to other forms of pollution, and indeed create pollution themselves.

Finally, it is evident that fish flesh can already be produced under some aquacultural systems more cheaply and more profitably than either capture fish or animal farming: Shang (1973) found a higher rate of return on aquaculture in Taiwan than on sea fishing or pig farming.

We should also note that, from the point of view of its role in developing an economy, aquaculture may offer certain general benefits in terms of broadening the protein supply base, stabilizing fish supplies, providing rural employment and creating exports, and these are discussed later in section 10.8.

10.2 CATEGORIES OF AQUACULTURAL PRODUCTION

So far we have tacitly implied that aquaculture is primarily for the production of fish for food. We must however recognize that the term covers a range of activities, categorized by Pillay (1973) as:

(a) Food production, from both fish and other organisms (e.g. seaweeds)
(b) Enhancement of natural stocks by artificial recruitment and transplantation
(c) Production of sport fish
(d) Production of bait fish
(e) Production of aquatic organisms for research or pet-keeping
(f) A means of recycling organic waste
(g) Production of industrial commodities (e.g. pearls, drugs)

Although the remainder of this chapter refers to category (a), we must note that production under other headings may be significant under certain circumstances. Much of the initial interest in culture in Europe in the late nineteenth century was for category (b), in the hope that man might 'seed the oceans' from artificial production to make good the overfishing of inshore stocks that was already apparent. This idea is still relevant today, with for example Japan releasing crabs and shrimps, France releasing lobsters and Norway considering releasing cod fry. Under heading (c), in the United Kingdom trout is raised not only for food but particularly for the restocking of 'put and take' rod fisheries for recreationalists: two-thirds of trout raised in Wales is for this purpose. Under (g), the culture of artificial pearls in Japan using oysters is a large and expanding activity. Finally, much current research in Europe and North America concerns aquacultural production as an adjunct to the recycling of domestic organic wastes (f), including integration with the hydroponic cultivation of land crops.

10.2.1 Aquacultural systems

As we shall see, there is an immense variety of aquacultural activities in the world; hence our aim here is to introduce some issues of particular concern to economists and likely to be relevant to aquacultural activities in general. Readers who are specifically interested in the 'economics' of any particular system (or species or country) will find the several aquacultural bibliographies and symposia useful (e.g. Vondruska, 1973; FAO, 1979b; Pillay and Dill, 1979; Pillay, 1981). To make generalizations, some analytical categorization is essential. Since almost all fish are candidate species for culture, and the purposes may be one or more of those identified above, the systems in use vary widely. We may however categorize on the following basis:

Intensive systems. Typified by the culture of fish in high densities within enclosures such as tanks, artificial ponds, cages and silos, in which a substantial water flow is provided to supply oxygen and remove wastes, and to which food is added. The fish may well be transferred to different enclosures as they grow.

Probably the most intensive system is that to raise salmonids in recirculating silo systems with heavy feeding, producing amazing yields of up to 6000 tonnes/hectare in the United States (Ackefors and Rosen, 1979). In Japan, yellowtail farmed intensively yield up to 280 tonnes/ha, while more typically shrimps in tanks produce 2–6 tonnes/ha, and in the United States pond-caged catfish produce 5–6 tonnes/ha. In each case it is, however, debatable whether a yield/*area* measure is particularly meaningful, for the essential element is heavy feeding in a small area.

Extensive systems. Typified by the culture of fish in low densities in natural open or semiopen situations, with primarily natural feeding and little environmental control. Examples are the stocking of carp in natural ponds, or the re-laying of oyster seed in suitable offshore areas, or possibly the 'ranching' of fish by releasing juveniles to fend for themselves until caught or, ideally, returning to their point of release when mature, as in salmon ranching. Yields under extensive systems are typically much lower, and often less than 100 kg/ha. Such extensive systems are widely used for example for pond carp in India and China, and trout in Taiwan. Environmental control usually involves predator exclusion. Also, a pond area will often be fertilized to promote the growth of natural algae, and some supplementary feeding may be given.

Intermediate or mixed systems. A grouping including intermediate intensities and systems that involve both intensive and extensive elements. Examples vary from systems where fish are fed but in naturally enclosed areas, to where fish are not fed but are held in artificial ponds, possibly with fertilizer added to improve natural productivity. Examples include carp farming in Germany, tilapia in Thailand and milkfish in the Philippines. Mixed systems sometimes involve the gathering and relocating of seed towards natural but controlled environments, such as mussel seed on-growing in bags in Europe, and oysters grown from rafts in the United States. Yield figures vary greatly with system, from perhaps 1 tonne/ha for pond carp to 100 tonnes/ha for some shellfish culture.

We should note however that the same fish may be cultured under different systems, even within one country. For example, carp is raised in India under extensive lake systems yielding 300 kg/ha as well as intermediate pond systems yielding 3 tonnes/ha; trout in Taiwan kept in ponds yields just 200 kg/ha, while in silos yields are up to one thousand times higher in the United States.

The classification above is widely employed and is based essentially on density/area relationships, but these are rather deceptive in terms of the resources that are used in production. We can attempt to be more precise by quantifying some of the parameters involved.

10.2.2 Resource requirements and aquacultural systems

The differences between the many systems in use throughout the world can usefully be simplified into an analysis of the resources employed under three headings: land, labour and energy. These three resources are used both *directly* and *indirectly*; thus the fish farm uses labour inputs directly in the form of labour employed in the operation of the farm, but also indirectly in the form of the labour that was used in producing essential non-labour inputs such as fertilizer, water pumps and concrete. Likewise the fish farm itself utilizes land, but in total resource terms we must also account for the land utilized to produce non-land inputs such as feedstuffs and cages. Labour inputs in total are then expressed as man-days per tonne produced, and land inputs as hectares per tonne produced. The third element is less obvious, but we may employ gross energy requirement (GER), expressed as gigajoules per tonne (GJ/tonne*), as a measure of those *non*-renewable resources used up in production in terms of all the primary energy required to make all the capital inputs (ponds, nets, pumps, etc.), plus the direct energy to operate the process. The three elements together describe the resource requirements of each system, and also reveal the important differences between systems. *Table 10.2* is a cross-section of different systems in different countries, and suggests, as expected, that labour requirements are higher for subsistence operations, and decline as production becomes more capital-intensive. On the basis of such data, we may now quantify tentatively the parameters of the different aquacultural systems in terms of economic resource usage (*Table 10.3*). It must be stressed that individual farms are greatly affected by local conditions, and that this classification is only broadly indicative.

*43 gigajoules is energy-equivalent to 1 tonne of oil.

TABLE 10.2 Aquaculture systems and resource use

System	*Manpower required* (man-days/t)	*Farm land required* (ha/t)	*Total land required* (ha/t)	*GER** (GJ/t)
Tilapia: ponds (Africa)	170	0.5	0.5	0.4
Tilapia/shrimp: ponds (El Salvador)	27	0.4	0.4	1
Milkfish: enclosures (Philippines)	92	0	0.1	2
Carp: net cages (Japan)	23	0	0.2	18
Carp: ponds (Germany)	13	1.3	1.6	25
Trout: ponds (U.K.)	22	0.04	0.2	56
Catfish: ponds (U.S.A.)	3	0.7	1.5	95

*Note: An overall range of 0.1 to over 300 GJ/tonne has been found (Thai subsistence tilapia/carp ponds through to Japanese recirculated water systems for carp).
Source: Edwardson (1976).

TABLE 10.3 Resource requirements and the classification of aquacultural systems

	Resource use			
Type of system	*Manpower* (man-d/t)	*Farm land* (ha/t)	*GER*	*Example*
Extensive	>90	>0.5	<10	Thailand carp/tilapia; Philippines milkfish
Intermediate	30–90	0.1–0.5	10–50	Thailand tilapia; Israeli carp
Intensive	<30	<0.1	>50	U.K. trout; Japanese recirculating carp unit; U.S. catfish

10.2.3 Monoculture, polyculture and integrated fish farming

A further important distinction may be made between those systems where one species of fish is the only crop gathered, which are termed *monoculture*, those producing more than one species, termed *polyculture*, and those where fish farming is linked to other forms of production, referred to as *integrated fish farming*.

Monoculture is perhaps the most typical form still, where production is limited to a single species, although that species may be sold at different ages and to different markets; for example, fingerling trout may be sold to restock recreation lakes or later as food. Polyculture involves farming several compatible species of fish or aquatic organisms simultaneously. The best-known example is that of Indian carp ponds, where three or four species of carp are raised, each occupying an ecological niche within the pond, and yields of up to 8.5 tonnes/ha with only modest feeding have been recorded. Carp have also been raised with tilapia, and mullet with prawns.

The term 'integrated fish farming' refers to the combination of fish and other forms of production, often farming. At its simplest, in China pig manure is used to fertilize fish ponds, and in the United States, cornfields provide cheap trout food. In India, fish-with-pigs gives a typical yield of 600 kg of fish and 420 kg of pig meat per 0.1 ha area. In Asia and Latin America, fish have been raised in ricefields during certain months; for example, in India, prawns-with-rice gives three crops a year, at 500–700 kg/ha. At a more directly integrated level, ducks may be raised on ponds above the fish; in East Europe 500 ducks may be raised on 1 ha of pond, yielding 3 tonnes of duck and increasing fish yields by 120–180 kg from the pond. In the Philippines, 4000 duck farms raise 700 000 ducks, fertilizing a lake that produced 3000 tonnes of fish, 27 500 tonnes of prawns and 100 000 tonnes of snails (Pullin and Shehadeh, 1981). Perhaps the most 'integrated' of all systems has hens *above* pigs *above* ponds, with the food and manure dropping down to produce fish and greenstuff in the pond! (*See* Pillay and Dill, 1979, for further detail.)

Aquaculture is also found integrated with non-farming activities, especially with irrigation and various forms of power production. Fish is farmed in waters associated with hydroelectric schemes and in the warm-water effluent of power stations. There are problems with such production, including difficulties concerning water quality, reliability of supply and costs in aquaculture use, but already in Europe tilapia, eels and turbot are all produced in power station effluent. The Soviet Union has thirty-four such farms (1983), with plans for a further seventy-two and eventual production of 1 million tonnes of fish per annum in power station reservoirs.

10.2.4 Sea ranching

Sea ranching is a particularly interesting recent development in systems involving the release of juvenile fish to grow, totally unprotected, on natural marine food supplies until harvested at marketable sizes. Species already in production or under consideration include salmon in several countries, crabs, lobsters and cod. The problems of survival and harvesting have so far restricted the major successes in this area to salmon ranching, as the salmon conveniently returns to the area of release and there also provides a supply of eggs. The proportion of fish released that eventually return is in the range 1–15%, occasionally touching 20%, and as a return of only 1% will probably cover production costs,* the viability prospects already look very favourable; the necessary artificial feeding of smolts covers only 1% of the fishes' lifetime needs, and a return of 2–50 kg of salmon per kilogram of smolts released is achieved (Thorpe, 1980). In Japan for example, where all hatcheries are operated by the state, chum salmon ranching over the period 1966–72 was astonishingly profitable. With an average cost (mean 1966–72) per returned fish of 85 yen giving an average cost of 24 yen/kg, compared to an average (mean 1966–72) landed price of 670 yen/kg, the fry production cost of (mean) landings of some 28 000 tonnes p.a. was only 3.6% of the landed value (Kobayashi, 1980), and hatchery fish now comprise 80% of the total salmon landings of 50 000 tonnes (Needham, 1981).

The success so far achieved has led to ambitious plans; Sweden releases 500 000 smolt annually into the Baltic, and the Soviet Union alone plans an annual salmon release of 5 billion p.a. by the year 2000. Already some 50 000–70 000 tonnes (20–30%) of the world salmon catch is based on hatchery-raised fish (Thorpe, 1980). However, Norway has achieved returns of only 1–2%, and the Soviet Union has failed in attempts to ranch pink salmon in the White and Barents Seas.

Limitations associated with environmental carrying capacity, predation and especially the establishment of ownership over wandering stocks even within 200 mile EEZs will cause problems for any substantial growth in ranching, and it is unlikely that ranching will become widespread very rapidly. In particular, the potential conflict with commercial capture fishing could be difficult to resolve (Stokes, 1982). Nevertheless, several governments are giving it substantial support, such as those of Canada and Japan. In Japan over thirty species are raised in fifty-five hatcheries for fisheries restocking (*Fish Farming International* **9** (6) (1982)). In 1982, there were twelve salmon ranches operating in Oregon, U.S.A. albeit all very small.

10.3 FIRMS IN AQUACULTURE AND THEIR OBJECTIVES

With such a variety of aquacultural activities, the basic form of the production unit—the 'firm'—also varies considerably. One basic difference lies in the distinction between aquaculture as a subsistence activity and as a commercial cash crop. Some writers have implied that the latter is the only important form: 'people start fish farms to make money' (Pitcher and Hart, 1982, p. 311). Yet while this view may be reasonable when it refers to Western economies, much of the aquaculture in south-east Asia and China is subsistence in nature. For example, carp in

*In North America and Japan; in the United Kingdom, a return of perhaps 6% with Atlantic salmon would be needed (Needham, 1981).

China and milkfish in the Philippines are frequently produced by family or cooperative groups, the fish not being marketed but providing a food input to the group.

10.3.1 Types of enterprise

However in general terms the trend is towards intensification and integration in production, and four basic forms emerge:

Individual and family units. Probably the most typical form, being common in for example central and southern Europe and the developing countries of Asia and Africa. It is typified by the fish farm run by an individual or as a family operation, often at the artisanal or subsistence level in developing countries. Usually only one 'farm' is operated, with personal control and management by the owner, and the operation is small-scale and labour-intensive.

Commercial firms. Increasingly aquaculture in Western Europe and America is being developed by commercial firms, frequently large companies. In many cases these companies enter into aquaculture from other activities, attracted by a combination of potential profits, fairly low barriers to entry (*see* section 10.7.2), an ability to use their size and resources to solve complex problems, and some linkage with their existing activities. Such firms only rarely come from traditional capture fishing, but usually have some other relevant interest. For example, BP Nutrition, a subsidiary of the British oil company BP, is Europe's largest producer of fish food and a major source of R & D knowledge, and has extended from this into active fish farming in Scotland, Norway, Portugal and the Ivory Coast. Other British companies involved include Unilever, Kraft, Shell, Fisons, Blue Circle Industries, Fitch Lovell and Amey Roadstone. In 1983 Unilever operated ten salmon farms in the United Kingdom and others in Sweden, and farmed prawns in Sri Lanka (Jardine, 1983). In the United States, Campbell Soups, the timber giant Weyerhauser Co., C. Brewer (sugar and chemicals), Dow Chemicals, Union Carbide, Coca-Cola and the Inmont Co. (chemicals) all have aquacultural interests, often internationally. In Ireland, Guinness farms oysters and in Belgium Tate & Lyle farms tilapia.

The extent of involvement in aquaculture by commercial companies has grown greatly over the last few years. For example, in 1975, Pillay (1979) reported 833 companies in twenty-six countries involved in fish farming; Banerjee (1981) reports that by 1980 there were over 6000 firms in the United States alone, including 3800 for catfish, 1550 for baitfish and 500 for oysters.

Cooperatives. The cooperative unit, where there is some element of joint ownership by individuals within a group, is frequently found in central and Eastern Europe, and in some developing countries. The cooperative gains from some of the economies of scale that a commercial firm enjoys, such as in bulk purchasing, specialization, and marketing, and also from the spreading of risk and managerial responsibilities. The cooperative is particularly typical in socialist economies, where the fishery 'kolkhozes' are group property with collective democratic decision-taking. Sysoev (1974) states that in 1968 there were over fifty aquaculture kolkhozes in the Soviet Union raising 3500 tonnes of pond fish out of a total of seventy fish farms; Pillay (1979) reports that total Soviet production had risen to 210 000 tonnes of pond fish, and expansion is continuing rapidly in the 1980s.

State agencies. While government agencies are involved in aspects of aquaculture in almost all countries, in most this is primarily in R & D and in extension support services. In some cases however, the government may operate hatcheries to provide seed, and in China and the Soviet Union the state operates fish farms as well. In France, many trout farms are government-sponsored. The support that the state provides via research and extension services includes the transfer of research results to the field via technicians, site assessment, seed supply, disease control, credit provision and personnel training.

Finally we must make the distinction between the 'firm' and the 'plant': a plant or establishment is the basic production unit at a single site, whereas a firm is the decision-taking unit, which may operate one or more plants. Thus the aquaculture firm may operate several fish farms, and may indeed operate plants in non-aquacultural activities. Although this may be a significant difference, for the most part the rest of this chapter will refer to the single-plant firm: the fish farm as a firm.

10.3.2 Objectives

With such a diversity of firms, not surprisingly we encounter a range of objectives. Although later analysis will be based largely on the traditional assumption in economics that the firm seeks to maximize its profits (*see* Chapter 1, section 1.3.5) and this aim is indeed probably typical of many small and most large firms in the private sector in developed, and to a lesser extent developing countries, certain other possible objectives are important:

(a) Maximization of production or of sales revenue: especially relevant to small-scale subsistence farmers and cooperative ventures, and possibly to the involvement of some very large diversified companies, albeit subject then to a minimum profit level restraint.
(b) Growth maximization: this may well be restricted to large companies diversifying into aquaculture from stagnant markets, although small firms might also have this objective.
(c) Satisficing behaviour: where the firm seeks satisfactory performance across a range of aspects (profits, growth, etc.) rather than maximizing any single one. It seems likely that many family or individual fish farms can be best understood in this light.

It must also be borne in mind that regional and national state agencies involved in aquaculture will tend to have non-profit objectives; maximization of food supplies in the short and/or long run may predominate, or aspects of community development, local income enhancement or trade may be part of a satisficing matrix.

10.4 THE ECONOMICS OF AQUACULTURE: REVENUES AND COSTS

The diversity of systems, environments and firms makes it impractical to analyse 'the economics' of aquaculture in holistic terms. There are, however, many studies of specific systems; these are usually 'costs-and-earnings' analyses, sometimes with some investment appraisal, such as those by Berge (1978), Lewis (1979) and Shepherd (1974). However some basic economic analysis has applicability across a fairly wide range of situations.

10.4.1 Revenues and costs

The analysis of the individual profit-maximizing unit has been undertaken by Shang (1981) and in other more specific studies. The essential elements are that the total profit (TP) received per area of land or water that is farmed is derived from the relationship between the total revenue received from sales of the fish produced (TR) and the total costs of producing the fish (TC), i.e.

$$TP = TR - TC \tag{10.1}$$

Since the TR element is based on the total physical production of the operation, y, and the average revenue received from selling that product, AR, and TC is based upon total production y and average cost incurred in producing this, AC, then

$$TP = y(AR - AC) \tag{10.2}$$

This gives us the essential elements, and we shall use this in order to examine important features of each. The farmer will, by his own actions, influence y and AC, and may be able to influence AR under certain circumstances. Let us first examine y, the physical production of the aquaculture unit.

10.4.2 Physical production

There are two principal elements involved in physical production; primarily we have the physical productivity of the fish farm's operations, but also we should recognize that farmers may have the ability to withhold their production from the market, perhaps allowing the fish to become larger before harvesting or freezing and storing after harvest. As we shall see, the quantity of fish that is sold is determined by the farm's market position also, but we are primarily concerned first with physical production per unit area; that is, the production function. The principal factors that underlie productivity per unit in the individual farm may be classified as follows:

Stocking rate. An area of water limited by space and natural food supply has an ECC (environmental carrying capacity) in terms of the physical weight of fish stock that is sustainable under natural conditions. In certain simple artisanal farms, it is only this ECC that is cropped, but typically aquaculture involves enhancing ECC by various methods, especially by fertilization to increase plankton production (e.g. in a pond), by supplementary feeding to increase food supply, especially of key nutrients, and by aeration, to increase the dissolved oxygen present, often by the constant renewal of the water supply, which will also remove waste products. In addition, stock management to optimize the combination of size groups of the species, especially by balancing the decline of growth rates at higher stocking densities and perhaps by periodic cropping or transferral to other enclosures, will be important. Polyculture to utilize the natural and enhanced productivity more fully by multi-species production will represent a different approach and offers potentially great scope. All these methods have cost implications, and the optimal farm unit will utilize any method up to the level at which the marginal cost is equal to the marginal revenue that is resultant from it.

Growth and survival rates. The rate at which fish grow and the mortality experienced are both susceptible to manipulation by the farmer, the principal means being selective breeding and hybridization. These techniques are usually based on scientific research by government or large firms, although the individual farm may operate selection of breeding stock for desirable growth and survival characteristics. Stocking rate must also be optimal in relation to available space and food. Overcrowding will affect growth and mortality rates, and may be a critical problem in territorial species such as lobsters or groupers. Fertilizer and/or food input quality and quantity are vital; feeding affects not only stocking rate but also growth rates. Generally the more intensive the system, then the greater the reliance on artificial feeding. As far as water quality is concerned, the satisfactory control of water temperature and dissolved oxygen within definable limits is one of the main determinants of success. Temperature can be controlled by windbreaks, water depth control and water input temperature; dissolved oxygen mainly by the supply of good-quality water and sound environmental management. Control of diseases, predators and parasites and so on is regarded as one of the most important factors. High stocking rates, pollution and poor environmental management tend to increase disease problems, affecting growth and mortality. Generally, the more intensive the system, the greater the efforts to remove predators completely.

The individual farm may have to strike a balance between stocking rate and growth and mortality rates, and will identify the ways in which costs are affected by the policies pursued. To illustrate, while it was demonstrated in the United States that tilapia grew 50% faster when fed on pellets than in a manured pond, the costs of production were $0.41/kg compared to $0.02–$0.21/kg respectively, thus favouring the more extensive system.

10.4.3 Costs

The costs of producing farmed fish may be divided into two main classes: *fixed* costs, the total amount of which do not vary with the quantity produced, and *variable* costs, which do vary with production quantity. In the long run of course all costs must by definition be variable, but in the short run the individual farm will have certain costs that have to be met regardless of total production, although sometimes payment can be postponed. Although the distinction between the two groups is sometimes somewhat arbitrary, we shall now discuss the principal elements of the two.

10.4.3.1 *Fixed costs*

Interest. The main element in fixed costs is usually that associated with paying interest on financial capital raised to construct and operate the farm. In addition to capital used to purchase equipment, etc., the farm will also need working capital to finance stocks of feedstuffs, fertilizers, fish in production, fish in storage, and so on. The firm will raise finance either internally or from external sources such as banks, money markets, etc., in the latter case either as debt or by selling an equity interest in the firm. External finance will involve the paying of interest and dividends, the amount varying with the amount raised and the inherent riskiness of the venture; as aquaculture is often seen as relatively risky, interest rates may be high, and Shang (1981) reports rates on aquacultural loans in developing countries in the range 12–30% p.a. Sometimes government agencies will make credit or capital available, often at reduced rates. Internal finance will involve an opportunity cost in terms of the interest foregone which it might have earned.

Land purchase or lease. Most farms will face the need to purchase or lease a land or shore area for their operations, and even those employing marine situations will normally pay some form of commercial rent to obtain exclusive rights. (For example, about 46% of the milkfish farms in the Philippines are established on leased land—*see* Shang (1981, p. 123).) The amount paid will be associated in part with alternative uses, but particularly important considerations in the value of a site for aquaculture include water quality, the topography of the area, soil quality, the location and ease of access to the site, and its proximity to markets.

Capital depreciation. The third principal element in fixed costs is associated with allowances for the depreciation of the capital stock. Aquaculture may involve substantial initial investment, especially in the case of intensive systems, and investment in ponds, cages, rafts, boats and suchlike must be written off, sometimes over a short period.

Indirect operating costs. There are certain operating costs that have to be met, whatever the production level, such as maintenance, office activities, insurance, land rates, and some part of power inputs. These may in fact vary somewhat with output, but this variation is often so small as to allow such costs to be regarded as fixed. Some permanent labour costs may very well be of this fixed-cost type; although we shall here regard labour as primarily a variable cost, many empirical studies take labour costs as mainly fixed and partly variable (e.g. Lewis, 1979).

10.4.3.2 *Variable costs*

Variable costs vary with production volume, given an initial capital investment. As in the long run all inputs are variable, since the *scale of plant* involving all inputs may be varied, then all costs are variable; however, for the individual firm operating annually, the principal variable costs are as follows.

Feedstuffs and fertilizers. These are often the most important element in total costs in intensive systems, typically comprising 50% of total costs, sometimes as much as 75% (e.g. EEC trout production). However the majority of world finfish production is still based on natural food supplies for the most part—Tang (1979) suggests 97%. The proportion of costs taken by food depends on the scale of operations (*see* section 10.5). The costs of feedstuffs per unit of fish produced, AC_{fs}, follow the form

$$AC_{fs} = f(p_{fs}, CR) \tag{10.3}$$

where AC_{fs} is the average cost of feed per unit of fish, p_{fs} is the unit price of the feed and CR is the conversion ratio of feed to fish flesh. p_{fs} is largely beyond the control of the individual firm, unless it also has interests in feedstuff manufacturing and can use this vertical linkage to obtain cheap inputs. The conversion ratio is a crucially important factor and will be discussed in section 10.4.4.

Supplies of seed/fry/spawn. A vital element in any system is obtaining supplies of seed, fry, fingerlings, etc. to grow-on, and these may comprise as much as 50% of total costs (Shang, 1981). There are two basic sources: collection from the wild,, benefiting from natural productivity, or production under controlled conditions in a hatchery. The latter may be owned by the firm, by another firm, or sometimes by local or national public bodies. The producer must decide the age at which to purchase, for while younger seed may be cheaper, older seed will have a higher survival rate and will involve lower total feedstuff costs.

As hatcheries may need to operate at a fairly substantial scale to be viable, they can sustain a large number of fish farms, and it is not unusual for hatcheries to develop a degree of monopoly power. Larger farms may extend operations backwards into fry production partly to avoid this kind of monopoly, and partly to obtain the desired quantity, quality and reliability of inputs.

As the problems of culturing many organisms have not yet been solved at a cost to compete with natural stocks, collection from the wild remains very important, for example for oysters, scallops, eels, turbot, bream and carp. The need to collect from the wild severely limits the commercial aquaculture of many marine finfish (Brown, 1977), and reduction of this problem is one key advantage in salmon ranching.

Labour. Labour costs arise from feeding, harvesting and maintenance, all of which are partially susceptible to mechanization. The producer will be influenced by the relative prices and productivity of labour and capital; thus in many developing countries, aquaculture is labour-intensive because of the cheapness of labour inputs in relation to scarce and expensive capital (*see* section 10.6).

Other production costs. A number of other production costs may be variable, and often the most important of these is energy consumption. This varies very greatly with the system employed, and highly intensive systems may have very high costs associated with water pumping, recirculation and aeration. Systems that involve boats will have fuel costs also.

Selling costs. Most producers will incur costs in marketing, and others may deliberately integrate vertically forward into marketing activities. The costs include transportation, preservation, processing, packaging, storing and advertising of the product. In developing countries, with often dispersed markets, poor distribution systems, and sometimes extremes of climate, preservation is especially important, permitting the product to reach a wider market and command a higher price.

Finally, we should note that the individual farmer may be able to deflect some of his costs onto the community in general, for there can be substantial externalities in aquaculture. In particular there is the question of how much of the pollution produced by a farm is dealt with by the farm (internal costs) or by the community (external costs). For example, while it might require perhaps just £1000 of capital investment per ton to farm trout in the United Kingdom (Lewis, 1981), a trout farm stocked with 35 tons will produce as much sewage as a village of 1000 inhabitants, and the water passing the farm will be comparable to the water consumption of a town with 200000 inhabitants (Christensen, 1974). The extent to which the farmer has to meet the associated costs is a direct function of the extent and adequacy of environmental legislation, and most fish farms do not in practice internalize the costs of effluent treatment.

10.4.4 Conversion ratios

The conversion ratio (CR) is the ratio at which fish convert inputs into output; that is, convert (dry) feedstuff into (wet) weight gain. As such, the

CR is central to the economics of any aquacultural operation, for the essence of culture is to convert low-grade, low-price inputs into high-grade, high-price outputs, and the CR will be a primary determining factor as to whether such an operation will be commercially viable.

Properly managed, correctly fed fish can have remarkably low CRs: often in the range of 4 : 1 or 3 : 1, sometimes as low as 1.5 : 1. In extreme cases with fingerlings, the CR can be between 1 : 1 and 0.5 : 1, this apparent impossibility arising from the fact that as much as 80% of the flesh gain is water content. Generally, aquacultural CRs compare favourably with those obtained in agriculture, although there is much variation associated with the quality of the input.

Achieving a low CR is an important factor in lowering overall production costs. It is partly a function of the species or subspecies farmed, partly of the age profile of the fish kept (generally CR declines with age), and partly with feeding specification and practice. Feedstuffs need to be carefully formulated, attractive in appearance and colour, available at correct times, and delivered such as to minimize wastage. For example, poor binding qualities in wet feeds will increase wastage. Product specification can be varied so as to produce desired characteristics in the final product. A further important factor is the stocking rate, for excessive density may not only reduce survival rates, but can depress the CR and reduce the average weight of harvested fish, all of which will tend to increase average costs. Conversely, understocking densities can result in the waste of feedstuffs as well as of space, again increasing average costs.

The basic principle of feeding is depicted in *Figure 10.1*. The two principal features are MC_{fs}, which is the marginal cost (*see* section 1.3.4) of feedstuffs being applied, and MR_{fs}, which is the marginal revenue being earned from the extra production arising from the application of the extra units of feedstuff. As a generalization, MC_{fs} will have a positive slope whereas MR_{fs} will have a negative slope, as extra feeding will increase

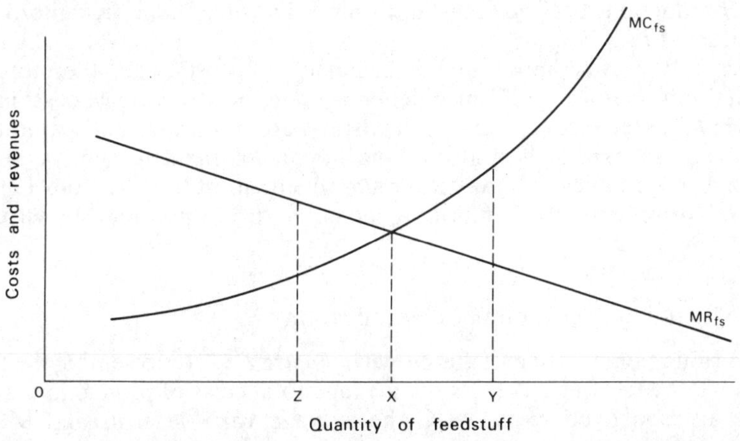

FIGURE 10.1 Optimal feeding stategy in aquaculture.

production but at a decreasing rate, such that total revenue is increasing but at a lessening rate. MR_{fs} will eventually become zero when additional feedstuffs fail to increase TR at all. The optimal strategy is to feed where $MC_{fs} = MR_{fs}$; that is, at quantity X. Feeding other quantities is sub-optimal: for example, at Y, the MC of the feedstuff applied exceeds the MR generated, so that total profits would be higher with lower quantities applied. At quantity Z, the reverse applies and more feedstuff should be used. Discovering this overall optimal level in practice may not be easy, for although MC_{fs} may be identifiable, there is much greater uncertainty concerning MR_{fs},which will be influenced by the nature of the market for the final product; it should be noted that the demand for feedstuff is thus a derived demand, dependent on the demand for the farmed fish.

Identifying the correct daily feeding rate is even more complex. It depends initially on the composition of the feedstuff itself in terms of proteins, fats and carbohydrates, and also on the species and age of the fish, stocking density, natural food availability (if any), water temperature and weather conditions, as well as the price of the feed (*see* Shang, 1981).

It is important to recognize that simple CRs can be rather misleading in overall terms. Thus while carp might achieve a ratio of 1.3–1.5:1 when fed with fish meal, with soybeans this might rise to 3–5:1. Yet the soybean feedstuff is produced at the lowest trophic level, whereas the fish meal might well be made from herring that have already fed at a higher trophic level. Given an inter-trophic level conversion ratio of 10:1, the conversion efficiency of 'non-preferred inputs' into 'preferred output' may in fact be 3 or 4 times better if the carp are fed on soybeans (Ackefors and Rosen, 1979).

To make meaningful comparisons, one should employ more specific food conversion ratios, although these may not be of practical significance to the individual farm. It is worth noting that more closely defined ratios tend to reveal clearly the innate advantages of fish farming: thus, the comparison is between a ratio of 0.53 calories of edible product per calorie of metabolizable energy of food for rainbow trout, and ratios of 0.3 for milk production, 0.25 for pigs and only 0.18 for poultry (Kinghorn and Gjedrem, 1982).

The CR is an important determinant of costs and therefore of profitability, but its significance depends upon the structure of costs in the individual enterprise. If artificial feedstuffs are not important within total costs (e.g. in extensive systems), the impact of the CR may be slight; perhaps more typically however, an improvement of the CR from 12:1 to 4:1 in Norwegian pondfish farming increased 'profit per hour' by virtually 100% (Berge, 1978).

10.4.5 Minimum cost output determination

The various elements of cost are shown in *Figure 10.2*, representing the firm in the short run, where ATC is the average total costs of production, AFC is the average fixed costs, AVC the average variable costs and MC is marginal costs.

The AFC curve has a distinctive shape known as a rectangular hyperbola, and depicts the process of 'spreading overheads' as greater production levels are compared on the particular scale of farm. The ATC curve is typically U-shaped; it follows the law of diminishing returns, which suggests that as units of variable inputs are applied to the fixed inputs, at low output levels average costs will decline but at higher levels

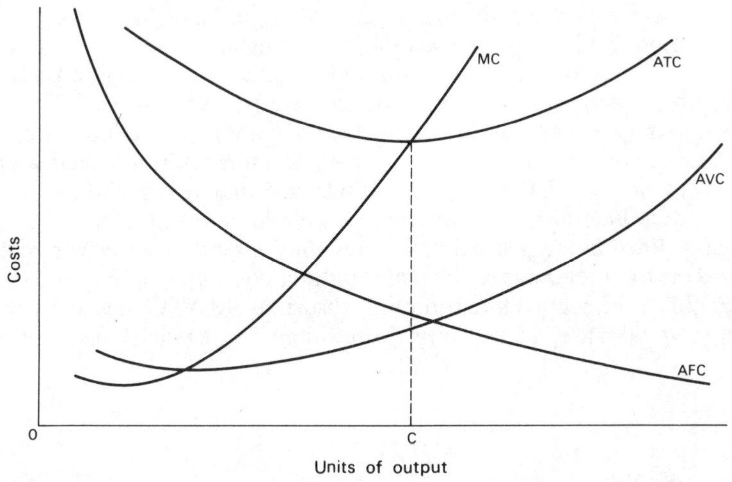

FIGURE 10.2 Costs of production in aquaculture: the short run.

average costs will tend to rise (*see* Chapter 1). The reason for this behaviour can be grasped intuitively if we consider a fixed pond unit, to which we add increasing quantities of fish fry and food, etc. At first the fixed costs of the pond are spread across the increasing quantities produced, so that although the total variable costs will tend to rise as more of these inputs are used, AFC falls faster and so ATC declines. However, beyond a certain optimum point, overcrowding, waste, competition, etc. will start to pull the AVC curve up more steeply than the AFC curve is falling, and so ATC will itself start to rise. The point at which ATC is at a minimum may be regarded as the optimum use, or 'capacity' in economic terms, of the farm given its fixed inputs, and is shown as output level C in *Figure 10.2*. We shall see later that production may not in practice take place at this level.

10.5 ECONOMIES OF SCALE IN AQUACULTURE

So far we have considered the farm with fixed costs, that is, one operating at a particular scale of plant. However, scale can of course be adjusted over time, such that we consider *all* costs as variable in the long run. What then happens to the average total costs of production? Will they tend to decline with larger scale (economies of scale) or perhaps beyond a certain scale tend to increase (diseconomies of scale)?

Before answering, we should recognize that scale is of considerable importance, particularly if we should find evidence of economies of scale, in the following ways. Economies of scale will confer the benefits of lower-cost production on the larger farm unit, giving it commercial strength as compared with smaller units. If significant, their presence will call for larger initial capital investments, posing a financial problem for the producer. In particular, the required capital for a larger plant may constitute a *barrier to entry* into aquaculture (*see* section 10.7.2).

As we compare costs at different scales of plant in production, then given a constant state of technology, the textbook interpretation is that we might expect to see an LRATC curve that is either U-shaped or possibly L-shaped, indicating that economies of scale are present as scale increases, bringing down average total costs, but they may then at larger scales be overtaken by diseconomies of scale, pulling costs up (*see Figure 10.3*). In *Figure 10.3*, we see a short-run plant shown as $SRATC_2$ has average total costs (C_2) that are, at capacity, lower than the capacity costs of either

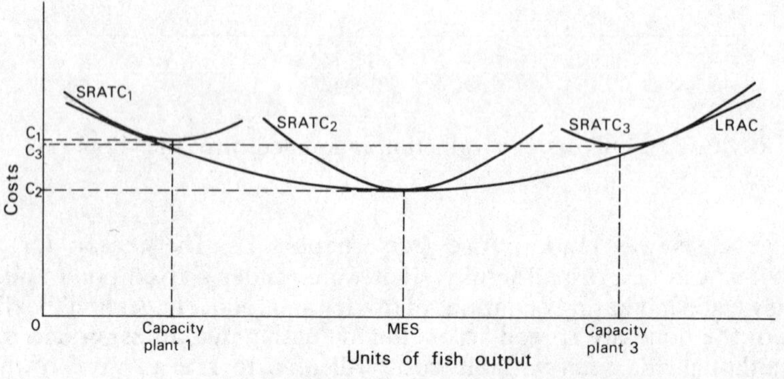

FIGURE 10.3 Economies of scale in aquaculture: costs in the long run.

$SRATC_1$ (C_1) or $SRATC_3$ (C_3). If we can imagine a continuum of plants of gradually larger scale, then we can construct the LRATC curve, which represents the least-cost manner of producing the various output levels. With economies of scale present, LRATC declines as scale increases; with diseconomies, LRATC increases with scale. Note that, with the exception of the optimum scale of plant ($SRATC_2$ above), production would *not* optimally take place at the capacity level of any plant; it will be possible to achieve lower ATC if a larger plant is built, but then used at less than capacity (that is, LRATC does not link up 'capacity' levels, except that of $SRATC_2$). The validity of this can be seen by imagining a plant somewhat larger than plant $SRATC_1$; this will have costs lower than C_1 at the capacity

LRATC = Long Run Average Total Cost

output of $SRATC_1$. The point at which LRATC is minimized is known as the minimum efficient scale (MES) and is the lowest level that either SR or LR costs can reach. If MES is substantial, in terms of the associated capital investment or as a proportion of total market size, then economies of scale may be considered to be significant. It is worth noting that, although we assume that the state of technical knowledge is given, at larger scales different technology may be selected from the available set of possibilities. Some empirical evidence is presented soon, but we must first identify the sources of potential economies of scale in aquaculture.

10.5.1 Sources of economies of scale in aquaculture

The principal economies of scale in aquaculture arise from seven sources:

Increased dimensions. The basic operation of most fish farms involves keeping fish in some form of container, and since the volume of any container, be it square, round or whatever, will increase at a faster rate than the area of its walls, then the capital construction costs per water volume will decline with scale.* In general engineering terms, the so-called six-tenths rule may apply, that capital costs increase by a factor of 0.6 with scale. It is also likely that greater efficiency in land and water management will be achieved, although conversely, smaller units may allow easier management and maintenance (Shang, 1981).

Labour costs. Although the total quantity of labour will increase at larger scale, the quantity per unit produced will almost certainly decline. One worker can feed very much larger quantities of fish with only a marginal increase in time and effort; Shang (1981, p. 32) suggests for example that the necessary labour per acre (= 0.41 hectare) in freshwater prawn farming in Hawaii declines from 0.25 man-years/acre on a 1-acre farm to 0.1 man-years/acre on a 100-acre farm. Lewis (1979, p. 39) suggests that for a British trout farm, labour costs per pound (lb) decline from 33.1 to 4.4 pence/lb as output size p.a. rises from under 5 tons to over 100 tons, and concludes that this decline in labour costs is the largest single contributor to scale economies. Weir (1979) confirms this by showing that average output per worker on these farms rises from 10 tons in small farms (0–10 tons per annum) to 40 tons on large farms (100-plus tons per annum).

Specialization. For a large farm, the functions undertaken can become more specialized, with an accompanying gain in expertise and lowering of costs. Specialization is especially relevant where the enterprise becomes vertically integrated, with involvements perhaps in feedstuff production, hatcheries, processing plant, ice plant, storage, distribution and marketing; larger scale overall will permit the achievement of scale in each separate activity, better planning, integration, and will release the farm from

*The volume of a vessel is roughly proportional to the cube of its radius, while its surface area is proportional to the square.

dependence on others for the activity, all of which will lower costs (*see* Cracknell, 1979; Gerhardsen, 1979).

Bulk purchase. Cost-saving gains may be made with scale in the purchase of a wide variety of inputs to the aquacultural unit. Particularly important are purchases of feedstuffs, fry, seed and boxes.

Risk spreading. Larger-scale operations permit the spreading of risk across a wider range of units, which can be a significant advantage. For example, with stocked cages for salmon production in the sea worth £20000 each, losses of two or three p.a. out of fifty owing to storm damage or vessel collisions may be acceptable, but would be disastrous in a five-cage unit (Nestel, 1981).

Advertising. The larger-scale operation is able to gain economies in its use of advertising, which always offers discounts to the larger user, who is also able to employ the more cost-effective regional and national media, and to have specialized marketing staff.

Research and development. A further cost-saving benefit from scale arises from the ability to operate in-house R & D activities to develop new ideas internally and to make more effective use of those from external sources.

10.5.2 Examples of economies of scale

Generally speaking, there are relatively few studies of economies of scale in aquaculture, although such evidence as there is clearly indicates that a downward-sloping LRATC is in fact typical. The example in *Table 10.4* is taken from Lewis (1979) and relates to a cross-section of trout farms in the United Kingdom; at each size of farm (scale), the contribution of average

TABLE 10.4 Economies of scale in trout production in the United Kingdom

	Size of farm (tons per annum)					
	0–5	*6–10*	*11–15*	*16–20*	*21–50*	*100+*
Variable costs* (pence/lb)	30	32	32	36	30	27
Fixed costs†	47	33	27	24	23	11
Total costs (pence/lb)	77	65	59	59	52	38

*This included contract and casual labour, fish purchases, food, packaging and transport costs.
†This included regular paid labour, unpaid manual labour, power and fuel, maintenance, insurance, administration and depreciation.
Source: Lewis (1979).

variable and average fixed costs to average total costs is also given. As can be seen, the total costs per pound decline appreciably as scale increases, associated in fact mainly with economies in fixed labour costs. It is also apparent that, as one might anticipate, the proportion of the declining average total costs that is attributable to the fixed-costs elements at each scale also declines from about 62% to 29%. The data imply that MES is a farm producing over 100 tons annually. Confirming this pattern, Gerhardsen (1979) reports that the total interest, depreciation and labour cost per kilogram of trout produced in Norway declined from 5.51 kroner to 4.01 kroner in farms producing below and above 15 tons p.a. respectively.

Moreover, the presence and importance of declining costs is reflected in evidence which suggests that generally the larger aquaculture farms make higher average profits per unit. *Table 10.5* is based on Berge (1978) and relates to fifty-two pondfish salmonid production plants in Norway for the year 1974.

It should however be remembered that any use of profit rates alone as an indicator of economies of scale would be unwise. Generally, large farms use bulk sales/markets and earn a lower average revenue per sale than

TABLE 10.5 Costs, productivity and profits in Norwegian salmonid production

	Production rate (tonnes)*				
	1–5	*5.1–10*	*10.1–20*	*20.1–50*	*Over 50*
Average total production costs (kr/kg)	25.4	17.7	14.5	14.1	14.9
Production per man/year (tonnes)†	5.6	10.9	14.1	15.6	19.3
Operating profit per man/hour (kr)	12.01	22.78	23.84	29.20	61.54

* The data may not be strictly comparable across scale owing to differences in techniques arising from vintage rather than deliberate selection, and from different species output; however a clear general pattern emerges, albeit with some indication of diseconomies of scale at over 50 tons (i.e. MES may lie in the 20.1–50 tonnes size range).

†The data also allow for some interesting international comparisons; for example, average productivity per man/year in British salmonid production was still only 1 : 12.3 tons by 1980, the main reason for this being the failure to achieve economies of scale (Munro and Waddell, 1982).

Source: Berge (1978).

smaller firms that use local retailers, restaurants, farm-gate sales. For example, in the United Kingdom, 80% of the trout goes to wholesalers and fish markets and earns perhaps 20–30% less per pound than that sold locally. Not surprisingly then, average returns may *decline* with size, despite lower costs although total returns increase (Lewis, 1981).

As a final illustration, evidence is presented (*Figure 10.4*) on mussel culture in the Netherlands, and clearly depicts declining average costs with scale, this time with average revenue (= price) unaffected. Once again, no clear MES emerges.

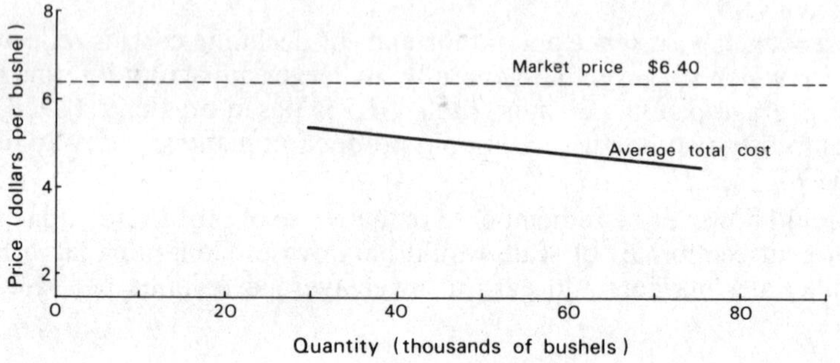

FIGURE 10.4 Economies of scale in Dutch mussel culture. Adapted from Clifton (1980) by courtesy of Elsevier.

In contrast, there appears to be very little empirical evidence of diseconomies of scale, although Berge (1978) suggests that increasing unit costs are experienced beyond 50 tonnes. Larkin (1982) does suggest however that economies of scale may be quickly exhausted in tropical aquaculture at least.

Three final points must be noted. First, the ability of the individual unit to achieve available economies of scale may be restricted by exogenous factors. The most obvious is the availability of suitable sites in terms of space and water quality, which in the United Kingdom has certainly affected both trout and salmon farms (Lewis, 1979).

Secondly, the potential may be restricted by the size and nature of market demand for the fish and/or the costs of transporting fish to new markets. Thus Clifton (1980, p. 331) found that, while increasing the scale of a mussel farm in the United States from 5000 bushels to 40000 bushels (1 U.S. bushel = 0.0352 m^3) would reduce average costs from \$25 to \$16, it was doubtful that the larger plant could sell all its output at a viable price. Very large rates of production may of course ultimately bring farms into competition not only with fish substitutes but other substitute foodstuffs.

Finally, as the state of technical knowledge changes, then it may be the larger firms that will be able to respond most quickly, adopt the newer systems, and thus reduce their production costs dynamically. Such large firms will also almost certainly benefit dynamically from the 'learning effect', whereby average costs will decline with *cumulative* production over time, as labour and management learn from past experience. Although untested as yet, it seems likely that learning will be a significant source of relative cost reductions over time in aquaculture.

10.6 CAPITAL-INTENSIVE VERSUS LABOUR-INTENSIVE PRODUCTION SYSTEMS

One of the most basic decisions to be taken in aquacultural production concerns the relative quantities to be employed of inputs of labour and capital. We may usefully identify the nature of this input mix with the aid of *Figure 10.5*. This figure employs two main types of curve: *production isoquants*, which are lines that link equal levels of production, and

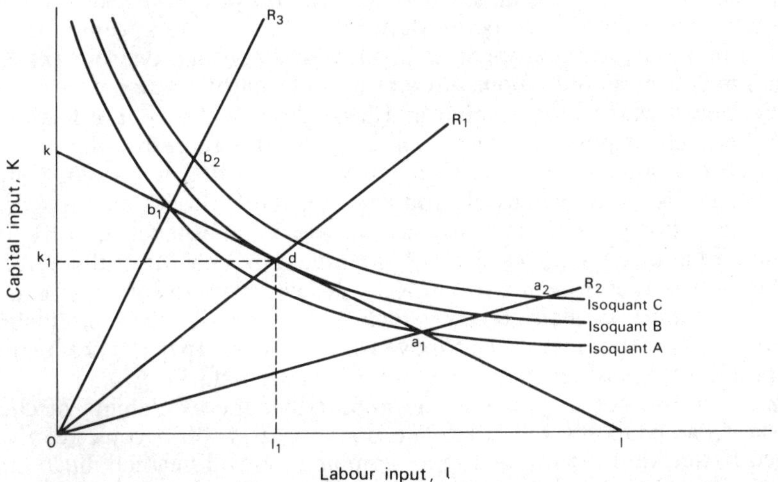

FIGURE 10.5 Optimal capital–labour intensities in aquaculture.

production isocost or *budget* lines, which link equal levels of production costs. To understand the model, we may relate it to one specific aquacultural activity, although it can be applied to any: we can employ it to analyse mussel production in the United States, as studied by Clifton (1980).

The isoquants represent increasing levels of production per period of time. Thus isoquant A represents, say, 4000 bushels of mussels produced per 15 months. As can be seen, this quantity can be produced with differing levels of inputs of labour and capital, different combinations of which will *each* produce that amount. Isoquant C represents greater inputs of *both* labour and capital, and traces combinations that will produce, say, 5000 bushels per 15 months. Each of these levels of production can be produced either by relatively labour-intensive methods (e.g. points a_1 and a_2) or relatively capital-intensive methods (e.g. points b_1 and b_2). The decision as to *how much* to produce and by *what capital/labour intensity* is taken with reference to the isocost line kl. This line represents by its distance from the origin the amounts of each factor input that the firm can afford to purchase. Given the market price (w) for labour inputs (l), then it could spend all its resources on labour (l); given the opportunity cost (r) of capital (K), then it could spend all on capital (k); more realistically, it will purchase some inputs of each, constrained therefore by kl as a budget line. The slope of this isocost/budget line is determined by relative factor prices, i.e. by w/r. A steep slope indicates that labour rates are relatively more expensive than capital, and the converse is also true.

The firm will decide to maximize output given its budget; that is, it will seek to produce on the isoquant as far from the origin as its budget will permit. This will be where an isoquant is tangential to the isocost line, in this case at point d on isoquant B. This isoquant will represent, say, 4500 bushels per 15 months, to be produced by l_1 labour and k_1 capital inputs. The firm *could* use its resources to produce 4000 bushels on isoquant A by combining capital and labour at point a_1 on kl, but the same expenditure redirected towards more capital and less labour will raise production to 4500 bushels at point d on isoquant B. Point d is therefore the point of

least-cost production for the firm, given the existing w/r ratio. Clifton (1980) in his study of mussel production in the United States suggested that the industry was in fact at point a_1, with capital per man at \$10 000 (compared incidentally to \$40 000 per man in U.S. agriculture). The industry was therefore inefficient, and should move towards point d by becoming more capital-intensive, such as to increase the capital/labour ratio to \$51 000 per man; such a move would increase (partial) productivity from 1333 bushels per man to 5000 bushels per man.

We can also see in principle the impact that the availability of cheap labour in an economy will have. The isocost line kl will become relatively much flatter, and the optimal input combination will become much more labour-intensive. Thus low-wage economies will optimize factor inputs along labour-intensive rays (such as OR_2). Conversely, high-wage economies will have a different w/r ratio, relatively steeper isocost lines, and might optimize factor inputs along rays such as OR_3. Note incidentally that more capital-intensive production techniques do not necessarily mean changed technologies, rather it is the application of more technology per worker in areas such as mechanical handling and feeding.

These variations in factor input intensity will of course be reflected in two ways. First, any *partial* productivity measure will be susceptible. For example, 'output per worker' in aquaculture can be as much a reflection of differing capital intensities in production systems as it is of 'efficiency' in the labour force. Secondly, the variations will be reflected in energy budgets as in section 10.2.2. Thus we can find (Richardson, 1976) a comparison clearly reflecting the factor input differences:

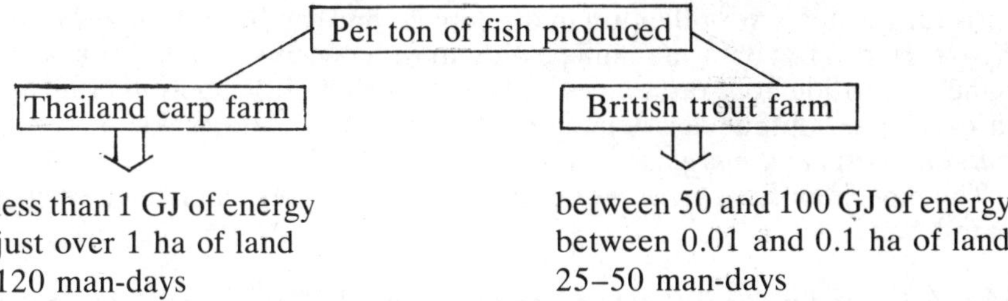

less than 1 GJ of energy
just over 1 ha of land
120 man-days

between 50 and 100 GJ of energy
between 0.01 and 0.1 ha of land
25–50 man-days

Finally, it is important to note that in some developing countries the high abundance of labour may mean that the marginal productivity of labour in other occupations (capture fisheries, agriculture) is very low indeed. Transfer of this labour to aquaculture may have virtually no effect on non-aquacultural production. In contrast, the transfer of capital from non-aquaculture to aquaculture may have very significant impacts elsewhere. Apart from favouring labour-intensive systems (i.e. kl would be very flat), this latter point is relevant to the question of the role of aquaculture in developing countries, for although there may be many general factors in its favour (*see* section 10.8), the opportunity cost of capital when used in aquaculture may be very high in terms of best alternative use foregone. Consideration of this 'opportunity cost' aspect of aquaculture is often omitted from some of the more optimistic overviews of its potential.

10.7 REVENUE

10.7.1 Revenue and the output decision: market structure

So far we have examined the elements y (physical productivity) and AC (average costs) in the model introduced in section 10.4.1, leaving AR (average revenue). Total revenue may be defined as the total income to the aquacultural unit, although more relevant parameters for optimum output decisions are average revenue and marginal revenue. The fish that are sold will be entering a market for fish where they will compete with other farmed fish, fish from traditional capture fisheries and non-fish products, with varying cross-elasticities against each of these (*see* Chapter 1). They may enter markets that are essentially local or regionalized, or national or international, or perhaps limited to certain socioeconomic groups. Thus we find almost every situation from the subsistence fish farmer selling a few surplus fish at the farm gate to local customers, through to multinational firms producing, distributing and selling in international markets.

Dependent upon the nature of competition, the producer may find that he has no choice but to accept the going market price (i.e. be a price-taker), or may be able to have some influence (a price-maker); he might be the sole seller of the fish within a certain market and thus have a monopoly, or be one of a group of a few sellers who to some extent recognize each other's existence (an oligopoly) in their behaviour. The fish farmer therefore will find himself in one of the market structures that are the traditional basis for the analysis of the firm in economics, and can be categorized as in *Figure 10.6*. (Readers unfamiliar with these concepts should look at a standard introductory economics text, such as that of Samuelson (1982).) In each case, output decisions are related to the relationships between *marginal* costs and *marginal* revenues.

The most important aspects of each situation may be summarized briefly as follows:

The fish farmer under perfect competition (Figure 10.6a). In these circumstances the farmer produces fish that are undifferentiated from those of his competitors and form a relatively insignificant part of total

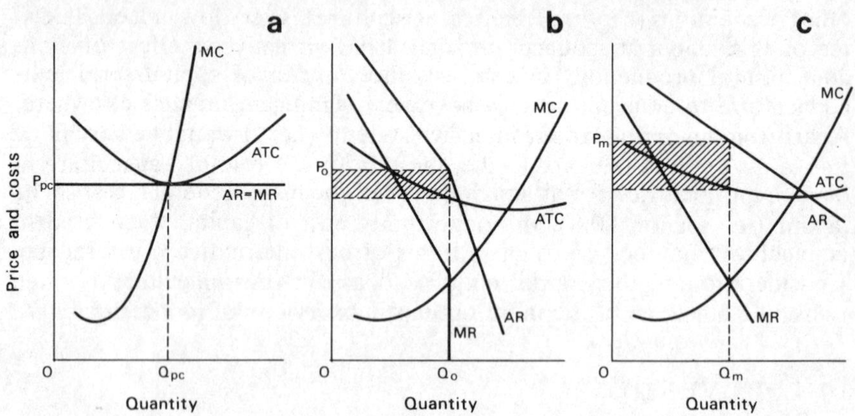

FIGURE 10.6 The fish farmer and market structure. (a) Perfect competition; (b) within oligopoly; (c) as a monopolist. The shaded areas indicate above-normal profit.

supplies. Here the market price is determined by the interaction of the forces of demand and supply. For the farmer, average revenue becomes a constant and is equal to market price ($AR = P_{pc}$), and his output decision is influenced by the relationship between this and his costs, which he can influence. To maximize his profits, he will need to produce where marginal cost equals marginal revenue (MC = MR), and as MR = AR, then he will produce where $MC = MR = AR = p_{pc}$. He will earn 'normal profits' only; if he earns less, he will have to leave this activity, and if he earns more in the short run then new firms will enter in the long run, pushing profits back to normal levels. As fish is customarily sold in a form undifferentiated by producer, perfect competition may well be typical of much aquaculture in general terms, although in practice firms tend to experience different cost structures and have a little localized price discretion. For perfect competition—or anything approaching it—to exist, it is crucial that barriers to entry are very low or insignificant (*see* section 10.7.2), thereby permitting easy entry if profits are sufficiently attractive.

The fish farmer within oligopoly (Figure 10.6b). There are four main features which suggest that fish farming might often be usefully analysed within an oligopoly framework. (i) Frequently there are relatively few fish farms competing within the relevant markets. (ii) Generally, the more fish that farmers wish to sell, the more they will have to lower their price; that is, they face a downward-sloping demand curve, reflected in the AR curve in *Figure 10.6b*. (iii) The products of individual farmers may be differentiated on a regional or national level; possibly by packaging and branding, or maybe by the localized nature of the market, giving the individual some local market power. (iv) Certain barriers to entry (*see* section 10.7.2) do exist to deter potential entrants.

Thus oligopoly is typified by a downward-sloping AR (and MR) curve, product differentiation to a degree, and fewness of sellers (that is, high seller concentration). The individual farm will again seek to maximize profits at MC = MR, but the exact nature of behaviour depends greatly on the extent and nature of the competition that does emerge. The diagram shows just one possible outcome, where the AR curve becomes kinked at the going price, p_0, as competitors would wish to match any price cuts the individual farm makes, but not any price increases (= differential price elasticity). Profits now will typically be above normal, as barriers to entry will be present here to deter potential competitors attracted by the profits.

The fish farmer as monopolist (Figure 10.6c). It is possible for a farm to enjoy monopoly power in being effectively the sole supplier of output to the market. To do so it would have to produce a clearly differentiated product (for example, to be the only supplier of hatchery seed). It may then set a price in relation to the market demand curve (which now becomes its demand curve) without reference to competitors, and the customary analysis suggests that it will set a higher price than the equivalent price under perfect competition, with lower total production; profits are however above normal, protected now by significant barriers to entry. Again, it seeks, as a profit maximizer, to produce where MC = MR, giving price p_m.

Market structures in aquaculture appear to vary widely, from those approximating quite closely to perfect competition to situations close to classical monopoly. For the most part however, intermediate market situations exist; for example, in the British trout industry, which in 1979 produced 4415 tonnes of table trout, the largest nineteen firms (= 13% of the total number) produced 62% of the total production, and indeed the largest five firms produced over 80% of trout sold in a frozen form (which was 16% of the total production) (Lewis, 1981). In contrast, there were 3800 firms producing catfish alone in the United States in 1981 (Banerjee, 1981), and overall in the United Kingdom there are an estimated 650–700 farms in operation (*Fish Farming International*, April 1982).

There can be little doubt that one of the key factors in the industrial structure of aquaculture is the existence, or otherwise, of barriers to entry, and these merit some specific attention.

10.7.2 Market structure: barriers to entry in aquaculture

Barriers to entry may be defined as factors that cause a potential entrant firm to face production costs higher than those of existing firms, or which prevent ('blockade') its entry.

Potential entrants are attracted to aquaculture by the existence of profits, acting as a 'signpost' that production can be profitable. However, what may constitute acceptable levels of profits is debatable, for in aquaculture a relatively high rate of return will be necessary to overcome the problems of market variation, operational problems and the various production hazards. For example, Saunders-Davies (1977) suggested that a rate of return on total capital of 30% p.a. was necessary in trout farming in the United Kingdom. The problems are compounded by the need to wait several years before profits emerge; Needham (1981) reports anticipated delays as long as ten to twelve years before profits became positive, and Kurtyanek (1982) suggests eight to ten years. During this period, cash flow problems would become critical, especially for the single-farm unit.

We can categorize the classes of barriers to entry as follows:

(a) Absolute cost advantages: where the costs of established firms are lower than those of a potential entrant whatever the scale of operation. Important reasons for cost advantages in aquaculture include the high cost and limited availability of capital, which puts new small firms at a marked disadvantage, and existing firms' control over the most favourable sites in terms of water supply and quality in relation to cost.

(b) Key input availability: the potential entrant is unable to obtain inputs in suitable quantity and at suitable prices to compete. For example, existing farms may have all the available skilled labour or control over the output of monopolistic hatcheries; or the entrant might be at a cost disadvantage in obtaining supplies of seed or fry, or feeds.

(c) Technology availability: the potential entrant is unable to acquire the relevant technology (or know-how), perhaps because it is patented, or held as a commercial secret, or based on skills acquired over time. For example, for some forms of salmon farming, knowledge of the marine engineering of sea cages is a crucial determinant of success.

(d) Economies of scale: if these exist, the entrant will face the need to invest in entry at a substantial scale or face higher costs at lower scales. Moreover, farmers entering on a small scale will face the risk of post-entry price cuts by existing firms to drive them out, especially if those firms have spare capacity available to absorb any increase in sales.

(e) Consumer loyalty and product differentiation: entrants face the twin problems of winning customers away from other farmers' fish and/or capture fish. Not only will brand loyalty have to be overcome but also their product may be seen as non-identical to capture fish (e.g. it may be seen as fattier, looser muscled, or have different colouring) and consumer resistance will have to be overcome in both cases (thereby increasing costs)—by advertising campaigns, for example. Any brand advertising by existing farmers will heighten this barrier.

(f) Legal barriers: these may be an important source of deterrent in the form of the various legal restrictions inhibiting or preventing the establishment of fish farms. These restrictions may concern factors such as waste disposal, disease control, or access to shore areas. Licences to produce may be needed (as for salmon in Norway), and there may even be problems with ownership of the fish themselves, such as in any ranching of salmon, and in obtaining any exclusive rights in inshore waters.*

(g) Entrepreneurial excellence: although less tangible, the excellence of the entrepreneur may itself confer such advantages to existing firms that potential entrants could not compete effectively. As aquaculture involves elements of craft as well as science, the combination of experience, knowledge and ability within the existing firms can be a very powerful barrier to others, especially in an increasingly high-technology industry.

Barriers to entry confer advantages on existing firms in, among other ways, allowing them discretion over prices. However such barriers may also inhibit the development of aquaculture as an industry in any country, and are therefore important on a wider level. Although such barriers as those above may be identified, there are other factors that tend to diminish dynamically the significance of barriers. These diminishing factors include especially the existence of expanding demand, permitting both old and newly established firms to prosper. Technological change, conferring an advantage on the *latest* investor, and the presence of fish supplies coming from wild fish or international trade, both diminish barriers. Entry by firms already established elsewhere, especially large firms, may overcome barriers, and government policies deliberately aimed at reducing them may operate, including active encouragement of new entry.

Thus for example Blue Circle was positively attracted into eel farming in the United Kingdom by a combination of the high level of demand and the fewness of competitors (*FFI*, March 1982). Many of the significant investors in intensive farming come from well established industrial bases elsewhere. Such firms may bring certain positive advantages with them in relation to the existing aquacultural firms: for example, BP with feedstuffs, Amey Roadstone with suitable quarries. Additionally, government may

*The Canadian Pearse Commission (*see* Chapter 8) recommended 'mariculture leases' to establish water property rights (Pearse, 1981, Chapter 11); in the United Kingdom, 'several orders' may be obtained, giving exclusive rights concerning sedentary fish species (*see* section 8.4.2).

help to break down barriers by making cheap credit available, supplying seeds, assisting with marketing and training personnel.

In contrast, it may also be possible for small firms to enter and survive even where they cannot enjoy the economies of scale of large units, for they may be able to sell their output at a higher unit price. Thus in the British trout industry, small farms have higher costs but sell at prices appreciably higher than large farms, who have to use wholesale markets or undertake processing. Lewis (1979) found that, in comparison to the data in *Table 10.4*, sale price per pound declined from 67 pence at the smallest scale to 52 pence at the largest. This situation puts considerable pressure in medium-sized units (21–50 tons per annum), who gain neither the production economies of scale nor the premium prices of the larger and smaller units respectively.

Thus in the dynamic situation barriers may be less important than they might seem. Nevertheless, it remains true that the lack of sufficient capital is a very widespread reason for the failure of fish farms throughout the world. Moreover the nature of the barriers underlies some of the reasons for aquaculture's relatively slow development in certain economies; for example, a lack of suitable natural sites appropriate for large-scale production units is an important factor in the British trout industry. In fact, the number of trout farms has increased in total from forty in 1970 to 520 by 1983; however, Lewis (1981) reveals that 62% of production came from units producing less than 20 tonnes annually, for large-scale production is not possible in many locations. Likewise, trout production in Denmark is not likely to expand greatly, primarily because of a lack of suitable sites (Kurtyanek, 1982).

10.7.3 Revenue, and increasing it . . .

Fish farmers will, under most circumstances, be interested in selling more fish and at higher prices. If they have some influence over the demand curve for their output, they may try to shift it bodily to the right; if not, they may consider moving down the curve by selling at a lower price. Only under perfect competition will the farmers theoretically accept price as given—and even there, they may well strive energetically to move towards developing more market power. In general terms, farmers can undertake a number of marketing activities to sell more and/or improve the price they will receive for their production:

(a) Maintenance of high and reliable quality, through from production to point of sale, whether in fresh or processed form.
(b) Processing to change the form and appeal of the product, for example by smoking, salting or freezing. Selection of species suitable for added value by such means is increasingly influencing investment decisions.
(c) By grading, sorting and careful handling during distribution and sale, for example to be able to offer retailers or restaurateurs boxes of fish of standard portion size.
(d) By gearing production to seasonal or regional demands, and/or maintaining a steady and reliable supply to outlets.

(e) By active product promotion; for example, the catfish market in the United States was developed only after changing the product's image away from that of a muddy-flavoured, ethnic food.

All these activities should, other things being equal, shift the demand curve to the right, so that the farmer can sell more fish at any price and/or charge a higher price. Simply reducing the price may not be a possible strategy (*see* section 10.7.1), but if it is, then the elasticity of demand for the product will be a crucial determinant as to whether total revenue will increase (*see* for example Gates and Matthiessen, 1971).

One significant advantage on the part of the fish farmer in relation to capture fish is that farmed fish is more highly standardized and has predictable characteristics ('built-in portion control'), involves lower risks, is produced reliably, and direct farm–shop linkages are feasible, perhaps leading to lower distribution and marketing costs. As a mark-up during distribution of capture fish is typically over 100%, cost reductions in this phase could significantly benefit farmed fish in the longer run.

We must also note that revenue will be affected by the final size at harvesting, and farmers may have several options open to them. For example, in salmon culture in the United Kingdom in sea cages, one cage will produce, say, 50 tonnes of fish over a two-year production cycle, but the farmer has an option of producing this yield either as 25 000 fish at 2 kg or as 10 000 at 5 kg. As larger fish attract a premium higher unit price, the latter seems more attractive, and costs would be lower as fewer smolts would be needed. However feed costs might be higher, because of less efficient conversion rates at larger sizes. In an empirical study of just such a decision choice, the recommendation tended towards a maximum-growth strategy, harvesting in fact at 4 kg (Crampton and Jackson, 1981). In other situations, farmers may more typically have the option to retain fish to harvest at larger sizes at a later date, and will have to balance the marginal revenues and costs involved, bearing in mind that shorter production periods tend to improve cash flows and reduce risks. In this case, they will also have to consider their time preference and discount future incomes accordingly.

Before leaving revenue, mention must also be made of the possible problem for farmers in that increasing total production may drive down market prices, affecting both farmed and capture fisheries. In Europe prices have already fallen in the case of salmon, eels and trout, and indeed recent evidence suggests that the British market for trout into the mid 1980s could well be oversupplied, with an associated drop in prices and possible impact on the structure of the industry. The response to such problems lies in market development, cooperative marketing, and the vigorous pursuit of possible new outlets in national and international markets.

10.7.4 Risk and uncertainty

Any consideration of aquaculture would not be complete without some mention of what is probably perceived by many farmers as the main feature of commercial fish farming: the presence of a relatively high level of risk and uncertainty. Aquaculture is, in its present form, a comparatively new industry and has attendant risks and uncertainties that require the best and most versatile level of management. Although they are interdependent, the main features have been itemized (Webber, 1973) as first, the biological elements such as disease and parasite attacks, predation and competition, the supply of seed/fry, nutrition, and inventory control and the prevention of overcrowding. Secondly, there are physical elements, including water quantity and quality, pollution and damage from natural hazards such as storms. Finally there are what he terms 'socioeconomic' elements, included within which are market fluctuations in demand and price, feedstuff costs and supplies, and labour supply difficulties. On a broader front, macroeconomic policy changes (as for example in the rate of interest or in exchange rates) and political stability may be difficult to predict. Poaching too is always a problem in farming.

Some of these constitute insurable risks, and there is a growing world industry in the insurance of aquacultural activities. Others can be guarded against by the prudent farmer, and indeed the similarity of this listing to that facing the agricultural farmer reminds us that natural renewable-resource production always involves a relatively high level of risk and uncertainty.

One notable feature in aquaculture is that, while such production will always face market uncertainty in terms of prices and inventories, the great uniformity in size and quality of farmed fish will undoubtedly tend to create a more stable pattern in prices, thereby reducing one element of risk relative to capture fisheries (*see*, for example, Clifton, 1980).

10.8 THE ROLE OF AQUACULTURE IN THE ECONOMY

Although in Western economies industries arise primarily from the drive for profits, even so each may play a number of roles within the economy; in socialist economies, industries may be created specifically with such roles in mind. Here we are concerned less with the nature of aquacultural outputs (*see* section 10.2), but rather with aquaculture's broader role. An important distinction may be made initially between developing as against developed economies, although a similar set of considerations may be applied.

We may identify three principal ways in which aquaculture contributes to social and economic welfare:

(a) The *production of fish as food* is important in both developed and developing economies, but especially so in developing countries, where fish is often a very significant source of such protein as is consumed (for example, in Africa and south-east Asia, fish represents 60–70% of all animal protein intake). Aquaculture is making and will continue to make an increasingly important contribution to food supply in developing countries, even though the average consumption per head in such countries of fish and other marine products was only 8.4 kg p.a. in 1979, compared with a world average of 12.5 kg p.a. Not only does aquaculture contribute to physical wellbeing by providing protein, vitamins and minerals, but it assists in achieving food self-sufficiency and produces food 'on the spot' for local consumption. In developed economies, the emphasis is more on the diversification of the sources of food supply, possibly low-cost products, and the production of highly valued species, which would be scarce and expensive from capture fisheries.

(b) In all economies, aquaculture has a *role in trade*, maybe in the creation of exports or in the saving of the need to import. In developed economies, farmed fish offers particularly an opportunity for import substitution and to replace fish or food supplies that have become uncertain or even unavailable, as for example after the reduction of some distant-water fleets following the developing of 200-mile EEZs. In developing economies the emphasis may sometimes be more on exporting certain species, especially highly valued shellfish species; thus in the Philippines we find subsistence-food milkfish culture alongside export-trade prawn culture aimed entirely at developed economies. This orientation towards export production in developing countries was also typical of the growth in their capture fisheries during the 1970s.

(c) In both types of economy, but particularly in the developing countries, aquaculture has a role as an important *stimulant to economic activity in rural areas*. Not only does it provide employment and income directly, as well as food, but it often generates fish processing activities. Even at the artisanal level the wives and children of the farmers may become involved in processing (filleting, smoking, etc.). This may all help to prevent migration, especially at the village level, and help to retain value-added within rural areas. Thus in the Philippines there are some 176 000 persons employed in milkfish culture, and in China, Thain (1981) reports over 10 000 farmers involved part-time in marine kelp farming alone. Experience in Asia has already proved that aquaculture, especially if combined with agriculture and/or animal husbandry (*see* Gerhardsen, 1979), is a very effective solution to the problems of rural underemployment and low farm incomes. A ratio of 1 job created per 4 tonnes of cultured fish produced is suggested (Shang, 1981), and a ratio of 1 man/5 hectares in a labour-intensive pond farm (as against 1 man/25 ha in a mechanized system) is mentioned by Pillay (1979). It has been suggested that the full development of aquaculture in India could lead to employment for over 8 million people. Although less significantly, aquaculture can play a useful employment- and income-generating role in rural areas in the developed economies too, taking up currently unused or underused resources.

Beyond these three principal roles, we can also identify other aspects of aquaculture. It can help to stabilize fish (and therefore, food) supplies within the national economy; commercial fishing tends to have seasonal fluctuations, and although fish farming itself may have a basic seasonal pattern, supplies can be organized with greater control and confidence. This may also relieve pressures on capture fish stocks, which may facilitate the improvement of fisheries management. It may also be possible to utilize aquaculture to support other fisheries, not only in the customary sense of supplementing natural stocks by re-seeding, but also by the farming of baitfish for capture fisheries and of re-stocking fish for recreational fisheries. Baitfish culture is already well established in the United States, and the supply of recreational fisheries is an important feature of the British trout industry. Finally, in the broadest of terms it can be argued that aquaculture will also tend to improve the overall quality of fish supplies offered to the market, in both developed and developing countries.

Within these broad roles for aquaculture, we can find it fulfilling widely differing functions under different circumstances. In Bangladesh, each acre (0.405 ha) must support in its cultivation all the life requirements for 3.5 persons, and with relatively little scope for the horizontal expansion of agriculture, the country is looking increasingly towards water-based production, where the natural advantages outlined in section 10.1.2 are quite crucial. In contrast, in the United Kingdom much of the culture of oysters (450 tonnes in 1978) and of eels (200 tonnes in 1980) is aimed at luxury export markets in the EEC and Scandinavia.

In the EEC, deliberate attempts have been made within the Common Fisheries Policy to develop aquaculture since the 1970s, partly as a supplement to capture fish but mainly as a growth industry likely to offer employment and income enhancement opportunities to disadvantaged areas of the Community. Assistance of various sorts has been given with this in mind since then, although in 1980 the EEC total aquaculture production was still only some 88 000 tonnes of fin fish (75% rainbow trout) and 340 000 tonnes of shellfish (71% mussels), compared to total fish landings of 5 million tonnes—although farmed fish were 15% of fish used directly for human consumption. Over the period 1971–82, the Community itself supported ninety-two aquaculture projects with aid worth 22.8 million ECUs (1 ECU = approximately £0.61), mainly in the form of construction and modernization grants. As the CFP is now agreed, it seems likely that this assistance will increase in future.

In Japan, aquaculture is rapidly becoming a major contributor to the supply of marine products, mainly for home consumption. Although culture raises only some 9% of total Japanese production, this is still around 1 million tonnes, for Japan is the world's top fish producer with some 11 million tonnes p.a. at the beginning of the 1980s. Aquaculture has reached this level from almost nothing thirty years ago: the main species farmed now are seaweeds, yellowtail, scallops, eels, carp, trout, sea bream and smelts. This has been achieved partly by private enterprise and fishermen's cooperatives, but also with massive state assistance in terms of direct state farming, grants for construction and releases, and governmental research. One reflection of Japanese success is the production of over 5000 tonnes annually of abalone (*Haliotis*), once regarded as being very difficult to culture, significantly reducing import levels. In addition, large quantities of red sea bream are produced, not only for cage culture for food but also to supplement natural stocks by releases to the wild—again sponsored by the state.

Generally, developed economies have tended to adopt intensive aquacultural systems because of limitations on land and water resource inputs, the high costs of labour, and the availability of technologically advanced systems, and then to produce high-valued species. Developing economies have tended to adopt more extensive systems, utilizing the more readily available land, water and labour resources. Such farms, even when small-scale, can play an important role in local food supplies and integrated rural development, often producing protein more cheaply than agriculture and with relatively fewer resource inputs.

China provides a good, albeit not perfectly documented, example of fish farming as essentially an extensive subsistence operation. With a history dating back three thousand years, Chinese aquaculture produces from freshwater ponds some 70% of the country's fish supplies, reaching 1.37 million tons in 1981. The various carp species are immensely important, and raised in a variety of ways: some as carefully planned polyculture with as many as seven species in one pond, some as integrated farming, with the fish feeding on the droppings and chrysalises of silkworms kept on mulberry trees on the embankments between ponds, and some in rice paddy fields. Despite this substantial production, fish consumption *per capita* is still low, and the government hopes to increase the areas and productivity of water in use for farming.

While aquaculture in China is essentially commune-based and virtually isolated from external economic influences, in other developing countries a different pattern is emerging. Many of the firms actively involved in aquacultural development in areas such as South America and Africa are fairly large commercial enterprises, and in some cases are already multinationals. In these circumstances, governmental assistance may well be drawn towards these firms rather than local artisanal farmers, as they have the necessary technology, capital, expertise, experience and markets, and thus the government aid may end up by supporting essentially export-orientated production. While this is not necessarily undesirable as the profits then made may be reinvested in the host economy, there is the risk that such profits will in fact be repatriated to the multinationals' parent countries by various means, while the firms themselves may gain an increasing hold over key resources for further aquacultural growth in the developing country. Thus while the host may derive some benefit in terms of job and income generation, and export trade, this may have little direct influence on the problems of the rural poor and protein deficiency. Indeed, it may even worsen it, in that these government funds or assistance might have been better spent instead on direct food production, possibly of products more readily accepted by the local community.

Finally, it is worth noting that, as populations and incomes grow in many developing countries where fish sometimes comes second only to rice in the diet, the demand for fish is likely to expand rapidly. Moreover, as perhaps 40–50% of farmed fish is consumed by humans directly (Shang, 1981) as against as little as 17% of capture fish (Ryther, 1975), aquaculture could play an increasingly important part in world food supply in the next century. However the movement of scarce resources into aquaculture has an opportunity cost, and in particular, capital in developing countries is likely to have high marginal productivity in alternative usages. It is therefore by no means axiomatic that aquaculture has substantial advantages over alternative food production systems—or indeed over alternative non-food usages of resources. The role of aquaculture in development and the associated problems encountered are fully explored in the literature (e.g. Smith and Peterson, 1982), although comparisons between aquacultural and non-aquacultural resource uses tend to be undertaken in rather superficial terms, if at all.

10.9 THE POTENTIAL OF AQUACULTURE: SOME LIMITATIONS

For several years, books and articles have explored and publicised the huge potential for aquacultural production on a world scale. Such figures have usually been based on loose estimates of 'areas suitable for production' multiplied by 'typical output per hectare' that might be achieved. Such estimates overlook the problems of scarce resources and opportunity costs, the difficulties of creating economically viable activities, and the question as to whether the desire to eat food can be translated into an effective demand for farmed fish. For example, while at present some 2.4 million hectares in Asia are used for aquaculture (Rabanal, 1977), a total of 30 million ha of swamp and tidal areas plus a further 100 million ha of lakes, lagoons, estuaries and the like might be considered suitable (Technical Advisory Committee, 1973). It would be most unwise to suggest that therefore Asian aquacultural production will increase *pro rata* from some 5 million tonnes in 1975 to the theoretically possible 270 million tonnes within any foreseeable future. However, undeniably a great potential exists, and technological advances may make all these areas, and others, even more productive than we can at present foresee. Moreover, in the developed economies there is also great potential, even perhaps, given intensive high-technology systems, an almost limitless potential—although the same could be said equally of intensive chicken production for example. Aquaculture should preferably be based near suitable water supplies, but with recycling and control systems even this requirement may become less crucial. Throughout, one should remember that it is already known that a hectare of water can produce as much or more food than a hectare of land.

There are, however, many problems with such optimistic viewpoints, and the pessimists see little hope that fish can help solve the world shortage of protein. At present much aquaculture does not in general produce cheap food, but rather, high-value or even luxury products, aimed not at feeding the masses but at feeding the high-income groups. At present many production systems are relatively high-cost, for a number of reasons. In many cases aquacultural systems have developed only very recently and are essentially experimental. By using fish meal as an important feedstuff, we are inserting another step in the food chain by feeding undesired fish to desirable fish; in Japan almost 500 000 tons of so-called 'trash fish, meal and other animal protein' was used to produce just 77 000 tons of yellowtail. Ryther (1975) reports a ratio of 5 tonnes of capture fish to feed 1 tonne of farmed. In Japan, shrimp fry are fed on minced clam meat, hardly a 'trash fish' (Shigueno, 1975). Perhaps the move in the early 1980s towards developing suitable foodstuffs from single-cell protein, produced for example from natural gas in the Barents Sea by the major chemical companies Hoechst and Saga Petroleum, foreshadows a significant trend (*FFI*, March 1982), especially as the waste heat from the single-cell protein plant may be used in any farm itself.

Throughout the 1970s the farming emphasis has been on fish that occur fairly high up in the food chain; maybe in the longer run production will have to move as close as possible to the phytoplankton on which marine life is based. Just one step away is to farm the marine filter-feeders such as oysters, scallops and mussels, all of which can be produced in convenient offshore areas, using a natural food supply but with control over predation and so on. Herbivorous carp and some tilapia species will fulfil a similar freshwater role. Polycultural and integrated systems in both cases can improve total yields substantially; the selection of fish with high conversion efficiencies will assist further.

The principal limitations on aquacultural development have been explored in the literature (e.g. Gerhardsen, 1979), but particularly important are site availability and legally enforceable property rights, which are a key element in the whole fish-farming process. Technology transfers from developed to developing countries, and from R & D to commercial operation, will have an influence on the rate of development, as will the availability of seed or fry, from both wild and cultured sources. Disease control is already recognized as one of the main problems, albeit not insuperable given time. Pollution in certain areas of the world will inhibit aquaculture. In developing countries especially, capital availability and its cost are important restraints. Like many other forms of production, including agriculture, aquaculture is vulnerable to changes in the cost of energy. We must also remember that the market acceptability of final outputs and their competitiveness with wild fish and other foods is an important restraint. To deal with these limitations, there is some role for domestic governments, especially in the provision of capital, credit, seed and fry stocks, and R & D, and also a role for international assistance, particularly flowing from developed to developing countries and including technology transfer, training and capital aid. Notwithstanding these limitations, aquaculture has a significant broad advantage in that it can often be complementary to, rather than competing with, other activities such as agriculture, forestry, energy production and irrigation.

The prospects for aquaculture in relation to capture fisheries are not easy to assess. One insight is gained by referring back to section 10.2.2, where we looked at resource usages in aquaculture. We can relate GER to both the fish protein quantities provided by various farming systems as well as whole-fish production, and compare this with comparable data for sea fishing as in *Table 10.6*. We can see that many subsistence systems compare favourably with even inshore fishing, although the most intensive systems compare unfavourably even with deep-sea fishing. However, the unfavourable comparison reflects the use of fish itself as a feedstuff input to aquaculture, and replacing fish meal with soybeans would for example cut the GER for trout to less than half. Production costs are related in part to GER via resource costs, which suggests that extensive systems, polyculture, and reformulated feedstuff inputs in intensive systems* will make aquaculture increasingly competitive with capture fisheries as non-renewable resource costs rise (for more detail and explanation, *see* Edwardson, 1976; Pitcher and Hart, 1982).

It is of course necessary to add that all the predictions made concerning the potential growth of aquaculture tend to be based, of necessity, on the assumption of constant prices. Clearly the price relationship between wild and farmed fish is absolutely critical to the development of aquaculture, especially in Western market economies. While farmed fish may be able to offer itself as a standardized, well processed and marketed product at a stable price and in certain supply, it is not clear that it is universally regarded as a perfect substitute for wild fish as regards flavour, and certainly the price differential between the two would be a critical determinant of demand growth. As fish farming often—not by any means always—takes place in relatively isolated areas, transport costs may themselves be an important constraint.

Finally, it is already clear that governments have a vital role in determining national policies towards aquaculture. While some have pursued a very active pro-culture policy (e.g. France), others have been lukewarm (e.g. the United Kingdom) and others positively unencouraging (e.g. in Denmark, in the face of pressure from commercial fishermen). In Europe the EEC has pursued a fairly positive policy, with assistance reaching £2.75 million in 1982; the intention here has been largely to help depressed regional economies, with aid given to Scotland, Ireland and Italy, mainly for culture but also processing. Governmental assistance in a variety of forms within a coherent policy will be most important in unblocking the bottlenecks that inhibit aquacultural development. In general terms, clarifying and simplifying the whole issue of property rights for individuals and firms in and under the sea, and overcoming the social difficulties that face a movement towards aquaculture are two particularly important areas that will require attention throughout the world.

*Salmon fed on 100% bacterial SCP show no appreciable loss of growth rate or quality (Parker, 1979).

TABLE 10.6 Gross energy requirements (GER) for unit protein and whole fish production on selected farms

	GER/tonne of protein	*GER/tonne of whole fish*
Extensive systems		
Tilapia in fertilized ponds (Africa)	5	0.4
Milkfish fed in pens (Philippines)	9	1
Carp fed in fertilized ponds (Philippines)	18	2
Milkfish fed in fertilized ponds (Taiwan)	52	7
Intermediate systems		
Tilapia fed in fertilized ponds (Thailand)	160	11
Carp fed in fertilized ponds (Germany)	250	25
Intensive systems		
Trout fed in earth ponds (U.K.)	389	56
Catfish fed in earth ponds (Thailand)	523	56
Catfish fed in earth ponds (U.S.A.)	891	95
Trout fed in aeration chambers (recirculation) (U.K.)	n.a.	280
Carp fed in recirculation tank (Japan)	n.a.	309
Polyculture		
Milkfish/prawns (Sri Lanka: intensive)	n.a.	170
Carp/mullet/tilapia (Israel: intensive)	n.a.	65
Tilapia/shrimp (El Salvador: extensive subsistence)	n.a.	1
Carp/tilapia (Thailand: extensive)	n.a.	0.13
Capture fisheries		
Herring: inshore fishing	26	3
Cod: deep-sea fishing	309	30

Source: Based on Edwardson (1976) and Pitcher and Hart (1982).

10.10 CONCLUSION AND OUTLOOK

There is an old adage concerning fishing which has often been quoted: 'Give a man a fish and he has food for a day: teach him to fish and he has food for the rest of his life.' Given the problems surrounding world capture fisheries, one might well modify the second phrase by inserting 'farm' before the word 'fish'. This would be an obvious oversimplification of the value of allocating resources to aquaculture in that it ignores resource availability and opportunity costs, yet it contains a basic truth. For there are many reasons to expect increasing pressures from both the demand and the supply side to be exerted on world capture fisheries in future. The growth in world population, and the rise in income levels, especially in developing countries, are likely to produce an increase in the demand for fish of some 2.0–2.4% p.a. in the period to 2000, compared with an estimated increase in supply of 1% p.a. (Robinson, 1982). This projection assumes constant relative prices. Within fish supply in total, one might anticipate a relative decline in production costs of farmed fish as against capture fish. Together these factors will tend to make aquaculture increasingly attractive over the next few decades.

The extent to which total world fish supplies can meet latent demand is not clear. Given the 'pessimistic' assumed rate of demand increase of 2.0% p.a., total world demand for fish will by 2000 have risen by 44 million tons as compared with the 1975 figure, some 75% of the increase occurring in developing countries, especially in the Far East. Given supply constraints this increased demand will certainly cause prices to rise, especially for those fish in restricted supply owing to resource constraints. Thus the capture-fish price of potential aquaculture species such as salmon, many crustaceans, and prime demersal fish such as turbot, halibut and sole can be expected to rise; this rise may be expected to bring forth further effort and more international trade, yet the potential capture supplies are limited. Indeed, the fixed resource base has already caused fish prices to increase relatively faster than other commodities in the 1970s in countries as diverse as Japan, the United Kingdom, Ghana and the Philippines (Robinson, 1982).

In the five years 1975–80, world aquacultural production rose from some 6.1 million tonnes to 9.4 million tonnes, a 54% increase, with farmed fish amounting to some 12% of the amount of capture fish landed (Pillay, 1981). This increase occurred despite a substantial revision downwards of estimates of aquacultural production in China, which was once thought to be producing as much as 50% of the 6.1 million tonnes but whose production level is now revised to only 1.2 million tonnes in 1978 (Zhu De-Shan, 1980). Moreover the make-up of world aquacultural production is shifting rapidly, away from the once predominant carp types towards shellfish, which rose from 17.5% of landed weight in 1975 to 37% in 1980 (Pillay, 1981). Almost certainly this shift must have involved an even faster rate of increase in the value of aquacultural production than in landed weight.

For many species, especially crustaceans, the technical problems for culture have been largely solved. As the supply of capture fish such as shrimp, lobster, oysters and turbot becomes increasingly inelastic with heavier exploitation, so market prices will tend to rise, and culture will become increasingly attractive. Given the control of pollution, adequate environmental management systems, the assured availability of seed or fry, and stability in the costs of inputs, especially feedstuffs, the prospects for many species are outstanding.

Many factors therefore are moving in favour of aquaculture: an upward trend in demand, especially in developing countries, with the prices of fish from traditional sources rising is an ideal backcloth. Yet aquaculture represents a different form of solution, more comparable with agriculture than with sea fishing. As such, it is difficult to predict just how fast the infant industry can expand. As we argued in section 10.9, the prospects look best for systems that are extensive and polycultural, for those where low-cost feedstuffs may be introduced into intensive production and for the production of high-value fish, and for those in the lower trophic levels such as the filter feeders. There is overall every reason to expect that the FAO estimates of reaping some 20–40 million tonnes from aquaculture by the end of this century is within realistic margins. This amount of fish will not 'feed the world', and it will be some years yet before farmed fish can compete in price terms directly with capture fish. However farmed fish already has begun to supplement supplies of popular, highly valued species from the wild, and further problems with capture fisheries will serve only to accelerate this trend.

10.11 SUMMARY

The problems encountered in conventional capture fisheries combine with the advantages of aquaculture to make the production of farmed fish a potentially important source of increased supplies of fish in the future.

Aquacultural systems may be categorized as intensive, extensive, and intermediate or mixed, and these types may be usefully compared on a resources-used basis. Firms taking part in aquaculture vary widely in type and objectives.

The essential elements in the economic analysis of the individual profit-maximizing unit may be analysed on the basis of TP = y(AR − AC). Physical production, y, is influenced especially by the stocking rate, and the growth and survival rates. Costs (AC) comprise both fixed cost elements and variable cost elements. Within these the cost of feedstuff is particularly important, in association with the conversion ratio (CR), as well as supplies of seeds and water quality control. Sources of potential economies of scale may be identified, and empirical evidence appears to support the probability of a downward-sloping long-run average total cost curve. Aquacultural production systems may be relatively capital-intensive or labour-intensive, depending primarily on the relative cost of the factor inputs.

Average revenue (AR) will be dependent on the nature of the market for the final product, and farmed fish may be sold under a number of differing market structures, with differing implications for the ability of the seller to increase total revenue. Barriers to entry, which tend to confer greater price discretion on the producer as well as inhibiting new entry, may be categorized, and the availability of suitable sites appears to be particularly important. Risk and uncertainty are key features of aquacultural production at the present time.

Aquaculture may be argued to have three principal roles in the economy, involving the production of fish (i) as food, (ii) for exporting and for import saving, and (iii) as a stimulant to economic activity in rural areas, as well as other minor roles. Despite a number of problems to be overcome in increasing supplies, the potential for aquaculture in terms of demand seems considerable, given projections of likely increases in world fish demand and problems with supplies both of conventional and non-conventional species. Already the relative price of capture fish is rising faster than that of other commodities, and aquacultural production will look increasingly attractive commercially as this trend continues, such that production may increase from the present 9.4 million tonnes towards perhaps 20–40 million tonnes by the year 2000.

10.12 BIBLIOGRAPHIC NOTES

The bibliography on aquaculture is expanding rapidly, probably even faster than aquaculture itself. In such a dynamic area, journals are particularly useful and *Fish Farming International*, *Fish Farmer* and *Aquaculture* are three particularly fruitful sources of general and specific information and analysis. The best general books on aquaculture are reports of conferences, which tend to be large and comprehensive: the reports edited by Pillay and Dill (1979), Pillay (1981) and Noel (1981) are especially rich in diverse papers, covering both general and very specific aspects. More manageable are the single-author books, but these tend to divide into rather descriptive works, such as that of Brown (1977), and analytical or theoretical books like that by Shang (1981)—although the latter is probably the best single source on economic analysis applied to aquaculture.

There have been several attempts to produce bibliographies on economic aspects, and those edited by Vondruska (1973) and the FAO (1979b) are the best. The latter part of Bell and Canterbury (1976, pp. 153–261) is a useful if dated bibliography by species. Lewis (1979) has a helpful chapter reviewing the literature on economic aspects. Most books on fish or fishing have a chapter on aquaculture, although often this starts with a general overview but soon becomes a case study of one or two species or systems—examples are the books by Pitcher and Hart (1982) and Avault (1980)—while other authors exclude economic aspects, such as Bardach (1978).

Readers pursuing the topic will find in addition to the general sources a number of useful sources that set out to examine economic aspects, usually in relation to one species or system: these include for example Shepherd (1974), Maclean (1975), Varley (1977), Clifton (1980), Goddard (1979–80), Lewis (1979, 1980) and Stokes (1982). There are other sources that are not aimed specifically at economic aspects but have good coverage or useful insights, including for example Shigueno (1975), Berge (1978), Sutterlin and Merrill (1979), and Thorpe (1980).

Finally, there are general review-type articles, covering aspects of the role and prospects of aquaculture, sometimes in relation to a particular region or group of countries. For example, Parker (1979), McAnuff (1979) and Kurtyanek (1982) cover some European aspects, Nash (1979) and Larkin (1982) some North American views, while Bell and Canterbury (1976), Pullin and Shehadeh (1981), Lam (1982), and Smith and Peterson (1982) look especially at aquaculture in developing countries. Pillay (1973a), Gerhardsen (1978) and Ackefors and Rosen (1979) take an overall viewpoint.

REFERENCES AND FURTHER READING

ACKEFORS, H. and C. G. ROSEN (1979). 'Farming the world's waters.' *Environment* **21** (9) : 16–20, 38–41.

ANDERSON, J. I. W. (1975). 'The aquacultural revolution.' *Proceedings of the Royal Society of London B* **191** : 169–84.

AVAULT, J. W. (1980). 'Aquaculture.' In R. T. Lackey and L. A. Nielsen (Eds), *Fisheries Management*, Ch. 16. Oxford: Basil Blackwell.

BANERJEE, T. (1981). 'Status of aquaculture in the U.S.A.' In S. Noel, (Ed.), *First International Fish Farming Conference, Brighton, England, 1981,* pp. 37–52. London: Andry Montgomery Conference Division, U.K.

BARDACH, J. (1978). 'The growing science of aquaculture.' In S. Gerking (Ed.), *Ecology of freshwater fish production*. Oxford: Basil Blackwell.

BARDACH, J. E., J. H. RYTHER and W. O. MCLARNEY (1972). *Aquaculture: the farming and husbandry of freshwater and marine organisms.* New York: Wiley-Interscience.

BELL, F. W. and E. R. CANTERBURY (1976). *Aquaculture for the developing countries.* Cambridge, Massachusetts: Ballinger Publishing.

BERGE, L. (1978). 'A study of costs and earnings in Norwegian pondfish farming in 1974.' In *Notes on the economics of aquaculture*. Bergen, Norway: Institute of Fisheries Economics.

BROWN, E. E. (1977). *World fish farming cultivation and economics.* Westport, Connecticut: AVI Technical Books.

CHRISTENSEN, N. O. (1974). 'Trout farming in Europe.' Lecture given at Conference on Fish Farming in Europe, London, December 1974.

CLIFTON, J. A. (1980). 'Some economics of mussel culture and harvest.' In R. A. Lutz (Ed.), *Mussel culture and harvest: a North American perspective*, pp. 312–38. Amsterdam: Elsevier.

CRACKNELL, T. J. (1979). 'Development of vertically integrated fish farming in Europe.' In T. V. R. Pillay and W. A. Dill (Eds), *Advances in Aquaculture*, pp. 34–9. Farnham, Surrey: Fishing News Books.

CRAMPTON, V. and A. JACKSON (1981). 'Large or small?' *Fish Farmer* **4** (4) (March) : 24–6.

EDWARDSON, W. (1976). 'Energy demands of aquaculture—a worldwide survey.' *Fish Farming International*, December: 10–13.

FAO (1979a). *World fisheries and the Law of the Sea: the FAO EEZ programme.* Rome: FAO.

FAO (1979b). *A selected bibliography on the economic aspects of aquaculture, 1969–1979*. Fisheries Circular No. 702. Rome: FAO.

GATES, J. M. and G. C. MATTHIESSEN (1971). In T. A. Gaucher (Ed.), *Aquaculture—a New England perspective,* pp. 22–50. Maine, USA: NEMRIP.

GERHARDSEN, G. M. (1978). 'Some aspects of economics as applied to aquacultural development.' In *Notes on the economics of aquaculture.* Bergen, Norway: Institute of Fisheries Economics.

GERHARDSEN, G. M. (1979). 'Aquaculture and integrated rural development, with special reference to economic factors.' In T. V. R. Pillay and W. A. Dill (Eds), *Advances in aquaculture,* pp. 10–22. Farnham, Surrey: Fishing News Books.

GODDARD, J. S. (1979–80). 'Economic and managerial aspects of trout farming.' *Farm Management* **4** (1) (winter) : 19–25.

JARDINE, C. (1983). 'Fish—the food of tomorrow?' *Unilever Magazine*, March: 9–13.

KINGHORN, B. P. and T. GJEDREM (1982). 'Farmed fish.' *Livestock Production Science* **9** : 263–9.

KOBAYASHI, T. (1980). 'Salmon propagation in Japan.' In J. Thorpe (Ed.), *Salmon ranching*, pp. 91–107. London: Academic Press.

KURTYANEK, D. (1982). *The European fishing industry*. SRI International: Datalog File 82–699 (*see also Fish Farming International* July 1982–83).

LAM, T. J. (1982). 'Fish culture in southeast Asia.' *Canadian Journal of Fisheries and Aquatic Science* **39** : 138–42.

LANDLESS, P. J. (Ed.) (1982). *Proceedings of the SMBA/HIDB Fish Farming Meeting, Oban, Scotland.* SMBA/HIDB.

LARKIN, P. A. (1982). 'Aquaculture in North America: an assessment of future prospects.' *Canadian Journal of Fisheries and Aquatic Science* **39** : 151–54.

LEWIS, M. R. (1979). *Fish farming in Great Britain: an economic survey with special reference to rainbow trout.* University of Reading, Department of Agricultural Economics and Management, Miscellaneous Study No. 67.

LEWIS, M.R. (1980). *Rainbow trout: production and marketing.* University of Reading, Department of Agricultural Economics and Management, Miscellaneous Study No. 68.

LEWIS, M. R. (1981). 'Trout: production and marketing trends in Europe.' In S. Noel (Ed.), *First International Fish Farming Conference, Brighton, England, 1981,* pp. 92–101. London: Andry Montgomery Conference Division, U.K.

MCANUFF, J. W. (1979). 'Towards a strategy for fish farming in the U.K.' *Food Policy* **4** (3) : 178–93.

MACLEAN, J. (1975). *The potential of aquaculture in Australia.* Australian Fisheries Paper No. 21. Canberra: Australian Government Publishing Service.

MILNE, P. H. (1976). 'Engineering and the economics of aquaculture.' *Journal of the Fisheries Research Board of Canada* **33** (4) : 888–98.

MISTAKIDIS, M. N. (1978). 'Marine fish culture in the Third World.' *Fish Farming International,* March: 30–5.

MOISEEV, P. A. (1977). 'Living resources of the world ocean: prospects of utilization and augmentation.' *Proceedings of the 5th Japan–Soviet International Symposium on Aquaculture, Tokyo and Sapporo,* pp. 14–18.

MUNRO, A. L. S. and I. F. WADDELL (1981). 'Survey reveals areas of growth.' *Fish Farmer (U.K.)* **4** (6) : 6.

MUNRO, A. L. S. and I. F. WADDELL (1982). 'Annual returns for 1981 from Scottish salmonid fish farms.' In P. J. Landless (Ed.), *Proceedings of the SMBA/HIDB Fish Farming Meeting, Oban, Scotland*, pp. 19–28. SMBA/HIDB.

NASH, C. (1979). 'Structure of U.S. aquaculture.' *Food Policy* **4** (3) : 204–15.

NEEDHAM, E. E. (1979). 'The future of fish farming including sea ranching.' In S. Noel (Ed.), *First International Fish Farming Conference, Brighton, England, 1981,* pp. 1–8. London: Andry Montgomery Conference Division, U.K.

NESTEL, B. L. (1981). 'Salmon: sea-pen culture of Atlantic salmon. In S. Noel (Ed.), *First International Fish Farming Conference, Brighton, England, 1981,* pp. 102–10. Andry Montgomery Conference Division, U.K.

NOEL, S. (Ed.) (1981). *First International Fish Farming Conference, Brighton, England, 1981*. London: Andry Montgomery Conference Division, U.K.

PARKER, R. G. B. (1979). 'Fish farming in Europe.' *Food Policy* **4** (3) : 194–203.

PILLAY, T. V. R. (1973a). *Technical Conference on Fishery Management and Development.* Rome: FAO.

PILLAY, T. V. R. (1973b). 'The role of aquaculture in fishing development and management.' *Journal of the Fisheries Research Board of Canada* **30** (12) : 2202–17.

PILLAY, T. V. R. (1979). 'The state of aquaculture, 1976.' In T. V. R. Pillay and W. A. Dill (Eds), *Advances in aquaculture*, pp. 1–10. Farnham, Surrey: Fishing News Books.

PILLAY, T. V. R. (1981). 'The state of aquaculture, 1981.' *World Conference on Aquaculture, Venice, Italy, 1981.*

PILLAY, T. V. R. and W. A. DILL (Eds) (1979). *Advances in aquaculture*. Farnham, Surrey: Fishing News Books.

PITCHER, T. J. and P. J. B. HART (1982). *Fisheries ecology*. London: Croom Helm.

PULLIN, R. S. V. and Z. H. SHEHADEH (1981). 'Integrated agriculture–aquaculture farming systems.' ICLARM *Conference Proceedings*. Manila: ICLARM–SEARCA.

REAY, P. J. (1979). *Aquaculture*. Studies in Biology No. 196. London: Edward Arnold.

ROBINSON, M. (1982). 'Prospects for world fisheries to 2000.' FAO Fish Circular No. 722. (Rev. 1).

RYTHER, J. H. (1975). 'Mariculture: how much protein and for whom?' *Oceanus* **18** (2) : 10–22.

SAMUELSON, P. (1982). *Economics,* 11th edn. New York: McGraw-Hill.

SHANG, Y. C. (1973). 'Comparison of the economic potential of aquaculture, land animal husbandry and ocean fisheries: the case of Taiwan.' *Aquaculture* **2** : 187–95.

SHANG, Y. C. (1981). *Aquaculture economics: basic concepts and methods of analysis.* London: Croom Helm.

SHEPHERD, C. J. (1974). 'The economics of aquaculture: a review.' *Oceanography and Marine Biology Annual Review* **13** : 413–20.

SHIGUENO, K. (1975). *'Shrimp culture in Japan.'* Tokyo: AIIP.

SMITH, L. J. and S. PETERSON (Eds) (1982). *Aquacultural development in less developed countries: social, economic and political problems.* Boulder, Colorado: Westview Press. (*see also Oceanus* **25** (2) : 1982, pp. 31–9).

SUTTERLIN, A. M. and S. P. MERRILL (1978). 'Norwegian salmonid farming.' Technical Report No. 779, Fisheries and Marine Service (Canada).

STOKES, R. L. (1982). 'The economics of salmon ranching.' *Land Economics* **58** (4) : 464–77.

SYSOEV, N. P. (1974). *Economics of the Soviet fishing industry.* Translation: U.S. Department of Commerce.

TANG, Y. A. (1979). 'Planning, design and construction of a coastal milk fish farm.' In T. V. R. Pillay and W. A. Dill (Eds), *Advances in Aquaculture,* pp. 104–16. Farnham, Surrey: Fishing News Books.

TECHNICAL ADVISORY COMMITTEE (1973). *Report of the TAC Working Group on Aquaculture.* Rome: FAO.

THAIN, B. (1981). 'Marine farming in China.' *Fish Farming International*, Sept.: 20–2.

THORPE, J. (Ed.) (1980). *Salmon ranching*. London and New York: Academic Press.

VARLEY, R. L. (1977). 'Economics of fish farming in the U.K.' *Fish Farming International* **4** (1) : 17–19.

VONDRUSKA, J. (1973). *Aquacultural economics bibliography.* NOAA Technical Report N.M.F.S. SSRF–703, Washington.

WEBBER, H. H. (1973). 'Risks to the aquaculture enterprise.' *Aquaculture* **2** : 157–72.

WEIR, A. (1979). 'Big producers trim costs—but small units find best markets for trout.' *Fish Farmer (U.K.)* **2** (6) : 48–9.

WHEATON, F. W. (1977). *Aquacultural engineering.* New York: John Wiley.

ZHU DE-SHAN (1980). 'A brief introduction to the fisheries of China.' FAO Fisheries Circular No. 726.

Author index

Subject index